The Company Corporation®

Incorporating Businesses Since 1899

...introduces an online calendar and reminder service that notifies you when Incorporation or Limited Liability Company (LLC) documents and actions are due.....

ComplianceWatch®

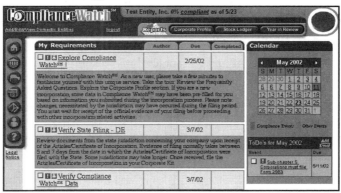

Let The Company Corporation® (TCC) help you manage the ongoing legal formalities associated with your LLC. ComplianceWatch® is an exclusive service of The Company Corporation®. It is designed to help protect your LLC in several important ways:

- access to a customized calendar and reminder service that can automatically notify you when it's time to hold your annual meeting, file annual reports, pay franchise taxes, and perform other duties to meet important deadlines

- access to sample documents and templates you can use to guide you through the preparation of your operating agreement

- the ability to record the official activities of your Limited Liability Company

To learn more about ComplianceWatch®, visit

www.compliancewatch.com

and take the tour.

Read This First

The information in this book is as up to date and accurate as we can make it. But it's important to realize that the law changes frequently, as do fees, forms and procedures. If you handle your own legal matters, it's up to you to be sure that all information you use—including the information in this book—is accurate.

We believe accurate and current legal information should help you solve many of your own legal problems on a cost-efficient basis. But this text is not a substitute for personalized advice from a knowledgeable lawyer. If you want the help of a trained professional, consult an attorney licensed to practice in your state.

The Company Corporation®
Incorporating Businesses Since 1899

Legal Guide for Starting & Running a Small Business

by Attorney Fred S. Steingold

edited by Ilona Bray

SEVENTH EDITION

Second Printing	AUGUST 2003
Editor	ILONA BRAY
Illustration	MARI STEIN
Book Design	TERRI HEARSH
Cover Design	TONI IHARA
Production	SARAH HINMAN
Proofreading	ROBERT WELLS
Index	JEAN MANN
Printing	ARVATO SERVICES, INC.

For information on bulk purchases or corporate premium sales, please contact the Special Sales Department. For academic sales or textbook adoptions, ask for Academic Sales. Call 800-955-4775 or write to Nolo, 950 Parker Street, Berkeley, CA 94710.

ACKNOWLEDGMENTS

Special thanks to Nolo Publisher Jake Warner—the cheerful perfectionist whose ideas infuse every page of this book—and to Nolo Editor Mary Randolph, who deftly whipped the early manuscripts into final shape.

Thanks, too, to the rest of the remarkable Nolo family for their invaluable contributions—especially Steve Elias, Robin Leonard, Barbara Hodovan, Jackie Mancuso, Tony Mancuso, Barbara Kate Repa, Beth Laurence and Ilona Bray.

In addition to the folks at Nolo, these other professionals generously shared their expertise to make this book possible:

- Attorneys Charles Borgsdorf, Larry Ferguson, Sandra Hazlett, Peter Long, Michael Malley, Robert Stevenson, Nancy Welber and Warren Widmayer.

- Certified Public Accountants Mark Hartley and Lonnie Loy.

- Insurance Specialists James Libs, Mike Mansel and Dave Tiedgen.

Finally, thanks to my small business clients, who are a constant source of knowledge and inspiration.

Table of Contents

INTRODUCTION

CHAPTER 1

Which Legal Form Is Best for Your Business?

CHAPTER 2

Structuring a Partnership Agreement

CHAPTER 3

Creating a Corporation

CHAPTER 4

Creating a Limited Liability Company

CHAPTER 5

Developing a Buy-Sell Agreement

CHAPTER 6

Naming Your Business and Products

CHAPTER 7

Licenses and Permits

CHAPTER 8

Tax Basics for the Small Business

CHAPTER 9

Raising Money for Your Business

CHAPTER 10

Buying a Business

CHAPTER 11

Franchises: How Not to Get Burned

CHAPTER 12

Insuring Your Business

CHAPTER 13

Negotiating a Favorable Lease

CHAPTER 14

Home-Based Business

CHAPTER 15

Employees and Independent Contractors

CHAPTER 16

The Importance of Excellent Customer Relations

CHAPTER 17

Legal Requirements for Dealing With Customers

CHAPTER 18

Cash, Credit Cards and Checks

CHAPTER 19

Extending Credit and Getting Paid

CHAPTER 20

Put It in Writing: Small Business Contracts

CHAPTER 21

The Financially Troubled Business

CHAPTER 22

Resolving Legal Disputes

CHAPTER 23

Representing Yourself in Small Claims Court

CHAPTER 24

Lawyers and Legal Research

Introduction

The law increasingly affects every aspect of a small business operation, from relationships with landlords, customers and suppliers to dealings with governmental agencies over taxes, licenses and zoning. Being surrounded by legal issues places most small business owners in an unhappy dilemma—either buy expensive legal help from a lawyer or go without.

Here is another alternative: a self-help book designed to answer most of the legal questions you're likely to ask in starting and running your business.

Fortunately, understanding and coping with most small business legal issues isn't akin to doing your own brain surgery. In truth, it's more like taking an aspirin when you feel a headache coming on.

No self-help law book, no matter how good, can eliminate the need to consult an attorney once in a while. But armed with the practical legal information you'll find here, you'll be able to make most day-to-day decisions on your own, seeking professional advice only when you truly need it.

If you understand basic legal issues, you can avoid basic legal problems. But staying out of trouble shouldn't be your only goal. Whether you're a retailer, professional, craftsperson, distributor or small manufacturer, a good understanding of the law can help you fashion policies and strategies that will pay off.

For example, suppose you want to lease a building. Typically, you'll have two worries. If you sign a long lease and your business doesn't succeed, you'll be stuck with an unneeded space. On the other hand, if you choose a very short lease and your business is the big hit you hope it will be, the landlord may jack up the rent.

Fortunately for the legally knowledgeable, there is an easy detour around this dilemma. It's called the lease option contract. Typically, for a small payment or a slightly increased rent, you can start with a short lease that gives you one, or even several, options to renew at an agreed-upon rental amount (often, the original rent plus an adjustment for inflation) if your business does well.

Dealing with customers is much the same. If you know the law that regulates advertising, refunds and warranties, you have a strong basis to establish policies that tell your customers you really do put their interests first. Seen this way, legal rules do not define how you'll treat customers. Instead, they form the foundation on which you build a more generous relationship, which will convert one-time customers into regulars and regular customers into advocates for your business.

Finally, a personal note. I'm a small business lawyer and legal writer based in Ann Arbor, Michigan. I advise many people with dreams and aspirations much like yours. Much of what I tell them day to day is in this book.

There is one thing I'd like to emphasize right here at the beginning. You're about to take charge of your legal decision-making in an exciting new way. In fact, you'll begin to look at law differently—not as an enemy to be feared but as a fact of business life that you can grasp and be comfortable with. In business, as elsewhere, knowledge is power, and this book helps you put the power of law in your hands.

ICONS

Throughout the book, these icons alert you to certain information.

Fast Track
We use this icon to let you know when you can skip information that may not be relevant to your situation.

Warning
This icon alerts you to potential problems.

Recommended Reading
When you see this icon, a list of additional resources that can assist you follows.

Cross-Reference
This icon refers you to a further discussion of the topic elsewhere in this book.

See an Expert
Lets you know when you need the advice of an attorney or other expert.

Tip
A legal or commonsense tip to help you understand or comply with legal requirements.

Recommended Forms
This icon refers you to a related chapter in Legal Forms for Starting & Running a Small Business, *by Fred S. Steingold (Nolo), which contains legal forms and checklists.* ∎

Which Legal Form Is Best for Your Business?

When you start a business, you must decide on a legal structure for it. Usually you'll choose either a sole proprietorship, a partnership, a limited liability company (LLC) or a corporation. There's no right or wrong choice that fits everyone. Your job is to understand how each legal structure works and then pick the one that best meets your needs. The best choice isn't always obvious. After reading this chapter, you may decide to seek some guidance from a lawyer or an accountant.

For many small businesses, the best initial choice is either a sole proprietorship or—if more than one owner is involved—a partnership. Either of these structures makes especially good sense in a business where personal liability isn't a big worry—for example, a small service business in which you are unlikely to be sued and for which you won't be borrowing much money. Sole proprietorships and partnerships are relatively simple and inexpensive to establish and maintain.

Forming an LLC or a corporation is more complicated and costly, but it's worth it for some small businesses. The main feature of LLCs and corporations that attracts small businesses is the limit they provide on their owners' personal liability for business debts and court judgments against the business. Another factor might be income taxes: You can set up an LLC or a corporation in a way that lets you enjoy more favorable tax rates. In certain circumstances, your business may be able to stash away earnings at a relatively low tax rate. In addition, an LLC or corporation may be able to provide a range of fringe benefits to employees (including the owners) and deduct the cost as a business expense.

Given the choice between creating an LLC or a corporation, many small business owners will generally be better off going the LLC route. For one thing, if your business will have several owners, the LLC can be more flexible than a corporation in the way you can parcel out profits and management duties. Also, setting up and maintaining an LLC can be a bit less complicated and expensive than a corporation. But there may be times a corporation will be more beneficial. For example, because a corporation—un-

like other types of business entities—issues stock certificates to its owners, a corporation can be an ideal vehicle if you want to bring in outside investors or reward loyal employees with stock options.

Keep in mind that your initial choice of a business form doesn't have to be permanent. You can start out as sole proprietorship or partnership and, later, if your business grows or the risks of personal liability increase, you can convert your business to an LLC or a corporation.

 For some small business owners, a less common type of business structure may be appropriate. *While most small businesses will find at least one good choice among the four basic business formats described above, a handful will have special situations in which a different format is required or at least is desirable. For example, a pair of dentists looking to limit their personal liability may need to set up a professional corporation (PC) or a professional limited liability company (PLLC). A group of real estate investors may find that a limited partnership is the best vehicle for them. These and other special types of business organizations are summarized in Section F at the end of this chapter.*

You may need professional advice in choosing the best entity for your business. *This chapter gives you a great deal of information to assist you in deciding how to best organize your business. Obviously, however, it's impossible to cover every nuance of tax and business law that applies to your business. This is especially so if your business has several owners with different and complex tax situations. And keep in mind that especially for businesses owned by several people who have different personal tax situations, sorting out the effects of "pass-through" taxation (where partners and most LLC members are taxed on their personal tax returns for their share of business profits and losses) is no picnic, even for seasoned tax pros. The bottom line is that unless your business will start small and have a very simple ownership structure, before you make*

WAYS TO ORGANIZE YOUR BUSINESS

TYPE OF ENTITY	MAIN ADVANTAGES	MAIN DRAWBACKS
Sole Proprietorship (Section A)	Simple and inexpensive to create and operate Owner reports profit or loss on his or her personal tax return	Owner personally liable for business debts
General Partnership (Section B)	Simple and inexpensive to create and operate Owners (partners) report their share of profit or loss on their personal tax returns	Owners (partners) personally liable for business debts
Limited Partnership (Section F)	Limited partners have limited personal liability for business debts as long as they don't participate in management General partners can raise cash without involving outside investors in management of business	General partners personally liable for business debts More expensive to create than general partnership Suitable mainly for companies that invest in real estate
Regular Corporation (Section C)	Owners have limited personal liability for business debts Fringe benefits can be deducted as business expense Owners can split corporate profit among owners and corporation, paying lower overall tax rate	More expensive to create than partnership or sole proprietorship Paperwork can seem burdensome to some owners Separate taxable entity
S Corporation (Section C)	Owners have limited personal liability for business debts Owners report their share of corporate profit or loss on their personal tax returns Owners can use corporate loss to offset income from other sources	More expensive to create than partnership or sole proprietorship More paperwork than for a limited liability company, which offers similar advantages Income must be allocated to owners according to their ownership interests Fringe benefits limited for owners who own more than 2% of shares
Professional Corporation (Section F)	Owners have no personal liability for malpractice of other owners	More expensive to create than partnership or sole proprietorship Paperwork can seem burdensome to some owners All owners must belong to the same profession
Nonprofit Corporation (Section F)	Corporation doesn't pay income taxes Contributions to charitable corporation are tax-deductible Fringe benefits can be deducted as business expense	Full tax advantages available only to groups organized for charitable, scientific, educational, literary or religious purposes Property transferred to corporation stays there; if corporation ends, property must go to another nonprofit
Limited Liability Company (Section D)	Owners have limited personal liability for business debts even if they participate in management Profit and loss can be allocated differently than ownership interests IRS rules now allow LLCs to choose between being taxed as partnership or corporation	More expensive to create than partnership or sole proprietorship State laws for creating LLCs may not reflect latest federal tax changes
Professional Limited Liability Company (Section F)	Same advantages as a regular limited liability company Gives state licensed professionals a way to enjoy those advantages	Same as for a regular limited liability company Members must all belong to the same profession
Limited Liability Partnership (Section F)	Mostly of interest to partners in old-line professions such as law, medicine and accounting Owners (partners) aren't personally liable for the malpractice of other partners Owners report their share of profit or loss on their personal tax returns	Unlike a limited liability company or a professional limited liability company, owners (partners) remain personally liable for many types of obligations owed to business creditors, lenders and landlords Not available in all states Often limited to a short list of professions

your final decision on a business entity, you'll want to check with a tax advisor after learning about the basic attributes of each type of business structure from this chapter and Chapters 2, 3 and 4.

A. Sole Proprietorships

The simplest form of business entity is the sole proprietorship. If you choose this legal structure, then legally speaking you and the business are the same. You can continue operating as a sole proprietor as long as you're the only owner of the business.

Establishing a sole proprietorship is cheap and relatively uncomplicated. While you do not have to file articles of incorporation or organization (as you would with a corporation or an LLC), you may have to obtain a business license to do business under state laws or local ordinances. States differ on the amount of licensing required. In California, for example, almost all businesses need a business license, which is available to anyone for a small fee. In other states, business licenses are the exception rather than the rule. But most states do require a sales tax license or permit for all retail businesses. Dealing with these routine licensing requirements generally involves little time or expense. However, many specialized businesses—such as an asbestos removal service or a restaurant that serves liquor— require additional licenses which may be harder to qualify for. (See Chapter 7 for more on this subject.)

In addition, if you're going to conduct your business under a trade name such as Smith Furniture Store rather than John Smith, you'll have to file an assumed name or fictitious name certificate at a local or state public office. This is so people who deal with your business will know who the real owner is. (See Chapter 6 for more on business names.)

From an income tax standpoint, a sole proprietorship and its owner are treated as a single entity. Business income and business losses are reported on your own federal tax return (Form 1040, Schedule C). If you have a business loss, you may be able to use it to offset income that you receive from other sources. (For more tax basics, see Chapter 8.)

Legal Forms for Starting & Running a Small Business *contains a checklist for starting a sole proprietorship.*

1. Personal Liability

A potential disadvantage of doing business as a sole proprietor is that you have unlimited personal liability on all business debts and court judgments related to your business.

EXAMPLE 1: Lester is the sole proprietor of a small manufacturing business. When business prospects look good, he orders $50,000 worth of supplies and uses them up. Unfortunately, there's a sudden drop in demand for his products, and Lester can't sell the items he's produced. When the company that sold Lester the supplies demands payment, he can't pay the bill.

As sole proprietor, Lester is personally liable for this business obligation. This means that the creditor can sue him and go after not only Lester's business assets, but his other property as well. This can include his house, his car and his personal bank account.

EXAMPLE 2: Shirley is the sole proprietor of a flower shop. One day Roger, one of Shirley's employees, is delivering flowers using a truck owned by the business. Roger strikes and seriously injures a pedestrian. The injured pedestrian sues Roger, claiming that he drove carelessly and caused the accident. The lawsuit names Shirley as a co-defendant. After a trial, the jury returns a large verdict against Roger— and Shirley as owner of the business. Shirley is personally liable to the injured pedestrian. This means the pedestrian can go after all of Shirley's assets, business and personal.

One of the major reasons to form a corporation or a limited liability company (LLC) is that, in theory at least, you'll avoid most personal liability. (But see Chapter 12, Section C, for a discussion of how a good liability insurance policy may be enough protection against personal liability for a sole proprietor.)

2. Income Taxes

As a sole proprietor, you and your business are one entity for income tax purposes. The profits of your business are taxed to you in the year that the business makes them, whether or not you remove the money from the business (called "flow-through" taxation, because the profits "flow through" to the owner's income tax return). You report business profits on Schedule C of Form 1040.

By contrast, if you form an LLC or a corporation, you have a choice of two different types of tax treatment.

- *Flow-Through Taxation.* One choice is to have the IRS tax your LLC or corporation like a sole proprietorship or partnership (discussed above). The owners report their share of LLC or corporate profits on their own tax returns, whether or not the money has been distributed to them.
- *Entity Taxation.* The other choice is to make the business a separate entity for income tax purposes. If you form an LLC and make that choice, the LLC will pay its own taxes on the profits of the LLC. And as a member of the LLC, you won't pay tax on the money earned by the LLC until you receive payments as compensation for services or as dividends. Similarly, if you form a corporation and choose this option, you as a shareholder won't pay tax on the money earned by the corporation until you receive payments as compensation for services or as dividends. The corporation will pay its own taxes on the corporate profits.

In Sections C and D of this chapter, I'll explain the mechanics of choosing between these two methods. For now, just be aware that this tax flexibility of LLCs and corporations offers some tax advantages over a sole proprietorship if you're able to leave some income in the business as "retained earnings." For example, suppose you want to build up a reserve to buy new equipment or your small label manufacturing company accumulates valuable inventory as it expands. In either case, you might want to leave $50,000 of profits or assets in the business at the end of the year. If you operated as a sole proprietor, those "retained" profits would be taxed on your personal income tax return at your marginal tax rate. But with an LLC or corporation that's taxed as a separate entity, the tax rate will almost certainly be lower.

You can share ownership of your business with your spouse and still maintain its status as a sole proprietorship. *If you choose to do this, in the eyes of the IRS you'll be co-sole proprietors. You can either split the profits from your business if you and your spouse file separate returns (and separate Schedule Cs), or you can put them on your joint Schedule C if you file a joint return. Only a spouse can be a co-sole proprietor. If any other family member shares ownership with you, the business must be organized as a partnership, corporation or limited liability company.*

3. Fringe Benefits

If you operate your business as a sole proprietorship, tax-sheltered retirement programs are available. A Keogh plan, for example, allows a sole proprietor to salt away a substantial amount of income free of current taxes. You can't really do any better by setting up an LLC or a corporation.

A regular ("C") corporation or an LLC that chooses to be taxed as a separate entity does have an advantage when it comes to medical expenses for the owner and his or her spouse and dependents. As a sole proprietor, you are limited as to how much you can deduct for medical expenses on your personal tax return: You can deduct only the amount that exceeds 7.5% of your adjusted gross income for the year. If you form an LLC or a corporation, however, and choose to have it taxed as a separate entity, you can have your business pay *all* of your family's medical expenses (so long as they're not covered by insurance) and then take these amounts as a business deduction. You won't be personally taxed for the value of this employment benefit.

In the past, sole proprietors could deduct only a portion of health insurance premiums for themselves and family members, while LLCs and corporations (if separate taxable entities) could deduct 100%. That sometimes provided a reason to form an LLC or corporation, but no longer. A self-employed person can now deduct 100% of those premiums.

If you form an LLC or a corporation, however, and choose to have it taxed as a separate entity, you can have the business hire you as an employee. The business can pay 100% of your family's health insurance premiums and uncovered medical expenses and then take these amounts as a business deduction; you won't be personally taxed for the value of this employment benefit.

Hiring Your Spouse Can Have Tax Benefits

If you choose to do business as a sole proprietor, there's a way you can deduct more of your family's medical expenses. First, hire your spouse at a reasonable wage. Then, set up a written health benefit plan covering your employees and their families. A sample form is shown below. Your business can then deduct 100% of the medical expenses it pays.

But balance whether such a plan can save you enough money to justify the effort. There may be some expense for setting up the plan and handling the associated paperwork. And remember that your business will be obligated for payroll taxes on your spouse's earnings. (See Chapter 8, Section C, for information on payroll taxes.) But this isn't all bad, since your spouse will become eligible for Social Security benefits in his or her own right, which can be of some value—especially if he or she hasn't already worked long enough to qualify.

If you're audited, the IRS will look closely to make sure your spouse is really an employee and performing needed services for the business.

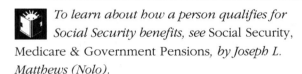 *To learn about how a person qualifies for Social Security benefits, see* Social Security, Medicare & Government Pensions, *by Joseph L. Matthews (Nolo).*

Sample Reimbursement Plan

Sam Jones, a sole proprietor doing business as Jones Consulting Services (the Company), establishes this Health and Accident Plan for the benefit of the Company's employees.

1. *Coverage.* Beginning January 1, 20XX, the Company will reimburse each employee for expenses incurred by the employee for the medical care of the employee and the employee's spouse and dependents, and for premiums for medical, dental and disability insurance. The medical care covered by this plan is defined in Section 213(d) of the Internal Revenue Code. Dependents are defined in Section 152.

2. *Direct Payment.* The Company may, in its discretion, pay any or all of the expenses directly instead of reimbursing the employee.

3. *Expense Documents.* Before reimbursing an employee or paying an expense directly, the Company may require the employee to submit bills and insurance premium notices.

4. *Other Insurance.* The Company will reimburse an employee or pay bills directly only if the reimbursement or payment is not provided for under any other health and accident or wage continuation plan.

5. *Ending or Changing the Plan.* Although the Company intends to maintain this plan indefinitely, the Company may end or change the plan at any time. This will not, however, affect an employee's right to claim reimbursement for expenses that arose before the plan was ended or changed.

Dated: December ___, 20XX

_____

Sam Jones, doing business as Jones
Consulting Services

4. Routine Business Expenses

As a sole proprietor, you can deduct day-to-day business expenses the same way an LLC, corporation or partnership can. Whether it's car expenses, meals, travel or entertainment, the same rules apply to all of these types of business entities.

You'll need to keep accurate books for your business that are clearly separate from your records of personal expenditures. The IRS has strict rules for tax-deductible business expenses (covered in Chapter 8, Section D), and you need to be able to document those expenses if challenged. One good approach is to keep separate checkbooks for your business and personal expenses—and pay for all of your business expenses out of the business checking account. But whatever your system, please pay attention to this basic advice: It's simple to keep track of business income and expenses if you keep them separate from the start—and murder if you don't.

B. Partnerships

If two or more people are going to own and operate your business, you must choose between establishing a partnership, a corporation or a limited liability company (LLC). This section looks at the general partnership, which is the type of partnership that most small businesses will be considering. The limited partnership is described in Section F1, below.

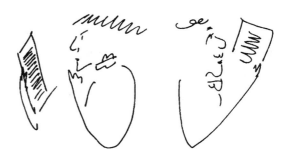

LAW IN THE REAL WORLD
First Things First

Ellen, Mary and Barbara Kate, librarians all, planned to open an electronic information searching business with an emphasis on information of special interest to women. They would hold on to their daytime jobs until they could determine if their new business could support all three women.

At a planning meeting to discuss buying personal computers and modems, Ellen said she wanted the business to be run as professionally as possible, which to her meant promptly incorporating or forming an LLC. The discussion about equipment was put off while the three women tried to decide how to organize the legal structure of their business. After several frustrating hours, they agreed to continue the discussion later and to do some research about the organizational options in the meantime.

Before the next meeting, Ellen conferred with a small business advisor who suggested that the women refocus their energy on the computers and modems and getting their business operating, keeping its legal structure as simple as possible. One good way to do this, she suggested, was to form a partnership, using a written partnership agreement. Each partner would contribute $10,000 to buy equipment and contribute roughly equal amounts of labor. Profits would be divided equally.

Later, if the business succeeded and grew, it might make sense to incorporate or form an LLC and consider other issues, like a health plan, pensions and other benefits. But for now, real professionalism meant getting on with the job—not consuming time and dollars forming an unneeded corporate or LLC entity.

The best way to form a partnership is to draw up and sign a partnership agreement (discussed fully in Chapter 2). Legally, you can have a partnership without a written agreement, in which case you'd be governed entirely by either the Uniform Partnership Act or the Revised Uniform Partnership Act (explained in Chapter 2).

Beyond a written agreement, the paperwork for setting up a partnership is minimal—about on a par with a sole proprietorship. You may have to file a partnership certificate with a public office to register your partnership name, and you may have to obtain a business license or two. The income tax paperwork for a partnership is marginally more complex than that for a sole proprietorship.

1. Personal Liability

As a partner in a general partnership, you face personal liability similar to that of the owner of a sole proprietorship. Your personal assets are at risk in addition to all assets of the partnership. In other words, you have unlimited personal liability on all business debts and court judgments related to your business.

In a partnership, any partner can take actions that legally bind the partnership entity. That means, for example, that if one partner signs a contract on behalf of the partnership, it will be fully enforceable against the partnership and each individual partner, even if the other partners weren't consulted in advance and didn't approve the contract. Also, the partnership is liable, as is each individual partner, for injuries caused by any partner while on partnership business.

> **EXAMPLE 1:** Ted, a partner in Argon Associates, signs a contract on behalf of the partnership that obligates the partnership to pay $50,000 for certain goods and services. Esther and Helen, the other partners, think Ted made a terrible deal. Nevertheless, Argon Associates is

bound by Ted's contract even though Esther and Helen didn't sign it.

EXAMPLE 2: Juan is a partner in Universal Contractors. Elroy, one of his partners, causes an accident while using a partnership vehicle. Juan and all the other partners will be financially liable to people injured in the accident if the car isn't covered by adequate insurance. The same would be true if Elroy used his own car while on partnership business.

In both of these situations, the personal assets (home, car and bank accounts) of each partner will be at stake, in addition to partnership assets. But remember that a partnership can protect against many risks by carrying adequate liability insurance.

2. Partners' Rights and Responsibilities

Each partner is entitled to full information—financial and otherwise—about the affairs of the partnership. Also, the partners have a "fiduciary" relationship to one another. This means that each partner owes the others the highest legal duty of good faith, loyalty and fairness in everything having to do with the partnership.

EXAMPLE: Wheels & Deals, a partnership, is in the business of selling used cars. No partner is free to open a competing used-car business without the consent of the other partners. This would be an obvious conflict of interest and, as such, would violate the fiduciary duty the partners legally owe to one another.

Unless agreed otherwise, a person can't become a new partner without the consent of all the other partners. However, in larger partnerships, it's common for partners to provide in the partnership agreement that new partners can be admitted with the consent of a certain percentage of the existing partners—75%, for example.

State laws regulating partnerships dictate what occurs if one partner leaves your partnership and you don't have a partnership agreement that provides for what happens. In about half the states, the partnership is automatically dissolved when a partner withdraws or dies; the business is then liquidated. In such a state, it's an excellent idea to put a provision in your partnership agreement that allows the business to continue without interruption, despite the technical dissolution of the partnership. A partnership agreement, for instance, may provide a "buy-sell" provision that calls for a buyout if one of the partners dies or wants to leave the partnership, avoiding a forced liquidation of the business.

EXAMPLE: Tom, Dick and Mary are equal partners. They agree in writing that if one of them dies, the other two will buy the deceased partner's interest in the partnership for $50,000 so that the business will continue. (Be aware that often a partnership agreement doesn't fix a precise amount as the buyout price but uses a more complicated formula based on such data as yearly sales, profits or book value.) To fund this arrangement, the partnership buys life insurance covering each partner in an amount large enough to cover the buyout. If Tom dies first, under the terms of the agreement, his wife and children will receive $50,000 from the partnership to compensate them for the value of Tom's ownership interest in the business. Technically, the remaining partners would operate as a new partnership, but the important point is that the business would keep functioning.

Other states—generally those that have adopted the revised version of the Uniform Partnership Act— follow a slightly different rule. In those states, if your partnership was created to last for a fixed length of time or was created for a specific project, and a partner leaves before the fixed time expires or the project is done, the partnership isn't automatically dissolved. Instead, the remaining partners have the opportunity to continue the existing partnership rather than having to form a new one. But even if your state follows this more flexible approach, you'll still want to use buy-sell provisions to specify how the departing partner—or the family of a partner who's died—gets compensated for his partnership interest.

 Chapter 5 discusses buy-sell provisions in greater detail.

3. Income Taxes

In terms of income and losses, the tax picture for a partnership is basically the same as that of a sole proprietorship. A partnership doesn't pay income taxes. It must, however, file an informational return that tells the government how much money the partnership earned or lost during the tax year and how much profit (or loss) belongs to each partner. Each partner uses Schedule E of Form 1040 to report the business profits (or losses) allocated to him and then pays income tax on his or her share, whether or not this income was actually distributed during the tax year. If the partnership loses money, each partner can deduct his or her share of losses for that year from income earned from other sources (subject to some fairly complicated tax basis rules—see Investment Partnerships, below).

Investment Partnerships

The above analysis assumes that the partner who deducts losses from other income actively participates in the business. If, instead, a partner is a passive investor (as is often the case in partnerships designed to invest in real estate) or receives income from passive sources (such as royalties, rents or dividends), any loss from the partnership business is treated as a passive loss for that partner. That means that for federal income tax purposes the loss can be deducted only from other passive income—not from ordinary income.

4. Fringe Benefits and Business Expenses

When it comes to retained earnings, tax-sheltered retirement plans and fringe benefits, a partnership is like a sole proprietorship, and the discussion in Section A3, above, applies to partnerships as well.

Likewise, business expenses can be deducted in the same way for a partnership as for a sole proprietorship; the discussion in Section A4, above, applies here as well.

Put it in writing. *If you go the partnership route, I strongly recommend that the partners sign a written partnership agreement, even though an oral partnership agreement is legal. The human memory is far too fallible to rely on for the details of important business decisions. Chapter 2 contains basic information on how to write a partnership agreement.*

C. Corporations

If you're concerned about limiting your personal liability for business debts, you'll want to consider organizing your business as either a limited liability company (LLC) or a corporation. (Of course, you may have other reasons in addition to limited liability for considering these two business structures.) Since the corporation has a longer legal history, I'll deal with it first, but the LLC—which is covered in Section D—may well be preferable for your particular business, despite its relative newness.

This book deals primarily with the small, privately owned corporation. I'll assume that all of the corporate stock is owned by one person or a few people, and that all shareholders are actively involved in the management of the business—with the possible exception of friends and relatives who have provided seed money in exchange for stock. Because there are many complexities involved in selling stock to the public, I don't discuss public corporations.

The most important feature of a corporation is that, legally, it's a separate entity from the individuals who own or operate it. You may own all the stock of your corporation, and you may be its only employee, but—if you follow sensible organizational and operating procedures—you and your corporation are separate legal entities.

All states have adopted legislation that permits a corporation to be formed by a single incorporator. All states permit a corporate board that has a single director, although the ability to set up a one-person board may depend on the number of shareholders. (See Chapter 3 for more details.) In addition, many states have streamlined the procedures for operating a small corporation to permit decisions to be made quickly and without needless formalities. For example, in most states, shareholders and directors can take action by unanimous written consent rather than by holding formal meetings, and directors' meetings can be held by telephone.

1. Limited Personal Liability

One of the main advantages of incorporating is that, in most circumstances, it limits your personal liability. If a court judgment is entered against the corporation, you stand to lose only the money that you've invested. Generally, as long as you've acted in your corporate capacity (as an employee, officer or director) and without the intent to defraud creditors, your home and personal bank accounts and other valuable property can't be touched by a creditor who has won a lawsuit against the corporation.

EXAMPLE: Andrea is the sole shareholder, director and officer of Market Basket Corporation, which runs a food store. Ronald, a Market Basket employee, drops a case of canned food on a customer's foot. The customer sues and wins a judgment against the business. Only corporate assets are available to pay the damages. Andrea is not personally liable.

Liability for your own acts. *If Andrea herself had dropped the case of cans, the fact that she is a shareholder, officer and director of the corporation wouldn't protect her from personal liability. She would still be personally liable for the wrongs (called torts, in legal lingo) that she personally commits. So much for theory. In practice, incorporating may not actually give you broad legal protection.*

In the real world, banks and some major corporate creditors often require the personal guarantee of individuals within the corporation. So the limited liability gained from incorporating isn't always as valuable a legal shield as it first seems.

EXAMPLE: Market Basket Corporation borrows $75,000 from a bank. Andrea signs the promissory note as president of the corporation, but the bank also requires her to guarantee the note personally. The corporation runs into financial difficulties and can't repay the debt. The bank sues and wins a judgment against the business for the unpaid principal plus interest. In collecting on the judgment, the bank can go after Andrea's assets as well as the corporation's property. Incorporation offers no advantage over a sole proprietorship when an owner personally guarantees a loan.

As mentioned in Sections A and B, above, liability insurance can protect against many of the risks of doing business. Because of this, many businesses can structure themselves as sole proprietorships or partnerships without worrying about unlimited personal liability. But if you operate a high-risk business—child care center, chemical supply house, asbestos removal service or college town bar—and you can't get (or can't afford) liability insurance for some risks that you're concerned about, incorporation may be the wisest choice.

EXAMPLE: Loren is afraid that a clerk at his After Hours beverage store might inadvertently sell liquor to an underaged customer or one who has had too much to drink. If that customer got drunk and hurt someone in a car accident, there might be a lawsuit against the business.

Loren contacts his insurance agent to arrange for coverage, but learns that his liquor store can afford only $50,000 worth of liability insurance. Loren buys the $50,000 worth of insurance, but also forms a corporation—After Hours Inc.—to run the business. Now if an injured person wins a large verdict, at least Loren won't be personally liable for the portion not covered by his insurance.

The lesson of these examples is clear: Before you decide to incorporate your business primarily to limit your personal liability, analyze what your exposure will be if you simply do business as a sole proprietor (or a partner in a partnership).

The limited liability feature of corporations can be valuable, protecting you from personal liability for:

- Debts that you haven't personally guaranteed, including most routine bills for supplies and small items of equipment.
- Injuries suffered by people who are injured by business activities not covered adequately by insurance.

Also, for a business with more than one owner, incorporating can offer a great deal of protection from the misdeeds or bad judgment of your co-owners. In contrast, in a partnership, as noted above, each partner is personally liable for the business-related activities of the other partners.

EXAMPLE: Ted, Mona and Maureen are partners in Mercury Enterprises. Mona writes a nasty letter about Harold, a former employee, which causes Harold to lose the chance of a good new job. Harold sues for defamation and wins a $60,000 judgment against the partnership. Ted and Maureen are each personally liable to pay the judgment even though Mona wrote the letter.

If Mercury Enterprises had been a corporation, Mona and the corporation would have been liable for the judgment, but Ted and Maureen would not. Ted and Maureen would lose money if the assets of the corporation were seized to pay the judgment, but their own personal assets would be safe.

LAW IN THE REAL WORLD
Going With Your Gut

Several years ago, John took over his dad's rug cleaning business as a sole proprietor. He didn't expect the business to ever grow beyond its status as a small local facility with six employees and $400,000 in annual sales. But grow it did—first to ten, then to 25 employees, operating in four suburban cities and taking in $3.5 million a year.

About this time, John and his wife bought a nice house, put a few dollars in the bank and finished paying off the promissory note to his dad for the purchase of the business. Things were going so well that John began to worry about what would happen to his personal assets if the business was sued for big bucks. He reviewed his insurance coverage and sensibly increased some of it. He reviewed his operations and improved several systems, including the one for storing, handling and disposing of toxics. Still, he felt vaguely disquieted.

Finally, even though he couldn't identify any other risks likely to result in a successful lawsuit against his company, John decided to incorporate, to limit his personal liability for the business's debts. He tried to explain his gut feelings of worry to his father, but felt he wasn't quite making sense. The older man interrupted and said, "I think you're trying to say that things have been going so well lately that something is bound to mess up soon. And if they do, you want as much of a legal shield between your personal assets and those of the business as possible."

"Precisely," John said. "But I've already protected myself against all obvious risks, so I can't logically justify a decision to incorporate."

His father replied, "C'mon, son, business decisions are like any other—if your gut tells you to be a little extra careful, go with it. Running a small business means being ready to trust your own intuition."

⚠ Payroll taxes. *Limited liability doesn't protect you if you fail to deposit taxes withheld from employees' wages—especially if you have anything to do with making decisions about what bills the corporation pays first. Also, because unpaid withheld taxes aren't dischargeable in bankruptcy, you want to pay these before you pay other debts (most of which can be wiped out in bankruptcy) in case your business goes downhill.*

2. Income Taxes

Federal taxation of corporations is a very complicated topic. Here I deal only with basic concepts.

The federal tax laws distinguish between two types of corporations. A regular corporation (sometimes called a "C corporation") is treated as a tax-paying entity separate from its investors and it must pay corporate federal income tax. By contrast, a corporation that chooses "S corporation" status doesn't pay federal income tax; instead, income taxes are paid by the corporation's owners.

a. S corporations

Electing to do business as an S corporation lets you have the limited liability of a corporate shareholder but pay income taxes on the same basis as a sole proprietor or a partner. Among other things, this means that as long as you actively participate in the business of the S corporation, business losses can be used as an offset against your other income—reducing, maybe even eliminating, your tax burden. The corporation itself doesn't pay taxes, but files an informational tax return telling what each shareholder's portion of the corporate income is.

> **EXAMPLE:** Paul decides to start an environmental clean-up business. Because insurance isn't available to cover all of the risks of this business, he forms a corporation called Ecology Action Inc. This limits Paul's personal liability if

there's a lawsuit against the corporation for an act not covered by insurance.

Paul is also concerned about taxes. He expects his company to lose money during its first few years; he'd like to claim those losses on his personal tax return to offset income he'll be receiving from consulting and teaching work. He registers with the IRS as an S corporation. Unless he changes that tax status later, his corporation won't pay any federal income tax. Paul will report the corporation's income loss on his own Form 1040 and will be able to use it as an offset against income from other sources.

For many years, if you wanted to limit the personal liability of all owners of your business and have the income and losses reported only on the owners' income tax returns, you would have no choice but to create an S corporation. Today, you can accomplish the same goal by creating a limited liability company (LLC), as explained in Section D, below. Because, in addition, an LLC offers its owners the significant advantage of greater flexibility in allocating profits and losses, it's generally better to structure your business as an LLC than as an S corporation. (But see Section E for a discussion of when it might be better to create an S corporation.)

Should Your Corporation Elect S Corporation Status?

For federal tax purposes, it's often best for a start-up company to elect to be an S corporation rather than a regular corporation. This is so even though recent changes in tax rates have made this decision a bit more complex. Still, to make sure an S corporation is best for you, speak to a knowledgeable accountant or other tax advisor. Also keep in mind that a limited liability company (LLC) may be an even better choice than either type of corporation. (See Sections D and E.)

Starting as an S corporation rather than a regular corporation may be wise for several reasons:

- Because income from an S corporation is taxed at only one level rather than two, your total tax bill will likely be less. (But be aware that the two-tier tax structure for regular corporations can sometimes be an advantage. See the discussion below on how a regular corporation can achieve tax savings through income-splitting.)

- Your business may have an operating loss the first year. With an S corporation, you generally can pass that loss through to your personal income tax return, using it to offset income that you (and your spouse, if you're married) may have from other sources. Of course, if you're expecting a profit rather than a loss—because, for example, you're converting a profitable sole proprietorship or partnership to a corporation—this pass-through for losses won't be an advantage to you.

- Interest you incur to buy S corporation stock is potentially deductible as an investment interest expense.

- When you sell the assets of your S corporation, you may be taxed less on your gain than if you operated the business as a regular corporation (because of the dual taxation structure of corporations).

- Your decision to elect to be an S corporation isn't permanent. If you later find there are tax advantages to being a regular corporation, you can easily drop your S corporation status, but timing is important.

Limits on deductions. *You can deduct S corporation losses on your personal return only to the extent of the money you put into the corporation (to buy stock) and any money you personally loaned to the corporation. Also, if you don't work actively in the S corporation, there are potential problems with claiming losses, because they might be considered losses from passive activities. For the most part, you can only use losses from passive activities to offset income from passive activities. See your tax advisor for technical details.*

Shareholders pay income tax on their share of the corporation's profits regardless of whether they actually received the money or not. If the corporation suffered a loss, shareholders can claim their share of that loss.

> **EXAMPLE:** Assume the same facts as above except that there are two other shareholders in Ecology Action Inc. Paul owns 50% of the stock, and Ellen and Ted each own 25%. Paul would report 50% of the corporation's profit or loss on his personal tax return, and Ellen and Ted would each report 25% on theirs.

Most states follow the federal pattern in taxing S corporations: they don't impose a corporate tax, choosing instead to tax the shareholders for corporate profits. About half a dozen states, however, do tax an S corporation the same as a regular corporation. The tax division of your state treasury department can tell you how S corporations are taxed in your state.

To be treated as an S corporation, all shareholders must sign and file IRS Form 2553. For more information on this and other requirements for electing S corporation status, see Chapter 8, Section B.

b. Regular corporations

Under federal income tax laws, a regular corporation is a separate entity from its shareholders. This means that the corporation pays taxes on any income that's left after business expenses have been paid.

As you saw earlier in this chapter, a sole proprietorship doesn't pay federal income tax as a separate entity; the owner simply reports the business's income or loss on Schedule C of Form 1040 and adds it to (or, in the case of a loss, subtracts it from) the owner's other income. Similarly, a partnership doesn't pay federal income tax; rather, the partnership annually files a form with the IRS to report each partner's share of yearly profit or loss from the partnership business. Each partner then adds his or her share of partnership income to other income reported on his or her personal tax return (the familiar Form 1040) or deducts his or her share of loss. And an S corporation is treated as a sole proprietorship or partnership for federal income tax purposes, depending on the number of owners.

A regular corporation is different. It reports its profits on Form 1120 and pays corporate tax on that income. In addition, if the profits are distributed to shareholders in the form of dividends, the shareholders pay tax on the dividends they receive (creating the much-feared "double taxation" scenario).

In practice, however, a regular corporation may not have to pay any corporate income tax even though it is a separate taxable entity. Here's how: In most incorporated small businesses, the owners are also employees. They receive salaries and bonuses as compensation for the services they perform for the corporation. The corporation then deducts this "reasonable" compensation as a business expense. In many small corporations, compensation to owner-employees eats up all the potential corporate profits, so there's no taxable income left for the corporation to pay taxes on.

EXAMPLE: Jody forms a one-person catering corporation, Jody Enterprises Ltd. She owns all the stock and is the main person running the business. The corporation hires her as an employee, with the title of president. The corporation pays her a salary plus bonuses that consume all of the corporation's profits. Jody's salary and bonuses are tax-deductible to the corporation as a corporate business expense. There are no corporate profits to tax. Jody simply pays tax on the income that she receives from the corporation, the same as any other corporate employee.

(1) Tax Savings Through Income Splitting

As an alternative to paying out all the corporate profits in the form of salaries and bonuses, you may want to leave some corporate income in the corporation to finance the growth of your business. You can often save tax dollars this way because, for the first $50,000 of taxable corporate income, the tax rate and actual taxes paid will generally be lower than what you'd pay as an individual. The federal government taxes the first $50,000 of taxable corporate income at 15%. The next $25,000 is taxed at 25%. Taxable income over $75,000 is taxed at 34% until taxable income reaches $10,000,000—at which point the rate becomes 35%. Additionally, to make larger corporations pay back the benefits of these lower graduated tax rates, corporate taxable incomes between $100,000 and $335,000 are subject to an extra 5% tax. (See the chart in Chapter 8, Section C1d.)

Here's an example of how, with proper planning, a small incorporated business can split income between the corporation and its owners, retaining money in the corporation for expenses and lowering the corporation's tax liability to an amount that's actually less than what would have to be paid by the principals of the same business if it were not incorporated.

EXAMPLE 1: Sally and Randolph run their own incorporated lumber supply company, S & R Wood Inc. One year their sales increase to $1.2 million. After the close of the third quarter, Sally and Randolph learn that S & R Wood is likely to make $110,000 net profit (net taxable corporate income) for the year. They decide to reward themselves and other key employees with moderate raises in pay, give a small year-end bonus to other workers and buy some needed equipment.

This reduces the company's net taxable income to $40,000—an amount that Sally and Randolph feel is prudent to retain in the corporation for expansion or in case next year's operations are less profitable. Taxes on these retained earnings are paid at the lowest corporate rate, 15%. If Sally and Randy had wanted to take home more money instead of leaving it in the business, they could have increased their salaries and paid taxes at a rate of at least 10% but more probably 25% or 28% or higher, depending on their tax brackets.

⚠ **Double taxation trap.** *Sally and Randy could have also declared a stock dividend. But because this would have subjected them to a double tax of 15% at the corporate level plus 5% or 15% at the personal level, it would have been a poor choice.*

EXAMPLE 2: Now assume S & R Wood is not incorporated but instead is operated as a partnership. Now the entire net profits of the business ($110,000 minus the bonuses to workers and deductible expenditures for equipment) are taxed to Sally and Randolph. The result is that the $40,000 (which was retained by the corporation in the above example) is taxed at their individual rate of 25% or 28% or higher rather than the 15% corporate rate.

For a more detailed explanation of how income-splitting can be an advantage to owners of small corporations, see *How to Form Your Own California Corporation*, or *Incorporate Your Business: A 50-State Legal Guide to Forming a Corporation*, both by Anthony Mancuso (Nolo).

The main point to remember is that once your business becomes profitable, doing business as a regular corporation allows a degree of flexibility in planning and controlling your federal income taxes that is unavailable to partnerships and sole proprietorships. To determine whether or not favorable corporate tax rates are a compelling reason for your business to incorporate, you'll need to study IRS regulations or go through an analysis with your accountant or other tax advisor.

Tax savings may be a largely theoretical advantage for the person just starting out. If your business is like many start-ups, your main concern will be generating enough income from the business to pay yourself a reasonable wage. Retaining profits in the business will come later. In this situation, the tax advantages of incorporating are illusory.

EXAMPLE: In its first year of operation, Maria's store, The Bookworm, has a profit of $25,000. As the sole proprietor, Maria withdraws the entire $25,000 as her personal salary, which places her in the 15% tax bracket after she subtracts her deductions and personal exemption. It doesn't make sense for Maria to incorporate to take advantage of income-splitting techniques—even if she could get by on say, $20,000 a year, if she left the remaining $5,000 in the corporation, it would be taxed at the 15% corporate tax rate, so her total tax bill would be the same.

Lower Tax Rates Not Available for S Corporations

The lower tax rates for retained earnings don't apply to S corporations, because, as discussed in subsection a, above, an S corporation does not itself pay taxes on earnings. Individual shareholders in an S corporation pay taxes on their portion of corporate earnings at their personal income tax rates (as if they were partners in a partnership). This is true whether or not those earnings are distributed to them, meaning that even if the shareholders do leave some earnings in the corporation, the shareholders will be taxed on them at their regular tax rates.

(2) Fringe Benefits

The tax rules governing fringe benefits are complicated. Generally, however, if your business will be offering fringe benefits to employees, you can enjoy a tax advantage if you organize as a regular corporation. The business can pay for employee benefits and then take these amounts as business expense deductions. You and the other shareholders who work as employees of your corporation can have the corporation pay for such employee benefits as:

- deferred compensation plans
- group term life insurance
- reimbursement of employee medical expenses that are not covered by insurance
- health and disability insurance.

But the real advantage is how these fringe benefits are treated on your personal tax return. As a shareholder, you won't be personally taxed for the value of this employment benefit. That's because none of the employees of a regular corporation—even if they're owners—have to pay income tax on the value of the fringe benefits they receive. So, for example, your corporation may decide to provide medical insurance for employees and to reimburse employees for uninsured medical payments. The corporation can deduct these payments as a business expense—including the portion paid for the owner-employees of the corporation—and you and the other owner-employees are not taxed on these benefits.

Other types of business entities can also deduct the cost of many fringe benefits as a business expense, but owners who receive these benefits will ordinarily be taxed on their value. That's because the tax laws distinguish between an employee and a self-employed person. The tax laws say that you're a self-employed person—and therefore are taxed on your fringe benefits—if you're a sole proprietor, a partner in a partnership, a member of an LLC that's taxed as a partnership or an owner of more than 2% of the shares of an S corporation. An owner-employee of a regular corporation, however, isn't classified as a self-employed person. So when it comes to the taxation of fringe benefits, owner-employees of a corporation enjoy a unique advantage.

This favorable tax treatment may seem like a powerful reason to organize your business as a regular corporation. Not so fast. Obviously, there's no benefit unless your business provides these benefits to employees in the first place. And that may be too expensive for some new businesses—especially because many types of employee benefits must be provided on a nondiscriminatory basis to a wide range of employees or to none, and must not be designed to primarily aid the business owner. If you put together a fringe benefit package that favors you and other owner-employees, the IRS will require owners to pay tax on their portion. Few new businesses can afford the cost of carrying expensive benefit programs—a cost that typically more than offsets any tax advantage to you as owner of a regular corporation.

Here are some of the IRS ground rules for fringe benefit plans:

- **Medical Reimbursement Plans.** If your business promises to pay those portions of your employees' medical expenses that are not covered by health insurance, your plan can also include the spouse and dependents of each employee. Usually you'll set a limit on the total amount that can be reimbursed during the year; this limit must be the same for all eligible employees. In the typical small business, if you include owner-

employees in the plan, your plan must benefit 70% of all employees or at least 80% of all employees who are eligible to participate. You can exclude employees who are under 25, work seasonally or less than 35 hours per week or have been employed less than three years. As long as you meet these rules, employees—even owner-employees—won't be taxed on reimbursements they receive. If you violate these rules, however, an owner may have to pay tax on all or part of the reimbursements that he or she receives under the plan. (These technical rules apply only to reimbursement of medical expenses—not to employer payment of medical insurance premiums.)

- **Group Life Insurance.** Your business can provide up to $50,000 of group term life insurance tax-free to employees (including yourself) if you meet certain conditions. As an owner-employee of a small corporation, you'll probably be a "key employee" under the tax laws. (A key employee is an officer who is paid more than $130,000 a year, an owner of at least 5% of the company or an owner of at least 1% of the company who is paid more than $150,000 a year.) If you are a key employee and want to deduct the cost of the insurance from your gross income, your plan must meet special rules: It must benefit at least 70% of all employees, limit the number of key employee participants to 15% of all group participants or meet other IRS guidelines for "non-discrimination." All benefits available to participating key employees must be available to all other participating members as well. You can provide different dollar amounts of life insurance to different employees without being "discriminatory" if the amount of coverage is uniformly related to compensation. Also, you can exclude employees who've worked for your company for less than three years.

Clearly, this is technical stuff. Let's say you open a video store and hire a bunch of students to work part-time during peak periods, and contract out for bookkeeping services. In such a case, you can set up a medical reimbursement plan without having to worry about covering a whole slew of employees. You could exclude the students because they're under 25 and work less than 35 hours a week. Your bookkeeper, being an independent contractor, wouldn't be an employee and wouldn't have to be covered. So perhaps your plan would cover only yourself and a few full-time employees, plus the families of all covered employees.

(3) Retirement Plans

It used to be that by incorporating you could set up a better tax-sheltered retirement plan than you could get as a sole proprietor, a partner or a shareholder-employee in an S corporation. There are no longer any significant differences.

3. Attracting Investors

To start and successfully run a small business, you may need more money than you can muster from your own savings or the cash generated by the enterprise. As explained in greater depth in Chapter 9, you have two basic options in raising money from outside sources: borrowing it or getting it from investors. If you expect to seek money from investors—even if they're family members, friends or business associates—there's a substantial advantage in forming a corporation.

Unlike a lender who, in return for providing money, receives a promise that you'll repay it with interest, an investor becomes a part-owner of the business. While it's possible to form a partnership and make an investor a partner or to form an LLC and make an investor a member, it's often more practical to form a corporation and make the investor a shareholder. That little piece of paper that the corporation issues—the stock certificate—is tangible proof of the shareholder's ownership interest in the business and it's something that most investors have come to expect. Put another way, if you offer an investor a partnership interest or an LLC interest,

you're more likely to run into resistance than if you offer her stock in a corporation.

Keep in mind that shareholders don't necessarily have to have equal rights to elect the board of directors or to receive dividends. To distinguish between various types of shareholders, you can issue different classes of stock with different rights, for example:

- common, voting shares to the initial owners who will be working in the business
- nonvoting shares for key employees to keep them loyal to the business
- nonvoting preferred shares to outside investors, giving them a preference if dividends are declared or the corporation is sold.

To repeat this key point, the fact that the corporate structure makes it relatively easy to distinguish between different investors by issuing different classes of stock is a real advantage.

Stock options can motivate employees. *Especially for a business that sells stock to the public or plans to do so before long, which allows the market to establish a price for the stock, issuing stock options to employees at a favorable price can be a great way to motivate them. That's because employees who hold options know that if the business is profitable and its stock price goes up, they'll be able to cash in their options at a substantial profit. This can motivate them to help make the business successful. Also, employees who get stock options are often willing to work for a bit less salary, making investment capital go farther in the early days of business life.*

Structuring your business as a corporation is not only advantageous but actually essential if—like many small business owners—you dream of someday attracting investors through a public offering. And, fortunately, it's become far easier than it used to be for a small business to do just that without turning to a conventional stock underwriting company. Congress and state legislatures have liberalized laws that enable a small corporation to raise from $1 million to $10 million annually through a relatively easy-to-use procedure called a limited public offering.

Consider using the Internet to sell shares. *You may decide to market your shares by placing your company's small offering prospectus on the Internet—something now allowed by the Securities and Exchange Commission (SEC), the federal agency that watches over securities laws. If your company creates a website to inform the public about your products and services, you can also use that site to distribute your prospectus and market your shares. Of course, you'll first need to take care of the paperwork required by federal and state securities laws.*

 Forming and running a corporation is discussed in more detail in Chapter 3.

Illusory Incorporation Advantages

What, in addition to limited liability and some marginal tax advantages, can you gain by incorporating? In drumming up enthusiasm for incorporating, lawyers and accountants often point to additional supposed benefits—but these advantages are rarely all they're cracked up to be.

Illusory Benefit: Easy Transfer of Corporate Stock If You Sell the Business. The sales pitch is that if you want to sell your interest in the corporation (which may be as much as 100% if you own all of the stock), you simply endorse your stock certificate on the back and turn over the certificate to the new owner. The corporation then issues a new stock certificate in the new owner's name to replace the one that you endorsed.

Reality: There's not much of a market for a small company's stock. And most small business owners go to great lengths to restrict the transferability of their stock. Moreover, in most sales of a corporate business, the corporate assets are transferred rather than the stock. (See Chapter 10.)

Illusory Benefit: Continuity of Business. A corporation continues even if an owner dies or withdraws. (Plus, there may be a buy-sell agreement—perhaps funded by insurance—in which co-owners of the corporation have the right to buy out your inheritors.) Either way, the corporation stays alive, in contrast to a sole proprietorship or partnership, which are automatically dissolved when the owner or a partner dies.

Reality: The death of a principal is traumatic whether you're a sole proprietorship, a partnership or a corporation. Usually the factors that allow a business to survive are personal and have nothing to do with its formal legal structure. You don't need to incorporate to ensure that your business will continue after your death. A sole proprietor can use a living trust or will to transfer the business to her heirs, and partners frequently have insurance-funded buy-sell agreements that allow the remaining partners to continue the business. (See Chapter 5.)

Illusory Benefit: Centralized Management. In corporations with a number of shareholders, management is typically centralized under a board of directors. With a partnership consisting of many partners, management can become fragmented.

Reality: If you are a partner in a partnership, it doesn't take a board of directors to centralize the management; chances are you and the other owners will make all decisions over a cup of coffee.

Conclusion: In weighing pros and cons of incorporation, concentrate on whether you believe you have a real need to limit your personal liability and also on whether you can get substantial tax benefits by retaining some earnings in the corporation and setting up fringe benefit plans. If you conclude that it would be beneficial to form a business entity that offers limited liability, the LLC (discussed in Section D) is often your best choice. And for many new businesses—especially those that won't run up significant debt or expose their owners to the threat of lawsuits—a sole proprietorship or partnership may be a perfectly adequate way to go, keeping in mind that you can always incorporate the business or form an LLC later.

D. Limited Liability Companies

The limited liability company (LLC) is the newest form of business entity. It has enjoyed a meteoric rise in popularity among both entrepreneurs and lawyers—and for good reason. It's often a very attractive alternative to the traditional ways of doing business, which are described in Sections A, B and C, above.

The state laws controlling how an LLC is created and the federal tax regulations controlling how an LLC is taxed are still evolving. Fortunately, the evolutionary trends are extremely favorable to small businesses. On the formation side, it's becoming simpler and simpler to set up an LLC. On the tax side, LLCs are benefitting from increased flexibility.

For an in-depth discussion of LLCs and step-by-step guidance on creating one, see Form Your Own Limited Liability Company, *by Anthony Mancuso (Nolo).*

Once you've decided that your business should be organized as an entity that limits your personal liability for business debts, you'll have to weigh the pros and cons of forming an LLC against the pros and cons of forming a corporation. Sometimes, one or the other will clearly emerge as the better choice.

Other times, the differences are more subtle—which often means that either will suit your needs equally well. After you've absorbed the information on both legal formats, you can look at Section E for help in choosing between the two.

1. Limited Personal Liability

As with a corporation, all of the owners of an LLC enjoy limited personal liability. This means that being a member of an LLC doesn't normally expose you personally to legal liability for business debts and court judgments against the business. Generally, if you become an LLC member, you risk only your share of capital paid into the business. You will, however, be responsible for any business debts that you personally guarantee (of course, you can reduce your risk to zero by not doing this) and for any wrongs (torts) that you personally commit (a good insurance policy should help here—see Chapter 12, *Insuring Your Business*).

By contrast, as discussed in Sections A and B above, owners of a sole proprietorship or general partnership have unlimited liability for business debts, as do the general partners in a limited partnership (and limited partners who take part in managing the business—discussed in Section F1, below).

Corporations and LLCs Use Different Terms		

Although there are many similarities between corporations and LLCs, there are many differences as well—especially when it comes to terminology, as shown in the following chart:

TERM	CORPORATION	LLC
What an Owner Is Called	Shareholder	Member
What an Owner Owns	Shares of Stock	Membership Interest
What Document Creates the Entity	Articles of Incorporation (or, in some states, Certificate of Incorporation or Charter)	Articles of Organization
What Document Spells Out Internal Operating Procedures	Bylaws	Operating Agreement

2. Number of Owners

Every state now allows single-member LLCs as well as multi-member ones. This means that if you plan to be the sole owner of a business and you wish to limit your personal liability, you have a choice of forming a corporation or an LLC.

3. Tax Flexibility

If you create a single-member LLC, it will not be taxed as a separate entity, like a regular corporation (see Section C), unless you elect to have it taxed in this manner. Normally, you won't choose corporate-style taxation, preferring to have your single-member LLC report its profits (or losses) on Schedule C of your personal return, just as a sole proprietorship would.

Similarly, if you have an LLC with two or more members, it will be treated as a partnership for tax purposes, with each partner reporting and paying income tax on her share of LLC profits unless you elect to have the LLC taxed as a corporation. Again, you normally won't elect to do this, preferring to have your multi-member LLC follow the partnership tax route. This means that the LLC will report its income (or loss) on Form 1065, an informational return that notifies the IRS of how much each member earned (or lost). Each member will then report his or her share of profits or losses on her personal Form 1040.

Occasionally, the members of an LLC will conclude that there's an advantage to being taxed like a corporation, with two levels of tax—one at the business entity level (for company profits) and another at the owners' personal income tax level (for salaries and dividends). LLCs that are taxed like corporations are able to split monies between business owners and the business itself, resulting in some situations in a significant overall tax saving. (See Section C2b(1), above, for a discussion of income splitting in the corporate context.)

If, after reviewing all the financial implications—and perhaps seeking the advice of a tax pro—you decide to elect corporation-style taxation, you'll do this by filing IRS Form 8832, *Entity Classification Election*. Where the LLC has two or more members, they can all sign the form or authorize one member or manager to sign.

Electing to have your LLC taxed as a corporation can be advantageous if you want to receive tax-free fringe benefits from the business. *If you follow the usual practice of having pass-through taxation for your LLC—meaning that the business isn't taxed as a separate entity—then as a business owner you'll be taxed on the value of the fringe benefits you receive from the LLC (unlike other employees). A different rule applies if you elect to have your LLC taxed as a corporation. In that situation, as long as you meet the IRS guidelines, you can receive fringe benefits as an owner-employee of the LLC and not have to pay tax on the value of those benefits. (For more on the tax treatment of fringe benefits, see Section C2b(2), above.)*

4. Flexible Management Structure

An LLC member may be an individual or a separate legal entity such as a partnership or corporation that has invested in the LLC. You and the other members jointly run the LLC unless you choose to have it run by a single member, an outside manager or a management group—which may consist of some members, some nonmembers or both. If you decide to form an LLC, I recommend that all the members sign an operating agreement that spells out how the business will be managed. Again, the details of how to do this are well covered in *Form Your Own Limited Liability Company*, by Anthony Mancuso (Nolo).

5. Flexible Distribution of Profits and Losses

The members of an LLC can decide to split up the LLC profits and losses each will receive any way they want. Although it's common to divide LLC profits according to the percentage of the business's assets each member contributed, this isn't legally required.

> **EXAMPLE:** Jim, Janna, Jill and Jerry—certified personal trainers—form Fit for Life LLC to operate a family fitness center. Each contributes $25,000 to the enterprise. Because Jim, who has a strong business background, has put together the LLC, set up a bookkeeping system, arranged for a bank loan to purchase necessary equipment and negotiated a very favorable lease at a good location, the owners state in their operating agreement that for the first two years, Jim will receive 40% of the LLC's profits and that Janna, Jill and Jerry will each receive 20%. After that, they'll share profits equally.

By contrast, rules governing corporate profits and losses are considerably more restrictive. A regular corporation can't allocate profits and losses to shareholders; instead, shareholders must receive dividends according to the number of shares they own—if they receive dividends at all. (But it is possible, although more cumbersome, to establish two or more classes of stock, each with different dividend rights.) Similarly, in an S corporation, profits and losses are attributed to the shareholders based on their shares: a shareholder who owns 25% of the shares in an S corporation ordinarily must be allo-

cated 25% of profits and losses—no more and no less. Sometimes, however, corporations can get away from this strict formula by adjusting the salaries of shareholders who work in the business.

The easy flexibility allowed to LLCs in distributing profits and losses permits businesses to be creative and even make distributions to members who have contributed no cash.

> **EXAMPLE:** Howard and Saul run a home repair business organized as an LLC. Howard puts up all the money to needed to buy a van, tools and supplies and to pay for advertising brochures and radio commercials. Saul, who has little cash but loads of experience in doing home repairs, will contribute future services to the LLC. Although the owners could agree to split profits and losses equally, they decide that Howard will get 60% for the first three years as a way of paying him back for taking the risk of putting up cash.

 Starting and operating an LLC is discussed in more detail in Chapter 4.

For forms to use in setting up an LLC, see Form Your Own Limited Liability Company, *by Anthony Mancuso (Nolo), and Nolo's* LLC Maker, *an easy-to-use software program that simplifies and automates much of the work of forming an LLC.*

E. Choosing Between a Corporation and an LLC

Let's assume that you've read all the earlier material in this chapter and that you now understand the chief legal, tax and financial characteristics of the main types of business entities. Let's also assume that you've concluded it would be advantageous to operate your small business through an entity that limits the personal liability of all the owners—even if following this strategy involves a bit more paperwork, complexity and possible expense.

For the reasons explained earlier in this chapter, you've probably narrowed your choice of entity to either the tried and true corporation or the new and streamlined LLC. Which is better? There's no answer to this question that applies to every business. Nevertheless, some general principles may be helpful.

For the majority of small businesses, the relative simplicity and flexibility of the LLC makes it the better choice. This is especially true if your business will hold property, such as real estate, that's likely to increase in value. That's because regular corporations (sometimes called C corporations) and their shareholders are subject to a double tax (both the corporation and the shareholders are taxed) on the increased value of the property when the property is sold or the corporation is liquidated. By contrast, LLC member-owners avoid this double taxation because the business's tax liabilities are passed through to them; the LLC itself does not pay a tax on its income.

But an LLC isn't always the best choice. Occasionally, other factors will be present that may tip the balance toward a corporation. Such factors include the following:

- **You'd like to provide extensive fringe benefits to owner-employees.** Often, when you form a corporation, you expect to be both a shareholder (owner) and an employee. The corporation can, for example, hire you to serve as its chief executive officer and pay you a tax-deductible salary, which, from a tax standpoint, is far better than paying you dividends, which can't be deducted by the corporation as a business expense and therefore wind up being taxed twice (once at the corporate level and once at the personal level). But corporate employees (including employees of a C corporation who are also owners) don't just receive pay—most also receive fringe benefits. These benefits can include the payment of health insurance premiums and direct reimbursement of medical expenses. The corporation can deduct the cost of these benefits and they are not treated as taxable income to the employees. Having your own corporation pay for these fringe benefits and then deduct the cost as a business expense can be an attractive feature of doing business through a regular corporation. These opportunities for you to receive tax-favored fringe benefits are somewhat reduced if you do business as an LLC. Also, a regular corporation may be able to offer slightly better retirement benefits or options under a corporate retirement plan.

- **You want to entice or keep key employees by offering stock options and stock bonus incentives.** Simply put, LLCs don't have stock; corporations do. While it's possible to reward an employee by offering a membership interest in an LLC, the process is awkward and likely to be less attractive to employees. Therefore, if you plan to offer ownership in your business as an employee incentive, it makes sense to incorporate rather than form an LLC.

Choosing Between an LLC and an S Corporation: Self-Employment Taxes Can Tip the Balance

You know that taxes are withheld from employees' paychecks. In 2003, for example, employers must withhold 7.65% of the first $87,000 of an employee's pay for Social Security and Medicare taxes, and 1.45% of earnings above that amount for Medicare taxes. The employer adds an equal amount (to match the employee's share of Social Security and Medicare taxes) and sends these funds to the IRS. The total sent to the IRS is 15.3% on the first $87,000 of wages and 2.9% on earnings above that amount. (See Chapter 8, Section C3). You may not be aware that the IRS collects a similar 15.3% tax on the first $87,000 earned by a self-employed person and a 2.9% tax on earnings above that amount for Medicare alone. For this reason, the Social Security and Medicare tax is often referred to as the "self-employment" tax.

For an S corporation, the rules on the self-employment tax are well established: as an S corporation shareholder, you pay the self-employment tax on money you receive as compensation for services—but *not* on profits that automatically pass through to you as a shareholder. For example, if your total share of S corporation income is $100,000 in 2003 and you perform services for the corporation reasonably worth $65,000, you will be taxed 15.3% on the $65,000 but not on the remaining $35,000.

By contrast, the rules for members of an LLC are more complicated, and, for now, somewhat unsettled. Proposed IRS regulations (which Congress has placed on hold) would impose the self-employment tax on your entire share of LLC profits in any of the following situations:

- You participate in the business for more than 500 hours during the LLC's tax year.
- You work in an LLC that provides professional services in the fields of health, law, engineering, architecture, accounting, actuarial science or consulting (no matter how many hours you work).
- You're empowered to sign contracts on behalf of your LLC.

Even though these proposed regulations do not have the force of law, the IRS says it won't challenge you if you use them in determining your liability for self-employment tax. This means that if you don't fall into one of the three categories listed above, you can use the same rules as apply to S corporation shareholders. But if you *do* fall into one of the above categories, you should assume that 100% of your income from the business will be subject to self-employment tax (although the amount that's over the current year's Social Security tax cut-off figure—$87,000 in 2003—will be subject only to Medicare tax).

The point is, that in some cases, an S corporation shareholder may pay less self-employment tax than some LLC members with similar income. You'll need to decide if these potential tax savings are more important than gaining such LLC advantages as flexibility in management structure and in distributing profits and losses.

F. Special Structures for Special Situations

It's very likely that the best organizational structure for your small business is either a sole proprietorship, partnership, corporation or LLC. (See Sections A, B, C and D, above.) There are, however, some situations in which other, less common entities will either offer some tax or other advantage or will be legally required. For instance, you and your tax advisor may decide that selecting a less common structure may be desirable for your business; for example, your real estate investment group may find some benefit in creating a limited partnership (described in Section 1, below). Or, you may find that the law in your state *requires* you to select a less common structure for your business; for example, if you're a doctor or an accountant and you want to limit your personal liability, state law may require you to form a professional corporation, a professional LLC or a limited liability partnership (all of which are described below in Section 2).

1. Limited Partnerships

The kind of partnership covered in Section B, above, is a *general* partnership. It's very different from another form of partnership known as a *limited* partnership, which, in certain circumstances, can combine the best attributes of a partnership and a corporation.

Most limited partnerships are formed to invest in real estate because of tax advantages for those who are passive investors; the passive investor is often able to personally write off depreciation and other real estate deductions. For the majority of other types of small businesses with more than one owner, chances are that forming either a general partnership, a corporation or an LLC will be the best way to go.

A limited partnership works like this. There must be one or more "general partners" with the same

basic rights and responsibilities as in any general partnership, and one or more "limited partners," who are usually passive investors. The big difference between a general partner and a limited partner is that the general partner *is* personally liable for the obligations of the partnership and the limited partner is *not* personally liable for them. The most a limited partner can lose by investing in a limited partnership is the amount that he or she:

- paid or agreed to pay into the partnership as a capital contribution; or
- received from the partnership after it became insolvent.

To maintain this limited liability, a limited partner may not participate in the management of the business, with a very few exceptions. A limited partner who does get actively involved in the management of the business risks losing immunity from personal liability, meaning he or she would have the same legal exposure as a general partner.

The advantage of a limited partnership as a business structure is that it provides a way for business owners to raise money from passive investors (the limited partners) without having either to take in new partners who will be active in the business or to engage in the intricacies of creating a corporation and issuing stock.

> **EXAMPLE:** Anthony and Janice's plan is to buy run-down houses, renovate them and then sell them at a good profit. All they lack is the cash to make the initial purchases. To solve this problem, they first create a partnership consisting of the two of them. Then they establish a limited partnership, with their own partnership as the general partner, and seek others who are willing to invest for a defined interest in the venture. Anthony and Janice figure that they need $100,000 to get started. They sell ten limited partnership interests at $10,000 each. The limited partners are given the right to a percentage of the profits for a specified number of

years, but they are not liable for any obligations of the partnership.

A general partnership that's been operating for years can also create a limited partnership to finance expansion.

EXAMPLE: Judith and Aretha have been partners in a small picture frame shop for two years. They want to expand into a bigger store in a much better location, where they can stock a large selection of fine art prints as well as frames. To raise money, they create a limited partnership, offering each investor an 8% interest in the total net profits of the store for the next three years as well as the return of the invested capital at the end of that period, in exchange for a $20,000 investment. They sell four limited partnership interests, raising $80,000.

There is a downside to limited partnerships: Doing business as a limited partnership can be at least as costly and complicated as doing business as a corporation. Although limited partnerships don't have to issue stock, state laws typically require that a limited partnership file registration information about the general and limited partners.

Watch out for confusing labels. *Despite the similarity in names, there are major differences between a limited partnership (discussed above) and a limited liability partnership (discussed below). To summarize:*

- *A limited partnership consists of at least one general partner and one or more limited partners. A general partner in a limited partnership is personally liable for all debts of and judgments against the business—regardless of who incurred the debt or other liability. A limited partner is generally not personally liable for any debts or judgments unless she actively participates in the business.*

- *A limited liability partnership (LLP) is a special form of general partnership and is usually reserved for professionals such as doctors, lawyers and accountants. Normally, a partner in an LLP isn't personally liable for the negligent acts of other partners but is liable for his or her own negligence and for other partnership debts.*

2. Choices for Professionals

If you are a professional, such as a doctor, lawyer or accountant, your choice of business structure may have to take into account certain additional factors. These include your need to avoid group liability, and state laws or rules of professional ethics governing your choices of business structure.

a. Professional corporations

Laws in every state permit certain professionals to form corporations known as "professional corporations" or "professional service corporations." In many states, people in certain occupations (for example, doctors, lawyers or accountants) who want to incorporate their practice can do so only through a professional corporation. In some states, some professionals have a choice of incorporating as either a professional corporation or a regular corporation (which can elect to be an S corporation).

The list of professionals eligible to incorporate is different in each state. Usually, though, professionals that must create a professional corporation include:

- accountants
- engineers
- healthcare professionals such as audiologists, dentists, nurses, opticians, optometrists, pharmacists, physical therapists, physicians and speech pathologists
- lawyers
- psychologists
- social workers
- veterinarians.

Call your state's corporate filing office (usually the Secretary of State or Corporation Commissioner) to see who is covered in your state.

Typically, a professional corporation must be organized for the sole purpose of rendering professional services and all shareholders must be licensed to render that service. For example, in a medical corporation, all of the shareholders must be licensed physicians.

Professional corporations aren't as popular as they used to be. The main reason for professionals to incorporate—favorable corporate taxation rules—has disappeared. Before 1986, professionals who incorporated could shelter more money from taxes than sole proprietors or partners could. This has all changed. Most professional corporations are now classified as "personal service corporations" by the IRS (see sidebar "Personal Service Corporations," below). Because the corporate income of personal service corporations is taxed at a flat rate of 35%, there's no longer any advantage to be gained by the two-tiered tax structure that allows ordinary corporations to save taxes on some retained earnings. Tax laws, however, still give favorable treatment to fringe benefits for corporate employees in professional corporations. (See Section C2b, above.)

Personal Service Corporations

Personal service corporations are defined under federal tax laws and have two basic characteristics:

- the professional employees of the corporation own the stock; and
- the corporation performs services in the fields of health, law, engineering, architecture, accounting, actuarial science, performing arts or consulting.

The other reason for professionals to consider incorporation is the limitation on personal liability. It's no secret that malpractice verdicts against professionals continue to climb. While incorporating can't protect a professional against liability for his or her negligence, it can protect against liability for the negligence of an associate.

EXAMPLE 1: Dr. Anton and Dr. Bartolo are surgeons who practice as partners. Dr. Bartolo leaves a medical instrument inside a patient, who bleeds to death. The jury returns a $2 million verdict against Dr. Bartolo and the partnership. There is only $1 million in malpractice insurance to cover the judgment. Dr. Anton (along with Dr. Bartolo) would be personally liable for the $1 million not covered by insurance.

EXAMPLE 2: Drs. Anton and Bartolo create a professional corporation. Dr. Bartolo commits the malpractice described in Example 1. Dr. Anton, a corporate employee, would not be personally liable for the portion of the verdict not covered by insurance. Dr. Bartolo, however, would still be personally responsible for the $1 million excess, because he was the one guilty of malpractice. (In some states, Dr. Anton would be free from personal liability only if the professional corporation carried at least the minimum amount of insurance mandated by state law.)

Insurance is a better alternative for most professionals than is the limited liability offered by incorporation. But with malpractice rates soaring for many professionals, it's often hard to afford all the insurance you could possibly need, so forming a professional corporation can be a useful back-up.

As an alternative to incorporating, professionals wishing to limit their personal liability should consider forming a professional limited liability company (PLLC) or limited liability partnership (LLP) as described below.

b. Professional limited liability companies

As explained above, licensed professionals are permitted to incorporate but, in most states, they can do so only by forming a special type of corporation—a professional corporation (PC). Similarly, in many states, licensed professionals who wish to form an LLC are required to use a special type of LLC known as a professional limited liability company (PLLC).

Lawyers or doctors in a group practice, for example, may find it advantageous to form a PC or PLLC so that each member of the group is legally liable for only his or her malpractice—not the malpractice of other members of the group, as would be the case in a partnership. Members of a PLLC also won't be personally liable for other business debts such as obligations owed to business creditors, lenders and the landlord.

Typically, state laws require that all members of a PLLC be licensed to practice the same profession—accounting, for example, or engineering.

Especially if the PLLC consists of lawyers, accountants, engineers, doctors or other healthcare professionals, state law may require that each member at least carry a specified amount of malpractice insurance or be bonded.

Check the law in your state before setting up a PLLC. *If you're a professional and considering the creation of a PLLC, you need to check your state's statute to learn which professionals can and can't form such an entity. There's wide variation from state to state. (For example, in California, many professionals, such as health professionals, therapists of any type and architects, cannot form any type of LLC.) If you're a member of a state professional society, its administrator may know the answer, or you can check the statute book at a nearby public library. (See Chapter 24 for information on doing legal research.)*

c. Limited liability partnerships

In a few states, laws or professional ethics rulings prevent accounting or law firms from doing business as corporations or LLCs. If you're an accountant or lawyer in such a state and would like some limitation on your personal liability for business obligations, look into forming a limited liability partnership (LLP). Unfortunately, the protection it offers is usually less than you'd get by forming a corporation or LLC—but it's better than nothing.

Available in some but not all states, a limited liability partnership is simply a general partnership whose partners enjoy some protection from personal liability. LLPs are authorized under state statutes and there's a bit of variation from state to state. Typically a partner in an LLP is personally liable only for his or her own negligence (malpractice) or that of an employee working directly under the partner's supervision; the partner isn't personally liable for the negligence of anyone else in the firm. That's helpful but, as a partner in an LLP, you're still personally liable for a large variety of partnership debts not involving your own negligent acts, for example, obligations owed to business creditors, lenders and the landlord—regardless of which partner incurred the obligation for the partnership.

EXAMPLE: Hillary, Edgar and Paula—all certified public accountants—want to form a new firm, but determine that ethics rules in their state prevent them from forming a professional corporation or PLLC. Instead, they form an LLP. Hillary, during a period of disarray in her personal life, messes up big time on a tax return for a major client, who has to pay huge penalties to the IRS. The client sues for malpractice and is awarded a $25,000 judgment. The LLP and Hillary are liable for paying the judgment. Edgar and Paula are not.

During the same period, Hillary also orders $15,000 worth of fancy office furniture, which the LLP can't afford. All three partners are personally liable for the furniture debt. (By contrast, if local ethics rules had allowed the three accountants to organize their accounting firm as a professional corporation or professional limited liability company and they had done so, none of them would be personally liable for the cost of the furniture unless they personally guaranteed payment.)

⚠️ **Check the law in your state before setting up an LLP.** *If you're a professional and considering the creation of an LLP, you need to check your state's statute to learn which professionals can and which can't form an LLP, because of the wide variation from state to state. (For example, only architects, accountants and lawyers can form LLPs in California, where LLPs are referred to as "registered limited liability partnerships," or RLLPs.) If you're a member of a state professional society, its administrator may know the answer, or you can check the statute book at a nearby public library. (See Chapter 24 for information on doing legal research.)*

3. Nonprofit Corporations

Each state permits people to form nonprofit corporations, also known as not-for-profit corporations. The main reason people form these corporations is to get tax-exempt status under the Internal Revenue Code (Section 501(c)(3)). To get tax-exempt status, the corporation must have been formed for religious, charitable, literary, scientific or educational purposes. If a corporation is tax-exempt under Section 501(c)(3), not only is it free from paying taxes on its income, but people and organizations who contribute to the nonprofit corporation can take a tax deduction for their contributions. Because many nonprofit organizations rely heavily on grants from public agencies and private foundations to fund their operations, attaining 501(c)(3) status is critical to success.

Tax-exempt status isn't the only benefit available to a nonprofit corporation. The nonprofit label seems to create an altruistic aura around the organization and the people running it. The message is, "We're not in this for the money—we really do love kids (or music or animals)." Also, an organization that plans to do some heavy mailing may be attracted by the cheaper postal rates that nonprofits are charged.

What kinds of groups should consider becoming nonprofit corporations? Here's a partial list:

- child care centers
- shelters for the homeless
- community healthcare clinics
- museums
- hospitals
- churches, synagogues, mosques and other places of worship
- schools
- performing arts groups
- conservation groups.

Most nonprofit corporations are run by a board of directors or trustees who are actively involved in the work of the corporation. Officers and employees (some of whom may also serve on the board) usually carry out the day-to-day business of the corporation and often receive salaries.

Keep in mind that if you put assets into a nonprofit corporation, you give up any ownership or proprietary interest in those assets. They must be irrevocably dedicated to the specified nonprofit purposes. If you want to get out of the business, you can't sell it and pocket the cash. If the nonprofit corporation does end, any remaining assets must go to another nonprofit.

📖 *This book is addressed primarily to people starting and running a business for profit, so you'll find little here on the peculiarities of nonprofit corporations. If you want to learn about such corporations in greater depth, see* How to Form Your Own Nonprofit Corporation, *by Anthony Mancuso (Nolo). That book provides step-by-step instructions for forming a nonprofit corporation in all states.*

4. Cooperatives and Cooperative-Type Organizations

Some people dream of forming a business of true equals—an organization owned and controlled democratically by its members.

These grassroots business organizers often refer to their businesses as a group, collective or co-op—but these are usually informal rather than legal labels. Everyone who starts a business with others needs to select a legal structure. Generally, this means picking one of the traditional formats described in this chapter: a nonprofit corporation, a partnership, a regular corporation or an LLC. However, some states do have specific laws allowing the formation of a "cooperative corporation." For example, in some states, a consumer "co-op" could be created to manufacture and sell arts and crafts.

If a co-op law exists in your state, it can help make the process of democratic ownership go more smoothly. Otherwise, you'll need to make sure your partnership agreement, corporate bylaws or LLC operating agreement contains the cooperative features that you and the other members feel are appropriate.

 To learn more about cooperative-type organizations and how to start one, I recommend that you visit the website of the National Cooperative Business Association at www.ncba.org. You can order many helpful publications there. Another fine resource is Co-op Incorporation Sourcebook *(Center for Cooperatives, University of California at Davis). It reviews business feasibility and legal requirements for starting a nonagricultural cooperative in California.* ■

Structuring a Partnership Agreement

There are two kinds of partnership: the general partnership and the limited partnership. This chapter discusses forming the more common kind, general partnerships. See Chapter 1, Section F1, for basic information about limited partnerships.

A. Why You Need a Written Agreement

When you form a partnership to run a small business, your partners will probably be family members, close friends or business associates. You may think it's unnecessary to sign a document with people you know quite well. Experience proves otherwise. No matter how rosy things are at the beginning, every partnership inevitably faces problems over the years. A well-thought-out written agree-

ment will help you preserve the business, as well as your friendships.

You can, however, have a legally valid partnership even without a written partnership agreement. If you don't sign an agreement, the laws of your state will dictate how the partnership is run. That isn't all bad. Every state except Louisiana has adopted either the Uniform Partnership Act (UPA) or the Revised Uniform Partnership Act (RUPA). States have sometimes made slight variations in these laws but there is still a remarkable amount of consistency from state to state. These laws solve many common partnership problems in a sensible way. For example, the UPA says that if you don't have an agreement, each partner shares equally in the profits and has an equal voice in management of the business. The UPA goes on to say that partners are not entitled to receive compensation for services they provide to the partnership.

While it's conceivable that the provisions of the UPA are exactly what you and your partners want, partners usually prefer to modify at least some of them. For example, if one partner contributes far more assets than others, that partner may deserve a greater share of the profits. Or you may want to allow one or more partners to receive a salary for their services. Or you may not want each partner to have an equal voice in running the business. Similarly, you may want to include customized provisions on how to value a partner's interest in the business if a partner dies or leaves. In that situation, many partners want to assign some value to the goodwill of the business for tax purposes—something that does not happen automatically under the UPA. With a written partnership agreement, you can tailor your partnership to fit your needs.

There are other benefits to working out the details in a written partnership agreement. You'll focus on issues you might not have thought of—issues about which you and your partners may have different opinions. For example, what if one partner wants special compensation above and beyond her share of the profits if she frequently works evenings or weekends on partnership business? By getting issues out into the open early, you can nip problems in the bud.

Most Partnership Information Is Confidential

The terms of a partnership agreement for a general partnership don't have to be made public. But, in some states, you must file a certificate of partnership, stating the names of the partners, with a county official (such as the county clerk) or state official (such as the secretary of state). (See Chapter 6, Section B3.)

B. An Overview of Your Partnership Agreement

It's up to you and your partners to decide what shape the partnership will take. A lawyer can help you focus on issues and suggest possible solutions, but you and your partners—not the lawyer—must make the basic choices.

This section goes through the clauses that are usually included in a partnership agreement for a small business.

Chapter 2 of Legal Forms for Starting & Running a Small Business *contains a sample partnership agreement.*

Where to Find Help With Partnership Agreements

The Partnership Book, by Denis Clifford & Ralph Warner (Nolo). It's the source of the clauses in this chapter, and contains extensive additional material on forming, managing and ending a partnership.

1. Name and Term

Although many partnerships do business using the last names of the partners, it's both legal and common for a partnership to have one name and to do business under another name. For example, the partnership of Jones, Gold and Sanchez could decide to do business as Seafood Express. The name Seafood Express would be an assumed name, or fictitious name, which you'd have to register with the appropriate state or county office.

 Chapter 6 contains a thorough discussion of business and product names.

Another issue is how long the partnership will last. If you want it to go on indefinitely, include a clause in your partnership agreement like this:

> The partnership shall last until it is dissolved by all the partners or a partner leaves, for any reason, including death.

On the other hand, if you plan to develop a particular piece of real estate or do some other finite task, you might want a clause with a definite date, such as one of the following:

> The partnership shall commence as of the date of this agreement and shall continue for a period of _____ years, at which time it shall be dissolved and its affairs wound up.

> or

> The partnership shall continue until _____ [specify an event such as "the completion and sale of The Commercial Office Plaza"], at which time the partnership shall be dissolved and its affairs wound up.

2. Purpose

The purpose of the partnership should be broadly stated in plain English. The advantage of a broad statement of partnership purposes is that you have flexibility if the business evolves. Here are two typical purpose clauses:

> The purpose of the partnership is to operate one or more stores for the sale of records, tapes, compact discs or other related merchandise.

> or

> The purpose of the partnership is to operate a bookkeeping and tax preparation service for individual clients and small businesses.

On the other hand, if you're sure you're creating your partnership for a short-term, specific purpose, such as presenting one trade show, it would be appropriate to use a more limited purpose clause, such as this one:

> The purpose of the partnership is to organize and present this year's Builders and Home Improvement Show at the Municipal Convention Center.

3. Contributions

Your partnership agreement should describe the initial contributions that you and your partners will make. Often, each partner contributes cash only. The amounts of contributions may be equal, but don't have to be. For example, one partner might contribute $5,000 while another contributes $1,000 and a third contributes a pickup truck. If a partner contributes property such as a vehicle, tools, a building, a patent or a copyright, you need to agree on the value of that property. You can also provide that one of the partners will contribute personal ser-

vices (perhaps painting the business headquarters) in return for a partnership interest. Keep in mind that a partner can sell, lend, lease or rent property to the partnership too.

a. Cash contributions

It's logically neat if each partner contributes an equal amount of cash to a new business. Otherwise, partners who invest more money than the others may feel entitled to a larger voice in making partnership decisions. But in the real world, not all partners are always able to make equal contributions of cash. One way to handle this is to have the partner who contributes more lend the extra amount to the business rather than contribute it outright.

> **EXAMPLE:** Ricardo and Alberta are opening a martial arts training center. Ricardo has just left a job at a corporation and received a handsome severance package. He's willing to put $40,000 into the business. Alberta, on the other hand, is a single mother who wants to start a business precisely because she is short of money. She can raise $10,000. Alberta could contribute $10,000 and Ricardo $40,000, with Ricardo having more say in partnership decisions than Alberta. But an easier and more democratic approach would be for each to contribute $10,000 in cash, with Ricardo lending the partnership the additional $30,000, to be repaid over three years at 10% annual interest.

A basic clause for equal cash contributions reads as follows:

> The initial capital of the partnership shall be a total of $_____. Each partner shall contribute an equal share amounting to $_____ no later than _____, 20____. Each partner shall own an equal share of the business.

If a partner can't initially contribute the desired amount of cash, another way to handle this problem is to agree that he or she will make payments over time. Here's a sample clause.

> Arthur Feldman shall be a partner upon making an initial contribution of $1,000 to the capital of the partnership. He will subsequently contribute to the partnership capital, and his capital account shall be credited, in the amount of $100 per month beginning July 1, 20__, until he has contributed the sum of $5,000 (including the initial $1,000 payment).

Interest on Partnership Investment: Should partners receive interest on their contributions of capital? Generally, no—after all, the money is already at work building a jointly owned business. But either way you decide this issue, cover it with a specific clause in the partnership agreement.

b. Contributions of services

Sometimes, a partner's contribution consists wholly or in part of services. In the above example concerning Alberta's contribution to the martial arts training center, another way to handle the disparity in available cash would be for Alberta to agree to work a certain number of hours more than Ricardo at a fixed rate (say $20 per hour) until the contributions were equalized. After that, the partners would work an equal amount of hours each week. If a partner is going to contribute services in return for an interest in the business, this should be spelled out in the partnership agreement.

EXAMPLE: Margaret and Alice form a 50/50 partnership for catering parties. Each will spend equal time on preparing the food and delivering it. Margaret contributes $10,000 to get the business going. Alice agrees to contribute unpaid labor as a bookkeeper and business manager for one year over and above the amount of time she spends on food-related work. Their intention is to equalize the contributions of the partners.

c. Contributions of property

Some or all of the partners may contribute property as well as, or instead of, cash. A clause covering this possibility might look like this:

> _____ shall contribute property valued at $_____ consisting of _____ _____ by _____, 20____. [If the property is difficult to describe, describe it in detail on a separate sheet of paper marked "Exhibit A" and add here, "and more particularly described in Exhibit A, attached to this agreement."]

Getting expert help. *If you're transferring property to your partnership, you may need the assistance of a tax expert. Such contributions raise questions about what tax basis (value) will be assigned to the property being transferred. The IRS looks at tax basis in determining how much profit you've gained when the property is later transferred or sold as well as the amount of losses you can claim on your tax return if the business is not profitable. These tax details are beyond the scope of this book.*

4. Profits, Losses, Draws and Salaries

How will partners be compensated? The first issue is how you'll divide profits once a year or at the end of some other fixed period. You should also determine if any partners can receive an early draw against their share of the profits—that is, be paid a portion of profits sooner than other partners. This might be appropriate if one partner is coming into the partnership with less savings than the others and is counting on partnership income for living expenses.

You'll also need to decide if any partners will receive a salary for work done in the business in addition to draws on their share of profits. If equal partners will all work a roughly equal number of hours, there's no need to pay salaries; an equal division of profits with or without a draw should be adequate. But if one partner will work more hours than the others, paying that partner a salary may be sensible. Or you could give the harder-working partner a larger share of the profits. If salaries are paid, they're a normal business expense and don't come out of profits.

If profits are shared equally, the following clause would be appropriate:

> The partners will share all profits equally, and they will be distributed [monthly, yearly, etc.]. All losses of the partnership will also be shared equally.

On the other hand, if profits and losses will be shared unequally, here are some sample clauses to consider:

> Partnership profits and losses will be shared among the partners as follows:
>
> | Name | Percentage |
> |------|------------|
> | _____ | _____ |
> | _____ | _____ |
> | _____ | _____ |
> | _____ | _____ |
>
> or
>
> Partnership profits and losses shall be shared among the partners as follows:
>
> | Name | % of Profits | % of Losses |
> |------|------------|-----------|
> | _____ | _____ | _____ |
> | _____ | _____ | _____ |
> | _____ | _____ | _____ |

> or
>
> Partnership profits and losses shall be shared by the partners in the same proportion as their contributions of capital bear to each other.

A draw is an advance of anticipated profits paid to a partner or partners. It's easiest if draws are to be made by all partners. But if you want to authorize draws for only certain partners, a clause like the following is appropriate:

> Partners _____ and _____ are entitled to draws from expected partnership profits. The amount of each draw will be determined by a vote of the partners. The draws shall be [monthly or on any other kind of schedule that you agree to].

You may also want to provide for the partnership to retain some profits in the business for new equipment, expansion or employee bonuses. Here's a sample clause:

> In determining the amount of profits available for distribution, allowance will be made for the fact that some money must remain undistributed and available as working capital as determined by [for example, "all partners" or "a majority of partners"].

Even though profits are reinvested, you and the other partners are taxed on your shares of them at your individual rates. (Chapter 1, Section C2b, discusses how a regular corporation may afford tax advantages over a partnership when a business has retained earnings.)

The Authority of Partners

Do you want each partner to be able to make decisions that bind the partnership in the normal operation of its business? Or do you want some limitations—for example, that large contracts or purchases must be approved in advance by a majority of the partners? You can address this issue in your partnership agreement. But remember that while a limitation on a partner's authority is binding among the partners themselves, it doesn't necessarily limit liability to outsiders who deal with the partner.

EXAMPLE: Peggy, Roger and Lisa run a bookkeeping and billing service for several doctors, dentists and clinics. Peggy, who is a computer whiz, believes that there's no such thing as too much electronic equipment. So in the partnership agreement, a clause provides that any purchase of equipment requires the approval of at least two of the partners. Peggy buys three notebook computers, two laser printers and assorted modems and fax machines for the partnership, without approval. The partnership and each partner are liable for the $12,000 bill, even though the partners limited liability among themselves. When Peggy purchased the equipment, the computer store didn't know what was in the partnership agreement—the usual case. And Peggy appeared to have authority to bind the partnership. The other partners, however, will have a legal claim against Peggy because she exceeded her authority under the partnership agreement.

LAW IN THE REAL WORLD
A Profitable Experience

Jan and Mike discussed forming a partnership to open a desktop publishing service aimed at helping small businesses design brochures, flyers and other promotional material. The idea of sharing the work and profits 50-50 appealed to both of them. There was only one major hangup: The partnership agreement form they looked at provided for profits to be divided at the end of the year. This was okay with Mike, who had received a generous severance package from a former job, but not for Jan, who was trying to put her daughter through college and had no financial cushion.

Recognizing their different circumstances, Jan and Mike agreed Jan would be allowed to take a monthly draw against her share of anticipated partnership profits of $3,000. And because they realized a new business needs all the cash it can get its hands on, Mike would wait and take the same amount at the end of the year. Then Mike and Jan would split any additional profits.

To guard against the possibility that Jan's draw would use up more than half of the profits and shortchange Mike, the partners, after checking the tax consequences with their tax advisor, also agreed that any amount Jan received over her 50% share would be considered a personal loan from the partnership, to be repaid out of her share of future years' profits.

5. Management Responsibilities

It's wise to pin down the basic way you'll operate the business. Commonly, in small business partnerships, all partners are involved in management and supervision, justifying a clause like the following:

> All partners shall be actively involved and materially participate in the management of operation of the partnership business.

You can go further if you want every partner to have a veto power:

> All partnership decisions must be made by the unanimous agreement of all partners.

Some small business partnerships distinguish between major and minor decisions, allowing a single partner to make a minor decision but requiring unanimity for major ones. If you decide to go down this road, you have to figure out how to define a major decision. The distinction between major and minor decisions—especially purchases or the undertaking of obligations—is often based on a dollar amount. A clause like this one would be appropriate:

> All major decisions of the partnership business must be made by a unanimous decision of all partners. Minor business decisions may be made by an individual partner. Major decisions are defined as all purchases and contracts over $5,000 [or other definition of major decisions].

If you want to provide for unequal management powers, here are some clauses to consider:

> Each partner shall participate in the management of the business. In exercising the powers of management, each partner's vote shall be in proportion to his or her interest in the partnership's capital.

> or

> In the management, control and direction of the business, the partners shall have the following percentages of voting power:
>
> Name   Percentage
>
> _____   _____
>
> _____   _____
>
> _____   _____
>
> _____   _____

If the partners are going to contribute different types of skills, you may also want to state that in your partnership agreement. And while it may seem unnecessary to list the hours to be worked, you may avoid possible problems through a clause such as the following:

> Except for vacations, holidays and times of illness, each partner will work _____ hours per week on partnership business.

Consider a clause on leaves of absence or sabbaticals. How much time off is allowed? And what happens to a partner's right to receive pay or profits while on leave?

Other financial matters to be dealt with in the partnership agreement may include the following:

- May partners borrow money on behalf of the partnership? Is there a dollar limit on how much a partner can borrow on behalf of the partnership without the prior consent of all partners?
- Are expense accounts authorized? If so, is there a limit on the amount?
- How many signatures are required on partnership checks and to withdraw money from the partnership bank account?
- How many weeks of paid or unpaid vacation each year are partners entitled to?

6. Partners' Outside Business Activities

A key partnership question is whether or not any partner can engage in outside business. In some instances, they must, at least at first, because the partnership business income isn't enough to live on. If a partner can engage in outside business, what types are permitted? You wouldn't want a partner to directly compete with the partnership. That would be a conflict of interest. But how do you define direct competition? If the partners are running a restaurant, can one of the partners own a catering business? Or work in a delicatessen? There are at least four different approaches to this issue. You can:

- Allow partners to engage in one or more other businesses except for those that directly compete with the partnership business.
- Allow partners to engage in other businesses without any other restrictions.
- List permitted activities.
- Prohibit partners from participating in any other business.

Here's an example of the first approach:

> Any partner may engage in one or more other businesses as well as the business of the partnership, but only to the extent that this activity does not directly and materially interfere with the business of the partnership and does not conflict with the time commitments or other obligations of that partner to the partnership under this agreement. Neither the partnership nor any other partner shall have any right to any income or profit derived by a partner from any outside business activity permitted under this section.

LAW IN THE REAL WORLD
Outside Interests

When Ted M. and Ted Y. formed a partnership and opened a bookstore (yup, they called it Two Teds), they didn't expect to make much, if any, money right away. According to their business plan, it would take two to three years for the store to be solidly profitable. In the meantime, both men would have to hold down second jobs. This led to a serious problem. Both men already worked in the book business (Ted M. managed a secondhand book shop, and Ted Y. was a sales rep for a large publisher) and wanted to avoid any hint of a conflict of interest between their personal and partnership interests.

Ted Y. explained his store plans to the publisher he worked for, who agreed to reduce his sales territory and let him work three days per week. (Ted Y. also promised to work 30 hours at Two Teds.) Because selling books to stores and selling them to the public aren't competitive operations, it was easy for the Teds to agree in writing as part of their partnership agreement that Ted Y.'s job didn't amount to a conflict of interest with the partnership.

Ted M.'s situation was tougher. No matter how much they thought about it, managing one store while owning part of another in the same city reeked of possible conflicts of interest. To solve this, it was decided that Ted M. would quit managing the other store. Initially, at least, he would work 55 hours per week at Two Teds and be paid a reasonable salary for the 25 hours per week he worked more than Ted Y.

7. Departure of a Partner—Buyouts

Now we're getting into one of the most essential—but complicated—areas of a partnership agreement: what you'll do if one of the partners voluntarily leaves, becomes disabled or dies. These things are not easy to think about when you're caught up in the excitement of starting a new business. Still, it's risky to postpone facing them. Sooner or later the partnership will change and fundamental issues will come up. A partner may want to leave for any number of reasons—such as to start another business or to move to another part of the country. Or maybe a partner will retire or die. Can the departing partner sell his or her interest? Do the remaining partners or partner have the right to buy it? How is the purchase price determined?

If one partner quits or dies, most partnership agreements very sensibly require a departing partner to give the remaining partners the chance to buy out his or her share and continue the business before selling or transferring it to outsiders. Here's a sample "right of first refusal" clause designed to accomplish this:

> If any partner leaves the partnership, for whatever reason, whether he or she quits, withdraws, is expelled, retires or dies, or becomes mentally or physically incapacitated or unable to fully function as a partner, he or she, or (in the case of a deceased partner) his or her estate, shall be obligated to sell his or her interest in the partnership to the remaining partners, who may buy that interest under the terms and conditions set forth in this agreement.

This option protects the remaining partners. But what if the departing partner has found a buyer who is willing to pay a hefty price for that partnership interest? Some partnerships don't compel a departing partner to take a lower price (as predetermined in the partnership agreement) than he or she would get from a bona fide outside buyer; their partnership agreements provide that the existing partners must pay the market price for the departing partner's share. Either way you resolve this issue, you should spell out your solution in the partnership agreement.

Here's a different approach:

> If the remaining partners do not purchase the departing partner's share of the business under the terms provided in this agreement within _____ days after the departing partner leaves, the entire business of the partnership shall be put up for sale and listed with an appropriate sales agent or broker.

a. Valuing a partner's share

One major issue in a buy-out clause is how you'll set the worth of the business—and the value of a partner's share. Let's look at some specific valuation methods.

The *asset valuation method* is based on the current net worth of the business (assets minus liabilities). As of the date the departing partner leaves, the net worth of all partnership assets is calculated and all outstanding business debts are deducted to determine net worth. Because goodwill isn't a tangible asset, it's not counted. The departing partner receives his or her ownership percentage of this amount, under whatever pay-out terms you agreed on.

The *book valuation method* is a variation of the asset valuation method. You calculate the value of all partnership assets and liabilities as they're set forth in the partnership accounting books, which basically means the acquisition cost. Because book value doesn't cover goodwill, in a successful business it has little relation to what the business is really worth. Furthermore, the acquisition cost of property is unlikely to be its current worth.

The *set-dollar method* involves an agreement by the partners in advance that if one partner departs from the partnership, the others will buy out his or her share for a pre-established price. Before adopting this method, be aware that the price selected may be arbitrary. Even if accurate for the present time, the worth of the business may fluctuate, making a predetermined value out-of-date. You might consider having the partners unanimously establish a value in writing for the partnership each year.

A *post-departure appraisal* means that you agree to have an independent appraiser determine the worth of the partnership when a partner departs. It sounds good in principle, but because many small businesses aren't amenable to precise valuation, even in the hands of an expert appraiser, it can lead to bitter arguments later.

The *capitalization of earnings method* determines what the business is worth based on what it earns. Unless there's an open market to set a price, the best estimate of what a business is worth often depends on its earning capacity. This method works best with a business that's been around for several years. First you need to measure the earnings of the business for a year or more. Then you must agree on a multiplier (often two to five) which, in effect, takes into consideration the fact that a buyer hopes to reap profits in future years. Finally, you multiply the earnings by your multiplier to arrive at a value. But how do you establish the multiplier? Often one is already loosely established in a particular industry. A consultant or trade magazine may tell you that profitable dry cleaning businesses are often sold on the basis of multiplying profits by a certain number. Be aware that this sort of information is at best an estimate which can change by industry, individual business and year. If you decide to use this method of valuing your business, you'll need expert advice.

You may want to have a different buyout price depending on when or why a partner departs. For example, a partner who leaves during the initial stages of a business (say, the first one or two years) may only be entitled to the balance in his or her capital account. After that initial period, the departing partner's interest could be calculated by a method that more accurately reflects the actual operation and success of the business.

You could also have varying formulas depending on why the partner leaves. For example, there might be one formula if the partner becomes disabled, retires over age 65 or dies, and another formula if the partner leaves under other circumstances.

b. Payments to departing partners

Your partnership agreement should provide for a payment schedule if there's a buyout. Otherwise, the departing partner would have the right to collect for the full value of his or her interest promptly. This could become a serious problem if a partner dies, since the deceased partner's family would likely insist on exercising this right.

Your decision on payment terms has a close relationship to the method you use for determining the buyout price. If the remaining partners can pay the price over a number of years, they're usually willing to pay a higher buyout price than if they must pay all the cash the day a partner leaves.

One of the best ways to finance the buyout of a partner's interest is through insurance. If a partner dies, the proceeds from the partnership-financed insurance policy are used to pay off his or her share, and partnership operating income doesn't have to be used. Many profitable partnerships buy insurance against each partner's serious illness, incapacity or death. This can be a sensible way of obtaining money to pay off a deceased partner's interest; a term policy, which is relatively cheap, is especially good.

8. Continuity of the Partnership

If a partnership has more than two members, the remaining partners usually want to continue the business as a partnership when a partner leaves. Here's a clause that you can use to assure the continuation of a partnership:

> In the case of a partner's death, permanent disability, retirement, voluntary withdrawal or expulsion from a partnership, the partnership shall not dissolve or terminate, but its business shall continue without interruption and without any break in continuity. On the disability, retirement, withdrawal, expulsion or death of any partner, the others shall not liquidate or wind up the affairs of the partnership, but shall continue to conduct the partnership under the terms of this agreement.

9. Noncompetition of Departing Partner

Another issue relating to a partner who leaves the partnership is future competition. You may want to prohibit the departing partner from competing against your firm. This may include the protection of your trade secrets and customer lists.

Legally, this is a touchy area. Forbidding a partner from engaging in his or her usual way of earning a living is a drastic act, and courts often refuse to enforce unfairly restrictive terms. To be legal, a noncompetition agreement normally must be reasonably limited in both time and geographical area and be otherwise fair. State laws vary in regard to noncompetition clauses, and it's not always possible to tell whether or not a judge will enforce one. If you're determined to include a noncompetition clause in your agreement, it makes sense to see a lawyer familiar with small business concerns.

This sample clause will give you an idea of how these clauses are often drafted:

> On the voluntary withdrawal, permanent disability, retirement or expulsion of any

> partner, that partner shall not carry on a business the same as or similar to the business of the partnership within the [describe area] for a period of [time period you've agreed on].

10. Control of Partnership Name

A business name can be valuable. The partnership agreement should spell out what happens to it if a partner leaves. There are a number of ways to handle this, including a clause stating that the partnership continues to own the name, that one partner owns the name, that control of the name will be decided on at a later date or, finally, that in the event of dissolution, the partnership business name will be owned by a majority of the former partners.

11. Resolving Partnership Disputes

Suppose there's a serious disagreement between the partners and you can't resolve it by personal discussions and negotiations. You may find yourself in court, which is a costly, time-consuming and emotionally draining way to deal with the dispute. Fortunately, there's a way around litigation as a means of resolving disputes. You can provide in your partnership agreement for mediation or arbitration or both. These subjects are treated in more depth in Chapter 22. Please read that discussion if you're not fully familiar with these methods.

Here's an example of a mediation clause:

> Any dispute arising out of this agreement or the partnership business will be resolved by mediation, if possible. The partners pledge to cooperate fully and fairly with the mediator in an attempt to reach a mutually satisfactory compromise to a dispute. The mediator will be _____. If any partner to a dispute feels it cannot be resolved by the

partners themselves, he or she shall so notify the other partners and the mediator in writing. Mediation will commence within _____ days of the Notice of Request for Mediation. The cost of mediation will be shared equally by all partners to the dispute.

To protect yourselves should mediation fail, you can follow up with an arbitration clause that takes over if a dispute can't be mediated to the satisfaction of the parties. The partners are bound by the arbitrator's decision, which can be enforced in court.

 See Chapter 22, Sections B and C, for additional mediation and arbitration clauses.

If you include both mediation and arbitration clauses in your partnership agreement, you need to decide whether the mediator and arbitrator should be the same person. If you have the same person playing both roles, you don't run the risk of having to present the case twice—first to the mediator and then, if mediation fails, to the arbitrator. On the other hand, the person who has ultimate power to make a decision as an arbitrator may be less effective as a mediator.

C. Changes in Your Partnership

As your business changes, your partnership agreement will have to change, too. For example, the addition of a new partner requires revision of at least the clauses listing the partners' names and those covering contributions and distribution of profits. Even if you admit no new partners, the growth of your business may require you to change your agreement. You and your partners may decide to run your expanded business differently than the original business. Or maybe more cash is required, and the partners decide that their contributions should be in proportions different from those originally agreed to. Any time you make a significant change in the structure or operation of your business, you should change the partnership agreement to reflect it.

The owners of most small partnerships specify that the partnership agreement may be amended only by the written consent of all partners. But you can create any amendment clause you choose. For example, you could specify that the agreement can be amended by vote of 51% of the partners or by 51% of the capital accounts.

At some point, your partnership may well decide to add another partner. You may need a new partner's contribution of cash or skills, or you may want to retain a key employee by making him or her a partner. Because a partnership technically is dissolved when a new partner joins it, it's helpful to include a clause in your partnership agreement such as the following one:

> Admission of a new partner shall not cause dissolution of the underlying partnership business, which will be continued by the new partnership entity. ■

3

Creating a Corporation

Chapter 1 introduced the basic business entities—the sole proprietorship, the partnership, the limited liability company and the corporation. This chapter tells you more about setting up a corporation. We'll start with the structure of a corporation, including the roles of the key players: the incorporators, shareholders, directors, officers and employees. Then we'll look at corporate finance—how you get money into the corporation and how you take it out. Next we'll walk step by step through the procedures for setting up a corporation. Finally, we'll examine some sound corporate business practices.

The material in this chapter applies to most, but not all, new corporations. Generally, this material will apply to you if your proposed corporation fits the following profile:

- A relatively small number of people—about ten or fewer—will own the corporate stock.
- All or most of the owners will participate directly in managing and running the business; investors who don't directly participate will generally be limited to friends or family members.
- All of the owners will live in the state in which you form your corporation and conduct your business.

Lawyers often call a small corporation that fits this profile a "closely held corporation." We'll borrow this term in its most general, nontechnical sense.

Classifying your corporation at the outset is important because if you're a closely held corporation and sell stock only to a few friends or family members, normally you'll be exempt from all but the most routine requirements of federal and state securities laws.

But if you sell stock in your corporation to outside investors—people who won't help run the business or aren't closely tied to people who are—you must comply with those laws. So if you want to sell stock to a wider range of people, especially if any of them live in a different state, you'll need to learn more about the requirements of the securities laws. In many states, there are generous exemptions

that allow sales of stock to as many as 35 investors without complicated paperwork. But because this is such a technical area and laws vary from state to state, you should seek legal advice from a lawyer knowledgeable about securities laws before you offer stock to outsiders.

A. The Structure of a Corporation

Corporations are controlled primarily by state, not federal, law. This means that 50 different sets of rules cover how corporations are created. Terminology differs from state to state. For example, most states use the term "articles of incorporation" to refer to the basic document creating the corporation, but some states (including Connecticut, Delaware, New Jersey, New York and Oklahoma) use the term "certificate of incorporation." Tennessee calls it a "charter," and Massachusetts uses the term "articles of organization." Fortunately, the similarities in corporate procedure outweigh the differences, so most of what you find in this chapter will apply to your own situation. Nevertheless, watch out for the differences.

People involved in a corporation traditionally play different legal roles: incorporator, shareholder, director, officer, employee. We'll look at those roles here. But, in virtually every state, there's a way that you can set up a corporation in which one or two people play all roles.

LAW IN THE REAL WORLD
Keeping a Hand in the Business

Anne opened a small business providing customized bookkeeping software for manicurists. For several years she struggled financially as she tried to convince small nail shops that buying her computerized system would ultimately be far cheaper than keeping records in a shoe box. Finally, when a trade magazine gave her system a rave review, business took off. Suddenly Anne found herself hiring employees, upgrading and customizing her software and greatly increasing her marketing activities.

It quickly became apparent to Anne that she couldn't do it all herself. Her key employees were increasingly critical to her success. To help ensure their loyalty and hard work, Anne realized it would be wise to give them an ownership interest in the business. She accomplished this by forming a closely held corporation, Digital Nail Inc. Initially Anne owned 100% of the stock, but under the terms of a shareholders' agreement, half a dozen or so key employees receive stock each year.

Although Anne will always remain the majority owner, over time, each longtime employee will gain a significant share. If an employee leaves the company, his or her stock will have to be sold back to Digital Nail at its book (asset) value—considerably less than its market value (assuming the business continued to prosper and was sold or went public). In short, not only does Anne's plan give key employees a stake in the success of the company, it provides a powerful incentive for them to stick with Digital Nail.

1. Incorporators

The incorporators (called the promoters in some states) do the preparatory work. This may include bringing together the people and the money to create the corporation. It always includes preparing and filing the articles of incorporation—the formal incorporation document that is filed with a state office such as the secretary of state. Although several people can serve as incorporators and sign the articles of incorporation, only one incorporator is required by law. Once the articles of incorporation are filed, the incorporator's job is nearly done. The only things that remain to be done are to select the first board of directors and to adopt the corporate bylaws (although, in some states, bylaws may be adopted by the directors).

2. Shareholders

The shareholders own the stock of the corporation. One person can own 100% of the stock. Among the things that only shareholders can do are these:

- Elect directors (although the initial board of directors is usually selected by the incorporator or promoter)
- Amend bylaws
- Approve the sale of all or substantially all of the corporate assets
- Approve mergers and reorganizations
- Amend the articles of incorporation
- Remove directors
- Dissolve the corporation.

State laws typically require that the shareholders hold an annual meeting. However, in many states, a "consent action" or "consent resolution"—a document signed by all of the shareholders—can be used in place of a formal meeting.

For the corporation to elect S corporation status under federal tax laws, all shareholders must sign the election form that's filed with the IRS. (For more on this, see Section F, Step 12.)

3. Directors

The directors manage the corporation and make major policy decisions. Among other things, the directors authorize the issuance of stock; decide on whether to mortgage, sell or lease real estate; and elect the corporate officers. Directors may hold regular or special meetings (or both). However, in many states, it's simpler and just as effective for the directors to take actions by signing a document called a "consent resolution" or "consent action."

The incorporators or shareholders decide how many directors the corporation will have. The number of directors is usually stated in the articles of incorporation or in the corporate bylaws. Most states specifically permit corporations to have just one director. In the remaining states, the requirement is that there be at least three directors, but there's an exception for corporations with fewer than three shareholders. If there are only two shareholders, the corporation can operate with two directors; if there's only one shareholder, the corporation needs only one director.

> **EXAMPLE 1:** Anita, Barry and Clint create a corporation in Michigan. They choose Anita to be the sole director. They can do this because the law in Michigan—as in many other states—permits a corporation to function with a single director regardless of the number of shareholders.

> **EXAMPLE 2:** Dustin, Erwin and Faye create a corporation in California. They would like Dustin to be the sole director, but California

law requires them to have at least three directors if there are three or more shareholders; they can have a single director only if the corporation has a single shareholder. Therefore, Dustin, Erwin and Faye create a three-person board of directors and appoint themselves to those positions.

4. Officers

The officers are normally responsible for the day-to-day operation of the corporation. State laws usually require that the corporation have at least a president, a secretary and a treasurer. The president is usually the chief operating officer of the corporation. The secretary is responsible for the corporate records. The treasurer, of course, is responsible for the corporate finances, although it's common to hand day-to-day duties to a bookkeeper. The corporation can have other officers—such as a vice-president—as well. In most states, one person can hold all of the required offices.

> **EXAMPLE:** Abdul forms a Texas corporation. He provides for the two corporate offices—president and secretary—that are required by Texas law. He appoints himself to both offices. This is legal in Texas and in most other states.

5. Employees

Employees work for the corporation in return for compensation. In the small corporations we're considering in this chapter, the owners (shareholders) are usually also employees of the corporation. It's through your salary and other compensation as a corporate employee that you'll receive most of your financial benefits from the business. Often the person who runs the business day-to-day gets the most compensation. This may or may not be the president.

6. How It All Fits Together

If you're new to all of this, the numerous components of a corporation may seem unduly complicated for a small business. Fortunately, it all fits together quite smoothly and easily.

> EXAMPLE: Al, Bev and Carla decide to form a corporation to run a fitness center. Their plan is to invest $10,000 apiece and be equal owners. Since state law requires only one person to sign the papers setting up the corporation, Bev signs the Articles of Incorporation for ABC Fitness Center Inc. and sends them to the Secretary of State's office along with the filing fee. Bev is the *incorporator*.
>
> Next, Bev adopts bylaws for the corporation calling for a three-person Board of Directors. She elects herself, Al and Carla to serve as the first *directors*. The three of them then elect Bev to be the president, Al to be the secretary and Carla to be the treasurer—so the three of them are then the *officers* of the corporation.
>
> When Al, Bev and Carla each pay $10,000 into the corporate bank account, they each receive a stock certificate for 10,000 shares of corporate stock; at that moment, they become shareholders.
>
> All three are active in running the business, working 50 hours a week and receiving a salary. Al and Bev, who have experience as personal trainers, take charge of training customers and supervising a small staff of other workers. Carla, who studied business in college, looks after the finances—billing customers, marketing, ordering supplies. So in addition to their other roles in the corporation, Al, Bev and Carla are employees.

B. Financing Your Corporation

It doesn't take an MBA degree to grasp the fundamentals of corporate finance in the typical small business. Assets come into the corporation in two forms: equity and debt. Let's look at each.

1. Funding Your Corporation With Equity

Basically, equity means shareholders contribute cash, valuable property or services to the company in exchange for stock in the company. The number of shares issued is somewhat arbitrary, but the customary practice in some places is for new corporations to issue one share for each dollar invested.

The most common way to pay for stock is with cash. For example, you may put $5,000 into the company in return for 5,000 shares of corporate stock. But money isn't the only thing that you can invest in a company in return for stock. You may also transfer physical assets, such as real estate or equipment, or a copyright, patent or trademark. Or you may receive stock in return for past services to the corporation.

> ⚠️ **Check before you transfer property for stock.** *Before you transfer property to your corporation in exchange for stock, check with your tax advisor. If you receive stock for property that has increased in value since you bought it, you may owe taxes.*

In some states, you can receive stock in return for promising to perform services to the corporation, or in return for a promissory note. In other words, you might receive 5,000 shares of stock in return for your promise to work for the corporation for 200 hours or to pay the corporation $5,000 six months later. Not all states, however, permit stock to be issued based on a promise of future services or money, so check the rules of your state.

2. Funding Your Corporation With Debt

The other major way to fund a corporation is through debt—that is, by borrowing money. But you should know that if your corporation borrows from a bank or other outside lender, the lender will probably expect you to personally guarantee to repay the debt should the business be unable to.

⚠️ **Lending money to the corporation.** *Until fairly recently, it was quite common for shareholders in some new corporations to lend money to the corporation or transfer assets from an existing sole proprietorship in exchange for a promissory note from the corporation. Shareholders gained tax benefits by dividing their initial investment between debt (represented by promissory notes) and equity (represented by stock certificates). Changes in the tax laws, however, have eliminated the shareholder loan as a viable option for purchasing equity in a new corporation.*

3. Leasing Property to the Corporation

Sometimes you'll want to retain ownership of property being used by the corporation. For example, maybe you own a garage or other small building your company will occupy. With real estate, it's usually better, from a tax standpoint, to have your corporation lease the property from you rather than to transfer the property to the corporation.

EXAMPLE: Nino forms New Age Innovators Inc. to develop some practical new technologies for the plumbing industry. He plans to work out of his garage. He leases the garage to his corporation for $500 a month. On his own personal Form 1040, Nino will report the rent as income and will deduct interest expense (for the mortgage on the building) and depreciation. On its corporate tax return, New Age Innovators Inc. will deduct its rent payments and operating expenses for the garage.

If you lease property to the corporation, have the directors adopt a board resolution approving a lease. Then have the corporation sign the lease as tenant with you, of course, as the landlord. This will be helpful in establishing the existence of a lease if the arrangements are questioned by the IRS.

C. Compensating Yourself

I've just discussed how you put money into the corporation. Now let's get to the fun part—how you take it out.

1. Salary and Bonuses

As a corporate employee, you can receive a reasonable salary plus bonuses which, for tax purposes, are lumped in with salary. (Many corporate owners prefer to pay themselves conservative salaries and then to reward themselves with a year-end bonus if it makes sense economically.) Salaries and bonuses are treated as business expenses of the corporation, which means that the corporation owes no tax on what it pays you. You, in turn, report what you receive as income on your personal income tax return just as you would if you worked for any other employer. The IRS has rules on how much salary is appropriate—the primary one is that the salary must be reasonable. This is a pretty loose standard and, as a practical matter, doesn't affect most small business people, because their businesses can't afford to pay them the sort of stratospheric salaries the IRS might consider unreasonable.

2. Interest on Loans to the Corporation

If you lend money or property to the corporation when it's underway in exchange for a promissory note, you'll receive interest on your loans. Hopefully, the corporation will repay you the principal amount of the loans as well. But you'll have to pay tax only on the interest you receive—not on the principal portion.

⚠️ **Minimum interest.** *Any loan between a corporation and an employee or stockholder for more than $10,000 must carry a minimum interest rate. The rate is based on U.S. Treasury Bill rates. The loan type also determines whether other requirements must be met. Check with your tax advisor for details.*

3. Fringe Benefits

Another way to profit from your investment in the corporation is through fringe benefits. For example, your corporation may purchase health insurance for employees and set up a plan under which the corporation reimburses employees for medical expenses not covered by insurance. Health insurance premiums and medical reimbursements paid by the corporation are tax-deductible business expenses for the corporation—and aren't taxable to the employee as personal income. By contrast, if you were to pay for medical expenses with no corporate help, only a limited amount would be tax-deductible on your personal income tax return.

S Corporations Note. S corporations are treated differently under the tax laws. Fringe benefits for an owner-employee who owns more than 2% of the stock of an S corporation are not given this favorable tax treatment.

4. Dividends

You've probably heard about corporate dividends paid to shareholders. This is another way that funds can be removed from a corporation for the benefit of its owners. Perhaps surprisingly, it is rarely done in a small corporation. Because the corporation can't deduct dividends as a business expense, dividends add up to double taxation. (This doesn't apply to S corporations; see Chapter 1, Section C.) The corporation is subject to tax on money paid as dividends, and then the shareholder is taxed a second time. To avoid this double taxation, it's much better to take money out of the corporation through the means previously discussed.

D. Do You Need a Lawyer to Incorporate?

It's possible to form your own corporation without professional help. Every day, many entrepreneurs do exactly that by using an incorporation kit. If you're inclined to go this route, check out *How to Form Your Own California Corporation* or *Incorporate Your Business: A 50-State Legal Guide to Forming a Corporation,* both by Anthony Mancuso (Nolo). These books provide information about incorporating, even if you decide not to do it yourself.

The obvious motivating factor for setting up a corporation on your own is to save on legal fees, which can range from $1,000 to $2,000 or more, depending on where you live. But be aware that there's a tradeoff: you're subjecting yourself to bureaucratic hassles and, unless you do your homework carefully, possible errors. The paper-filing phase, by itself, isn't all that difficult. But tax and legal liability problems may not be obvious to the do-it-yourselfer. And if you plan to issue stock to other than a few people who will work in the business or are close friends and relatives, securities laws can be troublesome. Still, dollars are often precious to people just starting out in business, and you may decide that it's worthwhile to attempt to form your corporation by yourself. If you choose that route, it's a good idea to have a lawyer experienced with small businesses look over the final documents before you file them. (Chapter 24 discusses finding, hiring and working with a lawyer.) You should be able to find a lawyer willing to do this at a fraction of the cost of having the lawyer handle the matter from beginning to end.

⚠️ **Beware of securities law.** *If you'll have a number of shareholders—especially people who won't be working in the business and who are not close relatives living in your state—consult a lawyer to see that you're in compliance with federal and state securities regulations. (See Section E, below.) While most small businesses are considered to be closely held corporations and exempt from these potentially complicated regulations, it's worth spending a few bucks to find out for sure. Anthony Mancuso's how-to-incorporate books, mentioned above, discuss this issue in detail.*

E. Overview of Incorporation Procedures

While there are differences from state to state, the basic procedures that you or your lawyer will follow in creating a corporation are these:

- Prepare and file the articles of incorporation
- Select a board of directors
- Adopt bylaws
- Elect officers
- Issue stock
- Decide whether or not you want to elect S corporation tax status.

In a moment, we'll walk through the incorporation process. Before we do, let's look at one additional step to consider before starting to incorporate: a pre-incorporation agreement. It may be unnecessary if you're planning a one-person corporation or if your corporation consists only of family members. Similarly, a pre-incorporation agreement is less necessary if you and your associates are incorporating an existing business or if you've done business together before. However, if you're going into business with relative strangers, putting your agreement in written form will help you avoid disputes later or, if an argument does arise, will provide a basis for resolving it through arbitration or litigation. (See Chapter 22.) Your written agreement should include these key points:

- the name of the corporation
- its purpose
- how much stock each person will buy and how he or she will pay for it
- what loans each person will make to the corporation and the terms of repayment
- what offices (president, vice-president, secretary, treasurer) each person will hold
- what compensation each of you will receive
- what expense accounts each of you will have
- what fringe benefits will be available.

If the corporation is going to lease real estate or other property from one of the owners, the agreement can also outline the terms of that transaction.

Another major topic to cover in either a pre-incorporation agreement or a separate buy-sell agreement is what happens if a shareholder wants to retire from the corporation or gets sick or dies or just wants to sell his stock. Will the corporation or the remaining shareholders be obligated to buy the stock? How will the price be set? Can the stock be sold to outsiders? These are difficult and important issues—and it's much better to think them through and arrive at a written agreement at the beginning of the corporation's life rather than wait until a crisis arises. If you don't have an agreement in place, you risk the pain of personal and business discord, and possibly even expensive, disruptive litigation.

I cover buy-sell agreements more in Chapter 5. Also, you can easily put together a solid agreement covering shareholder issues if you consult the Buy-Sell Agreement Handbook: Plan Ahead for Changes in the Ownership of Your Business, *by Anthony Mancuso & Bethany Laurence (Nolo).*

Chapter 2 of Legal Forms for Starting & Running a Small Business *contains a pre-incorporation agreement.*

Where to incorporate—beware the Delaware myth. *Many people are sold on the notion that there's something magical about incorporating in Delaware. The reality is that the best state to incorporate in is the state where your headquarters is located. For the vast majority of small business corporations, that means the state where you live. If you incorporate in Delaware you'll still have to register as an out-of-state corporation to do business in your own state.*

F. Twelve Basic Steps to Incorporate

The following outline will help you understand how to go about forming a corporation for your small business. The procedure for incorporating is similar—but not identical—in every state.

Step 1. Choose a Name

In Chapter 6, you'll find more detail about selecting a business name. But here are a few basics about naming a corporation.

In most states, to alert the public to your corporate status you must include certain words in your corporate name, such as *Incorporated, Corporation, Company* or *Limited*, or the abbreviations *Inc., Corp., Co.* or *Ltd.* And there are certain words you can't use in your name; for example, in California, the words *National, United States* and *Federal* are prohibited. In New York, you need the approval of a department of state government to use the words *Benefit, Council, Educational* or *Housing* in your corporate name. The quickest way to learn what words are required or prohibited in your state is to call or write to the office where you file the articles of incorporation—usually the Secretary of State or corporation commissioner's office. In the few states where they're unwilling to help you, the best approach (short of calling your lawyer) is to go to a law library and check the state statute ("code") sections dealing with corporations. For more on law libraries, see Chapter 24, Section D. Because you'll probably want to consult these laws frequently, you may want to buy a set from the state or a private publisher.

Most states will reject a corporation name that's the same as one already on file or one that's confusingly similar to the name of an existing corporation. But even if the Secretary of State accepts your corporate name (or tells you it's available in a pre-filing name reservation procedure), this doesn't guarantee your legal right to use it. An unincorporated business may already be using it as its trade name, or a business may be using it as a trademark or service mark to identify products or services. In short, as is discussed in Chapter 6, there is a good deal more to do to check out the availability of a particular name.

Before you file your corporate papers, check with your state's corporate filing office. Generally they can make a preliminary check and tell you if the name is available. If you expect some delay before the papers are actually filed, find out whether your state permits you to reserve a name. Many will reserve a name for you for a month or more.

What happens if you've got your heart set on a name but find that it's too similar to one already in use? One approach is to change it slightly. Most state's name records are computerized, and often a fairly small modification will turn rejection to approval. Or you can ask the owners of the other business to let you use the similar name. In many states you can use such a name if you get the written consent of the corporation that was established earlier.

In many states, a corporation can do business under an assumed or fictitious name. For example, if you incorporate as Miller Manufacturing Company but want to market some of your products under a more specific business name, you can simply file an assumed name certificate for Miller Appliances. Some states require that you file this paper at the same state office where you filed the articles of incorporation (such as the Secretary of State's office). In other states, you file your fictitious or assumed name certificate in the counties where your company does business. And some states require that you also publish notice of your assumed or fictitious name in a newspaper.

⚠ Using your corporate name as a trademark. *If you plan to use your corporate name as a trademark or service mark for products or services, you won't want a name that's very similar to someone else's. As explained further in Chapter 6, even if your name were approved by your corporate filing office, it might infringe the other user's trademark or service mark.*

Step 2. Prepare and File Articles of Incorporation

As noted above, in some states articles of incorporation are called certificates of incorporation, charters or articles of association. Here I'll stick with the term articles of incorporation.

In many states, the secretary of state can give you a printed form for the articles of incorporation; all you have to do is fill in some blank spaces. In other states, you must prepare the articles of incorporation from scratch.

Below is an example of articles of incorporation for a California corporation.

SAMPLE ARTICLES OF INCORPORATION

ARTICLES OF INCORPORATION
OF

_____

ONE: The name of this corporation is _____

TWO: The purpose of this corporation is to engage in any lawful act or activity for which a corporation may be organized under the General Corporation Law of California other than the banking business, the trust company business or the practice of a profession permitted to be incorporated by the California Corporation Code.

THREE: The name and address in this state of the corporation's initial agent for the service of process is:

_____

_____

FOUR: This corporation is authorized to issue only one class of shares of stock which shall be designated common stock. The total number of shares it is authorized to issue is _____ shares.

FIVE: The names and addresses of the persons who are appointed to act as the initial directors of this corporation are:

Name	Address
_____	_____
_____	_____
_____	_____
_____	_____
_____	_____

SIX: The liability of the directors of the corporation for monetary damages shall be eliminated to the fullest extent permissible under California law.

SEVEN: The corporation is authorized to indemnify the directors and officers of the corporation to the fullest extent permissible under California law.

IN WITNESS WHEREOF, the undersigned, being all the persons named above as the initial directors, have executed theseArticles of Incorporation.

Dated: _____   _____

_____

_____

_____

_____

The undersigned, being all the persons named above as the intial directors, declare that they are the persons who executed the foregoing Articles of Incorporation, which execution is their act and deed.

Dated: _____   _____

_____

_____

_____

_____

While details vary from state to state, the typical articles of incorporation include:

- the corporation's name
- its purpose
- the name of the "initial agent for service of process" (sometimes called a registered agent or resident agent)
- the number of shares authorized
- the names and addresses of the incorporators.

The purpose clause may seem confusing—it's as if you're being asked to define what your business will do until the end of time. Fortunately, this isn't necessary, because the statutes in many states allow you to use very general language, such as: "The purposes of this corporation shall be to engage in any lawful act or activity for which corporations may be organized under the business corporation law." If such a statement is permitted in your state, it's usually best not to be any more specific. This leaves you free to change the nature of your business without amending the articles of incorporation. It also helps you avoid questions of whether you're acting beyond the scope of your stated purpose if you go into a new business.

Most states require you to designate somebody as a resident agent or registered agent in the articles of incorporation. This is the person who is authorized to receive official notices and lawsuit papers. Normally, you designate the corporate president as this person. If you change the person named or there's a new address, you need to notify the secretary of state's office by filing a proper form.

It may take a few weeks for your articles of incorporation to be processed by the secretary of state's office. If you need quicker action, check to see if expedited handling is available. In some states, you can file your articles of incorporation in person and have the filing process completed within a day. Sometimes, articles of incorporation sent by UPS, Federal Express or other overnight means are treated as in-person filings and given expedited treatment.

If you need to sign contracts, such as a lease, even before the corporation has been formed, it's a good idea to state in the contract that you're acting on behalf of a corporation to be formed and that the contract is subject to ratification by the board of directors of the new corporation. Then, if for some reason the corporation is never formed or if the directors fail to ratify the document, you're free from personal liability. Here is sample language for such a lease.

> Landlord acknowledges that Martin Green is signing this lease on behalf of XYZ Corporation (a corporation to be formed) and that this lease is subject to ratification by the corporation's Board of Directors. If the corporation is not formed or if the Board of Directors fails to ratify this lease within 30 days of the present date, this lease will be void. In no event will Martin Green have any personal liability under this lease.

If this approach is not acceptable to the person with whom you're contracting, another possibility is to sign the contract in your own name—thereby assuming personal liability temporarily—but to specifically reserve the right to assign it to the corporation later.

Incorporation Fees

Each state imposes a fee or a combination of fees for incorporating. Some states also require an initial tax payment. The total amounts vary widely, from $50 to $1,000. To find out your state's fees, call the corporate filing office (usually a branch of the governor's office in your state capital). In some states the information is also available online: try exploring your state's website via www.50states.com. (Click on the name of your state, then, when an information screen pops up, click on the large box containing your state's name to be taken to your state's own government website.)

Landlord grants to Martin Green the right to assign this lease to XYZ Corporation, a corporation to be formed. Upon Landlord's receipt of written notice that such assignment has been made, Martin Green will automatically be released from any personal liability under this lease.

Step 3. Elect the First Board of Directors

In some states, initial directors are designated in the articles of incorporation. In other states, the incorporator or incorporators choose the first board of directors. If this is the practice in your state, be sure to document the appointment of directors with a statement or certificate signed by the incorporators. This statement or certificate, which will be inserted into your corporate record book, may look something like the one below.

SAMPLE DESIGNATION OF DIRECTORS BY INCORPORATOR

**ACTION BY INCORPORATOR
OF XYZ CORPORATION**

The Incorporator of XYZ Corporation, a Pennsylvania corporation, designates the following people to serve as the initial Board of Directors of the Corporation:

        Joyce Barker
        Lloyd Epstein
        Norton Phillips

Dated:_____   _____

                                  Joyce Barker, Incorporator

Step 4. Adopt Bylaws

The corporate bylaws contain much more detail than the articles of incorporation. They spell out the rights and powers of the shareholders, directors and officers of the corporation. Typically the bylaws state the time and place for the annual meeting of shareholders, how much notice of the meeting is given and what constitutes a quorum. There are also provisions for special meetings to consider issues so important they can't wait for the next annual meeting and a statement about what actions the shareholders can take by written consent without a formal meeting. Bylaws provide how many directors there are, how they're elected, what their powers are and if and how they're compensated. Titles of the corporate officers (generally, a president, secretary and treasurer) are listed in the bylaws.

The bylaws may also cover matters such as who is authorized to sign contracts, who has the right to inspect corporate books and records (and under what conditions), the fiscal year of the corporation and how the bylaws can be amended.

In a few states the incorporators must adopt the bylaws; in others, the directors must adopt them. And in still other states, you can choose between the two methods. If the incorporators adopt the bylaws, be sure to document this in a signed statement or certificate. If the directors adopt the bylaws (see below), reflect this action in your minutes of the first directors' meeting or, if you don't hold a meeting, in a written consent resolution of the directors.

 Chapter 2 of Legal Forms for Starting & Running a Small Business *contains sample bylaws.*

Step 5. Hold a Directors' Meeting

The directors must do a number of things at the beginning to get the corporation on the right track. Historically, corporations have recorded these actions in a document called "minutes of first meeting of the board of directors." These minutes were written in language reflecting a formal parliamentary procedure that really doesn't match the less formal style of most small businesses.

Fortunately, in most states, there's a streamlined method for accomplishing this. You or your lawyer can prepare a consent form to be signed by the board of directors such as the one below.

SAMPLE CONSENT FORM FOR DIRECTORS

XYZ Corporation consent of the board of directors

The directors of XYZ Corporation consent to the following:

1. BYLAWS: The attached bylaws shall be the bylaws of the corporation.

2. OFFICERS: The following people are elected to serve as officers of the corporation for the next year, or until their successors are elected:

    President:_____
    Secretary:_____
    Treasurer:_____

3. ISSUANCE OF STOCK CERTIFICATES: The President and Secretary are authorized and directed to issue stock certificates in the following amounts upon receipt of payment from the designated shareholders:

Name	Number of Shares	Amount to be Paid
1. _____	_____	_____
2. _____	_____	_____
3. _____	_____	_____

4. LEASE: The President is authorized and directed to enter into a three-year lease of space in The Village Green on the terms set out in the attached memorandum.

    Dated:_____,20_____
                                                   Director #1

    Dated:_____,20_____
                                                   Director #2

    Dated:_____,20_____
                                                   Director #3

What actions should the board of directors take at its first meeting, either in formal minutes or through a consent resolution? The following are typical:

- adopt bylaws
- designate corporate officers
- approve the form of stock certificate
- adopt the first fiscal year
- authorize issuance of stock
- approve lease
- approve employment contracts
- adopt a shareholders' agreement (buy-sell agreement—see Chapter 5).

Step 6. Set Up a Corporate Bank Account

Remember, your corporation is a legal entity separate from its shareholders, directors and officers. For that reason, the corporation needs its own bank account so that its finances can clearly be kept separate.

If you're incorporating an existing business that already has a bank account, I recommend that you start fresh and set up a new bank account for the corporation. The bank will ask for a corporate board of directors' resolution authorizing the new account and an Employer's ID Number. (Employer's ID Numbers are discussed in Chapter 8, Section A.)

If you decide to simply continue the old account, do the following:

- Find out the bank's procedures for changing a sole proprietorship or partnership account into a corporate account. Most likely, the bank will want your directors to adopt a specific resolution, using language the bank will supply. The bank will want to see your articles of incorporation and a copy of the banking resolution. You'll also be asked to provide your Employer's Identification Number (issued by the IRS). You may not have this immediately, and the bank will probably let you start using the account for the corporation if you assure them that you've applied for the ID number.

- Keep detailed records showing exactly how much money was in the account when it was changed over to the corporation. Also keep track of any checks that were written by your existing business but haven't cleared yet. These checks should be treated as expenses of the unincorporated business and deducted from the amount considered transferred to the corporation. Preparing and retaining these records will save you headaches a year or two down the road when you try to figure out exactly what was transferred to the corporation.

Step 7. Issue Stock

The corporation should issue a stock certificate to each shareholder. The certificate is evidence of the shareholder's ownership interest in the corporation. Filling out the stock certificate is simple. Your main legal concern is whether you need to do anything to comply with federal or state securities laws.

Federal securities laws are administered by the Securities and Exchange Commission (SEC). In addition, each state has its own law regulating the sale of securities, intended to protect passive investors—people who put money into a corporation but are not active in the day-to-day operations of the business.

The bad news is that both the federal and state requirements are very complicated. The good news is that, as discussed earlier, the typical small corporation—consisting solely of investors who are actively involved in the day-to-day operation of the company, and often their close relatives—is completely exempt from the complicated requirements. Nevertheless, some paperwork may be involved. For example, it's frequently advisable to give a "shareholder representation letter" to each prospective shareholder, even though it isn't strictly required under the state's securities laws. The letter gives you a way to confirm the purchaser's reasons for believing the transaction is exempt from the state's securities laws.

EXAMPLE: Edgewater Inc. has been formed to build and operate a restaurant on the shore of a scenic lake. Chester, a wealthy investor who has been a partner in three major deals with Todd, the president of Edgewater Inc., is going to invest $75,000 in the new corporation and receive 75,000 shares of stock. To qualify a stock purchase as exempt under the state's "limited offering exemption," the purchaser must be one of the following: an insider shareholder (a director, officer or promoter of the corporation); someone who's had a pre-existing business or personal relationship with the corporation or one of its officers; or a "sophisticated investor." (Sophisticated investors are those who, because of their business or financial experience, are in a good position to protect their interests when buying stock in a new corporation.) Chester qualifies as both a sophisticated investor and one who's had a pre-existing business relationship with the corporate president. Todd prepares a shareholder representation letter reciting these facts for Chester to sign.

Californians can obtain sample shareholder representation letters and reliable information on how to prepare them for their corporation (as well as blank stock certificates), from *How to Form Your Own California Corporation,* by Anthony Mancuso (Nolo).

Before you issue a stock certificate, make sure that the corporation has actually received payment for the shares. For example, if the shares are being purchased for cash, the corporation should receive the money before issuing the shares. If the corporation is issuing the stock in return for a promise of future payment by the shareholder (a practice allowed in some states but not others), the corporation should have in its possession a promissory note from the shareholder. If property is being transferred to the corporation in exchange for stock, the person transferring the property should sign a bill of sale for the property at the same time the corporate shares are issued.

Step 8. Complete Any Initial Financial Transactions

Tie up any other loose ends relating to the financing of the corporation. As noted earlier, your corporation may borrow some of its start-up money from friends, relatives or other lenders. The corporation should issue written promissory notes as evidence that loans have been made. In addition, if you're leasing a building or equipment to the corporation, sign a lease.

Step 9. Set Up a Corporate Record Book

You can create a corporate record book in an ordinary loose-leaf binder. A more official looking way to do it is to buy a corporate record book from Nolo or a local stationer. These usually come with stock certificates and an embossed corporate seal.

The main items that you'll keep in the corporate record book are the articles of incorporation, the

bylaws, the minutes of meetings (or consent resolutions) and the stock certificate stubs or ledger sheets showing who received the stock certificates and when. In many small corporations, shareholders prefer the convenience of simply leaving the completed stock certificates in the corporate record book even though each shareholder is, of course, entitled to possession of his or her certificate.

Step 10. Follow Through on State Government Requirements

Your state may require that you file documents in addition to the articles of incorporation. For example, in New York, you need to file a stock registration certificate certifying that you "keep a place for the sale, transfer or delivery of your corporate stock" at a certain address (normally your corporate offices). In California, you need to file a notice of stock transaction within 15 days after your first sale of stock and "an annual statement of domestic stock corporation" within 90 days after you file your articles of incorporation. To learn about requirements in your state, contact your corporate filing office.

Step 11. Comply With the Bulk Sales Act

If shareholders transfer assets of an existing business to the new corporation in return for stock, there may be some special requirements. About ten states have bulk sales laws designed to prevent business owners from secretly transferring their business assets to another company to avoid paying creditors. These laws apply mainly to retail, wholesale and manufacturing businesses. Basically, bulk sales laws require you to notify creditors that the assets of the business are being transferred.

Fortunately, state laws usually provide for some exemption or shortcuts when the assets are being transferred to a new corporation that will be taking over and continuing an existing business. A key element generally is that your new corporation agrees to take over the business debts of the existing company. If you're forming a corporation to take over and continue a business formerly run as a sole proprietorship or partnership, compliance with the bulk sales law should be relatively easy.

Step 12. File S Corporation Election

As discussed in some detail in Chapter 1, an S corporation is simply a corporation that decides to be taxed as a partnership. That is, it's not a separate tax entity like a regular corporation. Instead, the profits and losses of the corporation flow through to the individual shareholders who report them on their individual tax returns.

For purposes of incorporating under state law, the procedure is the same whether you're a regular corporation or an S corporation. But to become an S corporation, you need to file a form with the IRS. This is Form 2553, *Election by a Small Business Corporation*. All of the shareholders must sign this form. If you want to have S corporation status during the first tax year that your corporation exists, you need to file the election form before the 15th day of the third month of your tax year. In other words, you have a two-and-a-half month window during which you can file the election. When does your tax year start? For a new corporation, your tax year starts when your corporation (1) has shareholders, (2) acquires assets or (3) begins doing business, whichever happens first. If you miss the deadline, you have to wait until the next tax year to file the election form.

G. After You Incorporate

This chapter concentrates on steps you need to take to form your corporation. What must you do after incorporating? Obviously, you need to comply with federal and state tax filing rules. (See Chapter 8.) Your business may also need to get business licenses and permits. (See Chapter 7.) And it's smart to buy insurance before you begin doing business. (See Chapter 12.)

In addition, corporations must file an annual report with the state's corporate filing office. Typically this is a form sent to you by the corporate filing office which requires you to update information about corporate officers and location. Simply fill it out and return it with the necessary fee. If you forget to send the form back, your corporation may face fines and penalties and may even be automatically dissolved.

H. Safe Business Practices for Your Corporation

Last week you were the sole proprietor of a catering business you called Feasts On The Go. Today you own all the stock of a new corporation, Feasts On The Go, Inc. In addition, you're the corporation's director, president, secretary and treasurer.

Or maybe last week you and Emily were partners in a used record shop called Around Again. Today you each own 50% of the stock in a new corporation called Second Time Around, Incorporated, which is running the old partnership business. Emily's the president, you're the secretary-treasurer.

What has changed? On a day-to-day level, not much. You still show up at the same place each day and do the same kind of work you did before you incorporated. In fact, your before- and after-incorporation lives will probably be so similar that it will be easy to forget the fact that you're now working for a corporation that is a separate legal entity.

But forgetting can be risky. If you're careless about maintaining the separation between the corporation and yourself, you can jeopardize your tax benefits or your freedom from personal liability— the main reasons to incorporate in the first place. While it's rare for a judge to disregard a corporation and impose personal liability on a shareholder, it does happen. When it does, it's almost always in a small corporation where the owners have allowed the line between the corporation and the shareholders to get very fuzzy or disappear. Also, the IRS has the power to decide that a corporation is a sham if you fail to maintain it as a separate legal entity. Consider the following actual case:

> For 15 years, Walter Otto ran an export-import business in San Francisco. Then he incorporated his business. He filed articles of incorporation with the California Secretary of State for "Otto Sales Company Inc." Next he invested $50 in the corporation. A few years later, the business became insolvent. A salesman sued for unpaid commissions, naming both the corporation and Walter as defendants. After a trial, the judge ordered Walter himself to pay the salesman over $18,000. Doing business through a corporation didn't protect Walter from personal liability.

What did Walter do wrong? Several things:
- He never issued any stock certificates to himself or anyone else.
- He contributed only $50 to the corporation as his "equity" in the business. (For more on equity and how to structure the financial side of a corporation, see Section B, above.)
- He continued to use the same sales contracts that he used before he incorporated. These contracts said "W.E. Otto" at the top. At the bottom (for seller's signature), the contracts said: "W.E. Otto, by
_____, Sellers."

In the judge's view, Walter formed the corporation solely for his personal convenience and did not treat it as a real entity. So the judge "pierced the corporate veil" to make Walter personally liable for the debt. *Shafford v. Otto Sales Company,* 308 P.2d 428 (Cal. App. 1957).

Here are two more cases in which the owners of small corporations were found personally liable:
- J.C. Chou formed Oriental Fireworks Inc., a corporation that grossed from $230,000 to $400,000 annually. Its assets, however, never exceeded $13,000, and the company never bought liability insurance. Gregory Rice was seriously injured by fireworks distributed by the corporation. He sued and was awarded $432,000. Since the corporation lacked funds to pay the judgment—and didn't carry insurance—the court ruled that J.C. was personally liable.

J.C.'s Main Mistake: Failing to provide even minimally adequate funds to the corporation (in legal lingo, failing to adequately capitalize the corporation) or to carry proper insurance. *Rice v. Oriental Fireworks Co.,* 707 P.2d 1250 (Or. App. 1985).
- Dusty Schmidt and Terry Ulven were partners in a business called Western Oregon Christmas Trees. At Christmas time, the partnership rented tents from the Salem Tent and Awning Company to display their trees. Later, Dusty and Terry formed a corporation—Western Oregon Christmas Trees Inc. They continued to rent tents from Salem but didn't sign rental agreements or checks as corporate officers. When several tents were destroyed by a storm, Salem sued the corporation and was awarded a judgment of $12,500. The court ruled that Dusty and Terry also were personally liable for the judgment.

Dusty's and Terry's Main Foul-ups: Dusty and Terry made a $2,000 down payment on the tents using a check from their previous partnership—not from the corporation. Also, the pair commingled (mixed together) personal and corporate assets and failed to keep corporate records. *Salem Tent & Awning v. Schmidt,* 719 P.2d 899 (Or. App. 1986).

Even though these cases had unhappy endings for the owners of the small corporations, doing business as a corporation isn't all that dangerous. There are several simple steps you can take to preserve your corporate status so that you don't have to lie awake nights worrying about personal liability. These steps are not time-consuming—and they make good business sense.

1. Put Adequate Capital Into Your Corporation

Put in enough money and other assets to meet your foreseeable business requirements. The amount, of course, varies from business to business. What's reasonable to start a video store that requires a considerable inventory of films, a retail location and several employees may be vastly different than what's reasonable to start a typing service, which may need little more than a personal computer, printer, modem and copy and fax machines. See if you can get a recommendation from your accountant or someone in the same business.

2. Insure Against Obvious Risks

Try to determine if there's a substantial risk of customers or others being injured because of your business. If so, it's wise to obtain a reasonable amount of coverage. (See Chapter 12 for more on insurance.) There have been some cases—not many—in which a judge has felt that the failure of owners of a small corporation to buy insurance that was reasonably available was so reckless that it was a factor in disregarding the corporation and holding its owners personally liable.

> **EXAMPLE:** Eunice owns all the stock in a corporation called Roadside Enterprises Inc. The corporation sells and installs tires. It's obvious that an improperly installed tire can cause a serious accident. What if a Roadside employee forgets to tighten the lugs on a newly installed tire and the tire falls off, causing the driver to swerve into a tree? If the driver is killed, his or her family will probably sue Roadside. And if the corporation doesn't have reasonable insurance coverage (and hasn't set up a reasonable reserve fund), a judge could rule that Eunice has some personal liability—even though she wasn't even at the tire store when the employee was inattentive.

Basically, it's a matter of exercising reasonable business judgment. If your business involves the risk of injury and you can buy liability insurance at a reasonable price, I recommend that you do so. On the other hand, if affordable insurance isn't available—an unfortunate reality in some industries today—it's highly unlikely that a judge would find fault with the owners of the corporation for not insuring against the risks.

3. Observe Corporate Formalities

Another way to protect yourself from the possibility that your corporation could be disregarded by a court is to always take it seriously yourself. Issue stock certificates to the shareholders before your corporation starts doing business. Keep a corporate record book containing your articles of incorporation, stock records, bylaws and minutes of shareholders' and directors' meetings. Comply with state law requirements that you hold annual meetings of shareholders or act by signed consent actions or resolutions. Either way you should document all actions taken, such as election of officers for the next year.

Conference Calls. If it's not convenient for all the directors to meet at the same place, many states allow them to participate through a conference call. Follow up by documenting the telephone meeting in writing as soon as possible and sending a copy to each director.

Keep in mind that the annual meetings are minimum requirements. While it's not necessary or appropriate to write up minutes or consent actions for every conference you have with your colleagues, if you take significant corporate actions during the year, it's wise to document them through minutes of a special meeting or a consent action form. Keep the minutes and consent actions in your corporate record book.

Here are some types of business activities that you should document with minutes of a directors' meeting or a signed consent action form signed by the directors:

- authorizing corporate bank accounts and designating who is eligible to sign checks and withdraw funds
- determining salaries and bonuses of officers
- contributing to pension and profit-sharing plans
- acquiring another business
- borrowing money
- entering into major contracts
- buying, selling or leasing real estate
- adopting or amending employee fringe benefits plans
- applying for trademark registration.

Chapter 3 of Legal Forms for Starting & Running a Small Business *contains various forms for running your corporation.*

4. Separate Your Personal Finances From the Corporation's

The corporation needs its own bank account. (See Section F, Step 6.) Don't use the corporate bank account to pay your personal expenses. Get salary checks on a regular basis from the corporation (deducting employee withholding taxes); deposit the checks in your personal account; and then pay your own bills.

If you use personal funds to pay business expenses—for example, you pick up a ream of typing paper while you're out for lunch—you can have the corporation reimburse you, but be sure the corporation keeps the receipt for the paper to justify the payment as a proper business expense.

To further preserve the distinction between you and the corporation, document all transactions as if you were strangers. If the corporation leases property from you, sign a lease. If the corporation borrows money from you, get a promissory note. If you sell property to the corporation or use your property to buy stock, sign a bill of sale or other legal document formally transferring legal title to the corporation.

5. Use the Correct Corporate Name

Suppose the name of your corporation is The A.B. Smith Fitness Store Inc. Use that full business name in all your business dealings—on your stationery, business cards and phone book listings, on your signs, in catalogs and on the Internet. Be careful not to use a different or abbreviated version (such as Smith Fitness Center) unless you file an assumed name certificate or fictitious name certificate as permitted by state law. (For more on corporate names, see Section F and Chapter 6.)

6. Sign Documents As a Corporate Officer

In correspondence and on checks, sign your name as William Jones, President, along with the full name of your corporation, rather than just William Jones. This makes it clear to those who deal with you that you're acting as an agent or employee of the corporation and not as an individual. Follow this practice on any other documents you sign, such as contracts, order forms and promissory notes.

SAMPLE SIGNATURE OF CORPORATE OFFICER

JONES BAKERY INC.
By:＿＿＿＿＿＿＿＿＿＿＿＿＿＿＿＿＿＿＿
William Jones, President

In some cases, you may have to sign the contract or promissory note personally as a guarantor. For example, banks usually won't lend money to a small corporation without the personal guarantees of the principals, and some extra-cautious landlords may insist on similar guarantees for leases. But even if you have to accept personal liability for some corporate obligations, it's better to do this as a guarantor than as the main signer. The reason: The guarantee provides further evidence that you and the corporation are separate legal entities.

7. Assign Existing Business Contracts to the Corporation

If you incorporate an existing business (such as a sole proprietorship or a partnership), the old business may have contracts still in effect, which the corporation will take over. For example, maybe the prior business leased space and the lease still has a year to go. Or maybe you're a computer consultant and, as a sole proprietor, you'd just gotten started on a contract to design customized billing software for a medical clinic.

It's usually a good idea to formally transfer these contracts to the corporation. Generally, unless the contract expressly prohibits an assignment, you're free to transfer it to your corporation without getting the consent of the other party. But bear this in mind: Unless you get that consent and a release of personal liability, or unless your contract already specifically permits you to assign it to a new corporation and be free from personal liability, you're still going to be legally responsible for performance of the contract. This means that the landlord can turn to you if the corporation doesn't pay the rent, and the medical clinic can hold you personally responsible if you don't deliver the software you promised.

Important tax note. *If your corporation will derive income from passive sources, such as rents, royalties or dividends, or from the performance of personal services, get professional tax advice before you transfer contracts to the corporation. A transfer could lead to a personal holding company penalty—which could be quite substantial.*

To assign a contract, prepare a short document called "Assignment of Lease" or "Assignment of Computer Consultation Contract." A sample is shown below. Have the corporation agree to accept the assignment and to carry out the terms of the contract. From a business and legal standpoint, it makes sense to continue your business through a single entity—the corporation—rather than to do business simultaneously as a sole proprietor and as an employee of your corporation. Putting your eggs in one basket reduces the chances of blurring the distinction between the corporation and your personal business interests.

SAMPLE ASSIGNMENT OF CONTRACT

ASSIGNMENT OF RENOVATION CONTRACT

In consideration of the sum of $_____, receipt of which is acknowledged, Cecil Hardwick (d/b/a Hardwick Construction) assigns to Hardwick Building Company (a Nevada Corporation) all of his rights, duties and obligations under his contract with Plaza Building Associates dated _____, 20____, concerning the renovation of the Plaza Building.

Hardwick Building Company accepts this assignment and accepts all of Cecil Hardwick's duties under the assigned contract.

Dated:_____, 20___

ASSIGNOR:

ASSIGNEE:
Hardwick Building Company,
A Nevada Corporation

By: _____

_____
Cecil Hardwick d/b/a
Hardwick Construction

Cecil Hardwick
President

The Corporate Minutes Book, *by Anthony Mancuso (Nolo), shows how to hold and document necessary corporate meetings, and includes all forms on CD-ROM.* ■

CHAPTER

4

Creating a Limited Liability Company

Chapter 1 introduced the basic business entities—the sole proprietorship, the partnership, the limited liability company (LLC) and the corporation. This chapter tells you more about setting up an LLC.

As explained in Chapter 1, an LLC is often the best choice if you want to limit your personal liability as the owner of a small business. (Having limited liability means that being a member of an LLC doesn't normally expose you to legal liability for business debts and court judgments against the business.)

While forming a corporation will also give you and your co-owners (if you have any) limited liability, the structure of a corporation is somewhat more complicated than an LLC's. In even the smallest corporation, for example, you have a three-level organizational structure consisting of shareholders, a board of directors and corporate officers. It's true that the same people can fill all of these roles—in fact, in a one-person corporation, a single individual can do it all. But keeping track of what corporate hat you're wearing can be challenging when you have more pressing business matters to think about. And with an LLC, you may be able to avoid some of the legal and tax paperwork associated with a corporation. For example, an LLC needn't worry about getting signatures on stock subscriptions or issuing stock certificates or drawing up board of directors' resolutions—although an LLC whose members prefer a higher degree of formality are certainly free to issue membership certificates and to document all major company decisions. (See Section H8.) And when it comes to taxes, a one-member LLC that prefers pass-through taxation (as in a sole proprietorship) rather than corporate-style taxation can remain what the IRS calls a "disregarded entity"—which means the LLC itself needn't file any tax documents at all.

In addition to requiring less paperwork, an LLC can be far more streamlined and flexible than a cor-

poration. LLC owners can run their business with much less formality. For instance, the owners of an LLC (known as members) jointly manage the LLC (although they can instead designate one or more managers to manage it if they want to impose a separate level of management). And in most states, LLCs don't have to hold annual meetings of the members (although they can hold them if they choose). Finally, as discussed in Chapter 1, Section D, LLCs have the flexibility to choose to be taxed as corporations or as partnerships.

The paperwork requirements and legal rules governing LLCs are based on state laws. While these laws vary somewhat from state to state, LLCs do enjoy a surprising amount of consistency around the country. This chapter is based on the LLC state laws that are typical in most states. As you go through this chapter, you should keep in mind that the rules and practices for LLCs in your state may have some quirks that aren't covered here. It's your job to make sure that you're following the law in your state for creating an LLC.

 For comprehensive information and guidance on setting up an LLC, consult Form Your Own Limited Liability Company, *by Anthony Mancuso (Nolo). Among other things, the book contains complete details on preparing your LLC articles of organization and LLC operating agreement. The book also contains a CD-ROM to help you prepare these documents. Also, Nolo's* LLC Maker *software, by Anthony Mancuso, walks you through the process of creating an LLC.*

A. Number of Members Required

Every state now allows single-member LLCs as well as multi-member ones.

How one active business owner can form a two-member LLC. *If you're going to be the only person who's active in the business and you live in Massachusetts, there may be an easy way to meet the two-member legal requirement: If you're married, ask your spouse if he or she is willing to be the second member. Then, in the LLC operating agreement, assign a separate ownership (membership) interest to your spouse.*

B. Management of an LLC

As with any company, at least one person has to be in charge of managing the day-to-day business. In most states, unless you appoint one or more members or non-members to manage the LLC, you and all the other members are automatically responsible for managing the business. This is called "member-management." If you choose the other option and do appoint one or more people to manage the LLC, it's called "manager-management."

Chances are that your LLC will choose member-management rather than manager-management. That's because you probably won't want or need a separate level of management.

> **EXAMPLE:** Joyce, Phil and Nora form Cyber Networking LLC, a small consulting firm. All three members are experienced computer experts who actively work in the business and participate equally in running it. They meet weekly to review new project proposals and to decide whether or not to take on the new work. They are all member managers. Nothing could be simpler.

There are situations, however, in which a manager-managed LLC is the better way to go. This is most likely to be the case if you have passive investors who will feel more comfortable if the LLC appoints an active managing member (or perhaps several managing members) whose duties are explicitly defined.

> **EXAMPLE:** Terry, Bill and Chester form Wheel Wellness LLC, a bicycle repair business, built around Chester's years of experience in repairing exotic bikes. Terry and Bill contribute most of the money but, knowing little about bicycle repair, stay out of running of the business. Chester contributes a small amount of money to the LLC but his main contribution is his skill. Since Terry and Bill are passive investors, they agree that Chester will manage the company—but they carefully spell out his duties in the operating agreement so he knows what decisions require input from the investors. All three are happy with their manager-managed LLC in which the lines of authority are clearly defined.

If your LLC chooses to designate managers, you'll need to specify this choice either in your articles of organization or your operating agreement (see below), depending on your state law.

C. Financing an LLC

Assets come into an LLC in two forms: equity and debt. Let's look at each.

1. Capital Contributions (Equity)

Ordinarily, you and the other LLC members will make an initial financial contribution to the business. In return, you'll each get a percentage (capital) interest in the LLC. Among other things, this capital interest determines the portion of the LLC assets each of you is entitled to receive if the business is dissolved or sold. Also, this percentage is frequently used to determine how profits and losses will be allocated while the business is in operation.

Under most state statutes, your capital contributions can consist of cash, property or services—or the promise to provide any of these in the future.

⚠ **You may need to comply with securities laws.** *If an LLC membership is considered a "security," you'll need to register it at the federal or state level unless it's exempt from registration. Unfortunately, the rules for when LLC memberships are securities and when they're not haven't been well defined yet. Generally, if a member relies on his or her own efforts to make a profit—that is, the member actively engages in managing or working for the business—the interest probably won't be considered a security. It follows that most LLCs don't have to register before selling membership interests. If, however, a member relies on someone else's effort—that is, a member is a passive investor—that member's interest is probably a security, and must be registered.*

Because the law on whether LLC interests are securities is in flux, you may want to see an experienced business lawyer before you sell membership interests in your LLC to people who won't be active in the day-to-day business. You may want to make sure that the membership interests are not considered securities or, if they are, that they're exempt from government registration.

Normally, a capital investment in an LLC is tax-free. You and the other members don't pay tax on the membership interests you receive, and the LLC doesn't pay tax on the cash or property it accepts in exchange. The tax effects of paying capital into an LLC are deferred until a later time; as an LLC member, you'll be taxed on any profit you make when you sell your interest or you dissolve the business.

> **EXAMPLE:** Wendy makes a capital contribution of $10,000 to her new pet supply business, Puppy Love LLC. As the sole member, she receives a 100% capital interest in the business. She pays no tax at this time. Five years later when Wendy sells the business and receives $50,000 after all expenses are paid, she pays tax on the $40,000 profit.

Attracting Financing for Your LLC

In the past, corporations sometimes had an edge over other business forms in attracting investment capital because the corporate stock structure easily accommodates the issuance of shares to investors. These days, however, a growing number of venture capitalists are investing in LLCs because LLCs can be taxed as corporations or partnerships and they offer flexibility in how they're managed. For example, you can give majority voting power to a venture capital group in return for investing in your LLC. You simply amend your LLC operating agreement and issue voting membership interests to the group. What's more, if your LLC elects to be taxed like a partnership, the profits allocated to the investor-members won't be taxed twice (as corporate dividends are), but will pass through the LLC to the investors. They'll then report and pay taxes on the profits on their individual income tax returns.

2. Loans (Debt)

To supplement capital contributions, LLCs often borrow funds from time to time from their members or a member's family or friends. These loans help to increase the LLC's cash reserves or cover operational expenses. The money your LLC borrows isn't treated as business income—after all, it has to be paid back. As a result, neither the LLC nor the members pay tax on it.

These insider loans can benefit both the LLC and the lender. A loan payable with interest can result in an immediate investment return to the lender if repayments are made in monthly installments.

> **EXAMPLE:** Phil's mother lends $10,000 to Phil's one-person LLC. The interest rate is set at 8%— less than Phil would pay to a bank but more

than Phil's mother would earn from a government bond. The loan is repayable in monthly installments of principal and interest over a five-year period. Phil's mother receives a return on her money whether or not the LLC turns a profit in any given month or year.

To avoid IRS problems, your LLC should pay a lending member or other insider a commercially reasonable rate of interest—a rate that's close to what a bank would charge. When the LLC makes payments on the loan to the lending member, that member reports the interest payments received from the LLC on his individual income tax return, and pays taxes on them at his individual income tax rate. Of course, the repayment of principal by the LLC to the lending member is simply a return of loan proceeds, and isn't taxable income. The LLC deducts the interest payments that it makes to the lending member as a business expense. These deductions reduce the net profit of the LLC, which in turn reduces the profits allocated and taxed to members at the end of its tax year.

D. Compensating Members

We've looked at how money gets put into an LLC. Now let's get to the fun part and look at how you take money out. We'll assume that your LLC has chosen the usual course and opted for partnership-style rather than corporate-style taxation (discussed in Chapter 1, and in Section G4, below).

LLC management can choose to pay active members a regular salary or a share of LLC profits. (If a member is inactive, the LLC can only pay that member a share of the profits—see directly below). If the LLC does choose to pay an active member a salary, the salary must be reasonable in light of the services performed by the member—the IRS has rules on what an LLC can pay to its members as salaries and what must be paid out as profits (see IRS Publication 535, Chapter 2).

A salary paid in return for the performance of services (one that is not tied to net income of the

LLC) is classified as a "guaranteed payment." A guaranteed payment is taxed as ordinary income to the member, and the LLC will deduct it as a business expense before the net LLC income available for distribution to all members is computed.

EXAMPLE: Will and Peter each have 50% ownership interests in their home repair business, Fixer Upper LLC. Will works half-time in the business and receives guaranteed payments (a salary) of $30,000 annually for his services. Peter works full-time and receives guaranteed payments of $60,000 annually. During the year, the LLC earns $100,000 and has no expenses other than Will and Peter's salaries. After paying the salaries to the two members, the LLC is left with a $10,000 profit. That profit is allocated 50/50 between Will and Peter at the end of the year.

Now suppose you don't receive a "salary" for your services in the form of guaranteed payments during the year (or that you're an inactive member). In that case, your earnings are tied entirely to the net income of the LLC. An LLC's profits and losses are allocated to its members at the end of the LLC's tax year, according to the allocations in the LLC operating agreement. Typically, the share of profits and losses allocated to each member is based on each member's percentage, or capital, interest in the LLC. So, going back to the above example, if Will and Peter didn't receive guaranteed payments for their services, the LLC's $100,000 profit would be allocated equally between them at the end of the tax year. The capital accounts of both Will and Peter would be credited with $50,000.

Sometimes members decide, and state in their operating agreement, that one or more members may receive what's called a "draw"—a periodic payment against future LLC profits. In this case, members do not have to wait until the end of the LLC's tax year to take profits from the LLC. Each member takes a draw each month or quarter; that draw, or distribution of future profit, is subtracted from the member's capital account. When profits are allocated to each member at the end of the LLC tax year, the member's capital account balance goes back up.

In tax lingo, profits that are allocated to an LLC member are known as the member's "distributive share." An LLC member must pay income tax on her distributive share whether it's actually distributed to the member or retained in the LLC coffers.

Self-Employment Taxes for LLC Members

As mentioned in Chapter 1, the IRS collects a 15.3% "self-employment" tax on the first $87,000 earned by a self-employed person and a 2.9% tax on earnings above that amount for Medicare alone. While owners of S corporations do not have to pay the self-employment tax on the profits passed through the corporation to them, according to proposed IRS regulations (which Congress has placed on hold), as an LLC member you would have to pay self-employment tax not only on money you receive as compensation for services, but also on all profits passed through the LLC to you, in the following situations:

- You participate in the business for more than 500 hours during the LLC's tax year.
- You work in an LLC that provides professional services in the fields of health, law, engineering, architecture, accounting, actuarial science or consulting (no matter how many hours you work).
- You're empowered to sign contracts on behalf of your LLC.

The IRS says it won't challenge you if you use the proposed regulations to determine your liability for self-employment tax. If you fall into one of the three categories listed above, 100% of your income from the LLC will be subject to self-employment tax. Otherwise, you can apply the S corporation rules described at the end of Chapter 1.

E. Choosing a Name

Your LLC name will have to comply with state legal requirements. This usually means including an LLC designator such as "Limited Liability Company" or "Limited Company" in the LLC name. Many states allow abbreviations such as LLC or LC.

> **EXAMPLE:** You choose Andover Services as the name of your business. Depending on the state in which you're located, one or more of the following may be appropriate ways to indicate that your business is an LLC:
> - Andover Services Limited Liability Company
> - Andover Services L.L.C.
> - Andover Services LLC
> - Andover Services Limited Liability Co.
> - Andover Services Ltd. Liability Co.
> - Andover Services Limited Company
> - Andover Services Ltd. Co.
> - Andover Services L.C.
> - Andover Services LC.

You'll need to put the name of your LLC in the articles of organization that you'll file with your state's LLC filing office. If you pick a name that's already on file for an LLC in your state, your articles of organization will be rejected. The same thing will occur if your proposed name is not identical to but simply too close to one that's already on file. Some states will also cross-check your proposed name against names on file for existing corporations or limited partnerships. By planning ahead, you'll avoid the annoying setback of having to choose another name. In many states, if you call the LLC filing office, the clerk will make an instant computer check and let you know if there's a name conflict. A few states will ask you to request the information in writing.

⚠️ **Name availability check is only preliminary.** *Until you've reserved an LLC name (as explained below) or filed your LLC articles of organization and had your filing accepted, your proposed name isn't yours to use. The information* *on name availability that you receive by phone or in response to a written request for a name check is just preliminary. Until you definitely have the name reserved or filed and accepted, don't spend money on business stationery, signs or advertising using the proposed name.*

Be aware that even if your name is accepted by the LLC filing office, you may not have the full legal right to use that name to identify your products or services. The LLC filing office looks only at whether the name meets the requirements of the state LLC law and whether it's already in use by another LLC in the state. Some states will cross-check your proposed name against names on file for existing corporations or limited partnerships, but many will not even do that.

And, of course, legal conflicts may arise from other sources. Most important—especially if you'll use your name as a trademark or service mark to identify your goods or services—you'll need to make sure your proposed name isn't the same as or very similar to another well-known business name or trademark—Starbucks, Intel or Borders, for example (see Chapter 6). If it is, the owner of the famous name will insist that you drop it; if you don't, the name owner will very likely go to court and win. To avoid this complication, you may want to do a national name search—and perhaps register your name as a trademark or service mark if the name is clear for your use.

To learn more about trademark law in general and name searches in particular (including how you can do a simple name search yourself), read Trademark: Legal Care for Your Business & Product Name, *by Stephen Elias (Nolo).*

Suppose your LLC name is available but you're not quite ready to file your articles of organization. In most states, you can reserve the name for 30 to 120 days by paying a small filing fee. Many states have a preprinted form you can use for this purpose. After reserving a name, if you file your articles of organization within the reservation period, the name will be accepted by the LLC filing office.

You're not locked into your business name forever. *Your business can use a name that's different from the name used in your articles of organization. You can even use several alternative names. However, to use one or more alternatives with legal safety (in other words, to preserve the benefits of limited liability), you'll have to register each name as an "assumed" or "fictitious business name" at the state or county level or both. For more on this subject, see Chapter 6, Section B. It's also possible to change the name of your LLC by filing amended articles of organization.*

F. Paperwork for Setting Up an LLC

Setting up an LLC is simple. Typically, you must complete just two basic legal documents—the articles of organization (also called "articles of formation" or a "certificate of formation" in some states) and the operating agreement (called "regulations" in a few states).

Additional form for corporate-style taxation. *In the somewhat unusual event that you want to have your LLC taxed as a corporation, you'll also need to file a form with the IRS; it's IRS Form 8832, Entity Classification Election. See Section G4, below.*

1. Articles of Organization

In most states, preparing your articles of organization is surprisingly simple—especially if your LLC is a typical small business consisting of a handful of owners. Most states provide a printed form for the articles of organization; just fill in the blanks, sign the form and file it with the LLC filing office. The task is made even easier in the states that include instructions for filling in the blanks. Other states don't provide the actual articles of organization form but do furnish something almost as convenient: sample articles with instructions. You can prepare your own articles of incorporation by following the format and contents of the sample.

If your state is one of the few that provides neither fill-in-the-blank forms nor sample forms with instructions, you'll need to check your state's LLC statute to learn what to put into the articles of organization.

For step-by-step instructions on preparing articles of organization and other organizational documents for your LLC, consult Form Your Own Limited Liability Company, *by Anthony Mancuso (Nolo).*

Typically, your articles of organization will not need to include anything more than the following information:

- *The name of your LLC.* (See Section E, above, for more on picking a name.)
- *The name and address of your LLC's initial registered agent and office.* You'll probably name one of your members as your registered agent—the person who receives official correspondence relating to the LLC and who gets served with lawsuit papers if someone sues the business. You'll generally use the LLC's business location or the registered agent's home as the registered office address.

- *Statement of purpose.* In most states, you don't need to describe your business activity—a general statement of purpose will suffice. Example: "Purpose: To engage in any lawful business for which limited liability companies may be organized in this state."
- *Type of management.* You usually need to say whether your LLC will be member-managed or manager-managed. The difference between the two is explained in Section B, above. In most states, if you don't specify the type of management, your LLC will be managed by all the members (that is, member-managed). Typically, you'll also need to give the names and addresses of your initial members and, for manager-managed LLCs, your initial managers. (Note: In some states, the type of management is specified in the operating agreement rather than the articles.)
- *Principal place of business.* You'll give the address of your main business location. For most small businesses, it's also the only location.
- *Duration of the LLC.* In many states, your articles must specify how long your LLC will be active. You may be able to choose between a "perpetual" (unlimited) duration or a specific number of years. Some states put an upper limit on the number of years you can choose—30 or 50 years, for example. These statutory limits should cause no problem because when the time is up, you or your LLC successors can extend the life of the business for another long term of years.
- *Signatures of people forming the LLC.* Usually, state law allows one person to sign the articles as the organizer of the LLC. But if your LLC is member-managed, you'll probably choose to have all the initial members sign the articles of organization to give everyone a sense of participation.

After preparing your articles, you file them with your state's LLC filing office—usually the Secretary of State, located in your state's capital city. In a few states, before or after you file your articles of organization, you may need to put a legal notice in a local newspaper stating your intention to form an LLC.

⚠ There may be special requirements for licensed professionals. *In many states, if you're a licensed professional, you'll need to comply with additional rules for starting an LLC. For example, you may have to file special articles of organization for a professional LLC, and you may have to end your LLC name with special words or initials such as "Professional Limited Liability Company" or "PLLC." In a few states, such as California, many types of professionals, such as accountants, doctors and physical therapists, to name a few, are not allowed to form LLCs. For more on professional LLCs, see Chapter 1, Section F2b.*

2. Operating Agreement

Once you've filed your LLC articles of organization with your state's LLC filing office and the document has been accepted, you're officially in business. But if you have more than one member, don't overlook another important piece of LLC paperwork: the operating agreement. Although you can usually omit this document for a one-person LLC (except see "Ask your tax advisor about allocating goodwill payments in your operating agreement," below), it's very important to have one if your LLC has two or more members.

 Ask your tax advisor about allocating goodwill payments in your operating agreement. *If you plan to sell your LLC membership interest in the future, you may wish to specifically provide in your LLC operating agreement that part of the buyout price includes a reasonable payment for the selling member's share of the business's goodwill. (Goodwill is an intangible factor—often based on brand recognition or business reputation—that makes a business worth more than just the value of its physical assets.) You're probably aware that it's better to have income taxed as a capital gain rather than as ordinary income. By including such a goodwill allocation in an operating agreement, you ensure that the portion of the buyout price attributed to goodwill will be treated as a capital asset. This will save the selling member from having to pay tax on it at the higher, ordinary income tax rates. For this reason, if you set up a one-person LLC, you may want to create an operating agreement just for the purpose of making a goodwill allocation. See your tax advisor, as this is a complicated area of business tax law.*

The operating agreement serves a function similar to partnership agreements (Chapter 2) and corporate bylaws (Chapter 3). It sets the rules for how the owners will run the business and it defines their rights and responsibilities, such as the members' voting power and right to profits.

In a typical operating agreement for a member-managed LLC, provisions covering the following subjects are usually included:

- *Capital provisions.* One of the most important parts of an operating agreement sets forth how much money or property each member will contribute to the LLC and what additional contributions may later be required.
- *How a member's percentage interest is determined.* The operating agreement should state how members' percentage (capital) interests are computed. Typically a member's percentage interest will be based on how a member's capital account compares to the total of all

members' capital accounts. So if Ed has $25,000 in his capital account and the total of all capital accounts is $100,000, then Ed's percentage interest is 25%.

Capital Accounts Explained

In bookkeeping speak, a member's capital account represents the current value of that member's percentage of ownership interest.

When an LLC member contributes cash or property to the LLC, the member's capital account is credited with the cash amount or fair market value of the property contributed. Later, when profits are allocated at the end of the LLC tax year, the member's capital account balance goes up (the business owes the member this money); as distributions of profits are made, the capital account balance goes down (the business no longer owes this money to the member).

The capital account balance is also the amount of LLC assets that a member expects to be paid if the company is liquidated and split up among the members (assuming there's sufficient cash or other assets left after all creditors have been paid).

- *Type of management.* You may need to specify whether your LLC will be member-managed or manager-managed. Most small LLCs will opt for member-management, and in the majority of states, if you don't specify the type of management, your LLC will be managed by all the members (that is, member-managed). Typically, you'll also need to give the names and addresses of your initial members and, for manager-managed LLCs, your initial managers. (Note: In most states, you can elect the type of management either in your articles or your operating agreement.)

- *Membership voting.* Your agreement should also specify how issues will be voted on and decided. In the case of a member-managed LLC, you'll probably want a simple majority (51%) of membership interests to decide most issues, but you can also provide for a larger majority (two-thirds, for example) to decide some matters. You can also provide for per capita voting, where one member is given one vote.

- *Profits and losses.* You'll also want to cover how profits and losses will be allocated to members. Typically, it will be on the basis of each member's percentage (capital) interest in the LLC.

- *Distribution of money.* You may decide to put language in your operating agreement spelling out who will decide if and when LLC profits will be distributed to members. For example, you might provide that all members must agree on a distribution or, perhaps, that a majority of members can make that decision.

- *Tax election.* As noted above, an LLC is taxed as a partnership unless it elects to be taxed as a corporation. It's a good idea to state in your operating agreement how the LLC will be taxed initially.

- *Transfer of a membership interest.* Your operating agreement should provide for how a member can withdraw from the business and whether a member can transfer his or her interest in the LLC to someone else.

- *Addition of new members.* Your operating agreement should provide whether new members will be allowed into the LLC and how—that is, by a simple majority, a larger majority or a unanimous vote.

- *Buy-sell provisions.* Chapter 5 covers the important subject of what happens if a member dies, moves away, gets sick or simply wants to get out of the business. Can the LLC force the departing member to sell her interest to them? How will the interest of a departing member be valued? While you can cover these issues in a separate buy-sell agreement, it makes better sense for LLC members to deal with them in the operating agreement.

- *Other businesses.* Your operating agreement can provide, for example, that members are free to own interests in or work for other businesses that don't compete with the business of the LLC.

As mentioned above, most small businesses that operate as LLCs will prefer to have the business member-managed rather than manager-managed. If your business chooses the less popular option and decides to have a manager-managed structure, you'll need to include a special section in your operating agreement dealing with how managers are selected and replaced, and what authority they have.

 For excellent guidance on preparing your LLC operating agreement, consult Form Your Own Limited Liability Company, *by Anthony Mancuso (Nolo). It contains complete details for preparing an LLC operating agreement whether your LLC is member-managed or manager-managed. The disk that accompanies the book makes the task even easier.*

Have a lawyer review your operating agreement. *If you prepare your own operating agreement, it's a good idea to have an experienced small-business lawyer look it over before you and the other members sign it. That will help assure that the provisions are internally consistent and that you haven't made any technical errors that can cause legal, tax or financial problems later. A lawyer's fees for reviewing the operating agreement should be a fraction of what they would be if the lawyer drafted the document from scratch.*

G. After You Form Your LLC

Once your LLC articles of organization have been accepted by your state's LLC filing office and you've signed an LLC operating agreement dealing with such important issues as managing the business, allocating profits and losses and transferring membership interests, you're ready to start doing business. However, there are a few additional actions that are either legally required or worth considering to put your new company on a sound footing.

1. Set Up an LLC Bank Account

Remember, your LLC is a legal entity separate from its members and managers. For this reason, your LLC needs its own bank account so that its finances can clearly be kept separate.

If you're creating an LLC out of an existing business that already has a bank account—for example, your sole proprietorship or partnership business is now going to be run as an LLC—start fresh by opening a new bank account for the LLC. The bank may ask for a copy of your articles of organization and your Employer Identification Number (EIN), which is issued by the IRS. (EINs are discussed in Chapter 8, Section A.)

If you decide to simply continue the old account, you'll need to check with your bank to learn their procedures for moving a bank account from a prior business to a new legal entity. Again, the bank will probably want to see your articles of organization and your EIN. You need to keep detailed records showing exactly how much money was in the account when it was changed over to the LLC. Also, keep track of checks that were written by your prior business but haven't cleared yet. These checks should be treated as expenses of the prior business and deducted from the amount considered transferred to the LLC. If you don't prepare and retain these records, you can wind up with one big headache a few years from now when you try to reconstruct exactly what you transferred to the LLC.

2. Complete Any Initial Financial Transactions

Tie up any other loose ends relating to the financing of the LLC. For example, make sure that the members deposit their initial contributions of cash into the LLC bank account. If a member transfers property—computer equipment, for example—to the LLC in exchange for a membership interest, the member should sign a bill of sale confirming the transfer of property to the LLC. And if your LLC is borrowing start-up money from friends, relatives or its members, be sure to issue promissory notes from the LLC stating the interest rate and other terms of repayment. Finally, if you or another member will be leasing space to the LLC, prepare a lease as if the landlord were a complete outsider.

3. Comply With the Bulk Sales Law

If members are transferring assets from a pre-existing business to the new LLC in exchange for membership interests in the company, you may need to comply with your state's bulk sales law. These laws, currently on the books in about ten states, apply mainly to retail, wholesale and manufacturing businesses and are intended to prevent business owners from secretly transferring their business assets to another company to avoid paying creditors. Typically, under these laws, you have to notify creditors that the assets of the business are being transferred.

While the details of bulk sales laws differ somewhat from state to state, these laws usually have an exemption or shortcut that applies when you transfer assets from an existing business to a new LLC that will continue the business. Typically, to qualify, your LLC needs to agree in writing to take over the business debts of the existing company.

4. Inform the IRS If Your LLC Chooses Corporate Taxation

An LLC is normally taxed as a partnership (explained in Chapter 1, Section D). This means that for federal income tax purposes, the LLC itself does not pay a tax on its income. Profits or losses pass through to the individual members, who include their share of LLC profits or deduct their share of LLC losses on their personal tax returns. This is the route that the members of most LLCs prefer. If that's what you want to do, you don't have to let the IRS know. You'll automatically be treated as a partnership for federal income tax purposes.

The other tax option is to have your LLC treated as a corporation for tax purposes. Your tax advisor may recommend this if you expect your LLC profits will be substantial and the members are prepared to leave some of the profits in the business. The funds can be used in a later year, for example, to pay for a new building or the purchase of additional equipment. With corporate tax treatment, the income retained in the LLC is taxed at lower corporate tax rates (15% and 25% for taxable net income up to $75,000), instead of the top individual tax rates of 35% and 38.6% that might apply to income allocated to members of a LLC that has elected partnership-style taxation.

If your members want to have your LLC taxed as a corporation, the LLC will need to file IRS Form 8832, *Entity Classification Election*, within 75 days of the formation of the company. Otherwise, you'll have to wait until a later tax year to make the change.

For more on complying with federal and state tax filing rules, see Chapter 8.

H. Safe Business Practices for Your LLC

In a small LLC consisting of just one member or a few members, it's sometimes hard to keep in the front of your mind the fact that the LLC is a separate legal entity from you and the other members. You and your business are not the same. In the eyes of the law, you are an agent of the LLC. For example, when you sign contracts and other documents, you're signing them (or should be signing them) on behalf of the LLC and not as an individual.

Remembering this distinction between you and your LLC can seem especially burdensome if you've done business in the past as a sole proprietorship or partnership and have just changed over to an LLC. On the day-to-day level, it's really business as usual and, in many respects, nothing at all has changed. Yet, if you want to get the maximum protection from personal liability for debts of the business, you need to carefully observe the legal distinction between yourself and your LLC. Fortunately, as you'll see shortly, that task isn't as tough as you may think.

The reason why it's so important to always treat the LLC as a separate entity is that if you don't, a judge may decide that you're personally liable for a business debt or that you have to pay a lawsuit judgment out of your personal assets. It's becoming clear that in cases involving LLCs, judges will follow the same rules that they apply to corporations and will hold LLC owners personally liable for business debts if the owners haven't respected entity formalities. (See Chapter 3, Section H, for some examples of what courts have done when corporations have been sloppy.) So if you ignore the fact that your business is organized as an LLC, and you operate it more like a sole proprietorship or a partnership, you will needlessly face the risk of personal liability. It follows that many of the precautions that I recommend for protecting corporate shareholders from personal liability should help to shield LLC members.

1. Put Adequate Capital Into Your LLC

Put enough money and other assets into your business to meet business expenses that are likely to come up. If you don't, and there's a lawsuit, a judge may rule that the LLC is a sham—that it really isn't a separate entity from its owners—in which case you and the other members may be personally liable.

Each business has different financial needs. You can often legally fund a small home-based business such as a computer consulting operation on a shoestring. But opening a pizza restaurant would require considerably more money, since you'd need to lease space, outfit a kitchen and dining area and hire employees. Your accountant should be able to recommend a reasonable level of funding for your LLC.

2. Insure Against Obvious Risks

Think carefully about whether there's a substantial risk of customers or others getting hurt because of your business. If so, it's a good idea to buy a reasonable amount of liability insurance coverage. (See Chapter 12 for more on insurance.) In a few cases, judges have felt that the owners of a small corporation were acting recklessly because the corporation didn't buy liability insurance that was reasonably available. This recklessness played a part in the judges' decisions to hold the owners personally liable to people injured by the corporations' employees or products. It's likely the same principle will be applied to LLCs. So if liability insurance is available at a reasonable price, see to it that your LLC gets the proper coverage.

3. Separate Your Personal Finances From Your LLC's Finances

The LLC needs its own bank account (see Section G1). Don't use that account to pay your personal expenses. If you receive checks from the LLC for salaries or draws (see Section D, above), deposit the checks in your personal account and then pay your personal bills from that account.

If you use personal funds to pay business expenses—for example, you pick up a business book on the way home from work—you can have the LLC reimburse you. Be sure the LLC keeps a receipt for your purchase of the book to justify deducting the cost as a proper business expense.

To further separate you and other members from the LLC, document all transactions as if you were strangers. If the LLC leases a building from you, sign a lease. If the LLC borrows money from you, get a promissory note. If you sell equipment to the LLC, sign a bill of sale to formally transfer legal ownership to the LLC.

4. Use the Official LLC Name

Suppose the name of your LLC is Kitchen & Bath Designers LLC. Use that full business name in all your business dealing—on your stationery, business cards and phone book listings, on your signs, in catalogs and on the Internet. Don't use a different name or abbreviation (such as Kitchen & Bath Designers, without the letters LLC) unless you file an assumed name certificate or fictitious name certificate as permitted by state law. For more on LLC names, see Section E, above, and Chapter 6.

5. Sign Documents as An LLC Member or Manager

In correspondence and on checks, sign your name as Paula Smith, Member, or Paula Smith, Manager, along with the full name of your LLC, rather than just Paula Smith. This makes it clear to those who deal with you that you're acting as an agent or employee of the LLC and not as an individual. Follow this practice on any other documents you sign, such as contracts, order forms and promissory notes.

SAMPLE SIGNATURE OF LLC MEMBER OR MANAGER

Whole Grain Bakery LLC
By: _____
Paula Smith, Member

OR

Whole Grain Bakery LLC

By: _____
Paula Smith, Manager

In some cases you may have to personally sign an LLC document or promissory note as a guarantor. For example, a bank typically won't lend money to a small LLC unless the members personally guarantee repayment, and a super-cautious landlord may want you to guarantee the lease. But even if you have to accept personal liability for some LLC obligations, it's better to do this as a guarantor than as the main signer. The reason: The guarantee serves as further evidence that you and the LLC are separate legal entities.

6. File Annual State LLC Reports

In most states, you're required to file a one-page annual report on a form available from the LLC filing office. Usually, the form is automatically mailed to you. You'll have to pay a small filing fee in the range of $10 to $50—although the fee is higher in a few states. To avoid losing your legal status as an LLC and your protection from personal liability, it's important that you complete the form and return it along with the filing fee to the appropriate state office.

7. Assign Existing Business Contracts to Your LLC

If you've been doing business as a sole proprietorship or partnership and are now switching over to an LLC, you may have some ongoing contracts that you'd like the LLC to take over. For example, maybe your sole proprietorship signed a five-year lease for business space and there are still two years left to go under the lease. Or maybe the partnership you established for your lawn maintenance business has several contracts in force to service the lawns of major businesses in a local research park.

It makes sense to transfer these contracts to your LLC. You usually can do this without getting the consent of the other party to the contract, unless the contract specifically prohibits an assignment. But be aware that if you do assign a contract to your LLC, you'll still be personally liable for complying with it. There are basically only two situations in which this isn't true. The first is when the other party consents in writing to release you from liability. The second is when the contract contains language allowing you to assign it to a new LLC or corporation and be free from personal liability.

Unless you fall into one of these two exceptions, the landlord in the first example will be able to turn to you for the rent if the LLC doesn't pay it. Or in the second example, the businesses that contracted for your lawn maintenance services will be able to hold you personally responsible if your LLC doesn't perform and the businesses have to pay a higher price to get the work done by someone else.

Tax rules on passive investments are tricky. *If your LLC will receive income from passive sources (rents, royalties or dividends, for example) or from the performance of personal services, get professional advice before transferring contracts to the LLC. A transfer could lead to a personal holding company penalty—which could be quite substantial.*

SAMPLE ASSIGNMENT OF CONTRACT

Assignment of Contract

In consideration of the sum of $_____, receipt of which is acknowledged, WordSmith Associates (an Indiana partnership) assigns to WordSmith Media Consultants LLC (an Indiana limited liability company) all of its rights and duties under the contract with Smoke Stack Industries, Inc., dated

_____, 20__, for advertising, marketing and public relations services.

WordSmith Media Consultants LLC accepts this assignment and accepts all of WordSmith Associates' duties under the assigned contract.

Dated: _____, 20__

ASSIGNOR:	ASSIGNEE:
WordSmith Associates,	WordSmith Media Consultants LLC,
An Indiana Partnership	An Indiana Limited Liability Company
By:_____	By: _____
Cynthia Cardone	Cynthia Cardone
Partner	Member

8. Recordkeeping

If someone goes to court and asks the judge to disregard your LLC and hold you personally liable, you may be able to bolster your position if you can produce a record book that shows you've consistently treated the LLC as a separate legal entity. This is clearly the case when someone seeks to get behind a *corporation* and hold the owners (shareholders) personally liable. (See Chapter 3, Section H.) That's because by law and tradition, corporations are expected to observe a number of formalities such as holding annual meetings and documenting meetings of the board of directors. The paperwork requirements for an LLC are minimal compared with those for a corporation. Still, you may want to hold periodic meetings and document important LLC decisions—especially if you have more than two or three members. Depending on the degree of formality you choose for running your LLC, I recommend that you keep an LLC record book containing important paperwork, such as:

- the articles of organization
- the operating agreement
- a membership register listing the names and addresses of your members
- a membership transfer ledger showing the dates of any transfers of membership interests by a member
- membership certificates and stubs (if your LLC decides to issue certificates to members), and
- minutes of LLC meetings and written consent forms (if your LLC decides to hold formal meetings or to get written membership approvals for certain LLC decisions—see discussion directly below).

Even if your LLC has decided to proceed with a minimum amount of formal paperwork, you should consider documenting the members' approval of the most significant LLC actions, including:

- authorizing LLC bank accounts and designating who's eligible to sign checks and withdraw funds
- borrowing money, from a bank or from an LLC member
- amending the articles of organization or the operating agreement
- entering into major contracts
- buying, selling or leasing real estate
- electing corporate-style taxation or a tax year other than a calendar year
- authorizing distributions of profits to members
- admitting new members
- authorizing the LLC purchase of the interest of a departing member.

By staying on top of this simple paperwork, you'll have a paper trail of important LLC decisions that will help satisfy courts, the IRS and others that you've attended to all the legal and tax niceties and that you've treated the LLC as a separate legal entity.

 Your Limited Liability Company: An Operating Manual, *by Anthony Mancuso (Nolo), explains ongoing recordkeeping requirements and provides minutes, written consent forms and resolutions for a multitude of business decisions.* ■

5

Developing a Buy-Sell Agreement

If you're in business with others, there's a good chance that there will be ownership changes as the years go by. That's true whether you organize your business as a partnership, a limited liability company (LLC) or a corporation. Ownership changes may be the last thing you want to think about when the business is brand-new. However, the fact is that many things can happen down the road—or maybe only a few steps away—to affect the ownership of your business. For example, you or a co-owner may:

- decide to move out of state to pursue a new line of work
- become physically or mentally disabled—or even die
- seek to buy out a co-owner's interest in the business, or
- want to sell to an outsider.

What happens then? Will the transition proceed smoothly and fairly? Or will there be discord and, possibly, lawsuits? The answer may depend on how well you've planned for the future. Without careful planning, the business itself may be in jeopardy. In an extreme case, all the time and money that you and the other owners have put into the venture may evaporate as the business falls apart. Certainly, during the sunny, optimistic days when you're putting the business together, it's hard to focus on disruptive changes that you may face in the future. And it's equally difficult to do so when the business is humming merrily along. But planning ahead can save all involved from a ton of grief. To avoid anguishing problems, most businesses with two or more owners should put together a buy-sell agreement. This principle applies regardless of the legal format you've chosen for your business. Partners in a partnership, shareholders in a corporation and members of an LLC will all benefit from well-drafted buy-sell provisions.

First, let's get our terms straight. When I use the term buy-sell agreement, I'm not talking about a contract in which you promise to buy an outsider's business or an outsider promises to buy yours; that's a separate topic, covered in depth in Chapter 10. The buy-sell agreement we're looking at here is a binding contract among the owners of your business that controls the buying and selling of ownership interests in that business. When a co-owner is thinking about selling or giving away his or her interest, a good buy-sell agreement steps in to give the continuing owners some control over the transaction. Often, the agreement will regulate who can buy the departing owner's interest and at what price, or sometimes whether the co-owner can sell at all. Importantly, it helps assure that you and your co-owners aren't forced to work with strangers or other people you won't get along with. It can also help assure that if a co-owner leaves the business, she will receive a reasonable sum in exchange for her ownership interest—or if a co-owner dies, that her heirs will be paid fairly.

Typically a buy-sell agreement also gives the business and its continuing owners a chance to buy out an owner who's stopped working for the business or has died. This eliminates the possibility that active owners will be forced to share profits with an inactive owner or an unsuitable new owner. Some buy-sell agreements also say that if an owner dies, the surviving owners can force the deceased owner's estate representative or inheritors to sell back the deceased owner's interest to the company or to its surviving owners. Similar provisions may apply when an owner decides to retire after a certain period of time, or becomes disabled and can't actively participate in the business.

This chapter simply introduces you to the important concept of buy-sell agreements. For comprehensive coverage of the subject and precise guidance on how to develop your own agreement, be sure to consult Buy-Sell Agreement Handbook: Plan Ahead for Changes in the Ownership of Your Business, *by Anthony Mancuso & Bethany K. Laurence (Nolo). The book comes with a CD-ROM and a worksheet to walk you through the process.*

Check your agreement with an expert.
With the help of the comprehensive book and disk recommended above, you should be able to craft a respectable buy-sell agreement. However, as authors Mancuso and Laurence wisely note, even their book can't provide the depth of advice—especially in the tax and estate-planning realm—that a buy-sell or financial planner or tax expert can provide. And of course, their book can't customize an agreement for you that suits exactly your company's and each owner's individual needs. So if you do draft your own buy-sell agreement, be sure to take it to a small business tax or legal advisor before putting your finalized agreement into action.

A. Major Benefits of Adopting a Buy-Sell Agreement

If you *don't* have a buy-sell agreement, here are some things that can happen:

- You may be forced to work with and share control of the company with an inexperienced or untrustworthy stranger who buys the interest of a departing owner.
- You may be forced to work with the spouse or other family member of a deceased or divorced owner. While this might work out just fine, there's also a substantial possibility that the family member will lack the necessary business skills or the right personal qualities for working with you and the other co-owners.
- If you leave the company or die, you or your survivors may be stuck with a small business interest that no outsider wants to buy—and for which no insider will give you a decent price.
- You and your co-owners may argue with a departing co-owner or the inheritors of that co-owner over what price should be paid for

the interest that's changing hands. This can cause an angry deadlock that can wreak havoc on your business operations.

Now let's see how a buy-sell agreement can help your business avoid these situations.

1. Controlling Who Can Own an Interest in Your Company

An outsider who gains an ownership interest can disrupt the smooth flow of your business—especially in the case of major management decisions that require unanimous approval of the owners. Consider this example:

EXAMPLE 1: Joe and Cindy form a small corporation. Each receives 50% of the corporate stock. They don't foresee problems down the road so they don't bother with a buy-sell agreement. A few years later, Joe and Cindy have a serious disagreement over how to expand the business. To avoid further hassles, Joe sells his shares to Albert, whom Cindy has never met before. The two quickly reach an impasse on management issues and the business comes to a standstill.

A buy-sell agreement can prevent this from happening, by giving the owners the power to prevent outsiders from buying in. Sometimes this is accomplished by giving the remaining owner or owners the opportunity to meet any outsider's offer for an interest in the company. This type of provision is called a "Right of First Refusal." To better understand its purpose, see what happens if Joe and Cindy had a buy-sell agreement:

EXAMPLE 2: Joe and Cindy form a small corporation—and they wisely create a buy-sell agreement to deal with what happens if one of them wants to leave the business. A few years later when they disagree on how to expand, Joe decides to sell his shares. Albert offers to buy the shares for $10 each. The Right-of-First-Refusal provision in their buy-sell agreement requires Joe to offer the shares to Cindy at the same price. Rather than share control of the business with a stranger, Cindy buys Joe's shares. The business continues to run smoothly and prospers.

A buy-sell agreement can also give the surviving owners the power to purchase the interest of an owner who's died if the surviving owners don't want the inheritors of the deceased owner to become co-owners of the business.

Who Doesn't Need a Buy-Sell Agreement?

Although a buy-sell agreement can benefit most small businesses, there are situations where one isn't essential.

You're the 100% owner of the business. If you have a one-person business, obviously you won't have much interest in an agreement that controls who may own interests in the company, since you can do that yourself. But consider the possibility that you may want to plan for the future by agreeing to sell the business to a valuable employee who is willing and able to take it over. In that situation, you might decide to sign a buy-sell agreement with the employee. This will assure the employee that he or she will be taking over some day, and you'll know that you or your inheritors will receive payment when ownership of the company is transferred to the employee upon your death.

You own the business with your spouse. If you've been married a long time and have a good, solid marriage, you probably won't need a buy-sell agreement. It's unlikely that either of you will want to leave the company unless you both do. And if one of you dies, the other one probably will inherit the ownership interest. On the other hand, if you haven't been married long, or your future with your spouse is unsure, a buy-sell agreement can make sense.

You own the business with one of your children. If you plan to transfer part or all of your business to your child, a buy-sell agreement isn't required. You can arrange the transfer through a regular contract or your will or a trust. But even here, you may want to sign a buy-sell agreement. It's always possible, for example, that your child will die or want to leave the business before you do. A buy-sell agreement can address this and other possibilities.

2. Providing a Guaranteed Buyer for Your Ownership Interest

As we've seen, a buy-sell agreement can protect your company by making sure that an outsider does not disrupt the business by becoming an owner without the approval of the owners. But a buy-sell agreement can also help you individually if you ever reach the point where you want or need to sell your ownership interest.

Obviously, it can be quite difficult to sell a less-than-100% share of a small business. There may be no market at all for a minority interest. A person interested in buying into a small business will normally not find it attractive to be in business with strangers and to have very little say in how the business is managed. This lack of a true market for your interest can be a problem for you and your family. The time may come when you want to leave the business but your co-owners may be unwilling to pay you a fair price for your interest. If that happens, you may be stuck with a share of the company you can't sell. The same thing can happen if your heirs inherit your piece of the company.

> **EXAMPLE:** Norm, Betty and Phil form a small corporation, each receiving one-third of the shares. They neglect to sign a buy-sell agreement. Three years later, Norm dies unexpectedly. His wife and two children inherit his shares. They'd like to sell the shares to raise money for college and other living expenses but can't find an outside buyer. Knowing this, Betty and Phil buy Norm's shares for a pittance.

A good buy-sell agreement can avoid an unfortunate outcome like this by requiring the company or the remaining owners to pay a fair price if your inheritors want to sell your interest in the business. You accomplish this by putting a "Right-to-Force-a-Sale" provision in your buy-sell agreement, which requires the company or the continuing owners to buy you out if you die, and sometimes under other circumstances. (The agreement can also provide that the company purchase life insurance on its owners, to fund the future purchase of a deceased owner's interest.) This can protect you and your inheritors from taking a financial hit if the company or continuing owners refuse to buy your interest at a fair price or from becoming embroiled in bruising negotiations over what will happen to your ownership interest.

Let's see how a buy-sell agreement could have changed the grim outcome for Norm's family in the above example.

> **EXAMPLE:** Norm, Betty and Phil form a small corporation, each receiving one-third of the shares. Wisely, they sign a buy-sell agreement containing a Right-to-Force-a-Sale clause, which kicks in if one of them dies. The clause requires the surviving owners to buy the interest of an owner who's died, assuming the estate representative, trustee or inheritors want to sell it.
>
> Three years later, Norm dies unexpectedly. His wife, as representative of his estate, invokes the Right-to-Force-a-Sale clause. Since the agreement required the purchase of life insurance policies on each owner, Betty and Phil can easily buy out Norm's shares at the price in the agreement by using the insurance proceeds. Norm's wife spends the money for college expenses for the children and for other living expenses.

A buy-sell agreement can also require the company or remaining owners to buy your interest in other situations as well. For instance, you may want to retire or stop working, or you may become mentally or physically disabled. If you don't have a buy-sell agreement in these situations, there's no guarantee that you'll get a fair price for your business interest.

3. Setting a Fair Price and Providing a Workable Method for a Buyout

A well-prepared buy-sell agreement can set a price for interests in the business—or a formula for setting a price. This can eliminate lengthy disputes and unpleasant lawsuits about the value of an owner's interest. Equally important, the agreement can provide a mechanism for how the departing owner (or his or her family members) will be paid. Having to come up with a lump-sum payment for a departing owner's interest, for example, may create financial stress for the company or the remaining owners. As a solution, a buy-sell agreement may provide for payments to be made in installments over a number of years. Or maybe the payments will come from life or disability insurance that the company buys for each owner.

Be forewarned that figuring out a fair price in advance of a buyout scenario is no easy task. You and the other owners will be trying to arrive at a price that, years from now, will represent the true value of the company. You can't know today if your business will prosper in the years ahead or struggle to make a profit. And since there's no public market for small business interests, it's hard to make comparisons with interests in similar businesses—not that such information would be of great help anyway. Each industry and small business is different; comparative data from other companies has limited value. Still, picking a fair price—or a formula for setting the price—is essential if the buy-sell agreement is to do its job.

There are five basic methods for setting a buyout price—all of which are explained clearly and in great depth in *How to Create a Buy-Sell Agreement & Control the Destiny of Your Small Business,* by Anthony J. Mancuso & Bethany K. Laurence (Nolo). Typically, you'll set a price for the business as a whole—or a formula for determining that price, and the interest of an owner will usually be a percentage of that price. For example, if the entire business is worth $500,000, the interest of a 25% owner will be worth $125,000 for buy-out purposes. Let's briefly look at the most common methods for valuing a company for purposes of a buyout:

a. Valuation Method 1—Agreeing on a fixed price in advance

Using this method, you simply agree on a price for the business as a whole and put that number in your buy-sell agreement. This agreed-value or fixed-price method is simple and certain. However, it's hard to pick a price that will reflect the value of the business throughout its life—the price you decide on today can quickly become outdated. So if you use this method, you will want to provide that the number will be updated each year.

b. Valuation Method 2—Book value

The book value of a company is generally its assets minus its liabilities as shown on the company's most recent year-end balance sheet. Because the book value is basically a snapshot of the company's finances on a given day, it doesn't give information about the profitability of the business. Also, book value may not reflect assets such as customer goodwill that reflect the profit-making ability of the company. Compared to other formulas for determining value, the book value method usually results in the most conservative (lowest) value for a business.

c. Valuation Method 3—Multiple of book value

If a small business has been up and running for several years, its real value is probably greater than its book value. The multiple-of-book-value method takes into account intangible assets that add to the worth of the business—assets such as goodwill, patents, copyrights, brand names and trade names.

You might decide that the price of the business should be, for example, two times its book value or three times its book value.

d. Valuation Method 4— Capitalization of earnings

This method is best suited to established companies, since it measures the value of a business by its past profits. If your company is just starting out or hasn't been around very long, you can't use this method because you have no earnings history. But after your company has produced a good profit for several years, you may want to shift over to this method. Here's how it works. You first determine the company's annual earnings, or profit, by subtracting the cost of doing business from gross revenues. Next you multiply the earnings by a number called a multiplier. The number you choose should depend, to some degree, on your company's industry and also on prevailing interest rates. Generally, you'll apply the multiplier to your company's average annual earnings for a "base earning period" of three years or longer.

e. Valuation Method 5—Appraisal method

Your buy-sell agreement can simply provide that at the time of a buy-out, a professional business appraiser will establish the value of the business. Actually, you may want to provide for two appraisers. Typically, as part of the buy-out process, the buyer (usually the company or remaining owners) and the seller (for instance, the departing owner or the representative of a deceased owner's estate) each choose an appraiser to value the company. If they come up with the same price, that value is used. If they come up with close prices, the parties may be able to negotiate and agree on a price. But if the two appraisers are far apart on the price, the agreement may require them to choose a third appraiser

who will set the price. A drawback is that the appraisal method can be costly and time-consuming.

B. Where to Put Your Buy-Sell Provisions

You may be wondering what kind of document should hold your buy-sell provisions. Basically, you need to choose between putting the provisions in a separate buy-sell agreement and adding them to another document that may already be in existence—for example, your corporate bylaws, your LLC operating agreement or your partnership agreement. Here are my recommendations.

1. Corporations

If you do business as a corporation, you can add your buy-sell provisions to your organizational documents—either your articles of incorporation or, more likely, your bylaws. Or, you can adopt a separate agreement, often called a shareholders' agreement in the corporate context. I believe that the latter approach—adopting a distinct agreement—is best. You're emphasizing the importance of these provisions, so that an owner can't later claim surprise when another owner asserts the terms.

If you follow this recommendation, it's a very good idea to refer to the separate buy-sell agreement in the bylaws. This can help head off a legal challenge by someone looking for a legal way to escape from the buy-sell terms.

Whichever approach you take, make sure your buy-sell provisions don't conflict with the existing provisions of your articles of incorporation or bylaws. You may want a lawyer to help you with this consistency check.

To make sure that potential buyers of your corporate stock as well as potential creditors know about the buy-sell agreement, you should add language to each stock certificate stating that the share is subject to the terms of a shareholders agreement. This statement is called a stock certificate *legend*.

2.   LLCs and Partnerships

For a partnership—whether general or limited—the partnership agreement is the primary (and, usually, only) agreement among the business owners. Similarly, for an LLC, the operating agreement is the primary agreement between owners. So for partnerships and LLCs, I recommend that you place your buy-sell provisions in the partnership or LLC operating agreement itself. You'll want to make sure, of course, that the buy-sell terms mesh well with the other provisions of the agreement. A lawyer can help with this chore.

Perform a Consistency Check on Your Buy-Sell Provisions

Whether you adopt your buy-sell provisions as part of a separate agreement or add them to your bylaws, partnership agreement (discussed in Chapter 2) or LLC operating agreement (discussed in Chapter 4), make sure they do not conflict with the current provisions of those organizational documents. Mostly, you want to check to make sure an existing provision in one of those documents does not prohibit, or impose addition rules on, any of the buy-sell provisions that you're adding. For example, if your partnership agreement prohibits the transfer of ownership interests to outsiders, but the buy-sell provision you want to use allows an owner to sell to an outside buyer under certain circumstances, you will want to amend your partnership agreement to delete the restriction on transfers.

⚠ Prevent legal termination of partnerships and LLCs. *One area that partnerships and LLCs need to cover in their buy-sell provisions is what happens to the company when an owner leaves (sells out, retires or dies). Some state laws say that the part-*

nership or LLC automatically dissolves when an owners leaves unless the partnership agreement or LLC operating agreement says otherwise or unless the remaining owners vote to continue the company within 90 days. If the owners don't vote to continue the company in that period of time, the company is considered dissolved and must file dissolution papers with the state. To avoid risking the future of the partnership or LLC and having to take a vote after an owner leaves, as part of your buy-sell provisions state that the partnership or LLC continues without a vote of the owners when an owner leaves the company.

C. When to Create a Buy-Sell Agreement

The key to a successful buy-sell agreement is coming up with a reasonable plan early on, before anyone knows who will be most affected by it. At the outset, when you're just getting started, your concerns and those of the other owners will be roughly the same because no one knows who will be the first to leave. Because at that early point no one wants to sell out, everyone has the same interest in crafting an agreement that's fair to everyone. So the best time to create a buy-sell agreement is when you're setting up the business.

With a brand-new business, you and your co-owners can start by putting together a very simple buy-sell agreement. You can concentrate on giving your company or continuing owners the right to buy a selling or departing owner's interest at a fair price, or a price to be set according to a simple formula such as book or appraised value.

After you've been in business a few years, you may want to come up with a more complex agreement. The same holds true if your business's assets have become quite valuable or there's a concern about limiting estate taxes. While it's always a good idea to have a small-business lawyer look over your buy-sell agreement before it's final, it's especially important to get a lawyer's help in creating a more sophisticated agreement. ∎

Naming Your Business and Products

Trademark Terminology

Trademark: A word, phrase, design or symbol that identifies a product brand—such as Compaq computers, Nike shoes, Kodak cameras, Xerox photocopiers and Marathon gasoline.

Service Mark: A word, phrase, design or symbol that identifies the provider of a service—such as Burger King (fast foods), Roto-Rooter (sewer-drain service), Kinko's (copy centers) and Blockbuster (video rentals).

Mark: Sometimes used to refer to both a *trademark* and a *service mark,* because the terms are nearly, but not completely, interchangeable.

Corporate Name: The name of a corporation as registered with one or more states. *Examples:* Time Inc.; Sony Corporation. The corporate name refers to the corporation only, and not to any product or services it offers.

Trade Name or Business Name: The name used to identify a business, as distinct from the product or service it offers. It may be the same as the product or service name; for example, Sony Corporation sells electronic equipment under the Sony trademark; McDonald's Corporation uses the service mark McDonald's on its fast-food service. Or the trade name or business name may be different— for example, General Motors Corporation sells cars under the Buick trademark.

Assumed Name or Fictitious Name: A business name different from the owner's name. *Example:* Laura does business as Coffee Express. Partnerships and (in many states) corporations may also use assumed or fictitious names. In most places, you must register a fictitious name. (See Section B3.)

Federal Trademark Register: A list of all trademarks and service marks registered with the federal government. To be accepted, a trademark or service mark must be distinctive and not confusingly similar to an existing mark. All states maintain trademark registers too, and some maintain service mark registers; pre-existing federal trademark rights have priority.

N aming your business and products may not be as simple as it first appears. For one thing, you need to comply with legal procedures mandated by state law. If you incorporate, for example, or form a limited liability company, you must choose a corporate or LLC name acceptable to your state's business filing office. And all businesses—corporations, LLCs, partnerships and sole proprietorships—must comply with laws dealing with the registration and possible publication of assumed names or fictitious names. (See Section B.)

Other legal procedures having to do with business names are not mandatory, but it nevertheless makes good sense to follow them. For example, before using a cool sounding name—especially one that will also be used to identify your products and services—it's extremely smart to find out whether someone else already has rights to the name and, as a result, can legally limit how you use it or tell you not to use it at all. This normally involves at least two steps. To avoid a claim of unfair competition, your first step is to do a local name search to make sure that no local business in your field uses a similar name. Don't start Jimmy's French Laundry if there's already a Jenny's French Laundry a few miles away.

Step two involves making sure you gain maximum protection for your trademarks or service marks—names you'll use to identify your products or services. Especially if you're looking for comprehensive protection for a trademark or service mark, you'll want to first carefully check and then register the mark under federal and state trademark laws. (See Sections C, D and E.)

Just how much effort and expense should you sensibly invest in protecting the name of your business, product or service? The answer depends on many factors, such as: the size of your business, the size of the market that you'll operate in, the type of product or service and your expectations for growth and expansion. As a general rule, the more customers your business will reach, the more you need to be sure you have the exclusive right to use your chosen name within your business or product niche. For example, if you're starting a local computer repair service, you won't need as much business name protection as if you were planning to sell a new line of low-fat salad dressings in all 50 states. But be aware that because of the Internet and other electronic communication methods, the number of small businesses that compete with one another is rapidly growing, meaning the need to do in-depth name searches and to consider the implications of trademark law is also rapidly growing.

Business Names and Trademarks: They Are Not the Same

Legally, there are two main types of business names:

- the formal name of the business, called its trade name (Apple Computer Inc., for example), and
- the names that a business uses to market its products or services, called trademarks and service marks (Macintosh brand computer, for example).

Use of either type of business name can raise legal issues, but the most serious lawsuits tend to focus on the trademarks and service marks a business uses to market its products or services.

By being the first to use and register a trademark or service mark, a business can prevent another business from using the same or very similar mark. Laws that protect the integrity of trademarks and service marks are intended to prevent consumers from being unfairly confused about the source of products and services. A buyer should be able to rely on the fact that the source of a computer bearing the trademark "Macintosh" is Apple Computer Inc., which has registered Macintosh as a trademark.

Obviously, if you're choosing a name to use as a trademark or service mark, you need to conduct a full search to make sure no other business is already using that name as a trademark or service mark. What may be less obvious is that you need to make exactly the same kind of search if you plan to use your business name to identify your goods or services—as when Ford Motor Company markets cars under the brand name (trademark) Ford.

For a thorough discussion of business names, see Trademark: Legal Care for Your Business & Product Name, *by Stephen Elias (Nolo). That book discusses in great depth how to choose a legally protectable name and offers step-by-step instructions on how to file a federal trademark registration. Also check out the Nolo website (www.nolo.com) where you'll find extensive legal information on patents, copyrights and trademarks.*

A. Business Names: An Overview

Complying with the few mandatory legal procedures for naming your small business is relatively simple. (See Section B.) For some very small, local businesses, meeting these requirements and doing nothing more may be adequate.

> **EXAMPLE:** Jeff wants to start a local word processing service called "Speedy Typing for All." He'll be a sole proprietor. Since his is a small, unincorporated local business, he is probably safe enough if he registers the name as an assumed or fictitious name. In most states, he will register it at the county level, but some states require registration at the state level and also require publishing the name in a newspaper. (See Section B for more on assumed and fictitious names.) Jeff probably doesn't need to spend time and money to register the name as a state trademark or service mark. With a descriptive name and a small local business, there's little likelihood that the customers of any other business would be misled, so there's not much

to protect. However, Jeff should check to be sure there are no other word processing services in his area using the same or a very similar name. If there are, Jeff should change his name or risk a claim of unfair competition. If Jeff wants to go the extra legal mile, he should check his state's Trademark Register and the Federal Register to see if other "Speedy Typing" businesses are registered. (See Section F for how to do a trademark search.)

Until quite recently, a wide range of local businesses—small retail stores, repair services and craft studios, for example—didn't need to worry about registering a trademark or service mark. And to avoid possible claims that they were unfairly using another business's name, they could feel relatively secure if they checked for possible name conflicts in state and local business directories and Yellow Pages with no need to do a more formal state or federal trademark search. But today, the rules of the game are dramatically different. The reason is that in the world of the Internet, mail order and rapidly growing national chains, the idea of "local" isn't what it used to be. Today, even modest-sized businesses must consider taking name protection steps that used to be the sole concern of larger, more expansive enterprises. For example, you might think you have no problem if you're choosing a name for a shoe store in a small town. Think again. If you happen to pick a name that's similar to a shoe store that sells on the Internet, you are very likely to be accused of trademark infringement and probably forced to change your business name, even though the online store is located 2,500 miles away.

Doing Business on the World Wide Web

Like many other business owners, you may decide to operate a website. If so, you'll need to select a domain name—a unique address that computers understand and customers can use to find you. The issues involved in choosing a domain name range from getting your hands on an available one to avoiding trademark lawsuits based on your choice of name.

A good domain name should be memorable, clever, and easily spelled. Unfortunately, many of the best names are already taken. To see if the name you have in mind has been registered, go to www.networksolutions.com. This site allows you to search for a particular name. For example, if you are starting a speed typing business, you might check "speedy.com." If you find that speedy.com is already taken, the www.networksolutions.com website allows you to peruse other possibilities. After you enter relevant keywords (such as quick, speedy and typing), you'll get a list of related names that are still up for grabs.

Once you've found an available name, you'll need to make sure it doesn't conflict with someone else's trademark. If your choice will cause customer confusion between your company and another, you're safer choosing another name.

This is true even if the other business is halfway across the country. Once you've established a Web presence, you are in competition with businesses around the globe, and must address trademark issues equally broadly. A generic name such as "coffee.com" will keep you safest from lawsuits, but will also leave you unable to protect your name from use by other businesses—you'll need to strike a balance.

After you've chosen an appropriate domain name, you can register it online with a service such as Network Solutions, at the website mentioned above. Some businesses register under more than one name, or register common misspellings of their names.

Courts are still grappling with the issues surrounding domain names and trademark law, and there's much more to know than I can cover here. For detailed and up-to-date information on choosing and registering domain names, as well as avoiding domain name conflicts, check out Nolo's free Internet Law Center at www.nolo.com (on the home page, click "Legal Encyclopedia," then "Internet Law"). Also read *Domain Names: How to Choose & Protect a Great Name for Your Website*, by Stephen Elias & Patricia Gima (Nolo).

These days, about the only time you might be able to ignore thinking about trademarks and service marks is if you have a tiny, local business that uses your own name—or a very common name—to market goods and services locally. In short, if you plan to sell services using your own name (Harvey Walker Roof Repair) or if yours will be a one-person, home-based business such as a graphic design service (A+ Design), you're not likely to have a trademark problem. But if your business is just a little bigger, such as a large camping equipment store (Wilderness Outfitters), or sells goods or services beyond a very local or industry-specific niche (Lamps.com Online Lamp Store), you really should take time to understand the basics of trademark law (Sections C, D and E)—and conduct a name search to see if someone else in your field is already using your proposed name (Section F).

The reason to be absolutely sure you have the legal right to use your chosen business name is simple: You don't want to invest time and money in signs, stationery and ads for your business and then get a nasty letter from a large company that claims a right to the name you're using and threatens you with a trademark infringement lawsuit. Just defending such a case in federal court can cost you upwards of $100,000, meaning that even if you're sure that you're in the legal right, you'll probably wind up changing your name just to duck the lawsuit—no fun, given the investment you've already made.

If you decide that you want the protection of federal or state trademark registration, see Trademark: Legal Care for Your Business & Product Name, *by Stephen Elias (Nolo). You can probably handle the registration process yourself, but if you prefer to use a lawyer, the book will make you better able to take advantage of your lawyer's assistance.*

Relying on a State-Filing Search May Not Be Adequate

When you form a corporation or LLC, the state filing office will check to see if your proposed business name is the same as or confusingly similar to one already on file. If so, your name will be rejected. But just because your name is accepted by the state filing office doesn't mean your business name is safe to use. That's because these offices don't check state or federal *trademark* registers. In short, even though a name may be available in your state to identify your business, you may run into costly trademark infringement problems if you use it to also identify your products and services.

EXAMPLE: Tony and Lars form a corporation that will design state-of-the-art sound systems for restaurants and jazz clubs. Their name—The Ears Have It Inc.—has been cleared by the secretary of state for their state. Can they now safely use this name as a service mark to market their services? No. When the secretary of state cleared the corporate name, it simply meant that the name didn't duplicate the name of another corporation in that state. Another company may have already been using the name as a trademark or service mark. This wouldn't show up in the secretary of state's corporate name records.

Since Tony and Lars are hoping to market their services in several states, they (or a name search company they hire) should do a thorough search, including checking federal and state trademark registers. If they don't, they may inadvertently find themselves in conflict with a company that's already using the name. If they find that their proposed name is clear, they should think about registering it as a federal trademark or service mark.

B. Mandatory Name Procedures

As mentioned, there are name-related legal tasks that every business must pay attention to.

1. Corporations

As we saw in Chapter 3, part of the process of creating a corporation is choosing a corporate name. Most states require certain words or abbreviations in your corporate name, so the public can recognize that your business is a corporation. This puts them on notice that, in general, you're not personally liable for debts of the corporation. (See Chapter 1 regarding limitations on the liability of corporate shareholders.)

Each state has its own laws dealing with what words you must include in your corporate name, so check your own state's statute. Most states will send you an information packet along with a sample printed form for the articles of incorporation. If so, the instructions will probably tell you the required words. Typically, the state will require one of the following in your official corporate name: *Incorporated, Corporation, Company* or *Limited*, or the abbreviations *Inc., Corp., Co.* or *Ltd.* If the name doesn't include one of the required terms, the state won't accept your corporate filing.

The law in your state will also likely list some words that can't be included in your corporate name or that can be used by only certain types of businesses.

Words That Are Typically Limited or Prohibited

Bank, banking, co-operative, engineering, trust, National, Federal, United States, insurance, acceptance, guaranty, pharmacy, credit union, medical, architect, indemnity, thrift, certified accountant, Olympic, surveyor.

This is by no means a complete list. For example, in New York you need the approval of a department of state government to use the words *Benefit, Council* or *Housing* in your corporate name.

To learn about the prohibited or limited words in your state, start by calling the office where you file the articles of incorporation. This is usually the secretary of state or the corporate commissioner's office. If they can't or won't tell you, go to a law library or to Nolo's online legal research center (www.nolo.com) and look up the statute sections dealing with corporations.

Building Your Reference Library

Consider buying a copy of your state's corporation statutes; it will be handy for answering other legal questions as well. Of course, a lawyer can also let you know about your state's corporate name requirements.

Most states will reject a corporation name that's the same as one already on file or that's confusingly similar to the name of an existing corporation. If this happens to you and you've really got your heart set on the name you've picked out, there may be a way to get around the rejection. One approach is to change the name slightly or add something to it. Even a relatively small change may result in approval of the name. Or in some states, you can use a similar (but not identical) name if the prior holder of the name consents in writing. The document in which the other company gives its consent will have to be filed with the office that accepts corporate filings. Obviously, you're most likely to get cooperation from the other corporation if your business involves a completely different product or service.

> **EXAMPLE:** Country Squire Inc. sells wood-burning stoves in the southern part of the state. It consents in writing to the use of the name "Country Squire Inn Inc." by a new corporation that will run a bed-and-breakfast in the northern part of the state. With the consent on file, the state corporations commissioner accepts the Country Squire Inn Inc. incorporation papers.

To avoid filing your corporate papers and then receiving word three weeks later that your name has been rejected, in many states you can call the government office that receives incorporation papers and ask if your proposed name is available. They may give you preliminary clearance by phone if the records show that no other corporation in your state is using the same or a similar name.

Watch how you use the name. *The fact that the state filing office accepts your corporate name doesn't assure that you have the exclusive right to use the name in your state. An unincorporated business may already be using it as its trade name in your state. Or another business—whether incorporated in your state or elsewhere—may be using the name as a trademark or service mark. Depending on the situation, the prior use often gives the user the right to legally prevent your use of the name if your use of the name would be likely to confuse customers. It's always prudent to check further to avoid conflicts with other users. (See Section F for how to conduct a name search. For how to protect a name as a trademark or service mark, see Section C.)*

If you expect some delay between the time you choose a name and the time you file your incorporation papers, find out if your state lets you reserve your preferred corporate name. Many states allow you to tie up a corporate name for two to four months by simply filing a form and paying a small fee.

2. Limited Liability Companies

The procedures for LLC names are very similar to the procedures for corporate names, discussed in Section 1. When you prepare the Articles of Organization for your LLC, you'll need to include its name. If the proposed name—or one similar to it—is already in use by another LLC on file with the LLC filing office, your Articles of Organization will be sent back to you unfiled. To avoid this inconvenience, it's wise to check the availability of the name before you file the Articles.

Your LLC will have to include certain words or abbreviations that let people know its legal status. Examples include:

- Limited Liability Company
- Limited Company
- Ltd. Liability Co.
- L.L.C.
- LLC.

The list of words and abbreviations varies a bit from state to state, so you'll need to check the law in your state to learn all the possibilities.

Here's a shortcut for picking a required LLC designator. *Ending your LLC name with the words "Limited Liability Company" will meet the name requirements of all states except Florida and Iowa; in those two states, "Limited Company" or "L.C." is required.*

As with a corporation, your state law may prohibit you from using certain words in your LLC name—words, for example, that refer to banking, insurance, trust or financial services. And again, as with a corporation, your state filing office won't accept your proposed LLC name if it's the same as or very similar to an LLC name that's already on file. Your state may also cross-check the name against the names of non-LLC entities—such as corporations and limited partnerships—that are required to register with the state. Your name will be rejected if it's too close to one of these.

For an in-depth discussion of choosing a name for your LLC, see Form Your Own Limited Liability Company, *by Anthony Mancuso (Nolo).*

3. Assumed and Fictitious Names

Sole proprietors sometimes choose to do business under names different from their own names, and partnerships usually select a partnership name other than the full names of all partners. Corporations and limited liability companies may also decide to do business under names different from their official corporate names. Depending on state law, these adopted business names will legally be called "assumed names" or "fictitious names." If your business uses such a name, you probably must register it.

a. Sole proprietorships and partnerships

If you're a sole proprietor or partnership, in most states, you're required to file an assumed name or fictitious name certificate with the designated public office—usually at the county level—before you start doing business. Generally, there's a printed form for you to fill out, and you'll probably have to pay a small filing fee. In some states, the registration is good for a limited period, such as five years, and must be renewed. State law may also require that you publish notice of your business name in a local newspaper.

States require you to file the certificate for a simple reason: It lets members of the public know who is behind the name. If you don't register your assumed or fictitious name, you can have both legal and practical problems. For one thing, in many states, you may not be able to sue on a contract made or other transaction done under the business name. And in some states, you may be fined. In a number of states you can't open a bank account in the name of your business without filing.

Terminology

Some people refer to an assumed name or a fictitious name as a "DBA." That's short for "doing business as"—for example, Albert White doing business as Al's Cabinet Shop. On legal documents such as contracts and lawsuits, this may appear as: Albert White d/b/a Al's Cabinet Shop.

b. Corporations and LLCs

Most corporations and limited liability companies operate under their corporate or LLC name which, of course, is on file with their state filing office. If, however, a corporation or LLC decides to do business under a different name, many states require it to file an assumed or fictitious name registration. All you have to do is complete a simple form and send it to the state filing office with a modest filing fee.

> **EXAMPLE:** Miracle Widget Manufacturing Company, a corporation, wants to do parts of its business under the name "Widco" and other parts under the name "Industrial Innovators." In many states, it will have to register both of these names as assumed or fictitious names.

It's important to use your correct corporate or LLC name, since this makes it more difficult for anyone to claim that your business entity is a sham (believe it or not, lawyers call this "piercing the corporate veil") and impose personal liability on you. (See Chapter 3.) If you're going to do business under a name that deviates from the official name on your Articles of Incorporation or LLC Articles of Organization, it's essential that the name be properly registered. That way, you won't jeopardize the immunity from personal liability that's part of your reason for having a corporation or LLC.

If your state doesn't allow a corporation or LLC to register an assumed or fictitious name, there is sometimes an easy way to reach this same end while complying with state rules. You can use a preferred business name in conjunction with your official corporate or LLC name.

> **EXAMPLE:** Contemporary Home Furnishings LLC is established in a state that doesn't allow registration of assumed or fictitious names. The company wishes to operate a lamp store called "Bright Lights." It does this by calling the lamp store "BRIGHT LIGHTS" and then in smaller print adding "a division of Contemporary Home Furnishings LLC" or by saying "BRIGHT LIGHTS, owned and operated by Contemporary Furnishings LLC."

This puts everyone on notice that the business isn't a sole proprietorship or partnership—so you continue to enjoy the benefits of limited personal liability.

When it comes to products and services, a corporation or LLC is completely free to use names that are unrelated to its corporate or LLC name (as long as these names don't infringe someone else's trademark, of course). In fact, this is common. Apple Computers, for example, sells products under the name Macintosh, and the Ford Motor Company sells Taurus automobiles.

C. Trademarks and Service Marks

A trademark or service mark consists of two parts. In reverse order, they are:

- The noun that specifies what kind of product or service you're talking about. *Examples*: automobile; health plan.
- The word or words that function as an adjective to identify a product or service as being different from all others. *Examples:* Buick automobile; Saab automobile; Blue Shield health plan; Kaiser health plan.

Think of these as the first and last names of products and services. The last name identifies the group; the first name uniquely specifies a member of that group. As such, the trademark is used as a proper adjective and is always capitalized.

Trademark law is the main tool that businesses use to protect the symbols and words that identify the origin of services and products. The basic premise is that the first user of a distinctive (that is, creative or unusual) name or symbol gets the exclusive right to use it. If you're the first user, you can make that right easier to enforce if you register the name or symbol with the federal trademark agency. The principal purpose of registration is to protect rights that already existed because you used the mark first. But registration can also confer other rights. For example, if you're using an unregistered mark without knowing that someone else used it first, federal registration can give you priority in areas outside the first user's market territory. The twin goals of trademark law are:

- to prevent businesses from getting a free ride off the creativity of others in naming and distinguishing services and products, and
- to prevent customers from being confused by names that are misleadingly similar.

From a legal protection standpoint, the best trademarks are coined words, such as Kodak or Yuban, or arbitrary words such as Arrow for shirts or Camel for cigarettes, which have nothing to do with the product. Nearly as good are suggestive trademarks—ones that hint at some aspect of the product. For example, Talon suggests the gripping power of a zipper.

Trademarks that consist of creative, unusual or otherwise memorable terms are called "distinctive" and "strong." If you're the first to use such a name or symbol, you can legally stop others from using it in most situations.

Trademarks that consist of ordinary terms are called "weak," and competitors are free to use them. Merely descriptive words (such as Easy Clean for a cleanser) generally are not legally protectable. These weak marks can, however, become strong if they acquire a secondary meaning through prolonged usage. If that happens, they may be federally registered and may also be protected under the law of unfair competition if there's a local conflict with a similar mark. (See Section E.)

You can't acquire any rights in the name of the product itself; this is called a generic name. This means you can't adopt Bicycle or Refrigerator as your trademark for your version of those products. You can use the words as *part* of a distinctive name.

The law doesn't allow a business to claim the exclusive right to use descriptive words and generic names because competitors also need to describe their products. If you could tie up key words for your own exclusive use, your competitors would be unduly restricted in describing their goods. Also, descriptive terms aren't particularly memorable and don't further the purpose of trademarks and service marks.

D. Strong and Weak Trademarks

As noted earlier, with very few exceptions, only strong trademarks or service marks have the full protection of federal and state trademark laws. Remember, too, that trademark laws don't automatically protect a business name (the name of your company); to be considered a mark, a business name must be used to identify a product or service in the marketplace.

A trademark is considered weak when others can use it (or something similar) on products or services that don't compete directly with yours. Most ordinary trademarks are weak. *Examples:* Liquor Barn, Cuts Deluxe, Charlie's Auto Parts, 10-Minute Lube.

A trademark is considered legally strong when others can't use it or anything similar on related goods or services. There are two kinds of strong trademarks: ones that contain distinctive terms and ones that contain ordinary terms that have acquired distinctiveness through use.

1. Distinctive Terms

Distinctive trademarks are memorable, evocative, unique or somehow surprising—for example, 7-Up, Lycra or Cherokee apparel. The words themselves have little or no descriptive function; they serve to set the product or service off from others.

So if you're naming a service or product and want a strong mark, try for a name that is either unusual or used in an unusual way. A judge is likely to treat a distinctive name as a trademark or service mark and protect it from use by others—unless someone else has used a similar trademark on the same type of product or service first.

> **EXAMPLE:** "Buick" distinguishes a line of cars from others, and the name means nothing apart from its trademark use. It's a distinctive name. Conversely, "Dependable Dry Cleaners" merely tells you something about the business; it doesn't help you distinguish it from rivals who might also advertise their services as reliable or efficient. So the name would probably not qualify for trademark or service mark protection unless it had been in use for a long time and developed a sizable following—that is, a secondary meaning.

2. Ordinary Words

Generic terms can't be protected by trademark law; original and distinctive words can be protected. But what about other words used to identify products and services—ordinary words that are neither generic nor distinctive? This category covers place names (Downtown Barbers), surnames (Harris Sales), words that describe the product or service (Slim-Fast Diet Food) and words of praise (Tip-Top Pet Shop). Ordinary words receive limited legal protection as trademarks. It's more difficult to keep others from using them or something similar.

Even a weak trademark can acquire limited protection under unfair competition laws. For example, an ordinary name (a weak trademark) can be protected from someone else using the name in a confusing way. The law of unfair competition is generally based on state law (statutes and judge-made law) that supplements federal and state trademark laws. Owners of weak and unregistered names can get some relief from a rival's use of the identical name on the identical product or service in a competing market.

Weak trademarks can become strong ones through long use and extensive public familiarity with the mark. A trademark that starts out being ordinary or otherwise weak (like Dependable Cleaners) can sometimes, over time and through use, become identified in the public's mind with a specific product or service. When that happens, it can be transformed into a strong trademark.

> **EXAMPLE:** Chap Stick brand of lip balm was originally a weak trademark. It simply described the condition the product was designed to cure: chapped lips. But it became strong as advertising and word of mouth helped the public develop a clear association between the name and a specific product. Over time, the name developed distinctiveness based on familiarity rather than any quality inherent in the name.

Lawyers describe a trademark that has become distinctive over time as one that has acquired a "secondary meaning." McDonald's is another good example of a weak mark that developed a secondary meaning over the years—and now qualifies for broad protection.

E. How to Protect Your Trademark

What do the words aspirin, escalator, cellophane and shredded wheat have in common? They are all former trademarks that have entered our language as product names. These words have lost their status as trademarks and are now generic terms. Other examples of former trademarks include harmonica, linoleum, raisin bran, thermos and milk of magnesia. In each of these cases, a business lost its exclusive right to use a valuable trademark.

Here are some steps that your business can take to prevent this from happening to your trademark.

- Use your trademark as a proper adjective that describes your product. You'll notice that ads refer to a Xerox copier, Jell-O gelatin and Band-Aid adhesive strips. If people continue to use the words Xerox, Jell-O and Band-Aid alone, these marks can easily go the way of other trademarks like nylon, mimeograph and yo-yo.

- Always capitalize the first letter of your trademark. And at some place on each ad or package, say specifically that the trademark is owned by your company.

- If your trademark has been placed on the federal trademark register, consistently give notice of that fact by using the ® symbol. If a trademark isn't federally registered or is registered only by a state, you may use the letters "TM" or "SM" to give notice of your claims. You may not use ® unless your mark is in fact on the federal register.

- Take prompt legal action if other businesses use your trademark without permission. A trademark may become weakened or even generic if others use it to describe their products and you do nothing about it. You or your lawyer should send a letter by certified mail (return receipt requested) demanding that the infringement cease. If your demand is ignored, be prepared to go to court to seek an injunction—but first do a careful cost/benefit analysis to satisfy yourself that it's worth the expense.

- If you discover that a newspaper or TV program has improperly used your trademark, send them a letter. Keep a copy in your records as proof that you have consistently enforced your trademark rights.

F. Name Searches

There are compelling business and legal reasons to conduct a name search before you lock in the name of your business. As noted above, this is especially true if you choose an unusual or unique business name that will also be used to identify your products—Z Pop Inc., for example, will sell a new carbonated drink called Z. If someone else in your field is already using this name and may even have registered it as a state or federal trademark or service mark, you will really be an infringer if you start to use it (based on the fact that customers really are likely to be confused as to the source of two businesses' services and products). In such circumstances you can be forced to give up the name.

1. Conducting Your Search

Here are some self-help search techniques to see if others are using a business name like the one you have in mind:

- *Check state and county records where business names are filed.* To avoid a claim that you're unfairly competing with another local business by using their name, start with the records of your state's office where corporations and LLCs are registered—usually the Secretary of State or Corporations Commissioner—as well as the state office (if any) that maintains a list of assumed or fictitious names for corporations, LLCs, partnerships and sole proprietorships. In addition, if assumed or fictitious names are filed at the county or local level, check the lists for the counties and localities in which you plan to do business now or in the foreseeable future.
- *Check business directories and trade sources.* These include the phone books of all major metropolitan areas, general business directories and trade magazines for your industry. A reference librarian should be able to help you. Also, take a look at all online search engines such as Google, Yahoo!, AltaVista and Excite to see if anyone is using your name.
- *Check trademarks and service marks registered in your state.* The office that registers trademarks and service marks in your state should be able to tell you by phone if another business has registered a name that's the same as or close to the one you're thinking about. In some states, you may have to request the information in writing and pay a small fee for the search. It makes better sense, however, to mount an even broader search, checking on state registrations nationwide—a task made simple by using a computer database (see below).
- *Check the federal trademark register.* Since goods and services are widely marketed over

the Internet as well as through mail-order catalogs these days, your small business— even though you think it's local—may find itself competing with national companies. It makes sense to make sure you're not infringing on a trademark or service mark that's been federally registered. A large public library or special business and government library near you should carry the federal trademark register, which contains trademark and service mark names arranged by categories of goods and services. Check it for potential conflicts with your name. Also check the *Official Gazette* for the most recent filings.

Performing a full search of all registered and unregistered trademark sources involves time, effort and some cost. Also, since there is considerable skill involved in doing an in-depth search, it often makes sense to engage professional help. But fortunately, there are three different levels of searches and a small, local business can often get by with a somewhat shallower search. The three levels are:

1. **A direct hit federal register search,** which compares your mark with identical or very similar federally registered (and pending) marks in one or more trademark classes. This is the quickest, cheapest and most bare-bones type search. A direct hit search is especially helpful when you're trying to choose among several potential names or trademarks and want to narrow the field by discovering and eliminating obviously unavailable names or marks.

2. **An analytical search,** which compares your mark with all registered and pending marks (federal and state) that sound or look like your mark. The search also covers marks that mean the same thing or in some other way might lead to customers' confusion between them and your mark. This deeper type of search is more expensive and time-consuming than a direct hit search.

3. **A comprehensive trademark search,** which hunts for all possibly relevant unregis-

tered marks as well as for federal and state registered (and pending) trademarks. Because of its depth and breadth, this type of search is the trickiest to do well and, as a result, the most expensive and time-consuming.

For many businesses, especially those that plan to operate regionally or nationally, a direct hit search is only the first step to clearing a business name. If the proposed name is distinctive, a more thorough search—at least an analytical search—will be appropriate.

> **EXAMPLE:** Jamie is considering Geoscan as the name of her new company. She does a direct hit search and finds that no one else has registered that name. That's reassuring. But since Jamie plans to do business nationwide, she decides that she can't rely entirely on the direct hit search and needs to dig deeper.

Jamie has chosen a fairly distinctive name, so she is wise to take further steps. If your proposed name is less distinctive (a "weak" mark), or your business is small and local and you can live with the possibility that an undiscovered prior user will surface later, a direct hit search may suffice. A search firm can do a direct hit search for a reasonable fee. Or you can do the search yourself by using the federal government's trademark database, called TESS (for Trademark Electronic Search Service). You'll find it at the website of the U.S. Patent and Trademark Office, www.uspto.gov. To use TESS, you enter the business name you're interested in. The database will tell you if someone else is using the name, and if so, will give you the owner's name, the date of registration or application and the goods or services it represents.

A deeper, analytical search looks for synonyms, phonetic equivalents, alternative spellings, anagrams (rearrangements of letters) and other similarities that may create a potential conflict.

EXAMPLE: Jamie embarks on an analytical search. She starts out by looking at the marks that immediately surround Geoscan alphabetically (it turns out that Geoport and Geoscope have been registered). Then she checks out all the marks ending in -scan and all marks with the sounds -eo or -osc in the middle. She also searches for all the synonyms she can think of (earthspan), and then anagrams (scanoge, canesog) and alternative spellings (gioscan, jeoscan, geoskan). This gives her a better idea of potential conflicts.

It's essential to perform this deeper search if you want to make sure your business name or mark isn't likely to be challenged as being confusingly similar to, or evocative of, an existing name or mark. While in theory it's possible for you to do an analytical search using the TESS database, I recommend you use another Internet resource, SAEGIS by Thomson & Thomson at www.saegis.com. True, even here, there's a considerable learning curve—and you will have to pay some fees. But the SAEGIS search engine is simply better suited to analytical searching than TESS.

Often, it's wise to go beyond a direct hit search *and* an analytical search. If you have a small, local business, you should, in addition to a direct hit search, check the Yellow Pages, newspapers, trade and product journals and any other source that might show that another business is using the same or a similar name or mark locally. If your business elects to do a more comprehensive search, you'd include not only an analytical search of registered and pending trademarks, but also an examination of Yellow Pages, trade directories, the Internet, product catalogs and other industry sources. Because most disputes about names and marks are resolved in favor of the first actual user, you need to discover any actual use of the proposed name—whether or not it's officially registered.

Consider hiring a search firm. *You can reliably do a direct hit search yourself, but for an analytical or comprehensive search, a search firm is likely to produce more reliable results. It may be well worth the cost—especially if you have a strong and distinctive mark and will be investing heavily in promoting your products or services under that mark.*

Search firms—which, unlike lawyers, don't offer legal advice—generally charge as follows:

- *direct hit search (for identical marks)—from $30 to $100 per mark searched.*
- *analytical federally registered trademark search (for similar or related marks)—from $85 to $300 per trademark.*
- *common law search (for unregistered marks) —from $100 to $200 per mark searched.*
- *comprehensive search (combining analytical federal, state and common law)—between $185 and $500 per mark searched.*

The ranges of rates reflect variations in search coverage, the type of report you get, the experience of the searchers and economies of scale. Be on the lookout for firms that advertise an unusually low price to draw you in, but then add on charges so the overall cost becomes excessive. Shop sensibly to determine the true cost.

2. Analyzing Your Search Results

So now you've done your search, whether by hiring a search firm or performing the search yourself, and you have the results in hand. What do the results mean? There are a few things you should look for when you read through the names that were found in your search. First, did your search turn up any names that are identical to the one you are using or plan to use? Finding an identical name should make you pause, but doesn't automatically mean that you must scrap plans to use your name. If the identical name is being used for a very different product or service from the one you are producing or plan to produce, then you have good reason to move forward with your plans to use the name and register it as a trademark or service mark. For example, just because a plumbing business in Coos, Oregon, calls itself Z-Pop doesn't mean you, in Arizona, can't use Z-Pop as the brand name for your soda pop. That plumbing business in Oregon is not your competitor and your use of Z-Pop for your soda pop will not likely confuse customers into thinking that your soda pop is related to that plumbing business. On the other hand, if you find an identical name being used on an identical or closely related product or service, such as another soda pop product, then you really should consider choosing a different name. Even if the company using the name seems like a local outfit in a faraway place, it could have plans to expand its territory.

The second thing you should look out for is an identical (or very similar) name that is linked to a very famous company or product. This situation is often referred to, in trademark lingo, as dilution. Dilution occurs when a brand name has become so famous (like Coke) that not even noncompeting products or services can use the name. If it turns out that the mark you've had your eye on is famous and highly marketed, don't touch it. Let it go. Find another name.

Finally, the third thing you should look for is a name that is very similar to the name you want to use. If you find a similar name *and* it is being used to market the same type of product or service that you are planning to create or offer, then you should seriously consider choosing a different name. How close is close? That is a very tricky issue and is often a matter of considerable subjectivity on the part of trademark examiners and the PTO. If you're not sure and really want to use the name, consider hiring an attorney specializing in trademark law for the sole purpose of helping you decide if the two names are too close for comfort.

We've given you a few guidelines for evaluating your search results, but there is more to evaluating competing names than what we can provide in this chapter. If you think your situation is more complex and you need more information, please consult the recommended book below.

 For more information on conducting a thorough national search and on how to evaluate competing marks, see Trademark: Legal Care for Your Business & Product Name, *by Stephen Elias (Nolo).* ■

7

Licenses and Permits

Y ou'll probably need a license or permit— maybe several—for your business. In some locations, every business needs a basic business license. But whether or not that is required, your business may need one or more specialized licenses. This is especially likely if you serve or sell food, liquor or firearms, work with hazardous materials or discharge any materials into the air or water.

There are licensing and permit requirements at all levels of government—federal, state, regional, county and city. It's not always easy to discover exactly what licenses and permits you'll need. But it's very important. You should thoroughly research this issue before you start a business, complete the purchase of a business, change locations or remodel or expand your operation. If you don't, you may face huge expenses and hassles. In a worst case situation, you could be prevented from operating your planned business at a particular location but still be obligated to pay rent or a mortgage. For example, what if you sign a five-year lease for business space and then discover that the location isn't zoned properly for your business? What if you buy a restaurant and then find out that the liquor license isn't transferable? Or suppose you rent or buy business space thinking that you can afford to remodel or expand it, without realizing that remodeling means you must comply with all current ordinances? You might have to pay for $15,000 worth of improvements to comply with the federal Americans with Disabilities Act or $10,000 for a state-of-the-art waste disposal system.

Here are several examples that illustrate the types of licenses and permits many businesses need:

- Misook plans to open a new restaurant. Before doing so, she needs a permit from the department of building and safety for remodeling work and a license from the health department approving the kitchen equipment and ventilation system. She also needs a sign permit and approval of her customer and employee parking facilities from the city plan-

ning department. Finally, she has to get a sales tax license; even though in her state sit-down meals are not taxed, she must collect and report sales tax for take-out orders and miscellaneous items such as cookbooks.

- Leisure Time Enterprises, a partnership, buys a liquor store that also sells state lottery tickets. In addition to obtaining a basic business license issued by the city, the partners must have the state-issued alcoholic beverage license transferred to them. They also have to apply to the state lottery bureau for a transfer of the lottery license and to the state treasury department for a sales tax license.

- Electronic Assembly Inc., a corporation that assembles electronic components for manufacturers of stereo equipment, must obtain a conditional use permit from the planning and zoning board in order to conduct its "light manufacturing operation" in a commercial district. The company also needs clearance from a tri-county environmental agency concerned about possible air pollution and disposal of toxic chemicals. In addition, the new elevator must be inspected and approved by the state department of labor.

- Peaches and Cream, a new disco, has to get fire department clearance for its exit system and also must comply with the city's parking ordinance—which practically speaking means negotiating with the planning department for the number of off-street parking spaces the disco will provide for customers. The club also needs a liquor license from the state liquor control commission, a cabaret license from the city council and a sales tax license.

- Glenda needs an occupational license from the state department of cosmetology before she can open up her beauty shop. Because she carries a line of shampoos, conditioners and make-up, she needs a sales tax permit as well. In addition, because she's extending the front of her shop three feet into the front setback area, she needs a variance from the zoning board of appeals. Finally, because she's in an "historic preservation area," her sign must be approved by the local planning board.

In short, license and permit requirements can affect where you locate your business, how much you'll have to spend for remodeling and whether or not you'll have to provide off-street parking. If zoning requirements are too restrictive, you might even decide to avoid the hassle and move somewhere you don't have to fight City Hall for the right to do business. Similarly, if building codes require extensive—and expensive—remodeling to bring an older building up to current standards, you might want to look for newer space that already complies with building and safety laws.

Each state has its own system of licensing as does each unit of local government. Obviously, it's impossible to provide a comprehensive list of every permit and license in the United States. Fortunately, I can give you some general principles and a positive approach to help you learn about and comply with the licensing requirements that affect your business.

⚠ Double check license and permit rules.
When you investigate the type of licenses and permits you need for your business, check directly with the appropriate governmental agencies. Never rely on the fact that an existing business similar to yours didn't need a license or had to meet only minimal building code requirements. Laws and ordinances are amended frequently—generally to impose more stringent requirements. Often an existing business is allowed to continue under the old rules, but new businesses must meet the higher standards. Similarly, for obvious reasons, don't rely on the advice of real estate agents, business brokers, the seller of a business or anyone else with a financial interest in having a deal go through.

The Purposes of Licenses and Permits

Governments require licenses and permits for two basic reasons. One is to raise money; the whole point behind some licenses or permits is to levy a tax on doing business. In a way, these are the easiest to comply with—you pay your money and get your license.

The other basic purpose behind licenses and permits is to protect public health and safety and, increasingly, aesthetics. A sign ordinance that dictates the size and placement of a business sign or an environmental regulation that prohibits you from releasing sulphur dioxide into the atmosphere are two of many possible examples. Complying with regulatory ordinances can often be far more difficult than complying with those designed simply to raise money.

A. Federal Registrations and Licenses

Small businesses don't have to worry about federal permits and licenses, but all businesses must know about federal tax registrations.

1. Tax Registrations

On the federal level, there are two tax registrations that you should know about. The first is the application for an Employer Identification Number (Form SS-4), which should be filed by every business. The form is available online at www.irs.gov. If you're a sole proprietor, you may use your own Social Security number rather than a separate Employer Identification Number, but I generally recommend that even sole proprietors obtain an Employer Identification Number—especially if they plan to hire employees or retain independent contractors. It's one good way to keep your business and personal affairs separate. Employer Identification Numbers are covered in Chapter 8.

The second federal registration requirement applies if your business is a corporation and you want to elect status as an S corporation. In that case, you need to file Form 2553 (*Election by a Small Business Corporation*; also available at www.irs.gov). S corporations are discussed in Chapter 1, Section C2, and Chapter 3, Section A2; the requirements for filing Form 2553 are discussed in Chapter 8, Section B.

2. Federal Licenses and Permits

The federal government doesn't require permits from most small businesses, but it does get into the act when certain business activities or products are involved. Below is a list of the business operations most likely to need a federal license or permit, along with the name of the federal agency to contact.

Business	Agency to Contact
Investments advisors	Securities and Exchange Commission
Ground transportation business such as a trucking company operating as a common carrier	Federal Motor Carrier Safety Administration
Preparation of meat products	Food and Drug Administration
Production of drugs	Food and Drug Administration
Making tobacco products or alcohol, or making or dealing in firearms	Bureau of Alcohol, Tobacco and Firearms of the U.S. Treasury Department

B. State Requirements

It may take a little effort to discover which business permits and licenses your state requires. Fortunately, small-business assistance agencies set up in every U.S. state can help you cut through the bureaucratic thicket. (See Appendix A.) Most offer free or inexpensive publications that list the required state registrations, licenses and permits. Often the information is available online at the agency website.

Beyond contacting these general purpose agencies, it's wise to call all state agencies that might regulate your business and ask what they require. In addition, you can often get valuable information from the state chamber of commerce and from trade associations or professional groups serving your business, profession or industry.

1. Licensing of Occupations and Professions

It should come as no surprise that states require licensing of people practicing the traditional professions, such as lawyers, physicians, dentists, accountants, psychologists, nurses, pharmacists, architects and professional engineers. Most states also require licenses for people engaged in a broad range of other occupations. The list varies from state to state but typically includes such people as barbers, auto mechanics, bill collectors, private investigators, building contractors, cosmetologists, funeral directors, pest control specialists, real estate agents, tax preparers and insurance agents. Since you can't always guess the occupations for which licenses are needed, you'll need to inquire.

Some licenses are taken out by the business entity (for example, your partnership or corporation), while others must be issued to the individuals who work in the business. For example, licensing laws for professionals—including lawyers, doctors, accountants and architects—tend to place requirements on individual professionals rather than on the partnership or professional corporation that is the business entity.

The procedures vary, but to get a license for a profession or occupation, you'll probably have to show evidence of training in the field, and you may have to pass a written examination. Sometimes you must practice your trade or profession under the supervision of a more experienced person before you can become fully licensed. For example, a real estate agent usually must work under the supervision of a licensed broker for several years before the agent is eligible to become a broker. Usually there's a formal application process, which may involve a background check. A license may be good only for a limited period, after which time there may be retesting before the license can be renewed. License laws for some occupations and professions require evidence of continuing education, usually in the form of short professional seminars.

2. Tax Registration

In all but the few states that still assess no taxes on income, chances are you'll have to register under your state's income tax laws in much the same way that you do under the federal laws. The state agency in charge (such as the treasury department or the department of revenue) can tell you what registrations are necessary. In addition, if you're engaging in retail sales, you may need to register for or obtain a sales tax license. There may also be registrations for other business taxes.

3. Employer-Employee Matters

As an employer, you may have to register with your state's department of labor or with agencies administering the laws on unemployment compensation and workers' compensation. As explained in more detail in Chapter 15, workers' compensation is a method of paying the medical bills and lost wages of employees injured in the course of their employment—regardless of who is at fault. Some state laws allow a business to be self-insured under some circumstances, but for most small businesses this isn't practical, so you'll have to carry workers' compensation insurance.

In addition, if your state has its own version of the federal Occupational Safety and Health Act (OSHA), your business may need to meet certain state-mandated requirements to protect your employees in the workplace.

Finally, a number of tax requirements relate to a business that has employees or works with independent contractors. For example, you'll need to get Employer ID Numbers from both the IRS and state tax authorities. And you'll have to withhold income taxes and Social Security taxes from the paychecks of employees, and report the figures to both the employee and the government. With independent contractors, you need to report income annually on a Form 1099 which goes to the independent contractor and the government. For more on taxation, see Chapter 8. For more on employees and independent contractors, see Chapter 15.

4. Licensing Based on Products Sold

Some licenses for businesses are based on the type of products sold. For example, there often are special licenses for businesses that sell liquor, food, lottery tickets, gasoline or firearms.

5. Environmental Regulations

Governmental regulation of environmental concerns continues to expand. As the owner of a small business, you may have to deal with regulators at the state or regional (multi-county) level. It's unlikely that you'll become involved with environmental regulations at the federal level.

Here are several activities that affect the environment and may require a special permit.

- *Emissions into the air for an incinerator, boiler or other facility.* For example, if you're going to be venting your dry cleaning equipment into the outside air, you may need a permit.
- *Discharge of waste water to surface or ground water.* For example, you may need a discharge permit if byproducts from manufacturing are being disposed of in a nearby pond. And you may need a storage permit if materials that you store on your site could contaminate ground or surface water.
- *Handling of hazardous waste.* If your business has any connection with hazardous waste, it's likely that the environmental agency will require you to at least maintain accurate records concerning the waste. You may need special disposal permits as well. Environmental regulations may also require you to register underground storage tanks holding gasoline, oil or other chemicals. And if there's an underground tank on your business site that's no longer being used, you may be required to remove it.

Permits aren't just for big factories. *At first glance, the above list might suggest that only manufacturers or owners of large businesses need to worry about environmental regulations. Not so. Many small businesses need to obtain permits, or at least become informed about what they must do to avoid contaminating the environment. For ex-ample, if you create and sell leaded glass windows, you need to know if you can dump your lead-laced wastewater down the nearby storm sewer or need a permit for some other means of disposal. Similarly, dry cleaners, photo processors and others need to know the rules for handling and disposing of the hazardous substances used in their work.*

C. Regional Requirements

Increasingly, some environmental concerns are being addressed by regional (multi-county) agencies rather than by an arm of the state or local government. If so, you may need a permit or license from that regional body.

1. Environmental Regulations

In many areas, control of air pollution is now handled by a regional (multi-county or state) agency that issues permits and monitors compliance. For example, in northern California, the Bay Area Air Quality Control District covers at least seven counties. A regional body with environmental responsibilities may also have jurisdiction over waste water discharge or the storage or disposal of hazardous materials.

2. Water Usage

Questions affecting the use of water by a small business are usually dealt with at the local (city or county) level, but some issues may fall within the jurisdiction of a regional authority. For example, if your business is in a semi-rural area and plans to draw its water from a well rather than the public water supply, a regional health authority may test the purity of the water before you're allowed to use it. In scarce-water areas, a regional water management body may have authority to decide whether or not you may install a well or use an existing one.

Similarly, while regulation of septic systems typically is left to local health departments, in some areas permits may be under the control of a regional body.

D. Local Requirements

On the local level, begin by asking city and county officials about license and permit requirements for your business. A few larger cities that hope to attract economic growth may have a centralized office that provides this information. Otherwise, the city and county officials most likely to be of help are as follows:

- city or county clerk
- building and safety department
- health department
- planning (zoning) department
- tax offices (for example, tax assessor or treasurer)
- fire department
- police department
- public works department.

Nonofficial but often extremely helpful sources of information include local chambers of commerce, trade associations, contractors who have experience in building or remodeling commercial space and people who have businesses like yours. You can also consult a lawyer who's familiar with small businesses similar to yours.

1. Local Property Taxes

Your city may impose a property tax on the furniture, fixtures and equipment that your business owns. If so, you may be required by law to file a list of that property with city tax officials, along with cost and depreciation information. You may have to update this information annually. Sometimes there's also a tax on inventory—which leads many retail businesses to run a stock reduction sale a few weeks before the inventory-taking date mandated by the tax law.

2. Other Local Taxes

Some cities, especially larger ones, tax gross receipts and income. Check with the city treasurer for registration and filing requirements.

3. Health and Environmental Permits

If your business involves food preparation or sales, you'll need a license or permit from the local health department. The health ordinances may require regular inspections as well. Whether you run a sit-down or a fast-food restaurant or a catering establishment, you can expect the health department to take a keen interest in the type of cooking equipment you use, the adequacy of the refrigeration system and many other features of the business that can affect the health of your customers.

You may also run into health department regulations if you receive water from a well rather than a public water supply. In small towns or semi-rural areas, health departments routinely test well water for purity. Also, where septic systems are used for sanitary sewer disposal, the health department supervises the installation of new septic systems to make sure that there's no health hazard. (As noted in Section C, in some areas these matters are handled by regional rather than local authorities.)

Increasingly, local health departments are getting involved in environmental duties, including such things as radon tests and asbestos removal. Many other environmental problems, however, such as air and water quality, are still dealt with mainly at the state and regional level.

4. Crowd Control

If your business deals with large numbers of customers, you may need licenses or permits from the fire or police departments. These agencies are concerned about overcrowding and the ability of people to leave the premises in case there's an emergency. The role of the fire department may overlap with that of the building and safety department in prescribing the number of exit doors, the hardware on those doors, the lighting to be used and the maintenance of clear paths to the exits. The fire department will also be concerned about combustible materials used or stored on your business premises.

5. Building Codes

For anything but the most minor renovation (such as putting in track lighting or installing shelves), you're likely to need a permit—maybe several—from the building and safety department which enforces building ordinances and codes. Often, separate permits are issued for separate parts of a construction or remodeling project, including permits for electrical, plumbing and mechanical (heating and ventilating) work. If you don't have experience in these areas, you may need a licensed contractor to help you discover the requirements for your construction or remodeling project.

Building codes are amended frequently, and each revision seems to put new restrictions and requirements on the building owner. Municipalities often exempt existing businesses from laying out

money to retrofit their premises—at least for major items such as elevators, heating and ventilating systems and overhead sprinkler systems. This is sometimes called "grandfathering"—slang for not imposing new rules retroactively. Grandfathering can create surprises. You may look at space in an older building and figure that you'll have no problems in doing business there because the current business owner or the one who just vacated the premises didn't. You could be in for a surprise. The prior occupant may have had the benefit of grandfathering language which didn't require him or her to bring the space up to the level of the current codes. A change in occupancy or ownership may end the benefits of grandfathering, and a new occupant or owner may be required to make extensive improvements. An experienced contractor can help you determine the building and safety requirements that apply to a particular space—for example, a code section mandating that railings on outside stairs be 36 inches high.

If You Build or Remodel

For any building or remodeling project, it's essential that you learn the applicable rules. If your city uses all or part of the Uniform Building Code, get a copy of it.

Other municipal ordinances may be administered by the building and safety department or by another unit of local government. There's no uniformity in how the responsibility for administering these other ordinances is assigned. A large municipality or county might have several separate departments to act as the enforcing agency. A smaller city or county would probably leave everything to the building and safety department.

6. Zoning Ordinances

Before you sign a lease, you absolutely need to know that the space is properly zoned for your usage. If it's not, it's best to make the lease contingent on your getting the property rezoned or getting a variance or conditional use permit—whatever it takes under the ordinance to make it possible for you to do business there without being hassled by the city or county. In some communities, you must get a zoning compliance permit before you start your business at a given location. Other communities simply wait for someone to complain before zoning compliance gets looked at. Keep in mind that by applying for a construction permit for remodeling or by filing tax information with the municipality, you may trigger an investigation of zoning compliance.

Zoning laws may also regulate off-street parking, water and air quality and waste disposal, and the size, construction and placement of signs. In some communities, historic district restrictions may keep you from modifying the exterior of a building or even changing the paint color without permission from a board of administrators. Years ago, people tried to argue in court that such regulation of aesthetics wasn't a proper governmental function—that it wasn't related to the protection of the public health and safety. However, a carefully drawn ordinance seeking to preserve the special appeal of a historic district will very likely survive a legal challenge. So if you look at space in one of these protected neighborhoods, be prepared to suspend your freedom of choice and place the destiny of at least the exterior of the building in the hands of a panel of administrators.

In Chapter 14, dealing with home-based businesses, you'll find a discussion of zoning ordinances as they relate to businesses in the home. Take the time to review Chapter 14, Sections A and B, because zoning restrictions apply to all businesses.

E. How to Deal With Local Building and Zoning Officials

There's a certain amount of administrative discretion under building codes and zoning ordinances—enough, certainly, that it can help greatly to have the administrators on your side. Here are some ideas for accomplishing this.

1. Seek Support From the Business Community

If you employ local people and will contribute positively to the economy, it may pay to make contact with city or county business development officials or even the chamber of commerce. If they see your business as an asset and don't want you to locate in the next city, they may be helpful in steering you through the building and safety department and may even advocate on your behalf before zoning and planning officials. Trade associations and merchants' associations may also come to your aid if you need building and safety officials to decide in your favor in areas in which they have some administrative discretion. Finally, contractors, lawyers and others who are familiar with the system and the personalities often know how to get things done and can be helpful to you.

2. Appealing an Adverse Ruling

The decision of a zoning or building official isn't necessarily final. If you get an adverse decision from the local Planning Commission, for example, you may be able to have a board of zoning adjustment or board of appeals interpret the zoning ordinance in a way that's favorable to you. Alternatively, you may be able to obtain a variance (a special exception to a zoning law) if a strict interpretation of the ordinance causes a hardship. In some cases, you can get a conditional use permit, which lets you use the property in question for your kind of business as long as you meet certain conditions set down by the administrative panel.

In dealing with administrators and especially with appeals boards, it's important to have the support of neighbors and others in your community. A favorable petition signed by most other businesses in your immediate area or oral expressions of support from half a dozen neighbors can make the difference between success and failure at an administrative hearing. Conversely, if objectors are numerous and adamant, you may not get what you're after. So if you sense opposition developing from those living or doing business nearby, try to resolve your differences before you get to a public hearing—even if it means you must make compromises on the details of your proposal.

LAW IN THE REAL WORLD
Strategic Planning Pays Off

Shelby, owner of Small Universe Books, is delighted to learn that the drugstore next door is going out of business. He immediately seeks to buy or sign a long-term lease for the building so he can expand his profitable business. The future looks rosy.

Not so fast. Shelby learns that for his new business use of the building, he'll have to supply eight parking spaces to get a permit. Doing this in his desperately crowded neighborhood is totally impossible at anything approaching an affordable price.

Instead of giving up, Shelby asks the city planning commission for a variance to waive the parking spaces rule. A public hearing is scheduled. Shelby knows he has to put on a persuasive case, so he:

- Calls hundreds of local writers, publishers, critics, educators and book lovers to pack the hearing room and testify that an expanded book store will be a great community resource.
- Documents the prohibitive cost of buying or leasing the required parking spaces.
- Offers to validate parking at a lot four blocks away, just outside the worst of the congested area.
- Hires an architect who determines that a heavily used, nearby public garage can accommodate 20 more cars if the parking spaces are striped differently.
- Offers to pay for the restriping.

Shelby gets the variance.

3. Going to Court

Every day, hundreds if not thousands of interpretations and applications of building and zoning laws are worked out through negotiation with administrators and through administrative appeals. But if these channels fail, it's possible in many instances to go to court. This can be very expensive and time-consuming. What good is it if you win your battle for a permit to remodel your premises but you waste two years getting to that point? Still, there are times when what you're seeking is so valuable and your chances of success are so great that you can afford both the time and money to get a definitive ruling from the courts. And in some instances, you can get a court to consider your dispute fairly quickly. If, for example, you submitted plans to the city that complied with all building and safety codes, and the building official refused to issue a building permit unless you agreed to put in some additional improvements you believe are not required by the ordinance, you could quickly go to court asking for an order of "mandamus" based on the fact that the administrator wasn't following the law.

Before you consider court action, however, get as much information as you can about the cost of litigation, how long it will take (you can win in the trial court, but the city might decide to appeal), and the likelihood of your ultimate success. This is a specialized corner of the law, so you're going to need someone who's had experience in the field— and there may not be that many to choose from in any given location. Look for a lawyer who's represented a similar business in a dispute with the city or someone who formerly worked as a city attorney and knows all the ins and outs of the local ordinances. ■

8

Tax Basics for the Small Business

No matter whether your business is organized as a sole proprietorship, partnership, corporation or limited liability company, you've automatically got a silent partner: Uncle Sam. The federal tax laws make this unavoidable. To guard against interest and penalties, you need to know what tax forms to file and when to file them. And to succeed in business, you need at least a basic, working knowledge of the tax system.

On a more positive note, by being aware of the fine points of the tax laws, you can often legally save a bundle of money—not to mention aggravation. For example, having a clear picture of what the IRS regards as a proper business expense will allow you to take deductions that otherwise might not occur to you.

⚠️ **Get detailed information.** *The tax laws are vast and complicated, and you'll surely need much more information than you'll find in this chapter. Here I just hit the high points; it's up to you to deepen your knowledge. A good starting place is the IRS website at www.irs.gov.*

In addition to what you learn from books and other publications, you may have to hire a bookkeeper and an accountant. If you're operating a one-person word processing business out of your home, you may be able to keep your books and do your taxes with no professional help at all—or perhaps get help just the first time you file your annual tax return, to make sure you've correctly completed Schedules C (*Profit or Loss From Business*) and SE (*Self-Employment Tax*). On the other hand, if you've formed a corporation that's operating a good-sized dry-cleaning shop with eight employees, you may want an accountant to help set up your books and to prepare—or at least review—your business tax returns each year. And you may find that employing a part-time bookkeeper not only results in your records being well kept, but also frees you for more important tasks.

A word of caution about one other possible source of assistance: IRS employees. Most of them are hardworking and well-meaning, but their training and supervision are often inadequate. Unfortunately, it's common to receive poor oral advice in answer to questions. And if the advice proves to be so inaccurate that it results in your being assessed interest and penalties, the fact that you got it from an IRS employee won't get you off the hook. In short, it's often cheaper in the long run to rely on the advice of an experienced small business accountant than on a free oral opinion from the IRS.

State Taxes. In addition to federal taxes, you need to be aware of your state's tax scheme, which may include an income tax structured along the same lines as the federal version or one that has some major differences. Before you begin your business, contact your state's taxing authority to get detailed information.

A. Employer Identification Number

Even if your business has no employees, you must get an Employer Identification Number (EIN) from the IRS when you start a business that you've set up as:

- a partnership
- an S corporation
- a C (regular) corporation
- a limited liability company (LLC) with two or more members, or
- a single-member LLC that you've chosen to have taxed as corporation.

Technically, if you're a sole proprietor or the sole member of a limited liability company (LLC) which is not being taxed as a corporation (see Chapter 1, Section D) and you have no employees, you can use your personal Social Security number instead of an EIN. But even in those situations, it's a good business practice to get an EIN to differentiate cleanly between your personal and business finances.

You'll need your EIN before you file a tax return or make a tax deposit. In some cases, a bank will require you to have an EIN before you can open a business bank account.

APPLICATION FOR EMPLOYER IDENTIFICATION NUMBER

| Form **SS-4**
 (Rev. December 2001)
 Department of the Treasury
 Internal Revenue Service | **Application for Employer Identification Number**
 (For use by employers, corporations, partnerships, trusts, estates, churches, government agencies, Indian tribal entities, certain individuals, and others.)
 ► See separate instructions for each line. ► Keep a copy for your records. | EIN

 OMB No. 1545-0003 |

Type or print clearly.

1 Legal name of entity (or individual) for whom the EIN is being requested
Alpha Bean Cromwell

| **2** Trade name of business (if different from name on line 1)
 ABCD Plumbing | **3** Executor, trustee, "care of" name |

| **4a** Mailing address (room, apt., suite no. and street, or P.O. box)
 1234 Rooter Place | **5a** Street address (if different) (Do not enter a P.O. box.) |
| **4b** City, state, and ZIP code
 Nowheresville, CA 95555 | **5b** City, state, and ZIP code |

6 County and state where principal business is located
Somewheres County, California

| **7a** Name of principal officer, general partner, grantor, owner, or trustor
 Alpha Bean Cromwell | **7b** SSN, ITIN, or EIN |

8a Type of entity (check only one box)
- [X] Sole proprietor (SSN) 555 55 5555
- [ ] Partnership
- [ ] Corporation (enter form number to be filed) ►
- [ ] Personal service corp.
- [ ] Church or church-controlled organization
- [ ] Other nonprofit organization (specify) ►
- [ ] Other (specify) ►

- [ ] Estate (SSN of decedent)
- [ ] Plan administrator (SSN)
- [ ] Trust (SSN of grantor)
- [ ] National Guard   [ ] State/local government
- [ ] Farmers' cooperative   [ ] Federal government/military
- [ ] REMIC   [ ] Indian tribal governments/enterprises
- Group Exemption Number (GEN) ►

8b If a corporation, name the state or foreign country (if applicable) where incorporated | State | Foreign country

9 Reason for applying (check only one box)
- [X] Started new business (specify type) ►
- [ ] Hired employees (Check the box and see line 12.)
- [ ] Compliance with IRS withholding regulations
- [ ] Other (specify) ►

- [ ] Banking purpose (specify purpose) ►
- [ ] Changed type of organization (specify new type) ►
- [ ] Purchased going business
- [ ] Created a trust (specify type) ►
- [ ] Created a pension plan (specify type) ►

10 Date business started or acquired (month, day, year)
01/01/03

11 Closing month of accounting year
December

12 First date wages or annuities were paid or will be paid (month, day, year). **Note:** If applicant is a withholding agent, enter date income will first be paid to nonresident alien. (month, day, year) . . . . ►

13 Highest number of employees expected in the next 12 months. **Note:** If the applicant does not expect to have any employees during the period, enter "-0-." . . . . ►

Agricultural	Household	Other

14 Check **one** box that best describes the principal activity of your business.
- [ ] Construction   [ ] Rental & leasing   [ ] Transportation & warehousing
- [ ] Real estate   [ ] Manufacturing   [ ] Finance & insurance
- [ ] Health care & social assistance   [ ] Wholesale-agent/broker
- [ ] Accommodation & food service   [ ] Wholesale-other   [ ] Retail
- [ ] Other (specify)

15 Indicate principal line of merchandise sold; specific construction work done; products produced; or services provided.

16a Has the applicant ever applied for an employer identification number for this or any other business? . . . . [ ] Yes [X] No
Note: If "Yes," please complete lines 16b and 16c.

16b If you checked "Yes" on line 16a, give applicant's legal name and trade name shown on prior application if different from line 1 or 2 above.
Legal name ►   Trade name ►

16c Approximate date when, and city and state where, the application was filed. Enter previous employer identification number if known.

Approximate date when filed (mo., day, year)	City and state where filed	Previous EIN

Third Party Designee	Complete this section **only** if you want to authorize the named individual to receive the entity's EIN and answer questions about the completion of this form.	
	Designee's name	Designee's telephone number (include area code) (510) 555-5555
	Address and ZIP code	Designee's fax number (include area code) (510) 666-6666

Under penalties of perjury, I declare that I have examined this application, and to the best of my knowledge and belief, it is true, correct, and complete.

Applicant's telephone number (include area code) ( )

Name and title (type or print clearly) ►

Applicant's fax number (include area code) ( )

Signature ► *Alpha Bean Cromwell*   Date ► 1/1/03

For Privacy Act and Paperwork Reduction Act Notice, see separate instructions.   Cat. No. 16055N   Form **SS-4** (Rev. 12-2001)

1. How to Apply

To get an EIN, file Form SS-4, *Application for Employer Identification Number.*

The form isn't difficult to fill out if you follow the IRS instructions. Nevertheless, a few pointers may help.

Space 1. Insert your official corporate name if you're a corporation or your official company name if you're a limited liability company. If you're a partnership, use the partnership name shown in your partnership agreement. If you're a sole proprietor, insert your full name—the name you use on your personal tax return.

Space 11. Here you're asked to state the closing month of your business accounting year. Your answer, however, isn't binding. You make your binding election of a fiscal year-end on the first federal income tax return that you file for the business.

Sole proprietors, partnerships, S corporations, personal service corporations (see Chapter 1, Section F2a) and limited liability companies are generally required to use a calendar year—that is, a year ending December 31—for tax purposes. Personal service corporations have two basic characteristics:

- the professional employees of the corporation own the stock, and
- the corporation performs its services in the fields of health, law, engineering, architecture, accounting, actuarial science, performing arts or consulting.

To use a tax year other than a calendar year, an S corporation must demonstrate to the IRS that there is a substantial business reason to do so, such as the seasonal nature of the business. Basically, the IRS wants to make sure that permitting you to claim a tax year other than the calendar year won't substantially distort your income.

See IRS Publication 589, Tax Information on S Corporations, *and IRS Publication 538,* Business Purpose Tax Year, *for details.*

A regular corporation that's not a personal service corporation is freer to choose a fiscal year. Most small businesses find that where there's a choice, the calendar year is the most convenient way to proceed. Sometimes, however, there are tax planning reasons for a business owner to choose a different tax year for the business.

EXAMPLE 1: Radcraft Inc., a regular corporation, selects the calendar year for its fiscal year. In December 2003 it pays a $30,000 bonus to Jill, the president and sole shareholder. The bonus is included on Jill's 2003 income tax return, and tax on the bonus is due in April 2004.

EXAMPLE 2: Jill selects a fiscal year of February 1 through January 31 for Radcraft Inc. (On Form SS-4, she lists January in space 11 for the closing month of the corporation's accounting year.) In January 2003, the corporation pays Jill a $30,000 bonus. The bonus is included in Jill's 2003 income tax return. The tax on the bonus isn't due until April 2004—although Jill must keep track of it when computing her quarterly estimates in 2003.

An accountant or other experienced tax advisor can help you decide whether or not you and your corporation can realize a tax advantage by using a tax year other than a calendar year.

Space 12. The IRS will send you computer-generated payroll tax forms based on your answer to this question.

Space 13. These numbers can be estimated. It's usually best to estimate on the low side.

Space 17a. This question refers to the business, not the owner. Normally, a partnership, corporation or limited liability company has only one Employer Identification Number (EIN). A sole proprietor may have several businesses, each with a separate number.

After filling out the form, there are three ways to obtain the number.

- *By mail.* If you have enough lead time, you can mail Form SS-4 to the IRS and wait for the number to be mailed to you, which will take about four weeks.
- *By phone.* To get a Form SS-4 processed more quickly, use the TELE-TIN system operated by the IRS. Complete Form SS-4 and, before you mail it, phone in the information to the IRS at the phone number for your region. Phone numbers are listed in the form's instruction sheet. An IRS employee assigns an EIN, which you'll then insert in the upper-right corner of the form before sending it to the IRS.
- *By email.* The IRS has made it a snap to get your EIN online. Go to www.irs.gov/smallbiz for details.
- *By fax.* You can fax your Form SS-4. To obtain the fax number, inquire at the IRS office where you pick up your Form SS-4. You'll get your EIN in a day or two. This is slower than the phone method but it avoids the frustration of repeated calling because the TELE-TIN voice line is tied up.

Use your EIN on all business tax returns, checks and other documents you send to the IRS. Your state taxing authority may also require your EIN on state tax forms.

2. When to Get a New Number

If your S corporation chooses to change to a regular corporation—or your regular corporation chooses to change to an S corporation—it doesn't need a new EIN; the one you already have is still sufficient. However, you'll need to get a new EIN if any of these changes occur in your business:

- You incorporate your sole proprietorship or partnership.
- You convert your sole proprietorship or partnership to a limited liability company.
- Your sole proprietorship takes in partners and begins operating as a partnership.
- Your partnership is taken over by one of the partners and begins operating as a sole proprietorship.
- Your corporation changes to a partnership or to a sole proprietorship.
- You purchase or inherit an existing business that you'll operate as a sole proprietorship.
- You represent an estate that operates a business after the owner's death.
- You terminate an old partnership and begin a new one.

Filing Form SS-4 for an LLC

The IRS has some special rules applicable to LLCs completing Form SS-4, as follows:

- You have a single-member LLC, and you plan to run it as if you were a sole proprietor (using Schedule C to report business income). Your LLC won't need an Employer Identification Number (EIN). Therefore, you probably shouldn't file Form SS-4. Your name and Social Security number will normally be all you need to use for tax purposes. But if your LLC will have employees, you can, if you wish, get an EIN for the LLC for reporting and paying employment taxes. You can also get an EIN for non-tax reasons (such as a state requirement) or simply as a bookkeeping preference. If you do decide to get an EIN for the LLC, check the "Other" box in space 8a and write in: "Disregarded Entity—Sole Proprietorship."

- You have a multi-member LLC, and you plan to run it as if you were a partnership (using Form 1065 to report business income). You should apply for an EIN and, in space 8a, check the "Partnership" box.

- You have either a single-member or a multi-member LLC, and you plan to run it as a C Corporation. You should apply for an EIN and, in space 8a, check the "Corporation" box. Then, below the "form number" line, write in "Single-Member" or "Multi-Member." Also be sure to file Form 8832 to elect corporate tax status, as explained in Chapter 4, Section G4.

B. Becoming an S Corporation

Many corporations derive tax benefits from electing S corporation status. The difference between a regular corporation, which is a separate tax entity from its shareholders, and an S corporation, whose income is reported on the owners' tax returns, is described in some detail in Chapter 1. If you're not thoroughly familiar with this material, please re-read it before going on.

To become an S corporation, all shareholders must sign and file IRS Form 2553 (*Election by a Small Business Corporation*) with the IRS by the 15th day of the third month of the tax year to which the election is to apply.

EXAMPLE: Nancy, Jerry and Agnes form a corporation, Phoenix Ventures Inc. They start to do business on September 1, 2003, and, like most businesses, use the calendar year for accounting and tax purposes. Their 2003 tax year will be a short one: September 1 through December 31. To obtain S corporation status for that first tax year, they need to file Form 2553 by November 15, 2003, which is the 15th day of the third month of that tax year. If they miss that deadline, their corporation won't qualify for S corporation status in 2003. But if they file Form 2553 by March 15, 2004, their corporation will get S corporation status for 2004.

A number of technical rules govern which corporations can elect to become S corporations. Your corporation must meet these requirements:

- It must be a "domestic" corporation—one that's organized under U.S. federal or state law.
- It must have only one class of stock.
- It must have no more than 75 shareholders.
- It must have as shareholders only individuals, estates and certain trusts. Partnerships and corporations can't be shareholders in an S corporation.
- Its shareholders must be citizens of the United States. Nonresident aliens can't be shareholders.

There are other technical rules, but the vast majority of new, small corporations may become S corporations if they choose to do so.

To elect S corporation status, you need the consent of all shareholders. Unless yours is a one-person corporation, you should agree on this election before you form your corporation. An S corporation election doesn't have to be permanent. You can start out as an S corporation and then, after a few years, revoke your S corporation status and be taxed as a regular corporation. If you terminate your status as an S corporation, generally you'll have to wait five years until you can again become an S corporation—although you may be able to get permission from the IRS to shorten this waiting period.

Once the shareholders file a Form 2553, the corporation continues to be an S corporation each year until the shareholders revoke that status or it's terminated under IRS rules. What terminates S corporation status? For one thing, ceasing to qualify as an S corporation. For example, your corporation would no longer qualify if it had more than 75 shareholders or if you or another shareholder transferred some of your stock to a partnership.

C. Business Taxes in General

Three main categories of federal business taxes may apply to your business:

- income tax
- employment taxes
- self-employment tax.

This section looks briefly at each of these tax categories. Get IRS Publication 509, *Tax Calendars,* to see when to file returns and make tax payments. It's updated annually.

Excise Taxes. In addition to the three main business taxes, the federal government imposes excise taxes on a few specialized transactions and products. These taxes almost never are of concern to small businesses. To see if your business is affected, see IRS Publication 334, *Tax Guide for Small Business.*

1. Income Tax

You must file an annual federal tax return reporting your business income. Below is a list of the forms to use.

Business Income Tax Forms

Type of Legal Entity	Form
Sole Proprietorship	Schedule C (Form 1040)
Partnership	Form 1065
Regular Corporation	Form 1120 or 1120-A
S Corporation	Form 1120-S
LLC	Form 1065, 1120 or 1120-A

a. Sole proprietorship

If you're a sole proprietor, your business itself doesn't pay income tax. You report your business income (or loss) on Schedule C, and file it with Form 1040. Your Schedule C income (or loss) is added to (or subtracted from) the other income you report on your personal Form 1040. If you have more than one business, file a separate Schedule C for each business.

b. Partnership

A partnership Form 1065 is an informational tax return telling the IRS how much each partner earned. The partnership doesn't pay tax on this income. Each partner reports his or her share of income (or loss) on Schedule E, *Supplemental Income and Loss*, and files it with Form 1040. This Schedule E amount is added to (or subtracted from) the other income the partner reports on Form 1040. In other words, a partner's income is treated like a sole proprietor's income on Form 1040: It's listed in a separate schedule and then blended with other income listed on the first page of the 1040.

⚠️ **Passive losses.** *Losses from passive partnership activities—such as real estate investments or royalties, in which the partnership plays the role of a passive investor—can usually only be taken as a credit against income from other passive activities. This is explained in greater detail in IRS Publication 925.*

c. S corporation

The S corporation itself doesn't pay income tax. Form 1120-S filed by an S corporation is an informational return telling the IRS how much each shareholder earned. As a shareholder, you report your portion of income or loss on Schedule E and file it with Form 1040. Then you add that income to (or subtract a loss from) your other 1040 income.

d. Regular corporation

A regular corporation reports its income or loss on Form 1120 or 1120-A and pays a tax if there is income. But in many small corporations, the shareholders are employees who receive all profits of the business in the form of salaries and bonuses, which are

tax-deductible by the corporation as a business expense. In that situation, the corporation would have no taxable income. Not all small corporations, however, are able to pay out their income in the form of salaries and bonuses. If they don't, they must pay a corporate income tax.

> **EXAMPLE:** Jenny and her twin sister Janet are the sole shareholders in Neptune Corporation, which manufactures swimming pool supplies. In the second year of their corporate existence, to encourage growth, Jenny and Janet decide to pay themselves minimal salaries and to plow most of the corporate income into inventory and the purchase of rehabilitated but serviceable equipment. The money that the corporation puts into inventory and equipment isn't available for distribution to Jenny and Janet; moreover, most of that money isn't a currently deductible business expense, so it is taxed at corporate income tax rates. (The equipment will be capitalized; depreciation deductions will be spread over several years.)

Tax Rates on Taxable Corporate Income

Income Over	But Not Over	Tax Rate
$0	$50,000	15%
$50,000	$75,000	25%
$75,000	$100,000	34%
$100,000	$335,000	39%
$335,000	$10,000,000	34%
$10,000,000	$15,000,000	35%
$15,000,000	$18,333,333	38%
Over $18,333,333		35%

Note: Personal service corporations are subject to a flat tax of 35% regardless of the amount of income.

If you have a regular corporation that expects to have taxable income, your corporation needs to make periodic deposits of its estimated income taxes. And if you're an employee of your regular corporation (as is almost always the case with an owner of a small business corporation), taxes and Social Security payments must be withheld from your paychecks.

e. Limited liability company

A single-member LLC is normally taxed as a sole proprietorship, meaning that you'll report the income (or loss) on Schedule C and file it with Form 1040. The bottom line will be added to (or subtracted from) the other income you report on Form 1040.

An LLC that has two or more members, unless the owners choose to have the business taxed as a corporation, will be taxed as a partnership (tax liability passes through to the LLC members) and will use Form 1065—an informational return that tells the IRS how much each member earned. The LLC doesn't pay tax on its income but, as with a partnership, each member reports his or her share of income (or loss) on Schedule E, *Supplemental Income and Loss*, which is filed with Form 1040. This Schedule E amount is added to (or subtracted from) the other income the member reports on Form 1040.

An LLC that chooses to be taxed as a corporation will use Form 1120 or 1120-A. See subsection d, above, for a discussion of corporate taxes.

2. Federal Payroll Taxes

There are several types of employment-related taxes the federal government exacts from businesses.

a. Federal income tax withholding (FIT)

You must withhold income taxes from employees' paychecks based on:

- the employee's filing status (single, married or married but withholding at the higher single rate)
- the number of dependents (withholding allowances) declared by the employee, and
- the size of the employee's salary.

Each employee should give you a signed Form W-4 stating her withholding allowance. Save these forms. You needn't send them to the IRS unless the employee:

- claims more than ten allowances, or
- claims to be exempt from withholding and also normally earns more than $200 a week.

Use the tables in Circular E (referenced below) to figure out how much income tax to withhold.

• *IRS Publication 15, Circular E, Employer's Tax Guide, published by the IRS, explains employment-related taxes clearly and in great detail. Updated whenever the tax rates change, Circular E is available at all IRS offices (or at www.irs.gov) and is mailed automatically to all businesses with an EIN.*

- *IRS Publication 334, Tax Guide for Small Business and Keeping Records, and if you're just getting started, IRS Publication 583, Starting a Business and Keeping Records, are well worth reading. These publications are free from your local IRS office or can be obtained by calling the main IRS number: 800-829-3676 or by going to www.irs.gov.*
- Tax Savvy for Small Business, *by Frederick W. Daily (Nolo). An excellent guide to all the tax problems small businesses face. The audit material alone is well worth the price of the book.*
- Small-Time Operator, *by Bernard Kamoroff (Bell Springs Publishing), is a clearly written book that covers not only taxes but also many other practical aspects of doing business, including bookkeeping.*
- U.S. Master Tax Guide *(CCH, Inc.), is updated annually and available in law libraries, business school libraries and the reference departments of major public libraries. It features in-depth explanations of tax complexities.*
- The Kiplinger Tax Letter, *published by the Kiplinger Washington Editors, is a bi-weekly newsletter that does an excellent job of keeping you up-to-date on what's happening in the tax field. The breezy—some would say breathless—style is fun to read. Go to www.kiplinger.com or call 800-544-0155.*

Also, there is software that handles payroll, including tax computations. Look into QuickPay, OneWrite *and* Peachtree.

b.   Social Security tax (FICA)

You must withhold the employee's share of the Social Security tax and Medicare tax from the employee's pay. And you must also pay the employer's share. The amounts to be withheld are listed in the most current edition of Circular E. For 2003, for example, the employer and the employee are each required to pay 7.65% on the first $87,000 of the employee's annual wages; the 7.65% figure is the sum of the 6.2% Social Security tax and the 1.45% Medicare tax. There is no Social Security tax on the portion of the employee's annual wages that exceeds $87,000—only the Medicare tax; the employer and the employee each pay the 1.45% Medicare tax on the excess amount. The rates and the cut-off point for the Social Security tax change annually.

Withholding From an Owner's Paycheck

Money you earn from your corporation—whether it's an S type or a regular corporation—isn't limited to dividends you receive as a shareholder. If you perform substantial services for your corporation, you're considered an employee for tax purposes. This means you must complete and submit a Form W-4 to the corporation the same as any other employee, and the corporation must withhold income taxes and your share of Social Security and Medicare taxes from your paychecks.

These requirements may seem burdensome, but if you're an employee of a regular corporation the time you spend completing the paperwork is well worth it because the money you take out as an employee is taxed only once rather than twice. (See Chapter 1, Section C2.)

c.   Federal unemployment tax (FUTA)

Finally, you must report and pay the federal unemployment tax (FUTA). The employer is responsible for paying this tax; it's not withheld from the employee's pay. The FUTA rate through 2007 is 6.2% of the first $7,000 of the employee's wages for the year. Employers are given a credit for participating in state unemployment programs. The credit reduces the FUTA rate to 0.8% for most employers—which translates into $56 for an employee earning $7,000 or more per year. Use Form 940 or 940EZ to report federal unemployment tax. Sole proprietorships and partnerships don't pay the FUTA on the owners' compensation.

d.   Periodic deposits

You must periodically deposit the withheld income tax and the employer's and employee's shares of Social Security and Medicare taxes at an authorized financial institution—usually a bank. The IRS sends you coupons to use in making these deposits. It also provides instructions on how often you're required to deposit these funds, which depends on the size of your payroll and amounts due; a typical small business makes monthly deposits.

Deposit taxes on time. *Be sure to withhold taxes as required by the tax laws—and to deposit those taxes on time. There are substantial penalties if you don't. And if you're an owner of a small business and personally involved in its management, you can be held personally liable for these taxes and the additional penalties, even if the business has the funds to pay them. If your business suddenly runs into financial trouble, put the withheld taxes at the top of the list for payment. If that means not paying suppliers and others, so be it. The debts of the other creditors can be wiped out in bankruptcy if the business continues to go downhill. Not so with the withheld taxes. You can remain personally liable for these amounts even if the business goes through bankruptcy. However, passive investors—for example, those who merely own corporate shares and play no role in making business decisions—face very little risk of being personally liable for the taxes.*

Get a copy of IRS Publication 509, Tax Calendars, *to see when to file returns and make tax payments. It's available from your local IRS office, by calling the main IRS number: 800-829-3676 or by going to www.irs.gov. The publication is updated annually.*

Payroll Taxes Made Easy

If you're overwhelmed by the requirements for calculating payroll taxes and the fine points of when and where to pay them, you can pay a bank or payroll service to do the work for you. A reputable payroll tax service that offers a tax notification service will calculate the correct amount due, produce the checks to pay the employees and the taxes and notify you when the taxes are due.

One big advantage of a payroll service over a bank is that the bank will normally withhold the amount of the tax from your account when the payroll is done, even though the tax isn't due yet. That means the bank, not you, gets the use of the money for a while. If your payroll service offers tax notification, it will prepare the checks and tell you when they must be deposited. Depending on how often you must make payments, that can give you the use of the money an extra month or more.

At the end of each quarter, the payroll service will produce your quarterly payroll tax returns and instruct you about how to file them. At the end of the year, the service will also prepare W-2 forms and federal and state transmittal forms.

Payroll services can be cost-effective as compared to the hours it will take to handle your own tax reporting even for very small businesses. But when you look for one, it pays to shop around. Avoid services that charge set-up fees—basically, a fee for putting your information into its computer—or extra fees to prepare W-2 forms or quarterly and annual tax returns.

3. Self-Employment Tax

The self-employment tax applies to income you receive from actively working in your business—but not as an employee of that business. Technically, it's not an employment tax, but it's so closely related that you should be aware of it to fully understand employment taxes.

If you're a sole proprietor or a partner (or an LLC member, probably—see note below), you must pay the federal self-employment tax in addition to regular income tax. The self-employment tax is equal to the employer's and employee's portion of the Social Security and Medicare taxes that you and your employer would pay on your compensation if you received it as an employee.

Compute this tax each year on Schedule SE, which you then attach to your personal Form 1040. Add the self-employment tax to the income tax that you owe. For example, in 2003, the self-employment tax is set at 15.3% on earnings up to $87,000 and 2.9% on earnings over $87,000. The tax law lightens the burden of the self-employment tax somewhat by allowing you to deduct one-half of this tax in computing your adjusted gross income. You take the deduction on the first page of your federal tax return.

You may not owe the full self-employment tax on all of your business earnings. If you have income from another job that's subject to withholding—common for people just getting started in business—the income from your other job will reduce the tax base for your self-employment tax. So in computing your self-employment for 2003, for example, you'd reduce the $87,000 figure to reflect any of your job earnings that were subject to employer withholding.

> **EXAMPLE:** Morton works ¾ time as a chemistry instructor at a local college, where he receives an annual salary of $60,000. He also does consulting, as a sole proprietor, for several chemical companies and earns an additional $40,000 a year after expenses. The $60,000 salary at the

college—which is subject to withholding by the employer—is used to reduce the $87,000 cap on income that's subject to the 15.3% self-employment tax. So Morton computes the tax at the rate of 15.3% on $27,000 of his consulting business income ($87,000 less $60,000 = $27,000). On the remaining portion—$13,000 ($40,000 less $27,000 = $13,000)—he computes the tax at the rate of 2.9%.

⚠ LLC members may have to pay self-employment tax. *As explained in Chapter 1 and Chapter 4, Section D, LLC members may have to pay self-employment tax on all income they receive from the LLC, whether in the form of salary or allocations of profit.*

Computing Your Estimated Taxes

Many taxpayers receive income from sources other than paychecks—for example, from investments and royalties. These taxpayers often owe surprising amounts of income taxes on April 15. Sometimes, that's because they had no employer to withhold income tax during the year. Other times, it's because even though there was an employer, the amounts withheld were insufficient to cover the taxpayer's non-employment income.

As you may know, the IRS doesn't want you to wait until April 15 to pay. Instead, the IRS requires you to pay your taxes in advance in quarterly estimated installments if not enough is being withheld from your salary to cover your full income tax bill. To avoid interest and penalties, you must pay in advance at least 90% of this year's tax or an amount equal to 100% of last year's tax (or 110% of last year's tax if your adjusted gross income is over $150,000 (2003 figures)).

In figuring out what your tax bill will be and whether you need to pay any quarterly installments of estimated taxes, don't overlook the self-employment tax which is added to your regular income tax on your Form 1040 as part of your tax obligation. Make sure your quarterly installments are large enough to cover your self-employment tax as well as your usual income tax.

For more on this subject, see IRS Publication 505, *Tax Withholding and Estimated Tax,* available at the nearest IRS office or by going to www.irs.gov.

D. Business Deductions

Of all the federal taxes that may affect a small business, income tax is the one that business owners are most concerned about. The general formula is that you first figure out your gross profit—your gross receipts or sales less returns and allowances and the cost of goods sold. Then you subtract your other business expenses to find the net income or loss of your business. For an in-depth analysis of what business expenses can be deducted, see IRS Publication 535, *Business Expenses.*

In this section, we'll look at common categories of deductible business expenses.

Home-Based Businesses. If you have a home-based business, you'll find special tax pointers in Chapter 12.

1. IRS Guidelines for Business Deductions

The IRS has broad, general guidelines for what constitutes deductible expenses. For example, to be deductible, a business expense must be ordinary and necessary—something that's common in your type of business, trade or profession. If you have an expense that's partly for business and partly personal, you must separate the personal from the business part. Only the business part is deductible.

So much for generalities. Here's a partial list of the kinds of expenses that your business can normally deduct:

- advertising
- bad debts
- car and truck expenses
- commissions and fees
- conventions and trade shows
- depreciation on property owned by the business (discussed in Section 2, below)
- employee benefit programs
- insurance
- interest
- legal, accounting and other professional services

- office expenses
- pension and profit-sharing plans
- rent
- repairs to and maintenance of business premises and equipment
- supplies
- taxes and licenses
- trade publications
- travel, meals and entertainment
- utilities
- wages.

This list isn't all-inclusive. You can also deduct any other expenses that you believe—and can convince the IRS—are ordinary and necessary business expenses.

Now let's look at the rules affecting a number of specific expenses (deductions) in more depth.

2. Depreciation

If you buy equipment or machinery that has a useful life longer than one year, the IRS generally won't let you deduct the full cost in the year you buy it. Instead, you deduct a portion each year over the term of the item's useful life by using depreciation. Depreciation is the loss in the value of the property over the time the property is used—including wear and tear, age and obsolence. IRS tables list the useful life of various types of equipment and machinery for the purpose of depreciation.

You don't need to depreciate inexpensive items. *Exceptions are made for inexpensive items for which the cost of detailed recordkeeping would be prohibitive. For example, your $75 desktop calculator may last for five years but you'd undoubtedly be allowed to deduct its entire cost in the year you buy it. You'd probably treat it as part of your office supplies.*

You may choose one of two methods—straight-line or accelerated—for figuring depreciation.

a. Straight-line depreciation

The straight-line method means that you deduct an equal amount each year over the projected life of the asset. Actually, that's a bit of an over-simplification; something called the "half-year convention" makes things slightly more complicated. That rule allows only a half-year's worth of depreciation to be deducted in the first year.

> **EXAMPLE:** Norbert buys a $1,000 fax machine in 2003 which can be depreciated over five years according to the IRS table. Under a strict application of the straight-line depreciation method, he'd deduct $200 each year for five years. But the half-year convention allows him to deduct only a half year's worth of depreciation—$100—the first year. So Norbert would deduct $100 the first year; $200 a year for the next four years; and the final $100 in the sixth year.

(Exceptions to the half-year rule are explained in IRS Publication 946.)

b. Accelerated depreciation

Another method of depreciating assets—accelerated depreciation—is also available. Most small businesses will want to use the accelerated depreciation tables instead of the straight-line method. It allows them to write off a large amount of the purchase price in the years immediately following the purchase of the machinery or equipment. That, of course, makes the tax savings available sooner.

Generous rules apply to new assets that you buy for your business, if those assets would normally depreciate in 20 years or less. If you buy these assets after May 5, 2003, and place them into service by the end of 2004, you can deduct a whopping 50% of their cost in the first year. (In a few cases, you have until the end of 2005 to place the assets into service.)

c. Immediate write-offs

Thanks to another tax rule, many—perhaps most—businesses will not have to worry at all about depreciating machinery and equipment they buy in 2003, 2004 and 2005. During this time period, you can largely sidestep the normal depreciation guidelines. You can, if you choose, write off a substantial amount of depreciable assets in the year of purchase. You can, if you choose, write off up to $100,000 of depreciable assets (including off-the-shelf computer software) in the year of purchase.

> **EXAMPLE:** Bertha buys an $8,000 computer in 2003. Ordinarily, she'd have to use IRS depreciation tables and spread the cost over several years. But she has the option of deducting the cost all at once in the year 2003. This is known as a Section 179 capital-expense election.

There are a few important limitations to this deduction. The first, which doesn't affect many businesses that are just starting out, applies if you purchase more than $400,000 in depreciable assets in one year. If you do, the maximum amount you can deduct as a Section 179 capital-expense deduction is reduced, dollar for dollar, by the amount you exceed $400,000. For example, if you spend $405,000 on depreciable assets, you can write off—as an expense deduction—only $95,000 ($100,000 less $5,000). This $400,000 threshhold will be adjusted for inflation.

Second, the amount you write off can't exceed the total taxable income that your business received in that year. You may, however, carry forward any disallowed part of this write-off so that you get some tax benefit in future years.

Any depreciable assets that you don't write off under Section 179 can be depreciated and written off under the straight-line or accelearated methods of depreciation, above.

For further explanation of this complicated area, see Tax Savvy for Small Business, *by Frederick W. Daily (Nolo).*

To Take Business Deductions, You Need a Business

The tax laws don't allow you to take business deductions for a hobby. Sometimes, however, the line between a business and a hobby can get fuzzy. This can happen if your small business is more a labor of love than a dependable source of income. Let's say you're a chiropractor but your real passion is growing orchids. Occasionally, you sell your orchids to friends and neighbors. You can't possibly get rich doing this, but you are intrigued by the possibility of deducting the cost of your plant materials, gardening equipment, fertilizer, plant-related magazine subscriptions and the expenses of attending an orchid-growers convention. Can you legitimately deduct these items? Maybe—or maybe not.

The answer lies in whether you're profit motivated. To test for a profit motive, the IRS relies mainly on a simple "3-of-5" test. If your business makes a profit in any three out of five consecutive years, you're presumed to have a profit motive. That's true even if during the profitable year the profit was only $1. If you don't pass the "3-of-5" test, you may still be able to convince the IRS that you have a profit motive—but the going will be tougher. You'll have to use your ingenuity to establish that you have a real business. Some things that may help: Business cards, letterhead, well-kept books, a separate bank account, a separate phone line, business licenses and permits and expenses for marketing.

3. Employees' Pay

You can deduct salaries, wages and other forms of pay that you give to employees as long as you meet certain IRS tests listed below. If you're both an em-

ployee and a shareholder of your business, your own salary must meet the same tests for deductibility as salaries paid to any other executive or employee.

For a salary to be deductible, you must show that:

- The payments are ordinary and necessary expenses directly connected with your business.
- The payments are reasonable. Fortunately, you have broad discretion to decide what's reasonable. Short of a scam—such as paying a huge salary to a spouse or relative who does little or no work—the IRS will almost always accept your notion of what's reasonable pay.
- The payments are for services actually performed.

If you use the cash method of accounting (very common among small businesses), you can deduct salaries and wages only for the year in which they were paid. However, you can deduct employee taxes your business withheld in the year your business withheld them; you can't deduct (until paid to the government) the employer's matching portion of these taxes. Businesses using the accrual method have more latitude in when they can deduct salaries and payroll taxes.

You can also deduct bonuses you pay to employees if they're intended as additional payment for services and not as gifts; most bonuses qualify for deduction. If your business distributes cash, gift certificates or similar items of easily convertible cash value, the value of such items is considered additional wages or salary regardless of the amount. If a bonus is considered as part of an employee's wages or salary, it's subject to employment taxes and withholding rules.

Certain non-cash bonuses that *are* intended as gifts are deductible if they are less than $25 per person per year.

EXAMPLE: To promote employee goodwill, Pebblestone Partnership distributes turkeys, hams and other items of nominal value at holidays. The value of these items isn't considered salaries or wages, but the partnership can deduct their cost as a business expense.

4. Employee Benefits

A number of employee benefits can be deducted, including:

- health and dental insurance
- group term life insurance
- moving expenses
- qualified employee benefit plans, including profit-sharing plans, stock bonus plans and money purchase pension plans
- employee benefit plans that allow employees to choose among two or more benefits consisting of cash and qualified benefits.

If your business can afford these benefits, not only are they tax deductible by your business, but they are not taxed to the employee.

While these benefits sound attractive, there are two serious drawbacks. First, many small businesses—particularly those just starting out—can't afford them. Second, plans that mainly benefit the owners of the business are not tax-deductible. (See Chapter 1, Section C2b(2), for a more thorough discussion.)

5. Meals, Entertainment and Travel

To be treated as a business deduction, travel expenses need to be ordinary and necessary in your type of business. Basically, these are any reasonable expenses you incur while traveling for business. You (or your business) can't deduct expenses for personal or vacation purposes, or any part of business expenses that is lavish or extravagant.

(And deductible travel expenses don't include expenses for entertainment such as sports events and concerts.)

But if you're on the kind of tight travel and entertainment budget common to most small business people, you won't have to worry about this last restriction. Here are examples of deductible travel expenses:

- air, rail and bus transportation while traveling on business
- operating and maintaining your own car for business (see Section 6 for more on car expenses).
- taxi fares or other costs of transportation between the airport or station and your hotel, from one customer to another or from one place of business to another
- baggage charges and transportation costs for sample and display material
- meals and lodging while traveling on business
- cleaning and laundry expenses
- telephone and fax expenses
- public stenographers' fees
- tips incidental to any of these expenses.

You cannot deduct expenses for transportation while you're not traveling. The IRS says that you're traveling away from home if (1) your duties require you to be away from the general area of your tax home substantially longer than an ordinary day's work, and (2) you need to get sleep or rest to meet the demands of your work. (Napping in your car doesn't count.) Generally, your "tax home" is your main place of business regardless of where your family home is.

If a trip is entirely for business, you can deduct all of your ordinary and necessary travel expenses. If your trip was primarily personal, you can't deduct any travel expenses—even if you did some business at your destination. What if your trip was primarily for business but you took a vacation-like side trip? Then you need to allocate your expenses; see IRS Publication 463 for instructions. The IRS does give you one break; if you legitimately need to fly somewhere for business, you can write off the entire plane fare, even though you stay over for pleasure after your business is completed.

Meal and entertainment expenses have special rules and restrictions. You can generally deduct only 50% of your business-related meal and entertainment expenses. In addition, the IRS may disallow extravagant and excessive expenses. But short of fraud or obvious gross excess, the IRS doesn't monitor where you go for your business meals. So in practice, for most small business people, 50% of all business-related meal expenses are deductible. As an employer, this 50% limit applies to your business even if you reimburse your employees for 100% of their meal and entertainment expenses.

If you're a sole proprietor, deduct the allowable portion of your own business travel, meals and entertainment expenses on Schedule C of your Form 1040. Use Schedule C to also report the expenses that you reimburse or directly pay your employees. (Consult IRS Publication 463, *Travel, Entertainment, Gift, and Car Expenses*, for an in-depth treatment of this subject.)

If you're a partner or a shareholder of a corporation in which you play an active management role, it's usually best to have your partnership or corporation reimburse you for your business-related travel and entertainment expenses. The business can then deduct these amounts to the extent allowed by law.

⚠ **Excessive expenses may trigger an audit.** *Your overall travel and entertainment budget may result in a tax audit if these expenses are out of proportion to what the IRS thinks is reasonable, given your type of business and income. For most honest small business people, this isn't usually a problem unless they have some extraordinary need to travel.*

> **EXAMPLE:** *Ben starts a marble importing business and spends his first year visiting 200 prominent architects and interior designers from coast to coast to introduce his business. His high travel expense triggers an audit, but Ben is able to show that these trips were necessary to get his business off the ground.*

If you are audited, you'll need to show the IRS complete and accurate records of your travel and entertainment expenses, including actual receipts. Also, since you need to tie each trip and meal to a specific business purpose, it makes good sense to keep a log stating the purpose. Otherwise, if challenged, you may have trouble recalling the details.

6. Automobile Expenses

If you use your car for business, you may be able to deduct some or all of your car expenses. Deductible items include:

- gas
- oil
- tolls
- tires
- garage rent
- lease fees
- rental fees
- parking fees
- repairs
- licenses
- depreciation.

The following discussion assumes you use your car more than 50% for business. Special rules apply if you use your car 50% or less for business. For complete information about deductions for your car, again see IRS Publication 463.

If you use your car for both business and personal purposes, you must divide your expenses between business and personal use. (This rule applies to all items you use for both business and personal use.) The miles you put on your car driving from your home to your main place of business are considered to be commuting miles—a personal use, not deductible. The same thing applies to fees you pay to park your car at your place of business.

> **EXAMPLE:** Tricia has a catering business that requires her to call on customers. She drives 20,000 miles during the year: 12,000 for business and 8,000 for personal use (including her daily trips from home to her shop). She can

claim only 60% of the cost of operating her car as a business expense (12,000 divided by 20,000). The coins she fed the parking meter in front of her shop each day would be a personal (commuting) expense and not deductible; fees paid for parking while calling on customers would, however, be deductible.

What about depreciation? As with other business assets, you can deduct the cost of a car (but only the portion used for business), but you must spread the deductions over several years. IRS depreciation tables have special schedules for cars. In 2003, a new car that you placed into service before May 6th will be eligible for a maximum first-year deduction of $7,660. For a new car placed into service on or after May 6, 2003, the maximum first-year deduction is $10,710.

Depreciation for Employees' Cars. If your employees use their cars in their work, they can't take a depreciation deduction unless this use is for your convenience as their employer and you require it as a condition of employment.

If you don't want to keep track of your car expenses and you want to avoid the complexity of the depreciation rules, the IRS offers a second method for deducting car expenses. You can use the standard mileage rate for your business usage. In 2003, the rate is 36 cents per mile. The rate changes periodically, so check IRS publications for the latest figure. If you're going to use the standard mileage rate, you must start by using it in the year you begin using the car for business. If you don't use the standard mileage rate that first year, you can't use it for that car later on. If you use the standard mileage rate, you can also deduct tolls and parking fees that were paid while on business.

If you take a deduction for car expenses, you must file Form 4562 with your tax return. If you give an employee a car for business and personal use, the employee must report as income the value of the personal usage. For example, an employee who keeps a company car at home and drives to and from work must report that commuting usage—and any other personal usage—as income.

If you lease rather than own your car, you can deduct the part of each lease payment that's for your business use of the car. If you use your leased car 60% for business, you can deduct 60% of each lease payment. You can't deduct any payments you make to buy the car even if the payments are called lease payments. A lease with an option to buy may be a lease or a purchase contract, depending on its wording.

Keep accurate records of your car usage so that if you're challenged by the IRS, you can demonstrate the extent of your business use. The best procedure is to keep a daily log in your glove compartment to record the following about each business trip:
- date
- destination
- mileage
- business purpose.

E. Tax Audits

As a small business owner, you're three times more likely to be audited by the IRS than a regular employee-taxpayer would be. If you're audited, you have the burden of proving that your tax return is accurate. In over 80% of audits, the taxpayer winds up owing more taxes—usually because of poor recordkeeping rather than dishonesty.

If your business is facing an audit, you'll get excellent guidance from Tax Savvy for Small Business, *by Frederick W. Daily (Nolo)—which is the source of much of the material in this section. The* Tax Savvy *book goes through the audit process step by step and in great depth. And if, as commonly happens, the business audit turns into a personal audit as well, refer to* Stand Up to the IRS, *which is also by Frederick W. Daily (Nolo).*

1. How the IRS Audits a Small Business

The IRS conducts two kinds of audits of small businesses and their owners: *office* audits and *field* audits. There's a difference not only in where the audit is held, but also in the intensity of the process.

If you're a sole proprietor and gross less than $100,000 per year, the IRS is likely to ask you to come to their office for the audit. Usually an office audit lasts from two to four hours, and a typical business taxpayer is hit for additional taxes averaging about $4,000.

If you have a partnership or corporation, or a sole proprietorship that grosses over $100,000 a year, the IRS will probably order a field audit. The process will be much more intensive than an office audit. Field auditors—called revenue agents—are much better trained in accounting than are IRS office tax auditors. The average amount owed by a business after going through a field audit is over $17,000, including additional tax, penalty and interest.

An IRS field audit may be conducted at your business place, but doesn't have to be. If your business premises are very small, you might point out that having the audit conducted there would interfere with your operations. Ask that the audit be held elsewhere—at the IRS office, for example. Or if you plan to be represented by a tax professional—a lawyer or accountant with tax experience—you can request that the audit be conducted at the professional's office.

Even though you have the right to have an audit conducted elsewhere, an auditor has the power to enter your business if it's open to the public. But an auditor can't go into a private area—such as a storeroom or your private office—unless you consent. But if you have nothing to hide, there's no reason to raise suspicions by denying access. Offer the IRS auditor a complete tour.

If you have a home office, you don't have to let an auditor into your home unless there's a court order. But if you refuse entry, your home office depreciation or rental expense will probably be disallowed because you haven't proven you had a home office.

2. The IRS Inquiry

Wherever the audit is conducted, the auditor will want to see the business records you used to prepare the tax returns. This can include check registers, bank statements, canceled checks, receipts, invoices and a formal set of books.

To get still more financial information about you and your business, an auditor can require records from your tax preparer, banks, suppliers, customers and others.

3. Hiring a Tax Professional

Many small business owners can handle a run of the mill IRS office audit without professional representation. Often it's sensible to do this, since the cost of hiring professional help may be more than the IRS is likely to bill you. However, if you fear that some serious irregularity may come to light—perhaps you've taken a huge deduction and can't produce a receipt or canceled check to verify it—consult with a tax professional before the audit.

When it comes to a field audit where more money will almost surely be at stake, it's usually wise to bring in a tax professional from the outset. The IRS uses experienced auditors to conduct field audits, so you may be overmatched if questions come up about your documents or interpretations of the tax law.

4. Preparing for Your Audit

Thoroughly review the tax return that's going to be audited.

Make sure you can explain how you came up with the figures. Identify problem areas, such as how you reported particular items of income or expense.

Then find all the records you need to substantiate your tax return and organize them logically and clearly for the auditor. Among the items to gather up for the audit are:

- bank statements, canceled checks and receipts
- electronic records—for example, charge card statements
- books and records—which can range from a formal set of books to cash register tapes
- appointment books, logs and diaries
- car records, and
- travel and entertainment records.

If records are missing, you may still be able to prove a deduction by offering an oral explanation or by reconstructing records in writing. Business-related expenses of less than $25 each don't require substantiation.

Neatness counts. *It can be tempting to dump a pile of receipts on the table and require the auditor to search through them. This is one temptation you'll want to avoid. Neatness helps build credibility with the auditor who, when presented with well-maintained records, may even give you the benefit of the doubt on questionable items.*

5. What Auditors Look For

In auditing your business, the IRS will try to determine if you

- failed to report all of your business sales or receipts (income)
- skimmed cash from the business
- wrote off personal living costs—family travel, for example—as business expenses
- failed to file payroll tax returns on time or to make the required deposits, or
- improperly classified some workers as independent contractors rather than employees.

This isn't a complete list—just the things the IRS auditor will most likely scrutinize.

Be prepared for an analysis of your bank accounts. Office auditors don't always take the time to

do this, but field auditors do. This consists of adding up all the deposits in all your business bank accounts to see if the total is more than your reported income. The auditor will also want to see all of your personal account records to learn if the amounts deposited are consistent with your business cash flow. It's smart to review your bank accounts in advance to try to spot and be able to explain deposits that weren't income and therefore weren't reported on your tax return—loan proceeds, for example, or proceeds from the sale of assets (other than the capital gain portion), transfers from other accounts, inheritances, gifts or money held for relatives.

After confirming that your income figures are accurate, turn to your business expenses. The tax law makes you prove that your deductions were legitimate; the IRS doesn't have to disprove them. Be especially careful to have good documentation for deductions you took for travel and entertainment, a home office, thefts, bad debts, depreciation and car expenses—all prime targets during an IRS probe.

If you can't produce thorough records to back up your deductions, don't despair. You may be able to reconstruct the missing documents. For guidance on how to do this, see *Tax Savvy for Small Business,* by Frederick W. Daily (Nolo).

6. How to Behave at an Audit

Keep small talk to a minimum. An auditor is trained to listen for clues about your lifestyle—which may not seem affordable on your reported income. Raising suspicions in an auditor's mind can prolong the agony of an audit.

If you're asked a direct question, try to answer "yes" or "no." Don't over-explain or answer questions that weren't asked. If you don't have a ready answer, it's OK to say, "I don't know" or "I'll get back to you on that" or "I'll have to check with my accountant." Often the auditor will let it go. At the very least, you've bought some time, which can work to your advantage.

Most auditors are businesslike, but now and then you run into one who's impolite, hostile—or maybe is just having a bad day. You're entitled to courteous treatment from IRS auditors. If your auditor gets out of line, mention your right to courteous treatment and politely ask the auditor to lighten up. If that doesn't work, ask to speak to the auditor's manager and describe the unfair treatment you're receiving.

It's all right to ask for time out. *You can stop or recess an audit for just about any good reason—for a few minutes to go to the bathroom or eat lunch, or for the day because you feel ill or need to confer with a tax professional. If you ask for a recess, the auditor may find it more convenient to resume the audit in a week or two—giving you time to regroup or get professional advice.*

7. How to Negotiate With an Auditor

As Fred Daily explains in much greater depth in *Tax Savvy for Small Business* (Nolo), there's often room to bargain during the audit process—despite the official line that IRS auditors don't negotiate. One approach is to suggest that a disputed item be resolved by applying a percentage figure. Suppose you claimed the costs of a trip as a business deduction. The auditor, believing it was a personal trip, wants to disallow the deduction. You might say: "Perhaps, in fairness, the trip can be seen as being both for business and pleasure. How about agreeing that 70% of the expenses were for business and 30% for pleasure?" This may work. On the other hand, IRS auditors are instructed not to talk about compromising the dollars—so you may not get as far by using a more direct approach and proposing, for example, to pay $5,000 to settle a $10,000 IRS claim.

Another tactic in negotiating is to take the offensive. An audit isn't a one-way street. Auditors must make adjustments in your favor when you're legally entitled to one. Maybe you missed a deduction or were overly conservative on your return. When the auditor's review has been completed, bring up the items which entitle you to an adjustment in your favor. This can help offset the amounts the auditor claims you owe. ■

Raising Money for Your Business

To succeed in business, you'll need money to get started and to keep afloat until you become profitable—and, assuming you're successful, you'll probably need more money to expand than you can generate internally. How much you'll need and when you'll need it will depend on the nature of the business. However, unless you have a good-sized nest egg put aside or are starting a tiny, home-based business on a shoestring, finding money to finance your new enterprise is likely to be a major concern. Fortunately, there are many places to look for start-up funds. If one source doesn't pan out, you can try another and then another.

And there's no requirement that you get all your money from a single source. Often, you can tap a combination of sources—for example, savings, loans and equity investments—to provide the needed funds. In this chapter, we'll look at all of these sources—and the legal rules that apply.

⚠️ **Watch your pennies.** *Although you may be chomping at the bit to get your new business going, it can be a mistake to pour in too much money at the beginning. You need time to learn if the business is viable. Because a fair number of small businesses fail, raising and spending a pile of money for an untested business idea can lead to much grief—especially if you're personally on the hook for borrowed funds. While some small businesses require a great deal of cash or credit up front, my experience is that many others don't. Consider starting as small and cheaply as possible. If your concept works, more funds will become available. If not, you can move on and take advantage of the lessons you've learned—and you won't be burdened with a ton of debts.*

A Business Plan Can Help

Before you start searching for money, it's helpful to write a business plan—a statement that analyzes your proposed business and explains how it will become profitable. *How to Write a Business Plan,* by Mike McKeever (Nolo), offers step-by-step guidance. McKeever suggests that a simple plan include the following elements:

- business description
- your business accomplishments
- sales revenue forecast
- profit and loss forecast
- capital spending plan, and
- cash flow forecast.

For a more sophisticated plan, McKeever recommends that the following elements be added:

- marketing plan
- future trends
- risks your business faces
- personnel plan
- specific business goals
- your personal financial statement, and
- your personal background—including your strong and weak points.

A major part of your business plan should cover how much money you'll need to get started and how you'll pay it back. Be conservative in projecting income. It may take months before a significant amount of money starts flowing into the business. Obviously, you'll need sufficient funds to carry you through the start-up period. A cash flow analysis can help you decide how much money you should start out with so you can weather the lean, early days of the business and give yourself a reasonable chance to find out if the business can turn a profit.

Putting numbers on paper also forces you to focus on where the money will be coming from and how it will flow through your business. This is a valuable reality test for you and—equally important—it's something that lenders and investors will want to look at before shelling out money.

A. Two Types of Outside Financing

If you're starting a small business, chances are that at least part of the initial funding will come from your own pocket—savings, an inheritance or a severance check you received for taking early retirement. But you may also need to seek money from outside sources, so it's important to understand the two main categories of such funding and the differences between them. One category consists of loans; the other consists of equity investments.

1. Loans

As you know, a loan is based on a simple idea: someone gives you money and you promise to pay it back—usually with interest. Since you must pay back the lender whether your business is a fabulous success or a miserable failure, the entire risk of your new enterprise is placed squarely on your shoulders.

Of course, nothing in business—or in life, for that matter—is without risk. Nevertheless, a commercial lender will be unwilling to lend you money if it looks like there's much chance the money won't get repaid. And to help keep the risk low, a lender will very likely ask for security for the loan—for example, a mortgage on your house so that the lender can take and sell your house if you don't keep up your loan payments.

But as compared to selling a portion of your business to investors, there's an obvious plus side to borrowing money: If your business succeeds as you hope and you pay back the lender as promised, you reap all future profits. There's no need to share them. In short, if you're confident about the prospects of your business and you have the opportunity to borrow money, a loan is a more attractive source of money than getting it from an equity investor who will own a piece of your business and receive a share of the profits. Again, the downside

is that if the business fails and you've personally guaranteed the loan, you'll have to repay it. By contrast, you don't have to repay equity investors if the business goes under.

Loans are so common that you probably are familiar with the mechanics, but nevertheless it makes sense to review the basics.

a. The promissory note

A lender will almost always want you to sign a written promissory note—a paper that says, in effect, "I promise to pay you $XXX plus interest of XX%" and then describes how and when payments are to be made. (See Section C2 for a sample form.) A bank or other commercial lender will use a form with a bit more wording than our form, but the basic idea is always the same.

A friend or relative may be willing to lend you money on a handshake. This is a poor idea for both of you. It's always a better business practice to put the loan in writing—and to state a specific interest rate and repayment plan. Otherwise, you open the door to unfortunate misunderstandings that can unnecessarily chill a great relationship.

Sign only the original of the promissory note. When it's paid off, you're entitled to get it back. You don't want several signed copies floating around that can cast doubt on whether the debt has been fully paid. But you should keep a photocopy of the signed note—marked "COPY"—for your business records.

b. Repayment plans

If the interest rate on the loan doesn't exceed the maximum rate allowed by your state's usury law, you and the lender are free to work out the terms of repayment.

Typically, a state's usury law will allow a lender to charge a higher rate when lending money for business purposes than for personal reasons—in fact, in several of these state laws, there's no limit at all on the interest rate that can be charged on business loans, as long as the business borrower agrees to the rate in writing. In a few states, the higher limit or absence of any limit applies only when the business borrower is organized as a corporation. In other states, the higher rates permitted for business borrowers are legal even if the borrower is a sole proprietorship, partnership or limited liability company.

⚠ Check your state usury law. *As a general rule, if your business is a corporation and the terms of repayment are in a promissory note, the lender can safely charge interest of up to 10% per year and not have to worry about the usury law. But because there's so much variation in usury laws from state to state, you or the lender should check the law. Look under interest or usury in the index to your state's statutes. (For more on doing your own legal research, see Chapter 24.)*

Assuming there are no usury law problems, you and the lender can agree on any number of repayment plans. Let's say you borrow $10,000 with interest at the rate of 10% a year. Here are just a few of the repayment possibilities:

- *Lump sum repayment.* You agree, for example, to pay principal and interest in one lump sum at the end of one year. Under this plan, 12 months later you'd pay the lender $10,000 in "principal"—the borrowed amount—plus $1,000 in interest.
- *Periodic interest and lump sum repayment of principal.* You agree, for example, to pay interest only for two years and then interest and principal at the end of the third year. With this type of loan plan—often called a "balloon" loan because of the big payment at the end—you'd pay $1,000 in interest at the end of the first and second years, and then $10,000 in principal and $1,000 in interest at the end of the third year.

- *Periodic payments of principal and interest.* You agree, for example, to repay $2,500 of the principal each year for four years, plus interest at the end of each year. Under this plan, your payments would look like this:
  End of Year One:
    $2,500 principal + $1,000 interest
  End of Year Two:
    $2,500 principal + $750 interest
  End of Year Three:
    $2,500 principal + $500 interest
  End of Year Four:
    $2,500 principal + $250 interest.
- *Amortized payments.* You agree, for example, to make equal monthly payments so that principal and interest are fully paid in five years. Under this plan, you'd consult an amortization table in a book, on computer software or on the Internet to figure out how much must be paid each month for five years to fully to pay off a $10,000 loan plus the 10% interest. The table would say you'd have to pay $212.48 a month. Each of your payments would consist of both principal and interest. At the beginning of the repayment period, the interest portion of each payment would be large; at the end, it would be small.
- *Amortized payments with a balloon.* You agree, for example, to make equal monthly payments based on a five-year amortization schedule, but to pay off the remaining principal at the end of the third year. Under this plan, you'd pay $212.48 each month for three years. At the end of the third year after making the normal monthly payment, there'd still be $4,604.42 in unpaid principal, so along with your normal payment of $212.48, you'd make a balloon payment to cover the remaining principal.

⚠ Avoid loans with prepayment penalties.
Whenever you borrow money, you'd like to be free to reduce or pay off the principal faster than called for in the promissory note if you have the wherewithal to do so, since this reduces or stops the running of interest. In other words, if you have a three-year loan but are able to pay it off by the end of year two, you don't want to pay interest for year three. By law, some states always allow such early repayment and you only pay interest for the time you have the use of the borrowed money. In other states, however, the law allows a lender to charge a penalty (amounting to a portion of the future interest) when a borrower reduces the balance or pays back a loan sooner than called for. Because it seems unfair to have to pay anything for the use of borrowed money except interest for the time the principal is actually in your hands, try to make sure any promissory note you sign says you can prepay any or all of the principal without penalty. If the lender doesn't agree, see if you can negotiate a compromise under which you'll owe a prepayment penalty only if you pay back the loan during a relatively short period, such as six months from the time you borrow the money.

c. Security

Lenders, with the possible exception of friends or relatives, will probably require you to provide some valuable property—called security or collateral— that they can grab and sell to collect their money if you can't keep up with the loan repayment plan. For example, the lender may seek a second mortgage or deed of trust on your house, or may ask for a security interest or lien on your mutual funds or the equipment, inventory and accounts receivable of your business. Again, the reason for doing this is if you don't make your payments, the lender can sell the pledged assets (the security) to pay off the loan.

But it's important to realize that a lender isn't limited to using the pledged assets to satisfy the loan. If you don't make good on your repayment commitment, a lender also has the right to sue you. Typically, a lender will seize pledged assets first and then sue you only if the funds realized from those assets are insufficient to pay off the loan—but that's not a legal requirement. A lender may decide to sue you before using up the pledged assets. If the lender wins the lawsuit and gets a judgment against you, assets you haven't specifically pledged as security are at risk—as is a portion of your future earnings.

In short, before you borrow money—under either a secured or unsecured promissory note—think about what will happen if you run into financial problems.

d. Co-signers and guarantors

If you lack sufficient assets to pledge as security for a loan, a lender may try other methods to attempt to guarantee that the loan will be prepaid. One is to ask you to get someone who is richer than you to co-sign or guarantee the loan. That means the lender will have two people rather than one to collect from if you don't make your payments. When asking friends or relatives to co-sign or guarantee a promissory note, be sure they understand that they're risking their personal assets if you don't repay it.

If you're married, the lender may insist that your spouse co-sign the promissory note. Be aware that if your spouse signs, not only are your personal assets at risk, but also those assets that the two of you jointly own—a house, for example, or a bank account. What's more, if your spouse has a job, his or her earnings will be subject to garnishment if the lender sues and gets a judgment against the two of you because the loan isn't repaid as promised.

Community Property States

If you live in a community property state—Arizona, California, Idaho, Louisiana, Nevada, New Mexico, Texas, Washington or Wisconsin—you'll need to do a bit of research or consult briefly with a business lawyer to learn the legal effect of your spouse co-signing a promissory note. (See Chapter 24.) In researching Wisconsin law, you'd look under marital property, but the concept is the same as community property for all practical purposes.

In a community property state, debts incurred by one spouse are usually the legal responsibility of both—meaning that a couple's community property is at risk if the debt isn't paid.

In addition to community property, you or your spouse may have separate property—which, depending on the law of the particular community property state, is usually property owned by a spouse prior to marriage or acquired after marriage by gift or inheritance. The effect of your spouse co-signing a promissory note for a business loan is to obligate his or her separate property, as well, to repay the loan.

⚠ **Forming a corporation or LLC may not protect you from personal liability on a loan.** *As explained in Chapter 1, a virtue of doing business as a corporation or a limited liability company (LLC) is that corporate shareholders and LLC members aren't personally liable for paying business debts, including loans made by the corporation or LLC. But a small corporation or LLC—especially one just starting up—will find it impossible to borrow money from a bank or other sophisticated lender unless the shareholders or members personally guarantee repayment. And if this guarantee is made, the shareholders or members are just as obligated to repay the loan as if they signed as personal borrowers*

in the first place. Typically, lenders will continue to require that shareholders or LLC members guarantee repayment of a corporate or LLC loan—at least until the business is well established and has a long record of being profitable.

2. Equity Investments

Equity investors buy a piece of your business. They become co-owners and share in the fortunes and misfortunes of your business. Like you, they can make or lose a bundle. Generally, if your business does badly or flops, you're under no obligation to pay them back their money. However, some equity investors would like to have their cake and eat it too; they want you to guarantee some return on their investment even if the business does poorly. Unless you're really desperate for the cash, avoid an investor who wants a guarantee. It's simply too risky a proposition for someone starting or running a small business.

a. Limiting risk

Because equity investors are co-owners of the business, they may be exposed to personal liability for all business debts unless your business is a corporation, limited partnership or limited liability company. If you recruit equity investors for what has been your sole proprietorship, your business will now be treated as a general partnership. This means your equity investors will be considered to be general partners, whether or not they take part in running the business. And, as explained in Chapter 1, as far as people outside of the business are concerned—people who are owed money or who have a judgment against the business—general partners are all personally liable for the debts of the partnership.

Equity investors often want to limit their losses to what they put into the business. An investor who puts $10,000 into a business may be prepared to lose the $10,000—but no more. In short, the investor doesn't want to put the rest of his or her assets at risk. The investor will want to avoid being—or being treated as—a general partner.

Fortunately, there are three common ways to organize your business so that you can offer an investor protection from losses beyond the money being invested.

- *Corporation.* Form a corporation and issue stock to the investor. A shareholder who doesn't participate in corporate activities and decision-making is virtually free from liability beyond his or her original investment. A shareholder who does help run the company is liable to outsiders for his or her own actions—for example, making slanderous statements or negligently operating a piece of equipment—but isn't liable for corporate debts or the actions of corporate employees.

- *Limited Partnership.* Form a limited partnership and make the investor a limited partner. A limited partner's freedom from liability is similar to that of a shareholder, as long as the limited partner doesn't become actively involved in running the business.

- *Limited Liability Company.* Form a limited liability company and make the investor a member. The investor will be protected in much the same manner as a shareholder or limited partner.

Each of these business formats is described in much greater detail in Chapter 1.

⚠ Encourage investors to determine their own degree of risk. *As mentioned, an investor in a business organized as a corporation, limited partnership or limited liability company usually stands to lose no more than his or her investment. However, state laws must be followed carefully to achieve this result. To avoid having investors accuse you of giving misleading assurances, recommend that they check with their own financial and legal advisors to evaluate if their investment exposes them to the possibility of incurring additional losses.*

b. Return on investment

Someone who invests in your business may be willing to face the loss of the entire investment and not insist that you guarantee repayment. But to offset the risk of losing the invested money, the investor may want to receive substantial benefits if the business is successful. For example, an investor may insist on a generous percentage of the business profits and, to help assure that there are such profits, may seek to put a cap on your salary. The terms are always negotiable—there's no formula for figuring out what's fair to both you and the investor.

Here are just a few possibilities:

- John, a former police detective, decides to start a business to offer security training seminars to mid-sized manufacturing companies. He forms STS Limited Liability Company and invests $10,000, which is only part of his $20,000 start-up budget. His aunt Paula, recently widowed, invests $10,000 of her inheritance in the company. The STS operating agreement states that John will be in full control of day-to-day operations. John and Paula agree in writing that John will receive a salary of no more than $4,000 a month from STS for the first four years, and that Paula will receive 60% of STS profits during that period. After that, John's salary will be tied to gross receipts, and John and Paula will share profits equally.

- Stella wants to start a travel agency. She approaches Edgar, a friend from college days, who has just sold a screenplay to a major studio and is looking for investment opportunities. They agree that Stella will form a limited partnership and act as the general partner. Edgar will invest $60,000 in the business and become a limited partner. Stella will work for $3,000 a month and use the first profits of the travel agency pay back Edgar's $60,000 investment. After that, the profits will be split 50/50.

- Larry, an experienced carpenter, wants to become a general contractor so he can build custom homes and do major remodeling jobs.

He's able to invest his savings of $30,000 in his new venture, but needs another $20,000 to get started. Larry forms a corporation, Prestige Homes Inc., and invites his friend Brook, who owns a building supply business, to invest $20,000 in return for a 40% interest in Prestige Homes. Brook agrees, on the condition that the new corporation will buy all its lumber and other building materials from Brook's company—and, in addition, pay Brook $5,000 for each home that's built by Prestige Homes. They sign a shareholders' agreement containing those terms.

c. Compliance with securities regulations

The law treats corporate shares and limited partnership interests as securities. Issuing these securities to investors is regulated by federal and state law. In some cases, an investor's interest in a limited liability company may also come under these laws.

This means that before selling an investor an interest in your business, you'll need to learn more about the requirements of the securities laws. Fortunately, there are generous exemptions that normally allow a small business to provide a limited number of investors an interest in the business without complicated paperwork. Chances are good that your business will be able to qualify for these exemptions. In the rare cases in which the exemptions won't work for your small business and you have to meet the complex requirements of the securities laws—such as distributing an approved prospectus to potential investors—it's probably too much trouble to do the deal unless a great deal of money is involved.

For a first-rate introduction to securities laws and the exemptions for small businesses, see Incorporate Your Business: A 50-State Legal Guide to Forming a Corporation, *or* How to Form Your Own California Corporation, *both by Anthony Mancuso (Nolo).*

B. Thirteen Common Sources of Money

While there are many sources of money for a small business, some are more accessible than others. There are 13 that entrepreneurs tend to rely on most frequently.

1. Salary

"Don't give up your day job." That's the advice commonly given to aspiring actors and musicians—but it's equally applicable to many entrepreneurs who are testing the waters. If you start small enough, you may be able to stay afloat for many months by continuing your full-time job or cutting back to part-time. This steady source of income can reduce your need for turning to others for start-up funds and can help keep you solvent if the business doesn't succeed.

2. Personal Savings

Putting your own money into your business is the simplest way to get started or to expand your business. You avoid entanglements with others, keep your business affairs private and steer clear of possible legal complications.

If your business takes off, you'll own business assets—such as inventory, equipment and furniture—free of debt, making it easier to borrow money later or bring equity investors into the business.

Your money may come from savings that you've carefully accumulated over the years. Or it may come from a lump sum of money that's available all at once. For example, you may have received an inheritance from a relative or an attractive severance package from a job you've just left. Or perhaps you've sold your house and will be living in a less expensive one or in rented quarters. Investing this money in your own business may yield a bigger return than you could ever expect to receive by investing it in someone else's business.

⚠ Try to keep some cash in reserve.
Since no business is risk-free and the cash flow is usually unpredictable, it makes sense not to commit every last dollar to your business. Yes, this can be extremely hard to do. But if you can plan well enough to keep a reasonable amount of cash on hand to cover several months' worth of living expenses and possible medical emergencies, you'll improve your odds of succeeding in business. And you'll receive an added bonus of not having to worry constantly about how to pay personal bills.

If You're the Beneficiary of a Trust Fund

Another possible source of funds can be a trust fund established on your behalf at the death of a parent, grandparent or other relative. Often these funds provide the beneficiary with income for a number of years before the trust ends and all remaining funds are turned over to the beneficiary in a lump sum. However, in the meantime, the trustee often has the discretionary power to take additional money out of the trust for a good reason, such as education, health needs and possibly starting a business. Since the trustee's discretion will be tied to the specific wording of the trust document, you'll want to start by reading it carefully. But assuming that distributing money for a business venture would qualify as a proper purpose under the trust, you should present your business plan to the trustee. If the trustee agrees that your plan has merit, this can magically free up the cash you're looking for.

3. Equity in Your Home

If you own a home, you may be able to tap into a portion of the equity to raise cash. As you know, equity is the difference between what the home is worth and how much is left on the mortgage. Let's say you bought your home several years ago for $150,000 by paying $30,000 down and getting a $120,000 mortgage. Today, the house would sell for $200,000 and the mortgage balance is down to $100,000. You have $100,000 in equity—some of which you can use to help finance your business.

There are two ways to get your hands on a portion of the equity. One is to get a new, larger mortgage that will pay off the earlier one and still yield some cash. For example, if you get a new mortgage for $160,000—which is 80% of the home's current value and likely to be approved by a conservative lender—you'll have $60,000 after the earlier mortgage balance of $100,000 is paid off. Unfortunately, the actual amount you'll end up with will be significantly less because the bank will require you to pay some hefty costs for processing the mortgage. These transaction costs typically include an application fee, document preparation fees, closing costs known as points, fees for a personal credit check, an appraisal of the home and mortgage title insurance.

⚠ Plan carefully before applying for a new mortgage. *If your purpose in getting a new mortgage is to raise a relatively small amount of money for your business, make sure you understand all of the costs involved. Obviously, unless it's your only way to raise money, you don't want to plunk down $2,000 in expenses to get your hands on $10,000 which, of course, will also require you to pay interest. Before applying for a mortgage, ask the lender to itemize the costs involved. Also, if you're planning to quit your job or cut back to half-time to run the business, it may be wise to wait until after the mortgage loan has been made—especially if you don't have a spouse or significant other earning a decent income. This is because before approving the new mortgage, the lender will be looking at your ability to repay. Having a steady source of income from a job when you apply for and receive a mortgage loan can help convince the lender to approve the loan.*

The second approach is to apply for a line of credit based on your home equity. The bank will have a second mortgage on your home. Using the assumptions in the example, you may be able to obtain a line of credit for $60,000. Typically, the bank will give you a checkbook which you can use to write checks against the line of credit. Your monthly payment to the bank will depend on how much of the credit line you've used.

Deciding which method to use can be difficult. A line of credit will likely cost less to set up—perhaps there will simply be a $250 upfront fee rather than a few thousand dollars in closing costs for a mortgage—but the interest rate will likely be higher or,

if the loan has a variable interest rate, the bank will have the right to increase the interest rate if interest rates in the overall economy rise.

💡 Don't overdo borrowing against your house. *Whichever method you use to borrow against your house, you put your home at risk if you can't meet the repayment schedule. You don't want to lose your house to the lender or be forced to sell under pressure of an imminent foreclosure to save a portion of the equity. So don't borrow more than you absolutely need. Also, take time to figure out how you'll make the mortgage payments if your business is slow to get off the ground or you end up closing it. One good approach is to look for a loan with a long repayment window and, hence, lower monthly payments. If your business does well, you can always repay the loan sooner.*

4. Retirement Savings

If you have money in a retirement savings plan where you work, you may be able to borrow some of that money. As you know, income tax on the money you contribute to an IRS-qualified plan—such as a 401(k) plan—is deferred, allowing your retirement to grow faster. Check the plan language to see if loans are allowed for business purposes. If so, you should be able to borrow up to one-half of what you have in the plan—but no more than $50,000. Also check other conditions, such as the maximum term allowed for a loan (typically, five years), the interest rate and the loan fees. You will have to pay interest on the money you borrow from your plan, but that's not all bad. Because the money you're borrowing is yours, the interest goes back into your plan.

Generally, unless you've reached the age of 59½, you wouldn't be wise to simply take rather than borrow money from the tax-deferred plan. Early withdrawals are subject to a penalty tax. After age 59½, however, IRS rules allow you to withdraw funds without paying a penalty tax.

⚠️ **Don't borrow from an IRA.** *Unfortunately, if you borrow money from an Individual Retirement Account (IRA), it will be treated as a withdrawal and you'll have to pay a penalty tax if you're not yet 59½ years old.*

5. Credit Cards

You can use your credit cards to help finance your business. Plastic can quickly get you a computer and fax machine—and probably other business equipment and furniture as well. And for expenses such as rent, phone bills or money to pay employees, you can usually get a cash advance.

Credit cards are a convenient way to arrange for short-term financing because they're so easy to use. Over the long haul, however, they're less attractive—mainly because the interest charges are relatively high, often as much as 20% or more per year. If you're going to succeed in business, you shouldn't need me to tell you not to borrow very much for very long at those rates.

6. Buying on Credit

The companies from which you're buying goods or services may offer favorable credit terms to capture your business. Often this will mean you don't have to pay your bill for 30 or 60 or more days. Or you may be able to spread payments for a purchase over a period of several months with no finance charges as long as you pay each installment on time. And the interest rate that's charged may be substantially lower than that charged by a credit card company.

Don't be discouraged by the fact that the best credit terms usually go to established businesses and that new businesses typically have to pay up front. Credit decisions are somewhat subjective, leaving you room to convince the seller that your new business deserves special consideration. Espe-

cially if you'll need starting inventory as in the case of a retail store, call suppliers and ask for help. Show them a copy of your credit history and business plan. If they look good and you're persuasive, you may be able to get a fair amount of your inventory on favorable terms.

7. Leasing

If you need equipment—anything from computers and copiers to forklifts and trucks—consider leasing it. True, leasing doesn't put money directly in your hands but, almost as good from a cash flow point of view, it does reduce the amount of cash you'd have to come up with if you were to instead buy the same equipment. And many leases offer you the option to acquire the equipment for a nominal amount when the lease period is over. Over the long term, leasing usually costs a bit more than buying—but if the cash flow from your business will be tight for a few years, leasing can be an effective way to get the equipment you need now.

8. Friends, Relatives and Business Associates

Those close to you can often lend you money or invest in your business. This helps you avoid the hassle of pleading your case to outsiders and enduring extra paperwork and bureaucratic delays—and can be especially valuable if you've been through bankruptcy or had other credit problems that would make borrowing from a commercial lender difficult or impossible.

Some advantages of borrowing money from people you know well are that you may be charged a lower interest rate, may be able to delay paying back money until you're more established and may be given more flexibility if you get into a jam. But once the loan terms are agreed to, there's one thing that borrowing from friends, relatives or business associates doesn't do. It doesn't legally diminish your obligation to meet those terms.

In addition, borrowing money from relatives and friends can have a big downside. There's always the possibility that if your business does poorly and those close to you end up losing money, you'll damage a good personal relationship. So in dealing with friends, relatives and business associates, be extra careful to not only clearly establish the terms of the deal and put it in writing, but also make an extra effort to explain the risks. In short, it's your job to make sure your helpful friend or relative won't suffer a true hardship if you're unable to meet your financial commitments.

⚠ Don't borrow from people on fixed incomes. *Don't borrow or accept investment money from folks who can't afford to lose money. It's fine to borrow needed money from your Mom if she's well enough off that lending you $20,000 won't put her in the poorhouse if things go wrong and you can't repay the loan. But if your Mom lives on Social Security, don't borrow her last $10,000 no matter how badly you need it. If you do and your business fails, you'll be about as miserable as it's possible to be.*

Gifts Can Save Taxes

If you're likely to inherit money from a parent or grandparent in the future, it can make sense for them to make a gift now. Why? Because if a family member's estate exceeds a certain amount ($1.5 million in 2003, rising to $2 million in 2004), the excess will be heavily taxed by the federal government when that person dies.

By contrast, up to fairly generous limits, there will be no estate or gift tax on the money the relative gives away while alive. Specifically, an individual can make a gift of up to $11,000 per year per person free of any federal gift or estate tax—and a couple can give twice that amount. For example, your mother and father can each give $11,000 to you and $11,000 to your spouse—a total of $44,000—in one year. This has the effect of removing this money from their estates with neither a federal estate or gift tax. Obviously, gifts of that size can be a big boost to any small business since there is no worry about the need to repay.

💡 How to promote family harmony. *If your parents give you money for your business, it may make sense for them to make equal gifts to the other children. Or if the parent isn't financially able to do this, he or she can even things out by leaving the other children more in a will or trust. If this is done, the reason for the discrepancy can be explained in the will or trust, or in a separate letter.*

For detailed information on gifts and the tax laws, see Plan Your Estate, *by Denis Clifford & Cora Jordan (Nolo).*

9. Supporters

As Mike McKeever points out in *How to Write a Business Plan* (Nolo), many types of businesses have loyal and devoted followers—people who care as much about the business as the owners do. A health food restaurant, a women's bookstore, an import car repair shop or an art studio, for example, may attract people who are enthusiastic about lending money to or investing in the business because it fits in with their lifestyle or beliefs.

Their decision to participate is driven to some extent by their feelings and is not strictly a business proposition. These people can also be a source of great ideas—ideas that can be as valuable as money—and they'll be happy to share these with you at no charge.

The rules for borrowing from friends and relatives apply here as well. Put repayment terms in writing—and don't accept money from people who can't afford to risk it.

10. Banks

Banks are in the money business, so it's natural to look to them for start-up funds. It's hard to predict, however, whether the banks you approach will be willing to lend you money on reasonable terms. Historically, banks were reluctant to lend substantial sums to a new business, even if the owner was willing to pledge a house or other valuable asset as security (for example, by giving the bank a second mortgage) for repayment. Often this reluctance to lend was attributable to the fact that loan officers were looking for an established record of business profitability which, of course, a new business couldn't provide. Fortunately, that stand-offish attitude is starting to crumble. Many banks, in fact, have departments geared especially to the needs of small businesses—and some are even eager to establish a banking relationship with those just getting started. With a little luck, you may be able to locate such an enlightened, small-business-oriented bank in your community. As you might imagine, banks offer their best terms to businesses that appear the least risky and that are likely to maintain sizable deposits as the business grows.

Generally, banks respond more favorably to loan applications when the requested loan is guaranteed by the Small Business Administration (SBA). Check out the SBA's LowDoc program—so called because the paperwork requirements have been drastically cut to a one-page application. The SBA says its response time under the LowDoc program is only two or three days—a far cry from other programs in which the document review can take weeks or months. If you're approved for a LowDoc loan, a bank may lend you up to $150,000 and the SBA will guarantee up to 85% of the loan.

Under other programs, the SBA can guarantee a bank loan up to $1 million if the loan meets SBA standards. Typically, your business must show profits for at least two years. You must work full time in the business and be able to offer property as collateral. Some banks will help you complete the SBA form, but may charge a fee for this service.

Look into other SBA programs. *New programs emerge from time to time—and they're not always bank loan guarantee programs. For example, the SBA's Micro Loan Program provides business loans of up to $35,000 through designated nonprofit agencies. Women, low income and minority entrepreneurs are eligible for these funds, which can be used for working capital, inventory, supplies, equipment, expansion or job creation. Ask your nearest SBA office for details or go to the SBA's website at www.sba.gov. The SBA also offers loan information clinics which it co-sponsors with the Service Corps of Retired Executives (SCORE).*

For more details, see SBA Loans: A Step-by-Step Guide, *by Patrick D. O'Hara (John Wiley and Sons, Inc.). Also, order the free booklet,* The Credit Process: A Guide for Small Business Owners *(Federal Reserve Bank of New York), by calling the bank's Public Information Department at 212-720-6134. Or, you can view it online at www.ny.frb.org. Click on Publications, then Order Publications, then look under Community Development and click Small Business Resources, then scroll down until you find it.*

11. Other Commercial Lenders

If you can't get a bank loan, consider applying to other commercial lenders, such as Allied Capital Corp., the Money Store or GE Capital. More than one-third of the money loaned to small businesses comes from these nonbank sources. They're often less tight-fisted than banks and may give more weight to intangible factors like your business vision and personal integrity. You'll be in an especially good position to borrow from a nonbank lender if your loan qualifies for SBA backing.

The Five C's of Credit

Bankers like to speak of the five C's of credit analysis—factors they look at when they evaluate a loan request. When applying to a bank for a loan, be prepared to address these points.

- *Character.* Bankers lend money to borrowers who appear honest and who have a good credit history. Before you apply for a loan, it makes sense to obtain a copy of your credit report and clean up any problems.
- *Capacity.* This is a prediction of the borrower's ability to repay the loan. For a new business, bankers look at the business plan. For an existing business, bankers consider financial statements and industry trends.
- *Collateral.* Bankers generally want a borrower to pledge an asset which can be sold to pay off the loan if the borrower lacks funds.
- *Capital.* The borrower's net worth—the amount by which assets exceed debts—is scrutinized.
- *Conditions.* The current economic climate can influence whether a loan is given and the amount of the loan.

12. Venture Capitalists

There are companies and individuals looking to invest in extraordinary companies that can produce large profits. See if your city has a venture capital club which helps introduce new businesses to venture capitalists. If so, get in contact and find out how you can meet potential investors. Often you'll be afforded a chance to make a short presentation which can make an impression on someone with deep pockets. Your local or state chamber of commerce should be able to direct you to the closest club, or you can check with the instructor of a business school that offers courses in entrepreneurship.

13. The Seller of an Existing Business

If you're buying an existing business, you may be able to negotiate favorable payment terms—which can reduce the amount of cash you have to come up with. You have a number of variables to work with. Try to keep the down payment low and see if the seller will agree to below-market interest rates or will even charge no interest for the first year or two.

Try, too, to extend the payments over as many years as possible. As with a bank loan, you can always pay the debt off early if your business prospers. (For more on buying a business, see Chapter 10.)

C. Document All Money You Receive

In raising money for your business, you should be familiar with the basic paperwork and other legal requirements, a number of which I've already mentioned in this chapter.

Chapter 4 of Legal Forms for Starting & Running a Small Business *contains several promissory note forms and a security agreement.*

1. Gifts

If a family member gives you money for your business, it's smart to put it in writing. Strictly speaking, this isn't a legal requirement, but nevertheless I highly recommend that you do so. For one thing, it can help with taxes. An individual can make a gift each year of up to $11,000 to any number of people. These gifts won't be subject to either the federal estate or gift tax. (See Section B8.) If the giver states in writing that the money is a gift and not a loan, it will be clear to the IRS that no tax is owed.

A second reason to document the gift is to avoid possible future misunderstandings with other people who eventually inherit from the giver. Incredible as it may seem, brothers and sisters have sometimes gone to court to argue that a sum of money that a parent advanced to one child should be treated not as a gift, but as a loan to be repaid to the estate. And even where siblings haven't resorted to such drastic action, doubts about a parent's intentions can simmer beneath the surface for years, hurting the relationship.

2. Loans Without Security

The way to document a loan is through a promissory note. (See Section A1.)

Banks and other commercial lenders will have their own forms for you to sign. The following forms can be used if you borrow money from a relative or friend.

SAMPLE PROMISSORY NOTE FOR INSTALLMENT PAYMENTS THAT INCLUDE PRINCIPAL AND INTEREST

September 1, 20XX

For value received, I promise to pay to Leo Lender

$10,000 and interest at the rate of 10% per annum on the unpaid balance as follows:

1. I will pay 60 monthly installments of $212.48 each.

2. I will pay the first installment on October 1, 20XX, and a similar installment on the first day of each month after that until principal and interest have been paid in full.

3. Payments will be applied first on interest and then on principal.

4. I will pay the entire amount of principal and interest within five years from the date of this note.

5. I may prepay all or any part of the principal without penalty.

6. If I am more than 10 days late in making any payment, Leo Lender may declare that the entire balance of unpaid principal is due immediately, together with the interest that has accrued.

Bob Borrower

**SAMPLE PROMISSORY NOTE FOR ANNUAL
INTEREST PAYMENTS AND BALLOON PAYMENT
OF PRINCIPAL**

September 1, 20XX

For value received, I promise to pay to
Leo Lender

$10,000 and interest at the rate of 10%
    per annum on the unpaid balance as
    follows:

1. I will pay interest on September 1
   each year for five years beginning in
   20XX.

2. I will pay the principal five years
   from the date of this note.

3. I may prepay all or any part of the
   principal without penalty.

4. If I am more than 10 days late in making any payment, Leo Lender may declare that the principal is due immediately, together with the interest
   that has accrued.

_____

Bob Borrower

**SAMPLE PROMISSORY NOTE FOR LUMP
SUM REPAYMENT**

September 1, 20XX

For value received, I promise to pay to
Leo Lender

$10,000 and interest at the rate of 10%
per annum on the unpaid balance on [Insert
Date When the Entire $10,000 plus Interest
is Due]. I may prepay all or any part of
the principal without penalty.

_____

Bob Borrower

For additional promissory notes that cover several common transactions, see 101 Law Forms for Personal Use (with CD-ROM), *by Robin Leonard & Ralph Warner (Nolo). You'll find promissory notes that can be used for a loan repayable in a lump sum with no interest, a lump sum with interest, installments without interest, installments with interest, a lump sum secured by real or personal property and installments secured by real or personal property.*

3. Loans With Security

If you're pledging property as security for a loan, you can start with one of the sample forms given in Section C2, above—but the promissory note should also state that it's a secured loan and that additional documents have been prepared and are being signed to fully protect the lender. Commercial lenders will generally prepare these additional documents. When you're borrowing from a friend or family member, however, and pledging security for the loan, you and the lender will need to follow through on these details.

a. Note secured by personal property

Personal property is property that's not real estate—equipment and inventory, for example. If you're pledging personal property as security, here is sample language to include in a promissory note:

SECURED INTEREST PROVISION

I agree that until the principal and
interest owed under this note are paid in
full, the note will be secured by a security agreement signed today giving
(lender's name) a security interest in the
equipment, fixtures, inventory and accounts receivable of the business known as
(name of borrower's business).

You should prepare and sign a security agreement that gives the lender the right to take the specified assets if you don't repay your loan as agreed. You should also prepare and sign a Uniform Commercial Code Financing Statement—sometimes called Form UCC-1. This form should be available at office supply stores that serve lawyers. Generally, there will be a statewide office where the lender should file this form. In addition, in many states, the lender should also file a copy at the county office that keeps records of liens on personal property. The form notifies future creditors that the lender is a secured creditor and holds a lien on the listed assets. When you pay off the loan, the lender should release the lien—and, as with real estate liens, the release should be filed at the same public office where the Form UCC-1 was filed.

If you pledge a car or truck, check with the office in your state that handles motor vehicle titles to learn how to record the fact that the lender is obtaining a security interest in the car or truck.

b. Note secured by real estate

Here is sample language to include in a note secured by real estate:

SECURED INTEREST PROVISION

```
    I agree that until the principal and
interest owed under this note are paid in
full, the note will be secured by a mort-
gage [or deed of trust] to real estate
commonly known as ____(address or other
description)____, owned by
_____(name)_____ signed on _(date)_
and recorded at ____(place recorded)____.
```

You'll probably need professional help in preparing the mortgage or deed of trust. This is routine stuff for an experienced real estate lawyer, so you should be able to get it done by paying for a half-hour or less of a lawyer's time. The mortgage or deed of trust will have to be witnessed and notarized, and then get recorded for a small fee at a government office that handles real estate registrations. To learn the name and location of the correct government office, call the county clerk or inquire at a title insurance company.

⚠️ **Be sure the security interest gets canceled.** *You don't want to face problems ten years from now when you go to sell the real estate. So when you pay off the loan, don't forget to get a paper signed by the lender that releases or discharges the mortgage or deed of trust. The document, which will need to be witnessed and notarized, must be filed at the same place at which the mortgage or deed of trust was filed. Again, you'd be wise to consult briefly with a lawyer or check with a local title insurance company to make sure you're doing this correctly.*

4. Equity Investments

Equity investments in a limited partnership, corporation or limited liability company are usually treated as securities and may be regulated by federal and state laws. (See Section A2.) It's unlikely that this will be a problem for a small business with just a few owners and investors. Investments in these businesses are usually exempt from the regulations. If that's so in your case, you won't have to deal with the sometimes burdensome paperwork. If, however, you decide to go public—make a public offering of an interest in your business—then you definitely need to seek detailed legal advice.

Whether or not you must meet special requirements under federal or state laws regulating securities, you should always have a written agreement with an equity investor. The mechanics will depend on the legal structure of your business.

- **Sole Proprietorship.** By definition, a sole proprietorship is owned by just one person. Anyone else who invests in your business and acquires equity in it becomes a co-owner—

which means that, legally, your sole proprietorship is converted into a partnership. It makes sense to sign a partnership agreement outlining your responsibilities and those of the investor (see Chapter 2).

- **Partnership.** An equity investor in a partnership is a partner, so you should amend your partnership agreement to include your new partner and specify the financial relationships. All partners—old and new—should sign it. (Again, see Chapter 2 for help on partnership agreements and consult *The Partnership Book,* by Denis Clifford & Ralph Warner (Nolo).)

- **Limited Partnership.** Assuming that the investor will play a passive role and won't be actively involved in running the business, he or she will be a limited partner. The limited partnership agreement will define how a lim-

ited partner gets money from the business. The limited partner will receive a certificate recognizing his or her interest in the limited partnership.

- **Corporation.** The equity investor will be a shareholder. You, the equity investor and all other shareholders should sign a shareholders' agreement—or amend the existing agreement if there is one—to spell out the corporation's obligations to the investor. The corporation should issue a stock certificate in the investor's name.

- **Limited Liability Company.** The equity investor will be a member. You, the equity investor and all other members of the LLC should sign an operating agreement—or amend the existing operating agreement if there is one. ■

Buying a Business

For those who would like to own their own business, buying an existing business may be a better approach than starting from scratch. After all, there's something attractive about letting someone else find a location and sign a lease; test the market and develop a customer base; buy furniture, fixtures, equipment and inventory; hire employees; and perform the countless other chores that go with starting a business. In short, there's something very attractive about letting someone else prove that the business works.

If you find yourself looking for an existing business to buy, keep an open mind. It's not always possible to buy a business you'll be happy with at a price you can afford. Many people who buy existing businesses do very well, but others, having explored the opportunities and finding nothing to their liking, return to the idea of starting their own business. And some people pay too much money for a poor business or one they may never really enjoy operating.

This chapter first looks at how to find a business to buy. Then it turns to the nuts and bolts of actually buying a business, including how to structure the purchase, what to investigate before closing the deal and the legal documents needed for a business to change hands.

Selling a Business. This chapter focuses on buying a business, but a seller's concerns are also discussed briefly in Section I.

A. Finding a Business to Buy

Before you look for a business to buy, narrow your field of possible choices. First, decide whether you want to be in a service, manufacturing, wholesale, retail or food service business. Once you make this choice, consider the specific type of business you're interested in—perhaps a desktop publishing center, a management consulting business, a direct-mail processing business, a dance studio, a flower shop or a used book store.

Your choice of business should be motivated by the type of work you've done in the past, courses you've taken, special skills you've developed through a hobby or perhaps just a strong yearning to work in a particular field. It's almost always a mistake to consider buying a business you know little about, no matter how good it looks. For example, if you're confused by mechanical and electronic equipment, buying an auto tune-up shop or a business that installs security systems makes little sense even if the business looks irresistible from a financial point of view.

If you're currently employed by a small business you like, what are the chances of that business becoming available to you? Maybe the current owner wants to retire, is in bad health, is moving out of the city or is just getting bored. If you know the inner workings of the business and are sure that it's doing well—or at least that it has the potential to flower under your able leadership—that would be an ideal place to start. Failing that, perhaps business associates or friends can provide you with leads to similar businesses that may be available.

Here are some other time-tested ways to search for an available business:

- *Newspaper ads.* This is a traditional starting point and can quickly put you in touch with people who are actively seeking a buyer for their business. Unfortunately, ads are only the tip of the iceberg. Many of the best business opportunities never get into the papers but surface primarily by word of mouth.

- *Professionals who advise small businesses.* Bankers, lawyers, accountants, insurance agents and real estate brokers who regularly work with small businesses often know about available businesses before they go on the market. Think about who you know who is plugged into this network and get on the phone. A few well-placed phone calls may be enough to identify likely candidates in your area.

- *Business suppliers.* Another great way to tap into the grapevine is to contact the network of suppliers for that business. For example, if you're thinking of opening a flower shop, a floral wholesaler in your area will probably know who is thinking of retiring or selling out for other reasons.

- *Trade associations.* Almost every business has a local or regional trade association—for example, the Northern California Booksellers Association or the Michigan Pest Control Association. The secretary or a long-time employee of such a group may have heard about a business owner who's thinking of retiring.
- *The direct approach.* If there's a business that you've admired from afar, simply drop in and politely ask if the owner has ever thought about selling. Who knows? Maybe he or she has been thinking about moving to another part of the country or changing to a different type of business. Once in a while, you'll be in the right place at the right time. A long shot? Probably—but you have nothing to lose by trying it.
- *Business brokers.* Finally, there are business brokers—people who earn commissions from business owners who need help finding buyers. As is true in all endeavors, not all business brokers are created equal. A few are honest, ingenious and hardworking. Many more are adequate but nothing special when it comes to competence, energy and integrity. More than a few are sleazy, incompetent and interested almost exclusively in earning a commission. In short, before working with a broker, it pays to carefully check out his or her reputation. Several glowing recommendations from a banker, accountant or fellow small business person should raise your confidence level. On the other hand, if the feedback you get is lukewarm, look for someone else.

It's foolish to rely on a broker—who gets paid only if the deal goes through—for advice about the quality of the business or the fairness of its price. If you do, he or she is almost sure to paint an unrealistically rosy picture. Also, because the seller typically pays the broker, the broker's loyalty will be to the seller—not to you. Use a broker only to find a business, not to negotiate the purchase price and other terms. See Section G on drafting the documents involved, particularly the purchase agreement.

B. What's the Structure of the Business You Want to Buy?

If you find a business you're interested in, one important question is: What kind of legal entity owns the business—a sole proprietorship, partnership, corporation or limited liability company (LLC)?

1. Buying From a Sole Proprietor or Partnership

When you buy a business from a sole proprietor or a partnership, you never acquire the old legal structure of the business, only its assets (and possibly its liabilities, depending on how the business was structured).

Legally, it's simplest to buy a business from a sole proprietor, because one person owns the business and the assets are in his or her name. Buying from a partnership is almost as simple, although a partnership agreement typically requires the consent of all owners before the business can be sold. If you're dealing with only one partner in a partnership, to avoid disappointment, promptly ask to see the partnership agreement. Then make sure that the person negotiating the deal has received proper authority from the other owners. Beyond that, get a clear understanding early on about whether you'll only be buying the assets of the business, or whether the seller is also trying to get you to assume responsibility for all liabilities.

> **⚠ It's best to avoid assuming business liabilities.** *A major issue in buying any business is whether you'll be purchasing only its assets, or if, as part of the deal, you'll also be taking on its liabilities. You'll avoid many potential legal and debt entanglements if you insist on buying the assets only (even if this means you pay a higher price). But whatever you and the seller decide, it's vital that you clearly record your understanding in the purchase documents.*

> **💡 Changing a business's structure.** *A new owner is free to change the legal form of a business. For example, you can buy a business from a sole proprietor and then operate it through a partnership or corporation.*

2. Buying From a Corporation

When you buy a business owned by a corporation, you run into a special problem: figuring out the best way to structure your purchase. You can buy the corporate entity itself (the stock) or you can buy only its assets, leaving the seller still owning the corporation minus the assets you purchased.

In almost any purchase of a business, you'll be much better off buying the assets rather than the corporate stock (but see subsection c, below). Most sales of small businesses—a whopping 94%—involve the sale of assets rather than corporate stock. Buying assets has four distinct advantages:

- It helps you avoid the liabilities of the existing business.
- It gives you significant tax advantages.
- You can avoid acquiring unwanted assets from the corporation.
- You generally can get a higher tax basis for depreciable assets, which means there's less taxable gain to report if you later sell the assets.

EXAMPLE OF STOCK PURCHASE: Brown Manufacturing Inc. is a small corporation owned by Joseph Brown and his two sons. The company, which makes specialized computer circuit boards, owns a small factory, several machines, raw materials, an inventory of completed items, office furniture and equipment and two delivery trucks. The corporation owns all of the assets of the business. In a stock purchase, you'd buy 100% of the stock of the corporation from Joseph Brown and his sons. As the new owner, you'd elect yourself (and anyone else you choose) to the board of directors; the board would then typically appoint you to the office of president.

EXAMPLE OF ASSET PURCHASE: You want to buy the business operated by Brown Manufacturing Inc., but instead of buying the corporate stock, you have the corporation sell you all or most of its assets, such as the factory, the machines, the trucks and several patents and trade secrets associated with circuit board assembly. The seller would continue to own Brown Manufacturing Inc. minus its assets. You would use these assets to run the manufacturing business as a sole proprietorship or partnership (if you have one or more business associates), or perhaps you would choose to place the assets in a new corporation of your own.

Get the Consent of Shareholders When You Purchase Corporate Assets

Remember that a corporation is a separate legal entity from its owners—the shareholders. When you purchase the assets of a small corporation, you want to avoid the possibility of having to deal with disgruntled minority owners. Even though the corporation's bylaws or shareholders' agreement may permit the sale of its assets with the consent of a majority (or more) of the shareholders, it's legally far safer for you if you insist that all shareholders agree with the sale of the corporation's assets. Get this consent in writing by following a two-step process:

- Require that all shareholders sign the purchase contract.
- Ask that all of the corporation's shareholders and directors sign and give you a copy of an official Corporate Resolution Authorizing Sale of Assets.

A big bonus that comes with insisting that all shareholders sign the purchase contract is that they then become personally liable for the warranties and representations in the contract. Without their signatures, should things go wrong, your only recourse would be against the corporation, which by that time would probably be without funds. You can also include language committing each shareholder to any noncompetition clause in the agreement—but as with other noncompete covenants, you must pay the signer something to make the covenant legally binding.

a. Liabilities of the corporation

If you buy the stock of a corporation, you're buying not only the assets but any liabilities as well. This is fine if there aren't any, but this can be difficult to determine. Maybe the corporation owes federal income taxes that you don't know about or has a huge balance to pay on a bank loan. Or maybe a customer slipped in the entryway of the business three months ago, broke his leg and is right now visiting a lawyer to prepare a million-dollar lawsuit. Or maybe there's an underground storage tank quietly leaking into the earth below the corporation's main office. Hidden liabilities can surface for injuries caused by defective products, discrimination against employees or environmental or safety violations, to name but a few.

In addition, the business may have contracts that you don't want to assume. For example, the corporation may have a five-year maintenance contract for service on the computers it owns—and there may be four more years to go at a rate you consider exorbitant.

You can protect yourself against some unknown liabilities. A good investigation will uncover many (though not all) potential liabilities. And personal warranties from the seller guaranteeing payment of any liabilities not disclosed can give you someone to turn to if unknown or undisclosed liabilities suddenly surface. Insurance may cover some of these risks, such as claims for injuries caused by defective products. But the point remains—if you buy a corporation, it's almost impossible to get 100% protection from its obligations.

In contrast, by buying the assets of the corporation rather than the corporate stock, you can avoid virtually all of these liability problems as long as you notify creditors of your purchase under the terms of your state's bulk sales statute (see Section G10) and you don't lead creditors to believe that you're picking up the liabilities of the corporation.

It's important to realize, however, that under some circumstances, if you continue the business of the prior corporation, you or your new corporation may still be subject to some liabilities incurred by the old corporation even if you only purchase assets. Known in legal lingo as "successor liability," the most common area of concern is product liability—liability to a person injured by a defective product. This is particularly likely to arise if you buy the assets of a corporation that manufactured a potentially hazardous consumer product and you directly continue the business. Each state has its own legal rules governing what constitutes a sufficient link (often called continuity) between the first manufacturer and the second to hold the second liable. One court ruled that there may be such a link if:

- There is a continuation of the management, personnel, physical location, assets and general business operations of the selling corporation.
- The selling corporation quickly ceased its ordinary business operations and then liquidated and dissolved.
- The purchasing company assumed the liabilities and obligations of the seller ordinarily necessary for continuing the business operations of the selling corporation.

In addition, depending on state law, a company that's just a continuation of an earlier corporation may be liable for other legal problems of the earlier corporation—for example, a wrongful discharge case brought by an ex-employee—or even for contractual obligations such as a union contract. The good news is that if you're fully informed about the law in your state, you can usually anticipate any successor liability problems and structure your purchase to avoid them. Or you may be able to buy insurance—often called "tail coverage"—to protect you from the long tail of the old corporation's liabilities.

b.   Tax advantages

You may be able to get several kinds of tax advantages in an asset purchase because you can allocate the purchase price among various assets you buy. As long as this allocation is based on an arm's length negotiation between you and the seller, it's likely to be upheld by the IRS.

You want to allocate the greater portion of the purchase price to assets you can write off against earnings immediately or through depreciation. These include things like the inventory of the business, supplies, machinery, equipment and vehicles, furniture and fixtures. Normally, you'll also want to assign some value to the seller's noncompetition agreement. The value of the promise not to compete is spread over its duration (often three to five years), and an equal amount is deducted each year. On the other

hand, you'll want to assign minimally reasonable values to assets that can't be deducted as current expenses, depreciated or amortized. This includes such assets as goodwill, trademarks, customer lists and trade names. (How to allocate purchase price to different assets you're buying is discussed in Section G.)

In addition, by buying assets rather than corporate stock, you can depreciate assets that the seller has already fully depreciated.

> **EXAMPLE:** Arthur is buying a dry cleaning business. The business has dry cleaning equipment that's ten years old but in excellent condition. The owner has fully depreciated it. Arthur and the seller allocate $30,000 of the purchase price to the equipment. That way, Arthur can start to depreciate it a second time. If Arthur bought the corporate stock, he wouldn't be able to take any depreciation for this equipment.

c.   Exceptions: When you must or should purchase stock

In some situations you may not be able to swing a deal in which you only buy corporate assets. This can occur, for example, if the seller insists on a stock sale—perhaps because he or she believes there's a tax advantage in going this route. If you agree to this, see subsection d, below, "How to protect yourself if you buy corporate stock."

In some limited circumstances where the corporation has a uniquely valuable asset that can't be transferred, it may actually be better to buy the stock of the corporation rather than its assets. For example, the corporation may have tax benefits such as a net operating loss carryover (NOL) that you want to take advantage of. The NOL carryover would be lost if you purchased the assets rather than the corporate stock. Also, if a store had a favorable five-year lease with a five-year option to renew that wasn't freely assignable, that could provide an incentive to you to buy the corporate stock. Or suppose a computer retail business had a hard-to-get distributorship for a particular brand of popular computers. If the distributorship contract couldn't be assigned to you and you weren't sure you could qualify for a similar contract yourself, you might consider buying the corporate stock because the corporation would likely continue to have the rights to be a distributor.

⚠ Investigating distributorships. *Even in a stock purchase, you'd want to read the distributorship documents carefully and check with the manufacturer to confirm that the manufacturer didn't reserve the right to cancel the distributorship if the corporate stock changed hands.*

d. How to protect yourself if you buy corporate stock

If you do decide to purchase a corporation's stock instead of its assets, protect yourself to the maximum extent possible. Conduct an in-depth investigation of the corporation's financial affairs. Try to get a strong personal guarantee from the shareholders that things are as stated. You could also get a warranty from the seller that he or she will pay for certain types of problems such as tax liabilities, obligations to former employees or damage claims by the landlord. Then arrange to pay for the business in installments spread over a number of years. Most liabilities will come to light in the first few years after you purchase the business. If the seller fails to make good on his or her warranty, you can pay for these liabilities and then withhold the amounts from the balance you owe the seller. Also, as mentioned earlier, insurance may be in place or obtainable to protect against product liability and other personal injury claims.

3. Buying From an LLC

In buying a business from an LLC, you'll have to start by making the same decision as when buying from a corporation: Should you purchase the whole entity (the LLC) or just its assets? In my opinion, you're much better off buying the assets rather than the entity, for the reasons I listed in Section B2, above, Buying From a Corporation.

Buying the Entity. If you buy the LLC entity, you won't be buying shares of stock as you would with a corporation. An LLC doesn't issue stock. Instead, you'll purchase the membership interests of all the LLC members. By doing so, you'll wind up owning the LLC, which in turn owns the company's assets.

Buying the Assets. If you simply buy the business's assets, the LLC will transfer the assets to you, leaving the current LLC members with ownership of the LLC shell. (The shell is a company without any assets, except possibly your promissory note for the balance of the purchase price.) To avoid possible problems with dissatisfied LLC members, I recommend that you require all members to sign the sales agreement.

C. Gathering Information About a Business

Buying a business takes weeks or months. During that time you'll need to diligently gather information—lots of information—about the business so that you don't get stung on the purchase price or have surprises later about income, expenses or undisclosed liabilities. Eventually, this information will help you structure a sound sales agreement.

In most small business purchases, the buyer learns everything possible about the business before signing the sales agreement. By contrast, business brokers sometimes advise making a quick formal offer to purchase with a number of contingencies that allow you to terminate the deal if all the facts don't turn out as represented by the seller. I recommend against this approach. Why invest your time, effort and money in a complete investigation of the business if the preliminary review of records convinces you that this isn't the business for you or that the price is too high? Better to request early access to financial records that will help you decide if you're really interested in the business. Then if you're satisfied with the finances you can sign a sales agreement with appropriate contingency clauses or wait until closing (legal lingo for the transfer of the business) to sign.

If you and the seller are strangers to one another, however, the seller may be reluctant to turn over sensitive business information until he or she is confident that you're a serious buyer. The seller may suspect you have some secret plan in mind, like using the information in a competitive business or some other improper purpose. To allay these fears, consider giving the seller a confidentiality letter like the one below.

SAMPLE CONFIDENTIALITY LETTER

Carlos Mendez, President
Mendez Furniture Company Inc.

Dear Mr. Mendez:

   As you know, I am looking into the purchase of your furniture business. Our conversations have been helpful but I'm now at the stage where I would like to see your company's financial records, including your tax returns, for the past five years.

   I know that the information that I'm requesting is confidential and that improper use of the information could damage your business. Consequently, I will use this confidential information only to help me decide whether I want to purchase your business and the terms of that purchase. I will disclose this confidential information only to my co-investors, my lawyer and my accountant. I'll make sure that each of these people knows that this information is confidential, and I'll ask them to sign confidentiality agreements before I release the information to them.

   If I don't buy your business, I will return all of the confidential information, including any copies, to you and will continue to treat in confidence the information you have disclosed to me.

   I look forward to receiving this information.

Sincerely yours,

Suzanne Gerstein

That kind of letter will satisfy many sellers. But a few sellers may prefer a longer, more formal confidentiality agreement drafted by a lawyer. That's okay, but you (and perhaps your lawyer as well) should make sure that the proposed document contains no binding commitment to buy the business. It should be limited to your agreement to treat the information as strictly confidential and use it only to investigate the purchase of the business, and to the other terms set out in the letter. If the proposed agreement goes farther than that, find out why and get legal advice.

Don't be surprised if the seller wants to learn about your own financial status, job or business history. Remember that most purchases of a small business are usually done on an installment basis, where the seller receives a down payment and payments over a period of time. The seller is interested in your financial stability, your reputation for integrity and your general business savvy because the seller, in effect, will be extending credit to you.

D. Valuing the Business

Does it sound impossibly demanding to determine a fair purchase price for a business? It's really not—especially if you take the sales price with a grain of salt. Most sellers ask for way too much, and far too many inexperienced buyers don't bargain aggressively enough. Lots of little businesses are worth no more than the fair current value of inventory and equipment. Goodwill, over and above the value of the continuing hard work of the owner, is commonly a myth.

1. What Are You Buying?

Generally, the assets of a business consist of inventory, fixed assets (furniture, fixtures, equipment) and intangible assets (such as a lease, trade name, customer list and goodwill). The most important factor in establishing the fair market value of these assets is this: Given the realities of the business and the industry in which it operates, what kind of return would a buyer reasonably expect on his or her investment? To arrive at this number, an appraiser will look both at the business's earnings and what similar businesses typically earn.

2. Goodwill Can Be a Myth

Be very careful about what you pay for goodwill—the portion of the purchase price attributed to such intangible factors as the reputation of the business, its location and the loyalty of its customers. Despite what sellers will almost surely tell you, many small businesses have little or no value beyond the value of the hard assets such as furniture, fixtures and equipment. How can this be, if a business earns a good yearly profit? Easy. Most of the profit is commonly attributable to the hard work, clear vision and good judgment of the owner, not to the inherent value of the business. Think of it this way: Most rug cleaning businesses, hardware stores, print shops and restaurants don't make a substantial profit. Those that do are usually run by uniquely talented people. When these people move on, many of those businesses quickly lose their luster.

> EXAMPLE: Joe and Monte own Caretti Brothers, a highly successful produce store that they've operated for 20 years. They sell the business to Anna Marie, who pays $200,000, including $100,000 for goodwill. Anna Marie continues to run the business as Caretti Brothers and does her best to preserve the store's distinctive atmosphere. Nevertheless, in her first year she earns only one-third the profits generated by the former owners.
>
> Unhappily, she realizes that Joe and Monte succeeded because customers valued their extroverted personalities and their rare ability to select only the freshest and tastiest tomatoes and grapefruit. Too late, she understands that she should have paid little or nothing for goodwill, which was largely personal to the Carettis and couldn't be transferred to her.

Goodwill isn't always a myth. Some profitable businesses—usually those that have been established for years and have strong name recognition—are worth significantly more than the value of their tangible assets, because they have a good reputation. Even if the owner retires or sells out, this reputation will continue to bring in business. Unfortunately, deciding that a business has goodwill is easier than deciding how much. One approach is for buyer and seller to try to agree on a multiplier—the number by which earnings (or sometimes sales) must be multiplied to determine the value of the business.

Where does the multiplier come from? In some industries, there are rough norms. For example, certain types of businesses typically sell for five times earnings, while other often sell for ten or more. Construction companies, retail stores and restaurants are examples of businesses where you can often obtain standard multipliers from business evaluators or appraisers who specialize in that industry.

⚠️ **Be critical of all multipliers.** *Never accept a multiplier without loads of caution. The facts of a particular business, the state of the local economy and industry trends change so quickly that last year's sensible multiplier can be completely off base this year.*

3. Evaluating the Business's Financial Health

To properly evaluate the business, ask for access to the following documents:

- tax returns, profit and loss statements and balance sheets for the last five years
- loan documents, if you're going to assume any obligations of the business
- papers relating to specific assets; for example, the lease if you're taking over seller's space or title documents if you're purchasing the seller's building
- patents, trademarks, copyrights and licenses
- documents that relate to lawsuits, administrative proceedings and claims against the corporation
- all accountants' reports, including compilation reports, reviews and audit reports. (See "Types of Accountants' Reports," below.) A full-fledged audit report is the best, but not all small busi-

nesses have one available. Whatever type report the business has, specifically ask for a list of all assets and the depreciation schedules.

In addition, if you're purchasing corporate stock, ask for:

- corporate contracts with major suppliers, as well as contracts obligating the corporation to deliver goods or services
- employment agreements, union contracts and any other documents concerning wage levels and fringe benefit obligations.

Types of Accountants' Reports

Reports from Certified Public Accountants come in three basic varieties:

Compiled. The CPA compiles the balance sheet of the company and the related statements of income and retained earnings and cash flows for a specified year. The compilation simply presents, in the form of a financial statement, the information gathered by the owners of the company. The accountant doesn't audit or review the information or offer an opinion about it.

Reviewed. The CPA goes a step farther by asking questions of company personnel and analyzing the financial data presented by the owners. Short of a full-scale audit, the CPA certifies only that he or she isn't aware of any material modifications that should be made to the financial statements to conform to generally accepted accounting principles.

Audited. Here, the CPA examines, on a test basis, evidence supporting the amounts and disclosures in the financial statements. For example, the CPA may visit the warehouse to see if it really contains the inventory that's claimed. Also, the accountant assesses the accounting principles used by the owners and evaluates the overall financial statement. If everything is in order, the CPA signs an opinion that the financial statements are accurate and maintained in conformity with generally accepted accounting principles.

Once the books are in your hands, have an experienced small business accountant study them. You and your accountant should look especially hard at the years before the last one. It's relatively easy for a business owner to pump up earnings and depress expenses for a year or two, so assume that the results for the last year at least have been manipulated.

Tips for spotting exaggerated earnings. *One way to see if earnings have been exaggerated is to see if there are fewer employees now than previously—almost any business can operate shorthanded for a limited time. Also, check to see if equipment maintenance or replacement has been deferred by comparing maintenance and replacement costs for the last year with those of the years before.*

4. Expert Help

Consider hiring an experienced appraiser to appraise the business as a whole as well as the individual assets. Check references and be sure the person you pick understands the type of business you are entering. For example, if you're thinking of buying a traditional typesetting business, work with someone who thoroughly understands the mostly negative implications that the rapid improvement of desktop publishing techniques holds for this business. Appraisals do cost money, but it's money well spent if it saves you from overpaying for the business.

Where can you turn for an accurate assessment of the value of a business? Here are three suggestions:

- Consult a member of the American Society of Appraisers who specializes in business valuations. For a list of such appraisers, call 800-ASA-VALU or visit www.appraisers.org.
- Check with a respected firm of certified public accountants. Many CPA firms offer business valuation services.
- Seek guidance from an experienced business broker. But use caution. Brokers are best at making deals. They often lack the technical training needed for placing a value on a business.

E. Other Items to Investigate

Now let's look at some other items that are worth investigating before you close on the purchase of a business.

1. Title to Assets

If real estate is included in the sale, ask to see the deed and the title insurance policy. The title should be rechecked to make sure no new encumbrances appear, and the title insurance policy will need to be updated. Also ask to see ownership documents for any cars and trucks.

It's a good idea to check with the appropriate county or state offices to see if there are liens on any of the vehicles or other equipment or merchandise. Lenders who have taken a security interest in the business or suppliers who have extended credit may have filed a UCC (Uniform Commercial Code) financing statement with the appropriate state agency to record the fact that they have a security interest in some assets of the business. Any bank lending officer, small business lawyer or accountant should be able to tell you where and how to check in your state.

2. Litigation

Ask to see copies of any lawsuit papers and letters from any people threatening lawsuits. Also check with the court clerk in the main counties in which business is conducted. What you're looking for are actual or threatened lawsuits involving injuries or claimed breaches of contract. This type of investigation is particularly important when you're buying the stock of a corporation, but you may also turn up information that will be valuable to an asset purchase. For example, if the business manufactures or distributes aluminum stepladders, finding product liability lawsuits pending will help you determine whether the ladders are safe or need to be redesigned. Also, remember that in a few circumstances even those who purchase assets of a corporation may be held liable for the existing business's liabilities. (See Section B2.)

3. Warranties and Guarantees

If you buy the stock of a corporation, you want to know what types of warranties the corporation has extended to its customers so you can anticipate claims. For example, if you buy a business that writes customized computer software, you'll want to know what promises have been made should bugs be discovered in already-installed programs.

4. Workers' Compensation Claims and Unemployment Claims

Check with the workers' compensation insurance carrier to learn the claims history of the business and current insurance rates. Also check with the state office handling unemployment affairs to learn what rate is currently applied to the payroll of the business. These facts will be primarily of concern if you're planning to purchase the stock of a corporation, because they'll indicate how much you'll probably have to pay for workers' compensation insurance or unemployment coverage. But in some states, even purchasers of corporate assets may have their future workers' compensation insurance rates affected if it looks like the new business is simply a continuation of the old one.

5. Employee Contracts and Benefits

This is a concern primarily if you're buying the stock of a corporation and will be subject to its contracts. However, if you intend to keep the same employees, you need this information for other purchases as well so that you'll know the employees' expectations when they come to work for your new business entity. They won't be happy campers if you offer them less pay or benefits than they're currently getting. If it's a concern, ask the seller for permission to talk to key employees to see if they'll stick with you after you buy the business. (Strictly speaking, permission isn't required, but being polite helps bring about a smooth transition.)

6. Maintenance of Trade Secrets

Not every business has trade secrets, but if the one you're purchasing does—and those secrets are a valuable asset for which you're paying—you want to be sure they've been properly safeguarded. Ask what the business has done to protect its trade secrets and other proprietary information such as customer lists. Has this information been disclosed only to key employees? Have those employees signed confidentiality agreements and covenants not to compete? If not, and key employees leave and set up a competing business, you may be buying a lot less than you bargained for.

7. Taxes

Again, this applies primarily to a purchase of corporate stock because you want to know what tax liabilities are hanging over the head of the corporation. But whatever kind of purchase you're making, you can gain valuable information about the income and expenses of the business, including the kinds of items that have been tax-deductible in the past. Check on state and local property taxes and sales taxes, federal and state income taxes and any special taxes levied by federal and state governments.

8. Leases

Look carefully at all space and equipment leases. How long does the lease have to run? Is it renewable? And, most important, if you're purchasing the assets, is it transferable? If the lease isn't clearly assignable, check with the landlord or equipment lessor about taking over the lease. If they respond favorably, get a commitment in writing. (For more on real estate leases, see Chapter 13.)

9. Other Contracts

If the business has contracts with suppliers or customers, become familiar with their terms. In the case of an asset sale, the important question is whether or not the contracts are assignable by the seller. Often, you need the consent of the supplier or customer. For example, if you're buying a gas station, does the oil company have to approve your taking over the contract for that brand of gasoline? Where a contract is freely transferable if all the conditions have been met, make sure the seller isn't in default or otherwise in noncompliance. If he or she is, you may not be able to enforce the contract.

10. Patents and Copyrights

Many small businesses don't own patents or copyrights, but as information becomes a more and more valuable part of many businesses, they are cropping up fairly often. Of course, if you're interested in buying a book, software or music publishing company, you can be pretty sure that the business's most valuable assets will be its intellectual property.

If patents or copyrights are involved, get hold of the basic registration documents and any contracts that give the business the right to exploit these rights. If you're not fully familiar with these matters, have the documents and contracts reviewed by a lawyer who specializes in this area of law. These lawyers are usually listed in a separate category in the Yellow Pages under "Patent and Trademark."

11. Trademarks and Product Names

Trademarks, service marks, business names and product names may be important business assets. If so, make sure that you'll have the continuing right to use them. Ask about the extent of any searches for conflicting marks and names, and what has been done to register or otherwise protect the marks and names you'll be taking over. (See Chapter 6 for more on business and product names.)

12. Licenses and Transferability

Check into any special licenses that you'll need to continue the business. For example, if you're buying a restaurant with a liquor license, is the license transferable? Has the existing business obtained an environmental permit for disposal of its wastes? If so, what about transferability? (If not, look into your potential liability.) The same goes for other special permits the existing business has, such as a health department license, or a federal license for trucking or broadcasting. (For more on licenses and permits, see Chapter 7.)

13. Zoning

The existing business may be operating under a temporary zoning variance or a conditional use permit that has important limitations. Learn exactly what the requirements and conditions are and whether you can continue operating under the variance or conditional use permit. Also, if you buy the business assets rather than corporate stock, you may find that you're no longer covered by prior zoning or building preferences; you may, for example, need more parking, better access and different signs. (See Chapter 7, Section D, and Chapter 14, Section A, for more on zoning and related requirements.)

14. Toxic Waste

If the business must dispose of toxic waste, or if its activities have any possible adverse impact on the purity of water and air, look into what licenses or permits are needed. Also, especially if your purchase involves real property, check carefully to see how toxic waste has been handled in the past. You could find yourself stuck with liability for past improprieties.

15. Franchisor Approval

If you're looking at a business that's operating under a franchise, the seller undoubtedly will need the approval of the franchisor before assigning the franchise to you. Look at the franchise agreement to see exactly what's involved in obtaining the franchisor's approval and then speak directly to the franchisor to see how the approval process can be expedited. (For more on franchises, see Chapter 11.)

16. Availability of Credit

Find out whether banks and major suppliers will be willing to extend credit to you. Credit may mean the difference between success and failure in your business.

17. Scuttlebutt

Never rely entirely on documents and public records. You can learn a lot simply by talking to people who have had contact with the existing business—bankers, key customers, suppliers, neighboring businesses and former employees. When talking to key people, take your time and pay attention to subtleties. Many people may be reluctant to talk frankly until they've sized you up, and others will have ties of friendship to the seller or be worried about their own possible legal liability if they divulge unfavorable information about the business.

F. Letter of Intent to Purchase

If all goes well, you and the seller may eventually agree on most major aspects of the purchase. But you still may not be quite ready to put together a formal sales agreement. Perhaps you need time for additional investigation, or maybe your lawyer, business advisor or key lender is out of town for a week or two. One device that can be helpful to keep momentum is a nonbinding letter of intent to purchase. The same objective can be accomplished through a more formal "memorandum of intent to purchase"—but a memorandum usually turns out to be more legalistic and, therefore, more threatening to a seller.

Giving the seller a modest, earnest money deposit along with the letter of intent is also helpful, because it shows you're sincerely interested in pursuing the purchase and are not wasting the seller's time. But because details of the purchase have not solidified at this point, be sure to provide that the deposit is to be refunded if the purchase falls through.

A sample nonbinding letter of intent is shown below.

LETTER OF INTENT TO PURCHASE

Robert Tower, President
The Tower Mart Inc.
25 Glen Blvd.
Arlington Heights, IL

Dear Bob:

Thanks for meeting with me again last week. I continue to be interested in purchasing the assets of the Tower Mart Inc. If we reach an agreement regarding my purchase, I plan to transfer these assets to a new corporation that I'm forming. My new company would then run a convenience store similar to what you're currently operating.

I'm interested in purchasing the following assets: the inventory, fixtures, equipment, leasehold improvements and business name. In addition, I will need all necessary licenses and permits transferred to me. I will expect you to give me a covenant not to compete stating that for three years, you won't open a similar store in our city. The purchase price for all of the assets as well as the good will and your covenant not to compete would be $150,000, as we have already discussed.

[Before referring to a covenant not to compete, see the discussion of such covenants in Section G5, below]

As an indication of my good faith in pursuing this matter, I am enclosing a check for $1,000 as earnest money. I would pay an additional $49,000 in cash at closing. The balance of $100,000 would be amortized in equal monthly installments over a period of 10 years with interest at the rate of 10% per annum.

Regarding the inventory, we will check this at the time of closing. If the inventory is valued at less than $45,000, the purchase price would be reduced accordingly. Also, as you and I discussed, your corporation would remain responsible for all liabilities of the present business and these would not be assumed by my new corporation.

Before I have my lawyer draft a sales agreement, there are some things I need to investigate:

1. I want to meet with your landlord to make sure that I can take over the existing lease and that I can get an option to extend it for another five years.

2. I need to have my accountant review all of your tax returns and business records for the past five years so that I can satisfy myself regarding the financial condition of your business.

3. I want to make sure that the state liquor board will approve a transfer of the beer and wine retail license to my new corporation.

Assuming that I'm satisfied with these items and all other aspects of the proposed purchase, I will have my lawyer draft a sales agreement and then we can close approximately 45 days from now.

This letter states my intent but it is not a legally binding contract or commitment on either my part or yours. Upon further investigation I may change my mind. If the deal doesn't go through for any reason, I'd be entitled to my earnest money back.

If my letter has captured the essence of what we talked about and you're still interested in pursuing the sale, please let me know. I believe that we are moving toward a transaction that can be advantageous to both of us.

Sincerely,

Mary Beyer

⚠ **Don't commit yourself.** *Make it clear in a letter of intent that it is not intended to be a binding contract. You may or may not need your lawyer's assistance in writing a letter of intent, but I do recommend that you call your lawyer to at least check on the adequacy of the language you use to describe the nonbinding nature of the letter.*

G. The Sales Agreement

The sales agreement is the key legal document in buying business assets or an entire corporation or LLC. You should create a written outline of the terms that you and the seller have agreed on. Next, you may want to have your lawyer review it and help draft the next version of the agreement. Once you and your lawyer are satisfied, present the agreement to the seller.

Why take on the document drafting yourself, rather than letting the seller do it? Because even though it's more time consuming, this approach will almost surely give you more control over the overall shape of the transaction. By seizing the initiative, you may well wind up with 95% or more of what you want.

This section briefly reviews the principal types of clauses in a business sales agreement. Remember, as discussed earlier (Section B2), it's almost always better to buy the assets from the corporation than to buy its stock. Accordingly, these clauses are geared primarily to an asset purchase. If for some reason you decide to buy corporate stock, make corresponding changes in your sales agreement.

📄 *Chapter 5 of* Legal Forms for Starting & Running a Small Business *contains various forms for buying a business.*

1. Names of Seller, Buyer and Business

Your sales agreement will start with the name and address of the seller and the buyer. It will also identify the business by its current name.

- *Purchase from or by a sole proprietor.* Name the sole proprietor, adding the business name if it's different from the individual's. *Example:* Mary Perfect doing business as Perfect Word Processing Service.
- *Purchase from or by a partnership.* Use the partnership's legal name and the names of all partners. *Example:* Ortega Associates, a Colorado partnership of William Ortega and Henry Cruz.
- *Purchase from or by a corporation.* Simply use the corporate name and identify it by the state where it's registered. *Example:* XYZ Enterprises Inc., a Massachusetts corporation.
- *Purchase from or by an LLC.* Just use the LLC name and the state where it's registered. *Example:* ABC Associates LLC, an Illinois limited liability company.

If you're going to operate the business you're purchasing as a new corporation or LLC, I recommend either of two procedures: Set up the new corporation or LLC before signing the purchase agreement and name the new entity as the purchaser. Or list the purchaser as yourself as the agent of a corporation or LLC to be formed. Using either of these methods, the assets can go directly into your new corporation or LLC rather than having a two-stage process in which you receive the assets and then transfer them to the new entity. If you're going to be putting the assets into a corporation or LLC, the seller undoubtedly will want you (and probably your spouse as well) to personally guarantee the payment of any part of the purchase price that's being paid on an installment basis.

2. Background Information

Often, before a sales agreement gets into the terms of the transaction, it outlines some background facts. For example, the sales agreement might state that "Mildred Johnson currently owns a business in Cincinnati which produces ice cream, sorbet and other dessert products" and that the sales agreement "applies only to the portion of the business operated at seller's west side location at 123 Maple Street."

You can also include some statements about the buyer; for example, "the buyer is a building contractor licensed under the laws of the state of Maine." These statements aren't usually a key section of a purchase agreement, but if they are included, it's important to be accurate.

3. Assets Being Sold

This is where you list what you're purchasing. You can put the details, such as lists of equipment, on a separate page which is sometimes referred to in the body of the agreement as a schedule or exhibit and specifically made part of the contract. Here's an example of how a sales agreement might list assets being sold:

a. All furniture, trade fixtures, equipment and mis—cellaneous items of tangible personal property owned by seller and used in the business, listed and described in Exhibit A which is hereby made a part of this agreement.

b. Customer lists and all other files and records of the business.

c. Assignment of the seller's interest (as tenant) in the lease dated March 1, 2002, for the building located at 123 Main Street owned by Central Property Associates (landlord).

d. Assignment of the seller's interest (as lessee) in the computer equipment lease with CompuLease dated March 1, 2002.

e. All telephone numbers of the business and the right to use the business name, "The Tower Mart." Seller will cease using that name on the day of closing.

If you have so agreed, also include a statement that you're not acquiring any of the liabilities of the business or that you're acquiring only those that are specified.

> Except as otherwise specified in this agreement, buyer is not assuming responsibility for any liabilities of the business. Seller will remain responsible for all liabilities of the business not specified in this agreement, and will indemnify buyer and save buyer harmless from and against such liabilities.

4. Purchase Price and Allocation of Assets

After stating the purchase price, allocate the price among the different categories of assets. Some typical allocations are shown below.

Allocation for a Retail Business

Merchandise on Hand	$ 75,000
Tangible Personal Property	$ 30,000
Assignment of Lease Agreement	$ 4,000
Trade Name and Goodwill	$ 8,000

Allocation for a Small Computer Company

Inventory (Computers and Software)	$100,000
Covenant Not to Compete	$ 30,000
Trade Name and Goodwill	$ 20,000
Patents and Copyrights	$ 5,000
Building Owned by Seller	$100,000
Land	$ 30,000

For tax reasons, as a buyer, you want most of the price assigned to the assets that give you the fastest recovery of your investment. You want the least allocated to items like goodwill, which can't be depreciated and gives you no tax benefits until you sell the business. Here's a summary of the write-off rules:

Type of Asset	Normal Write-off Period
Inventory	As sold
Furniture, Fixtures and Equipment	5 to 7 years
Covenant Not to Compete	15 years
Trade Name and Goodwill	15 years
Buildings	39 years
Patents and Copyrights	Remaining Term of Patent or Copyright
Lease Assignment	Remaining Term of Lease
Land	No Write-off

The seller should be willing to accommodate you in allocating the price to achieve your maximum legal tax savings—there's only a small tax advantage, if any, to the seller in applying other allocation priorities. However, because some sellers will find a modest tax advantage in tilting the allocation toward items that are taxed at capital gains rates rather than ordinary income rates, they may try to push negotiations in this direction. These items include covenants not to compete, real estate and goodwill.

In the first example above, inventory and merchandise on hand are given as high a value as can be reasonably supported. In the second example, the seller's building and land could reasonably be valued at anywhere from $130,000 to $160,000 depending on whose appraisal is used. I've assigned the lowest reasonable value to the building and land because, under IRS guidelines, the building must be depreciated over a period of 39 years and the land can't be depreciated at all.

If the seller is going to provide consulting services to you for a year or so, consider assigning a portion of the purchase price to those services so that you can write off that amount quickly as a business expense. Better yet, remove an appropriate amount from the purchase price and put it in a separate agreement for consulting services.

5. Covenant Not to Compete

Especially if the seller is well known and would be a threat to your business if he or she opened a rival outfit, you want a covenant (promise) not to compete. In such a covenant, the seller agrees not to compete directly or indirectly with you in the operation of the type of business that you've purchased. If the seller violates the covenant, judges or arbitrators will usually enforce it unless it unreasonably limits the seller's ability to earn a living.

To increase chances that your agreement will be enforced, it's wise to place a reasonable geographic limitation on the seller's right to run a similar business (for example, within 25 miles of your business) and also a reasonable time limit (for example, three years). If you're purchasing a business from a corporation, have the individual operators of the business sign their own personal promises not to compete.

Obviously, whatever geographic limitations you and the seller agree on should fit the area. In New York City, a 25-mile zone would take in a huge chunk of New Jersey and some 15 to 20 million people—probably an unreasonable restraint on the seller's future ability to earn a living. In drafting a covenant not to compete, get help from a savvy lawyer who knows what the state courts enforce.

An example of a covenant not to compete is shown below.

Covenant Not to Compete

Seller shall not establish, engage in, or become interested in, directly or indirectly, as an employee, owner, partner, agent, shareholder or otherwise, within a radius of ten miles from the city of _____, any business, trade or occupation similar to the business covered by this sales agreement for a period of three years. At the closing, the seller agrees to sign an agreement on this subject in the form set forth in Exhibit B.

LAW IN THE REAL WORLD
Why You Need a Covenant Not to Compete

Sid is buying a travel agency from Mary Jones, who has been in the travel business for 25 years and is well known in the community. Part of the reason Sid is buying her business is the excellent reputation and following her business has earned.

Two months after Sid takes over the business, Mary—who quickly tired of retirement—opens a new travel agency four blocks away. Inevitably some, perhaps many, of her old customers will abandon Sid and patronize Mary's business. Sid should have included a covenant not to compete in the sales agreement to protect himself against this possibility.

---

6. Adjustments

You'll probably need to adjust the sales price slightly at closing. For example, you should reimburse the seller for payments the seller has made for such items as rent, utilities or insurance for periods after you take over. On the other hand, if salaries and wages are paid every two weeks and you take over the business halfway through that period, the purchase price should be reduced at closing to reflect the fact that you'll be paying salaries for a period when the seller still owned the business. Adjustments may also be made for license fees, maintenance contracts, equipment leases and property taxes. Your sales agreement should contain a clause spelling out what items will need to be adjusted at closing and the method for making the adjustments.

7. Terms of Payment

Nearly 80% of small business purchases are handled on an installment basis, with the seller extending all or most of the credit. Typically, a buyer puts down about one-third of the purchase price and pays the balance over four or five years. For example, in the purchase of a $250,000 business, you may negotiate a contract that requires you to make a $50,000 down payment at closing with the balance paid in five annual installments of $40,000 each plus interest at 10% per year.

At the closing, you'll sign a promissory note for the unpaid portion of the purchase price. The seller generally will want to retain an ownership (security) interest in the equipment and other assets of the business until the purchase price has been paid. Sometimes called a "lien," this is akin to a mortgage on your home. Just as the bank could sell your home to pay off your loan if you fell behind in your payments, the seller of a business who retains a lien on or security interest in your business assets could, if you were delinquent in making payments, take possession of those assets and sell them to cover the balance owing.

Here's a sample terms of payment clause:

Purchaser will pay seller $_____ at closing and will pay the balance of $_____ according to the terms of a promissory note purchaser will sign at the closing, in the form set forth in Exhibit ___. The promissory note will provide for monthly payments of $_____ each. The payments will include interest on the unpaid balance at the rate of ____% per annum from and after the date of closing. The first installment will be due on the first day of the month following the closing and the remaining installments will be due on the first of each month after that until the principal and interest is fully paid. Payments will be applied first on interest and then on principal. The unpaid principal and interest shall be fully paid no later than ____ years from the date of the note. There will be no penalty for prepayment.

Until purchaser has paid the full balance of principal and interest on the debt, seller will retain a security interest in the business assets being purchased. As evidence of such security interest, purchaser, at closing, will sign a security agreement in the form set forth in attached Exhibit __ and will also a sign a Uniform Commercial Code Financing Statement, to be recorded at the appropriate county and state office.

It's a good idea to attach the proposed promissory note as well as the proposed security agreement as exhibits to the sales agreement.

Tax and Usury: Charge Reasonable Interest

The IRS will accept the interest rate agreed to by the seller and buyer if it is reasonable in terms of the current financing market and the risk involved in extending credit. If the interest rate is outside the reasonable range, the buyer may not be able to deduct the excess interest paid. To avoid this, stick close to prevailing interest rates.

Also be aware that state usury laws limit the rate of interest that can be charged. Here, it's the seller rather than the buyer who runs the risk of running afoul of the law. Not only may the seller not be able to collect excessive interest, but he or she may also face criminal penalties.

8. Inventory

Because the inventory of salable merchandise is likely to fluctuate between the time you sign the sales agreement and the closing, consider putting a provision in the sales agreement that allows for adjustment. For example, you might say that you'll pay up to $75,000 for merchandise on hand at the closing based on the seller's invoice cost. You might also provide that if there's more than $75,000 worth of merchandise on hand when you close, you have the right to purchase the excess at the seller's cost, or to choose $75,000 worth and leave the rest in the hands of the seller.

Here's another way to handle this problem. Simply provide that a physical count of all merchandise will be made on the day of sale or another mutually agreeable date. You might define the word merchandise to include only unopened and undamaged merchandise. In a retail business, you can agree to value the merchandise at its current wholesale cost, or at the seller's current retail price less a certain percentage. If you don't have experience doing an inventory, you might also put in the sales agreement that you and the seller will split the cost of hiring an inventory service company to determine the amount of the purchase price of the merchandise.

In a manufacturing or service business, you may have the analogous problem of placing a value on work in progress.

9. Accounts Receivable

The business you're buying may have sold goods to or performed services for customers who haven't yet paid. These unpaid sums are called "accounts receivable." Usually the accounts receivable of an existing business remain the property of that business and aren't transferred to the buyer. But a seller who prefers to be free of collection problems may want to include them. Be very careful. When a business changes hands, accounts can be hard to collect. A considerable percentage will probably never be collected, so you should get a substantial discount. How much depends on how collectable these accounts are. By now you should know this through your close examination of the seller's books and, if most of the money is owed by only a few accounts, by checking with them personally.

10. Bulk Sales Compliance

If the business you're buying involves the sale of merchandise from a stock you'll keep on hand, you may have to comply with a "bulk sales" law. Every state used to have such a law, but today only about ten still do—and that number is diminishing. These laws apply to transfers of a major part of the seller's materials, supplies, merchandise or other inventory. Generally, they don't apply to transfers where the seller's business consists primarily of selling personal services rather than merchandise.

Typically, a seller covered under the bulk sales law must give you a list (sworn to under penalty of perjury) of all business creditors and tell you the amounts due each one. Also, the seller must tell you about any claims made by potential creditors, even if the claims are disputed. Then you send notice to the creditors so that they'll know that the business is changing hands. If these things are not done, the creditors of the old business will continue to have a claim against the merchandise that you're buying. Sending proper notices protects you from such claims.

Sometimes, to avoid the need to comply with the bulk sales law, a contract will say that the seller will pay all outstanding debts of the business before the closing or out of the proceeds of the sale at the time of closing, and will furnish an affidavit to that effect at closing.

For more information on your local bulk sales law and the legal forms used to comply with it, the best place to look is a legal newspaper or other major newspaper that publishes legal notices.

11. Seller's Representation and Warranties

In the sales agreement, the seller should guarantee the basic facts of your transaction. Here's an example of the guarantees when the seller is a corporation:

Seller and seller's shareholders represent and warrant that:

1. Andover Corporation is in good standing under the laws of Wisconsin.

2. Andover Corporation's board of directors has authorized (through board resolutions to be delivered to buyer at closing) the signing of this sales contract and all of the transactions called for in the contract.

3. Andover Corporation has good and marketable title to the assets that are being sold and will convey them to buyer free and clear of all encumbrances, except for the assets listed in Exhibit A which will remain subject to the encumbrances listed there.

4. The balance sheet that Andover Corporation gave buyer correctly reflects the assets, liabilities and net worth of the business as of October 31, 20__, and there will be no material changes between the balance sheet date and the closing.

5. The income statement that Andover Corporation gave buyer accurately reflects the income and expenses of the company during the period covered, and no significant changes in the level of income or expense will occur between the contract date and the closing.

6. The lease under which Andover Corporation occupies space at 789 Oak Avenue is in full effect and is assignable to buyer. Andover Corporation will take all necessary steps to assign the lease to buyer.

7. Between the contract date and the closing, Andover Corporation will operate the business as usual and will take no action out of the ordinary.

8. Andover Corporation has complied with all applicable laws and regulations of the federal, state and local governments.

9. There are no lawsuits or claims pending or threatened against Andover Corporation other than those listed in Exhibit __, and Andover Corporation does not know of any basis for any other lawsuit or claim against the business.

10. Andover Corporation has disclosed to buyer all material facts that would reasonably affect a prudent investor's decision to purchase the assets covered by this agreement.

In addition, if the seller made specific statements to you about the business and these influenced your decision to buy it, have the seller reiterate these statements in writing in this section of the agreement.

Don't rely on the seller's promises.
Never use the seller's warranties and representations as an excuse for not thoroughly checking all important facts yourself, as discussed in Section C, above. Enforcing a warranty against the seller or suing for a misrepresentation can involve a long and expensive lawsuit.

If you're buying a business or the assets from a corporation, have the principal owners sign the war-ranties as individuals in addition to signing them as officers of the corporation. That way, you'll be able to go after their personal assets if they've misrepresented facts or if their warranties are violated.

The contract should also say that the warranties survive the closing. This gives you the right to sue if you discover some unpleasant facts about the business several years after you purchase it. Here's some wording to consider:

The representations and warranties of the parties to this agreement and those of the seller's shareholders shall survive the closing. The act of closing shall not bar either party from bringing an action based on a representation or warranty of the other party.

12. Buyer's Warranties and Representations

The seller may expect the buyer to sign representations and warranties as well. For example:

Buyer represents and warrants that:

1. Buyer is a corporation in good standing under the laws of Wisconsin.

2. Buyer has the authority to enter into and perform the buyer's obligations under the sales agreement.

3. Buyer has had an opportunity to inspect the assets of the business and agrees to accept the assets as is, except for the items referred to in Exhibit C.

The first representation in this example assumes you've established a corporation. You wouldn't include this statement if you were buying as a sole proprietor or signing on behalf of a partnership.

In the second representation, a corporate buyer would agree to furnish the seller with a board of directors' resolution approving the terms of the sales agreement and authorizing the signing of the purchase documents.

The third representation says that you're accepting the assets "as is." If it turns out that some of the assets are defective, that will be your problem and not the seller's—unless the seller knew about and failed to disclose some hidden defect that you couldn't be expected to discover through an inspection. Before signing a sales agreement, make sure you have actually inspected all the assets. If there are some that you haven't looked at carefully or which you're *not* willing to take as is, list them in an exhibit that specifically excludes them from the "as is" clause.

13. Access to Information

By the time you sign the sales agreement, you should have seen a lot of financial information involving the business, but you may still want to see more to verify that everything is as promised. So it's a good idea to include a paragraph or two in the sales agreement covering your right to get full information. In exchange, the seller will probably want to include language assuring that you'll deal with the information in a responsible manner—that is, that you won't make unnecessary disclosures. (For a discussion of sellers' concerns about confidentiality, see Section C, above.)

Here's some language you might place in the sales agreement:

> Before the closing, seller will provide to buyer and buyer's agents, during normal business hours, access to all of the company's properties, books, contracts and records, and will furnish to buyer all the information concerning the company's affairs that buyer reasonably requests.

> Buyer acknowledges that the company's books, records and other documents contain confidential information, and that communication of

such confidential information to third parties could injure the company's business if this transaction is not completed. Buyer agrees to take reasonable steps to assure that such information about the company remains confidential and is not revealed to outside sources. Buyer further agrees not to solicit any customers of the company disclosed from such confidential information.

> The confidential information that may become known to buyer includes customer lists, trade secrets, channels of distribution, pricing policy and records, inventory records and other information normally understood to be confidential or designated as such by seller.

14. Conduct of Business Pending Closing

Unless the sales agreement is signed at the closing, be sure that the seller doesn't make any detrimental changes in the business between the time you sign the sales agreement and the time you close. We considered some commitments along this line in Section G11 dealing with the seller's warranties and representations. In addition, if you're purchasing the stock of a corporation, get a commitment that no change will be made in the articles of incorporation or in the authorized or issued shares of the corporation. Also, if you're dealing with a corporation, get a commitment that no contract will be entered into by or on behalf of the corporation extending beyond the closing date, except those made in the ordinary course of business.

Finally, have the corporation agree that it won't increase the compensation paid to any officer or employee and won't make any new arrangements for bonuses.

15. Contingencies

A contingency clause is a safety valve that lets you walk away from the transaction if certain things don't pan out. For example, if the location of the business is a crucial part of your decision to buy, you'll want to reserve the right to cancel the deal if you find out that the lease can't be assigned to you. The same thing might be true of a required license; if you're buying a bar, you would make the deal contingent on the state transferring the liquor license to you. If you plan to expand the business or move to a new location, make the deal contingent on your being able to get approval from the local zoning and building officials. Here's a sample contingency clause:

> This agreement is contingent upon buyer
> receiving approval, by _____ ,
> 20____ , from the landlord and the city's
> building and safety department for a remodel-
> ing of the premises leased by the business as
> shown in the plans and specifications attached
> as Exhibit __.

16. Seller to Be a Consultant

Sometimes it pays to have the seller stay on for a few months as a consultant or employee to help ease your transition into the business and reassure long-time customers and suppliers that the business is in good hands. If you make these kinds of arrangements with the seller, be sure to capture them in the sales agreement, using language such as the following:

> _____, as an independent
> contractor engaged by buyer, will provide
> consultation, customer relations, general
> assistance and information to buyer pertaining
> to the company for up to 20 hours per week as
> requested by buyer for a period of eight weeks

> following closing. For such services, buyer will
> pay _____ $_____ per week.

The consulting fees are tax-deductible as current business expenses.

17. Broker Fees

If a business broker is involved, specify who is responsible for paying the fee, unless you independently hired the broker to help you locate the business. Normally, the seller is responsible.

18. Notices

It's customary to state addresses for both the seller and the purchaser where any notices and demands can be sent—for example, if a payment is late or another contract term is not met. Typically, sales agreements provide that notices can be given by first-class mail, but it is appropriate to require notice by registered mail with a return receipt requested.

19. Closing Date

Include a date for the closing. That's when you'll make your down payment, and both parties will sign any documents that are necessary to transfer the business to you.

H. The Closing

Finally, the big day has arrived—you're about to become the owner of a business. In an ideal world, you'd simply give the seller a check and the seller would give you the keys. Unfortunately, there's lots of additional paperwork involved.

There's also a certain amount of stress and pressure at a closing (after all, it's not every day that you buy a business). Working with your lawyer or other advisor, make a checklist in advance listing all documents to be signed and other actions to be taken at the closing. Review this carefully a couple of days before the closing and be sure you have all your paperwork ready to go. If anything is unclear or doesn't make sense to you, ask your lawyer to redraft the language in plain English so that you and everyone else can understand it.

Checklist for a Typical Closing

☐ *Adjust purchase price* for prorated items such as rent payments or utilities, or changes in the value of inventory.

☐ *Review documents promised by seller*—for example, a corporate board resolution authorizing the sale or an opinion of the seller's lawyer stating that the corporation is in good legal standing and that the sale has been properly approved by the shareholders and/or directors.

☐ *Sign promissory note* if you're not paying all cash for the business. The seller may require your spouse's signature as well so that your joint bank account will be a source of repayment if the business doesn't produce enough income.

☐ *Sign security agreement* giving the seller a lien on the business assets if you don't pay the full price in cash at closing. (If you fail to keep up your payments as promised, the seller can take back the assets subject to the security agreement.) You may also be asked to sign a UCC Financing Statement to be filed with the county clerk or secretary of state, giving public notice of the seller's lien.

☐ *Sign assignment of lease* if you're taking over an existing lease. If the landlord's approval is required, be sure it has been obtained before the closing.

☐ *Transfer vehicle titles* if cars or trucks are among the business assets.

☐ *Sign bill of sale* transferring ownership of other tangible business assets.

☐ *Sign transfer of patents, trademarks and copyrights* if included in the sale.

☐ *Sign franchise transfer documents* if you're buying a business from a franchisee. This should include the signed approval of the franchisor.

☐ *Sign closing or settlement statement* listing all financial aspects of the transaction. Ideally, everything in the closing or settlement statement should be based on clear language in the sales agreement so that nothing need be negotiated at the closing table.

☐ *Sign covenant not to compete* if seller agreed to one.

☐ *Sign consultation or employment agreement* if the seller has agreed to stay on as a consultant or employee.

☐ *Complete IRS Form 8594, Asset Acquisition Statement,* indicating how the purchase was allocated among the various assets. You and the seller will attach a copy of the form to your respective income tax returns.

I. Selling a Business

Obviously, when you're just starting out in business, selling it isn't at the forefront of your mind. But there's a good chance that, sooner or later, you'll need to or want to sell. The reasons can vary widely—from not liking working for yourself, to a need to relocate, to one spouse selling to the other as part of a divorce, to retirement.

Let's look at some things you can do get a good price for your business and protect your legal position.

1. Valuing Your Business

When you contemplate selling all of a business or only part (which might occur if you take in a partner or sell out to your co-owner spouse as part of a divorce), your first task is to determine the value of your business.

> **EXAMPLE:** Pauline has built a thriving retail business with three locations and 24 employees. Now she's getting divorced. She and her husband have agreed that she'll keep the business rather than liquidate it. Pauline must put a value on the business so that she and her husband can arrive at a reasonable property settlement.

You can get help from an appraiser (see Section D, above) or a business broker. If you do use a broker to sell your business, carefully read the listing agreement. Consider these issues:

- Does the broker have the exclusive right to sell your business or can you sell it directly without paying a commission?
- Do you have the right to reject a proposed purchaser because of the purchaser's credit history or for other reasons without having to pay the broker's commission?
- If there's an installment sale, will the broker receive his or her total commission out of the down payment or in installments as you're paid?

If you do business through a corporation, you'll probably be selling only the assets the corporation owns—not the corporation itself—although, from a tax and liability standpoint it's more advantageous for you to sell the corporate stock.

Timing of a sale can be critical to getting the best price. Suppose your company has had earnings of $400,000 per year for the past three years. And suppose, too, that you have good reason to believe you'll jump to $600,000 next year. You can, of course, tell a prospective buyer why you expect an increase in profits. But there's often a better tactic: hang on to the business for another year so that you have actual numbers to point to—not just a theory.

Would-be buyers will have much more confidence in your figures if you can show them several years' worth of financial statements audited or reviewed by a CPA. (The distinctions between the types of CPA reports are discussed in Section D, above.) Also, keep detailed schedules of expenses so that buyers can compare your business with others in your industry.

Getting a Good Price for Your Business

- Show steadily increasing profits at or above the industry average. Plan ahead. To show strong profits, you may need to give up some hidden perks. Don't fret; you'll be handsomely rewarded at sale time.
- Put your business in good general condition. Everything should be neat, tidy and in good working order. Machinery should be in good repair; your inventory should be well balanced and current.
- Maintain adequate personnel. A buyer will be put off—and discount the price—if the first chore in running the business is to recruit and train new employees.
- Get a written appraisal supporting your sales price. This can help persuade the buyer that the price is right.

These suggestions are from *Valuing Small Businesses and Professional Practices,* by Shannon Pratt (Dow Jones–Irwin).

2. Read Your Lease

Your lease may say that a new business owner can't take over your space without the landlord's consent. If so, such consent will be needed if you signed the lease as a sole proprietor or partner. It will also be needed if the purchaser is buying the assets of your corporation or LLC rather than its stock or membership interests. Find out early whether your landlord will be an obstacle to selling the business and, if so, how you can get his or her support.

3. Protect Your Privacy

A prospective purchaser will want to investigate your business thoroughly before signing a purchase agreement. To protect your privacy, use a confidentiality or nondisclosure agreement in which the potential purchaser promises not to use or disclose confidential information about your business—unless, of course, he or she decides to buy it. (A sample agreement is shown in Section C, above.) A prospective purchaser who violates this agreement can be sued for damages and injunctive relief.

4. Sign a Letter of Intent

In Section F, we looked at the nonbinding letter of intent from the standpoint of a buyer. There's no reason why such a letter can't be drafted by a seller who wants to summarize the terms of the proposed transaction as part of testing whether a potential buyer is serious.

5. Draft a Sales Agreement

To understand the elements of a sales agreement, read the previous sections of this chapter, particularly Section G. Here are some points to consider from the seller's viewpoint:

a. Structure of the sale

The sales agreement structures the sale. As noted in Section B1, if you're doing business as a sole proprietor or partnership, the structure of the sale is a foregone conclusion: You'll sell the assets of the business to the buyer. But if you're doing business as a corporation or LLC, the matter is more complicated. It's almost always better for you to sell your corporate stock or LLC membership interests than to have your business sell its assets. But for tax and liability reasons, buyers prefer to buy assets rather than stock or membership interests—and, in practice, the vast majority of small corporate or LLC businesses are sold on an asset sale basis. (See Section B, above.)

b. Excluded assets

If you're selling the assets of the business or the business itself—whether it be a sole proprietorship, a partnership, a corporation or an LLC—the purchase agreement lists the assets being transferred. Typically, this includes furniture, fixtures, equipment, inventory and vehicles and the business name. Equally important, specify any items excluded from the sale, for example: cash, accounts receivable, life insurance policies or your personal desk or computer.

c. Allocation of purchase price

In Section G, we focused on the allocation of the purchase price from the buyer's standpoint. The buyer wants to assign relatively high value to items that can be written off immediately or depreciated quickly. It rarely makes any difference, tax-wise, to the seller. A tax pro can quickly size up your particular sale. Allocation of purchase price is usually a win-win situation in which you can accommodate the buyer's reasonable tax needs without penalty.

d. Adequate security for installment sales

In most purchases of small businesses, the buyer puts down 20% to 40% of the purchase price and pays the balance in installments over three to five years. Plan ahead in case the buyer doesn't keep up the payments as promised. Insist that the buyer's spouse sign all closing documents jointly with the buyer. That way, if you need to sue the buyer because of non-payment, you have a chance of collecting the judgment out of a house owned jointly by the buyer and spouse, or from bank accounts in their joint names. If the couple's credit is weak, insist that the documents be signed by an outside guarantor.

The purchase agreement should require the buyer to give you a security interest (also called a lien) in the business assets. A financing statement that's filed with county or state officials will give public notice that you have a claim on the business assets.

If you're doing business as a corporation and are selling your stock, consider placing the stock certificates in escrow. That way, the buyer won't receive the certificates until the purchase price has been paid in full.

e. Looking to the future

The buyer may want to hire you for several months or years as a consultant or employee. If so, spell this out in the sales agreement or in a separate document signed at the same time. Be specific about the types of services you'll be expected to render, the amount of time you're committing and the amount you'll be paid. Sometimes, compensation for a seller's post-sale services is simply folded into the purchase price so the seller receives no additional payment.

If you've agreed not to compete with the buyer, the terms should be specified in a covenant not to compete. Cover such matters as precisely what business or activities you won't engage in, being careful not to burn all of your bridges. Think carefully about how long you're willing to refrain from working in a competing enterprise and how large a geographical area should be barred during the noncompetition period. (See Section G5.)

f. Warranties

Sales agreements typically contain numerous warranties and representations by the seller and a few by the buyer. (See Sections G11 and G12 for examples.) Read your warranties and representations carefully to make sure they don't go too far. For example, suppose the proposed warranty language says: "Seller warrants that the business name does not conflict with the name of any other business." What happens if, the day after the sale, a business that you didn't know about surfaces and complains that it had the name first? With the warranty wording given here, you could be liable for damages whether or not you knew about the other company.

If you see a warranty that's too far-reaching, have it rewritten. In our example, you might say something like "Seller warrants that, to the best of seller's knowledge, . . ." Or perhaps you could say: "Seller warrants that it has received no notice that its business name conflicts with that of any other business." ∎

11

Franchises: How Not to Get Burned

merica's landscape is dotted with franchises: Take the first exit off any freeway, and you're likely to spot familiar ones offering fast food, gasoline, groceries, lodgings and more. So, you might conclude, they must be making money, or they'd pack up and disappear. And why shouldn't you buy into an established chain to get a jump on the learning curve and tap into an existing customer base? Not so fast. For most people hoping to own a small business, buying a franchise is a poor idea. Most of the franchises you see on the road—or on Main Street or at the mall—are just barely eking out a profit beyond the percentage they must pay to the franchise vendor (the "franchisor"). Worse yet, some of their owners would like to sell, but can't. Because of the legal and economic rules exerted by the franchisor, you may end up feeling more like an indentured servant than an entrepreneur. In my view, you'll be happier and farther ahead financially if you start a business from scratch or buy an existing one.

In this chapter, I'll explain how franchises work, and delve deeper into their pitfalls. Then I'll introduce you to the two most important legal documents that are involved in the purchase of a franchise: the Uniform Franchise Operating Circular (UFOC) and the Franchise Agreement.

For more insight into the perils of franchise ownership, read the chapter titled "Don't Buy a Franchise" in Drive a Modest Car & 16 Other Keys to Small Business Success, *by Ralph Warner (Nolo). Also see* The Franchise Fraud: How to Protect Yourself Before and After You Invest, *by Robert L. Purvin, Jr. (John Wiley & Sons, Inc.). You'll find additional information on the websites of two organizations dedicated to promoting the rights of franchises: The American Franchisee Association (www.franchisee.org) and The American Association of Franchisees & Dealers (www.aafd.org). Both contain valuable information to help you protect your legal and financial interests. Also, the website of the U.S. Small Business Administration* (www.sba.gov) *offers a helpful download, "Evaluating Franchise Opportunities."*

Get professional advice before you plunge in. *Don't wait until you find yourself trapped in a costly and frustrating relationship with a franchisor—at which time you may have little legal recourse. It's worth paying for some sound legal and financial advice before you get locked into a contract or pay the franchisor a cent.*

A. What Is a Franchise?

The most convenient analysis and definition of a franchise comes from the Federal Trade Commission (FTC)—the one government agency that has nationwide regulatory power in this field. The FTC recognizes two types of business relationships that qualify for regulation as franchises:

- *The Package Franchise.* The franchisor licenses you to do business under a business format it has established. The business is closely identified with the franchisor's trademark or trade name. Examples include car washes, fast food outlets, motels, transmission centers, tax preparation services and quick copy shops.
- *The Product Franchise.* You distribute goods produced by the franchisor or under the franchisor's control or direction. The business or goods bear the franchisor's trademark or trade name. Examples include gasoline stations and car dealerships.

This chapter deals primarily with package franchises, which are more common.

The FTC definition is broad. It covers all of the businesses that you and I would ordinarily think of as franchises. Generally, the FTC (and many state agencies that regulate franchises) will classify your business relationship as a franchise if three conditions exist:

- You have the right to distribute goods or services that bear the franchisor's trademark, service mark, trade name or logo.
- The franchisor significantly assists you in operating your business or significantly controls what you do. For example, your franchisor might assist in site selection, train you and your employees or furnish you with a detailed instructional manual. A franchisor might exercise control by telling you where your business must be located and how your shop must be designed, or by dictating your hours, accounting and personnel practices and advertising program.
- You pay a fee to the franchisor of more than $500 for the first six months of operations. (In the real world, you're going to be paying a franchisor much more—probably anywhere from $10,000 or $20,000 to $1 million.)

All of this can add up to a complex and expensive relationship between you and the franchisor.

EXAMPLE: Lila loves the idea of selling donuts, and buys a franchise from Munchin Donuts International. She pays Munchin Donuts $50,000 as a franchise fee plus an additional $5,000 for training for herself and an assistant. Lila and her assistant must travel to the Munchin Donuts headquarters in another state for the training. Munchin Donuts helps her find a suitable location for a donut shop, then prescribes the store layout and décor. Lila makes the necessary improvements, but can't use her favorite contractor—she must use one on Munchin Donuts' approved list. She buys the donut-making equipment and shop furnishings directly from Munchin Donuts, as required by her franchise contract. Munchin Donuts provides Lila with a 500-page operating manual called *Making Donuts the Munchin Way*. Lila is also given the right to use the Munchin Donuts logo in her signage and advertising. Lila must buy all of the donut mixes directly from Munchin Donuts, and

each month she must pay Munchin 8% of her gross sales, plus a hefty fee for participation in Munchin's co-op advertising program. She must keep the shop open from 7 a.m. to 9 p.m., six days a week, as required by the Munchin Donuts operating manual.

B. The Downsides of Franchise Ownership

During your negotiations to buy a franchise, while everyone is still smiling, the franchisor is likely to assure you that you won't be in business all by yourself, but will be part of a team selling a recognized product or service. Franchisors typically also tout three other supposed benefits:

- *A proven plan for running the business.* The franchisor will furnish an operations manual that can serve as a roadmap to get you started.
- *Help from the franchisor if you run into problems.* The franchisor promises to make people available who are experienced in real estate, personnel policies, accounting and day-to-day operations.
- *A national or regional marketing program to attract customers.* The franchisor promises to advertise in print and on radio and TV so that the brand will become famous and customers will flock to your door.

Even if the franchisor makes good on all of these commitments—and many won't—the price you'll pay to get these benefits may be back-breakingly high. Do you really need to pay a company month after month, year after year, in order to master the fundamentals of making pizza or cleaning houses? As for business help from the franchisor, can't you simply hire advisors on an as-needed basis to help you with real estate, marketing or accounting issues? (As a matter of fact, you can probably learn the basic management skills you'll need by taking a course or two at a nearby community college.) And will the franchisor really invest enough money to build the kind of brand recognition that translates into huge profits for you? It's highly unlikely.

It's true that some small business people have signed on for a franchise and found prosperity and happiness, but many more have lost their shirts and feel bitter about their franchise experiences. So before you're seduced by the glitter of the franchisor's glib promises, take a hard look at the downsides of investing in a franchise.

It takes money to make money. *Some franchises may have a high profit potential—but the better ones tend to be well beyond the reach of the small operator. As Ralph Warner convincingly explains in* Drive a Modest Car & 16 Other Keys to Small Business Success *(Nolo), national hotel and motel groups may offer fine franchise opportunities, since they provide a real service through their 800 phone numbers and reservation booking services. Ditto for auto rental franchises since they, too, offer something of value. And franchises with famous and respected brands such as McDonald's and Pizza Hut may be worth the high cost. But these blue-chip opportunities are expensive to buy into. If you're an ordinary entrepreneur with possibly $50,000 or $75,000 to invest, you'll probably be looking at lesser-known franchises for which the prospects are not nearly so bright.*

Let's look at some reasons why franchises are usually a worse option than starting your own business or buying an existing one.

1. The Franchisor Gets a Huge Chunk of the Pie

The franchisor will almost certainly insist on getting a thick slice of your financial action—often the lion's share. Franchisors have figured out many ways to make money on your business, including:

- *Franchise fees.* You must always pay up-front for the right to be a franchisee. These buy-in fees can verge on the astronomical, especially for a successful, nationally established franchise.

- *Royalties.* Commonly, the franchisor gets a percentage of the income your franchise earns. Income usually means gross sales, not profits. If your franchise takes in $200,000 from gross sales and your contract calls for a 10% royalty, the franchisor will be entitled to receive $20,000 whether or not your business earns a profit. Other operating expenses can easily eat up the remaining $180,000 of gross income, leaving nothing—or even less.

- *Markups on equipment, goods and supplies.* The franchisor may add dollars to the cost of equipment, goods and supplies that the franchisor furnishes. Many franchise agreements require you to buy certain items from the franchisor rather than from outside suppliers; others let you buy through outside sources if the items meet the franchisor's specifications. If, for example, you're required to purchase cooking equipment from the franchisor, you may pay a bundle more than you'd pay a restaurant supply store.

- *Training fees.* Often you must pay the franchisor to train you and your employees— whether or not you need the training.

- *Co-op ad fees.* These fees cover advertising for the entire group of franchises or a regional group. For example, you may have to contribute to a fund for national advertising or for advertising for all the franchisees in your metropolitan area—whether or not any of your customers are likely to see the ads.

- *Interest on financing.* You may have to pay for deferring payment of a portion of the franchise fee, the cost of improving your business premises or buying equipment.
- *Leases.* Your franchisor may charge you rent on real estate or equipment. Typically, the franchisor does not lease real estate or equipment to you at the franchisor's cost but adds on a profit factor. But because relatively few franchisors own the premises where their franchisees do business, real estate lease charges are relatively uncommon.

If it appears that I'm painting a grim picture, I am. After you've made all the required payments to the franchisor, there may be very little left for you.

LAW IN THE REAL WORLD
Going It Alone

Phil, a real estate broker, wanted to open his own shop. He first considered going it alone, but then decided he might do better by purchasing a franchise from one of the national organizations. He contacted several and was amazed to find that he couldn't buy a one-office franchise directly from them. Instead he was told that in his region a "master" franchise had already been sold and that he would have to contact this company to purchase a sub-franchise.

When he did, he learned that his region had been divided into hundreds of sub-regions or territories, each of which was for sale through a local real estate office. All training, quality control and recruiting was done by the master franchise holder, not the national organization.

Eventually, Phil decided not to purchase any of the local franchises he was offered, concluding that the territories had been divided too narrowly. In the meantime, he has opened his own office and is doing fairly well. He might still affiliate with a franchise organization, but only if he can find one that sells good-sized territories at a reasonable price.

2. The Franchisor Can Tell You What to Do

If you're like many entrepreneurs, part of the attraction of owning a business is that you're free to make your own business decisions, test new ideas, and change and improve the products and services you offer. Unfortunately, when you're a franchisee, you give up a great deal of that freedom. The franchisor typically prescribes a formula for running the business and, for the most part, you're locked into using it. Don't be surprised if you soon become frustrated and bored.

But the consequences of signing on as a franchisee can go much farther than just stifled creativity. There's a real chance that your bottom line will be affected. Small businesses normally enjoy a huge advantage over multi-state giants: they're nimble enough to respond quickly to local conditions. By contrast, large organizations can't react nearly as fast, meaning that opportunities for adding profits—or avoiding losses—can be missed. For example, if you own a pizza franchise and notice that everyone in town is going crazy for fresh shiitake mushrooms, you could wait years before your franchisor lets you put any mushroom atop your pizza that isn't straight from a can. You're just a cog in a huge machine.

3. The Franchise Contract Will Favor the Franchisor

When you buy a franchise, you'll need to sign a contract with the franchisor. Contracts aren't bad in and of themselves—they're useful tools for spelling out all the terms and conditions of the relationship. However, the contract that you'll be handed will have been drafted by a team of skilled lawyers hired by the franchisor and will most likely contain dozen of clauses aimed at giving the franchisor every conceivable advantage. And you'll probably be told to "take it or leave it," with no opportunity to negotiate any of the contract terms.

To give you an idea of how one-sided these contracts can be, here are some clauses you're likely to find in the typical franchise contract.

- **Competition.** The franchisor will usually protect its freedom to grant additional franchises without restriction. This means that if your operation is successful, the franchisor may decide to sell a franchise to someone else right down the street, cutting into your market share. By contrast, you'll be required to agree that after the franchise relationship ends, you won't compete with the franchisor—either directly or indirectly. This stops you from working or investing in a similar business. While it's reasonable for the franchisor to want to protect its trademarks and trade secrets, the franchisor already has plenty of legal protection in this area. The franchisor has no solid justification for interfering with your ability to earn a living doing similar work after you've stopped being a franchisee—but it has superior bargaining power. It can usually force even unreasonable restrictions on you as part of the price of buying the franchise.

- **Selling Your Franchise.** When you own your own business, you're free to sell it to whomever you wish. Not so with a franchise. Typically, you can't sell your franchise unless the franchisor approves of the buyer. This means that if you want to retire or move to another state or shift to a different line of work, you're at the mercy of the franchisor. If the franchisor is picky, you may be left with few—if any—prospective buyers, and you may have to settle for a fraction of what the business is worth. Worse yet, the buyer will have to sign a new franchise contract, which may call for even higher royalty charges than you've been paying, making it all the more difficult to sell the business.

- **Disputes.** The contract may require you to resolve any disputes with the franchisor in the courts of the franchisor's home state. If you do business in Oregon and the franchisor's headquarters are in New Jersey, that's a long and expensive trip.

- **Goods and Services.** The contract may force you to buy all your goods and services from the franchisor. If you have to buy your milkshake mix from the franchisor, and your marketing services as well, you'll probably end up paying much more than if you were free to buy from vendors of your choice.

For more on franchise agreements, see Section E.

4. The Government Won't Protect You

Franchisors become very adept at selling franchises—but aren't known for following through on what they promise in the sales presentations. Some franchisors are notorious for misrepresenting key facts about their organization. Many deftly inflate your expectations of the profits you'll bring in. And some are fly-by-night outfits operating entirely by smoke and mirrors.

Don't assume you can go running to the government for help if the franchisor's promises turn out to be puffery. Neither the state nor the federal government is going to thoroughly investigate the accuracy of information in the offering circular or bail you out if things go wrong. True, you may get limited help from a government agency to close down or even prosecute an operator whose actions constitute outright fraud. But even in the case of blatant dishonesty by the franchisor, you'll be pretty much on your own in trying to get back your money.

The time to be cautious is at the beginning, while you listen to the sales banter from the franchisor. Remember that you're almost surely not receiving a balanced, objective point of view. No matter what they say about peace, brotherhood and all prospering together, most franchisors look at their job as simply to sell as many franchises as possible, as fast as possible, at the highest price possible.

Some Sobering Statistics

Benefits touted by the franchise industry may be overblown. Timothy Bates, an economics professor at Wayne State University, studied the numbers for a four-year period. Here's his comparison of what happened to those who started an independent business from scratch versus those who started a franchised business:

	Started an Independent Business	Started a Franchised Business
Maintained Ownership	62%	54%
Shut Down	32%	38%
Gave up Ownership	6%	8%

Professor Bates also found that after four years, people who bought an independent ongoing business were doing better than those who bought an ongoing franchise business. He cites these figures:

	Bought Into an Independent Business	Bought Into an Ongoing Franchise Business
Maintained Ownership	68%	52%
Shut Down	18%	32%
Gave up Ownership	16%	15%

Professor Bates concluded that whether someone starts a new business or buys one that's already in existence, the risk of having to shut down is greater if the owner takes the franchise route.

Source: *Inc. Magazine*, July 1995

C. Investigating a Franchise

If you've done your research and have identified a few businesses in which you believe you could be successful as a franchisee, investigate the franchisors. A good track record counts. Find out how many franchises each franchisor has in actual operation—information that's readily available in the offering circular. (See Section D20.)

Next, carefully evaluate whether the specific franchise operation you're thinking about makes economic sense. Is there really a demand out there for the product or service that you'll be selling? Can you make a decent profit given how much you can charge and your cost of doing business? Don't forget to count all those franchise fees. The franchisor may give you actual or hypothetical projections of how much money a typical franchisee can earn. Distrust these. Chances are they're full of hype. Ask for financial details about individual franchise operations that are geographically and demographically similar to the one that you're considering.

Most important, speak to a number of other franchisees. The names and addresses of those in your state will be listed in the offering circular. (Again, see Section D20.)

The more you know about the franchisor, the better. Visit the home office, even if it's in another city or state. Get to know the people you'll be dealing with if you buy. What's the background of the owners, officers and management staff of the franchisor? Do they have the experience and competence to give you the promised technical support?

Be especially suspicious of franchises that promise big profits for little work and offer a money-back guarantee. Rarely do you get something for nothing in this world and almost never do you get your money back when business deals go awry.

Learn how much help you can expect from the franchisor in:

- selecting a site
- negotiating a lease
- writing and placing help wanted ads for employees

- interviewing prospective employees
- getting the necessary business licenses, and
- ordering equipment.

Make sure all key promises are in writing. Oral statements don't count: Often they're not legally enforceable, but even where they are, proving in court what someone said years before may be impossible. One good way to get things in writing is to take notes when you talk to the franchisor. Then write up your notes, review them with the franchisor and ask for the signature of someone in authority.

With a larger franchisor, many of your contacts will be with a district or regional manager. Meet these people and find out what they're like.

Ask about whether any franchise operations have closed. Obviously, this is a sensitive topic for a franchisor. Ideally, the franchisor will be honest in discussing failures with you, but you can't count on this. If the franchisor seems to be stonewalling, try to get the names of franchisees whose operations failed from existing franchisees and talk to them directly.

Investigate the area where your franchise will be located. Talk to people who work or live nearby to learn more about the behavior and tastes of potential customers. What do other business owners have to say about your customer base? How do they think your franchise will fit into the community?

D. The Uniform Franchise Offering Circular

The Federal Trade Commission requires franchisors to give prospective franchisees an offering circular containing details about the franchise. In addition, the franchisor must give you a copy of the proposed franchise agreement and related documents. But FTC rules don't dictate the terms of the deal you and the franchisor agree to. As long as there's full disclosure, the deal can be very one-sided in favor of the franchisor and still be legal.

The FTC does list the items that a franchisor must include in an offering circular and provides a format for the franchisor to follow. Most states that regulate franchise sales prefer a slightly different format called the "Uniform Franchise Offering Circular." Since the FTC says it's okay for a franchisor to use that format, practically every national franchisor does.

Although the FTC requires the disclosure, it doesn't verify or vouch for the information the franchisor discloses. It's up to you to check out anything you don't understand or that sounds too good to be true.

Under FTC rules, if you're a prospective franchisee, the franchisor must give you the offering circular at the earliest of either:

- your first in-person (face-to-face) meeting with the franchisor, or
- ten working days (not counting Saturdays and Sundays) before you sign a contract or pay money to the franchisor.

If a franchisor violates these or other FTC rules, it may face heavy civil penalties. Also, the FTC may sue the franchisor, on your behalf, for damages or other relief, including cancellation of a franchise contract and refunds.

State laws often provide other avenues of relief for violation of disclosure and other requirements. For example, in some states, you may have the right to sue a franchisor who fails to make disclosures properly. In other words, you won't have to rely on the state to make your case for you.

Knowing that these legal avenues are open to you may give you some peace of mind—but don't relax your guard too much. If the franchisor becomes insolvent or goes into bankruptcy, chances are you'll recover only a minuscule part of your loss, or maybe nothing at all.

Here are the 23 items included in the Uniform Franchise Offering Circular and brief comments about how to think about each:

1. The Franchisor, Its Predecessors and Affiliates

Here you'll learn the name of the franchisor and its predecessors and affiliates, as well as the name under which the franchisor does business. You'll also find out if the franchisor is a corporation, a partnership or some other type of business.

The franchisor then describes its businesses and the franchises being offered, and lists the business experience of the franchisor and its predecessors and affiliates. You can find out how long the franchisor has operated the type of business you'd be franchising. You can also learn whether the franchisor has offered franchises in other lines of business and the number of franchises sold.

Finally, the franchisor must describe any regulations that are specific to the industry in which the franchisee operates.

2. Business Experience

The franchisor must list its principal officers. For each officer, his or her job for the past five years must be disclosed.

3. Litigation

This is where you learn the legal history of the franchisor. If the franchisor or its associated people have a history of legal problems, watch out. If the franchisor follows the FTC rule, you'll discover, for example, whether or not there are administrative, criminal or civil cases alleging:

- violation of any franchise, antitrust or securities law
- fraud
- unfair or deceptive trade practices, or
- comparable misconduct.

If any such actions are pending, the offering circular must provide full information.

Furthermore, the franchisor must disclose whether, in the past ten years, the franchisor or its people have been convicted of a felony, pleaded no contest to a felony charge or have been held liable in a civil action involving any of the offenses listed above. And there's more: If the franchisor or associated person is subject to an injunction (court order) relating to a franchise or involving any laws on securities, antitrust, trade regulation or trade practice, the franchisor must disclose this information. This can provide an early warning of potential problems.

Don't rely on the franchisor's explanations of lawsuits involving the company. You can look at the court files, which are open to the public and will name all of the participants on both sides. Call the people on the other side and get their version of events.

4. Bankruptcy

The franchisor must state whether the franchisor or its officers have gone through bankruptcy or been reorganized due to insolvency during the past ten years. The information required is far-reaching. The franchisor must disclose if any officer or general partner was a principal officer of any company or a general partner of any partnership that went bankrupt or was reorganized due to insolvency within one year after the officer or general partner was associated with the company or partnership.

5. Initial Franchise Fee

Read this section carefully to learn how much you'll be charged before you open for business and whether you'll have to pay it in a lump sum or installments. The franchisor must also explain under what conditions your money will be refunded.

If the franchisor doesn't charge identical initial fees to each franchisee, the franchisor must tell how fees are determined, or state the range of fees charged in the past year.

6. Other Fees

Here's where you get detail about any required fees. Using a simple chart, the franchisor must tell you the formula used to compute fees and the conditions for refunds.

When any fees are set by the vote of a cooperative organization of franchisees—for advertising, for example—the franchisor must disclose the voting power of franchisor-owned outlets. If franchisor outlets have controlling voting power, the franchisor must disclose a range for the fees.

7. Initial Investment

These are estimates (or a high-low range) of expenses you'll be responsible for. You'll be told who the payments must be made to, when the payments are due and the conditions for refunds. If part of your initial investment may be financed, you'll learn the details, including interest rates.

Listed expenses include those for:

- real estate, whether it's bought or leased
- equipment, fixtures, other fixed assets, construction, remodeling, leasehold improvements and decorating costs
- inventory required to begin operation
- security deposits, utility deposits, business licenses, other prepaid expenses and working capital required to begin operation, and
- any other payments you must make to start operations.

⚠ Don't invest everything in a franchise.
These fees can add up to far more than you first expected and dangerously stretch your budget. Never put every last cent into a franchise. Even with an honest franchisor, there's a good chance you won't make any money the first year. Keep enough money in reserve to live on during the start-up phase. And always be wary about pledging your house for a loan needed to buy a franchise. It's one thing to risk your savings; it's quite another to risk the roof over your family's head.

8. Restrictions on Sources of Products and Services

Here, the franchisor states whether you're required to purchase or lease from the franchisor—or from companies designated by the franchisor—any of the following: goods, services, supplies, fixtures, equipment, inventory, computer hardware and software, or real estate.

The franchisor also must say if and how it may earn income from these required purchases or leases. As mentioned in Section B, many franchisors mark up the products they require their franchisees to buy from them.

9. Franchisee's Obligations

In a simple table, the franchisor lists each of your obligations and tells you where each is spelled out in the franchise agreement and offering circular.

10. Financing

Look for the terms and conditions of any financing arrangements offered to help franchisees afford the purchase. Also review the statement of your liability if you can't make the payments.

As you review these, bear in mind that after signing onto a promissory note or financing contract requiring you to make payments to the franchisor, you may find that some other company has acquired the right to collect the debt from you. This can happen if the franchisor sells or assigns (transfers) the promissory note or financing contract to the other company. In the offering circular, the franchisor needs to state whether or not it plans to handle the financing arrangement this way. It may seem like a minor detail, but it can affect you down the road. Here's why: If you're dealing directly with the franchisor in making your payments, you may be able to withhold payment if the franchisor isn't meeting its obligations to you. By contrast, if the note or financing contract has been transferred to somebody else, you'll probably be obligated to pay regardless of how poorly the franchisor is performing.

⚠ Beware of finance charges. *Paying finance charges and interest on notes held by the franchisor is a real financial burden. If you can't afford to pay all of the franchise fees up front, maybe you shouldn't buy the franchise. Think long and hard before you pledge your house as security for these obligations—and before you ask your spouse or a relative to be a co-signer or guarantor of the debt.*

11. Franchisor's Obligations

What are the franchisor's obligations to you before you open your franchise business? For example, will the franchisor select a location for your business? Will the franchisor help you:

- negotiate the purchase or lease of the site?
- make sure the building you'll occupy conforms to local codes?
- obtain required building permits?
- construct, remodel or decorate the premises?
- purchase or lease equipment, signs and supplies?
- hire and train employees?

And what kind of assistance will the franchisor give you once your business is operating?

Look for detailed answers to these questions as well as a description of the training program the franchisor will provide, including: the location, length and content of the training program; when the training program will be conducted; experience that instructors have had with the franchisor; any charges for the training; the extent to which you'll be responsible for travel and living expenses of people enrolled in the training program; and whether any additional training programs or refresher courses are available or required.

12. Territory

Here the franchisor describes whether or not you have any territorial protection. Check to see whether the franchisor has established another franchisee or company-owned outlet in your territory, or has the right to do so in the future. Obviously, your business will be in trouble if the franchisor defines your exclusive territory very narrowly and then floods the market with outlets offering similar products or services.

Even if you have exclusive rights within a territory, you may not be safe from direct competition. Some franchisors require you to achieve a certain sales volume or market penetration to keep those exclusive rights. Make sure you understand under what conditions your area or territory can be altered.

13. Trademarks

Most likely your franchise will require you to use the franchisor's trademarks, service marks, trade names, logos or other commercial symbols. Fine. In many ways, these represent much of the value of a franchise. In fact, you'll want to research whether the franchisor itself has an ongoing right to use these marks and symbols.

For starters, the franchisor must tell you in the offering circular whether or not the franchisor's trademarks and symbols are registered with the U.S. Patent and Trademark Office. The franchisor must also describe any agreements, administrative proceedings or court cases that may affect your right to use these trademarks and symbols.

Franchisors should stand behind their trade names and trademarks. Even if a trademark is properly registered, it can still be challenged in court by a company that used it before the franchisor used it or registered it. Make sure that your franchisor is obligated in writing to defend any challenges against its names and trademarks and to indemnify you against any damage awards for using them. The franchisor should also agree to reimburse you for out-of-pocket expenses if you have to replace signs and print new supplies because of an adverse court ruling regarding names or trademarks.

14. Patents, Copyrights and Proprietary Information

The franchisor must give full details about any patents or copyrights that relate to the franchise and the terms and conditions under which you can use them. Let's say, for example, that a tire store franchisor has published an excellent copyrighted booklet telling consumers how to choose the right tires for their cars. The franchisor needs to disclose whether there have been any administrative or other claims filed that might affect the continued use of the booklet. And the franchisor needs to state whether it can require its franchisees to discontinue use of the booklet in running their franchisees.

Also, the franchisor must state if it claims proprietary rights in confidential information or trade secrets.

15. Obligation to Participate in the Actual Operation of the Franchise Business

Some franchisors permit someone to own a franchise without actively participating in the operation of the business. Other franchisors want the owner to be fully involved. The franchisor must state whether or not it will obligate you to participate

personally in operating the franchise business. It must also state whether or not it recommends that you participate.

If the franchisor doesn't require you, as a franchise owner, to personally be present and run the business, it may require that you employ an on-site manager who has successfully completed the franchisor's training program.

16. Restrictions on What the Franchisee May Sell

If you're going to be restricted in the goods or services you can offer or the customers you can sell to, this must be spelled out in the offering circular. Find out if you'll be required to carry the full range of the franchisor's products. For example, with a food franchise, do you have to offer the full menu? Can you add items to the menu?

Also, check whether the franchisor has the right to change the types of goods and services you're authorized to sell.

17. Renewal, Termination, Transfer and Dispute Resolution

You're entitled to know the conditions under which you may renew, extend or terminate your franchise and also the conditions under which the franchisor may refuse to deal with you. (See Section E8 for more on termination.)

Look, too, for information on whether disputes must be submitted to mediation or arbitration in place of going to court.

Mediation or arbitration is usually a plus. *Fighting a franchisor in court can be prohibitively expensive for a franchisee. The franchisor usually has very deep pockets and can better afford to finance—or even drag out—the litigation. If a legal dispute can't be settled through negotiation, it's almost always better for you to submit the matter to* *mediation or arbitration rather than go to court. Mediation and arbitration proceedings are much less expensive than lawsuits—and speedier to boot. There's a trade-off, however: In a lawsuit you can compel the franchisor to show you key documents and to answer questions under oath (in what's called a pre-trial deposition). Mediation and arbitration offer only very limited opportunities for this type of information gathering. For more on resolving legal disputes, see Chapter 22.*

18. Public Figures

Some franchisors use celebrities to promote franchise operations. The franchisor must disclose any compensation or other benefit given or promised to any public figures for using their names or endorsements. You also need to be told the extent to which celebrities are involved in the actual management or control of the franchisor and how much—if anything—they have invested in the franchise operation.

19. Earnings Claims

The franchisor has a choice. It can disclose the actual or potential sales, profits or earnings of its franchisees. Or it can say nothing on the subject—which is what most franchisors choose to do. If the franchisor does make any earnings claims, the offering circular must describe the factual basis and material assumptions that underlie these claims.

For earnings claims to make sense, you need to know the franchise locations that the numbers are based on and the number of years that they have been in operation. Actual figures are, of course, more helpful than hypothetical projections. Before you buy a franchise, have your accountant go over the numbers with a fine-toothed comb. Also check with a number of existing franchisees to see how they're doing.

20. List of Outlets

The information in this part of the circular can be a gold mine if you take advantage of it. The franchisor must list the total number of franchise locations and state how many of them were in operation when the offering circular was prepared, as well as how many are covered by franchise agreements but are not yet in operation. The franchisor must also list the names, addresses and telephone numbers of all its franchises in your state.

A company with a hundred franchises up and running has had a chance to test its business formula and has experience in helping franchisees get started. A company with only eight or ten units in operation is relatively young and still has a lot to learn. But be leery of a franchise that's merely on the drawing board and isn't yet in actual operation. It may never open and, even if it does, may not prosper. Obviously, a franchise that's not yet open can't give you hard information about sales or profitability.

The franchisor must also tell you how many franchises it has canceled or terminated in the last three years; how many it has not renewed; and how many the franchisor has reacquired.

Contact franchisees in your state or in nearby states. Ask questions: "How's it working out? Was it a good deal? Would you do it again? Are you making a profit? How much?" Franchisees sometimes feel locked in and are reluctant to admit that they made a mistake in buying a franchise, but they might level with you if you ask, "Would you feel comfortable recommending that I put my life savings into this deal?"

Ask franchisees if they get help and support from the home office and how often they see someone from headquarters. Spend a day or two at a few franchises. Picture yourself in that setting. How does the system seem to be working? If there's a franchisee organization, see if you can attend meetings and get old newsletters. Don't rely on what one or two franchisees tell you—they could have unrevealed ties to the franchisor or be unrealistically positive because they're trying to unload their own franchise or will be paid a commission if they help reel you in.

21. Financial Statements

The franchisor must file audited financial statements showing the condition of the company. Unless you have experience in interpreting financial statements, get an accountant with experience with franchises to interpret the figures and help you develop tough questions. You want a franchisor to be financially strong enough to follow through on training commitments, trademark protection and support services. If a franchisor is financially weak—many are—and folds overnight, your franchise may not be worth much.

To find an accountant with the right experience, seek recommendations from owners of successful local franchises who have been in business for a while.

22. Contracts

The franchisor must attach to the offering circular a copy of all agreements that you'll sign if you purchase the franchise. This includes lease agreements, option agreements and purchase agreements. Read them carefully and don't sign until you understand everything.

23. Receipt

The last page of the offering circular is a detachable receipt, which you sign as evidence that you received the offering circular.

E. The Franchise Agreement

If you buy a franchise, you and the franchisor will sign a long document called a franchise agreement. There probably will be other documents to sign at the same time, but the franchise agreement is far and away the most important. Whether or not any terms of the agreement are negotiable depends on whether the franchisor is new or long established and on prevailing market conditions. A new franchisor eager to penetrate the market may be more flexible and willing to make concessions than an established franchisor whose franchises are in high demand.

Again, if the franchisor has made any promises to you, make sure that they're in the franchise agreement. Otherwise, chances are you won't be able to enforce them.

Joan, a legal secretary, inherited $200,000. To achieve her goal of financial independence, she decided to start a business. Drawing on the experience of her cousin Max, who had done very well running several franchised taco stores, Joan decided to look at franchise opportunities.

Because she couldn't afford a major franchise, she narrowed her search to small outfits. One, a Belgian waffle shop, particularly intrigued her. When she expressed interest and her solvency was documented, she was quickly:

- flown to corporate headquarters
- assigned to two enthusiastic "vice presidents"
- shown an exciting video featuring a waffle shop overflowing with happy customers
- taken on a tour of a "typical" waffle franchise outlet, and
- told there were only a few franchises left and she had to decide quickly.

It almost worked. But at literally the last minute before signing she decided she had better call her cousin Max. He yelled "stop" so loudly that she told the franchise she wanted a few days to investigate, even if it meant losing out on the deal.

The investigation showed that the franchise was almost broke, three lawsuits from disappointed franchisees were pending, and the supposedly successful franchise was owned by the parent company and looked successful because prices were kept artificially low to bring in customers. And, oh yes, the "vice presidents" who dealt with Joan were really sales reps working on commission.

Let's look at a few sensitive areas of a franchise deal that you must be aware of before you plunk down your money and sign an agreement.

1. Franchise Fee

The extent of your personal liability for the franchise fee and other franchise obligations is a crucial consideration for you in making this deal.

Does the franchise agreement allow you to avoid personal liability for franchise-related debts by forming a corporation to serve as the franchisee? Or does the franchisor require you (and perhaps your spouse as well) to be personally responsible for all franchise obligations? At the risk of being repetitive, I strongly recommend against pledging your house or other assets as security for payment of the franchise fee. (See Section D5 for how the franchise fee is dealt with in the offering circular.)

2. Advertising Fees

If the franchise agreement requires you to pay an advertising fee to the franchisor, make sure that part of that fee is earmarked for local advertising over which you'll have some control. Perhaps the franchisor will agree to match any money you spend on local advertising. This is especially important if your franchise will be in an area where there are only a few other franchise locations. Otherwise the franchisor may spend all the advertising money 1,000 miles away where there are more franchisees—and you'll essentially be paying to support someone else's business.

Be alert for arrangements that allow the franchisor to reap profits from the advertising fees it charges you. In one case, a federal court said it was legal for Meineke Mufflers to set up its own in-house ad agency and hire it to handle franchise system advertising—a scheme that profited Meineke to the tune of millions of dollars in fees. (*Broussard v. Meineke Discount Muffler Shops*, 155 F.3d 331 (4th Cir. 1998).)

3. Royalty Fees

Typically, the royalty fees you pay the franchisor are a percentage of your gross sales. (See Section B.) They may, however, be a flat weekly or monthly charge. Be cautious about a franchisor who charges a small initial franchise fee but then charges you a high percentage of monthly sales.

> **EXAMPLE:** Compare two fast food operations. Franchisor A charges an initial fee of $5,000 and monthly royalties of 8% (in addition to advertising fees). Franchisor B charges a franchise fee of $20,000 and monthly royalties of 5% (not including advertising). Let's say that each franchise has annual sales of $500,000. In the first year, each franchisee will pay $45,000 to the franchisor. But look at succeeding years. Franchisee A will pay $40,000 each year to its franchisor, while Franchisee B pays only $25,000.

⚠️ **Franchise royalties are costly.** *Remember that many franchises simply are bad business deals. In a world where it's very hard for any small business to make a 10% profit, giving a huge chunk of money to the franchisor as a royalty rarely makes sense.*

4. Hidden Costs

Read the franchise agreement carefully to uncover any hidden costs—many of which are mentioned earlier in this chapter. (See Section B1.) It's to your advantage if the income received by the franchisor is primarily based on royalties. That way, the franchisor has a direct interest in making your business profitable. The franchisor's incentive to promote your profitability is somewhat reduced if the franchisor begins to see itself as primarily your landlord or supplier rather than as a business partner.

If you must buy equipment, supplies or inventory from the franchisor, make sure that the prices you'll pay are competitive with those charged by outside sources. You don't want to sign up with a franchisor who plans to gouge you on these items—especially if they're of iffy quality. Yes, the franchisor has a legitimate interest in seeing that all franchisees run standardized operations, and this can require that certain items such as food supplies be exactly the same. But this need for specialization should be balanced against your need to make a decent profit. Franchisors often allow you to buy equipment and goods through an approved supplier, as long as the franchisor's specifications are met.

5. Quotas

Some franchise agreements require you to meet sales quotas. For example, your agreement might state that if you don't maintain a certain volume of business, you'll no longer have the right to an exclusive territory. In some cases, the franchisor may also reserve the right to terminate your franchise if quotas aren't met. Watch out for this one. If the quotas aren't realistic or it takes you longer than you expected to master the business, you face the horrible prospect of losing some or all of your investment.

6. The Franchise Term

Typically, a franchise agreement provides for a term of five to 15 years. Beware of an agreement that states that the franchise can be terminated "at will" by the franchisor upon written notice. See Section E8 for a further discussion of termination provisions.

Also carefully study your renewal rights. Is renewal entirely in the hands of the franchisor? If you do renew, will a renewal fee be charged? Will you have to sign a new franchise agreement containing whatever terms are in effect when you renew? This could change the whole ball game, because ten years from now, when you go to renew, a new franchise agreement could have higher royalties or advertising fees.

Under some franchise agreements, the franchisor can require a franchisee to install expensive improvements in the business premises—even beyond the start-up installations. If the franchise agreement doesn't grant you the automatic right to renew your franchise on the same terms, seek language limiting the franchisor's right to force you to put expensive improvements into the business beyond the initial alterations. You want to be sure that if you're forced to put more money into the premises, you have enough time to recover that investment.

7. Assignment

Usually, a franchise agreement says that you must get the written approval of the franchisor before you transfer or assign your franchise agreement to someone else. But what happens if you have a serious health problem that prevents you from running the franchise? Could you transfer the franchise to a family member? Or, if you were to die, would your spouse automatically be able to continue the business for you?

And if you die, is there a deadline (such as 90 days or six months) during which the franchise must be transferred to a new owner to avoid termination of the franchise by the franchisor? Find out how long it takes, if someone wants to buy your franchise, to learn whether the franchisor approves or disapproves of the sale.

One way of dealing with your possible death as an owner of a franchise is a clause allowing your survivors a period of time to elect to keep and operate the business, as long as they meet the franchisor's training requirements.

Assuming you remain hale and hearty, but want to be able to get out of the franchise, some franchisors may be willing to give you the right to sell,

subject to the franchisor's right to match any bona fide offer (called a right of first refusal). For example, if someone comes to you with an offer to buy your franchise, you would have to give the franchisor 30 or 60 days to meet the terms of the purchase.

8. Termination

Study carefully what the franchise agreement says about the franchisor's right to terminate the franchise. If the franchisor can terminate your franchise because you have supposedly defaulted upon or breached the agreement, you want to be notified in writing of the franchisor's intent and given at least 30 days in which to clear the defaults or correct the breaches. On the other side of the coin, you may want to have the right to terminate the agreement yourself if the franchisor is in default.

Commonly, the franchisor has the right to terminate the franchise if you either fail to operate the business, understate your gross revenues, don't pay royalties when due or participate in a competing business.

Termination without good cause. *Watch out for franchise agreements that give the franchisor the right to terminate the franchise whether it has a good reason or not. Such clauses are harsh and unfair—so much so that several states have enacted statutes limiting the right of a franchisor to unilaterally terminate a franchisee. Typically, under such statutes, the franchisor would have to show "good cause" before terminating you.*

9. Competition

It's critical to know where you stand in terms of competition with other franchisees. Typically, the franchisor grants you a protected territory for your franchise operations. Within your territory, your franchisor agrees not to grant another franchise or to operate its own competing business. If you don't have a protected territory, will the franchisor at least give you first crack at buying any proposed new location near yours?

A franchise agreement also usually restricts you from competing in a similar business during the term of the franchise and for several years after its termination. Generally, courts enforce these restrictive covenants if they're reasonable as to time and geographic scope. Franchisors want to make sure their trade secrets aren't misused. You, on the other hand, don't want to give up your right to earn a living in the field that you know best. So take a close look at the non-competition language and make sure that it doesn't restrict you too severely. Maybe you can live with a provision that says that you won't go into a competing business in the same county as your franchise for two years after a termination; but maybe you can't.

F. Resolving Disputes With Your Franchisor

If you do opt for a franchise, try to keep the lines of communication with your franchisor open. Talk about problems as soon as they begin to emerge. If you wait until a lawsuit is your only option, you'll discover how expensive, time-consuming and often frustrating or even hopeless litigating with a franchisor can be.

A better option may be for you to band together with other franchisees to try to work out your mutual grievances with the franchisor. You'll gain negotiating power by presenting your concerns as a group. Some franchisees even form a separate franchisee's organization to negotiate on their behalf. If such negotiation doesn't work, look into whether the FTC—or perhaps the attorney general who enforces the franchise laws in your state—will take up the cudgels for you.

As a final resort, hire a lawyer familiar with franchisee rights to evaluate your prospects of winning a lawsuit. Be aware that franchise law is a relatively specialized area; not all business lawyers are experienced in this field. ■

12

Insuring Your Business

A well-designed insurance program can protect your business from many types of perils. Consider the following:

- A fire destroys all the furniture, fixtures and equipment in your restaurant.
- Burglars steal $75,000 worth of computer equipment you use in your book publishing business.
- A customer visiting your yogurt store slips on the just-washed floor and shatters her elbow.
- On the way to an office supply store to pick up some fax paper, one of your employees runs a stop sign and injures a child.
- A house painter has a severe allergic reaction to a solvent that your company manufactures and distributes.
- One of your employees is hospitalized for four weeks with a severe back injury she received while trying to lift a heavy package.
- The building where you're located is severely damaged by a windstorm. You're forced to close your doors for two months while repairs are made. In addition to having to pay $35,000 for continuing business expenses, you lose the $25,000 of profits you expected for that period—a total loss of $60,000.
- A client installs a lawn sprinkling system based on specifications you recommended as a landscape architect. Because you hadn't checked soil conditions carefully, the system malfunctions, flooding your client's basement and ruining the antique furniture stored there. Your client sues you for professional negligence.

Maybe none of these will happen to your business—but unless you consider yourself permanently exempt from Murphy's Law ("If anything can go wrong it will"), don't bet on it. Fortunately, insurance is available to cover each of these events and for many, if not most of them, is reasonably cost-effective.

Not every small business needs every type of coverage. In fact, a business that tried to buy insurance to cover all insurable risks probably wouldn't have money left over to do anything else. Deciding on insurance coverage usually involves some difficult choices. Here are some general rules to start with:

- Get enough property and liability coverage to protect yourself from common claims. These are the most important kinds of insurance for a small business.
- Buy insurance against serious risks where the insurance is reasonably priced.
- Keep costs down by selecting high deductibles.
- Self-insure if insurance is prohibitively expensive or the particular risk is highly unlikely.
- Adopt aggressive policies to reduce the likelihood of insurance claims, particularly in areas where you're self-insured.

Sections B, C and D look at the standard types of insurance available to small businesses and how you can put together a reasonable insurance program.

A. Working With an Insurance Agent

Find and work with a knowledgeable insurance agent—one who takes the time to analyze your business operations and to come up with a sensible program for your company. Generally, it's best to work with a single insurance agent for all your business needs so that coverages can be coordinated. But be sure to find out whether any agent you're speaking to is locked into one insurance company. If so, it may be wise to look elsewhere. The agent you choose should be willing to obtain quotes from several companies so that you don't pay more than is necessary.

To find a competent insurance agent or broker, talk to local business people, particularly those in your line of work. Other people in the same field should be able to give you good leads on insurance agents. Working with an agent who knows your business is advantageous because that person is already a fair way along the learning curve when it comes to helping you select an affordable and appropriate package.

EXAMPLE: Louisa, who owns a plant nursery, wants insurance coverage for risks associated with bugs and toxic substances. She finds an insurance agent who already works with similar businesses. The agent knows what insurance is available for a plant nursery and how to tailor the coverage to Louisa's business so that it will be affordable.

Insurance Terminology

In some parts of the country, the term "insurance agent" refers to a person who represents a specific company, and "insurance broker" refers to a person who is free to sell insurance offered by various companies. Elsewhere, the term "insurance agent" is used more broadly to cover both types of representatives—and that's how it's used in this chapter.

Steer clear of an agent who, without learning the specifics of your business, whips out a package policy and claims it will solve all your problems. Yes, the insurance industry has developed some excellent packages that cover the basic needs of various businesses. For example, there are packages offered for offices, retail sales operations, service businesses, hotels, industrial and processing companies and contractors. One of these may meet your needs, but neither you nor your insurance agent will know for sure until the agent asks you a lot of questions and thoroughly understands your business. If the agent is unable or unwilling to tailor your coverage to your particular business, find someone else.

Be frank with your agent when discussing your business. Reveal all areas of unusual risk. If you fail to disclose all the facts, you may not get the coverage you need or, in some circumstances, the insurance company may later take the position that you misrepresented the nature of your operation and, for that reason, deny you coverage for exceptional risks. Make sure you have a clear understanding of what your insurance policy covers and what's excluded. Does the policy exclude damage from a leaking sprinkler system? From a boiler explosion? From an earthquake? If so, and these are risks you face, find out if they can be covered by paying a small extra premium.

Also ask how much the agent will help in processing claims if you do have a loss. Ideally, the insurance company should have a local or regional office that's readily accessible to you. That's normally a better arrangement and more personal than dealing with an insurance company that hires an independent claim service to investigate and deal with claims.

It's a good idea to talk to several agents before making a final selection. Ask for written recommendations on comparable coverage and what the cost will be. There should be no charge for providing this information, because the agents will be eager to get your business.

Is the Company Solvent?

In recent years, many insurance companies have become insolvent. If you wind up with a company that goes broke and you have a loss covered by a policy, you may receive only a paltry portion of the coverage that you paid for or none at all. The best way to minimize this risk is to work with a company that appears in good financial shape.

You can check out insurers in these standard reference works, which rate insurance companies for financial solvency:

- *Best's Insurance Reports* (Property-Casualty Insurance Section)
- *Moody's Bank and Financial Manual* (Volume 2)
- *Duff & Phelps* (Insurance Company Claims-Paying Ability Rating Guide)
- *Standard & Poor's.*

Each publication has strengths and weaknesses. In my opinion, the best overall sources on the list are *Moody's* and *Duff & Phelps*. Some commentators think that *Best's* is too lenient in its ratings. And *Standard & Poor's* is sometimes incomplete because some companies prefer not to pay the huge fee it takes for a listing. Your insurance agent should be able to give you the latest ratings from these publications. You can also check the reference department at a public library.

Also consider the services offered by Weiss Inc., which is reputed to be tougher (more conservative) in its ratings. Weiss offers a variety of low-cost reports on the solvency of an insurance company. You can call Weiss toll-free at 800-289-9222 or go to their website at www.weissratings.com.

B. Property Coverage

In considering property coverage, there are four main issues to think about:

- What business property should you insure?
- What perils will the property be insured against? In other words, under what conditions will you be entitled to receive payment from the insurance company?
- What dollar amount of insurance should you carry? (Obviously, the higher the amount, the higher the premiums. You don't want to waste money on insurance but you do want to carry enough so that a loss wouldn't jeopardize your business.)
- Should you buy coverage for replacement cost or for the present value of the property?

Section B6 outlines property insurance from a renter's point of view. Renters may want to skip ahead, then return here and read the general information on how property insurance works.

1. Property Covered

Your insurance policy will contain a section called Building and Personal Property Coverage Form, which lists exactly what property is covered. If you own the building you're occupying, be sure the building is covered, including:

- completed additions
- permanently installed fixtures, machinery and equipment
- outdoor fixtures (such as pole lights)
- property used to maintain or service the building (such as fire extinguishing equipment).

The policy may also cover additions under construction as well as materials, equipment, supplies and temporary structures on or within 100 feet of the main building.

Be sure that your business personal property is also covered. A typical policy covers the following items located on the business premises:

- furniture and fixtures

- machinery and equipment
- inventory
- all other personal property used in the business (such as technical books and cassette tapes)
- leased personal property, if you're contractually obligated to insure it
- personal property of others that's in your custody.

⚠ Be sure that everything is covered. *Check carefully to be sure the policy covers all the types of personal property that you own or expect to own: furniture, equipment, goods that you sell, products that you manufacture and raw materials used in the manufacturing process.*

Typically, various items are excluded, such as accounting records, currency, deeds and vehicles held for sale. If you need coverage on excluded items, you can usually arrange it, for an additional premium.

2. Perils Covered

More than 90% of the time, property insurance for small businesses is written in one of three forms: Basic Form, Broad Form and Special Form. Special Form coverage is the most common and affords the best protection.

Whichever policy you decide on, read it carefully before you pay for it—not just when you've suffered a loss. You may discover that some coverage is narrower than it first seemed. For example, smoke loss may refer only to loss caused by a faulty heating or cooking unit; it may not cover smoke damage from industrial equipment. Similarly, an explosion may not include a burst steam boiler. Fortunately, most insurance policies today are written in plain English so you should have little problem in understanding what's covered and what isn't. If you need coverage not provided in the policy, talk to your agent about how to add it on.

Basic Form coverage includes losses caused by fire, lightning, explosion, windstorm or hail, smoke, aircraft or vehicles (but not loss or damage caused by vehicles you own or operate in the course of your business), riot, vandalism, sprinkler leaks, sinkholes and volcanoes. The policy defines these perils—and also lists some exclusions, such as nuclear hazards, power failures or mud slides.

Broad Form coverage contains everything that's in the Basic Form and adds protection from a few more perils, including breakage of glass (that is part of a building or structure), falling objects, weight of snow or ice and water damage. Again, these terms are defined in the policy and, again, exclusions are listed.

Special Form policies are constructed differently than Basic and Broad Form policies and offer wider and slightly more expensive coverage. Instead of listing specific perils such as fire and lightning, Special Form policies simply say that your business property is covered against all risks of physical loss unless the policy specifically excludes or limits the loss. This type of policy offers the most protection. For example, it's a convenient way to insure against loss by theft, which isn't covered by Basic and Broad Form policies. (Section D2 discusses theft insurance.)

⚠ If you need additional coverage. *If you're concerned about property loss caused by perils not covered or, in the case of a Special Form policy, excluded from an insurance policy, you can often get the additional coverage through an endorsement (add-on page) to the policy by paying an additional premium. For example, such coverage is usually available for losses due to earthquakes and floods.*

💡 Consider getting insurance coverage for damage caused by terrorists. *The Terrorism Risk Insurance Act of 2002 requires insurance companies to offer such coverage. True, you'll be* *charged an additional premium, but it should be relatively small. The law that requires insurers to offer this coverage will be in effect through 2004, but it may be extended through 2005. If your business had an insurance policy in effect on November 26, 2002, and the policy excluded damage caused by terrorists, that exclusion has been temporarily suspended—in other words, the insurance company must pay for such damage. But the insurer can reinstate the exclusion if you don't pay the increased premium for terrorism coverage within 30 days after the insurer bills you for it.*

Earthquake and Flood Insurance

Earthquake insurance can be handled through a separate policy or an endorsement to Basic, Broad or Special Form coverage. Deductibles in an earthquake endorsement are typically stated as a percentage—such as 10%—rather than as a dollar amount. This means that the higher your policy limit, the bigger the deductible. As a result, some business people choose a $200,000 policy with a $20,000 deductible rather than a $400,000 policy with a $40,000 deductible. They reason that the deductible on the latter policy is so high they're unlikely to ever collect anything.

Flood insurance, by contrast, is usually handled through a separate policy called "Difference in Conditions."

Combining Property and Liability Insurance in One Policy. You can purchase property insurance as a stand-alone and buy a separate stand-alone policy for liability coverage (discussed in Section C), or you can buy a policy that combines both coverages. It's often—but not always—cheaper to buy a combination policy. Here's where comparison shopping definitely pays off.

3. Amount of Coverage

Be sure to carry enough insurance on the building to rebuild it. But there's no need to insure the total value of your real property (the legal term that includes land and buildings), because land doesn't burn. Especially if you're in an area where land is very valuable, this is a big consideration.

If you're in doubt as to how much it would cost you to rebuild, have an appraisal made so you know that your idea of value is realistic. Because the value of the building and other property may increase, it's wise to get a new appraisal every few years. Your insurance agent should be able to help you do this.

Usually it's best to insure your property for 100% of its value. If doing this is prohibitively expensive, consider a policy with a higher deductible rather than underinsuring.

Underinsuring to get a reduced premium is a false economy for several reasons. Not only are you not covered if you suffer a total loss, but it may also reduce your ability to recover for a smaller loss. This is because most insurance policies carry a co-insurance clause which states that to recover the full policy amount, you have to carry insurance to cover at least 80% (this percentage may vary) of the property's replacement cost or actual cash value. If you don't, you become a co-insurer if there's a loss, even if it's less than the policy maximum; the policy will only pay off a percentage of its face value.

EXAMPLE 1: Fluoro Corporation owns a $100,000 building. If Fluoro carries $80,000 worth of insurance or more, the insurance company will pay Fluoro for the full amount of any loss up to the policy limit. For example, if the loss is $50,000 Fluoro will get the full $50,000. If the loss is $90,000, Fluoro will receive only $80,000, the policy limit.

EXAMPLE 2: Pluto Associates owns a similar $100,000 building. To get a reduced premium, the partners decide to carry only $40,000 worth of insurance. If there's a fire and Pluto has a loss of $20,000, its insurance company will pay only $10,000. Because Pluto carried only half of the 80% figure mentioned in the policy, it's entitled to only a proportional payment.

4. Replacement Cost vs. Current Value

Historically, in case of a loss, a basic fire insurance contract covered the actual current value of the property, not its full replacement value. Today, policies are routinely available with replacement cost coverage. This is the coverage you want.

> **EXAMPLE:** Sure-Lock Corporation owns a 20-year-old building. The current cash value of the building (the amount someone would pay to buy it) is $150,000. But if the building burned down, Sure-Lock would have to pay $200,000 to replace it. If Sure-Lock buys insurance based on the building's cash value and the policy has an 80% co-insurance clause, the company will need to insure the building for $120,000. If Sure-Lock buys insurance based on replacement cost, it will need to insure for $160,000, which is 80% of $200,000.

The real cost of insurance is reduced when you consider that insurance premiums for a business are a recognized business expense—which means they are tax-deductible.

5. Ordinance or Law Coverage

If you're purchasing insurance for an older building—either because you own it or your lease requires it—understand that a normal Basic Form, Broad Form or Special Form policy designed to replace your existing building should it be destroyed probably won't be adequate. The problem is that legal requirements adopted since the building was constructed will normally require that a stronger, safer, more fire resistant building be constructed. Doing this can cost far more than simply replacing the old building. To cope with this possibility, you want a policy that will not only replace the building but pay for all legally required upgrades. This coverage is called "Ordinance or Law Coverage."

> **EXAMPLE:** Time Warp Inc., sells antique furniture and building materials removed from old homes. In keeping with its image of days gone by, Time Warp does business in a 100-year-old building in a historic part of town. Time Warp carries insurance for the full replacement cost, $100,000. One day a fire destroys 50% of the building. The insurance pays $50,000 toward reconstruction, but the Time Warp owners learn to their dismay that rebuilding will cost much more and that the additional costs are not covered by their insurance policy. The items excluded by their typical property insurance policy include the following:
>
> - *The cost of meeting current health and safety codes.* The old building was of wood frame construction and lacked an elevator and sprinkler system. That was OK before the fire. The building pre-dated the health and safety ordinances and was "grandfathered"—specifically exempted from the new construction requirements. After the fire, it's a whole new ball game. In rebuilding, Time Warp must spend an additional $100,000 for masonry construction, an elevator and a sprinkler system required by current health and safety codes.
>
> - *The cost of rebuilding the undamaged portion of the building.* The local ordinance requires that if a building built before current codes is destroyed by fire to the extent of 50% or more, the entire building must be replaced. The cost of replacing the undamaged 50% of the building is another $200,000.

- *The cost of demolition.* The local ordinance requires that, because of the extent of damage, the entire building—both the damaged and undamaged portions—must be torn down before reconstruction begins. That will cost another $25,000.

"Ordinance or Law Coverage" would pay for all of these items.

6. Tenant's Insurance

If you're a tenant, read the insurance portion of your lease. You may have agreed to insure the building and protect the landlord against any liability suits based on your activities, in which case you'll need the type of coverage an owner would carry. This is available through a renter's commercial package policy, which also provides routine product liability coverage for businesses not involved in hazardous activities and allows you to name your landlord as an additional insured.

Even if you haven't agreed to provide insurance coverage in your lease, a renter's commercial policy can make excellent sense. Not only will it cover any of your "leasehold improvements," such as paneling and partitions, but it will also cover damage to the premises caused by your negligence. For example, if the building you rent suffers fire or water damage as a result of an employee's negligence (a fire in an area where food is prepared spreads and damages the walls and ceiling), you may be liable. This is true even if the building owner is insured and recovers from his or her insurance company, because the owner's insurer has the right to try to recover.

What the insurer will pay you for loss to leasehold improvements is based not on replacement value but on what's called the "use interest" in the improvements. Basically, the insurance company looks at how long you would have had the use of the improvements and reimburses you for the use you lose.

EXAMPLE: Court Reporting Associates (CRA) installs $20,000 worth of paneling in their rented offices. They have a five-year lease with an option to renew for five more years—which, for insurance purposes, is treated as a ten-year lease. Two years into the lease, a fire destroys the paneling. Because CRA used up 20% of the lease before the fire, it will receive payment for only 80% of value of the paneling.

Insurance clauses in leases vary widely. (See Chapter 13, Section D13, for more on such clauses.)

C. Liability Insurance

The second major category of insurance coverage for a small business is liability insurance. Your business can be legally liable to people injured and for property damaged because you or your employees didn't use reasonable care. For example, if a customer falls on a slippery floor and then sues you, you may be liable because you negligently failed to provide safe premises.

As you probably know, when it comes to personal injuries, judges are broadening the scope of what people can sue for—and juries are increasingly generous in awarding damages. Because an injured person can collect not only for lost wages and medical bills but also for such intangibles as pain, suffering and mental anguish, a single personal injury verdict against your business has the potential to wipe it out. For that reason, unless you have a very unusual business that has no personal contact with customers, suppliers or anyone else, your insurance program should include liability coverage.

Some intentional acts not involving bodily injuries are also usually covered under the liability portions of an insurance policy. Examples are libel, slander, defamation, false imprisonment and false arrest.

Toxic Waste Clean-Up

Suppose the government orders your company to clean up a toxic waste problem on your property. This can and regularly does occur even if the pollution occurred years before you bought the property. Will your liability insurance policy cover the clean-up costs (called the "response costs")? Most courts that have considered this question ruled that response costs are covered by a liability insurance policy, but a significant minority have ruled otherwise. If you have a business or own property that by any stretch of the imagination could become involved in a toxic waste or pollution problem, try to find out exactly how far your liability coverage extends in environmental situations. You may need to buy supplementary coverage (if available and affordable) to cover this risk.

Keep yourself informed on this subject. It's likely that, faced with court decisions saying that general liability coverage requires insurance companies to pay for response costs under clean-up orders, insurance companies will tighten up their policy language to exclude these expenses. You may need to buy special coverage if your business faces the possibility of a clean-up order.

1. General Liability Policies

Liability policies are designed to protect you against lawsuit judgments up to the amount of the policy limit plus the cost of defending the lawsuit. They provide coverage for a host of common perils, including customers and guests falling and getting mangled by your front door or otherwise being injured. Liability policies usually state a dollar limit per occurrence and an aggregate dollar limit for the policy year. For example, your policy may say that it will pay $500,000 per occurrence for personal injury or a total of $1 million in any one policy year.

⚠️ **Excluded claims.** *Punitive damages— damages intended to punish your business for willful or malicious behavior rather than compensate the injured person—are not covered by the typical general liability policy. And liability coverage won't protect your business if an employee intentionally assaults a customer. In addition, a general liability policy doesn't cover injuries caused by defective products or motor vehicles, or by an employer's liability for injuries received by workers on the job. Special coverage for these types of liability is discussed in the next three subsections.*

As noted, both building owners and tenants may purchase liability coverage separately or as part of a package policy that also provides a number of other types of insurance, including fire insurance for the building itself.

2. Product Liability Insurance

Product liability insurance covers liability for injuries caused by products you design, manufacture or sell. You may be liable to a person injured by a defective product or one that came without adequate instructions or warnings. Product liability insurance can be very expensive, but if your business manufactures, distributes or sells a product that may injure people, you should seriously consider buying it. For example, if you manufacture medical instruments or chemicals, you'll probably want this coverage. If you're a retailer and sell products in their original packages and provide no product assembly or service or advice, your exposure is drastically reduced; the manufacturer is primarily liable and the product liability coverage provided by standard renter's commercial policies should be adequate.

The amount of product liability insurance that you need depends on the nature of your product and not on your gross sales. Obviously, a company that sells $2 million of paper clips a year will need less coverage than a firm that manufactures gauges critical to the safe operation of heaters and also has $2 million worth of sales annually.

3. Vehicle Insurance

Make sure your business carries liability insurance not only on its own cars and trucks but also on employees' cars and trucks when those vehicles are used for business purposes. This coverage is known as Employer's Non-Owned Automobile Liability and is relatively inexpensive—a premium of $65 to $100 may buy you coverage of $1 million for one year. Vehicle insurance isn't provided under general liability policies.

It wouldn't hurt to check your employees' driving records before you entrust company vehicles to them or send them on business errands using their own cars, but failure to check won't be a problem under most vehicle policies unless the insurance company has listed that employee as an excluded driver. To do this, insurance companies periodically ask businesses for the names of employees who are driving on company business. They then check the names against state driving records. If this results in the discovery of a poor driving record for a particular employee, the insurer will likely exclude that driver from coverage and notify you.

Coverage for injury or property damage while using leased vehicles can be added to either your motor vehicle policy or your general liability policy—which is what a company would do if it owned no vehicles. This is known as Hired Vehicle coverage.

Most vehicle policies also cover physical damage to the car or truck caused by collision, fire or theft.

4. Workers' Compensation Insurance

As the name implies, workers' compensation insurance covers your liability for injuries received by employees on the job. All businesses with employees are required to provide for some kind of workers' compensation coverage.

Usually, an injured worker can't sue your business for negligence. But as a trade-off, he or she can collect specified benefits from your business for work-related injuries whether or not the business was negligent. All the worker must prove is that the injury came about in the course of employment—a concept that has a very broad definition in many states. For example, an employee injured at a company picnic may have a valid workers' compensation claim.

The amount of money that the employee can recover is limited. The worker can recover for medical treatment and lost wages and, in serious cases, for impaired future earning capacity. But there are no awards for pain and suffering or mental anguish. A growing portion of workers' compensation claims, however, result from mental or emotional stress. In California, an employee who proves that as little as 10% of his or her disability was caused by job-related stress can qualify for worker's compensation benefits.

As a sole proprietor, you usually can't be personally covered by workers' compensation insurance for any work-related injuries you sustain; only your employees can be covered. Workers' comp coverage of a partner or of an officer of a small corporation usually isn't required but can be obtained if you choose.

Each state has a law setting out what an employer must do to provide for workers' compensation benefits. Sometimes an employer can self-insure. Usually, that isn't practical for small businesses because they can't afford the type of cash reserve required by state law. Most small businesses buy insurance through a state fund or from a private insurance carrier. Insurance rates are based on the industry and occupation, as well as the size of the payroll. Your business's safety record can also influence the rate; if you have more accidents than are usually anticipated, your rate is likely to be increased.

Although workers' compensation laws cover virtually all injury claims by an employee against an employer, in a few instances employees can still sue an employer for pain and suffering resulting from a work-related injury. For example, in some states, an employer whose gross negligence or intentional conduct caused an injury can be sued. A second part of a workers' compensation policy (sometimes called Coverage B or employer's liability) insures the employer against liability for these types of claims. I recommend policy limits of $500,000 for most businesses for this coverage.

Workers' compensation insurance is required only for employees—not for independent contractors. (Independent contractors are covered in greater detail in Chapter 15, Section P.) Small businesses sometimes buy services from independent contractors to save money on workers' compensation insurance, as well as taxes and other expenses normally associated with employees. That's fine as long as you correctly label people as independent contractors rather than employees. But if you make a mistake, and a person improperly labeled as an independent contractor is injured while doing work for your business, you may have to pay large sums to cover medical bills and lost wages which should have been covered by workers' compensation insurance.

In addition, you can sometimes have a problem with a properly classified independent contractor who hires employees to perform some work for you. If you hire an independent contractor who has employees, insist on seeing a certificate of insurance establishing that the employees are covered by workers' compensation insurance.

EXAMPLE: You hire Sharon, who is doing business as Superior Painters, to paint your store. Sharon will be doing the work along with two of her employees. If Sharon doesn't carry workers' compensation insurance for her employees, and any of them are injured on the job, they may be treated as your employees, which would increase your own workers' compensation premiums. Also, have Sharon show you that she has general liability coverage; if she or one of her employees injures one of your customers while painting your store, such injuries may not be covered by your own insurance.

The Expanding Boundaries of Workers' Comp

Premiums for workers' compensation insurance are on the rise—partly because judges are extending the types of claims for which workers can receive payment. A key factor in many cases is stressful working conditions. Money has been awarded to:

- A worker who suffered a heart attack after an argument with his boss.
- A truck driver who blacked out while driving and was then unable to drive because of anxiety that he might black out again.
- A worker who fainted, fell and suffered a head injury after his supervisor told him he would be transferred to a new department and had to take a pay cut.

Judges have also expanded the right to receive workers' comp in other situations. For example, benefits were awarded to the family of a convenience store clerk who died after getting into a fist fight with a disorderly customer. And a woman who bought a cold tablet from her employer received payments when the tablet caused her to have tremors due to a congenital condition.

In another case, a cocktail waitress at a resort was on her way home when she stopped to help a resort guest who was having car trouble. The guest sexually assaulted her. The waitress was awarded workers' comp for injuries she received in the assault. The court's reasoning: The waitress had been told to be "very cordial and nice to guests." Therefore, her offer of assistance on the road was related to her employment.

D. Other Insurance to Consider

There are many forms of business insurance on the market today. You won't need them all, but some specialized coverage may make sense for your business.

1. Bonds Covering Employee Theft

If you're seriously concerned that employees might embezzle money from the business, look into bonds that cover all workers, including those hired after the bond goes into effect. Then, if an employee steals from you, the bonding company reimburses you for the loss.

2. Crime Coverage

Crime insurance covers losses when the criminal isn't connected with your business. Your policy should cover not only burglary and robbery but also other thefts and loss or disappearance of property. Depending on the kind of business and the part of the country you're in, you may be more concerned about losses by theft than from fire. Computers and other high-tech equipment are relatively lightweight and easy to carry away. A mid-sized publisher or word processing company, for example, could easily suffer a $100,000 loss in a night if its computers were stolen.

Usually, your company's business insurance covers only property owned by the company, not your personal property.

> **EXAMPLE:** Management Concepts Inc., a small consulting firm, is using an expensive computer that's the personal property of Patricia, the corporation's president. If the computer is stolen from the corporate offices, the corporation's insurance policy normally won't cover it. To protect against this kind of problem, Patricia should sign a Bill of Sale formally transferring legal title to the computer to the corporation. Or she should make sure that the corporation has an insurance policy that specifically protects property of officers or employees that's used in the business.

Probably the most convenient way to insure your business against loss by theft is to purchase the Special Form of property insurance, which includes such coverage. (See Section B2.)

If property is stolen from your business, you will, of course, have to document the loss. I recommend that you keep a computerized list of your business property, updated periodically. And keep a copy at home or in a fireproof box in case the computer and your records get stolen or destroyed.

3. Business Interruption Insurance

If your business property is damaged or destroyed and you can't use it, your business losses will far exceed the cost of repairing or replacing the damaged property. Your business may be unable to function until you can find a new location and purchase more goods. For example, if you're in California and an earthquake levels your retail warehouse, or if your business is in Indiana and a tornado rips the roof off your store, or a fire burns you out, you may be out of business for weeks or months while your inventory is replaced and new buildings are located.

Business interruption insurance—a valuable but often overlooked kind of insurance—is intended to cover your lost income while your business is closed, as well as the expenses you incur in keeping your business going while the lost property is repaired or replaced. This insurance coverage also pays the cost of renting temporary quarters. It's also possible to guard against losses if your business is interrupted because disaster strikes someone else.

> **EXAMPLE:** Tom operates a small bakery. Half of his income comes from supplying bread, rolls and pastry to a large restaurant. If the restaurant burns down, Tom's income will be drastically reduced. He might sensibly look into business interruption insurance that covers not only losses that would occur should his property be damaged but also those that would result if a major supplier or customer were suddenly forced to stop or curtail operation.

Before you buy business interruption insurance, run through a contingency plan of what you'd do in case of a disaster. Let's say that your warehouse were destroyed by fire. Assuming the contents of the warehouse were covered by your fire or multi-peril insurance, you need worry only about how much it will cost you to be out of business until you can set up a temporary warehouse and get more merchandise. Could you replace key merchandise quickly and take other steps to minimize the harm? If it's reasonable to believe that you'll be partially back in business in a couple of weeks and be in fairly good shape within 30 days, business interruption insurance might not really be worth the cost.

Will Your Customers Come Through?

Ben runs a successful bookstore. His inventory is covered, by a multi-peril contract, from loss from most hazards. But he worries that if he is burned out of his historic building, it might take a year or more to get repairs approved and made. Ben asks his insurance broker whether or not business interruption insurance makes sense.

After establishing that Ben could get new merchandise within a couple of weeks because book wholesalers and publishers would be anxious to help (Ben's credit is good), the broker recommends against it, pointing out that within a mile of Ben's building there are a dozen empty stores that Ben could rent very reasonably and be back in business almost immediately. The fact that Ben's loyal customers would likely support him after a disaster might even mean that sales would go up.

4. Industry-Specific Insurance

Supplementary insurance policy packages are often available for retail or manufacturing businesses, or even for specific types of businesses—a bookstore, barber shop or restaurant—and can be well worth looking into. For example, a manufacturing policy may have broader coverage for losses caused by malfunctioning equipment and machinery than a standard Special Form policy.

These additional resources might be helpful:
• Insuring Your Business, *by Sean Mooney (Insurance Information Institute Press). This is a well-written and comprehensive resource that contains many helpful suggestions. The Insurance Information Institute also offers other publications and free online information—see its website at www.iii.org.*
• Insurance Law in a Nutshell, *by John F. Dobbyn (West Wadsworth), is a concise statement of the basic legal principles. It's written primarily for law students, but useful to business people as well.*

E. Saving Money on Insurance

This chapter is based on the sensible premise that few businesses can really afford to adequately insure themselves against every possible risk. You need to decide what types of insurance are really essential and how much coverage to buy. While this is no easy task, here are some guidelines that should help.

1. Set Priorities

Start by looking at what coverage is required by state law. For example, there may be minimum requirements for coverage on business-related vehicles, and you will almost surely be required to carry workers' compensation insurance if you have employees.

Next, if you rent, you'll need to purchase any insurance required by your lease. See Section B6, above, and Chapter 13, Section D13, for a discussion of insurance language in a lease.

Beyond the required coverages for your business, ask these questions: What types of property losses would threaten the viability of my business? What kinds of liability lawsuits might wipe me out? Use your answers to tailor your coverage to protect against these potentially disastrous losses.

Be less concerned about insuring against smaller losses. For example, if you're in the self-help publishing business, consider a package especially tailored to printers and publishers that includes liability coverage for errors and omissions (such as leaving some vital information out of an instruction booklet you publish), but be less concerned about protecting yourself against claims of libel—after all, your material never comments on personalities.

2. Increase the Amount of Your Deductibles

Deductibles are used primarily for real and personal property insurance, including motor vehicle collision coverage. The difference between the cost of a policy with a $250 deductible and one with a $500 or $1,000 or even higher deductible is significant—particularly if you add up the premium savings for five or ten years. For example, the difference between a $250 and a $500 deductible may be 10% in premium costs, and the difference between a $500 and $1,000 deductible may save you an additional 3% to 5%. Most businesses can afford to be out of pocket $500 or even $1,000—especially if taking this risk means you pay significantly lower premiums. Consider using money saved with a higher deductible to buy other types of insurance where it's really needed. For example, the amount you save by having a higher deductible might pay for business interruption coverage.

3. Initiate Loss Prevention and Risk Reduction Measures

Good safety and security measures may eliminate the need for some types of insurance or lead to lower insurance rates. Ask your insurance agent what you can do to get a better rate. Sometimes something simple like installing deadbolt locks or buying two more fire extinguishers will qualify you for a lower premium. Here are some other ideas to cut losses and premiums.

- Install a fire alarm system, if one can be found at a reasonable cost.
- Install fireproofing materials to minimize fire damage in susceptible areas of the premises.
- Isolate and safely store flammable chemicals and other products.
- Provide adequate smoke detectors.
- Install a sprinkler system.

Ideas for preventing theft include:
- Install tamper-proof locks.
- Purchase a secure safe.
- Install an alarm system.
- Install better lighting.
- Hire a security service to patrol your property at night.

Also consider placing bars on doors or windows. This may create a negative impression; an innovative architect or contractor may be able to help you design and install these security devices in ways that are not unsightly.

To prevent injuries to customers, employees or members of the public, you might:
- Check each applicant's driving record and not hire people to drive who have poor records.
- Give additional training to drivers you do hire.
- Set up a system for safer operation of machinery.
- Conduct fire drills.
- Give your employees protective clothing and goggles if necessary.

Although how to protect against some types of risks may be obvious to you, how to protect against many others won't be. Get help from people who are experienced in identifying and dealing with risks. One excellent resource is your insurance company's safety inspector; your insurance agent can tell you whom to contact.

Another good approach is to ask your employees to identify all safety risks, no matter how small. Also ask them to propose cost-effective ways to eliminate or minimize them—they may have cheaper and more practical ideas than you do.

EXAMPLE: Adventure Apparel Corporation sells recreational and travel clothing by mail order from its well-stocked warehouse. The 25 employees of the corporation all take turns serving on the safety committee, which meets regularly to discuss safety issues ranging from the best way to operate computer terminals to reduce the possibility of repetitive motion injuries to making sure that the electric pallet lifters are run only by trained people. The system works because the employees are in a unique position to monitor safety hazards and to suggest practical solutions.

In the long run, a safety program will reduce your losses and, in turn, lower your insurance rates. In the short term, simply putting these practices into effect and letting insurance companies know about them may put you in a lower rate category. And of course, your employees will appreciate the care you show for their well-being—a significant plus in a world where keeping good employees is a real business asset.

4. Comparison Shop

No two companies charge exactly the same rates; you may be able to save a significant amount by shopping around. But be wary of unusually low prices—it may be a sign of a shaky company (see Section A for information on how to check out an insurance company). Or it may be that you're unfairly comparing policies that provide very different types of coverage. Make sure you know what you're buying.

Review your coverage and rates periodically. The insurance industry is cyclical, with alternating phases of low prices and high prices. When competition for insurance customers increases in a particular field, you really can achieve savings. But don't dump a loyal agent for a few cents. Ask your agent to look around and meet or come close to meeting the competition.

You can make the cyclical nature of the insurance industry work for you. If you're shopping for insurance during a time when prices are low, try locking in a low rate by signing up for a contract for three or more years.

5. Transfer Some Risks to Someone Else

Here are some possibilities:

- *Indemnification by manufacturer.* Suppose you run a store that sells exercise equipment, and primarily from one manufacturer. If you're

buying a significant amount of equipment, the manufacturer may be willing to provide insurance that indemnifies your business from any claim by a customer injured by the equipment.
- *Leasing employees.* Some businesses lease employees at least in part because the leasing company takes care of carrying workers' compensation and liability insurance on the employees (among other things); but be cautious—the overall cost of leasing employees may be greater than if you hire directly. You may also to be able to transfer some risks by simply engaging independent contractors to handle the more hazardous aspects of your business operations. (See Chapter 15.)

6. Find a Comprehensive Package

Look for a small business package that includes a full range of coverage. This is often much cheaper than buying coverage piecemeal from several different companies. Group plans often offer these packages.

7. Seek Out Group Plans

Is there a trade association in your industry? If so, it may be a source of good insurance coverage. Trade associations often get good affordable insurance rates for the members because they have superior bargaining power.

8. Self-Insure

Using this technique, you simply don't buy insurance and hope to maintain your own reserve fund to cover likely losses or liabilities. There are two drawbacks. First, despite good intentions, most small businesses don't have enough funds to set aside for this purpose. Second, unlike insurance premiums, money put into a reserve fund isn't tax-deductible until or unless you spend it.

F. Making a Claim

As soon as a loss occurs, gather and preserve evidence to help prove your claim if it becomes necessary. (If you followed my suggestion and have a comprehensive list of your property, get it out now.) Take pictures of any damaged property. Collect documents such as receipts showing what you paid for the lost property. If you can, secure the damaged property in a safe place so that it will be available for inspection later and for possible use in a lawsuit. Gather names of any witnesses who can help substantiate how the loss occurred and the extent of the damage.

Your next step is to request a claim form from your insurance agent. For small, routine losses you or someone else in your company can probably complete the form, with a little help from your agent. If more money is at stake, a lawyer can help you structure and justify your claim. (See Chapter 24 for information on how to find and hire a good lawyer.)

Damage to Rented Space. If you're renting the space your business occupies, start by figuring out whose insurance policy covers the loss—yours or the building owner's. For example, if a pipe breaks, you'll have to look at both insurance policies to see which one covers this risk. Ideally, your insurance company will pay you for damage to your inventory and equipment, and the owner's insurance company will pay for damage to the building. To make this happen and avoid squabbles, it helps to have a "mutual waiver of subrogation" in your lease. Without it, you can get caught in the cross-fire between two insurance companies. (See Chapter 13, Section D13.)

Often there's a time limit on filing your claim, but you may need more time to analyze all of your damages. Don't feel rushed. Take the time you need. Simply file the claim form within the required time limit, listing the losses you're sure of at that time. Indicate that the list of losses is partial and that you're still gathering information.

If you're served with a lawsuit or are informed that an injured person is going to make a claim against your business, get the lawsuit papers and related information to your insurance company as soon as possible. Contact your agent promptly. ■

Negotiating a Favorable Lease

Almost all small businesses start out in leased premises; many businesses prefer to use leased space throughout their business lives. By leasing rather than owning, you avoid tying up valuable working capital. Also, it's easier to move to new quarters if your space needs change. This chapter looks at how to find the right place for your business and how to negotiate your lease.

For more information on commercial leases, see Leasing Space for Your Small Business, *by Janet Portman & Fred S. Steingold (Nolo).*

A. Finding a Place

Your first step is to find the right space. Begin by analyzing the specific needs of your business. Real estate professionals are fond of saying that the three most important factors in choosing a business space are location, location and location. For certain types of retail stores and restaurants, this may be true. For example, a sandwich shop requires a location with a high volume of foot traffic. Or maybe you'll benefit if you're near other businesses that are similar to yours; restaurants often like to locate in a restaurant district.

But for many other businesses, where you're located doesn't matter much. For example, if you repair bathroom tile, run a computer-based information search business, import jewelry from Bali or do any one of ten thousand other things, it won't help you to be in a high-visibility, high-rent district. Chances are your business can efficiently operate in a less pricey area, where you can negotiate a lower rent and the

landlord is likely to be far more flexible on other lease terms as well.

After you've analyzed what you need, it's time to begin searching for the right spot. Go to the neighborhoods where you might like to locate; spend a day or two driving or walking the streets to see what may be available. Don't just look for vacant space. A store, office, studio or workshop that's good for your business may be occupied by a tenant who is going out of business—or moving to larger quarters in a few months. If you find a desirable location, call the landlord to see if the space will be coming on the market soon. There's a lot of turnover among small businesses, and you may get lucky.

Because some of the best opportunities come to light through word of mouth, ask friends, associates and other business people if they know of available space. Business owners—particularly those in the part of town that you're interested in—may know of businesses that are moving or going out of business long before these vacancies are announced in newspaper ads. And if you get there early, the landlord, relieved that he or she can avoid a period of vacancy and uncertainty, may offer you a favorable lease.

For-rent ads in newspapers are an obvious place to look. If the selection there is limited, call a real estate office that deals primarily with business space. The agent's fee—usually, a percentage of the rent that you'll be paying—is generally paid by the landlord. If your space needs are special, consider hiring an agent to search the market for you. But if you follow this somewhat unusual approach, you'll probably have to pay the agent's commission.

B. Leases and Rental Agreements: An Overview

A lease is a contract between you and the landlord. A lease can be for a short term (as little as one month) or long term, and it can be written or oral—although a lease for more than a year must be in writing to be legally enforceable. Some people use the phrase "rental agreement" to describe a short or oral lease for which rent is typically paid once a month and the tenancy can be terminated on a 30-day written notice. (See Section C, below, for more on short-term leases.) To avoid confusion, I'll stick to the word "lease."

Terminology

Sometimes a written lease talks about the "Lessor" and the "Lessee." The lessor is the landlord; the lessee is the tenant. If you have a choice in terminology, go with the plain English "landlord" and "tenant"; you'll reduce the risk of typos!

In theory, all terms of a lease are negotiable. Just how far you can negotiate, however, depends on economic conditions. If desirable properties are close to full occupancy in your city, landlords may not be willing to negotiate with you over price or other major lease terms. On the other hand, in many parts of the country where commercial space has been overbuilt, landlords are eager to bargain with small businesses to fill empty units. Even in a tight market you may come across some acceptable space that, for one reason or another, the landlord is anxious to fill, giving you greater bargaining power. This is often true where there's a new building or one under construction and the landlord needs cash. Also, if you're one of the first tenants in the building, you may get an especially attractive deal, because your presence may help the landlord attract other tenants.

If you find a landlord willing to negotiate, what should you ask for? After you read Section D, you'll have a good understanding of the kinds of terms that usually go into a lease. Since you're not likely to get everything you want, it's important to get your priorities straight in your own mind and concentrate on achieving what's most important. What do you really care about? What would be nice to have but not essential? What benefits can you offer the landlord for things you really need?

A lower rent is likely to be high on everybody's bargaining list. But how about physical changes in the building? Would you want the landlord to redesign the entryway? Add some office space at the back of the warehouse? Customize the interior for your needs? More or better parking for your customers might be worth more than slightly lowered rent. Your priorities may be unique to your business, so think them through carefully before making proposals and counter-proposals to the landlord.

Let's look at how you might approach the matter of rent. A landlord who is reluctant to lower the basic rent may be willing make other adjustments—which may be even more valuable. The landlord might do this so he or she can truthfully tell other prospective tenants that you're paying a high dollar amount per square foot. (It may sound silly, but some landlords do play this game.) For example, in a slack market, the landlord may be willing to give you a move-in allowance. Also, check out what the landlord is willing to do in paying for improvements (often called build-outs) to the space. (See Section D9.)

C. Short-Term Leases (Month-to-Month Rentals)

Once you've found the space you want, the next step, usually, is to sign a lease. (See Section D.) Occasionally, a small business that's just starting out prefers an oral lease permitting the tenant to occupy the space from month to month. This might seem attractive if you just want to test the waters, have great uncertainty about the prospects for your business and wouldn't mind leaving on short notice if the landlord terminated the lease. But even if you only want to make a very short-term commitment, it almost always makes far more sense to negotiate a written month-to-month lease or rental agreement. A written lease clarifies what's been agreed to and helps avoid disputes.

Whether oral or written, the key feature of a month-to-month lease is that you can move—or the landlord can require you to move—on short notice.

You can negotiate how notice is required, but if you don't, the law in your state will dictate the amount of time. In many states, this is 30 days, although states don't always compute the time period in the same way. Some, such as California, allow either the landlord or tenant to give notice at any date during a month; the 30 days runs from the notice date. Other states require that the notice be given at least 30 days before the first day of the next monthly rental period; furthermore, the termination date must coincide with the beginning of a new period.

> **EXAMPLE:** Albert is a tenant under an oral month-to-month lease in Michigan. He and the landlord haven't agreed on a specific notice period, relying instead on the law in their state, which requires a 30-day notice. Albert pays his rent on the first of each month. On July 15, Albert's landlord notifies him that he's terminating the lease as of August 15. Does Albert have to move by August 15? No. He can stay until September 1. That's because under the court interpretations in his state, he's entitled to notice 30 days in advance of a full rental period. Because Albert's rental period begins on the first day of each month, he can't be kicked out in the middle of a month. He's entitled to stay for at least one full rental period. If the landlord wanted Albert out by mid-August, he should have given Albert his notice before July 1.

⚠ Notice requirements vary from state to state. *For information about what's required in your state, you'll need to check the statutes or case law. (Chapter 24 suggests ways to do basic legal research.)*

The clauses in a month-to-month lease, other than those dealing with the length of the tenancy, are much the same as those in any other written lease, so be sure to consult the following sections of this chapter.

D. Written Long-Term Leases

Many small businesses and landlords prefer the protection of a written lease that lasts a year or more. But when you talk to the landlord, you'll probably be presented with a typed or printed lease prepared by the landlord or the landlord's lawyer. Because the terms typically favor the landlord, consider it as no more than the starting point. Chances are excellent that you'll be able to negotiate at least some significant improvements. Keep in mind that you have two sometimes conflicting goals: to get a favorable lease and to have a good long-term relationship with your landlord. In the interest of long-term harmony, there are times when it makes sense not to fight for the last scrap of a concession as if you were a starving pit bull.

To eliminate a proposed lease's one-sidedness, ask for equal treatment for you and the landlord for all clauses where this is relevant. For example, if the lease requires you to cure your lease defaults within ten days after you receive notice from the landlord, it should also require the landlord to cure his or her defaults within ten days after you give notice. Similarly, if you're required to pay for your landlord's attorney fees in enforcing the lease, the landlord should be required to pay for your attorney fees if you have to enforce the lease.

Now let's look at some common lease terms and how you might approach them.

📄 *Chapter 6 of* Legal Forms for Starting & Running a Small Business *contains various commercial lease forms.*

1. Who Should Sign the Lease?

Leases begin by naming the landlord and the tenant. Make sure that the person, partnership or corporation named as landlord is the owner of the property. Although this may seem to go without saying, believe me, it often doesn't. A husband may not have legal authority to sign leases for space in a building owned solely by his wife. A management company or on-site manager may have only day-to-day management powers that fall short of the right to approve new leases. Or if they can sign a lease, they may be able to offer only certain terms and concessions. If you have any doubts about whom you're dealing with and what authority they have, ask to see a deed or title insurance policy to verify that the named landlord really owns the building. Here are the rules about who's authorized to sign a binding lease on behalf of the landlord:

- If a building owned is by an individual, that person (or an authorized agent) should sign the lease.
- If a building is owned by a general partnership, insist on the signature of one of the partners.
- If a building is owned by a limited partnership (not uncommon for rental properties), require the signature of a general (managing) partner; a limited partner usually lacks the power to bind the partnership.
- If a building is owned by a corporation, get the signature of a corporate officer or an executive with authority to sign leases.
- If you're dealing with a rental agent who will be negotiating the lease and signing it on behalf of the owner, ask for written confirmation from the owner that the agent has that authority. Obviously, you need to worry less about this step if the rental agent is part of an established and respected real estate management company, but it never hurts to request documentation.

Who should be named as the tenant? Before you sign a lease as an individual or a partner, be aware that you'll be personally liable for the rent if your business runs into financial problems. If your business fails, the landlord can (and probably will) go after your personal assets such as your car, home and bank account. To avoid this exposure, consider incorporating. Then you can sign the lease as President of XYZ Inc.—and you're personally off the hook. (Personal liability for business debts is discussed in Chapter 1.)

Beware of personal guarantees. *In addition to signing in your corporate capacity, you may be asked to personally guarantee the lease. Doing this makes you personally responsible for the rent and means that the corporation doesn't shield your personal assets. One approach is to offer to guarantee the lease only up to a maximum amount—say, three months worth of rent. For even greater protection, see if the landlord is willing to release you from your personal guarantee if all rent is paid on time during the first year.*

2. Defining the Space You're Leasing

The lease should identify the space that you'll be occupying. If you're leasing the whole building, that's easy: simply give the street address. If you're leasing less than the whole building, specify your space more precisely. One way is to refer to building or floor plan drawings. For example, you might say "Suite 2 of the Commerce Building as shown on the attached drawing" or "The south half of the first floor of the Entrepreneur Plaza."

In describing the space you'll be occupying, don't overlook the common areas—space you'll be sharing with other tenants. This often includes hallways, rest rooms, elevators, storage space and parking. Spell out in your lease that your business (and your customers) have the right to use these additional spaces and facilities. If your business keeps unusual hours, remember to define when you have access to your space and the common spaces. You don't want to find yourself locked out some evening or weekend.

Because commercial space is often priced by the square foot, find out what method is used to compute square footage. Sometimes it's measured from the exterior of the walls or from the middle of walls' thickness. If this is the case, you'll be paying for some space that's not really usable. This isn't necessarily bad. But you need to find out about it in advance, because it affects rent negotiations.

The square footage rate is usually stated in annual terms—$20 a square foot means $20 per square foot per year. However, it's sometimes stated by the month—$.60 a square foot means 60 cents per square foot per month. Obviously you need to know exactly what any numbers you're quoted mean. Also find out if the quoted figure applies only to the space occupied by your business or whether you're expected to pay for a proportionate share of the common areas. If your rent is computed on the basis of dollars per square foot, and if you're asked to pay for a share of the common areas, it's reasonable to seek a lower square footage rate for common areas.

If your landlord has agreed to set aside some parking spaces for your business or to let you use a storage building or other outbuilding, get it in writing in the lease. Also specify if indoor storage space will be shared or is reserved exclusively for your use.

3. Starting Date of the Lease

Your lease should clearly state its starting date. This can sometimes be a problem, especially if you're renting space in a building that's still under construction or space currently occupied. If you sign a lease before ground has been broken or if the building is only partially complete, what happens if your space isn't ready by the time you need it? This too should be addressed in your lease. Otherwise there may be little pressure on the landlord to meet deadlines. One possibility is to negotiate a cut-off date by which you have the right to cancel the lease if the building (or your unit) isn't ready for occupancy. You may also be able to collect damages from the landlord if you suffer losses because your space isn't ready on time. But in negotiating such a clause, remember it's always hard to prove lost profits—particularly if you're just starting out in business—so it's better to negotiate a pre-set amount for your damages.

Also, with a building to be constructed or under construction, state in your lease that until local building officials have issued a certificate of occupancy for the building, no rent will be due. You

may think that this is so obvious it doesn't need to be spelled out in your lease, but some landlords have actually tried to collect rent even before building officials have approved the building for occupancy.

In a slight variation on this problem, some leases call for the landlord to erect a shell building. Then you, the tenant, finish off your own space. Obviously, you want to avoid having to install improvements in a partially constructed building, which may not be completed for many months. One good solution: a lease clause saying you don't have to start work on your space until the building is enclosed and the common areas—such as hallways and rest rooms—are done. The lease could also require the landlord to have the building and safety department make a preliminary inspection of your space before you start making improvements. The inspection would make sure the landlord has correctly installed the electrical and plumbing lines, and heating, ventilating and air-conditioning facilities within your leased space. You don't want to risk the possibility that you'll have to rip out and redo your interior work because the landlord's contractor made a mistake.

With space that's currently vacant, ask the landlord to agree to let you have immediate access to decorate and install equipment. That way, you'll be ready to do business when you start paying rent. Spell this out in the lease.

4. Ending Date of the Lease

The lease should state its termination date, although you may have an option to renew. (See Section 5.) Some leases state that if the tenant remains in possession after the termination without exercising an option to renew, the tenancy is from month to month during the holdover period. (See Section C for information on month-to-month tenancies.)

5. An Option to Renew a Lease

When you first negotiate a lease, you can often bargain for a clause that gives you the right to renew or extend your lease when its term ends. Let's say you're negotiating a new two-year lease. You like the location, the rent is favorable and you'd like the right to stay for an extended period if your business is doing well. But at the same time, you're nervous about signing a four-year lease in case your business doesn't prosper. A two-year lease that includes an option to renew for two more years may be ideal. Typically, you exercise an option to stay by notifying your landlord in writing a set number of days or months before the lease expires. The amount of notice required is negotiable.

Getting the landlord to include an option in your lease may not be easy. Put yourself in the landlord's shoes. You might well go for a firm commitment from the tenant for eight years with adequate rent increases built in. You'd find it less attractive to grant a series of successive two-year options, which introduce an element of uncertainty—they allow the tenant the right to stay if the location turns out to be profitable but to leave if it's a dud. Not surprisingly, as a landlord, you'd look for some economic incentive to make the deal more attractive.

Now that you understand the landlord's point of view, you won't be too surprised if you find that the rent rate for a short lease with an option to renew is more than the rate you can lock in with a long-term lease. Also, the landlord will likely want a higher rent for the renewal period, either in a fixed amount or an increase tied to a cost-of-living index.

⚠ Drawbacks of options to renew. *An option to renew isn't always a good idea. If your business isn't particularly sensitive as to its location (maybe you publish a newsletter on how to raise fish or sell advertising for trade shows), think twice before you waste bargaining clout or pay extra for an option to renew. Sure, you may have to move, but in a high-vacancy climate, you might even find space with a lower rent.*

LAW IN THE REAL WORLD
Know the Fine Print

Charlie bought a copy shop in a high-traffic location. There was only one year left on the three-year lease, but the lease contained an option to renew for an additional three years at a slightly higher—though still favorable—rent. The landlord consented to an assignment of the lease and Charlie took over the business. Things went well. Charlie decided to stay at the location.

Nine months after Charlie took over the business, the landlord came by for a casual chat. Charlie mentioned his plans for the coming year, including some marketing ideas. "Sounds good," the landlord said, "but you'll have a new address. I'm planning to move you to a spot around the corner on the second floor." Charlie was stunned. The new space would be much less visible to the public—and Charlie's business depended on walk-in customers.

Fortunately, Charlie had the presence of mind to dig out his lease. There, nestled in the fine print, was an option clause. All that Charlie had to do was to notify the landlord in writing, at least 60 days before the original lease expired, that he was exercising his option to stay on in the same space. A quick look at the calendar confirmed that Charlie had more than enough time to give the written notice. To be on the safe side, he quickly sent his notice to the landlord by certified mail (return receipt requested)—and thereby averted a financial disaster. For Charlie, the option clause meant the difference between success and failure.

6. The Right to Expand

If future expansion is a good possibility, you may want the lease to give you the right to add adjacent space or to move to larger quarters in the building.

Sometimes this is done through a right of first re-fusal—the landlord promises in the lease that before any other vacant space is rented to someone else, the landlord must offer it to you on the same terms and conditions.

7. Rent

Leases usually state the rent on a monthly basis, for example, $1,000 per month, and indicate when pay-ment is due—typically the first of the month in ad-vance. The lease may also say that the rent for your two-year lease is $24,000 payable in monthly install-ments of $1,000 per month on the first of the month. Sometimes there's a late charge if you're more than a few days late.

This isn't the only way to compute rent. Depend-ing on the type of building and local custom, here are the main ways that the rental amount is set:

- *Gross leases*. These require the tenant to pay a flat monthly amount. The landlord pays for all operating costs for the building—taxes, insur-ance, repairs and utilities. Under one com-mon variation, the tenant pays for its own electricity, heat and air conditioning; if your lease uses this method and you are in a build-ing with other tenants, see if there are sepa-rate meters available so that you can control these costs. If not, ask to see copies of the bills—you don't want to agree to pay for utili-ties if someone else in the building runs up huge bills.
- *Net leases*. The tenant must pay a monthly base rent plus some or all of the real estate taxes. If you sign this kind of lease and you're leasing just a portion of the building, make sure that the portion of the real estate taxes allocated to your space is fair.
- *Net-net leases*. This type goes farther and re-quires the tenant to pay the base rental amount plus real estate taxes and the landlord's insurance on the space you occupy (which is different from your own liability insurance,

discussed in Chapter 12). In a standard lease, the landlord insures the entire building against property damage caused by fire, flooding and the weather, as well as negli-gence and vandalism. The landlord's insurance also covers claims against the landlord brought by people injured on the property. In a net-net lease, the cost of this insurance is allo-cated among the tenants, usually on the basis of the proportion of space each one occupies.

- *Net-net-net ("triple net") leases*. The tenant pays the base rental amount plus the landlord's operating costs, including taxes, insurance, repairs and maintenance. Such leases are not often used for space rented by a small busi-ness, but there are exceptions, such as store-fronts in popular areas of large cities.
- *Percentage leases*. These leases are used most commonly for retailers in a shopping mall. The tenant pays base rent plus a percentage of gross income. (See Section F for a discus-sion of shopping center leases.)

If the lease is for more than one year, the land-lord may want to build in a rent increase for future years. For example, a three-year lease may provide for rent of $1,000 per month in year one, $1,100 in year two and $1,200 per month in year three. Some-times the increase is tied to some external measure, such as the Consumer Price Index. If the CPI in-creases 5% during the base year, so does your rent in year two.

Some landlords want the rent to be increased if their taxes or maintenance costs go up. If you're moving into a new building and the landlord pro-poses this last kind of formula, be particularly care-ful. No one really knows what operating costs will be in this situation—they may jump 50%. You'll at least want to negotiate a cap on how much the rent can go up because of increased operating costs.

As emphasized throughout this chapter, leases are normally negotiable. For example, depending on market conditions, you may be able to convince the landlord to turn a triple net lease into a gross lease. Or the landlord may be willing to put a cap on the amount of taxes, insurance and maintenance costs you'll have to pay. If vacancies rates are high, the landlord may be willing to give you a few months of free rent in return for your agreeing to take the space on a triple net basis.

8. Security Deposit

Landlords commonly request a security deposit in the amount of the last month's rent plus an additional amount equal to a half month's or full month's rent. So if your rent is $1,000 per month, you may have to cough up $2,500 to $3,000 before you take possession—$1,000 for the first month and $1,500 to $2,000 for the security deposit. This is all negotiable.

Ask the landlord to hold the security deposit in an interest-bearing bank account for your benefit. If you're concerned about the landlord's solvency, you might go farther and suggest that the security deposit be held in escrow by a third party—but don't be surprised if the landlord balks at either suggestion.

The security deposit is intended to cover unpaid rent if you move out early and any damage you cause during your occupancy over and above normal wear and tear. Usually, your right to be free from liability for normal wear and tear is recognized under state law; you don't have to worry about this unless the lease the landlord proposes tries to make you responsible for it. So if your lease obligates you to return your space "in tip-top condition," you'll want to ask for a change. Similarly, it's normally considered unreasonable for the landlord to require you to pay to repaint the space before you move out or install new carpeting—unless, of course, you caused an unusual amount of damage.

9. Improvements by the Landlord

Unless you rent a recently remodeled space designed for a business such as yours, the space will often need to be fixed up or modified before it's suitable for your use. At the inexpensive end of the

spectrum, you may need only a few coats of paint on the walls, or perhaps to have the carpet cleaned. At the big bucks end of the spectrum, you might need hundreds of thousands of dollars' worth of improvements before you could open an elegant new restaurant (for up-to-date kitchen equipment and an appealing decor) or a small manufacturing facility (pollution control equipment and a loading dock). In between these two extremes, your business might need more lighting and electrical outlets, air conditioning or perhaps a partitioned office or work area. Who's going to pay for these things— you or the landlord? It's all negotiable.

Your lease should specify the improvements the landlord is to make. Ideally, the landlord should agree to have improvements in place before your move-in date. The next best thing is a stated deadline within the first months of your lease.

Try to get the landlord to agree to pay for all or most of these improvements. But be forewarned that the landlord's willingness to pick up the tab will depend on a number of factors including the condition of the building, your type of business, the extent and cost of the improvements, whether the improvements would be useful to a future tenant, the length of your lease and—very important—how much rent you'll pay. For example, if you're starting a fancy restaurant, the landlord isn't likely to make $200,000 of improvements—but this might change if you're a famous chef whom the landlord is counting on as an anchor tenant. But if you're opening a bookstore, the landlord may agree to install shelving for you. If the building is in bad repair, you can probably convince the landlord to put it in decent shape for you and maybe to make needed modifications in the process. If you're paying a hefty rent for five years, you can expect more than if you're signing up for one year at a low rent.

Improvements to leased space usually become the property of the landlord. (See the discussion of fixtures in Section 10.) This means that after you move out, future tenants will continue to use the space in its improved condition, and the landlord will continue to collect rent for the improved space.

In other words, if your improvements are sensible, the economic benefits to the landlord will outlast your lease. This is a good negotiating point; you shouldn't be expected to bear the major financial burden for improvements that have a long useful life. On the other hand, if you have specialized needs—for example, you're running a photo lab or a dance studio—and your darkroom or hardwood floor would be of limited value to most future tenants, don't expect the landlord to willingly pick up the costs of the improvements. The landlord may even want to charge you something to cover the cost of remodeling the space after you leave.

After you agree with the landlord on improvements, make sure the lease is clear on what's being done. Attach drawings and specifications so later there can be no doubt about what was promised. If extensive improvements are to be made, insist on drawings and specs prepared by an architect or construction specialist. Think about all your needs: partitions, special lighting, soundproofing, special floor coverings, painting, wall coverings, woodwork, cabinetry and so on. Many landlords can be very flexible and open to making improvements if you approach them before the lease is signed.

Here is some language you might include in the lease:

> Before the beginning of the lease term, Landlord, at its expense, will make improvements to the premises as set forth in Exhibit A (Plans and Specifications for Improvements). These improvements will be completed in a workmanlike manner and comply with all applicable laws, ordinances, rules and regulations of governmental authorities.

Improvements to raw space—particularly in a new building—are often called the "build-out." Sometimes the landlord offers a standard build-out to every tenant. For example, the build-out might include a certain grade of carpeting or vinyl floor covering; a particular type of drop-ceiling; a certain number of fluorescent lighting panels per square feet of floor space; and a specified number of feet of drywall partitions, with two coats of paint. Once you understand the landlord's standard build-out, see if you can get some upgrades or extras thrown in. You may wind up with better carpeting, more lighting or fancier woodwork.

If the landlord offers a build-out allowance based on the cost of the improvements (for example, up to $30 per square foot of rented space), see if you can negotiate a higher figure. Generally, the longer the lease, the better the deal you can negotiate on the build-out. This makes sense. With a lease of three or five years, the landlord has an incentive to do far more for you than if you sign up for only 12 months.

10. Making Improvements Yourself

You may want to make improvements or alterations that go beyond what the landlord is willing to provide. The lease proposed by the landlord may require the landlord's permission before you can make improvements or alterations to the premises. Meet this clause head on by submitting your plans to the landlord before you sign the lease—and don't sign unless you get approval.

Also, provide that the landlord won't unreasonably withhold consent to future improvements you may wish to make.

At the end of the lease, you may want to remove some of the items you've installed and take them to a new location. Leases sometimes prohibit the removal of improvements. The landlord has a legitimate concern in preventing you from removing items in a way that damages the space or impedes renting to a new tenant. If your lease doesn't spell out your rights, the state law on "fixtures" will normally say that anything you've attached has become part of the real estate and is therefore the landlord's property. This can lead to arguments. For example, who owns the window air-conditioner that you attached with metal brackets?

The best way to avoid argument is to specify what you can remove and what belongs to the landlord. List all items you'll want to remove—either in the lease itself (if there's room) or on an extra sheet attached to the lease. (See Section G for how to do this.) Even if you have permission to remove certain items, make sure that you install them so they can be removed later without damage to the building. It may cost a little more to install easy-to-remove shelves, cabinets, light fixtures and air conditioning units. In the long run, however, it will be well worth it, because you can keep these items without having to make extensive repairs to the landlord's property.

11. Compliance With the ADA

The federal Americans with Disabilities Act (ADA) makes both you and your landlord responsible for making the premises accessible to disabled people. You can work out the details in your lease. Here are some suggestions on how to proceed:

- Ask the landlord to state (lawyers say "warrant") that the building complies with the ADA, based on an ADA survey or audit performed by an engineer or architect.
- If the landlord will be making improvements, see if the landlord will agree to pay for fully complying with the ADA.
- Make sure that the costs of bringing common areas into compliance aren't passed along to you as part of the "CAM" (common area maintenance) charges.

To comply with the ADA, you or the landlord may need to provide accessible parking, and install ramps, wide entry doors and specially designed restrooms. Since some of these improvements may be costly, you'd like the landlord to foot as much of the bill as possible.

 Your obligations don't end with access to the building. *To meet ADA requirements, you may have to re-design your office's interior space to improve access for disabled customers and employees. For example, you may need to widen aisles so that people using wheelchairs, walkers and electric scooters have ample room to maneuver, and you may need to lower service counters for ease of access. Be sure to budget enough to cover these improvements—your landlord isn't likely to cover these costs. For more information on ADA compliance for business premises, check the U.S. Department of Justice website, www.usdoj.gov, where you can view or download several helpful publications.*

12. Zoning Laws, Permits and Restrictions on Use of the Space

If the lease says nothing about the use of the space, you can use it for any lawful purpose. However, leases are often quite specific about what you can and can't do. For example, if your business sells and repairs bicycles, the landlord may insist that the lease limit you to these activities. This may seem okay now, but what if you want to do other things in the future? Define the permitted uses broadly enough to encompass any needs you anticipate. A poster business, for example, might want to provide that the space can also be used for classes on making and framing posters. A private post office might want to be free to do photocopying, fax transmissions and the retail sale of greeting cards.

No lease or landlord can give you the right to do something that's prohibited under the zoning laws. So it's an excellent idea to check with your local building or zoning department to be sure your anticipated uses are permitted under the local zoning ordinance. A bicycle shop may not be permitted in an office zone, for example. In addition to zoning ordinances, other planning, building, safety and health ordinances can affect your intended use. An ordinance may require a certain number of off-street parking spaces for some types of businesses, an entrance accessible to handicapped people or a restroom for customers—a common requirement for a restaurant. (For more on this subject, see Chapter 7, Section D6.)

13. Required Insurance

Most landlords want their tenants to carry insurance to cover damage the tenant does to the building and injuries suffered by customers and other visitors on the premises. This is something that any business would be wise to do even if it weren't required by a lease. (Chapter 12 covers the types of insurance you should consider.) But when you get down to specifics, it can be one of the most complicated parts of the lease.

Look carefully at the policy limits the landlord wants you to carry. Is a $2 million liability policy reasonable for your business? Some landlords want you to buy a policy to cover the landlord's liability for injuries as well as your own. This is often considered unreasonable; bargain to eliminate such a requirement, if you can.

At the very least, your landlord should agree to pay for casualty insurance on the building so that funds are available to repair it if it's destroyed or damaged by a fire or windstorm. And if you're in an area where floods or earthquakes are common, insist that the landlord also include these nonstandard coverages.

With both you and your landlord buying insurance, there's always the possibility of unnecessary duplication of coverage. Ask for a copy of your landlord's policy and review it with your agent.

When a landlord and tenant each carry property insurance, you can run into complications because of the legal concept of "subrogation." Ordinarily, if an insurance company pays an insured business for damaged property, the company has the right to turn around and sue any third party that caused the damage. The insurance is said to be subrogated to the rights of the insured business to collect damages—in other words, the insurance company steps into the shoes of the insured business.

EXAMPLE: Pericles Corporation is a tenant in a building owned by Town Development Associates. Pericles carries insurance on its property and Town Development carries insurance on the building. One evening, employees of Pericles forget to turn off the coffee maker before leaving.

The coffee boils away, the machine overheats and a fire breaks out, seriously damaging the building, furniture and equipment of Pericles. Pericles' insurance company pays for replacement of the damaged furniture and equipment, and Town Development's insurance company pays for repair of the building. However, since the fire was caused by the negligence of a Pericles employee, Town Development's insurance company steps into the shoes of Town Development and sues Pericles to collect the money paid out to repair the building. In doing so, the insurance company is exercising its right of subrogation.

You can head off this kind of headache by including a clause such as the following in your lease:

> Mutual Waiver of Subrogation
>
> Landlord and Tenant release each other from any and all liability to each other for any loss or damage to property, including loss of income and demolition or construction expenses due to the enforcement of ordinance or law, caused by fire or any of the Extended Coverage or Special Coverage perils, even if such fire or other peril has been caused by the fault or negligence of the other party or anyone for whom such party may be responsible.

If you don't have such a clause in your lease and try to waive subrogation rights after a loss occurs, you may be out of luck. Most insurance policies provide that a waiver of rights is effective only if it is made in writing before a loss.

14. Subletting Your Space or Assigning the Lease

Someday you may want to share your space with another business. For example, if you run a toy store, you might want to rent a portion of your floor space to someone who sells children's books. You'd do this by subletting the space. When you sublet, you're still responsible to the landlord for paying the entire rent and honoring all other provisions of the lease. Obviously, subletting is of more concern with a long lease than with a short one.

Another possibility is that you'll want to move out of the space during the term of the lease, because you've found better space or you've decided to go out of business. If you found another tenant to take over your space, you could sublease the whole space to the new tenant; in that case, you'd still be responsible to the landlord under the lease. But ideally, you'd want to assign your lease to the new tenant. Assigning your lease takes you out of the picture entirely. The new tenant pays the landlord directly and you have no further liability under the lease.

Landlords often are reluctant to give tenants an unlimited right to assign their lease or sublet their space. They're afraid of winding up with an occupant who is a deadbeat or who may damage the property or who runs a business that will adversely affect the image of the building, making it harder to attract good tenants. A typical provision drafted by a landlord looks like this:

> Tenant agrees not to assign or transfer this lease
> or sublet the premises or any part of the
> premises without the written consent of Landlord.

In my opinion, such a clause is unfair from a tenant's point of view. To make it fairer, ask to add the following wording:

> Consent of Landlord will not be unreasonably
> withheld.

With this additional wording in your lease, if you find a reasonable occupant to sublet to, and the landlord refuses to let you sublet, courts will generally rule that you're off the hook for rent after you move out.

⚠ **Uncooperative landlords.** *If you find yourself with a landlord who objects to a subtenant you've found, check with your lawyer or do some research to learn your legal rights in your state.*

LAW IN THE REAL WORLD
When Corporate Status Comes in Handy

Elena formed a corporation called Elena's Mediterranean Deli Inc. As president of her new corporation, she signed a five-year lease for space in a popular food court. Buried in the lease's small print was a sentence that said the lease couldn't be assigned and the space couldn't be sublet without the landlord's permission.

A few years later, Elena wanted to sell her business to Arnold for a handsome profit. Arnold planned to continue running the business at the same location. Elena told the landlord about her plans to sell and sublet. The landlord, who wanted to install his nephew in Elena's space, objected, saying he wouldn't let Elena assign the lease or sublet the space. The landlord was willing to excuse Elena from the rest of the lease—but this wouldn't allow her to reap the profit from a sale of her business.

What to do? Fortunately, because the corporation rather than Elena was the tenant, the lease was legally a corporate asset. Elena realized that she didn't need to sublet or assign her lease. She sold the corporation to Arnold, which meant that the corporation—although owned by a new shareholder—was still the tenant. Elena used the profits to go to grad school.

---

15. The Landlord's Right to Enter Your Space

Some leases give the landlord a broad right to enter your premises at all times to make inspections or repairs. This is an unnecessary invasion of your privacy, and most landlords will settle for a more limited right of entry. It's reasonable to provide that the landlord can only enter your leased space during normal business hours, unless there's a genuine emergency, such as a burst pipe or electrical hazard.

Because repairs can be disruptive, you might also require the landlord to consult you before making repairs and schedule them for a mutually convenient time. For many businesses, this won't be a problem. But if repairs could be disastrous—for example, you're a doctor renting space for your allergy practice or the owner of a shop that assembles delicate electronic components—you'll want to tightly control when the landlord can repaint or install new carpeting.

A related issue comes up near the end of a lease. Does the landlord have an unlimited right to enter your place to show it to prospective tenants? Depending on the type of business you have, this can be disruptive and annoying. It's a good idea for your lease to limit this type of intrusion to a slow period (say, 9 a.m. to 11 a.m., Monday through Friday) and to require 24 hours' notice.

16. Signs

Many types of businesses need one or more external signs. Check the lease to see if it gives your landlord the right to disapprove signs before they go up. One way to be sure the landlord won't be unreasonable is to have your signs approved when you sign the lease. If you do, attach a drawing or photo of the signs to the lease so that there can't be any argument later about what you agreed on.

⚠ **Don't forget municipal sign ordinances.** *In some communities, signs are heavily regulated by ordinances which restrict their size, number, color and location. In a few communities, there are even limitations on the content of signs—for example, in a few places in Southern California, there are limits on the number of non-English words you can use. So besides providing for your signs in your lease, check with local building and planning officials to see what ordinances and regulations may affect you.*

17. Cancelling Your Lease

In general, you can't cancel your lease before it runs out without pointing to a specific reason stated in the document itself—unless, of course, your landlord agrees to end the lease early. The right to end your lease early is definitely something you should think about during your negotiations. The future of your business may look rosy, but especially with a new business, no one knows for sure.

One approach for a new business is to propose a provision that allows you to cancel your lease if your gross income projections haven't reached a stated level by a certain time—say, six months after you take occupancy. Although this would be a somewhat unusual clause, a landlord with vacant space and no other tenants in prospect might accept it.

An even more compelling reason for ending your lease early would be that the building has been damaged by a fire or flooding and you can't conduct your business there. In most states, if you rent space in just a portion of a building, the law provides that you can terminate your lease if the building is destroyed. But what if it's only heavily damaged? If the landlord doesn't make repairs promptly, state law may allow you to terminate based on "constructive eviction"; the landlord's inaction, you would argue, constitutes an eviction. But if the landlord disputes this, you'll be stuck with what a judge rules. A better approach is to provide in your lease that if you can't run your business in your space for 30 days because of damage that you didn't cause, you can cancel the lease. Also, if relevant, make sure your 30-day provision covers the possibility that you and your customers can't get access to your space because of damage to another part of the building.

For more information on getting out of a lease, see Section I.

18. Mediation or Arbitration

I recommend that all small business leases have a clause requiring mediation or arbitration of landlord-tenant disputes. With mediation, an outside party helps the disputants arrive at their own settlement, which can then be recorded as a legally binding agreement. Arbitration is more like a private court action with the arbitrator in the role of a judge listening to the dispute and rendering a decision. But because no court is involved, it tends to be far faster and cheaper than a full-blown lawsuit. (Mediation and arbitration are covered in Chapter 22.)

19. The Fine Print

Study the lease thoroughly so that you're sure your responsibilities and those of the landlord are clear and reasonable. In addition to the major items already discussed, make sure the lease deals with all possible costs, including any of the following that concern you:

- *Real estate taxes.* If nothing is mentioned in the lease, this is normally the landlord's responsibility.
- *Utilities—water, electricity, natural gas, heating oil, etc.* These are usually the tenant's responsibility if not specifically mentioned in the lease.
- *Maintenance of the building and of your premises.* Without a lease provision to the contrary, the landlord must pay for maintaining the building; you pay for maintaining your own space. If you're leasing an entire building, you are normally responsible for all maintenance unless the lease specifies otherwise.
- *Repair and maintenance of the interior walls, ceiling and floors in your space.* This is normally the tenant's problem in the absence of a lease provision.
- *Repair of malfunctioning plumbing, electrical and mechanical systems (heating, ventilation and air conditioning—commonly called HVAC).* Without a lease provision, payment responsibilities are debatable. Generally, the landlord is responsible for systems that affect

the entire building—although the opposite is usually true if you lease the entire building. When you rent less than an entire building, the responsibility for mechanical or electrical facilities within the four walls of your space isn't always clear; you could find yourself arguing over who must pay for replacing a defective light fixture or a thermostat that goes haywire if the lease doesn't cover it.

- *Janitorial services.* These are normally the tenant's responsibility unless the lease says otherwise. Landlords usually provide janitorial services for bathrooms and other areas used in common by several tenants.
- *Window-washing.* Without specific lease language, the landlord normally doesn't have to wash windows. In smaller buildings, leases usually leave window-washing to the tenant, with the possible exception of windows serving common areas such as hallways, entryways and storage areas. In larger, multi-storied buildings, the landlord usually accepts responsibility—at least for the exterior of the windows.
- *Trash removal.* Without lease language to the contrary, this is the tenant's chore.
- *Landscape care and snow removal.* This is generally the landlord's duty unless you lease the entire building, in which case the burden shifts to you. It's always wise to address this issue in the lease—particularly if you're a tenant in a professional or other building where projecting the right image is important.
- *Parking lot maintenance.* This is something the landlord usually must pay for unless the whole parking lot is under your control, in which case it's usually your job unless the lease provides otherwise. In addition to maintenance, be sure the lease is clear regarding the landlord's duty to make a certain number of spaces available, keep the lot or garage open during normal business hours and provide security.

On service items such as janitorial services and window-washing, specify how often this will be done.

If the landlord is responsible for heating and air conditioning, will these services be available weekends and at night? If your business keeps long hours, you want your space to be comfortable at all times.

Regarding repairs, you and your landlord may find it convenient to allow you to make certain minor repairs not exceeding a fixed sum (say $300) and to deduct those outlays from your next month's rent.

E. Additional Clauses to Consider

Most of the above lease clauses are relatively common. Here are a few more, which are seen less often but which can be valuable to you as a tenant.

1. Option to Purchase the Building

If the situation warrants, consider a clause giving you an option to buy the building someday. It could give you the right to buy at a specified future time at a specified price, or a right of first refusal, in which if your landlord receives an offer from someone else to purchase the building, you'll be given a chance to match that offer. Many landlords will give you this right because it doesn't cost them anything. If you decide not to exercise your right of first refusal, the landlord simply sells the property to the person who made the offer.

2. The Right to Withhold Rent

Suppose your landlord violates the lease by not furnishing air conditioning for a sweltering July—or heat for a frigid January. Can you withhold rent? The traditional legal view is that your obligation to pay rent is independent of the landlord's obligation to perform under the lease. In other words, tenants are expected to quietly pay their rent except in the most extreme circumstances. But in the last 25 years, a tenants' rights revolution has taken place—mainly in the area of residential leases. For example, in the case of housing, many states recognize an "implied warranty of habitability." This means that regardless of what the lease obligates the landlord to do, the landlord must put dwelling units in a habitable condition—and keep them that way throughout the lease. If the landlord fails to do so, the tenant can withhold all or part of the rent without fearing eviction. Unless the parties come to an accommodation, a judge will ultimately decide how much of a rent reduction (the technical term is "abatement") the tenant is entitled to.

Commercial tenants, however, have not fared as well. The courts in most states still say that a commercial tenant must continue to pay rent despite the landlord's failure to meet implied or expressed duties. But this may be changing. Courts in several states have shown concern for the rights of commercial tenants. For example, a Texas court ruled that there is an implied warranty by a commercial landlord that leased premises are suitable for their intended purpose. The ruling came in a case where the landlord didn't provide adequate air conditioning, electricity, hot water, janitorial services or security to a business tenant. The tenant stopped paying rent and moved out. The court upheld the action of the business tenant.

How far the courts will go to protect your rights as a commercial tenant is still uncertain. Certainly a one-day failure to provide air conditioning wouldn't be enough to let you withhold rent or move out. But what if you and your customers have to sweat it out for two weeks? Or six weeks? That may be enough in some states, assuming you've given the landlord prompt notice of the problem and a chance to make repairs.

I recommend that you deal with all this legal uncertainty by requesting a lease clause giving you the right to withhold rent if, after reasonable notice, the landlord violates the lease in a way that seriously interferes with your ability to do business. Here's a sample clause:

> If, within ten days after notice from Tenant,
> Landlord fails to cure a default by Landlord that
> materially affects Tenant's ability to conduct its
> business, Tenant shall be entitled to a reason-

able abatement of rent for the period of default and may withhold all rent until Landlord has cured the default.

F. Shopping Center Leases

Leases for space in a shopping center are a special breed of animal. They often charge a percentage of sales as part of the rent and restrict competing businesses, to mention just two major differences.

It can be hard to read a shopping center lease and decide whether it offers a square deal or not. So, in addition to reading the lease language carefully, one of your first steps should be to check if the shopping center has a tenants' association; many shopping centers have them, and it can be a source of invaluable information. If there's no formal association, drop in on some current tenants. Either way, learn as much as you can about the center's management and how tenants are really treated. Also, try to find out which lease clauses the owner considers negotiable. This sort of information as to problems and opportunities will give you a definite advantage in your lease negotiations.

Now let's look at a typical shopping center lease. Many of the lease clauses discussed earlier in this chapter also appear in a shopping center lease, but there are likely to be a number of different wrinkles you should know about.

1. Percentage Rent

Retail businesses moving into a shopping center often find that the landlord expects to receive a percentage of gross sales in addition to a fixed "base rent." For example, the lease might provide:

a. The landlord will receive $2,000 a month as base rent.

b. In addition, if your gross sales exceed $200,000 a year, the landlord will receive 5% of the amount of your gross sales over the $200,000 figure.

c. The amount received by the landlord under the percentage rent clause won't exceed $25,000 a year.

In addition to trying to negotiate more favorable terms, be specific in how you define gross sales. Depending on your type of business, certain items should be deducted from gross sales before the percentage rent is determined. Here are some possibilities:

- returned merchandise
- charges you make for delivery and installation
- sales from vending machines
- refundable deposits
- catalog or mail-order sales
- sales tax.

In short, make sure your lease excludes all items that overstate your sales from the location you're renting.

2. Anchor Tenants

You may be attracted to a certain shopping center because one of the tenants is a major department store or supermarket. These superstars, known as anchor tenants, attract customers to the shopping center. Insist on a provision letting you out of the lease if an anchor tenant closes or, with a new shopping center, if the center never opens. Also seek the right to cancel your lease if center occupancy falls below a certain percentage. There's nothing worse than having a store in a half-empty mall.

3. Competing Businesses

How many record or running shoe stores can a mall support? You may want to negotiate a limit on the number of competing businesses allowed in the mall. Similarly, the landlord may want you to agree not to open a second store within a two-mile radius of the mall; the fear is that a second store too close might decrease gross sales from your mall location—thereby reducing the money the landlord gets under the percentage rent clause. At any rate, remember that these issues are usually negotiable. Many shopping centers (especially older ones) can no longer afford to dictate coercive terms to small businesses, and you may find much more landlord flexibility than you expect.

4. Duty to Remain Open

Your lease may compel you to remain open for business during all mall hours—typically 10 a.m. to 9 p.m. Monday through Saturday, and noon to 5 p.m. on Sunday. With a small business, think about whether you can afford to run your business during all of those hours or if it's appropriate to do so. For example, not many people buy children's shoes at 8:45 on Tuesday evening, but there is often a line on Saturday morning that justifies opening at 8:30 or 9 a.m. instead of 10, when the rest of the mall opens. If you need reasonable changes, ask for them.

G. How to Modify a Lease

As discussed in this chapter, there are a number of constructive ways to modify the lease presented by the landlord. The most important thing is to put the changes in writing. Never rely on oral understandings. In this day of computers and word processing software, the simplest method for making changes may be to have the landlord or landlord's lawyer print out a revised version of the lease—or you can make small changes on the lease itself by crossing out unacceptable wording and adding new language. You and the landlord should initial each of these changes.

If changes are extensive and it's not practical for the landlord to include them in a fresh draft, it's best to prepare an addition to the lease—in legal parlance, an "addendum." The addendum should refer to the main lease and state that in case of any conflict, the terms of the addendum supersede the original lease. A sample addendum is shown below.

Addendum

This is an Addendum to the Lease dated

_____, 20__, between

_____ (Landlord) and _____

_____ (Tenant) for commercial

space at

_____.

The parties agree to the following changes and

additions to the Lease:

[Insert changes and additions]

In all other respects, the terms of the original

Lease remain in full effect. However, if there is

a conflict between this Addendum and the

original Lease, the terms of this Addendum will

prevail.

Keep in mind that a lease can be modified even after it's been signed. For example, if six months into your lease your landlord agrees to install some partitions for $2,000, you can sign an addendum then.

H. Landlord-Tenant Disputes

There's almost no limit to the kinds of disputes that landlords and tenants can have. Your landlord may claim that you're damaging the building, or that you're consistently late paying rent or that you or your customers or visitors park in other tenants' spaces. You may feel that your landlord hasn't been furnishing services that were promised, such as security, janitorial or landscaping, or that your landlord is failing to attend to the leaky roof or having the windows washed frequently enough.

No matter what the cause, it's usually best to compromise a landlord-tenant dispute through negotiation. Sometimes a frank discussion and a little give and take by each side can resolve what seems like an impossible problem. If the dispute is serious and not amenable to face-to-face negotiations, have your lawyer help you analyze your legal rights. They may be stronger than you think. Legal trends in many parts of the country have improved the tenant's position.

If your lease has a mediation or arbitration clause, this is the obvious next step. But even if it doesn't, you may wish to suggest one or both of these approaches. Going to court can be expensive and time-consuming—something the landlord probably wants to avoid. In short, a sensible landlord has good reason to listen to your complaints and to mediate or arbitrate disputes. (See Chapter 22 for more on mediation and arbitration.)

1. Put Your Complaints in Writing

If you think your landlord has violated the lease, put your concern in writing in a straightforward, non-hostile way. State specifically what the violation is and what part of the lease it involves. Deliver your notice or letter to the landlord either in person or by certified mail (return receipt requested). Putting a landlord on early notice can help bolster your legal position if the dispute ever goes to court. If rent withholding is allowed in your state or by a specific clause in your lease (see Section E), you may want to write a letter or two to the landlord before you hold back on the rent. An example of such a letter is shown below.

SAMPLE LETTER TO LANDLORD

August 5, 20____

Arnold Ace
Ace Real Estate Associates
1234 Main Street
Anytown, U.S.A. 12345

I am writing to you about some problems we are having with our store space at 567 Enterprise Drive.

As you know, paragraph 12 of our lease specifically says that Ace Real Estate Associates will maintain the heating and air conditioning system and keep it in good repair. I have called your office twice this week and left word that the air conditioning is not working. No one has come to fix it or given us a date by which the work will be done. Our customers have complained, and on Tuesday we had to close early.

Also, under paragraph 14 of our lease, the Landlord agreed to replace the broken floor tiles in the entry area within two weeks after we took possession. We have been here for six weeks now and nothing has been done about the tiles. The broken tiles are hazardous.

These are serious violations of our lease. I am requesting that you immediately repair the air conditioning and promptly replace the broken floor tiles. We cannot operate without the air conditioning during this hot weather. Its lack has already caused us to lose substantial revenues and has damaged customer relationships.

If you do not take care of these matters within five days, I plan to have the work done myself and to deduct the cost from next month's rent.

If the cost of fixing the air conditioning is excessive, I may choose to terminate the lease and to sue your company for damages caused by your breaching the lease, including moving expenses and lost profits.

I hope that this will not be necessary. Please proceed at once to make the repairs as required by the lease.

Very truly yours,

Peter Olsen

2. Coping With the Threat of Eviction

Many leases contain stern language that appears to give the landlord the right to enter your space and regain possession if you don't pay your rent on time or fail to live up to some other lease obligation. Don't be intimidated. No matter what the lease says, in most states a landlord can't evict you without going to court and getting a court order first. This process requires that you be given notice and an opportunity to present your side of the dispute.

A hearing by a judge—or, if your lease so provides, by a mediator or arbitrator—gives you a chance to explain any legal defenses you have. For example, perhaps the reason you didn't pay your rent by the first of the month was that the landlord failed to repair the air conditioning as required by the lease. The right to a court hearing also gives you valuable time to develop your case and perhaps resolve the dispute. Court hearings don't take place instantly. You usually have some breathing space in which to build your legal response.

I. Getting Out of a Lease

Suppose that your business doesn't work out or—more optimistically—that you outgrow the space that you've leased. How free are you to simply vacate the space and walk away from the lease? Unless your landlord has done something to make your space unusable, you're legally responsible for the entire rent for the remaining portion of the lease if the landlord can't find another suitable tenant.

But especially if you have desirable space and a favorable lease, getting out of it—or most of it anyway—may be less difficult than you think. If you find that you need to move out, you have two options:

- *Buy your way out.* Try working out a deal in which the landlord keeps all or a part of your security deposit (including, perhaps, the last month's rent) in return for releasing you from the lease. If the lease still has a fairly long time to run or it will be hard to find a new tenant, you might need to sweeten the deal by offering an additional month or two of rent.

- *Find a new tenant.* Find a new tenant to take over the space. Present the new tenant to the landlord along with information about the person's credit and business history. Especially if your lease says that your landlord can't unreasonably refuse to consent to a sublease, you're in a strong legal position if the new tenant has good financial credentials and runs a business of a type permitted by your lease. But again, even without this provision (or if your lease flat out prohibits subletting or assignment), the law in your state may recognize the landlord's duty to mitigate damages—that is, try to find a replacement tenant and minimize his or her loss. If so, you're in a pretty good legal position. If the landlord accepts a new tenant who agrees to pay as much or more than you do, you're free of the lease at no further cost. If the landlord turns down the new tenant and then sues you for lost rent, you can argue that the landlord acted unreasonably and that the landlord—not you—should absorb any losses.

In addition, in states that recognize the landlord's duty to mitigate damages, usually the landlord must make a good faith effort to fill the space. Some landlords claim to meet this duty by placing a few ads in the newspaper and listing the property with a real estate agent (why should they do more since you're still obligated?). You're better off to use your own efforts to find a new tenant if possible.

J. When You Need Professional Help

A basic lease that sticks to routine clauses like those listed earlier in this chapter and is written in clear English should be no problem to negotiate yourself. However, it still may be prudent to have a lawyer with small business experience look over the final draft of the lease before you sign it. A visit of one-half hour or less should be sufficient. A real estate or small business expert may also be able to assist you. But make sure the person you check with doesn't stand to profit from putting the deal together—a circumstance that all but guarantees you won't get objective advice.

For nonroutine leases, seek assistance earlier in the game. You may need considerable help in negotiating and drafting some critical clauses. This may cost a few dollars, but compared to a confusing or landlord-slanted lease, a fair, well-drafted lease that contains the provisions you need is almost always a bargain.

For more on leases, see Leasing Space for Your Small Business, *by Janet Portman & Fred Steingold (Nolo);* Every Tenant's Legal Guide, *by Janet Portman & Marcia Stewart, (Nolo);* Every Landlord's Legal Guide, *by Marcia Stewart, Ralph Warner & Janet Portman (Nolo); and* Leases & Rental Agreements, *by Marcia Stewart & Janet Portman (Nolo).* ■

14

Home-Based Business

Ah, Home Sweet Home. Or is it Home Sweet Workplace? One of the major business trends is the dramatic increase in the number of consultants, artists, craftspeople, therapists, mail order specialists, professionals and others who use their homes as a business base.

One reason for this trend is the amazing array of electronic equipment that makes it possible to be productive and in touch with the rest of the world without leaving the comforts of home. By investing in a computer, a copier, a fax and an extra phone line or two, you can now duplicate conditions that until recently were practical only in leased commercial space.

But the upsurge in home-based businesses also reflects a new emphasis on the quality of life. Working at home gives you the chance to spend more time with your family, to be more flexible in the hours that you work and to avoid the gridlock of the highway.

From a legal standpoint, a home-based business isn't much different from any other business. You still need to pick a business name; decide whether to be a sole proprietor or to form a partnership or corporation; purchase insurance; pay taxes; sign contracts; and collect from customers. But a few special legal issues are peculiar to the at-home business, including land use restrictions, insurance and special tax provisions.

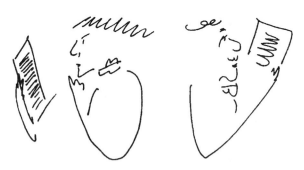

A. Zoning Laws

> *Planned communities and condominiums often have their own detailed rules affecting home-based businesses. Typically, these rules are stricter than local zoning ordinances. Skip ahead to Section B if your home is subject to these rules.*

Is it legal to run a business in your home? The answer depends on where you live and what you do. To understand how this works, let's start with the case of Bob Mullin, (*Metropolitan Development Commission v. Mullin,* 339 N.E.2d 751 (Ind. App. 1979), whose plight made its way into the lawbooks. Bob ran his insurance business from his two-bedroom home in Indianapolis. He thought he was on safe legal ground. After all, unlike in some cities, the local zoning ordinance allowed people to use their homes for "home occupations." As long as a home was used primarily as a residence, it could also be used for "professions and domestic occupations, crafts or services." The ordinance specifically allowed homes to be used for such occupations as law, medicine, dentistry, architecture, engineering, writing, painting, music lessons and photography. Also, people could use their homes for such businesses as dressmaking, tailoring, hair grooming, washing, ironing and cabinetmaking. So why not an insurance business?

Bob Mullin used his living room as a reception room and office, complete with a secretary's desk and filing cabinet. He put his own desk in the dining room in place of a dining room table. The photocopier stood in the kitchen next to the stove and refrigerator, and he converted one of the bedrooms into an office.

The zoning board took Bob to court, claiming he'd gone too far. The Indiana Court of Appeals agreed. The court ruled that it was okay for Bob to conduct an insurance business at home, but that Bob's usage was excessive. The business had taken over the house to the point that the primary use was no longer residential. The court told Bob to cut back or close down.

This case demonstrates but one of the many ways that local zoning ordinances can have a devastating effect on a home-based business. The good news is that by learning the law and using discretion, you may find that zoning isn't a real problem for your business.

1. How Zoning Ordinances Are Organized and Applied

Most cities have zoning ordinances. Areas outside of cities are usually covered by zoning ordinances adopted by county, village or township governments. Zoning ordinances come in many shapes and sizes, but they all do basically the same thing: they divide the area into districts in which various types of activities are allowed or prohibited. For example, there are usually residential districts for single-family and two-family homes and other districts for apartments. Other areas or zones are earmarked for commercial usage. Ordinances often break down the types of commercial usage; in some zoning districts, only offices or retail and service businesses are allowed. Usually some part of town is reserved for manufacturing operations, which are typically broken down into light and heavy industrial.

In some areas, more than one use is allowed in a district; for example, commercial and light industrial, or residential and commercial. Outside of cities, zones allow various types of agricultural activities.

Some zoning ordinances, especially in affluent areas, exclude home-based businesses. More commonly, zoning ordinances restrict—but don't prohibit—using a home for a business. An ordinance might say, for example, that in general you can't run a business from your home, but then go on to list several types of business that are permitted. The Indianapolis ordinance mentioned earlier specifically allowed professions such as law, medicine and architecture, as well as painting, music lessons and photography. Some ordinances are vague, simply

allowing "customary home occupations"—a term that must be interpreted by a judge if a given use is challenged.

Zoning ordinances that regulate home businesses frequently also limit:
- the amount of car and truck traffic
- outside signs
- on-street parking
- the number of employees
- the percentage of floor space devoted to the business.

It's not always easy to tell whether or not a particular business is allowed in a home under the zoning ordinance you're looking at. Some zoning ordinances were written years ago and don't adequately deal with many contemporary businesses that people wish to operate from home—especially sophisticated businesses that depend on high-tech communications equipment.

The level of enforcement varies widely. In more enlightened communities, zoning officials recognize that residential zoning is intended primarily to preserve the residential character of a neighborhood—not to prohibit low-profile businesses. Officials don't go out looking for violations but take their cues from the neighbors: If people living near a home-based business don't complain, why search for a possible technical violation? Even where it's clear that there's a violation, these officials work with the business owner to see if changes can be made to make the business conform to the ordinance before ordering the owner to end the business or taking administrative or court action.

On the other hand, you may have the misfortune of living in a community that believes in strict enforcement of all ordinances. In such a community, your home-based business may be at the mercy of fairly rigid bureaucrats—although, as we'll see, you may fight arbitrary or unreasonable action.

If municipal officials are determined to close down your home-based business, their first step is to write you a cease and desist letter. If you ignore this, you'll probably get another letter or two followed eventually by a misdemeanor prosecution (seeking a fine or, in an extreme case, a jail term) or a civil lawsuit requesting an injunction—a court order prohibiting future violations of the ordinance. If you violate such an injunction, the judge can fine you for contempt of court or even put you in jail.

2. Investigating Zoning Laws

Before setting up a home-based business, it's a good idea to learn not only what your local zoning ordinance provides but also to find out about enforcement attitudes. If you're in a strict enforcement community and you file for a local business license or tax permit, this may trigger an inquiry about whether you comply with the zoning ordinance. Talk to people who run other home-based businesses, local contractors, your city's business development office, small business advisors and lawyers about how to make the fewest legal waves.

You may find yourself in a gray area. Your planned home-based business may or may not violate a vaguely worded local ordinance—for example, a computerized information searching business in an area that allows traditional home-based businesses. It's hard to predict whether the local zoning officials will take action against you or not. One approach is to just go ahead and chance it. If you're simply planning to set up your desk and computer in an unused room in a home you already own, you have little to lose. This approach is far less sensible if you plan to buy or renovate a house to accommodate your business. Before you spend a significant sum to house your business, you want assurance that you won't be closed down. It's best to approach the city, explain your plans and ask for an official green light. If a purchase is involved, put a clause in your offer making the deal contingent on getting approval from the zoning authorities. Then, if your use isn't approved, you're free to cancel your purchase.

If you plan to operate out of your existing residence and decide that your business is doubtful legally, or that you could be closed down if the ordinance were strictly enforced, you can minimize the risks. Start by being a good neighbor. Make sure that your business has little if any impact on the people who live around you. For example, if all you do is convert one room to an office equipped for a consulting business, it's unlikely that anyone will complain—as long as you have no employees and see only an occasional client or customer at your home. This is true even if you generate $1 million a year in gross income. You'll also be in a better position if you cleared your plans with your neighbors or if several of them also have home-based businesses.

What kinds of things are most likely to get you trouble? Anything that a neighbor can see, hear or smell outside of your home that causes inconvenience or smacks of a commercial venture. Increased traffic, parking problems, signs, outside storage of supplies, noises or unpleasant odors emanating from your home—any of these can lead to neighborhood complaints. Pollution is another red flag.

EXAMPLE: A craftsman who worked at home with stained glass and even taught classes there was doing quite well until he started dumping lead-laced fluids down a storm drain. The neighbors properly insisted that the city attorney put him out of business.

Look for alternatives to frequent deliveries. *A daily procession of FedEx, UPS and U.S. Post Office trucks making deliveries to your house can annoy the neighbors. Consider having mail and packages sent to a private mailbox service such as the one run by Mail Boxes Etc. or a similar operation—especially if there's one located nearby.*

Ted operates a business in his home helping non-lawyers prepare their own divorce and bankruptcy forms. Several customers come and go each day, often in the early evening and on Saturdays. One of Ted's neighbors, who has no idea of what Ted is doing, jumps to the conclusion that he's dealing drugs.

She calls a meeting of other neighbors and convinces the others that there can be no other explanation for all the coming and going. They complain to the police and zoning board. When the truth comes out, the police laugh and leave.

The zoning officials are another matter. They cite a local ordinance prohibiting businesses that generate traffic and tell Ted to close down. Eventually, when Ted gets all his chagrined neighbors to sign a statement saying a few cars a day aren't a problem, the zoning officials reverse their position.

Ted could have avoided this time-consuming, anxiety-producing process if he'd simply told folks what was going on when he began his business.

3. Dealing With Zoning Officials

Suppose you receive a complaint from the city. What steps can you take? Start by going to City Hall and talking to the person who administers the zoning law—someone in the Zoning or Planning Department. There are both practical and legal reasons for attempting to resolve zoning matters without filing a lawsuit. On the practical level, administrative (agency) relief is quicker, less expensive and often more flexible than a judicial solution. And the law usually requires you to pursue your available administrative solutions before you go to court; this is known in legal lingo as "exhausting your administrative remedies."

The kind of response you can hope for at City Hall depends greatly on community attitudes. If some home-based businesses are allowed, you clearly want to show that yours meets the spirit of the criteria for allowing businesses. Emphasize how small and unobtrusive your business is. When faced with the facts, the city may become more reasonable. Or you may be able to negotiate a settlement under which you scale down your operations. For example, you might agree to limit your business to weekdays from 8 a.m. to 5 p.m. and to provide off-street parking for your one employee.

If you can't negotiate with the city staff, there are more formal approaches. Most places have a planning or zoning board with power to grant exceptions (variances or conditional use permits) if compliance with an ordinance would cause unreasonable hardship. For example, a zoning board might allow a physically handicapped person to operate a therapy practice at home even though some traffic is generated. The board may also have power to overturn a zoning official's interpretation of an ordinance. If you appeal to a local zoning or planning board, try to get neighbors to attend the hearing to speak on your behalf. If that is too inconvenient, ask as many neighbors as possible to write letters or sign a petition stating that they support your business use. Neighborhood support or opposition is likely to be crucial to the success or failure of your appeal. Also, come to the hearing with any photographs or documents that accurately show the nature and extent of your business.

In many cities, if you're turned down by a zoning or planning board or commission, you can appeal to a second board—often the city council itself. While it's less likely that you'll prevail at this level, it does happen.

Going beyond administrative channels, you may be able to get the zoning ordinance amended by the city council or county legislative body. For example, in some communities moves are afoot to change ordinances that allow "traditional home-based businesses" to include those based on the use of computer and other high-tech equipment—businesses that are unobtrusive, but hardly traditional.

To push through an ordinance change, you'll probably have to lobby some city council members or planning commissioners. You may also need to enlist the local chamber of commerce and other groups representing business people. With increased use of homes for businesses, the time may be ripe in your community for ordinance revisions of this sort. It's politically attractive to revamp an archaic ordinance to allow more home-based businesses, especially if the city is struggling with traffic and parking problems.

Also consider trying to get your property rezoned. This works best if your home is on the edge of a commercial district. Ask the city to move the boundary line separating the two zoning districts so that your home falls within the commercial district—which, of course, would give you much greater latitude to run your business out of your home.

4. Going to Court

If you decide municipal officials are being unreasonable in attempting to close down your home-based business and you can't get administrative relief or an ordinance amendment, you may want to take the matter to court yourself before the city starts a prosecution or requests an injunction. By acting first, you have a chance to frame the factual and legal issues more favorably, putting the municipality on the defensive. At this stage, you'll probably need a lawyer's help; zoning cases are relatively complicated and specialized. Consulting and perhaps hiring a lawyer who works in this area

regularly will be well worth the fee. Make sure you find a lawyer who's familiar with zoning practices (see Chapter 24 for more on finding and working with lawyers). You needn't turn the whole case over to a lawyer—there's plenty you can do to organize support from neighbors and other home-based businesses as well as researching how courts have decided other similar cases.

You can assert several legal theories in a zoning lawsuit, including the following:

- The city's legal interpretation of its zoning ordinance was incorrect. For example, you might claim that your word processing business is a "home occupation" even though the zoning officials decided that it isn't. You'd ask the judge to issue a judgment declaring that your business does qualify as a home occupation.

EXAMPLE: Dr. William Brady lived in Beverly Hills, California. He wrote a syndicated column and, with the help of secretaries, mailed out 150,000 pamphlets a year from his home office. The city tried to close his business because the local zoning ordinance prohibited home businesses that involved the purchase or sale of materials for profit. But the court ruled that the doctor wasn't violating the zoning ordinance; sending out the pamphlets was basically the same as a person answering his or her mail. *City of Beverly Hills v. Brady,* 215 P.2d 460 (Cal. 1950).

- The ordinance is invalid because it violates the state statute (called an "enabling law") that gives cities authority to enact zoning ordinances. For example, you might claim that the zoning ordinance is invalid because it doesn't permit homeowners to have "reasonable accessory uses" or "home occupations" as required by the state enabling law.
- The ordinance is invalid because the city didn't use proper procedures in adopting or

enforcing it. For example, the city may not have held the necessary public hearings before it amended the zoning ordinance to prohibit certain types of home-based businesses.

- The authorities have acted in a discriminatory manner by enforcing the ordinance against you. For example, they've allowed similar home-based businesses for years but now have singled you out for special treatment.

You aren't limited to just one legal theory. Your lawsuit can allege as many theories as apply.

Lawsuits are expensive, but yours may be settled before there's a full-scale hearing or trial. The city may agree on an acceptable compromise to avoid the expense or inconvenience of fighting your lawsuit, or may not want to put its zoning ordinance in jeopardy just for the sake of closing down one in-home business.

B. Private Land Use Restrictions

Zoning ordinances are not the only source of potential problems for a home-based business. You must also check out private restrictions on your use of your home, condo or co-op unit. Depending on the part of the country and the type of ownership arrangement, use restrictions commonly are found in the following documents:

- property deed (the restrictions are called "restrictive covenants")
- a subdivision's declaration of building and use restrictions or covenants, conditions and restrictions (CC&Rs)
- planned unit development (PUD) rules
- condominium regulations
- co-op regulations
- leases.

Language in these and similar documents is likely to restrict or even prohibit business uses. If your residence is covered by a title insurance policy (virtually every piece of real estate is), use restrictions may be identified there. If you've lost your deed or your subdivision, condo or co-op restrictions, get a copy from your association or go to the county office where title papers are recorded (usually the county recorder or register of deeds) and purchase a copy.

If your neighbors believe you're violating these restrictions, they may take action to stop you. Often—especially for condo, co-op or PUD units—they can take you before an owners' association board empowered to enforce regulations. If you don't come into compliance, you may lose privileges and face other penalties. Beyond these private sanctions, your neighbors can take you to court and try to stop your business. Judges can be very strict in enforcing these private restrictions. Here are three real-life instances where a judge sided with the neighbors.

> **EXAMPLE 1:** Salvador, a field manager for a brush manufacturer, supervised a staff of door-to-door salespeople and supplied them from his residence in Metairie, Louisiana. He interviewed prospective salespeople at his home and received stored merchandise in his garage. The court ruled that merely receiving samples wouldn't violate the restrictive covenants in the deed to Salvador's property. But Salvador had a problem because he used his home to hire and outfit new employees with samples stored at home. He wasn't using his home "for residential purposes only" as required by the restrictive covenants. *Woolley v. Cinquigranna,* 188 So.2d 701 (La. App. 1966).

> **EXAMPLE 2:** Sheldon and Raye practiced psychotherapy in their home in Illinois. The subdivision restrictions covering their home said that "No lot shall be used except for single residential purposes." Their neighbors took them to court, claiming a violation of that restrictive rule. The judge ordered Sheldon and Raye to discontinue their professional use of their home even though the exterior appearance of the home as

a single-family home hadn't been altered. *Wier v. Isenberg,* 420 N.E.2d 790 (Ill. App. 1981).

EXAMPLE 3: Myrtle operated a part-time beauty parlor in her Sunnyvale, California, home, receiving six customers per day. Myrtle didn't advertise her services, there was no external evidence of her business, and neighbors weren't inconvenienced. Still, the judge ruled that Myrtle violated the subdivision restriction that said "No lot shall be used except for residential purposes." *Biagini v. Hyde,* 3 Cal. App. 3d 877, 83 Cal. Rptr. 875 (Cal. App. 1970).

If you're taken to court, you have two main lines of defense. The first is that your neighbors or the condo association are misinterpreting the restrictions and that your business use is allowable. Second, if the neighbors did not object to prior business uses, they have, in legal effect, waived the right to do so now. In other words, their inaction in the past has nullified the restrictions.

Judges are often sympathetic to homeowners seeking to enjoy the use of their property. If neighbors have been lax or the restriction is vague, you have a good chance of getting a favorable ruling if your business use doesn't really hurt your neighbors or change the residential character of your neighborhood. On the other hand, if the legal restrictions are tightly drafted and your neighbors acted swiftly to enforce them whenever a violation came to their attention, even a sympathetic judge won't be able to help you.

But slugging it out in court should be a last resort. If you're both dogged and diplomatic, you may be able to find a way to operate your home-based business. Look first at the rule to see how restrictive it is. Some specifically allow certain types of home-based businesses while others simply adopt the standard in your municipality's zoning ordinance (see Section A, above), which in turn may be fairly permissive. If you don't qualify under the rules, consider trying to change them. Other people in your subdivision may also feel they are too restric-

tive. Often the document creating restrictive covenants says that restrictions can be changed if a certain number—say 70%—of the homeowners in the subdivision agree. Similarly, condo regulations can often be changed by agreement of a specified number of owners.

Leases. If you live in a rented house or apartment, read your lease carefully. Your landlord may have the right to evict you if you use the premises for business. It's best to get clearance in advance and have it written into the lease. Most landlords won't care if you use the property partly for business as long as you don't cause any damage or create any problems with your neighbors.

C. Insurance

Chapter 12 discusses insurance coverage for small businesses. The same general principles apply to home-based businesses, but there are also some special considerations you should be aware of.

Never rely exclusively on your normal homeowner's policy. If you do, bad things can happen:

- After your computer is stolen, you may find out that it's not covered by your homeowner's policy because business property is excluded.
- After your house burns down, you may find that the fire coverage is void because you didn't disclose your business use to the insurance company.
- After the UPS delivery person slips on your front porch and breaks his back, you may find you're not covered for injuries associated with business deliveries.

It's easy to avoid these nasty surprises. Sit down with your insurance agent and fully disclose your planned business operations. It's relatively inexpensive to add riders to your homeowner's policy to cover normal business risks. You may need separate policies for other business-related coverage.

When it comes to business equipment and furnishings, figure out how much it would cost for replacements after a fire, theft or other disaster. Don't overlook things such as the specialized business software you run on your computer. Depending on the nature of your business, replacing equipment and furniture could run into many thousands of dollars. Ask your insurance agent what it takes to insure this valuable property, allowing for a good-sized deductible to keep costs down. (See Chapter 12, Section E, on how to buy affordable insurance.) Make sure that the coverage on equipment and furnishings is for the full replacement cost—not just the depreciated value, as can be the case in some homeowner's policies.

Your homeowner's policy may also not adequately protect you from liability to business visitors. Accidents—such as people getting hurt when they trip and fall—are more likely to happen at home than in a well-planned office building. Your homeowner's policy probably protects you if you're sued by a social guest or someone at your home for a non-business purpose—a florist's truck driver delivering flowers or the meter reader who's checking on gas usage. But it may not cover a business associate, employee, customer or delivery person who is injured on your property.

Some home-based businesses need special kinds of insurance. If you render professional services, look into professional liability insurance. If you manufacture, distribute or sell products that may hurt someone, think about product liability insurance. Also, if you have employees, you'll need to provide workers' compensation coverage. (All this is covered in Chapter 12.)

If you do some business away from your home, be sure that your car insurance covers injuries that occur while you're on business errands. And see about the extent of your general liability coverage if you should accidentally injure someone or damage their property while away from home on business. You may need a rider or special policy to cover this risk. The Insurance Information Institute reports that many insurance companies are offering such riders for less than $200.

Policies to cover both your home and home business. *Several insurance companies have developed special policies that cover both your home and a business run from your home. Typically, these policies cover your computer equipment and other business property—whether used in your house or elsewhere—and protect you from business liability lawsuits and loss of income. These policies can be less expensive than either adding riders to your home insurance or buying separate policies for home and business. But check the coverage carefully, as these policies tend to primarily address home offices and may not adequately insure you if, for example, you're a small manufacturer or a wholesaler who stores inventory in the basement.*

Operating as a separate entity can affect your insurance coverage. *While the typical home-based business is organized as a sole proprietorship or partnership, you may have organized yours as a corporation or an LLC to get the benefit of limited personal liability. That's fine, but remember that your homeowner's policy—even if it has riders—insures you personally and may not insure a separate business entity. This can present a coverage problem if your corporation owns the $3,000 computer that gets stolen or the delivery person falls down your front stairs while delivering an overnight letter to your LLC. Check with your insurance agent or broker to make sure your business entity is covered in the insurance policy—as well as yourself. It's usually just a simple matter to have your business added as an insured party.*

D. Deducting Expenses for Business Use of Your Home

You may be able to take a tax deduction for business use of your home. The deduction is available not only for a home office but for other business uses as well, such as a workshop or studio at home.

Basically, if you meet the technical requirements of the tax law, you can deduct the cost of utilities, rent, depreciation, home insurance and repairs when you use part of your home for business. For a detailed explanation, see IRS Publication 587, *Business Use of Your Home,* which also spells out the limitations on the amount you can deduct. It's available on-line at www.irs.gov.

Keep in mind that whether or not you can deduct expenses that relate specifically to your home, such as rent, utilities, home insurance and repairs, you can still take a deduction for regular business expenses, such as photocopies, stationery, paper clips, wages, travel, equipment, professional memberships and publications. (See Chapter 8.) You can also deduct the cost of long-distance calls you make from home and a separate phone line used for business calls.

According to the IRS, your "home" can be a house, condo or apartment unit—or even a mobile home or boat. But wherever you live, before you can deduct expenses for using part of your home as a business, you must meet two tax law requirements.

Requirement #1: You must regularly use part of your home exclusively for a trade or business (see Section 1).

Requirement #2: You must be able to show that:
- you use your home as your principal place of business (see Section 2), or
- you meet patients, clients or customers at home (see Section 3), or
- you use a separate structure on your property exclusively for business purposes (see Section 4).

For more coverage of tax issues for home-based businesses, see Tax Savvy for Small Business, *by Frederick W. Daily (Nolo).*

1. Regular and Exclusive Use

The first requirement for taking deductions related to your home is that you regularly use part of your home exclusively for a trade or business. The notion of regular use is a bit vague. The IRS says it means you're using a part of your home for business on a continuing basis—not just for occasional or incidental business. A few hours a day on most days is probably enough to meet this test.

Exclusive use means that you use a portion of your home only for business. If you use part of your home for your business and also use it for personal purposes, you don't meet the exclusive use test.

EXAMPLE: Brook, a lawyer, uses a den in his home to write legal briefs and prepare contracts. He also uses the den for poker games, watching TV and hosting a book club. Result: Brook can't claim business deductions for using the den.

Ways to Document Your Home-Business Deduction

Here are some steps you can take to help establish your legal right to deduct home-related business expenses.
- Photograph your home office and draw a diagram showing the location of the office in your home.
- Have your business mail sent to your home.
- Use your home address on your business cards and stationery and in all business ads.
- Get a separate phone line for the business.
- Have clients or customers visit your home office—and keep a log of those visits.
- Keep track of the time you spend working at home.

2. Principal Place of Business

In addition to using part of your home regularly and exclusively for business (see Section 1), to take deductions relating to your home, your home must be your "principal place of business"—or, alternatively, if your home isn't your principal place of business, you can qualify for the deduction if you meet clients or customers at home (see Section 3) or if you use a separate structure on your property exclusively for business purposes (see Section 4).

Establishing that your home is your principal place of business is simple if you have only one type of business and conduct it only at home. It gets more complicated if you have several businesses or conduct a business from more than one location.

The IRS says that you can have a principal place of business for each trade or business in which you engage. This means that if you use your home for a part-time enterprise, it may qualify as a "principal place of business" for that business.

> **EXAMPLE:** Alma teaches school. As a teacher, her principal place of business is the school where she teaches. She also runs a public relations consulting company and uses a part of her home as the headquarters for that business; her expenses for this business use of the home should be deductible.

If you have more than one business location, including your home, for a single trade or business, you must figure out if your home is your principal place of business for that enterprise. Again, if it isn't, you can't take a deduction for the business use of your home.

Your home qualifies as your principal place of business if:

- you conduct the administrative or management activities of your business there, and
- you have no other fixed location where you conduct those activities.

Your home doesn't have to be the place where you generate most of your business income. It's enough that you regularly use it to do such things as keeping your books, scheduling appointments, doing research and ordering supplies. As long as you have no other fixed location where you do such things—for example, an outside office—you can take the deduction.

> **EXAMPLE:** Ellen, a wallpaper installer, performs services for clients in their homes and offices. She also has a home office which she uses regularly and exclusively to keep her books, arrange appointments and order supplies. Ellen is entitled to deduct expenses for that part of her home.

Home-connected expenses. *As noted earlier, the IRS rules discussed in this chapter apply only to home-connected expenses such as utilities, rent, depreciation, home insurance and repairs. You needn't conform to these rules in order to deduct other business expenses. If you have a bona fide business and don't qualify for deducting home-connected expenses, you can still deduct many other business expenses—for example, the cost of supplies, postage, advertising and long-distance phone calls.*

3. Meeting Clients or Customers at Home

If your home isn't your principal place of business, you may still be entitled to deduct expenses for business use of your home if you regularly use part of your home exclusively to meet with clients, customers or patients. Doing so even one or two days a week is probably sufficient. You can use the business space for other business purposes as well—doing bookkeeping, for example, or other business paperwork—but you'll lose the deduction if you use the space for personal purposes, such as watching movie videos.

> **EXAMPLE:** Julie, an accountant, works three days a week in her downtown office and two days a week in her suburban home office, which she uses only for business. She meets clients at her home office at least once a week. Since Julie regularly meets clients at her home office, she can take a home office deduction. This is so even though her downtown office is her principal place of business.

Keep a log of the clients or customers you meet at home. *Good records can be key if the IRS challenges your right to deduct home-related business expenses. Maintain an appointment book in which you carefully note the name of the client or customer and the date and time of each meeting at your home. Save these books for at least three years; they can be crucial to documenting business usage if your tax return is audited by the IRS.*

4. Using a Separate Building for Your Business

If your home isn't your principal place of business, and you don't meet clients or customers at home, you can deduct expenses for a separate, freestanding structure that you use regularly and exclusively for your business. This might be a studio or a converted garage or barn, for example. The structure doesn't have to be your principal place of business or a place where you meet patients, clients or customers. But be sure you use the structure only for your business: you can't store garden supplies there or, at least in theory, even use it for the monthly meeting of your investment club.

> **EXAMPLE:** Norm is a self-employed landscape architect. He has his main office in a professional center near a shopping mall, but most weekends he works in his home office, which is located in a converted carriage house in his backyard. Since Norm uses the carriage house regularly and exclusively for his landscape architect work, it qualifies for the home office deduction.

Storing Inventory or Product Samples at Home

If you sell retail or wholesale products and you store inventory or samples at home, you can deduct expenses for the business use of your home. There are two limitations, however: First, you won't qualify for the deduction if you have an office or other business location away from your home. Second, you have to store the products in a particular place—your garage, for example, or a closet or bedroom. It's OK to use the storage space for other purposes as well, as long as you regularly use it for inventory or samples.

> **EXAMPLE:** Jim sells heating and air conditioning filters to small businesses. His home is the only fixed location of his business. Jim regularly stores his inventory of filters in half of his basement. He sometimes uses the storage area for working on his racing bikes. Jim can deduct the expenses for the storage space even though he doesn't use that part of his basement exclusively for business.

5. Amount of Deduction

If you meet the tests for deducting expenses for business use of your home, you need to figure out how much you can deduct. The tax law lets you deduct only a portion of your home expenses—not 100%. Begin by determining how much of your home you use for business. There are two common methods for doing this.

Square Footage Method. Divide the number of square feet of space used for your business by the total number of square feet in your home. For example, if your home contains 1,200 square feet and you use 240 square feet for your business, then your business percentage is 20%.

Number of Rooms Method. If the rooms in your home are about the same size, figure the business percentage by dividing the number of rooms used for business by the number of rooms in the home. If you use one room in a four-room home for business, then 25% of the total area is used for business.

The deduction for business use of your home has several components. Using the percentage arrived at by either of the above methods, you can deduct from your gross income the business portion of:

- your rent, if you rent your home, or
- depreciation, mortgage interest and property taxes on your house, if you own your home—although you may prefer to deduct all of your mortgage interest and property taxes as part of your itemized personal deductions.

In addition, as either an owner or renter, you may deduct this same percentage of other expenses for keeping up and running an entire home. The IRS calls these *indirect expenses*.

They include:

- utility expenses for electricity, gas and heating oil
- service expenses for snow removal and trash pick-up
- homeowner's or renter's insurance

- home maintenance expenses that benefit your entire home, such as roof and furnace repair and exterior painting
- casualty losses if your home is damaged—for example, in a storm
- security system maintenance.

You may also deduct the entire cost of expenses you incur for the part of the house you use for business. The IRS calls these *direct expenses*. They include, for example, painting your home's business area or paying someone to clean it. If you pay a housekeeper to clean your entire house, you may deduct your business percentage of the expense.

> **EXAMPLE:** Rudy rents a 1,600-square-foot apartment and uses a 400-square-foot bedroom as a home office for his newsletter publishing business. His percentage of business use is 25% (400 divided by 1,600). He pays $12,000 in annual rent and has a $1,200 utility bill for the year. He also spends $200 to paint his home office. Rudy can deduct 25% of his rent and utilities and 100% of the painting expenses, allowing him to write off a total of $3,500.

You're always able to deduct the normal business expenses not associated with your home use. *Remember that this section addresses only the expenses you can deduct for business use of your home. As discussed earlier, whether or not you qualify for or take a home-business deduction, you're able to claim as business expenses—and deduct from gross income—the cost of such items as supplies, postage, long-distance charges and so on. You don't need to qualify to take deductions for your business use of your home in order to write off these items. And you can also depreciate or expense (under Section 179) the cost of office furniture, computers, copiers and other tangible property you use for your business and keep at home.*

⚠ **If you're a homeowner, deducting expenses for business use of your house can sometimes be a poor idea.** *Assuming you're eligible to deduct home business expenses on your current tax return, the next question is, should you? As you may know, most people no longer have to pay income tax on the profit they make when they sell their house. That's because as long as you owned and used the house as your principal residence for at least two years of the five years preceding the sale, $250,000 of capital gains is excluded from taxation if you're a single taxpayer and $500,000 is excluded for married couples. But there's a catch: You can't exclude the part of your gain that's equal to any depreciation allowed or "allowable" for the business use of your home after May 6, 1997. In other words, if you later sell your house for a profit, you volunteer to pay tax on your gain (in the amount you've depreciated) that you wouldn't otherwise have to pay. And you may fare no better even if you don't deduct depreciation but do deduct such expenses as a portion of your utility bills and homeowner's insurance on IRS Form 8829, Expenses for Business Use of Your Home; a strict reading of the law requires you to pay tax on any depreciation you could have taken! Does this mean you shouldn't claim depreciation or a portion of utility bills and homeowner's insurance? Not necessarily. To determine if you should or should not deduct for depreciation and other expenses of doing business at home, you need to care-fully analyze your tax situation. If you're in a higher federal and state tax bracket and don't expect to sell your home soon, it may make sense to lower your current tax bill by deducting depreciation and home-related expenses, investing the dollars you save. But if your income is low and you may sell your house soon, it's better not to take these deductions. (Also remember that if you itemize deductions on Schedule A, you're already able to deduct there the full amount of your home property taxes and the interest on your home mortgage—so the slight additional tax savings from deducting depreciation and other home business expenses on Form 8829 may not be worth the hassle.)*

📖 • Working from Home, *by Paul & Sarah Edwards (Jeremy P. Tarcher Inc.). This encyclopedic volume by the reigning gurus of home-based businesses covers everything from how to live with computers, faxes and voice mail to juggling family, friends, children and work.*

• The Home Office and Small Business Answer Book, *by Janet Attard (Owl Books). Using a reader-friendly question-and-answer format, this hefty book guides you through such essential issues as how to find customers, manage your home-based business and—most important of all—get paid.* ∎

Employees and Independent Contractors

This chapter deals with how to hire and fire employees and how to comply with laws that affect them. We'll also look at hiring independent contractors, instead of employees, for certain tasks.

As we go through the technical legal rules for hiring and firing, don't lose sight of three even more important concepts:

- hire qualified people
- treat them well, and
- create a workplace where employers and employees cheerfully combine their energies for the common good.

 Chapter 9 of Legal Forms for Starting & Running a Small Business *contains forms for hiring employees and independent contractors.*

For an in-depth treatment of your legal obligations, see The Employer's Legal Handbook, *by Fred S. Steingold (Nolo).*

A. Hiring Employees

You can steer clear of most of the legal perils of hiring employees by following the guidelines outlined below.

1. Avoid Illegal Discrimination

Federal and state laws prohibit you from discriminating against an applicant or employee because of race, color, gender, religious beliefs, national origin, physical disability—or age if the person is 40 years old or older. Also, many states and cities have laws prohibiting employment discrimination based on marital status, sexual orientation and a variety of other characteristics.

But anti-discrimination laws don't dictate whom you must hire. You remain free to hire, promote, discipline and fire employees and to set their salaries based on their skills, experience, performance and reliability.

Some illegal practices should be obvious, such as advertising a job for people ages 20 to 30 only—which on its face violates age discrimination laws—or paying lower wages to women than men for the same work in violation of equal pay laws. But more subtly, anti-discrimination laws also can bar employment practices which seem innocent but end up having a disproportionate and discriminatory impact on certain groups. For example, if your main means of seeking candidates is through word of mouth and your workforce consists entirely of white men, the word-of-mouth recruitment can be illegal discrimination if it produces only white male applicants.

To avoid violating anti-discrimination laws at the hiring stage:

- advertise job openings in widely read newspapers so they come to the attention of diverse people
- determine the skills, education and other attributes that are truly necessary to perform the job so that you don't impose requirements that unnecessarily exclude capable applicants, and
- avoid screening techniques that have an unfair impact on any group of applicants.

2. Respect the Applicant's Privacy Rights

While it's wise to screen potential employees, there's a potential problem in mounting intensive background checks. Your attempt to assess applicants by gathering information about their past can conflict with their right to privacy. Before you send for high school or college transcripts and credit reports, obtain the applicant's written consent. If the applicant won't consent, you're free to drop him or her from further consideration—as long as you follow that policy with all applicants.

3. Avoid False Job Security Promises

Employees have no legal rights to their jobs. This harkens back to a doctrine holding that an employee's continued employment is at the will or discretion of the employer, meaning that the employer can fire the employee at any time for any reason—or for no reason at all—absent a written or implied contract guaranteeing a fixed term of employment. The flip side is that the employee is free to quit at any time.

Of course, the at-will employment doctrine doesn't free you from complying with anti-discrimination laws. You can't fire someone for an illegal reason—because of the color of the employee's skin, for example, or because you prefer to put a younger person in the job.

The at-will relationship gives you considerable freedom to fire employees, but it may take some planning to preserve that freedom. One reason for this is that courts in many states have ruled that as a result of promises made at an employment interview or in an employee handbook, an employer has implied that an employee has a long-term work contract and will only be fired if there's a good reason such as poor performance or excessive absenteeism. Fortunately, if you follow commonsense business practices, you normally can retain a great deal of control over the firing process.

Don't give an applicant or employee any long-term assurances about employment that you may not be able to honor. Make sure your application forms, employee handbooks and offers of employment state that the job is at will and that oral statements can't act as a binding contract. Have the applicant acknowledge this in writing. Then you'll have an excellent chance of choosing whether and when to fire an employee on your own terms and without legal repercussions.

Full disclosure in hiring. *Recent legal developments indicate that in some circumstances you may have some legal responsibility to provide new employees with some measure of job security even if your employee handbook and other written statements say there is none. Specifically, if you're encouraging an applicant to leave an existing job or to move to your city from elsewhere, some courts have ruled that you have an affirmative duty to disclose negative information about the future of your business. Failure to do so may allow an employee who suffers adverse consequences from your failure to tell the whole truth to sue and recover damages. For example, if your business is in shaky financial shape or you're planning to downsize and eliminate many jobs, it's your responsibility to tell job candidates about it before they leave their presently secure jobs or move from New York to Los Angeles to work for you. Be especially forthright if you're already planning or considering eliminating the position you're hiring for.*

4. Prevent Negligent Hiring Claims

You have a legal duty to protect your customers, clients, visitors and the general public from injuries caused by employees who may harm others. When you hire someone for a position that may expose customers or others to danger, you must use special care in checking references and making other background checks. If someone gets hurt or has property stolen or damaged by an employee whose background you didn't check carefully, you can be sued for negligent hiring. Be especially vigilant when hiring maintenance workers and delivery drivers, whose jobs give them easy access to homes and apartments.

If you hire people for sensitive jobs, investigate their backgrounds as thoroughly as possible and look for any criminal convictions. If an employee will be driving, make sure he or she is currently licensed and has a decent driving record. And where state laws require an occupational license—for asbestos removal, for example, or tending bar—check to see that the applicant is properly licensed.

Contact all previous employers. Insist that the applicant explain any gaps in employment history. Consider turning over the pre-hire investigation to professionals with experience in screening job applicants.

To learn more about negligent hiring cases, see Employer's Guide to Workplace Torts, *by Ronald M. Green & Richard J. Reibstein (Bureau of National Affairs).*

5. Protect Against Unfair Competition

Employees sometimes leave to start a competing business or go to work for a competitor. Obviously, you needn't be too concerned about the employee you hire to scoop ice cream or the clerk you hire to work behind the counter at your dry cleaning shop. But employees who have access to inside information about product pricing or business expansion plans, for example, may pose competitive risks. The same goes for employees who handle valuable and hard-won customers—a salesperson, perhaps, who handles a $200,000 account.

Consider asking new hires to sign agreements not to take or disclose trade secrets or other confidential information. Also, you might ask selected employees to sign covenants not to compete with your business. (See subsection b.)

a. Trade secrets

Some business owners need to protect their unique assets from misuse—assets such as:

- a restaurant's recipes for a special salad dressing
- muffins that draw people from miles around
- a heating and cooling company's list of 500 customers for whom it regularly provides maintenance, or
- a computer company's unique process for speedily assembling computer boards.

If they are treated as such, the recipes, the customer list and the assembly process are all trade secrets. Other examples are an unpatented invention, engineering techniques, cost data, a formula or a machine. To qualify for trade secret protection, the business information you seek to protect must meet two requirements:

(1) **The information must truly be secret.**
The information must not be freely available from other sources. If the recipe for a restaurant's award-winning custard tart can be found in a standard American cookbook or recreated by a competent chef, it isn't a trade secret. On the other hand, if the restaurant's chef found the recipe in a medieval French cookbook in a provincial museum, translated it and figured out how to adapt it to currently available ingredients, it probably would be considered obscure enough to receive trade secret protection. That's because the recipe isn't available to other American restaurants.

(2) **You must have protected the secrecy.**
You must show that you've taken steps to keep the information secret—for example, by:
- keeping it in a secure place such as a locked cabinet
- giving employees access to it on a need to know basis, and
- having employees acknowledge in writing that the information is a trade secret.

EXAMPLE: Sue works at Speedy Copy Shop. She has daily access to the list of larger accounts that are regularly billed more than $2,000 per month. She quits to open her own shop. Before she does, she copies the list of major accounts. One of her first steps in getting her new business going is to try to get their business away from her former employer. Speedy sues Sue for infringing on its trade secret. At trial, Speedy shows that it keeps the list in a secure place, permits access only to selected employees who need the information and has all employees—including Sue—sign nondisclosure agreements. In light of these precautions, the judge orders Sue not to contact the customers on the list and requires her to compensate Speedy from any profits she's already earned on those accounts.

b. Covenants not to compete

It's always disappointing and often quite costly when a high-level employee leaves your business and begins competing with you—especially if you've trained the employee and shared valuable, inside information. Consider having such employees sign a covenant not to compete. In a typical covenant, the employee agrees not to own or work in a business that competes with yours for a specific time and within a specific distance from your established business.

The best time to secure a covenant not to compete is when you hire an employee. An employee who is already on the payroll may be more reluctant to sign anything—and you'll have less leverage to negotiate the agreement.

Battles over the legality of these agreements must usually be resolved in court. Judges are reluctant to deprive people of their rights to earn a living, so the key to a legally enforceable covenant not to compete is to make its terms reasonable. Focus on three questions.

- Is there a legitimate business reason for restricting activities of the particular employee? There probably is if you expect to spend significant time and money training a high-level employee and plan to trust him or her with sensitive contacts or lucrative accounts.
- Is the covenant reasonably limited in time? Courts tend to favor short covenants—the shorter the better. A one-year covenant may be reasonable for a particular employee. A three-year limit might not be.
- Is the covenant reasonably limited as to geographical scope? For a local business, a 50-mile limit or one that excludes competition in a few counties may be reasonable. For a regional business, a limit spanning several states may be deemed reasonable.

EXAMPLE: When Mary hires Sid to be the office manager for her profitable travel agency, she realizes that Sid will have access to major corporate accounts and daily contact with the corporate managers who make travel arrangements. Mary also knows that she'll spend considerable time in training Sid and invest more than $4,000 in specialized seminars that she'll require Sid to attend. She has Sid sign a covenant not to compete in which Sid promises that while working for Mary and for two years afterwards, he won't work for or own a travel agency within 50 miles of Mary's agency. After six months, Sid quits and starts a competing agency one mile from Mary's. The judge enforces the covenant not to compete by issuing an injunction forbidding Sid from operating his new business and by awarding damages to Mary as well.

Computers may defeat geographical limits. *As the travel and other industries begin doing more business through computer link-ups, geographical limits will become a less effective way to control competition by former employees. Through computer technology, a former worker may be able to compete with you from halfway across the country.*

For a guide on creating noncompete covenants for your employees to sign, see How to Create a Noncompete Agreement, *by Shannon Miehe (Nolo).*

B. Job Descriptions

Write a job description for each position. This will make the hiring process more objective, which in turn will reduce the possibility that you can be successfully accused of discrimination. Focus on qualifications, such as necessary skills, education, experience and licensure.

Be careful in setting requirements for education and experience. If set at an unnecessarily high level, your requirements may have the unintended effect of excluding a disproportionate number of racial minorities or other applicants who are part of other groups protected by anti-discrimination laws. Requiring a high school diploma or college degree may be discriminatory in some job categories because members of some minority groups are less likely than members of the general population to have completed high school or college. To require evidence of educational attainment may create an unnecessary barrier to getting a job. Of course, in many cases, a diploma, degree, certificate or license is a legitimate requirement because the job requires more than basic skills.

Also, specify the essential job functions. The Americans with Disabilities Act (ADA) forces you to decide what really is the core of each job so you don't exclude someone simply because he or she can't perform some marginal duties. Suppose your job description for a file clerk includes answering the phone, but the basic functions of the job are to file and retrieve written materials. Other employees usually answer the phone. Someone whose hearing is impaired may have trouble handling phone calls but be perfectly able to file and retrieve papers. Phone answering isn't an essential job function and shouldn't be listed as one.

C. Job Advertisements

After you write a job description, summarize it in a job advertisement. Be careful, because nuances in an ad can be used as evidence of discrimination against applicants of a particular gender, age or marital status.

There are a number of semantical pitfalls to avoid in job ads.

Don't Use	Use
Salesman	Salesperson
College Student	Part-time Worker
Handyman	General Repair Person
Gal Friday	Office Manager
Married Couple	Two-Person Job
Counter Girl	Retail Clerk
Waiter	Wait staff
Young	Energetic

In any ad, stick to the job skills needed and the basic responsibilities. Some examples:

"Fifty-unit apartment complex seeks experienced manager with general maintenance skills."

"Mid-sized manufacturing company has opening for accountant with tax experience to oversee interstate accounts."

"Cook trainee position available in new vegetarian restaurant. Flexible hours."

D. Job Applications

Develop a standard application form to make it easy to compare applicants. Use the form to let the job-seeker know the basic terms and conditions of the job. Because the applicant signs the application, it can be a valuable piece of evidence if a question comes up later about what you actually promised.

You can also use the job application to obtain the employee's consent to have you conduct a background investigation and reference check. If the applicant consents to your investigation, he or she will have a tough time later claiming an invasion of privacy. (See Section G.)

Limit the form to job-related information that will help you decide who's the best person for the job. Consider requesting the following information:

- Name, address, and phone number
- Are you legally entitled to work in the United States?
- What position are you applying for?
- What other positions would you like to be considered for?
- Can you work overtime?
- If you are hired, when can you start work?
- Education—high school, college, graduate and other (including school names, addresses, number of years attended, degree and major)
- Employment history—including name, address and phone number of each employer, supervisor's name, date of employment, job title and responsibilities and reason for leaving, and
- Special training or achievements.

If the job involves handling money or calling on customers at home, ask if the applicant has ever been convicted of a crime and the details of the conviction. Similarly, in an application for a job which requires driving, ask about the applicant's driving record.

1. Pre-Employment Inquiries

The chart below outlines the type of information you can ask for in applications and during job interviews as specified in federal laws. The chart may also be sufficient for complying with the laws of your state, but double-check with your state's civil rights department.

In addition to the areas covered in the chart, the Americans with Disabilities Act (ADA) prohibits you from asking any pre-employment questions about a disability—including medical history or treatment— or requiring a medical exam. However, before you make a job offer, you may ask questions about an applicant's ability to perform specific job functions.

PRE-EMPLOYMENT INQUIRIES

SUBJECT	LAWFUL PRE-EMPLOYMENT INQUIRIES	UNLAWFUL PRE-EMPLOYMENT INQUIRIES
Name	Applicant's full name. Have you ever worked for this company under a different name? Is any additional information relative to a different name necessary to check work record? If yes, explain.	Original name of an applicant whose name has been changed by court order or otherwise. Applicant's maiden name.
Address or Duration of Residence	How long have you been a resident of this state or city?	
Birthplace	None	Birthplace of applicant. Birthplace of applicant's parents, spouse or other close relatives. Requirements that applicant submit birth certificate, naturalization or baptismal record.
Age	Are you 18 years old or older? This question may be asked only for the purpose of determining whether applicants are of legal age for employment.	How old are you? What is your date of birth?
Religion or Creed	None	Inquiry into an applicant's religious denomination, religious affiliations, church, parish, pastor or religious holidays observed.
Race or Color	None	Inquiry regarding applicant's race, complexion or color of skin.
Photograph	None	Any requirement for a photograph prior to hire.
Height	None	Inquiry regarding applicant's height.
Weight	None	Inquiry regarding applicant's weight.
Marital Status	Is your spouse employed by this employer?	Requirement that an applicant provide any information regarding marital status or children. Are you single or married? Do you have any children? Is your spouse employed? What is your spouse's name?
Gender	None	Mr., Miss, Ms. or Mrs. or an inquiry regarding gender. Inquiry as to the ability to reproduce or advocacy of any form of birth control. Requirement that women be given pelvic examinations.

PRE-EMPLOYMENT INQUIRIES (continued)

SUBJECT	LAWFUL PRE-EMPLOYMENT INQUIRIES	UNLAWFUL PRE-EMPLOYMENT INQUIRIES
Disability	These [provide applicant with list] are the essential functions of the job. How would you perform them?	Inquiries regarding an individual's physical or mental condition which are not directly related to the requirements of a specific job and which are used as a factor in making employment decisions in a way which is contrary to the provisions or purposes of the Civil Rights Act.
Citizenship	Are you legally authorized to work in the United States on a full-time basis?	Questions below are unlawful unless asked as part of the federal I-9 process. Of what country are you a citizen? Whether an applicant is naturalized or a native-born citizen; the date when the applicant acquired citizenship. Requirement that an applicant produce naturalization papers or first papers. Whether applicant's parents or spouse are naturalized or native-born citizens of the United States: the date when such parent or spouse acquired citizenship.
National Origin	Inquiry into language applicant speaks and writes fluently.	Inquiry into applicant's lineage; ancestry; national origin; descent; parentage or nationality (unless part of I-9 process). Nationality of applicant's parents or spouse. Inquiry into how applicant acquired ability to read, write or speak a foreign language.
Education	Inquiry into the academic, vocational or professional education of an applicant and public and private schools attended.	
Experience	Inquiry into work experience. Inquiry into countries applicant has visited.	
Arrests	Have you ever been convicted of a crime? Are there any felony charges pending against you?	Inquiry regarding arrests which did not result in conviction. (Except for law enforcement agencies.)
Relatives	Names of applicant's relatives already employed by this company.	Address of any relative of applicant, other than address (within the United States) of applicant's father and mother, husband or wife and minor dependent children.
Notice in Case of Emergency	Name and address of person to be notified in case of accident or emergency.	Name and address of nearest relative to be notified in case of accident or emergency.
Organizations	Inquiry into the organizations of which an applicant is a member, excluding organizations the name or character of which indicates the race, color, religion, national origin or ancestry of its members.	List all clubs, societies and lodges to which you belong.

Source: *The Employer's Legal Handbook*, by Fred Steingold (Nolo).

2. Post-Offer Inquiries

After you make a conditional job offer, you're free to gather more details on health matters. You can at that point require a medical exam or ask health-related questions— but only if you require this for all candidates who receive conditional offers in the same job category.

E. Interviews

Before interviewing applicants for a job opening, write a set of questions focusing on the job duties as listed in the job description (see Section B) and the applicant's skills and experience. Some examples:

"Tell me about your experience in running a mailroom."

"How much experience did you have making cold calls on your last job?"

"Explain how you typically go about organizing your workday."

"Have any of your jobs required strong leadership skills?"

By writing down the questions and sticking to the same format for all interviews for the position, you reduce the risk that a rejected applicant will later complain about unequal treatment.

During an interview, focus on job requirements and company policies. Suppose you're concerned that an applicant with young kids may spend too much time talking with them on the phone. You can't ask: "Do you have children?" or "Who watches the kids when you're at work?" But you can say to the applicant: "We don't allow personal phone calls during work hours. Do you have a problem with that?" The applicant then knows the ground rules and will let you know if a problem exists. Just make sure you apply your phone policy to all employees.

For additional suggestions on interviewing, see Stay Out of Court: The Manager's Guide to Preventing Employee Lawsuits, *by Rita Risser (Prentice-Hall).*

F. Testing

Testing job applicants—which can include skills testing, aptitude testing, honesty testing, medical testing and drug testing—is most common in larger businesses. But even if your business is small or mid-sized, you may have needs you feel could best be met by testing. If so you should know the legal limitations.

1. Skills Tests

Most small businesses—especially new ones—operate on a slim profit margin and need to know that employees will be up to speed from day one. If you're hiring a computer operator, you may want to test the applicant for speed and accuracy in entering information. If you're hiring a person to be a clerk in your bookstore, you may want to test the applicant's knowledge of literature. If you're hiring a driver for a delivery van, a road test would be appropriate—and a cooking test for a chef is quite reasonable. As long as the skills you're testing for are genuinely related to job duties, a skills test is generally legal.

2. Aptitude Tests

Few small employers are tempted to use written tests to get additional insight into an applicant's abilities or psyche. That's fortunate, because these tests are usually a poor idea. A written aptitude test may discriminate illegally against minority applicants because it really reflects test-taking ability rather than actual job skills. A personality test can be even riskier. In addition to its potential for illegal discrimination, such a test may invade an applicant's protected privacy rights—by inquiring, for example, into religious beliefs or sexual practices.

If you do decide to use aptitude or personality tests, make sure they've been screened scientifically for validity and are related to job performance.

Get professional advice. *Because testing is such a sensitive legal issue and it's easy to make mistakes, it makes sense to check with an experienced employment lawyer before testing applicants. (See Chapter 24.)*

3. Honesty Tests

Lie detector or polygraph tests—rarely used by small businesses anyhow—are virtually outlawed by the federal Employee Polygraph Protection Act. With just a few exceptions, you can't require job applicants to take lie detector tests and you can't inquire about previous tests. The only private employers who can use lie detector tests to screen applicants are businesses that offer armored car, alarm and guard services or that manufacture, distribute or dispense pharmaceuticals—and even in those situations there are restrictions on which applicants can be tested and how the tests must be administered.

About the only time the typical employer can use a lie detector test is when an employee is reasonably suspected of being involved in a workplace theft or embezzlement.

Some employers are intrigued by written "honesty tests" as a way to screen job applicants. Because these tests are often inaccurate and sometimes invade an applicant's privacy or have a discriminatory impact on some minority groups, their legality is doubtful in most states.

4. Drug Tests

You have a legal right to insist on a drug-free workplace. Most small employers don't test for drugs, preferring to use background checks and personal interviews to try to screen out serious drug users. However, some employers want to be sure employees are drug-free and want to test.

The only problem is that testing to weed out drug users may conflict with workers' rights to privacy. The laws on drug testing vary widely from state to state and are changing quickly. Statutes regulating drug testing are summarized in the chart below. In states having such statutes, your right to test for drugs may turn on whether or not the employee's job poses an unusual risk of danger to the employee, co-workers or the public.

Check your state law on drug testing.
Before you initiate any program of testing job applicants or employees, be sure you know exactly what your state law provides. Like all laws, the laws summarized on the chart are subject to amendment—and states currently without drug-testing laws may decide to adopt them. A trade association may have information about the current status of the drug testing laws in your state or you can do your own legal research. A brief consultation with an experienced employment lawyer should also give you the information you need. (See Chapter 24.)

State Drug and Alcohol Testing

Alabama

Ala. Code §§ 25-5-330 to 25-5-340

Employers affected: Employers who establish a drug-free workplace program to qualify for a workers' compensation rate discount.

Testing applicants: Must test upon conditional offer of employment. Must test all new hires. Job ads must include notice that drug and alcohol testing required.

Testing employees: Random testing permitted. Must test after an accident that results in lost work time. Must also test upon reasonable suspicion; reasons for suspicion must be documented and made available to employee upon request.

Employee rights: Employees have 5 days to contest or explain a positive test result. Employer must have an employee assistance program or maintain a resource file of outside programs.

Notice and policy requirements: All employees must have written notice of drug policy. Must give 60 days advance notice before implementing testing program. Policy must state consequences of refusing to take test or testing positive.

Drug-free workplace program: Yes.

Alaska

Alaska Stat. §§ 23.10.600 and following

Employers affected: Voluntary for employers with one or more full-time employees. (There is no state mandated drug and alcohol testing.)

Testing employees: Employer may test:
- for any job-related purpose
- to maintain productivity and safety
- as part of an accident investigation
- upon reasonable suspicion.

Employee rights: Employer must provide written test results within 5 working days. Employee has 10 working days to request opportunity to explain positive test results; employer must grant request within 72 hours or before taking any adverse employment action.

Notice and policy requirement: Before implementing a testing program employer must distribute a written drug policy to all employees and must give 30 days' advance notice. Policy must state consequences of a positive test or refusal to submit to testing.

Arizona

Ariz. Rev. Stat. § 23-493

Employers affected: Employers with one or more full-time employees.

Testing applicants: Employer must inform prospective hires that they will undergo drug testing as a condition of employment.

Testing employees: Employees are subject to random and scheduled tests:
- for any job-related purpose,
- to maintain productivity and safety,
- upon reasonable suspicion.

Employee rights: Policy must inform employees of their right to explain positive results.

Notice and policy requirement: Before conducting tests employer must give employees a copy of the written policy. Policy must state the consequences of a positive test or refusal to submit to testing.

Drug-free workplace program: Yes.

Arkansas

Ark. Code Ann. §§ 11-14-105 to 11-14-107

Employers affected: Employers who establish a drug-free workplace program to qualify for a workers' compensation rate discount.

Testing applicants: Must test upon conditional offer of employment. Job ads must include notice that drug and alcohol testing required.

Testing employees: Employer must test any employee
- on reasonable suspicion of drug use
- as part of a routine fitness-for-duty medical exam
- after an accident that results in injury
- as follow-up to a required rehabilitation program.

Employee rights: Employer may not refuse to hire applicant or take adverse personnel action against an employee on the basis of a single positive test that has not been verified by a confirmation test. An applicant or employee has 5 days after receiving test results to contest or explain them.

Notice and policy requirements: Employer must give all employees a written statement of drug policy and must give 60 days' advance notice before implementing program.

Drug-free workplace program: Yes.

State Drug and Alcohol Testing (continued)

California

Cal. Lab. Code §§ 1025, 1026

Employers affected: No provisions for private employer testing. An employer with 25 or more employees must reasonably accommodate an employee who wants to enter a treatment program. Employer may fire or refuse to hire an employee whose drug or alcohol use interferes with job duties or workplace safety.

Connecticut

Conn. Gen. Stat. Ann. § 31-51t

Employers affected: Any individual, corporation, partnership or unincorporated association.

Testing applicants: Employer must inform job applicants in writing that drug testing is required as a condition of employment.

Testing employees: Employer may test:
- when there is reasonable suspicion that employee is under the influence of drugs or alcohol and job performance is or could be impaired
- when authorized by federal law
- when employee's position is dangerous or safety-sensitive
- as part of a voluntary employee assistance program.

Employee rights: Employer may not take any adverse personnel action on the basis of a single positive test that has not been verified by a confirmation test.

Florida

Fla. Stat. Ann. §§ 440.101 to 440.102

Employers affected: Employers who establish a drug-free workplace program to qualify for a workers' compensation rate discount.

Testing applicants: Must inform job applicants that drug and alcohol testing is required as a condition of employment.

Testing employees: Must test any employee:
- on reasonable suspicion of drug use
- as part of a routine fitness-for-duty medical exam
- as part of a required rehabilitation program.

Employee rights: Employees who voluntarily seek treatment for substance abuse cannot be fired, disciplined or discriminated against, unless they have tested positive or have been in treatment in the past. All employees have the right to explain positive results within 5 days. Em-

ployer may not take any adverse personnel action on the basis of an initial positive result that has not been verified by a confirmation test.

Notice and policy requirements: Prior to implementing testing, employer must give 60 days' advance notice and must give employees written copy of drug policy.

Drug-free workplace program: Yes.

Georgia

Ga. Code Ann. §§ 34-9-410 to 34-9-421

Employers affected: Employers who establish a drug-free workplace program to qualify for a workers' compensation rate discount.

Testing applicants: Applicants are required to submit to a substance abuse test after they have been offered employment.

Testing employees: Must test any employee:
- on reasonable suspicion of drug use
- as part of a routine fitness-for-duty medical exam
- as part of a required rehabilitation program.

Employee rights: Employees have 5 days to explain or contest a positive result. Employer must have an employee assistance program or maintain a resource file of outside programs.

Notice and policy requirements: Employer must give applicants and employees notice of testing; must give 60 days' notice before implementing program. All employees must receive a written policy statement; policy must state the consequences of refusing to submit to a drug test or of testing positive.

Drug-free workplace program: Yes.

Hawaii

Haw. Rev. Stat. § 329B-1

Testing applicants: Same conditions as current employees.

Testing employees: Employer may test employees only if these conditions are met:
- employer pays all costs including confirming test
- tests are performed by a licensed laboratory
- employee receives a list of the substances being tested for
- there is a form for disclosing medicines and legal drugs
- the results are kept confidential.

State Drug and Alcohol Testing (continued)

Idaho

Idaho Code §§ 72-1701 to 72-1706

Employers affected: Voluntary for all private employers.

Testing applicants: Employer may test as a condition of hiring.

Testing employees: May test as a condition of continued employment.

An employer who follows drug-free workplace guidelines may fire employees who refuse to submit to testing or who test positive for drugs or alcohol. Employees will be fired for misconduct and denied unemployment benefits.

Employee rights: An employee or applicant who receives notice of a positive test may request a retest within 7 working days. If the retest results are negative, the employer must pay for the cost; if they are positive, the employee must pay.

Drug-free workplace program: Yes (compliance is optional).

Illinois

775 Ill. Comp. Stat. § 5/2-104(C)(3)

Employers affected: Employers with 15 or more employees.

Testing employees: Employer may prohibit all employees from using or being under the influence of alcohol and illegal drugs. Employer may test employees who have been in rehabilitation. Employee may be held to the same standards as other employees, even if the unsatisfactory job performance or behavior is due to drug use or alcoholism.

Indiana

Ind. Code Ann. §§ 22-9-5-6(b), 22-9-5-24

Employers affected: Employers with 15 or more employees.

Testing employees: Employer may prohibit all employees from using or being under the influence of alcohol and illegal drugs. Employer may test employees who have been in rehabilitation. Employee may be held to the same standards as other employees, even if the unsatisfactory job performance or behavior is due to drug use or alcoholism.

Iowa

Iowa Code § 730.5

Employers affected: Employers with one or more full-time employees.

Testing applicants: Employer may test as a condition of hiring.

Testing employees: Employer may test employees:
- as a condition of continued employment
- upon reasonable suspicion
- during and after rehabilitation
- following an accident that caused a reportable injury or more than $1,000 property damage.

Employee rights: Employee has 7 days to request a retest. Employers with 50 or more employees must provide rehabilitation for any employee who has worked for at least one year and has not previously violated the substance abuse policy; no adverse action may be taken if employee successfully completes rehabilitation. Employer must have an employee assistance program or maintain a resource file of outside programs.

Drug-free workplace program: Yes (compliance is optional).

Louisiana

La. Rev. Stat. Ann. §§ 49:1001 and following

Employers affected: Employers with one or more full-time employees. (Does not apply to oil drilling, exploration or production.)

Testing applicants: Employer may require all applicants to submit to drug and alcohol test. Employer does not have to confirm a positive result of a pre-employment drug screen, but must offer the applicant the opportunity to pay for a confirmation test and a review by a medical review officer.

Employee rights: Except for a pre-employment test, employer may not take adverse personnel action on the basis of an initial screen. Employees with confirmed positive results have 7 working days to request access to all records relating to the drug test. Employer may allow employee to undergo rehabilitation without termination of employment.

State Drug and Alcohol Testing (continued)

Maine

Me. Rev. Stat. Ann. tit. 26, §§ 681 to 690

Employers affected: Employers with one or more full-time employees. (Law does not require or encourage employers to conduct substance abuse testing.)

Testing applicants: Employer may require applicant to take a drug test only if offered employment or placed on an eligibility list.

Testing employees: Employer may test for probable cause, but may not base belief on a single accident; must document the facts and give employee a copy. May test when:

- there could be an unreasonable threat to the health and safety of coworkers or the public
- an employee returns to work following a positive test.

Employee rights: Employee who tests positive has 3 days to explain or contest results. Employee must be given an opportunity to participate in a rehabilitation program for up to 6 months; an employer with more than 20 full-time employees must pay for half of any out-of-pocket costs. After successfully completing the program, employee is entitled to return to previous job with full pay and benefits.

Notice and policy requirements: All employers must have a written policy approved by the state Department of Labor. Policy must be distributed to each employee at least 30 days before it takes effect. Any changes to policy require 60 days advance notice. An employer with more than 20 full-time employees must have an employee assistance program certified by the Office of Substance Abuse before implementing a testing program.

Maryland

Md. Code Ann., [Health-Gen.] § 17-214

Employers affected: Law applies to all employers.

Testing applicants: May use preliminary screening to test applicant. If initial result is positive, may make job offer conditional on confirmation test results.

Testing employees: Employer may require substance abuse testing for legitimate business purposes only.

Employee rights: The sample must be tested by a certified laboratory; at the time of testing employee may request laboratory's name and address. An employee who tests positive must be given:

- a copy of the test results
- a copy of the employer's written drug and alcohol policy
- written notice of any adverse action employer intends to take
- statement of employee's right to an independent confirmation test at own expense.

Minnesota

Minn. Stat. Ann. §§ 181.950 to 181.957

Employers affected: Employers with one or more full-time employees. (Employers are not required to test.)

Testing applicants: Employers may require applicants to submit to a drug or alcohol test only after they have been given a job offer and have seen a written notice of testing policy. May only test if required of all applicants for same position.

Testing employees: Employers may require drug or alcohol testing only according to a written testing policy. Testing may be done if there is a reasonable suspicion that employee:

- is under the influence of drugs or alcohol
- has violated drug and alcohol policy
- has been involved in an accident
- has sustained or caused another employee to sustain a personal injury. Random tests permitted only for employees in safety-sensitive positions. With 2 weeks' notice, employers may also test as part of an annual routine physical exam.

Employee rights: If test is positive, employee has 3 days to explain the results; employee must notify employer within 5 days of intention to obtain a retest. Employer may not discharge employee for a first-time positive test without offering counseling or rehabilitation; employee who refuses or does not complete program successfully may be discharged.

Notice and policy requirements: Employees must be given a written notice of testing policy which includes consequences of refusing to take test or having a positive test result. Two weeks' notice required before testing as part of an annual routine physical exam.

State Drug and Alcohol Testing (continued)

Mississippi

Miss. Code Ann. §§ 71-7-1 and following; 71-3-205

Employers affected: Employers with one or more full-time employees. Employers who establish a drug-free workplace program to qualify for a workers' compensation rate discount must implement testing procedures.

Testing applicants: May test (must test, if drug-free workplace) all applicants as part of employment application process. Employer may request a signed statement that applicant has read and understands the drug and alcohol testing policy and/or notice.

Testing employees: May (must test, if drug-free workplace) require drug and alcohol testing of all employees:
- on reasonable suspicion
- as part of a routinely scheduled fitness for duty medical examination
- as a follow-up to a rehabilitation program
- who have tested positive within the previous 12 months.

Employee rights: Employer must inform an employee in writing within 5 working days of receipt of a positive confirmed test result; employee may request and receive a copy of the test result report. Employee has 10 working days after receiving notice to explain the positive test results. Private employer who elects to establish a drug-free workplace program must have an employee assistance program or maintain a resource file of outside programs.

Notice and policy requirements: 30 days before implementing testing program employer must give employees written notice of drug and alcohol policy which includes consequences
- of a positive confirmed result
- of refusing to take test
- of other violations of the policy.

Drug-free workplace program: Yes.

Montana

Mont. Code Ann. §§ 39-2-205 to 39-2-211

Employers affected: Employers with one or more employees.

Testing applicants: May test as a condition of hire.

Testing employees: Employees may be tested:
- on reasonable suspicion
- after involvement in an accident that causes personal injury or more than $1,500 property damage
- as a follow-up to a previous positive test
- as a follow-up to treatment or a rehabilitation program.

Employer may conduct random tests as long as there is an established date and all personnel are subject to testing.

Employer may require an employee who tests positive to undergo treatment as a condition of continued employment.

Employee rights: After a positive result, employee may request additional confirmation by an independent laboratory; if the results are negative, employer must pay the test costs.

Notice and policy requirements: Written policy must be available for review 60 days before testing.

Nebraska

Neb. Rev. Stat. §§ 48-1901 and following

Employers affected: Employers with 6 or more full-time and part-time employees.

Testing employees: Employer may require employees to submit to drug or alcohol testing and may discipline or discharge any employee who refuses.

Employee rights: Employer may not take adverse action on the basis of an initial positive result unless it is confirmed according to state and federal guidelines.

North Carolina

N.C. Gen. Stat. §§ 95-230 to 95-235

Employers affected: Law applies to all employers.

Testing employees: Employer must preserve samples for at least 90 days after confirmed test results are released.

Employee rights: Employee has right to retest a confirmed positive sample at own expense.

North Dakota

N.D. Cent. Code § 34-01-15

Employers affected: Any employer who requires a medical exam as a condition of hire or continued employment may include a drug or alcohol test.

State Drug and Alcohol Testing (continued)

Ohio

Ohio Admin. Code § 4123-17-58

Employers affected: Employers who establish a drug-free workplace program to qualify for a workers' compensation rate discount.

Testing applicants: Must test all applicants and new hires within at least 90 days of employment.

Testing employees: Must test employees:
- on reasonable suspicion
- following a return to work after a positive test
- after an accident which results in an injury requiring offsite medical attention or property damage over limit specified in drug and alcohol policy.

Employee rights: Employer must have an employee assistance plan. Employer must offer healthcare coverage which includes chemical dependency counseling and treatment.

Notice and policy requirements: Policy must state consequences for refusing to submit to testing or for violating guidelines. Policy must include a commitment to rehabilitation.

Drug-free workplace program: Yes.

Oklahoma

Okla. Stat. Ann. tit. 40, §§ 551 to 565

Employers affected: Employers with one or more employees. (Drug or alcohol testing not required or encouraged.)

Testing applicants: Employer may test applicants as a condition of employment; may refuse to hire applicant who refuses to undergo test or has a confirmed positive result.

Testing employees: Before requiring testing employer must provide an employee assistance program. Random testing is allowed. May test employees:
- on reasonable suspicion
- after an accident resulting in injury or property damage over $500
- as part of a routine fitness-for-duty examination
- or as follow-up to a rehabilitation program.

Employee rights: Employee has right to retest a positive result at own expense; if the confirmation test is negative employer must reimburse costs.

Notice and policy requirements: Before requiring testing employer must:
- adopt a written policy
- give a copy to each employee and to any applicant offered a job
- allow 30 days' notice.

Oregon

Or. Rev. Stat. §§ 659.225 to 659.227; 438.435

Employers affected: Law applies to all employers.

Testing applicants: Unless there is reasonable suspicion that an applicant is under the influence of alcohol, no employer may require a breathalyzer test as a condition of employment. Employer is not prohibited from conducting a test if applicant consents.

Testing employees: Unless there is reasonable suspicion that an employee is under the influence of alcohol, no employer may require a breathalyzer or blood alcohol test as a condition of continuing employment. Employer is not prohibited from conducting a test if employee consents.

Employee rights: No action may be taken based on the results of an on-site drug test without a confirming test performed according to state Health Division regulations. Upon written request test results will be reported to the employee.

Rhode Island

R.I. Gen. Laws §§ 28-6.5-1 to 28-6.5-2

Employers affected: Law applies to all employers.

Testing employees: May require employee to submit to a drug test only if there are reasonable grounds, based on specific observations, to believe employee is using controlled substances that are impairing job performance.

Employee rights: Employee who tests positive may have the sample retested at employer's expense and must be given opportunity to explain or refute results. Employee may not be terminated on the basis of a positive result, but must be referred to a licensed substance abuse professional. After referral employer may require additional testing; may terminate employee if test results are positive.

State Drug and Alcohol Testing (continued)

South Carolina

S.C. Code Ann. §§ 41-1-15; 38-73-500

Employers affected: Employers who establish a drug-free workplace program to qualify for a workers' compensation rate discount.

Testing employees: Must conduct random testing among all employees. Must conduct a follow-up test within 30 minutes of the first test.

Employee rights: Employee must receive positive test results in writing within 24 hours.

Notice and policy requirements: Employer must notify all employees of the drug-free workplace program at the time it is established or at the time of hiring, whichever is earlier. Program must include a policy statement that balances respect for individuals with the need to maintain a safe, drug-free environment

Drug-free workplace program: Yes.

Tennessee

Tenn. Code Ann. §§ 50-9-101 and following

Employers affected: Employers who establish a drug-free workplace program to qualify for a workers' compensation rate discount.

Testing applicants: Must test applicants upon conditional offer of employment. Job ads must include notice that drug and alcohol testing required.

Testing employees: Employer must test upon reasonable suspicion; must document behavior on which the suspicion is based within 24 hours or before test results are released, whichever is earlier, and must give a copy to the employee upon request. Employer must test employees:
- who are in safety sensitive positions
- as part of a routine fitness-for-duty medical exam
- after an accident that results in injury
- as a follow-up to a required rehabilitation program.

Employee rights: Employee has the right to explain or contest a positive result within 5 days. Employee may not be fired, disciplined or discriminated against for voluntarily seeking treatment unless employee has previously tested positive or been in a rehabilitation program.

Notice and policy requirements: Before implementing testing program, employer must provide 60 days' notice and must give all employees a written drug and alcohol policy statement.

Drug-free workplace program: Yes.

Texas

Tex. Lab. Code Ann. §§ 411.091 to 411.093

Employers affected: Employers with 15 or more employees who have a workers' compensation insurance policy.

Notice and policy requirements: Must adopt a drug abuse policy and provide a written copy to employees.

Drug-free workplace program: Under current law the Workers' Compensation Commission is conducting a study about implementing a drug-free workplace requirement. Report due to the legislature in February 2003.

Utah

Utah Code Ann. §§ 34-38-1 to 34-38-15

Employers affected: Employers with one or more employees.

Testing applicants: Employer may test any applicant for drugs or alcohol as long as management also submits to periodic testing.

Testing employees: Employer may test employee for drugs or alcohol as long as management also submits to periodic testing. Employer may also require testing to:
- investigate an accident or theft
- maintain employee or public safety
- ensure productivity, quality or security.

Employee rights: Employer may suspend, discipline, discharge or require treatment on the basis of a confirmed positive test result.

Notice and policy requirements: Testing must be conducted according to a written policy that has been distributed to employees and is available for review by prospective employees.

Vermont

Vt. Stat. Ann. tit. 21, § 511

Employers affected: Employers with one or more employees.

Testing applicants: Employer may not test applicants for drugs or alcohol unless there is a conditional job offer, 10 days' advance notice and test is part of a comprehensive physical examination.

State Drug and Alcohol Testing (continued)

Testing employees: Random testing not permitted unless required by federal law. Employer may not require testing unless:

- there is probable cause to believe an employee is using or is under the influence
- employer has an employee assistance program which provides rehabilitation
- employee who tests positive and agrees to enter employee assistance program is not terminated.

Employee rights: Employer must provide an informal meeting for employee or applicant to explain a positive test result. Employee or applicant has right to an independent retest at own expense. Employee who successfully completes employee assistance program may not be terminated; may be suspended for up to 3 months to complete program. Employee who tests positive after completing treatment may be fired.

Current as of March 12, 2001

You generally have much more leeway in screening job applicants than in testing employees who are already on board. If your state permits testing applicants or employees and you plan to do such testing, use the job application form to inform applicants of this policy. In addition, it's a good idea—and required by the law of some states—to give applicants a written drug testing policy statement that's separate from the application. When applicants are told up front about drug testing, it's harder for them to later claim that your drug testing program is a violation of their privacy.

Once an applicant becomes an employee, drug testing gets stickier. Testing is usually permitted when employees have been in an accident or you've seen them bring illegal drugs to work. Your legal right to test at random and without prior notice is unclear—and questionable.

Drug Testing and the ADA

The Americans with Disabilities Act (ADA) forbids you from testing an applicant for drugs until you've made a conditional offer of employment.

After you've made a conditional offer of employment and as part of a pre-employment medical screening, you may discover that the applicant had a drug problem in the past. The ADA prohibits you from discriminating against people because of past drug problems. This includes people who no longer use drugs illegally and are receiving treatment for drug addiction and those who have been rehabilitated successfully.

To make sure that drug use isn't recurring, however, you may request evidence that a person is taking part in a drug rehab program. You may also ask for the results of a drug test.

You can refuse to hire someone with a history of alcoholism or illegal drug use if you can show that the person poses a direct threat to health or safety. You must show that there's a high probability that the person will return to the illegal drug use or alcohol abuse, and a high probability of substantial harm to the person or others—harm that you can't reduce or eliminate by making reasonable changes in the workplace. Unfortunately, the EEOC offers no guidance on the type of evidence that would suffice to show the high probability of a problem arising.

G. Investigating Job Application Information

Since some people give false or incomplete information in their job applications, it's a good idea to verify their application information. To reduce the risk of an invasion of privacy claim, inform the applicant in the job application that you will be requesting information from former employers, schools, credit reporting sources and law enforcement agencies.

Ask the applicant to sign a consent form as part of the application process.

1. Former Employers

Contact as many former employers as possible to get the inside story about an applicant. But understand that former employers are often reluctant to say anything negative for fear that if they speak frankly, they may be hit by a lawsuit for defamation.

In speaking with former employers, you'll often have to read between the lines. If a former employer is neutral, offers only faint praise or repeatedly overpraises a person for one aspect of a job only—"really great with numbers" or "invariably on time"—there's a good chance some negative information is hiding in the wings. Ask former employers: "Would you hire back this person if you could?" The response may be telling. If the person pauses or equivocates, you have your answer.

If references aren't glowing and don't take in all aspects of the job, consider calling back the applicant for a more directed interview.

 Reference checks may become more informative. *States are starting to pass laws that allow employers to speak more frankly about their former employees without fear of being sued. Under a Kansas law, for example, an employer is presumed to be acting in good faith when responding to reference checks. The Kansas law says that to collect damages, a former employee must show by "clear and convincing evidence" that the former employer acted in bad faith in providing job-related information. Laws such as this help the former employer cope with a troubling legal bind: the possibility of being sued by the former employee for speaking too freely or, alternatively, being sued by the potential new employer for not disclosing seriously negative information.*

Find out if your state has a law or a court decision requiring employers to disclose seriously negative information about a former employee or absolving employers from liability for doing so in good faith. If so, don't assume that the former employers you call for reference checks know about it. Telling them about their responsibility and the protection they have under your state's law may lead to your getting a fuller picture of a prospective employee.

2. School Transcripts

On-the-job experience generally is more relevant to employment than an applicant's educational credentials. Still, you may have good reasons for requiring a high school diploma or college degree for some jobs—especially for younger employees who don't have a lot of job experience. If so, you may want to see proof that the applicant really received the diploma or degree or took the courses claimed in the job application.

3. Credit History

Credit information may be relevant in the rare cases when you hire someone who will handle money. Someone with large debts, for example, may be inclined to skim money from your business. And an applicant who can't keep his or her personal finances in order is probably not a good choice for a job requiring management of your company's finances. For these types of jobs, a credit check is sensible.

In most situations, however, a credit check is an unnecessary intrusion into an applicant's personal life. What's more, unless you have a good reason for doing a credit check for a particular job, you may run afoul of anti-discrimination laws. According to the EEOC, requiring an applicant to have good credit may subtly discriminate against some minority groups. State laws, too, may limit your use of credit information in deciding whether to hire someone.

Assuming that you have a good business reason to order a credit report on a job applicant, it's always a good idea to get the applicant's consent first. Some states, in fact, require such consent. In addition, the federal Fair Credit Reporting Act requires you to let an applicant know if he or she has been denied employment because of something in a credit report.

 Authoritative information about the Fair Credit Reporting Act is available at the Federal Trade Commission's website, www.ftc.gov.

4. Criminal History

Asking an applicant about his or her arrest record or making a hiring decision based on that record can violate state and federal anti-discrimination laws. Criminal charges are often dropped or found to be without merit.

Convictions are another matter. Anti-discrimination laws generally allow you to inquire about an applicant's conviction record and to reject an applicant because of a conviction record that suggests the applicant wouldn't be a good fit for the job. If you're hiring a delivery truck driver, for example, it wouldn't violate anti-discrimination laws to reject an applicant based on a drunk driving conviction.

In some states you can't ask about convictions for minor offenses or misdemeanors that go back more than five years if the applicant has had a clean slate since that time.

5. Driving Records

When a job requires an employee to drive, it's wise to inform applicants that you'll be checking on their driving record—and to actually do so. You usually can obtain driving records for a modest cost from the state authority that issues driver's licenses. Check, too, with your insurance company to be sure you meet the requirements for bringing new employees under your vehicle insurance coverage.

H. Immigration Law Requirements

Immigration laws, enforced by the Department of Homeland Security (DHS), prohibit hiring aliens who don't have government authorization to work in the United States. There are specific procedures you must follow when hiring employees—even those who are born and raised in the town where your business is located. Specifically, you and the new employee must complete Form I-9, *Employment Eligibility Verification.* This one-page form is intended to ensure that the employee can work legally in the United States and has proof of his or her identity.

 Form I-9 and further information are available on the website of DHS's Bureau of Citizenship & Immigration Services (BCIS) at www.bcis.gov.

I. Personnel Practices

The vast majority of job disputes can be resolved within the workplace if you listen patiently to what employees have to say and are prepared to make adjustments when legitimate complaints surface. However there's always the chance a dispute will get out of hand and that an employee will sue your small business for some perceived abuse of his or her rights. Or an unhappy employee may file a complaint with a government agency alleging that you violated a statute or an administrative regulation. If that happens, you'll have to prove to a judge, jury, arbitrator or investigator that you met your legal obligations to the employee. That can be harder than you think. Key paperwork may have been lost—or never prepared in the first place. And witnesses may have forgotten what happened or have moved on and not be locatable.

To maintain a solid, legal footing, establish good written policies and then maintain a paper trail indicating how they are implemented. Written policies and an employee handbook explaining employee benefits and responsibilities provide cogent points of reference when you discuss problems with an employee—and increase the likelihood of reaching an amicable resolution.

1. Employee Handbooks

An employee handbook can be of practical help in running your business. Once you give it to an employee, there can be no dispute over whether you gave the employee a list of paid days off or explained your vacation policies. It's all there in writing and everyone has the same information. If yours is a very small business, keep your handbook short and sweet at the start. At that stage, it's easy to involve all employees in writing it so that it accurately covers their concerns. Then, as your business grows, the framework necessary for a more detailed version will be in place.

If your handbook is good, you get a bonus: a measure of legal protection if you're challenged by an employee in a court or administrative proceeding. A handbook can be an objective piece of evidence showing that you've adopted fair and uniform policies and have informed your employees of exactly where they stand in their employment.

A good handbook should tell your employees how to let you know if they have a workplace problem. This gives you a chance to react before a small misunderstanding erupts into a full-blown legal dispute.

Even a tiny business with six to ten employees can benefit from an employee handbook—and you can produce one quickly and cheaply by using a self-help book or software program as a starting point. Modify the sample wording to fit your own needs.

Then check with your state department of labor to make sure your handbook complies with the laws in your state. Keep the handbook up to date as laws change. If you have specific legal questions, a brief consultation with a lawyer should be sufficient to clear them up.

Make sure your handbook doesn't promise more than you can deliver. *Your handbook may be treated as a contract that can actually limit your right to fire employees. To avoid that result, state in the handbook that:*

- *employees don't have employment contracts— and can't have them in the future—unless they're in writing and signed by the company president, and*
- *your company reserves the right to terminate employees for reasons not stated in the handbook or for no reason at all.*

2. Employee Performance Reviews

Most large companies review and evaluate their employees periodically. This is a sound management practice and one which many small companies should consider—especially for new employees. Evaluating new employees periodically gives them a chance to improve if they're not performing well. If you later find it necessary to discipline or fire an employee, it won't come as a surprise to the employee. By putting your evaluations in writing and saving them in the employee's file, you normally have a credible history of documented problems you can use if an employee claims that he or she was fired for an illegal reason. If your business has fewer than half a dozen employees, formal evaluations may be unwieldy—but it's still important to let employees know if they're not measuring up to what's expected of them. Keeping a short note of what you told the employee and when can be helpful as evidence that you gave the employee a chance to improve before you fired him or her.

J. Illegal Discrimination

To give workers a fair opportunity to get and keep jobs, Congress and state legislatures have passed laws prohibiting discrimination in the workplace.

1. Title VII of the Civil Rights Act

Title VII (42 USC § 2000 and following) applies to your business if you employ 15 or more people—either full-time or part-time. State laws, with similar prohibitions against discrimination, generally cover smaller employers, too.

Under Title VII, you can't use race, color, religion, gender or national origin as the basis for decisions on hirings, promotions, dismissals, pay raises, benefits, work assignments, leaves of absence—or just about any other aspect of employment. Title VII applies to everything from Help Wanted ads, to working conditions, to performance reviews, to giving references to other prospective employers.

2. Sexual Harassment

Sexual harassment in the workplace is a form of prohibited sexual discrimination. Illegal sexual harassment occurs when unwelcome sexual advances, requests for sexual favors and other verbal or physical conduct of a sexual nature creates a hostile or abusive work environment. The harassed employee is entitled to legal relief even without proof that the offending behavior has injured the employee psychologically.

Under federal law, it's clearly sexual harassment for an employer or a manager to make unwelcome sexual advances or to demand sexual favors in return for job benefits, promotions or continued employment.

But sexual harassment in the workplace can consist, as well, of many other activities including:

- posting sexually explicit photos that offend employees
- telling sex-related jokes or jokes that demean people because of their gender
- commenting inappropriately on an employee's appearance
- requiring employees to dress in scanty attire
- repeatedly requesting dates from a person who clearly isn't interested

- having strippers perform at a company gathering, and
- stating that people of one gender are inferior to people of the other gender or can't perform their jobs as well.

In short, any hostile or offensive behavior in the workplace that has a sexual component can constitute sexual harassment—and is illegal.

Your business can also be held responsible for sexual harassment if you or a supervisor know, or should know, it's being committed by one co-worker against another—or even by customers or vendors on your premises. You're also under a legal duty to take all necessary steps to prevent sexual harassment. No matter the size of your business, start by adopting a formal policy stating clearly that sexual harassment won't be tolerated. Post it on a bulletin board and place it in your employee handbook. Let employees know who within your company they can complain to if they've been sexually harassed.

Common Sense From the Supreme Court

People sometimes have taken extreme positions on the laws prohibiting sexual harassment. Fortunately, in 1998, the U.S. Supreme Court offered some practical advice to both employers and employees: Act reasonably and use common sense.

For example, in a case involving claims of same-sex harassment, the Court suggested that drawing the line between horseplay or flirtation and discrimination on the job isn't all that hard, even though men and woman may play differently. The Court said: "Common sense and an appropriate sensitivity to social context will enable courts and juries to distinguish between simple teasing or roughhousing among members of the same sex, and conduct which a reasonable person in the plaintiff's position would find hostile or abusive."

In other decisions, the Court has said that people who know about sexual harassment should let the employer know so that steps can be taken to stop it. An employee who doesn't cooperate with an employer's attempts to take corrective action may have a relatively weak case. The Court recognizes that, as an employer, you can defend against sexual harassment charges by showing you used reasonable care to address the problem—by having a strong written anti-harassment policy, for example, and a sound procedure for receiving and investigating complaints. Three cheers for common sense!

For an excellent in-depth explanation, see Sexual Harassment on the Job: What It Is & How to Stop It, *by William Petrocelli & Barbara Kate Repa (Nolo).*

3. Age Discrimination

The Age Discrimination in Employment Act or ADEA (29 USC § 623(a)) prohibits discrimination against those 40 years old or older. It applies to businesses with 20 or more employees—but similar state laws generally apply to businesses with fewer employees. As with the rest of Title VII, age discrimination is prohibited in all aspects of employment—hiring, firing, compensation and all other terms of employment.

Another law, the Older Worker's Benefits Protection Act, makes it illegal to use an employee's age as the basis for discrimination in benefits. Like the ADEA, this act covers employees who are 40 years old or older. Under this law, you cannot, for example, reduce health or life insurance benefits for older employees, nor can you stop their pensions from accruing if they work past their normal retirement ages. The law also discourages your business from targeting older workers when you cut staff.

The law also regulates the legal waivers that some employers ask employees to sign in connection with early retirement programs. For details, see *The Employer's Legal Handbook*, by Fred S. Steingold (Nolo).

4. Pregnancy

The Pregnancy Discrimination Act or PDA (92 USC § 2076) applies to businesses with 15 or more employees. Under the PDA, it's a form of gender discrimination to treat an employee differently because of pregnancy, childbirth or related medical conditions. If a woman is affected by such a condition, you must treat her the same as you treat other people in the workforce who are either able or unable to work.

You violate the PDA, for example, if you fire a woman whose pregnancy keeps her from working, but you don't fire other workers who are temporarily unable to do the job because of other physical problems. Similarly, if a pregnant worker is able to do the job, you can't lay her off because you think it's in her best interests to stay home. On the other hand, you don't violate the PDA if you apply medically based job restrictions to a pregnant woman— as long as you apply those same policies to employees who are not pregnant but who are under medical restrictions.

5. National Origin

The Immigration Reform and Control Act of 1986 makes it illegal to discriminate against a person because he or she isn't a U.S. citizen or national. The law forbids you from discriminating against aliens who have been lawfully admitted to the U.S. for permanent or temporary residence—and aliens who have applied for temporary residence status.

6. Gay and Lesbian Workers

Federal law doesn't specifically prohibit workplace discrimination based on sexual orientation, but several states have such laws—including California, Connecticut, the District of Columbia, Hawaii, Massachusetts, Minnesota, Nevada, New Hampshire, New Jersey, Rhode Island, Vermont and Wisconsin. Over 120 cities prohibit discrimination based on sexual orientation. If you're not sure what the local law is, call the municipal clerk where your company does business, or your state labor department or fair employment office.

K. Wages and Hours

Federal and state statutes regulate workplace wages and hours, imposing strict requirements on employers. Since fines and back wage awards can be expensive, it pays to know the law.

1. The Fair Labor Standards Act

The main law affecting worker's pay is the Federal Fair Labor Standards Act or FLSA (29 USC §§ 201 and following) which Congress passed in 1938. In addition to setting a minimum wage, the FLSA requires premium pay for overtime work and equal pay for men and women doing the same work. The law also contains special rules for hiring young workers.

Virtually all businesses and employees are covered. There are just a handful of specific exemptions, including most small farms. For details, check with the nearest office of the U.S. Labor Department's Wage and Hour Division. Even though your business is covered by the FLSA, some employees may be exempt from that law's minimum wage and overtime pay requirements.

Most employees who are exempt from the minimum wage and overtime pay requirements fall into one of five categories:
- executive employees
- administrative employees
- professional employees
- outside salespeople, and
- people in certain computer-related occupations.

There are a few miscellaneous categories of workers who are exempt as well.

The fine points of these exemptions are explained in Fact Sheet #17: Exemption for Executive, Administrative, Professional, and Outside Sales Employees under the Fair Labor Standards Act (FLSA), *available at the Department of Labor website, www.dol.gov.*

Who's Exempt and Who Isn't?

Job titles alone don't determine whether someone is an exempt executive, administrative or professional employee. The actual work relationship is what counts. Still, it's possible to make some generalizations about who's exempt and who isn't. Typical exempt jobs include such positions as department head, financial expert, personnel director, credit manager, account executive and tax specialist. Typical nonexempt jobs include such positions as clerk, bank teller, secretary, warehouse worker, errand runner, data entry person, bookkeeper, inspector and trainee.

2. Pay Requirements

If your business is covered by the FLSA, you must pay all covered employees at least the minimum wage—$5.15 an hour. Federal law allows you to pay a "training wage" of $4.25 an hour to employees under 20 years of age during their first 90 days on the job.

The amount will be higher if your state has established a higher minimum wage. In Alaska, for example, the minimum wage must remain 50 cents higher than the federal minimum. In California, the minimum wage is $6.75 an hour. In the few states that have a lower minimum, the federal rate controls. Each state has its own—often complex—rules for who's covered by its minimum wage law. A person who's exempt from the federal minimum wage requirements may be entitled to a minimum wage under the state law. To learn the details, call your state's department of labor.

The Equal Pay Act, an amendment to the FLSA, requires you to provide equal pay and benefits to men and women who do the same jobs, or jobs that require equal skill, effort and responsibility. Job titles aren't decisive in assessing whether two jobs

are equal; it's the work duties that count. The Act makes it unlawful, for example, for the owner of a hotel to pay its janitors (primarily men) at a different pay rate than its housekeepers (primarily women) if both are doing essentially the same work.

The Equal Pay Act doesn't prohibit pay differences based on:

- a seniority system
- a merit system
- a system that pays a worker based on the quantity or quality of what he or she produces, or
- any factor other than the worker's gender—starting salaries, for example, that are based on the worker's experience level.

3. Overtime Pay

The FLSA requires you to pay nonexempt workers at least one and one-half times their regular rates of pay for all hours worked in excess of 40 hours in one week. The FLSA doesn't require you to pay an employee at an overtime rate simply because he or she worked more than eight hours in one day. Generally, you calculate and pay overtime by the week. Each workweek stands alone; you can't average two or more workweeks. And you can't manipulate the start of the workweek merely to avoid paying overtime.

For more information on the overtime rules, see Fact Sheet #23: Overtime Requirements of the FLSA, available at the Department of Labor website, www.dol.gov.

4. Compensatory Time Off

The practice of granting hour-for-hour compensatory time—for example, giving a worker six hours time off one week as compensation for six hours of overtime work the previous week—isn't usually allowed for private sector employees covered by the FLSA. The rule is different for public employees.

Employers and employees are often puzzled when they learn that comp time isn't permitted in the private sector, because it seems like a sensible and mutually beneficial way to handle overtime in many situations. You do, however, have a few options for avoiding premium overtime pay by giving a worker time off instead of money. One way is to rearrange an employee's work schedule during a workweek.

> **EXAMPLE:** Margaret, a paralegal at the law firm of Smith and Jones, normally works an eight-hour day, Monday through Friday. One week, Margaret and the lawyers need to meet a deadline on a brief due in the court of appeals. So that week, Margaret works ten hours a day, Monday through Thursday. The law firm gives Margaret Friday off and pays her for a 40-hour week at her regular rate of pay. This is legal because Margaret hasn't worked any overtime as defined by the FLSA; only the hours over 40 hours in a week count as overtime hours.

If an employee works more than 40 hours one week, it's sometimes possible to reduce the worker's hours in another week so that the amount of the employee's paycheck remains constant. This is legal if:

- the time off is given within the same pay period as the overtime work, and
- the employee is given an hour and a half of time off for each hour of overtime work.

> **EXAMPLE:** Frames and Things, a shop that specializes in framing pictures, employs Jared and pays him $560 at the close of each two-week pay period. Because a week-long street art fair is expected to generate a great demand for framing services, the shop's owner wants Jared to work longer hours that week. However, the owner doesn't want to increase Jared's paycheck. She asks Jared to work 50 hours during

art fair week and gives him 15 hours off the next week. Since Jared is paid every two weeks, Frames and Things may properly reduce Jared's hours the second week to keep his paycheck at the $560 level.

Since state regulations may further restrict the use of comp time, check with your state's labor department and get a copy of all publications touching on wages and hours.

5. Calculating Work Hours

You must pay covered employees for all of their time that you control and that benefits you. In general, time on the job doesn't include the time employees spend washing themselves or changing clothes before or after work, or meal periods when employees are free from all work duties.

You needn't pay employees for the time spent commuting between their homes and the normal job site, but you do have to pay for commuting time which is actually a part of the job. If you run a plumbing repair service, for example, and require workers to stop by your shop to pick up orders, tools and supplies before going out on calls, their work day begins when they check in at your shop. Otherwise, just about the only situation in which you must pay workers for commuting time is when they've completed a day's work and are then called at home to do an emergency job for one of your customers.

You must count as payable time any periods when employees are not actually working, but are required to stay on your premises while waiting for work assignments. If you require employees to be on call, but you don't make them stay on your premises, then two rules generally apply.

- You don't count as payable time the on-call time that employees can control and use for their own enjoyment and benefit.
- You do count as payable time the on-call time over which employees have little or no

control and which they can't use for their own enjoyment or benefit.

EXAMPLE: AirTec provides mechanical services for small private planes at a local airfield. The company designates one of its mechanics to be on call each Saturday. A mechanic who is on call must remain at home near the phone and, for safety reasons, can't drink any alcohol. Since designated mechanics aren't free to use their on-call time as they please, it's payable time.

Unless there's an employment contract that states otherwise, you can generally pay a different hourly rate for on-call time than you do for regular work time. But keep in mind that employees must be paid at least the minimum amount required under the wage and hour regulations.

Nearly half the states have laws requiring employers to provide meal and rest breaks and specifying minimum times that must be allowed. You don't have to pay a covered employee for time spent on an actual meal. But the key is that the employee must be completely relieved from work during that period so that he or she can enjoy a regularly scheduled meal. If, for example, you require employees to remain at their desks during the meal period or keep an eye on machinery, you must pay for the meal time.

6. Child Labor

The FLSA (29 USC § 206) has special rules for younger workers. Those rules are designed to discourage young people from dropping out of school too soon and to protect them from dangerous work such as mining, demolition, wrecking, logging and roofing. Check with the local Wage and Hour office of the U.S. Department of Labor for the current rules and a list of jobs that are considered to be hazardous to young people. State laws—available from your state department of labor—may impose additional restrictions in hiring young workers.

L. Occupational Safety and Health

The Occupational Safety and Health Act or OSHA (29 USC §§ 651 to 678) is designed to reduce workplace hazards. It broadly requires employers to provide a workplace free of physical dangers and to meet specific health and safety standards. Employers must also provide safety training to employees, inform them about hazardous chemicals, notify government administrators about serious workplace accidents and keep detailed safety records.

Although there can be heavy penalties for not complying with OSHA, such penalties are usually reserved for extreme cases in which workplace conditions are highly dangerous and the employer has ignored warnings about them. If your workplace is inspected, OSHA will work with you to eliminate hazards. Inspections of small businesses are rare unless the business is especially hazardous—an auto paint shop, for example, or a welding business.

The OSHA law won't apply to your workplace if you're self-employed and have no employees, or if your business is a farm that employs only your immediate family members. Similarly, you won't be covered if you're in a business such as mining which is already regulated by other federal safety laws.

OSHA requires that you provide a place of employment that's "free from recognized hazards that are causing or likely to cause death or serious physical harm to employees." The Occupational Safety and Health Administration—also called OSHA—enforces the OSHA law and has set additional, more specific, workplace standards covering concerns such as:

- exposure to hazardous chemicals
- first aid and medical treatment
- noise levels
- protective gear—goggles, respirators, gloves, work shoes, ear protectors
- fire protection
- worker training, and
- workplace temperatures and ventilation.

Most small businesses are inspected by OSHA only if:

- an employee has complained to OSHA
- a worker has died from a job-related injury, or
- three or more employees have been hospitalized because of a workplace condition.

In each state, there's an agency funded mostly by the federal office of OSHA that offers free, on-site consultations about how you can comply with the law. In addition to consultants, a trade association in your industry may often be able to provide advice on complying with OSHA.

M. Workers' Compensation

The workers' compensation system provides replacement income and medical expenses to employees who suffer work-related injuries or illnesses. Benefits may also extend to the survivors of workers who are killed on the job.

Workers' compensation is a no-fault system, meaning an employee is usually entitled to receive stated benefits whether or not the employer provided a safe workplace and whether or not the worker's own carelessness contributed to the injury or illness. But the employer, too, receives some protection, because the employees are limited to fixed types of compensation—basically, partial wage replacement and payment of medical bills. The employee can't get paid for pain and suffering or mental anguish.

Each state has its own workers' compensation statute. While the details differ among those laws, one thing is clear: If you have employees, you generally need to obtain workers' compensation coverage. Your state workers' compensation office can tell you about any legal requirements for informing employees of their rights—generally by displaying a poster.

To cover the cost of workers' compensation benefits for employees, you usually are required to pay for insurance—either through a state fund or a private insurance company. While self-insurance is a possibility in some states, the technical requirements usually make this an impractical alternative for a small business.

Premiums are based on two factors: industry classification and payroll. If your premium is above a certain amount—$5,000 in many states—your actual experience with workers' compensation claims will affect your premiums. Your rate can go up or down, depending on how your claims compare with other businesses in your industry. The number of claims filed by your employees affects your premium more than the dollar value of the claims. That's because if you have a lot of accidents, it's assumed that you have an unsafe workplace and the insurance company eventually will have to pay out some large claims.

To keep your workers' compensation costs down, try to prevent accidents in the workplace by emphasizing safety. Provide proper equipment, safety devices and protective clothing. Train and retrain your employees in safe procedures and in how to deal with emergencies. Consider setting up a safety committee made up of both managers and workers. And promote employee health by offering wellness and fitness programs.

You may also be able to save money by reclassifying a worker—which may involve slightly changing the worker's job duties. For example, if you have five people in a warehouse assembling and packing products, consider assigning two as assemblers (perhaps in a separate area) and three as warehouse workers. The cost of workers' compensation for the assemblers should be lower since they don't need to lift heavy loads or work with equipment.

N. Termination

Firing someone—even a person who is demonstrably incompetent—can be a risky endeavor. Do it for the wrong reason or in the wrong way and you can be obligated to pay substantial money in damages, or to rehire the worker.

Cases in which former employees claim they were terminated for an improper reason or that an employer bungled the process are known as wrongful discharge cases—and they're based on such legal theories as violation of an anti-discrimination law, breach of contract, failure to deal in good faith with an employee and violation of public policy.

1. Guidelines for Firing Employees

As noted in Section A3, the at-will doctrine theoretically gives you the right to fire an employee at any time as long as it's not for an illegal reason. Even so, the safest approach any time you fire someone is to make sure that you have a legitimate business reason for the termination—reason that you have thought out and documented. If a fired employee sues you and the case goes to trial, jurors won't be too impressed if your main defense is, "I own the business and I don't have to give a reason for firing anyone." Most jurors feel that the at-will doctrine is unfair and they'll look for ways to hit you with damages if there's a way they can do it and still comply with the judge's legal instructions.

Another reason to always have a good, legitimate basis for firing someone is that a former employee—shocked by the firing—may be looking for a way to retaliate against you. The employee may claim that your business ignored a sexual harassment complaint or that the firing was motivated by racial discrimination. When challenged on a firing, you should be able to show, for example, that the employee did not adequately perform specific job duties or violated a clearly stated company policy.

Some Employees Have Contract Rights

Before you fire an employee, check into whether you've made an oral or written contractual commitment that may limit your right to fire. Consider the following:

- Is there a written or oral contract that promises the employee a job for a fixed period of time?
- When you hired the employee, did you make any oral commitments about job security?
- Have you assured the employee that you'd only fire him or her for good cause?
- Have you listed causes for termination—in a contract, employee handbook or elsewhere—in a way that limits you to those specified causes?
- Does your employee handbook or do other written policies or memos make any promises about job security?
- Does your company have written or customary procedures that must precede firing?

Your answers to these questions will help you identify whether you've limited your ability to fire the individual. If your employee handbook or your handouts to new employees restate your right to fire a worker at any time and say that all contracts must be in writing, you're usually in good shape.

Written employment contracts can be a two-way street. *While they may limit your right to fire an employee, the flip side is that they usually spell out the employee's obligations to your business. If the employee isn't performing well,* *chances are that he or she is in breach of the contract, giving you the legal right to terminate the relationship. Because the interpretation of contract terms can involve legal subtleties, consider having a brief conference with a lawyer before firing an employee who has a written contract.*

To head off the possibility that an employee may try to base a wrongful termination action on alleged illegal conduct or motives in your workplace, be prepared to show the real reason for the firing.

Reasons that may support a firing include:

- performing poorly on the job
- refusing to follow instructions
- abusing sick leave
- being absent excessively
- being tardy habitually
- possessing a weapon at work
- violating company rules
- being dishonest
- endangering health and safety
- engaging in criminal activity
- using alcohol or drugs at work
- behaving violently at work
- gambling at work, and
- disclosing company trade secrets to outsiders.

Depending on the nature of your business, you may have other legitimate reasons to fire employees as well. Whatever reasons you use as a basis for firing people, it's absolutely essential that you treat your employees evenhandedly. That is, if you regularly let some employees engage in prohibited conduct, you'll be on shaky legal ground if you claim good cause for firing others for the same reason.

EXAMPLE: Andrew, a black patient attendant, is a half-hour late for work three days in a row. His employer, a medical clinic, fires him. In suing for wrongful discharge based on illegal discrimination, Andrew shows that two white attendants had been similarly tardy in recent weeks, but received only a verbal warning to shape up. Even though excessive tardiness is a valid business reason for firing someone, the

jury awards damages to Andrew because the employer applied the rules unevenly and unfairly.

2. Final Review

Since firing is such a drastic and traumatic step— and one having potentially serious legal consequences for a small business—it makes sense for the owner or president to have the final say. If you're unsure about any aspect of the firing, seek advice from an experienced employment lawyer— especially if the employee may claim illegal discrimination or other legal violation.

Your final review should verify that:

- the firing wouldn't violate anti-discrimination or other statutes
- the firing wouldn't be a breach of contract, including oral assurances of job security or statements made in an employee handbook
- your company has given the employee adequate and documented warnings that he or she faced being fired—except where the conduct would clearly warrant immediate firing
- you have followed your stated personnel practices, and
- you have followed the same procedures in similar situations involving other employees.

For more on firing practices, see Dealing With Problem Employees: A Legal Guide, *by Amy DelPo & Lisa Guerin (Nolo).*

O. Unemployment Compensation

State laws generally require employers to contribute to an unemployment insurance fund. Your rate is normally based on the size of your payroll and the amount of unemployment benefits paid from your account. Employers with smaller payrolls and low levels of unemployment claims will, over time, pay lower taxes.

Employees who are terminated because of cutbacks or because they are not a good fit for a job are generally entitled to payments from the unemployment fund. Employees who are fired for serious misconduct—stealing or repeated absenteeism, for example—or who voluntarily leave a job without good cause are not entitled to unemployment payments.

Applying these categories to a particular termination isn't always easy. For example, suppose you and an employee get into an argument and she leaves shortly afterward. If she has quit, benefits are not legally due. If she was fired, however, she's entitled to unemployment benefits absent truly bad conduct such as selling illegal drugs in the workplace. It's sometimes difficult to discern whether a termination is a quitting or a firing.

The details of the claims process vary in each state. Pick up the applicable rules at the unemployment office closest to you. Typically, the process starts when a former employee files a claim with the state unemployment agency. You receive written notice of the claim and can file a written objection—usually within seven to ten days.

The state agency makes an initial determination of whether the former employee is eligible to get unemployment benefits. You or the former employee can appeal the initial eligibility decision and have a hearing before a referee—a hearing officer who is on the staff of the state agency. Additional appeals may also be available.

⚠ **Serious charges may be raised.** *The referee's decision sometimes influences what happens in a related civil lawsuit. For example, if the referee rules that the employee quit because he or she was being sexually harassed, that ruling may be decisive in a later case that the employee brings against your business. Consult a lawyer if you anticipate that complicated legal issues—such as sexual harassment, illegal discrimination or retaliation for complaining about a workplace hazard—may surface at the hearing.*

Think Twice Before Fighting Claims

Contesting all questionable claims may not be the wisest policy. Lots of claims you think are questionable probably are allowed under unemployment compensation laws, which are made deliberately lenient to give unemployed workers a transitional source of income and keep them off welfare. Unless there's strong evidence that the employee pilfered from the company or engaged in other fairly extreme conduct such as quitting for no reason, he or she will usually win in a claims contest.

What's more, fighting a claim can be time consuming, emotionally draining and costly for you—especially when balanced against the fact that a few unemployment claims spread over several years are unlikely to greatly increase your insurance rate.

Perhaps most important, fighting an unemployment claim will guarantee an angry former employee—a person far more likely to file a lawsuit or harm you or your business in some other way, such as bad-mouthing you among friends who remain on your payroll. This might happen anyway. But your challenge to the employee's right to receive unemployment benefits may be the irritant that prompts the former employee to strike back.

Balance the benefits of saving on unemployment taxes against the trouble it takes to fight the claim and the risk of inviting a lawsuit against your business.

P. Independent Contractors

Independent contractors differ from employees in two main ways:

- Independent contractors control not only the outcome of a project but also how the job gets done.
- Independent contractors control their own economic destiny to a large extent, making decisions and business investments that affect how much profit they'll earn and whether they'll suffer a loss.

Typically, a small business hires many independent contractors. Common examples are a lawyer or accountant, a painter who spruces up your office or a computer consultant who installs specialized software at your store and teaches employees how to use it.

Generally, independent contractors have special skills that you need to call on only sporadically. But sometimes your company may have ongoing needs that can be filled equally well by an employee or an independent contractor. (Section 1, below, describes the advantages and disadvantages of independent contractor status.) If you weigh both possibilities and conclude that you can save money and reduce paperwork by using an independent contractor rather than an employee, fine. But be sure he or she really qualifies for independent contractor status.

The IRS strongly prefers that workers be treated as employees and not as independent contractors. This is because employers must collect taxes on employee earnings through payroll withholding, assuring that the funds flow quickly and surely to the government. By contrast, an independent contractor receives his or her entire earnings without taxes being withheld and is responsible for paying taxes on those earnings. Contributing to the IRS bias against independent contractor status is a belief that some independent contractors may under-report or even fail to report their earnings, which results in a loss of tax revenue. State tax agencies, as well, tend to discourage businesses from classifying workers as independent contractors.

If you classify a worker as an independent contractor when the worker should have been treated as an employee, and the IRS or a state unemployment or labor commissioner's office investigates and rules against you, you can wind up having to pay the taxes that should have been withheld, together with interest and penalties. Section 2, below, discusses how you can reduce the risk of being challenged by the IRS—and other agencies—over whether you properly classified someone as an independent contractor.

 Hiring Independent Contractors, *by Stephen Fishman (Nolo), provides clear and comprehensive guidance on all aspects of using independent contractors in your business.*

1. Advantages and Disadvantages of Independent Contractor Status

By hiring a person as an employee, you assume financial burdens that you don't have if you hire the same person as an independent contractor. For example, you must make an employer's contribution for the worker's Social Security. You're also responsible for withholding federal and state income taxes, and for keeping records and reporting these items to the federal and state governments. Each year, you must send the employee a Form W-2 showing how much he or she earned and how much was withheld. (See Chapter 8, Section C2, for details on an employer's tax responsibilities.)

That's not all. As an employer, you must carry workers' compensation insurance for the employee and may have to make payments into an unemployment protection fund. Health insurance, retirement plans and other fringe benefits may add to the cost. Finally, although not legally required, most employers provide paid vacations and sick leave for employees, further driving up costs.

Now, contrast this situation with hiring an independent contractor. When you use an independent contractor, you're not required to withhold taxes from the amount you pay the worker, and you don't have to pay any portion of the worker's Social Security taxes. Your only responsibility is to complete a Form 1099-MISC at the end of the year if you paid the independent contractor $600 or more during the year. The form is sent to the IRS and the employee.

By hiring an independent contractor rather than an employee, you normally also save the expense of providing an office or other work space for the worker and the ongoing expenses of fringe benefits and insurance. Furthermore, if you become unhappy with the person's work, you can turn to another independent contractor without going through the trauma often associated with firing an employee who works each day on your premises. Another benefit of hiring someone as an independent contractor is that your company generally won't be liable for the negligence of the person you hire. If you hire employees, however, you would be liable if, for example, the employee carelessly injured someone while at work.

Of course, there are tradeoffs. A business doesn't enjoy as much day-to-day control over the work of an independent contractor. And not having the person always available may also be inconvenient. Furthermore, because an independent contractor must charge enough to cover the costs of doing business and still make a profit, he or she may charge a higher price for services than the hourly rate paid to an employee. And if an independent contractor is injured because of some dangerous situation at your business premises or in a place that you have control over, the independent contractor can sue your business, claiming negligence. By contrast, an employee in the same situation would be limited to often lower workers' compensation benefits. But if you carry adequate liability insurance to protect you from claims by any injured person who is not an employee, this isn't a significant drawback.

Given a choice, many workers prefer to be treated as independent contractors rather than employees. Some like the fact that there's no withholding of taxes; they feel that they have a better cash flow, even though they're ultimately responsible for paying their taxes, and the employer isn't picking up any part of the Social Security tax. Workers may also see benefits in being treated as independent contractors because of the opportunity it affords them to charge a higher rate and to deduct business expenses, including money spent on cars, home offices and travel and entertainment. On the other hand, some workers prefer employment status that gives them paid vacations, medical care and other fringe benefits at the employer's expense—and freedom from worry about the paperwork required of people who are in business for themselves.

2. How to Avoid Classification Problems

Because the IRS is the government agency most likely to challenge your classifying a worker as an independent contractor, we'll focus here on how to stay within the IRS guidelines. Fortunately, a worker who qualifies as an independent countractor under the IRS tests will almost certainly qualify as well under the rules of most state agencies, even though the state rules may be slightly different.

For a full treatment of the various legal tests for independent contractor status as well as contracts you can tear out and use to hire independent contractors, see Hiring Independent Contractors, *by Stephen Fishman (Nolo).*

It may surprise you to learn that there's no law or court case to precisely guide you in deciding if it's legally safe to treat a worker as an independent contractor for federal tax purposes. In fact, the most authoritative guidance is found in an unlikely place—the manual the IRS uses to train its audit examiners. Fortunately, by following a few basic rules derived from the principles discussed in this manual, you're likely to steer clear of most problems.

a. The easy cases

As a practical matter, you can hire a wide range of independent contractors with virtually no worries about whether they should be treated as employees. These "no sweat" situations involve workers who clearly are in business for themselves, demonstrated by the fact they share most of the following characteristics:

- The worker is available to perform services for many businesses.
- The worker has a fixed base of operations—a commercial or office location perhaps, or a room at home—and ongoing business expenses.
- The worker lists the business in the phone book and may also drum up business through newspaper ads, radio commercials and circulars.
- The worker undertakes a job based on the results the client wants, but remains free to decide how to get the job done.
- The worker hires and pays for assistants, as needed.
- The worker has invested significant money in the business for equipment, vehicles and supplies.
- Depending on how the business goes, the worker may earn a large profit, a small profit or none at all—perhaps even suffering a loss.
- The worker incurs expenses in doing a job that won't be reimbursed by the client.

A few examples will help you identify what a classic, easy-case independent contractor looks like.

EXAMPLE 1: Lydia runs a billing service for a number of law firms. She purchases a speedy computer for her home office, along with sophisticated billing software which she upgrades from time to time. Lydia advertises her business in a newspaper that serves lawyers, does work for several law firms and is continually looking for more clients. She goes to lawyers' offices weekly to collect their time and expense records so she can enter them into her computer system and produce bills and reports. During these visits, she sometimes consults with the managing partners about their special problems and needs, but she's free to devise solutions to meet the lawyers' needs. She pays for billing paper and other supplies and for her transportation to and from the lawyers' offices—and isn't directly reimbursed for these expenses.

EXAMPLE 2: Joe does lawn maintenance work in the summer and snow removal in the winter for local businesses, advertising for clients by sending out a circular twice a year to members of the chamber of commerce. He owns a truck, two lawn mowers, a leaf blower, fertilizer spreader, two shovels and a snow blower, as well as a scraper that attaches to the front of his truck. Joe has a schedule of charges based on the size of the grounds to be serviced and the number of times he provides his services. Sometimes, to meet his commitments to clients, Joe hires his brother to help mow grass or remove snow, paying him as his part-time employee. During a mild winter, when Joe gets fewer calls, he may have trouble covering his expenses.

EXAMPLE 3: Elsie, a catalog designer, works out of a studio in her apartment. She does freelance work for three local ad agencies, who have major retail clients. The ad agencies pay her a flat fee for each catalog she lays out. The agencies send her basic materials to be featured and suggest a theme for each catalog, but rely on Elsie's judgment on how best to present the material. She uses her own cameras, computers and art supplies to produce the camera-ready pages for the catalogs. In busy times, she farms out some of the artwork to colleagues in a nearby town, and pays them herself.

In each of these examples, the small business people (Lydia, Joe and Elsie)—not the companies that hire them—determine how to do the work. In addition, Lydia, Joe and Elsie control how they run their business. It's highly unlikely that a business hiring any of these three as an independent contractor would have any difficulty justifying its position if challenged.

b. The tougher cases

Other workers may be harder to classify as independent contractors. Not infrequently, a worker may be in an ambiguous area where the distinction between an employee and an independent contractor gets fuzzy. While you may see some advantages in treating the worker as an independent contractor, you may at the same time feel nervous about the legal risks involved, since any penalties for misclassification will fall squarely on your shoulders and not those of the worker.

The possible ambiguity in a worker's status can be seen in the following examples.

> **EXAMPLE 1:** During the week, Rocco is employed as a custodian at a research firm. Hoping to earn additional money, he checks the help-wanted ads where he sees that a small company is looking for someone to come in every Sunday to perform janitorial services. Rocco applies for the work and learns that the company would provide mops, brooms and pails, but that Rocco would be expected to bring his own vaccuum cleaner. The company would pay Rocco $100 per cleaning session, and would reimburse him up to $10 per session for cleaning supplies. The company would provide Rocco with a checklist of cleaning duties and the sequence in which they were to be performed. If the company president were to decide that the work on a given Sunday wasn't satisfactorily performed, Rocco would have to come back on Monday night to touch up.

> **EXAMPLE 2:** Alice is offered work delivering flowers and plants for a local florist shop from 2 p.m. to 5 p.m., Monday through Friday. The deal is that Alice will drive her own van and be responsible for gas and maintenance, which is offset by the fact that she'll earn $13 an hour for her work. The business owner will give Alice a delivery list each day, indicating the priority deliveries which need to be accomplished first. Otherwise, Alice will be free to decide the timing of the deliveries and to choose what route to follow. The business will also provide Alice with a cellular phone to take with her on her deliveries so she can call in periodically to see if she needs to return to the shop to pick up last-minute orders. While making deliveries, Alice will have to wear a jacket bearing the name of the florist shop.

> **EXAMPLE 3:** Edgar teaches art and design at a community college. He is approached by a clothing store owner who has a highly visible downtown location and is known for eye-catching window displays that change weekly. The store owner wants Edgar to come in each Tuesday—a day when Edgar doesn't teach—and change the window display under the owner's supervision. This is similar to work that Edgar is already doing for a bookstore on Saturday mornings. Edgar would be expected occasionally to construct some of the displays in his basement shop, since there's limited space at the clothing store to do so. He'd be reimbursed for the supplies used in the displays, but not for the tools he'd need to do the work.

In these three examples—and thousands of similar cases—the work arrangements share some characteristics of an employment relationship and some characteristics of an independent contractor relationship. It's difficult to predict if the IRS would agree with the business owner's decision to treat the worker as an independent contractor. The IRS pronouncements are not exact enough to allow you to accurately predict the outcome.

In these ambiguous situations, you have two safe ways to proceed—and a third way that involves a measure of risk.

Treat the Worker As an Employee. If you want to be super-safe and avoid any risk that the IRS—or other governmental agencies—will determine that you've mistakenly classified the worker as an independent contractor, follow a policy of always treating the worker as an employee. This will protect you from possible penalties. The problem is that both you and the worker will lose the advantages that can flow from an independent contractor relationship.

Require the Worker to Incorporate. If you and the worker are both motivated to go the independent contractor route in an ambiguous situation, there's a way to do it that's virtually as free from problems as hiring the person as an employee: simply have the worker incorporate. The IRS will almost always treat this as a valid arrangement and accept the fact that the worker isn't your employee but an employee of his or her own corporation. As described in Chapter 1, it's legal in every state to form a one-person corporation—and the process can be simple and relatively inexpensive.

Here are the details about how this strategy works:

- The worker forms a corporation under state law and obtains an Employer Identification Number from the IRS.
- You sign a contract with the corporation under which the corporation agrees to provide specified services for your business.
- The corporation hires the worker (who owns the corporate shares) as an employee to perform the services required by your contract with the corporation.
- The corporation bills you as services are performed for your business under the contract.
- You pay the corporation—not the employee—for the services billed to your business.
- Each time the corporation issues a paycheck to its employee, the corporation withholds federal income taxes, along with the employee's share of Social Security and Medicare taxes, as outlined in Chapter 8.
- Periodically, the corporation (using its own Employer Identification Number) pays the IRS the withheld taxes along with the employer's share of Social Security and Medicare taxes.

You'll find numerous easy-to-use contracts in Hiring Independent Contractors, *by Stephen Fishman (Nolo). In filling out these contracts, be sure to indicate that you're hiring the corporation as an independent contractor. The corporation's owner should sign the contract in a corporate capacity (as president, for example) rather than as an individual.*

Accept a Measure of Risk. Suppose the worker's status as an independent contractor is ambiguous and, for one reason or another, the safer courses of action—treating the worker as an employee or requiring the worker to incorporate—are not practical. Then you must recognize that if you move ahead and hire the worker as an independent contractor, you're opening yourself up to some legal risk.

One way to reduce the risk is to get professional advice. See a tax expert—a lawyer or accountant who's familiar with the worker classification issues.

Another way to reduce the risk is to follow as many of the following suggestions as you can:

- Sign a contract with the independent contractor spelling out the responsibilities of each party and how payment is to be determined for each job. The contract should allow the independent contractor to hire his or her own assistants and to have as much say as possible as to how the work is to be performed. A sample contract is shown below.
- Require the independent contractor to furnish all or most of the tools, equipment and material needed to complete the job.
- Avoid a commitment to reimburse the independent contractor for his or her business expenses; if necessary, pay the independent contractor a little more, but have him or her assume that responsibility.
- If feasible, arrange to pay a flat fee for the work rather than an hourly or weekly rate.
- Don't provide employee-type benefits such as paid vacation days, health insurance or retirement plans.
- Make it clear that the independent contractor is free to offer services to other businesses.

- Specifically state in your contract that the contractor will carry his or her own insurance, including workers' compensation coverage.
- Keep a file containing the independent contractor's business card, stationery samples,

ads and Employer Identification Number. These items can help show that the contractor has an established business.

SAMPLE CONTRACT WITH INDEPENDENT CONTRACTOR

AGREEMENT

This AGREEMENT is made on _____, _____, between _____
                                                                                            Client

of _____and _____
                    Business Address   Contractor

of _____.
                    Business Address

1. Services to Be Performed. Contractor agrees to perform the following services for Client:
    [Description of services]

2. Time for Performance. Contractor agrees to complete the performance of these services on or before
_____, _____.

3. Payment. In consideration of Contractor's performance of these services, Client agrees to pay Contractor as follows:
    [Description of how payment will be computed]

4. Invoices. Contractor will submit invoices for all services performed.

5. Independent Contractor. The parties intend Contractor to be an independent contractor in the performance of these services. Contractor shall have the right to control and determine the method and means of performing the above services; Client shall not have the right to control or determine such method or means.

6. Other Clients. Contractor retains the right to perform services for other clients.

7. Assistants. Contractor, at Contractor's expense, may employ such assistants as Contractor deems appropriate to carry out this agreement. Contractor will be responsible for paying such assistants, as well as any expense attributable to such assistants, including income taxes, unemployment insurance and Social Security taxes, and will maintain workers' compensation insurance for such employees.

8. Equipment and Supplies. Contractor, at Contractor's own expense, will provide all equipment, tools and supplies necessary to perform the above services, and will be responsible for all other expenses required for the performance of those services.

CONTRACTOR   CLIENT

_____   _____

Date _____

⚠️ **Trade secrets.** *In some situations, you may disclose trade secrets of your business to an independent contractor. If so, include a clause in the agreement prohibiting the independent contractor from disclosing or making any unauthorized use of the trade secrets.*

3. Special Categories of Workers

In most situations, the status of a worker is determined by the guidelines described in Section 2 above. Certain workers, however, fall into special categories, and the usual IRS criteria don't apply to them. For example, the federal tax law says that the following workers are automatically treated as employees as far as Social Security taxes, Medicare taxes and federal unemployment taxes (FUTA) are concerned:

- officers of corporations who provide service to the corporation
- food and laundry delivery drivers
- full-time salespeople who sell goods for resale
- full-time life insurance agents working mainly for one company
- at-home workers who are supplied with material and given specifications for work to be performed.

For these workers, you must withhold the worker's share of Social Security and Medicare taxes and you must also pay the employer's portion of those taxes. But you may or may not have to withhold income taxes for a statutory employee; it depends on whether the worker qualifies as an employee or independent contractor under the usual IRS guidelines.

Federal law also provides that for tax purposes, licensed real estate agents and door-to-door salespeople are generally treated as "nonemployees"—which is another way of saying they're independent contractors. People in these occupations may, however, be treated as employees for the purpose of state payroll taxes and workers' compensation coverage.

As a sole proprietor or partner in your own business, you're neither an employee nor an independent contractor. You're responsible for paying your own income tax and Social Security self-employment tax. If you're a shareholder in a corporation but provide services to the corporation, you're generally an employee.

4. Additional State Rules

The IRS analysis of who qualifies as an independent contractor is similar to the standards followed in most states for state taxes and unemployment rules, but there can be some differences. For example, in California, a person working for a licensed contractor who performs services requiring a license (for example, erecting a building) is considered to be an employee unless the worker also has a valid contractor's license. In short, if you plan to hire independent contractors, check with the employment office in your state to see if special rules are in effect.

5. The Risks of Misclassification

There are at least three ways for the IRS to learn about your hiring and classification practices. First, the IRS may look into the affairs of an independent contractor who hasn't been paying his or her income taxes. Second, disgruntled employees may complain to the IRS if they think independent contractors are getting favored treatment. Third, during tax audits, the IRS routinely checks to see if workers have been misclassified as independent contractors.

The presumption is that the worker is an employee unless proven otherwise. If the status of a worker is questioned, it's up to you to prove that the worker is an independent contractor rather than an employee.

If it turns out that an employee was in fact misclassified, the cost to your business will be heavy. You'll be responsible for paying the employee's Social Security tax, federal income tax and federal unemployment insurance for up to three years. In addition, the IRS can add penalties and interest.

State government officials are also interested in businesses that misclassify employees as independent contractors. A state employment office may audit your business to see if there's been any misclassification. The audit can be the result of a spot check by the state employment office or a request by an independent contractor for unemployment or workers' compensation benefits. You may wind up owing money to a state unemployment insurance fund. And if the IRS learns of the state's action, you'll probably face a federal audit as well.

A Worker's Status Might Change

Don't assume that once you've determined that a worker is an independent contractor, you can forget about the matter. If there's a shift in the working arrangements, you may have to reclassify the worker.

EXAMPLE: John operates a small desktop publishing shop specializing in writing and designing brochures, flyers and other promotional materials for small businesses. At first, John does most of the work himself, turning any overload over to others with similar skills. John collects from the customer and pays these people as independent contractors. So far, so good.

As John's business grows, he arranges for part-time help on a fairly regular basis. Sue, Ted and Ellen regularly handle the overflow, working in John's offices under his broad supervision an average of about two days per week each. The rest of the time they work for themselves. John continues to treat them as independent contractors. By law, he shouldn't.

Since John is exercising significant control over these workers and using their services in-house on a regular basis, he's tempting fate—and the IRS. To be safe, John should treat them as part-time employees, which requires that he withhold income taxes and pay the employer's share of Social Security taxes as well as carry workers' compensation insurance and pay into the state's unemployment fund.

16

The Importance of Excellent Customer Relations

Customers (you may call them clients or patients) are the lifeblood of any small business or professional practice. To thrive, you not only need a steady stream of people who keep coming back for more goods or services; you also need them to enthusiastically recommend your business to their friends. To build a loyal following, you must do more than just give people what the law requires. Yes, knowledge of your legal rights and those of your customers is important, but it's even more important not to let legal technicalities take priority over a key objective of your business: to keep happy customers coming back and sending other people your way.

EXAMPLE: When Sandra brought her white wool blazer home from the dry cleaner's, she was dismayed to see that it had a very slight pink tint. Sandra reported the problem to Milt, the owner of the cleaning shop. Milt could have legally responded in a number of ways, including the following:

- "The problem is scarcely noticeable. You're being fussy."
- "How do I know the blazer wasn't like this when you brought it in?"
- "Didn't you see our sign? We're not responsible for any problems once you take the cleaned garment from the shop."
- "That's a two-year old blazer. Used clothing isn't worth much. I'll pay you $20 for the damage—not a penny more."
- "I've never had this type of complaint before. I want to send the blazer to an independent testing lab to see if the fabric is substandard. If it is, it's your problem—not mine."

But Milt was a wise business person. He didn't stand on his legal rights. Instead he told Sandra: "I'm sorry this happened. We use state-of-the-art cleaning processes, but apparently something went wrong. In any case, we guarantee your complete satisfaction. Since we can't fix this type of damage, let me know the purchase price of an equivalent new blazer." Sandra did, and Milt reimbursed her the full amount.

As a result of his enlightened attitude, Milt had a happy customer. In the two years since the blazer problem, Sandra and her husband have taken more than $500 worth of cleaning business to Milt's shop. They not only continue to be loyal customers, but—even more important—every time Sandra wears her new blazer, she tells the story of how Milt bought it for her and she recommends his business. Because Milt treated Sandra well, the blazer now ranks as one of Milt's all-time best investments.

Now consider what would have happened if Milt had responded with a strictly legalistic approach, offering Sandra the value of a two-year-old blazer. Sandra might have grumbled and accepted the $20 payment, or she might have taken Milt to small claims court and perhaps have won a few dollars more. But this much is certain: Sandra and her husband would never have taken any more cleaning to Milt's place. Even worse, they'd likely have told others about Milt's inadequate service for years to come and might have complained to local better business and state regulatory agencies. So while Milt was thinking of himself as a tough business person who knows his legal rights and never lets customers rip him off, he actually would have foolishly lost many thousands of dollars of business.

Whether you run a restaurant, a hardware store or a sand and gravel business, if a customer complains about your product or service, don't quibble. It's much smarter to point to your customer satisfaction policy as you eliminate or reduce the charges—and maybe even give the customer something extra as a reward for putting up with the problem. Maybe you won't make any money on that transaction; you'll probably even take a small loss. And yes, once in a blue moon someone will take unfair advantage of your policy. So what? When you consider the good feelings that customers will have about your business—and the fact that you'll receive positive rather than negative word-of-mouth from everyone you treat generously—it's a bargain. Consider, too, that a customer whose problem you resolve is unlikely to complain to any agency or board with power to license or otherwise oversee your business. Anyone who has had to cope with an investigation knows that even if the complaint that triggered the inquiry has no merit, the process can be worrisome and, if lawyers are involved, expensive.

Legal relationships with customers are covered in the next three chapters. Chapter 17 covers the legal rules for handling advertising, retail pricing, returns, warranties and other customer transactions. In Chapter 18, you'll find information about checks and credit cards. Chapter 19 explains how to extend credit and get prompt payment.

A. Developing Your Customer Satisfaction Policy

Whether you're selling products or services, go farther than is legally required in anticipating and responding to the problems of your customers. How you do this depends in part on the nature of the products or services you offer. But for starters, consider the policy of Eddie Bauer—a highly successful national company that sells outdoor goods through its catalog and retail outlets:

OUR GUARANTEE

Every item we sell will give you complete satisfaction or you may return it for a full refund.

OUR CREED

To give you such outstanding quality, value, service and guarantee that we may be worthy of your high esteem.

Over the years, my family and I have bought many items from Eddie Bauer. We've never had to return anything for a refund. But just knowing that the company stands behind what it sells has given us confidence in Eddie Bauer products. And that, of course, is the point: By reassuring customers in advance that they control the resolution of any problems, Eddie Bauer's good customer service is a marketing advantage.

Some department store chains such as Nordstrom's have also built solid businesses based in large part on their guarantee of customer satisfaction. But it's not just the big-time operators who successfully use a customer recourse policy as a business-building technique. Nolo—the small California company that published this book—has more than held its own in the highly competitive book business in part because of consumer-oriented policies such as this one:

OUR NO-HASSLE GUARANTEE

Return anything you buy directly from Nolo for any reason and we'll cheerfully refund your purchase price. No ifs, ands or buts.

Short and simple. No legal technicalities. No complicated rules. As additional evidence of its desire to serve its customers, Nolo offers another customer satisfaction policy almost unheard of in the industry: Nolo gives people 35% off on any current title if they return the cover of a prior, out-of-date edition. Why? Because out-of-date law books can be dangerous, and a customer who uses them is poorly served.

Businesses that treat customers generously can reap an unexpected dividend: higher morale among workers. Employees are not robots. They hate defending miserly policies that result in stressful confrontations with customers. They make great ambassadors for businesses they truly feel good about.

LAW IN THE REAL WORLD
Listening to Your Employees

Rose, the owner of a retail store, overhears clerk Ned tell an unhappy customer that there is nothing he can do—the time to return a particular item ran out yesterday. Rose intervenes to solve the customer's problem by graciously taking the merchandise back. Now, Ned is unhappy. "I was just following your policy," he tells Rose. "You undercut me and made me feel really stupid." Rose realizes it is unwise to adopt a strict policy and then throw it out on a whim. After all, if she hadn't overheard the conversation, she would have lost a customer and made an employee feel bad about being a tough guy. Rose meets with her employees, and together they come up with a much more customer-friendly policy. They post it conspicuously in the store so that everyone knows what the new, fairer rules are.

Businesses that offer services have different problems than restaurants and retail outlets. But they still have many opportunities to enhance customer satisfaction and favorable word-of-mouth. On longer-term jobs, you can set time-performance standards in advance so that both you and the customer can judge if everyone's expectations are being met. Often this consists of little more than committing yourself to meeting interim deadlines. For example, a toxic materials contractor removing asbestos from heating ducts in a three-story building might agree to get the entire job done in 30 days with the first floor clean and ready to reoccupy in ten days and the second floor in 20 days. A home remodeling or painting company might go farther and commit to meticulously cleaning up its work area each day.

Another good approach is to regularly ask for feedback from customers or clients. For example, if you run a bookkeeping service, a copy shop or a janitorial service that does regular business with larger accounts, ask your customers from time to time if your high standards—and the customer's needs—are being met. I was favorably impressed when the landlord who owns the building where my law firm practices asked me to evaluate the interior and exterior maintenance services we were receiving. There's currently a glut of office space in my town. When my lease is up I'll have a choice of many new buildings. But I'll remember that my current landlord seemed sincerely concerned about keeping this building spic and span.

You may think that a business offering a service as intangible as a seminar would have a hard time developing an effective customer-satisfaction policy—but you'd be wrong. Here's a guarantee from the American Management Association that serves as an excellent model:

A SIMPLE GUARANTEE FOR A COMPLEX BUSINESS WORLD

At AMA, we guarantee the quality of our seminars. It's that simple. More than 98% of our seminar attendees say they would recommend the course they have taken to their colleagues. But if for any reason you are not satisfied with a seminar for which you have paid, AMA will give you credit toward another course of comparable price or will simply refund your fee. That's it! No hassles. No loopholes. Just excellent service. That's what AMA is all about.

Here are some other examples of service businesses that use guarantees as a way of building a customer base:

- If you're unhappy with your hotel room, Hampton Inn will refund your money.
- If you get transferred from phone to phone while seeking an answer to an insurance question, Delta Dental Plan of Massachusetts will send you a $50 check.
- If your mini-pizza takes more than five minutes to be served, Pizza Hut gives you a free one.
- If you're not satisfied with a lawn treatment applied by Green Valley Lawn Care, the company will reapply the treatment at no cost—or, if you prefer, refund the cost of the treatment.

Elements of an Effective Customer Satisfaction Policy

The following ideas for developing your customer satisfaction policy come from *Marketing Without Advertising*, by Michael Phillips & Salli Rasberry (Nolo):

- Customers should be encouraged to tell you about any problems.
- Customers should know their rights and responsibilities from the beginning.
- Customers should know the circumstances under which they are entitled to get their money back and how to take advantage of other rights.
- Customers—not you—should feel in control. It's far better to provide a full refund if the customer is dissatisfied than to demand that the customer come up with a "good reason" for the refund.
- A refund, or any other recourse you offer, should be prompt.

B. Telling Customers About Your Policies

Every communication between you and your customers is an opportunity to let them know that you're sincerely interested in their complaints and comments. Show your concern through signs in your business place, questionnaires and surveys mailed to them and by simply inquiring from time to time if their needs are being met. Use your imagination. Labels, receipts, catalogs and packaging afford you the chance to let people know what their rights are and exactly how you'll deal with any problems. And don't use small print. Although it's sometimes hard to accept, you want your customers to know that you welcome the chance to fix problems. Also see Chapter 17, Section E, for advice on how your website can best convey your policies to customers.

And now, a few words on how not to communicate with customers. We've all seen stores that have negative signs next to the cash register, with unfriendly messages like:

No returns without receipt

No cash refunds

No out-of-town checks

Often, the owner has then added a few Scotch-taped signs with more negative messages such as "$10 is charged for every returned check—no exceptions" or "If you break it, you own it." Not only is this offensive—it's stupid. Your statement of a customer's responsibilities doesn't have to be put in confrontational language. To take one example, even if you decide not to give cash refunds (a policy you may want to re-think), there are friendlier ways to state your policy, such as:

We are pleased to accept all returns

within 30 days for full store credit.

This statement has a positive tone but makes the customer responsible for returning the goods within 30 days to receive credit.

The law in many cities and a few states requires that you post your policies on returns and other customer recourse. In many of those locations, if you don't post your policy, your customers have the right to a full cash refund. But even if the law doesn't require you to post your policy, it makes excellent business and legal sense.

Get Help to Solve Customer Disputes

Sometimes, despite your best efforts to treat customers fairly, a dispute starts to get out of hand. At that point, consider bringing the Better Business Bureau or other respected third party into the picture. I recommend the BBB because according to various national polls, it's usually the first agency that consumers turn to for help when they're trying to solve a problem with a business.

Your local government may also offer mediation as a means of resolving consumer-business disputes without going to court. This is true, for example, in many counties in California. Also, many communities have neighborhood dispute programs that may be helpful for some types of small business disputes.

For more on dispute resolution techniques, including negotiation, mediation, arbitration and litigation, see Chapter 22.

Legal Requirements for Dealing With Customers

Many legal problems can be avoided by adopting enlightened policies for dealing with your customers. Customer-friendly policies, however, can't anticipate every problem. Consequently, you must understand the legal rules that apply. This chapter covers advertising, retail pricing and return practices, warranties and consumer protection laws.

A. Advertising

Before we get into the legal rules for advertising, consider a more fundamental question: Do you really need to advertise?

1. Is Advertising Necessary?

People starting a small business often assume they must advertise to attract customers. This always made good sense to me—until I read and thought about some eye-opening ideas in *Marketing Without Advertising,* by Michael Phillips & Salli Rasberry (Nolo). Phillips and Rasberry argue convincingly that for small businesses, most money spent on conventional advertising—radio and TV spots and

display ads in newspapers—is wasted. You're competing with thousands of other advertisers, and your message is unlikely to be noticed by enough potential customers to produce a profitable level of sales.

Here's more from *Marketing Without Advertising:*

> The best and most economical way to attract and hold customers is through personal recommendation. A customer who is pre-screened and prepared for what you have to offer is far more likely to appreciate you and use your business than is someone responding to an ad offering a low price. The essence of marketing without advertising is to encourage personal recommendation. How do you do this? Lots of ways, all of which start with creating an atmosphere of trust. Central to doing this is to run an honest business.

Phillips and Rasberry recommend marketing strategies that don't rely on traditional advertising. For example, they discuss the importance of the physical appearance of your business (insist on scrupulous cleanliness and avoid clutter and unpleasant smells). They point out that listing your products or services where customers expect to find them—such as the Yellow Pages, local business directories, trade publications and, depending on the business, the classifieds—is often extremely cost-effective. Interestingly, Phillips and Rasberry distinguish between advertising and listings not on the basis of cost (although advertising does usually cost considerably more), but on whether customers are pre-screened to see your message. For example, someone who checks the Yellow Pages or a local free classified newspaper for a drain cleaning service needs that type of business. By contrast, someone who reads a display ad or hears a radio spot for the same business is unlikely to need that service immediately or to remember the ad months or years later when the need does arise.

2. Legal Standards for Advertising

Advertising is regulated by both federal and state law. Under the law, your ad is unlawful if it tends to mislead or deceive. This means the government doesn't have to prove at an administrative hearing or in court that the ad actually fooled anyone—only that it had a deceptive quality. Your intentions don't matter either. If your ad is deceptive, you'll face legal problems even if you have the best intentions in the world. What counts is the overall impression created by the ad—not the technical truthfulness of the individual parts. Taken as a whole, your ad must fairly inform the ordinary consumer.

In addition, if your ad contains a false statement, you have violated the law. The fact that you didn't know the information was false is irrelevant.

The Federal Trade Commission (FTC) is the main federal agency that takes action against unlawful advertising. State and local governments also go after businesses that violate advertising laws; usually this is the responsibility of the state attorney general, consumer protection agency and local district attorney. Consumers and competitors may also be able to proceed directly against the advertiser.

Over the years, the FTC has taken action against many businesses accused of engaging in false and deceptive advertising. A significant number of those administrative actions have been tested in court. By and large, courts have upheld even the most stringent FTC policies. For the most part, the FTC relies on consumers and competitors to report unlawful advertising. (See Appendix B for addresses and phone numbers of FTC offices.) If FTC investigators are convinced that an ad violates the law, they usually try to bring the violator into voluntary compliance through informal means. If that doesn't work, the FTC can issue a cease-and-desist order and bring a civil lawsuit on behalf of people who have been harmed. The FTC can also seek a court order (injunction) to stop a questionable ad while an investigation is in progress. In addition, the FTC can require an advertiser to run corrective ads—ads that state the correct facts and admit that an earlier ad was deceptive.

Most states have laws—usually in the form of consumer fraud or deceptive practices statutes—that regulate advertising. Under these laws, state or local officials can seek injunctions against unlawful ads and take legal action to get restitution to consumers. Some laws provide for criminal penalties—fines and jail—but criminal proceedings for false advertising are rare unless fraud is involved.

Consumers often have the right to sue advertisers under state consumer protection laws. (See Section D.) For example, someone who purchases a product or services in reliance on a false or deceptive ad might sue in small claims court for a refund or join with others (sometimes ten of thousands of others) to sue for a huge sum in another court.

A competitor harmed by unlawful advertising, or faced with the likelihood of such harm, generally has the right to seek an injunction and possibly an award of money (damages) as well, although damages are often difficult to prove. Such cases usually are based on one of two legal theories: unfair competition or commercial disparagement.

3. How to Stay Out of Trouble

The following rules will help keep your ads within safe, legal limits.

Rule 1—Be Accurate

Make sure your ads are factually correct and that they don't tend to deceive or mislead the buying public. Don't show a picture of this year's model of a product if what you're selling is last year's model, even if they look almost the same.

Be truthful about what consumers can expect from your product. Don't say ABC pills will cure headaches if the pills offer only temporary pain relief. Don't claim a rug shampooer is a wizard at removing all kinds of stains when in fact there are some it won't budge.

Waterproof or fireproof means just that—not water resistant or fire resistant under some circumstances. The term polar, when attached to winter gear, suggests that it will keep people warm in extreme cold, not that it's just adequate when the temperature drops near freezing.

Rule 2—Get Permission

Does your ad feature someone's picture or endorsement? Does it quote material written by someone not on your staff or employed by your advertising agency? Does it use the name of a national organization such as the Boy Scouts or Red Cross? If so, get written permission.

Under U.S. copyright law, the "fair use" doctrine allows limited quotations from copyrighted works without specific authorization from the copyright owner. In some circumstances, this doctrine provides legal justification for the widespread practice of quoting from favorable reviews in ads for books, movies and plays—and even vacuum cleaners. However, with the exception of brief quotes from product or service reviews, you should always seek permission to quote protected material. For more on the fair use doctrine and many other aspects of copyright law and practice, see *The Copyright Handbook: How to Protect & Use Written Works,* by Stephen Fishman (Nolo).

Rule 3—Treat Competitors Fairly

Don't knock the goods, services or reputation of others by giving false or misleading information. If you compare your goods and services with those of other companies, double-check your information to make sure that every statement in your ad is accurate. Then check again.

Rule 4—Have Sufficient Quantities on Hand

When you advertise goods for sale, make every effort to have enough on hand to supply the demand that it's reasonable to expect. If you don't think you can meet the demand, state in your ad that quantities are limited. You may even want to state the number of units on hand.

State law may require merchants to stock an advertised product in quantities large enough to meet reasonably expected demand, unless the ad states that stock is limited. California, for example, has such a law. In other states, merchants may have to give a rain check if they run out of advertised goods in certain circumstances. Make sure you know what your state requires.

Rule 5—Watch Out for the Word "Free"

If you say that goods or services are "free" or "without charge," be sure there are no unstated terms or conditions that qualify the offer. If there are any limits, state them clearly and conspicuously.

Let's assume that you offer a free paintbrush to anyone who buys a can of paint for $8.95 and that you describe the kind of brush. Because you're disclosing the terms and conditions of your offer, you're in good shape so far. But there are pitfalls to avoid.

- If the $8.95 is more than you usually charge for this kind of paint, the brush clearly isn't free.
- Don't reduce the quality of the paint that the customer must purchase or the quantity of any services (such as free delivery) you normally provide. If you provide a lesser product or service, you're exacting a hidden cost for the brush.
- Disclose any other terms, conditions or limitations.

For more information on the use of the word "free," see Section B1, below.

Rule 6—Be Careful When You Describe Sales and Savings

You should be absolutely truthful in all claims about pricing. Because this point is so important, I discuss it in more detail in Section B1, below.

Rule 7—Observe Limitations on Offers of Credit

Don't advertise that you offer easy credit unless it's true. A business that's not careful in this area can be charged with engaging in an unfair or deceptive practice that violates the FTC law. You don't offer easy credit if:

- You don't extend credit to people who don't have a good credit rating.
- You offer credit to people with marginal or poor credit ratings but you require a higher down payment or shorter repayment period than is ordinarily required for creditworthy people.
- You offer credit to poor risks, but once all the fine print is deciphered, the true cost of credit you charge exceeds the average charged by others in your retail market.
- You offer credit to poor risks at favorable terms but employ draconian (although legal) collection practices against buyers who fall behind.

If you advertise specific credit terms, you must provide all relevant details, including the down payment, the terms of repayment and the annual interest rate.

B. Retail Pricing and Return Practices

In addition to regulating advertising, the federal government and most state governments have laws and rules that address several types of retail practices.

1. Deceptive Pricing

The Federal Trade Commission (FTC) has jurisdiction over deceptive pricing practices. At the state level, usually the attorney general's office or, in bigger cities, the district attorney's consumer fraud unit enforces laws dealing with deceptive trade practices. The two biggest problems they encounter concern retailers who (1) make incorrect price comparisons with other merchants or with their own "regular" prices, and (2) those who offer something that is supposedly "free" but in fact has a cost. (See Section A.)

Offering a reduction from your usual selling price is a common and powerful sales technique. But to satisfy legal requirements, it's essential that the former price be the actual, bona fide price at which you offered the article. Otherwise, the pricing is misleading.

EXAMPLE: WizWare Inc. produces computer software and announces a new product for $129. But the company sells the product to wholesalers as if it were a $79 product and similarly discounts it to direct customers. The $129 price has never really existed, except to mislead customers into thinking they were receiving a discount.

Price comparisons often use words such as "Regularly," "Usually" or "Reduced." For example, it's common to see a price tag that says, "Regularly $200, Now $150." Or sometimes a sign says "⅓ off our regular price." These comparisons are fine legally—if you in fact offered the sale merchandise at the old price for a reasonable length of time. They're not okay if you've brought a special batch of merchandise especially for the sale and created a fictional "regular" price or one you adhered to for only a day or two.

If your ad compares your price with what other merchants are charging for the same product, be sure of two things:

- The other merchants are selling the identical product; and
- There were a sufficient number of sales at the higher price by merchants in your area so that you're offering a legitimate bargain.

In other words, make sure that the higher comparison price isn't an isolated or unrepresentative price.

Regarding offers of "free" products or services, you can offer gifts only if there are no strings attached. (See the discussion of "free" offers in Section A.)

2. Sales Away From Your Place of Business

A customer has three days—a "cooling-off period"—to cancel any sale not made at a normal business place. For details, see the FTC's trade regulation rule called "Cooling Off Period for Door-to-Door Sales," 16 CFR § 429. Here's how the FTC defines a door-to-door sale:

> The sale, lease or rental of consumer goods or services with a purchase price of $25 or more, whether under single or multiple contracts, in which the seller or his representative personally solicits the sale, including those in response to or following an invitation by the buyer, and the buyer's agreement or offer to purchase is made at a place other than the place of business of the seller.

Pay attention to the words "other than the place of business of the seller." They cover a lot of ground. Legally, a door-to-door sale is one made at a customer's home, but it's also one made at a sales presentation at a friend's home, a computer fair, hotel, restaurant, convention or similar site.

If you do any selling covered by the FTC definition, you must do two things. First, give the buyer a fully completed receipt or a copy of the sales contract. These documents must contain everything that you promised orally, as well as the date of the transaction and your name and address. Also, you must have the following words in large boldface type near the signature on the contract or the front of the receipt:

> You, the buyer, may cancel this transaction at any time prior to midnight of the third business day after the date of this transaction. See the attached notice of cancellation form for an explanation of this right.

LAW IN THE REAL WORLD
Selling at Trade Shows

Do you sell consumer goods at trade shows or fairs? If so, you should give customers notice about their right to cancel their purchases. Otherwise, you may be violating the FTC's three-day cooling-off rule.

The FTC devised the rule to protect homebound, unsophisticated consumers from fast-talking door-to-door sales people. (If you've seen the movie *Tin Men*, you know what I mean.) At the time, most transactions at trade shows and fairs were business-to-business; the cooling-off period didn't apply. Over the years, however, trade shows and fairs have expanded considerably. In fact, many shows—featuring everything from computer software to outdoor equipment and housewares—are geared primarily toward consumer sales.

The FTC has "prosecutorial discretion" in pursuing merchants who sell at trade shows and fairs without giving customers a notice of cancellation rights. In most instances, the FTC doesn't stroll the halls of convention centers to shut down noncomplying businesses. But it has that power. And an unhappy (and savvy) customer could report you to the agency, which would investigate and could take action against you.

Second, you must give the buyer at the same time a completed form, in duplicate, labeled "NOTICE OF CANCELLATION." It must be attached to the receipt or contract and easily detachable. Here's what the notice must say:

NOTICE OF CANCELLATION

(Enter date of transaction)

You may cancel this transaction, without any penalty or obligation, within three business days from the above date.

If you cancel, any property traded in, any payments made by you under the contract or sale, and any negotiable instrument executed by you will be returned within ten business days following receipt by the seller of your cancellation notice, and any security interest arising out of the transaction will be canceled.

If you cancel, you must make available to the seller at your residence, in substantially as good condition as when received, any goods delivered to you under this contract or sale; or you may if you wish, comply with the instructions of the seller regarding the return shipment of the goods at the seller's expense and risk.

If you do make the goods available to the seller and the seller does not pick them up within 20 days of the date of your notice of cancellation, you may retain or dispose of the goods without any further obligation. If you fail to make the goods available to the seller, or if you agree to return the goods to the seller and fail to do so, then you remain liable for performance of all obligations under the contract.

To cancel this transaction, mail or deliver a signed and dated copy of this cancellation notice or any other written notice, or send a telegram to [name of seller], at [address of seller's place of business] not later than midnight of _____.

I hereby cancel this transaction.

_____   _____

Date   Buyer's Signature

⚠️ **State laws and regulations.** *Most states also have laws and regulations dealing with door-to-door sales. Some of them go beyond the federal requirements. For example, in some states, the cooling-off period is five days. Also, some states require that the notice of cancellation and contract be in the same language as the oral presentation.*

3. Refunds

Strictly speaking, once a sale (other than a door-to-door sale) is complete, you don't have to give a refund to a customer who changes his or her mind. This is based on traditional contract law, which says that a sale is a completed contract. In short, unless there's been a significant breach of the contract (for example, the goods or services you sold were seriously flawed) or some provision allows one of the parties to cancel, you're both stuck. So a customer who buys a product from you doesn't have the legal right to cancel the "contract" later and automatically get a refund. By the same token, if you discover that you could have charged a higher price, you can't cancel the sale either.

So much for the legalities. In real life, most retailers give customers the option of returning merchandise for either a cash refund or at least a store credit. Sometimes retailers impose conditions. For example, the customer must return the merchandise within a certain number of days; the merchandise must be unused; the customer must show a receipt or other proof of purchase.

A liberal refund policy can give your customers confidence in your business and can be an effective marketing technique. (See Chapter 16.) Whatever you decide to do about a customer recourse policy, word your rules as positively as possible and post them conspicuously in your store.

California's Refund Statute

In what appears to be the beginning of a trend, California (which is often a legal leader) has adopted a statute about refunds. New York, Virginia and Florida also have refund posting laws.

Under California Civil Code § 1723, a business is not required to give a cash refund or even a store credit to a customer who wants to return a product. You must, however, conspicuously post your policies if you don't meet the following minimum standards for merchandise returned within seven days after the sale:
- You don't give either a cash refund or credit refund; and
- You don't allow an equal exchange for such merchandise.

The California law doesn't apply to sales of food, plants, flowers or other perishable goods. And it doesn't apply to merchandise marked "as is," "no returns accepted" or "all sales final," or goods used or damaged after purchase, special goods received as ordered, goods not returned in their original package and goods which can't be resold due to health reasons.

4. Mail Orders

If you take orders through the mail, you need to become familiar with the Federal Trade Commission's "Rule Concerning Mail Order Merchandise," 16 CFR § 435. The rule is explained in an easy-to-read booklet, *Businessperson's Guide to the Federal Trade Commission's Mail or Telephone Order Merchandise Rule,* available on the FTC website at www.ftc.gov (click on "For Business Guidance," then "Business Publications" then "Advertising"). Here are some basic features of that rule:

- You must ship the merchandise within 30 days after you receive a properly completed order and payment, unless your ad clearly states that it will take longer.
- If there's going to be a delay, you must notify the customer in writing. You must give the customer the option of a new shipment date (if known) or the opportunity to cancel the order and receive a full refund. You must give the customer a postage-free way to reply. You may assume that a customer who doesn't reply has agreed to the delay.
- If the customer cancels, you must refund the customer's money within seven days after you receive the canceled order. If the customer used a credit card, you must issue the credit within one billing cycle.
- A customer who consents to an indefinite delay can still cancel the order any time before it's shipped.
- A customer who cancels or never receives the ordered merchandise doesn't have to accept a store credit in place of a refund, but is entitled to a cash refund or credit on the charge card.

The mail order rule doesn't cover mail order photo finishing; spaced deliveries such as magazines (except for the first shipment); sales of seeds and growing plants; COD orders; or orders made by telephone and charged to a credit card account.

5. Unordered Merchandise

With only two exceptions, federal law (and the law in most states) makes it illegal to mail unordered merchandise. The exceptions:

- free samples that you clearly and conspicuously mark as such
- merchandise mailed by a charitable organization to solicit contributions.

It's illegal to send the recipient a bill or dunning letter for any unordered merchandise. The FTC applies this law as well to unordered merchandise de-

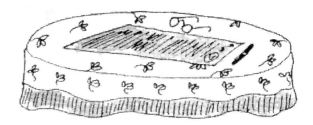

livered by means other than the mail. A person receiving unordered merchandise can treat it as a gift.

C. Warranties

Basically, a warranty is a guarantee. It's a commitment that the manufacturer and retailer will stand behind a product. Sometimes a warranty is made through an oral or written statement of the seller. This is called an express warranty.

Even if you don't make an express warranty, however, a warranty may be imposed by law; this is called an implied warranty. In other words, the law holds the manufacturer or retailer responsible for some warranties even if they've said nothing on the subject. Sometimes you can get rid of an implied warranty by making a disclaimer.

The law of warranties comes from two main sources. The first is a law called the Uniform Commercial Code (UCC), which has been adopted in every state. The second is the Magnuson-Moss Warranty Act, a federal law designed to protect consumers. In addition, some states have laws that go beyond the provisions of the UCC or Magnuson-Moss.

Although I focus on the sale of goods, it's also possible for services to be warranted. For example, a TV fix-it service may warrant that a repair job will be good for at least six months; an auto mechanic may warrant the repairs on a car's electrical system for one year; and a lawn maintenance company may warrant that certain weeds won't reappear during the current season. Warranties for services are almost always express and not implied, and they're not widely regulated by statute.

**Plan Ahead to Avoid
Warranty Problems**

If you're a retailer who sells big-ticket items,
try to work out a procedure with manufacturers for handling repair and replacement of defective products and making refunds. Obviously, you'll have better customer relationships
if you deal quickly and smoothly with warranty
problems.

If you're a retailer and you help customers
select, assemble or install products, or give advice or instructions about their use, carry product liability insurance. (See Chapter 12.)

---

1. Express Warranties

Express warranties are statements and promises that
a manufacturer or retailer makes about a product or
about a commitment to remedy defects and malfunctions in the product. If the statements are untrue or if the stated commitments are not honored,
the manufacturer or retailer may be legally liable to
the buyer for breach of warranty.

Express warranties take a variety of forms, from
advertising claims to a printed certificate that accompanies the product and specifically guarantees
it. Express warranties can be made either orally or
in writing.

a. Oral warranties

If a seller makes an oral promise to a buyer, that is
an express warranty.

> EXAMPLE: A seller says, "This TV set is new"
> or "This oven heats to over 600 degrees." If the
> TV set is used, or if the oven heats only to 500
> degrees, the seller will be liable for breach of

warranty, whether or not the seller knew that
the claims were false.

If the seller shows a customer a sample or a
model of goods being sold, there's an express
warranty that the goods the customer purchases
will be basically indistinguishable from the
sample. For example, if a salesperson shows a
customer some samples of fax paper and the
customer orders a dozen packages based on the
sample, the entire order must conform to that
sample. And if a dealer shows a customer a
small scale model of a garage door, the door
the customer receives must look like and be
constructed like the model.

But not everything that a seller says as part of a
sales transaction is a warranty. Merely giving an
opinion about the goods or praising them doesn't
create a warranty.

- Martha is at a drugstore looking at hair color-
  ing products. The clerk says: "I recommend
  this brand. It works very well, and I believe
  you'll be satisfied with it." Martha uses the
  product and develops a severe allergic reaction on her scalp.

- Phillip tries on a new suit. The store owner
  says: "It looks good on you. You'll be wearing it for a long time." In fact, the suit is a
  size too big and wears out after a year.

These statements would be considered opinions,
not promises or statements of fact. They wouldn't
constitute express warranties.

b. Written warranties

A statement doesn't have to be called a warranty or
guarantee to be legally treated as such. And warranties needn't be part of a formal written contract.
Statements made in product literature distributed by
the manufacturer or retail store, in advertisements or
orally by salespeople can constitute binding warranties.

If a sales contract or order form contains a description of the goods, that constitutes an express warranty by the seller that the goods will be as described. So if the product is described as an Ear Play Model 400 stereo receiver and it turns out to be a different brand or model, the seller has breached an express warranty.

Written warranties on consumer products are covered by state laws and a federal law, the Magnuson-Moss Warranty Act. That law is designed to make it easier for consumers to understand and deal with warranties. It doesn't replace state warranty laws but does add certain requirements.

The Magnuson-Moss Warranty Act covers consumer products normally used for personal, family or household purposes. It doesn't require a manufacturer or seller to give any written warranty at all. But if a written warranty is given, it must comply with the statute and with rules of the Federal Trade Commission.

For a product costing the consumer $15 or more, the written warranty must be in simple, understandable language. Also, the seller must make the terms of the warranty available to the buyer before the sale occurs. There are four ways you can comply with this requirement:

- Clearly and conspicuously display the warranty "in close conjunction to" the warranted product.
- Keep copies of warranties in readily available loose-leaf binders in each department of your store.
- Display packages so that the warranty is clearly visible to customers at the point of sale.
- Place a notice containing the warranty near the product in a way that clearly tells prospective buyers the product to which the warranty applies.

If a product costs $10 or more, the written warranty must state either that it's a full warranty or limited warranty. Naturally, a consumer who sees the words "full warranty" believes that he or she is getting a large measure of protection. To qualify as a full warranty, a written warranty must include at least the following coverage:

- A defective product will be repaired or replaced for free (including removal and installation, if necessary) during the warranty period.
- The product will be repaired within a reasonable time.
- The consumer won't have to do anything unreasonable to get warranty service (such as return a heavy product to a store or service center).
- The warranty is good for anyone who owns the product during the warranty period.
- If the product hasn't been repaired after a reasonable number of tries, the customer gets a replacement or a refund.
- The customer doesn't have to return a warranty card for the warranty to be valid.
- Implied warranties can't be disclaimed or denied or limited to any specific length of time.

Any written warranty that doesn't qualify as a full warranty must be labeled as a limited warranty. You can restrict the duration of implied warranties, as long as the restrictions are not unconscionable (that is, shockingly unfair). Restrictions must be stated clearly, and the implied warranties must last for a reasonable time.

The Magnuson-Moss Warranty Act doesn't supersede state laws that give consumers even greater rights and laws that permit people to recover damages for injuries caused by defective products, despite a disclaimer of liability. For example, in California the Song-Beverly Consumer Warranty Act contains more stringent warranty provisions than the Magnuson-Moss Warranty Act. Among other things, the California statute provides that a manufacturer who provides a written warranty (full or limited) must maintain service and repair facilities in California reasonably close to all areas where its products are sold. The manufacturer can delegate repair and service facilities to retailers or independent repair shops. Repairs must be completed within 30 days, except in unusual circumstances.

2. Warranties Imposed by Law

Implied warranties don't come from anything a seller says or does. They arise automatically when a product is sold. Under the Uniform Commercial Code, there are two kinds of implied warranties:

- that the product is fit for its ordinary use, and
- that the product is fit for any special use the seller knows about.

Each of these is explained below.

a. Fitness in general

A seller automatically makes an implied warranty that new (not used) goods sold "are fit for the ordinary purposes for which such goods are used"—in other words, that the product will work the way similar products ordinarily work. This implied warranty is also called a warranty of merchantability.

Here are some examples:

- A lawnmower will cut grass that is four inches tall.
- A stepladder will support a 275-pound person.
- A toaster will make both dark and light toast.
- A bicycle's brakes will work in a light rain.
- A bottle of ginger ale won't have loose glass in it.

The manufacturer and retailer of a product that's not fit for ordinary purposes are liable to the purchaser for breach of the implied warranty.

b. Fitness for a particular purpose

There's a special implied warranty if the seller has reason to know that (1) the goods are required for a particular purpose, and (2) the buyer is relying on the seller's skill or judgment to select suitable goods. In that situation, the seller is bound by an implied warranty that the goods will be fit for that purpose.

- Joanne goes to a paint store and asks for two gallons of white paint that will work well on plaster walls. The store owner selects paint for her. Unfortunately, it's intended solely for metallic surfaces and ruins her walls.
- Morton asks an air conditioning contractor to pick out and install an air conditioning unit for a part of his plant. He explains that the room contains extensive electronic equipment and must be kept at 55 degrees or cooler at all times. The air conditioner is installed but leads to costly problems, because in hot weather it can't keep the temperature below 62 degrees.
- Wilma goes to a sports retailer and asks for a sleeping bag that will be adequate to 10 degrees Fahrenheit. The retailer selects a certain model for Wilma, and she buys it, but it won't keep a normal person warm below freezing.

In these examples, each seller is liable to the buyer for breach of the implied warranty of fitness for a particular purpose. That's because each seller knew the buyer needed the goods for a particular purpose and that the buyer was relying on the seller's skill or judgment to furnish suitable goods.

This is different from the implied warranty of general fitness discussed in the preceding section. An air conditioner that cooled a room to 62 degrees in hot weather would be fit for the ordinary purposes for which an air conditioner is used. It wouldn't violate the implied warranty of general fitness. But because the seller in the second example knew the buyer had special requirements and was relying on the seller to meet them, this special implied warranty took effect.

c. Disclaimers of implied warranties

The Uniform Commercial Code allows sellers, in many cases, to disclaim implied warranties through a conspicuous written notice. Typically, to disclaim implied warranties, you must inform consumers in a conspicuous manner, and generally in writing, that you won't be responsible if the product malfunctions or is defective and that the entire product risk falls on them. To do this, you must specifically state that you don't warrant "merchantability," or use a phrase such as "with all faults" or "as is."

There are, however, major exceptions to the general rule, which may make it impossible to make a disclaimer.

Exception 1: State Law Restrictions. In some states, you may not be able to avoid implied warranties. Despite its name, the Uniform Commercial Code isn't completely uniform; several state legislatures have tinkered with parts of it, including the part about disclaiming implied warranties. Some states (including Connecticut, Massachusetts and Kansas) don't let you sell consumer products "as is."

Exception 2: Injuries. A disclaimer of implied warranties won't shield you from legal liability if your product is so defective it injures someone. Courts consider such a disclaimer "unconscionable."

Exception 3: Federal Law Restrictions. If you offer a written warranty for a consumer product or offer a service contract on it, you can't disclaim any implied warranty. (This restriction is imposed by the Magnuson-Moss Warranty Act.)

Implied warranties are difficult to disclaim. *If you're going to enter this legal thicket, you'll likely need a lawyer's advice on whether you can disclaim implied warranties in your situation and, if so, how best to do it. Even if the law permits a disclaimer of warranties, if you and a customer slug it out in court, you'll find that judges often tend to be pro-consumer—that is, to rule that unless a seller is absolutely clear, this warranty disclaimer will be disallowed.*

Sometimes a seller is interested not in getting rid of implied warranties entirely but only in limiting the remedies in case of a breach. For example, the seller may want to say that in case of a product defect, the buyer can either (1) return the goods and get a refund, or (2) have any defective parts replaced or repaired—but not collect monetary damages. But while a limitation on damages is normally effective, this isn't always true, especially where the limitation is found to be highly unreasonable. Suppose the seller of a $2,000 stereo set puts this language in the warranty: "Seller is obligated only to replace defective parts." After Mildred buys a stereo, a protective circuit fails, causing it to overheat. This destroys several key parts and ruins the stereo. Will a court allow the seller merely to replace the $5 part that didn't work? Perhaps not. The buyer may be able to convince the court that the limitation shouldn't be enforced because (under these circumstances) the limitation deprived her of the "substantial value of her bargain" or because the limitation is unconscionable (that is, shockingly unfair). And remember that a disclaimer can't shield you from liability for personal injury to a consumer hurt by a defective product.

3. What Happens If a Warranty Is Breached

Federal and state laws give consumers certain rights when an express or implied warranty is breached.

a. The buyer's options

Under the Uniform Commercial Code, if there's a breach of warranty, the customer usually can return the merchandise and get a full refund. The manufacturer or retailer bound by the warranty, however, has the right to cure the breach by fixing the merchandise or replacing it with nondefective merchandise. A customer who prefers to keep the merchandise can do so and sue for the direct economic loss—generally, the reduced value of the product because it's defective.

In addition to damages for the reduced value of a defective product, a buyer is also entitled to damages for:

• Consequential economic losses (such as lost profits) resulting from the product's failure to meet requirements and needs that were foreseeable at the time of sale.

EXAMPLE: Meadowbrook Golf Course buys 12 golf carts, all of which are defective. As a result, Meadowbrook loses $20,000 in profits over the eight-week period it takes to get the carts fixed. (It proves impractical to get substitute carts on short notice.) It can successfully recover these losses.

• Injury to people and damage to property caused by the defective product.

EXAMPLE: Millie buys a CutAbove power lawnmower. One day when her teenage son Reggie is mowing the lawn, the mower propels a small stone into one of his eyes. Reggie loses his sight in that eye. Because the mower doesn't contain normal safety features, Reggie is entitled to collect damages for his injury.

b. Who is liable?

Who is liable if a customer buys a product from a retailer and the product fails to live up to the warranty? Sometimes the manufacturer, sometimes the retailer and sometimes both. Although liability depends on the circumstances, here are some general rules:

• *Manufacturer's Express Warranty.* If an express warranty made by the manufacturer was breached, the manufacturer is responsible for making good on the promise. The retailer usually isn't liable, unless it "adopts" the manufacturer's warranty by its conduct at the time of sale.

EXAMPLE: Maria goes to Pete's Fitness Mart and looks at HomeBody, a $3,000 set of exercise machines manufactured by Health Horizons

Inc. She's interested, but wants to be sure it's backed by a broad warranty. To clinch the sale, Pete calls the president of Health Horizons and has the company send an extensive written warranty.

Nine months after Maria buys the HomeBody, it fails; meanwhile, Health Horizons has gone out of business. Pete's Fitness Mart is bound by the warranty, because it was part of the inducement that Pete used to convince Maria to buy Home-Body.

• *Retailer's Express Warranty.* If the warranty was made independently by a retailer, the retailer is liable. The manufacturer isn't bound unless the retailer was acting under the authority (in legal lingo, as an agent) of the manufacturer in making the warranty.
• *Breach of Implied Warranty of General Fitness.* If there is a breach of the implied warranty that the goods are fit for ordinary purposes, both the manufacturer and the retailer are liable—but if the customer sues the retailer, the retailer in turn will usually have the right to recover against the manufacturer for supplying a defective product.
• *Breach of Implied Warranty of Fitness for a Particular Purpose.* If the customer relied on the retailer to select the goods for a particular purpose and the goods aren't satisfactory for that purpose, the retailer is liable.
• *Personal Injury.* A buyer who's injured by an unfit product can usually sue the manufacturer, even though the injured person didn't deal directly with the manufacturer. What's more, not only the buyer can sue for personal injuries from a defective product. In most states, members of the buyer's family or household, or house guests who are injured, can also sue the manufacturer if it's reasonable to expect that these persons would use or be affected by the product.

Whether or not an injured person can sue the retailer as well as the manufacturer depends on court decisions in your state and the extent of the retailer's involvement in the sale. In many states, a retailer who simply sells an unopened box and makes no statements about the product is immune from liability if the product later injures someone. But some states hold the retailer liable even under these circumstances.

⚠️ **Get legal advice.** *Liability for breach of warranties is one of the most complex areas of commercial law. Because liability depends on many factors and because the law is somewhat unsettled, use this book for general background only. Also, it's important to understand that in a lawsuit, a person who has suffered a serious injury or significant economic loss because of a defective product will probably assert additional theories of legal liability (such as negligence and strict liability) besides breach of warranty. See a lawyer for specific legal advice.*

D. Consumer Protection Statutes

Remember "caveat emptor"—let the buyer beware? That used to be the law of the marketplace. Not anymore. Today, consumers have clout.

Case 1. In Florida, a Chevrolet dealer promised a "free four-day, three-night vacation to Acapulco" to anyone who bought a car or van. Relying on this special promotion, Peter bought a van from the dealer. When the vacation voucher arrived, Peter found that the so-called free vacation was really a time-share sales promotion. The vacation trip was loaded down with conditions, restrictions and obligations. Believing he'd been cheated, Peter sued the dealer. The jury awarded Peter $1,768 in compensatory damages (the value of the trip) plus $667,000 in punitive damages. (*Bill Branch Chevrolet, Inc. v. Burkert*, 521 So. 2d 153 (Fla. App. 2 Dist., 1988.)

Case 2. In New Jersey, Kenneth ordered some furniture from a store. When it arrived, Kenneth noticed numerous defects. He rejected the order and demanded a return of his deposit. The furniture store refused, and Kenneth sued. The jury awarded him three times the amount of his deposit and ordered the furniture store to pay his attorney fees. (*DiNicola v. Watchung Furniture's Country Manor*, N.J., Middlesex County Superior Court, No. L-80734-35, 1988.

Both cases were brought under state consumer protection statutes. These statutes are meant to protect consumers from unfair or deceptive practices and often go beyond the traditional legal remedies available for breach of warranty. Laws like these are on the books in nearly every state, although the details vary.

Consumer protection laws place a potent weapon in the hands of buyers. In an ordinary lawsuit, a plaintiff can recover only his or her actual losses. For example, without the benefit of a consumer protection law, the man who sued to get back his furniture deposit would be entitled to no more than his $600 deposit. But under the statute in his state, he received triple damages plus attorney fees. Similarly the man who sued the car dealer about the free vacation won punitive damages amounting to many times the value of his trip. The potential for large verdicts gives buyers and their lawyers an incentive to sue if it looks like a law has been violated.

"Big deal," you may say. "I'm an honest and ethical business person. None of this affects me." Well, that may not be so. For one thing, you need to know the details of your state's consumer protection laws so that you can tell your employees about practices that could get you in trouble. Furthermore, these state laws often allow a customer to sue even if the violation was not intentional. If you sell a product manufactured by a U.S.-based company (say, a Schwinn bike) and mistakenly advertise that the product was made in the U.S. when in fact it was made in Taiwan, you may be liable under the statute.

Hundreds of cases have been brought under consumer protection laws, including these:

- A man sued a department store that ran out of an advertised waffle iron and didn't give him a rain check—a violation of the consumer protection law in his state.
- A homeowner sued a roofing contractor who falsely advertised that it could arrange financing for roof repair jobs.
- A woman sued a health spa that reneged on its promise to return her deposit and cancel her contract if she changed her mind within three days.

Health spas, incidentally, have been singled out for special regulation; if you're going to start one, get the FTC pamphlet on this subject.

Most consumer protection laws contain a broad prohibition on "unfair or deceptive practices." In addition, many statutes list specific practices that are forbidden such as bait-and-switch and deceptive pricing, discussed above in Sections A2 and B1.

E. Dealing With Customers Online

For the most part, the same legal rules apply when you do business online as when you sell to customers in a brick-and-mortar store or by mail. As long as you don't overstep federal and state statutes and regulations, you have quite a bit of latitude in establishing your business policies and making them legally binding on your customers. You can set rules covering issues such as what sort of currency you accept, when and how customers can return items and what warranties you offer. In a store, you might do this by posting your policies in a prominent place or by having customers agree to them on an order form. When selling by mail, you can include your policies in your catalog or, again, on an order form. But obviously, the mechanics of informing customers of your policies are different when you're selling over the Internet.

In this section, I'll provide information to help you establish legally enforceable policies for your website. These online policies go by many different names, such as: *Terms and Conditions, Customer Conditions* or *Terms of Service*. The label you attach to them is not important; the content is.

For more on this subject, see How to Get Your Business on the Web: A Legal Guide to E-Commerce, *by Fred S. Steingold (Nolo). The book also explains how to choose and protect a domain name, how to create a website and how to limit your legal liability when doing business online.*

1. Why Bother to Post Policies?

With just one major exception, there are no laws requiring e-commerce websites to post their terms and conditions or mandating how and where such conditions should appear. The exception is the Children's Online Privacy Protection Act (COPPA), which requires you to post a privacy policy if your Web content is directed at children. The Federal Trade Commission enforces COPPA, so check its website for more information (www.ftc.gov).

Even with no general requirement that a business post its policies, posting can offer both business and legal benefits. On the business side, being straight with visitors and customers builds trust, credibility and loyalty. On the legal side, a well-thought-out set of terms and conditions can help limit your legal liability and avoid disputes over the details of transactions.

True, if a disgruntled customer sues you, your terms and conditions may not give you 100% protection, but at least you and your lawyer should have some solid arguing points to present to the judge.

2. Policies Worth Posting

If you'll be selling goods or services online, here are some topics you may want to cover in the policies you post:

Credit card use. If your website will offer direct sales via credit cards, it's wise to reassure customers that their credit card information will be kept confidential. Advise them of any steps you've taken to ensure the security of their credit card purchase. Also, under federal law, a credit card user is liable only for the first $50 of unauthorized purchases—assuming that the user promptly notifies the credit card issuer about the unauthorized use. Some businesses offer to pay up to the $50 limit if the credit card issuer fails to do so.

Warranties. You may already be offering a warranty that explains what you will and will not do for the customer if there's a problem with the products you sell. Your warranty can both reassure the customer and limit your liability, so I recommend that you post your warranty on your website. When you sell goods that carry a *manufacturer's limited warranty* and the goods sell for more than $15, federal law requires you to post the warranty or tell customers how they can view it.

Returns and repairs. It's important to develop a return and repair policy and post it online. For example, perhaps you're prepared to give a full refund, but only if the product is returned within 30 days and is in salable condition. If customers know this in advance, they won't be surprised if you refuse to give a refund 45 days after the purchase. While you have a great deal of discretion in how you deal with returns and repairs, a generous policy can build tremendous goodwill among present and prospective customers.

Legal jurisdiction. Since people from all over the country—or the world—may buy from you online, you may want to say that the law of your state will apply to any dispute, and that the courts of your state will have exclusive jurisdiction. Be aware, however, that some judges balk at enforcing this type of restriction, especially in a consumer transac-

tion involving a claim of $50 or more. Still, posting this type of provision can do no harm.

Sales limited to USA. You may wish to limit your exposure to laws (and lawsuits) in distant places by selling only to people in the United States. If so, you can post a notice to that effect—but also take polite and reasonable steps to reject orders from people outside the country.

Limited liability. You can use your postings to limit the financial damages for which your business will be legally responsible if there's a problem with the products, services or information you offer online. Understand that language limiting your liability won't always have the desired effect; judges may balk at limitations that are grossly unfair or that try to cut off the amount a person can receive for bodily injuries. But in most situations, judges do enforce limitations that customers have agreed to. Your posting may include language such as this: "Protobiz LLC will not be liable to a customer for any damages beyond what the customer has actually paid to Protobiz."

 Do some no-cost research: read the terms and conditions posted on websites that you respect. *The sites that you've personally used and come to trust will probably have well-written, customer-friendly policies that you can adapt for your own site. If you've never studied their fine print before, now's the time to do so. Then, after you've drafted your own set of policies, consider having a lawyer look over your handiwork and possibly tweak it for maximum legal impact.*

3. How and Where to Post Your Terms and Conditions

Easy navigation will be important throughout your website, and access to your terms and conditions is no exception. You'll want to provide prominent links that take customers right to your postings. This, by itself, provides a reasonable level of legal protection. If you want a higher degree of confidence that your terms and conditions will be binding, add an "I Accept" button by which customers must agree to your terms.

a. How to link prominently

Linking to your terms and conditions on your site's home page is a good place to start. You might also add links on other important pages, including the order page. You can call your link *Terms and Conditions* or anything else that's reasonably descriptive—for example, *Our Policies, Customer Policies,* or *Terms of Service.*

Here are some other ways to make your links and other information grab the customers' attention:

- Put the home page link where users can see it without having to scroll down.
- Put the link in large type and a distinctive color.
- Include a link on all other pages, if possible. But at a minimum, put the link on the pages where customers place orders so they can read your terms and conditions first.

- Write your terms and conditions in plain English so customers can easily understand their meaning.
- Put your terms and conditions in large type that's easy to read.

b. Requiring actual assent

If a dissatisfied customer sues you, you'd like the judge to treat your terms and conditions as a binding contract. Some judges will find a contract if you've followed the above guidelines—the assumption being that the customer read and accepted your terms. But other judges may rule that a conspicuous posting is not enough. They'll find a contract only if the customer specifically accepted your terms.

Currently, the most practical way to protect yourself is to present your terms to your customers, then require them to click a button at the end that says "I Accept" or "I Agree" before they can complete the transaction. That way, if a dispute ever ends up in court, you'll have evidence that the customer not only could have read your terms and conditions by clicking a link, but presumably did read them, right before actually agreeing to them. ■

18

Cash, Credit Cards and Checks

This chapter considers the three most common ways that businesses get paid for the goods and services they sell: cash, credit cards and checks. If you extend credit directly to customers, clients or patients, you should also read Chapter 19, which explains how to avoid collection problems.

A. Cash

Cash includes not only currency but also equivalents that are as good as cash—certified checks, cashier's checks, traveler's checks and (less common these days) money orders. Personal and business checks are quite another matter. (See Section C.)

If you have very large cash transactions, you may have to report them to the IRS. The reporting requirements are intended primarily to deter money-laundering schemes by customers (often drug dealers) who want to conceal income.

If you receive more than $10,000 in cash in one transaction or two or more related transactions, traveler's checks or money orders (but not certified, cashier's or business or personal checks), you're required to provide information about the transaction to the IRS—including the name, address and Social Security number of the buyer. In addition, if you're a retail merchant, you must report:

- cash transactions in which you receive more than $10,000 in installment payments in one year
- transactions of more than $10,000 in which part of the payment is in cash, traveler's checks or money orders; and
- any "suspicious transaction," no matter what the amount.

In calculating whether a transaction or related transactions involve more than $10,000 in cash, you must include not only cash, but also each cashier's check, traveler's check, bank draft or money order that's made out for $10,000 or less.

EXAMPLE 1: Gloria buys a boat from Todd, a boat dealer, for $16,500. She pays Todd with a $16,500 cashier's check payable to him. The cashier's check isn't treated as cash because the face amount is more than $10,000. Todd doesn't have to report this sale to the IRS as a cash transaction.

EXAMPLE 2: Donald buys gold coins from Maryanne, a coin dealer, for $13,200. Donald pays Maryanne $6,200 in $100 bills and a $7,000 cashier's check that he's purchased. Because the cashier's check is less than $10,000 it's treated as cash, so Maryanne must report this to the IRS as a cash transaction.

Use IRS Form 8300 (*Report of Cash Payments Over $10,000 Received in a Trade or Business*). You must also provide a copy of the completed form to the customer. The form must be filed within 15 days after a $10,000 or more transaction occurs, or within 15 days after a customer's transactions over a 12-month period add up to $10,000.

B. Credit Cards

Depending on the business you're in, your customers or clients may want to pay with plastic—the familiar Visa, MasterCard, Discover, American Express and other cards. Technically, there's a distinction between "credit cards" (such as Visa or MasterCard) and "travel and entertainment cards" (such as American Express and Diners Club) also called "charge cards." Credit cards are administered through banks; charge cards are usually administered through the issuing company. For most practical purposes, the same legal concepts apply, so I'll simply use "credit card" to cover both types.

In deciding which credit cards to recognize, take into account the preferences of your customers and clients, as well as the size of the discount exacted by the credit card issuer and how quickly you get paid.

When a customer charges goods or services using a bank-administered credit card, the bank credits your account with the amount of the sale less a discount—usually 3% to 5%—which is the bank's fee for handling the transaction and accepting the risk that the customer doesn't pay. In addition, the bank may charge you a start-up fee and an annual rental fee for the imprinting machine you use to record credit card information on sales slips.

If you're in a retail or other business where customers or clients expect to pay on credit, credit cards are often more cost-effective than directly extending credit. In general, if you follow the bank's rules—such as checking the credit card to make sure it hasn't expired and getting approval for all or at least larger transactions—the credit card issuer (not you) absorbs the loss if the customer doesn't pay up. Some of the newer electronic systems used by credit card issuers do most or all of the checking for you and get the money into your bank account almost immediately.

But whether you check credit cards the old-fashioned phone-in way or rely on the new systems, there are still a few exceptions to this general rule that if you follow the bank's procedures, you're sure to get your money. For example, if the goods are defective and the customer refuses to pay the bank, you may have to bear the loss. This will be spelled out in your contract with the bank. Read it carefully.

About a dozen states restrict your ability to record personal identification information about a credit card holder. The laws on this subject differ from state to state, but the California statute provides a good illustration of the kinds of restrictions that may apply to you. In California, in most circumstances you can't require the cardholder to give you personal identification information such as an address or phone number. There are, however, a few exceptions. You can require the cardholder to provide this information if:

- The bank or other agency that issued the credit card requires it to complete the transaction; or
- You need the information for a special purpose related to the transaction, for example, shipping, delivery, servicing or installation of the merchandise or for special orders.

There can be hefty penalties for violating these statutes, so learn the rules in your state and make sure that your employees know them.

But even if your state does permit you to record this information, ask yourself if you really need it. After all, if the customer doesn't pay the bill, it's a problem for the bank that issued the credit card, not for you. And because some customers regard the request for personal information as an invasion of their privacy, doing so may be poor marketing. If your main reason to gather this information is to build a mailing list, it's better simply to ask your customers if they'd like to be added to your list.

C. Checks

In any business—and especially in a service or wholesale business—you're likely to find that many customers or clients want to pay for goods and services using personal or business checks. Obviously, accepting payment by check is riskier than accepting payment by cash or credit card. Approximately 450 million bad checks are written each year.

1. Avoiding Bad Check Problems

Checks can be no good for a number of reasons. Here are the main ones:

- There are insufficient funds in the account to cover the amount of the purchase. Unless the check writer has overdraft protection, the check will be returned to you unpaid.
- The account has been closed—or perhaps it's a fictitious account that never existed.
- The signature of the person who signed the check is a forgery, in which case the bank will refuse payment.
- In the case of a third-party check (such as a paycheck) names or dollar amounts on the check have been altered, or the endorsement is a forgery.
- A person signing or endorsing a check on behalf of a partnership or corporation doesn't have legal authority to sign for the business.

Faced with these many possibilities for losses, some retail businesses adopt a simple policy: No checks. But such a policy often carries its own risks—mainly that you may lose perfectly solvent customers or clients who like the convenience of writing checks. After all, it's customary for most retail, wholesale, service and manufacturing industries to accept checks. And because with checks the bank doesn't keep a percentage of each transaction (as is the case with credit cards), you may actually want to encourage regular customers to pay by check rather than credit card.

No matter what type of business you're in, the best way to approach the potential bad check problem is to adopt sensible rules and stick to them. How stringent you want to be depends on the nature of your business, and how well rules will be accepted by your customers and clients. It boils down to a business decision about how much risk you're willing to accept.

If yours is a retail business, here are some policies to consider:

- Require that checks be written and signed in your presence.
- Accept checks drawn on local banks only.
- Be sure the checks have the customer's name, local address and phone number pre-printed on them.
- Don't accept checks written for more than the purchase price; in other words, don't give change for a check. (Some small businesses, such as grocers, build customer loyalty with minimal losses by issuing check-cashing cards allowing regular customers to write a check for up to $20 more than the price of goods purchased.)
- Wait until the check has cleared before giving a cash refund for returned goods.
- Don't accept third-party checks—paychecks, Social Security checks and other checks that someone else has made out to the customer who then endorses them.

EXAMPLE: Laurie offers you a check made out to her from her employer, Amalgamated Products. She endorses it on the back. The check may be a forgery, or maybe the company doesn't have funds in the account to cover the check.

- Don't accept post-dated checks.
- Set a limit on the check amount you will accept. Or at least call the bank and verify that larger checks are good.
- Require a manager's approval for checks over a certain amount. Better yet, hire clerks whose judgment you trust.
- Write the customer's phone number on the check, if the law in your state allows it.
- Ask to see ID—including something that contains a photo and signature. A driver's license is a good choice. Record key information (such as the driver's license number) on the check; it will help you locate the customer if the check is no good.

⚠️ **Restrictions on ID requirements.** *Find out if your state has a law restricting the kind of ID you can require. In some states, for example, you can't require a customer to show you a credit card as condition of accepting a check. However, if a customer voluntarily shows you a credit card as ID, state law may permit you to record the type of card, the issuer and the expiration date—but you can't write down the card number. If you violate laws of this type, you may face a fine, a civil lawsuit or both. No matter what your state law is, avoid using credit cards as a form of ID. For one thing, you can't charge the client's credit card account if the check bounces. For another, bank personnel or others seeing a credit card number may use this information improperly. Why subject your customers to this risk?*

If you're presented with a check drawn on a business account, be sure that the person signing it has authority to do so. If a check is signed by someone other than the owner, a partner or a corporate officer, call the bank to see if the person presenting the check is an authorized signer.

Some businesses post a sign saying that they charge a specified fee for any check that bounces. The legal reasoning is that in many states you can't collect such fees without advance warning to customers. And some business owners think that such notices deter bad check writers. Still, I generally recommend against posting signs. It's insulting to the customer, and there's no evidence that it will cut down the bad checks you receive. And remember, your main goal is to avoid getting bad checks in the first place—not to try to collect them later plus a $10 fee. But if you do post such a sign or charge such a fee, check the law in your state to see how much you can legally charge.

📖 Money Troubles: Legal Strategies to Cope With Your Debts, *by Robin Leonard (Nolo), is addressed primarily to people who owe money, but the information on bad check laws is also helpful to businesses receiving money.*

Once you accept a check, stamp it with an endorsement stamp (available from your bank) and deposit it in your business account the same day. Every day you wait increases the chances that the check-writer will have emptied or closed the account. Under the Uniform Commercial Code, a statute adopted in every state and which governs most banking transactions, there's a presumption that a check becomes "stale" six months after the date it's signed. The bank may refuse to honor it after that period—although in actual practice, they'll usually honor older checks as long as the account is solvent.

2. Dealing With Bad Checks

Even though you take all reasonable precautions, a bad check will occasionally slip through your system. A bank may return a check to you with the notation "insufficient funds" or "NSF," which means the same thing: the customer has an active account but there's not enough in it to cover the check. Or a bank may inform you that the account has been closed.

Here are some steps you can take—many of which apply primarily to bad checks from individuals. Other techniques may be more appropriate when the bad check comes from another business. (See Chapter 19.)

Step 1. Call the Customer

Call the customer and ask that he or she make the check good or pay you in cash. (This is one reason it's good to write down the customer's phone number when you take a check, if permitted by state law.) But be careful about when you call the customer—and how often. Laws in several states limit what you can do to collect debts. (See Chapter 19, Section D.) To avoid problems, call only between 8 a.m. and 9 p.m., don't discuss the debt with the customer's employer and make sure your request for payment is polite. Threatening a debtor that you'll publicize his or her name or notify his or her employer is illegal.

Step 2. Write a Letter

Send a certified letter—return receipt requested—making the same demand. This sets the stage for a possible criminal prosecution if the check-writer intentionally attempted to defraud you. Also, 35 states (including Arizona, California, Colorado, Florida, Illinois, Montana, New York and Washington) have bad-check laws that are particularly favorable to businesses. In such states, if you send a written demand for payment, you may be able to collect extra damages in court (often two or three times the value of the check) if the check-writer doesn't come through.

> **EXAMPLE:** Monica, the owner of a Florida gift shop, receives a bad check from Norbert. She sends Norbert a notice demanding payment in full plus a service charge of $15 or 5% of the check, whichever is greater. If Norbert doesn't pay within seven days, Monica can sue him under Florida law for the amount of the check plus additional damages of three times the amount of the check (at least $50). This is in addition to court costs, reasonable attorney fees and any bank fees that she incurs.

The sample notice and demand for payment shown below here is derived from the Florida bad-check statute (*Crimes,* § 832.07). Because the law in each state is different, find out the specific requirements where you do business. (See Chapter 24, Section D, for information on doing legal research.)

Sample Bad Check Notice (Florida)

You are hereby notified that a check, numbered _____, issued by you on _____, ____, drawn upon <u>(name of bank)</u>, and payable to _____, has been dishonored. Pursuant to Florida law, you have seven days from receipt of this notice to tender payment of the full amount of such check plus a service charge of $15 or an amount of up to 5% of the face amount of the check, whichever is greater, the total amount due being $_____ and cents. Unless this amount is paid in full within the time specified above, the holder of such check may turn over the dishonored check and all other available information relating to the incident to the state attorney for criminal prosecution. You may be additionally liable in a civil action for triple the amount of the check, but in no case less than $50, together with the amount of the check, a service charge, court costs, reasonable attorney fees and incurred bank fees, as provided in Florida Statutes Title VI, Civil Practice and Procedure, § 68.065.

State Bad Check Laws

State	Code Section	Maximum Damages Under State Bad Check Laws
Alabama	8-8-15	$30
Alaska	09.68.115	$100 or three times the amount of the check, whichever is greater, not to exceed the amount of the check by more than $1,000.
Arizona	13-1809	Twice the amount of the check or $50, whichever is greater.
Arkansas	4-60-103	Two times the amount of the check, but in no case less than $50.
California	CC 1719	Three times the amount of the check, not less than $100 nor more than $1,500.
Colorado	13-21-109	Three times the amount of the check, but not less than $100.
Connecticut	52-565a	If the customer wrote a check for which there was no account, damages can't exceed the amount of the check or $750. If check was written on an account with insufficient funds, damages can't exceed the amount of check or $400, whichever is less.
Florida	68.065	Three times the amount of the check or $50, whichever is greater.
Georgia	13-6-15	Two times the amount of the check, but in no case more than $500.
Hawaii	490:3-506	Three times the amount of the check or $100, whichever is greater, but not more than $500.
Idaho	1-2301A	Three times the amount of the check or $100, whichever is greater, but not more than $500.
Illinois	720 ILCS 5/17-1a	Three times the amount of the check or $100, whichever is greater, but not more than $1,500.
Indiana	26-2-7-6	Three times the amount of the check for checks up to $250. For checks over $250, the amount of the check plus $500.
Iowa	554.3513	Three times the amount of the check, but not more than $500.
Kansas	60-2610	Three times the amount of the check or $100, whichever is greater, but not more than $500.
Louisiana	9:272	Twice the amount of the check or $100, whichever is greater.
Maine	14-6071	Not more than $50.
Maryland	CL 15-802	Twice the amount of the check, not to exceed $1,000.
Massachusetts	93:40A	Not less than $100 and not more than $500.
Michigan	600.2952	Two times the amount of the check or $100, whichever is greater.
Minnesota	332.50	$100 or the value of the check, whichever is greater.
Mississippi	11-7-12	For checks up to $25, $30; for checks between $26 and $200, 50% of face amount, not to exceed $50 nor to be less than $30; if check is over $200, 25% of face amount.
Missouri	570.123	Three times the amount of the check or $100, whichever is greater, but not more than $500.
Montana	27-1-717	Three times the amount of the check or $100, whichever is greater, but not more than $500.
Nevada	41-620	Three times the amount of the check, not less than $100 nor more than $500.
New Hampshire	544-B:1	Court, service and collection costs; a debtor who fails to pay judgment immediately must pay $10 per business day up to $500, from date of judgment until debt paid.
New Jersey	2A:32A-1	Three times the amount of the check or $100, whichever is greater, but not more than $500.
New Mexico	56-14-1	Three times the amount of the check or $100, whichever is greater, but not more than $500.

State Bad Check Laws (continued)

State	Code Section	Maximum Damages Under State Bad Check Laws
New York	GOL 11-104	If the customer wrote a check for which there was no account, two times the amount of the check or $750, whichever is less. If a check was written on an account with insufficient funds, two times the amount of the check or $400, whichever is less.
North Carolina	6-21.3	Three times the amount of the check or $500, whichever is less, but not less than $100.
North Dakota	6-08-16.2	Three times the amount of the check or $100, whichever is less.
Oregon	30.701	Three times the amount of the check or $100, whichever is greater, but not more than $500.
Pennsylvania	42-8304	Three times the amount of the check or $100, whichever is greater, but not more than $500.
Rhode Island	6-42-3	Three times the amount of the check, not less than $200, not more than $1,000.
South Carolina	34-11-75	Three times the amount of the check or $500, whichever is less.
South Dakota	21-57-1	Three times the amount of the check, but not less than $100 or more than $200.
Tennessee	47-29-101	Three times the amount of the check, not to exceed $500.
Vermont	9-2311	Court costs, service fees, the amount of the check, interest, attorneys' fees and damages of $50.
Virginia	6.1-118.1	$10 to cover the returned check fee, the amount of the check and lost wages, to a total of $250.
Washington	62A.3-515	Three times the amount of the check or $300, whichever is less.
Wisconsin	943.245	Actual damages; three times the amount of the check and attorneys' fees, not to exceed $500.
Wyoming	1-1-115	Three times the amount of the check, but not less than $100, plus court costs.

Step 3. Contact the Bank

If the customer's bank account is still active, wait a few days and then inquire to see if the check is now good (the customer may have deposited a paycheck after the check was dishonored). You can normally check the status of an account by calling the bank and saying you hold a check for a certain dollar amount and asking if there is enough in the account to cover it. If so, take the returned check to the bank and draw out the cash. Another alternative is to ask the customer's bank for "enforced collection." If the bank offers this service, the bad check will be held in a special category. The next money deposited in the customer's account will go to you. Procedures and costs vary; get details from the bank.

Step 4. Request Prosecution

Intentionally writing a bad check is a crime. As noted above, before you contact the local district attorney's or prosecuting attorney's office to request prosecution, you may have to give the check-writer a written notice. After all, the bad check may have been an innocent mistake. The police department or district attorney can tell you if you must send a notice as a prelude to a prosecution (generally you must) and what the notice must contain. But again, in any oral or written communication with the customer who passed the bad check, avoid the temptation to threaten prosecution. Such a threat may constitute harassment or extortion under some state statutes.

What are the chances of law enforcement officials taking action? Some police departments and prosecuting officials drag their feet on these kinds of cases, saying that they don't want to be used as a collection agency. Others are far more cooperative. Some of the best have bad-check programs under which the person who has written the check is contacted and given a chance to avoid being prosecuted by making the check good and, in some counties, by attending special classes under a "diversion" program.

Step 5. Use Small Claims Court

If you still haven't been paid, consider suing in small claims court, as long as the check is less than the maximum amount you can sue for in small claims—or close enough that you don't mind waiving the excess. Most states have limits between $3,000 and $15,000. (See Chapter 23 on how to represent yourself in small claims court.) As noted in Step 2, if you've followed the bad-check procedures in your state, you may be entitled to two or even three times the amount of the check as damages as well as your court-filing and service-of-process costs. And if the check-writer has a job, you'll generally be able to use post-judgment proceedings to get paid out of the worker's wages—although it's difficult to collect from the wages of low-income people. You might also be able to collect from bank or other deposit accounts. In most states, you can also cheaply and easily put a lien against the debtor's real estate. Chances are you'll ultimately be paid when the property is voluntarily sold or refinanced.

Step 6. Use a Collection Agency

Turning a bad check over to a collection agency is often worth considering. For smaller checks, going to small claims court may not be worthwhile. Or perhaps, despite the huge cut a collection agency takes, you might want to put your time and energy elsewhere. And while some states make small claims court fairly friendly to businesses (for example, you may be able to send an employee to court with business records), other states make the business owner appear to testify in person. That may make suing the check writer more trouble than it's worth. So if you want to keep to a minimum your personal involvement in the collection process, keep open the possibility of letting a collection agency do most of the work.

When the Customer Stops Payment

Sometimes a customer stops payment on a check, claiming that the goods you sold were defective. If there's a legitimate dispute, the customer's good faith will be a valid defense to a prosecution or a civil lawsuit for multiple damages. And if it turns out that the goods were in fact defective, the customer will be entitled to a reduction of the amount owed—or even, in extreme cases, a cancellation of the debt. But if the customer's allegations are a trumped-up excuse to get something for nothing, you'll be entitled to your full legal remedies in court. Often, however, in dealing with a customer who is unhappy with the merchandise purchased, the best policy is simply to have the customer return the goods and to call it a day.

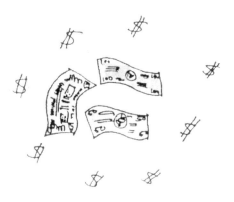

Payment in Full

Be careful about accepting and depositing checks that say "Payment in Full" or something similar. If the check writer owes more, you may be barred from collecting the additional amount.

Where there's a good faith dispute about how much the check writer owes you, depositing a full-payment check usually means that you accept the check in complete satisfaction of the debt. Crossing out the words "Payment in Full" generally won't help you. You'll still be cut off from suing for the balance.

However, a number of states have changed this rule to help creditors. In those states, if you cash a full payment check and explicitly reserve your right to sue for the balance, you can go after the check writer in court. States that have this modified rule include Alabama, Delaware, Massachusetts, Minnesota, Missouri, New Hampshire, New York, Ohio, Rhode Island, South Carolina, South Dakota, West Virginia and Wisconsin.

If your state has modified the rule, you normally can preserve your right to sue for the balance by writing the words "Under Protest" or "Without Prejudice" with your endorsement. California simply lets you cross out the full-payment language, cash the check and sue for the balance—but the check writer may be able to get around this by following certain procedures specified in the statute (California Civil Code § 1526). The statute was created to protect creditors, not debtors, however, so in most instances you can defeat a "Payment in Full" check.

■

19

Extending Credit and Getting Paid

I n this chapter, you'll find out how to establish credit practices that help ensure that you get paid when you should. You'll also learn how to comply with federal and state credit laws and what to do if customers, clients or patients don't pay when they're supposed to.

A. The Practical Side of Extending Credit

Some businesses give customers 30 or 60 days to pay for goods and services. They may even let customers make installment payments over a longer period. For example, a small wholesaler of children's music products might require retail customers to pay at the time of sale, but extend 30 days' credit to wholesale customers. Similarly, many professionals and other service providers extend

short-term credit to clients and customers, who are expected to pay after receiving a monthly invoice.

If you extend credit, you need to set up a well-organized, accurate, easy-to-use system of accounts, send out bills periodically and keep after those who pay slowly or not at all—all of which takes time, money and effort. Many small business people fantasize about avoiding the whole mess by requiring customers to pay cash. Unfortunately, this sort of day-dreaming is normally just that; in many businesses and professional practices it's almost impossible to operate if you don't extend credit.

1. Professional and Personal Service Businesses

In many professional or consulting practices, it used to be considered unusual to require a client or patient to complete a formal credit application. No longer. Today, credit applications are becoming routine, because businesses simply can't afford to work for deadbeats. But if you shy away from a formal application, you can still gather much pertinent information from your new client or patient intake sheet. Ask where the person works and banks. Ask for the name of the "nearest relative not living with you"—useful information if the client or patient skips out.

Healthcare professionals will, of course, want to inquire about insurance or Medicaid/Medicare coverage. Consider offering a modest discount (say, 5%) for payment at the time services are rendered—it usually leads to prompt payment. And think about posting a dignified sign saying: "If it's convenient, payment is appreciated when the bill is presented." If you accept credit cards, there's really no reason for the patient not to pay on the spot.

Lawyers, accountants, appraisers, engineers, dentists and other professionals may appropriately ask for advance payment to be applied against the first batch of services, especially if a new client or patient needs extensive services. One way to do this is to present a fee letter to each new client. The letter might state that new clients are asked to pay a retainer and that future payments are due ten days from billing. (See "Putting Professional Relationships on a Sound Financial Footing," below.)

Another positive thing a professional or consultant can do is to routinely record bank account data about the client or patient as payment is received. Then, if you have to sue the client or patient, you have one more place to turn to try to satisfy your judgment.

If you're worried that someone isn't creditworthy—particularly if the bill is likely to mount rapidly—you can run a quick credit check with a credit reporting agency. Credit checks are so routine these days that this won't drive away business. However, you should notify the client or patient beforehand. Also, before using credit reports, familiarize yourself with the Fair Credit Reporting Act and similar state laws. (See Section B.) For example, if you reject credit for a client or patient based on a credit report, you need to disclose this to the person, as well as the name, address and phone number of the credit reporting agency that gave you the negative information.

Putting Professional Relationships on a Sound Financial Footing

If you have a professional practice or run a consulting or personal service business, consider giving each client or patient a written statement of your billing procedures, so that they know what to expect.

It is also businesslike and inoffensive to prepare a letter of retention spelling out the services you'll be performing, how much you'll be charging, when you'll be billing and when payment is due. Such letters may even be legally required. In California, for example, lawyers and clients must sign a fee agreement if the expected fee is more than $1,000 or the fee is contingent on the outcome of a lawsuit.

You could even take the retention letter one step farther by providing payment envelopes for the patients to use in sending their monthly checks. This approach works for professionals where fairly predictable services are delivered over a defined time period.

Your letter should state when you expect to be paid—usually within ten days of the statement date. Also, list the amount of any interest or finance charges you'll assess (as permitted by state law) if payment is late, and reserve your right to stop rendering services. (In a few professions, rules of professional ethics may affect how and when you can terminate the relationship.) Have the client or patient acknowledge in writing that he or she has received your letter and agrees to its terms.

To find out legal limits on interest or finance charges, check the index to the annotated statutes (sometimes called a "code") for your state—available in any good law library. Look under the terms "interest," "usury" or "finance charges." Also, your professional or trade organization should have helpful information.

2. Wholesale and Manufacturing Businesses

If you're a shoe wholesaler, software company or clothing manufacturer—or if you're in any other wholesale or service business—you should have a credit policy, and you should insist that customers complete a formal application for credit. The details of your credit policy will depend on the kind of business you're in and the type of customers you serve. Here are some issues to think about:

- How many days after billing is payment due?
- Is there a discount for early payment?
- Do you require pre-payment or COD terms for certain classes of customers?
- Do you add interest or finance charges? If so, how much?
- When are credit checks required? (For example, you obviously wouldn't require a credit check if the customer is the government, and probably wouldn't for a major, well-established company. On the other hand, you likely would want to check on the credit of a new small business or an individual making a large purchase.)
- How are credit limits determined?
- When and how often do you send past due notices and follow up with phone calls?
- Do you keep selling to a customer whose account is overdue?
- At what point will you begin aggressive credit efforts?

When you approve credit for new trade accounts, let them know the maximum credit you're allowing and when they're expected to pay—as well as other relevant features of your credit policy.

Should You Charge Interest?

Most businesses don't charge interest or impose finance charges in exchange for granting credit. More typically, interest is charged when bills aren't paid within the agreed time, often between ten and 30 days. If you decide to impose these charges, you must inform the customer how the charges will be computed. The Truth in Lending Act (see Section B), which applies primarily to sales to consumers, prescribes the disclosures you must make—but not the rates you can charge. That's done by state law.

One reason to consider adding interest or finance charges after a certain date is that customers who are short of cash tend to pay first the bills that carry such charges. Other incentives for early payment include:

- Discounts for prompt payment—for example, 5% off if the customer pays his or her bill on the spot or within ten days.
- Free shipping and handling (a big item these days) for customers who pre-pay.
- Making the customer responsible for paying for court costs and reasonable attorney fees required to enforce collection if the customer doesn't pay as agreed. The customer must agree to this, either in a credit application or a separate contract.

A sample credit application form designed for trade accounts is shown below.

SAMPLE CREDIT APPLICATION

CREDIT APPLICATION

The undersigned company is applying for credit with ABC ELECTRICAL INC. and agrees to abide by the standard terms and conditions of ABC ELECTRICAL INC. as printed on the reverse side.

Company Name _____

DBA (if different) _____

Contact Person _____

Address _____

Phone (___)_____ Fax (___) _____

Federal Tax ID or Social Security No. _____

Type of Business _____ No. of Employees_____

Date Business Established _____

Types of Products You Will Purchase _____

Amount of Credit Requested $ _____

Are You a:

☐ CORPORATION

State of Incorporation _____

Names, Titles and Addresses of Your Three Chief Corporate Officers _____

Name and Address of Your Resident Agent _____

☐ LIMITED LIABILITY COMPANY (LLC)

State Where Formed _____

Names, Titles and Addresses of Your Three Chief Managers or Members _____

_____

_____

_____

Name and Address of Your Resident Agent _____

_____

☐ PARTNERSHIP

Names and Addresses of the Partners

_____

_____

_____

☐ SOLE PROPRIETORSHIP

Are you sales tax exempt? Yes ___ No ___

Have you ever had credit with us before? Yes ___ No ___

If yes, under what name? _____

Authorized Purchasers _____

_____

Purchase Order Required? Yes ___ No ___

SAMPLE CREDIT APPLICATION (continued)

TRADE REFERENCES

Reference #1 Name _____

Address _____

Phone (   ) _____

Reference #2 Name _____

Address _____

Phone (   ) _____

Reference #3 Name _____

Address _____

Phone (   ) _____

BANK REFERENCES

Bank #1 Account # _____ Phone (   ) _____

Contact Person _____

Name of Bank _____

Address _____

Bank #2 Account # _____ Phone (   ) _____

Contact Person _____

Name of Bank _____

Address _____

I represent that the above information is true and is given to induce ABC ELECTRICAL INC. to extend credit to the applicant. My company and I authorize ABC ELECTRICAL INC. to make such credit investigation as ABC ELECTRICAL INC. sees fit, including contacting the above trade references and banks and obtaining credit reports. My company and I authorize all trade references, banks and credit reporting agencies to disclose to ABC ELECTRICAL INC. any and all information concerning the financial and credit history of my company and myself.

I have read the terms and conditions stated below and agree to all of those terms and conditions.

Authorized Signature: _____

Printed Name: _____

Title: _____ Date: _____

GENERAL TERMS AND CONDITIONS AND PERSONAL GUARANTEE

1.   Bills are sent on the first day of each month. You may take the 5% discount as indicated on the bill if you pay the invoice by the 10th of the month.

2.   All bills become payable in full on the 11th day of the month and, if not paid by the end of the month, are considered past due.

3.   A service charge of 2% per month will be added to all amounts billed if not paid by the end of the month.

4.   No additional credit will be extended to past due accounts unless satisfactory arrangements are made with our credit department.

5.   PERSONAL GUARANTEE: If the credit customer is a corporation or LLC, then those signing this application, whether or not signing as an officer or manager, personally guarantee payment for all items purchased on credit by the corporation or LLC.

Personal guarantees can be a problem.
See the discussion in Section 3, below.

3. Extending Credit to Businesses

When the customer is another business, it's wise to get information about whom you're really dealing with—especially if the business wants a substantial amount of credit. Is the customer a sole proprietor? A partnership? A corporation? The answer determines who's liable for the debt. If the business is owned by an individual (for example, Bill Jones doing business as Jones Products), the owner's own assets—as well as those of the business—are available to satisfy the debt. With a general partnership, you can go after the assets of the individual partners, if necessary, so it's a good idea to have the names of all the partners listed on the credit application. A limited partnership, on the other hand, consists of general partners and limited partners; only the assets of the general partners are available to satisfy the debts of a limited partnership. (See Chapter 1, Section B.)

With a corporation, you usually are limited to collecting from the business assets. Because you can't collect from the personal bank accounts of the officers and shareholders, there's good reason to seek personal guarantees when dealing with a new or small corporation that wants substantial credit. In some businesses, however, it's completely against trade practices to ask for a personal guarantee. It's your job to learn the practices in your industry before using a clause like number 5, in the sample credit application above. If you do decide to seek personal guarantees, check out whether or not a signature on a credit application is sufficient in your state. The law may require that you obtain a new guarantee each time you extend credit to a company.

You may also want to ask for the personal guarantees of others if someone who applies for personal credit has a weak financial status. Maybe a friend or family member will agree to be responsible if the customer doesn't pay on time. This is often called co-signing. You can obtain the personal guarantee or co-signature on the credit application form or on a separate document called "Guarantee of Payment." As noted above, in some states, a personal guarantee on an application form or a one-time separate document may not suffice. You may need to get a signature from the guarantor each time you extend credit.

4. References and Credit Checks

Your credit application should provide space for the applicant to list several other businesses who will vouch for the fact that the applicant pays on time. Check these references carefully, even though the credit applicant is sure to list people who will say positive things. Your job is to try to penetrate the facade many credit applicants are sure to present that everything is just fine. One way to do this is to ask offbeat questions such as, "You mean ABC's credit is so good you'll take me to lunch if they stiff me?"

If the amount of credit you're extending is large, don't stop with checking a few references. Purchase a credit report on an individual from a national credit reporting agency such as Trans Union, Experian or Equifax or, on a business, from Dun & Bradstreet. You'll find them listed under "Credit Reporting Agencies" in the Yellow Pages, or check for a toll-free number or website.

To get a report on an individual, most agencies want the name, address, phone number, Social Security number and date of birth, if possible, of the person you're asking them to search—information you should get on your credit application form.

Be wary of negative information in credit reports, which may be inaccurate or out of date. If an individual seems to be otherwise well qualified for credit, consider giving him or her a chance to explain the negative stuff before you deny credit.

5. Signatures for Receipt of Goods

Have customers sign receipts when they receive merchandise on credit. If you provide services, have customers sign an acknowledgment of services performed. This avoids arguments about whether or not the customer actually received the goods or services.

B. Laws That Regulate Consumer Credit

Many small businesses don't extend credit directly to consumers. With the widespread availability of credit cards, this is often the safest and most cost-effective way to go. However, if yours is a business where credit must be granted, you must comply with federal laws affecting credit sales to consumers for personal, family or household purposes. States are also beginning to adopt consumer credit laws that mirror many provisions of federal law.

Here's an introduction to the major federal laws that affect consumer credit:

1. The Truth in Lending Act

This statute requires you to disclose your exact credit terms to people who apply for credit, so they'll know what they're expected to pay. It also regulates how you advertise consumer credit. Among the items you must disclose to a consumer who buys on credit are the following:

- the monthly finance charge
- the annual interest rate
- when payments are due
- the total sale price—cash price of the item or service plus all other charges
- the amount of any late payment charges and when they'll be imposed.

2. The Fair Credit Billing Act

This law dictates what you must do if a customer claims you made a mistake in your billing. The customer must notify you within 60 days after you mailed the first bill containing the claimed error. You must respond within 30 days after you receive the letter unless the dispute has already been resolved. You must also conduct a reasonable investigation and, within 90 days after getting the customer's letter, explain why the bill is correct or correct the error. If you don't follow this procedure, you must give the customer a $50 credit toward the disputed amount—even if your bill was correct. Until the dispute is resolved, you can't report to a credit bureau that the customer is delinquent.

> **EXAMPLE:** Ron notifies CompuCo that he wasn't properly credited for a payment he sent in on his computer system. Under the Fair Credit Billing Act, CompuCo must acknowledge Ron's notice within 30 days. And within 90 days, CompuCo must either agree with Ron and correct his account or, after conducting a reasonable investigation, send Ron a letter explaining why the company feels his bill was correct. While this is happening, Ron doesn't have to pay the disputed amount. And he can't be penalized for withholding payment. During this period, CompuCo can't tell a credit reporting agency that this is a delinquent bill. CompuCo can charge interest on the disputed bill, but if Ron turns out to be right, the interest must be dropped.

State laws may also deal with billing disputes. Generally, if a state law on this subject conflicts with the federal statute, the federal statute will control—but there's one exception: a state law will prevail if it gives a consumer more time to notify a creditor about a billing error. For example, as explained above, the federal law gives a consumer 60 days after receiving a bill to notify you of a billing error. If a state law gives a consumer 90 days to notify you, the consumer will be entitled to the extra 30 days.

In addition to telling you how to handle billing disputes, the Fair Credit Billing Act requires you, in periodic mailings, to tell consumers what their rights are.

3. The Equal Credit Opportunity Act

You may not discriminate against an applicant on the basis of race, color, religion, national origin, age, sex or marital status. The Act does leave you free to consider legitimate factors in granting credit, such as the applicant's financial status (earnings and savings) and credit record. Despite the prohibition on age discrimination, you can reject a consumer who hasn't reached the legal age in your state for entering into contracts.

4. The Fair Credit Reporting Act

This law deals primarily with credit reports issued by credit reporting agencies. It's intended to protect consumers from having their eligibility for credit thwarted by inaccurate or obsolete credit report information. The law gives consumers the right to a copy of their credit reports. If they feel something is inaccurate, they can ask that it be corrected or removed. If the business reporting the credit problem doesn't agree to a change or deletion or if the credit bureau refuses to make it, the consumer can add a 100-word statement to the file explaining his or her side of the story. This becomes a part of any future credit report.

5. The Fair Debt Collection Practices Act

This statute addresses abusive methods used by third-party collectors—bill collectors you hire to collect overdue bills. Small businesses are more directly affected by state laws that apply directly to collection methods used by a creditor. (See Section D3.)

 An excellent resource regarding consumer credit is Consumer Law: Sales Practices and Credit Regulation, *by Howard J. Alperin & Roland J. Alperin (West Publishing Co.). It should be available at most law libraries. Also helpful is* Manual of Credit and Commercial Laws *(National Association of Credit Management).*

A fine Nolo book discusses these issues from the perspective of the consumer: Money Troubles: Legal Strategies to Cope With Your Debts, *by Robin Leonard.*

Also very helpful are two booklets published by the Federal Trade Commission:
- How to Advertise Consumer Credit: Complying With the Law
- How to Write Readable Credit Forms.

Both are available at www.ftc.gov. See Appendix B for additional FTC contact information.

Finally, you may find helpful information in Bankruptcy and Other Debtor-Creditor Laws in a Nutshell, *by David B. Epstein (West Publishing Co.).*

You may be able to get information from a local trade association (such as a contractors', restaurant or tax preparers' association) or Chamber of Commerce.

C. Becoming a Secured Creditor

If you sell major amounts of merchandise or equipment to a customer on credit, look into becoming a secured creditor. If the debt is secured by property of the customer, you can seize that property if the customer doesn't pay the debt as promised. A common arrangement is for a business to take a security interest in the goods it sells on credit. For example, a store that sells furniture on credit keeps a security interest in the furniture. If the buyer gets behind on payments, the store can take the furniture back. Under federal and state laws dealing with billing problems, you may be subject to penalties for failing to comply with the required procedures.

1. Sales of Merchandise or Equipment

The Uniform Commercial Code (UCC), which has been adopted by all states, provides a method for you to acquire a legal (security) interest in the property that you sell to the customer—or in other property of the customer—that will let you sell or take back the property if the customer doesn't pay. Typically, you have the customer sign a financing agreement and a UCC Financing Statement. You then file the UCC Financing Statement with the appropriate public office, such as the county clerk or the secretary of state (it varies from state to state).

Also, if the customer files for bankruptcy, you'll have a big advantage over general (unsecured) creditors—those who didn't take a security interest in the customer's property. The property in which you have a security interest will be earmarked for your benefit. Unsecured creditors get only a share of the bankrupt's unsecured assets—which may repay only a tiny portion of what's owed or (often) nothing at all.

Obviously, it takes time and requires some paperwork and expense to create a security interest. It may not be worth it if you sell someone a $500 washing machine (it's a lot easier to take credit cards and require full payment)—but definitely worth doing when the product is a $10,000 computer system. Banks routinely obtain a security interest when they lend money to a customer to purchase equipment.

Incidentally, as an alternative to extending credit on larger purchases, one option is to refer the customer to a bank or leasing company—particularly one with whom you've established a working relationship. These organizations are in business to take credit risks and can absorb losses better than you can.

2. Special Rights for Those in the Construction Business

A lien is a legal claim on someone's property. Under state law, you may have a mechanic's, materialman's or construction lien on real estate if you provided materials or labor on a construction or renovation project—for example, if you supplied the lighting fixtures or installed the roofing for a new house. If your bill isn't paid, you can foreclose on your lien. This means the real estate can be sold to pay your bill.

Unfortunately, in many states to take advantage of this powerful weapon to protect your rights, you have to file certain legal documents claiming (perfecting) a lien within a short time after you complete your work or supply the materials. Speak to a construction industry trade association or, if necessary, a lawyer about how to do this.

D. Collection Problems

Despite your best efforts to screen your customers, if you extend credit, sooner or later you're going to run into people or businesses who are slow in paying. It can be one of the most frustrating aspects of running a business. Part of the reason is that you may be pursuing several objectives that are not compatible. Here's what I mean:

- You want to be paid in full, of course, but—
- You'd also like to continue doing business with the customer, if possible. What's more—
- You don't want to run afoul of laws that restrict or prohibit aggressive collection tactics, and
- You don't want waste your resources on a wild goose chase.

It's not an easy problem, but a number of techniques can help keep your losses to a minimum.

1. Strategies for Avoiding or Reducing Losses

Following these suggestions should help you hold down your losses on credit transactions:

- Send bills promptly and re-bill at least monthly. There's no need to wait for the end of the month.
- Make sure your bills clearly state the goods sold or the services provided. It's a great idea to include on the bill a request to the customer to contact you if there are problems with the goods or services. If the customer fails to do so and later tries to excuse the failure to pay by claiming the goods or services were unsatisfactory, you have a good argument that the customer is fabricating a phony excuse. Another benefit is that if your goods or services are in fact prone to problems, you open up lines of communication and usually can keep the customer happy.
- Enclose a self-addressed envelope (preferably stamped) to facilitate payment.
- Keep a record of the checking account that the customer uses to pay you.
- Send past due notices promptly when an account is overdue. Ask clearly for payment. Many people worry that the word "pay" sounds too blunt. Here are a few alternate phrases, courtesy of collection expert Leonard Sklar, author of *The Check Is NOT in the Mail* (Baroque Publishing):
  "We'd appreciate it if you would *clear your account*."
  "You can *take care of this* by cash or check, whichever you prefer."
  "Please *bring your account current*."
- If this doesn't work, promptly telephone to ask what's wrong. The customer needs to know that you follow these matters closely. Do not extend more credit, no matter what the hard luck story. This is particularly important. Lots of businesses facing tight finances pay only when they need more merchandise.

If you let them have it without payment, you're teaching them that you're a pushover.
- Have a series of letters to use in routine cases. These letters should escalate in intensity as time goes by. (See the discussion of collection letters later in this section.)
- If the customer has genuine financial problems, find out what the customer realistically can afford. Consider extending the time for payment if the customer agrees in writing to a new payment schedule. Call the day before the next scheduled payment is due to be sure the customer plans to respect the agreement.
- Save copies of all correspondence with the customer and keep notes of all telephone conversations.
- Watch out for checks for less than the full amount that say "Payment in Full." In some states, if you deposit the check—especially if the amount owed is in dispute—you may have wiped out the balance owing. (See Chapter 18, Section C2.) Learn the law in your state before you deposit such a check.
- Continue to keep in contact with the customer—but don't harass him or her. (See Section D3.)
- If an account is unpaid for an extended period and you're doubtful about ever collecting, consider offering in writing a time-limited, deep discount to resolve the matter. This way, the customer has the incentive to borrow money to take advantage of your one-time, never-again offer to settle.
- When collection starts to put heavy demands on your time, and your chances of recovery are slim because you know the customer is on the skids, consider turning the debt over to a collection agency so you can get on with more productive activities. (But first consider the collection alternatives described in Section E.)

2. Collection Letters

You may find it useful to develop a set of past due notices to use when customers fall behind. Although these are form letters, it's easy to customize them using your computer and word processing software. In writing to an individual customer, use the customer's name. In writing to a company, address your letter to the owner or chief operating office. It's less effective to start out with "Dear Customer" or "Dear Accounts Payable Supervisor."

Your first letter may suggest that perhaps the bill was overlooked, and that payment should be sent now so that the customer can maintain a good credit rating. Your second and third letters should be polite but increasingly firm. Vary the format of your letters. Each one should look a little different. Samples are shown below.

Letter 1

```
          Account No. _____


     Dear _____:


     Our records show that you have an outstanding balance with our company of $450.00.
This is for  (describe the goods or services) .

     Is there a problem with this bill? If so, please call me so that we can resolve the
matter. Otherwise, please send your payment at this time to bring your account current.
I'm enclosing a business reply envelope for you to use.

     Until you bring your account current, it's our policy to put further purchases on a
cash basis.

     Sincerely,




     P.S. Paying your bill at this time will help you to maintain your good credit rating.
```

Letter 2

Re: Overdue Bill ($_____)

Account No._____

Dear _____:

Your bill for $450.00 is seriously overdue. This is for the _(describe the goods or services furnished)_ we supplied to you last _(state the month)_. More than 60 days have gone by since we sent you our invoice. You did not respond to the letter I sent you last month.

We value your patronage but must insist that you bring your account up to date. Doing so will help you protect your reputation for prompt payment.

Please send your check today for the full balance. If this is not feasible, please call me to discuss a possible payment plan. I need to hear from you as soon as possible.

Sincerely,

Letter 3

Re: Collection Action on

Overdue Bill ($_____)

Account No._____

Dear _____:

We show an unpaid balance of $450 on your account that is over 90 days old. This is for the _____ that we supplied you over _____ days ago.

I have repeatedly tried to contact you, but my calls and letters have gone unheeded.

You must send full payment by _(date)_ or contact me by that date to discuss your intentions. If I do not hear from you, I plan to turn over the account for collection.

As you know, collection action can only have an adverse effect on your credit rating, and, according to our credit agreement, you will be responsible for collection costs. I hope to hear from you immediately so that the matter can be resolved without taking that step.

Sincerely,

3. Prohibited Collection Practices

Because of abuses, Congress passed the Fair Debt Collection Practices Act to regulate the activities of collection agencies. The federal law doesn't cover small businesses that collect their own bills. Many state laws, however, do crack down on the aggressive collection techniques of such businesses. And in states where the legislature hasn't yet acted, court decisions often penalize businesses that harass debtors or use unfair collection tactics.

Most business owners know intuitively the kind of behavior that's out of bounds. Here are some debt collection practices specifically outlawed by California's Fair Debt Collection Practices statute:

- Using or threatening to use physical force to collect a debt.
- Falsely threatening that the failure to pay a consumer debt will result in an accusation that the debtor has committed a crime.
- Using obscene or profane language.
- Causing expense to the debtor for long distance calls.
- Causing a phone to ring repeatedly or continuously to annoy the debtor.
- Communicating with the debtor so often as to be unreasonable and to constitute harassment.
- Communicating with the debtor's employer regarding a consumer debt unless the communication is necessary or the debtor has consented in writing. (A communication is necessary, according to the statute, only to verify the debtor's employment, to locate the debtor or to carry out a garnishment of wages after you have sued and won a judgment.)

The list goes on and on. If there's a similar statute in your state, get a copy and read it carefully. Like California's, most state laws in this field are modeled on the federal law. Some statutes, however, are more specific than others; for example, some list specific hours during which you can call the debtor.

E. Collection Options

Suppose you can't get the customer to pay up voluntarily. What next? If you're not willing to write off the debt (which is sometimes the wisest thing to do), you have three collection options:

- sue in small claims court
- hire a lawyer
- turn the account over to a collection agency.

Each choice has pros and cons.

Small claims court (see Chapter 23) is inexpensive and speedy. The downside is that it can take a good chunk of your time. Furthermore, any judgment that you receive may be worthless if the debtor lacks a job or bank account.

Lawyers can be effective, but they're expensive. Consider using a lawyer to write dunning letters. Many lawyers are willing to do this for a nominal charge.

Collection agencies are good at tracing elusive debtors, but they take a big percentage of what they collect for you. ■

Put It in Writing: Small Business Contracts

As the owner of a small business, it's likely that you'll often encounter both written and oral contracts. The most important piece of advice about contracts is obvious: Put all important agreements in writing. This chapter shows you how, and tells you what to do if something goes wrong.

A. What Makes a Valid Contract

A valid contract requires two and sometimes three elements:

- An agreement (meeting of the minds) between the parties.
- "Consideration"—a legal term meaning the exchange of things of value.
- Something in writing, if the contract covers certain matters, such as the sale of real estate and tasks that can't be completed in one year. (See Section D.)

For example, suppose you're opening a new store. You meet with Joe, a sign maker, to discuss the construction and installation of a five-foot by three-foot sign. Joe offers to do the work for $450 and to have the sign ready for your grand opening on June 15. "It's a deal," you say. You now have a legally binding contract, enforceable in court or by arbitration. All the necessary elements are present:

- **An Agreement.** Joe offered to build and install the sign at a certain price by a certain date. You accepted the offer by telling Joe, "It's a deal."
- **Consideration.** The two of you are exchanging something of value. You're giving your promise to pay $450. Joe is giving his promise to build and install the sign.
- **Written Agreement Not Required Here.** Normal business contracts that can be performed in less than a year don't have to be in writing to be enforceable.

To understand why "consideration" is important, let's explore the difference between a contract and a gift. Assume that Joe installs the sign on time and you pay him $450 as agreed. Impressed by the high quality of his work, you say: "Joe, to thank you for the great job you did, I'm going to send you a $100 bonus next week." Can Joe enforce your promise to pay the bonus? No. He got what he bargained for— the $450 payment. He didn't promise you anything (consideration) for the extra $100 payment. If you pay it, fine. If not, Joe can't force you to.

1. Negotiations

Negotiations, which may or may not lead to an agreement, do not constitute a contract. So if instead of meeting face to face with Joe, you call him and describe the job, and he says he can probably do it for about $450, you don't have a contract.

2. Offer and Acceptance

If after negotiations, two people reach an agreement, a contract is formed. Say that after discussing the job with you by phone, Joe promptly sends you a letter in which he says: "I can build and install the sign shown on the enclosed sketch for $450. I'll have it in place by June 15 when you open. You can pay me then." You send back a fax saying: "Sounds good. Go ahead." This is a valid contract. Joe has made a clear offer. You've just as clearly accepted that offer. The fact that you and Joe didn't meet face-to-face and didn't even use the same type of communication medium doesn't alter this conclusion.

In this example, you accepted Joe's offer promptly. But what if you'd waited two weeks or two months to accept? The legal rule is that an offer without a stated expiration date remains open for a reasonable time. What's reasonable depends on the type of business and the facts of the situation. If you're offered a truckload of fish or flowers, it might be unreasonable to delay your acceptance more than a few hours or even minutes, while an offer to sell surplus wood chips at a time when the market is glutted might reasonably be assumed to be good for a month or more. But there's really no need to tolerate any uncertainty in this regard. Include a clear deadline for acceptance when you present an offer. If you want to accept an offer, do it as promptly as possible.

3. Counter-Offers

In the real world, negotiations aren't usually as simple as making an offer and having it accepted. And until an agreement is reached, there's no contract.

For example, say Joe sends you the letter offering to provide your sign for $450. You call his office and leave a message on his voice mail saying: "Go ahead, but I can only pay $400." So far, there's no contract. By changing the terms of Joe's offer, you've rejected it and made a counter-offer. The two of you are still negotiating. If Joe calls back and says, "Okay, I'll do it for $400," you now have a binding contract. Joe has accepted your counter-offer. Again, the fact that you and Joe weren't in the same room or never spoke to each other isn't significant. What is key is that one of you made an offer (in this case, in the form of a counter-offer), and the other accepted it.

4. Revoking an Offer

Until an offer is accepted, it can be revoked by the person who made it. So if you're about to write Joe a letter accepting his offer, and Joe calls to revoke his offer because he's decided $450 isn't enough, you're out of luck. Joe revoked his offer before you accepted it, so there's no contract.

How an Offer to Contract Ends

- The person who made the offer revokes it before it's accepted.
- The offer expires.
  EXAMPLE: "This offer will expire automatically if I don't receive your acceptance by noon on May 10." But unless you've been paid something to keep the offer open (as is common for an option to buy real property—see next section), you (the offeror) can still revoke the unaccepted offer before the period for acceptance expires.
- A reasonable time elapses. As discussed in Section 2, above, there are no hard and fast rules as to what's reasonable. It all depends on circumstances and the practices in your industry.
- The offer is rejected. If you reject an offer and then change your mind, it's too late. To get the deal going again, you'll need to make an offer to the other party.
- Either party dies before the offer is accepted.

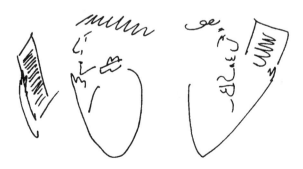

5. Option to Keep Offer Open

If you want someone to keep an offer open while you think about it, you may have to pay for the privilege. If you do, and the person who made the offer agrees to keep it open, your agreement (which is itself a contract) is called an "option." Options are commonly used when real estate or businesses are sold.

To stay with our sign example, say that when Joe sends you the letter offering to provide your sign, you tell him you're not ready to respond yet, but you want to be sure the offer will stay open while you think about it. Joe responds that if you pay $100 now, he'll keep his offer open for two more weeks. You pay the $100 and accept the offer within the two-week period. The resulting contract would be valid even if Joe tried to withdraw his offer before the end of the two-week period. You and Joe already have a contract (an option), which consists of your right to purchase his services at the $450 price if you act within the two-week period. He received something of value (your $100) in return for granting you this option.

6. How Offers Are Accepted

Usually, offers are accepted either in writing or orally. But that's not always necessary. It is an area of considerable legal complexity, but generally an offer can be accepted by a prompt action that conforms with the terms of the offer. For example, you might leave the sign builder Joe a note at his workshop, saying "Please add a red border to this sign today; I'll pay you an extra $100." Joe comes back that afternoon and adds the red border. You're obligated to pay him.

7. An Advertisement As an Offer

Under traditional contract law, ads are considered only invitations to negotiate or to make an offer; you have no obligation to go through with the deal just because someone offers to meet your advertised price. So if a customer appears and says she wants to buy the house, land or business that you advertised in the classifieds for $200,000, there's no binding contract. One major exception to this rule involves rewards. Generally, an ad offering to pay a reward is binding if someone performs the requested act.

Consumer protection laws have also changed this traditional rule. For example, the law in many states requires merchants to stock advertised items in quantities large enough to meet reasonably expected demand, unless the ad states that stock is limited. And some states require the merchant to give a rain check allowing the consumer to purchase the same merchandise at the same price at a later date. (See Chapter 17 for more on consumer transactions.)

B. Unfair or Illegal Contracts

What if a person makes a bad bargain? Suppose you agree to pay $800 for a used laser printer that's worth only $200. Can you call off the deal on the ground that the contract was grossly unfair? Probably not. As long as there's a valid contract, it doesn't usually matter whether or not the item is objectively worth the price paid for it.

Sometimes, however, a court sets aside a contract if the terms are unconscionable—that is, shockingly unfair. For example, a judge or arbitrator may release an unsophisticated consumer (say a recent immigrant with a language problem) from a grossly unfair contract extracted by a sophisticated, high-pressure salesperson. Applying this principle of law, a contract to sell a $500 television for $5,000 might be set aside. But even though a judge might cite contract law, the decision would probably be based more on the doctrine of fraud or misrepresentation. Or the decision might be based on a state consumer protection statute that prohibits taking advantage of someone who can't protect his or her interests because of disability, illiteracy or a language problem. (See Chapter 17, Section D, for more on this type of statute.)

When it comes to reasonably experienced business people working out contracts with each other, however, unfairness is rarely if ever a legal ground for setting aside a contract. Usually, a party who negotiates a bad deal is stuck with it.

If a contract clause is illegal or against public policy, a judge or arbitrator won't enforce it. For example, a remodeling contract stating that neither party will obtain a legally required building permit would be void as a violation of public policy, as would a similar contract obligating a party to bribe a building inspector.

C. Misrepresentation, Duress or Mistake

If before you sign a contract the other person tells you a false statement about something important, and you rely on that statement in signing the contract, you can go to court and have the contract rescinded (canceled). This is so even if the other person doesn't realize that the fact is untrue. For example, say you buy a pickup truck for your business, relying on the seller's assertion that the truck can carry loads up to two tons. It turns out that the

seller got the numbers wrong, and the truck can only carry one-ton loads. You can have the contract rescinded. If you have a contract rescinded, you must return any benefits you already received. In this example, you'd have to return the pickup truck to the seller to get your money back.

If you accept "an offer you can't refuse"—because, for example, the offer is made at gunpoint—the contract isn't legally enforceable. The same is true of any other contract made as a result of unlawful threats. For example, if one party threatens to report the other party to the IRS or a state agency if a one-sided contract isn't signed, the contract isn't enforceable.

A mistake is the other ground for rescission of a contract. You thought you were buying a two-year-old computer. The seller thought you were buying her five-year-old computer. If you were both acting in good faith and simply miscommunicated, a judge or arbitrator would probably set aside the contract. But you can't avoid liability if you simply used bad judgment and paid too much for a five-year-old computer that doesn't provide the quality or speed you need.

Breach of Warranty

Sometimes a buyer can return goods to the seller and get a refund based on a breach of warranty. While the practical result in such cases may be the same as setting aside a contract for the reasons mentioned in this section, a different legal concept is at work.

An action for breach of warranty assumes that there's a valid contract. When a buyer seeks a refund based on breach of warranty, he or she is saying: "I acknowledge that we have a binding contract. I want to enforce my rights under that contract for breach of warranty." (See Chapter 17.)

D. Must a Contract Be in Writing?

Unless a contract falls into one of several specific categories, it is binding even if it's not in writing. You should put all important contracts in writing anyway. Otherwise, you run the risk of a dispute as to exactly what was promised, how much was to be paid, when the contract was to be performed and on and on and on. And if you argue so long that you end up in court, it can be somewhere between difficult and impossible (not to mention expensive) to prove the existence and terms of an oral contract.

1. Contracts That Must Be in Writing

Each state has a statute (usually called the Statute of Frauds) listing the types of contracts that must be written to be valid. A typical list includes:

a. Contracts involving the sale of real estate or an interest in real estate

Examples are a contract to purchase a building or parking lot or a contract to sell someone the right to use part of your land for a certain purpose (an easement).

Chapter 7 of Legal Forms for Starting & Running a Small Business *contains forms for buying real estate.*

b. Leases of real estate lasting longer than one year

An example is a three-year lease for retail space in a neighborhood shopping plaza.

Chapter 6 of Legal Forms for Starting & Running a Small Business *contains forms for commercial leases.*

c. A promise to pay someone else's debt

This generally involves guarantees of payment. Examples are the president of a corporation personally guarantees to pay for any goods you sell to the corporation; or an uncle guarantees to pay the rent for his nephew's new store.

d. Contracts that will take more than one year to perform

This provision of the Statute of Frauds applies only to contracts that cannot be performed within one year; for example, a contract to provide landscaping services to a hotel for a two-year period.

If performance of a contract is possible within one year, the contract doesn't have to be in writing. How about a contract to plant three maple trees within the next two years? Since the trees could be planted right away, the contract doesn't have to be in writing to be enforceable. Here are several more examples of oral contracts performable within one year (and therefore enforceable):

- A contract to teach four new employees within the next 18 months how to use a software program.
- A contract to cater a total of ten sales banquets for a corporation at dates to be selected by the corporation during the next three years.
- A contract to remove debris from the sites of five new homes to be completed within the next two years.

e. Contracts for the sale of goods (tangible personal property) worth $500 or more

A contract to sell you a notebook computer for $2,000, for example, must be in writing to be enforceable. If you call a computer store and they agree over the phone to sell you the computer for $2,000 but raise the price to $2,500 when you get there, you don't have an enforceable contract.

Under the Uniform Commercial Code (UCC), however, the written contract doesn't have to state the price or time of delivery—only that the parties agree on the sale of goods and the quantity of goods being sold. And in some cases, if the seller simply sends a written confirmation of an oral order and the buyer doesn't promptly object, a contract has been formed. These UCC exceptions are very important; be sure to read Section 3, below, which explains them in more detail.

There's an important exception to the rule that contracts for the sale of goods worth $500 must be in writing. If an oral contract is partially performed, the whole contract becomes binding. For example, say a salesperson offers to sell you a notebook computer for $2,000 and to throw in a modem when the store gets its next shipment in a week. You pay the $2,000 and take the computer home. When you return to the store the next week to pick up your modem, the store denies that it owes you one. You could sue successfully for breach of contract even though you don't have a written contract for a sale of goods over $500. The reason is that partial performance of the oral contract (your payment and the store's partial delivery of the merchandise) removes the transaction from the written contract (Statute of Frauds) requirements. Of course, as a practical matter, it would have been better to get the whole deal in writing.

Chapter 8 of Legal Forms for Starting & Running a Small Business *contains forms for buying, selling, manufacturing, renting and storing goods.*

2. What Constitutes a Written Contract

When state law does require a contract to be in writing, it doesn't mean you need a long-winded document labeled "contract" or "agreement" and signed by both parties. Especially in a business context, judges recognize and enforce writings that contain few details. All that's typically required is a letter, memo or any other writing signed by the party against whom the contract is being enforced. The writing must identify the parties and generally describe the subject and the main terms and conditions of the agreement. That's all. The rules for what the writing must contain are even more relaxed for transactions covered by the Uniform Commercial Code, which automatically fills in many missing details. (See Section 3, below.)

I don't recommend that you settle for the bare-bones legal requirements. Because business people's memories—like everyone else's—are imperfect, and because putting a contract in writing tends to highlight erroneous assumptions, and because not everyone you deal with is completely trustworthy, you want important contracts to contain a reasonable amount of detail.

EXAMPLE: Arnie, a fish shop operator, meets Phyllis, a phone equipment salesperson, at a trade show. Arnie becomes enthusiastic about purchasing a new telephone system for $3,000, which he believes covers the installation, including all wiring and control panels. Phyllis, the sales rep for FoneTek, thinks her company is providing just the phones themselves. If they go ahead on the basis of an oral contract, disaster clearly looms. If, however, Arnie and Phyllis sit down to write up a contract, the issues that haven't really been agreed on are sure to come out, and Arnie and Phyllis will have ample opportunity to make necessary adjustments or call the deal off.

See Section E, below, for suggestions on writing a business contract.

3. The Sale of Goods: Special Uniform Commercial Code Rules

The Uniform Commercial Code (UCC) contains special rules affecting contracts for the sale of goods. It loosens up the requirements for creating a binding contract when goods are being sold.

The UCC requires you to produce something in writing if you want to enforce a contract for a sale of goods and the price is $500 or more. However, the UCC says that this writing can be very brief—briefer than a normal written contract. Under the UCC, the writing need only:

- indicate that the parties have agreed on the sale of the goods, and
- state the quantity of goods being sold.

If items such as price, time and place of delivery, or quality of the goods are missing, the UCC fills them in based on customs and practices in the particular industry.

⚠ **Don't rely on sketchy contracts.** *Just because the UCC makes legal some very sketchy contracts for the sale of goods doesn't mean it's a good idea to routinely use such contracts. It's far better to follow the outline in Section E, below, to put together a good written contract.*

Remember, if a customer comes to a store, pays for merchandise and takes it away, there's no need for a formal written contract—the deal is done. (For larger purchases, it makes sense for the retailer to have the customer sign a receipt acknowledging delivery of the goods.) Under the UCC, having some writing is important when the seller merely promises to deliver the goods.

In most situations, the UCC requires that when a contract must be in writing to be enforceable, it must be signed by the person against whom the other party is seeking to enforce the contract. Stated another way, if A wants to sue B for breach of contract and a writing is required, A must show that B signed something showing an intent to be contractually bound.

But when merchants—people who sell goods—are involved, there doesn't always have to be a signed document. If a seller sends a confirmation of an order and the buyer doesn't object in writing within ten days after receiving it, nothing more is required to satisfy the written contract requirement.

EXAMPLE: Nandita owns a retail store that sells shoes. Runner's Choice Inc., a manufacturer, sends Nandita a notice saying: "This is to confirm that you agreed to buy 1,000 pairs of men's jogging shoes from this Company." Under normal written contract rules (see Section B, above), this wouldn't be enough to permit Runner's Choice to enforce a contract against Nandita, because she's signed nothing. But under the UCC, if Nandita doesn't object in writing within ten days after receiving the notice, she can't complain about the lack of a written document bearing her signature.

In this example, the notice from Runner's Choice satisfies the requirement that the contract be evidenced by a writing. However, if Runner's Choice sues Nandita for rejecting the shipment of shoes, it will still have to convince the judge or arbitrator that before Runner's Choice sent Nandita the notice, the parties actually reached an oral agreement regarding the shoes. In short, the notice, by itself, is not conclusive evidence that the parties reached a meeting of the minds. A contract signed by both sides is always preferable.

Where the UCC Came From

In 1940, someone came up with a brilliant idea: Why not put together a comprehensive code (statute) covering all the branches of commercial law and get it adopted in all states? That way, businesses in Michigan, Illinois, Georgia and Oregon would all follow the same rules.

It took 11 years to carry out this proposal, which resulted in a set of model statutes called the Uniform Commercial Code, or UCC. Every state except Louisiana has adopted it; Louisiana has adopted key portions of it. It covers these areas of law:

- Sales (including Warranties; see Chapter 17, Section C)
- Commercial Paper (drafts, checks, certificates of deposit, promissory notes)
- Bank Deposits and Collections
- Letters of Credit
- Bulk Transfers
- Warehouse Receipts, Bills of Lading and Other Documents of Title
- Investment Securities
- Secured Transactions.

Checking Out the UCC

Your state laws (statutes) should be available in any law library in your state, as in the reference section of many public libraries, and via Nolo's Legal Research Center at www.nolo.com. The Uniform Commercial Code is probably indexed under Uniform, Commercial or Commerce. Another good Web source is www.law.cornell.edu/uniform/ucc.html. For most small businesses, the section on Sales (Article 2) is the most helpful part of the UCC. The UCC changes fairly often; be sure you have the latest version that's been adopted in your state.

Valid Contracts With No Writing at All. Where specially manufactured goods are ordered, the UCC says you don't need something in writing to enforce a sales contract if the seller has already made a significant effort toward completing the terms of the contract.

EXAMPLE: A restaurant calls and orders 500 sets of dishes from a restaurant supply company. The dishes are to feature the restaurant's logo. If the supply company makes a substantial beginning on manufacturing the dishes and applying the logo, the restaurant can't avoid liability on the contract simply because it was oral.

E. Writing Business-to-Business Contracts

Whatever your business, you'll need to write contracts from time to time. You'll probably need a written contract if you want to:

- buy or sell goods
- perform services as an independent contractor or consultant
- lease real estate or equipment
- manufacture, distribute or license products
- enter into joint ventures
- grant credit
- advertise.

1. Checklist of Contract Clauses

The content of a contract depends, of course, on the type of transaction you're getting into. This checklist includes items to consider when you draft a contract:

- *Names and addresses of the parties.*
- *Date that the contract is signed.* (See Section F for suggestions about signing a contract.)
- *A short preamble ("recitals").* This provides some of the background of the agreement. For example, a contract might recite that Discs Unlimited is a retailer of compact discs and has three stores in the metropolitan area; that Stewart has an inventory management business; and that Discs Unlimited wishes to retain Stewart as an independent contractor to establish and maintain the company's computerized inventory control system.
- *What each party is promising to do:* Pay money, provide a service, sell something, build something or so on. Often this section of the contract—particularly if it involves a product or a construction project—is labeled "specifications." In many situations, such as designing software, constructing a building or providing consulting services, the specifications require an attachment that can run on for pages and may include drawings, formulas or charts. (See Section 3, below, for how-to information.)
- *When the work will be done or the product delivered.* If strict compliance with contract deadlines is important, be sure to include the words, "Time is of the essence." Otherwise, a judge would probably allow reasonable leeway in enforcing the deadlines.
- *How long the contract will remain in effect.*
- *The price—or how it will be determined.*
- *When payment is due.* Will there be installments, and will interest be charged? In contracts for consulting and other services, it's common to have a payment schedule tied to interim completion deadlines. For example, a contract for architectural services might provide for payment of one-third of the architect's fees when drawings and specifications are finished and approved; one-third after bids have been received on the construction project and a contract signed with the general contractor; and one-third when the project is completed and a certificate of occupancy is issued by the building department.
- *Warranties.* If one party guarantees labor and materials for a certain period of time, what steps will be taken to correct warranty problems?
- *Conditions under which either party can terminate the agreement.*
- *"Liquidated damages" if performance is delayed or defective.* In cases where actual damages for breach of contract would be difficult to compute, the parties can establish in advance a fixed dollar amount (called liquidated damages) to be paid by a party who fails to perform its contractual obligations properly. (See Section H, below.)
- *Whether or not either party can transfer (assign) the contract to another person or company.* A contract that allows assignment of contract rights may be okay if it involves just the right to receive money, but not if it means that some other, unknown party will wind up performing skilled services called for by the contract.
- *Arbitration or mediation of disputes.*
- *Whether or not a party who breaches the contract is responsible for the other party's attorney fees and legal costs.*
- *Where notices of default or other communications concerning the contract can be sent.* Typically, the notices are sent to the business headquarters of the contracting parties.
- *What state law applies if questions about the contract arise.* If the parties have operations in different states or the contract is to be performed in more than one state, you may avoid potentially knotty legal issues if you specify in advance which state law applies.

2. Additional Requirements for Specialized Contracts

Many states require specific provisions in contracts that cover certain types of transactions. Areas where special requirements are likely include:

- sales of new and used vehicles and mobile homes
- home improvement services
- motor vehicle repairs
- apartment and home rentals
- door-to-door sales
- funerals, burials and cremations.

If you're in one of these regulated businesses, you not only need to use a written contract; you also need to make sure it conforms to your state's legal rules. Among other things, you may have to put certain information or warnings in type of a certain size, including a statement about the customer's right to cancel the deal under certain conditions. In some states, you may have to print the contract in Spanish as well as English.

EXAMPLE: In Michigan, a statute requires a funeral director to insert the following language in bold-faced type in every prepaid funeral contract:

> "This contract may be canceled either before death or after death by the buyer or, if the buyer is deceased, by the person or persons legally authorized to make funeral arrangements. If the contract is canceled, the buyer or the buyer's estate is entitled to receive a refund of __% of the contract price and any income earned from investment of the principal less administrative or escrow fees."

3. How to Design Your Contracts

You need contract forms that reflect the specialized nature of what you do, be it creating software, selling produce, publishing books or cleaning buildings. This is especially true if your business is subject to consumer laws that require specific contract language. Typically, you'll need several basic types of contract for your business, each with spaces to fill in the details of the specific transaction.

EXAMPLE: Brian is setting up a direct mail consulting business. He plans to work with local businesses to show them how to stay in better contact with customers by announcing sales, new merchandise and seasonally extended hours. Brian needs a contract that covers what he'll do, when he'll do it, what he expects his small business clients to provide, warranties, responsibilities for proofreading and signing off on mailings, and payment.

Brian will also need to hire independent contractors, graphic designers, artists and computer wizards to help him carry out his contracts, so he'll also need a basic "work-for-hire" contract. Finally, Brian plans to use his experience to develop customized software for sale to similar businesses and so will need a basic software licensing agreement.

If you're new to your business, start by gathering copies of contracts used by other people in your field. Some kinds of contracts, such as commercial leases, are widely available. For other kinds, you may have to dig a bit. Trade associations, which commonly publish material containing sample contracts, are one good source. Other people in your line of work may be willing to share their contracts with you. Form books published for lawyers are an excellent starting point for developing your own specialized contract. Talk to the librarian at any major law library to find some suitable books. (See Chapter 24 for tips on finding and using a law library.)

Once you find a simple contract that's more or less suitable, make sure that you understand every word. Obviously, contracts written in plain English are better than those filled with legalese—but if the latter type is all you can find, it may not be too difficult to rewrite it. Next, write a rough draft of any additions you may need.

Professional help. *If you plan to use a form contract for major transactions, consider reviewing it with a lawyer who has small business experience—ideally, one who knows something about your field. It can help you see whether or not the contract does what you want it to do and includes everything you need. Because you have done most of the work, your advisor's advice should be reasonably priced. (See Chapter 24 for how to hire and work with a lawyer.)*

4. Attachments to Contracts

It's common to use attachments (often called exhibits) to your contract to list lengthy details that don't fit neatly into the main body of the contract. For example, in drawing up a contract with a sign maker, you could attach a sketch of the sign and a list of detailed specifications, including materials to be used. Simply refer in the main contract to Attachment A or Exhibit A and note that you "hereby incorporate it into your contract." By referring to the attachment in the contract itself, you make it a part of the contract.

If you're a consultant or routinely contract for your services, consider using a short basic contract and then adding your performance specs in an attachment. That way you can use the same basic contract form over and over with only slight modifications.

 Materials Written Primarily for Individuals
• 101 Law Forms for Personal Use, *by Robin Leonard & Ralph Warner (Nolo). This book, which includes promissory notes and agreements to sell, lease and store property, also contains contracts for service providers (child care, home repair contractors) that are of use to small business people in these fields.*

Materials Written Primarily for Business People
• Legal Forms for Starting & Running a Small Business, *by Fred S. Steingold (Nolo). The book, accompanied by a CD-ROM, will make it easy for you to prepare a variety of business contracts and legal forms, including leases, contracts for the purchase of a business or real estate and contracts for hiring employees and independent contractors.*

Materials Written Primarily for Lawyers and Law Students
• Contracts in a Nutshell, *by Claude D. Rohwer & Gordon D. Schaber (West Publishing Co.). An overview of contract law.*
• Sales and Leases of Goods in a Nutshell, *by John M. Stockton and Frederick H. Miller (West Publishing Co.). Legal analysis of the Uniform Commercial Code sections dealing with sales.*
• Basic Legal Forms with Commentary, *by Clifford R. Ennico & Marvin Hayman (West Publishing Co.). Clear and comprehensive forms. This one-volume work is found in many law offices. It's more expensive than the other books on the list, but well worth the price if you draft a lot of contracts.*

F. The Formalities of Getting a Contract Signed

Many contracts take the form of a single document containing a series of numbered clauses. Both parties sign in duplicate, and each keeps a copy. But as discussed throughout this chapter, some written contracts are much less formal. Commonly they're in two—or more—parts. For example, A sends B an offer; B accepts by a separate letter or fax. Or A sends B an offer; B sends back a counter-offer; A accepts the counter-offer by letter or fax. As pointed out in Section A, as long as there's a genuine meeting of the minds, a contract contained in several documents is valid.

Another form of contract is a letter that pulls together the details of your deal and is accepted by the other person by a signature at the bottom. This is typical when you and the other party (perhaps someone you've worked with often) have worked out the deal over lunch or through a series of phone calls and don't feel the need for a formal contract. An example is shown below.

```
September 10, 20__


Dear Mary:


    I'd like to summarize our agreement for you to redecorate our store at 123 Main Street.
We agreed that for $2,000 you'll apply wall covering to the south wall of our sales areas
and apply two coats of paint to the remaining walls. The paint will be XYZ brand latex
semi-gloss, and the wall covering will be ABC brand vinyl, pattern #66.


    In addition to the $2,000 payment, I'll promptly reimburse you for the paint and wall
covering at your cost (when you present invoices from RacaFrax Wall Coverings), but you'll
be responsible for the cost of all other tools, equipment and supplies.


    I'll pay you $1,000 before you start work and the balance within 7 days after the work
is completed. You'll do the work on the next two Sundays so that our business isn't
interrupted. The quality of your work will meet or exceed the job you recently completed
for the Ski Shoppe next door.


    We also agreed that if any problems come up about this job and we can't resolve them
ourselves, we'll submit our dispute to Metro Mediators Inc. for mediation and, if that
doesn't resolve the problem, to binding arbitration—and we'll split the cost 50/50.


    If I've accurately stated our agreement, please sign the enclosed copy of this letter
and return it to me by noon Wednesday.


    Sincerely,


    Jim Dalton
    d/b/a Jim's Fitness Shop

    The above terms are acceptable to me.


    Date:                    Mary Walz
```

Be sure to read Section D3, above, for special rules affecting contracts governed by the Uniform Commercial Code.

1. Revising a Contract Before You Sign

In negotiating a contract, it's common for the parties to go back and forth through several drafts, refining the language. Using a computer with word-processing software, it's simple to crank out a fresh version of the contract each time revisions are made. But that's not the only way to handle changes in wording. For minor changes, you can simply cross out the old wording and write in the new, using a typewriter or pen. If you use this method, each party should initial each change when the contract is signed to establish that the changes were properly consented to and not illegally added later.

Still another way to handle changes—particularly if the changes are extensive—is to put them in an addendum. If you use an addendum, state that in case of a conflict between the addendum and the main contract, the wording in the addendum prevails. Both parties should sign the addendum and the main contract.

If a contract has gone through several revisions, it's a good idea to have both parties initial each page so that you're sure everyone has a correct copy of the final draft.

2. Signatures

Business people are sometimes confused as to how best to sign a contract. It depends on the legal form of your business.

- **A sole proprietor** can simply sign his or her name, because a sole proprietorship isn't a separate legal entity. But there are two other ways to do it, either of which is just as legal.

Method 1:
Jim Dalton
D/B/A Jim's Fitness Shop
(D/B/A means "doing business as.")
Method 2:
Jim's Fitness Shop
By:_____
    Jim Dalton

- For a **partnership,** the following format is commonly used:
ARGUS ELECTRONICS,
A Michigan Partnership
By: _____
    Randy Argus, a General Partner

Only one partner needs to sign on behalf of a partnership.

 Chapter 2, Section B, contains a discussion of the authority of a single partner to bind the partnership and each of the individual partners.

- For a **limited liability company,** use this format:
REALTY APPRAISAL SERVICES, LLC
By:_____
    Shela Martin, Member [or Manager]
- For a **corporation,** use this format:
KIDDIE KRAFTS INC.,
A California Corporation
By: _____
    Madeline Arshak, President

A person signing as a corporate officer doesn't assume personal liability for meeting contractual obligations. (See Chapter 1, Section C, for a discussion of how using the corporate form of doing business can limit the personal liability of people operating the corporation.) If the other party to a contract is a corporation, you may (particularly in a major transaction) want to see a board of directors' resolution or corporate bylaws authorizing the particular officer to sign contracts on behalf of the corporation. You can omit this step if the contract is signed by the corporate president; a president is presumed to have authority to sign contracts for a corporation.

If you're entering into a contract with a corporation and want someone (such as a corporate officer or major shareholder) to sign a personal guarantee, you can use a clause like this one at the end of the contract:

> In consideration of Seller entering into the above contract with Starlight Corporation, I personally guarantee the performance of all of the above contractual obligations undertaken by Starlight Corporation.

_____

Liz Star

Chapter 1 of Legal Forms for Starting & Running a Small Business *contains additional information on signing business contracts.*

3. Witnesses and Notaries

Notarization means that a notary public certifies in writing that:

- You're the person you claim to be, and
- You've acknowledged under oath signing the document.

Very few contracts need to be notarized or signed by witnesses. The major exceptions to this rule are documents that are going to be recorded at a public office charged with keeping such records (usually called the county recorder or registrar of deeds). These documents are described in the next section. Occasionally—but very rarely—state laws require witnesses or notaries to sign other types of documents.

4. Recording

The great majority of business contracts don't have to be publicly recorded—and, in fact, are usually ineligible for recording. Here are the exceptions:

- Documents that affect title to or rights in real estate. This includes deeds, mortgages, trust deeds (a form of mortgage used in many states) and easement agreements.
- Long-term real estate leases, or memoranda summarizing them.
- Some documents dealing with tangible personal property, such as UCC financing statements or chattel mortgages, when the seller or a third party is financing part of the purchase price and receiving a security (contingent ownership) interest in the property. Banks, for example, routinely record security interests when making equipment loans.

5. Dates

When you sign a contract, offer, counter-offer or acceptance, include the date—and make sure the other person does too. This helps to establish that there was agreement (remember, a meeting of the minds is an essential element of any valid contract). A simple way to do this is to always put a date line (Date: _____, 20__) next to the place where each person will sign. Don't worry if the dates of signing differ by a few days or even a week, as is common when the parties exchange documents by mail.

> **EXAMPLE:** If you sign on Monday and the other party signs a week later, you have a valid contract unless (1) you revoked your signature before the other person signed, or (2) you stated in the contract or offer that the other person must accept the offer before that date.

6. Originals and Photocopies

A contract is an "original" as long as the signatures are originals. So a photocopied document which both parties then sign is an original. So is a carbon copy or computer-printed copy which both parties sign.

If you enter into a traditional written contract—one document that contains the full agreement of the parties and is signed by both of them—it's best if each party has a copy of the contract with the original signatures of both parties. This is easy if you sign at the same session; simply sign two originals, so each party can keep a fully signed one.

A photocopy or faxed copy of a signed contract can still be enforced as long as the judge or arbitrator is convinced that what you have is an accurate reproduction of the original.

Storing Contracts

Store your contracts and other important documents in a fireproof safe or file cabinet. Another precaution is to keep photocopies of all important documents at another location. This may seem like overkill—but not if you have to prove what's in a contract and all copies have been destroyed, stolen or lost.

---

7. Revising a Contract After Both Parties Sign

Once a contract has been signed, any changes must be agreed to by both parties. In essence this means they're forming a new contract. The simplest way to make fairly minor revisions to a signed contract is through an addendum—or a second or third addendum if necessary. When you write an addendum, follow these steps:

- Refer to the earlier contract by date, names of the parties and subject matter.
- State all of the changes.
- State that in case of a conflict between the terms of the original contract and the addendum, the terms of the addendum prevail.
- Make it clear that all terms of the original contract, except those that you're changing, remain in effect.

- Sign and date the addendum and keep it with the original.

LAW IN THE REAL WORLD
Writing Contracts the Simple Way

Galen owns a small publishing company that specializes in local guide books. Henry, one of Galen's long-time authors, is late in delivering a manuscript for a book on 50 off-beat family adventures in the Northern Rocky Mountains. When he finally turns it in, the computer-printed manuscript is full of nearly incomprehensible handwritten additions.

Galen calls Henry and points out that their contract requires Henry to submit the manuscript neatly typed. Henry is furious. "You told me to get it done fast, no matter what," he says. "I stayed up half the night for two weeks to make the deadline and this is the thanks I get."

Galen prudently waits a few days and then invites Henry to lunch. Once both men look at the plain language of the contract, "Author shall submit all manuscript material neatly typed," Henry has to agree that Galen is right. Galen then offers to have someone on his staff do the typing work and subtract the cost from Henry's future royalties. They scribble the contract addendum on a paper placemat and both sign it. Later, Galen photocopies the placemat and mails it to Henry.

G. Enforcing Contracts in Court

Often, if there's a dispute about a claimed breach of contract, you can resolve it through negotiation. If that doesn't work, you'll need to use one of the other methods of resolving legal disputes: mediation, arbitration or litigation. (See Chapter 22 for an overview on how each works.)

Here is how a contract dispute is likely to be resolved if mediation doesn't work and you resort to more formal proceedings—arbitration or a lawsuit.

Most lawsuits and arbitrations involving contracts focus on two basic questions:

- Was there a breach of contract?
- If so, what relief should be awarded to the non-breaching party?

We'll tackle the first question here, and the second one in Section H.

Suppose your business sues or is sued for an alleged breach of contract or such a claim is taken to arbitration. What defenses can the defendant assert? Here are the main ones:

- **No valid contract was formed.** If there was no meeting of the minds (no legally binding offer and acceptance) in the first place, or no consideration was given in exchange for one party's promise, no contract even exists. (See Section A.) It's a lot easier to establish such a claim if neither side has begun to follow and rely on the so-called contract.
- **There's no written contract, and because of the subject of the contract, one is required by law.** (See Section D.)
- **The contract is void because it's illegal or against public policy.** Contracts that call for criminal or immoral conduct may be unenforceable. (See Section B.)
- **The contract should be rescinded (canceled) because the other side misrepresented the facts in inducing you to sign it.** (See Section C.)
- **The contract was induced by duress.** (See Section C.)
- **There was a mutual mistake.** (See Section C.)
- **There was no breach of contract.** The defendant admits entering into a valid contract with the plaintiff, but fully complied with its terms.
- **The other party suffered no damages.** The breach of the contract was minor or technical and didn't cause the plaintiff any actual loss or damage. For example, if your store delivered a conference table and six chairs to a lawyer's new office a week later than promised, there's likely been minor inconvenience but no real damage—nothing serious enough to make you liable for breach of contract.
- **The plaintiff failed to limit (mitigate) the damages.** All parties to a contract have a legal duty to act reasonably and keep any damages to a minimum (called "mitigation of damages" in legalese). Or, put another way, it's not legally permissible to sit back and let damages add up when reasonable steps could be taken to stop or limit them. For example, suppose your company services refrigerators, and you signed a two-year contract with a butcher. While you're on vacation, the butcher calls your company and requests that you immediately repair a breakdown in his refrigerator. Your chief assistant is sick, so the job doesn't get done until you return ten days later. The butcher sues for damages, claiming he lost $5,000 worth of meat due to lack of refrigeration. You can point out that the butcher could have mitigated his damages by calling another company to fix his refrigerator. Had he done this promptly, his loss might have been limited to $500 of particularly temperature-sensitive meat plus $300 for the extra service charged. You should be responsible for $800 in damages and not the full $5,000.

Chapter 13, Section I, explains how the concept of mitigation of damages applies where a lease is involved. This information is generally applicable to all contracts.

Enforcing Lost Contracts

What if a party wants to legally enforce a written contract, but neither party can find a signed copy? The contract is still legally enforceable if you can prove to the satisfaction of an arbitrator or judge that:

- A written agreement was actually signed, and
- It contained the specific terms you're seeking to enforce.

You may be able to reconstruct the terms from an unsigned photocopy or from a final draft stored on your computer.

H. What Can You Sue For?

In a breach-of-contract case, the court may award the plaintiff money damages and may also, in some cases, order the defendant to do—or stop doing—something.

1. Compensatory Damages

If a plaintiff proves that a defendant breached a contract, the usual approach is for the judge or arbitrator to award the plaintiff "compensatory damages." The goal is to put the parties in the same position as they would have been in if the contract had been performed—or to come as close to that as possible.

Let's return to the contract with Joe, the sign maker we discussed in Section A. If Joe failed to build the sign for your business, and it cost you $750 to have someone else do it, you'd be entitled to recover $300 from Joe for breach of contract. This is the difference between the contract price you and Joe agreed on ($450) and what you had to pay to get the job done ($750). This assumes that you made a reasonable effort to limit or mitigate your damages. In this situation, you'd have to show that you made a reasonable attempt to find a second sign maker to do the job at a fair price. You couldn't just go to the most expensive sign maker in the state and expect Joe to reimburse you for the top dollar. (Mitigation of damages is discussed in Section G, above.)

2. Consequential Damages

A plaintiff may also be entitled to "consequential damages." These are damages that arise out of circumstances that the breaching party knew about or should have foreseen when the contract was made.

For example, what if Joe built your sign for you but didn't get around to installing it until a month after your business's grand opening? Can you sue for the profits you lost because potential customers didn't know your store was there? The usual rule is that you can recover for lost profits only if this issue is covered by your contract or if it was foreseeable to both parties when you signed the contract that you'd lose profits if the other person didn't carry out the contact. Whether or not a judge will award you damages for Joe's failure to install your sign on time is anybody's guess—unless you specifically dealt with the issue in the contract.

If the contract did provide for lost profits, there's another problem: The amount of lost profits you claim must be ascertainable with reasonable certainty. With a new store, you have no earnings history. This makes it difficult to prove and recover lost profits. But you may able to show how much similar stores at similar locations earned when they first started and get a judge to accept this as a reasonable estimate of your losses.

Let's look at one more example. Say that the sign you ordered from Joe was to contain your store name plus the name of a major manufacturer of merchandise you planned to carry. You had a deal with the manufacturer that entitled you to a 10% discount if you put the manufacturer's name on your sign. Because Joe put up the sign a month after the store opened, you didn't receive the discount on the first batch of merchandise, which cost you an extra $1,000. Can you collect this money from Joe? Only if Joe knew about your deal with the manufacturer when you and he entered into your contract. Otherwise, Joe would have no reason to expect you to suffer this additional loss if he installed the sign late.

3. Liquidated Damages

In addition to or in place of compensatory and consequential damages, a plaintiff may be able to recover "liquidated damages." These are damages that the parties agree in the contract will be paid if there's a breach. That is, instead of trying to determine the money damages for a breach of contract after the fact, you do it in advance.

For example, because actual losses caused by late installation of your sign would be difficult to determine, you and Joe could agree in your contract that for each day of delay, Joe would owe you a $25 late fee. If the liquidated damages are a reasonable attempt to estimate the losses you'd suffer and are not intended as a penalty, a judge or arbitrator will enforce this clause.

Contracts for the purchase of real estate commonly contain a liquidated damages clause. For example, if you put down $5,000 in "earnest money" when you sign a contract to purchase a building, the contract will likely allow the seller to retain the $5,000 as liquidated damages if you later back out for no good reason.

4. Injunctions and Other Equitable Relief

In addition to monetary damages, a judge may order "equitable" relief in some circumstances. This can come in a variety of forms, depending on the facts of the case and the ingenuity of the judge. The idea is to reach a fair result and do justice in a way that can't be done simply by an award of money. Here are some equitable remedies that a judge may order:

- **Injunctions.** An injunction is an order issued by a judge prohibiting a person from performing specified activities. Occasionally, a judge issues an injunction to prevent a party from violating a contract. When time is of the essence, a judge may issue an emergency injunction (sometimes called a temporary restraining order) without a hearing to freeze matters until a court hearing can be held.

EXAMPLE 1: Aggie accepts a job as the accounts manager for DDS Innovations, a dental supply house. As part of her employment contract, she signs a covenant not to compete in the same business in a four-county area for two years after leaving the company. After 18 months on the job, Aggie quits and starts a business in the same city, competing directly with DDS Innovations. The company sues Aggie for breach of her covenant not to compete. The judge, after conducting a trial, finds that the covenant not to compete is reasonable and legally valid, and enjoins Aggie from continuing in that business for two years.

EXAMPLE 2: Maurice and Albert are business partners who have a falling out. Unable to resolve the dispute, Maurice sues Albert, claiming a breach of the partnership agreement. Albert counter-sues. The judge holds a preliminary hearing and issues a preliminary injunction—in force while the lawsuit is pending—prohibiting both partners from removing any property from the offices of the partnership and from taking any money from the partnership bank account.

EXAMPLE 3: Gilda and her landlord Archie have a dispute over who is to pay for electricity to Gilda's restaurant. On Friday afternoon, Archie threatens to shut off the power to Gilda's restaurant, which would ruin a private banquet for 200 guests that night. Based on Gilda's affidavit (sworn statement) showing the likelihood of immediate damage, the judge issues a temporary restraining order (TRO) prohibiting Archie from shutting off Gilda's power. The judge schedules a hearing for 9 a.m. Monday, at which time the TRO may be dissolved or continued. Because a TRO is usually issued based on the statements of one party only ("ex parte" in legal lingo), such an order is signed only if there's an emergency. A court hearing is always scheduled promptly.

- **Specific Performance.** If a contract concerns a unique or special asset—such as a piece of real estate, a work of art or a uniquely valuable item of jewelry—the judge may order the losing party to deliver the property to the other party to carry out the agreement. This remedy is rarely used in any other type of commercial transaction.

- **Rescission.** In an appropriate case a judge may rescind (cancel) a contract and order restitution of any money already paid. This unusual remedy is generally reserved for situations where one party's breach has completely frustrated the objectives of the other party, making enforcement of the contract unfair. To obtain rescission, the party getting a refund must give up any benefits already received. (Grounds for rescission of a contract are discussed in Sections B and C.)

If a judge orders you to perform a contract or stop doing something that violates a contract, you can find yourself in deep trouble if you don't obey the order. You can be held in contempt of court, which is punishable by fines and even time in jail. ■

The Financially Troubled Business

new business doesn't come with a guarantee. Even with the best planning, there's a possibility that your business will go through hard times and maybe even fail. Many an entrepreneur has weathered a number of shaky ventures before landing in a business that proved solidly successful. So if your business becomes troubled, or even if it needs to be put out of its misery, it shouldn't be viewed as the end of the world.

And, although it's always unpleasant—and can be heart-breaking—to have your business go bad, it's important to understand that there are many steps you can take to limit your losses so that you can get back on your feet and move on to other, more productive ventures. Especially if faced promptly, business troubles don't have to be long-term financial disasters.

A key economic preservation strategy is to protect your personal assets from business debts to the greatest extent possible. How you organize and run your business can make a decisive difference in whether you're able to do this. (See Section A.) In addition, if your enterprise should find itself in financial trouble, your day-to-day management decisions should be guided at least in part by your knowledge of what legal and business actions can help or hurt your personal situation. (See Section B.) Finally, if your financial troubles become so severe that you consider ending your business and maybe even declaring bankruptcy, you'll need to know exactly what legal options and protections are available.

A. Thinking Ahead to Protect Your Personal Assets

Perhaps you own a home, a valuable car, stocks and bonds or a savings account. Or maybe you own a second business or other valuable assets. Whatever you own, one thing is sure: You don't want to see everything you've acquired gobbled up by debts resulting from a failed business. Fortunately, with some advance planning, you can often protect many of your personal assets from your business creditors.

⚠ Early planning is essential. *It's crucial that you develop your asset protection plan as early as possible—preferably before rather than after you begin doing business. Once your business is in operation—and especially after it runs into financial trouble—you'll be greatly restricted in the steps you can take to protect your personal assets.*

1. Choice of Business Entity

As discussed in Chapter 1, when you start your business, insulating yourself from personal liability for business debts and liabilities is one important consideration. This is especially true if there's a strong possibility that failure of the business would leave a huge stack of bills or lawsuits for uninsured liabilities. If you organize your business as a sole proprietorship or partnership, you'll be personally liable for all obligations of the business. If, however, you organize your business as a corporation or a limited liability company (LLC), your personal liability will be substantially limited. Or to put this more bluntly, corporations and LLCs offer the greatest opportunity for protecting your personal assets from business obligations.

2. Beware of Penniless Partners

Another good reason to start your business as a corporation or LLC rather than a general partnership—or to switch your existing partnership to a corporation or LLC—is to protect yourself from the possible insolvency of any co-owners which could leave you stuck with all the business liabilities. The potential problem of working with co-owners in the context of a partnership is that if your business goes bad, you and your partners will be liable "jointly and severally" for business debts. This legal jargon means if one partner can't pay his or her share of business debts, the others will each owe the whole amount. So if you operate as a partnership, at least make sure your partners have enough assets to pay their share of any partnership debts.

> **EXAMPLE:** Ginny has two partners when her partnership business fails, leaving $30,000 in unpaid bills. Creditors get a judgment for $30,000 against all three partners. Unfortunately, Ginny's partners don't have any assets. Under the doctrine of joint and several liability, Ginny is legally on the hook to pay the entire judgment.

Assuming that Ginny pays the entire $30,000 judgment and the partnership agreement makes all the partners equally liable for business debts, she'll be able to collect $10,000 from each of the other partners if they come into some money in the future.

3. Personal Loan Guarantees

Even if you form a corporation or LLC which insulates your personal assets from business debts, you're likely to find yourself asked to put your personal assets on the line if your business applies for a bank loan or line of credit. Commercial lenders particularly won't make a loan or extend a line of credit to new corporations or LLCs unless the business owners personally guarantee to repay it. Unfortunately, if you agree to do this and your business later is unable to make payments as they come due, the lender has a right to get a judgment and collect it from your personal assets exactly as if you hadn't formed a corporation or LLC in the first place.

In some cases, the requirement that you personally guarantee a potential loan may be enough to dissuade you from borrowing the money in the first place. In unusual circumstances, a lender may agree to put a cap on the amount of your guarantee so your assets aren't fully at risk. Or, if you can't sell that idea, try for a written commitment that your personal guarantee will expire after a pre-established period of time—perhaps two years—if the corporation or LLC has made all payments on time and is profitable.

4. Having Your Spouse Sign Too

If a lender asks you to personally guarantee a line of credit or a loan for your corporation or LLC, the lender may also ask for your spouse to be a co-guarantor. A lender may make a similar request if you open a line of credit or take out a loan as a sole proprietor or partner. Be aware of the additional risk this entails. In most states—except for the nine that follow the community property system—if you alone sign for a line of credit or a loan and don't pay on time, the creditor can get a judgment against you but not your spouse. This means that, ordinarily, a creditor will be able to reach the property that you own in your own name, but not the property that you and your spouse own in both your names.

If you and your spouse both sign on the dotted line, the creditor's rights will be much greater. Now if you and your spouse own property in your joint names—a home or bank account, for example—the creditor will be able to sue and get a judgment against both of you if the debt isn't paid. In addition, the creditor can then enforce the judgment by seizing your joint bank account or jointly owned securities or home in addition to property you own in your name alone. The creditor will also be able go after property that's in your spouse's name alone—and even be able to garnish your spouse's paycheck.

⚠️ **Both spouses are liable for most debts in community property states.** *Nine states follow the community property system: Arizona, California, Idaho, Louisiana, Nevada, New Mexico, Texas, Washington and Wisconsin. In those states, a married couple's property accumulated after marriage is primarily community or jointly owed property regardless of the names in which it's held. Each spouse can also own separate property but, especially in longer marriages, this tends to be less important. In most instances, the rights of creditors vary, depending on the type of property involved.*

- **Community Property.** *Usually, property earned or acquired by either spouse after marriage—except by gift or inheritance—is at risk for a debt incurred by either spouse. This means a creditor can go after the community property of you and your spouse to pay off a debt, even if only you signed for the loan. In other words, you can't shield the community property from a creditor by not having your spouse sign for the loan.*

- **Separate Property.** *This usually is property a spouse owned before getting married, acquired later by gift or inheritance or agreed in writing would be kept separate. It's also property—such as a business—acquired from separate assets. If, for example, someone gets married owning a piece of real estate, sells it and uses the proceeds to open a business, the business is separate property. If your spouse has separate property and signs for a loan, his or her separate property will be at risk if you default—but if your spouse declines to sign, his or her separate property will normally be beyond the creditor's reach. Your own separate property, of course, will be at risk whether or not your spouse signs.*

5. Pledging Collateral for Loans

In addition to asking you to personally guarantee a loan by signing a promissory note, a lender may ask you to pledge a personal asset—typically, your home—as collateral for a business loan. In the case of your home, this would be done through a second mortgage or deed of trust. Think long and hard before you agree to do this, since it means you'll lose your home if you can't repay the money and the lender exercises its right to foreclose.

A key point is to understand that there can be a big difference between simply putting your personal signature on a promissory note (see Section A3, above) and giving the lender a security interest in property such as your home. The reason is that states have debtor protection laws (called homestead laws) that protect your investment in your home. This means that being unable to pay a personal debt—one, for example, based on a promissory note that's not secured by your home—won't automatically put you at risk of losing your home. By comparison, however, if you pledge your house as security for a loan, these homestead laws won't protect you.

⚠ Check the law in your state. *In many states the homestead exemption is low—or even nonexistent. This means that if an unsecured creditor sues and gets a judgment, the creditor could possibly force the sale of your home to collect.*

So much for the law. In the cold world of trying to raise money for your business, you may have no practical alternative to putting your home at risk. The truth is that the equity in your home may be your most accessible source of cash. The point is to ponder seriously what you and your family would do if you lost your home due to business reverses.

⚠ Be careful in using a home equity line of credit to finance your business. *A home equity line of credit, of course, amounts to a second mortgage. Don't overlook the fact that if you write a $15,000 check against your line of credit to cover business expenses and can't later make your payments on time, the bank can enforce its lien rights and force sale of your home.*

6. Maintain Adequate Insurance

You never know when an injured person may sue your business, claiming that you or an employee acted negligently—for example, a customer who falls in your parking lot and fractures her hip may claim that you were negligent in not keeping the area properly lighted. A jury may agree that you were negligent and sock your business with a huge judgment. There are many other risks as well—such as an injured consumer suing your manufacturing business for producing a defective product or a suit by a pedestrian injured by one of your employees who was driving a company truck. In short, you absolutely need to carry adequate insurance because if you don't, your investment in the business could be wiped out by a huge verdict. Even if your personal funds or house aren't at risk, you'll have suffered a stunning financial loss.

If you're a sole proprietor or partner, be especially careful to carry adequate business risk insurance since you're personally liable for paying the judgment. Another way to say this is if insurance proves too expensive or difficult to get, you'll almost certainly want to form a corporation or LLC to at least limit your personal liability. (For more on insurance, see Chapter 12.)

B. Managing the Financially Troubled Business

So far this chapter has reviewed things small business owners can do in advance to limit potential liability. Now let's shift gears and assume your business is currently facing financial problems. My focus here is to present several practical strategies that will help legally protect both you and your personal assets.

1. Keep Taxes Current

Rule Number One for the owner of any struggling business is to meticulously pay on time all taxes withheld from employees' paychecks. (See Chapter 8, Section C.) Even if you operate your business as a corporation or LLC, the IRS and state tax authorities can hold you personally liable for these taxes—plus penalties—if they're not paid. And you're still legally on the hook to pay these taxes, even if the business goes bankrupt.

So if your business starts having financial problems, stave off the other creditors as best you can—and use whatever cash is available to take care of employment taxes. Paying these taxes is so crucial that if your business is financially disorganized, you should pay for any accounting help you need to be sure these taxes are computed accurately and paid on time.

And remember that you don't have to wait until the last day to deposit employment taxes. It's often wise to deposit the employment taxes as soon as you know the figures so the money will be out of your bank account and legitimately beyond the reach of any other creditor who is attempting to collect a court judgment against your business.

⚠️ **Don't pay employment taxes with a charge card.** *If possible, use a check or cash to pay employment taxes, since this means they're really paid. By contrast, if you use your personal charge card and can't pay the bill later, you'll continue to be responsible to the charge card company for the amount you charged for taxes—even if you go through personal bankruptcy. A discharge in bankruptcy won't cancel your personal liability for the portion of your credit card debt that's attributable to the tax payments.*

2. Don't Lie About Debts

When a business starts to have financial troubles, its owner may frantically try to borrow more money.

Before doing this, think carefully about whether your business is really likely to do better in the near future or if you're only likely to compound your debt problems. If you apply for a new loan or to consolidate old ones, be forthright in disclosing the financial condition of your business. If you misrepresent your debts to get a loan, you may not be able to get rid of your personal liability for the debt—even if you go through bankruptcy—because the law will regard your new debt as being obtained by fraud. Where big bucks are involved, the debt could haunt you for many years.

The key to avoiding trouble with lenders is to be very careful that all facts appear—and appear accurately—on any financial statement you give a potential creditor. Even if you borrow money or have credit extended to you without having to fill out a financial statement, it can be treated as fraud if you knew that the business was having financial trouble and didn't make all the facts clear to your creditor.

⚠️ **Don't rely on shortcuts suggested by the lender's agent.** *Some finance company employees have been known to deliberately tell people—orally, of course—that they don't need to list all their debts. Often this is done because the person in the finance company office is under pressure to make loans and therefore has a motive to bend the rules to qualify you. Don't fall for this. If you later default on the loan and the company claims you obtained the money by fraudulently withholding information about your finances, chances are the employee will either be long gone or will say, "Of course I didn't say to deliberately omit debts." Either way, chances are you'll be unable to discharge the "fraudulent" debt in bankruptcy.*

Also, be aware that the bankruptcy laws take a broad view of what constitutes fraud. Not disclosing negative financial information may be considered fraudulent even if you acted with the best of intentions.

EXAMPLE: Jimmy, a sole proprietor, owns a secondhand furniture store. One day, the landlord raises the store rent by 50%. Based on past performance, Jimmy knows that with the rent increase, he'll have difficulty making a profit. Nevertheless, he decides to stay at that location because it would cost even more money to move elsewhere. At this time, he has a line of credit for $25,000 with a local bank of which only $10,000 has been used. A month later, already feeling the sting of the higher rent, he draws against the additional $15,000 and uses it to keep afloat. Because Jimmy neglected to tell the bank about the significant rent increase that put his business in a precarious financial condition, the additional draws can be considered to be a fraudulent use of credit and may well not be discharged in bankruptcy. If the bank sues Jimmy in bankruptcy court after he's gone through bankruptcy, Jimmy may still be liable for the $15,000.

This doesn't mean that drawing on a line of credit to meet the ordinary ebb and flow of business constitutes fraud. It doesn't. After all, the bank expects that you'll use your line of credit to cover leaner times. But you do need to disclose significant changes in your business such as a lawsuit or the bankruptcy of your largest customer that threatens the financial well-being of your business.

3. Be Careful About Transferring Business Property

Occasionally, out of desperation, a business owner will consider trying to protect personal assets by hiding them. Since creditors are used to ferreting out such tactics, by and large they prove ineffective and are likely to give rise to civil and perhaps even criminal charges of fraud. Specifically, a business owner shouldn't:

- transfer assets to friends or relatives in any effort to hide them from creditors or from the bankruptcy court, or
- conceal property or income from a court.

4. Avoid Preferential Payments to Creditors

The Bankruptcy Code frowns on your preferring certain creditors over others by making what are called "preferential payments." If you file for bankruptcy, all payments you make during the year before the filing will be scrutinized by creditors to make sure that some creditors weren't given an unfair advantage by being paid while others received little or nothing. If you did improperly single out some creditors for more favorable treatment by paying money or transferring property to them, the bankruptcy judge can order those creditors to return the money or property so it can be added to the total (called your bankruptcy estate) available to all of your creditors.

Fortunately, most payments you make as part of your business's ordinary operations won't be considered to be illegal preferences should you declare bankruptcy. Here's a brief overview of the types of payments that are safe and those likely to cause problems.

- *Payments in the ordinary course of business.* Neither you nor the payee has to worry about the payments you make in the ordinary course of business. These payments are considered to be safe and won't be undone—even if you made them the day before you filed for bankruptcy. Examples of payments you can safely make include:
- utilities
- rent
- payroll deposits
- retirement plan contributions
- insurance premiums
- payments to suppliers whom you pay on delivery or with 30 to 60 day terms, and

- salaries—as long as they're kept at the same level you've been paying right along.
- *Payments to family members or insiders.* If you repay money or transfer property to a family member or insider and then you file for bankruptcy within one year after the payment or transfer, the family member or insider will probably have to return the money or property to the bankruptcy court so it can be divided among your creditors. (An insider is someone who's in or close to your business such as a partner, a corporate director or a corporate officer.)
- *Payments to other creditors.* When you repay money or transfer property to someone who's neither a relative nor an insider and the payment isn't in the ordinary course of business, the 90 days before you file for bankruptcy are crucial. (Example: Paying off a bank loan that's not due for six months.) If you make such payments or transfers of property during the 90-day period, the recipient may have to return the money or property to the bankruptcy court to be added to the pool of funds available to your creditors.

5. Protect Your Bank Account

If you face serious financial problems and owe money to a bank, it's often wise to keep most of your checking and other accounts elsewhere. This is because typically your loan agreement gives the bank the right to take your funds without prior notice if the bank thinks you're in financial trouble. (This is called a setoff.) To put it mildly, it can be a rude surprise to learn that your favorite lender has suddenly drained your account.

6. Plan for Ongoing Insurance Coverage

If your business winds up in a Chapter 11 or Chapter 13 reorganization under the Bankruptcy Code (see

Section F), you may have a tough time finding a carrier that's willing to renew your business coverage or one that's willing to issue a new policy. So if you're planning to seek protection under either of those bankruptcy sections, make sure you have insurance in place that extends at least 12 months into the future. You'll need to make payments on the policy as payments become due, but as long as you pay on time, the insurance can't be canceled and you'll enjoy some peace of mind as you continue in business.

7. Don't Panic About Utilities or Your Lease

If you declare bankruptcy, the utility companies can't use your filing as an excuse for shutting off services—although they can require you to post a reasonable deposit if you want to keep the lights, phone service and heat.

Similarly, as long as you continue to pay your rent, your landlord can't kick you out. Don't be spooked by the scary clause commonly placed in commercial leases that says you're automatically in default if you file for bankruptcy. You can't believe everything you read. These clauses are not enforceable.

8. Consider Returning Some Leased Property

If you're leasing equipment and know you won't want to retain it after you file for bankruptcy, consider giving it back to the leasing company before you file. If you do so and the equipment is currently worth less than what you owe under the lease, the deficiency will get discharged in bankruptcy.

On the other hand, if you prefer to keep the leased property, you'll need to continue making your lease payments on time. When you choose to hang onto leased property, the obligation to make lease payments isn't discharged by your going through bankruptcy.

C. Seeking an Objective Analysis

A business can get into financial trouble for a long list of reasons. One of the most common is simply that the business owner, over time, becomes less attentive to the needs of the business—perhaps as a result of getting tired of dealing with problems which have become tedious. It may help to think of a business much as you would a child: No matter how much work you put in early in life, both continue to need constant attention and are unlikely to thrive if that attention is absent for any extended time.

Early signs of financial trouble usually include the following:

- You've routinely begun to ask creditors for more time to pay bills.
- Creditors are beginning to require you to pay COD.
- Your bank line of credit is routinely maxed out.
- You need to delay cashing your own paycheck a few days because the money isn't there.

And red flags are obviously flying if:

- Impatient creditors are calling you repeatedly.
- You're getting cash advances on your credit card to keep your business afloat.
- You're starting to miss payments to your landlord.
- You're being sued or threatened with lawsuits.
- You're having trouble paying employment taxes.
- Other tax bills are piling up.

The fact that your business is having financial problems doesn't mean it will fail. Even a seriously ailing business may be savable if you recognize the true extent of its problems and seek help soon enough. One good approach is to get objective advice to help you determine how deep your financial problems are and what options are open to you. Maybe you're just facing a temporary downturn that you should be able to weather by cutting costs and fine-tuning your business operations. But it's also possible that your problems may be more serious, requiring you to take more drastic steps to avoid a complete financial disaster that eats up not only your investment in the business but your personal assets as well.

Turn first to an experienced accountant. A small business accountant can usually review your business numbers—your debt-to-equity ratio, for example, or the time it's taking you to collect receivables—and quickly take your business's financial temperature. Then, he or she will try to identify some problem areas—such as overhead that's too high given your volume of sales. And an experienced business accountant often can provide practical advice for getting the business back on a solid financial track by suggesting, for example, ways to collect more of your receivables or quickly convert assets to needed cash.

If you conclude your financial problems are especially serious, you'll also normally want to consult an experienced small business lawyer or self-help law book. For starters, the lawyer will probably have a good idea about what the creditors are thinking—insights that can be very valuable in managing these strained relationships. In addition, after information about your business's financial problems and legal structure is on the table, an experienced lawyer should be able to help you sensibly decide whether it's best to try to buy more time through negotiations with creditors, try to sell the business, use a bankruptcy proceeding to keep creditors off your back while you try to rebuild the business or simply shut the business down and liquidate any remaining assets.

Seek out a good small business consultant. *If you can find the right one, a small business consultant can often suggest more meaningful business operation strategies than an accountant or lawyer—new strategies, for example, for your product mix, marketing, location and pricing. But check references carefully to be sure the person you're considering working with really helped others in similar circumstances. Almost anyone can set up shop as a business consultant and the last thing you want is bad advice.*

It May Pay to Have Your Business Appraised

It can often make sense to hire an appraiser to place a value on the business's real estate, equipment and inventory. For one thing, a solid appraisal will provide realistic values for your business assets and therefore help you and your accountant analyze your financial predicament. Especially if you're considering trying to sell your business, this information can be extremely helpful.

An appraisal may also be helpful if you try to negotiate a nonbankruptcy "workout" with your creditors. Even though you're not legally required to disclose the results of an appraisal at this stage, doing so can definitely be in your interest if the appraisal shows you have valuable assets. This information is likely to reassure unsecured creditors and convince them to give you some breathing room. (See Section D on workouts.) What's more, knowing the value of business assets can be extremely helpful in making decisions about bankruptcy, if matters come to that. You'll have a good idea, for example, of how much debt will remain if the assets are liquidated in a Chapter 7 business bankruptcy and whether the remaining debt—which you may be responsible for paying—will force you into personal bankruptcy.

How a Good Consultant Can Help

Ben opens an instant typography business, borrowing from his family to purchase necessary phototype equipment and software and leasing the rest. Although his business is busy from the start and Ben is working long hours, after nine months it's obvious he's losing money. Trying to figure out what to do, Ben considers increasing his sales or cutting his overhead. But since he and his employees are already overworked, this doesn't promise to solve the problem.

Finally, Ben turns to Sarah, a local small business consultant highly recommended by a neighboring business owner. After examining Ben's books for less than two hours, Sarah spots the problem. Ben isn't charging enough for his services.

After listening to Ben explain that producing type for local businesses is a very competitive business and that he will lose customers if he institutes a general price increase, Sarah helps Ben come up with a plan which involves keeping his current prices in effect for about one-half of his volume. But she also suggests that he raise prices significantly for rush orders and specialty work. With some adjustments over time, Sarah's plan works brilliantly. Customers remain loyal, since prices for routine work haven't changed. On rush orders and specialty work, it turns out that Sarah's insight that customers focus more on speed and quality and less on price is correct. Ben's customers pay his higher prices without much complaint and within a month his business is making money.

D. Workouts

In developing a plan of action for your financially troubled business, your objectives probably include one or more of the following:

- keeping the business alive
- salvaging as much as possible from your investment
- minimizing or eliminating your personal liability for business debts
- avoiding personal liability for IRS or other tax penalties
- retaining certain property—such as your house—that's been pledged as security to a creditor
- preserving your ability to get personal or business credit in the future, and
- protecting the assets of relatives and friends who have helped you financially.

Fortunately, several nonbankruptcy ways to try to cope with a failing business are worth considering. In this section, I explain one of these which is commonly called a workout. This normally involves developing a voluntary plan under which your creditors and others make concessions so you can keep your business in operation as you continue to zealously address its financial problems so that eventually your creditors can hope to receive all or most of their money.

But workouts aren't your only choice. Section E, below, briefly covers two other nonbankruptcy possibilities: selling your business or simply shutting it down.

Finally, Section F summarizes the bankruptcy alternatives of liquidating your business under Chapter 7 of the Bankruptcy Code or keeping it in operation under the protection of Chapter 11 or Chapter 13. You'll want to read all of these sections for an overview of the full range of choices available.

Sometimes it's hard to remember this when your business is going badly: There are bound to be a number of people who are pulling for your business to succeed—people such as creditors, suppliers, employees, customers and even neighboring business owners who will benefit if you can stay in operation. Bruce Ballenger, a Los Angeles CPA, refers to these people as stakeholders since they have a stake in whether your company lives or dies. Given their long-term self interest, some of these folks may be willing to lend a helping hand. To take an example, creditors may be willing to make some financial concessions—usually as part of a well-defined business recovery plan (the workout)—to help you through your financial difficulties.

Creditors who will give you more time to pay or otherwise help you probably won't do it for altruistic reasons but because they understand that their chances of getting paid on past debts are better if they cut you some slack, such as extending the time for debt payment or even agreeing to forgive a portion of your debt. Valued customers who rely on the availability of your goods and services may also be willing to help out. For example, they may be willing to speed their payments to you so they won't have to turn to a less satisfactory business to fill their needs. Similarly, suppliers may realize that they need your future business as much as you need their supplies. As long as you can convince them that your business can be viable in the long run, they may extend the time for you to repay old debts and even extend more credit.

Your employees are obviously among your business's key stakeholders. Some may agree to work reduced hours or accept reduced wages and benefits until your business gets healthy again. After all, a job in the hand is worth two in the want ads.

Finally, local authorities may be willing to give you more time to pay property taxes—a better alternative than trying to squeeze cash from a defunct business, unless there are statutory tax sale deadlines.

To get all your stakeholders to work together, you typically need to create a "workout plan." This is an out-of-court agreement under which your major creditors agree to hold off on suing your business, collecting on court judgments they've already obtained or forcing you into bankruptcy. Possibly,

creditors may even agree to extend more credit while you try to jointly devise a realistic payment schedule. For creditors to go along with your proposal, they must at a minimum be convinced that they're likely to come out better financially under your workout plan than they would if they sued you or pushed you into bankruptcy.

To prepare a workout package, you'll need to start by opening your books to your creditors. A good way to begin the full disclosure process is to prepare a list of all creditors and how much each is owed. Then, list the assets of your business along with estimates as to their value both if you liquidate and if you stay in business. It makes sense to include financial statements—and property appraisals if you have them—in your workout package so that creditors can see what you're worth and what your problems are. Also, if you have created a business turn-around plan either on your own or working with a small business advisor, include it in your package.

Next, you'll normally want to compare what the creditors will receive if you have to liquidate the business in a Chapter 7 bankruptcy with what they're likely to receive if your workout plan succeeds. To do this, you may need some help from a bankruptcy lawyer or experienced accountant in putting together the liquidation scenario. Give time and thought to showing why your alternative proposal—your long-term workout plan—is likely to eventually put far more money in each of your creditor's pockets as compared to the meager returns they are likely to receive if you go through bankruptcy. While it makes sense to emphasize why your plan to turn around your business has a good chance of succeeding, you'll also want to be realistic. Creditors will be justly suspicious of any plan that's based on wishful thinking.

💡 Put the facts on bankruptcy forms.

For extra psychological leverage in trying to get creditors to negotiate a livable workout plan, you may want to prepare official bankruptcy forms (available from an office supply store) as if you actually planned to file. The filled-in forms will list your business debts and the value of your business assets. Show the forms to your creditors along with your workout plan. This sends the message that you're really prepared to file for bankruptcy if you can't achieve a compromise. It also dramatically highlights how little the creditors will wind up with if they push you into bankruptcy.

In negotiating with creditors who have a mortgage or other security interest in real property, vehicles or business equipment in your possession, be prepared to show them that you're continuing to keep the property in good condition. Otherwise, they'll likely conclude that they're better off to move quickly to repossess it. Also realize that while suppliers may be willing to extend your time for paying past debts, most will expect you to pay in advance or COD for any new goods delivered to your business. To avoid this inconvenience, you'll need to convince them that your business is in the black on the basis of current operations and that you're routinely paying all new bills promptly.

Be sure your employees support you. If your long-time managers and other key employees are willing to take a temporary pay cut, it will go a long way towards convincing creditors that your business can slim down enough to become profitable. Also be sure that disgruntled employees aren't badmouthing your recovery plan. Remember that most long-term creditors will almost surely know some of your employees and are very likely to contact them for the true lowdown on your business.

Try to get 100% of your major creditors to agree to your plan. Unfortunately, if there are a significant number of holdouts among your major creditors, your workout plan is probably doomed to failure. The holdouts will drain your time and energy—not to mention your checking account—as they push ahead with lawsuits and other collection efforts.

Once your creditors agree to your plan, quickly put the terms in writing. Each written agreement should state specifically that if you make agreed workout payments on time, the creditor will hold off on filing lawsuits and will terminate collection actions. In addition, if the creditor has agreed to accept less than 100% of what's owed, there should be a clear statement that if you pay the agreed amount, you and your business will be fully released from the debt.

⚠️ Make your peace with the IRS first.

If you owe back taxes, pay them or come to terms with the IRS before you approach the other creditors. They're unlikely to agree to a workout if there's a chance the IRS may close down the business.

Ideas for Business Workouts

Here are a number of common elements of workout packages.

- *Partial Liquidation of Assets.* You agree to sell specific business assets that are not essential to your current business and to use the money to partially pay creditors on a pro rata basis.

- *A Creditor Takes the Collateral.* You turn over to a secured creditor the property you pledged as security for the loan or line of credit. The creditor agrees that your total obligation is wiped out—even if the property is worth less than you still owe. Normally, the creditor will do this only if he or she concludes that repossessing and selling the used property is likely to net more than letting you keep it and holding onto your debt. Or put another way, if the creditor really sees you as a long-term deadbeat, he or she will be more likely to take the property and forget about the debt.

- *Lump Sum Payback.* The creditor accepts a lump sum payoff that's less than the full debt and in full satisfaction of the entire debt. This scenario can particularly make sense when you have a family member or friend who will lend you some new money only if your creditor will accept a partial payment. The important thing is to make creditors realize they may get little or nothing if they don't agree.

- *Monthly Payments.* You agree to make monthly payments on your debts and the creditors agree to hold off on lawsuits and other collection actions. The total amount they agree to accept may be less than the amount owed—but if the debt is reduced, the creditors will probably want a larger monthly amount than they'd settle for on a lump sum payoff.

- *Creditors Become Owners.* In unusual situations, creditors may agree to take ownership rights—such as stock in your corporation—in exchange for forgiving some or all debts owed to them.

Source: *Holding Onto the American Dream: How Small Businesses Can Conquer Financial Problems,* by Marguerite M. Kirk (Odenwald Press).

E. Selling or Closing the Business

Although selling your financially troubled business may seem like a long shot, it's always worth a try. (See Chapter 10, Section I.) Naturally, you won't get top dollar for your business when it's in distress—but if you arrange a sale, it may give you enough to pay creditors and come away with a few bucks. Selling an operating business, even one that's in trouble, almost always brings more money than closing it down and selling off the assets.

Before you give up and conclude that no one will buy your business, consider that people buy businesses—even those with financial problems—for all sorts of reasons, including:

- The buyer may have lower personal financial needs and expectations and may be willing to squeak by on a modest return that's wholly unacceptable to you.

- The buyer may have a similar business and by combining the two operate more efficiently than you can.

- The buyer may be extremely anxious to take over one or more of your business assets—its location, key employees or name.

- The buyer may have better access to needed financing than you do and therefore be able to stay the course until your good business idea ultimately proves itself.

- The buyer may have greater expertise in your business than you do and see a way to turn a profit by changing how the business is run.

- The buyer may conclude that it's cheaper to buy your business and turn it around than to start a similar business from scratch.

Value is in the eye of the beholder.

Even if you believe it is an illusion, the fact that the buyer merely thinks that he or she has greater expertise than you do or that the business has unrecognized potential may be enough to produce a purchase offer. Don't let your ego get in the way of making the deal by defending your business decisions and strategy so forcefully that you talk the potential purchaser into withdrawing his or her offer.

If you have an opportunity to sell your business but the proceeds of the sale won't yield enough money to pay off all the business debts, look carefully at what remaining debts you'll be personally responsible for and what personal assets have been pledged as security for the business debts. Merely selling the business won't be enough to relieve you from your personal liability to creditors or the risk that creditors may take property that you've pledged as security. To reduce or eliminate your personal liability or the danger of losing pledged property, there are some solutions worth looking into. On debts for which you're personally liable, see if the bank or other creditor is willing to substitute the purchaser of your business on the indebtedness and release. The creditor may be willing to do this if the person buying your business is financially stronger than you are or, in the case of a currently unsecured debt, is willing to pledge security. A buyer who's enthusiastic about the prospects of the business may be willing to be substituted for you.

If the creditor won't let you off the hook, another way of dealing with unsecured debts that you'll be personally liable for is to ask the buyer to agree in writing to pay the specified debts and to indemnify and save you harmless from those obligations. This means that if the bank or other creditor comes after you because the debt isn't paid, the buyer guarantees to pay the debt and protect you from any liability. Of course, this kind of guarantee is only as

good as the buyer's financial condition, so you won't want to rely on such a guarantee if you have any reason to believe the buyer is financially shaky.

Where you've secured a business debt by pledging your personal property as collateral—for example, your home, car or stocks—see if the creditor is willing to release your property as security if the buyer substitutes property of equal or greater value. The buyer, for example, may have as much or more equity in his or her home than you do in yours and the bank may be willing to substitute that home as security in place of yours, if the buyer consents.

So much for selling your financially troubled business. If you can't sell it, consider closing it down. Even if you can't pay all your debts immediately, this option at least allows you to avoid running up more. In addition, you'll normally want to negotiate with your creditors to pay them off for less than the full amount the business owes. Why should creditors accept this? It's often a better choice than either of their other options: suing you and chasing down your assets to collect every last dollar or taking what's available in a bankruptcy liquidation. Trying this approach can be particularly sensible, too, if you have a corporation or LLC and have personally guaranteed some business debts. If you can reach a negotiated settlement, you'll not only avoid a business bankruptcy but also you won't have to go through personal bankruptcy to get out from under the debts you've guaranteed.

If you haven't personally guaranteed any debts of the corporation or LLC, one option is to simply close the business and pay the debts on a prorata basis to the extent the business has funds. Then, let the corporation or LLC die on its own. Since any remaining debts aren't your personal responsibility, this should, in theory at least, end matters. Sometimes, however, you may want to consider having the business file for bankruptcy in this situation. If the corporation or LLC hasn't gone through bankruptcy, some creditors may go ahead and sue the business and get judgments against it. If that happens, you may be subpoenaed and have to go to court to explain that the business used up all its assets. That can be a nuisance. So if you have a number of creditors who are likely to pursue you to the bitter end, putting the business through bankruptcy may make sense since it will save you from having to testify in multiple lawsuits. Creditors, of course, lose their right to sue once the corporation or LLC is bankrupt.

⚠️ **Watch out for preferential treatment.** *If at first you decide simply to close down your business but later decide to file for bankruptcy, you may have backed into trouble. If your business eventually has to file for bankruptcy, giving preferential treatment to some creditors in the months before you file by paying off all or part of their bills can create a problem. Creditors who didn't receive preferential treatment may complain, in which case the favored creditors will have to return the money or property they received so it can part of an asset pool available for equitable distribution among all creditors. (See Section B4, above.) So even if you hope not to file for bankruptcy, try to work out similar deals with all creditors.*

F. Understanding Bankruptcy

If your business is in serious financial trouble, you'll want to consider the possibility that you'll eventually need to file for bankruptcy if the other strategies mentioned in this chapter won't work for you. Fortunately, thoroughly understanding how bankruptcy works and how you can best cope with it if it becomes inevitable can result in major savings later on.

1. Different Types of Bankruptcy

Bankruptcy is a legal proceeding handled in the federal court system. It's based on the federal Bankruptcy Code, which is divided into different chapters, each covering a different type of bankruptcy as described below. Bankruptcy is usually voluntary, but be aware that one or more creditors may force

you into bankruptcy by filing an involuntary bankruptcy petition against you. Because lawyers and others with bankruptcy knowledge refer to the various types of bankruptcy protection by their chapter numbers, you too will need to learn this jargon which I explain below.

⚠️ **Expected changes to bankruptcy law didn't happen.** *Despite years of intense lobbying and campaign contributions from the credit card and banking industry, recent efforts to change the nation's bankruptcy laws died in Congress in November 2002. Any further efforts to change the federal bankruptcy law will have to start from scratch when the108th Congress convenes in 2003. For the latest information, keep watch on the national news and the Legal Updates section of Nolo's website (www.nolo.com).*

💼 **Legal advice may be essential.** *If you're a sole proprietor and have a relatively small amount of business debt, you may be able to handle a bankruptcy yourself or with a limited amount of professional help. But be forewarned: a number of issues (property exempt from being taken to pay debts, for one example) can be complicated when business and personal affairs are intertwined. For sole proprietors with significant debt and for partnerships, corporations and LLCs, it generally makes sense to seek advice from a lawyer who specializes in small business bankruptcy. Professional help is essential for corporations and LLCs because you can't represent these entities in a bankruptcy proceeding unless you're a lawyer. Seek out an experienced bankruptcy lawyer who will take the time to explain all your options—both bankruptcy and nonbankruptcy—before he or she files papers for you. Be wary of any lawyer who instantly assumes that you should proceed with a Chapter 7 liquidation which, in many cases, will prove to be a poor choice.*

2. Liquidating the Business Under Chapter 7

A Chapter 7 filing is sometimes called a "straight bankruptcy." It's available to businesses organized in all the usual ways—sole proprietorship, partnership, corporation and LLC. Under Chapter 7, your business property is sold and the proceeds are used to pay off debts to the extent funds are available.

If your business is a partnership, each partner is personally liable for all partnership debts. Putting the partnership through Chapter 7 won't do away with your personal liability for these debts. To accomplish that, you'd need to file for personal bankruptcy.

If your business is a corporation or LLC, you're generally not personally liable for debts of the business, unless you've personally guaranteed a business debt, in which case you're liable for repaying it. And if you've put up any property as collateral, that property can be taken unless you pay the creditor—known as a "secured creditor"—the value of the property or agree to have the debt survive the bankruptcy. To escape from personal liability for business debts, you'll have to file for personal bankruptcy after the corporate or LLC bankruptcy is wound up.

A personal filing under Chapter 7 will free you from personal liability for most business debts—but it bears some potential disadvantages. The fact that you've filed for personal bankruptcy remains on your credit record for ten years. This can cause trouble when you apply for a mortgage, a bank loan, a charge account or a credit card. What's more, employers sometimes use credit information to screen job applicants as do some landlords in checking out potential tenants.

⚠ Co-signers and guarantors are still on the hook. *If a friend or family member has co-signed for a business loan or guaranteed payment of a business debt, putting the business or yourself through Chapter 7 bankruptcy won't relieve the co-signer or guarantor from personal liability for the debt. This can be an added reason to try to resolve your debt problems through a workout or other non-bankruptcy alternative. (See Section D.)*

For in-depth guidance, including forms and instructions for filing, see How to File for Chapter 7 Bankruptcy, *by Stephen Elias, Robin Leonard, Kathleen Michon & Albin Renauer (Nolo).*

Two Kinds of Creditors

Bankruptcy law distinguishes broadly between two types of creditors: secured and unsecured.

A secured creditor is either one to whom you or your business has pledged collateral in exchange for a loan or line of credit (voluntary secured creditor) or one who has filed a lien (tax, judgment or mechanic's) against your property (involuntary secured creditor). Pledged collateral to a voluntary secured creditor may consist of business property such as inventory and equipment or your own property such as your house, car or boat. Either way, the creditor ends up with a lien on the property. This means that if you or the business can't pay back the debt, the creditor can take the property to satisfy the debt.

An unsecured creditor is either one to whom no collateral has been pledged or one who hasn't filed a lien. Typically, these debts will include amounts your business owes for inventory, office supplies, minor equipment and furnishings, rent and advertising, as well as what's owed for services such as maintenance contracts, equipment repair and professional advice. Credit card charges, too, are unsecured.

In bankruptcy, the secured creditor is in a much more favorable legal position than one who is unsecured. If the bankrupt business has little or no money, the unsecured creditor is likely to wind up with little or nothing, whereas the secured creditor walks away with whatever the collateral is worth. A Chapter 7 bankruptcy gets rid of the debt but not the security interest.

3. Reorganizing Your Business Debts

As an alternative to liquidation under Chapter 7, you may prefer to reorganize your debts under Chapters 11, 12 or 13 so that you can continue to operate your business while the bankruptcy court protects you from the demands of creditors. In a reorganization, you can often reduce the amounts you must pay back to unsecured creditors. In addition, under a court-approved repayment plan, you can spread your payments over a number of years.

Among the situations in which Chapters 11, 12 and 13 are worth considering are these:

- You want to retain all your assets and keep the business going.
- You want to partially liquidate your assets and then keep the business alive on a scaled-down basis.
- You want to totally liquidate the business by selling it either as a going concern or by selling any remaining assets.
- You want to buy time to put the business in decent shape so that it's more attractive to potential purchasers.
- You want to pay your taxes in installments to stave off the IRS or state or local tax collectors who are poised to seize your assets, which would put you out of business.

In each case, a Chapter 11, 12 or 13 proceeding may offer the possibility of helping you achieve your objectives.

a. Chapter 11

A Chapter 11 reorganization allows your sole proprietorship, partnership, corporation or LLC to continue doing business while often reducing or even eliminating the amounts you must pay back to unsecured creditors. Under a court-approved repayment plan, you can spread your payments over a number of years. Five years is typical.

If you file for a Chapter 11 reorganization, you'll immediately receive the protection of the bankruptcy court. All lawsuits and other collection actions against your business will come to a screeching halt. You'll then have 90 days in which to submit a plan—called a reorganization plan—showing how you propose to pay past-due debts while keeping up to date on current ones. If your business debts don't exceed $2 million, you can use a new, fast-track version of Chapter 11 that simplifies procedures and gives the creditors less control than they have in a regular Chapter 11 reorganization.

Your plan will have to meet a few legal guidelines; for example, it must show that back taxes will be fully paid within five years. And secured creditors—those to whom your business has pledged collateral—must receive the collateral or the current value of the collateral or the current value of the debt. Your plan doesn't have to include payment to unsecured creditors unless those creditors would receive some payment if your business were to file for liquidation under Chapter 7.

After you file the plan, creditors vote on it. Secured and unsecured vote separately and, to be adopted, the plan must be approved by 51% of the creditors in each class. If your plan is carefully crafted, the creditors will likely accept it. But if the creditors reject the reorganization plan, all may not be lost. A solution may be found in the "cram down"—a phrase used to describe the last-resort powers of the bankruptcy court. If your plan is basically fair and equitable, the judge can cram it down the throats of all the creditors.

To help your business stay alive, the judge can terminate burdensome or unprofitable leases or contracts. If, for example, your business is occupying expensive space under a lease that runs for seven years, your business is contractually obligated to keep paying rent throughout those seven years. But in Chapter 11, the judge can allow your business to move to a less costly location, with no further obligation to your current landlord.

With these many benefits, Chapter 11 sounds like a good deal for a financially troubled business, but the grim truth is that it rarely succeeds. It's usually an overwhelming task for a typical business owner to keep up with current bills while simultaneously chopping away at large past-due debts and paying chunky administrative and legal fees. The result is that more than 90% of businesses that file under Chapter 11 eventually switch to Chapter 7 and liquidate their assets—although the new, fast-track procedures may lead to a higher success rate.

Compare the payoffs to creditors.
Basically, if you're convinced that you can get more money for the creditors by reorganizing under Chapters 11, 12 or 13 than by filing for a straight liquidation under Chapter 7, then reorganize. Otherwise, don't waste your time, energy and money. Proceed directly with a Chapter 7 filing. Why worry about how much the creditors get? Because the more they get, the less you may be personally liable for.

b. Chapter 12

A Chapter 12 bankruptcy is available to family-owned farming businesses. As in a Chapter 11 proceeding, the total amount of debt owed to unsecured creditors may be reduced in the Chapter 12 plan. In addition, the financially ailing farm operation is allowed to continue doing business under a court-approved plan for repaying its remaining debts over a number of years. A court-appointed trustee serves as the intermediary between the farm and its creditors. Because this book is primarily for nonfarm businesses, Chapter 12 won't be treated further.

c. Chapter 13

Businesses, per se, are not permitted to file for Chapter 13 bankruptcy. A sole proprietor, however, may file as an individual and include the business debts for which he or she is personally liable. There are financial limits, which are adjusted annually based on a cost-of-living index. You can file for Chapter 13 bankruptcy if you have no more than $871,500 in secured debts and no more than $290,525 in unsecured debts. (These limits will be automatically adjusted effective April 1, 2004 to reflect changes in the Consumer Price Index.) Contingent or unliquidated claims—such as a sexual harassment claim against you that's not yet resolved—don't count against these limits. As in a Chapter 11 reorganization, the amount you must pay back to unsecured creditors is reduced (sometimes to as little as zero) and, under a court-approved plan, you continue to run the business while paying off debts over a period that can last up to five years. A court-appointed trustee—whose fees you pay—makes payments to creditors under the pay-back plan.

As noted in the next section, there can be advantages to filing under Chapter 13 rather than Chapter 11 if your business qualifies. Prospects for keeping your business afloat over the long term are better with a Chapter 13.

See Chapter 13 Bankruptcy: Repay Your Debts, *by Robin Leonard (Nolo), for a clear and in-depth look at how to get a court-approved repayment plan—either with or without a lawyer.*

d. Choosing between Chapter 11 and Chapter 13

All types of business entities—sole proprietorships, partnerships, corporations and limited liability companies—can choose to file under Chapter 7 for a straight liquidation bankruptcy or under Chapter 11 for a reorganization of their business debts. Since Chapter 11 and Chapter 13 both allow a business to remain in operation under a court-approved plan, a sole proprietor who qualifies for both may face the dilemma of choosing between the two. Generally, it's more advantageous to choose Chapter 13, for a number of reasons:

- A Chapter 13 reorganization plan is usually approved by the court in less time than a Chapter 11 plan.

- You don't have to deal with a creditors' committee—a committee that's appointed in a Chapter 11 filing to represent the interests of the unsecured creditors. This means you'll expend a lot less time and energy on paperwork, meetings and possibly attorney fees. Creditors may object separately to your Chapter 13 plan, but they don't carry the same weight as a committee would in a Chapter 11.

- You'll be able to pay less than 100 cents on the dollar for unsecured debts. The bankruptcy judge in a Chapter 13 can approve a plan which provides for partial debt repayment.

- If you meet the terms of the court-approved payment plan, virtually all remaining, unpaid debts will be wiped away even if some of them were obtained under circumstances the law might consider fraudulent. For example, if you obtain credit by misrepresenting your credit history, the debt probably won't be discharged under either Chapter 7 or 11 and the creditor will be able to sue you personally—but under Chapter 13, if you make all payments as called for by the plan, the creditor can't sue you for that debt.

- A Chapter 13 filing will stop collection action against a co-signer or guarantor if the Chapter 13 plan treats creditors fairly. In short, this option can help you protect friends and relatives who have obligated themselves to pay your debts.

- Going the Chapter 13 route is usually less expensive than the Chapter 11 alternative. That's because the filing fees are lower and, if you hire a lawyer to help you, the legal fees will be lower too,

There is, however, one area in which Chapter 11 may be a better choice. In a Chapter 13 reorganization, you generally can't modify the terms of a mortgage loan or other credit agreement which is secured by your home. This means that even if your house is worth less than what you owe, you must still pay the balance. There are a few technical exceptions to this rule, but they're of little practical value to most people. A different rule applies to Chapter 11 filings, creating the possibility of reducing the loan if the value of your home has dropped. So if you have a huge mortgage on your home and the value of the property has dropped, then Chapter 11 is probably better for you than Chapter 13.

4. Who's Who in Bankruptcy

In addition to understanding the various types of bankruptcy, you'll quickly need to understand who the major players are and at least some of the jargon involved in a bankruptcy proceeding. Here's a brief overview.

- *Debtor.* The debtor is the person or business entity that owes the money. This can be you or your business or both. If your business isn't a sole proprietorship, you and your business each need to file separate sets of bankruptcy papers. Generally, it's the debtor that files for bankruptcy, although creditors can sometimes start the ball rolling, in which case it's called an involuntary bankruptcy.

- *Creditor.* This can be any person, business or governmental agency that has or may have a claim against you or your business. A secured creditor is one that has a lien (claim) against specific property—usually either in the form of a real estate mortgage or a security interest in a vehicle or other equipment. A secured creditor is usually in a better legal position than an unsecured creditor, because if money isn't available to pay the debt, the secured creditor is entitled to grab the assets pledged as security.

- *Trustee.* A bankruptcy trustee takes possession of the debtor's business assets in a Chapter 7 proceeding and liquidates them to pay creditors. In a Chapter 7 personal bankruptcy, the trustee gathers the debtor's nonexempt property (a second home, for example), liquidates it and distributes the proceeds to the unsecured creditors. In a Chapter 11 proceeding, the debtor usually retains control over the business assets while the business continues to operate. But, especially if the business owner has committed fraud or seriously mismanaged the business, the court may appoint a trustee to take over in a Chapter 11 proceeding so that the creditors' interests are better protected. In a Chapter 12 or 13 bankruptcy, the debtor remains in possession of the property; the trustee collects monthly payments and distributes them to creditors. Trustees are appointed by the bankruptcy judge unless the district has a U.S. Trustee—a full-time federal employee with a staff of assistant trustees who serve as trustees in Chapter 11 cases and appoint and supervise outside trustees in Chapter 7, 12 and 13 cases.

- *Judge.* A bankruptcy judge is part of the federal district court and has broad control over bankruptcy proceedings, including authority to resolve all disputes between the business and its creditors, as well as any issues involving the business's property. Despite this broad authority, the judge may abstain from trying issues that can be litigated in a state court—for example, actions to foreclose on real estate or to gain possession of cars and equipment, and cases involving environmental cleanups. Bankruptcies are supervised, for the most part, by the trustee where one's been appointed—but debtors and creditors who disagree with a trustee's decision can seek a ruling from the bankruptcy judge who can overrule the trustee.

- *Creditors' committee.* In a Chapter 11 proceeding, an unsecured creditors' committee may be appointed to represent the interests of all the unsecured creditors. If the proceeding

is complicated, there may be additional creditors' committees representing special interests—for example, pension and profit-sharing recipients, under-secured creditors and secured creditors. A creditor's committee may object that a proposed plan writes off too much of the debt owed to its members or that it gives the debtor too much time to pay.

5. Key Bankruptcy Concepts

Unfortunately, your mini-education in how bankruptcy works isn't quite complete. Since bankruptcy law is unique, with its own concepts, procedures and jargon, it's crucially important to understand the legal basics.

a. Bankruptcy estate

Once you or your business file for bankruptcy, the property—called the bankruptcy estate—is controlled by the bankruptcy proceedings. Creditors can't get their hands on it without the court's permission. Property subject to court control includes not only the property your business owned when you filed the bankruptcy papers, but also money your business earned but hadn't collected before you filed for bankruptcy. Also, in a Chapter 11, 12 or 13 proceeding, if your business acquires property after your case is filed, that property becomes part of the bankruptcy estate. However, if your business holds money in trust for third parties—such as withholding taxes that are to be paid to the IRS—that money isn't part of the bankruptcy estate.

⚠ You may need a separate bank account. *If you don't pay the employment taxes immediately, keep them in a separate bank account designated as a trust account so that it's clear that these funds are separate from other funds of the business. Then you'll be able to use these funds to* *pay the taxes and avoid personal liability and penalties. In a Chapter 11 filing, you'll probably need to set up several separate accounts—for example, accounts for payroll and general operations, in addition to the one for employment taxes.*

b. The automatic stay

As soon as your business has filed a bankruptcy petition, creditors are stayed (stopped) from continuing their collection efforts against the business. In addition, creditors can no longer seize any property owned or leased by the business that secures its debts, such as a car, building or equipment. Further, it's illegal for creditors to contact you to push for payment, start a lawsuit against you or pursue any other collection action without permission of the bankruptcy court. Utilities such as the power, phone and water company must continue to serve your business as long as you can guarantee payment for future services—for example, by posting a deposit. Be aware that the IRS can continue an audit, issue a tax deficiency notice, demand a tax return, issue a tax assessment and demand payment, but can't record a lien or seize your property.

c. The bankruptcy filing

To start a bankruptcy case, your business must file a form called a Petition for Relief with the clerk of the federal bankruptcy court. To learn the location of the bankruptcy court, call the clerk of the U.S. District Court that's nearest your business.

A list of creditors (everyone your business owes money to) and their addresses should accompany your Petition, using a special format so that copies of your creditor list can be used as a mailing list. Within 15 days, you must also file lists of debts, assets and a history of your business. In bankruptcy jargon, these lists are called bankruptcy schedules and Statement of Financial Affairs. You'll want to include all debts your business may owe and any claims that creditors may have against your business—even those you have some doubts about or you dispute.

d. Claims

Once notified of your bankruptcy, creditors may file claims for payment of their debts with the bankruptcy court. Your business—and, in a Chapter 7 or Chapter 13 filing, the bankruptcy trustee—can challenge a claim that seems to be improper. The judge will decide if the claim is valid. In a liquidation of a business, since there's almost never enough money to pay all allowed claims, the law establishes priorities. Your bankruptcy estate (any money or property salvaged from your business) is used to pay the highest priority claims first, then the next highest priority, and so on as long as the money lasts. Creditors in the lowest category, to actually receive any money, will typically have to take much less than the amount they're owed, since by definition there isn't enough money to go around. In fact, it's not uncommon for unsecured creditors to receive nothing.

Some creditors can obtain a super-priority status. In a Chapter 11, 12 or 13 bankruptcy where the trustee or debtor must borrow new money to keep the business running, the lender of these funds would obtain a super-priority claim and be first in line when assets are distributed. Next come the secured creditors who have liens on specific real estate, vehicles, equipment or other property. After that come such claims as the expenses of administering the bankruptcy, wages and commissions earned during the 90 days before the bankruptcy started, money owed to an employee benefit plan, deposits made on consumer goods and most taxes. At the bottom of the heap are general, unsecured claimants who, if they're lucky, receive a pittance. Often, unsecured claimants get a few cents for each dollar they were owed or come away entirely empty-handed. In a Chapter 13, secured creditors with liens and priority debts could be paid simultaneously through the Chapter 13 plan.

e. The effect of bankruptcy on secured debts

If you go through a Chapter 7 personal bankruptcy, the creditor will lose the right to get a personal judgment against you requiring you to pay the debt that's owed. But even though the creditor can no longer demand that you repay the debt, if you've pledged property as collateral, the creditor will still have a lien on that specific property. Because the creditor will be able to enforce the lien and take or sell the property, you need to be aware of the three options available to you—which can be summarized as The Three Rs:

- *Relinquishment.* You can simply give up the house, car or other property on which the creditor has a lien.
- *Redemption.* You may buy it by paying the creditor, usually in a lump sum, the value of the property. If there's a dispute about how much the property is worth, the bankruptcy judge will determine the value.
- *Reaffirmation.* You may reaffirm your obligation to pay the debt secured by your property before the debt is discharged in bankruptcy. Then, you continue to make payments as you had agreed before the bankruptcy. Of course, the lien will remain on the property and, if you later miss payments, the creditor will be able to enforce the lien by taking back property to pay for the balance of the reaffirmed debt.

f. Exempt property

If you go through a Chapter 7 personal bankruptcy where your assets are liquidated to pay your debts, you don't have to give up all of your personal property to pay back creditors. The law allows you to keep some items (called exempt property) to help you get a fresh start. Exempt property is listed in the federal bankruptcy code, but states also have laws listing exemptions. Generally, you'll rely on your state law exemptions—either because the state law exemptions are more advantageous or because, as is the case in most states, the state law gives you no choice. If you do have a choice, check the homestead allowance carefully as it's usually more generous under state law.

Most state exemptions allow you to keep property in these broad categories:

- motor vehicles, to a certain modest value
- clothing other than furs
- household furnishings and goods
- household appliances
- jewelry such as a wedding or engagement ring and a watch
- personal effects—personal possessions that don't fall into the categories of clothing and jewelry
- life insurance (cash or loan value, or proceeds) to a certain value
- pensions for public employees or pensions that qualify under ERISA
- part of the equity in your home
- tools of your trade or profession, to a certain value
- portion of unpaid but earned wages, and
- public benefits (welfare, Social Security, unemployment compensation) accumulated in a bank account.

For detailed state-by-state lists of exemptions, see Money Troubles: Legal Strategies to Cope With Your Debts, *or* Bankruptcy: Is It the Right Solution to Your Debt Problems?, *both by Robin Leonard (Nolo).*

LAW IN THE REAL WORLD
Carl and Phyllis Save Their Home

Carl starts a neighborhood restaurant, organizing his business as a one-person corporation. To raise capital, Carl and his wife Phyllis borrow $50,000 from a bank on their signature and additionally secure the loan by giving the bank a second mortgage on their home.

In its first year, the business runs up a pile of debts. With prospects of becoming profitable looking bleak, Carl decides to close down. Carl considers putting the corporation through bankruptcy to make a clean break with creditors. Unfortunately, this won't help with the bank loan since Carl and Phyllis are personally liable for that debt and their home is at risk if they can't pay it. Since this is a secured debt, even if they go through personal bankruptcy they'll lose their home.

So Carl and Phyllis reduce the bank loan with $10,000 of personal savings that Phyllis had set aside from her salary as a school teacher. They then refinance their home by getting a new first mortgage that pays off both the old mortgages. (Fortunately, Carl is able to get his old job back, so he and Phyllis have income to qualify for the new mortgage.) Carl and Phyllis now have 30 years to pay off the new mortgage in monthly installment payments.

Carl closes the business, sells the corporation's few remaining assets and, before dissolving the corporation, distributes the proceeds pro rata to the business's unsecured creditors.

The business failed but with this small-scale workout, Carl and Phyllis saved their home.

Resolving Legal Disputes

L egal disputes—actual and potential—come in all shapes and sizes when you run a small business. Consider these examples:

- The phone company puts your Yellow Pages ad in the wrong classification and refuses to do anything about it.
- A former employee claims that you wrongfully fired her.
- Your landlord puts off repairing a leaky roof. As a result, valuable merchandise is ruined in a rainstorm.
- Your insurance company offers a ridiculously low settlement when one of your trucks is totalled.
- You refuse to accept a dozen custom-built display cases because they don't meet your specifications. The shop that constructed them threatens to sue.
- You want to stop a former employee from opening a competing business two blocks away and soliciting customers using a copy of your customer list.
- Just when your business begins to do well, your partners claim that you're not doing everything you promised to do in the partnership agreement. They want to terminate the agreement and continue the business without you.

How you handle such disputes can have a profound effect on your bottom line, not to mention your mental health and the morale of your employees. Fortunately, you usually have a number of options available, giving you some control over the time, energy and money that you spend on resolving legal problems.

We live in a litigious society. Often, the first reaction to a business dispute is, "I'll see you in court!" But rarely is litigation the only method for resolving a dispute. Litigation is enormously expensive and almost always results in hard feelings that prevent the contending parties from ever doing business with one another again, so it's always smart to think about alternatives. Commonly available options include negotiation, mediation and ar-

bitration. These noncourtroom approaches to handling legal disputes are often referred to as Alternative Dispute Resolution or ADR. This chapter explores the various types of dispute resolution so that, whether or not you work with a lawyer, you'll be better able to take charge of tactical and settlement decisions.

A. Negotiating a Settlement

In most situations, a negotiated solution is far better and cheaper than one imposed by an arbitrator or a judge. A settlement often can be reached speedily and at minimum expense. Litigation (and, to some extent, arbitration) can not only empty your wallet—they can also eat up an amazing amount of your time and that of your employees.

Always seek a negotiated settlement before you sue, even if you're so angry you don't want to speak to the other party. Try to evaluate the legal and financial realities objectively. Your goal should be to achieve the best result at the lowest cost. If instead you act on the conviction (whether it's right or wrong makes no difference) that you're being victimized by the other side, chances are you'll end up fighting for the last dollar because of the principle involved. A business person who is controlled by this sort of emotional reaction is almost sure to get ensnared in a lawsuit that will take too long and cost too much.

Here are some helpful pointers for negotiations:

- Listen closely to what your opponent says. Acknowledge that you hear the points your opponent is making even if you disagree with them.
- Avoid personal attacks. This only raises the level of hostility and makes settlement more difficult. Equally important, don't react impulsively to the emotional outbursts of your opponent.
- Try to structure the negotiation as a mutual attempt to solve a problem. Jointly seek solutions that recognize the interests of both parties.
- Learn your opponent's priorities. Maybe dollars are less important than a formula for future business relations. You may not be as far apart as you think.
- Put yourself in your opponent's shoes. What can you offer to make the settlement more palatable? The best settlements are those in which both sides feel they've won (or at least not given up anything fundamental).
- When you propose a specific settlement, make it clear that you're attempting to compromise. Offers of settlement (clearly labeled as such) can't be introduced against you if you ever go to trial.
- If a settlement is reached, promptly write it down and have all parties sign it. You or your lawyer should volunteer to prepare the first draft. That way, you can include protective language that, once included, your opponent may see as too minor to quibble about.
- Money is a powerful incentive to settlement. If your business is going to have to pay something eventually, come to the negotiating table with your checkbook or a wad of $100 bills. The other side may settle at a surprisingly low figure if they can walk away from the bargaining table with payment in hand. Of course, if you pay with cash, be sure to get a receipt.

 Getting to Yes, *by Roger Fisher & William Ury (Penguin Books).*

Getting Past No: Negotiating With Difficult People, *by William Ury (Bantam Books).*

B. Understanding Mediation

Many people confuse mediation with arbitration (discussed in Section C). While both are nonjudicial ways to resolve disputes, there's a huge difference: arbitration is binding; mediation isn't. The mediator simply helps the parties work out a solution to their dispute. Neither side is committed in advance to accept the mediator's advice.

Where to Find a Mediator

You and the other party can choose anyone you both respect to act as mediator. Local small business or community groups may provide trained mediators, as do the arbitration services listed in Section C.

"Turbo-charged negotiation" is how one lawyer describes mediation. In mediation, you ask the mediator, as a neutral expert, to help both sides negotiate. If you follow the classic model—used by big business for, say, a labor-management dispute—the mediator typically meets separately with each side. Everything said in those meetings is confidential. The mediator helps each party analyze its needs. When both sides get close to a settlement, everyone meets together to work out the details.

Mediators in small business disputes often prefer a much less formal approach. More likely than not, the mediator will have everyone sit down together from the very beginning and allow both parties to express all their issues—even emotional ones. Often this works because the people are mad at each other for reasons that go well beyond the legal issues that are supposed to define the dispute. Once everything is on the table, a good mediator helps the parties find a mutually acceptable solution.

LAW IN THE REAL WORLD
Getting at the Real Problems

Doug rents a storefront from Tom for five years. Although they occasionally have their differences over Tom's duty to keep the building in good repair and Doug's to maintain the grounds, they get along reasonably well. Then Doug has a bad financial month and is late with the rent. Tom, who has given Doug an extension several times in the past, threatens to begin eviction proceedings immediately. Doug responds by pointing out that Tom failed to fix a roof leak that damaged some of his inventory. Clearly, the stage is set for a nasty court fight. To head this off, a neighboring business owner suggests that Tom and Doug mediate their dispute under a program co-sponsored by the Chamber of Commerce.

At the mediation, Doug wants to know why Tom is being so unreasonable. The answer, it turns out, is simple. Doug has repeatedly left the gate open in the yard behind the building letting Tom's beloved dog run into the street. Tom finds it hard to forgive such carelessness and is ready to punish Doug by using whatever legal leverage is available. When Doug and Tom work out the dog problem (Tom will put in a better gate, Doug absolutely guarantees to keep it closed), the rest of the issues are quickly resolved, and a lawsuit is avoided.

But does mediation work? Perhaps surprisingly, given the fact there's no one to impose a solution, the answer is yes, in as many as 80% of mediations. One reason is apparently that by agreeing to medi-

ate a dispute in the first place, you and the other side must cooperate to establish the rules which, in turn, sets the stage for cooperating to find a solution to the dispute.

Sample mediation clauses that you can include in your business contracts are shown below.

Sample Mediation Clause 1

If a dispute arises relating to this agreement, the parties will follow this procedure before pursuing any other remedy:

1. The parties will promptly meet to attempt in good faith to negotiate a resolution of the dispute.

2. If, within 30 days after that meeting, the parties have not resolved the dispute, they will submit the dispute to good faith mediation in accordance with the rules of the (name of organization such as American Arbitration Association) and to bear equally the costs of the mediation.

3. After a mediator is appointed, the parties will participate in good faith in the mediation. If the dispute is not resolved within 30 days, it will be settled by arbitration in accordance with the rules of (name of organization), and judgment upon the award rendered by the arbitrator may be entered in any court having jurisdiction.

Sample Mediation Clause 2

If a dispute arises between the parties to this contract, the parties agree to participate in at least four hours of mediation in accordance with the mediation procedures of United States

Arbitration & Mediation, Inc. The parties agree to split equally the costs of mediation. The mediation will be administered by [designate either the specific USA&M office or a local USA&M office designated by the USA&M National Headquarters].

If your original contract is silent on the subject of mediation or arbitration, you and the other party still can agree to use either or both of these methods to resolve a dispute. Chances are good that your adversary (if a business person) will be as receptive as you are to some method of avoiding the expense and delay of litigation. Even if a negotiating impasse has led to a lawsuit, you can change horses in midstream; you can agree to mediation or arbitration, and cancel the lawsuit when you reach a settlement.

 For in-depth guidance, read How to Mediate Your Dispute, *by Peter Lovenheim (Nolo).*

C. Arbitration

With arbitration, you get a relatively quick, relatively inexpensive solution to a business dispute without going to court. Like a judge, the arbitrator—or arbitration panel—has power to hear the dispute and make a final, binding decision. Where does this power come from? From you and the other party. You agree to submit to arbitration and to be bound by the arbitrator's decision.

Almost any commercial dispute that can be litigated can be arbitrated. Disputes with employees can be arbitrated, as can disagreements with a landlord, supplier, business partner, franchisor, architect, builder, customer or equipment rental company.

Arbitration clauses are becoming a part of most commercial contracts. Insurance contracts, for example, frequently provide that any dispute over the amount of benefits to be paid by the insurance company will be decided by arbitration rather than litigation. The same goes for construction contracts: There's often a clause that requires arbitration for any contractual disputes. Through such clauses, you can provide in advance for arbitration to be used. You and the other party can also decide to use arbitration after a dispute arises.

If the losing party doesn't pay the money required by an arbitration award, the winner can easily convert the award to a court judgment, which can be enforced like any other court judgment. Unlike a judgment based on litigation, however, you generally can't take an appeal from an arbitration-based judgment. (An exception is when there was some element of fraud in the procedures leading to the arbitration award.)

Here are the chief advantages of arbitration:

* Arbitration is usually much less expensive than litigation. The American Arbitration Association, for example, charges on a sliding scale, based on the amount of the claim:

Amount of Claim	Filing Fee	Case Service Fee
Up to $10,000	$500	N/A
$10,001 to $75,000	$750	N/A
$75,001 to $150,000	$1,250	$750
$150,001 to $300,000	$2,750	$1,000
$300,001 to $500,000	$4,250	$1,250
$500,001 to $1,000,000	$6,000	$2,000
$1,000,001 to $7,000,000	$8,500	$2,500
$7,000,001 to $10,000,000	$13,000	$3,000
Above $10,000,000	Contact Regional Office	

* You're likely to receive an arbitrator's decision within six months after the demand for arbitration is submitted. And, under certain circumstances, the American Arbitration Association has expedited procedures leading to a quicker decision. Lawsuits, on the other hand, usually aren't decided for a year or often much more—and an appeal may add several more years of delay.

- Unlike a trial, arbitration proceedings are private. There's no need for your competitors or the general public to know your business.
- The rules of evidence are relaxed in an arbitration proceeding. This makes it easier to get to the heart of the matter. Courtroom trials often get bogged down in evidentiary arguments that obscure rather than clarify the facts.
- Arbitration often avoids the bitter acrimony that can affect the parties in a lawsuit. It's not unusual for parties to resume their normal business relationship after their dispute has been arbitrated.

How Arbitration Works: An Example

Smooth Shift Transmission hires Better Builders to add two service bays to its transmission shop for a total of $60,000. The contract calls for a $30,000 down payment. The balance is due when the job is completed. However, after the work is done, Smooth Shift isn't satisfied with the job. There are several large cracks in the concrete floor installed by Better Builders. On the advice of its architect, Smooth Shift delays making the final payment.

A few weeks later the floor begins to settle, creating several gaps where it meets an outside wall. Better Builders claims that these problems are minor and threatens to sue Smooth Shift for the final payment of $30,000. But Smooth Shift points to a clause in the construction contract: "All disputes concerning this project will be submitted to arbitration."

Better Builders sends a "demand for arbitration" to the American Arbitration Association (AAA), a nationwide organization that administers many of the arbitration proceedings in this country. In response, the AAA sends a list of five proposed arbitrators to each side. The parties agree on one of the listed people to serve as their arbitrator. (If parties can't agree, the AAA makes the selection.) A hearing is scheduled a month later.

During the hearing, which takes only three hours, each side makes a brief opening statement describing the controversy. Smooth Shift's owner then shows the arbitrator the construction contract, the plans and specs for the job and photographs of the floor. The architect hired by Smooth Shift testifies that the floor problems are serious, and that the floor must be replaced.

Now it's Better Builders' turn. The president of Better Builders testifies that the floor problems are minor and can be fixed with $1,000 worth of patching material. A week later, the arbitrator sends the parties his findings and his decision: The floor needs to be replaced at a cost of $18,000. That amount is to be deducted from the $30,000 final payment owed to Better Builders, meaning Smooth Shift owes Better Builders only $12,000. End of case.

How to Find an Arbitrator

- *The American Arbitration Association.* The oldest and largest organization of its kind, with regional offices in 38 U.S. cities. The main office is in New York City. Contact at www.adr.org or 212-484-4181.
- *Judicial Arbitration and Mediation Services, Inc./Endispute.* This is the largest private dispute resolution company with offices nationwide; mediates and arbitrates a wide range of commercial disputes. Contact at www.jamsadr.com.
- *U.S. Arbitration and Mediation.* A network of nationwide offices provides general arbitration and mediation of commercial disputes. Contact at www.usam.com or 800-318-2700.

Keep in mind that you are not required to use an organization for arbitration. You and the other party are free to choose your own arbitrator or arbitration panel, and to set your own procedural rules. Just remember that for arbitration to be binding and legally enforceable, you need to follow the simple guidelines set down in your state's arbitration statute. You can usually find the statute by looking in the statutory index under arbitration or checking the table of contents for the civil procedure sections.

Here's a sample clause you can use in a contract to provide for the arbitration of disputes:

Sample Arbitration Clause 1

Any controversy or claim rising out of or relating to this contract, or the breach of this contract, shall be settled by arbitration in accordance with the rules of the American Arbitration Association. A judgment of a court having jurisdiction may be entered upon the arbitrator's award.

Here's an example of an agreement you and the other party should sign if you want to go to arbitration with a dispute that has already arisen and that isn't covered by an arbitration agreement in an existing contract:

Sample Arbitration Clause 2

We agree to submit the following controversy to arbitration under the rules of the American Arbitration Association: _(describe the controversy)_

We further agree that a judgment of a court having jurisdiction may be entered upon the arbitrator's award.

If you and the other party want to choose an arbitrator on your own to act outside the administrative framework of an organization, use a clause like this one:

Sample Arbitration Clause 3

We agree to submit the following controversy to arbitration by (name of arbitrator): _(describe the controversy)_

We further agree that the arbitration procedures shall be as prescribed by the arbitrator and the costs of arbitration shall be as apportioned by the arbitrator.

Consider using arbitration for employment disputes. *Lawsuits by former employees claiming wrongful discharge or illegal discrimination can be costly and extremely contentious. By planning ahead, you should be able to avoid these lawsuits and use arbitration instead. The key is to have employees agree in writing that all disputes will be submitted to arbitration. True, some courts have rejected these agreements, believing that the agreements weren't really voluntary or else were calculated to help the employer avoid the full impact of civil rights laws. Still, if you draft the arbitration* *agreement carefully and the employee signs it before being hired, it will probably be enforceable. The agreement should use plain language to tell what disputes are covered and what rights (such as the right to a jury trial) the employee is giving up. Give employees a few days to review the agreement before they have to sign. Try for a balanced agreement that benefits both you and the employee. If it's tipped too far in your favor, a court may rule that it's unconscionable and refuse to enforce it.*

D. Going to Court

If your attempts at settling a dispute fail and you end up in a lawsuit, you'll need more help than this book can offer. Unless you go to small claims court, in fact, you'll probably need to hire a lawyer to represent you.

Despite its ample drawbacks, litigation may offer advantages in some situations. For example, you may decide you want a jury trial if you're the underdog. If you're a small franchisee going toe to toe with a multinational corporation, and the factual questions are pretty evenly balanced, the jury's sympathy may tip the scales of justice in your direction.

Another reason for considering litigation is that various procedural safeguards can help ensure that only trustworthy evidence is presented. The judge will only consider evidence that has been submitted according to a strict set of rules. In addition, using various methods of pretrial discovery, such as depositions, you can force the other side to disclose the evidence it plans to offer at trial and can also uncover evidence helpful to you. Of course, discovery is a two-way street. The other side can force you to disclose information you'd rather keep to yourself.

1. The Federal and State Court Systems

In the United States, two court systems operate side by side: the federal and state courts. Most business lawsuits (in fact, most lawsuits of every kind) are handled in state courts.

Broadly, federal courts have jurisdiction over only two types of cases. The first type involves what lawyers call federal questions: cases based on provisions in the U.S. Constitution, treaties and federal laws. This includes such things as discrimination cases arising under federal civil rights laws, and bankruptcy, patent, copyright and trademark cases arising under specific federal statutes.

The second type of case heard by federal district courts involves controversies between citizens of two different states; in these cases, the amount in controversy must exceed $50,000 before a federal court can get involved. This authority of the federal courts is called diversity jurisdiction because the litigants come from different (diverse) states. When a federal court exercises diversity jurisdiction, it's not necessary for a federal question to be involved. The court applies the law of the state in which the case arose.

EXAMPLE: A truck owned by an Arizona corporation is in an accident on a California freeway with a truck owned by a California corporation. Valuable computer equipment in the Arizona company's truck is ruined. If the ruined equipment was worth more than $50,000, the

Arizona corporation can sue the California corporation in either the California state courts or in a federal district court located in California. If the Arizona company sues in federal court, the judge will apply California law relating to vehicle accidents.

In handling cases based on diversity of citizenship, a corporation—a fictional legal person—is treated as a "citizen" of the state where it's incorporated.

As a practical matter, it often doesn't make much difference whether a business case proceeds in federal court or state court. When there's a choice between going to state or federal court, the decision is usually a tactical one based on comparisons between the caliber and philosophy of the state and federal judges, as well as comparisons between the likely composition of the juries in the two courts. Delay may also be a consideration; sometimes one court may have less of a backlog than another.

2. The Litigation Process

In a typical commercial case, the plaintiff (the person or company who sues) asks the judge to issue a judgment against the defendant (the person or company being sued). In many business cases, the plaintiff wants a money judgment—or, in legal parlance, damages.

But judges have power to grant many other kinds of relief to the plaintiff. For example, in a civil (that is, noncriminal) case, a judge may:

- Order a building official to issue a permit allowing the plaintiff company to expand its office building.
- Issue an injunction (order) prohibiting a former corporate officer from improperly disclosing or benefiting from trade secrets.
- Require a seller to transfer legal title to real estate in accordance with a purchase agreement.
- Have the sheriff remove a tenant from business premises and restore possession to the landlord.

- Place business assets in the hands of a receiver for short-term management.
- Order a business to stop infringing on a patent owned by another business.
- Require a partner to make an accounting to other partners.
- Order a state administrative board to issue a license.
- Interpret the meaning of a contract or declare a contract void.
- Force a corporation to open its books and records to all shareholders.

This is just a partial list; the point is that judges have broad powers. The powers of a small claims court (and some other local courts) are more limited. For example, in small claims court, you're generally limited to seeking a judgment for money damages—although the judge may have some additional limited authority such as requiring one of the parties to return goods to the other party as a condition of receiving payment. (For more on small claims court, see Chapter 23.)

It may surprise you to learn that most commercial lawsuits never go to trial. Frequently, a business starts a lawsuit mainly to get the attention of an adversary after attempts at a negotiated settlement have broken down. The message is, "We're serious. This thing can't drag on forever. We've got to resolve it on realistic terms." As costs mount and both parties gain a clearer picture of what they'll be able—or unable—to prove in court, and judges make rulings in preliminary courtroom skirmishes (known as "motions"), the parties often decide to compromise and settle the case.

Never lose sight of the fact that you can reach a negotiated settlement at any time. Any experienced lawyer can recite examples of cases settled "on the courthouse steps" just before the trial was to begin. And many cases have been settled after the evidence was presented and the jurors were in the jury room discussing what the verdict should be.

The High Cost of Justice

We all know lawsuits are expensive. But did you know just how expensive? The business lawyer's meter typically runs at $150 to $250 an hour for a long list of legal chores, including:

- conferences and telephone calls with you, witnesses and other lawyers
- legal research
- drafting documents such as a complaint, answer, counter-complaint, motions, requests for production of documents, briefs and jury instructions
- taking the depositions of witnesses or potential witnesses
- arguing motions in court (including many that affect only the litigation process and not the merits of the case)
- attending conferences in the judge's chambers
- driving to the courthouse and waiting for his or her turn to argue pre-trial motions
- conducting the trial.

Other costs include paying the public stenographer to take down depositions and type up the transcripts, jury fees, investigator costs and expert witness fees.

In most situations, each party pays its own attorney fees, although you can provide in a contract (such as a lease) that if a contract-related dispute goes to court, the losing party pays the fees of the winner's lawyer. If you don't have such a clause, the cost of winning may be so high that it's a hollow victory.

3. Getting Speedy Relief Through an Injunction

With clogged dockets and rules that allow extensive pre-trial discovery (depositions, interrogatories and other devices aimed at learning the facts of the other party's case), it's not always easy to get a speedy hearing in a commercial case. A case may be tied up in court for months or even years before it's decided. These built-in delays generally work to the advantage of the defendant and the disadvantage of the plaintiff. (It's the plaintiff who's taken the case to court and wants some action.)

In some instances, however, a plaintiff can go to court and get prompt attention. Two key elements must be present:

- The defendant must be causing irreparable harm to plaintiff's business—harm that can't be rectified by monetary damages; and
- There must be a need for immediate relief.

EXAMPLE: The grand opening of Trudy's new store in a neighborhood shopping plaza is scheduled for Saturday. Trudy's lease gives her the right to use the adjoining parking lot for customer parking. On the Monday before the grand opening, Trudy is stunned to see that a contractor, who is about to build an addition to the plaza, has occupied 16 of the plaza's 20 parking spaces with trucks and a large construction shed. Unable to convince her landlord or the contractor to move the equipment, Trudy goes to court for an injunction.

The judge orders a quick hearing (scheduled for the following day) to hear arguments on whether a preliminary injunction should be issued immediately to prevent harm to Trudy's business, pending a full-scale hearing.

In a case that involves an urgent threat to health or safety, or imminent damage to property, a judge also has the power to issue a temporary restraining order (TRO) to keep any harm from occurring or continuing until a hearing on a preliminary injunction can be scheduled. Because a TRO is issued without a hearing at which both sides can be heard (ex parte), it's a radical remedy. So, before issuing a TRO, the judge has to be convinced that the circumstances are extreme; even then, the restraining order will be in effect only for a day or two—just long enough to make arrangements to bring both sides to court.

To go back to Trudy's situation, if earth movers were about to dig up the pavement of the parking spaces, a judge might issue a TRO for a day based mostly on Trudy's sworn statement (affidavit) that she was about to suffer irreparable harm (once the pavement was gone, it would be difficult to use the parking spaces). The TRO would last until a hearing was held, at which point the court would decide whether or not to issue an injunction.

4. Testifying in Court

Especially if you're not paying the bill, a lawsuit can be a fascinating experience. Our system of trying cases has evolved and been tested for many hundreds of years. And, although some of the conventions of a trial can seem quaint, litigation remains a largely effective (although not necessarily cost-effective) way to ferret out the truth and reach a just result.

Even if you hire a lawyer to handle your lawsuit, you still need to understand some of the nuts and bolts of the system to make it work for you. You may well be called on to testify in a legal proceeding—either as a plaintiff, a defendant or a witness. Here are some suggestions to help you do it effectively.

- Treat pre-trial discovery—especially depositions—seriously. At a deposition, a party or witness is put under oath and cross-examined by the opponent's lawyer in the presence of a public stenographer. A transcript is typed up. Cases are frequently settled on the basis of deposition testimony. The other lawyer will

not only be listening carefully to your testimony but will be sizing you up as a witness. What will the jury think about you? Will you get flustered easily? Can you be baited into an argument? Do you project confidence or fear? In addition, if the case does go to trial, you'll have a lot of explaining to do if your testimony at trial differs from what you said at your deposition. Be accurate.

- Watch what you wear. Your clothing at a deposition or in court should indicate that you treat the case seriously. It should be conservative—not sporty, flashy or obviously expensive.

- In court, you're always "on stage"—not just when you're on the witness stand. If there's a jury, you'll be studied continually, at the counsel table or relaxing in the corridor. So maintain a serious demeanor, and be careful about conversations that the judge or jury may overhear.

- Before testifying, carefully review the typed transcript of your deposition as well as any written statements you've given about your case. You'll be embarrassed on cross-examination if you say something on the witness stand that differs from your earlier statements.

- If your business is incorporated, go to extra lengths to let the jury know that you're a small business—not General Motors. This is particularly important if your opposition is not a corporation. You don't want the jury to think of this as a battle between David and Goliath, with you cast as Goliath.

- On the witness stand, give the lawyer time to complete the question before you attempt to answer. If you're unsure or didn't hear the question, ask the lawyer to repeat it. If you still don't understand what he or she is seeking, ask for clarification.

- Keep your emotions under control during cross-examination. If you get angry, lose your temper or try to meet a lawyer's sarcasm with sarcasm of your own, you'll hurt your case. Be courteous even if the lawyer isn't.

- If possible, answer with a simple yes or no. This is particularly important on cross-examination. If more than a yes or no answer is needed, give only the requested facts. Then stop. Be careful about volunteering information just because you think it will be helpful. Such information may suggest whole new areas of questioning to the cross-examiner.

- Conversely, if the lawyer cross-examining tries to limit you to answering yes or no to a question that you feel you can't properly answer in a single word, say that you're unable to give a yes or no answer. The judge probably will let you explain.

- Unless you're testifying as an expert witness (someone with specialized knowledge who can give opinions in court), limit your testimony to facts—things you've personally seen or heard or done or said. Your opinions and conclusions usually aren't admissible.

- A definite answer is desirable. For example, "It was 10 p.m." is better than "I think it was about 10 p.m." But if you can't speak with such assurance, it's perfectly acceptable—and

advisable—to qualify your answer. And there will be times when the only honest answer is "I don't know," or "I don't remember."

- Watch out for words like "always" and "never." Sometimes in cross-examination a lawyer will try to get you to agree with an overly broad statement. For example: "Is it your testimony that your company never extends credit to first-time customers?" "Are you saying that you always send confirming letters?" Chances are the lawyer is setting the stage for further questions that will require you to back off from such an absolute statement. This can undermine your testimony. So your answer might be: "Our general policy is to not extend credit to first-time customers, but we have made some exceptions." Or, "We almost always send confirming letters but I can remember a few times when we did not."

Represent Yourself in Court: How to Prepare & Try a Winning Case, *by Paul Bergman & Sara J. Berman-Barrett (Nolo). Explains how to handle a civil trial yourself, without a lawyer, from start to finish.* ■

Representing Yourself
in Small Claims Court

You might think that paying a lawyer is unavoidable when you file a lawsuit. But that's not necessarily so. There are many times when you, as a business owner, can represent yourself in court. Of course, you wouldn't want to be your own lawyer in defending a $100,000 contract case or a $1 million personal injury suit. But how about suing customers for unpaid bills or a supplier for $5,000 for a breach of contract?

In cases like those, consider using a court designed for nonlawyers: small claims court. In a few states, other names are used, but the purpose is the same: to provide a speedy, inexpensive resolution of disputes that involve relatively small amounts of money. The jurisdictional limits (the amount for which you can sue) in these courts are rising fairly quickly. You may be surprised to learn that in a number of states you can sue for $5,000 or more. (A chart listing each state's small claims court limit is in Section C.)

A business person can use small claims court to collect bills, to obtain a judgment for breach of contract or to seek money for minor property damage claims—for example, suing someone who broke a sign in your parking lot. Small claims court offers a great opportunity to collect money that would otherwise be lost because it would be too expensive to sue in regular court. True, for very small cases, it's not always cost-effective, and occasionally you'll have problems collecting your judgment. But small claims should still be part of the collection strategies of many businesses.

Before you start a lawsuit in small claims court, investigate alternatives. If your case involves a written contract, check to see if the contract requires mediation or arbitration of disputes. (See Chapter 22, Sections B and C.) If so, this may limit or cut off your right to go to any court, including small claims court. Second, consider other cost-effective options such as free or low-cost publicly operated mediation programs. If you're in a dispute with a customer, or perhaps another business, and you still have hopes of preserving some aspect of the relationship, mediation—even if not provided for in a contract—is often a better alternative than small claims court. Any litigation tends to harden peoples' feelings. (See Chapter 20.)

Everybody's Guide to Small Claims Court, *by Ralph Warner (Nolo), goes into great depth on all of the topics covered in this chapter. It will be especially valuable in helping you prepare evidence and present your case to the judge.*

A. Deciding Whether to Represent Yourself

Most people who go to small claims court handle their own cases. In fact, in some states, lawyers aren't allowed to represent clients in small claims court. In any case, representing yourself is almost always the best choice—after all, the main reason to use the small claims court is because the size of the case doesn't justify the cost of hiring a lawyer. (The second benefit of using small claims court may be to satisfy any courtroom fantasies inspired by shows such as "L.A. Law"—although this one wears out pretty quickly.)

If you're doing business as a corporation and wish to proceed on your own, check the law in your state. In a few states, even if you're the president and sole shareholder of your corporation, you aren't allowed to represent the corporation. The reasoning is that the corporation legally is a separate entity and, therefore, appearing in court for a corporation amounts to practicing law without a license. Most states, however, allow a corporation to designate an officer or employee to appear for the corporation in small claims court. Even better, in some states, you can send your bookkeeper to testify in a small claims matter involving unpaid debts—the most common type of case. The clerk of the court can tell you what the rules are in your state.

Viewed strictly in terms of dollars and cents, if you can spare time away from your business, it's almost always better to represent yourself in small claims court than to hire a lawyer. To see just how great the savings can be, let's value your time at $30 an hour and assume that a typical small claims case takes 15 hours from filing to collection.

Lawyer's Time at $150 an hour
x 15 hours = $2,250
Lawyer's Time at $250 an hour
x 15 hours = $3,750
Your Time at $30 an hour
x 15 hours = $450

Clearly, we're looking at more than pennies here. And several studies show that people who represent themselves in small claims court do just as well as those represented by a lawyer. So it's hardly surprising that many business people who regularly use small claims court swear by it.

On the other hand, if your business is keeping you so busy that you can't easily afford the time to deal with a small claims case (chances are you'll still have to show up in court), you may have no choice but to hire a lawyer. In some states, this can be done in small claims court; in others, such as California, Idaho, Michigan and Nebraska, lawyers can't appear in small claims. The case will have to go to formal court, where chances are that more complicated procedures will add considerably to the time it takes. In that situation, you might want to seek a lawyer willing to take the case on a contingent fee basis. This means the lawyer gets a percentage of your recovery if you win and nothing if you lose. A lawyer who takes a $5,000 case on a contingent basis calling for a legal fee of one-third will receive $1,667 if there's a verdict for the full amount of the claim and if (sometimes a big if) the full amount is actually collected. This is substantially less than the $2,250 or $3,750 you'd be obligated to pay the lawyer—win or lose— under a straight hourly arrangement.

Another alternative is a partial contingent fee arrangement. Following this approach, you might find a lawyer who would charge you $100 an hour plus 15% or 20% of the amount actually recovered. Under such an arrangement, you spread between yourself

and the lawyer some of the risks of not recovering the full amount of your claim. (For more on lawyers and fee arrangements, see Chapter 24, Section B.)

A far less costly approach is to represent yourself but have a lawyer occasionally give advice on legal points or help with strategy.

LAW IN THE REAL WORLD
Using a Lawyer Wisely

George is a skillful, honest and hard-working real estate appraiser. While most of his customers pay their bills promptly, each year a dozen or so drag their feet. It drives George up the wall to think that people are ripping him off by not paying their bills. Several years ago, he decided to pursue every nonpaying customer if the amount involved was significant and there was a reasonable chance of collection.

Initially, he spent some time with his lawyer to become familiar with court procedures and to discuss pre-court strategies such as sending an effective collection letter. He also spent $15 for a complete copy of the court rules that apply in all courts of the state. (George is more ambitious than most business people and sometimes ventures into the regular courts, where legal matters can get a bit more complicated.)

Over the years, George has done very well in collecting unpaid accounts. Occasionally, if matters get complicated, he calls or visits his lawyer. Phone calls rarely last longer than 15 minutes, and visits rarely last longer than a half-hour. Wisely, George groups together several problems so he can discuss them at the same time. Occasionally, George has his lawyer draft a legal pleading or a notice or letter.

(See Chapter 24 for more on effective ways to work with a lawyer.)

B. Learning the Rules

Small claims court procedures are simple and easy to master. Basically, you pay a small fee, file your lawsuit with the court clerk, see to it that the papers are served on your opponent, show up on the appointed day and tell your story. Check with the court clerk for the specifics. The court rules are usually published in a booklet or information sheet.

In addition, clerks in small claims court are expected to explain procedures to you. They may even help you fill out the necessary forms, which are quite simple anyhow. If necessary, be persistent. If you ask enough questions, you'll get the answers you need to handle your own case comfortably. Also, in some states such as California, you can consult a small claims court advisor for free.

C. Meeting the Jurisdictional Limits

How much can you sue for in small claims court? The maximum amount varies from state to state. Generally, the limit is between $3,000 and $15,000. Check your state's limit on the chart below, but also ask the court clerk to see if the limit has been increased since the chart was prepared; state legislatures regularly increase these limits.

Don't assume that your case can't be brought in small claims court if it's for slightly more than the limit. You may want to ask for the jurisdictional limit and forget about the rest. For example, suppose you're in the wholesale lighting fixture business, and a local retailer owes you $3,650 for some lamps. If the jurisdictional limit in your state's small claims court is $3,000, in the long run, it may be less expensive for you to forget about the $650 excess. Hiring a lawyer and going to regular court would be even more expensive.

SMALL CLAIMS COURT LIMITS

State	Amount	State	Amount
Alabama	$3,000	Montana	$3,000
Alaska	$7,500	Nebraska	$2,400
Arizona	$2,500	Nevada	$5,000
Arkansas	$5,000	New Hampshire	$5,000
California	$5,000	New Jersey	$3,000
Colorado	$7,500	New Mexico	$10,000
Connecticut	$3,500	New York	$3,000
Delaware	$15,000	North Carolina	$4,000
District of Columbia	$5,000	North Dakota	$5,000
Florida	$5,000	Ohio	$3,000
Georgia	$15,000	Oklahoma	$4,500
Hawaii	$3,500	Oregon	$5,000
Idaho	$4,000	Pennsylvania	$8,000
Illinois	$5,000	Rhode Island	$1,500
Indiana	$3,000*	South Carolina	$7,500
Iowa	$5,000	South Dakota	$8,000
Kansas	$1,800	Tennessee	$15,000**
Kentucky	$1,500	Texas	$5,000
Louisiana	$3,000	Utah	$5,000
Maine	$4,500	Vermont	$3,500
Maryland	$2,500	Virginia	$2,000
Massachusetts	$2,000	Washington	$4,000
Michigan	$3,000	West Virginia	$5,000
Minnesota	$7,500	Wisconsin	$5,000
Mississippi	$2,500	Wyoming	$3,000
Missouri	$3,000		

* $6,000 in Marion County and Allen County
** $25,000 in Shelby County and Anderson County
Source: *Everybody's Guide to Small Claims Court*, by Ralph Warner (Nolo).

D. Before You File Your Lawsuit

Before you start your lawsuit by filing papers in small claims court, ask yourself some questions to figure out if a small claims court suit is right for you.

1. Do You Have a Good Case?

First, you want to be relatively sure of your legal position. You must have a valid legal basis for a lawsuit. Do you have a decent chance of proving in court that the defendant refused to pay a fair and just bill, or broke a contract or negligently damaged your property? If not, any talk about going to small claims court is just an idle threat that will hurt your credibility. *Everybody's Guide to Small Claims Court*, by Ralph Warner (Nolo), has a good chapter on how to analyze common types of cases, including breach of contract, personal injury, property damage and breach of warranty.

2. Can You Sue the Defendant in Your State?

If you conclude that your case is legally sound, next determine whether or not you can sue the defendant in your state. In legal terms, you must find out whether or not your state courts have jurisdiction over the defendant. Generally, you can sue in your state if the defendant resides there or regularly does business there.

If all your contacts with an out-of-state defendant have been by mail and telephone, and the defendant doesn't have an office, warehouse or sales staff in your state, you may not be able to sue that defendant in your local courts. You could sue in the defendant's home state, but unless it's right next door, it's probably more trouble than a small claims case is worth.

3. Can You Settle Out of Court?

Your next step is to call the other side to see if the matter can be settled without going to court. Mention that you're planning to go to court if the matter can't be resolved. The other side may decide to pay the claim or suggest terms for a fair settlement.

If the response to your call is negative, follow up with a demand letter in which you state your claim, demand payment by a certain date and again inform the other side that you'll go to court if the matter isn't promptly settled. In your letter, restate the facts in the dispute even though the other side knows them. That way, if you do go to court later, you can use the demand letter to show the judge that you made every reasonable effort to collect the bill. In some states, a demand letter is required before you can sue. In any state, it's a good idea. A sample letter is shown below.

SAMPLE DEMAND LETTER

```
December 12, 20__


Sonya Renaud
Chez Posh
54 Lakeshore Ave.
Seattle, WA

Dear Sonya:


It's been three months since I finished installing the sound system at your new
restaurant, Chez Posh. As you know, our deal was that you'd pay me $1,000 before I
started work, with the balance ($3,500) to be paid when the job was done. All I've
received so far is the down payment.

You've told me several times that the sound system works perfectly. But when I
press you for payment, you keep putting me off. As the owner of a small business, I
need a steady flow of cash to keep going. I'm making this final request for payment
before I take this matter to small claims court. Please bring me your check for
$3,500 by Thursday. If I don't receive it by then, I will file a lawsuit.


I think it's in your best interest to pay voluntarily. If I have to sue, I'm sure
the judge will order you to pay my court costs, as well as interest. Also, a law-
suit may hurt your credit—something a new business can't afford. So please bring
your check to me by Thursday.


Sincerely,


Bill Presley
Owner, King Sound Company
```

4. Could You Collect If You Win?

Before you actually file your papers, determine if you're likely to collect if you win. If you won't be able to collect, there's no point in throwing good money after bad in a small claims court lawsuit. If you think the defendant might not pay a small claims court judgment voluntarily, ask yourself these questions:

- Is the defendant employed? If so, usually it is fairly easy to collect from (garnish) the defendant's paycheck unless he or she has a very low income job or lots of other judgment creditors are already in line. However, you can't collect from a welfare, Social Security, unemployment, pension or disability check.
- Does he or she have a bank account? Do you know where? And are you confident that it will stay open? If so, you'll be able to collect the judgment from funds in the account.
- Does the defendant own a home or other real estate? If so, you can place a lien (legal claim)

on the property. The lien must be paid off when the property is sold. And if you want to go to a lot of trouble, you can force the sale of the property to pay the judgment if the defendant's equity exceeds prior debts (such as mortgages) and protected amounts called "statutory exemptions."

- Is the defendant a solvent business, or at least one with a positive cash flow? If so, you can probably collect a judgment.

If the defendant is unlikely to pay a judgment voluntarily and lacks a job, a bank account or other assets that you can go after to satisfy the judgment, you should probably forget about suing—unless you're reasonably sure the defendant will be solvent soon, as might be the case with a college student or someone who stands to inherit money. Although judgments can usually be collected for five to ten years, depending on the state (and can sometimes be renewed), a significant number of small claims judgments are never collected.

E. Figuring Out Whom to Sue

Normally, it makes sense to sue all defendants who are reasonably likely to be legally liable to you. This increases the chances of getting a collectible judgment from at least one person or business. For example, if a husband and wife purchased some merchandise for their house and owe you money, sue both of them—that is, name both of them as defendants in your lawsuit. Similarly, if an employee of a computer repair company damaged your equipment while repairing it, sue both the employee and the company.

When suing a business, check to see if it's a sole proprietorship, a partnership, a corporation or an LLC.

- If it's a sole proprietorship, the defendant would be "John Smith doing business as Smith Furniture Company."
- In a partnership, name all of the individual partners and also give the name of the partnership. For example: "Smith-Jones Software

Specialists, an Indiana partnership, John Smith and Ida Jones, jointly and severally."

- In the case of a corporation, name the corporation as the defendant: "Rackafrax Inc., a California corporation." The lawsuit papers can be served on the resident agent—the person designated by the corporation as the official recipient of lawsuit papers—or on one of several officers of the corporation.
- If it's a limited liability company, name the LLC, for example, Garth's Film Scores, LLC. As with a corporation, you can serve papers on the resident agent or LLC officer.

You may need to do a little research to find out who owns a business or what its correct legal name is. Check the county office that accepts filings of assumed or fictitious names. They'll tell you the owner or owners of a sole proprietorship. Corporate names and corporate assumed names are usually on file with the a state office such as the secretary of state's office.

Don't worry if you're not 100% accurate when you name a business or the owners in a lawsuit. In most states if you name a business defendant incorrectly (you sue Joe's Bar, which is owned by Abdul Irani), you can correct it in court. And in some states, such as Michigan, you can sue a business in small claims court in any name used in an advertisement, sign, invoice, sales slip, register tape, business card, contract or other communication or document used by the business.

F. Handling Your Small Claims Court Lawsuit

Small claims court is designed to be used without lawyers—that's one of its best features. You shouldn't have any trouble going it alone.

1. File Your Complaint

The first formal step in starting your small claims case is to fill out a form known as a "complaint" or "statement of claim" or "affidavit and claim." These forms are available from the court clerk. You'll write a brief statement (perhaps one or two sentences) describing your claim and why the defendant is liable. You'll also state how much money you're asking for. If you're suing on a written contract—as would be common if the defendant failed to pay a bill—you may be asked to attach a photocopy of the contract to the court papers. The court clerk will issue a document called a "summons," which informs the defendant that the suit has been filed and where and when to appear for the hearing.

2. Serve Your Papers

Every state has rules on how the defendant must be notified of a lawsuit. If you don't follow the rules carefully, the court cannot rule against the defendant. In many states, papers can be served on (delivered to) the defendant by registered or certified mail. Also in many states, the clerk's office takes care of sending the papers to the defendant, often by certified mail with a return receipt requested. If state law requires that the papers be given to the defendant in person (or if he or she refuses to accept certified mail), this can be done at modest cost by a private process server or by a public officer, such as a sheriff or marshal. Depending on the law in your state, you may be able to recover the costs of doing this only if you first try to serve the papers by mail.

About half of defendants refuse to accept registered or certified mail, so you'll probably have to turn to personal service a good deal of the time.

3. Prepare for Court

Many small claims cases involve only an unpaid bill, and there's no dispute about the amount owed. You may win such a case by default because the defendant doesn't bother to show up for the hearing. In more complicated cases, your success in court may turn on how well you prepare. You need to think carefully about how you're going to convince that judge that you're right.

Since there's lots of truth to the old saying that a picture is worth at least 1,000 words, bring pictures to court whenever possible.

> **EXAMPLE:** Rosalie, suing ABC Contractors for damage they did to her roof, brings photos showing the condition of her building before and after ABC workers damaged it.

You may be able to make a point effectively by preparing a drawing or chart. For a few dollars, you can pick up a huge piece of poster board on which you can create a chart or diagram with a felt tip pen. You can use a drawing to show how a room is laid out or how a complicated piece of machinery works. Judges, like everybody else, focus their attention on pictures, graphs and charts.

Incidentally, if your business provides custom goods or services, consider routinely taking pictures of your completed jobs and products. If you later must sue for an unpaid bill, this will make it more difficult for the customer to concoct a bogus claim that he or she failed to pay because the job was badly done. Another good technique is to include a request on every invoice that the customer notify you immediately if there is any problem with the goods or services. Then, if you have to sue to collect on an unpaid bill and the defendant shows up and says that there were problems with the goods or services, you can argue convincingly that the customer never complained before you pressed for payment.

It's almost always helpful to have an eyewitness testify on your behalf. In an undisputed case involving the collection of a bill, you or your bookkeeper can testify about past billings and how much the customer or supplier still owes. Be sure to have copies of the bills. In a contested case, you may want to line up appropriate witnesses. For example, if the unpaid bill is for your company's installation of a telephone system, you might arrange for the person who actually installed the system to come to court. You're entitled to subpoena witnesses, but usually you won't want to use that power to compel a reluctant witness to appear. A person who is hostile can do you more harm than good. A subpoena is useful, however, so that a friendly witness can show it to his or her employer and not have any problems getting off work to come to court.

You may want to present an expert opinion, such as an appraisal of a car repair. As long as it can easily be presented in written form, many states allow this type of evidence in the form of a letter, even though technically it's hearsay—a type of evidence that's not admissible in most other courts. This special treatment recognizes that it's not economic to have expert witnesses standing by in small claims court. If you're in doubt as to the rules in your state ask the court clerk.

> **EXAMPLE:** Cyril pays $3,000 to have Roxanne build some laminated countertops for his kitchenware shop. He later has to pay someone else $2,000 to repair the job because Roxanne botched it. Cyril sues Roxanne in small claims court to recover the extra $2,000 he had to pay. He contacts another countertop contractor to testify, as an expert witness, that the original job was well below usual standards.

Business records (including letters you sent the defendant) can be very useful at the hearing. Be prepared with all contracts and other records and papers that relate to the transaction involved in the lawsuit. It's better to come with too many papers than too few.

4. Present Your Case at the Court Hearing

Many small claims court defendants simply fail to show up for the trial. Normally, that means the plaintiff can probably get a judgment (by default) after briefly stating his or her case. A default judgment that grants you the relief you want is as valid as any other. But if the properly served defendant comes into court a few days later with a good reason for not showing up (illness, emergency business trip, transportation problems), the judge may be willing to set aside the default judgment and hold a new hearing. However, if the defendant waits more than a month to ask for relief, the judge probably won't grant the request.

In small claims court, the rules of evidence and procedure are informal. Especially if no lawyer is involved, each side simply stands and tells the judge its story and presents its witnesses and other evidence.

Begin your presentation by telling the judge in a sentence or two what the case is about, for example: "My company sells and installs telephone systems. We installed a system for Dr. Jones, a veterinarian. He owes us $2,800 and refuses to pay." Or: "We have a video rental store. Superior Decorating Service signed a contract to paint our store for $2,500. They didn't show up and we had to hire somebody else. It cost us $4,000 to complete the job."

After the short summary of the case, be prepared to lay out the important facts in chronological order. This will be much more helpful than a long rambling presentation that skips back and forth. During the hearing, you can present your photographs and drawings. Usually you do this by showing them to the other party and then handing them to the court clerk or bailiff to give to the judge. Most courts have blackboards if you need to improvise during the hearing.

Be sure to bring to court a copy of the demand letter you sent to the defendant and present it to the judge. This not only shows that you made a reasonable effort to resolve the dispute without a hearing in court, but is another way to present the facts as you see them.

Address your testimony to the judge, not to the other side. Avoid arguing with the other side. Often small claims judges interrupt and ask questions. Always respond directly to the point the judge is inquiring about; then go back to making your points. If the judge keeps interrupting and throws you off balance, politely ask for a moment to review your notes to be sure you've covered all key points. At the end of the case, it's appropriate to point out inconsistencies or fallacies in your opponent's testimony. But stick to the facts and never put your argument on a personal basis.

As you conclude your presentation, ask the judge to award you the amount you're suing for plus court costs. If you win, you're normally entitled to have the other side pay your filing fee, any fees for service of papers and any fees that you paid to witnesses you had to subpoena.

Judges sometimes give their decisions at the end of the hearing. It's also common for the judge to mail out a written decision a few days after the case has been heard. If the case goes against you, check out your appeal rights. (See Section H, below.)

G. Representing Yourself If You're the Defendant

If you receive small claims papers naming you as the defendant, read the papers carefully. In most states, a written answer is not required. You just show up in court and tell your story. When in doubt, call the court clerk or check the local rules. Also, based on your time and energy constraints, decide whether you want to hire a lawyer (lawyers are prohibited in a few states) or perhaps exercise your option to transfer the case to regular court where formal rules of evidence and procedure apply and you always have the right to be represented by a lawyer.

Consider calling the plaintiff with an offer to settle. Often the person suing will accept far less than the amount claimed in the complaint. If you do arrange for a compromise, be sure to get the lawsuit formally dismissed and get a written release from any further liability. Local practice varies, but a common phrase is that the lawsuit is "dismissed with prejudice." This means that the plaintiff can't sue you again over the same transaction.

If the case can't be compromised, think about filing a counterclaim. Suppose the Acme Rug Cleaning Company sues you for $500 for failing to pay them for cleaning the carpets in your office. Let's assume you had two reasons for not paying their bill. First, they did a terrible job of cleaning the rug, and, in your judgment, aren't entitled to any payment. Second, they destroyed an antique chair valued at $1,000. In addition to denying liability for the $500 cleaning bill, you may want to file a counterclaim for $1,000 for the ruined chair. If your counterclaim is over the limits of the small claims court, the case will be transferred from small claims to the regular court.

Even if you don't have much of a defense, it may pay you to show up in court if you wish to pay a judgment in installments. In a number of states, a judge can order a small claims judgment to be paid over time if you so request.

If you don't show up for a hearing, the plaintiff can get a default judgment. And if you, as a defendant, show up at a hearing but the plaintiff doesn't, you're entitled to have the case dismissed. If this happens, ask the judge to dismiss the case "with prejudice." As noted above, this means that the plaintiff can't start up the case against you later on. However, if the plaintiff had a good reason for not showing up in court, the judge may set a new hearing date and keep the case alive.

H. Appealing Small Claims Decisions

In a few states, one price you pay for going to small claims court is the loss of your right to appeal. In most, though, you can appeal a decision of a small claims court to a higher court. In some states, such as California and Massachusetts, only the defendant is permitted to appeal. Where an appeal is allowed, check with the court rules to see whether you're entitled to a complete new trial on the facts of what happened or whether the higher court simply reviews the small claims judgment to see if the judge applied the correct legal rules.

As a practical matter, the right to take an appeal may not be all that important. Especially in smaller cases, spending time on an appeal is usually not cost-effective.

I. Collecting Your Judgment

Winning a judgment in small claims court will make you feel good. But you haven't really won your case until the other side pays up. Fortunately, many individuals and most reputable businesses pay voluntarily after a judge renders a decision. People recognize that they've had their day in court and that an outsider (the judge) has determined they truly owe the money.

When the losing party does pay you, you must give that person a "satisfaction of judgment" form. This form is usually available from the court clerk and simply acknowledges that you've been paid. It helps the losing party maintain good credit. One word of caution: Don't sign a satisfaction of judgment form until you're sure you've been paid in full. Because the person who pays you may be tempted to stop payment on a personal check, wait until the check clears or insist on cash, a certified or cashier's check or a money order.

Unfortunately, a significant number of debtors refuse to pay even after a court enters a judgment against them. There are many ways that debtors can protect themselves and, in effect, become "judgment-proof." Many people who are not completely without assets are still beyond the reach of your efforts to collect from them. For example, a creditor can't legally take the food from a debtor's table, or the TV from his living room, or even (in many cases) the car from his driveway.

If the defendant (now called a "judgment debtor") has a job and a bank account, garnishment may be the answer if the defendant refuses to pay you. By filing certain forms with the court where you obtained your judgment, you can require the debtor's employer to pay the judgment out of wages, or the debtor's bank to pay it out of a bank account. If you garnish wages, you'll be able to obtain only a portion of the person's paycheck. You may have to go through repeated garnishments.

Judgments can also be collected from other sources. For example, you may be able to use the debtor's motor vehicles and real estate as a collection source. The procedure is called "attachment." But many types of property are exempt from attachment. For example, in many states a portion, or all, of the equity in a debtor's home is exempt under a "homestead" exemption. In Alaska this amount is $250,000; in Massachusetts, it's $100,000.

If the judgment debtor is a going business, you may be able to impose a "till tap"—that is, a right to collect a certain part of the daily receipts of the business. You'll have to check the procedures in your state.

If you don't know where a judgment debtor works or has assets, you can file forms requiring the person to come back into court and disclose these things to you. After being put under oath, the judgment debtor will have to reveal information that may lead to collection of the judgment, including:

- where he or she works and the amount of wages he or she receives
- the location and extent of bank accounts
- any personal property, such as stocks and bonds or cars
- real estate holdings, and
- business assets.

Then, through garnishment and other proceedings, you may be able to obtain enough money to satisfy your judgment. Most of the time, however, if you have to force the judgment debtor into court to disclose assets, you'll find yourself wasting a lot of valuable time with very little likelihood of ever getting full payment.

For more on debt collection, see Chapter 19.

LAW IN THE REAL WORLD
Big Pay-Off From Small Claims

Tim operates Tree Craft, a tree planting and trimming business. At the end of each year he writes off about $10,000 in bad debts—accounts that customers haven't paid after receiving numerous invoices and at least one phone contact. Since this is only 3% of Tim's total annual billings, he doesn't worry about it.

Jennifer, Tim's wife, who handles the books, decides she isn't going to put up with it any more. "The money for the winter vacation to Hawaii that we have never had is sitting in those deadbeats' pockets, and I'm going to do something about it," she declares.

She writes each debtor saying that small claims actions will be filed pronto if the check isn't in the mail PDQ. Much to Tim's surprise, 10% of the deadbeats pay. But he's really flabbergasted when, after the small claims cases are actually filed and papers served, another 20% pay. Even better, a further 10% pay at (or just before) the small claims hearing—some of them because Tim and Jennifer agree to reduce the bill slightly after listening to a hard luck story.

Although 20% of the defendants have moved and can't be reached and a few have gone bankrupt, wiping out their debt, Tim and Jennifer get judgments against the rest—many of whom don't show up in court. (Those that do they confront with photos showing Tim's good work.) Since most have real estate and don't want judgment liens filed, all but a few judgment-proof debtors pay up. The final tally is that Tree Craft collects all or part of the fee from over 60% of the nonpayers.

And later, when Jennifer sees Tim eyeing new pickup trucks, she laughs and says, "Forget it. You and I and the kids are spending two weeks in Hawaii—and we'll toast the deadbeats who made it all possible."

24

Lawyers and Legal Research

When you own or run a small business, you need lots of legal information. Lawyers, of course, are prime sources of this information, but if you bought all the needed information at their rates—$150 to $250 an hour—you'd quickly empty your bank account. Fortunately, as an intelligent business person, there are a number of efficient ways you can acquire on your own a good working knowledge of the legal principles and procedures necessary to start and run a small business.

But can you run your business without ever consulting a lawyer? Probably not. Lawyers do more than dispense legal information. They also offer strategic advice and apply sophisticated technical skills. How frequently you'll need professional help is hard to say. It depends on the nature of your business, the number of employees you hire, how many locations you have and the kinds of problems you run into with customers, suppliers, landlords, contractors, the government, the media, insurance companies and a host of other people and entities. Your challenge isn't to avoid lawyers altogether but rather to use them on a cost-effective basis.

Ideally, you should find a lawyer who's willing to serve as a legal coach and help you educate yourself. Then you can often negotiate legal transactions on your own and prepare preliminary drafts of documents, turning to your lawyer from time to time for advice, review and fine-tuning.

In working with a lawyer, remember that you're the boss. A lawyer, of course, has specialized training, knowledge, skill and experience in dealing with legal matters. But that's no reason for you to abdicate control over legal decision-making and how much time and money should be spent on a particular legal problem. Because you almost surely can't afford all the legal services that you'd benefit from, you need to set priorities. When thinking about a legal problem, ask yourself: "Can I do this myself?" "Can I do this myself with some help from a lawyer?" "Should I simply put this in my lawyer's hands?"

How a Business Lawyer Can Help You

Here's a brief checklist of ways that a lawyer can help you:

- Assist with the start-up of your business (review a partnership agreement or incorporation documents, for example).
- Look over a proposed lease.
- Analyze land use regulations in zoning ordinances and private title documents.
- Review employment agreements and sensitive employee terminations.
- Represent you before governmental bodies and help to cut through bureaucratic red tape.
- Assist you with "intellectual property" issues—patents, copyrights, trademarks, trade secrets and business names.
- Coach or represent you in lawsuits or arbitrations where the stakes are high or the legal issues particularly complex.
- Review or draft documents for the purchase or sale of a business or real estate.
- Check or draft estate planning documents—wills, trusts and powers of attorney.
- Advise on public offerings of corporate stock (compliance with Blue Sky laws).

A. How to Find the Right Lawyer

Locating a good lawyer for your small business may not be as easy as you think. The fact is that most lawyers lack in-depth experience in working for small businesses. Of about 900,000 lawyers in America today, probably fewer than 50,000 possess sufficient training and experience in small business law to be of real help to you.

1. Compile a List of Prospects

Don't expect to locate a good business lawyer by simply looking in the phone book, consulting a law directory or reading an advertisement. There's not enough information in these sources to help you make a valid judgment. Almost as useless are lawyer referral services operated by bar associations. Generally, these services make little attempt to evaluate a lawyer's skill and experience. They simply supply the names of lawyers who have listed with the service, often accepting the lawyer's own word for what types of skills he or she has.

A better approach is to talk to people in your community who own or operate truly excellent businesses. These people obviously understand quality in other ways, so why not in lawyers? Ask them who their lawyer is and what they think of that person. Ask them about other lawyers they've used and what led them to make a change. If you talk to half a dozen business people, chances are you'll come away with several good leads.

Other people who provide services to the business community can also help you identify lawyers you should consider. For example, speak to your banker, accountant, insurance agent and real estate broker. These people come into frequent contact with lawyers who represent business clients and are in a position to make informed judgments. Friends, relatives and business associates within your own company can also provide names of possible lawyers. But ask them specifically about lawyers who have had experience working for business clients and consider carefully whether they really know enough about business and human nature to know what they're talking about.

In some types of specialized businesses—software design, restaurants, plant nurseries—it can pay to work with a lawyer who already knows the field. That way you can take advantage of the fact that the lawyer is already fairly far up the learning curve. Besides having knowledge about a certain type of business, a specialist may have experience with specific types of legal problems; for example, a lawyer may have special expertise in zoning law, liquor licenses or intellectual property matters. Sometimes specialists charge a little more, but if their specialized information is truly valuable, it can be money well spent. Trade associations are often a good place to get referrals to specialists.

Here are a few other sources you can turn to for possible candidates in your search for a lawyer:

- The director of your state or local chamber of commerce may know of several business lawyers who have the kind of experience that you're looking for.
- A law librarian can help identify authors in your state who have written books or articles on business law.

- The director of your state's continuing legal education (CLE) program—usually run by a bar association, a law school or both—can identify lawyers who have lectured or written on business law for other lawyers. Someone who's a "lawyer's lawyer" presumably has the extra depth of knowledge and experience to do a superior job for you—but may charge more.

- The chairperson of a state or county bar committee for business lawyers may be able to point out some well-qualified practitioners in your vicinity.

Once you have the names of several lawyers, a good source of more information about them is the *Martindale-Hubbell Law Directory*, available at most law libraries and some local public libraries. This resource contains biographical sketches of most practicing lawyers and information about their experience, specialties, education and the professional organizations they belong to. Many firms also list their major clients in the directory—an excellent indication of the types of practice the firm is engaged in. In addition, almost every lawyer listed in the directory, whether or not he or she purchased space for a biographical sketch, is rated "AV," "BV" or "CV." These ratings come from confidential opinions that *Martindale-Hubbell* solicits from lawyers and judges. The first letter is for "Legal Ability," which is rated as follows:

"A"—Very High to Preeminent

"B"—High to Very High

"C"—Fair to High

The "V" part stands for "Very High General Recommendation," meaning that the rated lawyer adheres to professional standards of conduct and ethics. But it's practically meaningless because lawyers who don't qualify for it aren't rated at all.

(*Martindale-Hubbell* prudently cautions that the absence of a rating shouldn't be construed as a reflection on the lawyer; some lawyers ask that their rating not be published, and there may be other reasons for the absence of a rating.)

I believe that the rating system works remarkably well. Don't make it your sole criterion for deciding on a potential lawyer for your business, but be reasonably confident that a lawyer who gets high marks from other business clients and an "AV" rating from *Martindale-Hubbell* knows what he or she is doing.

You can reach *Martindale-Hubbell* online at www.martindale.com. Another excellent source of information about lawyers is West's Legal Directory at www.lawoffice.com.

2. Shop Around

After you get the names of several good prospects, shop around. If you announce your intentions in advance, most lawyers will be willing to speak to you for a half hour or so at no charge so that you can size them up and make an informed decision. Look for experience, personal rapport and accessibility. Some of these characteristics will be apparent almost immediately. Others may take longer to discover. So even after you've hired a lawyer who seems right for you, keep open the possibility that you may have to make a change later.

Pay particular attention to the rapport between you and your lawyer. No matter how experienced and well recommended a lawyer is, if you feel uncomfortable with that person during your first meeting or two, you may never achieve an ideal lawyer-client relationship. Trust your instincts and seek a lawyer whose personality is compatible with your own.

Your lawyer should be accessible when you need legal services. Unfortunately, the complaint logs of all law regulatory groups indicate that many lawyers are not. If every time you have a problem there's a delay of several days before you can talk to your lawyer on the phone or get an appointment, you'll lose precious time, not to mention sleep. And almost nothing is more aggravating to a client than to leave a legal project in a lawyer's hands and then have weeks or even months go by without anything happening. You want a lawyer who will work hard on your behalf and follow through promptly on all assignments.

Try to find a lawyer who seems interested in your business and either already knows a lot about your field or who seems genuinely eager to learn more about it. Avoid the lawyer who's aloof and doesn't want to get involved in learning the nitty-gritty details of what you do.

Some lawyers are nitpickers who get unnecessarily bogged down in legal technicalities. They point out a million reasons why something can't be done. Meanwhile, a valuable business opportunity slips away. You want a lawyer who blends legal technicalities with a practical approach—someone who figures out a way to do something, not one who offers reasons why it can't be done.

B. Fees and Bills

When you hire a lawyer, have a clear understanding about how fees will be computed. And as new jobs are brought to the lawyer, ask specifically about charges for each. Many lawyers initiate fee discussions, but others forget or are shy about doing so. Bring up the subject yourself. Insist that the ground rules be clearly established. In California, all fee agreements between lawyers and clients must be in writing if the expected fee is $1,000 or more, or is contingent on the outcome of a lawsuit. Perhaps this will be common everywhere soon.

1. How Lawyers Charge

There are four basic ways that lawyers charge. The first is by the hour. In most parts of the United States, you can get competent services for your small business for $150 to $250 an hour.

Sometimes a lawyer quotes a flat fee for a specific job. For example, the lawyer may offer to draw up a real estate purchase agreement for $300. Or to represent you before a state licensing board for

$3,000. You pay the same amount regardless of how much time the lawyer spends.

In some cases, a lawyer may charge a contingent fee. This is a percentage (such as 33⅓%) of the amount the lawyer obtains for you in a negotiated settlement or through a trial. If the lawyer recovers nothing for you, there's no fee. However, the lawyer does generally expect reimbursement for out-of-pocket expenses, such as filing fees, long distance phone calls and transcripts of testimony. Contingent fees are common in personal injury lawsuits but relatively unusual in small business cases.

Finally, you may be able to hire a lawyer for a flat annual fee (retainer) to handle all of your routine legal business. You'll usually pay in equal monthly installments and, normally, the lawyer will bill you an additional amount for extraordinary services—such as representing you in a major lawsuit. Obviously, the key to making this arrangement work is to have a written agreement clearly defining what's routine and what's extraordinary.

Comparison shopping among lawyers will help you avoid overpaying. But the cheapest hourly rate isn't necessarily the best. A novice who charges only $80 an hour may take three hours to review a consultant's work-for-hire contract. A more experienced lawyer who charges $200 an hour may do the same job in half an hour and make better suggestions. Take into account the lawyer's knowledge in your field, his or her reputation and personal rapport.

2. Ways to Save on Legal Fees

There are many ways to hold down the cost of legal services. Here's a summary.

- *Group together your legal affairs.* You'll save money if you consult with your lawyer on several matters at one time. For example, in a one-hour conference, you may be able to review the annual updating of your corporate record book, renewing your lease and a noncompetition agreement you've drafted for new employees to sign.

- *Help out.* You or your employees can do a lot of work yourselves. Help gather documents needed for a real estate transaction. Line up witnesses for a trial. Write the first couple of drafts of a contract; give your lawyer the relatively inexpensive task of reviewing and polishing the document.

- *Ask the lawyer to be your coach.* Make it clear that you're eager to do as much work as possible yourself with the lawyer coaching you from the sidelines. Many lawyers find it gratifying to impart their knowledge and experience to others, but they're used to clients who simply drop their problems on the lawyer's desk to solve. Unless you specifically ask for coaching, you may never tap into your lawyer's ability to help you in that way.

- *Read trade journals in your field.* They'll help you keep up with specific legal developments that your lawyer may have missed. Send pertinent clippings to your lawyer—this can dramatically reduce legal research time—and encourage your lawyer to do the same for you.

- *Show that you're an important client.* The single most important thing you can do to tell your lawyer how much you value the relationship is to pay your bills on time. Also, let your lawyer know about plans for expansion and your company's possible future legal needs. And if your business wins an award or otherwise is recognized as being a leader in its field, let your lawyer know about it—everyone feels good when an enterprise they're associated with prospers. Also, let your lawyer know when you recommend him or her to your business colleagues.

- *Use nonlawyer professionals.* Often, nonlawyer professionals perform some tasks better and at less cost than lawyers. For example, look to management consultants for strategic business planning; real estate brokers or appraisers for valuation of properties; accoun-

tants for preparation of financial proposals; insurance agents for advice on insurance protection; and CPAs for the preparation of tax returns. Each of these concerns is likely to have a legal aspect, and you may eventually want to consult your lawyer, but normally you won't need to until you've gathered information on your own.

A tax tip. *If you visit your lawyer on a personal legal matter (such as reviewing a contract for the purchase of a house) and you also discuss a business problem (such as a commercial lawsuit you've been threatened with), ask your lawyer to allocate the time spent and send you separate bills. At tax time, you can easily list the business portion as a tax-deductible business expense.*

C. Problems With Your Lawyer

Relations between lawyers and clients are not always perfect. If you see a problem emerging, nip it in the bud. Don't just sit back and fume; call, visit or write to your lawyer. The problem won't get resolved if your lawyer doesn't even know there's a problem. Sure, it's hard to confront someone whom you may need to rely on for future help and advice—but an open exchange is essential for a healthy lawyer-client relationship.

Whatever it is that rankles, have an honest discussion about your feelings. Maybe you're upset because your lawyer hasn't kept you informed about what's going on in your case or has failed to meet a promised deadline. Or maybe last month's bill was shockingly high or lacked any breakdown of how your lawyer's time was spent.

One good test of whether a lawyer-client relationship is a good one is to ask yourself if you feel able to talk freely with your lawyer about your degree of participation in any legal matter and your control over how the lawyer carries out a legal assignment.

If you can't frankly discuss these sometimes sensitive matters with your lawyer, get another lawyer. Otherwise, you'll surely waste money on unnecessary legal fees and risk having legal matters turn out badly. Remember that you're always free to change lawyers and to get all important documents back from a lawyer you no longer employ.

Your Rights As a Client

As a client, it's reasonable to expect that you'll:
- be treated courteously by your lawyer and the members of his or her staff
- receive an itemized statement of services rendered and a full explanation of billing practices
- be charged reasonable fees
- receive a prompt response to phone calls and letters
- have confidential legal conferences, free from unwarranted interruptions
- be kept informed of the status of your case
- have your legal matters handled diligently and competently, and
- receive clear answers to all relevant questions.

If any of these expectations aren't met, consider going elsewhere for legal services.

D. Do-It-Yourself Legal Research

Law libraries are chock full of valuable information—information that you can easily ferret out on your own. All you need is a rudimentary knowledge of how the information is organized.

1. Finding a Law Library

Your first step is to find a law library that's open to the public. You may find such a library in your county courthouse or at your state capitol. Public law schools generally permit the public to use their libraries, and some private law schools grant access to their libraries—sometimes for a modest user fee. The reference department of a major public library may have a fairly decent legal research collection. If you're lucky enough to have access to several law libraries, select one that has a reference librarian to assist you.

Finally, don't overlook the law library in your own lawyer's office. Most lawyers, on request, will gladly share their books with their clients.

Legal Research: How to Find & Understand the Law, *by Stephen Elias & Susan Levinkind (Nolo). A nontechnical book written for the average person and covering basic legal materials. Among other things, it explains how to use all major legal research tools and helps you frame your research questions.*

2. Federal and State Law

Every business is governed by both federal law and state law. If yours is a typical small business, you'll be concerned primarily with state law. For example, the law dealing with how you form a sole proprietorship, partnership or corporation is almost entirely based on state sources, as is the law controlling buying a business, leasing space, hiring employees, forming contracts and resolving disputes through arbitration or small claims court. Federal law deals with federal taxes, trademarks, consumer protection and equal opportunity standards. In some areas of business (such as consumer protection and equal opportunity legislation) federal and state laws may overlap.

3. Primary and Secondary Sources

In doing legal research, you'll refer to both primary and secondary sources. Primary sources are statements of the law itself, including:

- *Constitutions* (federal and state)
- *Legislation* (laws—also called statutes or ordinances—passed by Congress, your state legislature and local governments)
- *Administrative rules and regulations* (issued by federal and state administrative agencies charged with implementing statutes)
- *Case law* (decisions of federal and state courts interpreting statutes—and sometimes making law, known as "common law," if the subject isn't covered by a statute).

A small business rarely gets involved in questions of constitutional law. You're far more likely to be concerned with law created by a federal or state statute, or by an administrative rule or regulation. At the federal level, that includes the Internal Revenue Code and regulations adopted by the Internal Revenue Service; regulations dealing with advertising, warranties and other consumer matters adopted by the Federal Trade Commission; and equal opportunity statutes such as Title VII of the Civil Rights Act administered by the Justice Department and Equal Employment Opportunities Commission. At the state level, you'll likely be interested in statutes dealing with licensing, partnership law, corporate law, commercial transactions (your state's version of the Uniform Commercial Code), employment matters and court procedures. You may also need to get into local laws dealing with zoning, health and building and safety regulations.

Depending on the type of business you have, you may also want to research statutes and regulations dealing with other legal topics such as the environment, labor relations, product liability, real estate, copyrights and so on.

4. How to Begin

Obviously, primary sources—statements of the "raw law"—are important. But most legal research begins with secondary sources—books that comment on, organize or describe primary materials.

It often makes sense to start with one of the two national encyclopedias, *American Jurisprudence 2d* (cited as *AmJur2d*) or *Corpus Juris Secundum* (cited as *CJS*). If your state has its own encyclopedia, check that too. These encyclopedias organize the case law and some statutes into narrative statements organized alphabetically by subject. Through citations in footnotes, you can locate the cases and statutes themselves.

It's also helpful if you can find a treatise on the subject you're researching. A treatise is simply a book (or series of books) that covers a specific area of law. I've always been impressed by the Nutshell Series published by West Publishing Co. You may want to look at *Contracts in a Nutshell*, by Claude D. Rohwer & Gordon D. Schaber, and *The Law of Corporations in a Nutshell*, by Robert W. Hamilton.

Law reviews published by law schools and other legal periodicals may also contain useful summaries of the law. The *American Bar Association Journal* as well as the journal published by your state bar association should be available in the law library that you use. In these journals, you'll often find well-written and timely articles on legal issues that affect small businesses. You can locate law review and bar journal articles through *The Index to Legal Periodicals*. Be warned, however, that law school reviews contain articles by law professors and students, and are of more academic than practical interest.

I highly recommend *The Practical Lawyer*, published by the Joint Committee on Continuing Legal Education of the American Law Institute and American Bar Association (ALI-ABA). Each edition contains half a dozen clear and practical articles—many of which address topics of interest to small businesses. The checklists and forms are superb. This resource is virtually unknown outside the legal profession. If you get hooked on the law, consider subscribing.

Finally, practically every state has an organization that provides continuing legal education to practicing lawyers. Especially in the more populous states, these organizations publish excellent books on business law subjects which, unlike nationally published treatises, focus on the law in your state and contain state-specific forms and checklists. You can also find a wealth of relevant information in the course materials prepared for continuing legal education seminars.

5. Online Research

For the computer savvy, online research can be speedy and inexpensive.

Be sure to stop at Nolo's own site, www.nolo.com, where you'll discover valuable online information, including loads of material on small business law and legal research links.

Lawyers who do computer research rely primarily on two systems—Westlaw and Lexis. A small but growing number of public law libraries offer these services. Those that do offer them usually require a sizable advance or a credit card; you pay as you go. Ask a law librarian for details, but be prepared for sticker shock. You can end up paying as much as $300 an hour.

It's more practical to use other online sources which cost you nothing other than the usual charges for online access time. For an introduction to the vast amount of cyber-info that's out there, you might sample these sites:

- Lawyers Weekly at www.lawyersweeklyusa.com. Here you'll find up-to-date news on a wide range of legal topics.

- Martindale-Hubbell at www.lawyers.com. As with the martindale.com site described in Section A, this site will help you locate a lawyer, but it contains other very helpful features as well. For example, by clicking on "Ask a Lawyer," you can pose a question of general interest and receive an online answer from a practitioner on Martindale-Hubbell's panel. Or you can browse fascinating articles on current legal topics.

- Findlaw, at www.findlaw.com. Their business section has a number of interesting articles and guides, as well as useful forms and checklists for business use.

- The Thomas Legislative Information site at http://thomas.loc.gov. Named for Thomas Jefferson, this site contains a wealth of information on bills pending in Congress and laws recently adopted.

- Lectric Law Library at www.lectlaw.com. This is a good place to explore a wide range of business law issues. Many business law topics are covered in reasonable depth.

- The Internal Revenue Service at www.irs.gov. You can download tax forms, instructions and a wide range of IRS publications.

- National Federation of Independent Business at www.nfibonline.com. If you want to check on small business news and get practical tips, try this site.

- U.S. Small Business Administration at www.sbaonline.sba.gov. Here you'll find information on starting and financing your small business.

Tips for Researching Business Law

- When looking up statutes, use an annotated version. It comes in a multi-volume set and contains the laws themselves plus references to court and administrative decisions interpreting the statutes and often to treatises and articles that discuss the law.

- Statutes are frequently amended. Always check the pocket-part supplement at the back of statute (code) books to make sure you have the latest edition.

- When you look up a state court decision (case), use the regional reporter published by West Publishing Co. if it's available. Before the text of the case begins, an ingenious system of notes (called the "key number" system) helps you tap into other similar cases. Ask the reference librarian to explain, or consult one of the books on legal research referred to earlier.

- Use the Shepard Citation system to see if and where the court case you're looking at has been relied on, discounted or overruled by a later court. *Legal Research: How to Find & Understand the Law,* by Stephen Elias & Susan Levinkind (Nolo), has a good, easy-to-follow explanation of how to use the Shepard's system.

- A relatively unknown resource for quickly locating state business laws is the United States Law Digest volume of the *Martindale-Hubbell Law Directory*. There's a handy summary of laws, including statutory citations, for each state. Dozens of business law topics are covered, including Commercial Code, Consumer Protection, Corporations, Employer and Employee, Insurance, Landlord and Tenant, Leases, Partnership, Principal and Agent, Real Property, Statute of Frauds and Trademarks, Trade Names and Service Marks. But you may need a magnifying glass: the print is minuscule.

- The Gigalaw site at www.gigalaw.com specializes in Internet law issues—perfect if you're considering taking your business online.

- Findlaw at www.findlaw.com is well named. Here you'll find a rich collection of forms, articles and links to statutes and court decisions. Be sure to visit the business section.

Appendix A

STATE OFFICES THAT PROVIDE SMALL BUSINESS START-UP HELP

Alabama
Department of Revenue
Sales, Use & Business Tax Division,
Severance & License Section
50 Ripley Street
Montgomery, AL 36132
334-353-7827
www.ador.state.al.us/licenses/index.html

Alaska
Department of Community and
Economic Development
Division of Occupational Licensing
333 Willoughby Ave., 9th Floor,
State Office Bldg.
Juneau, AK 99801
907-465-2534
www.state.ak.us/local/bus1.html

Arizona
Department of Commerce
Business Connection
3800 N. Central Ave., Ste. 1500
Phoenix, AZ 85012
602-280-1480
www.azcommerce.com/smallbus

Arkansas
Department of Economic Development
One Capitol Mall
Little Rock, AR 72201
501-682-1060
www.aedc.state.ar.us

California
Office of Small Business
Department of Commerce
801 K Street, Suite 1700
Sacramento, CA 95814
800-303-6600, 916-322-5790
www.ss.ca.gov/business/resources.htm

Colorado
Small Business Development Center
1625 Broadway, Suite 1700
Denver, CO 80202
303-892-3840, 800-333-7798
www.state.co.us/gov_dir/oed

Connecticut
Connecticut Economic Resource Center, Inc.
805 Brook Street Bldg. #4
Rocky Hill, CN 06067
800-392-2122
www.ct-clic.com/business/business.htm

Delaware
Division of Revenue
820 North French Street
P.O. Box 2340
Wilmington, DE 19899-2340
302-577-5800
www.state.de.us/revenue/obt/obtmain.htm

District of Columbia
Department of Consumer and Regulatory
Affairs
941 North Capitol Street, NE
Washington, DC 20002
202-442-4515
http://dcra.dc.gov

Florida
Enterprise Florida, Inc. (EFI)
390 North Orange Ave.
Suite 1300
Orlando, FL 32801
407-316-4600
www.eflorida.com

Georgia
Secretary of State
First Stop Business Information Center
Suite 315, West Tower
2 Martin Luther King, Jr. Drive
Atlanta, GA 30334
404-656-7061
800-656-4558
www.sos.state.ga.us/FirstStop

Hawaii
Department of Commerce and
Consumer Affairs
Business Registration Division
1010 Richards Street
Honolulu, HI 96813
808-586-2744
www.businessregistrations.com

Idaho
Economic Development Division
Department of Commerce
P.O. Box 83720
Boise, ID 83720-0093
208-334-2470
www.idoc.state.id.us

Illinois
Department of Commerce and
Community Affairs
100 West Randolph St., Suite 3-400
Chicago, IL 60601
312-814-7179
www.commerce.state.il.us/doingbusiness/
First_Stop/Permits.htm

Indiana
Community Development Division
Department of Commerce
One North Capitol, Suite 700
Indianapolis, IN 46204-2288
317-232-8800
www.in.gov/doc/businesses/index.html

Iowa
Bureau of Small Business Development
Department of Economic Development
200 East Grand Avenue
Des Moines, IA 50309
800-532-1216* 515-242-4750
www.state.ia.us

Kansas
Division of Business Development
1000 SW Jackson, Suite 100
Topeka, KN 66612
785-296-5298
www.accesskansas.org

Kentucky
Cabinet for Economic Development Business
Information Clearinghouse
2200 Capitol Plaza Tower
Frankfort, KY 40601
800-626-2250* 502-564-4252 x4317
www.edc.state.ky.us

Louisiana
Secretary of State
First Stop Shop Division
P.O. Box 94125
Baton Rouge, LA 70804-9125
800-259-0001
www.sec.state.la.us/comm/fss-index

Maine
Business Development Division
Department of Economic and Community
Development
59 State House Station
Augusta, ME 04333
800-872-3838* 207-624-9804
www.econdevmaine.com

Maryland
Department of Business Development and
Employment Development
217 East Redwood Street
Baltimore, MD 21202-3316
410-767-6300
www.blis.state.md.us

Massachusetts
Office of Business Development
10 Park Plaza, Ste. 8720
Boston, MA 02108
617-727-3206, 800-5-CAPITAL
www.mass.gov

Michigan
Economic Development Corp.
300 N. Washington Square
Lansing, MI 48913
517-373-9808
www.mi.gov/emi

Minnesota
Small Business Assistance Office
Department of Trade and Economic
Development
500 Metro Square Building
121 E. 7th Place
St. Paul, MN 55101-2146
800-657-3858, 651-282-2103
www.dted.state.mn.us/01x00f.asp

Mississippi
Development Authority
P.O. Box 849
Jackson, MS 39205-0849
601-359-3593
www.mississippi.org

Missouri
Department of Economic Development
Business Assistance Center
301 West High St., Rm. 720
P.O. Box 118
Jefferson City, MO 65102-0118
888-751-2863
www.ecodev.state.mo.us/mbac

Montana
Department of Commerce
Small Business Development Center
P.O. Box 200505
Helena, MT 59620-0505
406-841-2747
http://commerce.state.mt.us

Nebraska
Department of Economic Development
301 Centennial Mall South
P.O. Box 94666
Lincoln, NE 68509-4666
402-471-3111 800-426-6505
www.neded.org

Nevada
Department of Business and Industry
555 E. Washington
Suite 4900
Carson City, NV 89701
775-486-2758
http://dbi.state.nv.us

New Hampshire
Small Business Development Center
670 N. Commercial St.
Manchester, NH 03101
603-624-2000
www.nhsbdc.org

New Jersey
Division of Revenue
225 West State Street
Trenton, NJ 08608-1001
609-292-9292
www.state.nj.us/njbiz

New Mexico
Economic Development Department
1100 St. Francis Drive
Santa Fe, NM 87503
505-827-0300
www.edd.state.nm.us

New York
Governor's Office of Regulatory Reform
Governor Alfred E. Smith Bldg.
P.O. Box 7027, 17th Floor
Albany, NY 12225
800-342-3464
518-474-8275
www.gorr.state.ny.us/gorr/startbus

North Carolina
Department of the Secretary of State
Business License Information
P.O. Box 29622
Raleigh, NC 27626-0622
919-807-2166
800-228-8433
www.secretary.state.nc.us/blio

North Dakota
Business Information Center
700 E. Main, 2nd Floor
P.O. Box 5509
Bismarck, ND 58506
701-328-5850
www.discovernd.net/business

Ohio
Small Business Development Center
37 North High Street
Columbus, OH 43215-3065
614-225-6910
www.ohiosbdc.org

Oklahoma
Tax Commission
2501 North Lincoln Blvd.
Oklahoma City, OK 73194
Connors Bldg., Capitol Complex
405-521-3160
www.oktax.state.ok.us/oktax/busreg.html

Oregon
Business Information Center
Public Service Bldg., Suite 151
255 Capitol St. NE
Salem, OR 93710-1327
503-986-2200
www.sos.state.or.us

Pennsylvania
Department of Community and Economic
Development
Center for Entrepreneurial Assistance
Commonwealth Keystone Bldg.
400 North St., 4th Floor
Harrisburg, PA 17120-0225
800-280-3801
717-783-5700
www.inventpa.com

Puerto Rico
Commonwealth Department of Commerce,
Box S
4275 Old San Juan Station
San Juan, PR 00905
809-721-3290
www.puertorico.com

Rhode Island
Economic Development Corp
One West Exchange St.
Providence, RI 02903
401-222-2601
www.riedc.com/sab/sabframe.htm

South Carolina
Small Business Development Center
1705 College St.
Columbia, SC 29208
803-777-5118
http://sbdcweb.badm.sc.edu

South Dakota
Governor's Office
of Economic Development
Capital Lake Plaza
711 East Wells Avenue
Pierre, SD 57501-3369
800-872-6190, 605-773-5032
www.sdgreatprofits.com/start-up/resource.htm

Tennessee
Department of Economic and Community
Development
312 8th Avenue North
11th Floor
William R. Snodgrass TN Tower
Nashville, TN 37243-0405
615-741-2626
www.state.tn.us/ecd/res_guide.htm

Texas
Department of Economic Development
1700 North Congress
SFA Building
Austin, TX 78711
512-936-0100
www.tded.state.tx.us

Utah
Department of Community and Economic
Development
324 South State St., Suite 500
Salt Lake City, UT 84111
801-538-8700
www.dced.state.ut.us/nav/library/bizutah/
title.htm

Vermont
Department of Economic Development
National Life Bldg., Drawer 20
Montpelier, VT 05620-0501
800-VERMONT
802-828-3080
www.thinkvermont.com/start/index.cfm

Virginia
Department of Business Assistance
Department of Economic Development
P.O. Box 446
1021 E. Cary Street
11th Floor
Richmond, VA 23218-4446
804-371-8200
www.yesvirginia.org/smallbuscorner.asp

Washington
Department of Licensing
Master License Service (MLS)
405 Black Lake Blvd., Bldg. 2
P.O. Box 9034
Olympia, WA 98507-9034
360-664-1400
http://access.wa.gov

West Virginia
Secretary of State
1900 Kanawha Blvd. E., Bldg. 1, Suite 157-K
Charleston, WV 25305-0770
304-558-8000
www.wvsos.com/common/startbusiness.htm

Wisconsin
Department of Commerce
PO Box 7970
201 West Washington Avenue
Madison, WI 53707
800-HELPBUS* 608-266-1018
www.commerce.state.wi.us

Wyoming
Small Business Development Center
P.O. Box 3922
Laramie, WY 82071-3922
307-766-3505
www.uwyo.edu/sbdc/starting.html

---

*In-state calling only.

Appendix B

FEDERAL TRADE COMMISSION OFFICES

Headquarters
Federal Trade Commission
6th and Pennsylvania Avenue, NW
Washington, DC 20580
202-326-3175
www.ftc.gov

Regional Offices
Western Region
10877 Wilshire Boulevard, Suite 700
Los Angeles, CA 90024

Western Region
901 Market Street, Suite 570
San Francisco, CA 94103

Southeast Region
225 Peachtree Street, NE
Atlanta, GA 30303

Midwest Region
55 East Monroe Street, Suite 1860
Chicago IL 60603

Northwest Region
1 Bowling Green
New York, NY 10004

East Central Region
1111 Superior Avenue, Suite 200
Cleveland, OH 44114

Southwest Region
1999 Bryan St., Suite 2150
Dallas, TX 75201

Northwest Region
2896 Federal Building
915 Second Avenue
Seattle, WA 98174

Index

M

N

O

Renewal options, leases, 13/7
Rent
    methods of calculating, 13/5–6, 13/8–9, 13/17
    withholding, 13/16–17, 13/19
Rental agreements, 13/2–3. *See also* Leases
Renter's insurance, 12/8, 12/17, 13/12
Reorganizing a business. *See* Chapter 11 bankruptcy; Chapter 12 bankruptcy; Chapter 13 bankruptcy
Replacement cost coverage, 12/7
Rescission of contracts, 17/6–8, 20/5, 20/20
Resident agent, 3/11, 4/8
Retained earnings, 1/5
Retainers, 19/2–3, 24/5
Retention letters, 19/3
Retirement plans
    corporations, 1/19
    general partnerships, 1/5, 1/10
    sole proprietorships, 1/5
    as source of start-up funds, 9/10–11
Return and repair policies, 16/6, 17/17
Revised Uniform Partnership Act (RUPA), 1/8, 2/2
Right of first refusal, 2/10, 5/3, 13/16
Right to force a sale provision, sales agreements, 5/5
RLLPs. *See* Registered limited liability partnerships (RLLPs)
Royalties, franchises, 11/16

S

SAEGIS, 6/15
Safety and health issues, 7/5, 12/15–16, 15/29–30
Salary, as source of start-up funds, 9/8. *See also* Compensation
Sales agreements
    when buying a business, 10/5, 10/15–23
    when selling a business, 10/26–27
Sales taxes, 7/5
Satisfaction of judgment forms, small claims court, 23/12
Savings, as source of start-up funds, 9/9, 9/10–11
SBA. *See* Small Business Administration (SBA)
SCORE. *See* Service Corps of Retired Executives (SCORE)
S corporations
    advantages and disadvantages, 1/3
    electing tax status as, 1/14, 3/4, 3/17, 8/6–7
    fringe benefits, 1/18, 3/7
    profit/loss distribution, 1/23
    and self-employment tax, 1/25, 4/6
    taxation, 1/13–15, 1/17, 1/25, 8/7, 8/8
    tax year, 3/17, 8/4
    terminating S corporation status, 8/7
    vs. LLCs, 1/25

Section 179 deductions, 8/15
Secured creditors, 19/9–10, 21/16, 21/17, 21/19, 21/20, 21/21, 21/22
Secured loans, 9/5, 9/16–17, 20/15, 21/4
Securities and Exchange Commission (SEC), 1/20, 7/4
Securities laws
    corporations, 3/2, 3/7, 3/15, 9/8
    limited partnerships, 9/8
    LLCs, 4/4
Security agreements, when buying a business, 10/18, 10/24, 10/27
Security deposits, leases, 13/9
Self-employment taxes, 1/25, 4/6, 8/12–13
Self-insurance, 12/2, 12/10, 12/16, 15/30
Selling a business, 10/24–27
    corporations, 1/20, 10/25, 10/26, 10/27
    financially troubled businesses, 21/13–15
    franchises, 11/6
    LLCs, 4/4, 4/9, 10/26
    sales agreement, 10/26–27
    sellers retained as consultants, 10/17, 10/23, 10/27
Separate property, 21/4
Service businesses
    contracts, 20/12
    credit policies, 19/2–3
    warranties, 17/9
Service Corps of Retired Executives (SCORE), 9/13
Service marks, 6/2, 6/10–11. *See also* Trademarks
Services
    as partnership contribution, 2/5
    stock issued in return for, 3/5
Set-dollar valuation method, 2/11
Settlements, 22/2–3, 22/9, 23/6, 23/11
Sexual harassment, 15/24–25
Sexual orientation discrimination, 15/26
Shareholder representation letters, 3/15–16
Shareholders
    annual meeting, 3/3, 3/13, 3/19
    consenting to sale of corporate assets, 10/5
    corporate role of, 3/3–4
    income taxes, 1/5, 1/13, 1/15–16
    loans to corporation, 3/6–7
    profit/loss distribution, 1.23. *See also* Dividends
Shareholders' agreements, 5/7
Shopping center leases, 13/8, 13/17–18
Signatures
    corporate officers, 3/20, 20/14–15
    leases, 13/4–5
    LLC members/managers, 4/14, 20/14
    partnerships, 20/14
    for receipt of goods or services, 19/8

Here are answers to the most frequently asked questions about Registered Agent and ComplianceWatch®

1. Q. What is a Registered Agent?

A. It is an "agent" of the corporation or Limited Liability Company (LLC) who is officially "registered" with the state to be responsible for receiving and forwarding vital legal documents, such as tax forms and notice of litigation (also known as service of process or SOP), on behalf of your corporation or LLC.

Most states require corporations and Limited Liability Companies (LLCs) to designate and maintain a Registered Agent to receive and forward this correspondence on behalf of your company. The Registered Agent for your corporation or LLC must be located at a legal address (not a PO Box) within that state, hence they are sometimes referred to as a "Resident" Agent.

2. Q. What are the benefits of having a third party Registered Agent?

A. Most business owners choose a third party to serve in this critical capacity. There are several good reasons for this, including:

◆ If you are frequently out of the office and no one is available during regular business hours to receive notice of litigation on your behalf, you could be defaulted for failing to answer a claim in a timely manner.

◆ If you aren't sure your address will stay the same in the future, having a Registered Agent allows you to change the location of your company easily without filing a costly change of address with the state.

◆ A third party Registered Agent offers a layer of privacy, protecting you from publicly being served litigation papers while in the presence of customers and employees.

3. Q. Why choose The Company Corporation® for my Registered Agent Service?

A. Most importantly, we will forward, via FedEx®, a notice of litigation when it arrives in our office. This notice details who is suing you, in what court, when process was served, the nature of the case and how much time you have to respond.

We also will receive and forward official state and federal documents as well as state franchise tax or annual reports when required.

The Company Corporation's® Registered Agent Service also includes ComplianceWatch®, a FREE online service that notifies you when critical corporate activities are due.

If you file a Change of Agent form with your state, you must send a copy of the document to The Company Corporation® to officially cancel your Registered Agent Service.

4. Q. How does ComplianceWatch® help me maintain my corporate status?

A. Other service companies simply help only with incorporating or forming the LLC. ComplianceWatch® helps manage the ongoing legal formalities associated with your corporate entity.

This service, offered exclusively by The Company Corporation®, helps protect your personal assets by keeping your business on track in a number of key ways:

◆ state-specific features help assure accurate record-keeping and reporting compliance

◆ automatic notification when it's time to file annual reports, pay franchise taxes and hold annual meetings

◆ convenient email messaging capabilities help you save time when communicating with your directors, officers and shareholders or LLC members

5. Q. How do I register for ComplianceWatch®?

A. It is easy to activate your ComplianceWatch® Service. Login to www.ComplianceWatch.com and take the "virtual tour" to learn about Compliance Watch features. Then, go to "Register for Compliance Watch," click on the link, fill in the User Information and you're on your way.

It's that easy!

6. Q. My corporation or LLC is no longer active. What should I do now?

A. There are benefits to officially terminating your corporation or LLC with your state. You avoid having to pay franchise taxes or file annual reports. In some states, there could be penalties involved should you try to restart your old company or even start a new one without having officially terminated the company with the appropriate Secretary of State's office. The Company Corporation® can provide the forms and assistance you need to dissolve or withdrawl your company from the state.

Keep in mind that formal dissolution usually does not relieve the Registered Agent of its statutory responsibilities. For example, in Delaware, as your Registered Agent, we must continue to receive and forward your notice(s) of litigation for three years after a formal dis-solution of a business.

If you wish to discontinue receiving invoices, you must complete certain business-closure activities, in writing, and signed by an authorized individual. You may not cancel over the phone. The document should state that you:

◆ have ceased operating your corporation or LLC

◆ are not going to pay for Registered Agent Service

◆ are instructing The Company Corporation® to reject any Service of Process

◆ are holding The Company Corporation®

About Registered Agent *and* ComplianceWatch® Service

The Company Corporation®
Incorporating Businesses Since 1899

7. Q. **What is the duration of Registered Agent Service?**

A. It is a 12-month service, annually renewed. Failure to renew your Registered Agent Service may affect your company's good standing with your state.

8. Q. **Is multi-year Registered Agent Service available?**

A. Absolutely! You can save money and time by choosing the two or three-year option for Registered Agent Service. Save up to 20% when you lock in today's prices and take advantage of the substantial two and three-year discounts. To learn more, just login to: www.aboutregisteredagent.com

9. Q. **How can I contact The Company Corporation® to pay the enclosed invoice to renew my Registered Agent Service?**

A. There are four easy ways to pay your annual invoice for Registered Agent Service - online, by phone, by mail, or by fax.

Direct online payment:
Click on:
www.aboutregisteredagent.com.

Direct phone payment:
Call toll-free:
1-800-792-2131

Direct mail payment:
Send completed invoice form to:
The Company Corporation
P.O. Box 13397
Philadelphia, PA 19101-3397

Direct fax payment:
Fax invoice with complete credit card information and length of service option selected to:
302-636-5454

Help ensure your good corporate standing. Don't delay. Renew your Registered Agent Service today!

The Company Corporation®
Incorporating Businesses Since 1899

The Company Corporation®
2711 Centerville Road, Suite 400
Wilmington, DE 19808
800-877-4224
www.incorporate.com

rev 3/03

Phaidon Encyclopedia
of
Decorative Arts
1890–1940

PHAIDON ENCYCLOPEDIA
OF
DECORATIVE ARTS
1890-1940

Edited by Philippe Garner

PHAIDON · OXFORD

A Quarto Book

Published by Phaidon Press Limited
Littlegate House
St Ebbe's Street
Oxford

First published in Great Britain in 1978
First paperback edition 1988

Copyright © 1978 Quarto Publishing plc

ISBN 0 7148 2534 4

This book was designed and produced by
Quarto Publishing plc
The Old Brewery
6 Blundell Street
London N7 9BH

Managing Editor: Robert Adkinson
Art Editor: Roger Daniels
Designers: Gillian Allan, Peter Laws, Linda Nash
Editorial Assistant: Corinne Molesworth
Picture Research: Annette Brown

Phototypeset in England by
Filmtype Services Limited, Scarborough

Cover illustrations originated in Italy by
Starf Photolitho SRL, Rome

Printed in Hong Kong by
Leefung-Asco Printers Limited

Contents

Introduction

THE LAST TWENTY YEARS have witnessed a strong awakening of interest in, and academic and professional approval of, the decorative arts of the period 1890–1940, as a result of which there have been many exhibitions, books and articles on aspects of the period. There has been a confusing proliferation of reference works on specific topics; confusing, because it detracts from the appreciation of the overall picture and the fluidity of design history, the often subtle phases of transition from one style to another; confusing, also, because of the inability of certain authors to agree on points of terminology — one author's Modernism can easily become another's Art Deco.

The aim of this encyclopedia has been to cover the whole period in detail from the dual viewpoints of style and theory and of actual production. The introductory chapters, through both their text and illustrations, should establish distinctly the predominant styles and trends around which evolved the detailed history of the period. It has been particularly satisfying to see, at last, Art Deco identified and isolated as the exotic and elusive style it was, a peculiarly French swansong to feminity, luxury and refinement before the onslaught of the international Modernist style.

It has also proved interesting, in discussing certain schools or theorists or designers, to realise how the pen can prove mightier than the craftsman's tasks and the artifacts can fall short of their ideals. In German design, for instance, the history of design school theory and administration has proved often more relevant to the history of decorative art than the artifacts themselves.

Perhaps the most valid driving force behind the encyclopedia, however, has been the enthusiasm for the period felt by all those involved in its production, an enthusiasm which hopefully this work will help to communicate.

PHILIPPE GARNER

PART ONE

STYLES
AND
INFLUENCES
IN THE
DECORATIVE
ARTS

1890-1940

Art Nouveau *by Roger-Henri Guerrand*

The birth of a modern style

THE STYLE IN THE decorative arts which eventually came to be known as Art Nouveau was made possible by a number of outstanding writers on aesthetics during the nineteenth century, notably John Ruskin and William Morris in Britain, and Léon de Laborde and Eugène-Emmanuel Viollet-le-Duc in France. What these writers had in common was a rejection of the crass materialism which had reached its apogee in many of the exhibits at the Great Exhibition held in London in 1851. The long-forgotten truth that art should be in harmony with the age which produces it was rediscovered around 1850 by these men whose love of the past was, nevertheless, beyond dispute.

In the field of aesthetics Ruskin especially was responsible for numerous advances. He rejected the fine distinction between the so-called major and minor arts; interior decoration, therefore, which had formerly been entirely in the hands of artisans, now took on the dimensions of a major social and artistic mission to be accomplished. According to Ruskin, the decorative arts should once again assume the central position in artistic concern they had occupied at the time of the Renaissance. Lecturing at Bradford in 1859, he reminded his audience that Correggio's finest work is to be found in the domes of two churches he decorated in Padua, that Michelangelo's mas-

terpiece is the decorated ceiling of the Pope's private chapel, that Tintoretto decorated the ceiling and walls of a benevolent society in Venice.

It was also Ruskin who called on architects to draw their inspiration from the lessons taught by nature, a concept which was to be central to movements in the decorative arts at the end of the nineteenth century. The ambition to translate the secret truths of nature in architecture and interior design can be seen in the works of Horta in Brussels, of Guimard in Paris and of Gaudí in Barcelona.

At the first international industrial exhibition of modern times, the Great Exhibition of 1851 held in London, there were 1,756 French participants, many of whom gained awards. This success delighted French officialdom, with the exception of Count Léon de Laborde, who had been in charge of organising French participation in the exhibition. In his report on the exhibition, published in 1856, he made a number of criticisms which show him to have been one of the most perceptive men of his time and one of the prophets of future developments in the decorative arts.

Léon de Laborde was an eminent archaeologist, a member of the Institut and director of the Archives Nationales during the Second Empire. He had travelled widely and studied the great monuments of antiquity. Unlike some of his contemporaries, however, he did not make a cult of the past and roundly criticized artists who killed art by making a fetish of copying the masterpieces of past ages. At the beginning of his report on the Great Exhibition he made the following revolutionary statement: 'The future of the Arts, of the Sciences and of Industry lies in their association'. According to Laborde, artists should concern themselves much more with the settings and surroundings of everyday life; we should be able to attend concerts or plays in auditoriums decorated by Ingres or Delacroix. In the creation of fine architecture, fine streets and the organisation of performances and manifestations, the government would introduce town dwellers to the beauties of nature.

he report of Count de Laborde was not unfamiliar to those who supported the idea of an artistic revolution in which the state would play an important role. The Belgian workers party, for instance, included the promotion of art in its programme at the end of the nineteenth century, and its leader Emile Vandervelde, regularly attended the social gatherings given by the daughter of William Morris. In Brussels Victor Horta constructed the first 'cathedral of socialism' in the form of the new Maison du Peuple. Laborde

Portrait of John Ruskin by T. B. Wirgman.

Parisian silverwork exhibited at
the 1851 Great Exhibition.

Above French bronze *vide-poche, c.* 1900.

Right Silver and cast glass pendant-brooch by René Lalique, *c.* 1900.

would have appreciated this incarnation of his dreams which was so far removed from the Neo-classical monuments so much favoured during his lifetime.

Only the restoration work carried out by Viollet-le-Duc and his writings on Gothic art have been the subject of serious study hitherto. Little remains to be said about the way he was virtually possessed by the Gothic style. His discussions of the nature of architecture are, however, amazingly clear-sighted. His *Entretiens sur l'Architecture* appeared between 1863 and 1872 and were translated into English between 1877 and 1881. They were to become key works for all those who wished a change in the accepted attitude to architecture and the decorative arts in the nineteenth century. 'It is barbarous,' he suggested, 'to reproduce a Greek temple in Paris or London, for a transplanted imitation of this monument reveals an ignorance of the basic principles governing its construction, and ignorance is barbarism.'

On the subject of interior decoration, Viollet-le-Duc, who was to teach for several years in the Ecole des Arts Décoratifs in Paris, professed exactly the same ideas as Ruskin and Laborde: 'Interior decoration', he wrote, 'has lost any semblance of unity. The architect never gives a

Gilt and silver-bronze
statuette by E. Barrias, 'La
Nature se dévoilant devant
La Science', 1890s.

DE LA COUR DU CHATEAU DE CHARLEVAL

Above Illustration from
Viollet-le-Duc's *Entretiens
sur l'Architecture*, 1863–72.

Above right German
advertisement for Samuel
Bing's Maison de l'Art
Nouveau, 1895.

Right Vaulted hall from
Viollet-le-Duc's *Entretiens
sur l'Architecture*.

second thought to what sort of paintings are to
decorate the rooms he has designed, the painter
never takes into consideration the architecture of
the rooms where he hangs his works, the furniture-
maker completely ignores what both the painter
and the architect have done, and the man who
supplies the curtains takes great pains to ensure
that his products are all that you notice in a room.'

The twenty *Entretiens sur l'Architecture* run to
about a thousand pages in which Viollet-le-Duc
reveals an extensive knowledge of the architecture
of the past, while offering countless new ideas. He
did not, however, succeed in shaking the faith of
his established colleagues who, for many more
years, continued to copy the methods of past
architecture and persisted in their attempt to dress
up modern building programmes in classical
forms.

Thanks to Ruskin, Laborde and Viollet-le-Duc,
however, the artistic expression of life in the
nineteenth century was soon to appear in the social
landscape. Through their writings they had a
determining influence on the formation of the new
modern style for which they had so passionately
pleaded. Although they often contradicted themselves they had the great merit of trying to resolve
the dichotomy between Art and Industry, which

Above left Hotel Solvay in Brussels by Victor Horta, 1894–8.

Above centre Antoni Gaudí, Barcelona, Casa Milá, 1905–7.

Left Antoni Gaudí, Barcelona, detail of window, Casa Milá, 1905–7.

Above right Paris Métro, Victor Hugo, by Hector Guimard, 1900.

Right Paris Métro, Bois de Boulogne, by Hector Guimard, 1900.

Printed fabric designed by
Alphonse Mucha, *c.* 1900.

was the major problem of their age.

Samuel Bing, the well-known expert on Far-Eastern Art, did not invent the expression 'Art Nouveau' when he chose it as the name of the shop he opened, at the end of December 1895, in the Rue de Provence in Paris. The term had already been coined by the Belgian lawyers, Octave Maus and Edmond Picard, who created the review *L'Art Moderne* in 1881.

As early as 1884 these two men proclaimed themselves 'believers in Art Nouveau,' an art which refused to accept the prevailing cult of the past. At first they attached the label to the works of painters who rejected academicism. The more specialised use of the term, for architecture and art objects, was only to come later when the painters were given various other labels. At the same time different countries were quick to create their own specific version of the term: Jugendstil, Sezessionstill, Modern Style, Arte Joven, Nieuwe Kunst, Style Liberty.

These movements have a number of common features which can be grouped under four major headings or aspirations.

First of all, there was a total rejection of the academic traditions which dominated teaching in art schools throughout the whole of the nineteenth century. For anyone wishing to create 'Art Nouveau' the cult of classical antiquity was a thing of the past and only to be found in the work of careerists. The Parisian Métro is a perfect illustration of this point. Jules Formigé, who built the overhead lines in a neo-doric style was covered with honours and made a member of the Institut, while Hector Guimard, who created a distinctive organic style for the stations, suffered the misfortune of seeing his work defaced – something which has continued to the present day – and being considered unworthy of mention in reference books for many years to come.

The rejection of antiquity went hand in hand with a return to the observation and imitation of nature. This was the advice given by Horta to Guimard when the latter came to visit him in Brussels. It was also one of the principles governing Gaudí's architecture, Morris's wallpapers, and Gallé's vases. It meant that the straight line was abandoned in favour of the curve and that there was a considerable vogue for Gothic or Japanese forms. These innovations were soon to become new conventions for second-rate artists.

Finally, many of the designers and architects of 1900 wished to take part in the movement for social reform and to join in the struggle of the European working class. Jean Lahor, a French disciple of William Morris, became the apostle of cheap housing, the creation of which would have kept Art Nouveau artists more than busy. Some of these men actually became members of socialist parties while others professed their sympathy to the socialist cause.

Thus it seemed possible that a form of art in keeping with a democratic society might now emerge, transforming the streets, the décor of the home, and everyday objects. Perhaps the wish expressed by Viollet-le-Duc could now come true: 'It is only possible for the Arts to find their true place, to develop and to progress in the living heart of the nation. . .'

Left Necklace in gold and pearls by Edward Colonna for Samuel Bing, *c.* 1900.

Below left Tiffany peacock lamp, *c.* 1900; Tiffany glass and lamps were promoted in Europe by Samuel Bing in his Rue de Provence shop in Paris.

Art Deco *by Martin Battersby*

The triumph of 1925

THE INTERNATIONAL EXHIBITION of Decorative and Industrial Arts held in Paris during the summer of 1925 was the occasion for a number of publications by leading French art critics and historians dealing with various aspects of contemporary applied arts. From these it is possible to trace the emergence and development of the style known today as 'Art Deco', a name bestowed as a result of the exhibition held at the Musée des Arts Décoratifs in 1966 entitled 'Les Années 1925'. The style was not so named during its existence when it was referred to as 'moderne' or 'contemporain' for, as is usually the case, a definitive name was applied only long after in retrospect.

The general consensus among these writers, Gabriel Mourey, Gaston Quénioux, Emile Bayard and Emile Sedeyn and others was that Art Nouveau became 'une fantaisie passagère, tôt démodée, vouée au bienfaisant oubli' as early as 1901 when, due to the inevitable commercialisation and consequent decline in artistic standards following the 1900 Exhibition, the style was abruptly dropped by both the influential patrons and the majority of artists and craftsmen who had championed its cause with such energy a few years before.

While this categorical statement was in the main true, Art Nouveau lingered on in favour for some years with those not in the inner circles of taste-makers. A number of buildings in Paris, some dated as late as 1913, show typical Art Nouveau motifs incorporating whiplash curves and floral motifs, and Louis Majorelle continued creating designs for furniture with elaborate decorations of carving and gilt-bronze appliques on themes of waterlilies and orchids which have been dated well after 1901. There is justification however for the contemporary comment that between 1901 and 1910 there was little or no original work produced and that for the most part decorative artists were working 'dans l'ombre'.

Art Nouveau had exerted a liberating influence in freeing design from the historicism which had debased so much of nineteenth-century creative activity, but the fact of its having no links with the past (the occasional references to Louis-Quinze and Louis-Seize styles can be discounted) proved to be a disadvantage. Art Nouveau could only be seen at its best in a complete ensemble, something only a limited number of patrons desired or could afford. Single pieces did not harmonise with furniture of previous periods in the way that, for instance, those of the eighteenth century did, even if in different styles. It is difficult to see how Art Nouveau could have developed logically with the passage of time as the works of past epochs had done, for the alternatives were either greater eccentricity or a simplicity which would have destroyed its essence.

This lack of a natural development, combined with its abandonment by artists and patrons alike, left many wary of novelty and, to the pleasure and profit of antique dealers and the many manufacturers of reproduction eighteenth-century furniture who had been bitter opponents of Art Nouveau from the start, the trend in interior decoration turned to versions of Louis-Quinze and Louis-Seize styles which, if lacking in originality, were pleasing and guaranteed not to become

Enamelled glass flask with stopper by Delvaux, *c.* 1920.

Lalique glass figure,
'Suzanne au bain', *c.* 1925.

Centre Bronze hand mirror by René Lalique, *c*. 1915.

Below Lithograph by Jean Dupas for *Toi*, an advertisement for Fourrures Max, *c*. 1925.

unfashionable overnight – a serious matter in taste-conscious Paris. During this period, when design seemed almost to lie fallow, a number of critics advocated a return to the principles of the last period of French design, that of about 1820, when there had been a logical development of taste before the growing mass-production had combined with showy pastiches of past historical styles to atrophy original inspiration. The dangers of slavish imitation were recognised and what was advocated was a development of 1820 styles as though the intervening years had not existed, at the same time recognising and adapting the technical improvements of the last eighty years.

A complaint often voiced in the previous two decades had been of the lack of co-operation between designers and manufacturers. Even more serious were the lamentably low standards of tuition in the decorative arts in technical schools. Equal concern was expressed at the vast quantities of low-priced German imports such as lighting fixtures from Nuremberg, furnishing fabrics from Gladbach and Leipzig and furniture from Darmstadt and Munich. These imports seriously threatened French manufacturers and imperilled the vaunted supremacy of Paris as the arbiter of taste. This influx of German goods had started even before the founding in 1907 of the Munich Deutscher Werkbund, with its aim of bringing together artists, craftsmen and manufacturers for the production of well-designed and inexpensive products for the home market and for export to other countries.

This purpose had been spelled out in the introduction to the catalogue for the Munich Werkbund Exhibition of 1909 in Brussels. In the hope that similar collaboration could result from the German example and that French designers and manufacturers could profit to their mutual advantage, an invitation was extended to the Munich Werkbund to exhibit in Paris at the 1910 Salon d'Automne. An important element in the creation of Art Deco was the result of this exhibition.

French critics were at best lukewarm in their comments on the rooms and objects displayed. Cultured Parisian taste, chauvinistic to the last, had never found much to admire in German design and not without reason. In this case, the verdict on the furniture was that it lacked elegance and was too obviously derived from the more cumbersome types of Biedermeier – itself a style flourishing about 1820 – while the colour schemes were found to be garish. However, the more observant visitors were impressed by a general unity of concept, a sincerity of purpose and the benefits of a collaboration between the artist and the manufacturer. The influential writer Gabriel Mourey commented that the greatest merit of German decorative art was that it was 'profoundly and congenitally German', and from it the lesson could be drawn that it was the duty of French decorative art to be as French as possible and that nothing should be neglected in accentuating this quality. In other words, the qualities of craftsmanship, elegance and originality which had characterised the best of the eighteenth-century work should be renewed.

The lesson of co-operation was quickly learned

and, as a result of this exhibition, several large Parisian department stores opened specialised departments under the direction of established designers for the sale of contemporary furniture, textiles and artifacts manufactured in quantity, but stamped by the personal taste of the designer and his collaborators. These shops within shops were important in introducing Art Deco to a much wider public.

Paradoxically, it was yet another foreign influence – and the most important – which crystallised the Frenchness of Art Deco. Again to quote Gabriel Mourey, 'there is no doubt that the influence of the Ballets Russes not only in the arts of the theatre but the arts of the book, textiles, in fact on all the decorative arts, appeared as dominating as that of Japanese art in former years'.

Paris had little or no knowledge of Russian decorative art of any period before the arrival of Serge Diaghilev and his compatriots in 1909. Since the early years of the eighteenth century the traffic had been in the opposite direction with French architects, sculptors and painters being sought after by Russian royalty and aristocracy and with news of the latest Parisian fashions being eagerly awaited in the Russian capital. The impact therefore of the Ballets Russes was all the greater on an audience knowing little or nothing of contemporary artistic trends in Russia. The greatest sensation was caused by the ballets on Oriental themes and the premières of *Schéhérazade* and *Thamar* caused a furore with their blending of unfamiliar music, exciting choreography and the performances of inspired dancers interpreting erotic and sadistic tales, so different from the badly danced and insipid ballets to which Parisian audiences were accustomed at the Paris Opera House.

Apart from the genius of the leading dancers, the most significant impact upon the audiences were the designs of Léon Bakst (the more restrained but no less brilliant work of Alexandre

Above Stone sculpture by Joseph Bernard, included in the 1925 Paris Exhibition.

Left André Groult: Chambre de Madame in the Pavillon d'un Ambassadeur at the 1925 Paris Exhibition.

Below Walnut *chiffonnier* by Süe et Mare, made in 1923 and exhibited in the Rotonde du Pavillon de la Compagnie des Arts Français at the Paris 1925 Exhibition.

Right Marquetry panel designed for the Compagnie Internationale des Wagons-Lits, 1920s.

Above left Printed fabric
border by André Mare,
c. 1920.

Above Fabric by
Benedictus, *c*. 1928.

Benois tended to be overshadowed) and overnight the pale subdued tones – 'la chanson grise' – which were a legacy of Art Nouveau were swept away by a dazzling spectrum of jewel colours, vermilion, violet, citron, crimson, orange, emerald and ultramarine enhanced by a liberal use of gold and silver. Equally exciting were the combinations of clashing colours, red with orange, blue with green or violet with yellow, all considered vulgar and unused since the heyday of the Second Empire. Bakst's interpretations of a legendary Orient opened exciting prospects for artists and designers.

In 1910 Paul Poiret was at the outset of a brilliant though chequered career as a couturier, decorator and patron of the arts. Two years previously he had revolutionised fashion and fashion illustration with his production in a limited edition of *Les Robes de Paul Poiret* illustrated by drawings by the young Paul Iribe in which an Oriental influence can be seen. This was intensified in the volume presented by Poiret in 1911 which had even more spectacular illustrations by Georges Lepape. The new craze which swept Paris for all things Persian and reminiscent of the Arabian Nights Entertainments exactly coincided with Poiret's own tastes. In a ceaseless search for new ideas, Poiret toured Germany and

Austria visiting art schools, exhibitions, theatres and studios and meeting the leading figures in avant-garde circles. At the Wiener Werkstätte he met Josef Hoffmann, Bruno Paul, Gustav Klimt, he exchanged ideas with Max Reinhardt and his company of actors and designers and was welcomed by Prince Eitel, the cultured and informed third son of the German Kaiser.

He found much to admire and emulate, and returned from his travels replete with ideas to be transmuted into French terms. Impressed by the high standards and the results of the training in German and Austrian art schools and technical colleges, he nevertheless deplored the somewhat pedantic approach to teaching and in 1911 put his own ideas into practice by founding the Atelier Martine where the pupils, completely untrained young girls, were encouraged to express their individuality in designs for textiles, wallpapers and furniture. Their lack of technical knowledge was made up for by skilled overseers who translated their designs into practical terms, carefully preserving the original concept. In addition, he encouraged the young and still unsuccessful painter Raoul Dufy to embark on textile design as a result of seeing his woodcut illustrations for *Le Bestiaire* of Guillaume Apollinaire with the happy result that Dufy created some of the most beautiful printed fabrics of this century, first for Poiret and later for the firm of Bianchini-Férier.

A similar use of untrained talent was made in the studio organised in Paris by François Ducharne in 1922, under the leadership of the brilliant designer Michel Dubost. Some thirty young boys and girls were maintained to produce sketches and ideas and again their freshness and spontaneity were considered to benefit from not being hampered by the technical needs of the actual processes of silk weaving, and technicians in Lyons adapted their ideas with successful results.

The accent on youth was characteristic of the generation of versatile designers mostly in their early twenties who, through the encouragement and active patronage of Paul Poiret, Lucien Vogel the publisher and others, created Art Deco. In the four years preceding the First World War, Paris was the brilliant centre of European culture at a time of feverish activity. It was as though French society was obeying an instinct to enjoy every aspect of life to the full.

Artists and designers were given opportunities for exercising their versatility which they generally seized with enthusiasm. To take only one example, Paul Iribe revolutionised fashion illustration in his work for Poiret, designed beautiful fabrics, which can still be seen at the Musée des Tissus in Lyons, furniture for the discriminating couturier Jacques Doucet, who had been Poiret's mentor, and even wallpapers and jewellery. His 'rose Iribe' was widely imitated and in its various transformations became a key motif in the ornamental repertoire of Art Deco – a repertoire which drew from the colours of the Ballets Russes, the forms of early nineteenth-century furniture and applied ornament, and which in turn owed a lot to the Viennese designers. All these elements were welded together and transformed by a characteristic French sense of style and elegance.

Iribe's rose, a highly conventionalised version of the bloom, bears a close resemblance to a similar treatment found in the work of Viennese designers. This in turn was derived from the roses of Charles Rennie Mackintosh and his followers of the Glasgow School. Mackintosh had a considerable influence in Austria and Germany in the early years of the century although when exhibited in Paris his work had met with minimal appreciation.

Very different from the slightly morbid and sometimes even sinister blooms of Art Nouveau, the conventionalised Art Deco roses, marguerites, dahlias and zinnias appear as a constant theme, sometimes as an allover design, sometimes in an oval panel (the oval itself being a favourite shape), or in a swag of drapery with ropes of pearls, ribbons, doves, fawns and formalised fountains. The spiral is a recurring motif, especially in ironwork. During the war years Iribe's rose became more than just a decorative motif: it symbolised the spirit of France. In 1930, when Art Deco was no longer fashionable, Iribe mourned the passing of his rose with the words 'for thousands the flower is as necessary as the machine – shall we sacrifice the flower on the altar of cubism and the machine?'

It was in 1911 that the term *ensemblier* appeared and with it the indication that a new factor in

Above right Cabinet in macassar ebony and inlaid ivory by Emile-Jacques Ruhlmann, 1919.

Right Interior by Primavera, c. 1920.

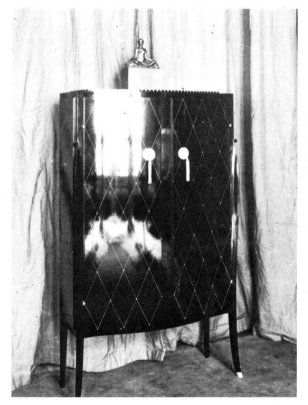

Above left Commemorative silver medallion for the Paris 1925 Exhibition by P. Turin.

Above Metal-mounted, decorated pottery vase, marked 'd'Argyl', *c.* 1925.

Far left Cabinet in macassar ebony by Emile-Jacques Ruhlmann, early 1920s.

Left Wrought-iron mirror frame by Edgar Brandt, *c.* 1925.

Below Silvered bronze clock designed by Paul Follot for Pomone at the Bon Marché, *c.* 1925.

La Soie, Boulogne glazed
pottery figure by Marcel
Renard, exhibited at the
Paris 1925 Exhibition.

interior decoration had emerged, to have a definite effect on designers and patrons alike. For the greater part of the nineteenth century fashionable styles of furniture and decoration had ceased to develop in a logical and orderly manner. With the coming of the Industrial Revolution, the rise of new social classes and the increasing use of machinery, taste veered to uninspired pastiches, however inappropriate to their function, of the previous centuries. These *ameublements de style* were largely mass-produced and were supplied from firms of *tapissier-décorateurs*. Art Nouveau itself had been a revolt against this obsession with historicism and from it one concept remained: the interior or *ensemble* contemporary in feeling, original in design, with no references to the past and preferably the creation of either a single designer or a group working in close collaboration. It was this lesson that the French designers had to relearn from the example of the Munich Werkbund.

The foremost upholders of this principle were Paul Follot and Maurice Dufrêne. Both had worked in the Art Nouveau manner for Julius Meier-Graefe's La Maison Moderne and both had reacted strongly against Art Nouveau soon after the 1900 Exhibition. Dufrêne was particularly vehement in his condemnation in the introduction to the catalogue of his exhibits at the Salon des Décorateurs in 1906. While both designers sought new idioms of expression, each developed in a different way. Follot's inclination was towards rich surface ornament applied to simple and elegant forms using rare figured veneers, lacquer and gilded carvings. As versatile as any of his contemporaries, he designed wallpapers, metalwork, ceramics and textiles, which formed part of his ensembles, and in 1923 his prolific talents were employed at Pomone, a department at the Bon Marché devoted to his work. Dufrêne on the other hand was less interested in the luxurious aspects of interior decoration, favouring an almost rustic simplicity in much of his work which increasingly showed his interest in the application of industrial techniques to furniture. In 1921 he set up a special shop, La Maîtrise, at the Galeries Lafayette.

The painter André Mare turned his attention to interior decoration in 1910 and, after working with the architect Louis Süe on the decorations to celebrate the end of the war in 1918, they founded the Compagnie des Arts Français, working with Boutet de Monval, the painter, Gustave-Louis Jaulmes, who specialised in tapestry design and mural paintings, Paul Véra, a versatile painter, sculptor and wood engraver, Maurice Marinot, a distinguished glass worker, and André Marty, a graphic artist whose work was much in demand for fashion periodicals such as *La Gazette du Bon Ton*, *Vogue* and *Fémina* among others. This group was concerned less with creating startling and fashionable interiors than with an adherence to traditional values of sobriety and elegance. It dispersed in 1928 when Art Deco had given way to a starker idiom of decoration alien to their ideas.

Léon Jallot had been the director of Bing's Art Nouveau workshops and like many of his contemporaries rebelled against the style when he opened his own studio in 1903 after Bing's death. He was joined by his son Maurice after the war in the creation of furniture characterised by simplicity of line enlivened by rich surface textures of veneers and lacquer.

Undoubtedly the most celebrated of the designers working along traditional lines was Emile-Jacques Ruhlmann, who first won attention in 1913 and soon became known for the luxurious elegance and exquisite craftsmanship of his furniture which could compare with that of the greatest *ébenistes* of the eighteenth century. Fortunate in very soon acquiring an extremely rich clientèle to appreciate the magnificent quality of his work, he produced until his death in 1933 furniture restrained in shape and veneered in exotic and rare woods, enhanced by delicate inlays of ivory combined with shagreen and tooled leather. Designed in collaboration with other craftsmen of the first rank, Edgar Brandt, Jean Dunand, René Lalique and Stephany, the Hôtel d'un Collectionneur Ruhlmann created for the 1925 Exhibition proved the most notable representative of the best of contemporary French decorative art.

The outbreak of war in 1914 did not necessarily mean a complete stoppage of artistic activity in Paris, but shortages of materials and labour diminished production considerably. But despite the continuing shortages after the end of the war, the major concern was to reassert the position of Paris and French craftsmanship in every field of decorative art, now that the threat of German competition had been removed. Apart from being a matter of national pride, the export of French luxury goods brought into the country extremely large amounts of money and was a mainstay of the economy. With little or no competition, France was in a position to dictate to the rest of the world and to supply luxury and style for which there was an increasing demand after the grim war years. Paris was a magnet for the rich and pleasure-seeking from every continent who flocked to buy from the great French design houses.

There was no immediate change of direction as far as the decorative arts were concerned. On demobilisation some artists resumed where they had left off in 1914; for those who had not been involved in the war it had been a period of marking time. Two significant art movements now arose: Dada in Switzerland and De Stijl in Holland, but in 1919 they were little known in Paris beyond a limited circle and no one could foresee that they were to contribute to the counter movement which would sweep away Art Deco. In the meantime, the creative artists who had made their mark before the war still ruled as arbiters of taste, notably Paul Poiret whose elaborate styles typified the fashions of the first five years of the 1920s. Once again, the Ballets Russes appeared to renew the excitements of prewar seasons, reviving the repertoire which had made such an impression and adding new productions designed principally by French painters.

Immediately after the war new names appeared in the art journals – names of designers trained before the war and now qualified to satisfy in their individual manner the growing demands, such as the two metalworkers, Raymond Subes and Edgar Brandt, the latter working to the designs of his partner Louis Favart and making major contributions to the 1925 Exhibition.

In 1920 the highly individual worker in metal and lacquer, Armand-Albert Rateau opened his own studio and during the next ten years produced a body of work for illustrious clients which was inspired by the patinated bronzes of Pompeii and the Near Eastern countries. In 1922 Jules Leleu followed suit, specialising in furniture entirely veneered in blond shagreen ornamented with a version of the Iribe rose. In the same year André Domin and Marcel Genevrière combined to open the firm of Dominique and René Joubert and Philippe Petit opened D.I.M. (Décoration Intérieure Moderne).

The majority of illustrations of interiors of this period were not of actual houses but of the temporary installations at the annual Salons des Artistes-Décorateurs and the Salons d'Automne where, in addition to the work of the *ensembliers,* that of specialised designers and craftsmen was exhibited. Ceramics by René Buthaud, Emile Decoeur, Raoul Lachenal and Emile Lenoble, metalwork by Luc Lanel for the firm of Christofle, Raymond Subes and Paul Kiss, glass by Gabriel Argy-Rousseau, Maurice Marinot, François Décorchemont, Marcel Goupy, Jean Luce and the firms of Daum, Baccarat and, pre-eminently, Lalique, bookbindings by Rose Adler, Paul Bonet and Pierre Legrain – also a creator of individual pieces of furniture – textiles and carpets by Eric Bagge, Sonia Delaunay, and Hélène Henry and jewellery by Cartier, Boucheron, Lacloche, Jean and Georges Bastard. Many more could be cited to witness the galaxy of original talent working in the Art Deco style, the apotheosis of which was the 1925 Exhibition. It was also its swan song – a curious parallel with the demise of Art Nouveau soon after the 1900 Exhibition.

The element of change was an essential factor in the structure of fashion in Paris. Just as women's fashions changed from season to season so did the fashions in interior decoration, but necessarily at a slower tempo: elegant women could change their clothes more rapidly than their surroundings. Two new enthusiasms, Cubism and Negro Art, were important factors in the decline of Art Deco. The former had been the subject of experiment before the war in a very limited circle of painters, but in the early twenties began to acquire a certain chic not unconnected with the new craze for jazz music which had been introduced into France in 1919. Negro art had been known and admired by a number of artists before the war, but they were mostly unrecognised at the time and it took the 1922 exhibition of art from the French colonies to awaken a wider interest in a form of expression totally alien to the refined elegance of Art Deco. But the latter had been in vogue for a number of years, while the new angular forms had the attraction of novelty. Other factors rendered Art Deco unfashionable after 1925: women's clothes became simpler as they began to take a more active role in life and indulged in sports of which they had previously been spectators; machines and especially automobiles came to symbolise the new doctrines of functionalism, and the new and revolutionary steel furniture began to appear from the Bauhaus. The elegance of Art Deco with its gracious curves and pretty ornaments of flowers and garlands was replaced by the hard chic of steel and angular and unadorned surfaces.

Modernism *by Gillian Naylor*

An international style

FOR THE PURPOSES of this survey, the roots of Modernism must be located in the nineteenth-century consolidation and questioning of Enlightenment attitudes. For the ideal of progress, the cult of individualism, the celebration of nature, and the challenge of science and technology, which all contribute, to a greater or lesser degree, to nineteenth-century theories of design, are protean and ambiguous concepts, their impact and interpretation varied from country to country, and from generation to generation; their acceptance or rejection depended on social, political and philosophical developments.

Several generalisations, however, can be made about nineteenth-century attitudes which are relevant to the emerging concept of 'modernity'; for the major theorists of the nineteenth century were concerned, above all, with the problem of 'style', and in their investigations and recommendations certain themes or obsessions emerge that were to be developed and, in some cases, transformed by their twentieth-century successors. On the most simplistic level, the preoccupation with a new focus for commitment was prompted by the rejection, or reinterpretation of the classical canons of form and beauty; and this assault on classicism, or more specifically, on the rule of the academies, was conducted on various fronts.

A growing sense of nationalism had contributed to the re-interpretation and celebration of the Gothic, and Gothic, the native style of Northern Europe, was promoted on both moral and rational grounds (most typically by Ruskin in England and Viollet-le-Duc in France – Ruskin celebrating its humanistic virtues, while Viollet-le-Duc demonstrated the style's allegiance to the laws of structural necessity). And at the same time, Darwin's evolutionary theories, reinforced by botanists' and biologists' investigations into the determinants for organic growth and form, prompted similar investigations into the nature and development of style. Style, which obviously varied according to country and culture, could now be seen to be determined by the nature and availability of materials and techniques, as well as by social and symbolic needs.

Two conflicting ideologies emerged from this concentration on objective analysis, as well as on social and symbolic priorities. For while the 'scientific attitude' led to demands for a new architecture to meet the needs of a new age, the growing dissatisfaction with the materialism of the nineteenth century led to that nostalgia for the past and celebration of the vernacular associated with the British Arts and Crafts Movement's ideals for design reform.

Following Nikolaus Pevsner's seminal works, most historians of modern design locate the initial impulse for reform in the theory and practice of British designers in the nineteenth century. For their crusade in the cause of craftsmanship established an ideal of commitment which no subsequent generation could ignore. Starting from the premise that man-made forms both reflect and shape society's values, they campaigned for a new humanism in design. This concern for the ethics as well as the aesthetics of design involved first an attempt to revive the philosophies of service, apprenticeship and quality that were associated with the medieval guild system; second, a respect for natural and organic form, and third the conviction that the designer should promote spiritual rather than commercial values. Such ideals, however quixotic, led to a renaissance in British design that was admired and imitated throughout Europe. The various 'secessions' in Europe looked to Britain for a lead in both the theory and practice of design reform.

The British approach to design tended to be emotional and empirical, while Continental designers were heirs to a more rigorously intellectual tradition. Both Viollet-le-Duc and Semper, whose books formed the corner-stone of Continental theory, were analytical and objective in their assessments of the nature of design. Their observations were based on attempts to define the laws of structure and the nature of materials, and their definitions of design were related to scientific rather than spiritual 'truths'. Designers attempting to forge a 'modern' style at the turn of the century inherited, then, a complex set of values from their nineteenth-century predecessors – values that were reflected in the ambiguous achievements of Art Nouveau. For in their search for new and symbolic forms of expression, Art Nouveau architects, while remaining faithful to the spirit of Viollet-le-Duc, demonstrated revolutionary concepts of space, form and structure; and the designers, drawing inspiration from nature, from the discovery, or re-discovery of earlier or alien cultures as well as from their determination to demonstrate craftsmanship as an art, achieved the now familiar transformation and fusion of form and decoration. At the same time, however, the majority of the designers and architects associated with Art Nouveau acknowledged social as well as aesthetic priorities. Their campaign was for beauty in the service of humanity, so that the cost, and inevitable élitism of the style had either to be justified or avoided.

Several strategies were evolved in order to overcome the problem. In France, for example,

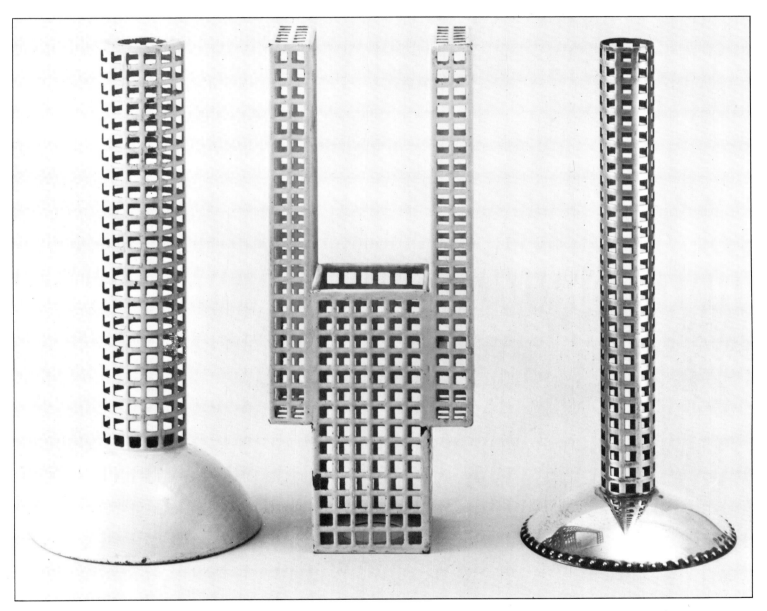

Metal baskets designed by
Josef Hoffmann *c.* 1905,
which strongly anticipate
the stylistic preoccupations
of the Modernist designers
of the twenties and thirties.

Hector Guimard had demonstrated in his designs for the Métro stations how individuality of form and expression could be reconciled with mass-production techniques. In Austria Otto Wagner, who had been appointed head of the School of Architecture in the Vienna Academy of Fine Art as well as artistic adviser to the Viennese Transport Commission in 1894, was involved with similar problems. Wagner, however, believed that 'modern' problems required 'modern' solutions, and his inaugural address to the academy (*Moderne Architektur*, 1895) was based on this theme. 'All modern forms', he stated, 'must reflect the new materials and the new requirements of our time: if they are to meet the needs of modern man, they must express our improved, democratic, clear-thinking selves. . . .'

Wagner was, of course, the *éminence grise* of the Vienna Secession movement, and the Wiener Werkstätte (1903), whose founder members included his pupil Josef Hoffmann, was the most prestigious of the various guilds, societies and artists' collaboratives that were set up throughout Europe at the turn of the century.

The majority of these were inspired by British Arts and Crafts precedents, and the Wiener Werkstätte was originally modelled on C. R.

Ashbee's Guild of Handicraft (1888). Hoffmann, however, did not share the Arts and Crafts anxiety about designing for an élite. From the outset the workshops served a rich, sophisticated and cosmopolitan clientèle, producing furniture, fabrics, metalware and ceramics in forms and patterns that anticipate the stylistic preoccupations of the 1920s and 1930s.

Similar workshops had been established in Germany during the 1880s and 1890s; their subsequent development, however, was very different from that of their Viennese counterpart. From the turn of the century, German craft societies, unlike those in Britain, were concerned with the problem of serial, as opposed to craft production. Within a few years of helping to found the Werkstätte in Munich in 1897, for example, Richard Riemerschmid was designing furniture from standardised components (Typenmöbel), and the Deutscher Werkbund (1907), whose founder members included industrialists as well as representatives from the Werkstätte, was established with the specific programme of promoting standards for industrial design.

The establishment of the Werkbund marks a watershed in the history of modern design, for in the bitter debates that surrounded its formation all

Above Emile-Jacques Ruhlmann: modernist desk, *c.* 1930.

Right Adjustable *chaise longue* with a steel tube frame, designed by Le Corbusier and manufactured by Thonet Brothers, 1928.

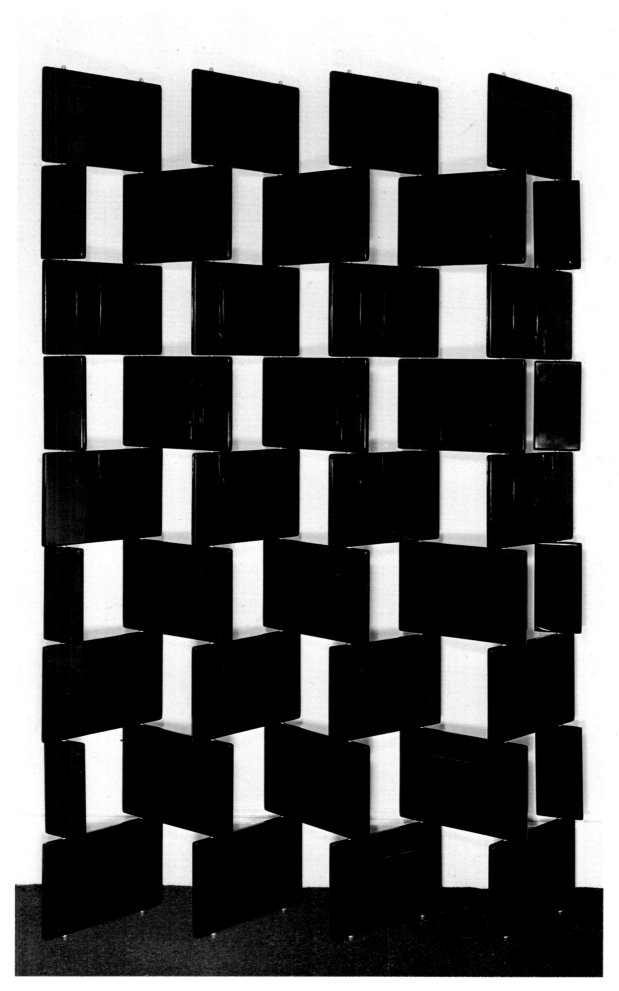

Black lacquer screen,
c. 1924, designed by Eileen
Gray, whose lacquer
furniture was exhibited by
Le Corbusier in the
Pavillon de l'Esprit
Nouveau at the 1925 Paris
Exhibition.

the conflicting ideologies that underlie twentieth-century design theory were either aired or anticipated. The first and most controversial issue involved the need to define the nature and role of the designer: should he continue to consolidate the British tradition and work as an artist and an individualist, or should he dedicate himself to the service of industry, evolving a style and a standard for mass-production? Each point of view had its champion within the organisation, and the issue came to a head in 1914 in the now famous debate between Henry van de Velde and Hermann Muthesius.

By this time, however, Van de Velde seemed to be fighting a rear-guard action, and the practical as well as ideological implications of Muthesius' theories were reflected in design developments throughout Europe. For in the decade leading up to the First World War, European countries were recognising the need to establish or improve standards in industrial design, and it is significant that during this period several organisations with similar aims were established. Austria, for example, set up its Werkbund in 1910, and a Swiss Werkbund was founded in 1913; the Svenska Slöjdföreningen was reorganised along Werkbund lines during the war, and the British Design and Industries Association was founded in 1915.

These organisations were primarily concerned with the practical problems of improving standards for mass production, and each country evolved its own methods and ideals for training designers and proselytizing industry. But the problem of form, or style, remained, and definitions of style were complicated by moral and aesthetic imperatives as well as practical considerations. As Muthesius put it in 1911, in a speech outlining the aims of the Werkbund: 'Higher than purpose, material and technique stands form. The first three aspects [of design] might be impeccably achieved, but if form is

Interior of the Berlin apartment designed by Marcel Breuer in 1927 for Piscator, one of the leading avant-garde theatrical directors of the twenties.

ignored we are still living in a brutish world.' For Muthesius, as for several of his contemporaries at this time, the concept of 'ideal form' had obvious platonic, or classical connotations, and the 'call to order' which followed in the wake of Art Nouveau frequently involved a return to classical forms or a renewed interest in classical canons of order and harmony. At the same time, however, such preoccupations, paradoxically enough, were reinforced by a widespread admiration for what Le Corbusier was to call the 'Engineer's Aesthetic' in *Towards a New Architecture*. For ships, locomotives and aircraft were designed in a 'style' that was both determined by and expressive of function and materials. Modern life was, in fact, according to Le Corbusier, creating 'its own objects: its costume, its fountain pen, its eversharp pencil, its typewriter, its telephone, its admirable office furniture, its plate glass, and its "innovation" trunks, the safety razor and the briar pipe, the bowler hat and the limousine, the steamship and the airplane.'

The conviction that design should be determined by need and function, and at the same time achieve that 'state of platonic grandeur, mathematical order, speculation [and] the perception of the harmony that lies in emotional relationships' was fundamental to Modern Movement theory during the 1920s and 1930s. It was, of course, clearly expressed in Le Corbusier's work during this period, and was also latent in the teaching at the Bauhaus (1919–33). Although Walter Gropius, who assumed the directorship of Van de Velde's Craft School in Weimar in 1918, maintained that the school never sought to achieve or to express a 'style', its work, both at Weimar and Dessau, reflects the school's preoccupation with the formal expression, or interpretation, of a platonic ideal of architecture and design. For, following the post-war 'Expressionist' period, in which materials were used to demonstrate per-

The spread of the
International Style: an
American Modernist
interior, *c.* 1930.

sonal, and in some cases, idiosyncratic ideologies, the school embarked on its now familiar crusade for 'the creation of standard types for all the practical commodities of everyday use'; and its programme produced a 'style', or form-language similar to that achieved by avant-garde designers throughout Europe during this period. For designers from within both the Russian and Dutch Constructivist movements formulated similar ideals and a similar aesthetic. It is significant, however, that the Dutch had no reservations about conducting their campaign under the banner of 'style', or, more specifically 'the style' (De Stijl), defined by Theo van Doesburg, the movement's most active theorist, as 'the universal, collective manner of expression.'

These aspirations towards unity and universality, however, were challenged on various levels during the 1920s and 1930s. From within the Bauhaus itself, Hannes Meyer, the Swiss architect who was appointed as successor to Gropius in 1928, campaigned for a more rigidly functionalist approach to architecture and design, and for the elimination of the 'stylistic' preoccupations of 'inbred theories', which 'closed every approach to right living'. 'Thus my tragi-comic situation arose: as Director of the Bauhaus I fought against the Bauhaus style. I fought constructively through my teaching: Let all life be a striving for oxygen + carbon + sugar + starch + protein. All design, therefore, should be firmly anchored in the world of reality . . .'.

The 'world of reality', however, especially in the post-Freudian era, could never be satisfactorily defined or expressed in terms of economy, efficiency and logic, for as Salvador Dali pointed out: 'The subconscious has a symbolic language that is a truly universal language, for it speaks with the vocabulary of the great vital constants – sexual instincts, feeling of death, physical notions of the enigma of space – those vital constants are echoed in every human being.' And the Surrealist vision, with its subversive questioning and undermining of the contemporary striving for efficiency and competence, re-invested the object with those ambiguous levels of meaning that had been inherent in Art Nouveau design, and in the Utopian ideals formulated by Expressionist architects and designers following the First World War. 'Has the useful ever made us happy?' wrote Bruno Taut in his *Alpine Architecture* (1919), 'Comfort, Convenience, Good Living, Education, knife and fork, railways and water-closets: and then – guns, bombs, instruments for killing! . . . We must

Chaise longue in laminated beech and plywood, designed by Marcel Breuer for the Isokon furniture company of London, 1935.

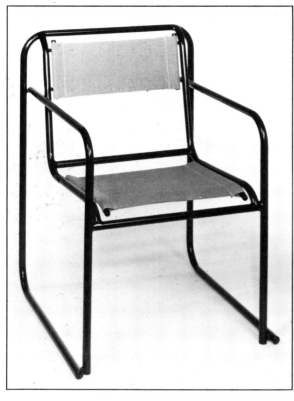

Left The influence of the Bauhaus: armchair in tubular steel and canvas manufactured *c.* 1931 by PEL (Practical Equipment Ltd.) of London.

Below Bar table in glass and steel from the villa Le Roc at Cannes, designed for the Marquis of Cholmondely, 1934.

always strive for the unattainable if we are to reach the attainable.'

In their striving for the unattainable, however, Expressionist architects and designers demonstrated their ideas in forms that were either crystalline or amorphous, and these 'crystalline' visions were expressed in shapes and suggested structures that are now associated with the Modernist style in decorative design. The use of shiny materials, angular or geometric forms and exaggerated symmetries became stylistic clichés among the 'Modernist' (as opposed to 'modern') designers of the 1920s and 1930s.

The existence of what was felt to be a 'pseudo-modern' style of design first became apparent in the 1925 Exhibition in Paris, which, according to its sponsors, was 'open to all manufacturers whose produce is artistic in character and shows clearly modern tendencies'. These 'clearly modern tendencies', however, could be and were, widely interpreted. For, apart from Corbusier's Pavillon de l'Esprit Nouveau, a number of French exhibits revealed a spurious and superficial 'modernity'.

'It was the ominous Paris Exhibition of 1925 which must be held responsible for the introduction of bad "Modernism" into the trade', wrote Nikolaus Pevsner in his *An Enquiry into Industrial Art in England*, published in 1937. The majority of promoters of 'good' design in the 1920s and 1930s shared Pevsner's conviction that 'Modernism' in its 'jazz forms' had 'spoiled the market for serious modern work.' The assumption that 'nothing of vital energy and beauty can be created unless it be fit for its purpose, clear, straightforward and simple' had, as we have seen, a long pre-history. It was founded on the fallacy of progress, the conviction that man is capable of achieving an ordered and efficient society and that such order and efficiency could be expressed in the forms he created. Such optimism, of course, was to be challenged by twentieth-century realities.

Surrealism and Neo-Baroque *by Martin Battersby*

Reaction to Modernism

THE 1929 EDITION of *Répertoire du Goût Moderne*, an album with coloured drawings of interiors and accessories by Pierre Chareau, Dominique, Guévrékian, André Lurçat, Mallet-Stevens and Louis Sognot, amply demonstrates the full extent of the reaction against Art Deco. The interiors illustrated are devoid of any decoration in the sense the word would have possessed a few years before. The furniture has become angular, with no mouldings or carving, and in many cases incorporates tubular metal elements; paintings and ornaments have been reduced to a minimum and often the only note of relief from the predominating severity is a rug of geometrical design.

This cult of simplicity, so alien to the principles of Art Deco, had been advocated as early as 1920 in the first issue of the avant-garde manifesto *L'Esprit Nouveau*, and was followed in 1921 by Le Corbusier's famous dictum, 'une maison est une machine à habiter'. Functional simplicity and harmony were the aims of the new generation of architects and decorators for whom *L'Esprit Nouveau* was the spokesman. L'Union des Artistes Modernes, an association with Robert Mallet-Stevens, Pierre Chareau, René Herbst and François Jourdain as leading figures, was equally firm in the belief that the interior of the future should be suited to the needs of contemporary life – as they imagined it to be – with no concession to unnecessary ornament to distract from functionalism. The tubular steel furniture originating from the Bauhaus designs of Marcel Breuer had its imitators in France even before the exhibition of work from the Bauhaus at the Salon des Artistes-Décorateurs in 1930, some French writers even claiming the concept as being French.

The machine, particularly that type of machine giving an impression of pent-up power and speed, had a fascination for many designers and they expressed this preoccupation in abstract geometrical terms with straight lines or circles arranged in interlocking patterns. The desire to dissociate their work from any trace of traditional design is obvious.

This new idiom of decoration with its emphasis on plain unadorned surfaces, sombre or neutral colours relieved only by the use of mirrors or the sharp glitter of chromium plate, undoubtedly by reason of its novelty had its followers in both France and England. For one thing, this modernistic effect could be obtained relatively inexpensively, which was an important consideration in the early 1930s when the effects of the depression following the Wall Street crash of 1929 made economy a necessity. It was in harmony with the

current fashions dictated by Parisian couturiers with their emphasis on elongation and the use of the bias cut in the new long skirts, mandatory for both day and evening wear.

Yet the financial stringencies which made this simplicity a fashion also meant that Modernism was comparatively little used in private houses and was mainly to be found in public buildings such as hotels, showrooms and restaurants. Also, just as there had been those resistant to the attractions of Art Nouveau and Art Deco, so there were many who found Modernism without charm.

Although Baroque painters had to wait until after the war to receive academic approval on a large scale, the architecture and sculpture began to find adherents about 1930. As far back as 1909 the Ballets Russes had presented *Le Pavillon d'Armide* with Louis-Quatorze décor and costumes by Alexandre Benois on their first appearance in Paris, but the more exotic Oriental fantasies of Léon Bakst had overshadowed this production. The brilliant revival of *La Belle au Bois Dormant* by Diaghilev in 1921, with its masterly designs by Bakst in the most lavish and exuberant Baroque style, had been a short-lived failure, and was only produced in London. However, music lovers were attracted to the Mozart festivals at Salzburg and were exploring the Baroque monasteries and churches in Austria.

This combination of circumstances gave an impetus to the reversal of taste against Modernism – an impetus fostered by the growing number of interior decorators, the majority of whom could no longer be classed as *ensembliers* designing every element in an interior. The new type of decorator was more versed in commercialising his personal taste, choosing antiques and fabrics to form a pleasing décor. As the opportunities for any kind of training in interior decoration were at that time non-existent, decorators were not adept at designing either furniture or decorations and consequently relied upon the use of antiques rather than modern furniture.

The apartment in Paris of Carlos de Bestigui demonstrates the trend away from Modernism to a more decorative treatment incorporating neo-Baroque motifs. In the early 1930s de Bestigui had commissioned Le Corbusier to design an apartment near the Arc de Triomphe in Paris. Consisting of a drawing room, dining room, bedroom and a roof garden, with, of course, a bathroom and kitchen, it was on two floors. Le Corbusier's treatment resulted in plain white walls, large windows from floor to ceiling, and a free-standing spiral staircase connecting the upper and lower

Drawing room in the Paris
apartment of Carlos de
Bestigui, designed by Le
Corbusier, showing the
spiral staircase, before 1936.

floors, positioned in the living room.

Figures of blackamoors fashionable in the eighteenth century and revived in the sixties and seventies of the nineteenth century became extremely popular in the 1930s. Christian Bérard ranged them against the blood-red colonnades in the second scene of the 1936 ballet *Symphonie Fantastique*. Beyond the columns could be seen winged sphinxes – another much collected ornament. These were not the Egyptian type but based on eighteenth-century models which were coquettish portraits of contemporary beauties – La Belle Omorphi, mistress of Louis XV, or Camargo the dancer.

Two further theatrical productions reflected this new interest in the Baroque. In 1932 Charles B. Cochran presented the Max Reinhardt production of Offenbach's operetta, renamed *Helen*, with designs by Oliver Messel which owed inspiration to the work of the Bibbienna family. The all-white bedroom – an innovation in theatrical décor – was particularly praised. Max Reinhardt had a strong preference for the Baroque as he demonstrated in his film version of *A Midsummer Night's Dream*, again inspired by the Bibbiennas and Tiepolo and with Surrealist touches in the treatment of the fairy scenes. Incidentally, Hollywood designers also favoured Baroque elements, particularly in décors for musicals, the best example being the spectacular sequence designed by John Harkrider for the film of *The Great Ziegfeld* in 1936.

The second major theatrical production was Rex Whistler's décor for the ballet *The Wise Virgins* in 1940 which confirmed the masterly command of period interpretation, design and draughtsmanship which had already been revealed by his previous graphic work and mural paintings, which incorporated references to the Baroque.

The Surrealist exhibitions held in London and New York in 1936 and in Paris two years later caused a furore of praise and abuse. Surrealism was not a new movement in 1936 – it had its origins, according to some, before the First World War – but the exhibition revealed to an astonished public a large quantity of work previously known only to limited circles. Anyone who attended the opening in London will remember the mingled delight and repulsion forcibly expressed by those present, together with the realisation that there were surreal elements in so much of the artistic creativity of the past. The fantastic dream-like works of William Blake, Hieronymus Bosch, 'Douanier' Rousseau, Arcimboldo, Fuseli and a host of others were claimed as forerunners of the movement.

Furthered by publicity stunts by Salvador Dali, Surrealism was taken up by advertising, photographers, window dressers and interior decorators. In fashion, Elsa Schiaparelli interpreted designs by Dali and Cocteau, creating the much publicised but little-worn hats in the form of a shoe, a hen sitting on a nest and a lamb cutlet with a paper frill. Dali's version of the Venus de Milo as a chest of drawers became a walking suit with *trompe l'oeil* drawer fronts, and for evening wear, a series of short jackets were beautifully embroidered with Surrealist motifs. With the more macabre and hallucinatory aspects removed, Surrealism invaded interior decoration in the shape of Mae

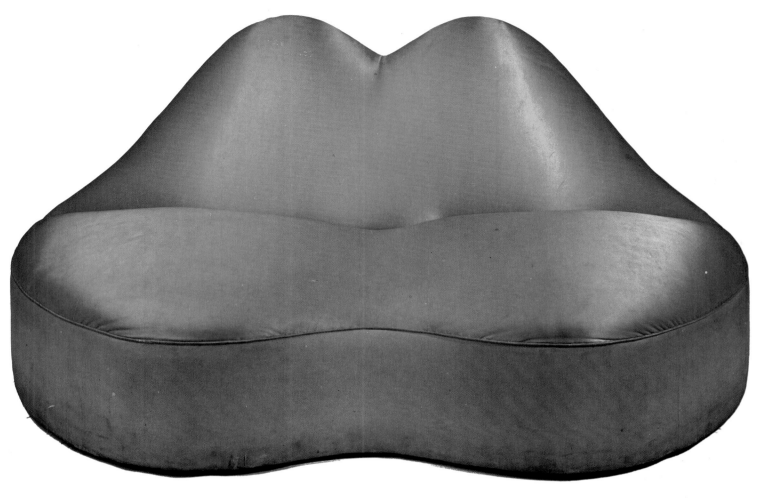

Above Mae West lips sofa by Salvador Dali, 1936.

Left Setting for *The Great Ziegfeld*, 1936.

Far left top Roof garden of Carlos de Bestigui's apartment.

Far left centre Rex Whistler's design for the setting of the ballet *The Wise Virgins*, 1940.

Far left Room setting exhibited at the Surrealist exhibition held in Paris in 1938.

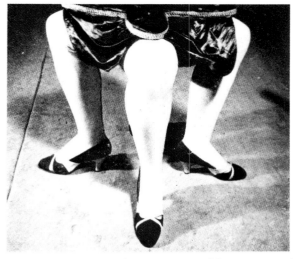

West's mouth made into a settee, tables supported by giant hands or stools with three lifelike legs of acrobats. Hands as a motif were to be seen in fashion photographs, holding jewels, cosmetics — in fact anything a hand could hold. Victorian marble hands created as souvenirs or *memento mori* were brought once more to light and occupied places of honour, often with the nails varnished in the fashionable shade of shocking pink.

Other Victorian bric-à-brac, such as marble obelisks and glass domes, encasing the stranger products of nineteenth-century imagination, were eagerly sought after in the newly discovered Caledonian Market in London and the flea market in Paris, both these markets having been found to be fruitful sources for the fashionable Baroque and mid-nineteenth century pieces. With the break-up of many large houses as a result of the depression of the early thirties the contents of attics and drawing rooms alike flooded the market and could be found at extremely low prices.

The main sources for spreading this fashion, which combined Surrealism, Baroque and Victoriana, were the fashion magazines. *Vogue* with its supplement on decorating – issued separately as *House and Garden* at a later date – and *Harper's Bazaar* all influenced taste and fashion by the editorial text and by the advertising more than any other periodicals. Both looked to Paris for ideas, as they were primarily concerned with fashion. Paris was still the leader in this field and both employed the best photographers and artists to illustrate fashion, the rivalry between the two periodicals ensuring that only the most original and imaginative treatment was used by each. To add variety to the editorial text, the best of interior decoration was included and as one succeeded in obtaining an exclusive coverage of a house decorated by Elsie de Wolfe the other would reply by an article on Syrie Maugham.

Vogue had an advantage in the services of Christian Bérard, acknowledged as an arbiter of taste in Parisian society. From his fertile imagination there issued designs for covers of the magazine, evocative drawings of the important fashions from the leading couturiers as well as original ideas for interior decoration, needlework or printed fabrics. His romantic outlook, preference for period derivations and exquisite sense of colour cannot be underestimated as an influence on taste in the period before the war.

Above Lobster chair, mid-1930s.

Above right The 'Ultra-meuble' by Kurt Seligmann, exhibited at the Paris Surrealist Exhibition of 1938.

Revivalism *by Malcolm Haslam*

Alternative styles and tastes

WHAT OCCURRED DURING the period 1890–1940 was a rare event in the history of art: the emergence of styles which depended hardly at all on precedent. Even the Renaissance, as its name implies, was to a large extent a historical revival. Perhaps the advent of Gothic in the twelfth and thirteenth centuries had been the last time that an entirely modern style had appeared, as it were, from nowhere.

All the art historical glamour of the last decade of the nineteenth and the first half of the twentieth century belongs to the designers and architects celebrated in Nikolaus Pevsner's *Pioneers of Modern Design* and it is easy to forget that Modernism was regarded by a vast majority of their contemporaries with suspicion and scorn, and that much the greater part of the architecture and decorative art produced during the period was traditional in style – or rather styles.

It is not to be supposed that every Modernist rejected out of hand his entire artistic heritage. On the contrary many had a profound understanding of past styles and applied their knowledge to their art. The pottery of William de Morgan, a close friend and disciple of William Morris, seemed and still seems today something original and progressive; but in 1888 De Morgan wrote to his partner from Italy: 'I hope to find when I come back a mine of pots that might be Greek, Sicilian, Etruscan, Moorish, Italian Renaissance – anything but Staffordshire.' De Morgan's remark indicates an attitude shared by many of the avant-garde decorative artists: that considerations of manufacture and materials came above style. The corollary, which was recognised by a small but increasing number of architects, designers and craftsmen was that style *depended* on materials and manufacture, and this idea became an integral principle of the Bauhaus ideology.

At the same time there were all those who regretted this down-grading of style – in the art historical sense – and who turned with a defensive ardour to the traditional criteria of good taste. Even some Modernists seem to have looked askance at the monsters they had spawned; for instance Josef Maria Olbrich was apparently only saved by an early death from dedicating himself entirely to a revived Rococo, and Arthur Heygate Mackmurdo, one of the creators of Art Nouveau, had effectively bowed out of the Modern Movement by the turn of the century with a series of designs in imitation of Wren or Sansovino.

The inversion of this process, which can hardly be documented, involves all those young art-school dreamers whose Modernist aspirations were soon drowned in the very muddy waters of commercialism and financial necessity and profit.

There were many designers who accepted their clients' taste, whether their client was a private patron or the public at large. Outside a small circle of enlightened individuals, men like Güell or Rathenau, most people clung to the styles they understood or, more importantly, the styles which had the 'correct' national, social or economic significance. Over the last hundred years Modernism in art and design has so often been identifiable with radical opinion that a healthy demand for historical styles from those wishing to declare their ideological orthodoxy, or simply their wealth, has always been maintained. From Morris to Le Corbusier the ethos of Modernism often demanded a socialist orientation in politics. The world would only become a more beautiful place when the poor were richer and the rich were less vulgar.

At the Great Exhibition of 1851, however, Prince Albert had helped to establish Renaissance as the style of commercial prosperity. Baron Haussmann had rebuilt Paris for Napoleon III in the styles of the periods during which the French monarchy had enjoyed its greatest degree of absolutism; he had made the boulevards too wide to be barricaded by a discontented populace.

Similarly, the Ringstrasse in Vienna had been planned by Franz Josef in order to avert any recurrence of the events of 1848 when the vulnerability of the imperial residence had become frighteningly apparent. The Ringstrasse had created a quasi-moat between the imperial government and the proletarians who lived in Vienna's suburbs. The new road had been lined along its inner edge by government offices, which were in effect fortresses, built in a variety of historical styles recalling the might and majesty of the Hapsburg Emperors.

Seldom during the period under review was there a public building erected in an avant-garde style. It is also noticeable how often Modernism flourished in provincial cities, away from the seat of national government. Art Nouveau, for instance was nurtured in Nancy, Barcelona, Glasgow, Turin, Munich and Chicago, cities with a degree of commercial prosperity but with something less than awe for the central administration. It does not seem fanciful to argue that the more authoritarian governments were the more relentlessly opposed to Modernism was the style of their buildings. Henry Bacon's Lincoln Memorial, Washington D.C., completed in 1917, and Sir Edward Lutyens' Viceroy's House, New Delhi, completed in 1931 were both as frankly revivalist as Albert

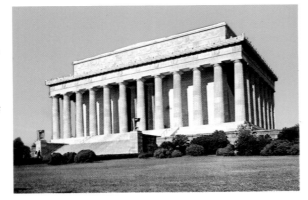

Right The Lincoln Memorial, Washington DC, designed in classical style by Henry Bacon, 1917.

Far right English Edwardian revivalism in the staircase of Belfast City Hall, designed by Sir A. Brumwell Thomas, 1906.

Below The Neo-Baroque domed hall of the World Exhibition, Paris, 1889.

Speer's model for a new Berlin or Marcello Piacentini's Terza Roma.

The antipathy to Modernism which characterised totalitarian governments is endorsed by the Nazis' closure of the Bauhaus and by the Kremlin's promulgation of Social Realism. If this argument seems a little exaggerated it is only putting in terms of political history the innate conservatism of the higher echelons in society, which is neatly expressed by the wording of a 1908 advertisement for a leading firm of British cabinet-makers: 'Persons of taste who desire to furnish their town houses or country houses in the English or French Period Styles may entrust themselves with complete confidence to the guidance of Warings', Decorators to H. M. the King'. Even in the early twentieth century much western art remained in one important respect the same as it had been since the middle ages – it was art designed for courtiers.

What styles, then, were revived between 1890 and 1940? The brief answer is any if not all. 'Eclecticism' is the English word applied to Victorian revivalism of the latter half of the nineteenth century and there is no reason why it should not be used for the continuation of the same phenomenon in the twentieth century. It is less descriptive than the German term 'Historismus', but its innuendo of selection from a repertoire is more revealing about contemporary attitudes, one of which claimed that the biological analogy of 'natural selection' invalidated any fundamental break with earlier modes.

The bible of British eclecticism was for at least half a century Owen Jones' *Grammar of Ornament*, first published in 1856. Here, presented in fine chromo-lithographic plates, is a wide choice of historical styles of decoration ranging from ancient Greek and Celtic to Louis Quinze and late Stuart; there are even illustrations by Christopher Dresser of the geometrical adaptation of flowers, but that is the book's only concession to Modernism, and the Baroque, Rococo, Adam, Louis Seize, Empire and Regency were omitted because their frivolity offended mid-Victorian high-mindedness. But Thackeray's novels and the architecture of Nesfield and Shaw cast a more demure light over the eighteenth century so that by 1890 the designer's range of choice was practically comprehensive.

Similarly in France, during the reign of Emperor Napoleon III, as we have seen, those styles most readily identifiable with autocracy had been reinstated after decades of neglect following the Revolution of 1789. As Germany moved towards unification the principal criterion operating in choice of historical style was nationalism, tempered only by a perennial infatuation with the classicism of the south. In America, where the country's own artistic past would hardly be appreciated until the twentieth century, a catholicity of taste reflected the variety of European nations from which the immigrants hailed.

This rapid survey shows that during the period under review the designer's (or his client's) choice was practically unlimited, or at least that the permissible certainly outweighed the taboo. Moreover the formalisation of architectural training, which occurred in most nations of the western world at the turn of the century and was due to the

Left A Neo-classical cabinet made in England, *c.* 1905.

Below An English Edwardian interior in the Neo-classical style.

ever increasing amount of technical and legal information to be assimilated by the student, produced a breed of architect versed not only in the minutiae of plumbing and electric lifts but also in the niceties of the acanthus scroll and the gargoyle.

Thorstein Veblen in his book *Theory of the Leisure Class* published in 1899 coined the phrase 'conspicuous waste' to describe the ostentatious affluence of the European and American rich, and it is a phrase which may be neatly applied to so much of the architecture and the decorative arts produced during the two decades before the First World War. 'Edwardian' and 'Wilhelminisch' have entered their respective languages as pejorative terms implying profligate luxury; this was *la Belle Epoque* or, as it became known in Veblen's America, the Gilded Age.

Nowhere was the waste more conspicuous than in New York. Along Fifth Avenue there sprang up the palaces which were ironically labelled 'houses' – Senator Clark house, William K. Vanderbilt house, A. T. Stewart house, Andrew Carnegie house, John Jacob Astor house and more.

Their style was usually that of the grandest seventeenth- or eighteenth-century French *châteaux* and American architects like Richard M. Hunt, who had attended the Ecole des Beaux-Arts

in Paris, France, were much in demand. Even when Duveen was in full flight it was not possible to furnish these mansions throughout with more or less genuine antiques, so all over Europe and America craftsmen were at work making replicas or creating period pieces. The Franco-British Exhibition at the White City, London, in 1908 included immaculate reproductions by Edouard Poteau of Oeben and Riesener furniture and a complete Marie Antoinette boudoir. H. C. Marillier, writing in the *Illustrated Review of the Exhibition*, compared these reproductions with 'the new art,' and no doubt expressed conventional opinion on both sides of the Channel and on both sides of the Atlantic when he concluded: '. . . . but in common honesty I am bound to confess that of the two, I am more inclined to admire the splendid workmanship exhibited by these copies of the antique than the striving after original effects exhibited by the new school'.

It is too easy to forget that Tiffany's iridescent glass was only a sideline and that far greater resources went into the manufacture of such objects as the Adams vase presented in 1895 by the stockholders and directors of the American Cotton Oil Company to Edward Dean Adams, chairman of the board. An elaborate confection in the manner of Cellini, it inspires statistical rather

The John Jacob Astor house on Fifth Avenue, New York, designed in French château style, 1898.

than aesthetic appreciation; for instance, three draughtsmen, fifteen modellers, eighteen goldsmiths, twenty-one chasers, twelve finishers, four moulders, three turners, two enamellers, three stonecutters and two lapidaries were involved in its production.

Opulence and Rococo splendour had not been unknown during the second half of the nineteenth century. The Rothschilds, for example, in London, Paris and Vienna had established Louis Quinze as a style de luxe and the firms catering for the taste of the wealthy had provided the bankers and their imitators with appropriate accessories. But the American tycoons of the Gilded Age outstripped their European counterparts in the lavish grandeur of the surroundings which they demanded. They came to Europe to acquire the heirlooms of a declining aristocracy and on their sallies into the old continent in search of tapestries or titled marriage partners they had to be accommodated in hotels built in the manner to which they were accustomed. Thus, beside Green Park in London rose the Ritz, designed by the Anglo-French partnership of Davis and Mewès, the latter supplying the inevitable Beaux-Arts panache.

In Paris and on the Riviera the same sort of monuments appeared, and to ferry the 'Innocents' across the Atlantic, liners were built which had public rooms fitted out like Renaissance or Baroque palaces such as those designed by Gustavo Pulitzer Finali for the Italia Line. Before the industrial buildings of America began to impinge on progressive architects, before Hollywood spectaculars had begun to flicker on the screens of European cinemas and before jazz imprinted its crazy rhythms on the culture of the Old World, the first wave of transatlantic influence was an imposing heap of flotsam and jetsam, in styles which were elaborately historical but unmistakably Yankee.

At the same time other, less sumptuous styles were being revived. In France, despite rapid assimilation of iron and ferro-concrete technology, decorative art appeared in the styles associated with most of the French monarchs from François Premier to Louis Seize; particularly favoured round the turn of the century was the Rococo of Louis Quinze, as curly and flippant as Art Nouveau without being offensively modern. But almost everywhere Art Nouveau itself provoked a flight to the more sober styles of the past.

Sir Reginald Blomfield was typical of a generation of English architects bred in the neo-gothic tradition who despised 'the swirl and the blob' (to quote his description of Art Nouveau), and turned to a rather jaded Georgian. The 'Wrenaissance' which had begun in the 1880s was still a style sometimes preferred to Georgian for office buildings, either commercial or municipal, and for some domestic work. Generally, however, 'Jacobethan' remained the popular style for private houses, occasionally on a grand scale when Sir Edward Lutyens used it for some of his country mansions, but mostly in a more modest version which particularly found favour with the garden-city planners. The style was taken up by speculators who built in the suburbs of most large English cities, and a huge market was created for the appropriate furnishings.

In an age when nationalism pervaded all levels of society, vernacular styles were in vogue not only in England but throughout most of Europe. In Scotland, the Scottish Baronial prevailed; Mackintosh's original development of the style was a mutation which met with very limited approval. Similarly, the Dutch architect Berlage transformed the medievalism of the Rundbogenstil into something modern, but for every Berlage there were several others happy to follow historical detail with the pedantry of P. J. H. Cuypers whose Rijksmuseum and railway-station in Amsterdam had established the popularity of the revival.

Nowhere was the reaction against Art Nouveau more vehement than in Germany, where the new style was known as Jugendstil. C. F. Schinkel's architecture, the most severely monumental style with a claim to being considered national, was an appropriate corrective. Peter Behrens and a few others could doff their caps to Schinkel and still design factories and electrical fittings that were truly modern, but many more were happy to retrieve their pattern-books and recreate the world of Frederick Wilhelm III. Among the latter, Heinrich von Tessenow was to be Speer's tutor, and Wilhelm Kreis and Paul Ludwig Troost were, like the style in which they were adepts, to have a new lease of life during the 1930s.

Cultivated German taste which disapproved of Jugendstil but found the Neo-classical monotonous and frighteningly plain, sought relief in the northern Baroque, the old standby which always afforded the ornamental carver plenty of opportunity for angst-ridden intricacies of decoration; and the furniture in this style was more solid, more burgerlich.

The Rundbogenstil also had its followers in Germany and a notable construction was the Wertheim department store in the Leipziger Strasse, Berlin, designed by Adolf Messel and completed in 1899; on a framework of iron and hung in places with enormous plate-glass windows the full height of the façade, the building was liberally spread with Gothic carved stone decoration, but the elevations were articulated in a Schinkelesque repetition of unitary bays, and the edifice was topped off with mansard roofs. It looked like the plates from a history of German architecture, superimposed one over another.

In Scandinavia the same sort of historicisms appeared as were being perpetrated by architects and designers in the rest of Europe. Martin Nyrop's Town Hall, Copenhagen, built between 1892 and 1902 is in the revived Rundbogenstil which prevailed in Holland and Germany during the 1890s, and Ragnar Ostberg's Town Hall, Stockholm, was built between 1909 and 1923 in the local version of Baroque (with Gothic embellishments).

A revival of Romantic Classicism which started in Denmark round 1910 and in Sweden about a decade later has affinities with neo-Schinkelism in Germany. Just as an admiration for Schinkel led some German designers to a severe functionalism, so Romantic Classicism in Scandinavia was gradually transformed into the international Modern Style of the late 1920s. In Denmark the revival included an enthusiasm for Sheraton's furniture designs, which lies behind the elegance of modern

Right The swimming bath at the Royal Automobile Club building, London, built in 1908–11 to designs by Arthur J. Davis and Charles Mewès.

Below Revivalist styles were widely used in the interior designs for the great transatlantic liners; the main lounge of the Italia Line's *Conte di Savoia* (1932), designed by Gustavo Pulitzer Finali, was a combination of Neo-classical and Baroque elements which contrasted strangely with the 'modern' covering of the furniture.

Danish furniture, perhaps the country's most felicitous contribution to the Modern Movement.

Gradually during the 1920s and 1930s Modernism became more acceptable in Europe and America. The Bauhaus message was disseminated, and the attention of the world was caught at the 1925 Exhibition in Paris. But reviewing this exhibition the Surrealist poet Louis Aragon commented: 'Well, personally, after all, I prefer *le Grand Art*'. The barren geometry of modern design put off many less profound critics than Aragon; they clung tenaciously to the more homely, less sophisticated styles of their forbears or the more pompous, less restrained styles which bore authority's seal of approval – just as the Surrealists might yearn for decoration which was more the stuff that dreams are made of. Hybrids began to appear: Palladian windows with Crittal metal frames, bakelite boxes with classical reliefs moulded on the lid. Sometimes it is called Kitsch and it has had its own revival in the recent past.

Times were changing. But Liberty's, the London department store, must have reassured those who felt that progress was inexorably swift. In 1924 they opened their new (if that is the right word) premises on Great Marlborough Street. It was a pious offering to the buccaneering genius of the Elizabethan era, the spirit of commercial

Left The Neo-classical design of the Royal Automobile Club's swimming bath was repeated by Davis and Mewès in their design for the German liner *Vaterland*.

Below The tea foyer at the Ritz Hotel, London, designed in 1904 by Arthur J. Davis and Charles Mewès.

enterprise which had made Britain so rich and powerful. The half-timbered façade, the oak-beamed interior and the shopgirls' medieval uniforms testified to the middle-class's undying faith in the right-mindedness of their yeomen forbears. One wonders whether it was a deliberate touch of irony to have had carved, on the keystone of the archway bearing the famous clock, this couplet:

No minute gone comes ever back again
Take heed and see ye nothing do in vain.

Perhaps since 1920 stylistic revivals have changed in character. One cannot be quite sure whether Libertys' Tudor building of 1924 was historical revivalism or nostalgia for happier days before the First World War. The same doubt is raised when considering Hitler's classicism; was it an evocation of the Roman Republic or a re-miniscence of the pride of Germany before the Second Reich collapsed? Perhaps a new category of revivalism had emerged. There had been the antiquarianism of the earlier nineteenth-century revivals; then there had been the political, social or economic symbolism of most revivals up to the First World War; and now there were revivals induced by nostalgia, which seem to have begun between the Wars and are still with us now.

Above Reception room by Wilhelm Kreis, Bremen, 1911; reproduced in the Deutscher Werkbund yearbook for 1912.

Right and below Sculpted window surrounds by Karl Gross, Dresden, 1911; reproduced in the Deutscher Werkbund yearbook for 1912.

Above Cabinet made in the workshops of Liberty & Co., *c.* 1908.

Right Liberty & Co. dress, made *c.* 1929.

Industrial Design 1890–1940 *by Stuart Durant*

An aesthetic for technology

IN 1890 THE STEAM AGE was drawing to its close. The exalted position of steam, which had seemed so permanent at the time of the 1851 Exhibition, was to be usurped in barely more than a generation. At its zenith, steam could propel screw or paddle ships, a single steam engine could turn many lathes or operate many looms. The steam locomotive had appeared early in its final and perfect form, but within a short time steam had ceased to be the prime field for the innovator. With the exception of the development of the steam turbine in the 1880s and 1890s, steam technology had changed remarkably little throughout the whole steam age.

The advance of nineteenth-century technology was so swift that by 1879 Werner von Siemens was able to demonstrate electric traction with his miniature passenger-carrying railway at the Berlin Trade Fair. The death knell had sounded for steam. In December 1879, Thomas Edison, having perfected the carbon filament lamp, demonstrated the practicability of electric lighting to New Yorkers. Electricity was clean, it could be produced at centralised generating stations and, above all, it was versatile. It could provide motive power, illumination and heat. By 1884 Siemens and his partner Halske had constructed an electric

tramway between Frankfurt-am-Main and Offenbach. The earliest of the London electric underground railways was begun in 1887.

Over twenty-five million people witnessed the marvels of electricity at the Paris Universal Exhibition of 1889. The electric beacon at the top of Gustave Eiffel's three-hundred-metre tower – the centre-piece of the exhibition – was seen from vantage points on the cathedral of Orléans, some seventy miles distant. Searchlights on the Eiffel Tower picked out buildings over six miles away on the outskirts of Paris. At the Telephone Pavilion visitors listened to singers performing at the Opéra, or the Opéra Comique – a clumsy foretaste of the radio broadcast some thirty years away. Electrically-driven viewing gantries gave visitors an aerial view of the unprecedented array of machinery displayed along the length of Ferdinand Dutert's Palace of Machines, the largest nineteenth-century steel and glass building. The 1889 Exhibition was entirely illuminated by electricity and had its own generating stations operated by rival contractors. There were 20,000 Edison electric lamps in the Palace of Machines alone. In England the gardens of the Royal Horticultural Society in South Kensington had been illuminated with 9,700 electric lights for the

Far left A contemporary impression of the electric searchlights placed on the Eiffel Tower for the 1889 Paris Universal Exhibition.

Left The Palace of Machines at the 1889 Paris Universal Exhibition by Contamin and Dutert, showing the curtain wall of stained glass.

Colonial and Indian Exhibition of 1886.

The invention of the petrol-powered internal combustion engine, together with the introduction of the electric motor, was to prove an important factor in the eventual displacement of the steam engine. The precursor of the petrol engine was the gas engine in which a mixture of gas and air was combusted by an electric spark. The Parisian engineer Etienne Lenoir had succeeded in producing such an engine in 1859. Lenoir's engine was, however, too expensive to be operated commercially. But, in 1878, the German Nikolaus Otto developed a four-stroke gas engine that was comparatively economical to run. In principle Otto's gas engine is close to the modern petrol engine. At the 1889 Exhibition, one of the electricity-generating stations was operated with Otto engines. In 1885 Gottlieb Daimler fitted a high-speed petrol engine of his own design to a rudimentary motor car.

Henry Ford brought the motor car within reach of considerable sections of the American proletariat. Ford achieved this not by making improvements to the design of the motor car itself, but by concentrating on bringing down the costs of production. Ford reduced costs by the introduction of production-line assembly, first introduced for the Model T Ford in 1913, although the car itself had been first launched in 1908.

It is ironical that the Great War could not have been fought upon the vast and terrifying scale which it was, had it not been for the adoption of assembly-line production by manufacturers of military equipment. The obverse side of this dispiriting picture was that mass-production soon made it possible for many ordinary people to possess mechanical domestic equipment which made their lives a good deal more enjoyable. In *Vers une Architecture* (1923) Le Corbusier could speak of houses 'built on the same principles as the Ford car'. He looked forward to the coming of the 'house-machine' – 'the mass-production house, healthy – and morally so too – and beautiful'.

Ford and his methods epitomise the unfettered spirit of American industry. American industry had, in fact, been making spectacular progress since the middle of the nineteenth century, this was amply confirmed by the scale of the great American industrial exhibitions – the Philadelphia Centennial Exhibition of 1876, the World's Columbian Exhibition of Chicago of 1893 and the St. Louis Exhibition of 1904.

However impressive was American industrial growth, that of Germany was equally so. German mercantilism was, like America's, allied to a vigorous technology. The rise of Germany as an industrial giant is readily demonstrated by a few statistics. During the years 1881–5, Britain's share of world trade was approximately 38 per cent while Germany's share was just over 17 per cent. By 1913, however, the gap had narrowed and Britain's share of world trade had fallen to just over 27 per cent while Germany's had risen to nearly 22 per cent. The German figures for steel production are especially impressive, for by 1913 Germany's steel production was within sight of being three times that of Britain's. By 1914 Germany's national wealth had surpassed Britain's. These figures were achieved despite the facts that Germany lacked a ready-made imperial market and that she had emerged late as a unified nation. Much of Germany's industrial progress can be attributed to the importance which she attached to scientific and technological research.

The Germans responded not only to the technological challenges of industrialization but also to its aesthetic challenges. Although Britain, as exemplified by Richard Redgrave's *Supplementary Report on Design (1852)*, a critical assessment of the art manufactures at the Great Exhibition, had been concerned at a comparatively early date with mass-produced products, no viable kind of British machine aesthetic had been formulated. The Deutscher Werkbund typified Germany's far-sighted approach to the issue of the machine. Traditionally the response to the machine of the academically-trained architect or the designer, had been to ignore it. However, the Werkbund was to draw into its orbit the leading German architects.

The Deutscher Werkbund was founded in 1907 and represents the first large-scale attempt to reconcile the arts with industry. Membership of the Werkbund was by invitation and open to manufacturers, architects and industrial artists. Among distinguished Werkbund members were: Peter Behrens, who had been appointed design co-ordinator for the great electrical combine AEG in the same year that the Werkbund was founded; Walter Gropius, who was to be Director of the Bauhaus from 1919 to 1928; Richard Riemerschmid, who had planned the garden city – a British idea – at Hellerau, near Dresden; and Henry van de Velde who had been initially inspired by the Utopianism of Ruskin and Morris but who had come to the conclusion that the modern artist should collaborate with commerce and industry. Among Austrian members of the Werkbund were Josef Hoffmann, Otto Wagner and, somewhat unexpectedly, Gustav Klimt.

The Werkbund had been founded by Hermann Muthesius as the outcome of a furore after he had publicly condemned German manufacturers for their mindless filching of historic styles with which to clothe their products. Muthesius, a Prussian architect and civil servant, had already established a reputation with two immensely ambitious surveys of British Arts and Crafts and progressive architecture – W. R. Lethaby called him 'the historian of English free architecture'. (Muthesius' studies are – the four-volume *Das Englische Baukunst und Gedenwart*, completed in 1904, and the three-volume *Das Englische Haus* – the better known of the two works – completed in 1905.) During the six years, from 1896, that he spent in Britain, Muthesius became fully acquainted with the philosophy of the Arts and Crafts Movement. However, he saw that the Arts and Crafts Movement, with its emphasis on the revival of traditional craft values, was fostering an entirely negative attitude towards the machine.

The first yearbook of the Werkbund was published in 1912. It illustrates Behrens' powerfully monumental AEG factories as well as his light-fittings and ventilating fans for AEG. Worker's houses by Riemerschmid are also shown, as well as designs for wooden toys, tombs, ceramics and linoleum. Many of the Werkbund designs do not differ very greatly from contemporary Arts and

Opposite German industrial advertising, 1914; Germany was the first nation to apply industrial design on a large scale to manufactures, especially those of the automobile industry.

Crafts-inspired designs shown in contemporary publications like *The Studio*, the emphasis being upon simplicity and appropriateness of ornamentation.

A significant feature of the Werkbund yearbooks was the high standard of their theoretical debate. In his address at the Werkbund convention at Dresden in 1911, *Wo Stehen Wir*? (Where do we stand?), which was published in the 1912 yearbook, Muthesius indicated his own position. He stressed the importance of quality, form – in its pure and abstract sense – and standardization.

The interest in form seems peculiarly German and stems from the idea of the Platonic archetype, the governing form which transcends transitory forms, that had been so prevalent in the thinking of Goethe and his contemporaries. As a theorist Muthesius has an obvious importance, as a designer he lacked the inventiveness of Werkbund colleagues like Behrens or Hans Poelzig.

The 1913 Werkbund yearbook was in great part devoted to factory design. Behrens' famous turbine assembly building for AEG is illustrated. This building represented, in its classical refinement, the most potent Werkbund ideals. There are also factories by Hans Poelzig – romantic and almost Piranesi-like – as well as Walter Gropius'

Fagus shoe-last factory, a harbinger of Bauhaus architecture. Muthesius' factory is Neo-classical and altogether undistinguished. A number of North American factories are also shown, including the Ford factory at Detroit. A lesser portion of the yearbook is devoted to illustrations of shop fronts and window displays. Gropius, Muthesius and August Endell, a survivor from the Jugendstil era, contributed articles. No true Werkbund style – as there was a Bauhaus style – can be said to have emerged, although there seems to have been a distinct preference for monumentality.

One of the most interesting examples of collaboration between a Werkbund designer and the manufacturer is to be found in the work of Ernst Neumann illustrated in the 1914 Werkbund yearbook. Neumann designed elegant and functional limousines, while his commercial car body (for Bussing Braunschweig) is very sculptural. Other designs for vehicles, locomotives, ships and aircraft are anonymous. Among these are the Zeppelin *Sachsen* – the first airship to operate commercially and an advanced-looking monoplane by the Luftverkehrs Gesellschaft, Johannistal. The locomotives shown are light and compact and there is clear visual evidence of a concern for aerodynamic form in some of the designs –

Below Limousine coachwork designed by Ernst Neumann, 1914.

Bottom Commercial vehicle body designed by Ernst Neumann for Bussing Braunschweig, 1914.

Above The Ford factory at Detroit, illustrated in the 1913 Werkbund yearbook, one of the first factories specially built for production-line techniques.

Right Interior of the glass pavilion designed by Bruno Taut for the 1914 Werkbund Exhibition.

funnels, domes and cabs are unmistakably flared, if not streamlined.

In 1914 the Werkbund mounted a large-scale outdoor exhibition at Cologne. Unfortunately its full impact was to be greatly diminished by the outbreak of war. The Cologne exhibition is documented in the 1915 Werkbund yearbook. Among the buildings of note were Gropius' model factory and administration building in which the influence of Frank Lloyd Wright is very evident in the main façade. In the rear courtyard façade Gropius further developed the idea of the window-skin with which he had experimented in the Fagus factory. Bruno Taut designed an exquisite little proto-expressionist glass pavilion with an ingenious, almost geodesic, roof structure. Henry van de Velde's Werkbund Theatre has certain curvilinear features and decorative details that remind one of his affinities with Art Nouveau. Peter Behrens' conference hall is Neo-classical and confirms the impression of classicism latent in the work of many Werkbund designers. Josef Hoffmann's Austrian pavilion is also Neo-classical, but in a chic Viennese way. Apart from railway carriage design, and Hermann Muthesius' interiors for the Hamburg-Amerika Line steamship *Bismarck*, transport design was not represented at Cologne. Although the Werkbund continued in existence after the 1914–18 war, it was to be overtaken by the Bauhaus as an influence in the future direction of design.

Although there was a good deal of anti-German feeling in Britain after the outbreak of war on 4 August 1914 the lessons of the Werkbund were carefully studied. In May 1915, the Design and Industries Association was founded. 'Where an enemy has a noble lesson to teach', said Clutton Brock, one of the founders of the D.I.A., 'it can only be learned from him nobly'. The D.I.A. published a number of yearbooks, but at two-yearly intervals, in emulation of the Werkbund. The first of these came out in 1922, seven years after the D.I.A. had been founded.

C. H. Collins Barker, Keeper and Secretary of the National Gallery, in the 1922 yearbook's introduction asserted that the chief article of the creed of the D.I.A. founders was 'fitness for purpose'. If 'a thing were unaffectedly made to fulfil its purpose thoroughly, then it would be good art'. Collins Barker also remarked that 'the disease of modern design and industry was not due to machinery, but to the imperfect comprehension of its limitations and possibilities'. Apart from this introduction there is no theoretical content in the first D.I.A. yearbook. We must look at the illustrations if we are to understand the ideals of the D.I.A. in its early stages.

Work illustrated in the 1922 D.I.A. yearbook comes from Heal and Sons, good, sensible, 'cottage furniture'; Dryad Handicrafts, excellent cane furniture inspired by German models; Josiah Wedgwood and Sons, refined, traditional pottery; W. Foxton, bold fabrics designed by Lovat Fraser and Gregory Brown; Leslie Mansfield's house style for Macfisheries, restrained and purposeful – a series of designs that were outstanding for their day. Motor cars by Lanchester, Bentley and bodywork by Hooper are illustrated as examples of 'fitness for purpose'. London Underground

Above Leslie Mansfield's design for the shop fronts of the Macfisheries chain of shops, 1922.

Left Interior of a London Underground carriage, 1922.

rolling-stock and aircraft by Bristol and Vickers are also used to emphasise the same point, and an airman's costume is praised for its functional beauty. The contents of the D.I.A. yearbook for 1924–5 are similar to the first D.I.A. yearbook. The London Underground is featured again as well as a number of rather unadventurous stands at the British Empire Exhibition, 1924.

John Gloag in his introduction to the D.I.A. yearbook for 1924–5, is cautious in his prognosis of the role of the D.I.A., 'It is a great temptation to dream of imposing plans that will recast the world and destroy all the foolish legacies of bad custom from past generations, the cramping traditions and other obstacles that stand in the way of an orderly and beautiful civilization; but the improvement of even one section of industry is a much more serviceable contribution to general betterment than a thousand Utopias – on paper'.

The D.I.A., then, was modest in its aims and its early work was admittedly unexciting. However, in the spring of 1932 the D.I.A. was to publish a journal, *Design in Industry*, to be superseded by *Design for Today* in 1933. The specialist editor of the first issue of *Design in Industry* was a pioneer of the Modern Movement in Britain, E. Maxwell Fry, and from this time onwards the D.I.A. was to be associated with the burgeoning British Modern Movement. Typographically *Design in Industry* is somewhat uncomfortable, the typefaces are sans-serif but arranged without the Bauhaus aplomb, but the journal itself was by no means fusty. Lethaby is quoted on the cover: design did not 'involve some strange originality . . . . it should be just the appropriate shaping and finish for the thing required'. The D.I.A. in many ways spanned the gulf between the Arts and Crafts Movement and Modernism.

Le Corbusier's *Vers une Architecture*, published in Paris in 1923 and in London in 1927 as *Towards a New Architecture*, is a key work. Many of Le Corbusier's ideas were to penetrate to the very subconscious of a generation. As a polemicist he was quite the equal of predecessors like Pugin or Viollet-le-Duc. The Argument from *Towards a New Architecture* is justly famous. Here is the opening paragraph: 'The Engineer's Aesthetic, and Architecture, are two things that march together and follow one from the other; the one being now at its full height (the engineer's), the other (the architect's) in an unhappy state of retrogression'.

The argument based on the analogy of the aeroplane shows Le Corbusier as a machine age

romantic: 'The airplane is the product of close selection . . . . . The lesson of the airplane lies in the logic which governed the statement of the problem and its realization. The problem of the house has not yet been stated. Nevertheless there do exist standards for the dwelling-house. Machinery contains in itself the factor of economy, which makes for selection. The house is a machine for living in.' Le Corbusier's ideas were demonstrated in his L'Esprit Nouveau pavilion at the Paris 1925 Exhibition. The L'Esprit Nouveau pavilion was merely a single apartment, taken like a drawer from a chest-of-drawers, from a large block of flats from his city of 3,000,000 inhabitants of 1922. The apartment, with its colour-washed walls, was furnished with cheap bentwood chairs and mass-produced equipment. A model monoplane was hung on a wall like a trophy.

Some of Le Corbusier's ideas, glossily packaged, appear in Norman Bel Geddes' *Horizons* which was published in 1932. Bel Geddes was a film and stage designer – he also wrote and directed for the film and stage – who, in the 1930s, had built up a successful industrial design practice. Bel Geddes tells us: 'We are entering a new era which, notably, shall be characterised by design in four specific phases: Design in social structure to insure the organization of people, work, wealth, leisure. Design in machines that shall improve working conditions by eliminating drudgery. Design in all objects of daily use that shall make them economical, durable, convenient, congenial to everyone. Design in the arts, painting, music, literature, and architecture, that shall inspire the new era.'

There was nothing really new in the principle of streamlining and in the First World War some of the later Zeppelins had comparatively sophisticated aerodynamic forms. Even before the war, some of the locomotives illustrated in the 1914 Werkbund yearbook approached the streamlined form.

Although there were other excellent designers in the streamlined idiom – Henry Dreyfuss, Otto Kohler and Raymond Loewy, for instance – Bel Geddes, in *Horizons*, did more than any one else to propagandise the streamlined form.

Bel Geddes said in *Horizons* that he had decided in 1927 to cease to work only for the theatre. Henceforward he would design for sources 'more vitally akin to life to-day'. He then worked on projects for streamlined ocean liners, motor cars, motor coaches and steam locomotives, most of which were never to exist even in prototype form. Bel Geddes' transatlantic airliner, inspired by Claude Dornier's giant Do X of 1929, had twelve engines and a cruising speed of 100 mph. There was to be luxurious accommodation in the wings and the twin hulls for 451 passengers and a crew of 155. Refuelling was to take place, in flight, over Newfoundland. The fact that Bel Geddes could jettison a respected 'high art' – the theatre – in order to embrace industrial design is highly significant. Since Behrens, the Werkbund, the Bauhaus or Le Corbusier industrial design had become an increasingly esteemed activity. The 1930s were the heroic age of industrial design. The outbreak of war in 1939 brought that age which had such faith in design to an end.

Below Theatre project by Norman Bel Geddes, 1932.

Right Pierce-Arrow car exhibited outside the House of Tomorrow at the Century of Progress Exposition, Chicago World's Fair.

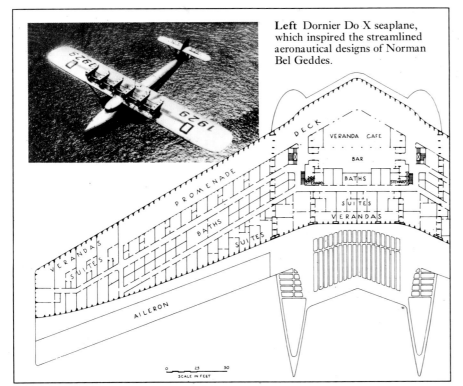

Left Dornier Do X seaplane, which inspired the streamlined aeronautical designs of Norman Bel Geddes.

PART TWO

DESIGNS
AND
DESIGNERS

1890-1940

France

Furniture and Interior Design *by Philippe Garner*

THE 1890s SAW THE DEVELOPMENT in France of Art Nouveau, the fully evolved characteristics of which enjoyed their greatest success at the 1900 Exhibition, combining the threads of naturalism, abstraction from nature and Japanese-inspired refinement that had been at the roots of the style. From the various displays at the 1900 Exhibition the concept of Art Nouveau furnishing emerges as a total one – designers were seen as *ensembliers*, rather than as creators of individual pieces of furniture, and it is perhaps the overpowering effect of a complete French Art Nouveau interior that made the fashion fairly short-lived.

During the Art Nouveau period, France had two centres for furniture and interior design: Paris, naturally, as the capital, and also the town of Nancy, where Emile Gallé encouraged local artists to work in the more naturalistic version of Art Nouveau which he favoured. In Paris, one of the most significant names in the evolution and success of the Art Nouveau style interior was that of Samuel Bing.

Bing, dealer, patron and publisher, was an enthusiastic admirer of Japanese art through the last quarter of the nineteenth century. Much travelled, Bing had visited the Far East he so much admired; he also met Louis Comfort Tiffany in the United States and returned filled with Tiffany's ideals of allying industrial methods of production to high standards of artistic creativity. In 1888 Bing had launched a monthly magazine, *Le Japon Artistique*. At the Galeries de l'Art Nouveau which he opened at 22 Rue de Provence in December 1895 Bing exhibited the work of the artists he admired, including Tiffany, Aubrey Beardsley, René Lalique and Emile Gallé. During the late 1890s Bing sponsored the work of a number of artists whose potential he admired, notably Georges de Feure, Edward Colonna and Eugène Gaillard and it was with their contributions to his Pavillon de l'Art Nouveau at the Paris Exhibition of 1900 that he was to achieve his greatest success. By the time of Bing's death five years later in 1905 the style to which he gave a name had begun to decline. Colonna had ceased to work for Bing in 1903 and neither Gaillard nor de Feure was to create anything to equal their contributions of 1900.

The suite of rooms which constituted the Pavillon de l'Art Nouveau are amongst the most important interiors created in the style and deserve particular attention. The entrance itself was a seductive promise of the delights within, in the form of panels by the talented Dutch-Belgian Georges de Feure depicting life-size female figures in elaborate peacock-skirted dresses. De Feure had a distinctive graphic style, comparable in its colours, emphasis on outlines and elegant harmonies of women and flowers, to that of Alphonse Mucha, but with a more sophisticated flavour. His graphic talent found expression in the design of textiles, papers and stained glass, examples of which, together with his furniture, a Sitting Room and a Dressing Room, were to be found in Bing's Pavillon. The Sitting Room was certainly one of the most refined rooms created in the Art Nouveau style. With its use of embroidered silk upholsteries and gilt wood furniture delicately carved with stylised floral motifs the room achieved an aristocratic flavour in the best traditions of the French eighteenth century.

Eugène Gaillard exhibited two rooms, a Dining Room and a Bedroom. In the Dining Room, Gaillard contrived to use elegant whiplash motifs everywhere, on the tooled leather upholstery of chairs, on the carved panels of the cabinet that dominated the room, woven in the design of the carpet, in the metalwork ornamental frieze which adorned the *boiseries* beneath murals by José Maria Sert and in the carved limbs of the furniture. Gaillard's passion for the undulating line was given a free rein in the Bedroom where the lines of heavily figured wood panelling emphasised the fluid concept of the furniture. Edward Colonna's Drawing Room had more of the refinement of de Feure than the exuberance of Gaillard. Muted green plush walls set off the lines, elegantly abstracted from nature, of Colonna's furniture.

Julius Meier-Graefe played a role similar to that of Bing as entrepreneur and patron. His interest was in applying modern ideas in a cohesive way to every aspect of domestic design. Setting up workshops and commissioning work from a wide range of designers, both from France and abroad, Meier-Graefe opened La Maison Moderne in 1898 in the Rue des Petits Champs as a showcase and retail outlet. The shop-front was designed in his characteristic abstract dynamic style by the Belgian artist Henri van de Velde, whose work strongly influenced Abel Landry, head of the Maison Moderne furniture atelier. Paul Follot and Maurice Dufrêne both designed furniture and other items for Meier-Graefe. The success of La Maison Moderne was short-lived as was that of a group formed in 1898 and calling itself 'les Six.'

The six included three artists who achieved distinction as furniture designers, Alexandre Charpentier, Charles Plumet and Tony Selmersheim. Charpentier designed furniture with strong yet fluid lines and would incorporate the low-relief

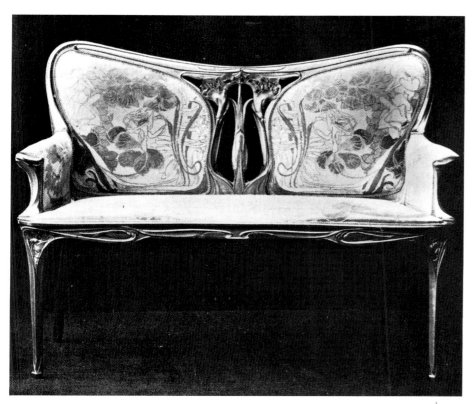

Left Giltwood and silk *canapé* designed by Georges de Feure for his sitting room in Bing's Pavillon de l'Art Nouveau in the 1900 Paris Exhibition.

Below Mahogany table designed by Edward Colonna for his drawing room in Bing's Pavillon de l'Art Nouveau.

Bottom Bedroom designed by Eugène Gaillard for Bing's Pavillon.

Pearwood cabinet designed
by Hector Guimard, *c.* 1900.

Carved wood chair by
Rupert Carabin, 1896.
Collection Mr. and Mrs.
Robert Walker, Paris.

carved panels at which he was so talented. Plumet and Selmersheim designed furniture on elegant abstract organic lines in the Paris mode and continued to work together on architectural and interior design schemes after the dissolution of the original group. Decorator Georges Hoentschel distinguished himself with his naturalistically carved furniture and *boiseries* in his *ensemble*, La Salle du Bois, at the Pavillon de l'Union Centrale des Arts Décoratifs in 1900.

Architect-designer Hector Guimard was one of the most important practitioners of the principle of total environment. Active as an architect from 1888, he evolved his Art Nouveau style towards the mid 1890s. Guimard's high Art Nouveau period lasted until about 1905 when his work mellowed into a more restrained, more elegant phase. He designed every detail of his interiors, plasterwork, stained glass, tiles and fireplaces, light fittings, woodwork, handles and lock-plates as well, of course, as the furniture. During his high Art Nouveau period, his furniture was truly eccentric, with energetic lines sweeping over fireplaces, and filling corners, echoing the relief of wall mouldings and fitted woodwork and emphasising the sense of unity. At a later date, between about 1905 and 1912, whilst still employing interplays of sculpted, abstract curvilinear forms, Guimard showed greater restraint in the more subdued carving of the steamed pearwood which he favoured.

An isolated but significant talent working in the 1890s was that of Rupert Carabin. He carved slightly bizarre pieces of furniture incorporating full-relief allegorical female nudes. Carabin was his own craftsman and a feature of his furniture is the rich patina achieved by soaking in linseed oil and long and patient rubbing.

The school of furniture design encouraged by Emile Gallé in Nancy had its origins in the 1880s, when Gallé first discovered the qualities of exotic woods and added furniture design to the crafts of glass and faïence which had been the mainstay of his family's business. Gallé spent the late 1880s in the preparation of his first major furniture exhibit, for the Paris Universal Exhibition of 1889. Although in these early years of furniture production the forms tended to be ponderous and uninspired, the details of his work were already full of invention. He revitalised the craft of marquetry, using a wide variety of fruitwoods and exotic woods in their natural hues, often with details carved in relief. Plant and animal life inspired this rich marquetry with which he filled flat areas and the shapes he gave to limbs and framework. Gallé's debt to Japanese art was evident in the elegant abstract designs which he created within the tenets of his naturalism. An example is to be found in his chair 'aux ombelles' the back of which represents the plant theme in the style of a Japanese *tsuba*.

Gallé's principles of furniture design were set out in an essay, 'Le Mobilier Contemporain orné d'après la Nature', published in the November/December 1900 issue of the *Revue des Arts Décoratifs*. Here he explained the logic of Nature as a source of inspiration and emphasised the importance of choosing a theme relevant to function. The dining table 'aux herbes potagères' of 1892 is a good illustration of Gallé's principles.

Below 'Les Fleurs du Mal', carved wood and fruitwood marquetry cabinet on a theme from Baudelaire, designed by Emile Gallé, 1896.

Below right Carved fruitwood *sellette*, designed by Emile Gallé, *c*. 1900.

Bottom Gallé carved wood and fruitwood marquetry tray, *c*. 1900.

Gallé's masterpiece is the magnificent bed, *Aube et Crépuscule*, made in the last year of his life, 1904, with its spectacular panels of marquetry work, carved in relief and incorporating glass and mother-of-pearl.

The most important cabinet-maker to come under Gallé's influence in the 1890s was Louis Majorelle, whose career would otherwise have been spent in the manufacture of the Louis-Quinze style pieces in which his family business specialised. Majorelle followed in Gallé's footsteps in the application of natural themes to furniture design and many of his naturalistically carved pieces with marquetry decoration on the panels bear a very strong affinity to Gallé's work. At his best, however, Majorelle showed a distinctive personal style, escaping from the often cloying naturalism preached by Gallé to a more plastic, more abstract style that is amongst the strongest, purest expressions of French Art Nouveau and somehow avoiding the provincialism of much Nancy furniture. Majorelle's major works were the suites 'aux nénuphars' and 'aux orchidées', created between 1900 and 1908, in which the undulations of the design, fluidly carved in rich mahogany, are emphasised by the sensual lines of stylised gilt-bronze orchids, lily-pads and stems.

Other Nancy furniture designers of note were Jacques Gruber, Eugène Vallin and Emile André, all of whom became members of the 'Ecole de Nancy, Alliance Provinciale des Industries d'Art' founded by Gallé in 1901. Gruber, during the late 1890s, showed an interest both in glass and in furniture, working for a few years for the Daum brothers and designing furniture for Majorelle. He ran his own cabinet-making business for ten years between 1900 and 1910, creating pieces which, at their best, exploited to the full the abstract sculptural possibilities of French Art Nouveau, but which, at their worse, mixed heavy sculptural themes with naturalistic motifs with an overpowering effect in a ponderously provincial style in certain complete room designs. Gruber's interest in glass can be seen in his use of cameo glass panels in his furniture. After 1910 he devoted all his energies to work in another favoured medium, stained glass.

Eugène Vallin was, like Majorelle and Gruber at their best, interested in the plastic possibilities of wood. His furniture seems to grow from the ground in liquid, unbroken lines. Abandoning furniture design, Vallin turned full-time to architecture and satisfied his sculptural interests in work in poured concrete. Emile André, architect and furniture designer, was a founder member of the Ecole de Nancy. Victor Prouvé, friend and associate of Gallé, and, after Gallé's death, artistic director of his factory, created designs for marquetry panels for Gallé and for Majorelle.

The reaction against Art Nouveau and the evolution towards the style and motifs of Art Deco can be traced back to the years between 1905 and 1908. The flowing lines of Art Nouveau were subdued into more sober forms whilst more disciplined bouquets of stylised flowers, garlands and ribbonwork replaced the lush and convoluted motifs of the Art Nouveau style in the carved or inlaid details of furniture. A number of Art Nouveau furniture designers and decorators were able to change with the times and evolve towards the emerging Art Deco style; others, such as Guimard, mellowed their Art Nouveau style or, indeed, seem to have completely abandoned their work, unable or unwilling to adapt. Gallé died in 1904, Bing in 1905, and two leaders of taste were lost. Majorelle had, by 1910, evolved the more sober style in which he worked until his death in 1926.

Maurice Dufrêne and Paul Follot, leading contributors to Meier-Graefe's La Maison Moderne, did some very notable work in this transitional phase and emerged as leading designers in the Art Deco style in the early 1920s when, in 1921, Dufrêne assumed responsibility of the La Maîtrise ateliers for the Galeries Lafayette and, two years later, Follot took charge of the Atelier Pomone at the Bon Marché. The first such atelier of Art Deco design concerned with every aspect of furniture and the interior was the Atelier Martine opened by Paul Poiret in 1911. Journals of the pre-war years show a confusion of styles in furniture, but the recurrent thread is the restraint and Neoclassicism of the emerging Art Deco style which found one of its most perfect expression in the years immediately after the war in the work of Louis Süe and André Mare, whose Compagnie des Arts Français was founded in 1919. Süe et Mare, as they became known, created furniture in rich, highly-polished woods, of simple, slightly bulbous form with conventionalised floral Art Deco motifs carved in low-relief or inlayed in mother-of-pearl. They also created textile and paper designs using similar motifs and enjoyed the opportunity to present their total style in various exhibits including their Musée d'Art Contemporain at the 1925 Exhibition.

Léon Jallot and François Jourdain were amongst the more successful designers of the transitional phase, the latter favouring a rather advanced angular style. Paul Iribe, better known as an illustrator, designed a few exceptional items of furniture in the Art Deco style for the couturier Jacques Doucet, notably a commode in mahogany, sharkskin and ebony of about 1912, carved with Neo-classical garlands and inlaid with a highly stylised spray of flowers, and a series of *fauteuils-gondole* of about the same date. Clément Mère made furniture in the Art Deco style, elaborately inlaid and incorporating panels of tooled leather in their design.

The greatest *ébéniste-décorateur*, however, working in the Art Deco style was undoubtedly Emile-Jacques Ruhlmann, probably the most important cabinet-maker of the twentieth century. Although Ruhlmann had exhibited at the Salon d'Automne in 1910, it was at the Salon of 1913 that his work attracted attention when he introduced the slender tapered leg which was to become his hallmark. His pre-war successes included the *meuble d'encoignure* of 1916 inlaid in ivory with an elaborate bouquet of flowers in pure Art Deco taste. Shortly after the war Ruhlmann launched his Etablissements Ruhlmann et Laurent which, in the years up to his death in 1933, became the most prestigious decorating firm in France. At the Salon of 1919 Ruhlmann showed a superb cabinet in dark, figured wood, raised on his now characteristic slender tapered legs and inlaid in ivory with a

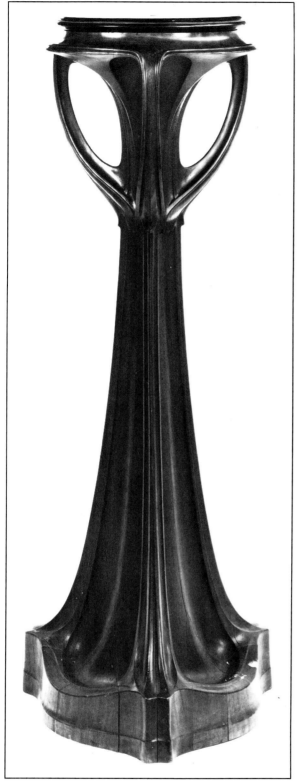

Above Mahogany desk and chair with gilt-bronze mounts 'aux orchidées', designed by Louis Majorelle, *c.* 1905.

Left Carved oak armchair, designed by Louis Majorelle, *c.* 1900.

Far left Carved mahogany *sellette*, designed by Jacques Gruber, *c.* 1900.

Pair of chairs and occasional table produced by the Compagnie des Arts Francais, Süe et Mare, early 1920s.

stylised motif of a classical god in a chariot. The Neo-classicism was evident the following year in his major work exhibited, a large cabinet in finely figured wood inlaid with overlapping circles of ivory and with a central panel of Neo-classical figures. Ruhlmann was gradually evolving the distinctive repertoire of forms and decorative motifs that were the elements of his personal style.

The obvious features of Ruhlmann's work, in addition of course to the prodigious labour required to achieve the perfection he demanded, were his simple, at times monumental shapes, perfectly proportioned and often raised on slender tapered legs, his use of rich exotic woods, notably *ébène de macassar* and amboyna, and the decorative use of rich materials, inlays of ebony or tortoiseshell and ivory used for key plates, *sabots* and plaques or inlaid in filets or rows of minute spots.

Ruhlmann's work was a central feature of the 1925 Exhibition where he decorated the Hôtel d'un Collectionneur and designed a Study in the Pavillon d'un Ambassadeur. In the creation of grand public rooms Ruhlmann was in his element, and here could be seen the full range of his skills. The grandiose schemes were judiciously enhanced by the heavy Neo-classical paintings of Jean Dupas and sculptures of Joseph Bernard.

In the last few years of his life Ruhlmann made

Opposite page Interior design by Emile-Jacques Ruhlmann, 1925.

Left *Meuble d'encoignure* in macassar ebony inlaid in ivory, designed by Emile-Jacques Ruhlmann, 1916.

Below left The Grand Salon d'un Collectionneur designed by Emile-Jacques Ruhlmann. The mural on the right is by Jean Dupas.

Below Cabinet covered in sharkskin with ivory lock plates, *sabots* and decorative details, designed by André Groult, and included in his Chambre de Madame in the Pavillon d'un Ambassadeur in the Paris 1925 Exhibition. Collection N. Manoukian, Paris.

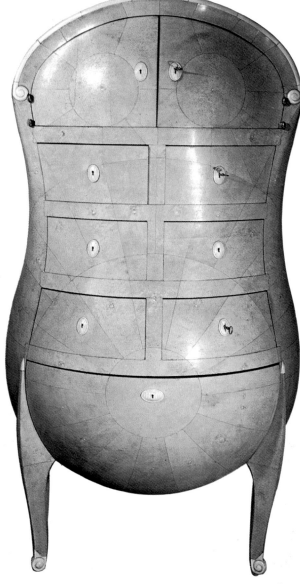

certain concessions to the taste for Modernism, designing a bar on chromium-plated metal skis, a kidney-shaped desk fitted with telephone, chromium-plated metal lamp, handles and foot-rest and, in the early thirties, a spectacular polished metal bed for the Maharajah of Indore in pure Modernist style.

After Ruhlmann's death his nephew Porteneuve took over his ateliers and worked from his designs for a limited period. From the early twenties, however, he had many imitators. These included Jules Leleu, who began to exhibit regularly at the Salon des Artistes Décorateurs after 1922 and who figured quite prominently in the 1925 Exhibition; the firm of Dominique, founded in 1922 by André Domin and Marcel Genevrière, which decorated the Salon in the Pavillon d'un Ambassadeur in 1925; the firm of Joubert et Petit and countless other Paris and provincial firms made a heavy-handed version of Ruhlmann's style, the ubiquitous bourgeois furniture of the late twenties and the thirties.

The twenties was a rich and varied decade in furniture and interior design and brought forth a number of talents too individual to be grouped under the blanket label of Art Deco. These included André Groult, Armand-Albert Rateau, Clément Rousseau and Eugène Printz. Groult, who had been exhibiting at the Salon des Artistes Décorateurs since 1910, worked at first in a style evocative of Louis-Seize and the Restauration, but is best remembered for his use of sharkskin. His most remarkable creation was the furnishing of the Chambre de Madame in the Pavillon d'un Ambassadeur, the swollen forms and softly curving lines of each piece completely covered in pale sharkskin. Groult incorporated wallpaper designs by Marie Laurencin into his decorative schemes.

Rateau's most interesting work is the furniture he designed in bronze, inspired from the antique. His work in the twenties included a series of commissions for Jeanne Lanvin, a highly individual bathroom for the Duchesse d'Albe's Madrid home, the home of the Baronne Eugène de Rothschild and various other commissions. He participated in the decoration of the Pavillon de l'Elégance in 1925.

Clément Rousseau used rich materials, ivory, sharkskin, ebony and palm-wood in small pieces of furniture and decorative objects of considerable refinement and simplicity. His patrons included Jacques Doucet and Robert de Rothschild.

Eugène Printz specialised in the use of metal, not in the functionalist style of the Modernist movement, but richly oxydised, or burnished and contrasted with panels of rich lacquer.

The design of textiles and wallpapers enjoyed very specific attention during the Art Deco period, before the austerity that characterised the Modernist movement ousted exotic patterning in avant-garde circles in favour of the purity of unadorned surfaces. Raoul Dufy designed fabrics and papers for Paul Poiret before going under contract in 1912 to the textile firm of Bianchini et Ferier, a contract which lasted until 1930 and was responsible, especially in the early years, for a series of delightful designs. After 1912 André Groult supervised the manufacture of textiles and papers to his own designs and to those of various other artists including Laurencin and Iribe. Paul Véra and André Mare designed fabrics for the Compagnie des Arts Français. The published folios of designs by Edouard Benedictus for the firms of Tassinari & Châtel, Brunet and Meunié & Cie. bear witness to his considerable talent. The Lyons silk works of François Ducharne, founded in 1920, produced rich fabrics under the artistic direction of Michel Dubost.

The revival of the craft of lacquer in the 1920s can be credited almost exclusively to the craftsmanship of one man, the Swiss-born Jean Dunand whose first encounter with lacquer was in 1912. He first used it to patinate the metal vases he was then making. By 1920 he had extended its use to furniture and this became his major area of work. During the 1920s he expanded his Rue Hallé ateliers as demand for his work increased until he occupied almost an entire block. Although Dunand lacquered furniture for other designers or cabinet-makers, including Printz, Ruhlmann and Pierre Legrain, he did not rely on outside cabinet-makers for his own creations, as furniture had to meet specific requirements of construction if it was to be successfully lacquered. Dunand designed many pieces himself but he also enlisted the help of artists who contributed their own designs and this accounts for the very wide range of motifs with which he is associated.

Dunand's most exciting works exploit the richness of large expanses of undecorated lacquer, relieved perhaps by painted or incised angular motifs or the inlaid particles of crushed eggshell, clustered like a miniature crazy paving or scattered like a snowstorm, which became his speciality. His stark black and silver lacquer Smoking Room in the Pavillon d'un Ambassadeur was amongst the highlights and surprises of the 1925 Exhibition. In 1929 he executed furniture and wall decorations for an extraordinary apartment in San Francisco for a Mr. Templeton-Crocker. In the twenties he had created furniture for Madeleine Vionnet, in the early thirties he worked on giant panels for the *Normandie* and was active until the closure of his workshops at the outbreak of war in 1939.

Amidst the diversity of furniture and interior design in the 1920s there emerged a distinct trend among a small but important group of artists towards a style which found its main inspiration in Cubism and primitive African art. The most distinguished and successful exponents of this style were Pierre Legrain, Marcel Coard and Eileen Gray and its most significant and enlightened patron was *couturier* and *mécène* Jacques Doucet.

Doucet's story is fascinating and remarkable. One of the foremost talents in the profession of *couture*, a profession only recently made socially acceptable, he emerged as one of the most perceptive art collectors and connoisseurs of his generation, amongst the first to appreciate the revolutionary work of Cubists, Picasso and Braque, of Modigliani, Ernst, Miro, de Chirico. After years spent collecting the finest works of the French eighteenth century, he sent the entire collection for sale at auction in 1912 to devote himself to forming a collection of contemporary works. Paul Iribe was commissioned to redecorate Doucet's apartment and he, in turn, enlisted the

Smoking room, lacquered
walls, ceiling and fittings,
by Jean Dunand, for the
Pavillon d'un Ambassadeur.

Opposite page Lacquer screen by Jean Dunand, *c.* 1925.

Left and below Lacquer screen and *meuble d'appui* designed by Léon and Maurice Jallot, 1929. Collection Hervé Poulain, Paris.

help of Pierre Legrain. In 1914 Iribe left for America and thus ended his work for Doucet. The next ten years or so were spent by Doucet in commissioning and acquiring works of art and furnishings that he found exciting and it seems likely that his own passion for Cubism and African art encouraged his protégés to follow the new source of inspiration.

Doucet's energy was extraordinary. Already into his seventies, he decided in the late 1920s to create a spectacular setting for his collection and entrusted Pierre Legrain with the *aménagement* of a villa at Neuilly that was to be a shrine to contemporary artistic achievement. Doucet died in 1929, the villa barely completed.

Entering one room through massive cast glass doors by René Lalique one sees, beneath Douanier Rousseau's *Snake Charmer*, a remarkable sofa, banded in ivory, by Marcel Coard, beside it a lacquer table of primitive inspiration by Eileen Gray, behind the table a gold lacquered ornamental cube by Pierre Legrain supporting a stone sculpture by Joseph Czaky, to the right a small table by André Groult, the sharkskin top supporting a primitive sculpture, and a sharkskin and lacquered wood stool by Pierre Legrain, its form inspired by the ceremonial stools of the Ashanti

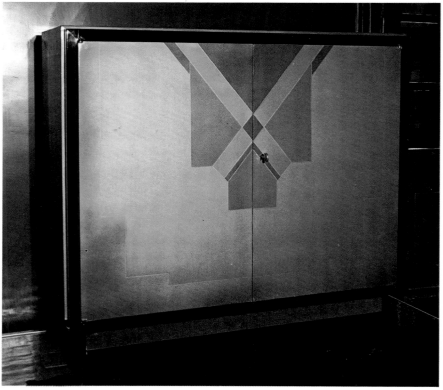

people of Central Africa. Other artists whose furniture and furnishings filled the villa included Rose Adler, Clément Rousseau, Paul-Louis Mergier, Gustave Miklos and Etienne Cournault. Doucet was an exception and as a rule such highly individual designers as Gray, Legrain and Coard found relatively limited success, requiring from their patrons a rare combination of wealth and discernment, and it is therefore not surprising that their clients should often be creative artists themselves, including several *couturiers*, or from artistic or intellectually strong backgrounds.

Eileen Gray's work in lacquer was noticed as early as 1913 by Doucet, who bought the screen *Le Destin* from her in that year. This Irish-born designer who had studied at the Slade before settling in Paris in 1907 created several pieces for Doucet, including a beautiful lacquered table, the legs conceived as giant lilies on stems. However, her most important interior was created in 1924 for Mme. Mathieu Lévy, known professionally in the fashion world as Suzanne Talbot. Here Miss Gray combined the luxury of her lacquer with certain elements that reflected the influence of Doucet and other, purer, more sculptural elements derived from her interest in the ideas of the Dutch De Stijl group. Among the remarkable features of this elegant apartment were the screens and panels of articulated rectangles of lacquered wood. The sophisticated lines of the furniture were contrasted with genuine African stools and objects and wild animal skins. In the late twenties, Miss Gray abandoned lacquer and worked in collaboration with architect Jean Badovici creating furniture that was at once functionalist and eccentric, using such materials as tubular and sheet metal and cork in its manufacture.

Pierre Legrain's patrons included Maurice Martin du Gard, Pierre Meyer, the Vicomte de Noailles and Mme Jeanne Tachard, a milliner friend of Doucet. Legrain was the designer most

directly influenced by African art and the strong and aggressive styles of central African furniture and carving are a prominent feature of his work. He also loved to use and to mix unusual textures and materials: open-grained palmwood or limed oak were used with areas of gilt or coloured lacquer, polished chromed metal, parchment, etched glass and ivory. Legrain's career was cut short by his death in 1929 at the age of forty.

Marcel Coard had trained as an architect at the Ecole des Beaux Arts, but found his vocation as a decorator and designer. Like Legrain, he loved and exploited rich materials, rich woods, mother-of-pearl, and lapis lazuli and was one of the first to cover furniture in parchment and leather. His forms were bold and inventive and his feeling for African art is often reflected in the concept or carved details of his furniture.

The late twenties saw the pendulum swing against the highly decorative aspects of Art Deco, against the rich patterns and the multiplicity of opulent woods and materials. The growing taste for simplicity could be seen even in the work of expensive decorators. Jean-Michel Frank was foremost amongst Parisian decorators to abandon pattern, relying on the more subtle luxury of fine materials and plain forms in mellow, neutral tones of cream, ivory and beige. The relative austerity of Pierre Chareau's Bureau Bibliothèque in the Pavillon d'un Ambassadeur of 1925 foreshadowed the tastes of a few years later, by which time Chareau was deeply involved in the design of functional iron-framed furniture and sculptural light fittings.

The principles and achievements of the Bauhaus school were a significant formative influence on French designers, notably in the field of tubular metal furniture. The chairs of Le Corbusier, notably his *chaise longue* of 1928, have become accepted as classics of design and are still in production. The changes that were in the air

Opposite page and above Salon for Mme. J.–Suzanne Talbot, designed by Paul Ruaud, using glass and white cellulose paint to create a Modernist setting for furniture by Eileen Gray, certain elements of which were included in the original Eileen Gray design for the Suzanne Talbot apartment in 1924. *L'Illustration*, May 1933.

Left Chromed tubular-metal and sheet-metal adjustable table, designed by Eileen Gray.

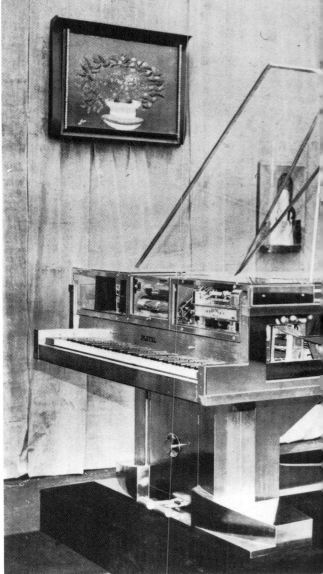

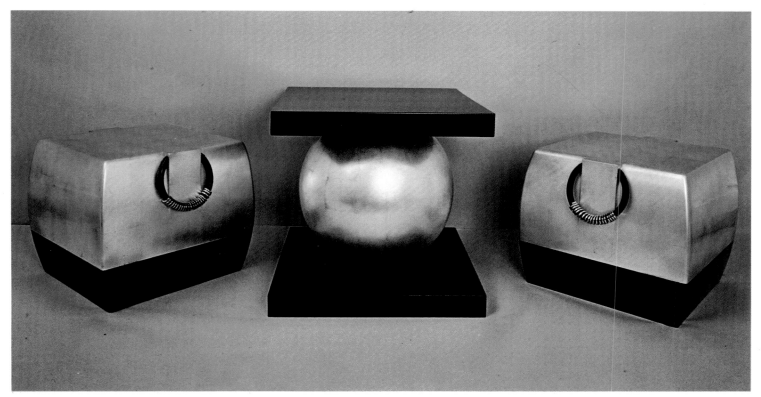

Above Metal and glass piano designed by Pierre Legrain for Pleyel. *Mobilier et Décoration*, April 1929.

Above left Gilt and lacquered wood corner *bibliothèque*, designed by Pierre Legrain.

Left Pair of stools and table designed by Pierre Legrain for Mme. Tachard. Made of silvered and lacquered wood. Collection Mr. and Mrs. Robert Walker, Paris.

Above right *Bureau-bibliothèque* in a modern apartment designed by P. Chareau for Jacques Doucet. The desk, desk stool, table and chairs are by Pierre Legrain, *c.* 1923. *Art et Décoration*, 1924.

Right An interior view of the Doucet villa at Neuilly, 1929.

Above Coco Chanel photographed by Cecil Beaton with fashionable blackamoor props, 1937.

Right Detail of the apartment of Mme. Helena Rubinstein, late 1930s.

affected every aspect of domestic design. Modernist rugs by artists such as Jean Lurçat, Eileen Gray or Bruno da Silva Bruhns replaced the florid rugs and carpets associated with the Art Deco style; wall decorations were virtually eliminated. The designers and decorators working in this new style saw themselves as purists, as rationalists, though their brand of functionalism by no means precluded a sense of style. On the contrary, the best Modernist interiors were totally chic, though their icy perfection and often clinical appearance suggest that their designers have somehow overlooked their ultimate function as living spaces for imperfect humans. The welcome virtues of Modernist interiors were in their sense of space and their emphasis on light and cleanliness.

The rallying point for French Modernism was the Union des Artistes Modernes founded in 1930 with, as *Comité Directeur*, Hélène Henry, René Herbst, François Jourdain, Robert Mallet-Stevens and Raymond Templier. The Union was a high-principled organisation whose fecund membership came to include some of the foremost designers in France, several of whom had now outgrown the more decorative style in which they had previously worked. The 1934 list of active members included Rose Adler, Pierre Chareau, Paul Colin, Etienne Cournault, Joseph Czaky, Jean Lambert-Rucki, Jacques Le Chevalier, Le Corbusier, Pierre Jeanneret, Jean Lurçat, Jan and Joël Martel, Gustave Miklos, Charles Moreaux, Charlotte Perriand, Jean Puiforcat and Gérard Sandoz.

There is a law of physics which states that to every action there is an equal and opposite reaction. This law might well be said to apply also to tastes in decorating, and the reaction against Modernism in the mid and late 1930s was as strong as the ideals that had originally fostered the U.A.M. Although the principles of functionalism by no means died a complete death, and, indeed, the U.A.M. enjoyed a renewed lease of life after the Second World War, fashionable decorators reacted against the bareness of interiors. The desire for *fantaisie* allied to the Surrealist taste for the *imprévu*, the *objet trouvé* was responsible for some very remarkable interiors. One of the best known is that of Carlos de Bestigui, particularly interesting because Bestigui had commissioned Le Corbusier to design the structure as the height of the fashion for Modernist simplicity. De Bestigui, a leader of fashion, reacted immediately against the austerity of Le Corbusier's concept by filling the rooms with Baroque furniture and ornaments, blackamoors, elaborately carved mirror frames and fireplaces, dripping chandeliers and well-rounded deep-upholstered seats.

The neo-Baroque taste was also perfectly represented in the apartment decorated in the late thirties for Mme. Helena Rubinstein. In the bedroom, walls, doors and the bed itself were covered in quilted satins, the furniture heavily inlaid with mother-of-pearl. In the salon was a bizarre mixture, carved Indian furniture, a suite of Venetian eighteenth-century shell seat furniture, the inevitable blackamoors. On the walls were paintings by Dali and other Surrealists, including an extraordinary sequin-spangled study of Mme. Rubinstein herself by Pavel Tchelitchew.

Glass *by Philippe Garner*

FRENCH LUXURY GLASS PRODUCTION had, by the 1890s, reached a remarkably high standard of technical and creative inspiration. This achievement can be traced back to the innovations of a small but significant number of talented artists, notably Philippe-Joseph Brocard, Auguste Jean, Ernest Léveillé and Eugène Rousseau, but above all the genius of one man, Emile Gallé, who inspired a whole generation of artisans and made the Paris Universal Exhibition of 1900 the showcase for creations in glass of an unprecedented technical virtuosity.

If the 1900 Exhibition was a high point for glass elaborately wrought into works of art, it was also the occasion for the prediction by Eugène Houtart that, 'Steel and glass are without doubt the two elements which will characterize the twentieth century and will give their name to it.' The prediction seemed to find its fulfilment after the First World War, when glass became the chosen material for designs of every scale, from the mass-produced luxury of René Lalique's scent bottles to Pierre Chareau's Maison de Verre, undertaken in the late 1920s and completed in 1931. After the First World War, whilst a few artists such as Maurice Marinot continued the tradition of glass object as work of art, established by Emile Gallé, though in a quite different stylistic vein, glass found wide favour with designers and decorators. Madame Lipska created an eccentric home for Antoine, the hairdresser, in which virtually every feature was of glass; Pierre Legrain designed a piano where glass replaced wood, laying bare the internal mechanism.

Léon Rosenthal, writing in 1927 in *La Verrerie Française depuis Cinquante Ans*, pinpointed the Paris Universal Exhibition of 1878 as the dawn of a revival in glass production. Here, beside the grandiose but predictable displays from such large and well-established glassworks as Baccarat and Saint-Louis, were fascinating and innovative exhibits. Brocard showed the fresh and colourful results of his experiments in enamelling, though his debt to Islamic models was still very evident. Jean showed enamelled pieces, but his most notable innovation was in his free-form applications of glass and in his vases of free-blown organic form. Gallé enjoyed his first major opportunity to exhibit. It was Rousseau, however, who attracted most praise and attention for vases of Japanese inspiration, both in their form and in their decoration, but more especially for his glass decorated in the mass, glass imitating agates, jades and other semi-precious stones and often enhanced with internal *craquelé* effects.

Emile Gallé took over the family glass and faïence works in 1874. He had enjoyed the benefit of an extensive education, including a technical apprenticeship in glassworks at Meisenthal and was eager, on taking over the family business, to experiment and extend the range of production. During the late 1870s he built new workshops and experimented with techniques. His exhibit of 1878 was predominantly of enamelled wares in styles of historical inspiration. In 1884 he sent an exhibit to Paris that included his first significant experiments with the internal chemistry of glass itself. His *notice* of exhibits itemises examples of 'Colorations nouvelles du verre, doublés, triplés, verres marbrés, imitation de pierres précieuses, emploi de feuilles métalliques, bulles d'air.'

The sources of Gallé's inspiration were rich and varied. As with so many of the avant-garde of his generation, Gallé's introduction to Japanese art was an important step in creating a new visual language. The ability to create elegant, often almost abstract graphic designs from the plant and insect life that were his most constant fund of motifs, owes a strong debt to Japanese art. Many creations bear witness to this source of inspiration, a taste that Gallé's acquaintance with Count Robert de Montesquiou no doubt did a great deal to foster. Nature was Gallé's great source of

Cameo glass vase by Eugène Rousseau, 1880s.

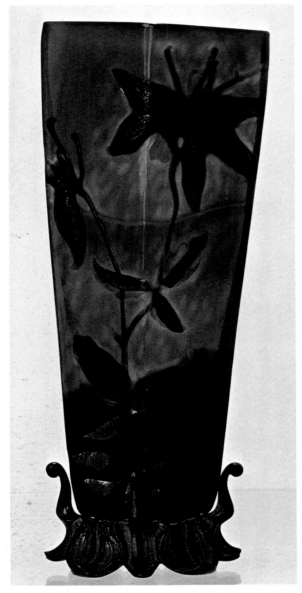

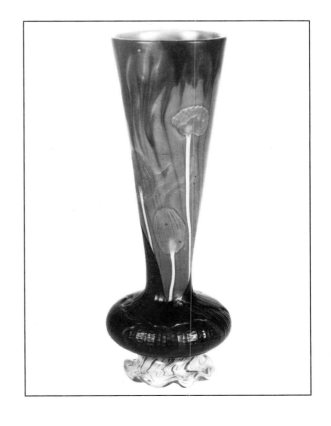

Top Glass vase by Emile Gallé, the decoration in *marqueterie-sur-verre c.* 1900.

Top right 'Rose de France' glass vase by Emile Gallé, *c.* 1900.

Above Emile Gallé in 1889.

Right Enamelled glass bottle by Emile Gallé, 1880s.

Far right 'Onion' vase by Emile Gallé, 1900.

inspiration as the enthusiasm aroused by the botanical studies of his school days hardened into an aesthetic discipline.

Gallé's more personal creations also reflect his poetic ideas, often culled from his extensive reading of contemporary French poets. His *vases parlants* were inscribed with extracts from the verses which had inspired the decoration, verses from Hugo, Baudelaire, Maeterlinck, Gautier, Rimbaud and others, or lines from sources as far apart as Shakespeare and the Bible, the latter in response to Gallé's urge to imbue many of his works with a quasi-religious mysticism.

Triumph at the Paris Exhibition of 1889, where Gallé won a gold medal and the Grand Prix, crowned the growing success of the 1880s. His major innovation in 1889 was his cameo glass, glass of two or more layers carved or etched back, leaving the design in relief in one or more colours against a contrasting ground. The technique was copied from that of Chinese Chien Lung cased glass studied by Gallé in the South Kensington Museum. It was on a debased, mass-production, acid-etched version of his cameo technique that Gallé was to base the prosperity of his business, expanding during the 1890s to the point where, around 1900, he employed some three hundred people with retail outlets as far afield as Frankfurt and London (opened 1904). Gallé's status as an artist of national importance was confirmed by the award in 1889 of the Légion d'Honneur and by major public commissions such as the vases presented by the nation in 1896 to the Tsar and Tsarina of Russia.

The year 1897 saw the introduction by Gallé of a new technique, *marqueterie-sur-verre*, which involved inlaying semi-molten glass details of decoration into the semi-molten body of the piece being worked on. The 1900 Paris Exhibition was perhaps Gallé's finest hour, his last major showing before his death from leukaemia in 1904. He at last escaped from his tendency to make vases fascinating in the detail, but pedestrian in form. In 1900 he showed more sculptural freedom with pieces of completely organic form or worked in high relief with fluid applications of glass. Two of his greatest masterpieces date from his post-1900 Exhibition period, the *Main aux Algues* and the extraordinary lamp, *Les Coprins*, of 1904.

Gallé's influence on contemporary glassmakers was considerable, as indeed was his influence on craftsmen in other media in his home town of Nancy. A group of artists allied themselves in 1901 as the 'Ecole de Nancy, Alliance Provinciale des Industries d'Art'. Gallé, naturally, was their president and guiding light; Louis Majorelle, Eugène Vallin and the Daum brothers were vice-presidents. The Ecole de Nancy style of glass became prevalent in France, produced by local firms, such as that of the brothers Désiré and Eugène Muller and the Verrerie de Nancy of the Daum brothers, and by other firms such as that of Auguste Legras who had taken over the Cristalleries of Saint Denis and of Pantin. The Muller brothers had started as craftsmen working in the Gallé ateliers before setting up their own business in the late 1890s, a business that was to prosper through a succession of styles until finally closing down in 1936.

Carved cameo and applied glass vase from the Daum workshops, with gilt-bronze base, *c.* 1900.

Above Daum glass bowl, overlaid and etched, 1920s.
Above right *Pâte-de-verre* medallions by Henri Cros, 1880s. Collection of Roger Marx.

Right *Pâte-de-verre* bowl by François-Emile Décorchemont, 1920s.

Alphonse-Georges Reyen, after an apprenticeship, first with Gallé in the 1870s and then with Rousseau, produced cameo vases of fine quality in the Nancy idiom around 1900. Eugène Michel, who had worked with Rousseau and subsequently with his associate and successor Ernest Léveillé, produced a few exceptional cameo vases worked in high relief. The Frères Pannier created a series of fine carved cameo vases for the Escalier de Cristal in Paris, again showing a strong debt to Gallé.

Though the largest glassworks operating in the shadow of Emile Gallé was that of Legras, employing at the turn of the century some fifteen hundred people, the most notable rivals to Gallé were the Daum brothers, Auguste and Antonin, who, by the 1890s, shared the responsibility of the family business. They were more dependent than Gallé on the creativity of their employees and this was to their advantage. When Gallé died there began a steady decline in his factory's production until its final closure in 1935. The broader creative basis of the Daum works, however, ensured their success through several generations, with the result that Daum is still today an important name in French glass production.

Though the Daum works were never able to produce *tours de force* as extraordinary as the best of Gallé's creations, they were capable of a very high technical and artistic standard. They made their own a particular style of broad surface faceting, an effect described as *martelé*. They counted amongst their collaborators Jacques Gruber, who worked with them between 1894 and 1897 before turning his interest to cabinet-making, Eugène Goll, their most talented glassworker, responsible for some of the most sculptural and inventive pieces that bear the Daum mark, and Walter who had his own atelier within the Daum works between about 1906 and the First World War for the creation of *pâte-de-verre*, a process which the Daum brothers were the first to exploit commercially.

After the hiatus of the war the Daum works went back into production and worked through the twenties and thirties in a new decorative idiom. Natural motifs fell out of favour, to be replaced by abstract geometric designs. Amongst the factory's most impressive creations during this period were the deep-etched angular table lamps in colourless glass that marked so strong a contrast with the warmth and femininity of the cameo glass table lamps of the early years of the century.

The *pâte-de-verre* process used by Walter *chez* Daum involved the firing of a body built up in a mould from a paste of powdered glass and metallic oxides to give colour. The technique was first revived in the nineteenth century by artist-sculptor Henri Cros. The classical themes he favoured reflected his original source of inspiration, ancient glass paste creations exhibited in Paris in 1878. Cros' work, characterised by a rough, pitted surface, weak, pastel colours and a total opacity, became more ambitious after 1892, when the Manufacture de Sèvres put a workshop at his disposal, and included such projects as the mural fountain of 1893 for the Musée du Luxembourg. His son Jean continued in his father's footsteps and produced similar work.

Two other artists of note worked independently through the 1890s to perfect their own *pâte-de-verre* techniques. Albert Dammouse, working at Sèvres, turned his attention from porcelain to glass, exhibiting his first fragile, brittle and opaque *pâte-de-verre* bowls and vases in 1898. The next few years saw the perfection of his skills as his glass achieved a more translucent quality and he undertook daring works combining motifs of translucent *pâte-d'émail* within an opaque tracery of *pâte-de-verre*. Dammouse worked in *pâte-de-verre* until his death in 1926. Georges Despret achieved his first successes around 1900. His hallmark was work in relief, *pâte-de-verre* fish, masks or figures, vases modelled with scarabs or seahorses. He worked through the 1920s and 1930s, changing his style to suit the times and collaborating with sculptors, such as Pierre Le Faguays, on the creation of fashionable themes.

Walter similarly employed sculptors to design subjects for execution in *pâte-de-verre* in the new workshops he set up in 1919. His collaborators included Henri Bergé, whose taste was still unfashionably confined to the stylised motifs from nature of Nancy Art Nouveau, and the sculptor J. Descomps. This same lingering-on of Art Nouveau motifs was evident in the post-war output of the most commercial of *pâte-de-verre* artists, Gabriel Argy-Rousseau, though he proved himself equally capable of interpreting current tastes, including the mid and late twenties taste for Egyptian motifs.

The major talent to work in *pâte-de-verre* was perhaps François-Emile Décorchemont, whose first pieces date from 1903. His earliest pieces were evocative of Dammouse with their mat, thin and brittle bodies and trailing Art Nouveau motifs, but after 1908 he found a more personal style when he started to cast his vases by the *cire perdue* process. Between 1908 and 1914 Décorchemont produced a series of semi-translucent, heavy-bodied vases cast with scarabs or natural motifs such as seaweed. The chunky self-confidence of these vases was much admired as was the quality of the more sober forms, sometimes enhanced with geometric decorations, which he created after the war. During the 1930s his work became more ponderous, more mechanical and less inspired.

The Art Deco style found expression in the feminine and decorative glass designs of a number of artists and was most successfully captured in the enamelled glassware very much in evidence in contemporary illustrated folios on the French decorative arts during the early and mid twenties. The names that recur are those of Marcel Goupy, Decuper-Delvaux, Quenvit, Jean Luce, Georges Chevalier working for the Cristalleries de Baccarat and Mme Cless-Brothier for Louis Vuitton; the most usual motifs were sprays of blossom, highly formalised flowers, figure or animal subjects in a restrained Neo-classical taste.

The trade marks Le Verre Français, Déguy and Schneider, the latter representing the Cristalleries de Schneider founded by Charles Schneider, an old pupil of Emile Gallé's, became known during the twenties and into the thirties for etched glass, usually in harsh colours, and decorated with rigidly stylised flowers, insects, or the geometric motifs that were becoming increasingly popular. The names of Déguy and Schneider also became

Left *Pâte-de-verre* dish by Gabriel Argy-Rousseau, 1920s.

Right 'L'Oiseau de Feu', Lalique glass and bronze lamp, 1920s.

Below left *Pâte-de-verre* vase by Gabriel Argy-Rousseau, 1920s.

Below Lalique glass 'Serpent' vase, 1920s.

Below right *Cire perdue* glass vase by René Lalique, *c.* 1905–10.

Below far right Perfume bottles, powder boxes and an eagle's head seal, from Lalique's and other factories, 1920s.

Deep etched glass vase by
Maurice Marinot, 1920s.

associated with the mottled glass regularly used for shades in ornamental lamps, often in elaborate mounts by *ferronniers* such as Edgar Brandt.

French art glass production between the wars was dominated, however, by two strong yet contrasting talents, René Lalique and Maurice Marinot, the former responsible for combining modern techniques of mass-production with a consistently high level of artistic involvement, the latter for raising glasswork to the level of a fine art in an idiom as appropriate to the twentieth century as that of Gallé had been to the *fin-de-siècle*.

René Lalique's interest in glass dated back to the 1890s and his use of cast glass in multi-media works of art; around 1900 he first began to use glass in his exquisite jewellery, caring nothing for its lack of intrinsic worth if its qualities were appropriate to the design. It is from about this time that date his earliest experiments in the creation of all-glass *cire perdue* pieces, including vases and panels such as those used by Lalique in the decoration of his 40 Cours de la Reine home.

In 1902 he set up a small glassworks, employing four workers, at Clairfontaine. Lalique's first commission for commercial glass was from the parfumeur Coty who approached him to design scent bottles. Between 1907–8 these were made for Lalique by the firm of Legras.

Lalique's growing interest in glass encouraged the opening of his own glassworks at Combs-la-Ville in 1909. By 1912 his career as a jeweller was over and a new career lay open to him. Between 1918 and 1922 he supervised the construction of enlarged works, the Verrerie d'Art – René Lalique & Cie., at Wingen-sur-Moder. Through the 1920s and until the final close of production in 1939 the Lalique factory produced an extensive range of vases, glasses and other tableware, clocks, lamps, scent bottles, brooches, pendants, dressing table sets, even motor car mascots and items of furniture. Produced in very large quantities in clear, opalescent or, more rarely, coloured glass, the Lalique output was of good but not remarkable quality; its greatest distinction was in the stylish repertoire of designs, ranging from elegant evocations of Lalique's Art Nouveau phase, through pretty renderings of all the typical Art Deco themes to more aggressively modern motifs, most of them Lalique's own creation.

Lalique triumphed at the Paris Exhibition of 1925 with examples of his factory's work in many of the French pavilions, notably glass beams, panels and furniture for the Pavillon de la Manufacture Nationale de Sèvres. Amongst his most

Enamelled glass *coupe* by
Maurice Marinot, *c*. 1920.

prestigious commissions was the decoration of the grand dining saloon of the *Normandie*, launched in 1932. Lalique's success inevitably spawned imitators at various levels of the market, from Sabino, whose creations could on occasion rival those of Lalique, to Hunebelle, Verlys and others.

Maurice Marinot ranks in a category of his own. A painter working in the *fauve* style, he first became intrigued by the possibilities of glass during a visit to the Bar-sur-Seine glassworks of his friends the Viard brothers in 1911. Nineteen-thirteen marked the beginning of his serious concentration on glass as he decorated in brilliant enamels glass bodies made up to his designs by the Viard's gaffers. Writing in 1920 in *L'Amour de l'Art* on 'Le Métier du Verre Soufflé' Marinot expressed his feeling, in strong contrast to the ideas of Art Nouveau glassworkers, that 'the two essential qualities of glass are its translucence and its brilliance.' His interest in enamelled decoration waned with the growth of his passion for the intrinsic qualities of glass.

By 1922 he had abandoned enamelling and started to learn the skills of glass-blowing at a furnace put at his disposal by the Viard brothers. He blew heavy-bodied clear glass vases and flasks, often enhanced by internal flights of minute air bubbles, which he would then decorate, cold, with strong angular motifs achieved by deep and rough etching and wheel carving. In his pursuit of the ultimate purity in glass creation Marinot, about 1927, showed greater interest than before in what he called 'modelage à chaud'; all the creative work was done at the furnace on semi-molten glass. Internal effects were achieved by metallic oxides on the surface which would then be sheathed in a gather of clear glass; heavy applications were worked deftly around the semi-molten glass with rudimentary but effective tools.

The film made in 1933 by Jean Benoît Lévy of Marinot at work well conveys the magic and confidence of his sculpting the liquid metal in this method of 'modelage à chaud' that characterised his mature phase. He abandoned glass in 1937 to revert to painting, but it is on his glass and not his canvases that his reputation rests.

Marinot's strong personal style found considerable success with contemporary critics and bred the inevitable crop of imitators. The Daum works produced a series of deep-etched vases in a more decorative version of the Marinot style; Henri Navarre and André Thuret were perhaps his most gifted imitators, though, even at their best, their work lacked the brilliance of Marinot's.

Ceramics *by Lynne Thornton*

THE CERAMISTS OF THE LATE NINETEENTH CENTURY remained, to a certain extent, outside the mainstream of the applied arts of the time, for temperamental, stylistic and geographical reasons. The two main centres of Art Nouveau, except for ceramics, were Paris and Nancy. The designers, who did not carry out the work with their own hands, were generally part of artistic, literary or fashionable circles, or closely connected with them. The members of the circles not only bought the objects, but also helped the designers to be better known through their social connections.

The ceramists, on the other hand, although they participated in international exhibitions and Paris salons, were scattered around France, using local clays and, for the most part, themselves throwing, turning, glazing and firing, selling only to close friends or personal customers. They were passionately involved with the fusion of earth and fire, going through poverty or ill-health with a dogged determination. There was none of the *fin-de-siècle* intellectualism of the other branches of Art Nouveau, but a profound love of the craft, a sensual contact with the grain of a glaze or the form of a vase, which had taken shape through the potter's skill and artistic impulsion, which came from the heart rather than from the brain.

By the twentieth century, there were many more retail outlets. There was also a closer collaboration between the large manufacturers and ceramic designers. By the late twenties and thirties, things had gone to the extreme; many ceramists believed that there was no longer place for unique pieces, but that ceramics should be made to be distributed on a wide scale. The split became so great between the ideals of the artist-potter of the late nineteenth century and the ceramic industrialisation of the twentieth, that nowadays in France there are very few studio potters; on the one side there are the factories, and on the other, artisans working in a traditional manner in the provinces.

The first stirrings of the modern art pottery movement began in France in the 1830s, with Avisseau, Pull, Barbizet and Sergent, who were inspired by the naturalism of the sixteenth-century potter, Palissy. At the same time, Ziegler was making heavy saltglazed stoneware in archaic forms. We then come to Théodore Deck, a remarkable technician who made brightly-coloured faïence with motifs drawn from Japan, Turkey, Egypt and China. The 1870s were notable for the Haviland workshops in Auteuil, directed by Ernest Chaplet. Although this short-lived enterprise was not a great success financially, the red earth vases decorated in coloured liquid clay (*barbotine*) were an important stand against the ostentation and impersonality of factory-produced ceramics.

In 1881 the Haviland workshops moved to Rue Blomet in Paris, where Chaplet, together with Edouard and Albert Dammouse, Ringel d'Illzach, Hexamer and others, made dark-brown stoneware with incised decoration, the coloured glazes encircled with gold in the manner of *cloisonné* enamels. It was at this time that Paul Gauguin started making ceramics, fired by Chaplet, who had bought the business from Haviland's in 1885. Two years later, Chaplet sold it to Auguste

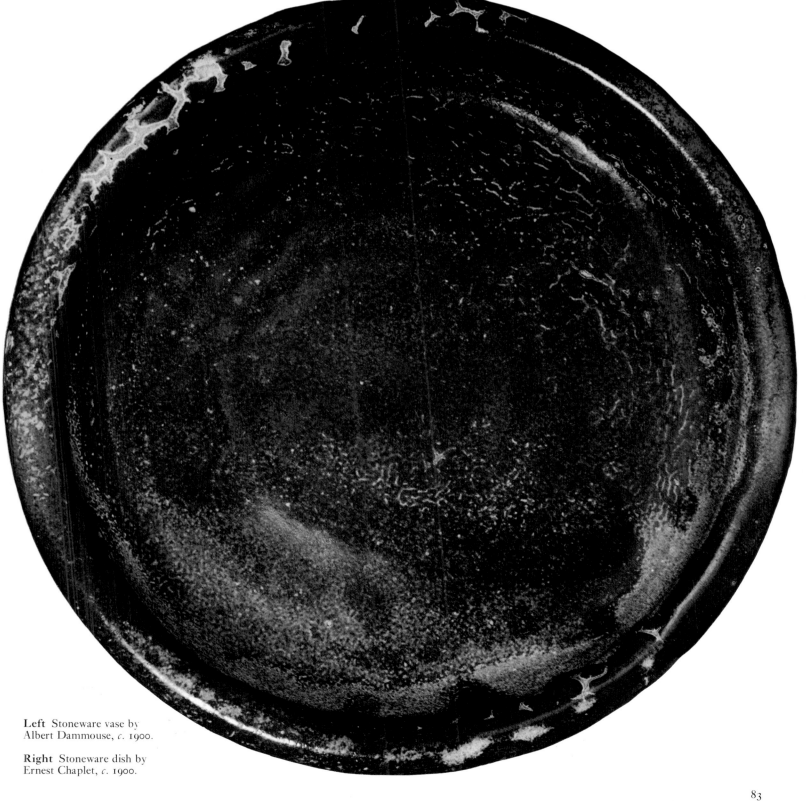

Left Stoneware vase by
Albert Dammouse, *c.* 1900.

Right Stoneware dish by
Ernest Chaplet, *c.* 1900.

Auguste Delaherche
drawing his ceramics from
the kiln. Illustrated in *Les
Arts*, Paris 1920.

Delaherche and it was with Delaherche that Gauguin continued to work on his return from Martinique in 1887.

The main purpose of Chaplet's decision to move from Paris to Choisy-le-Roi was to continue his research into *flambé* glazes on porcelain. The remarkable results ranged from shiny *sang-de-boeuf* to veined, spotted and jaspered turquoise and white. He also made vases and dishes with thick glazes whose granular surfaces resembled pitted orange peel. Although porcelain became his great passion, he went on making stoneware, some in collaboration with the sculptor Jules Dalou. Chaplet went blind in 1904 and left the direction of the studio to his grandson, Emile Lenoble.

Auguste Delaherche was more prolific than Chaplet, and it is perhaps because his work is to be found in relatively large quantities, that his masterpieces are overshadowed by the earlier rustic work. He came from the Beauvaisis, a traditional ceramic making area. Between 1883 and 1886 he worked in saltglaze stoneware, but his aim to sell art ceramics at low prices met with little success. In Paris, he began to use drip glazes which he had seen on Japanese stoneware, with engraved or raised floral decoration, eventually winning a gold medal at the 1889 Universal Exhibition. In 1894, Delaherche moved to Armentières, in the Beauvaisis, and in the following ten years he relied for effect on deep, pure monochrome glazes on simple forms. After 1904, he made unique pieces, only keeping those which were perfect, refusing to accept any result, however beautiful, if it was by accident and not entirely controlled by himself. At the age of sixty-eight, Delaherche began to make delicate white porcelain vases with a pierced decoration of stylised flowers, now very rare.

Of Chaplet's collaborators, Albert Dammouse is of particular interest. Son of a Sèvres sculptor, he began his career by decorating in *pâte-sur-pâte*. After having worked with Chaplet, he set up his own studios in the village of Sèvres in 1892, where he made stoneware, faïence and porcelain ornamented with flowers, leaves or seaweed. Dammouse then turned to making vases and bowls in translucid paste, which he first exhibited in 1898.

François-Emile Décorchemont, painter and later famous glass-maker, also made fragile objects in *pâte-d'émail* and *pâte-de-verre* around 1900. His first experiments, however, were in stoneware, which he fired in his own room. A more professional ceramist was Adrien-Pierre Dalpayrat. As a Master Potter, he travelled all over France, settling in 1889 in Bourg-la-Reine, where he worked with his wife and three sons. Although he made some porcelain and faïence, Dalpayrat is best known for his stoneware vases, sculpted either in strange twisted shapes or in the form of animals, fruit or vegetables. He perfected a *sang-de-boeuf* glaze called 'rouge Dalpayrat', which he mixed with spinach green, lapis blue, purple and white. Together with Adèle Lesbros and Voisin, Dalpayrat made ceramics for wide distribution at a low cost, but he also created unique pieces, sometimes mounted in ormolu. Many of his best pieces were bought by European museums.

Edmond Lachenal was a painter, sculptor and decorator. After having worked with Théodore Deck for ten years, he set up his own ceramic workshops at the age of twenty-five, at Châtillon-sous-Bagneux. He first of all made faïence decorated in the Isnik taste, then, perfecting a technique of metallo-ceramics by electrolysis and using hydrofluoric acid to obtain matt *velouté* glazes. Lachenal's faïence and stoneware vases ornamented with flowers or animals had a certain success, but he became particularly known for his stoneware editions of sculptures by Rodin, de Frumerie, Dejean, Fix-Masseau and Saint-Marceaux. Lachenal, in the first years of the twentieth century, abandoned ceramics for the theatre, leaving his workshops to his wife and son Raoul. In 1911, Raoul set up on his own in Boulogne, where he made ceramics, either in series or unique pieces, with geometric or stylised floral designs in chestnut, red, black, green and white.

This editing of sculptures in ceramics and the application of stoneware to architecture was an important feature of Art Nouveau. Besides Dalpayrat, Lachenal and Jeanneney, the two leading figures in this field were Bigot and Muller. Alexandre Bigot, inspired by the Japanese ceramics at the 1889 Universal Exhibition, set up a kiln at Mer in the Loire-et-Cher. From 1894 on, he showed his plates with newts, frogs and mermaids in low relief swimming among deep translucid glazes. After 1900, he turned towards making stoneware for both inside and outside buildings (including Guimard's Castel Béranger), and editing sculpture. He got into financial difficulties and his workshops closed in 1914.

Emile Muller's factory at Ivry was more commercial in every sense. In his published catalogue there were lists of all the stoneware sculpture available, including the well-known portrait of Yvette Guilbert by Toulouse-Lautrec. Muller, together with the firms Gentil et Bourdet and Hyppolyte Boulanger, made much of the architectural ceramics of the time.

Japan can be said to have been one of the major influences in Art Nouveau ceramics, but there were in fact two streams of influence. Firstly, there was the Japan of blue and white porcelain, fans, kimonos and woodcuts enjoyed by the Goncourts, Bing, Whistler, Vever and the Impressionists. Among the ceramists who used these superficial motifs of the Orient were Deck, the Cazin family, Moreau-Nelaton and Gallé. Jean-Charles Cazin, who had been employed on a freelance basis by the Fulham Factory in England in 1872, decorated his stoneware with incised branches of flowers and leaves in the Japanese manner. His son Michel, painter, engraver, sculptor, medal-maker and ceramist, worked with his wife Berthe in his father's studios. His squat vases in monochrome glazes have leaves and shells in low relief, sometimes mounted in bronze.

Etienne Moreau-Nelaton was a well-known writer, painter and collector. While his first pieces were of rustic simplicity in grey-yellow and blue, his later work, vases and bottles in faïence and stoneware, were decorated with flowers. This observation of nature in close-up, learnt from the Japanese, was particularly marked in the work of Emile Gallé. During the 1890s, he covered faïence with insects and flowers on gold grounds. His earlier ceramics, though, had shown none of this realism, being at first closely based on eighteenth-

century models and then decorated with historical subjects or Egyptian motifs.

The other aspect of the Japanese influence, the rough stoneware, the impurities of natural ingredients, the drip glazes and, indeed, the Oriental philosophy, touched many Art Nouveau ceramists, but most notably the School of Saint-Amand. The leader was Jean Carriès, a man of humble origins, who had painfully made a career for himself sculpting in a realist manner quite opposed to the current academic style. Although he had been impressed by the Oriental ceramics at the 1878 Universal Exhibition, it was those pieces in the collection of his friend, Paul Jeanneney, which struck him like a divine revelation. Carriès settled in Saint-Amand-en-Puisaye in the Nièvre where he learned the rudiments of ceramic making from the local potters. He worked like a man inspired, strenuously fighting against technical and financial difficulties making vases with *gris*, *cendré* and *ciré* glazes over which he poured pink or gold enamels. Out of his hands grew grotesque masks, hare-eared toads, squat grinning goblins, like malevolent manifestations of the devil driving

Grotesque mask in stoneware by Jean Carriès, *c.* 1890.

Right Stoneware vase with ormolu mounts by Georges Hoentschel, *c.* 1900.

Below Stoneware vases and pears by Georges Hoentschel, Emile Grittel and Henri de Vallombreuse, *c.* 1900.

Opposite page Stoneware bust, *Flore*, by Louis Chalon and Emile Muller, *c.* 1900.

him on. In 1889 the Princess of Scey-Montbéliard commissioned from him a doorway for a library containing the partition of Wagner's *Parsifal*, but Carriès, tubercular from an early age, exhausted by the demands of his chosen craft and harrassed by his patron's demands, died before it could be finished.

All Carriès' work was left to his great friend, Georges Hoentschel, a celebrated interior decorator, collector and man of the world. Hoentschel bought Carriès' house, the Château de Montriveau, and began to make stoneware himself. His work is closer to the Japanese originals than to Carriès; the vases, in sober blue, green, grey and beige, were sometimes finished with ivory stoppers, sometimes mounted in ormolu, revealing his taste for the Orient and the eighteenth century. In the last few years of his life, he worked mostly in the studio in Clichy belonging to Emile Grittel.

Grittel, who had worked for Hoentschel's large decorating company, had joined him at Saint-Amand and probably himself executed much of the ceramics signed with Hoentschel's monogram. Grittel made vases, pears and gourds with coloured or gold drip glazes on coral, olive-green and deep brown grounds. His name was scarcely mentioned in the art press of the time and his work has only recently been rediscovered. Carriès' great passion for ceramics inspired others to go to Saint-Amand after his death, including Paul Jeanneney, who made stoneware with bamboo shapes, cut-out bodies and dripped or 'curdled' glazes. He was followed by William Lee, Henri de Vallombreuse and Count Nils de Bark, who were little more than dilettantes.

Lustreware is another piece in the jig-saw of nineteenth-century ceramics. Less important than in England (Maws, Pilkingtons, De Morgan), there was nonetheless a most interesting production made at Golfe-Juan by the Massier family, Clément, Delphin and Jérôme. Some of the best stoneware with shimmering blue, violet, mauve, silver and green lustre glazes was signed by Lucien Lévy-Dhurmer, famous pastellist, who was at one time the artistic director of the works.

The making of French Art Nouveau porcelain remained almost exclusively in the hands of the Manufacture Nationale de Sèvres and Limoges. Sèvres, having reached the peak of technical perfection, had been trying for some years to shake the state-supported artists out of their torpor. Experiments were made with new pastes and glazes and models were provided by Frémiet, Chéret, Léonard, Guimard, and others. With an administrative and artistic shake-up in preparation for the 1900 Universal Exhibition, Sèvres began to come into line with the Modern Movement.

One of the most interesting Sèvres ceramists was Taxile Doat who, besides his work for the factory, fired in his own kiln in Paris and, after 1898, in the village of Sèvres. Internationally famous for his *pâte-sur-pâte* medallions applied to porcelain bodies, Doat published a technical treatise on high-fire ceramics in the United States and in 1909 taught at the St. Louis University City. With the opening of hostilities, he returned to France, where he continued to work until the early 1930s. As for the Limoges porcelain, this was designed by Georges de Feure and Edward Col-

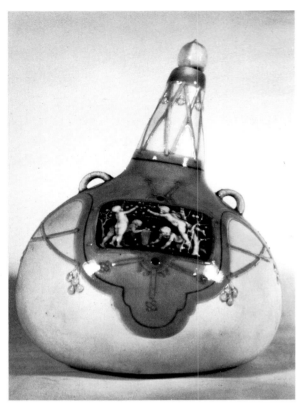

Right and far right
Porcelain gourds decorated in *pâte-sur-pâte* by Taxile Doat, *c.* 1902.

onna for Samuel Bing's shop, L'Art Nouveau, the delicate white bodies painted with sophisticated designs in pink, powder-blue and green, which are typically Parisian in feeling. Both Bing and Meier-Graefe, owner of La Maison Moderne, were helpful in bringing Art Nouveau ceramics to the public's notice.

If the late nineteenth century was marked by the influence of Japan and the revival of stoneware, then the early twentieth century was notable for the interest in Chinese and Islamic ceramics, and the importance of brightly-coloured painted faïence. Emile Decoeur was perhaps the greatest purist of the 'Chinese' ceramists. At the age of fourteen he was employed by Edmond Lachenal with whom he worked for ten years; many pieces of faïence are marked with both their monograms or names. Decoeur eventually left Lachenal's workshops and, after a brief collaboration with Rumèbe, set up on his own. A great admirer of Carriès, he began to work exclusively in stoneware but was later to consider the Art Nouveau decoration on these early vases as 'youthful mistakes'.

In 1907, Decoeur settled at Fontenay-les-Roses. The thin or 'clotted' glazes on his stoneware and later porcelain vases and bowls became completely monochrome, in pink, pale green, yellow, white and black. His pure Oriental forms and the perfection of his glazes made Decoeur the best known ceramist in France of the 1920s and 1930s.

Another notable ceramist of the twenties was Emile Lenoble. After seven years in an industrial ceramic factory, in 1903 Lenoble went back to the home of his grandfather, Ernest Chaplet, in Choisy-le-Roi. Around 1910 he began to paint his stoneware, something usually done only to porcelain or faïence. His vases were later overlaid with slip engraved with friezes of chevrons, spirals, zig-zags, arabesques and stylised leaves and flowers in broken white, bronze-brown and black. Lenoble

had been inspired by Japanese and Korean ceramics seen in the collection of the engraver Henri Rivière, but after the war, he became attracted to China. Between 1919 and 1930, he widened his palette, using wallflower-yellows and browns, celadon-green and lapis-blue, azure and turquoise, the *sgraffito* decoration becoming secondary to the depth and quality of the glaze.

Henri Simmen studied ceramic techniques with Lachenal. His first personal pieces of stoneware were with black and brown abstract motifs on salt-glazed grounds, with occasional touches of gold enamelling. On his return from the Far East after the war, he modelled his stoneware by hand and used only natural ingredients to make his remarkable glazes in *aventurine*, imperial yellow, celadon, white and brilliant red. His Japanese wife, Madame O'Kin Simmen, sculpted stoppers, bases or handles in ivory and horn.

Séraphin Soudbinine, a Russian from Novgorod, had become one of Rodin's favourite assistants. However, after seeing the Far Eastern ceramics in the Metropolitan Museum in New York, he began to create archaic-looking vases sculpted with grotesque monsters in matt stoneware on brown shiny grounds, and animals and dishes in retractory, 'wickerwork' or 'curdled' glazes. He kept only the perfect pieces and struggled for three years to obtain a black glaze. A bomb destroyed Soudbinine's studio during the war; ill and ruined, he died in 1944, leaving only a few pieces, all of exceptional quality.

Georges Serré was an apprentice at the Sèvres factory from 1902 until the beginning of the First World War. During the war, he was sent to Saigon, where he taught ceramics in the native art schools. He participated at the Colonial Exhibition of Marseilles, (1922) and Paris (1931), remaining attached to Chinese and Khmer art all his life. He engraved geometric patterns on the half-dried grounds of his unique pieces, fired in his studio in

Left Stoneware bowl by Georges Serré, *c.* 1934.

Below left Faïence vase by Edouard Cazaux, *c.* 1930–5.

Below Stoneware pot and cover by Séraphin Soudbinine, *c.* 1930–5.

A group of stoneware
vessels; behind: plate
(*c.* 1914) and vase
(*c.* 1925) by Raoul
Lachenal; front (l. to r.):
two vases (*c.* 1930) by
Emile Decoeur; vase by
Emile Lenoble (*c.* 1913).

the village of Sèvres. His talent was recognised at an exhibition at Rouard's (Rouard had replaced Bing and Meier-Graefe as patron and dealer of contemporary applied arts). Sculptors such as Dejean, Gimond, Niclausse, Comtesse, asked him to edit their works in brown granular stoneware.

Paul Beyer was very much involved in the revival of stoneware in France during the twenties and thirties, but his stylistic sources were very different from those of Serré. Working in Lyons, Beyer made objects for everyday use with salt-glazes, in the manner of the traditional country potters. Besides these pieces, often with zoomorphic forms and concentric engraved surfaces, he sculpted hierarchic statues of saints with their attributes. In the mid-1930s, Beyer was lent a mill by Sèvres where he went on experimenting, moving even further towards simplification. In 1942, he settled at La Borne, near Bourges, and gave a new lease of life to this village of potters.

One of the most marked features of early twentieth-century ceramics was the taste for decorated faïence. The leading exponents were Fernand Rumèbe, Edouard Cazaux, Jean Mayodon, René Buthaud and Andrè Metthey. While Rumèbe was influenced by Middle Eastern ceramics and Khmer art, the others ornamented their work

with figures and animals in a Neo-classical style. Metthey had become renowned for his ceramics decorated by the Fauve artists; this lasted only a few years, and he began himself to paint, using thick polychrome glazes with a crackled gold finish, which were especially popular at the time. While Metthey, in chronic ill-health, died in 1920, Mayodon was to continue decorating pools, fountains and transatlantic liners, while Buthaud, from 1939 to 1955, made statues in stanniferous glazed faïence.

During the 1920s and 1930s, many ceramists and decorators were employed by manufacturers or received commissions from them, while those working individually were no longer willing to make rare and unique pieces at the price of continual effort and sacrifices of time, money and health. They preferred to make or design ceramics which, through casting or other methods, could be made on a large scale. Sèvres, now financially independent, could no longer impose its taste on the public, but had to join the Modern Movement in order to survive commercially: they opened a faïence section under Etienne Avenard, experimented in new pastes, asked well-known painters for models to decorate services and edited sculpture by popular artists.

Jean Luce and Marcel Goupy designed elegant and useful tableware, and Maurice Gensoli made pieces with zoomorphic finials sculpted in porcelain paste and covered with crystalline glazes of great purity. Sèvres participated in the decoration of the *Normandie* launched in 1932, and exhibited giant ceramic murals designed by Zadkine, de Chirico, Gromaire, and others, at the 1937 Paris Exhibition. Limoges too, commissioned independent artists, including Luce and Goupy. Nearly all the large Parisian department stores and decorators had their own ceramic section; Louis Süe and André Mare (La Compagnie des Arts Français) sold Baroque faïence with thick white slip glaze; Claude Lévy, Colette Guéden and Jean and Jacques Adnet designed for Primavera (Printemps). The Adnet brothers also supplied models to La Maîtrise (Galeries Lafayette).

Among the ceramists working on their own were Jean Besnard, who began by making robust primitive pottery with moulded or incised geometric decoration. During the 1930s, he made vases with lacy surfaces (*dentellés*) and humorous figures with retracted glazes (*crispés*). Jacques Lenoble, son of Emile Lenoble and great-grandson of Ernest Chaplet, worked with his wife, Hélène, daughter of the painter Henri Lebasque. The white clay bodies of his vases and bowls were covered with creamy slip in turquoise, white, black, coral, burnt ochre; all surprise results of firing or glazing were to be eliminated. Lenoble, like so many others during the 1930s, turned towards the decoration in ceramics of transatlantic liners, swimming pools and buildings. André Fau, who had worked in the faïence section of Sèvres, became an 'industrial art ceramist', believing in 'selection and diffusion'; Pierre Lebasque, brother of Hélène Lenoble, modelled fish; Henri Chaumeil made moulded and pierced faïence in crackled glazes; Luc Lanel and his wife Marjolaine, whose first pieces were fired by Chaumeil, made stanniferous faïence fountains, light fittings, radiator covers and panels to be applied to furniture; Guidette Carbonnel tiles with flowers, animals and figures in low relief; and Georges Jouve, vases with gun-metal glazes and ceramic panels for interior decoration.

Of course a new generation of ceramists with different aesthetics and priorities of production began to work after the Second World War, but never again were French ceramics to reach the heights and magnificence of its Art Nouveau and Art Deco artists. The exhibition of 1925 had heralded a decline in the French applied arts.

Above left Stoneware vase with an *aventurine* glaze by Henri Simmen. Ivory stopper carved by Mme. O'Kin Simmen, *c.* 1925–30.

Above Low-relief panel in Sèvres stanniferous faïence after a drawing by Ossip Zadkine. Executed for the 1937 Paris International Exhibition.

Silver, Jewellery and Metalwork *by Philippe Garner*

THE CRAFTS OF SILVER, jewellery, metalwork and small-scale sculpture and the allied skills of enamelling and, of course, design, make a rich and significant study in the period from 1890 to 1940. The standards of French craftsmanship within these areas were very high indeed, unrivalled in any other country, and the period was rich in its constant variety of invention. Tastes in jewellery most notably, so susceptible to the vagaries and whims of fashion, serve as an expressive mirror of the period, reflecting in turn the hot-house decadence of the *fin-de-siècle*, the world of Boldini's frothy aristocrats, and the brittle austerity of Modernism.

The Art Nouveau period was a truly great one for French jewellery, and there was no greater single talent than René Lalique. At the age of sixteen, on the death of his father, Lalique was apprenticed to the celebrated goldsmith Louis Aucoc, whilst simultaneously pursuing his studies at the Paris Ecole des Arts Décoratifs. A period of study in England in the late 1870s completed his education. On his return to France he worked freelance for the prestigious houses of Cartier, Boucheron, Renn, Gariod, Hamelin, and Destape, the latter becoming his full-time employer. By 1885 Lalique was in charge of the Destape workshops and in 1886 Destape handed over the atelier to his talented protégé.

Lalique's success dates from his first major exhibition, at the Paris Salon of 1894. He had, by that time, already designed jewels for Sarah Bernhardt and was evolving his distinctive style. His considerable success earned him the Légion d'Honneur in 1897 and brought forward such significant but diverse patrons as Calouste Gulbenkian and Count Robert de Montesquiou. The former became enamoured of Lalique's artistry and offered him a virtual carte-blanche commission, while at the same time buying many fine examples of his work from exhibitions.

The resulting collection of over one hundred and forty works, displayed in the Gulbenkian foundation in Lisbon, is undoubtedly the finest in the world and includes such major pieces as the oft-illustrated *parure de corsage* of a giant *plique-à-jour* enamelled, grotesque dragonfly with the carved chrysoprase body and head of a woman. Montesquiou, in an essay 'Orfèvre et Verrier' (the *verrier* being Gallé) from the *recueil* of 1897, *Les Roseaux Pensants*, wrote with rapture of a visit to Lalique's shop and of the fantastic treasures to be found within. His career as a jeweller lasted until about 1910 by which date Art Nouveau was démodé and Lalique's passion was for glass.

A daring innovator with a total disdain for traditional ideas on the concept and substance of jewellery, Lalique extended the palette available to jewellers through his passion for semi-precious stones and non-precious materials. He would devote to work in carved horn, mother-of-pearl and enamels the care that others might reserve exclusively for gold, platinum and diamonds. He incorporated his first nude figure in a jewel in 1895 and first used carved horn in 1896. His skill with enamels, and, most notably translucent, *plique-à-jour* enamels, was remarkable.

But what was perhaps most striking about Lalique's jewellery, and, indeed, the multi-media works of art which he also created, was the fertility of their graphic invention. Lalique's motifs reflected perfectly the often morbid aspects of *fin-de-siècle* taste; he devised refined, graphic designs from the Medusas, the Ophelias, the drugged, poppy-wreathed maidens, the grotesque creatures, half-animal, half-human of Symbolist literature and painting; he froze into exquisite and precious works of art the literary world of a Des Esseintes, the visual world of Khnopff, Delville or Schwabe. And, always, whatever the motif, Lalique's graphic ability created distinctively personal linear patterns that could be visualised as an abstract art in themselves. Critic Roger Marx writing in *Les Modes* in 1901 noted, 'Lalique has laid open new and unknown possibilities for jewellery – the evolution of jewellery design today owes its sole debt to him.'

The brothers Paul and Henri Vever and Lucien Gaillard were the most gifted of the jewellers influenced by Lalique. The Vever brothers were the inheritors of a family business, as indeed was Gaillard, and first attracted attention at the 1900 Exhibition. They exploited the style and the techniques made fashionable by Lalique and their workshops became particularly adept at the *plique-à-jour* and other enamel work so much in favour. The brothers acted as entrepreneurs and many of their designs were commissioned from artists such as Edward Colonna, whose jewellery designs were also sold in Bing's Maison de l'Art Nouveau, and Eugène Grasset. Lucien Gautrait, who had worked for the Maison Vever, was one more talented jeweller in the Lalique tradition. Henri Vever also wrote a major documentary work, *La Bijouterie Française au XIXe Siècle*.

Lucien Gaillard became director of his family's firm in 1892, and his primary interest was in metalwork until, around 1900, Lalique encouraged him to design jewellery. Despite the evident Lalique influence, Gaillard's jewellery was

Above Gold enamel and carved ivory brooch by René Lalique, *c.* 1900.

Right Hair ornament, carved horn and seed pearls, by Lucien Gaillard, *c.* 1900.

Far right Chalice in silver and blown opalescent glass by René Lalique, *c.* 1900.

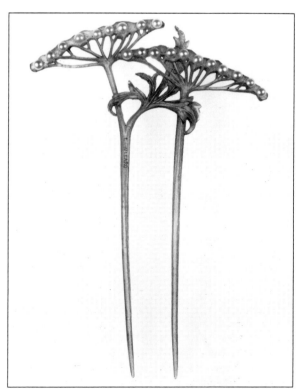

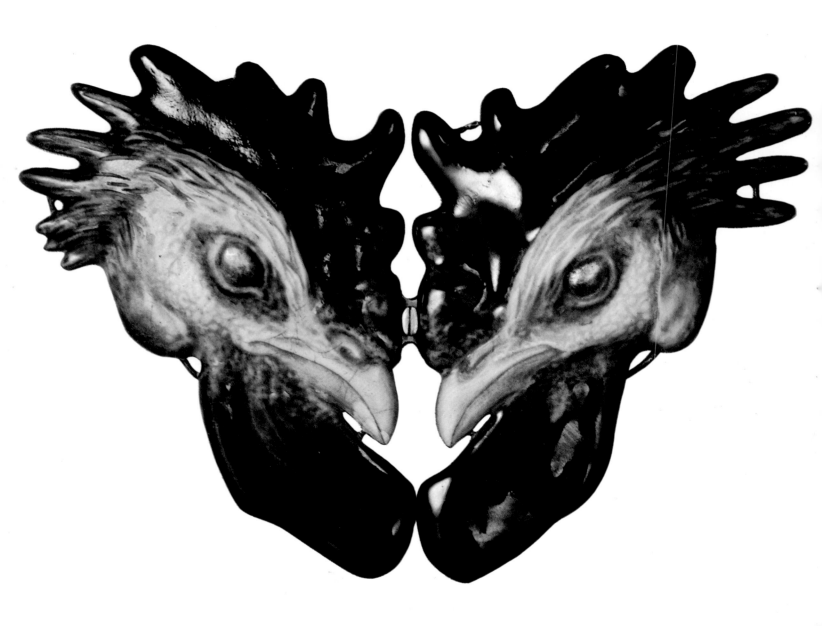

Belt buckle by René
Lalique, enamel on copper,
gold clasp, *c.* 1900.

very successful, winning him first prize at the Société des Artistes Français in 1904. He made a distinctive series of carved horn hair combs as stylised sprays of honesty, ombellifers or mistletoe, often set with small Baroque pearls as flowerheads or berries.

Georges Fouquet, who took over the family firm in 1895 and was anxious to express himself in the fashionable Art Nouveau style, found an ideal collaborator in Alphonse Mucha, the graphic artist whom he commissioned in 1901 to design his new Rue Royale shop. This combination of Mucha's luscious and refined graphic sense with Fouquet's ability to translate the artist's designs into exquisite works of art was responsible for only a limited number of jewels, but they are amongst the most extraordinary works created in the Art Nouveau period. The major known examples of this collaboration are works of pure fantasy, jewels of theatrical proportions. These include a bizarre bracelet conceived for Sarah Bernhardt, a grotesque enamelled and articulated gold griffin encircling the forearm and hand and incorporating a ring; a giant *parure de corsage* incorporating a carved ivory face surrounded by carved ivory and gold arabesques of hair, an enamelled halo, pendant Baroque stones and a pendant painted panel, watercolour on ivory within a gold border, and a

recently rediscovered *devant de corsage*, the centrepiece of a concoction that included decorated chains and shoulder pieces, incorporating a similar but larger painted ivory panel within an exquisite, part-*plique-à-jour* enamelled, openwork border. Alphonse Mucha's published folio, *Documents Décoratifs*, includes delightful designs for jewels that were never executed.

La Maison Moderne retailed jewellery in high Art Nouveau taste by Paul Follot, Maurice Dufrêne and Manuel Orazi. More traditional firms such as that founded by Frédéric Boucheron in 1858 made certain concessions to the fashions of 1900 as can be seen for example from the designs of L. Hirtz for Boucheron, published in the winter 1901 *Studio* special number on jewellery and fans.

Eugène Feuillâtre left the Lalique workshop in 1899, having mastered the skills of enamelling. Though he designed and exhibited jewellery, examples of which are illustrated by Vever, his forte was in large-scale *tours de force* of enamelling including *plique-à-jour* creations of unprecedented daring. The 29 cm. diameter dish from the Charles Handley-Read collection with its vigorous design of a grotesque fish in polychrome enamels in a silver framework, is perhaps the finest surviving example. He joined the Société des Artistes Français and exhibited with them until 1910.

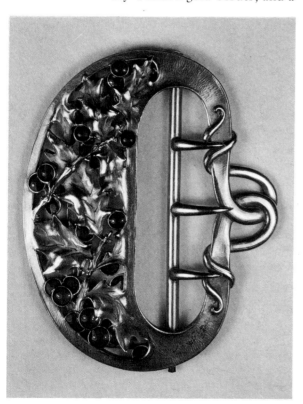

Above Gold and enamel belt buckle, *c*. 1900.

Right Enamelled bottle and stopper by Eugène Feuillâtre, *c*. 1900.

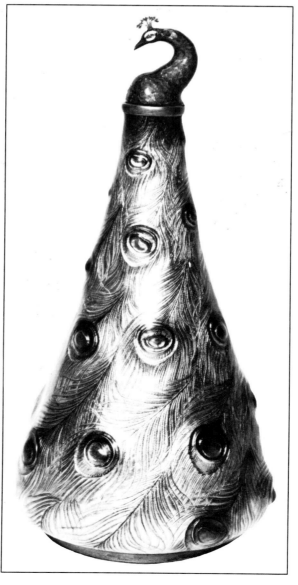

Chocolatière in silver-gilt by
Cardeilhac, *c.* 1900.

The firm of Cardeilhac produced a number of exciting designs in the Art Nouveau taste. The firm's involvement in fine *orfèvrerie* dates back to the late 1880s and stems from the enthusiasm of Ernest Cardeilhac, grandson of the founder. His entries won a silver medal in 1889 and he distinguished himself in 1900 with objects executed by his firm to the designs of Lucien Bonvallet. Cardeilhac created a series of attractive mounts for vases by leading glass-makers and potters. The most characteristic Cardeilhac pieces were those in silver or silver-gilt decorated with stylised yet restrained plant motifs and with details such as handles and finials in carved wood or tinted ivory.

The firm of Falize, directed after 1897 by André Falize, grandson of the founder, was another of the major *orfèvres* active at the turn of the century and its diverse output included works in the Art Nouveau taste made up to the designs of various artists including Lucien Lévy-Dhurmer.

Lucien Gaillard's output was by no means restricted to jewellery. He studied in depth the various aspects of metalwork, patination, plating, alloying as well as Japanese techniques of decoration and produced a variety of objects from parasol handles to hairpins which combined fine and unusual workmanship with a strong sense of design, using precious and non-precious materials with equal respect.

Dinanderie, work in non-precious metals, came into its own in the early years of the twentieth century, partly perhaps as a result of exposure to Japanese works of art. Bonvallet exhibited vases in 1902 in *repoussé* copper. Two years later the Swiss-born craftsman Jean Dunand exhibited his first examples of *dinanderie*. Dunand, who was to achieve considerable renown between the wars as a lacquer artist first came to the notice of critics with a series of vases of organic form, gourds, marrow forms, and other semi-naturalistic shapes meticulously hammered from flat sheets of metal. Gradually Dunand abandoned these forms in favour of vases of simple silhouette with decoration achieved by inlays or contrasting patinations; although the forms of this period immediately preceding the First World War were no longer naturalistic, the decorations often were, with Dunand recreating the appearance of snake-skin or inlaying the elegant lines of peacock feathers.

A branch of the decorative arts which enjoyed a particular vogue around 1900 and subsequently, in different styles, in the twenties and thirties, was decorative sculpture. Small, domestic-scale sculptures were to be found serving a variety of functions, from vide-poches to table lamps, as well as being created in a purely ornamental capacity. The main source of inspiration to Art Nouveau sculptors was undoubtedly Loïe Fuller. This American dancer who first appeared at the Folies Bergère in 1893 and triumphed at the Paris Exhibition of 1900 was hailed as the living embodiment of the Art Nouveau style. The greatest sculptural tributes are probably the two versions of her in the full flight of her dance by Raoul Larche, cast in bronze by Siot-Decauville. Pierre Roche, Théodore Rivière and Rupert Carabin were among the sculptors who attempted to

Bronze table lamp modelled as the dancer Loïe Fuller by Raoul Larche, *c*. 1900.

of a woman, gilded and crowned with a diadem', and another was a symbolic sculpture for the Bosnia-Herzegovina pavilion. From 1900 also dates the large bust of a woman, her hair swirling to form the stylised base in typical Mucha graphic style, of which four casts are now known; from 1901 dates a softer interpretation of the same concept cast as part of the furnishings of the Fouquet shop. From about 1900 dates the beautiful wall-applique preserved in a private Brussels collection. Representing the part-veiled head of a young woman, it is hung with amethysts, malachite and enamelled details. The bare light bulbs at the centre of giant flowerheads either side of the face harmonise in a way that could only have been possible in 1900, contemporary taste finding an acceptable harmony between the magic of electric lighting and the mysticism of the subject.

A remarkable but somehow isolated talent in the realm of Art Nouveau metalwork was Paris architect-designer Hector Guimard, perhaps best known for his inventively organic cast-iron entrances to the Paris underground, designed in 1900, which have been described as '. . . gateways to a subterranean Venusburg such as Beardsley described so vividly in his story *Under the Hill.*' Between 1907 and 1910, Guimard designed small objects, vases, frames, a cane handle to be cast in bronze or silver, giving rein on a reduced scale to his characteristic abstract organic motifs. His most important metalwork venture, however, were his cast-iron architectural details, the designs for which were published in 1907 under the title *Fontes Artistiques pour Constructions, Fumisterie, Articles de Jardins et Sepultures, Style Guimard* by the Fonderies de Saint-Dizier.

Sculptor and decorator Alexandre Charpentier modelled low-relief, sensitive allegorical nude figures for door handles and lock plates and was regarded as one of the best medallists during his active period at the turn of the century.

After the interruption brought about by the First World War, altogether new styles and techniques of metalwork came into prominence. Lush and extravagant examples of Art Nouveau had seemed *passé* as early as 1905, though more restrained versions, such as the taut elegance of Guimard's metalwork, were still in evidence up to just a few years before the war. For certain artists the transition into Art Deco was a natural and easy one. The close of the war, however, heralded the emergence of a host of new talents.

Not least among them was Edgar Brandt, master *ferronnier* and largely responsible for the sudden and tremendous popularity after 1920 of wrought iron work. René d'Avril, writing in 1925, recorded the claim that Brandt was already a competent iron worker at the age of fifteen. He was in his late thirties, however, when, in 1919, after the war, he finally set up his own atelier. His success in the early 1920s was immediate as he forged his metal into the stylised motifs, the scrolls, ribbonwork, Neo-classical figures and formalised flowers of Art Deco. By 1925 and the International Paris Exhibition, Brandt, working in collaboration with his partner, designer-architect Louis Favier, emerged as one of the major contributors, to whom was entrusted the creation of the Porte d'Honneur to the Exhibition. The

Above *Parure de corsage*, designed by Alphonse Mucha and executed by Georges Fouquet, in gold, enamels, emeralds, watercolour and metallic paint on ivory, and hung with a Baroque pearl, *c.* 1900.

Opposite page Gilt-bronze bust by Maurice Bouval, *c.* 1900.

capture in bronze the fluid magic of her dance movements.

Maurice Bouval modelled some of the most sensual decorative Art Nouveau sculptures. His works, which were conceived as paper knives, dishes, door-handles, appliques or purely decorative objects, were usually in gilt-bronze and always on the theme of the dream-maiden or *femme-fleur* so dear to French Art Nouveau. Leo Laporte-Blairsy designed a clever series of lamps as female figures holding giant pierced flowers or carved glass shades that concealed light fittings. Louis Chalon, Charles Korschann, G. Flamand, Max Blondat, Agathon Leonard and Villanis were amongst the more gifted of the decorative sculptors to work in the Art Nouveau style.

Alphonse Mucha designed only a few decorative sculptures but they are amongst the most impressive of the Art Nouveau period. Although dependent for the translation of his ideas into bronze on the help of the sculptor Auguste Seysses, his few ventures into three-dimensional work bear his own unmistakable hallmark. Mucha's interest in sculpture covered the period 1899 to 1903 and at least two of his sculptures were conceived for the Paris Exhibition of 1900. One, for the Houbigant stand, he describes as '. . . a bust

major work on show in 1925 was the magnificent five-fold screen, *L'Oasis*, which summarised the motifs that Brandt helped popularise. The central panel represented a stylised fountain, whilst the remaining area was filled with stylised leaves and the repeated flower-like scroll that became a leitmotif of French Art Deco. *L'Oasis*, like many of Brandt's larger-scale works, was enlivened with a warm-coloured patination, thus avoiding the sombre effect of large areas of blackened metal.

The Brandt workshops made decorative radiator covers, jardinières, floor, wall and table lamps, the glass shades usually from the Daum factory, firescreens, mirror frames, console tables, indeed any item of furnishing that could successfully be wrought in iron. Brandt also, on occasion, worked in bronze as was the case for his serpent lamps.

Brandt's style and techniques were adopted by a number of imitators including Charles Piguet in Lyons, Paul Kiss, Edouard, Marcel and Charles Schenck, Nics Frères and Raymond Subes. Emile Robert has been given credit for teaching the skills of ironwork; it was undoubtedly Brandt's talent, however, that led and encouraged French Art Deco metalwork.

When Jean Dunand resumed his activity in 1919, he had already evolved a new personal style in his *dinanderie*. By its quasi-oriental simplicity and dependence on totally abstract geometric design it placed him apart from and chronologically in advance of artists such as Brandt. Dunand, having perfected the techniques of inlaying and patinating his metal, had now introduced the use of lacquer in his metalwork, either providing a rich even surface or crisp contrasts of red and black in strong geometric designs. Although his growing interest was in the use of lacquer on wood, metalwork, now usually lacquered, remained a constant area of his output through the 1920s and 1930s. Amongst his most successful vases were those with free-standing lacquered fins. Dunand's workshops in the Rue Hallé also produced a variety of small-scale lacquered metalwork items such as cigarette cases, and jewellery.

Claudius Linossier, a former apprentice with Dunand, set up an atelier in Lyons and his hammered, patinated and inlaid metal dishes and vases, evocative of the work of Dunand, earned regular mention in contemporary surveys of the decorative arts in the twenties. Jean Serrière worked in a similar vein.

Decorative sculptures in the styles of the twenties and thirties enjoyed the popular success that Art Nouveau sculptures had enjoyed at the turn of

Above *L'Oasis*, an elaborate wrought metal screen by Edgar Brandt, 1925.

Right The *porte d'honneur* to the 1925 Exhibition, wrought iron, by Edgar Brandt and Louis Favier.

the century. They ranged from top quality artifacts in bronze and carved ivory to stylish but cheaply-made figures that must have been manufactured in substantial numbers. Sculptors whose work has strong claims to be categorised as fine rather than decorative art include Gustave Miklos, Joseph Czaky and Joseph Bernard, though each of these artists collaborated with leading decorators. Miklos created models to be decorated in lacquer by Dunand; for Doucet he made a remarkable pair of andirons in gilt and enamelled bronze, and the bronze mounts and sabots of a pair of *tabourets*; he designed a piece of jewellery executed in gold in 1927 by Raymond Templier. Czaky incorporated one of his sculptures into a cabinet designed for Doucet by Marcel Coard; he also designed the sculptural stair-rail for Doucet's new Neuilly home. Bernard's Neo-classical sculptures, in stone or cast in bronze, provided a decorative counterpoint to Ruhlmann's rich but austere furniture in his room schemes at the 1925 Paris Exhibition.

Edouard Marcel Sandoz and François Pompon modelled heavily stylised animals in stone or to be cast in bronze. The twin brothers Joël and Jan Martel, working as one, abandoned their early monumental style and evolved a more fashionable style in the twenties, as they translated the visual language of Cubism into a decorative idiom. Their work was well represented at the Paris 1925 Exhibition where they designed bas-reliefs for the Pavillon du Tourisme and the Porte Concorde and sculpted details in the bathroom for the Pavillon de la Manufacture de Sèvres. The brothers Jean and Jacques Adnet created decorative bas-reliefs and sculptures in a style similar to that of the Martels.

Purely ornamental figures as domestic decoration enjoyed considerable popularity and the genre was successfully exploited by a wide range of artists. The Rumanian-born sculptor Demetre Chiparus, working in Paris, proved his pre-eminence in the creation of figures in painted bronze and carved ivory. The complete absence of reference to his work in contemporary folios on the decorative arts, however, seems to suggest that he was considered somewhat bad taste by more serious critics. He created totally lifelike figures of exotic dancers, often in brief, jewelled costumes that revealed large areas of ivory flesh, or in more elaborate costumes that reflected such fashionable fads as the quasi-oriental exoticism of the Ballets Russes or the taste for all things Egyptian which followed the discovery of Tutankhamen's tomb. J. Descomps and R. Philippe created figures in

Below left Josephine Baker wearing lacquered bracelets by Jean Dunand; photograph taken in 1926 when Josephine was nineteen.

Below Decorative sculpture, signed 'J. Martel', in polished metal, 1920s.

Below Wrought and inlaid metal vase by Jean Dunand, *c.* 1920.

Below right Eggshell lacquer vase by Jean Dunand, 1929. Formerly in the collection of Edgar Brandt.

bronze and ivory, though less extravagant than those of Chiparus. Pierre Le Faguays and Bouraine also mixed bronze and ivory, but are better known for works fully cast in bronze; typical of their work are their stylised semi-naked female figures with formalised, almost two-dimensional draperies. Bouraine sculpted memorable Amazon warriors and a group of Leda and the swan. The mark Le Verrier appears on stylish figures cast in spelter.

The inter-war years provided an equally varied range of jewellery, from the ostentatious creations of the great traditional jewellery houses, through the more intellectual and artistic creations of a small group of designers who treated jewels as miniature sculptures, to the vast range of cheaply-produced costume jewellery, designed to be briefly worn, and as rapidly discarded as fashion dictated, the popularisation of which is generally credited to Coco Chanel in the late 1920s.

The Establishment of the jewellery world was represented in Paris by the *grandes maisons* such as Boucheron, Cartier, Van Cleef and Arpels, and Lacloche Frères. In the 1920s these firms found a style that combined elements of Art Deco, the vibrant colours and Orientalism of the Ballets Russes and a love of chinoiserie motifs. They used

Above left Patinated
bronze figure, marked
'Fringue', 1920s.

Above Silvered metal
figure, modelled by Fayral
and cast by Max le Verrier,
1920s.

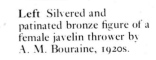

Left Silvered and
patinated bronze figure of a
female javelin thrower by
A. M. Bouraine, 1920s.

Below Bracelet by Raymond Templier in platinum, white gold, onyx and diamonds, late 1920s.

Right Pendant in platinum, coral, jet and brilliants by Jean Fouquet, late 1920s.

Tea service in silver and wood by Jean Puiforcat, late 1920s.

onyx, carved coral and jade, frosted crystal and brilliants. Typical of their creations are cigarette or vanity cases mixing exotic materials, elaborate diamond-studded brooches, tassels of seed pearls or brilliants. Cartier also produced remarkable clocks, including their celebrated 'mystery' clocks. The 1920s was a very successful time for such firms. The Crash of 1929 and the depression that followed, however, had an inevitable effect on such a high-luxury industry, as, of course, did the social acceptance of costume jewellery. During the 1930s the most ubiquitous jewel, exquisitely created in diamonds by Cartier or mass-produced in paste, was the double dress clip. The Surrealist fashions of the late 1930s inspired a series of *fantaisie* brooches, typical of which were the carved ebony negro heads or coral hands holding gold flowers made by Cartier.

Perhaps the most exciting phase in jewellery design between the wars, however, is to be found in the late 1920s work of a select group of artists, notably Raymond Templier, Gérard Sandoz, Jean Fouquet and Paul Brandt. Templier, Sandoz and Fouquet were second generation jewellers, the sons of Paul Templier, Gustave Sandoz and the George Fouquet who had enjoyed such success around 1900. They each combined a background

of technical involvement with an acute sensitivity
to the emerging aesthetic of Modernism. The most
important document on their work is the folio
Bijoux et Orfèvrerie published *c.* 1930 by Charles
Moreau in the series 'L'Art International
d'Aujourd'hui.' Here can be found the motifs and
materials which these artists employed. The motifs are almost invariably abstract, tough geometric
forms that evoke the dynamism of machinery, a
sophistication of Futurism. The materials are cold
and the works are finished with the perfection of
precision-engineering. Platinum, silver and white
gold are allied with black areas of onyx, jet or
enamel. Black, red or other brilliant lacquers
emphasise the graphic elements of designs, sometimes incorporating areas of crushed eggshell to
provide a counterpoint to the otherwise total
austerity. The Moreau folio illustrates Templier's
extraordinary *parure* created for Brigitte Helm's
role in *L'Argent* of 1927, Fouquet's split bullet-
form frosted crystal pendant, a display of Brandt's
dynamic eggshell lacquer cigarette cases in a
setting by René Herbst.

The silversmith Jean Puiforcat adapted the
abstract, geometric elements of Modernism to the
creation of fine quality work in which he would
contrast the texture of the silver with emphatic

handles, finials and details of dark rich woods or
rock crystal. His best pieces date from the mid and
late twenties. Sandoz designed silverware along
similar lines in addition to creating decorative
costume jewellery.

The Modernist style was adapted to work in
non-precious metals, perhaps more appropriately
since an important element of Modernism was the
tradition of functionalism which somehow seemed
at odds with work in precious materials. The
Union des Artistes Modernes, established in 1930,
led the field in France in the design of Modernist
metalwork. Members such as René Herbst and
Jacques Le Chevallier worked on new ideas for
light fittings, those of Le Chevallier often with
self-consciously exposed screwheads in the functionalist tradition.

In the early 1920s, designer Jean Perzel specialised in the creation of light fittings. He won
first prize in the lighting section at the 1928 Salon
des Artistes-Décorateurs and perfectly reflected
the ideals of Modernism in his elegant, discreet
designs for floor, wall and table lights in chromed
metal and glass. Desny used the geometric
language of Modernism in clever metalwork
designs such as his double cone drinking vessels,
and in a series of glass and metal table lamps.

Graphic Art *by Martin Battersby*

FROM THE CLOSING YEARS of the nineteenth century, the graphic arts in France showed a steadily improving standard in design and production. As a result of this new excellence, there arose a corresponding enthusiasm on the part of bibliophiles for collecting limited editions of contemporary illustrated books, thus giving a greatly increased field of work for artists, typographers, makers of fine papers and bookbinders. In 1820 the Société des Bibliophiles Français had been founded, and for the next fifty years informed its members about the comparatively small number of *éditions-de-luxe* being produced, as well as of antiquarian books. Developments in technical processes and a consequent increase in the number of volumes published gave rise to the founding of the Société des Livres in 1874, the Société des Cent Bibliophiles in 1895, the Société des XX two years later and the Société du Livre Contemporain in 1904. In the 1920s, the number of these associations increased still further both in Paris and the provinces as edition after edition of classics and modern works were produced for this exclusive market.

These associations of book lovers and, more especially, those formed in the latter years of the century were also concerned with raising the standard of book production and of the graphic arts, which with few exceptions had degenerated below the standards set during previous centuries. Encased in bindings which, like the furniture and architecture of the mid 1800s, were timid pastiches of past historical styles, the texts, often difficult to read, were set in badly-designed types and printed on paper of indifferent quality. The illustrations were reproduced from pen and ink drawings transferred to boxwood blocks and subsequently engraved by skilled technicians, upon whose dexterity artists unversed in the actual techniques of wood engraving imposed almost impossible demands. It was surprising that so much of the character of the original drawings survived, but this was only due to the craftsmanship of the engravers who painstakingly reproduced the slightest nuances of line of the originals. One of the best examples of this translation of one medium into another were the engravings of Gustave Doré's drawings by Sotain and Pisan.

Other methods of reproduction, such as steel-engraving, *eau-forte* or lithography in the main failed to satisfy the high standards of book production demanded by collectors aware of the excellence of the eighteenth century. It was William Morris as the producer of the volumes from his Kelmscott Press, founded in 1891, who proved influential in restoring the essential features of a well-produced book – a perfect balance and harmony between the text and the illustrations, the text being well-designed and sympathetic to the spirit of the words.

Even before the appearance of the Kelmscott Press, the teachings of Morris and of Walter Crane had considerable influence in France. The designer Eugène Grasset with his specially designed type and illustrations for *Les Quatre Fils Aymon*, published in 1883, had shown the way to a renaissance in book production after overcoming a lack of enthusiasm from critics and public. Grasset continued his pioneering efforts in designing new original and legible types – his 'Grasset' fount appeared in 1898 and was widely used – and his example was followed by George Auriol, Bellery-Desfontaines and Naudin. The illustrator Bracquemond, already well-known as a water-colourist, agreed with William Morris in advocating the use of original woodcuts to achieve, as he wrote in his *Etude sur la Gravure sur Bois*, published in 1897, 'the unity of the elements on a printed page'. The woodcut should, he main-

Right Poster by Eugène Grasset for Sarah Bernhardt as Jeanne d'Arc.

Opposite page *Le Retour*, lithograph by Georges de Feure, *c*. 1900.

Numéro 1   Mai 1897

L'ESTAMPE
Moderne

Directeurs :

CH. MASSON & H. PIAZZA

★

Publication Mensuelle

Contenant

Quatre estampes originales inédites

en Couleurs et en Noir

des

principaux Artistes Modernes

Français et Étrangers

éditée par

L'IMPRIMERIE CHAMPENOIS

ABONNEMENTS D'UN AN :	LE NUMÉRO :
Paris 40 frs.	Paris 3 frs. 50
Dépar⁶ et Étranger 43 frs.	Dépar⁶ et Étranger 4 frs.

SOMMAIRE

Femme du Riff.	Automne.
L. A. GIRARDOT	R. MÉNARD
Marchande de Lacets.	Corinne.
L. MALTESTE	M. HBALDIR-DUMAS

Direction et Administration : 66, Boulevard Saint-Michel, Paris.

Mucha

Cover to the first issue of
L'Estampe Moderne,
incorporating a design by
Alphonse Mucha, May
1897.

tained, be true to itself and should not be forced into a facsimile of a steel engraving, a pen drawing or even a photograph. From a practical viewpoint the woodcut had an advantage in that it could be printed simultaneously with the type on a wider choice of paper, thus obviating the use of the coated papers needed for half-tone or process blocks. The editor, Bracquemond considered, should be 'the architect of the book', choosing a type which suited the feeling of the author's intention, the paper upon which it was printed, the binding and even the design of the endpapers – all refinements which had been too often disregarded for decades.

The editor who first realised these aims to the fullest was Pellatan who achieved European renown from 1896. For each of his publications, which included titles from authors as diverse as Alfred de Musset, Theocritus, Jean Lorrain, François Villon and Molière, a different type was used – many being designed by Grasset – while illustrations were commissioned from Grasset, Daniel Vierge, Bellery-Desfontaines, Jeanniot and Bellenger.

Grasset, Bracquemond and Pellatan were later realised to have been the pioneers whose creative efforts had a profound influence on the graphic arts in France. The standards they set gave encouragement to others to follow their example, giving hitherto unrealised opportunities to young and promising painters to extend their talents to book illustration. As the critic Raymond Cogniat commented in 1929 when the fashion for collecting illustrated *éditions-de-luxe* was at its height, 'the modern book offers an amateur of the arts unlimited scope for possessing works by artists which no collector of paintings could own even if he were endowed with an enormous fortune. Who could unite in one gallery hundreds of canvases or drawings signed by Matisse, Picasso, Rouault, Laboureur, Maurice Denis, Chagall and Dufy? The book allows the greatest eclecticism of taste and the right to indulge contrary tendencies in art. Realism and Surrealism, abstract and concrete, can be juxtaposed in a collector's library'.

The number of illustrated *éditions-de-luxe* produced in the 1920s was so large that several periodicals devoted a regular monthly feature to new publications, but paradoxically, while giving so many opportunities to graphic artists, their work in these volumes was little known to the general public. For an explanation of this it is necessary to describe the system by which the books were distributed. Each volume was produced in an edition limited to anything between one hundred and fifteen hundred copies – generally the more lavish the presentation, the smaller the edition, as only the highest standard could justify the extremely high prices. While the text and the illustrations were constant there were different categories. A small number would be printed on an extremely costly hand-made paper of which there were many kinds both made in France and imported from Holland, China and Japan. The cost of this paper could account for as much as a fifth of that of the book. Extra loose plates of illustrations signed by the artist and in some cases one or more of the original drawings were included. In all likelihood this edition would be rebound by a leading artist bookbinder, thereby increasing its artistic and financial value.

A rather larger number would be printed on less costly paper with fewer loose plates, while the bulk of the edition would be on still less expensive fine quality paper, the entire edition being signed and numbered. This last category could be priced at a fifth of that of the first, while being exactly the same in appearance and quality of printing. Very often the entire edition was sold as soon as an advance notice was given, and without even being examined by the purchaser.

The entire edition was frequently distributed solely through the bibliophile societies to their members, and thus the general public had no opportunity of buying or even seeing a copy. They were regarded more as works of art with a possibly increasing financial value than as books to be read for enjoyment.

In many cases *éditions-de-luxe* were left with the sections unsewn with a protective covering of card necessitating rebinding to ensure their preservation. Private collectors would commission artist-binders to provide this protection for their libraries, generally with uninspired versions of eighteenth century bindings. It was Henri Marius-Michel who, in his *La Reliure Française* published in 1880, advocated that the binding should echo the feeling of the text rather than conform to conventions of traditional bindings with their tooled and gilded ornaments.

Woodcut by Mariano Andrieu for *Amphitryon 38* by Giraudoux.

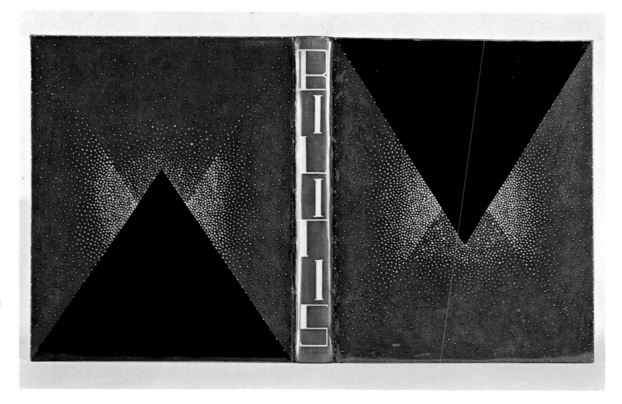

The work of William Morris and Walter Crane in this field played a considerable part in this revolutionary concept and the break with conventional ideas gave limitless opportunities for decorative bindings to designers working in the Art Nouveau manner, whether using expensive leathers for single copies or cloth ornaments with stamped or printed designs for large editions.

About 1920 a further innovation was introduced by Pierre Legrain already well-known as a designer of interiors and furniture inspired by African primitive art. Hitherto the front and back covers and the spine of the book had been treated as separate entities, but Legrain spread his design over the entire cover so that when the book was fully opened a complete composition was revealed. In addition to the usual coloured leathers – and in the 1920s a range of brilliantly hued skins were utilised – he incorporated wood, ivory, mother-of-pearl and shagreen as decorative elements. Legrain's influence can be seen in the work of Rose Adler who, with René Kieffer, Robert Bonfils, Georges Cretté, Gruel, Louis Creuzevault, Paul Bonet and even Jean Dunand, raised bookbinding in France to new heights of originality of design combined with consummate technical excellence in its execution.

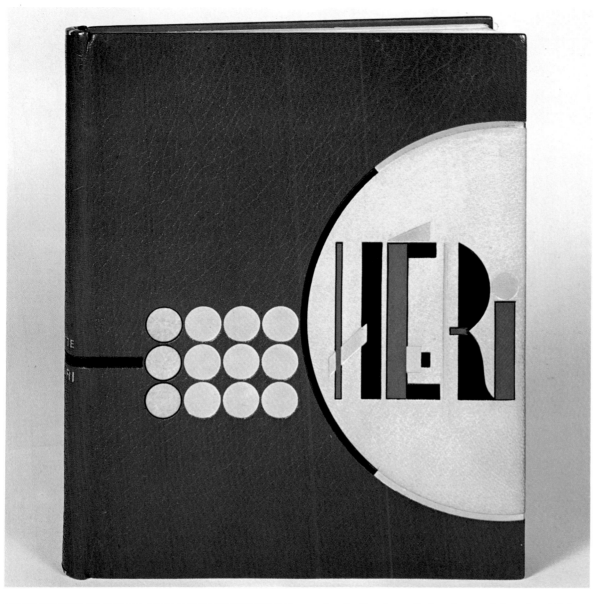

Left Binding by Rose Adler for *Chéri* by Colette, late 1920s.

Below left Binding by Greuzevault, late 1920s.

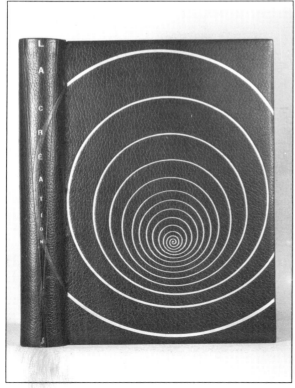

An indication of the demand for the *éditions-de-luxe* can be gauged from the fact that, while in 1905 there were fifteen publishers specialising solely in this type of book, the number in 1920 was estimated to be well over sixty. Inevitably this led to a scarcity of books suitable for presentation in an illustrated version and a consequent duplication, particularly of the classics. This particularly happened in the case of *Les Fables de la Fontaine*. Illustrated in the eighteenth century by Jean Baptiste Oudry, in 1802 by Percier the official architect to Napoleon I, in 1833 by Gouget in the romantic Gothic revival manner, no less than three versions were planned during the 1920s in as many years. The magnificent version with decorations by Paul Jouve appeared in 1929.

Jouve had first attracted attention when at the age of sixteen he had sculpted an important frieze of animals for the 1900 Exhibition. Specializing in the portraiture of animals and particularly the larger wild fauna of the jungle he was an obvious choice to illustrate *Le Livre du Jungle* by Rudyard Kipling in 1919. Kipling, indeed, enjoyed considerable popularity in France, more perhaps than any other English contemporary author – his original drawings being interpreted in wood engravings by François-Louis Schmied. Jouve was not interested in depicting humans, so Schmied was commissioned to illustrate *Kim* in the following year. In 1930, Jouve and Schmied again collaborated on *Le Pélerin d'Angkor* by Pierre Loti. In the same year Jouve decorated *La Chasse de Kâa*, an episode from *Le Livre du Jungle*, and in 1932 *Paradis Terrestres* by Colette.

Another edition of La Fontaine's *Fables* was that of Joseph Hemard, but this seems to have aroused little enthusiasm. The third version was the cause of a remarkable scandal, when in 1927 Ambroise Vollard commissioned illustrations from Marc Chagall. The choice of an artist so closely identified with mystical Russian folklore caused a furore of protest in the press and the general indignation was so intense that it caused a special debate in the Chambre des Députés. Unperturbed, Chagall produced a hundred drawings over the next four years, but the delays which seemed to be a matter of course with Vollard's publications put off publication when the latter died in 1939. *Les Fables*, together with another project for Chagall, *Les Cinq Livres du Bible*, had to wait until after the war, when they were published by Tériade.

Two versions of *Les Contes de Perrault* appeared, the first in 1922 with magnificent etchings by Etienne Drian, and the second in 1929, illustrated by no less than thirty-three artists including Marie Laurencin, Alexeieff (who was much in demand for translations of Russian classics), Pierre Pinsard, Hermine David, Dignimont, Laboureur and Laborde. It was commended more as a compendium of the leading artists of the book than as an integrated work of art.

Kees van Dongen, whose *fauve* portraits of society beauties convey so much of the spirit of the 1920s was an appropriate choice to illustrate *Deauville*, written by Paul Poiret, and *La Garçonne* by Victor Margueritte, a novel which had been a *succès de scandale* in 1923 with its frank treatment of drugs and lesbianism. Van Dongen's travels in

Right Illustration by Paul Jouve to *Le Livre du Jungle* (The Jungle Book) by Rudyard Kipling, 1919.

Below right Illustration by Etienne Drian to *Les Contes de Perrault*, 1923.

the Near East resulted in a series of colourful drawings for *Les Contes des Mille et une Nuits* and for another Kipling book, *Les plus beaux Contes*.

Georges Rouault undertook the illustrations for *Réincarnation du Père Ubu* written by Ambroise Vollard in 1918, but again this too had to wait until 1932 for publication. Rouault's own book *Cirque de l'Etoile Filante* with characteristic drawings of tragic clowns was published by Vollard in 1936.

The Symbolist painter Maurice Denis had a similar experience with Vollard and his illustrations for Verlaine's *Sagesse*, for although Denis started work in 1889, twenty-two years elapsed before publication. In the meantime Denis had created 216 illustrations for *L'Imitation de Jésus Christ*, which were engraved by Tony Beltrand and published in 1903. One of the great masterpieces of French graphic art and book production was *Les Eclogues de Virgile*, edited by Count Kessler (who did so much to raise the standards of typography), and illustrated with woodcuts by Aristide Maillol. Started in 1912, the project was abandoned for some years and was finally published in 1926.

These excessive delays were obviously exceptional in view of the constantly increasing demand, and some artists like Charles Laboureur turned out no less than thirty books between 1917 and 1929, a prolific output which gave rise to the criticism that his illustrations were so alike as to be interchangeable.

A complete catalogue of the graphic artists working in the field of book illustration would need several volumes and would include much work that was negligible by deservedly forgotten artists. The most talented were recorded in a series of booklets *Les Artistes du Livre* produced in the 1920s, each volume being devoted to the work of a single artist. Carlègle, Charles Martin, Hemard, Laboureur, Herman Paul were some of the more notable names celebrated. The work of Pablo Picasso for *Les Métamorphoses d'Ovide* and Balzac's *Le Chef d'œuvre Inconnu*, of Raoul Dufy for *Le Bestiaire* and *Le Poète Assassiné*, both by Guillaume Apollinaire, of Sylvain Sauvage for *Contes Antiques* by Pierre Louÿs, of Maxime Dethomas, Alexeieff, Dunoyer de Segonzac and Daragnès are among those who in their different ways made important contributions to the renaissance of book production in France.

On a far more modest scale the collection *Le Livre de Demain* with its distinctive orange and black covers produced well-printed books, with woodcuts by notable artists, within the reach of a wider public. Issued at an extremely low price, printed on inexpensive paper, with the woodcuts reproduced mechanically, the monthly volumes by well-known authors first appeared in 1921 and continued until well after the war.

The woodcut, whether an original by an artist or a rendering by another hand, was not of course the only method of reproducing graphics. A photographic copy of an original drawing in colour or black and white could be made by a process invented in 1886 by Gillot, but the generally poor quality of photography, particularly in colour, together with the necessity of printing on a paper heavily coated with kaolin, which was liable to stick together and deteriorate in damp conditions,

Illustration by Silvain Sauvage to the *Contes Antiques* by Pierre Louÿs, 1929.

Right Illustration by Pierre Brissaud to *Les Malheurs de Sophie*, 1923.

Centre Illustration 'Dans la grotte', by George Barbier to Verlaine's *Les Fêtes Galantes*, 1928.

Far right Lithographic plate from Alphonse Mucha's folio, *Documents Décoratifs*.

rendered this method unsatisfactory. Techniques of drypoint, acquatint, steel engraving, mezzotint and lithography were often used, but had the disadvantage of needing a separate printing from the text and were generally used for *hors-texte* illustrations.

For the connoisseur the ideal method of reproduction was the *pochoir* process by which the colour was stencilled by hand. Early playing cards and the popular prints of the eighteenth century were crude examples of this, but by the first decade of the century the technique had become more sophisticated, enabling the printers to reproduce drawings with great accuracy. By the 1920s the process had become mechanised, but the hand method was still being used for the best of the *éditions-de-luxe*.

Prior to 1908, information about the latest fashions was communicated either by photographs or by conventionalised pen drawings characterised by elongated doll-like figures with vapid expressions. Of a low standard of draughtsmanship and amateurish in execution, these drawings showed a sad degeneration from the charming fashion plates of the nineteenth century.

This was abruptly changed in that year by the appearance of a slim booklet *Les Robes de Paul Poiret* issued in a limited edition of 250 copies which were sent to Poiret's clients as an advertisement for his new and revolutionary ideas of fashion, and the drawings in black-and-white with added colour by the *pochoir* process had a far-

Poster by Jules Chéret for
Loïe Fuller at the Folies
Bergère, 1893.

reaching effect which neither Poiret nor the young artist could have foreseen.

Iribe, then twenty-five-years-old, interpreted Poiret's ideas rather than actual dresses, and his lifelike animated models, which even betrayed private amusement, were as much of an innovation as the uncorseted bodies advocated by Poiret.

The small number of copies of the album, which included no text, were more than enough to spread the idea that a serious artist could, without demeaning his art, depict the latest fashions to the advantage of himself as well as the couturier. No longer were the insipid drawings acceptable in the better periodicals. Coincidentally, the influence of the Ballets Russes and of Bakst confirmed the changes Poiret was effecting in *haute couture*: women were wearing the new high-waisted line or Oriental tunics and draped dresses in brilliant colours, reminiscent of odalisques from an Arabian Night's harem.

There also emerged a new generation of young and extremely talented artists eager to record the new feelings permeating both fashion and the decorative arts in general. Advertisers and, in particular, the makers of the new exotic scents created to enhance the Oriental mood were among the first to employ Iribe to represent their products with evocative drawings, and soon the editorial pages were enlivened with similar drawings.

Even before the appearance of a second album, *Les Choses de Paul Poiret*, in 1911, this new trend was firmly established. This time the illustrations were by Georges Lepape; again, there was no text, but the treatment was more sumptuous with drawings reproduced in colour by the *pochoir* method and heightened with gold and silver to accentuate the more pronounced Oriental flavour of the drawings and the fashions, while the debt to Japanese prints, discernible in the Iribe drawings, was more noticeable. Lepape's drawings are the embodiment of the craze for Oriental luxury and colour pervading fashion and interior decoration in the years immediately before the First World War.

His contemporary Georges Barbier was equally obsessed with this overcharged atmosphere of a legendary Orient and many drawings of the Ballets Russes dancers in their roles bear witness to the fascination the world of ballet had for him. After the war Barbier was more attracted by the eighteenth century and his designs for Maurice Rostand's play *Casanova* were published by Lucien Vogel.

Not enough credit has been given in the past to Vogel, through whose taste and judgment so many of the graphic artists of the time are indebted in the exquisitely produced volumes he published. His most notable achievement was undoubtedly *La Gazette du Bon Ton*, issued between 1912 and 1925, which remains the most beautifully produced periodical ever concerned primarily with fashion, although it also dealt with the decorative arts, music, ballet and the theatre. In 1925 it was acquired by Condé Nast and incorporated into *Vogue*. The colour plates and the decorations interspersed through the text gave full rein to the individual treatment of fashion by the many contributing artists. Of these the most notable were Lepape, Charles Martin, Pierre Brissaud and André Marty, whose work could also be found in *Vogue*, *Fémina*, *House and Garden*, *Le Jardin des Modes* and *Comoedia Illustré*. Occasional contributors included Benito, Guy Arnoux, Drian, Valentine Gross, and Brunelleschi.

After 1925, with the decline of Art Deco and with radical changes in fashion, many of these artists gave up this work. Photography began to occupy more space and the number of drawings decreased. However, to bring variety to the layouts, fashion editors still used artists for the more dramatic creations of important couturiers, and during the thirties Erik, Willaumez, Jean Cocteau, Jean Hugo, Reynaldo Luza and particularly Christian Bérard conveyed the feeling of the latest collections. Mention should be made of two albums designed for a Parisian furrier as examples of the best of graphic work. *La Dernière Lettre Persane* was issued by Fourrures Max about 1923 with striking drawings by Benito and an equally distinguished work for the same firm, *Toi*, featured drawings by Jean Dupas of nude female statues draped with extravagant furs as an accompaniment to poems by Colette.

Lithography was a medium ideally suited for printing posters, whether from an original drawing on the stone by the artist himself and printed under his close supervision, as Toulouse-Lautrec often did, or whether reproduced by a mechanical process involving light sheets of metal which replaced the cumbersome blocks of lithographic stone. The effervescent Watteau-style fantasies of Jules Chéret, the richly patterned intricacies of Alphonse Mucha with the use of gold and silver to enhance the luminous colouring, the mordant line of Steinlen, the Japanese inspired exoticism of Orazi and the sedate elegance of Grasset enlivened the walls of Paris and were seriously discussed and collected by enthusiasts. Among the best examples of Art Nouveau as interpreted by different artists, they gradually disappeared from the hoardings of

Illustration by Jean Cocteau to *Opium*, 1930.

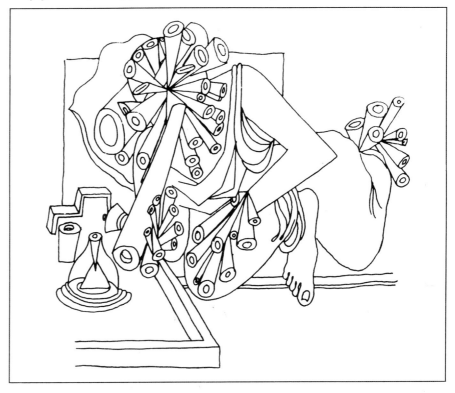

Poster by Cassandre
for the French Line
c. 1930.

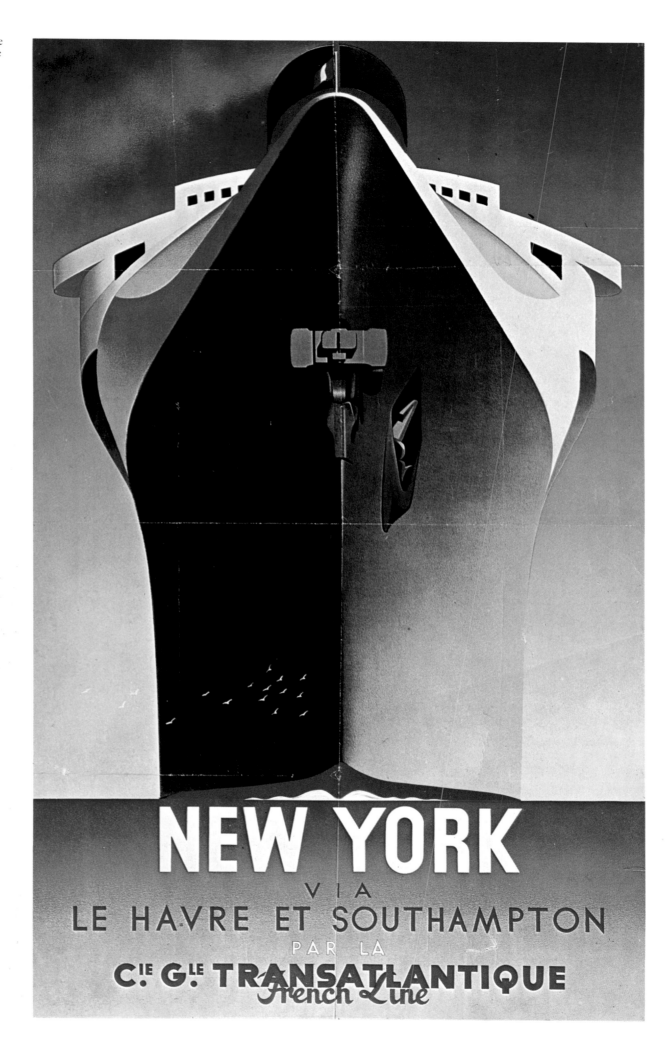

Below Painting by Paul Colin of Josephine Baker, 1926.

Right Poster by Zig for Mistinguett at the Casino de Paris, 1931.

Paris with the decline of that effervescent style.

After this short period of brilliance, poster art reverted to a mediocrity which with few exceptions was general through the twenties and thirties. The explosion of graphic talent which marked the early years of Art Deco seemed not to have extended to posters, although exception must be made for those advertising the Ballets Russes. André Marty designed the first for the company, while Cocteau's portraits of Karsavina and of Nijinsky in *Spectre de la Rose* and that of Anna Pavlova by Valentin Serov were brilliant by any standards. George Barbier, Drian, Benedictus, Bonfils and Jean Dupas, all so active in other branches of graphic art, designed occasional posters for art exhibitions, for charity balls and similar occasions with an appeal to a more sophisticated public, but were rarely, if ever, commissioned by manufacturers. Jean Dupas's work was in fact more popular in England and the United States than in his own country.

In the late twenties and the thirties the pace of life in Paris, as in every capital, increased and, with the growing use of motor cars, the function of a poster became increasingly that of a *télégraphiste*, as a contemporary writer commented. The bold Cubist-inspired styles of Cassandre – one of the great masters of the poster – Coulon, Loupot, and Gio Ponti were ideally suited to convey the advertiser's message at a glance. Paul Colin, influenced by Negro art, and Gesmar were particularly successful in their posters for the theatre and music hall.

Theatre and Ballet *by Martin Battersby*

THE STANDARD OF DESIGN in the French theatre during the closing years of the nineteenth century was extremely low, partly from indifference on the part of theatrical directors, but mostly because there were few if any designers willing to submit to the megalomania of most of the leading actors of the time. It had become the custom to order scenery from firms of scene painters who were often talented painters in a debased *trompe l'oeil* manner but were lacking in design sense or a feeling for historical accuracy.

Costumes were ordered in a similar fashion from theatrical dressmakers, especially made for the leading characters and hired from stock for minor parts. In historical dramas the leading actresses made no concessions to period feeling and their clothes were modern in line with applied details of dubious authenticity. For modern plays the stars would be dressed *gratis* by a well-known couturier, regardless of the character played, on the understanding that she would be photographed for the fashion journals.

In the small experimental theatres, however, new seeds of theatrical presentation were germinating. In 1887 Antoine founded the Théâtre Libre on the principles of historical accuracy, combined with an overall unity of design. Wherever possible he used the real thing, substituting for papier-mâché imitations real joints of meat in a butcher's shop, a real fountain in a woodland scene and even real cobwebs in a dungeon setting. Lugné Poé took a diametrically opposite attitude at his Théâtre de l'Oeuvre, reducing the décor to the minimum of a few draperies arranged in an empty space and having the costumes designed to express the character portrayed and to harmonise with each other. He commissioned designs from painters, including Pierre Bonnard, Odilon Redon, Edouard Vuillard and Paul Serusier, and among his innovations were a sloping stage for Ibsen's *Solness* and a projected production of a Shakespearian play set in a circus. In parenthesis it should be noted that Loïe Fuller, the American dancer who caused a furore on her debut at the Folies Bergère in 1893, invented a glass stage lit from below and a setting of large sheets of mirrors which reflected multiple images of her as she danced.

The literal realism of Antoine and the poetic realism of Poé influenced innovators outside France: Stanislavsky and Meyerhold in Russia, and Max Reinhardt in Germany. It was from Russia that there emerged a company destined to revolutionise theatrical design in France and subsequently most other countries, besides contributing an important element to the new style of Art Deco which made its appearance about 1910.

The unique personality and talents of Serge Diaghilev found expression in the founding of the Ballets Russes with the help of two of the greatest painter-designers of the time, Alexandre Benois and Léon Bakst. The Ballets Russes were able to propagate new concepts in theatrical design to a greater extent than the small experimental theatres which were often little known outside a small circle of admirers and were financially handicapped. The technical demands of ballet – the need for an uncluttered stage and the use of little more than a painted backcloth and wings – gave the designer greater scope for unity of concept. In addition, ballet has no language barrier but uses a universal language of movement and thus can be shown with equal effect in many different countries. In the case of the Ballets Russes there was a shrewdly organised publicity campaign before the first night.

It is difficult to imagine the impact upon Parisian audiences of the Ballets Russes, for later generations have become almost over-familiar with reproductions of the original designs and with generally mediocre revivals. Accustomed to insipid and third-rate performances at the Paris Opéra the new company overwhelmed audiences by the dazzling artistry of the dancers, the originality of the staging and, above all, the masterly designs.

In particular, the visions of a legendary Orient depicted by Bakst in *Schéhérazade* and *Thamar*, with their sumptuous settings and brilliant costumes, had an immediate effect upon every branch of the decorative arts besides theatrical design, as contemporary writers on the arts testify, justifying the comment that life could be divided into two parts – before and after seeing the Ballets Russes.

Paul Poiret, then the rising couturier, his collaborators Paul Iribe and Georges Lepape, Georges Barbier and André Marty all added to their reputations as painters by embarking upon stage design. Poiret's elaborate Oriental masquerades were in the nature of theatrical presentations, with costumes designed for each guest. In his memoirs, he describes his collaboration as dress designer with the painter Ronsin for the production of an Oriental fantasy *Le Minaret* at the Théâtre de la Renaissance. The first act was in tones of blue and green, the second in red and violet, the only note of colour in the black and white third act being a vivid apple-green costume. Barbier's most notable production was *Casanova* by Maurice Rostand in 1919 the success of which led to his being asked to design the costumes for

A drawing by
Georges Barbier of
Nijinsky in
Schéhérazade.

Above Design for setting by André Derain for *La Boutique Fantasque*, 1919.

Right 'La chambre à coucher d'un libertin': design for setting by Georges Barbier for *Casanova*, 1919.

Previous page Design by Leon Bakst for the décor of *Schéhérazade*, probably executed after the first Paris production of 1910.

Rudolph Valentino's film *Monsieur Beaucaire*. Iribe went to Hollywood in 1914 and worked extensively for Cecil B. de Mille while Lepape and Marty had extensive careers designing for plays and revues in Paris. It is likely that none of these careers would have been so successful had not the Ballets Russes shown the way.

In 1912, Diaghilev established his company in Monte Carlo and increasingly engaged the services of young French painters and of foreigners based in Paris. Picasso, Braque, Rouault and Derain were employed in preference to his original Russian collaborators, though Bakst was recalled to design the superb settings and costumes for *La Belle au Bois Dormant* in 1921, unfortunately a financial failure.

The success of the Ballets Russes forced the authorities at the Paris Opéra to bring their productions up to date, and in 1914 a new director, Jacques Rouché, was appointed. He was thus enabled to realise on a wider scale the ideas formulated by his previous experience as manager since 1910 of the Théâtre des Arts where he had worked with Dunoyer de Segonzac, Edouard Vuillard, Poiret and Dresa as designers. 'It is necessary', he had written in 1910, 'that a painter should advise the producer, designing costumes, settings and properties, sitting in at rehearsals with the author and indicating in agreement with him the gestures and movements of the actors'. Although this function is taken for granted today, the need for such a statement is an indication of the lack of cohesion prevalent in the theatre in the early years of the century.

Rouché's first task was to jettison the old-fashioned and shabby décors, and to commission designs for the classics and for new productions from painters including Maxime Dethomas, Drésa, René Piot, Derain, de Chirico, Pruna, Brianchon and Cassandre. Similar reforms took place at the Théâtre Chatelet under the direction of Ida Rubinstein, the creator of the leading role,

Zobëide in *Schéhérazade* and now, with the help of a large personal fortune, in management in her own right. The founding of the Théâtre du Vieux Colombier by Jacques Copeau in 1913, with a repertory which included Shakespeare and other Elizabethan playwrights, brought an English influence by Copeau's admiration of the work of William Poel and Granville Barker, and led to his asking Duncan Grant to design the clothes for *Twelfth Night* against a setting by François Jourdain.

In post-war years, a short-lived rival to the Ballets Russes was the Ballets Suèdois company, started in 1920. The standard of design in the productions was higher than that of the dancing. Bonnard devised a new version of Debussy's *Jeux*, Jean Hugo returned to the fashions of 1900 for *Les Mariés de la Tour Eiffel* and Picabia designed the avant-garde *Relâche* with its interpolated film extracts by René Clair. Most notably Fernand Léger made use of Negro art as an inspiration in *La Création du Monde* to a score by Darius Milhaud. Negro artifacts from the French colonies in Africa had been exhibited the previous year, and this ballet had a considerable influence on the decorative arts, reinforced later by the presentation of the Revue Nègre, starring Josephine Baker, by Rolf de Maré in 1925 after the failure of his Ballets Suèdois.

During the 1920s the Ballets Russes spread its influence even more widely by its extensive tours and its repertoire demonstrated Diaghilev's search for greater novelties as diverse as the witty and elegant *Les Biches*, with the Marie Laurencin designs perfectly complementing the music of François Poulenc and *La Chatte* in a Constructivist setting with costumes of talc and black American cloth.

The 1920s gave opportunities to two remarkably talented young men who played a decisive part in both French theatre and ballet. Jean Cocteau had provided the scenarios for ballets for

Design for setting by A.–M. Cassandre for the Ballet Russe production of *Aubade*, 1936.

'Arlequin': costume design
by Georges Lepape, 1915.

Diaghilev's company, including the unsuccessful *Le Dieu Bleu* in 1912, the scandal-provoking *Parade*, with its designs by Picasso in 1919, and *Train Bleu* costumed by Chanel in 1924. In 1922 he turned his attention to the theatre with an adaptation of Sophocles' drama *Antigone* presented at the Théâtre de l'Atelier, again with costumes designed by Chanel. This production began his long preoccupation with the themes of classical mythology, which was carried further in 1926 in his original play *Orphée*, designed by Jean Hugo and Chapel.

Christian Bérard first attracted attention as a painter in 1925 when he exhibited as a member of the short-lived 'neo-romantic' group, which included Pavel Tchelitchew and Eugene Berman, both destined to make notable contributions to theatre design. In 1930 Cocteau and Bérard collaborated for the first time on the former's one-act play *La Voix Humaine* to be followed in 1934 by *La Machine Infernale*. Tentative plans for a ballet by Bérard had been made by Diaghilev before his death in 1929 but it was not until 1933 that the unforgettable *Cotillon* – in the opinion of many one of the most perfect ballets – was first performed by the Ballets de Monte Carlo.

Diaghilev's death threw the world of ballet into confusion and it seemed as though an era of

Left 'Romeo': costume design by Jean Hugo.

Below Design for setting by Lanvin for the Theatre Daunou.

Above Design for setting
by Christian Bérard for the
Ballet Russe production of
The Seventh Symphony,
1938.

Right Design for setting
by Eugène Berman for
Devil's Holiday, 1939.

greatness had come to an end. The Ballets 1933 lasted only some six weeks as a company, but during its brief career approximated the panache of the Diaghilev company with a brilliant assemblage of talent, much of it in fact drawn from the Ballets Russes. With Balanchine as choreographer, Bérard as designer for *Mozartiana*, Tchelitchew for *Errante*, Derain for *Fastes* and *Songes* and Tilly Losch, Tamara Toumanova, Roman Jasinsky among the dancers, not to mention Lotte Lenya in a speaking role, success should have been assured had not difficulties intervened.

A reassembly of many of the former Diaghilev company with a repertoire of revivals and new productions started in 1932 and under different names due to internal shifts of power toured extensively until the outbreak of war. Apart from revivals of Diaghilev's creations, and particularly the early ballets with their predominantly Russian feeling, the considerable number of new productions had an entirely French influence and reflected the current trends of the artistic world of Paris. Surrealism was represented by André Masson's designs for the first symphonic ballet of Léonide Massine, *Les Présages*, and those of Miro for *Jeux d'Enfants*. Bérard, already recognised as an arbiter of taste in Paris, combined masterly economy of means and a sure sense of colour in the neo-romantic ballets *Cotillon*, *Symphonie Fantastique* and *Seventh Symphony*, the two last-named to symphonies by Berlioz and Beethoven respectively. Raoul Dufy also designed the enchanting *Beach*.

In addition to his settings for Cocteau plays, Bérard designed in 1935 *La Reine Margot* by Bourdet, Jouvet's production of Molière's *L'Ecole des Femmes* in 1936, another Jouvet production of Corneille's *L'Illusion Comique* in 1937, and in the following year *Cyrano de Bergerac* and *Le Corsair*.

One of the main tourist attractions since the 1900s has been the French music hall which presented spectacles devoted mainly to a glorification of the female form, either over-dressed in feathers and diamanté-embroidered chiffon, or the opposite – a nude Marie Antoinette and Empress Theodora being particularly memorable.

With minimal differences, the style of presentation remained unchanged, with the main attractions of 'historical tableaux' designed to include as many female nudes as possible, interspersed with conventional music hall acts. A specialised genre of design, it attracted a host of imitators of Gesmar and Erté, the two most celebrated exponents. Gesmar designed almost exclusively for the shows featuring Mistinguett and her celebrated legs. The talents of Erté (Romain de Tirtoff), a much better designer than Gesmar, were ideally suited to this type of design where he could give full rein to his ingenuity and taste for elaborate ornament. On the whole the world of the music hall was an enclosed one and few if any of the designers working for the straight theatre or for ballet entered it.

It will be seen that between 1900 and 1940 there were radical changes in theatrical production in France and that the painter as designer played an increasingly important part, adding crucial elements to the magic and fantasy which is an essential part of any theatre.

Below Design for setting by Christian Bérard for Molière's *L'Ecole des Femmes*, 1936.

Bottom Design for a theatrical curtain by Erté, *c*.1920s.

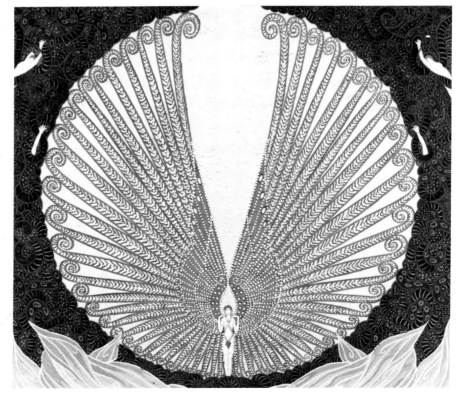

Fashion *by Philippe Garner*

THE FASHION INDUSTRY is a twentieth-century phenomenon. The growth of the industry, the commercial necessity for a fairly rapid turnover, helped along greatly by the profusion of rival fashion magazines, have had the snowball effect of accelerating the evolution of fashion and encouraging a fertile and rapid turnover of ideas.

The *fin-de-siècle* styles involved only small variations on a mode of dress that had, in its essentials, dominated female fashion for several decades, a mode that combined the stiffness of a tight-fitted boned bodice with the impracticality of a full, floor-length skirt. Woman's role as object in a male-dominated world was reflected in the restrictions imposed by the fashionable trussing of the bodice and the cumbersome fullness of skirts. Georges de Feure's illustrations of fashionably dressed ladies of the turn of the century reflect clearly that the decorative element predominated to the virtual exclusion of any sense of practicality.

A significant aspect of the fashion history of the period was the evolution of the creative *couturier*. It was Charles Frederick Worth who, in the last quarter of the nineteenth century, had given the role of the *couturier* social acceptability; no longer was he merely regarded as a tradesman not to be invited to one's home other than on business. The second generation of *couturiers*, after Worth, be-

came a new aristocracy of taste and included important patrons of the arts such as Jacques Doucet. The best known amongst the talented designers of this generation were the Callot sisters, Chéruit, Dœuillet, Drecoll, Paquin and Doucet.

The most exciting talent to emerge in the early years of the century, as a liberating force, and one of the major influences in contemporary fashions and tastes was Paul Poiret. After starting his career in the house of his great hero, Doucet, Poiret set up his own *maison de couture* in 1903. He was far more than a dress designer. The fastidious concern he showed for costume extended to every aspect of his lifestyle, his Atelier Martine had a strong influence on interior design, whilst Poiret's lavish entertaining and the exotic fancy-dress soirées in his garden-club, L'Oasis, became legendary. His publications of 1908 and 1911, *Les Robes de Paul Poiret racontées par Paul Iribe* and *Les Choses de Paul Poiret vues par Georges Lepape*, revitalised the art of fashion illustration.

In his role as *couturier*, Poiret's major influence was in liberating women from the stiff and restricting corsetry in which they had been trapped for so long. In 1906 he introduced his distinctive loose coats, often fur-trimmed, the sleeves lost in the amorphous gathers of cloth. Iribe's drawings of 1908, however, show the more revolutionary idea of looseness in day and evening dresses. The new fashion launched by Poiret was evocative of the Empire period with the softness of its lines and the *style Empire* high waist. In 1910, as if from a perverse desire to assert his total control over fashion, Poiret launched the hobble skirt, restricting, in a new way, the women he had sought to liberate. The fashion enjoyed only a brief success.

Poiret's major fashion success was in launching his own orientalised designs at the time of the dazzling Paris stage success of the Ballets Russes in 1909. Poiret's turbans, aigrettes, harem pants and skirts were an immediate and total success with a public delighted and inspired by Bakst's designs for *Schéhérazade*.

Despite the brave front maintained by fashion writers, the First World War was a lean time for Paris *couture*. Many houses, including that of Poiret, were forced to close their doors. The period immediately after the war was one of confusion in fashion. Women were reluctant to sacrifice the ease of the mid-calf length which had become popular during the war years; designers were uncertain whether to revert to the luxurious Oriental pre-war styles for afternoon or evening wear. Dipping hems provided a compromise. A

Right French gown *c.* 1907.

Opposite page A drawing by Georges Lepape of Paul Poiret's design, 'Au Clair de la Lune', 1913.

Above Erté in fancy dress in Monte Carlo, 1922.

Opposite page Mme. Poiret wearing a dress designed by her husband.

drawing of 1919, *Au Thé Dansant, Schéhérazade*, by Marthe Romme, well illustrates the lingering taste for Poiret's Orientalism, together with the new use of draped cloth and full wings over the hips. Amongst the most exquisite drawings of the Paris fashions of this period are those of Russian émigré Erté who, since 1914, had been supplying the American *Harper's Bazaar* with refined, meticulously drawn ink and gouache illustrations of the latest Paris trends in fashion. Amongst the most delightful creations of this period were the tightly-pleated, clinging velvet dresses of Mariano Fortuny, introduced before the war and still in evidence in virtually the same, classic styles through the twenties.

It was about 1922 that there emerged the silhouette popularly associated with the 1920s; the bust was eliminated and dresses fell in a straight line past a waistline that had dropped to the hips. Spanish-born illustrator Benito, in his 1922 drawing 'Florentin' for Poiret, shows his female subject as virtually rectangular. About a year later other fashions emerged which are so closely linked with the accepted image of the 1920s, the 'Cloche' hat, the shingle and the short-lived cropped hairstyle that became known in England as the 'Eton' crop.

By 1925, skirts were being worn a little higher, but it was only for a brief season in 1926 that hems reached a record height, stopping just below the knee. Gabrielle 'Coco' Chanel was the rising star of Paris *couture* with her timely, and commercially successful, emphasis on easy pleated skirts and soft jackets and 'sports' clothes. By 1927 Chanel's casual, lean, tanned look for daytime was law and Jean Patou, Lucien Lelong and Madeleine Vionnet successfully followed her lead. A softer, more feminine element, however, was ousting the short, straight dress for evening wear.

After a brief spell of uncertainty between the shorter or longer dresses for evening wear, an uncertainty which certain designers tried to resolve with the somewhat unsatisfactory compromise of handkerchief skirts with irregular hems, the late twenties and early thirties emerged as a period of almost unequalled elegance in evening wear.

The new full-length line was smooth, sleek and figure-hugging, the cleverly-cut dresses, often deceptively simple sheaths of cloth without fastening, simply fitted where they fell and required a flawless slender body if they were to look as stunning as they did in the photographs of Edward Steichen or George Hoyningen-Huené. Two designers excelled in the creation of evening dresses in a fashion conceived in perfect harmony with the streamlined chic of the Modernist interiors so much in vogue. Foremost was Madeleine Vionnet who is acknowledged as the originator of the bias cut so essential for the clinging effect she now achieved with consummate mastery. Vionnet created her designs and worked out their complex cutting directly in cloth on a half-life-size dummy.

The other great specialist of the new sleek silhouette was Alix, later known as Madame Grès, who opened her *maison de couture* in 1933 and enjoyed an immediate success with her distinctively personal interpretation of the fashion. Alix specialised in clinging evening dresses with tightly tucked drapes of cloth, seemingly inspired by

Right Schiaparelli quilted jacket from the 'Circus' collection, 1938.

Below right 'Florentin', drawing for Poiret by Edouard Garcia Benito, 1922.

Hellenistic sculpture. The fashionable fabrics were shiny and clinging, satins, silk jersey and *crêpe*. In 1934 Alix created a sleek cellophane evening dress described in *Vogue* as 'glistening like a magnificent black scarab.'

Just as the clean, uncluttered lines of Modernism were ousted in the mid thirties by a phase of revivalism tinged with a taste for Surrealism, so there was a movement in fashion away from the sleek glamour of the Vionnet style towards a more romantic phase. Spanish-born Cristobal Balenciaga scored an immediate success on opening in Paris in 1937 with a collection of neo-Victorian dresses. The trend was towards a more elaborate style, full-skirted and wide-shouldered, which found its most delightful graphic expression in the drawings of Christian 'Bébé' Bérard. Some of the wittiest *Vogue* covers and illustrations of the late thirties bear Bérard's signature and often lightheartedly caricature the imagery of fashionable Surrealist painters.

The most exciting talent to emerge in the thirties was the unpredictable Italian Elsa Schiaparelli who had opened in Paris in 1928 and won immediate acclaim for her imaginative knitwear and 'sports' clothes. Typical of her inventiveness was the 1928 knitted jumper with a *trompe*

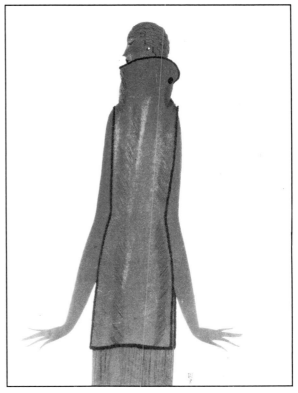

Left Knitted jumper with *trompe l'oeil* cravat by Elsa Schiaparelli, 1928.

Below left The sleek lines of the mid 1930s.

l'oeil knotted cravat incorporated into the pattern of the knit. The element of surprise was ever-present in 'Schiap's' work. She made 'Shocking' pink her colour, launched her 'Shocking' perfume and ultimately wrote her autobiography, *Shocking Life*. After 1935 and the opening of her Place Vendôme Boutique the name of Schiaparelli became synonymous with amusing ideas in fashion. Her collections followed a succession of novel themes and she had particular success with her 'Circus Parade' of 1938. She popularised the short, box-shouldered jacket, quilted or encrusted with mirror, sequin or embroidered designs. Her most memorable clothes, however, are those which bear witness to her collaboration with Salvador Dali and Jean Cocteau.

Cocteau made witty drawings of faces and hands to be applied to evening dresses. Dali inspired such designs as the dress printed with *trompe l'oeil* rips and tears or yet another dress printed with a life-size lobster and salad over which he was persuaded with some difficulty to restrain from splashing mayonnaise.

The highly individual fabrics and luxurious silks and satins created by artists and manufacturers of the early years of the fashion industry contrast sharply with today's man-made fibres.

United Kingdom

British Design 1890–1940 *by Isabelle Anscombe*

The Arts and Crafts Movement

FROM THE 1860S ONWARDS Britain rose to a prominent position in European decorative arts. The founding of Morris, Marshall, Faulkner & Co. in 1861 had been the beginning of a new movement in reaction to the allegorical flourishes of design in the 1851 Great Exhibition. The Arts and Crafts Movement, absorbing the tenets of the Gothic Revival, was committed to honest and simple design for domestic use. Inspired by the teachings of John Ruskin and Pre-Raphaelite art, it was an intellectual movement, the majority of the designers being professional architects, which

captured the imagination of its time. Arts and Crafts furniture and artifacts laid stress on the honest presentation of materials, structure and production, taking as its highest principle Ruskin's and William Morris's belief that only the highest good could come from man transforming his own environment by the work of his own hands. The machine was despised, as was any decorative idiom which slavishly copied past styles. Handicrafts flourished, especially in the fields of embroidery, metalwork, stained glass and art pottery.

All over the country handicraft guilds were

Below Sideboard and furniture designed by Snell & Co. and exhibited at the Great Exhibition of 1851.

Below right Earthenware vases showing the over-elaborateness of design typical of many exhibits at the Great Exhibition of 1851.

founded to involve both the working man and the hitherto unemployable young lady in the practical creation of their own environment. The most influential of these guilds were the Century Guild, founded in 1882 by Arthur Heygate Mackmurdo, the Art-Workers' Guild founded in 1884, Charles Robert Ashbee's Guild of Handicraft formed in 1888, the same year as the Arts and Crafts Exhibition Society, and, in 1900, the Birmingham Guild of Handicraft.

The original impetus of the Arts and Crafts ideals gave rise to considerable activity which was chronicled in the pages of *The Studio*.

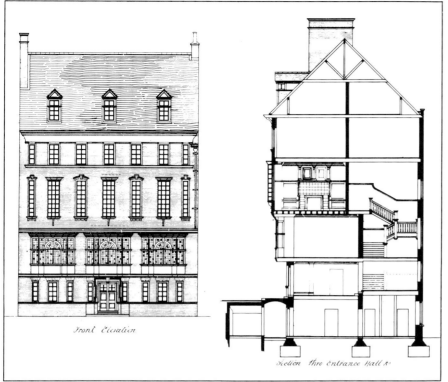

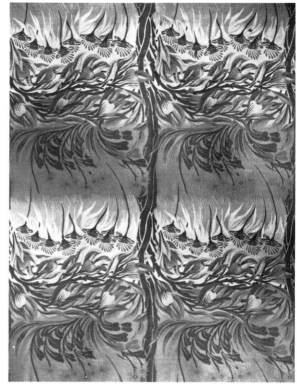

Top left Designs for Old
Swan House, Chelsea, by
R. Norman Shaw, 1875–6.

Top Woven hanging
designed by A. H.
Mackmurdo, *c.* 1882.

Left Desk designed by
A. H. Mackmurdo, 1886.

Above Title page from
Wren's City Churches by
A. H. Mackmurdo, considered
to be one of the first
examples of Art Nouveau.

The magazine was frankly propagandist for the movement and through its pages the inspiration of British design was made known in Europe and America. Another outcome of the reaction to the Great Exhibition was that some industrial design almost underwent a revolution, notably in the work of Dr. Christopher Dresser or William Arthur Smith Benson, who became the director of Morris & Co. after Morris's death in 1896. The Arts and Crafts Movement was the start of an entirely contemporary design idiom.

The Arts and Crafts home was eclectic. Houses built by Philip Webb, Norman Shaw or Charles Francis Annesley Voysey stressed the architectural qualities of wood and stone. Morris & Co. wallpapers or woven hangings presented a backdrop for Gothic-inspired, sturdy oak furniture. Every detail, from light fittings to carpets, was chosen to reflect an internal coherence which was as much intellectual as aesthetic. As Walter Crane wrote: 'The great charm of the Morrisian method is that it lends itself to either simplicity or splendour. You might be almost as plain as Thoreau, with a rush-bottomed chair, piece of matting, and oaken trestle table; or you might have gold and lustre (the choice ware of William de Morgan) gleaming from the sideboard, and jewel-

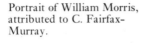

Portrait of William Morris, attributed to C. Fairfax-Murray.

led light in the windows, and walls hung with arras tapestry.'

The Aesthetic Movement

The 1890s in Europe reflect an almost conscious sense of *fin-de-siècle* decadence. In England the writings of Swinburne, Wilde or Beardsley mirrored the preoccupations of the French poets who wrote of the inexorable birth of the modern city at the zenith of capitalism, and the legal feuds between Whistler and Ruskin or Buchanan and D. G. Rossetti accentuated the fact that feelings were running high.

The decorative arts entered this arena under the

banner of the Aesthetic Movement, with Oscar Wilde in the front line. The Aesthetic Movement depended, in the eyes of a public educated by the lampooning it received in the press, on a handful of beings who declared themselves for Art, and nothing but Art. Wilde summed up this popular image in a lecture given on his American tour when he said, tacitly referring to Du Maurier's *Punch* cartoons, that his audience no doubt regarded him as 'a young man . . . whose greatest difficulty in life was the difficulty of living up to the level of his blue china – a paradox,' he added, 'from which England has not yet recovered.'

The Aesthetic Movement had successfully assi-

milated the Japanese taste which had been seized upon after the first Japanese artifacts had been displayed at the 1862 International Exhibition. Japanese motifs, asymmetry and delicacy were absorbed into the Arts and Crafts ideals in the work of Edward William Godwin, Bruce J. Talbert or Thomas Jeckyll, the Art Pottery of Minton & Co. under the direction of William Stephen Coleman, or the fabrics and wallpapers by Walter Crane or Lewis F. Day. In the 1860s and 1870s Godwin and Norman Shaw had introduced an architectural style known as Queen Anne, using red brick in a form of domestic, secular architecture removed from the earlier Gothic, in their

houses at Bedford Park, the first garden suburb begun in 1876, and Tite Street, Chelsea.

Into houses such as these came the blue and white china, the emblems of the peacock, lily or sunflower which were to symbolise the Aesthetic Movement. Art had reached the middle class home with new fabrics for women's dresses and new books, such as those by Kate Greenaway, to entertain in the nursery. This movement only had credence in England and America and was made much fun of within the context of a final flourish before the new century was ushered in. Yet even those who set out to ridicule it gave it respect; for example, the costumes for *Patience, or Bunthorne's*

The William Morris Room at the Victoria and Albert Museum, London.

139

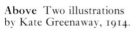

Above Two illustrations by Kate Greenaway, 1914.

Right Carpet, 'Green Pastures', designed by C. F. A. Voysey, 1896.

Bride: An Aesthetic Opera were designed by W. S. Gilbert using 'authentic' Liberty & Co. fabrics.

In 1890 William Morris began his last great enterprise, the Kelmscott Press, which was to lead to British domination in the art of fine printing and typography for many years to come. In 1894 *The Yellow Book* was published with illustrations by Aubrey Beardsley. In 1897 Pilkington's established their pottery with designs by Walter Crane, Voysey and Lewis F. Day. Also in 1894 the Belgian Henry van de Velde designed four rooms for Samuel Bing's new shop, La Maison de l'Art Nouveau in Paris, influenced by his visit to Liberty & Co. in 1891. In 1898 the Grand Duke of Hesse commissioned designs from C. R. Ashbee and Mackay Hugh Baillie Scott for furniture, made by the Guild of Handicraft, for the artists' colony set up at Darmstadt. Britain's lead was beginning to have its effects abroad.

The 1890s in Great Britain

In 1894 Liberty & Co., which had opened in 1875 selling Japanese and Oriental goods, went public and the new shares were eagerly bought. In 1890 Liberty's had an entire section in the Paris Exhibition, where Arthur Liberty was himself a juror. He had always been aware of the importance of remaining slightly ahead of changes in taste and during the 1890s began new ventures, ably supported by the Welshman John Llewellyn, who had been appointed to the board in 1898 after his success in the fabrics department where he had commissioned designs by Voysey, Jessie M. King and Arthur Silver, founder of the Silver Studio. In 1899 a new silver range, Cymric, was introduced with designs by Bernard Cuzner, Rex Silver (Arthur's eldest son) and Jessie M. King. It is probable that the name itself was bestowed on the range by Llewellyn.

In 1901 a new company, Liberty & Co. (Cymric) Ltd., was formed in conjunction with the Birmingham silver firm W. H. Haseler, and around the same time the Manxman Archibald Knox, probably introduced to Liberty by his friend Christopher Dresser, began his work in the Cymric range and quickly came to dominate the design of the silver.

From 1900 Liberty's had stocked German Kayser-Zinn pewter, but from 1903 their own Tudric range, with designs by Knox, was introduced, probably on the suggestion of William Haseler of the Birmingham firm. Liberty's fabrics and wallpapers and especially Knox's metalwork designs give the most coherent suggestion in England of the Art Nouveau forms which were beginning to appear in Europe. However, British designers always remained adamantly opposed to Art Nouveau and although Arthur Liberty had welcomed a new style, he would have agreed with Lewis F. Day that the Continental work showed 'symptoms . . . of pronounced disease.'

After Britain's lead in the decorative arts it seems strange that from this time on she was to strongly oppose any new influences, from Art Nouveau to the Bauhaus and the Modern Movement, and to remain firm in her adherence to the simple functional lines and country morals of the Arts and Crafts Movement. Within her own boundaries artists such as the Glasgow Four, who

Above Interior of Hill House, Dunbartonshire, Scotland, designed by C. R. Mackintosh, 1904.

Far left Charles Rennie Mackintosh as a young man.

Left Margaret Mackintosh photographed in the Mackintosh's flat in Mains Street, Glasgow.

Woven silk designed by Arthur Silver for Liberty & Co., c. 1895.

were acclaimed abroad, were to be virtually ignored by critics and public alike.

The Glasgow Four were Charles Rennie Mackintosh, Herbert McNair and Margaret and Frances Macdonald, all of whom studied at the Glasgow School of Art in the early 1890s. Mackintosh, an architect, had produced his first furniture designs in the early 1890s and this early work already shows an avoidance of reference to period design and a sparseness in the absence of applied ornament. His designs were dictated by the problems of the arrangement of interior space and he laid stress on vertical elements, his high-backed chairs giving a variety of height within a room, despite the acknowledged criticism of their impracticality. When the Macdonald sisters (Margaret married Mackintosh and Frances married McNair) left the Glasgow School of Art they opened their own studio for embroidery, gesso, leaded glass, *repoussé* metalwork and book illustration, which quickly became a meeting place for other Glasgow designers, such as Jessie M. King, Ernest Archibald Taylor and Talwin Morris.

In 1896 the Four were invited to send furniture, craftwork and posters to the Arts and Crafts Exhibition Society show where their work, especially the posters, met with a puzzled and shocked reaction. However, the editor of the *Studio* made a visit to Glasgow and in 1897 published two appreciative articles on their work. This was quickly picked up in Europe and the following year the Darmstadt magazine *Dekorative Kunst* contained an article on the Glasgow School.

Earlier, in 1895, work from Glasgow Art School had been sent to the Liège Exhibition where it was received enthusiastically, although Mackintosh himself never favoured the Belgian and French excesses of Art Nouveau. It was in Vienna that he found like minds. In 1900 he visited the 8th Vienna Secessionist Exhibition, which was devoted to the work of foreign designers, including Mackintosh and his wife, C. R. Ashbee and Van de

Velde. There he met Josef Hoffmann with whom he was to remain in contact for many years, warmly supporting the decision to found the Wiener Werkstätte. Mackintosh received two commissions in Vienna, including the design of a music room for a house for the banker Fritz Waerndorfer, who was to finance the Werkstätte, where a dining room was commissioned from Hoffmann. Mackintosh also exhibited successfully at the Turin Exhibition of 1902. It must have been a sore disappointment to Mackintosh to find his work received so sympathetically abroad while being almost ignored in England.

His most important commissions in and around Glasgow were for the Glasgow School of Art (1896), the series of tea rooms designed for Miss Cranston, on which he at first collaborated with George Walton, and a few private houses, notably Hill House, Helensburgh (1902). These projects where he designed almost every element, from cutlery for the tea rooms to rugs for Hill House, demonstrate his remarkable creation of a distinctive style totally removed from the influences of the preceding century.

Further south another geographical area was to give its name to a style of craftsmanship which owed its being more directly to the Arts and Crafts Movement: the Cotswold School. In 1890 Kenton & Co. was formed by Ernest Gimson, Sidney Barnsley, Alfred Powell, Mervyn Macartney, Reginald Blomfield and W. R. Lethaby. In 1891 the company held an exhibition at Barnard's Inn.

The company gave these architects a taste for furniture design, and in 1893 Gimson and Barnsley moved out of London to Ewen, near Cirencester, to look for a suitable place to found a workshop. Ernest Barnsley left his Birmingham architectural practice to join them. In 1901 they employed Peter Waals, an experienced Dutch cabinet-maker. They began a workshop at Pinbury and in March 1902 settled permanently in workshops of their own building at Sapperton. *The*

Above Wall panels and mirrors for the Willow Tea Rooms, Glasgow, by C. R. Mackintosh, 1904.

Far left Detail of the doors for the Willow Tea Rooms, designed by C. R. Mackintosh.

Left Metal lampshade designed by C. R. Mackintosh, *c.* 1900.

Studio naturally warmly supported the work they produced, although other critics condemned their use of dovetail joints which could be felt when one sat down upon a chair, or, as in a review in *The Builder* of a bow-fronted oak dresser exhibited by Sidney Barnsley in 1899: '. . . the turn-buttons to the small top cupboards look like the work of a savage; the wooden handles to the lower doors . . . are actually nailed on at one end, the rough nail head showing at the top. This is not only not artistic, it is not even good taste.'

However, they would have defended their work by reference to the Arts and Crafts ideals of

The work of the Cotswold School, which influenced Ambrose Heal and Gordon Russell, demonstrates the continuance of the Arts and Crafts antipathy to the machine. As Gordon Russell noted in his autobiography, when considering art education, no schools existed which recognized the need for particular training for machine production. It was this legacy of the Arts and Crafts Movement which led to the culpable ignorance in England of the co-ordination, as at the Bauhaus, of technical and art trainings. As late as 1927 Harry Peach, who started the Dryad Workshops and was a militant member of the

The Pinbury workshop shared by Ernest Gimson and Sidney and Ernest Barnsley, *c*. 1895.

honesty of materials and production and their solid wardrobes and dressers all show beautiful workmanship in the treatment of the wood, allowing the material to stand alone, or in contrast with different inlaid woods. Gimson himself never executed his designs, except some turned ash chairs; the work was carried out by the various craftsmen they employed and the metalwork – handles and the like – were made by the local blacksmith, Alfred Bucknell, to Gimson's designs. Gimson died in 1919 and the Barnsleys in 1926, but Waals continued until 1937, moving to his own workshops at Chalford in 1920, still using some of Gimson's designs.

Design and Industries Association, could organise the D.I.A. display for the Leipzig Exhibition as a show of country crafts. From the First World War England began to lose her place among the leaders of European design.

The Design and Industries Association
In many ways the period under discussion, 1890–1940, is divided by the founding, in 1915, of the Design and Industries Association. The foundation of the D.I.A. followed a visit to the Werkbund Exhibition in Cologne in 1914 by Harold Stabler, Harry Peach, Ambrose Heal and other founder members of the D.I.A. who had for

long been concerned about the lack of good design for ordinary manufactured household items. The Arts and Crafts Movement had treated manufacturers with disdain and the manufacturers unsurprisingly reacted by ignoring any overtures made in their direction. Despite the enthusiasm of the original 199 members of the D.I.A., this antipathy to the machine remained, hidden in their Ruskinian approach to design.

William Richard Lethaby, for example, who had founded the Central School of Art in 1896, for long regarded as the most progressive school in Europe, still championed the idea that the idioms of craftwork should inspire the machine and that

design should be for people and not for the sake of theoretical concepts such as those held at the Bauhaus or in the French review, *L'Esprit Nouveau.* In 1913 he had written: 'Although a machine-made thing can never be a work of art in the proper sense, there is no reason why it should not be good in a secondary order ... Machinework should show quite frankly that it is the child of the machine; it is the pretence and subterfuge of most machine-made things which make them disgusting.'

His definition is of art and not of design in the modern sense and it is hardly surprising that the D.I.A. was never to champion an attitude to the

Top left Unpolished oak furniture designed by Ambrose Heal for houses in Letchworth, the first English garden city, *c.* 1901.

Top Steel firedogs designed by Ernest Gimson, *c.* 1910.

Above Extendable oak dining table by Peter Waals, *c.* 1924.

Right Dresser designed by Ambrose Heal and exhibited at the Royal Academy, London, 1935.

Below Table and chairs designed by Ambrose Heal, c. 1920.

Letterhead for the Omega Workshops, probably designed by Wyndham Lewis.

machine which would allow it an order of its own. The new reformers were not only designers, but manufacturers and retailers as well, such as Ambrose Heal, Gordon Russell or James Morton, of Morton Sundour textiles, who advocated plain, sturdy 'cottage' furniture.

The Omega Workshops

Just before the First World War a group of artists, under the leadership of Roger Fry, came together who combined the Arts and Crafts ethic with the impetus of Post-Impressionist art. On 8 July 1913 the Omega Workshops opened at 33 Fitzroy Square. The artists involved, Duncan Grant, Vanessa Bell, Wyndham Lewis, Frederick Etchells, Cuthbert Hamilton and Edward Wadsworth, produced painted screens and furniture, hand-dyed textiles, pottery, designs for murals and a miscellany of smaller items. The Omega was shortlived, mainly due to the war, which removed

Grant and Bell from London, the walk-out over a disagreement on a commission for a Post-Impressionist room at the Ideal Home Exhibition of Lewis, Etchells, Wadsworth and Hamilton, and competition from Heal's. The Omega closed in 1919.

From the beginning it had been clear that Wyndham Lewis found it hard to suppress his love of machinery and aggressive attitude to art within the rule of anonymity which ensured the domination of the more temperate Bloomsbury charm, but his artistic preoccupations did lead the others into conveying non-representational abstract designs into their fabrics and screens. His mural designs for Lady Drogheda's Futurist dining room, 1913–14, showed how different were his aspirations from the pastel colours, dancing figures and vases of flowers of Grant and Bell, who also absorbed the influence of Bakst into their interiors. Duncan Grant and Vanessa Bell were in the forefront of mural design, which flourished with artists such as Douglas Davidson, Eric Ravilious, Rex Whistler's murals for the Tate's tea room or Mary Adshead's designs for Bank Underground station, John Banting who painted a wall in Fortnum & Mason's new decoration department and Boris Anrep who produced mosaic pavements.

Modernism in Britain

The 1920s were the years of the interior, whether the very English intellectuality of Grant and Bell or Francis Bacon's 'constructivist room', with white walls, circular glass tables and mirrors and neutral coloured rugs woven in 'thought patterns'. In 1927 Syrie Maugham uncovered her 'all-white room' in her seventeenth-century Chelsea house, decorated with white flowers according to the season; some said she had originated the all-white idiom, others claimed it was Arundell Clarke, while yet more have it as Da Silva Bruhns; whatever the truth, the scheme was widely adopted, as in Claridges all-white restaurant.

The turning-point for interior design had come with the 1925 Paris Exhibition. Germany, and therefore the Bauhaus, had been excluded from exhibiting and it was not until 1930–1 that the Salon des Artistes-Décorateurs included a Bauhaus section.

The 1925 Exhibition was dominated by the work of Ruhlmann, Süe et Mare and Lalique, but England's reaction was summed up by the *Architectural Review* of that year: 'Unquestionably every Englishman who visits the pavilions and stands of the modern French *ensembliers* will ask himself whether he would care to live among such impeccable surroundings from which cosiness is markedly absent. . . . But little doubt that our Englishman, mindful of fireside joys, of capacious easy chairs, will, perhaps, admire, then turn aside and leave such artificialities to the exhibition and to France.'

The exhibition did influence one important aspect of British design, the Modernist rug. The American poster designer Edward McKnight Kauffer, encouraged by Marion Dorn, first used Cubist abstract designs in rugs and from 1928 their work was hand-woven at the Wilton Royal Carpet Factory, which also commissioned Marian Pepler, John Tandy and Ronald Grierson. Also in

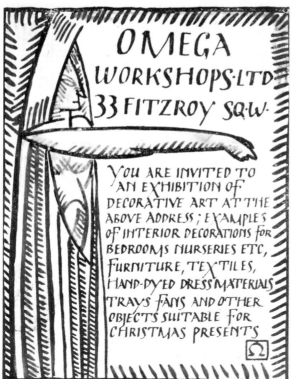

1928 James Morton started the Edinburgh Weavers as a specialist branch of Morton Sundour Fabrics Ltd.

Gradually the new ideas did begin to find expression in England. The influence of modern Scandinavian design reached the British public; Fortnum & Mason's held an exhibition of the furniture of Alvar Aalto. In 1928 Shoolbred's, the decorating firm, held an exhibition of work by the French Décoration Intérieure Moderne which had exhibited in the 1925 Paris Exhibition. Steel frame furniture by PEL was exhibited at the Ideal Home Exhibition, although it was criticised in comparison to the work of Marcel Breuer, and in 1933 Gordon Russell began making steel frame chairs. In 1933 the Dorland Hall Exhibition was organised by the architects Oliver Hill, Wells Coates, Serge Chermayeff and Raymond McGrath. In 1931 Jack Pritchard of Isokon had visited the Bauhaus and in 1934, under his aegis, Walter Gropius came to England. However, like Breuer, Chermayeff and Moholy-Nagy, he did not stay for long before departing for America. Although Britain no longer rejected Modernism out of hand, it was still a minority taste, held by many to belong only to left-wing intellectuals. As Herbert Read wrote in 1934, in *Art and Industry*: '. . . the real

Above Interior designed by Serge Chermayeff, *c*. 1930.

Left Advertisement for an exhibition at the Omega Workshops.

problem is not to adapt machine production to the aesthetic standards of handicraft, but to think out new aesthetic standards for new methods of production.' This the English were loathe to do.

The design of the late 1920s and 1930s divides itself between the architects who had to depend mainly upon state commissions, such as the excellent work done by Frank Pick for London Transport or Raymond McGrath's work as Decoration Consultant to the BBC, and the design shops which owed their custom mainly to educated Mayfair or, as with Duncan Miller, to the financial support of film companies. Architects such as Chermayeff, Max Fry or Wells Coates found their work in short demand, although Brian O'Rorke's designs for the R.M.S. *Orion* stood in obvious contrast to the Edwardian excesses lauded in the *Architectural Review* of 1914 for the Cunard liners which included 'genuine antiques and replicas of Old Masters as part of the decoration'.

The real discipline of the Bauhaus furniture, founded upon geometry, was scarce, but modern design, square furniture or the later rounded curves in plain veneer, were to be found at Curtis Moffat's Fitzroy Square galleries, at Betty Joel Ltd. at 25 Knightsbridge, at Arundell Clarke's in Bruton Street or at Heal's.

Opposite Interior at Claridge's Hotel, London, showing rugs designed by Marion Dorn, *c.* 1935.

Left and below Modernist interiors by Serge Chermayeff, *c.* 1930.

Furniture *by Isabelle Anscombe*

Glasgow cabinet designed by E. A. Taylor, *c.* 1900.

IN 1859 PHILIP WEBB had designed and built the Red House for William Morris at Upton in Kent. Together with Dante Gabriel Rossetti and Edward Burne-Jones they also designed and painted the furniture; solidly constructed in native woods, according to Morris's tastes, panels were painted with medieval scenes not unlike Morris's own romances. On the founding of Morris, Marshall, Faulkner & Co., Webb became chief designer, continuing to produce solid oak trestle tables and other furniture in the sturdy British tradition. His most successful houses, Clouds, at East Knoyle in Wiltshire, furnished by Morris & Co., and Standen, at East Grinstead, both reflect a new awareness of elegance without grandeur, using wood panelling as interior decoration.

Morris & Co. was capable of producing decorative schemes for houses such as these, or for Stanmore Hall, where furniture by W. R. Lethaby was commissioned from Kenton & Co., and also items such as the simple rushed Sussex chairs based on traditional designs. Mervyn Macartney, W. A. S. Benson and Frank Brangwyn also designed furniture for Morris & Co., the latter two also working for J. S. Henry & Co. who specialised in simple inlaid furniture based on Art Nouveau lines. Benson also designed silver mounts and hinges for Morris & Co. Brangwyn continued to produce inlaid furniture with simple lines, such as his decorated screens for the Rowley Gallery. In 1890 George Jack became the chief designer for Morris & Co. and he introduced a quasi-eighteenth-century style with large cabinets with intricate inlaid decoration, mainly in mahogany.

In 1882 A. H. Mackmurdo founded the first of the influential guilds, the Century Guild. Using mahogany, oak and satinwood, Mackmurdo's designs are true precursors of Art Nouveau with asymmetrical patterns of vigorous stems, leaves and flowers running aslant his pieces giving an almost harsh impression of growth. His proportions were carefully and simply planned for a severe impression relieved by painted panels, fretwork or brass detailing. His idioms dominated the work of the Century Guild. Another designer who developed an idiosyncratic style approaching Art Nouveau was C. F. A. Voysey. His own house, The Orchard, built at Chorley Wood, Hertfordshire, in 1900, showed a more restrained style with little surface decoration, relying mainly on a juxtaposition of lines and the qualities of wood. In 1931 an exhibition of Voysey's work was held at the Batsford Gallery where even the retrospective pieces compared favourably with the best contemporary design.

In 1897 M. H. Baillie Scott was commissioned to design the dining room and drawing room for the Grand Duke of Hesse's Palace at Darmstadt. He collaborated with C. R. Ashbee, whose Guild of Handicraft carried out their designs for furniture and metalwork. This commission, along with the British exhibits at foreign exhibitions, did much to make known the work of English Arts and Crafts designers in Europe and was to inspire many European designers.

Baillie Scott's elaborate inlays and Ashbee's enamels enhanced the almost eccentric shapes of some of the designs and created a rich and luxurious interior, demonstrating, as did Ashbee's silver designs, that the Arts and Crafts Movement was not dedicated solely to the revival of 'cottage' crafts. Ashbee's house, Magpie and Stump, in Cheyne Walk, Chelsea, had been completed by the Guild of Handicraft in 1895; a true demonstration of their many accomplishments with tooled leatherwork, metalwork and carving. From 1898 Baillie Scott designed furniture for John White of Bedford which was sold to Liberty & Co.

The work of Norman Shaw, who had introduced the Queen Anne style at Bedford Park, shows the link between the Gothicism of early Morris or William Burges and the craftsman tradition of Ernest Gimson. Gimson used simply proportioned structures to show his mastery of geometric pattern and delicate inlay, using different woods, metals or mother-of-pearl. An architect by training, Gimson's first craft work was with plasterwork and gesso, which he continued to use in his houses and also as a decorative feature on his woodwork, using simple motifs such as the English rose.

Gimson's designs were produced by his workmen at Sapperton but his intricate designs for inlaid patterns, beading or stringing show an intimate understanding of his materials. His particular idiom has remained unsurpassed, but the work of his colleagues at Sapperton, Ernest and Sidney Barnsley, influenced the later work of Ambrose Heal and Gordon Russell. His own designs were still produced after his death by Peter Waals, although Waals adopted the larger sense of geometry rather than Gimson's smaller intricate designs. The work of the Barnsleys was in the tradition of British woodwork, giving attention to the effects of handwork in total opposition to the possibilities of machine finishes. A border decorated with gouging shows the man at work, although their work was sometimes criticised for a roughness of finish.

In Glasgow George Walton had his own firm of

Above left Rosewood
cabinet inlaid with
purplewood, tulipwood and
ebony, designed by W. A. S.
Benson and made by
Morris & Co., *c.* 1899.

Above Table and chair
with stencilled canvas back
by C. R. Mackintosh, *c.* 1901.

Left Dining room of the
Red House, built by Philip
Webb for William Morris,
1859.

decorators and George Logan and E. A. Taylor designed for Wylie & Lockhead. Walton left Glasgow for London in 1897, where he designed for Liberty & Co. and E. A. Taylor went to Manchester in 1908, where he designed for George Wragge Ltd. All three were inevitably influenced by the work of the Glasgow Four although, because they were designing for commercial production, their designs necessarily are more conventional than the elongated shapes of Mackintosh's furniture. Mackintosh's interiors show a concern for an integral whole, as for example in the furniture for the Willow Tea Rooms, designed for Miss Cranston in 1903, where the high-backed chairs were for look rather than comfort or practicality. They were designed to solve a specific artistic problem within the conception of filling the interior space in the best possible manner and the high, spindly backs suggest the young trees after which the rooms were named.

For the Ingram Street Tea Rooms Mackintosh designed the screens, murals, lampshades and even the cutlery to fulfil his overall design. He never used veneers for his furniture, preferring a black, dark or light green stain or the use of a white enamel-like surface obtained by a coach-painting technique, which he first used for his own flat in Mains Street in 1900. Where the designs of the contemporary Cotswold School could be used in almost any setting, fitting into the long tradition of English woodwork design, Mackintosh's work required the total interior, devoid of any reference to past traditions, perhaps the reason why his work was opposed in England. Mackintosh left Glasgow in 1914 but completed little work after that date.

For the first quarter of the twentieth century the idioms essential to the Arts and Crafts Movement declined in favour either of reproduction furniture and the eighteenth-century models such as those produced by George Jack or of the craftsman tradition maintained by Heal's and Gordon Russell, supported by the doctrines of the Design and Industries Association. Dunbar-Hay (and to some extent the Dryad Workshops which sold caneware) continued to market solidly made pieces which relied on the qualities of the wood with little ornamentation.

Following the vogue for mural decoration, the Omega Workshops produced painted furniture; mainly using second-hand furniture, Roger Fry prided himself on incorporating any original pattern within the applied design, with the result, however, that the Omega furniture was not destined for survival. The historical models admitted by designers changed from Gothic and medieval to the more classical lines of the Adam Brothers, praised in the *Architectural Review* by Paul Nash. The rich decoration of the French exhibits at the 1925 Paris Exhibition was ignored in England in favour of the 'cottage' tradition, as was the use of new materials introduced by Le Corbusier and the Modernist design ethic promoted by the masters of the Bauhaus.

In 1925 Marcel Breuer designed his first steel chair but it was not accepted in England until PEL introduced a steel chair at the Ideal Home Exhibition, which even then failed to comprehend the true theory of the structure. Designers such as John Tandy or Eileen Gray sought more congenial surroundings in Paris. As Herbert Read wrote in 1934 in *Art and Industry*: '. . . in many cases when a good design is discovered in this country, it can be traced to a foreign prototype.'

The most serious of the new designers and architects realised that they owed their new aesthetic to the machine, and in so doing turned their attention to machine design. Both Heal's and Gordon Russell introduced steel and laminated wood furniture and in 1931 Russell designed his first Murphy Radio cabinet. Serge Chermayeff also designed a wireless cabinet, Jack Gold electric

Below Fruitwood armchair designed by Ernest Gimson, *c.* 1900.

Below right Single door oak wardrobe with three rows of bevelled panels *c.* 1930, and oak chest of drawers with walnut handles, *c.* 1930, designed by Gordon Russell.

Top Oak dresser designed by Ambrose Heal, *c.* 1910.

Above left Altar chair from Queen's Cross Church, Glasgow, in oak and horsehair, designed by C. R. Mackintosh, 1897.

Above High chair of stained wood, exhibited by C. R. Mackintosh at the Secessionist Exhibition in Vienna, 1900.

Left Piano designed by M. H. Baillie Scott, *c.* 1898.

Above Painted virginals by Roger Fry for the Omega Workshops.

Right Silvered wood cabinet designed by Serge Chermayeff, *c.* 1930.

light fittings, Wells Coates an electric radiator, Raymond McGrath was commissioned to design for the BBC and designed not only studios and sets but also microphone stands and other equipment and a Nobel prizewinner, Dr. Dalen designed the Aga cooker. Equally, modern architecture was largely limited to G.L.C. housing and other official commissions; there are very few Modernist houses built for private use in the English countryside. Herbert Read went on to say that: 'If we decide that the product of the machine can be a work of art, then what is to become of the artist who is displaced by the machine? Has he any function in a machine-age society, or must he reconcile himself to a purely dilettante role – must he become, as most contemporary artists have become, merely a social entertainer?'

Apart from Roger Fry's 'little group of Post-Impressionists', few artists concerned themselves with furniture design, although Edward James commissioned work from Salvador Dali, such as the famous lobster telephone receivers. As abstract art rose in importance above the applied arts, the artists themselves saw their importance as being political, especially as Fascist régimes in Europe gradually gained a stranglehold on art. In many ways, in the field of the decorative arts, Read's statement bore more than a grain of truth. When, in 1936, the first ten Designers for Industry were appointed by the Royal Society of Arts, they included new designers such as Eric Gill and Keith Murray, but also such central Arts and Crafts figures as Harold Stabler and C. F. A. Voysey. The majority of new furniture designers worked out of exclusive shops.

Betty Joel Ltd. at 25 Knightsbridge was perhaps the most exclusive new designer, selling signed rugs and expensive furniture, far from functional, with large rounded curves and patterned veneers. As the *Architectural Review* noted in 1935: 'Laminated wood frees the cabinet maker (perhaps to his regret) from the tyranny of frame and panel. Doors can be cut out like so much cardboard. Ornament is sought in the grain of veneer, the direction of which need no longer bear any relation to the construction.'

Betty Joel's work is a perfect example of this freedom. More simple, functional lines were achieved by Arundell Clarke who, it is reputed, was the first to introduce the large square armchair. His furniture fitted into a plain decorative scheme with pattern employed only on the floor with commissioned signed rugs, the big upholstered armchairs and curved veneered furniture. The use of veneers on the walls was also popular. Curtis Moffat, who opened in 1929, followed much the same style as Arundell Clarke, while J. Duncan Miller used more dramatic effects.

All these decorators catered very much for an élite; cheaper furniture was available from Plan Ltd., who produced basic units for built-in furniture, which became more and more of a necessity as people moved into smaller houses and flats, or PEL Ltd., who produced steel frame chairs and steel and glass furniture, or The Makers of Simple Furniture who produced items in plywood. A friend of Walter Gropius, Jack Pritchard of Isokon, produced steel frame furniture which was probably the best available in England.

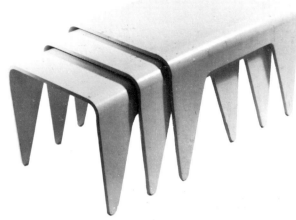

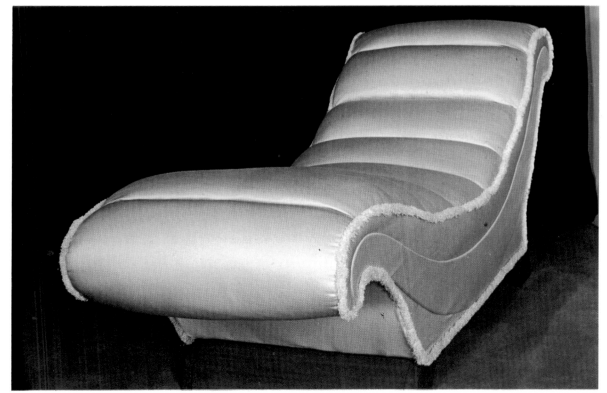

Top left Cocktail cabinet in coromandel ebony and walnut on a mahogany frame, designed by Serge Chermayeff, *c.* 1930.

Above left Plywood chair designed by Gerald Summers, *c.* 1930.

Top Nest of tables designed by Marcel Breuer and made by Isokon of London, *c.* 1936.

Above Painted table from the Omega Workshops.

Left *Chaise longue* by Betty Joel, *c.* 1930.

Ceramics *by Ian Bennett*

THE SECOND HALF of the nineteenth century was an age of stylistic eclecticism in the arts. The expansion of empires, combined with a conscious historicism, created an amazing variety of influences. In the applied arts, Gothicism, *japonisme* and Islamic art were the three principal influences. The ceramics of the late nineteenth century show these three very strongly. The willowy 'whiplash' style of French Art Nouveau had a very minor effect, and when its presence is seen in English applied art, it is usually in a somewhat debased and commercialised form, as in certain of the Moorcroft Florian and Flammarian wares and Minton's Secessionist wares.

The influence of Japan on late nineteenth-century European applied art is of the utmost importance. Indeed, it is questionable whether the Aesthetic Movement in English decorative arts or French Art Nouveau could have existed without it. The French artist and designer Félix Bracquemond is credited with being the agent behind the spread of Japanese motifs in European art. In 1856, Bracquemond had discovered a volume of Hokusai's *Manga* in the studio of the Paris printer Auguste Delâtre, a volume which he purchased subsequently and showed to a number of his friends, including Manet, Degas, Fantin-Latour, Whistler and the Goncourts.

As a direct result of this discovery, Bracquemond himself, in collaboration with the designer and retailer Eugène Rousseau, designed a famous dinner service, known as the Bracquemond-Rousseau service. Individual images of birds, flowers and insects were transfer-printed asymmetrically on to plain white blanks, these blanks being in an eighteenth-century revival style.

Despite the incongruity of image and ceramic shape, an incongruity pointed out by several contemporary critics, this service was to have a profound influence both in France and the rest of the Western world. Similar wares were produced by Maria Longworth Nichols at her newly founded Rookwood Pottery in Cincinnati in 1881. In England, W. S. Coleman designed a transfer-printed service for Milton's in 1870 and five years later, the same factory registered its Bamboo and Fan service. Worcester also began marketing similar wares including a service decorated with scenes after Ando Hiroshige's *Fifty-three Stages of the Tokaido Road* in 1873 and the Sparrow and Bamboo pattern in 1879.

Such wares represented one aspect of the Japanese influence, the transference of what were originally woodcut images to ceramic surfaces. There was also much porcelain made in styles simulating Japanese metalwork and ivory, including Minton pieces based on enamel, and the Worcester Factory's sculptural pieces, many of which were modelled by the extremely gifted James Hadley.

The 1860s and 1870s also saw the founding of a number of art potteries which attempted to produce ceramics based upon new ideas in design and individual inspiration within a more intimate atmosphere than that found in the large industrial factories. Of these, the most important were: Milton's Art Pottery Studio, founded in 1871 in Kensington Gore, London, under the directorship of William Coleman; the De Morgan Pottery, which began producing ceramics on a commercial scale around 1872; the Linthorpe Pottery of Middlesbrough, Yorkshire, founded in 1879 by John Harrison and Christopher Dresser, and the Doulton Factory of Lambeth, London, which was originally founded in 1815, but only began making artistic stoneware in the 1860s.

The work of Doulton's and C. J. C. Bailey's Fulham Pottery was concerned principally with the revival of medieval saltglaze stoneware (*grès de Flandres*). Doulton's also produced painted wares called Faïence and Impasto, and it was this type of painted pottery which was also the main product of the Minton Art Pottery Studio, which lasted for only four years.

The saltglaze revival took place largely as the result of the presence in England of the French painter-potter Jean-Charles Cazin, who had arrived in 1871 to take up the Directorship of the South Kensington Art School in succession to Alphonse Legros; he was also employed on a freelance basis as a ceramic designer by the Fulham Pottery and taught drawing and ceramics at the Lambeth School of Art. The head of the Lambeth School, John Sparkes, had been the man principally responsible for persuading Henry Doulton to employ ex-students in his factory, and among those taught by Cazin were Walter and Edwin Martin. Their elder brother Robert Wallace joined the Fulham Pottery in 1872 as a modeller, and he too was influenced by Cazin.

Cazin had been a teacher at Tours in France, and was thus in touch with the Palissy revival of the French potter Charles Avisseau. Certainly the medievalism of the Fulham Pottery's wares, as well as that of Doulton and early Martin ware, combined with a strong element of Renaissance decoration, point to Cazin's influence, and the realism of much of the modelling at Doulton and Fulham has faint echoes of Avisseau.

Left Vase by Mark V. Marshall, made at Doulton's in 1904.

Right Isnik ware vase by William de Morgan and painted by Fred Passenger, *c.* 1906.

Bottom left Collection of painted underglaze earthenware tiles by William de Morgan, late nineteenth century.

Bottom Plaque designed by W. S. Coleman for Minton's, 1872.

An example of the
grotesque birds made by
Robert Wallace Martin in
the 1890s.

By 1890, the first major phase of the English art pottery movement was over. Doulton had produced much of its best work, although fine things were still being done by Mark Marshall and Frank Butler, the most successful of only a very few English artists who made use of the French 'whiplash' style of Art Nouveau. Painted Doulton faïence was also produced in a style apparently based on Alphonse Mucha's poster art.

William de Morgan, who had begun producing pottery on a commercial scale in about 1872, had fully developed his range of Isnik inspired designs and colours and his range of metallic lustres based on Hispano-Moresque prototypes. He had moved to Merton Abbey in 1882, and then to Sand's End in Fulham in 1888. He took as a partner the architect Halsey Ricardo. During this period, all the hollow wares were thrown by De Morgan's workmen (previously he had purchased blanks from industrial factories) and the production of the lustres, although improved technically, was reduced to a quarter of the firm's output.

During the 1890s De Morgan spent six months of every year in Florence; while there, he made contact with the Cantagalli Factory, at which some of the first nineteenth-century revivals of lustre had been made under the directorship of Ulisse

Cantagalli. De Morgan designed several pieces, which were fired by the factory, and recent evidence suggests that these continued to be made, bearing only the factory mark, long after the designer's death in 1917. In 1898, De Morgan entered into a new partnership at the Sand's End factory with three of his long-serving workmen, the thrower Frank Iles and the brothers Charles and Fred Passenger who were decorators. This partnership, during which some splendid work was produced, lasted until 1907 and is known generally as the Late Fulham Period. The Passengers and Iles carried on making pottery at Sand's End until 1911. From 1923 to 1931, Fred Passenger was employed by Ida Perrins at the Bushey Heath Pottery, making ceramics in a debased De Morgan style.

In 1873, Robert Wallace Martin and his brothers Walter and Edwin had established the firm of R. W. Martin at Pomona House, Fulham. They were joined later in the same year by the fourth brother, Charles Douglas, who remained essentially a somewhat inefficient business manager, although occasionally turning his hand to designing or even modelling. In 1877, the brothers set up a workshop at Southall and a shop in Brownlow Street, London, as an outlet for their wares.

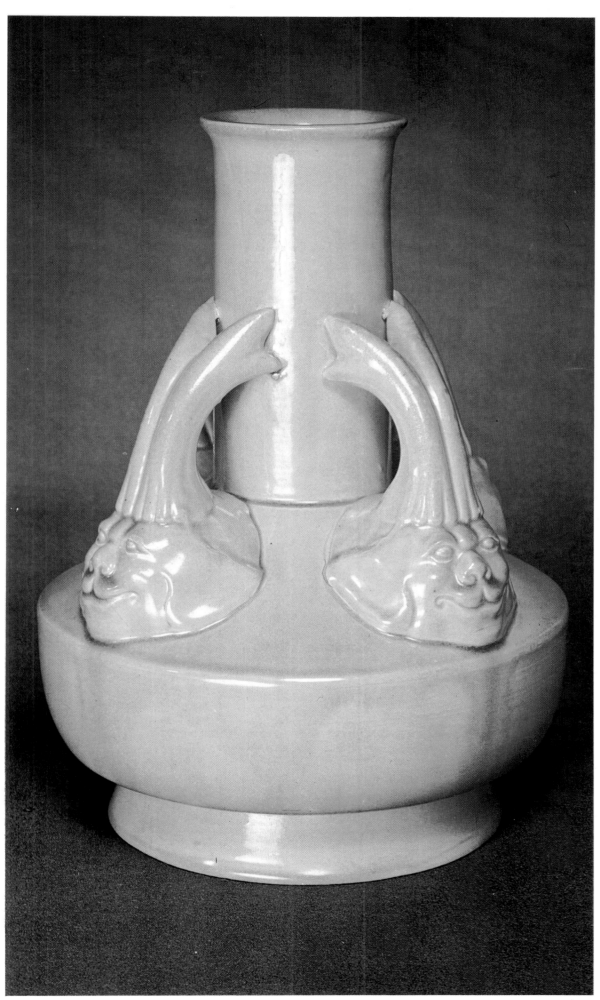

Grotesque vase designed by
Christopher Dresser for
William Ault, *c.* 1892.

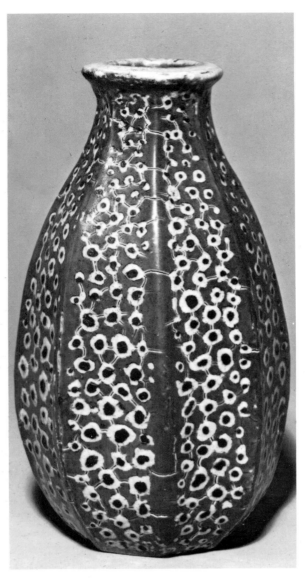

Saltglaze stoneware gourd vase designed by Edwin Martin, 1906.

pottery. In 1900, Edwin and his brother Walter, in company with the collector S. K. Greenslade, who had been enthusiastic about the new abstract glazed pieces, visited the Paris International Exhibition. Many of Edwin's subsequent pieces, which continued to be made well into the twentieth century, were obviously influenced by the techniques of the Japanese folk pottery which he saw there, but there is evidence that the brothers were unimpressed by the French studio pottery.

After two years of severe mental illness, Charles Douglas Martin died in 1910. In 1912, Walter died of thrombosis, which virtually ended the active life of the pottery since he had been the only one of the brothers with a technical knowledge of glazing and firing. Edwin lived until 1915 and the elder brother Robert Wallace until 1923. After 1923, Robert Wallace's son Clement, with a Captain Butterfield as partner, glazed and fired the surviving biscuit pieces, and also produced pieces from the surviving moulds.

One of the most important industrial designers in the second half of the nineteenth century was Christopher Dresser. Born in 1834, Dresser began his career as a botanist. In the 1860s, he began designing metalwork for some of the leading firms of Sheffield and Birmingham, and also designed ceramics for Minton's in the 1870s. It is probable that he designed for several other industrial and art potteries (his connection with some of the Devon potteries has not yet been documented), as well as designing glass, metalwork, furniture, wallpapers and fabrics for many different companies.

He visited Japan in 1876, one of the first European designers to make this trip, and in 1879 he started the Linthorpe Pottery at Linthorpe Village, near Middlesbrough, Yorkshire, with John Harrison, a wealthy local landowner. The motivation for this venture was partly philanthropic and partly artistic, this area of Yorkshire being then, as now, economically very depressed.

The Linthorpe Factory lasted until 1889, when Harrison became bankrupt. Dresser's association, however, is thought to have ceased in about 1883. In the Dresser period, most of the pieces were designed by him and bear his facsimile signature. The dark green-brown streaky abstract glazes, which largely characterised the firm's wares, were influenced by Dresser's knowledge of Japanese pottery, as some of the monochrome green, blue or yellow wares were influenced by Chinese ceramics. Recent evidence suggests that much of the glaze palette of Linthorpe Pottery was developed by the factory's brilliant manager Henry Tooth.

Tooth left Linthorpe in 1882 and in the same year opened a pottery with William Ault at Woodville, near Burton-on-Trent. This was called the Bretby Art Pottery. Ault severed his connections with Tooth in 1887 and opened his own pottery at Swadlincote, not far from Woodville. This factory was known as Ault Potteries Ltd. until 1922 when the Ashby Potter's Guild of Pascoe Tunnicliffe was absorbed; from 1923 until it ceased production in 1947, the firm was known as Ault and Tunnicliffe Ltd.

The pottery produced in both the Bretby and Ault factories were obviously closely influenced by that of Linthorpe. Dresser himself designed a range of pieces for Ault in the 1890s; some of these

The Martin Brothers produced a wide variety of ceramics. The grotesque animals and birds are mainly the work of Robert Wallace. In the early years Gothic and Renaissance themes predominate, but in the 1880s and 1890s, first natural history, insects and marine life, and then mythological beasts such as dragons and animals and fishes with strange gargoyle faces, began to appear either incised or in low relief on vases, jugs and other ware. Much of the inspiration for such themes came from Japanese woodcuts and illustrated books, examples of which were in the brothers' possession. From 1880 until 1895, the brothers employed Edward Willey as an assistant, and it is obvious from his surviving sketchbooks that he was responsible for much of the designing during this period.

In the late 1890s, following Willey's departure, Edwin Martin began producing gourd vases, usually very small, based on vegetable forms and certain types of marine life. The surfaces of these pieces are inspired by the various natural substances – tortoise-shell, sea-shells, mother-of-pearl, dried sea-urchins – which the brothers are known to have collected. It is probable that the sudden appearance of this type of decoration was hastened by Willey's departure and arose out of the detailed decorative work on which Edwin had been engaged during the time Willey was at the

UN CHEVALIER SANS PEUR ET SANS REPROCHE

are almost indistinguishable from Linthorpe, although a few outrageous, grotesque, Gothic pieces are immediately recognisable as Ault, and remain among Dresser's most famous ceramic designs. Also in the north, a Leeds firm, Wilcox and Company, opened an art pottery studio called Burmantofts Faience in 1880. Some of the Linthorpe decorating staff moved there and influenced some of the factory's products. However, Burmantofts also produced a range of pieces painted in the Isnik palette, often of very high quality, which were obviously inspired by the work of William de Morgan.

Although the connection has never been clearly documented, it is certain that De Morgan's revival of lustre also influenced the products of the Pilkington Factory. The latter came into existence as the result of the discovery of clay by the Clifton

and Kersley Coal Company in 1889 while sinking mine shafts at Clifton in Lancashire. The owners of the company, four brothers called Pilkington, consulted an expert chemist at Wedgwood's, William Burton, and in 1891 the Pilkington Tile and Pottery Company was formed under the management of William and his brother Joseph. It was not, however, until after 1903, when the art pottery was called Lancastrian Ware (Royal Lancastrian after 1913) that the famous lustre was produced.

Although Lancastrian lustre reached a very high technical standard, the designs and colours are frequently vulgar and garish, and suffer generally from too mechanical a handling. In the early years of the twentieth century, a number of talented decorators were recruited, including Richard Joyce, who had worked at Bretby, in 1905,

Lancastrian Ware wall plaque painted in silver lustre by Richard Joyce after a design by Walter Crane for Pilkingtons, 1907.

Top Linthorpe bowl designed by Christopher Dresser, *c.* 1880.

Above Bowl designed by William Moorcroft.

Above right Pot with lid made by Charles Cox at the Mortlake Pottery, 1912.

Gordon Forsyth, who became art director of the factory, in 1906, and William S. Mycock, Charles Cundall and Gladwys Rogers in 1907. Designs were also commissioned from three of the leading Arts and Crafts designers and artists: Charles Voysey (tiles only), Lewis F. Day and Walter Crane. Both Day and Crane had previously designed ceramics for a number of different factories, including Maw and Company, a Shropshire firm which began producing art pottery in the 1870s; they made about six pieces to Crane's designs, these usually being decorated with copper lustre.

The Pilkington Factory continued the production of art pottery until 1957, except for a break between 1938 and 1948. In the early years of the factory, the production of wares with streaked and monochrome glazes: Ultramarine Blue (later renamed Kingfisher Blue), Uranium Orange, Orange Vermilion, as well as pieces with crystalline glazes, equalled or outnumbered those pieces with the more expensive and hazardous lustre glazes. In 1928, Joseph Burton developed Lapis ware, a process for abstract or pictorial decoration in soft muted colours. Some of these latter pieces are of good quality.

In the last decade of the nineteenth century and the first decade of the twentieth, the obsession with various high temperature metallic-oxide glazes which had been a feature of the French, German and Danish industrial factories and some studio potteries in those countries since the 1870s, spread to England.

Considerable controversy exists over the chronology of European and American high-temperature transmutation glazes. The German glaze chemist and potter Hermann Seger began experimenting in the early 1870s and developed fine *flambé* glazes while technical director of the Royal Porcelain Factory, Berlin, from 1878 to 1890. In France, Théodore Deck at Sèvres and the studio potter Ernest Chaplet each had produced

successful copper red glazes by the early 1880s, although the Sèvres factory had produced isolated examples as early as the 1830s, and more pieces under the supervision of the glaze chemist Ebelman in the 1850s. In 1884, several soft-paste porcelain pieces with copper red (*sang-de-boeuf*) glazes made by Lauth and Vogt at Sèvres were exhibited at the Exposition de l'Union Centrale in Paris, an exhibition which also contained the first successful examples of Seger's Berlin *sang-de-boeuf* seen in public. By an extraordinary coincidence, 1884 is also the year in which Ernest Chaplet in France and Hugh C. Robertson at the Chelsea Keramic Works in the United States produced their first successful stoneware decorated with high temperature *flambé* glazes.

In England, the earliest experiments seem to have taken place in the 1890s, although, typically, not by any of the major industrial factories. It seems probable that the first English ceramist so engaged was Bernard Moore. Moore's family firm was disbanded in 1905, and from 1906 to 1915, he headed his own small art pottery at Wolfe Street, Stoke-on-Trent. The majority of Moore's pieces are low-temperature, red *soufflé* glazes (as are those by Doulton, Howson and many other factories, both large and small, which produced such work in the early years of the twentieth century). However, a few genuine high-temperature glazed pieces were produced by Moore, although these were probably not made until the last years of his factory's existence.

For the production of high-temperature glazes based principally on Chinese porcelains of the Ch'ing dynasty, the most important English potter must be William Howson Taylor, who founded his Ruskin Pottery at West Smethwick, near Birmingham, in 1898. The Ruskin Factory, which lasted until 1935 (although it closed its doors officially in 1933) produced a wide range of glazed wares – low temperature *soufflé*, monochrome lustres, some with simple painted decoration, crystalline glazes

Above Pots designed at the Omega Workshops, *c.* 1917.

Left Earthenware vase with matt green glaze by Keith Murray for Wedgwood, *c.* 1933.

Far left Earthenware coffee set with Moonstone glaze by Keith Murray for Wedgwood, *c.* 1934.

Below left Example of early twentieth-century glazed ware from the Ruskin Factory, Birmingham.

and some unpleasant matt glazes made in the late 1920s and early 1930s, these last being the factory's only concession to the prevailing English version of sub-Art Deco taste.

However, the factory is best remembered for its high-temperature *flambé* glazes, which achieved a range of colour and brilliance unknown in the work of any other Western potter or factory. Many such pieces are gaudy and violent in their effects; at their best, however, they are of an extraordinarily high quality.

As in the nineteenth century, the major industrial factories in the present century have shown little interest in new approaches to ceramics. One notable exception were Wedgwood's pieces commissioned from the New Zealand architect Keith Murray in the 1930s, which compensate for the artistically cheap Fairyland Lustre produced by Daisy Makeig-Jones at the factory in the previous two decades. The latter wares inspired a somewhat tasteless movement in English ceramic decoration which could be described as 'Twenties Chinoiserie'. Murray's designs, in contrast, are a genuine attempt to interpret in ceramics the spare, clean lines of the new Functionalist architecture; combined with the high quality of Wedgwood's glazes and bodies, they are particularly handsome and their true importance has not yet been fully recognised nor reflected in saleroom prices.

Other attempts by Staffordshire factories to produce work in a new idiom were generally lamentable. The Newport Factory of A. J. Wilkinson Ltd. in Burslem, under the influence of Clarice Cliff, produced pottery painted with designs by many leading British artists, including Laura Knight, Duncan Grant, Vanessa Bell, John Armstrong, Frank Brangwyn (who had also designed a range of wares for Doulton), Barbara Hepworth, Paul Nash, Ben Nicholson and Graham Sutherland. Their work, although cheaply produced, is a relief from the aptly named Bizarre designs of Cliff

Above Stoneware vase made by Shoji Hamada at the St. Ives Pottery, *c.* 1922.

Right Guru stoneware vase made by W. Staite-Murray, *c.* 1935.

herself, which have, unfortunately, come to be considered a major British contribution to Art Deco; they were not, at the time, held in much esteem, nor should we afford them much today. Cliff also designed vases and jars painted in strident colours, involving gold.

In England, the predominant influence in the history of twentieth-century ceramics has been the work of Bernard Leach. Leach, however, was not the first English studio potter nor was he the first to seek inspiration from Japan and, more importantly, from Chinese ceramics of the T'ang and Sung dynasties. The Martin Brothers might be considered the first English studio potters and in the first decades of the twentieth century, several individuals, notably George Cox and Reginald Wells, and one or two small potteries, of which the most important was Upchurch, began making earthenware and stoneware with thick monochromatic glazes based on early Chinese models.

Leach made his first pots in Tokyo in 1911. By the time he returned to England to found his own pottery in 1920, he had come into contact with Soetsu Yanagi, the brilliant Japanese scholar who was instrumental in founding the Japanese Folk Craft movement. Leach's ideas from then on were based on a notion of anonymous craft combined with the Zen discipline of repetition.

His work, which spans the years from 1911 to 1972, when increasingly poor eyesight forced him to give up pottery, was an attempt to synthesise Oriental ideas and techniques with English traditional ceramics. Certainly the work most admired by Japanese connoisseurs is that in which the English influence is predominant. Ironically, such connoisseurs find little to admire in Leach's work when it is most self-consciously Oriental in flavour.

In the early years of the 1920s, the St. Ives Pottery took on a number of pupils. Shoji Hamada had come to England with Leach as a budding potter and spent three years at St. Ives. He returned to Japan to become perhaps the most distinguished exponent of the *Mingei* (folk) school of ceramics. The first English pupils included Michael Cardew, Katherine Pleydell Bouverie and Norah Braden. Cardew's work from the beginning was rooted in the English slipware tradition and has always been less 'Japanese' than that of Leach himself. In the late nineteenth century, several small art potteries had started in Devon and Cornwall making earthenware and slipware (Charles Brannum's Barum Ware being the most accomplished) and it was these and such surviving country potteries as that of Edwin Beer Fishley at Fremington, which may be said to have guided Cardew as a potter.

The main alternative to the Leach tradition in English ceramics in the late 1920s and 1930s was the work of William Staite-Murray. Murray had collaborated with the Vorticist painter Cuthbert Hamilton at the Yeoman Pottery during the First World War and was throughout his comparatively short career (he emigrated to Rhodesia in 1939 and gave up potting thereafter) concerned with relating his pottery to current developments in painting and sculpture. He thought of himself primarily as an artist and it is this aspect of his philosophy, quite apart from the magnificent body of work he

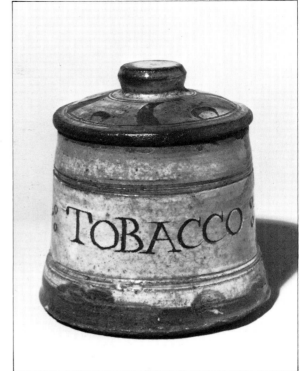

produced, which has caused the great revival of interest in his career in recent years. As head of the ceramics department of the Royal College of Art from 1925, Murray taught many gifted students, including Thomas Haile, Henry Hammond, Reginald Marlow, Heber Matthews and Helen Pinkham, all of whom subsequently became distinguished studio potters.

English studio pottery in the two decades preceding the Second World War was dominated by two great potters, Bernard Leach and William Staite-Murray, although there were other brilliant individuals. The work of Charles and Nell Vyse, for instance, can be divided into three main groups – figure subjects, which were executed from 1919 onwards, pots closely influenced by T'ang and Sung ceramics (in many cases such pieces were actual copies of known Chinese pieces), and wares painted either with figure subjects or with an abstract decoration based on Cubist-Vorticist painting. The earliest examples of the 'Chinese' wares seem to have been executed in the late 1920s. In terms of the techniques of Oriental glazes – *chun, celadon, tenmoku,* etc. – the Vyses were supreme among English studio potters, although much of their work in these idioms lacks individuality.

The coming to power of Hitler in 1933 caused the migration of many artists from Europe. Among those who came to England were Lucie Rie and Hans Coper, the former from Austria and the latter from Germany. Rie had attended Polowny's ceramic classes at the Vienna Kunstgewerbeschule and was before the war an accomplished potter who had been represented in many exhibitions. She taught Coper ceramics in England and their real significance lies in the work they have produced, and the extraordinary influence they have had, during the past twenty-five years on many studio and art potters in the United Kingdom.

Top left Chelsea stoneware vase made by Charles Vyse, *c.* 1934.

Top right Tobacco jar made by Michael Cardew, *c.* 1923.

Above Tile panel in stoneware by Bernard Leach, *c.* 1938.

Glass *by Isabelle Anscombe*

A single light stained glass window designed by Henry Holiday for James Powell, *c*. 1875.

WITHIN THE ARTS AND CRAFTS Movement the two most renowned firms making decorative glass were Powell's of Whitefriars and James Couper & Sons of Glasgow. From 1890 to 1900, under the influence of Harry J. Powell, the Whitefriars firm had pioneered forms of glass which relied more upon firing techniques and upon the form itself rather than decoration. The firm had earlier produced stained glass for Morris & Co. and simple uncut table glass for Philip Webb, and were happy to absorb the ideas of beauty lying in shape and method of production rather than applied decoration. Frank Brangwyn also designed glass-ware for the firm.

The Glasgow firm produced a range called Clutha glass and although George Walton designed for them from 1896–8, the true spirit of the Clutha glass was developed by Christopher Dresser from the mid 1890s. Freed by the nature of the material from his adherence to strict utility or scientific principle, Dresser shows a rare sensuousness in his glassware which reflects a profound reaction to the force and beauty of natural forms. His forms are irregular, following the sinuousness and rhythm of organic growth which was to become the central motif of Art Nouveau, and lack the aggression of some of his silver designs, although one still sees the influence of his botanical studies. The blown Clutha glass uses opaque green glass, often shot with translucent streaks of gold or cream, perhaps the result of Dresser's interest in Roman or Middle-Eastern ancient glass. The Art Nouveau forms were also utilised by Stuart & Sons of Stourbridge with furnace decoration and Stevens & Williams, also of Stourbridge, experimented with crackled glass or silver-deposit decoration and were known for their Japanese-style work in which the glass was cased and decorated.

In its early years the firm of Morris & Co. had depended financially on their stained glass, meeting the demand for ecclesiastical glass created by the Gothic Revival. D. G. Rossetti, Henry Holiday and William Morris designed stained glass, but the firm's most notable designer was Edward Burne-Jones who used the same delicate figures and pensive faces with borders of acanthus leaves or flowers not unlike Morris's designs. Morris himself was concerned with the qualities of colour in the glass. Holiday's glass is much stronger in its design, often using two layers of glass to give the required texture of a more painterly conception. There were many firms making stained glass, such as Hardman's, Powell's or Heaton, Butler & Bayne, who also made glass mosaics.

Gradually the conception of stained glass changed, as the designs in the *Studio Yearbooks* testify. Stained glass was used to add an element of depth and fantasy to a room and the designs became simpler, less pictorial and more true to the medium. The work of the Glasgow designers Oscar Paterson and E. A. Taylor shows a greater use of the lead lines to delineate figures or landscapes of imaginative style: fewer colours were used to greater effect.

E. A. Taylor began designing stained glass around 1900 when he began work for the Glasgow furniture-makers Wylie & Lochhead and he and designers such as Walter J. Pearce, Alex Gascoyne or Selwyn Image firmly established the fashion for plain leaded glass begun by the Arts and Crafts designer Christopher Whall. Frank Brangwyn was commissioned by Samuel Bing to design windows for the opening of his shop, L'Art Nouveau, in Paris, as was L. C. Tiffany. Stained glass became a major feature of the Art Nouveau home.

In the 1920s and 1930s the lack of good table glass was criticised. In 1933 John Gloag, while praising the architectural adaptations of glass, wrote: 'Glass which is often beautiful in shape is tortured with ornament: its merit as a design dies the death of a thousand cuts. . . . The cocktail has much to answer for . . .'

Most glass of good design, and reasonable price, sold in England in the thirties was Czechoslovakian, such as that sold at the newly opened Primavera. Keith Murray designed plain glass in simple shapes for Stevens & Williams of Stourbridge and Arundell Clarke stocked some interesting designs, but there seemed to be little else available apart from the classic cut glass.

As a building material glass now found a new importance as the technology of modern architecture allowed for walls to be filled in free from the dictates of structural necessity: plate glass and glass bricks were used and the *Daily Express* building was the first to be faced entirely on the exterior with glass panels. In 1933 Oliver Hill designed the Pilkington Brothers' stand at the Dorland Hall Exhibition, showing glass floor tiles, mosaics, mirrors and engraved panels and even glass furniture. In the same year Paul Nash designed a bathroom for Mrs. Edward James using panels of different coloured and textured glass and mirrors in an abstract design. Lawrence Whistler and Eric Gill also used glass decoratively and it was most popular for modern cocktail bars and lounges. Raymond McGrath designed the interiors of Fischer's restaurant in New Bond Street and of the Embassy Club.

Right and below Clutha vases designed by Christopher Dresser for James Couper & Sons, 1890s.

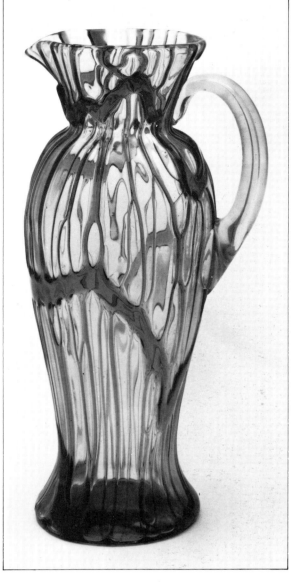

At Fischer's the space was divided by white circular pillars with the floor patterned with abstract squares of different coloured rubber reminiscent of Marion Dorn rugs. The furniture picked up the circular lines as did circular pieces of glass set into the counter. The walls were mirrored. The Embassy Club was decorated with panels of cut and polished glass. McGrath also used engraved glass which was made by Pugh Brothers.

Glass-topped tables and mirrors were an asset in renovating old London houses, enlarging small flats and enabling the occupiers to create modern surroundings. *The Studio* of 1930 commented that: 'Instead of sitting in dignified but disconsolate fashion on chairs designed apparently for the mortification of the flesh we sprawl at full length at so low an elevation that it has become necessary to introduce special low tables so that we can reach our cocktails or cigarettes without any serious physical exertion. . . . Here may be noted a significant change in our social habits affecting the character of our furnishing.'

The lightness and luminosity of glass in the home reflected the change from the 'horrors' of Victorian clutter and stuffiness.

Above Green on clear glass jug by Harry Powell, *c.* 1905.

Left Design for a stained glass window by E. A. Taylor, *c.* 1900.

Silver, Jewellery and Metalwork *by Isabelle Anscombe*

SILVER AND JEWELLERY were two of the media which received renewed attention due to the Arts and Crafts Movement. Silver design was taken out of the hands of the established manufacturers, whose productions at this time were of a deplorably low standard, as artists and architects turned their hand to silversmithing. One group of designers emerged who were to meet at the premises of Montague Fordham, House Furnisher, Jeweller and Metalworker at 9 Maddox Street in London. Fordham was a solicitor and successful businessman who had been the first director of the Birmingham Guild of Handicraft, founded in 1890. He left Birmingham in 1896 and opened his showrooms in 1898–9, acquiring also the Artificers' Guild in 1903, when Edward Spencer succeeded Nelson Dawson as artistic director.

The work of John Paul Cooper and Henry Wilson was sold through Montague Fordham and the Artificers' Guild, 1902–10 being J. P. Cooper's most intense period of activity. Both men were articled to the architect J. D. Sedding, and occasionally their work can be almost indistinguishable. It shows the influence of Sedding's Gothic designs in the combination of ivory and crystal with gold and silver and in certain motifs. Cooper's first departure into craftwork, en-

couraged by Wilson, was a number of gesso boxes of various shapes and similar boxes covered in shagreen with silver mounts which were to remain popular until the 1930s. Spencer's work was also influenced by Cooper. These designers all incorporated fine gems, mother-of-pearl, ivory and other materials into their intricate settings and employed the various motifs of the Arts and Crafts Movement.

Arthur Dixon, who had been a director of the Birmingham Guild, and Arthur Gaskin and his wife, Georgina Cave France of the Birmingham Group of painters, must also have been known to Fordham. Mrs. Gaskin had designed silverwork while still a student at Birmingham School of Art and from 1899 she collaborated with her husband, marking their pieces with a capital 'G'. Arthur Gaskin became head of the Vittoria Street School for jewellers and silversmiths in Birmingham.

The craft of enamelling was propagated by the work of Alexander Fisher, who had studied the technique in France and opened his own school in 1904. In 1901 he had worked briefly with Nelson Dawson, who was then to teach his wife Edith the art and she carried out most of the enamelling on their silver and jewellery. Other designers at this time were Harold Stabler, a founder member of the Design and Industries Association, who had

Silver cup with wirework handles by C. R. Ashbee at the Guild of Handicraft, *c.* 1900.

been a director at the Keswick School of Industrial Art from 1884 until 1902, when he left to join Richard Llewellyn Rathbone, a relative of W. A. S. Benson, in Liverpool. Omar Ramsden and Alwyn Carr worked together from 1898 until the outbreak of the First World War, although their partnership was not formally dissolved until 1919; Carr continued to work until the 1920s and Ramsden until 1939.

All these designers worked recognizably within the Arts and Crafts idiom, although each had an individual attitude towards his treatment of the medium. During the 1890s the Japanese taste was absorbed, most markedly by the Birmingham firm, Elkingtons, who were the first to adapt Japanese designs, such as Komai. The most idiosyncratic of the Aesthetic Movement designs were in cast-iron, made by Barnard, Bishop and Barnard to Thomas Jeckyll's designs.

Perhaps the best known of the Arts and Crafts metalwork designers was C. R. Ashbee. He had founded the Guild of Handicraft in 1888 and John Pearson was their first metalwork instructor. Himself self-taught, probably through the manuals of the American Charles G. Leland, the Guild began by producing simple embossed platters of brass and copper. John Pearson also supplied Morris & Co. with his embossed metal dishes, which was probably a contributing factor in his resignation from the Guild in 1892. In his last years he ran his own workshop.

The Guild of Handicraft first began working in silver and electroplate in 1889, although Ashbee did not register a mark until 1896. The first work, in keeping with the aspirations of the Guild, shows that the craftsmen – John Williams, W. A. White and William Hardiman – were self-taught, although Ashbee hated the mechanical finish of commercial silverwork and encouraged his silversmiths to leave the impression of hammer marks on the surface of their work. From 1890 they began using gems and enamelling, mainly done by Arthur Cameron who worked on Ashbee's Chelsea house, Magpie and Stump, and their best work was done while the Guild was at Essex House between 1890 and 1902. Ashbee's own work is most recognizable from his wirework, which he perfected around 1897, and the delicacy of his designs, often using green glass and silver together.

The work of Dr. Christopher Dresser represents the highest achievement in design for industrial manufacture. A doctor in botany, he based his design ethic upon the principles of Owen Jones and upon a scientific elegance for 'fitness for purpose' more akin to the design of the Modern Movement than to the Victorian 1880s. Most of his designs were executed in electroplate, due as much to his concern for an economic use of materials as to the manufacturers' financial preference. He designed for Elkington & Co. from 1875 to 1888, for Hukin & Heath from 1878 and for James Dixon & Co. from 1879. Although one of the few designers of his time to have visited Japan, his metalwork designs show a sparseness and complete absence of decoration in total opposition to the eclectic leanings of other designers. He wrote: 'In order to justify its existence a vessel must be constructed, but when formed it need not of

Left Pendant designed by C. R. Ashbee, 1903.

Below Electroplated soup tureen, cover and ladle with ebony handles and knop, designed by Christopher Dresser for Hukin & Heath, 1880.

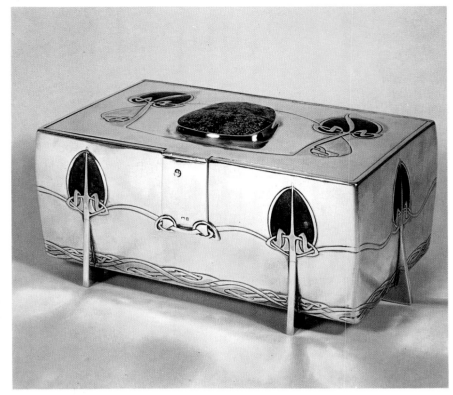

Top left Guild of Handicraft silver christening mug made for Lord David Cecil, 1902.
Top right Liberty & Co. silver and enamel casket designed by Archibald Knox, 1903.
Above Candlestick in painted copper, brass and wood by Christopher Dresser made by Perry & Co., 1883.
Right Enamelled triptych by Alexander Fisher, *c.* 1900.

necessity be ornamented; ornamentation must ever be regarded as separate from construction.' This was a revolutionary view at the time. Other designers for industrial production were rare, although the work of W. A. S. Benson, who set up his own workshop in 1880, was for mass production. His metal lamps, firescreens and light fittings, in brass and copper, have a starkness unusual in Arts and Crafts designs, although his kettles and teapots are nearer in their shape to that ethic. C. F. A. Voysey also designed metal light fittings for machine production.

The designs for silver, jewellery and metalwork for Liberty & Co. were commissioned from various designers, including Rex Silver, Oliver Baker, Bernard Cuzner, Arthur Gaskin and Jessie M. King.

The most outstanding of Liberty's designers was Archibald Knox, who was to determine the Liberty style. Knox had studied Celtic design at Douglas School of Art on the Isle of Man and applied the Runic interlacing of forms in his designs for silver and pewter. There is an affinity between the Celtic forms used by Alexander Fisher and those by Knox, but where Fisher used the style by way of decoration, Knox employed the form in a more integral, structural manner. The use of gems or enamel was often dependent on the commission of the purchaser and the price rose accordingly.

After the flourish of activity in this field of the Arts and Crafts Movement, interest in silver and jewellery design seems to have declined, leaving the field once again to the established manufacturers who continued to produce reproduction styles. Apart from the work of Keith Murray, perhaps the first freelance designer for industry since Dresser, for Mappin & Webb there is a sad lack of notable designers, most modern design being carried out in stainless steel.

Above left Silver-mounted jug by C. R. Ashbee at the Guild of Handicraft, c. 1900; green glass by Powell's of Whitefriars.

Above Liberty & Co. Cymric silver and enamel covered box, 1900.

Left Brooch-pendant, enamelled and set with a moonstone with three pendants of crystal, enamel and moonstone, by Henry Wilson, c. 1913.

Textiles and Graphic Art *by Isabelle Anscombe*

THE GOTHIC REVIVAL had inspired the increasing use of Gothic patterns and motifs in textiles, hangings and tiles, but the formation in 1861 of Morris, Marshall, Faulkner & Co. caused an enormous change in taste towards a new use of such items in the home. William Morris produced his first hand-blocked wallpaper designs in 1862 and in 1875 branched out into experiments with dyeing fabrics with Thomas Wardle in Leek. There are many stories of Morris with permanently blue hands from the indigo vats and he spent much of his time perfecting the use of natural dyes in his private war against the use of commercial chemical colours.

In 1883 he moved his fabric works to Merton Abbey where he had already set up looms for weaving his 'Hammersmith' rugs and carpets. The entwining floral designs of Morris's wallpapers and chintzes are too well known to require description, but it is interesting to note that despite his mastery of conveying the sense of growth in his designs he never mastered the art of drawing animals and birds, which were usually executed by Edward Burne-Jones. John Henry Dearle, who worked with Morris at Merton Abbey, also designed some wallpapers, fabrics and tapestries.

Above Tile by Pilkington, 1902.

Right Fabric design by Morris & Co.

Carpet designed by E. McKnight Kauffer, *c*. 1934.

Morris encouraged all forms of workmanship and his daughter May became known for her embroideries; she took over the embroidery section of the firm in 1885. William de Morgan had met Morris at Red Lion Square in the early days of the firm and in 1869 started his kiln in the basement of 40 Fitzroy Square, coming closer to Morris in 1874 when the firm was reorganised as Morris & Co. Between 1882 and 1888 he worked at Merton Abbey, producing tiles which were mainly for interior use, adapting Morris's favoured Persian models and echoing Morris in his use of floral forms. The colours of his birds, animals, ships and grotesques show the same concern for purity and brightness which all but obsessed Morris.

Following the example of Morris & Co. and in line with the Arts and Crafts ethic, many designers whose primary interests perhaps lay elsewhere also worked on flat designs. In 1870 Lewis F. Day began his own business making stained glass, embroidery, textiles, wallpapers and carpets; A. H. Mackmurdo, whose work was to influence C. F. A. Voysey, produced fabrics and rugs through his Century Guild; Christopher Dresser, although few of his flat designs have survived, filled *Studies in Design* (1875) and *Modern Ornamentation* (1886) with wallpaper designs, friezes and dadoes and his studio was mainly concerned with textile design during the 1890s. Many firms commissioned Arts and Crafts designers: Jeffrey & Co. (wallpapers) employed Walter Crane, Lewis F. Day, E. W. Godwin, Mackmurdo and George Walton. Both Maw & Co. and Pilkingtons (tiles) commissioned Lewis F. Day and Walter Crane, who also designed for Mintons and Wedgwood. Alexander Morton – later Morton Sundour – produced designs by Voysey and George Walton for fabrics, hangings and carpets. Voysey designed hand-printed wallpapers for Essex & Co. and fabrics for many companies, including the Glasgow firm Wylie & Lochhead.

Liberty & Co. naturally kept pace with their competitors and sold designs by Crane, Day, Voysey, Arthur Silver and Jessie M. King. In comparison to the fulsome naturalistic patterns which had predominated at the 1851 Exhibition, the smaller, neater repeating motifs of these fabrics and papers and more restrained designs for carpets, all executed in subtler colours, must have been a welcome relief to the woman of taste. It proved also that the leading designers of the time could, when they chose, co-operate quite happily with large manufacturers, thus realizing one of the principal ambitions of the later Modern Movement: bringing good design to industry.

Embroidery enjoyed a new vogue at this time, encouraged by the newly founded ladies' guilds and stimulated by the example set by Morris & Co. The Glasgow School of Art also gave rise to a local community of embroiderers, led by Jessie R. Newberry, the wife of the Principal. She taught embroidery at the School from 1894 to 1908, as did Ann Macbeth. Their two most famous pupils were Frances and Margaret Macdonald.

At this time *The Studio* magazine contained models for needlework and held competitions for designs and work; what had been revived as an interest in craft became an art. The interest was continued into the wave of Post-Impressionism by the needlepoint designs of the Omega Workshops, especially in the work of Vanessa Bell and Duncan Grant, whose designs were executed by his mother. They used needlepoint, in vivid colours and bold patterns not only for chair seats, but for mirror frames and screens.

Another successful offshoot of the Arts and Crafts Movement was the art of fine printing. The first achievement was *The Hobby Horse*, a quarterly magazine of A. H. Mackmurdo's Century Guild, which was printed on hand-made paper and supervised by Emery Walker. It first appeared in 1884 and was followed in 1890 by Morris's

Kelmscott Press. He had earlier planned, with Burne-Jones, to issue an edition of *The Earthly Paradise*, so the idea of following the model of medieval illuminated manuscripts was already in his mind by the time he came to his Kelmscott *Chaucer*, for which he designed his own type and decorated the pages. Lewis F. Day, in *The Easter Art Journal* of 1899 criticised Morris's typefaces as being too heavy and bemoaned the fact that, for a socialist, the books immediately became collectors' items.

Lewis F. Day himself, in company with the artists Walter Crane, Jessie M. King and Kate Greenaway, instituted a new style of illustration for children's books. Kate Greenaway especially adopted many of the colours and motifs of the Aesthetic Movement, while Jessie M. King, with the stylisation of line peculiar to the Glasgow School, portrayed the classic fairy stories in fine detail with attention to trees and landscapes and the differing textures of an Art interior. Colour and an element of fantasy opened new realms of nursery reading.

A rather more sinister fantasy element dominated the work of Aubrey Beardsley which appeared in *The Yellow Book*, running for thirteen volumes before disappearing in the midst of the Wilde scandal. It had done much, however, to introduce the French decadents to England. Fine printing was again encouraged in 1912, the year in which *Imprint* appeared, owing much in its typography to the work of Edward Johnston.

'Long Live the Vortex!' was the next cry to be heard, in total opposition to the gentle art that typography had been until April 1914 when *Blast No. 1* was issued under the editorship of Wyndham Lewis. The anarchic presentation of the Vorticist manifesto, containing work by the artists of the Rebel Art Centre, destroyed any hope for an apolitical art and made other efforts at private presses, such as Bloomsbury's Hogarth Press, seem all too unrealistically gentle. The excesses of this review foresaw the future of poster design and is reminiscent, in its violence on contemporary taste, of the posters produced by the Glasgow Four.

Meanwhile the gentler arts still continued. Frank Brangwyn, who combined nineteenth-century elements with a more modern taste, designed carpets, fabrics and pottery. Charming tiles were designed by Bernard Leach, Edward Bawden and Vanessa Bell and Duncan Grant, who continued to work on their almost Italianate interiors and artifacts. Their fabrics were used successfully for costumes when Grant designed the set for Jacques Copeau's production of *Twelfth Night*.

While the fortunes of British design tended to decline from the twenties into the thirties, England led in one important aspect of the complete interior, in the field of textile and rug design. During this time women began to enter the scene as designers in their own right, conscious of their recent emancipation and eager to be regarded as professional in their chosen spheres. Among the new designers, many of whom worked for Allan Walton Fabrics Ltd., were Elspeth Little, Dorothy Larcher, Phyllis Barron, Enid Marx, Sonia Delaunay, Margaret Stanfield and Riette Moore.

'The Angel of Night', gesso and mother-of-pearl panel by Frederick Marriott, 1904.

Top Tapestry by William
Morris and Edward Burne-
Jones, *Love Leading the Pilgrim*.

Left Poster for the London
Underground by Frank
Pick, 1930s.

Above Illustration by
Kate Greenaway.

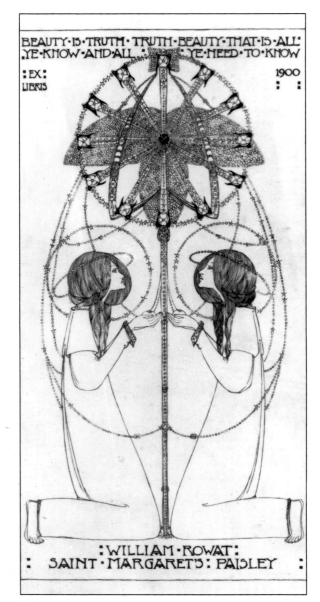

BEAUTY·IS·TRUTH·TRUTH·BEAUTY·THAT·IS·ALL'
·YE·KNOW·AND·ALL · · ·YE·NEED·TO·KNOW

:EX:
LIBRIS
1900
: :

:WILLIAM·ROWAT:
SAINT·MARGARET'S·PAISLEY

Right *Ex libris* design by Jessie M. King, 1900.

Below Music room designed by Vanessa Bell and Duncan Grant, 1933.

In *The New Interior Decoration* (1929) by Dorothy Todd and Raymond Mortimer, the authors wrote that: 'Roughly speaking, there are two schools of modern textile design: that which employs purely geometric patterns, and that which is generally more free and fanciful, in which trees, horses, the human figure, and so on, are freely and often amusingly introduced.' Raymond Mortimer's tastes lay more with the latter style, but it was the geometric patterns which were probably the more popular at the time, reflecting the absorption of Cubist art. During the late twenties strong colours and a mass of detailed decoration were considered inadmissible in the interior and it was often curtains or rugs alone which introduced an element of movement into the otherwise calm environment. Allan Walton, Tamessa Fabrics Ltd. or Arundell Clarke all sold the new fabrics and artists and architects also either designed their own fabrics or commissioned them especially for their interiors. Other designers were Edward Bawden, Marion Dorn, McKnight Kauffer, Paul Nash, Bernard Adeney, Raymond McGrath, Evelyn Wyld, Ashley Havinden or Serge Chermayeff.

The most revolutionary change in design came in the area of rugs. James Morton of Morton Sundour and Edinburgh Weavers expressly wanted a new form of decorative textile to complement modern architecture and both his company and the Wilton Royal Carpet Factory led the field in rug design. Some artists employed the Irish designer Jean Orage, based in Chelsea, to weave their designs. Others sent their designs out to India or China to be made up and Ronald Grierson even taught himself the technique. Duncan Miller Ltd. sold rugs made by the Edinburgh Weavers to designs by John Tandy, Ashley Havinden, Terence Prentis, Jean Varda and Marion Dorn; Gordon Russell Ltd. sold rugs by Marian Pepler, who was married to Richard Russell, Gordon's brother; in 1934 Simpsons held an exhibition of Ashley Havinden's rugs, a departure from their usual style perhaps due to his directorship of Crawford's, Simpsons advertising agency; Fortnum & Mason also held a show of Modernist rugs; Betty Joel sold her rugs exclusively through her own showrooms.

While McKnight Kauffer and Marion Dorn had instituted the plain background, often in neutral shades, and lack of border, their strong abstract designs differ from the more fanciful designs of Ronald Grierson or John Tandy. There is a distinction to be made between those rugs designed by interior designers as a part of a decorative whole and those designed by artists whose true interests lay elsewhere.

The alternative to the sparseness of the modern home was the mural, although most artists worked mainly in the houses of friends for special commissions. In 1933 Duncan Grant and Vanessa Bell painted a music room, featured in the *Architectural Review*, where the walls were painted with panels of flowers and even the piano was decorated with abstract shapes. However, in 1935 Grant was commissioned to decorate a lounge in the new Cunard liner RMS *Queen Mary*, but when the painted panels were erected they were vetoed by the company director.

MAY 31
COLLECT FOR
THE FEAST OF S. ANGELA MERICI

DEUS, QUI NOVUM PER BEATAM
ANGELAM SACRARUM VIRGINUM
COLLEGIUM IN ECCLESIA TUA FLOR-
ESCERE VOLUISTI: DA NOBIS, EIUS
INTERCESSIONE, ANGELICIS MORI-
BUS VIVERE; UT, TERRENIS OMNIBUS
ABDICATIS, GAUDIIS PERFRUI MERE-
AMUR AETERNIS · PER DOMINUM NOSTRUM
IESUM CHRISTUM FILIUM TUUM QUI TECUM
VIVIT ET REGNAT IN UNITATE SPIRITUS SANCTI
DEUS PER OMNIA SAECULA SAECULORUM

ABCDEFGHIJJKLMN
OPQQRRSTUV
WXYZ

Raymond Mortimer commented that such a decorative scheme would have been out of place within so lavish a setting which catered for people perhaps more at home with the luxurious Art Deco or Hollywood style. Other murals depicted more modern themes, such as John Armstrong's gesso panels for the restaurant of Shellmex House which showed cars, horses and aeroplanes symbolising the speed of modern life, John Banting's Surrealist interiors with huge abstractions of the human figure, or Ben Nicholson's decorative carved reliefs.

Industry benefited from the new designers in the fields of advertising and typography. In 1925 Eric Gill was drawing alphabets for Stanley Morison, the director of the Monotype Corporation's typography section, which were then adapted as the Perpetua typeface. Gill had trained as an architect and then studied typography under Edward Johnston. Johnston had been influenced by W. R. Lethaby, who supported craft above art, the commonplace above genius, and Gill also retained a sense of the importance of commonplaceness and normality in his work.

He and Johnston also refined a second type for the Monotype Corporation, the Sans Serif alphabet, which was widely used for lettering in public notices. Johnston was commissioned by Frank Pick to design the lettering for London Transport, where McKnight Kauffer was also employed to design posters. Disregarding Gill's masonry sculpture, for which he is now justly better known, his work in typography almost revolutionised the art. The work of Frank Pick for the London Underground and of Jack Beddington for Shellmex, equally, is now daily taken for granted, but at the time was a vital innovation. Many leading artists of the time were concerned with poster design and new ways of presentation, each bringing their own 'ism' to bear upon their work; most notable are Rex Whistler, Eric Ravilious, John Piper and Graham Sutherland.

Top An example of text set in the Sans Serif face designed by Eric Gill.

Above 'The Peacock Skirt', illustration by Aubrey Beardsley for Oscar Wilde's *Salome*, 1894.

Right Poster for *The Scottish Musical Review* by C. R. Mackintosh, 1896.

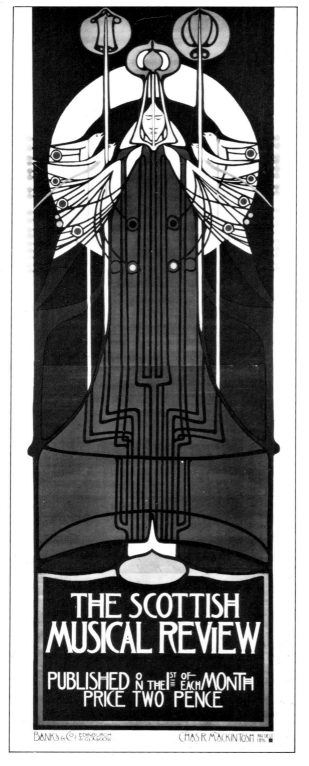

United States

by Isabelle Anscombe

American Design 1890–1940

IN THE MAIN, the decorative arts in America in the nineteenth century took their lead from Europe, whether from Greek classicism or Louis-Quinze, and these revivalist tendencies were adopted also in architecture. The United States, however, led in technical virtuosity, as in various types of spring revolving chairs or John H. Belter's bentwood chairs, or in the far-sightedness of some individuals to collect the best of ancient cultures. Louis Comfort Tiffany collected ancient glass and his father commissioned Christopher Dresser to collect Japanese objects for Tiffany & Co. while in Japan in 1877. The American Institute of Ar-

Cover of *The Craftsman* magazine.

chitects was founded in New York in 1857 and gradually a more coherent American style was evolved by men such as Frank Furness in Philadelphia or Henry H. Richardson in Boston. The development of the shingle style is even thought to have influenced the work of C. F. A. Voysey in England.

However, contemporary movements in Europe tended to reach the United States somewhat anachronistically and haphazardly. The Gothic Revival of Pugin and Ruskin reached America merely as a style adopted by a few designers, such as Isaac Scott, and lacked both the emotional and nationalistic impact of the English movement. Although the Eastlake style swept the East Coast it was misinterpreted because Eastlake's book was taken out of context and the work of similar designers, Bruce Talbert or Norman Shaw, was little known.

The opening up of Japan, however, and the resultant Aesthetic Movement, did catch the American imagination, perhaps not least because it had an able and flamboyant preacher in the figure of Oscar Wilde who lectured throughout the United States in 1882–3. Japanese ceramics were shown at the 1876 Philadelphia Centennial Exposition and influenced the course of art pottery and also book design and graphics. Indeed, the Aesthetic Movement was an English-speaking phenomenon.

By 1890 the most important foreign importation of style was the Arts and Crafts Movement of Morris and Ruskin. Many Americans visited England and even met Morris personally and returned fired with his ideals, dedicated to handicrafts and the rejection of the machine in art. Publications such as *International Studio, House Beautiful, The Ladies Home Journal* or *The Craftsman* spread the word to a wider audience. What was largely lost in translation across the Atlantic was the political background to the movement. When Walter Crane, a member of the Socialist League, spoke in Boston in 1891 in support of the Chicago Anarchists, he was banned from several clubs and a dinner in his honour was cancelled. A kind Bostonian lady warned him that if he persisted in such views his whole trip – and he depended on American commissions to finance himself – would be ruined.

The vast continent of America was not so concerned with problems of labour or class; the 'land of opportunity' offered different solutions to such problems in concepts of the frontier and freedom. Gustav Stickley began publication of *The Craftsman* in 1901 and for the first few years

Top 'When Hearts are Trumps' by Will H. Bradley, 1895.

Above left A library bookcase from *Hints on Household Taste* by Charles L. Eastlake, 1868.

Above A Craftsman living room illustrated in *The Craftsman*.

Left Poster by Maxfield Parrish.

Below left Sullivan's
Guaranty Building in
Buffalo (1894–5). Below
right The Bayard Building,
probably the last building
by Sullivan still in existence
in New York State, dating
from 1897–8.

Bottom Interior of the
Darwin Martin house,
Buffalo, by Frank Lloyd
Wright, 1904.

invited socialist guest writers to contribute. He upheld the doctrine of a truly democratic art in rejection of past styles of extinct civilisations. By 1906 his views were changing; his bankruptcy in 1916 was hastened by his earlier admission that he had never built the 'Craftsman' houses whose plans he published and that he knew their cost to be higher than stated.

The Arts and Crafts Movement was important in America not only for the fine workmanship it encouraged from individuals, but also for the growing awareness it developed among Americans that they should also find a truly national art. It should be noted, however, that the concepts of a national art differed across the country. On the East Coast Morrisian communities were founded and furniture and other decorative items made which have a direct resemblance to the British movement. In California, however, the climate and landscape and also the impact of the destruction of San Francisco in 1906 led to different interpretations. Morris's romantic return to the medieval European past was supplanted by the recognition of California's own past in Spanish-Mexican culture and Indian culture, as in Charles F. Lummis's publication *Land of Sunshine*.

Chicago was perhaps the most important centre of Arts and Crafts activity but was also an area most affected by frontier concepts. A style had to be evolved which no longer took its lead from the commercial and organisational centres of the East Coast, rooted as they were in European traditions. The high office buildings of Louis Sullivan almost foretold the future of the machine age of the automobile centre of the world which was to grow in Detroit. The mid-west relied on modern machines and means of communication for its survival and could, even in the 1890s, ill afford to espouse the microcosmic ideals of the Arts and Crafts Movement. The movement did, however, supply the impetus for a freedom of style.

As in England, the movement broke the barriers of traditional imitation in commercial areas such as wallpaper and fabric design and graphics. The adoption of Art Nouveau styles by firms such as the York Wallpaper Co. or M. H. Birge & Sons allowed people to see for the first time that contemporary design was available. Similarly, the art of the book was transformed by the output of Morris's Kelmscott Press. (Roberts Brothers of Boston were Morris's American publishers.) Dard

Hunter at Roycroft produced books on handmade paper, hand-bound in leather, which proved immensely popular. And the practice of illuminated lettering, floral borders and Gothic typefaces was adopted by many publishers. Will H. Bradley had adopted Beardsley's influence by the 1890s and went on to form his own idiosyncratic style, using Art Nouveau and Aesthetic motifs. Where Maxfield Parrish also reflects the self-conscious poses and dreamy light of Art Nouveau, his young ladies look out over landscapes of truly American proportions.

Despite the flourish of individual design brought about by the spread of Arts and Crafts ideals, by 1925 the United States found that it could not contribute to the Paris Exhibition where the rules of admission stipulated that work had to be both original and modern. Although in 1876 American exhibits at Philadelphia had relied on over-adorned copies of past styles, by 1893 at the Chicago World's Fair there was much new and original work to admire and American potters especially had won prizes at foreign international exhibitions.

The lesson of the 1925 Paris Exhibition flooded the American market with 'Art Moderne', reflecting the lavish decoration of the French exhibits. The United States led the world in architecture with the development of the skyscraper, and the ornamentation of buildings appeared to take precedence over domestic decoration. Not only skyscrapers but theatres, factories, churches, the Bay bridges or the Hoover Dam became the showpieces of American design. Geometric motifs replaced the sinuous curves of Art Nouveau; the zig-zag, sun-ray, bolt of lightning, waterfall or Aztec motifs and the stylised human figure, birds or leaping deer signified the 'speed' of Futurism as America began to 'go somewhere'. Steel grid buildings, reinforced concrete and the first working elevator, developed by Otis in 1889, all contributed to the new style.

Every aspect of a building was decorated, from the façade to the elevators, the ceiling to the mail boxes, the floors and doors to the radiator grilles. Coloured marbles, bronze, glass and many reflective surfaces were used to augment the powerful image of the skyscraper. In New York the Chanin Building, Radio City, the Chrysler Building, with an automobile motif picked out in brick on the exterior walls and repeated in Van Alen's interiors, or Donald Deskey's interior decoration for the Rockefeller Center are all examples of a style which glorified economic growth and technological advance. The Niagara Mohawk's office building in Syracuse was given a façade of stainless steel with horizontal strips of frosted glass; above the main entrance is a helmeted, winged figure in stainless steel, 'The Spirit of Power', and in the main entrance are four glass wall panels depicting 'Gas', 'Generation', 'Transmission' and 'Illumination'. Diego Rivera's murals in the RCA Building depicted the decadence of capitalism and included portraits of Communist leaders: they were replaced. In Michigan Eliel Saarinen (Eero's father) employed his wife to design the upholstery and rugs for his interiors.

By 1930 the American economy was in deep depression. The lavish scale of decoration which signified the glories of the capitalist system at its zenith had to give way to a vocabulary which expressed the utilisation of that technological knowledge and gave the consumer not just abundant ornamentation but also value for money. Industrial designers were recruited from the realms of theatrical design and advertising; new products had to show evidence of the benefits of science. Luxury could still be had, but under the banner of scientific economy and reductivism.

Designers such as Norman Bel Geddes, Henry Dreyfuss, Raymond Loewy and Walter Dorwin Teague introduced streamlined forms into automobile, ship, railroad and aeroplane design. Exterior styling was gone, integral design became the rule. On the surface, the new science of design was comparable to the theories of the Bauhaus which defined the house as a machine for living, but the decorative idiom of streamlining was misapplied and became a symbol of scientific progress rather than a true theory, the expression of an attitude rather than an understanding.

Walter Dorwin Teague designed Kodak cameras, again employing the horizontal parallel, and showed a plain interior, again using curves, in his lounge for the Ford Exposition at the 1939 New York World's Fair. Raymond Loewy turned from graphics for *Harper's Bazaar* and *Vogue* to designing refrigerators and trains and Henry Dreyfuss worked on objects as disparate as perfume bottles and telephones.

By 1940 the style had been discredited. The Depression had heightened commercial competition and style became an element of obsolescence. The mythologies of Hollywood sets encouraged the idea of streamlining as an element of decoration rather than a scientific principle. In England in 1935 the *Architectural Review* had

Below Modernist interior by A. L. Kocher and G. Ziegler, New York, *c*. 1930.

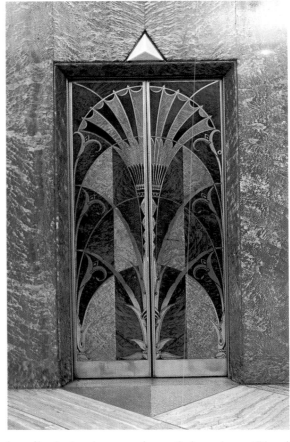

described the importation of American 'Plaza' architecture in cinemas by saying: 'They are around us on every side like a nightmare of pale, expressionless film faces fringed with impossible Garbo eyelashes.'

But whatever the criticisms, both social and aesthetic, of the American style, the idioms of power, the United States had shown that it could develop a national style, in the automobile and the skyscraper façade as much as in the home, and could stand apart from European historicism.

Above Radiator grill by Jacques Delamarre in the foyer of the Chanin Building, New York, 1929.

Above right Elevator door by William van Alen in the Chrysler Building, New York, 1930.

Right S. L. Rothafel's private suite by Donald Deskey in Radio City Music Hall, 1933.

Furniture

DURING THE 1850s and 1860s American furniture design was dominated by historical revivals, culminating in an excess of eclecticism in the exhibits at the Chicago World's Fair in 1893. In the 1850s the most popular cabinet maker in New York was John Henry Belter, a German, who worked in the Rococo style and also Louis-Seize. By the 1860s a French Renaissance style was a favourite, although some makers, such as Isaac Scott, did absorb the Gothic idiom from England, as shown in the work of Daniel Pabst, the leading Philadelphia cabinet maker, also German-born. The influence of Christopher Dresser, who lectured in Philadelphia in 1876, is clear in Pabst's work after that date. Most American furniture therefore, although perhaps dignified, was rather heavy and imposing, with an excess of carving and added ornamentation, or was admirable by virtue of its technical inventiveness, as in the work of the American Chair Company of New York.

A more sobering and elegant influence was the work of the Shakers who had first settled in America at the end of the eighteenth century. In 1852 they had founded a chair factory to produce their craftsmanship for outside sale and by 1860 the simple designs and materials of the Shaker philosophy had become fashionable on the East coast. Another element of simplicity was added in the 1860s with the publication in America of Charles Eastlake's *Hints on Household Taste*, which was extremely successful and gave rise to a so-called 'Eastlake style' which the author himself was forced to disavow in the fourth edition of the book. Eastlake advocated Gothic ornamentation, although with restrained, conventionalised motifs and an absence of clutter in the decoration of the home. However misinterpreted, the book led the way to an alternative to the earlier heaviness of mahogany and relief carving.

In 1882 Oscar Wilde lectured in America, accompanying Gilbert and Sullivan's 'aesthetic opera' *Patience* and preaching not only the aesthetic ideals for which he was lampooned but also a healthy attitude for a relatively new country, that America should find the inspiration for her art in her own lands and not attempt to copy past or dissimilar civilisations. Both Wilde and the styles of the Aesthetic Movement were clearly heard and even the established New York firm of Herter Brothers, who had been making furniture in light walnut in the Rococo manner, now designed Japanese-inspired furniture in ebonised wood with delicate inlays. However, the 1890s vogue for Orientalism led away from the delicacy of Japanese designs and also introduced Turkish

Left An illustration from *Hints on Household Taste* by Charles Eastlake, 1868.

Below Bed, bureau and mirror, and night table by Daniel Pabst *c.* 1876.

Interior of Frank Lloyd Wright's house, Taliesin, built in 1911.

craftsmen. His woodwork reflects both the Mission style of California and Art Nouveau in elaborate carving and detailing, mainly in oak, the most delicate work carried out by George Thiele. In the Arts and Crafts tradition joints or pegging are included as features of the overall design. He exhibited at Turin in 1902, was elected a member of the Royal Society of Arts in London and even commissioned to design furniture for Buckingham Palace. He retired in 1920.

Charles Rohlfs often lectured at the Roycroft community at East Aurora which had been started by Elbert Hubbard in 1895, following a visit to Morris's Kelmscott Press in Hammersmith. Previously Hubbard had been a successful soap salesman and Roycroft was run along good business lines, beginning with a press and book bindery and gradually incorporating other crafts; the furniture shop was started around 1901. Janet Ashbee, when she visited East Aurora in that year, criticised the work there for a lack of organic unity and although the Roycroft furniture is solidly and honestly made, generally in oak or mahogany, it does lack the presence of a true designer's form. Some of the first productions were slightly heavier versions of Morris & Co. chairs and later pieces bear a resemblance to the Craftsman style of Gustav Stickley.

Stickley had trained as a stonemason and then been apprenticed to relatives who were furniture makers within the general style of the period. However, in 1898 he visited France and England and returned full of the desire to create a new American style, totally divorced from European traditions and, following his debt to Ruskin, absorbing the principles of architecture. In 1901 he founded *The Craftsman* magazine in which he upheld the social aims of the British Arts and Crafts designers and called for a truly democratic national art. He held a quasi-psychological view that simpler surroundings would lead to a spiritual regeneration, especially in the industrial cities, and his solid, severe furniture would seem to reflect his social aims more than any artistic genius.

In 1900 the company was enlarged and changed its title from the Gustav Stickley Company to the Craftsman Workshops and also acquired a timber mill in the Adirondacks to supply the oak which was most generally used. From 1903–4 Harvey Ellis worked for the company, ornamenting the furniture with inlaid metals, the only decoration ever employed. In 1915 the company was declared bankrupt and taken over by his two brothers as the Stickley Manufacturing Company, which still exists today, but 'craftsman' had already become synonymous with a certain style of furniture.

Other communities were founded with the same aims as Roycroft, one by an Englishman who had been a pupil of Ruskin's at Oxford and one inspired by the ideals of Morris's *News From Nowhere* and modelled on Ashbee's Guild of Handicraft. Ralf Ratcliffe Whitehead's colony, Byrdcliffe, at Woodstock was founded in 1902 which produced some furniture; the Elverhoj Colony near Washington was started by a Dane named Anderson and the Rose Valley Community was founded in 1901 by the Philadelphia architect William L. Price. Price, like Stickley, was concerned with the morality of the honesty of

or 'Moorish' themes with upholstered divans generously tufted, tasselled and fringed; a style especially popular for the smoking room. It is interesting to note that an early photograph of a room in Frank Lloyd Wright's house depicts just this Victorian clutter of the Aesthetic Movement influence.

Towards the end of the nineteenth century many contacts were made across the Atlantic in the field of the decorative arts. In the same year that Oscar Wilde toured America, the Boston architect Henry H. Richardson visited England and met William Morris and Burne-Jones; in 1889 an exhibition of American arts, including Rookwood faïence and designs by John La Farge, was held in London; the following year Walter Crane visited the States, lecturing and designing and in 1891 an exhibition of C. F. A. Voysey's work was held in Boston.

In 1893 Samuel Bing visited America and two years later published *La Culture Artistique en Amérique*. In 1896 C. R. Ashbee made his first visit to America and in 1901 met Frank Lloyd Wright, forming a friendship which was to last for many years. Both Gustav Stickley and Elbert Hubbard, perhaps the foremost Arts and Crafts designers, visited Europe and England and returned inspired by the ideals they had met with. Gradually Arts and Crafts and handicraft societies were founded across America and magazines such as *House Beautiful* and the *International Studio* promoted Arts and Crafts aims and designs.

One of the first to assimilate European trends in design was Charles Rohlfs. Rohlfs was originally an actor, a profession disliked by his wife and, encouraged by her, he opened a small workshop in Buffalo in 1890. He worked independently on commission, never employing more than eight

Left Morris chair by Gustav Stickley, *c.* 1905.

Centre Teak storage bench designed by Charles and Henry Greene for the Blacker House, Pasadena, 1906.

Below Maple cabinet with silver inlay made for the Gamble House, California, by Charles Sumner Greene, 1908.

Below Oak chair by Charles Rohlfs, 1898.

Bottom left The Craftsman Workshops illustrated in *The Craftsman* magazine, 1904.

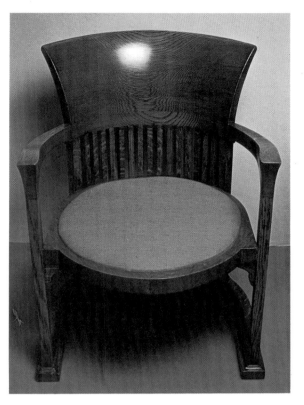

Far left Side chair by Frank Lloyd Wright for the Aline Barnsdell House, Los Angeles, 1920.

Below left Redwood side chair by Frank Lloyd Wright for the Paul R. Hanna House, Palo Alto, California, 1937.

Centre left Armchair by Frank Lloyd Wright for the B. Harley Bradley House, Kankaki, Illinois, 1900.

Centre right Oak armchair by Frank Lloyd Wright for the Darwin T. Martin House, Buffalo, 1904.

Left Carved and painted wood hexagonal box by Lucia K. Mathews c. 1910.

Below Interior of the Kaufmann House by Frank Lloyd Wright, 1936.

Right An arrangement of objects by The Furniture Shop (1906–20), now in the Oakland Museum, California: pair of carved and painted cylindrical candlesticks by Arthur F. and Lucia K. Mathews; gold-leafed and painted wooden jar with lid by Lucia K. Mathews; portrait of Lucia Mathews, *c.* 1899, oil on canvas, by Arthur F. Mathews; carved and painted chest by Arthur F. and Lucia K. Mathews.

Above Drawing of a desk by Frank Lloyd Wright for the rear guest room in the Avery Coonily House, Riverside, Illinois, 1908.

production, an echo of the Shakers, and sold the furniture made in the community's workshops through an outlet in Philadelphia where it was hoped that the simply constructed and decorated pieces would influence contemporary taste.

In California the Arts and Crafts ideals were interpreted with new emphases. The work of Charles Sumner Greene and his brother Henry absorbed the local Mission style and also a Japanese influence. All their furniture (mostly designed by Charles) was commissioned, generally for the interiors of the houses they built around Pasadena in 1907–9. Ashbee visited them in 1909 and admired their work above everything he had seen in America, but noticed with regret that the craftsmen who executed their furniture designs were mostly elderly men who had been trained in the tradition of hand craftsmanship, before the generalised use of machines. Their work, often inlaid with fine metals or carved panels with Japanese motifs, although inspired by a visit to England in 1901 shows an elegance and eclecticism lacking in the work of the East Coast designers.

The work of The Furniture Shop (1906–20) reflects a truly Californian style. It was founded in 1906 after the Great Fire in San Francisco by Arthur F. Mathews, the Director of the Art Institute of California, and his wife (and one-time pupil) Lucia. *Philoplis* magazine was founded at the same time, dedicated to the formulation of a new style, influenced by A. F. Mathews's Beaux-Arts training as a painter in Paris, for the rebuilding of the city. Thirty to forty craftsmen were employed and the furniture reflects A. F. Mathews's own work as a muralist and decorator rather than

the preoccupations of a craftsman-designer. The carved inlay and painting work was carried out by Lucia using the bright colours – orange, yellow and green – of the California landscape to depict local flowers, plants and trees.

The arrival of European influences in America tended to be anachronistic and the Arts and Crafts, or Craftsman, idiom was scarcely established before a genuine American style was forged through the work of Louis Sullivan and Frank Lloyd Wright in Chicago. Sullivan had introduced Art Nouveau forms in a system of architectural ornament, holding that the outward form of a building should express its function. His best work was for office buildings, but his ideas were taken and expanded in residential buildings by the younger architects who worked in his offices.

Frank Lloyd Wright worked as a draughtsman in the offices of Adler & Sullivan from 1888–93, leaving to join D. H. Perkins, Myron Hunt and R. C. Spencer at Steinway Hall. His first independent commission was the Winslow residence in 1893 and his style reached its peak during his period of work at his own Oak Park studio. Wright believed in integral design for his houses and his furniture was designed to solve specific problems within a particular interior, as in the Hanna house where the polygonal furniture reflects the hexagonal design of the house. Each house also had a particular ornamental theme and any added decoration was to echo that chosen motif; decoration generally relied on positioning geometric shapes.

Chicago had been quick to absorb the influences of the Arts and Crafts Movement – the Chicago Arts and Crafts Society was founded in 1897 and

Left Modernist furniture and interior by Jean-Michel Frank for the Templeton-Crocker apartment in San Francisco.

an Englishman, Joseph Twyman, did much to publicise Morris & Co. goods – but although Wright was involved with the movement through his friendship with C. R. Ashbee he held that it was the machine that was to determine a truly American art for the future. While Sullivan wrote for *The Craftsman* from 1905 onwards, and although Wright knew designers such as Elbert Hubbard his style moved forward on into the twentieth century and away from his original influences.

At the Paris Exhibition of 1925 there was no American work shown; it was suggested that the only representative object of American decorative arts would be the skyscraper. It is true that the major innovations in America at this time were in architecture, although changes obviously brought with them alterations in decorative styles.

In 1923 the Austrian Richard Neutra came to America to join his old associate Rudolph Schindler, who had worked with Frank Lloyd Wright. Neutra had studied under Adolf Loos who had seen Sullivan's buildings in Chicago in the early 1890s. His pupil Neutra went on to California where in 1928 he build the Health House, experimenting with new building techniques and technologies. Influenced by a visit to the Bauhaus in 1930 he returned to experiment with prefabricated housing and, in 1936, a model house using plywood. This influence took Wright's principles one step further and created plain interiors using much glass, uniform surfaces or exposed interior brick.

Until the 1925 Exhibition the main decorative styles were again historical revivals and the econ-omic stringencies of the 1929 Wall Street Crash doomed any real expansion of the new 'Art Moderne' influence, although geometric forms in exotic woods or new materials were introduced. In 1931 the American Institute of Interior Designers was founded and women enjoyed a heyday of importance in this profession. The best-known New York designer was Elsie de Wolfe, an actress turned designer, whose style based on eighteenth-century furniture and floral chintzes was extremely popular in the twenties and early thirties. Her dining room at the Colony Club introduced lattices as an indoor device which, combined with floral fabrics, produced a garden-like interior. Rose Cummings also used clear colours.

The all-white idiom, known as the 'White Look' also had its vogue, especially in Hollywood which also favoured the jazzy zigzags and black outlines of the modernistic idiom. Streamlining, motifs from Hollywood film sets, Art Deco, 'Cunard' lines all found some expression in both domestic and commercial interiors.

In the 1930s Swedish Modern became popular, with functional forms in blond woods. Knoll International made furniture in this style designed by Florence Knoll, Mies van der Rohe and Eero Saarinen. This style also absorbed the tenets of the Bauhaus and Charles Eames and Saarinen experimented with new materials; in 1939 they won first prize in an International Furniture Design Competition for a moulded plywood chair with a light metal frame, based on Marcel Breuer's prototype. As Frank Lloyd Wright had predicted, the machine and scientific theory had come to stay in furniture design.

Ceramics

Opposite

Top right A glazed
earthenware bottle
decorated in high relief
designed by Isaac E. Scott
for the Chelsea Keramic
Art Works, 1879.

Top centre Two Losanti
ware vases designed by
Mary Louise McLaughlin,
c. 1901.

**Right and top
left** Two Rookwood
vases which were exhibited
at the Paris 1900
Exhibition.

Bottom left Glazed
earthenware vase by one
of the Robertson family,
c. 1877.

Below Plate and pilgrim
jar by Mary Louise
McLaughlin, 1877.

ART POTTERY was perhaps the area of design where Arts and Crafts ideals were most widespread in America. Practically and financially it was, and is, a form where the artist-designer and craftsman could be one and, it is interesting to note, potteries in America were often set up either for therapeutic reasons or to provide some useful, but ladylike, occupation for women. The initial stimulus for American pottery came with the Philadelphia Centennial Exposition of 1876 where the first Oriental exhibits were seen as well as work from Doulton and examples of Ernest Chaplet's barbotine slip-painted technique. Both the Robertsons and Mary Louise McLaughlin visited the exhibition of ceramics and returned to their native states of Massachusetts and Ohio to put what they had seen into practice.

From the 1870s art pottery was dominated by the method of underglaze decoration. In 1872 the Chelsea Keramic Art Works was formed by James Robertson and his three sons, George, Alexander and Hugh. Specialising first in Greek terra cotta forms, in 1877 Chelsea faïence was introduced using simple shapes and glazes in soft colours. The process known as barbotine, similar to Haviland faïence, – painting with coloured slips, generally on a blue or green ground – was introduced; about the same time Mary Louise McLaughlin produced her first slip-decorated ware, also inspired by the Philadelphia exhibits.

In 1884 Hugh C. Robertson, then the only member of his family remaining at the Chelsea Works, achieved his first oxblood glaze. He had been experimenting with various Oriental glazes, including a mustard yellow, sea and apple greens and turquoise, all used with no ornamentation on simple stoneware shapes. His experiments however almost led him to bankruptcy and he closed the pottery in 1889. It was reopened in 1891 with support from Boston businessmen along more commercial lines and in 1895, upon the move to a new site, became the Dedham Pottery, best known for Robertson's crackleware, the blue in-glaze borders decorated with a variety of flora and fauna, the most popular being the rabbit.

The other exponent of the underglaze technique, Mary Louise McLaughlin, developed her Limoges glaze – to become known as 'Cincinnati Limoges' – in 1877. She had herself exhibited some china painting in 1876 and in 1879 she formed the Cincinnati Pottery Club to follow her faïence experiments and encourage other women, firing the work at the Coultry Pottery. From 1881 the Club used the facilities at Rookwood, but in 1882 these were refused and Miss McLaughlin had to cease work on her underglaze decoration. In 1895 she resumed work using inlaid clays, but abandoned this in 1898 in favour of hard-paste decorative porcelain. In 1901 the best results were achieved with her high-fired translucent creamy-white Losanti ware, on which she herself prided her reputation. She abandoned ceramics completely in 1906, but remains the most important of all the Cincinnati ceramists.

There were over thirty potteries in the state of Ohio after the initial impetus of the Philadelphia Exposition, the most famous being the Rookwood Pottery in Cincinnati. Rookwood was started by Maria Longworth Nichols Storer with financial help from her father and support from some of the ladies from the Cincinnati Pottery Club. Mrs. Nichols had already accomplished some china painting before she tried her first experiments in ceramics.

From 1880 to 1884 the work at Rookwood was mainly the ladies' experiments, with heavy relief or incised decoration and much gilding, but from 1884 due to Laura Fry's work with underglaze decoration the 'Standard' Rookwood ware became the best known feature of the firm, with brown, red, yellow or orange slips under a yellow-tinted high glaze. In 1883 William Watts Taylor had been employed as manager of the firm to establish Rookwood on a more commercial footing, but the pottery always retained its philosophy of allowing

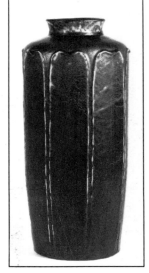

Above Rookwood earthenware vase by Albert R. Valentien, 1890.

Centre left Vase by S. A. Weller, *c.* 1905.

Centre right Earthenware vase by the Grueby Faience Co. of Boston, *c.* 1899.

Above right Vase by George E. Ohr made at the Biloxi Art Pottery, *c.* 1900.

individual artists a free hand in their designs. Several designers later left Rookwood to found their own potteries, such as Albert Valentien and Artus Van Briggle. Rookwood was also the first pottery in America to have a chemist on the staff, Karl Langenbeck, who joined them in 1885.

In 1886–7 Rookwood carried out the first experiments with a matt glaze but, due to concentration on the development of the elusive Tiger Eye glaze, it was not until the St. Louis Exposition in 1904 that the first Vellum matt glazes were seen, to be followed in 1910 with a second grey or brown matt glaze known as Ombroso. Also in the early 1900s unsigned ornamental wares were produced, cast in moulds, and in 1915 a range of soft porcelain. Rookwood, unlike so many other potteries, survived both the Depression and the Second World War.

The first serious rival to the domination of underglaze decoration came with the introduction of the matt glaze, which was most fully developed in the work of William H. Grueby of Boston. The Grueby Faience & Tile Company had been incorporated in 1891, but it was the work of Delaherche exhibited at the Chicago World's Fair of 1893 which probably inspired the forms of Grueby's work. Grueby vases are distinguished not only for the quality of the glaze but also for the simplicity of the shapes, decorated with incised relief motifs, usually of leaves.

Artus Van Briggle, who had worked with Karl Langenbeck at the Avon Pottery, was sent by Rookwood to France where he too studied the use of a matt glaze. In 1899, forced by tuberculosis to move to Colorado Springs, although he himself only survived until 1904, he set up his own pottery, where he perfected his glaze, using Art Nouveau motifs. Most of the work which employs matt glazes shows an austerity of form, in contrast to the reliance on ornamentation of the technique of underglaze painting. Van Briggle fused the arts of sculpture and ceramics, as in his famous Lorelei vase, in a manner reminiscent of the work of Emile Gallé. Charles Volkmar, of the Volkmar Kilns, New Jersey, also experimented with matt glazes.

In 1902 an Englishman Frederick H. Rhead began work with William P. Jervis at the Vance/Avon Faience in Ohio, then moving to the Weller Pottery in Zanesville. There he introduced a technique (which he called Jap Birdimal) of using a squeeze-bag to pipe the outline of a decoration in white slip, generally on a grey or blue ground, and then filling in the design with a contrasting colour. From 1904–8 Rhead worked at the Roseville Pottery in Zanesville where he added the Della Robbia line – using a *sgraffito* process – to their line of underglaze decorated ware known as Rozane, comparable to Standard Rookwood, Lonhuda Pottery or Weller's Louwelsa range. Rhead himself considered the process of inlaid decoration the most effective as it gave the potter the most control over his design, and he produced some beautiful work at the Arequipa Pottery in California – set up, as was Marblehead in Boston, as a therapeutic centre for tuberculosis patients – between 1911 and 1913, when he left to found his own pottery. He left his own company in 1917, abandoning also his newly founded journal, *The Potter*, and returned to Zanesville. Rhead was also obsessed with finding the technique for the Chinese mirror or reflecting black glaze and as late as 1934 he was honoured for his experimentation and success.

Perhaps the most distinctive style using the inlaid process was achieved at the Newcomb College Pottery. Newcomb College was the women's college of Tulane University in New Orleans and the pottery was set up by Ellsworth Woodward to provide both a technical and artistic training for women. A succession of potters were

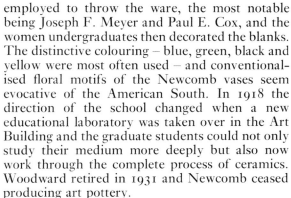

employed to throw the ware, the most notable being Joseph F. Meyer and Paul E. Cox, and the women undergraduates then decorated the blanks. The distinctive colouring – blue, green, black and yellow were most often used – and conventionalised floral motifs of the Newcomb vases seem evocative of the American South. In 1918 the direction of the school changed when a new educational laboratory was taken over in the Art Building and the graduate students could not only study their medium more deeply but also now work through the complete process of ceramics. Woodward retired in 1931 and Newcomb ceased producing art pottery.

One of the most remarkable examples of the ascendancy of American art pottery in the eyes of the world is the University City Pottery in Missouri. The pottery belonged to the Art Institute of the People's University started by the opportunist entrepreneur, Edward Gardner Lewis, who had launched the American Women's League in 1907. Lewis himself was interested in ceramics, self-taught using Samuel Robineau's translation of Taxile Doat's *Grand Feu Ceramics*, and in 1903 an extremely fine porcelain clay had been found in the area, fine enough to tempt Taxile Doat to leave his native Sèvres, with his ceramic collection, for University City in 1909. There he was joined by Samuel Robineau and his wife Adelaide, who had in 1899 published the *Keramic Studio*, Frederick H. Rhead and Kathryn E. Cherry. The school specialised in correspondence courses.

The first kiln was fired under Doat's supervision in April 1910 and many different glazes were used, most notably high-fired porcelain with *flambé* and crystalline glazes. The pottery won many prizes, the greatest being the Grand Prize awarded to Mrs. Robineau's scarab vase at the Turin International Exhibition in 1911.

Louis Comfort Tiffany first began experimenting with pottery in 1898 at his Corona works, New York, although the pottery bases for his lamps and other items were purchased from the Grueby Pottery. Tiffany exhibited his Old Ivory ware in 1904 and again the following year, but no ceramics were offered to the public until 1905. The majority of the work was moulded using a high-fired white clay which gave a light yellow-green glaze from which the name 'old ivory' was derived. He also experimented with mat, crystalline and iridescent glazes and from 1911 he introduced Bronze Pottery, probably influenced by the work of Clewell Metal Art which had opened in 1906 and by 1909 was producing ceramics with a metal coating of copper or silver. Tiffany's pottery was, from its inception, overshadowed by his Favrile glass and shows the same concern for flowing Art Nouveau lines and idioms. Production ceased between 1917 and 1920.

The many other potteries of this period are too numerous to name, although worth mentioning are the Paul Revere Pottery in Boston, Pewabic in Detroit, in New York the Volkmar Pottery, Buffalo Pottery and Fulper Pottery, which introduced its Vasekraft art pottery in 1909 with a multitude of glazes on stoneware bases which continued until 1930, Kenton Hills in Kentucky, Cowan Pottery in Ohio which from 1920 to 1931 produced limited edition moulded porcelain figures in addition to their art pottery, which proved extremely popular. In contrast was the Biloxi Art Pottery where George E. Ohr produced individual pieces, some paper thin in tortured shapes.

Art pottery was the area where, perhaps more than any other, America demonstrated that she could learn from the examples provided at the 1876 Philadelphia Centennial and create an American art by the time of the Chicago World's Fair seventeen years later.

Above left Vase from the Newcomb College Pottery, New Orleans, late 19th century.

Top centre Vase from the Fulper Pottery Company, *c.* 1910.

Top right Cast ceramic tile by Ernest Batchelder, *c.* 1910.

Centre Four vases from the University City Pottery characteristic of the work of Taxile Doat, *c.* 1912.

Above Art Nouveau vase by Artus Van Briggle, 1902.

Glass

THE MIDDLE OF the nineteenth century in England had seen a considerable revival in the art of stained glass. America had not had a Gothic Revival, bringing with it the re-emergence of ecclesiastical art, and it was not until later in the century that stained glass was seen as a promising art form. In 1872–3 the illustrator and watercolourist, John La Farge, visited France and England where he not only admired medieval glass, but also met some of the Pre-Raphaelites and saw the work of Morris & Co. He produced his first stained glass in New York in 1876 and worked with the Boston architect Henry H. Richardson and also Stanford White; he designed the panels for Richardson's Holy Trinity church in Boston, perhaps the finest example of 'Richardson Romanesque'. Around 1887 he began experimenting with different techniques and developed an opalescent glass which lent itself to Art Nouveau forms, no longer requiring etching or painting for effect. La Farge died in 1906, by which time his work had been widely copied.

It is interesting to note that even by the 1890s there was a 'revival' of the old technique of colouring pot-metal glass. Otto Heinigke formed a partnership with Owen J. Bowen, who had previously worked with both La Farge and Tiffany, and they produced church glass using painted leaded glass, influenced by Heinigke's visit to Europe in 1896. In 1913 they were joined by Oliver Phelps Smith and in 1915 he and Heinigke's son formed a new partnership, Heinigke & Smith, continuing to produce church glass for several years. Charles J. Connick of Boston also produced church glass in the traditional style.

The undoubted leader of the medium, however, was Louis Comfort Tiffany. He was the son of the founder of Tiffany & Co. and had studied painting under George Innes and travelled in Europe before he set up L. C. Tiffany and the Associated Artists in 1879 with the help of Candace Wheeler. By the early 1880s they were the most successful New York decorating firm and were commissioned in 1882 to decorate President Arthur's White House. By 1885 however the association had come to an end and the independent Tiffany Glass Company was founded. At the same time Tiffany moved into the top floor of his father's mansion where he created his own studio.

In 1892 Tiffany acquired his own glass furnaces at Corona and in 1895 the first Tiffany lamps were offered to the public. On bronze stands, the shades were leaded with varying qualities of glass, usually in floral designs. Amongst the successful designs were Clara Driscoll's dragonfly lamp and Mrs. Curtis Freschel's wisteria lamp, both produced around 1900. The lamps incorporated the best elements from Tiffany's glass which, with mosaics, he had begun to produce as early as 1876. Tiffany himself saw a social need for decorative stained glass to create interiors full of warmth and light, where perhaps otherwise a window might have looked out only on to a brick wall. It did not take long for every artistic household to own a lamp or window.

The first Favrile (meaning hand-made) glass was offered for sale from the Corona works in 1896. The first year's production had gone straight to museums. Tiffany owned an extensive collection of ancient glass which provided him with his fascination for texture and integral decoration. The workshops first produced plain gold lustre ware, followed by peacock blue and then other colours. This work was commercial in comparison to Tiffany's own experiments in achieving iridescent finishes or the Paperweight decorated glass, the Cypriote or Lava glass. From 1900 until his retirement from the firm in 1919 Tiffany Studios were best known for their art glass.

The John Harvard Memorial Window by John La Farge in St. John's Chapel, Southwark Cathedral, London, c. 1905.

The popularity of Tiffany glass obviously led many other manufacturers to follow his lead. The Quezal Art Glass and Decorating Co. of Brooklyn was started in 1901 by two former employees of the Tiffany Studio and in 1893 Handel & Co. of Connecticut began producing cheaper versions of the Tiffany lamps. In 1904 the New York Steuben Glass Works first produced their Aurene glass which was based on the Favrile glass, in Art Nouveau forms. Other companies were the Fostoria Glass Speciality Co. and Imperial Glass Co. of Ohio, Fenton Art Glass Co. of Virginia, Lustre Art Glass Co. of New York or Vineland Flint Glassworks of New Jersey.

Frank Lloyd Wright used leaded glass in his decorative schemes, using plain glass in totally geometric designs which picked up the central motifs used within a specific house. As skyscraper design took over from the more sinuous forms of Art Nouveau, glass was used as much in a structural capacity as in a decorative manner. As in England in the twenties and thirties, glass was used, etched, plain or mirrored, in interiors for bars and theatres; it was used in the home, especially in bathrooms.

Top right A collection of Tiffany iridescent glass vases, *c.* 1900.

Top centre Tiffany 'Jack-in-the-pulpit' glass vase, *c.* 1900.

Far right Tiffany miniature wisteria lamp, *c.* 1900.

Right Tiffany poppy lamp, *c.* 1900.

Right Tiffany acorn lamp, *c.* 1900.

Far right Hanging lamp in leaded glass by Frank Lloyd Wright for the Susan Lawrence Darner House, Springfield, Illinois, 1903.

Bottom right Leaded art glass ceiling lamp by Charles Sumner Greene, 1907.

Silver, Jewellery and Metalwork

Silver and jewellery in the United States tended to be dominated by the work of old, established firms such as the Gorham Manufacturing Co. or Tiffany & Co. Jabez Gorham founded his firm in Rhode Island around 1815 and Charles L. Tiffany's company took the name Tiffany & Co. in 1853, forming a silver department in 1868. Both firms were influenced by the changes in style of the craft revival and Art Nouveau, but on the whole their stock was conservative in design.

The director of Gorham, Edward Holbrook, organised a group of silversmiths with high technical skill to carry out the designs of William C. Codman, an Englishman who came to Providence in 1891. The silver and jewellery produced was sold under the name of Martele from about 1900 and embraced the new styles. The jewellery was mainly in silver, with some copper, set with pearls, quartz or mother-of-pearl. In other fields, the company was known for being the first to introduce mass production of silver items.

Tiffany & Co. was known for its wealth of precious stones and gems and when L. C. Tiffany, the founder's son, began to design jewellery he was able to use materials not generally found in designs stemming from the craft ethic. Tiffany silver derived its designs from Japanese art, following the ideals of the Aesthetic Movement; L. C. Tiffany sent silver from the company as a wedding gift to Mucha in Paris in 1906. When L. C. Tiffany became vice-president of the firm a separate department was set up under Julia Munson to make artistic jewellery, often following his own designs, which tended to be only a rough sketch, a model from his own extensive collection of Eastern and European objects, or just the suggestion of a flower or other natural form which could be adapted. Few pieces were made and production ceased in 1916.

L. C. Tiffany also worked with Julia Munson at his own Tiffany Studios where, in the late 1890s, experiments began with enamels, often used on *repoussé* copper bowls or vases. Opaque and translucent layers were used, fired separately, and often finished with a final iridescent coat, leaving an effect similar to his glassware.

As in England the Arts and Crafts Movement inspired many individuals to turn to the professional practice of their particular craft. In Boston, where Arts and Crafts first took hold in America, Elizabeth E. Copeland, after studying in England, combined silverwork and enamelling, her work showing clearly the handicraft of the maker. Following Miss Copeland, Edward Everette Oakes designed jewellery in Boston and showed at the Arts and Crafts Society Exhibition in 1923.

In Chicago also several individuals set up shop. There the work was more elegant in design, inspired by the powerful influence of the Prairie School architects. Around 1910 Florence Koehler made jewellery in the Art Nouveau style, owing more to France than to England for her designs. Her work was extremely popular in Chicago intellectual circles. The Kalo Shops were opened

Right Copper lamp by Dirk van Erp, *c.* 1911.

Below and centre Two examples of Gorham silverware illustrated in *The Craftsman* of 1904.

by Clara Barck Welles and sold extremely simple and elegant silverware; they continued until 1970, although Mrs. Welles retired in 1940. Robert R. Jarvie was listed as a silversmith in Chicago from 1893 until 1917 and was principally known for his simple copper candlesticks, but from 1912 he also designed commissioned trophies for cattle shows in Chicago and the surrounding area. His work was also known on the Eastern seaboard.

The style in jewellery between 1895 and 1910 was predominantly Art Nouveau, which combined either a form of stylised sculpture, as in some of Tiffany's work, or the mixture of precious metals and perhaps worthless stones, where the overall design becomes of more importance than the value of the piece. The Art Nouveau influence was to give way to a far more geometric style with patterns of small dots, circles and triangles, rather after the fashion of Josef Hoffmann.

Margaret de Patta, a painter and sculptress, began jewellery design in 1929, originating a structural style and introducing cuts which widened the visual scope of transparent gems. Paul Flato designed jewellery in Hollywood in the thirties with pieces such as 'shooting stars', a brooch made up of a spray of diamante stars. After 1930 the sculptor Alexander Calder designed some jewellery using hammered or twisted silver and brass wire. Man Ray also designed some jewels.

The Arts and Crafts communities fostered a revival in metalwork. The Roycrofters made wrought iron and the Roycroft Copper Shop was headed by Karl Kipp, from Vienna, helped by Dard Hunter who was primarily concerned with the book bindery. Kipp designed bookends, candlesticks, trays, vases and other household items which were then made by the other members of the Shop. The hammered copper was decorated with stylised designs, usually of flowers or trees. The work sold well, advertised through the Roycroft catalogues. Up to thirty-five men were employed in the Copper Shop. Kipp left Roycroft for a short period around 1912 when he founded his own Tookay Shop in East Aurora, although he continued many of the Roycroft designs.

In California Dirk van Erp opened the Copper Shop in Oakland in 1908, moving in 1910 to San Francisco. He had begun by making vases out of brass shell casings which he sold to a San Francisco gallery in 1906. At the Copper Shop he produced a range of copper lamps with mica shades as well as vases, trays and other items. His work was simple and he left the hammer marks to demonstrate the handmade qualities of his work. He retired in 1929 although he still continued to design some pieces until his death in 1933.

Top left 'American Beauty' vase in hand-hammered copper, made by the Roycroft Copper Shop, c. 1912.

Top right Inkpot, c. 1926, in hand-wrought copper with sprayed-on lacquer finish, made by the Roycroft Copper Shop.

Left Desk lamp in hand-hammered copper with mica shades made by the Roycroft Copper Shop, c. 1908.

Below Tiffany & Co. inkwell in carved ivory with crocidolite eyes, gilded leaves and enamelled top, c. 1900.

Germany and Austria

by Ian Bennett

Movements and Influences 1890–1940

OF ALL THE MAJOR MANUFACTURING countries, it was Germany which made the most serious attempt before the First World War to resolve the problems of designing machine-made products. Although the machine-versus-craftsman debate was carried on as vociferously as elsewhere, the solution was realised to lie not in the 'either-or' framework created by Morris in England or even the somewhat vague compromise of the Wiener Werkstätte in Austria, but in a realistic attempt at synthesis.

Art historically, the Germans were better prepared for such a synthesis than were the English or Austrians (the debate hardly touching the mainstream of French applied art at this time). A typical German interpretation of the English Arts and Crafts Movement can be found in the writings of Hermann Muthesius, one of the most influential architects and designers in the pre-Bauhaus era. Muthesius had spent seven years in England between 1896 and 1903 with the official task of observing and reporting on the developments in English architecture and design.

As a result of his English sojourn, Muthesius published *Das Englische Haus* between 1904 and 1905, in which he analyzed the architectural achievements of Richard Norman Shaw, William Godwin and others, architects who, in the 1890s, had already influenced many of the younger generation of Germans, including Spalding, Grenander, Hans Poelzig, Ernst Eber and Muthesius himself.

The concept of the *Gesamtkunstwerk* is strong in Muthesius' book, in which he devotes as much space to the integral fitments of buildings – lights, door handles, heating, plumbing, furniture – as he does to the architecture itself. However, in one crucial respect, he differed from the attitude expressed by the Arts and Crafts Movement: 'Let the human mind think of shapes the machine can produce. Such shapes, once they are logically developed in accordance with what machines can do, we may certainly call artistic. They will satisfy because they will no longer be imitation handicrafts but typical machine-made shapes.'

In *Das Englische Haus* and other works, such as the essay 'Kunst und Maschine' which appeared in *Dekorative Kunst* in 1902, Muthesius was the first and most important spokesman for the industrialization of design at the beginning of the century. There was, however, one very significant precursor of his arguments; this was the book entitled *Wissenschaft, Industrie und Kunst* published in Braunschweig in 1852 by the architect and critic Gottfried Semper. Like his English contemporaries, Semper was dismayed by the quality of work shown at the Great Exhibition of 1851 and believed that design would not flourish again on a worthwhile aesthetic level until the machine was used to its full potential.

The two magazines primarily responsible for the propagation of the Art Nouveau concept of design were *Pan*, founded by Julius Meier-Graefe in 1895, and *Jugend*, which began publication the following year, and gave its name to the stylistic movement in Germany. In Darmstadt, two was published *Deutsche Kunst und Dekoration*. In 1897, there appeared not only the three Darmstadt journals mentioned previously, but two others also, *Kunst und Handwerk* and *Dekorative Kunst*, both of which were published in Munich, the latter by Meier-Graefe again.

The Munich group designed metalwork, furniture and graphics. Paul and Pankok collaborated on interior schemes for the German Pavilions in the Paris 1900 and Turin 1902 International Exhibitions; Riemerschmid exhibited a room in Paris on the ubiquitous theme of a 'Room for an Art Lover', and at Turin Behrens exhibited the living-room interior he had designed for the home of Ludwig Alter. Members also worked on architectural commissions, the most important of which, with regard to Art Nouveau, was the Atelier Elvira, a photographic studio in Munich, the façade of which was decorated by August Endell between 1897 and 1898 with dramatic, swirling forms obviously influenced by Obrist. Two commissions won by Endell in 1901, the Sanatorium at Föhr and the Bunder Theatre, Berlin, both of which are of a more restrained appearance than the Atelier Elvira.

Most modern authors hold the view that the 'whiplash' Art Nouveau style all but disappeared from the work of the Munich group after about 1902–3. Pankok left for Stuttgart in the former year, while Behrens had settled at the Mathildenhöhe colony in 1899.

At Darmstadt in 1901, Behrens designed his own house, including every detail of the interior fitments down to the domestic crockery. Although possibly less organic than, for instance, Mackintosh's designs, there is an obvious curvilinearity about the interior and some of its appointments.

Another important influence on the curvilinear style of German Jugendstil was the Belgian-born architect, painter, designer and teacher Henry van de Velde. He had studied painting at the Antwerp Academy between 1880 and 1884, and in the latter year went to Paris, where he remained for a year.

Cover for *Deutsche Kunst und Dekoration* designed by Margaret Macdonald Mackintosh.

He made some personal contact with the Impressionists and Symbolists. He was invited to join Les Vingt, a Brussels Secessionist group, in 1889, at which time he began to paint in a Divisionist style. Four years later, however, encouraged by his fellow Belgian Willy Finch, he abandoned painting to devote himself to designing for the applied arts, to architecture and to codifying his theories of design.

In 1894–5, he moved to Uccle, near Brussels, designing both the architecture and interior furnishings of his house Bloemenwerf; into the façade of the building, he incorporated ceramics made by local craftsman under his supervision to the designs of Willy Finch; his fiancée, Maria Sethe, who had visited England, where she had interviewed William Morris, purchased English Arts and Crafts furniture and wallpapers for the interior, which blended well with the pieces designed by Van de Velde himself.

At this time, Van de Velde met both Bing and Meier-Graefe, the two most important entrepreneurs of Art Nouveau design; he exhibited work in Dresden in 1897 and decorated the Paris offices of *Dekorative Kunst* in the Rue Pergolese in 1898. In the latter year he also established his own decorating firm in Brussels with financial help from Count Harry Kessler. Largely through the

efforts of Meier-Graefe, his work and ideas became widely known in Germany.

In 1899, Van de Velde moved to Berlin, exhibiting at the salons of Keller and Reiner. He lectured extensively in Germany and Austria between 1900 and 1901 and in the latter year published *Die Renaissance im Modernen Kunstgewerbe*. In 1902, he published a collection of his lectures under the title *Prinzipielle Erklärungen*; it was in these lectures that he expressed one of the principles of his aesthetic philosophy: 'Ornament and its shape should express – symbolise – the object's function and nothing more. Through its shape it should clarify the aim of the object and allude to its function – always based on reason'.

In 1900, he collaborated with Willem Hirschwald, owner of the Hohenzollern Kunstgewerbehaus, on designs and in 1901, he was employed by the Grand Duke Wilhelm Ernst of Sachsen-Weimar 'to raise the artistic level of design' and to establish workshops in Weimar in which to train artisans. Work was successfully exhibited at the Leipzig annual fair and the Weimar Kunstgewerbeschule created a new approach to teaching and design – the artisans were encouraged not to produce 'one-off' pieces but to develop a new concept of design for mass-production.

Until 1907, the Weimar venture had been

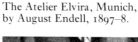

The Atelier Elvira, Munich, by August Endell, 1897–8.

private, but in that year the school became state-run and collaborated with commercial firms in the dukedom. Wilhelm Ernst did not, however, approve of the way in which the school was run and Van de Velde, as an alien, was forced to resign on the outbreak of war in 1914.

Throughout his career at Weimar, Van de Velde's work showed the influence of some of the leading German and Austrian designers, including Behrens, Olbrich and Hoffmann. Also, in the Villa Hohenhof, which he designed for the industrialist Karl-Ernst Osthaus in 1908, he showed that he was influenced by the English designers such as Baillie Scott and Mackintosh, the Villa itself being clearly based (as were many German houses at this time) on Baillie Scott's 'House of an Art Lover' scheme of 1900–1. On his resignation from Weimar, Van de Velde moved to Switzerland for the duration of the war. His recommendations for a successor included the young Walter Gropius, and it was Gropius who was given the appointment in 1919, the name of the institution changing its name officially on April 11 of that year to the Staatliches Bauhaus in Weimar.

The Deutscher Werkbund
In 1906–7, most of the Secessionist groups formed themselves into a single design association which

Left Bloemenwerf, Van de Velde's residence in Uccle, Brussels, 1895–6.

Bottom Project for Restaurant Webicht, Weimar, by Henry van de Velde, 1904.

Above The Tietz store in Dusseldorf, designed by Josef Olbrich, 1907–9.

Right Airship passenger saloon designed by Bernhard Pankok and illustrated in the Deutscher Werkbund yearbook of 1914.

Below Richard Riemerschmid's·furniture workshop of the Deutscher Werkbund at Hellerau.

called itself the Deutscher Werkbund (DWB). The instigator of this amalgamation was Karl Schmidt, who in 1898, had formed the Dresdener Werkstätte für Handwerkkunst, a workshop with a markedly commercial outlook, and one which was concerned primarily with designing for industry. Schmidt was a cabinet-maker by profession and furniture was the principal product of the workshop; he was also the brother-in-law of Richard Riemerschmid, who began designing standardized furniture units for the Werkstätte in 1905, units which were machine-made and designed for easy assembly.

The majority of leading designers in Germany, including Behrens, Riemerschmid, Pankok, Paul, Gropius and Van de Velde worked for the Werkbund and outside contributors showed at the great exhibition of 1914 in Cologne, including Hoffmann, who produced a somewhat decadent pavilion in a style reminiscent of nothing so much as Regency, which appeared a little strange in such surroundings. By 1909, the Werkbund could claim 731 members, including 360 artists and 267 manufacturers and retailers.

The DWB established itself at Hellerau, a garden suburb near Dresden. The idea of the garden city itself was the product of that peculiar mixture of nationalism, sociology and arts and crafts which runs through much German architecture and design at this time.

It was also the theme of numerous books, including the Austrian Camillo Sitte's *Der Städtebau nach seinen Kunstlerischen Grundsätzen* of 1889, one of the first and most important, and Muthesius' *Landhaus und Garten* of 1907. The nationalistic element was to be found most strongly expressed in the influential book by Julius Langbehn published anonymously in 1890 under the title *Rembrandt als Erzieher*, in which the blatant historicism of German nineteenth-century art and architecture was attacked, especially as the majority of historical models were not German but French and English.

At the same time, many of the leading young German designers were influenced by a series of books by Friedrich Ostendorf, in which the importance of geometry in architecture was stressed, and by a work published in 1907 by A. G. Meyer, *Eisenbauten; ihre Geschichte und Aesthetik*. Meyer's book was symptomatic of a move towards industrial processes in architecture first made truly apparent in Adolf Messel's Wertheim Department Store in Berlin, which was built between 1897 and 1904.

In the early part of the century, a number of architects, including Adolf Messel, Frans Schwechten and Otto Eckmann, were employed by Emil Rathenau, head of AEG, to design his company's buildings and some of its products. In 1907, however, Paul Jordan, technical director of the company, asked Peter Behrens to take on overall responsibility for design, and to bring a sense of corporate identity to AEG's products. At the same time, he was asked to design the company's new Turbine factory building on the Huttenstrasse in Berlin in collaboration with the engineer Karl Bernhardt, and to design and coordinate AEG's new factory complex on the Brunnenstrasse site in the suburbs of Berlin.

Working in Behrens's office as an assistant on the AEG projects was Walter Gropius; encouraged by the critical success enjoyed by the AEG buildings, Gropius contacted Karl Benscheidt, founder of the Fagus Shoe firm in Berlin. Benscheidt had commissioned a new factory building from Eduard Werner in 1909 but was known not to be satisfied with the proposed exterior. Gropius submitted a series of plans which was eventually accepted, and the building was erected between 1911 and 1914; Gropius worked in collaboration with A. G. Meyer to achieve this new advance in industrial architecture.

Nevertheless, at the Werkbund Exhibition in Cologne in 1914, in which over 100 members of the group and invited guests showed work, the strong hint of a compromise was to be seen. The exhibition included a model factory, with seventy working machines, designed by Gropius and a pavilion in glass and steel by Bruno Taut. Behrens's pavilion, however, was in a strongly Neo-classical style and Van de Velde's theatre remained in the 'organic' style associated with almost all his work. Even Gropius's furniture was of a sort one would not associate readily with his name – lush, veneered pieces in a style somewhat similar to French Art Deco.

Above The Wertheim Department Store in Berlin, designed by Adolf Messel and built between 1897 and 1904.

Left The administrative buildings (rear elevation) of the 1914 Werkbund exhibition, designed by Walter Gropius.

Below left Model factory designed by Walter Gropius for the 1914 Werkbund exhibition.

Bottom left Theatre designed by Henry van de Velde for the Werkbund exhibition of 1914.

Right Electric kettle designed by Peter Behrens for AEG, *c.* 1908.

Bottom The Fagus factory, built between 1911 and 1914, designed by Walter Gropius.

The Wiener Werkstätte

In 1897, Josef Hoffmann, Koloman ('Kolo') Moser and Josef Maria Olbrich were the protagonists in the founding of the Vienna Secession; its motto was *Der Zeit ihre Kunst – der Kunst ihre Freiheit* (Art for the times – Art must be Free). All three had studied under the Austrian architect and designer Otto Wagner who, from 1894, had been a professor at the Academy of Arts in Vienna and was regarded by the Secession as a father-figure.

Hoffmann's first attempts at furniture design for the Secession building in 1898 were simple, plain pieces with lattice decoration, which owed much to English Arts and Crafts woodwork. Only in the Paris 1900 Exhibition did he begin to produce pieces in a geometric style combined with rich materials. In 1898, Wagner himself designed the Majolika Haus, with its ceramic decoration in a curvilinear Art Nouveau style which owed much to French and Belgian precedents; in the same year, the Secession held its first group show and also launched yet another *The Studio*-type publication, *Ver Sacrum*. This was followed in 1900 by *Das Interieur*.

In 1903, with the backing of a young banker, Fritz Warndorfer, the Wiener Werkstätte-Produktiv-Gemeinschaft von Kunsthandwerkern in Wien was founded, with Hoffmann and Moser as artistic directors (Moser resigned in 1906). At one time, the Werkstätte employed 100 workers, among them being thirty-seven masters who signed their work. Joseph Eduard Wimmer joined in 1912 and Dagobert Peche in 1915.

In the early years, all the designing was carried out by the two artistic directors, including bookbinding, leatherwork, gold and silver, lacquer, furniture, enamels, jewellery and, of course, the complete designing of buildings. By the end of the decade, however, other artists and architects were regularly submitting designs for a wide range of objects; they included Gustav Klimt, Adolf Loos, Otto Wagner, Carl Otto Czeschka, Otto Prutscher, Michael Powolny and Berthold Löffler.

Adolf Loos, mentioned above, was one of the most important and accomplished architects of his day. From 1893 to 1896, he was resident in Chicago and thus had first-hand experience of Sullivan's architecture and teaching. He was one of the initial members of the Secession but after 1898, when he had a disagreement with Hoffmann, who refused to allow to exhibit a complete room in the Secession's exhibition, he ceased to be an official member of the group, although he continued his association with it and subsequently exhibited with the Werkstätte.

He published important books in the 1900s,

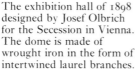

The exhibition hall of 1898 designed by Josef Olbrich for the Secession in Vienna. The dome is made of wrought iron in the form of intertwined laurel branches.

including *Ornament und Verbrechen* (1908) and *Architektur* (1910). He became one of the few Austrian supporters of Muthesius' ideas.

In 1904, the Wiener Werkstätte received its most important commission, which was possibly the most significant awarded to any of the European Secessionist groups before the First World War: the Brussels house of Adolphe Stoclet. This was for the building and interior.

The interior of the Palais Stoclet is almost a vocabulary of the early Wiener Werkstätte; all the leading designers worked on every aspect, from Klimt's mosaic frieze in the dining room, entitled 'Expectation' and 'Fulfilment' to the light fittings and door handles. The Werkstätte was given absolute freedom to choose the richest materials, and the house was filled with marble, glass and highly polished hardwoods. Apart from Hoffmann, Moser and Klimt, others who designed work for the interior included Carl Otto Czeschka, the ceramists Michael Powolny and Berthold Löffler, the sculptors Richard Luksch and Franz Metzner and the painters Leopold Forstner and Ludwig Heinrich Jungnickel.

Klimt's mosaic frieze, perhaps his most famous single work, was executed in materials which are ample testimony to the almost Byzantine extravagance of the interior – enamel, coral, semi-precious stones, gold and silver.

Poster advertising one of the annual exhibitions held by the Vienna Secession.

Above Silver tea service designed by Josef Wimmer, 1912.

Left Lamp designed by Josef Hoffmann, *c.* 1905.

Above Metal baskets designed by Josef Hoffmann, founder of the Wiener Werkstätte and a member of the Secession, *c.* 1905.

Right Box in various woods, designed by Kolo Moser, co-founder with Hoffmann of the Wiener Werkstätte, *c.* 1905.

Below Sitting room of the Palais Stoclet, designed by Hoffmann, rising through two storeys of the house.

Right Exterior view of the Palais Stoclet, Brussels, designed by Josef Hoffmann and begun in 1905.

Below Dining room of the Palais Stoclet, designed by Hoffmann, incorporating marble veneers and mosaics by Klimt.

The Weimar Bauhaus 1919–24

In 1915, Henry van de Velde recommended a number of successors to his post as director of the Weimar Kunstgewerbeschule, including Walter Gropius. Gropius had already formulated his theory of the unity of art and technology, and the unification of all the arts and crafts within an architectural whole – again the *Gesamtkunstwerk*. In 1916, he submitted a report to the Grand-Ducal State Ministry on his proposals for the school.

Gropius' appointment to the directorship was confirmed in 1919, and on 11 April the school officially changed its name to the Staatliches Bauhaus im Weimar. In the same year, Gropius published his *Programm*, in which he stated most clearly the principal of the *Gesamtkunstwerk* which was to be the Bauhaus goal: 'The ultimate aim of all visual arts is the complete building! . . . Architects, painters and sculptors must recognise anew and learn to grasp the composite character of a building both as an entity and its separate parts.'

The teaching programme at the Bauhaus included 'all practical and scientific areas of creative work'. The three principal areas were architecture, painting and sculpture, to which all other branches of the crafts were considered adjuncts. The various crafts taught at Weimar included stonemasonry, stucco and plaster, woodcarving, ceramics, all forms of metalwork, including blacksmithing and locksmithing, cabinet-making, stained glass, enamels, mosaics, etching, wood engraving, lithography, chasing, weaving, typography, interior and exterior design, stage design and landscape gardening.

In addition, students were expected to take courses in art history, the science of materials, anatomy and 'the physical and chemical theory of colour'. There was even a course on 'basic concepts of book-keeping, contract negotiations, personnel'.

It was realised immediately that there was a

Left Vases made in the ceramics workshop of the Bauhaus by Gerhard Marcks, *c.* 1922.

Below Silver tea service, made by Christian Dell in the metal workshop of the Bauhaus, 1925.

conflict between the attempts of the craft workshops to teach students how to make things and the fact that the Bauhaus masters (this term being adopted in preference to the more academically formal professor) had no personal experience of manufacturing. Thus, in each workshop, there was a master of form, who was responsible for aesthetic and functional theory and for designing, and one or two masters of craft, who could actually work with their hands.

At the Weimar Bauhaus, Gropius was the master of form in the cabinet-making workshop, Georg Muche and Oskar Schlemmer in the wood-working workshop and Johannes Itten from 1919 to 1923 in the metal workshop, being succeeded by László Moholy-Nagy from 1923 to 1927. Georg Muche was master of form in the weaving workshop from the founding of the Bauhaus, and he was one of the few masters to continue in the same position after the move to Dessau, remaining in charge of weaving until 1927.

In the sculpture workshop, Ittens was master of form until 1922, in which year he was succeeded by Schlemmer; the stage workshop, begun in 1921, was run by Lothar Schreyer until 1923, when Schlemmer took over. The mural workshop was run at Weimar by Ittens initially, who was succeeded in 1923 by Schlemmer and Kandinsky. Book-binding was run as an independent workshop for Bauhaus students by Otto Dorfner, while the printing workshop was run by Feininger, although the prime influence after 1923 was Moholy-Nagy.

The architecture classes at the Weimar Bauhaus were, ironically, the least practical. Gropius himself had his own practice, which he continued to run; occasional theoretical lectures were given by Adolf Meyer, while after 1923, some classes were taught by Muche and Marcel Breuer.

Students at the Bauhaus were first required to attend the basic course, of which the most important parts were the *Vorkurs*, the classes taught initially by Itten on the characteristics of materials and the processes of arts and crafts. After completing this basic course, they could then join the craft workshop of their choice, first as 'apprentices', then as 'journeymen' and finally, after having taken examinations, they were awarded the title 'master'.

From the beginning, the products of the Bauhaus workshops were well received by art critics. In 1923, the Bauhaus held an exhibition of its products, which Walter Passarge, in *Das Kunstblatt*, described favourably: 'Very beautiful textiles, ceramics, and metalwork . . . in all these works, one perceives the thorough training in craftsmanship.' However, it was not art critics which the Bauhaus had to attract, but the leaders of industry.

The Dessau Bauhaus 1925–32

In 1924, when it became apparent that the days of the Bauhaus at Weimar were numbered, the council for the school began discussions with the local government of Dessau, a heavily industrialised town. The response was encouraging and it was agreed that the school could be moved there, new buildings would be financed and the school would be given a generous annual subsidy. Many of the leading German art critics, museum directors and art historians came forward in support of the Bauhaus, but the Dessau city council instituted its own investigation of the school as it had existed at Weimar.

The investigators were greeted by a slide lecture given by Gropius. One of the team, Master Carpenter Wagner, Chairman of the Guild Committee of Dessau, wrote a detailed report of what he had seen and heard; perhaps unconsciously, he discerned that the flaw in the Bauhaus argument was exactly the same flaw as had undermined the high ideals of Morris and Co. in England. The public was not interested in art, a fact presumably well-known to commercial manufacturers; as a result, any commercially made piece of 'artistic' design was not likely to sell and therefore had to be marketed in small numbers at high prices. Most crucially, the products of the Bauhaus workshops were essentially individualistic, hand-made crafts not suitable for mass production.

On the move to Dessau, many of the criticisms voiced by Wagner and others were heeded, even if Gropius did not openly admit to have considered them. There is, for instance, a new air of reality about his *Principles of Bauhaus Production* published in 1926: 'The products reproduced from prototypes that have been developed by the Bauhaus can be offered at a reasonable price only by utilization of all the modern, economical methods of standardization (mass production by industry) and by large scale sales.'

At Dessau, the workshops were subjected to a thorough reorganisation. Ceramics, which at Weimar, had been taught in a separate building in Dornburg, with Gerhard Marcks as master of form, were dropped, as were woodwork, stained glass and bookbinding. After 1928, the cabinet-making and metal workshops were amalgamated into the new Department of Interior Design under Josef Albers and Alfred Arndt (the distinction

between master of form and master of craft was also abandoned). The weaving workshop, which had been one of the few commercially successful departments at Weimar, continued at Dessau with the same staff, Gunta Stölzl succeeding Georg Muche in 1927; Stölzl was succeeded as head of department by Anni Albers in 1931, who was herself succeeded by Lilly Reich in 1932. The sculpture workshop was renamed the plastic workshop, in charge of which was Joost Schmidt. The printing workshop was renamed the printing and advertising department and was under the joint directorship of Schmidt and Herbert Bayer, although the latter resigned in 1928. The mural department was run by Hinnerk Scheper, although from 1928 to 1931 when he was in Moscow, Arndt deputised.

Architecture remained on a somewhat insubstantial footing. The Dutch architect and town planner Mart Stam was invited to lecture between 1928 and 1929, and in the last year of the Dessau Bauhaus, Marcel Breuer was in charge of the department. A new workshop at Dessau was photography, started by Walter Peterhans in 1929. The stage workshop ceased to exist officially in 1929 after Schlemmer resigned.

Although the emphasis on art remained strong at Dessau, the teaching staff made a great effort to make the much-needed breakthrough into industry. Although the Weimar Bauhaus had had some successes, notably with furniture, typography and textiles, the Dessau Bauhaus proved far more commercially minded and enjoyed a greater success.

Its most notable achievements were the designing of a wide range of light fixtures, including the Kandem range of desk lamps, and also textiles, both woven and printed, and wallpapers. The first wallpapers were not produced commercially until 1929, but thereafter proved one of the Bauhaus' main sources of income.

Magazine storage shelves in cherrywood and mirror plate, designed by Walter Gropius at the Bauhaus, 1923.

Despite these commercial successes, the history of the Bauhaus after 1928 was not a happy one. The Dessau Government, like that at Weimar, was becoming strongly loaded with right-wing political groups, of whom the most powerful were the National Socialists. The old accusations of socialist leanings were hurled against the school, and more specifically at Gropius, at every discussion of the Bauhaus' budget, and Gropius took the view that his position as head of the school had become untenable.

His eventual resignation also prompted the resignation of Breuer, Moholy-Nagy and Bayer, followed by Schlemmer in 1929. His place was taken by Hannes Meyer, who has been described as having a 'fanatical commitment to a functionalist view of architecture'.

Meyer was sacked in 1930 by Fritz Hesse, Mayor of Dessau, who had always been the staunchest supporter of the Bauhaus, and who believed that only by taking such a drastic measure could he save the school from closing under fascist pressure.

On the recommendation of Gropius (an unconstitutional move – directors were supposed to be appointed only by a full council of the Bauhaus masters), Hesse appointed Ludwig Mies van der Rohe as the new director. Mies had first met Gropius when they were assistants in Behrens' office (a third assistant was Le Corbusier) and since 1926, he had been vice-president of the Deutscher Werkbund, with which organisation the Bauhaus had always maintained close links.

Throughout the 1920s, Mies had proved himself one of the foremost German architects; he had undertaken numerous important commissions, including the Weissenhof housing development in 1927 (for which he had designed the famous Weissenhof cantilever chair) and the German Pavilion in the Barcelona World's Fair of 1929 (for which he had designed the Barcelona chair).

Under Mies, architecture flourished at the Bauhaus, and the various departments which had proven to be of financial worth continued to be successful. However, by 1932, the position of the Dessau Bauhaus was untenable and the school was forced to close. In October, Mies managed to reopen what remained of it as a private institution in a disused telephone factory in Berlin. However, it still did not escape the attentions of the National Socialists and on 10 August 1933 Mies announced the final dissolution of the Bauhaus. It had existed a mere fourteen years, but despite its economic success between 1928 and 1930, it never had the same impetus after Gropius' departure. He had conceived it and perhaps no one else properly understood it.

Expressionist Design in Germany

Although the interwar years in Germany were naturally dominated by the Bauhaus, the Deutscher Werkbund continued to exist as a strong influence, and there were other important, although perhaps less permanent, movements. The most significant was Expressionism, the major impact of which was upon painting, but which also influenced music, architecture and films.

Gropius and Bruno Taut had been under the spell of Expressionist ideas before the First World War (and to a certain extent remained so afterwards), as can be seen from Gropius' design for a diesel locomotive in 1913. Hans Poelzig, an influential industrial architect, designed a chemical factory at Luban in 1911 which, like his watertower executed at Posen in the same year, is one of the few realised Expressionist architectural projects.

The most bizarre and extraordinary, however, was Rudolf Steiner's Goetheaneum 11, built of concrete in 1925–8 at Dornach to replace an identical wooden building erected in 1913 but destroyed by fire in 1925.

Below Adjustable ceiling lamp designed by Marianna Brandt and Hans Przyrembel at the Bauhaus, 1926.

Below right Chemical factory at Luban, designed by Hans Poelzig, 1911.

Opposite Slit gobelin with linen warp and cotton woof, woven in the weaving workshop of the Dessau Bauhaus by Gunta Stölzl, 1927–8.

Furniture

IN GERMANY, there was little furniture made in a purely Art Nouveau idiom. Van de Velde had designed a number of chairs and desks between 1897 and 1898 before moving permanently to Germany. These are curvilinear and organic, with a frequent use in the large pieces of inset stained glass. Although more restrained than the majority of French Art Nouveau furniture, it is arguable that Van de Velde's designs owe at least as much to the less florid pieces by designers such as Majorelle as they do to Mackintosh. Van de Velde's influence can be seen in the work of several German designers in the early part of the present century, especially that of Bruno Schmitz of Berlin.

In Germany itself, as we have mentioned before, a certain amount of commercial Art Nouveau furniture was produced, particularly by the Möbelfabrik Olbernau in Saxony, for whom Otto Weinhold worked as a designer. Heinrich Vogeler of Worpswede also designed interesting pieces but, with their obvious rusticity, they are closer to the 'nationalistic', 'peasant' furniture associated with many Eastern European designers.

The most important German designer of furniture in the early years of the twentieth century was probably Richard Riemerschmid. Like the work of other designers associated with the Werkbund – Karl Bertsch, Bruno Paul, Adolf Schneck and Paul Schmitthenner, for instance – Riemerschmid's furniture as a whole represents a strange stylistic mixture which it is difficult to categorise.

Some of his earliest pieces are in a plain English Arts and Crafts idiom, while others may be compared to the early furniture of the Prairie School architects.

Riemerschmid's associate in the Munich Secession, Bruno Paul, was capable of even greater variety, although it has to be said that there was always an element of richness in his work which is absent from Riemerschmid's most characteristic Typenmöbel designed for the Werkbund. In 1914, for instance, Paul designed a bizarre blue lacquer commode in an elongated version of German Baroque, and even as late as the 1930s, he was designing pieces for the Werkbund with thick, glossy veneers, although the forms were decidedly uninspired.

August Endell produced interesting furniture in traditional materials such as elm, but mixed with modern elements such as forged steel. Bernhard Pankok designed furniture which, of all that produced by Munich designers, was perhaps the closest to the more outrageous products of the Nancy and Paris Art Nouveau schools.

Although the emphasis at Hellerau was on simplicity, some designers, such as Karl Bertsch produced pieces that could be described as late Biedermeier. Adolf Schneck was responsible for the simplest, most carpenter-like, pieces, although the most characteristic early Werkbund designs are those associated with Riemerschmid. All of his furniture was designed to be made by machine, the joints overlapping and held together by screws. There were three price ranges, depending on the quality of the wood used, the cheapest being pine. Domestic furniture, especially fitted elements, were designed in such a way that the shape could be altered or expanded by the addition or subtraction of separate elements.

Karl Schmidt, who was responsible for marketing these and other products of the Werkbund, would market a design for only a year, thus avoiding the sense of *déjà vu* usually associated with mass-produced objects. By 1909, Riemerschmid and Bertsch between them had produced a vast quantity of designs, including over 800 varieties of chair. Many of the same architects and artists also produced designs for carpets, curtains and other domestic textiles; these included several of the designers connected with the Werkbund including Bruno Paul, Van de Velde, R. Grimm, A. Grenander, and Gropius, while E. Seyfried specialised in wall-papers. Peter Behrens was employed by the Anker Linoleum Company as a designer and several of the Darmstadt group also designed wallpapers for Alexander Koch.

The early furniture of the Wiener Werkstätte, despite its frequent use of expensive woods and various inlaid materials, was comparatively simple, Hoffmann's designs in particular owing much to Mackintosh and the more restrained elements of English Arts and Crafts. Later pieces, however, while still remaining angular, tend to become richer and several writers have commented on the fact that the Werkstätte furniture of the period between about 1908 and 1915, with its rich veneers, inlays and lacquers, foreshadows French Art Deco furniture of the 1920s. Even Otto Wagner's furniture is suprisingly rich in taste.

Almost all the Werkstätte furniture was made by outside Viennese firms, including the Kunstmöbelfabrik August Ungethium, the Werkstätten für Wohnungseinrichtung, M. Niedermoser und Söhne (with upholstery by Wilhelm Niedermoser) and Porteis und Fix. In the 1920s, some weird carved and painted pieces were designed by Dagobert Peche, although the majority of Werkstätte furniture of this late period, notably that designed by Hoffmann for his Austrian Pavilion at the Paris 1925 Exhibition, did not differ

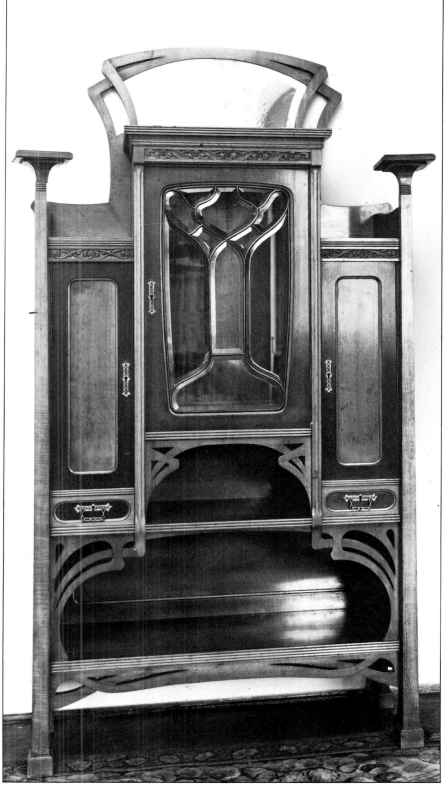

Left Longcase clock designed by Richard Riemerschmid, 1902–3.

Far left Cabinet designed by Otto Weinhold, *c*. 1900.

Below Round veneered table designed by Bruno Paul, 1935.

Left Dining chair designed by Richard Reimerschmid, *c*. 1900.

Far left Blue lacquered commode designed by Bruno Paul, 1914.

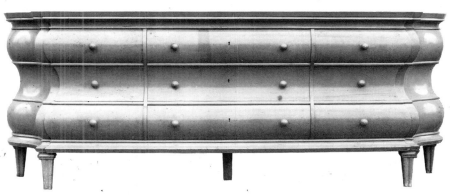

Above Armchair veneered in amboyna wood, designed by Koloman Moser, 1904.

Left Desk and chair designed by Josef Hoffmann, 1905, showing the influence of Charles Rennie Mackintosh and the English Arts and Crafts Movement.

much from pre-First World War examples; if anything it was richer and more ornate.

Following the war, the major impetus in furniture design in Germany came from the Werkbund and the Bauhaus. In the late nineteenth century, the Thonet factory, which had been producing elegant bentwood furniture for several decades, had farmed out its patents to some sixty factories all over Europe, employed a total workforce of around 35,000. Thonet continued to bring out new designs in the 1920s and 1930s, including examples designed by Ferdinand Kramer and Josef Frank. In 1927 Thonet marketed the chairs designed for the Weissenhof housing project by Mies van der Rohe in cantilevered tubular steel, with cane-work designed by Lilly Reich, the latter subsequently head of the Bauhaus weaving workshop.

The Weissenhoff development itself was probably the most architecturally prestigious enterprise of the twentieth century; the seventeen architects who each designed buildings included Behrens, Le Corbusier, Poelzig, Taut and Oud.

The major development in furniture design, and specifically of chairs, was the use of steel and other metals. In 1921, Adolf Schneck of the Werkbund, who worked in Stuttgart, and who was also involved on the Weissenhof project, designed a desk with chromium-plated legs. Schneck was also a pioneer in the use of inexpensive laminates, plywood and fibre-board, later used to good effect by the firm of Heinz and Bode Rasch, Josef Albers and Alvar Aalto.

The most influential period for Bauhaus furniture was the period immediately after the move from Weimar until 1928, during which time Marcel Breuer was in charge. Breuer's earliest furniture of 1922–3 was obviously inspired by Gerrit Rietveld and De Stijl – the famous Rietveld Berlin chair was first produced in 1917. By 1924–5, Breuer was using tubular steel for furniture and in 1925–6, as a private commission, produced in tubular steel and leather one of the most famous twentieth-century furniture designs, the Wassily chair. This was manufactured commercially by Standard-Möbel from 1926.

In 1926–7, Mart Stam and Mies van der Rohe both designed, apparently, cantilevered tubular steel chairs; evidence as to which came first is controversial, but there is some evidence that it may have been that of Stam. Mies' chair, the MR, was the first version of the Weissenhof chair and was manufactured by Berliner Metallgewerbe. The Weissenhof chair itself was marketed by Thonet, while Stam's design was manufactured by L. & C. Arnold. Breuer's tubular steel furniture designed for the Bauhaus Refectory was manufactured by Standard-Möbel from 1927, followed by the dining chair designed for the Bauhaus masters' private apartments and the chairs for the Bauhaus auditorium. Other Breuer designs were produced by Thonet.

In 1929, Mies van der Rohe designed what many would consider the single most brilliant piece of industrial furniture of the twentieth-century, the forged steel-strip and leather Barcelona chair which, despite its apparent simplicity, is a design which requires complicated and careful production techniques; it is extraordinarily luxurious in effect and has always been very expensive. Other, almost equally well-known Mies chairs are the cantilevered Brno and Tugendhat of 1930, both of which were designed for the Tugendhat house in Brno, Czechoslovakia; the former was produced in either steel-strip or tube, the latter in tube.

In the late 1920s, several other designers were working in tubular steel in Germany, including Mart Stam, Adolf Schneck, the firm of Heinz and Bode Rasch, Heinrich Bredendieck, Per Bücking, Heinrich Lauterbach (ex-Bauhaus students) and Walter Gropius.

Below The Wassily armchair in tubular steel and leather, designed by Marcel Breuer, 1925.

Below left The Barcelona chair in forged steel-strip and leather, designed by Mies van der Rohe, 1929.

Ceramics

GERMAN CERAMICS of the period 1890 to 1940 followed much the same pattern as in most other European countries. There were a few studio potters experimenting with new techniques, many small art potteries and some fine work done by some of the large established firms: in the case of Germany, by Meissen and Berlin.

Several individuals established themselves as potters in Germany in the 1880s and 1890s. The Von Heider family, Max and his three sons, Hans, Fritz and Rudolf, experimented with lustres at a kiln in Schongau, Bavaria. Max had established himself as a potter in Munich before moving to Schongau and his three sons were successful painters. Like many European potters, the Von Heiders were influenced indirectly by Hispano-Moresque lustres but it seems likely that their main source of inspiration was the work of Clement Massier in France and possibly Zsolnay in Hungary. Rudolf began working as an independent potter sometime after 1905, while his two brothers taught ceramics at the Magdeburg Kunstgewerbeschule.

Another German potter working in lustre was Franz Anton Mehlem of Bonn, who was given a special room in the German Pavilion at the Paris 1900 Exhibition; many of his pieces were painted by Frilling, and included panels composed of earthenware tiles.

Probably the most important German potter working towards the end of the nineteenth century was Hermann Mutz who had established his own factory at Altona on the Elbe in 1871. He was joined by his son Richard, who was also to become a distinguished potter, in 1893. Hermann's early pieces in earthenware have a rustic flavour but also show the influence of Japanese folk pottery, examples of which had been collected by Mutz's friend, Justus Brinkmann, first director of the Kunstgewerbe Museum in Hamburg. The Mutzes were also influenced by the stoneware of the French potter Jean Carriès and the lustreware by the Danish potter, Herman Kahler. The first stoneware was fired in about 1902, with abstract drip glazes in browns, blues and greens.

In 1904, Richard Mutz set up an independent workshop in Berlin. At this time, he began to collaborate on stoneware sculpture with his friends Ernst Barlach, their first commission being a portrait plaque of Brinkmann to celebrate the twenty-fifth anniversary of the Hamburg Museum in 1902. Barlach designed a number of pieces which were fired by Mutz, including a vase with grotesque handles which bears a remarkable resemblance to Christopher Dresser's designs for the Ault factory in the 1890s.

Barlach, although one of the great German sculptors of the twentieth century, also had a great influence on the development of ceramics in that country. In 1904, he had been appointed a Professor at the Staatliche Fachschule für Keramik at Höhr-Grenzhausen, Westerwald, and in 1908 wrote *Keramic, Stoff und Form* which was widely read. Apart from his work with Mutz, some of his sculptures of peasants and beggars were cast in white porcelain by the Schwarzburger Werkstatten für Porzellankunst. In the 1920s and 1930s, others were cast by Meissen, some in white porcelain and others in red Böttger stoneware.

In 1899, the painters Wilhelm Sus and Hans Thoma founded the Grossherzogliche Majolika Manufaktur at Karlsruhe in the Black Forest on the orders of the Grand Duke Friedrich I of Baden. The artistic director was one of Germany's best-known potters, Max Laeuger, who had studied painting in Paris at the Académie Julien in the early 1890s. Other ceramic designers working under him at Karlsruhe included Franz Blazek, who specialised in animal sculptures, Emil Pottner, a painter and printmaker from Berlin, and Fritz Behn, a Munich sculptor. Laeuger himself became an important member of the Darmstadt group, designing furniture, silver, carpets and posters in addition to ceramics. He also cast sculpture in stoneware for other artists.

Two other important German potters were Elizabeth Schmidt-Pecht and Julius Diez. The former was interested in neo-Rococo based on Dutch Delft. At the La Libre Esthétique Exhibition in Brussels in 1900, she showed vases in earthenware decorated in polychrome slip and with *sgraffito* decoration of flowers in an Art Nouveau style. Diez, known primarily as a book illustrator and poster artist, produced ceramics in much the same style as Schmidt-Pecht.

Many of the artists and designers connected with the Munich Secession and the Darmstadt group were involved with ceramics, either as makers or designers. Of these, the most important was Johann Julius Scharvogel, who had begun his career as a ceramist with the firm of Villeroy and Boch in the Saar in 1883, a firm which marketed its products, usually medieval and Renaissance inspired salt-glazed wares under the name Mettlach after the factory in the Rhineland originally owned by Jean-François Boch and which was one of the three factories which merged in 1839 to form Villeroy and Boch. Scharvogel remained at the factory until 1898. Later he became one of the founder members of the Deutscher Werkbund.

In 1906, Scharvogel was made head of the Grossherzogliche Keramischen Manufaktur at

White porcelain figure by Ernst Barlach, *c.* 1908.

Darmstadt, executing not only his own pieces but also those designed by other members of the artists' colony. Other factories also produced work designed by the Darmstadt artists, including Bauscher of Weiden, Krautheim & Adelberg, Josef Bock, Ohme, Meissen, Serapis, the porcelain factory at Burgau, Reinhold Hanke, the Waechtersbacher Steingutfabrik and many others.

Among other Darmstadt artists, Peter Behrens designed porcelain tableware for his own home around 1901, which was manufactured and marketed commercially by Bauscher Bruders of Weiden. In a delicate, angular Art Nouveau style, these pieces are in strong contrast to the overblown stoneware he designed for Franz Anton Mehlem of Bonn around 1900. More interesting are the medievally inspired jugs, usually with pewter mounts, he designed for the firm of Reinhold Hanke of Höhr-Grenzhausen around 1903.

Richard Riemerschmid designed very similar stoneware for Reinhold Merkelbach, another factory in Höhr-Grenzhausen, pieces which are easily confused with those of his colleague Paul Wynand, who had studied with Barlach at the Staatliche Fachschule für Keramik, from 1905. In 1906, Riemerschmid also designed a porcelain table service for Meissen, more traditional in shape than a similar service designed for the same factory by Van de Velde, and with rather clumsy and ugly handles.

Around 1902, Van de Velde designed some superb *flambé* stoneware which was executed by Reinhold Hanke. These pieces, with smooth, rounded bodies and angular but flowing handles, are in contrast to the work of the Darmstadt designers, seeming to bear no allegiance to past styles and reflecting the influence of such architects as Guimard and Horta, who were much admired by Van de Velde. Between 1903 and 1905, he was commissioned to design porcelain tableware by Meissen; these beautifully restrained pieces have moulded decoration and underglaze blue painting and gilding. They must rank among the most successful and beautiful industrial ceramics of this period.

Josef Emanuel Margold designed ceramics for Josef Bock's factory in Vienna and for Ernst Wahliss's Serapis factory in the same city. Ernst Riegel designed figure models which were made by Waechtersbacher Steingutfabrik.

Ceramics were taught at the Weimar Bauhaus, but the workshop was closed on the move to Dessau; it was felt that the teaching of ceramics exemplified a somewhat 'folksy' attitude which was far removed from the school's philosophy. Also, the use of architectural ceramics as an integral part of a building, which had become popular around 1900, was not well regarded by the majority of serious architects in the 1920s.

The Bauhaus pottery workshop was run as a separate studio at Dornburg. The master of form was the sculptor Gerhard Marcks and the master of craft Max Krehan. From 1923, Otto Lindig and Theodor Bogler were given their own design studio. This was when the pottery workshop itself was divided into the workshop for instruction and the workshop for production. Both Lindig and Bogler were Bauhaus journeymen.

Early Bauhaus pottery is surprisingly traditional, both in shape and decoration. Gerhard Marcks' designs in particular are based on traditional German and Flemish salt-glazed stoneware, embellished with 'naive' pictures on cobalt. Many of these pieces are, however, extremely attractive and may be compared with similar work done by numerous traditional American 'crock' houses in and around New York throughout the nineteenth century.

Bogler and Lindig were more concerned than Marcks with producing prototypes for mass production. Although interesting, their table wares do not compare with some of the products of the established factories such as Meissen. Some of Bogler's designs were produced by Velten-

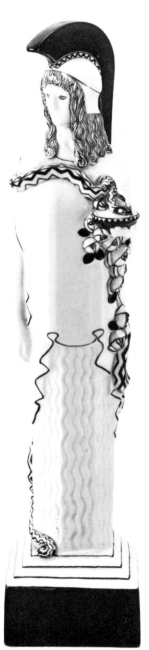

Above Ceramic figure designed by Michael Powolny, *c.* 1906.

Left Covered pottery jug, designed by Reinhold Hanke, *c.* 1906.

Vordamm and others by the Staatliche Porzellan-Manufaktur of Berlin. The majority, however, were produced in quantity from moulds by the production workshop of the Bauhaus itself.

The Staatliche Porzellan-Manufaktur in Berlin was one of the main producers of new design during the 1920s and 1930s. Apart from its association with some of the Bauhaus potters, it manufactured an extremely famous and widely selling porcelain service in 1930 designed by Trudi Petri and called Urbino. Another important service was the '1382' designed by Hermann Gretsch and manufactured by the Porzellaneschirr. Arzberg and first shown at the 1930 exhibition of the Deutscher Werkbund in Paris.

Throughout the period under discussion, the work of the major German factories was of considerable importance. Like Sèvres in France, Meissen and KPM (the Königlichen Porzellan-Manufaktur of Berlin, later the Staatliche Porzellan-Manufaktur) were at the forefront of new techniques and employed many talented outside designers and artists.

Berlin was probably the first factory in Germany to concern itself with new ideas. In 1878, it established a chemical and research department under the directorship of one of the most gifted European ceramic chemists, Hermann Seger, who is remembered primarily today for his invention of Seger cones in 1886, small ceramic pyramids which melted at different temperatures and thus enabled the heat within the kilns to be far better controlled than in the past. Seger also developed a very fine porcellaneous body capable of taking the extremely high temperatures required for the superb range of metallic oxide *flambé* glazes he had perfected. This body was known as Seger-Porzellan; *flambé*-glazed examples were exhibited for the first time in 1880 but were not manufactured commercially until 1883.

Seger continued working at Berlin until 1890. His colleague in the chemical department was Albert Heinicke who had joined Berlin in 1873. His speciality was crystalline glaze, which he had developed to a commercially viable stage by 1885. Sometime after 1900, Heinicke developed a fine porcelain body suitable for underglaze painting. He remained at the factory until 1910.

The artist directorship of the factory was under Alexander Kips from 1888 to 1908, being succeeded in the latter year by Scharvogel's erstwhile partner at Munich, Theodor Hermann Schmutz-Baudiss. The latter retained his directorship until 1926. Under the influence of its chemical and artistic directors, the work of the Berlin factory can be divided into four groups – glaze effects, sculptural Art Nouveau pieces and later figures in the Art Deco style, more formalised pieces which are close in feel to the Viennese work of Powolny, Löffler and others, and table wares.

Schmutz-Baudiss, known for his atmospheric, 'underglaze' paintings, was responsible primarily for the formalised, Viennese approach. In the late 1890s, he had worked at the Ganser factory at Diesen-Ammersee with two other distinguished Hermann potters, Paul Dresler (whose work was influenced by Middle-Eastern ceramics) and Auguste Papendieck. In 1897, he had become a member of the Vereinigten Werkstätten of Mu-

Opposite top Vase with putto filial made at the Königlichen Porzellan-Manufaktur of Berlin, modelled by Fritzsche and decorated by Flad, *c.* 1900.

Opposite bottom A pair of Seger porcelain vases with ormolu mounts, *c.* 1890.

Left Two figures produced by the Serapis Fayence factory in Vienna, *c.* 1925.

Below Stoneware bottle designed by Gerhard Marcks and executed by Max Krehan at the Bauhaus pottery workshop at Dornburg, *c.* 1922.

Bottom Stoneware jar and lid made in Vienna by Lucie Rie, 1930s.

nich. Designers at Berlin who were greatly influenced by Schmutz-Baudiss' style included Emil Rutte and Adolf Flad. Later modellers of figures, some of whom worked right through to the Second World War and after, included Paul Schley, Adolf Amberg, Hans Schwegerle, Anton Puchegger, Karl Himmelstross and Eduard Klabena; the last named is particularly well-known for his superbly modelled and brightly coloured birds.

Encouraged by the initiative of the Secessionist potters, Meissen began to produce interesting new work around the turn of the century. In 1903–4, they commissioned tableware from Henry van de Velde, having in 1896 been gratified by the popularity of their first important Art Nouveau service, Krokus, which was designed by Julius Konrad Hentschel.

Other freelance designers included Richard Riemerschmid and C. Paul Walther, and Meissen also cast figures by Ernst Barlach. Their most celebrated modeller during the years between about 1910 and 1930 was Paul Scheurich, who, in the 1920s, modelled attenuated, almost Mannerist, figures which were often cast in white porcelain. He is famous for a series of figures based on dancers in the Ballets Russes which were executed around 1914.

Above Three Meissen figures modelled by Paul Scheurich, *c.* 1920.

Right Ceramic clock designed by Michael Powolny, *c.* 1910.

Other factories which should be mentioned here are Nymphenburg, whose artistic director from 1906 to 1909. Josef Wackerle, was one of the best-known German ceramic modellers, and Rosenthal, which was founded in 1879. The latter factory made fine domestic wares, including three famous services, Darmstadt (1905), Donatello (1907) and Isolde (1910).

The involvement of the Wiener Werkstätte with ceramics began initially with the founding of the Wiener Keramik studio in 1905 under the joint directorship of Michael Powolny and Berthold Löffler. Powolny had been a pupil at the Vienna Kunstgewerbeschule and was one of the founders both of the Secession and the Werkstätte. He specialised in faïence figures of cherubs in white, yellow and black, as well as producing large, neo-Mannerist figures and animals. Löffler's work is similar. In 1912, the Wiener Keramik amalgamated with the Gmündner Keramik of Franz Schliess to form the Vereinigte Wiener und Gmündner Keramik GmbH.

The role of the Vienna Kunstgewerbeschule was crucially important in the development of Austrian ceramics at the turn of the century. In 1876, it had established a separate ceramic workshop with its own technical and chemical laboratory. Around 1900, special ceramic courses were arranged with workshops for decoration and glazing under Hans Macht. Moser and Hoffmann taught design, while at the same time having their own ceramics made by outside firms, of which the most important was probably the Josef Bock porcelain factory in Vienna.

From 1909 to 1932, the ceramic classes at the Kunstgewerbeschule were taught by Powolny, Löffler and Robert Obseiger, the last named having been a pupil at the school from 1909 to 1914. Thus the ceramic department of the Kunstgewerbeschule and the Wiener Keramik of the Werkstätte were linked by the same directors, who were also instrumental in gaining the patronage of outside firms for the potters they taught in the school.

Between 1900 and 1905, before Powolny and Löffler began teaching, pupils at the Kunstgewerbeschule included Jutta Sikka and Helena Johnova; at this time, they produced somewhat crude abstract glazed pots. In the period between 1910 and 1915, there was an immediate change of style. Pupils like Obseiger, Ludwig Schmidt, Julie Sitte and Rosa Krenn began to produce stylised figure models with subtle colouring. At that same time, these and other Kunstgewerbeschule pupils such as Fritz Dietl, Anton Kling, Emil Meier, Wilhelm Schleich and Anton Kleiber began designing for the Wiener Keramik. Two pupils, Emilie Schleiss-Simandl and W. Schuhl designed Gmündner Fayence.

Of the industrial factories associated with the Kunstgewerbeschule and the Werkstätte, the most significant was that of Josef Bock. This had been founded originally by Johann Kutterwatz in 1828 and was taken over by Bock in 1871; he remained the director of the factory until 1935. Among those who are known to have produced designs for the factory are Hoffmann, Moser, Rudolf Hammel, Antoinette Krasnik, Jutta Sikka, Therese Trethan, Hans Kalmsteiner, Johanna Poller-Hollmann, Otto Prutscher, Emanuel Margold and Dagobert Peche.

Particularly good tableware was designed by Therese Trese Trethan and Jutta Sikka around 1900–5 in angular, functionalist shapes. Tableware with simple black geometric ornament on white was designed by Hoffmann around 1908. Eduard Klabena, whose bird figures were produced by Berlin, modelled some pieces for Bock before he started his own Langensdorfer Keramik factory in 1911.

In 1885, Friedrich Goldscheider founded the Goldscheider'schen Porzellan-Manufaktur und Majolika Fabrik, with factories in Vienna and Pilsen. Some of the earliest figures were modelled by Arthur Strasser, who specialised in Middle Eastern subjects and Negro busts. Other figures included draped female forms holding shell-form lamps, some of which were signed 'Doebrich'. Many Kunstgewerbeschule graduates were employed on a permanent or freelance basis.

In 1892, the firm of Reissner, Stellmacher and Kessel was founded in Turn-Teplitz. The wares produced here were marketed under the trade-name Amphora; some of the porcelain is simple, with *flambé* glazes. However, the factory also produced elaborate figure sculpture, some of which was decorated with gold and inset with stones (Juwelenporzellan); these reached the height of vulgarity. Kunstgewerbeschule graduates included Michael Mörtl, who modelled animals, some of which were also produced by the firm of A. Förster & Co.; Arthur Strasser also produced designs for Amphora.

Another important Viennese factory was founded by Ernst Wahliss in 1863. Under his sons Hans and Erich, this factory began producing Serapis-Fayence around 1911. The best-known designers were Karl (Charles) Gallé, Franz Staudigl, Karl Klaus and Willibald Russ. Tableware was decorated with scrolling geometric motifs, usually in black and green, with profuse gilding; stylised figure subjects were also produced.

The Kunstgewerbeschule and the various factories described above continued in importance throughout the 1920s and 1930s, with the style of their products varying very little from the prewar pieces. The inter-war years also saw the founding of a small number of important factories, the best known of them being the Wiener Porzellanmanufaktur Augarten, founded in 1922–3. This factory, which produced both table and decorative wares, exhibited a large group of pieces at the 1925 Paris Exhibition, which was awarded a Gold Medal. Designers for Augarten included Hoffmann, Powolny, Prutscher and Valerie Wieselthier. Much important work was also produced by the Wiener Kunstkeramische Werkstätte Busch & Ludescher, which had been founded in 1908. Modellers included Bruno Emmel, Johanna Meier-Michel, Michael Mörtl, Anton Puchegger and Olga Sitte.

The 1930s saw a movement in Austrian ceramics away from the elaborate figure modelling which had by then become characteristic of the Kunstgewerbeschule and its admirers. Although Moser's students at the Kunstgewerbeschule at

Head of a girl, ceramic by Valerie Wieselthier, *c.* 1925.

the beginning of the century had produced simple pieces with strong forms and monochrome glazes, Powolny and Löffler had been responsible for a move towards figure modelling which gradually took on a more elaborate style, finally becoming quite Baroque.

This development reached both its high point and its culmination with the work of Susi Singer and Valerie (Vally) Wieselthier in the mid 1920s. Around 1930, Robert Obseiger, who had by then become the most influential teacher at the Kunstgewerbeschule, began to produce small vessels decorated with matt glazes of rich colour. These pots stand out from the surrounding mass of often whimsical figure modelling, as do those of one of the most brilliant pupils of the Kunstgewerbeschule during the 1920s, Lucie Marie Gomperz, who, as Lucie Rie, became internationally famous as one of the greatest studio potters after she had settled in England in 1938.

Other notable figures in Vienna in the mid-1930s were Gertrud and Otto Nazler, almost self-taught except for a few lessons with the Viennese figurative potter Franz Xavier Iskra. Like Lucie Rie, they had their first international success in Paris; Rie had shown her work in the 1925 exhibition and again in the 1937 show; in the latter, the Nazlers received a silver medal. Their work, like that of Rie and Obseiger at this time, is concerned with glaze and form.

Lucie Rie herself has indicated that the influence of some of the English studio potters, notably Bernard Leach, had spread to Vienna by this time and the English approach to pottery may have had more than a little to do with this new direction in Viennese ceramics. The Nazlers, like Rie, left Austria in 1938, settling in the United States. This new direction in ceramics, begun in England, can also be seen in the work of one or two German studio potters in the inter-war years, notably Richard Bampi and Jan Bontjes van Beek.

Glass

Loetz vase with pewter mount, c. 1900.

THE THREE GREAT NAMES connected with Art Nouveau glass are Gallé in France, Tiffany in the United States and Loetz in Austria, although many other factories and individuals were active as makers and designers in the period between approximately 1880 and 1914. Of these three, the least highly regarded today, in terms of the art market, is Loetz, possibly because the glass itself remains 'anonymous' and relates not to an individual but to a corporate image.

The Loetz factory was founded at Klostermühle in 1836 and was named Glasfabrik Johann Loetz-Witwe in 1848 by Suzanne, widow of Johann Loetz. In 1879, Max von Spaun became head of the factory, appointing Eduard Prochazka as works manager. Over the next eleven years, the factory produced seven varieties of decorative glass, many of which attempted to imitate the surface appearance of different hardstones. The first iridescent pieces were produced in the 1880s, and in 1898, the firm showed a major group of iridescent glass in the Vienna Jubilee Exhibition designed by Max von Spaun. Hoffmann, Moser, Prutscher, Peche and Powolny are all known to have designed pieces on commission for the factory, while Loetz executed pieces on commission for the Werkstätte.

Not surprisingly, members of the Werkstätte were involved as designers with most of the leading Austro-Hungarian glass houses at this time, as they were with most of the potteries. Apart from those mentioned in the previous paragraph, other important Werkstätte glass designers included Olbrich, Moser, Wimmer, Löffler, Jutta Sikka, Hilda Jesser, Vally Wieselthier, Reni Schaschl, Mathilde Flögl, Ludwig Jungnickel, Fritzi Löw-Lazar and Julius Zimpel.

Firms for whom the Werkstätte designed, or whom the Werkstätte commissioned to execute their pieces, included Loetz, Meyr's Neffe, Johann Oertel, Ludwig Moser & Söhne, Carl Goldberg and J. & L. Lobmeyr. They also designed pieces made by various glasshouses on commission for the important retailers, Bakalowitz of Vienna.

Of all the major Austrian firms, J. & L. Lobmeyr was considered the most prestigious, followed by Graf Harrach. Both these firms were located in Vienna. Lobmeyr produced table glass of very high quality; they also marketed decorative pieces, including engraved and etched work and superb enamelled pieces in the Middle-Eastern taste, the quality of the enamelling being far superior to that found on similar pieces being produced contemporaneously by Brocard in France.

Around 1910, the firm produced its first pieces designed by members of the Werkstätte. Hoffmann designed what is probably his best known range of decorated glass for Lobmeyr, pieces with opaque black or grey motifs on clear or matt glass, a type of decoration called 'bronzitdecor', which was taken up by other Werkstätte designers, especially Jungnickel. The factory continued to produce new designs by members of the Werkstätte throughout the 1920s and 1930s and even during the Second World War held an exhibition in Vienna which included pieces newly designed by Adolf Loos.

The Harrach glass house is less interesting. In 1898, it exhibited a group of attractive pieces in the Vienna Jubilee Exhibition which were obvious imitations of Tiffany, and in 1900, its display had widened its scope to include cameo glass in the style of Gallé and enamelled pieces decorated with designs after Alphonse Mucha. In 1901, the painter Julius Jelinek became artistic director and he commissioned designs from a number of the leading Czech Secessionists, including Jan Kotěra.

The Wiener Werkstätte was also closely connected with the firm of Ludwig Moser & Söhne of Karlsbad, which had been founded in 1857. Before the First World War, Hoffmann had designed pieces in opaque black or purple glass, faceted or moulded with human figures or foliate decoration.

After the war, other Werkstätte members, including Hilda Jesser, Wimmer, Peche and Zimpel also designed for the firm. Meyr's Neffe, founded originally in 1814, exhibited pieces in the Paris 1900 Exhibition; many of these were iridescent and of Persian shapes. Designers included Moser and Olbrich. In the 1920s, they produced pieces designed by Hoffmann and Moser, and a particularly extensive group by Prutscher. However, by this time they had become part of the Karlsbad Kristallglaswerkshutte of Ludwig Moser & Söhne. Two other firms producing good iridescent and cameo glass were Wilhelm Kralik & Söhne, which until 1881 had been one of the three factories known collectively as Meyr's Neffe, and Pallme-König & Habel.

The firm of Bakalowits in Vienna was the most prestigious retailer of glass, for whom many factories did exclusive work. In the late 1880s, Bakalowits began selling iridescent glass designed by Richard Bakalowits and Kolo Moser, this being made by Loetz. By 1889, they had commissioned designs from a number of younger German artists, including Olbrich, who designed a pair of crystal glass candlesticks. In the Paris 1900 Exhibition, Bakalowits showed pieces designed by Olbrich, Moser and Bertold Löffler, and iridescent glass lamps in curvilinear Art Nouveau metal mounts by Gustav Gurschner. A large group of pieces designed by Moser were shown in an exhibition in London in 1902 organised by *The Studio*.

Kolo Moser himself had spent six months in a glass manufactory before the Werkstätte was formed and had practical experience of production methods. Many of his tableware designs showed the hand of an innovator, his wine glasses, for instance, being made in one piece, as opposed to the usual three-section production. He designed much decorative iridescent glass for Bakalowits which was executed by Loetz, Meyr's Neffe and the Reinische Glashütten.

In Germany, there were a number of important Art Nouveau designers, the most significant of whom was probably Karl Koepping. He had trained as a painter and etcher in Munich but began experimenting with glass around 1895. He first took on Friedrich Zitmann, an expert glass blower, to execute his designs, but after a policy disagreement in 1896, his pieces were made by the Grossherzogliche Sächsische Fachschule und Lehrwerkstätte für Glasinstrumentmacher und Mechaniker. His tall, spindly pieces, with extraordinary curvilinear stems, were greatly admired and were retailed by Bing in Paris; he also produced elegant and beautifully coloured wine glasses in less outrageous shapes.

Koepping's erstwhile partner Zitmann began producing pieces in a somewhat coarsened version of Koepping's style, which also proved very popular, and around 1897 began making iridescent glass with bubbling and pitting. This was intended to imitate the surface effects of excavated Roman glass, the shapes of which Zitmann also copied exactly. Roman glass of this type was also the inspiration for Tiffany Cypriote glass, first made around 1895–6 (Zitmann may well have been inspired as much by this as by originals), and the Frankfurt firm of P. A. Tacchi was making direct copies of Roman glass with iridescence in the late 1870s. Good Art Nouveau glass was also designed by Desiré Christian for the Meisenthal factory in Lothringia.

The German Seccessionist involvement in glass was not as important as it was in Austria. WMF established a glass factory in 1881, principally to produce the glass liners for its metalwork. However, in 1883 they established a serious factory although the production of art glass did not begin until the 1920s; at this time, they marketed iridescent pieces called Ikora-Kristall and Myra-Kristall.

In the 1920s and 1930s, WMF commissioned designs from, among others, Richard Riemerschmid, Wilhelm Wagenfeld and Paul Haustein.

A collection of Loetz iridescent glass, *c.* 1900.

Above Set of glasses designed by Josef Hoffmann for Lobmeyr, *c.* 1910.

Right Decorated glass beakers designed by Hilda Jesser, *c.* 1920.

Below 'Islamic' enamelled glass vase by Lobmeyr, *c.* 1900.

Below right Two vessels in violet glass, designed by Josef Hoffmann, 1915.

Riemerschmid also designed glass for Ferdinand von Poschinger's Buchenau Glashüttenwerke in Bavaria. This firm produced many examples of Art Nouveau glass around 1900 in different techniques, which owed much to Gallé, Tiffany and Loetz. Another important designer for Buchenau was Betty Hedrich.

A series of tall-stemmed wine glasses produced by the Reinische Glashütten of Cologne around 1900 and similar set by Peill und Söhne datable to around 1910 have been attributed by some writers to Riemerschmid; a glass of the same type is illustrated in the Deutscher Werkbund yearbook for 1912. Some tall simple glass bottles were designed by Behrens around 1898 and may have been made at the glass factory established at Darmstadt, the Grossherzoglichen Hessisches Edelglasmanufaktur. From 1907, this factory was under the directorship of Josef Emil Scheckendorf, a member of the Munich Secession who had exhibited glass with the Vereinigten Werkstätten in 1901.

Another important German glass designer was Wilhelm von Eiff, who had studied briefly under Pankok at Stuttgart in 1913. In 1921, he worked for a short while for a firm established by Stefan Rath, a nephew of the Lobmeyr brothers, at Steinschönau, and in 1922 he became professor of engraving on glass and gemstones at the Stuttgart Kunstgewerbeschule. His engraved glass is of a very high quality, similar in style to that of Orrefors. Glass of the same type was produced by the Sachsischen Landesstelle für Kunstgewerbe, designed by Richard Sussmuth, Walter Nitschke, Anton Witt and Imgard Kotte-Weidaner.

In the 1930s, one of the most important designers of glass in Germany was the ex-Bauhaus student Wilhelm Wagenfeld. Glass was not a subject specially taught at the Bauhaus, although Wagenfeld saw, and was obviously influenced by, the glass table wares with metal and wood mounts designed in the metal workshop at Weimar by Krajewski, Tümpel and, most successfully, by Albers.

Wagenfeld remained at the Bauhaus until 1931, after which he became an independent designer specialising in glass and ceramics. In 1932, he designed a fireproof glass tea service for Jenaer Glaswerke Schott und Gen.

This firm had for long been one of the leaders of modern glass in Germany, having produced a simple glass tea service for the Werkbund in 1912 designed by Ilse Decho. If anything, the earlier tea service is of a more satisfactory form, although Wagenfeld's development of heat-resistant glass is of crucial importance. Wagenfeld also designed for the Vereinigte Lausitzer Glaswerke factory, Weisswasser/Oberlausitz, of which he became director, his facet-cut pieces being called Rautenglas; other designs were made for the Rosenthal Porcelain Factory glass division (the actual building for which was designed by Gropius), for the glass division of WMF and for Peill & Putzler. He established the Werkstätte Wagenfeld in 1954 and one of his best-known commissions of recent years was for the cutlery, crockery and trays on Lufthansa airlines. He will probably be remembered as one of the greatest Functionalist architects and interior designers.

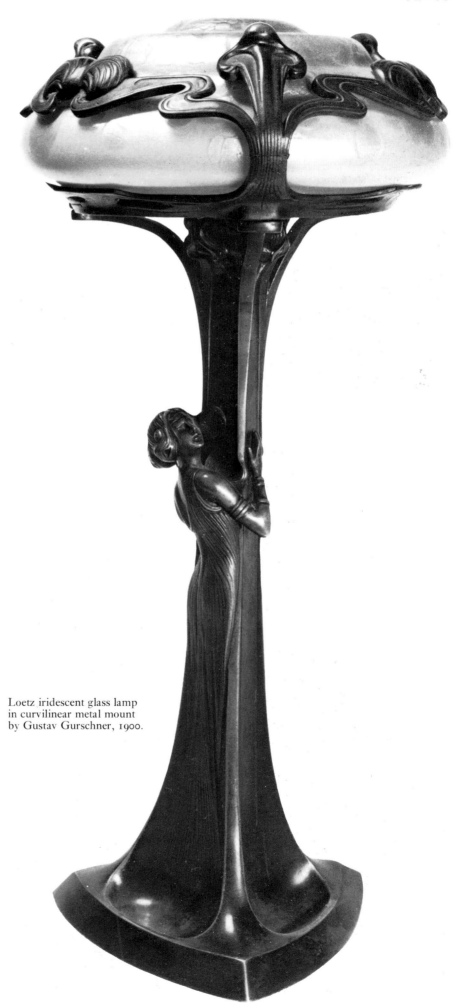

Loetz iridescent glass lamp in curvilinear metal mount by Gustav Gurschner, 1900.

Silver, Jewellery and Metalwork

AS WITH FURNITURE, the majority of the members of the main German and Austrian Secessionist groups designed in both precious and base metals, and the Wiener Werkstätte produced a wide range of jewellery, usually designed by Hoffmann, Moser, Prutscher, Czeschka, Peche or Wimmer; known workers (or actual makers) for the Werkstätte included Alfred Meyer, Alfred Wertnik, Konrad and Josef Hessfeld, Adolf Erbrech, Karl Medl, Josef Wagner, Theodor Quereser, Konrad Schindel, Konrad Koch and Karl Ponocny, the last named of whom seems to have made the majority of jewellery designed by Hoffmann and Moser. Another maker was Anton Pribil, who produced many of Czeschka's designs.

The Wiener Werkstätte's metalwork was made in an extraordinary range of styles. This is especially true of Hoffmann's designs. The earliest examples, dating from 1903-4, are often very formal, with simple, very 'modernist' shapes; in some cases, the pieces have a hammered finish. Pieces such as the silver tea service designed in 1904, with its monumental samovar, must rank among the greatest metalwork of the twentieth century. Much of this early work by both Hoffmann and Moser shows the obvious influence of Mackintosh, Ashbee and Van de Velde and, especially in the placement of handles and feet, of Christopher Dresser. Mackintosh's influence can be seen clearly in the open-lattice baskets designed by Hoffmann, which are strongly geometric, and Ashbee's in some flattened covered dishes designed also by Hoffmann and which date from 1908.

The influence of Ashbee on Moser can be seen in a tall stemmed covered cup in silver and lapis-lazuli designed in 1908, and the influence of Dresser most strongly in pieces such as the plain silver sugar bowl of perfectly spherical shape with four smaller spherical feet designed in 1905.

Hoffmann continued to design metalwork throughout his long career. In 1912, he founded the Österreichisches Werkbund and in 1920, he moved more into the realm of industrial design as head of the Gruppe Wien of the Deutscher Werkbund. In the 1920s, he produced many designs of similar monumentality to his prewar pieces but also designed some extraordinary fluted silver, much of which is gilt and some of which reaches the height of neo-Rococo extravagance. He produced many cutlery designs for the Solingen firm of Carl Pott, founded in 1906, and for the last of which he was awarded posthumous gold medals at the Brussels World Fair of 1958 and the Milan Triennale of 1960.

Czeschka also designed some very extravagant silver before the First World War, which is often inset with precious and semi-precious stones and ivory. The inspiration for such pieces seems Romanesque or Byzantine. Wimmer's early style often appears to have a strong Cubist element overlaid with an Expressionist exaggeration of form. This is particularly true of a faceted silver tea service designed in 1912.

In Germany, there was much very ornate Art Nouveau metalwork, especially by firms such as J. P. Kayser Söhne of Krefeld, who manufactured a wide range of pewter under the trade name Kayser-Zinn from 1874, and the Württembergische Metallwarenfabrik or WMF, which was founded in Geislingen in 1853 by Daniel Straub. Around 1900, under the directorship of Carl Haegele, WMF produced some of the most outrageously curvilinear Art Nouveau metalwork, usually in either pewter or nickle-silver, and often with green glass liners, to be found anywhere in Europe. The designer Hugo Leven was responsible for the finest Kayser-Zinn, while Beyschlag was the chief designer for WMF.

Several other firms produced interesting pewter, including the Metallwaren-Fabrik Eduard Hueck of Lüdenschied which founded in 1864 and which employed around 100 workers by 1900. The firm commissioned work from many of the leading Secessionists, including Peter Behrens, Josef Maria Olbrich and Albin Müller, the last named of whom had gone to Darmstadt in 1906, where he remained for the rest of his career. In Cologne, the Kunstgewerbliche Metallwaren-Fabrik H. Feith and A. Floch produced interesting designs under the trade-name Electra and in Nuremburg, an historic centre for the production of pewter, was the Kunstgewerbliche Metallwaren-Fabrik Orion of G. F. Schmidt and Friedrich Adler. The Weihlund had its own pewter workshop at Helltrau, designers of which included K. Kretschmer, Karl Kross, Konrad Hentschel, Paul Hanstein and Wolfgang von Wevin. Much good Art Nouveau jewellery was produced under Georg Kleemann at the Staatliche Fachschule für Edelmetall at Pforzheim.

Other commercial firms producing Art Nouveau silver and plate include M. H. Wilkens & Söhne of Bremen, founded in 1810. In the early years of the present century, they made ornate pieces designed by Heinrich Vogeler, and also simpler pieces by Behrens and Müller. Another Bremen firm, Koch & Bergfeld, employed many designers in its own studio and outside designers included Hugo Leven and Albin Müller. One of

Below Silver-gilt tea service designed by Josef Hoffmann, 1904.

Bottom left Silver teapot, sugar bowl and milk jug, designed by Henry van de Velde, 1903.

Bottom right Pewter tea service designed by Hugo Leven for J. P. Kayser Söhne of Krefeld and marked with the trade name of Kayser-Zinn, c. 1900.

Right WMF silvered metal liqueur set, *c.* 1900.

Below right Jewellery designed by Josef Hoffmann, *c.* 1904.

Below far right Edelzinn pewter jug designed by Josef Maria Olbrich, 1901.

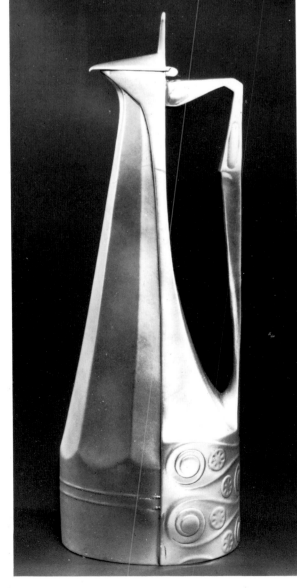

the largest and most important firms was P. Bruckmann & Söhne of Heilbronn, which had been founded in 1805. Designers included Behrens, Friedrich Adler, Paul Haustein, Josef Emanuel Margold, Franz Borès, Rudolf Rochga, George Roehmer and Bernhard Wenig. Bruckmann was also one of the major industrial firms to produce the designs of the Deutscher Werkbund.

The range of metalwork designed by Behrens for AEG should not be forgotten in this context; around 1900 Behrens also designed several ranges of cutlery for the firm of M. J. Rückert of Mainz, as did Richard Riemerschmid. The latter's designs tend to be simpler than those of Behrens, which retained strong elements of curvilinearity.

Possibly the most impressive of metalwork designers active in Germany in the first half of the twentieth century was Henry van de Velde. His early silver is in a style which can perhaps be described as 'geometric-curvilinear'; it may be compared to some of the earliest designs of Georg Jensen. A particularly fine group of Van de Velde's silver is in the Zürich Kunstgewerbemuseum and is of exceptional quality; the majority of it was made by the Grand-Duke's court jewellers at Weimar, Hans and Wilhelm Müller, or by Van de Velde's pupil Albert Feinauer.

Right Bronze lamp with nautilus shell by Gustav Gurschner, 1900.

Left High silver vase decorated with lapis-lazuli (1908) and spherical silver sugar bowl (1905), designed by Koloman Moser.

Below Brass ebony and silver teapot produced by Marianne Brandt at the Bauhaus workshop, *c.* 1924.

One of the most distinctive German silver-smiths in the early part of the century was Ernst Riegel who worked at Darmstadt between 1906 and 1912, after which he became head of the Staatliche Werkschule in Cologne. He designed much ecclesiastical silver in an ornate, monumental style, which seemed to owe much to Byzantine or medieval models.

The inter-war years saw few noteworthy developments in the design of German metalwork except at the Bauhaus. The firm of Treusch in Leipzig produced pieces influenced by French designers and by Jensen, and a few individuals, such as Bettina Krumbholtz, who was also active in Leipzig, made simple items often embellished with enamelling.

The metalworkshop at the Bauhaus was started at Weimar by a craftsman called Kopka; he proved unsuitable, however, and his place as master of craft or technical supervisor was taken by Christian Dell. The masters of form were Johannes Itten from 1919 to 1923 and László Moholy-Nagy until 1928; after the latter date, the workshop was incorporated into the Department of Interior Design, although Wilhelm Wagenfeld was placed in charge of metalwork production. From its earliest days, the metal workshop had a number of extremely gifted pupils, including Otto Rittweger, K. J. Jucker, Wolfgang Tümpel, Wolfgang Rössiger, Friedrich Marby, Josef Knau, Marianne Brandt, Josef Albers and Wagenfeld himself. Many of the best Bauhaus designs are associated with the names of Jucker, Brandt and Wagenfeld, the last named of whom subsequently became one of the most important industrial designers in Germany, his work in glass being particularly significant.

The earliest products of the Bauhaus workshop were not far removed from that of a normal craft studio, being principally in precious metals. This ceased after Moholy-Nagy took charge, and from

Below Silver duck on stand with semi-precious stones, designed by Ernest Riegel, *c.* 1910.

Right 'Flame Leaper', figure in ivory and metal by Frederick Preiss, *c.* 1930.

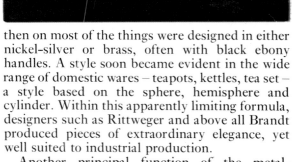

then on most of the things were designed in either nickel-silver or brass, often with black ebony handles. A style soon became evident in the wide range of domestic wares – teapots, kettles, tea set – a style based on the sphere, hemisphere and cylinder. Within this apparently limiting formula, designers such as Rittweger and above all Brandt produced pieces of extraordinary elegance, yet well suited to industrial production.

Another principal function of the metal-workshop was the designing of interior fittings, notably lamps and various lights. The light-fixtures designed at the Bauhaus did become one of the school's most valuable commercial assets. Extremely elegant examples designed by Mari-anne Brandt, Hans Przyrembel and Karl Jucker were industrially produced by a number of firms, including Schwintzer & Graff and Körting & Matthiesson, the latter marketing the Kandem range.

Attached to the metal workshop was a jewellery workshop which was run autonomously by Naum Slutzky; not surprisingly, it ceased to exist after Moholy-Nagy assumed overall responsibility for Bauhaus metalwork. Slutzky's extremely func-tional pieces – he designed a ring with a setting which enabled the stone to be changed at will – have had considerable influence, especially on Scandinavian jewellery design, during the years since the Second World War.

Weaving

WEAVING and later wallpapers were two of the most commercially successful fields of Bauhaus production. One of the principal departures of the Bauhaus weaving style was its rejection of the pictorial mode which had dominated late nineteenth-century and Art Nouveau hangings, the majority of which were in traditional tapestry weave. Many of the Bauhaus weavings were designed under the influence of Paul Klee, who took a particular interest in the workshop, but while these and other 'artist' designed pieces show a strong individualism, they are all in abstract patterning.

The products of the weaving workshop can be divided into four groups – individual pieces, commissioned works, series designs made in quantity at the Bauhaus itself and, fourthly, prototypes for industrial mass-production. The workshop was taken over by Gunta Stölzl in 1927 (she had been a Bauhaus student), followed by Anni Albers in 1931, and finally by Lilly Reich in 1932. These three, and other talented designers, including Lies Dienhardt, Martha Erps, Gertrud Hautschk, Ruth Hollos, Benita Otte and particularly Otti Berger all produced splendid work. Firms which produced Bauhaus textiles included Poly-textil Gesellschaft of Berlin and Pausa of Stuttgart. Wallpapers were produced by Rasch in 1930–1.

Above Woven silk tapestry made by Anni Albers at the Bauhaus weaving workshop by Anni Albers, 1926.

Left Cotton carpet designed for a nursery by Benita Otte at the Bauhaus, 1923.

Belgium

by Philippe Garner

Belgian design 1890–1940

BELGIUM, PERHAPS MORE than any other country, in the period 1890–1940, shows the very direct influence on the decorative arts of prevailing political circumstances. In the years before the First World War, under the kingship of Leopold II, Belgium enjoyed a strong and flourishing economy, backed by the wealth in natural resources of her extensive colonies. This new prosperity which was reflected around 1900 in the wealth of Belgian creativity and the strength of her luxury crafts, emerged from a period of considerable social unrest in the 1880s. After the fall of Belgium's Liberal government in 1884, the working class had rallied in 1885 under the banner of the Parti Ouvrier Belge and there had followed a disruptive succession of riots and strike threats.

After 1886, the Belgian socialist cause attracted the support of a number of middle-class liberal intellectuals, professional men such as the lawyer Max Hallet, who were to play a crucial role in the economic growth of the country and also in the conversion to the socialist cause of young artists, architects and designers. They created a rational link between their own socialist ideals and the emergent theories of design that were to harden into a version of Art Nouveau that was propagated and flourished as a truly socialist art, 'L'art du peuple'.

The principles of William Morris thus came to fruition in Belgium whilst failing to have any profound effect in his own country in the somewhat misguided realities of the British Arts and Crafts Movement. Max Hallet and his likeminded colleagues Jules Destrée and Emile Vandervelde formed close links with Henry van de Velde, perhaps Belgium's most important theorist and designer during the 1890s, and it was as a result of their lobbying that the Parti Ouvrier Belge was persuaded to employ the revolutionary architect Victor Horta to create their Maison du Peuple, built between 1895 and 1899. Despite Horta's protest that his selection as architect for the project was not political, the building stood as a monument to the democratisation of the Belgian applied and decorative arts.

The avant-garde of Belgian art had first manifested itself in the 1880s. Octave Maus, a spokesman for the movement, founded his progressive journal, *L'Art Moderne*, in 1881, whilst the most progressive artists formed themselves into the Groupe des Vingt in 1884 under the guidance of Maus. Les Vingt involved themselves at first in the promotion and exhibition of the avant-garde in the fine arts and showed works by Redon, Seurat, Lautrec, Gauguin, Cézanne, Van Gogh and others. The election to their ranks in 1888 of Henry van de Velde marked the beginning of their involvement in the applied arts, which they exhibited after 1891 at the annual salons alongside examples of the fine arts. In 1894 the group reformed as the Libre Esthétique and, at their first salon, the designer Gustave Serrurier-Bovy exhibited a complete range of domestic furnishings.

The Libre Esthétique formed the backbone of Belgian ideological Art Nouveau, embracing notably the work of Van de Velde, Serrurier-Bovy and Horta and reflecting both the principles of pioneer designer Viollet-le-Duc and the English theorists, and the prevalent stylistic preoccupations with Japanese art and with organic form. The import of Japanese artifacts into Belgium, as in England and France, can be traced back to the 1860s and notably to the opening of La Maison Japonaise in Brussels in 1866. Serrurier-Bovy retailed imported Japanese wares through his decorating business, opened in Liège in 1884. The crystalisation during the 1890s of these various elements combined with the rich and fertile thread of symbolism running through art and design, made turn of the century Belgium a major international centre for the arts.

The tide began to turn in the early years of the century. Van de Velde moved to Weimar where, in 1906, he supervised the foundation of the Kunstgewerbeschule. A new generation of designers came very strongly under the influence of the Austrian Secession style and turned their backs on Belgium's own dynamic organic style. In so doing they sacrificed Belgian independence and it seems a highly appropriate symbol of this new lead from Austria that one of Josef Hoffmann's major achievements, the Palais Stoclet, should have been commissioned by a Belgian and built between 1905 and 1911 in Brussels. The circumstances of the First World War made the Belgian arts the victims of political factors just as, in the 1890's, political factors had helped revitalise the applied arts. After 1918 Belgium became a follower rather than a leader in the applied arts; her foremost architects, men such as René Braem and L.-H. de Koninck, showed a very strong debt to the Viennese school; French decorating firms such as Dominique found a market for their designs; it is symptomatic that Herbert Hoffman's seminal 1930 study of international modern interiors devotes only two pages to Belgian designs, illustrating two uninspired Modernist Brussels interiors, one by Victor Bourgeois, the other interior by L.-H. de Koninck.

Left The dining room of the Hotel Solvay, designed by Victor Horta and constructed between 1894 and 1898.

Above Interior by the architect L.–H. de Koninck, 1930.

Below Dining room of a house in the Hague designed by Henry van de Velde, 1898.

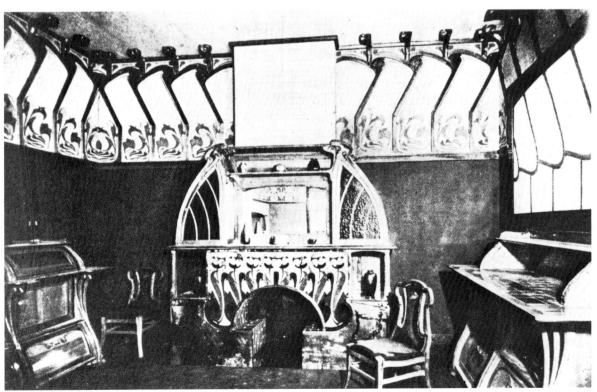

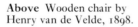

Above Wooden chair by
Henry van de Velde, 1898.

Above right Interior of
the Paris shop, La Maison
Moderne, designed by
Henry van de Velde for
Julius Meier-Graefe in 1898.

Right Two women's
gowns designed by Henry
van de Velde, 1900.

Furniture and interiors

Belgium's foremost designers of the Art Nouveau
period were architects of total environment,
concerned with every aspect of design from
architectural structure to the smallest details of
furnishings and domestic utensils. Henry van de
Velde took this to the extreme of designing the
clothes to be worn in his interiors. Their schemes
can be compared, despite superficial national
distinctions of style, to the concepts of Hector
Guimard in Paris, Charles Rennie Mackintosh in
Glasgow and Josef Hoffmann in Vienna.

Henri van de Velde was perhaps the most
versatile Belgian designer of his generation and the
influence of his theories were to help shape the
direction of European design through the first
quarter of the twentieth century. A self-taught
architect, Van de Velde had started his career as a
painter working in a broad graphic style reminiscent of Maurice Denis and showing the strong
influence of Japanese wood blocks. He expounded
and published his theories of design and put them
into practice when he designed and fitted out his
own home, Bloemenwerf, at Uccle in 1894, achieving an organic whole that made it the embodiment
of his principles and a landmark of modern design.
Van de Velde's use of robust organic lines,

abstracting not the entire plant form, but only the essential stem from nature, created a distinctive new style. The commissions received by Van de Velde to create four room settings for Bing's Maison de L'Art Nouveau in 1895 and to design Julius Meier-Graefe's influential Paris shop La Maison Moderne in 1898 are evidence enough of its success. The tobacco shop designed by Van de Velde in 1898 in Berlin for the International Havana Company is a perfect example of his fully-developed Art Nouveau style. There is a sense of total unity between the dynamic abstract rhythms of the furniture, the fitted cabinets and woodwork and the stencilled wall decorations.

Victor Horta underwent a formal training as an architect and became a fervent disciple of Viollet-le-Duc's principles of structural honesty. Although his Maison du Peuple served as his most perfect credo, Horta was at his best in the design of private houses with few budgetary restrictions. Like Van de Velde, he conceived both structure and furnishings and, like Van de Velde, he made full use of the abstract curving line. Horta's style was more lush, however, than that of Van de Velde and could create an ambiance of luxury which one does not associate with the more spartan 'honesty' of Van de Velde's furniture and interiors. Horta

Far left The dining room of the Horta House in Brussels, begun in 1898.

Top right Detail of the dining room door moulding.

Above Entrance hall of the Emile Tassel House, by Victor Horta, 1893.

Left Fireplace in the Van Eetvelde house designed by Victor Horta from 1895–7.

was at his peak for a period of some ten years which began with his design of a home for the engineer Emile Tassel in 1893.

Horta's interiors were full of light and the vitality of his ever-present patterns of whiplash curves never detracted from the sense of space which he always conveyed. The metal structure of his interiors was laid bare, but Horta's skill was such that the structure itself came to play a role within the decorative concept of the whole, its lines echoed in the metal whiplashes of light fittings and furniture, in the graphics of window-leading or mural decoration. Horta's masterpiece was his Hôtel Solvay, constructed between 1894 and 1898. His major works include the Van Eetvelde house of 1895–7, his own home, now the Musée Horta, undertaken in 1898, the Aubecq house of 1899–1902 and the house commissioned by Max Hallet in 1902.

Paul Hankar was amongst the more talented of the second rank of Belgian architect-designers working in the shadow of Horta and Van de Velde. He designed homes for a number of artists including a villa for his friend Philippe Wolfers in 1900. Others worthy of note are Paul Saintenoy, Gustave Strauven, a former apprentice chez Horta, Emile van Averbeke and Paul Vizzavona.

Aside from the architect-decorators, the most important furniture designer and decorator was Gustave Serrurier-Bovy. A true product of his age, brought up on the teachings of Viollet-le-Duc and the English Arts and Crafts Movement, Serrurier-Bovy devised a personal, honest style of furniture design in the early 1890s akin to that of Van de Velde and characterised by simple yet emphatic organic lines. He exhibited at the London Arts and Crafts Exhibition in 1896 and at the Paris Salon du Champ de Mars between 1896 and 1903, and, in 1899, opened a factory at Liège for the large-scale manufacture of his designs.

Glass

In the *arts du feu* Belgium's foremost factories in the period 1890–1940 were the glassworks of Val-Saint-Lambert and the Kéramis potteries founded by the Boch family in 1841. With both ceramics and glass, as with other areas of the applied arts in Belgium, it was only before the First World War that production was inventive and worthy of international attention. The successful growth of the Val-Saint-Lambert works dated back to the formation in 1826 of the Société Anonyme des Verreries et Cristalleries du Val-Saint-Lambert. By 1890 the works were featuring prominently in international exhibitions and, during the period 1890–1910, under the artistic direction of Léon Ledru, produced a wide variety of exciting glass-ware ranging from the functionalist pieces designed by Van de Velde to more elaborate coloured and decorated glass showing the influence of innovations made by Emile Gallé in Nancy.

The Kéramis works enjoyed the benefit of the creative directorship of Alfred William Finch for a brief period between 1890 and 1893. Finch, a painter, had been a founder member of Les Vingt and, in 1891, included Kéramis ceramics in the group's Salon. He injected a new vitality into Belgian pottery design and the wares made under his direction reflect the prevailing avant-garde taste for simple graphic motifs abstracted from nature. It is a typical reflection of the international stature of pre-First World War Belgian decorative art that Finch's ceramics were retailed in one of the most adventurous shops in Paris, La Maison Moderne. The Vermeren-Coché potteries, around 1900, made a series of stoneware masks inspired from Belgian folklore after models by the sculptor Isidore de Rudder.

Metalwork and jewellery

Only during the first phase of the period 1890–1940 did Belgium produce any designers or craftsmen of note in the area of metalwork, silver, jewellery and decorative sculpture. Belgium's most distinguished craftsman-designer of the Art Nouveau period, whose work is comparable in quality to the best contemporary French creations and whose technical versatility compares with that of René Lalique, is Philippe Wolfers.

Wolfers was born into a family of jewellers and learned the skills of the craft in his father's workshop. During the 1880s he worked on pieces in eighteenth-century taste before evolving a personal style in the early 1890s. Along with others of his generation he turned to nature for inspiration, stylising plant forms in a manner that betrayed the debt to Japan. Wolfers used plant, animal and human forms in his jewellery designs which were often given extra piquancy by their Symbolist allusions. His jewels could include such details as a medusa mask in carved ivory and gold with staring opal cabochon eyes or a carved ivory nude restrained by gold serpents. Another jewel, for example, a pendant entitled *La Nuit* of 1899, incorporates a naked figure carved in carnelian, with enamelled butterfly wings. Wolfers was a master of the techniques of enamelling and used the *plique-à-jour* process that was enjoying such a vogue in Paris. He favoured unusual contrasts of materials and exploited the colours and irregularities of semi-precious stones. He designed models to be cast in bronze, elaborate contorted Art Nouveau silver mounts for glass vases from the Cristalleries du Val-Saint-Lambert and silver vessels to be richly decorated with enamels. After 1904 he abandoned jewellery to concentrate on the extraordinary multi-media sculpture in which he had started to specialise during the 1890s.

A regular feature in Wolfers' scuplture and in the work of other Belgian decorative sculptors after 1893 was the incorporation of carved ivory. The vogue was encouraged by King Leopold II after the first importation of ivory from the Belgian Congo in 1893. Leopold made gifts of ivory to a group of prominent sculptors and craftsmen and the earliest results of this sponsorship were exhibited at the Exposition Universelle held in Antwerp in 1894. Examples of such work include the symbolist bust, *Sphinx Mystérieux*, of 1897 by Charles van der Stappen; *Orchidée*, Arthur Craco's fluid sculpture in ivory and gilt-bronze of 1894, originally included in the 1894 Antwerp exhibition, and the extraordinary candlestick conceived by Franz Hoosemans as a carved ivory figure of a woman entwined in giant thistles.

Henry van de Velde's dynamic graphic style was well adapted to the design of a variety of metalwork from luxury silverware to the more functional objects that were to become a more major preoccupation during his years in Germany. The design of silver jewellery allowed the opportunity for the unrestrained exercise of his principles of dynamic rhythm and interplays of organic lines and forms. His metalwork masterpiece is perhaps the electro-plated candelabrum exhibited at the Libre Esthétique in the late 1890s and purchased in 1900 by the Musées Royaux d'Art et d'Histoire. In its total synthesis between form, function and decoration this object can be cited as a perfect resolution of the stylistic and theoretical problems which Art Nouveau designers sought to resolve. Van de Velde's designs for domestic metalware ranged from elegant flatware to somewhat cumbersome stoves. Horta and Serrurier-Bovy designed metal furniture and fittings as part of their total vision as *ensembliers*. In future, designers were not to see their artifacts singly, as isolated objects, but as part of a total planned environment.

The architect Antoine Pompe produced a series of designs around 1900 for metal tableware, ironwork and jewellery in a refined Art Nouveau style, but his concepts were never executed. Fernand Dubois created silverware and other luxury objects in a more naturalistic version of Art Nouveau. He had been the pupil of Charles van der Stappen and became a friend of Horta who built a house for him between 1901 and 1906. Like so many other leading Belgian designers he regularly incorporated carved ivory into the works he exhibited at the Libre Esthétique between 1894 and 1899.

Amongst the few exponents of the luxury crafts in Belgium after the First World War was Philippe Wolfers' son Marcel who became an accomplished artist in lacquer. He experimented with the medium on vases and other vessels of simple traditional Oriental forms, achieving unusual effects of texture, unusual natural patternings and added refinements of gilding and mother-of-pearl inlays.

Above Henry van de Velde's electro-plated candelabrum, late 1890s.

Left Lacquered pot and cover by Marcel Wolfers, 1920s.

Right Ivory and bronze head by Julien Dillens, *c.* 1895.

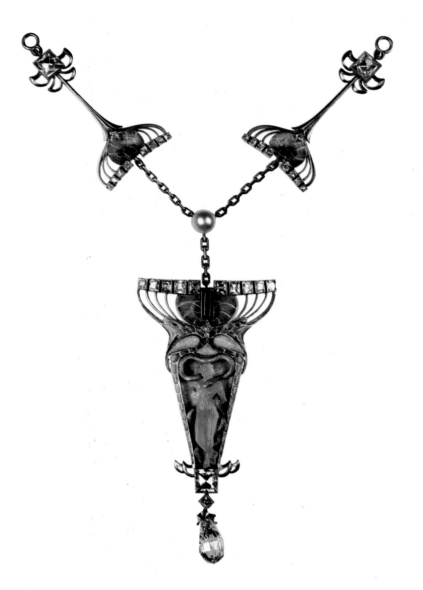

Graphics

Belgian graphics were dominated around the turn of the century by a decorative Art Nouveau style that showed strong affinites with the Paris style as epitomised by Alphonse Mucha. Foremost of the Belgian artists in this decorative vein was Privat-Livemont. He had studied in Paris and returned to Belgium in 1889 to work as a decorator. His first commission to design a poster came in 1890 from the Cercle Artistique de Schaerbeek and during the nineties he showed his strength in such posters as those for 'Absinthe' 'Robette' designed in 1896, 'Bec Auer' of the same year, 'Cacao Van Houten' of 1897 and 'Café Rajah' of 1899. Privat-Livemont's style used themes very similar to those of Mucha, notably Art Nouveau women with arabesques of stylised hair, and as a result he has been accused of plagiarism. However, the two artists evolved independently and Privat-Livemont's graphic motifs and colour schemes were distinctive and personal. The craze for collecting posters developed in Belgium as it did in Paris and the leading retailer, Dietrich, would supply collectors with the work of the foremost designers who included Privat-Livemont, Victor Mignot, Henri Meunier, Adolphe Crespin and Fernand Toussaint. Meunier's style was strong, simple and confident, as can be seen at its best in his poster *Rajah* of 1897. Crespin is perhaps best remembered for his association with the architect Hankar for whom he designed a poster in 1894. Theo van Rysselberghe was a close friend of Octave Maus and figured prominently in Les Vingt and the Libre Esthétique, designing several of their exhibition posters. Armand Rassenfosse founded the *Caprice Revue* with Emile Berchmanns and Auguste Donnay and all three exhibited their graphics at the Libre Esthétique. Perhaps the most significant Belgian poster, certainly the most characteristically Belgian, was Henry van de Velde's 'Tropon' of 1898.

Above 'Eve', a pendant designed in 1901 by Philippe Wolfers; opals, diamonds, emeralds and pearls set on gold.

Right Lithograph by Privat-Livemont, 1900.

Opposite The 'Tropon' poster by Henry van de Velde, 1898.

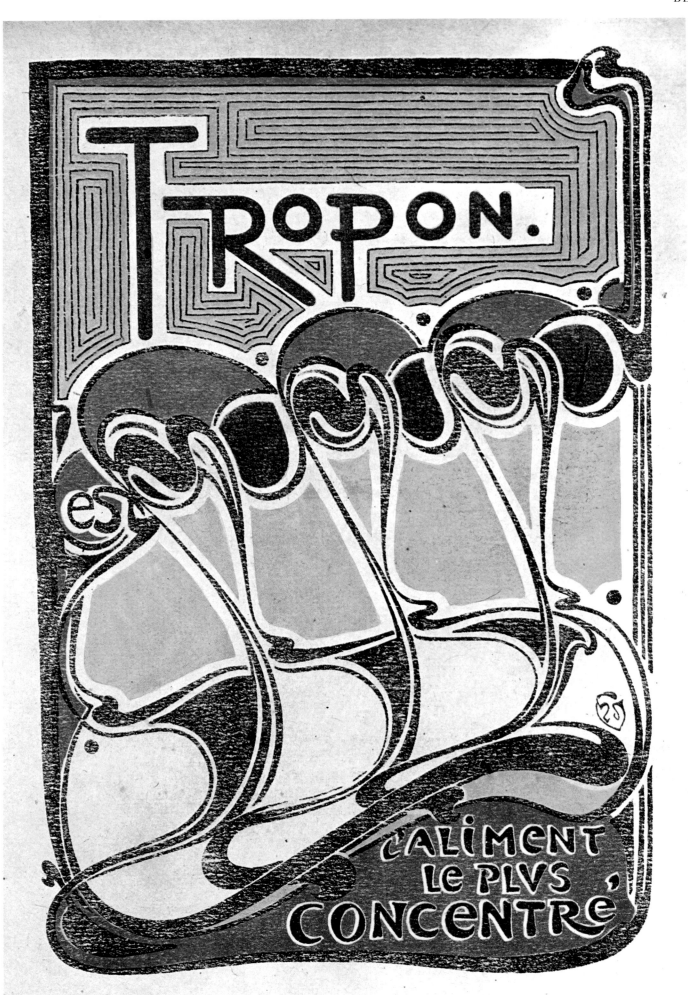

The Netherlands

by Gillian Naylor

The 1890s in the Netherlands

THE IMPETUS FOR DESIGN innovation and reform in Holland, as in most West European countries, stemmed partly from the expansion of trade and industry during the nineteenth century and partly from the activities of a growing and articulate architectural profession. Throughout the period under review, Dutch architects were active as designers, theorists and teachers, demanding and achieving standards appropriate to their various philosophies of form and structure.

The first attempts to examine and establish standards for applied design, for example, came in the 1870s, when the architect P. H. J. Cuypers began working on two important commissions in Amsterdam – the Rijksmuseum (1876–85), which now houses an important collection of Dutch Art Nouveau, and the Central Station (1886–9). Soon after he had started work on the Rijksmuseum, Cuypers, who had studied under the French architect and theorist Viollet-le-Duc, founded the Quellinus school (named after a seventeenth-century Flemish sculptor) in order to train the craftsmen needed for work on the museum; and in 1881 he established two further museum schools: the Rijksnormaalschool voor Teekenonderwijzers, to train drawing teachers, and an Arts and Crafts School (Rijksschool voor Kunstniverheid).

These schools helped to fulfil a need for professional training that had been growing more acute in Holland during the nineteenth century, and were the first of many similar organisations, societies and associations that were founded from the 1870s onwards in order to promote better standards in design, architecture and craftsmanship. In 1871, for example, the Association for the Promotion of Industrial and Handcrafts (Vereeniging tot Bevorderung van Fabrieks-en Hand-nijverheid) had organised an exhibition in Amsterdam on the theme of 'Art applied to Industry', with such disastrous results that in that same year a Museum of Industrial Art was founded in Haarlem. In 1893, several architects who had worked in Cuypers' office (including K. P. C. de Bazel, J. M. L. Lauweriks and J. M. de Groot launched the *Architectura et Amicitia* society, which brought together artists working in various fields; and in 1904 V. A. N. K., the influential Dutch Society of Arts and Crafts (Nederlandsche Vereeniging voor Ambacts-en Nijverheidskunst), was set up in order to combat what was felt to be the 'pernicious' influence of Art Nouveau.

For by this time Art Nouveau, inspired by Belgian precedent, was spreading throughout Holland; and its forms, as well as its philosophy, ran counter to the social and aesthetic ideals established by the Dutch design reformers, ideals which were reinforced by the work and theory of that remarkable and frequently underestimated architect, H. P. Berlage.

Berlage, like Cuypers, was not trained in Holland, and had studied at the Institute of Technology in Zurich, in the department of architecture founded by Gottfried Semper. Although Semper had left Zurich four years before Berlage began to study there, his influence, naturally enough, still predominated. From Semper, Berlage inherited the conviction that architecture aspires to order and objectivity, and that 'style' is determined by structure, which itself is determined by materials and purpose. Semper's thesis, elaborated in his seminal book *Der Stil in den technischen und tektonischen Kunsten* (1860–3), that man-made forms, like natural forms, should be determined by the logic of fitness, function and adaptability, was reinforced in Berlage's case, by the latter's study of contemporary botanists and zoologists, most notably Ernst Haeckel, whose book, *Kunstformen der Natur*, published in 1899, drew analogies between fine art and craft forms and natural forms in marine organisms. Again a further, and in view of subsequent developments, influential dimension was added to Berlage's theory through his preoccupation with Hegelian philosophies, which convinced him of the necessity for 'style', which he defined as the essence, rather than the appearance of architecture. So that Berlage, a Utopian Socialist in the tradition of Ruskin and Morris, campaigned through his work and writing, for the demonstration of a new philosophy of form: a universal 'style' in art, architecture and design that would reflect as well as promote the achievement of social and aesthetic harmony.

Such a style, however, could not, in Berlage's opinion, encompass the vagaries and eccentricities of Art Nouveau which, at the turn of the century, were being promoted by disciples of Henry van de Velde, the Belgian painter turned architect, designer and theorist. In 1898, for example, J. Thorn Prikker, the Symbolist painter (who also worked as an interior designer, producing wallpapers and fabrics, including batik work), and Chris Wegerif, a furniture designer, had opened Arts and Crafts, a shop in The Hague, which, in spite of its British name, sold furniture and objets d'art which Berlagian theorists condemned as 'unhealthy'.

In 1900 Berlage opened t'Binnenhuis, his own

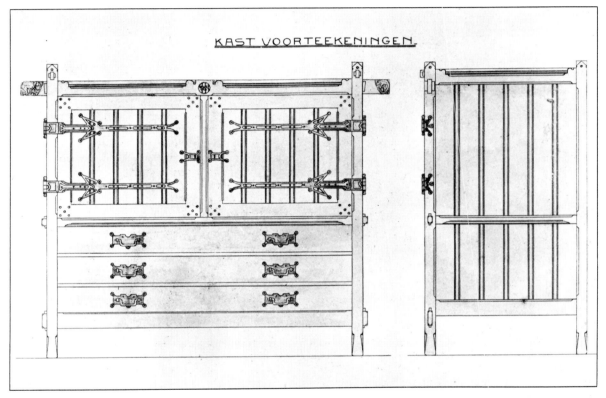

KAST VOORTEEKENINGEN

Above left Cabinet
by H. P. Berlage, *c.* 1900.
Above Chair designed by
H. P. Berlage *c.* 1904.
Below Linen damask,
by Chris Lebeau, *c.* 1895.

shop in Amsterdam, in order to sell furniture and furnishings designed to demonstrate his belief in the demonstration of structure and truth to materials. His approach to furniture design, which was derived from Semper's *Der Stil*, and which anticipates that of Gerrit Rietveld, was defined in *Over Stijl in bouw-en meubelkunst* (On Style in Architecture and Furniture Design) published in Amsterdam in 1904: 'A piece of furniture', he wrote, 'consists of the composition of parts into a firm whole, of which the parts serve as a framework for the panelling.'

The influence of Berlage on subsequent generations in Holland is obvious; for on the one hand the De Stijl group inherited his preoccupation with the structure and symbolism of space and form, while the Amsterdam School, also working in the 1920s, shared his confident demonstration of materials and texture.

Dutch design 1890–1920

At the same time, however, the achievements of the Dutch Art Nouveau designers, in spite of contemporary condemnation, were remarkable, not only for their invention and refinement, but for their demonstration of a specifically national variant of the style. Art Nouveau elements,

Above 'Delftsche Slaolie'
poster by Jan Toorop, 1895.

Right 'Narcissus' design
for fabric, by Michel Duco
Crop, 1890.

Far right Vase by the
Zuid Holland Pottery at
Gouda, c. 1900.

predictably enough, first began to appear in the work of Dutch Symbolist painters, most notably Thorn Prikker and Jan Toorop who were both associated with the Belgian Les Vingt group; and Art Nouveau tendencies in graphic design and illustration were re-inforced following an exhibition of British graphic art in The Hague in 1893. Toorop, for example produced his famous posters for 'Delftsche Slaolie' in 1895, and these designs, with their tense line, and obsessively two-dimensional vitality, demonstrate a quality of abstraction unique in Art Nouveau graphic design at that time.

A similar abstraction is also evident in Dutch textile design during this period, and a source for these exotic and proto-expressionist patterns can no doubt be traced to Holland's long-established trading links with Java and Indonesia. Dutch traders had, of course, been bringing in work from the colonies in the East Indies since the late sixteenth century; as in other European countries, however, the Art Nouveau renaissance in Holland prompted a new interest in the work of alien cultures (most notably of course, as far as France, England and Austria were concerned, in Japan), and during the last decades of the nineteenth century, several Dutch designers and textile manufacturers 'rediscovered' Javanese batik work, on the one hand experimenting with the traditional craft methods, and on the other adapting and simplifying the complex processes involved for mass-production. Thorn Prikker, for example, produced batik-inspired work for the Arts and Crafts shop in The Hague, and Agatha Wegerif-Gravesteyn, the wife of Chris Wegerif, also experimented with batik in their workshops in Apeldoorn. Several other leading designers, most notably Theodorus Colenbrander, C. A. Lion Cachet, the architect K. P. C. de Bazel and Juriaan Kok also worked in batik, while Michel Duco Crop designed machine-printed textiles for P. F. van Vlissingen & Co. of Helmond in the 1890s; dress fabrics, damasks and moquettes were also produced, those by Jaap Gidding and Jacob Jongert for Leo Schellens of Eindhoven being characteristic of Dutch Expressionist design in the 1920s.

Dutch ceramics, glass and silverware were also remarkable for their variety and invention at the turn of the century. The most celebrated designer specialising in ceramics during this period was Th. A. C. Colenbrander who, in spite of Berlage's dismissal of him as a 'craftsman of little importance', produced a wide range of unique and individual designs throughout his career. His bizarre and delicate work for the Rozenburg pottery in The Hague is well known, and towards the end of his life he designed an equally idiosyncratic collection for the Ram pottery at Arnhem – work which is distinguished by its flame-like and abstract patterning. Juriaan Kok, J. Schellink and R. Sterken also worked for Rozenburg. Other potteries which produced interesting work during this period include that of Wed N. Brantjes at Purmerende, the Zuid Holland at Gouda and the Amstelhoek factory, the latter introduced designs by C. J. van der Hoef at the turn of the century: vases etc, decorated with simple, almost naive, geometric patterns a

Top Tea-set designed by Juriaan Kok for the Rozenburg pottery in the Hague, 1903.

Above Clock by L. W. Nieuwenhuis, c. 1904.

Above right Rozenburg eggshell earthenware vase, c. 1900.

complete antithesis to the sophisticated delicacy of Rozenburg. Among Dutch silversmiths, Jan Eissenlöffel was probably the most inventive, but Frans Zwollo and the architect Johannes Lauweriks also worked in silver, while Berlage and de Bazel designed glassware, the latter for Leerdam.

In comparison with contemporary work in Belgium and France, Dutch furniture design at the turn of the century seems sober, restrained and even monumental, the designers achieving richness and variety from their choice of materials and decoration, rather than from plasticity of form. Dutch bourgeois traditions no doubt influenced design in this area, as well as that respect for sound construction and the honest use of materials recommended by Cuypers and Berlage. The work of Chris Wegerif, for example, for the Arts and Crafts shop in The Hague, has hardly a hint of mannerism, and is reminiscent of that of Voysey, while that of Gerrit Wilhelm Dijsselhof obviously also derives some inspiration from English Arts and Crafts achievements. Dijsselhof designed this furniture for a private client, Dr. van Hoorn, and much of the 'luxury' furniture produced during this period was for special commissions. The Rijksmuseum, for example, has furniture designed by Th. W. Nieuwenhuis, and C. A. Lion Cachet who were working for Van Wisselingh of Amsterdam. The most prestigious of these pieces were for Th. G. Deutz van Schaik, who had a house on the Frederiksplein in Amsterdam.

There is a direct stylistic link between this furniture, with its sobriety of form and richness of decoration, and that produced by the Amsterdam school designers and architects of the 1920s. For the design philosophy of architects such as Michel de Klerk and Piet Kramer was derived as much from the Art Nouveau stress on individualism and experiment, as from Berlage's demonstration of

the nature of materials. So that while the Dutch variant of Art Deco is as lively, idiosyncratic and inventive as its French equivalent, Dutch design in the 1920s was motivated by an ideal of social purpose rather than the demonstration of luxury, 'taste', and conspicuous consumption.

De Stijl and after

A very different interpretation and demonstration of the ideal of social purpose in design, however, was developing in Holland during the First World War, based on concepts of form and commitment that were also derived from the theories of Berlage. For the De Stijl group of architects and designers, who issued their first manifesto in November 1918, believed that art, architecture and design should aspire to universality rather than individuality, and that a universal 'style' was, in fact, emerging, that would both symbolise and precipitate universal harmony.

The initiator and most articulate member of the group was Theo van Doesburg who edited the *De Stijl* magazine from its inception in 1917 until his death in 1931. Van Doesburg was trained as a painter, but in the period immediately prior to the First World War, he worked as an art critic, reporting on the activities of the European avant-garde in various Dutch magazines and newspapers. The revelation of the work and philosophy of the painter Piet Mondrian, however, convinced him that universality and objectivity were attainable in design and architecture as well as painting. (Mondrian, who had been working in Paris, returned to Holland just before the outbreak of the 1914–18 war, and was painting his *Pier and Ocean* series at Scheveningen when Van Doesburg encountered him and his work.) This conviction was reinforced by his discovery of the contemporary work of architects such as J. J. P. Oud, Jan Wils and Robert van t'Hoff, who were all designing buildings with strongly stressed horizontals and

Right Chair by C. A. Lion Cachet, *c.* 1904.

Far right Armchair designed by M. de Klerk, *c.* 1913.

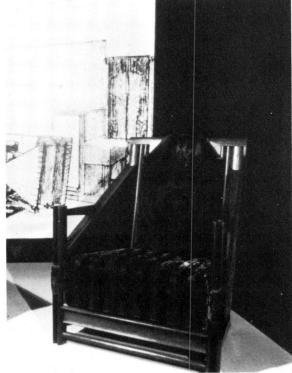

verticals. (Wils and van t'Hoff returned from the States just before the war with first-hand knowledge and photographs of the work of Frank Lloyd Wright, while Oud came back from Germany, renouncing his former Arts and Crafts allegiances for what he described as 'Cubist' architecture.)

The De Stijl belief that progress and perfection, on both a material and metaphysical level, could be demonstrated by means of the new formal and spatial harmonies made possible by the use of materials such as steel, concrete and glass, was of course, shared by designers and architects in France, Germany and Russia, and Van Doesburg travelled widely throughout Europe in the 1920s, exchanging ideas with other like-minded theorists. By 1925, for example, De Stijl had an international membership, Van Doesburg having recruited campaigners from Russia, Austria and the Bauhaus.

The most remarkable and influential of the De Stijl designers, however, was Gerrit Rietveld, a carpenter by training, who studied architecture in evening classes and who designed two of the most famous 'icons' of the Modern Movement: the Red-Blue chair in 1917, and the Schroeder house in Utrecht in 1924.

Rietveld, who was the son of a cabinet maker, set up his own furniture workshop in 1911; his early work is simple and carefully hand-crafted, in keeping with the Dutch Arts and Crafts tradition. In 1916, however, he was introduced first to the painter Bart van der Leck, at that time a member of the De Stijl group, and then to the architect Robert van t'Hoff, who asked him to copy, from photographs, furniture by Frank Lloyd Wright for the *Huis ter Heide* (1916). The Red-Blue chair was designed a few months after this, its formal and spatial innovations no doubt inspired by Rietveld's recent encounters with new attitudes to materials and form. The chair was, in fact, designed as a personal experiment but, following

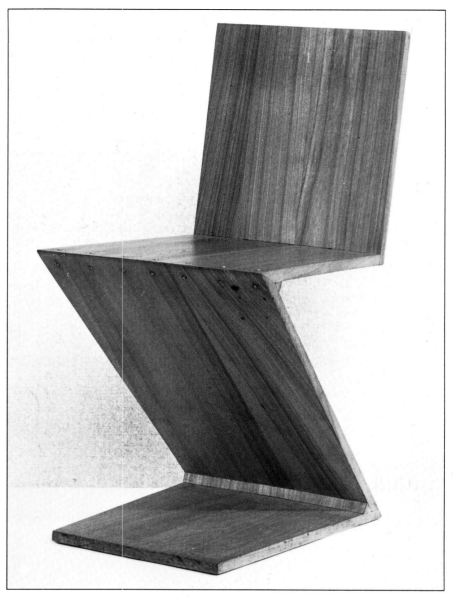

Above Zig-zag chair by Gerrit Rietveld, 1936.

Left Crate chair by Gerrit Rietveld, 1936.

its illustration in *De Stijl* magazine, it became widely known in avant-garde circles throughout Europe. 'The so-called Red–Blue chair,' Rietveld subsequently wrote, 'the chair made of two boards and a number of laths, that chair was made to the end of showing that a thing of beauty, e.g. a spatial object, could be made of nothing but straight machined materials. So I had a plank sawn into strips and laths; the centre part I sawed into two halves, so I had a seat and back, and then, with the laths of various lengths, I constructed the chair. When making that thing, it never occurred to me that it would prove all that meaningful for myself and possibly for others; that it would even have an impact on architecture.'

Rietveld continued to work as an architect and furniture designer throughout his career (his final work, completed after his death, was the Stedelijk Van Gogh Museum in Amsterdam).

The majority of his furniture designs were experimental, but several, including the 'crate' chair and table (1934), the zig-zag chair (1934), and an upholstered armchair (1935) were manufactured by the Metz retail store well known for its support of modern design and designers.

The need to demonstrate the new ideologies through designs for mass-production was, of course, a primary aim of Modern Movement designers, who also campaigned for the use of materials that would, in their opinion, be light, efficient, durable, and, if produced in sufficient quantities, inexpensive. Tubular steel, which fulfils all these requirements was widely promoted during the 1920s and 1930s, and Rietveld designed several chairs using the material. It was Mart Stam, the Dutch functionalist architect, however, who produced one of the first cantilevered chairs in tubular steel (1924–6), and W. H. Gispen, originally an 'art' metalworker who had opened his own small factory in Rotterdam in 1916, was producing designs for serial production in tubular steel by 1925, as well as promoting functionalist philosophies.

One of the most interesting of the design organisations that has survived since the 1920s, however, is the Weverij de Ploeg, which was first established as an idealistic agricultural community at Best, in Brabant, in the years following the First World War. The original community was dissolved, and in 1923 some of its members, believing that industry must supplement the ideal of agricultural self-sufficiency, set up a small weaving mill in the village of Bergeyk. Their efforts and endeavours were recognised and supported by several cosmopolitan designers, including Mart Stam; and Otti Berger, a weaving instructor at the Bauhaus designed many of their early fabrics. The firm has maintained a remarkably high standard of design since the 1920s, and in 1956 commissioned Gerrit Rietveld to design a new factory, which produces printed textiles as well as weaves, the majority designed in their own studios.

Since the turn of the century, therefore, Holland has produced an active and inventive design profession, whose achievements, while reflecting European as well as international developments, remain essentially national, demonstrating the profession's ability to relate its idealism to practical requirements.

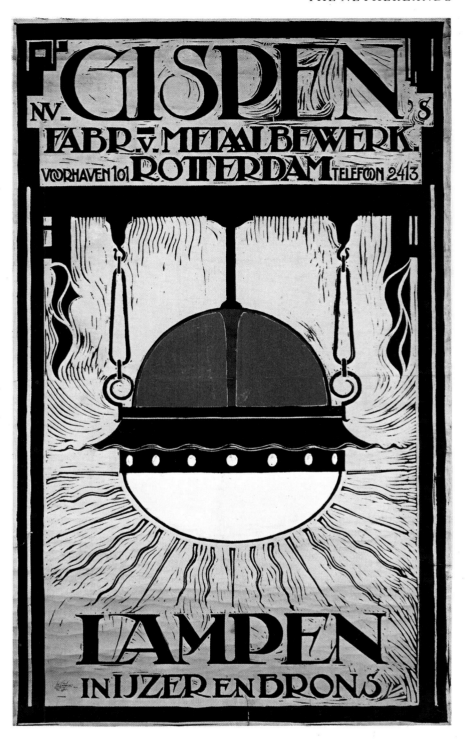

Opposite The Red–Blue chair by Gerrit Rietveld, 1917.

Above Poster by W. H. Gispen, 1921.

Left Hanging lamp of glass and metal by W. H. Gispen, *c.* 1925.

Scandinavia

by Ada Polak

IN THE COURSE OF THE PERIOD from 1890 to 1940, the Scandinavians emerged from being mainly imitative in the decorative arts to holding an important position in European design; in some fields and at certain periods their influence spread beyond their own countries. During the 1930s the expression 'Scandinavian design' came to imply a whole new way of living within the home, widely adopted all over the Western world.

These developments were led by Denmark and Sweden, which could build on centuries of independent nationhood and courtly life, and the high standards of taste and craftsmanship which are the precious adjuncts of a long and stable history. No similar traditions existed in Finland and Norway, which both gained their national independence in the course of our period (the political union between Norway and Sweden being dissolved in 1905, that between Finland and Russia in 1917). Finns and Norwegians were apt to look to their neighbours in general questions of style, though individual artists from both countries could, in inspired moments, produce the very best.

Throughout the period, but especially after the First World War, artists and designers in Denmark and Sweden worked purposefully together to explore the technical and stylistic possibilities of the decorative arts of the age and also to define their role in the modern world and adapt their products to it.

Ceramics before 1920

The first symptoms of rebellion against the expensive style and pomp of European historicism could be seen at the Scandinavian Exhibition in Copenhagen in 1888. Here Bing & Grøndahl's Porcelain Factory (founded in 1853) showed its famous Heron service, which was exhibited in Paris the following year. Designed by the painter Pietro Krohn, it struck a fine balance between the complexities of a naturally observed theme and stylized and disciplined form. The service was produced with the technique of underglaze painting, which had been worked out in 1885 by Arnold Krog for the Royal Porcelain Factory of Copenhagen (founded in 1779). Krog stood as artistic leader of the factory from 1884 to 1916. He had used the new technique himself in a series of vessels of marked Japanese inspiration, and the soft, gentle colouring under the faultless, shiny glaze was finely attuned to the lyrical taste of the *fin-de-siècle*. The underglaze technique did, of course, become an enormous commercial success, and its soft blue-white-grey harmonies are to this day most people's immediate association with the name of Royal Copenhagen porcelain.

In preparation for the Paris Exhibition in 1900, Bing & Grøndahl engaged the painter J. F. Willumsen to do some creative work for them. During his short period as ceramic designer, Willumsen produced some powerful models in high-fired stoneware, which were realized with great technical mastery by the factory's technical staff.

But the most original talent in Danish ceramics at this stage was undoubtedly Thorvald Bindesbøll. He began as a painter, but between 1893 and 1904 he worked primarily with pottery. His exuberant mind overflowed with ideas which he sketched down rapidly on paper, and then realized in earthenware, sometimes with his own hands, sometimes with the assistance of professional potters. Bindesbøll worked first at the pottery of J. Wallman in Utterslev, and later at the Københavns Lervarefabrik (G. Eifrig) in Valby near Copenhagen. He formed his clay into large, simple, powerful forms, and decorated them with wavy lines which divided one large colour area of slip from another. But there is no fashionable dreaminess about Bindesbøll's wavy lines; they are not inspired by mysterious algae or the tresses of sorrowing maidens, but by the clouds of the skies and the waves of the sea.

During the 1890s, the two great Swedish factories, Rörstrand and Gustavsberg, both engaged artists to design for them, in preparation for the great Scandinavian and international exhibitions. Alf Wallander worked for Rörstrand from 1896 onwards and Gunnar Gunnarson Wennerberg for Gustavsberg from 1895 to 1908. The architect Ferdinand Boberg and his wife Anna worked for Gustavsberg from 1909 to 1914 and periodically also for Rörstrand. All these artists produced charming and attractive, though sometimes very complex models of excellent quality in an idiom strongly influenced by international Art Nouveau. They also designed excellent models for serial production.

Between 1897 and 1902, the Anglo-Belgian designer Alfred Finch produced some strikingly simple and well-made pottery for the Iris workshops in Helsinki. The creator and leader of this enterprise was Count Louis Sparre, and some good quality furniture and metalwork, as well as ceramics, were produced there, all in a simple, unaffected style, influenced by progressive tendencies on the Continent. At the Paris Exhibition in 1900, the Iris Room in the Finnish pavilion created quite a sensation by its quiet, inexpensive intimacy, which contrasted strikingly with the opulence of the surroundings.

The ceramic factory of Arabia in Helsinki was

founded in 1876 as a subsidiary of Sweden's Rörstrand. In 1916 it passed into Finnish hands. Thure Öberg had been head designer since 1895, and he produced some very fascinating lamps and vases in a complex and sophisticated Art Nouveau style. The Fennia series of vessels produced from 1902 onwards, have hand-painted decorations in angular, abstract patterns, a curious kind of Art Deco far in advance of its time. It was designed by the progressive architect Eliel Saarinen, but he was most probably initially inspired as a ceramic designer by the painter Akseli Gallen-Kalela, the great moving spirit behind so much of what happened in radical directions in all the arts of Finland at the turn of the century.

Glass before 1920
About the turn of the century, both the two main Swedish factories for tableware and decorative glass, Kotsa (founded in 1742) and Reijmyre (founded in 1810) engaged many of the same artist-designers who had worked in the ceramic industry. Gunnar G. Wennerberg worked for Kosta from 1898 to 1902 and again in 1908. Alf Wallander designed for Kosta from 1907 to 1911 and sporadically for Reijmyre between 1908 and 1914. Ferdinand and Anna Boberg also designed

for Reijmyre. All these artists worked mainly in complex cased glass technique invented by Emile Gallé which was by now being copied all over Europe. Wennerberg in particular had grasped the spirit of the style and gave it a fine and poetic personal interpretation.

Silver and metalwork before 1920
The great name in Scandinavian silver was of course Georg Jensen. He began by making jewellery in a handsome international Art Nouveau style. In 1904 he opened his own workshop in Copenhagen, where he produced vessels and tableware, assisted from 1906 by Johan Rohde, and eventually by several other goldsmiths and designers. The style that gained Georg Jensen international fame was robust and richly decorated, with the ornaments borrowed directly from nature and with a wide use of sculptured detail. Famous models in this style are the teapot with the rose on the cover from 1905 (a complete tea and coffee service with the rose as the common motif grew from the initial model), and the five-branched candlestick of 1921, with its energetic curves and tight clusters of fruit motifs. In 1915 Johan Rohde designed a set of table silver, which is still in production, and which to many people

Earthenware dish produced at Valby by Thorvald Bindesbøll, 1901.

seems to represent the very essence of the George Jensen style.

Thorvald Bindesbøll produced sketches for silver models, some of which were realised before the turn of the century by the Copenhagen firm of A. Michelsen. But Bindesbøll really thought in ceramic terms, and his silver designs had to be substantially adjusted by working goldsmiths to be put into production.

In Sweden Javob Angmann began his career as silversmith soon after 1900, and worked with great integrity in a personal version of the Art Nouveau style throughout his career. Most of his designs were realised by the big Stockholm firm of Gullsmeds Aktie Bolaget (GAB) (founded in 1867). The Norwegians did their most spectacular work in coloured enamels. Both the great Oslo firms of J. Tostrup (founded in 1838) and David Andersen (founded in 1876) produced some elegantly fragile stemmed cups in *plique-à-jour*, which won both praise and medals in Paris in 1900.

Furniture before 1920

Throughout the period of 1890 to 1920, the Danes were world leaders in this field, and they looked to eighteenth-century England for models. Both Johan Rohde and Thorvald Bindesbøll worked within this idiom, each according to his temperament, Rohde's designs being elegant, simple, exclusive, and Bindesbøll's heavy, robust and intensely personal. The Swedes were more orientated towards the contemporary styles of the Continent. Ferdinand Boberg produced some very fine and expensive furniture for King Oscar's Room in the Swedish pavilion in Paris in 1900 in an international Art Nouveau style. The architect Carl Westman designed interiors complete with furniture and fittings, all in an austere style, with a stress on the rectilinguar, which shows an affinity with the work of Charles Rennie Mackintosh. Of great originality is the furniture in the Thonet bentwood technique, designed by another architect, Carl Bergsten, which makes use of purely geometrical elements.

Textiles before 1920

In Denmark and Sweden, traditional techniques of weaving and embroidery were being rediscovered in and around the new museums, and successfully adapted for use in modern homes. Large-scale tapestries with figure compositions of quality were being produced by two Norwegian artists, Frieda Hansen and Gerhard Munthe.

Frieda Hansen was both designer and weaver. In her workshop in Oslo she created a series of large compositions, many of which were shown at international exhibitions and acquired by museums abroad. She was also technically inventive; her transparent curtains with flower patterns, in which the warp is only partly covered by the woollen weft, came to figure among her most admired products.

Gerhard Munthe, an Impressionist painter of some note, developed advanced ideas on the use of stylization which he put into practice in a long series of cartoons derived from folklore subjects. The tapestries were then made up by professional weavers. He is also notable as a creator of handsome books. When a newly translated edition of the thirteenth-century national epic *Heimskringla* (the sagas of the Norwegian kings) by Snorre Sturlasson was produced in 1898, it was planned by Munthe, who also directed the printers and illustrators, while providing many illustrations and all the borders and vignettes himself.

The Functionalist Ideal 1914–40

Though neutral during the war, the Swedes experienced great restrictions, hardships and changes in their material life, which in their turn led to a deepened consciousness of many social problems. At the same time, echoes of radical new

Below left Vignette by Gerhard Munthe for the 1899 illustrated edition of Snorre Sturlasson's *Heimskringla*.

Below right PH-lamp in copper and brass, designed in 1927 by Poul Henningsen for Louis Poulsen, Copenhagen.

Folding deck chair in teak designed by Kaare Klint for Rudolph Rasmussen, 1933.

made considerable advances in the analysis of the true function of furniture. As professor in furniture design at the Kunstakademi from 1924 and as designer for the highly reputed furniture-making firm of Rudolph Rasmussen from 1928, he had a first-hand knowledge and understanding of theory and practice alike, and enjoyed widespread influence in Sweden as well as in Denmark. Another architect, Poul Henningsen, analysed the table lamp and its functions, and produced a model which won a gold medal in Paris in 1925. Two years later a perfected version was put into production in Copenhagen, and thousands of models of the PH-lamp have served down the years, both in Scandinavia and in many other countries.

Ceramics 1920–40

Patrick Nordström, a potter born in Sweden in 1870, spent a number of years around 1900 in Paris, where he worked closely with the great makers of stoneware, including Delaherche, Chaplet, Carriès and others. He was not the only Scandinavian to be acquainted with these developments, but partly by chance and coincidence, he became the main transmitter of their ideas to the northern countries. By 1911 he was himself making stoneware, and in 1912 he settled in Copenhagen where he spent the rest of his life. In the exciting ceramic circles of Copenhagen, Nordström found the stimulus he needed to put into practice the ideas he had brought back with him from Paris. Between 1912 and 1922 he was attached to the Royal Copenhagen Porcelain Factory, where he began production of stoneware vessels and figures, partly inspired by the Paris potters, but with distinct echoes of Chinese Sung, which have continued to be produced to this day.

In 1930 Axel Salto, one of the most imaginative of Danish potters, as well as an all-round designer of note, began a long partnership with the firm, producing stoneware vessels in a powerful and highly personal style.

During the 1920s some stoneware sculpture was produced, probably influenced by the work of the German sculptor Ernst Barlach in pre-war Berlin. Jais Nielsen and Knud Kyhn, both painter-sculptors, produced an impressive series of figures in stoneware, many of large dimensions and glazed in oxblood red. One of Denmark's most famous sculptors, Gerhard Henning, modelled charming figures to be produced in milky white porcelain between 1909 and 1914 and again between 1920 and 1925. Bing & Grøndahl had produced porcelain models sculptured by Kai Nielsen in the years immediately preceding the war, while Ebbe Sadolin, perhaps most famous as an illustrator, designed some fine tableware for the factory.

The purest expression of Functionalist style in ceramics, however, were the stoneware goods, produced between 1929 and 1969 at the Saxbo workshops in Copenhagen. Its leader and inspiring force was Nathalie Krebs, a chemical engineer who had worked for some time for Bing & Grøndahl, specialising in coloured glazes. When she started her own workshop, she first moved into premises which had been vacated on the death of Patrick Nordström, and where he had worked privately since 1922. For the formation of her pots

ideas on production and style reached Scandinavia from other European countries, and the Swedes began to rethink their ideas on housing and the furnishing of homes within the context of their own situation.

A small group of individuals was instrumental in the thinking out and practical promotion of the new thoughts on style and design in many areas of the decorative arts in Scandinavia.

Gregor Paulsson had spent his formative years in Germany and became the main 'ideologist' of the group, promoting the aims of the group with slogans like 'Better Household Goods' and 'Let the Artists Design for Industry'. Paulsson also inspired the radical reform of the Svenska Slöjdföreningen (Swedish Crafts Association) founded in 1845). In its new guise it became the main instrument for reform in design and production.

Another promoter of the new ideas was Erik Wettergreen, Director of the Nationalmuseum of Sweden, an impassioned lover of the Franco-Swedish styles of the eighteenth century.

Third in the central group of reformers was Elsa Gullberg, a textile designer of note and the only practising artist-craftsman among them. In 1917 the group presented its ideas to the public in tangible form at the Housing Exhibition at the Liljevalchs Konsthall in Stockholm. Here for the first time a series of interiors were shown, not as artists dreamt they might be in some ideal and utopian world, but as homes for ordinary people, furnished with goods of taste and quality. The exhibition drew an enormous and enthusiastic public. The spectacularly beautiful Swedish show in Paris in 1925 introduced the ideas of the group to a wider European public.

A similarly thoughtful approach to design and production can also be found in post-war Denmark, but there the new ideas were spread largely by single individuals, rather than as a part of a national programme. The architect Kaare Klint

Right Lion's head in *chamotte* stoneware by Gunnar Nylund for Rörstrand, 1933.

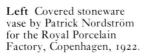

Left Covered stoneware vase by Patrick Nordström for the Royal Porcelain Factory, Copenhagen, 1922.

Below left 'Argenta' vase with green glaze and silver inlay, designed by Wilhelm Kåge for Gustavsberg, 1930.

Below Stoneware vessel by Axel Salto for the Royal Porcelain Factory, Copenhagen, 1931.

'The Potter', sculpted figure in stoneware with oxblood glaze, by Jais Nielsen, 1925.

Nathalie Krebs sought the assistance of professional potters, such as Gunnar Nylund, the Swede, who worked at Saxbo during the first year of its existence, and the sculptor Erik Rahr and others.

The longest and closest partnership, however, was that with Eva Stæhr-Nielsen, which lasted from 1932 to 1969. Mrs. Stæhr-Nielsen adapted her models brilliantly to carry the exquisite glazes invented by Nathalie Krebs. Paradoxically, these most Functionalist of potters' products are not very useful; at best they can hold a bunch of flowers, and their main function is indeed to stand and look beautiful.

This account of Danish ceramics would be incomplete without a mention of the family firms of potters with a long history and tradition. In such companies modern ideas could be accepted and taken up in the discipline and controlled context of a practical pottery business. Herman A. Kähler learned the craft from his father in the family workshop at Næstved (founded in 1839), and has again taught it to his son, H. J. Kähler, who now carries on the firm. They work mainly in glazed stoneware. The island of Bornholm has rich clay deposits, and has for centuries been a centre for good anonymous pottery-making. In 1859 L. Hjorth set up a small factory for the production of terracotta, figures and vessels, in a Neo-classical style. His son and his sons and daughters still produce fine quality work at Bornholm in a restrained modern idiom.

Gunnar Nylund left Saxbo in 1931 to become head designer of the Rörstrand-Lidköping factory in his native Sweden, where he produced some excellent designs for mass-produced household goods. His co-operation with Nathalie Krebs however, had given him more ambitious ideas and he also produced a series of porcelain and stoneware designs. Some of these are in the austere purist style of his Danish colleague, while others

are directly modelled on Sung ware. He has also produced some impressive sculpture. At the factory of Gustavsberg Wilhelm Kåge worked as designer from 1917, and remained the decisive artistic influence throughout our period and beyond.

According to the Functionalist programme, he began by reforming the serial production of household goods in a modern idiom. But his activities also included the creation of more ambitious genres of decorative ware. He created his Argenta series of green glazed stoneware inlaid with silver for the Stockholm Exhibition in 1930, as well as the Farsta series of stoneware vessels in painted faïence, and his series of large dishes painted with fashionable women's heads was particularly impressive. In 1937, Kåge was joined at Gustavsberg by Stig Lindberg. He introduced a more strikingly modernistic style to the serial production, but his many contributions to Swedish pottery came after the end of our period.

Porsgrunds Porselænsfabrik (founded in 1885) in Norway produced some good porcelain and pottery in a modern idiom, especially during the years from 1927 when Nora Gulbrandson was chief designer. The 1930s also saw the beginnings of original work in Finnish ceramics at the Arabia factory, but the great period in the history of the Arabia factory came after the Second World War.

Glass 1920–40

By far the most spectacular and original contribution in Scandinavian design was in Swedish glass. The new developments were from the first centred on the factory of Orrefors (founded in 1898). In 1916, stimulated by the call from Stockholm of 'Let the Artist Design for Industry', the management engaged Simon Gate as designer, and in the following year Edward Hald also joined them. Both Gate and Hald were painters and neither had previous knowledge of glass. Under

Top Saxbo stoneware vase, *c.* 1930.

Above Early Graal glass by Edward Hald, 1917.

Right Glass vase by Simon Gate, *c.* 1930.

Below left Early Graal glass by Simon Gate, 1917.

Below right Furnace-worked vase of clear glass, with black foot and rim, by Simon Gate for Orrefors, 1930.

the expert guidance of the experienced glass-blower, Knut Bergqvist, they soon began to see the potential of the material.

From the very start they worked along three main lines, which were to be followed up to the end of our period with ever greater confidence and sophistication. There were the models in pure furnace work, often produced in one or two colours, black and clear being a fashionable combination. Over the years many handsome table services were also produced, some expensive for Orrefors itself, and others simple and cheap but pleasing to look at and good to handle, for the sister factory of Sandviken. The second line was glass decorated with engraved figures and ornaments. With the help initially of one craftsman, Gustaf Abels, a cutter from Kosta, they began producing patterns for engraving. Gate worked mainly with Neo-classical subjects to be executed in deep and finely graded relief; these had a distinct flavour of Lobmeyr, but possessed a crisp vitality all of their own. Hald chose his subject frequently from contemporary life and had them executed in a sketchy manner, with the engraver's wheel producing more a matting of the surface than deep incisions. There was a gay Parisian air about many of Hald's decorative patterns – he had after all studied with Matisse. The third and final line in Orrefors art glass had coloured patterns inlaid into the glass, the genre being given the proud name of Graal as early as 1916.

The starting point for the Orrefors Graal was Gallé's standardized cased glass vases with flower decorations cut out of the surface, but as the motifs on Graal were enclosed in the glass and received a final heating within its clear casing, they acquired a fluidity and glassiness which made them something quite new and startling. In 1930 the supporting technique of Ariel was worked out.

Compared to what the Swedes did, the contribution to the development of the art of glass-making of the other Scandinavian countries was modest. In Denmark, the architect Jacob E. Bang worked as designer at the factory of Holmegaard (founded in 1825) from 1928 to 1942.

In Finland, Henry Ericsson designed engraved glass for the factory of Riihimäki (founded in 1910) in a style clearly inspired by Edward Hald, and so did Sverre Pettersen for Hadeland in Norway from 1928 until the end of our period and beyond. Arttu Brummer made some good but modest glass with inlaid air bubbles in the style of Marinot, again for Riihimäki. Gunnel Nyman was the pioneer of the great Finnish expansion within the field of art glass during the 1950s and 1960s, although her first experiments with glass had been interrupted by the Second World War. Alvar Aalto, the famous architect, designed glass vases in plain metal, sometimes tinted into one colour, most famous among them being the Savoy series created in 1937.

Silver and metalwork 1920–40
Stylistically speaking, the purest Functionalist silver was made by Wiven Nilsson in his workshop in Lund in Sweden, with an almost Cubist look in his most characteristic pieces. Ernst Fleming in his Atelier Borgila in Stockholm also worked in a radically modern style.

In Denmark Kay Bojesen trained in Georg Jensen's workshops, made extremely shapely models in plain and unadorned silver, and also some very fine table silver. He also worked in wood, making some of the most attractive toys of the period. Kay Bojesen employed outside designers in his silversmith's workshop, among them the architects Magnus Stephensen and Ole Wanscher, the latter more famous as a furniture designer. Sigvard Bernadotte of the Swedish royal family was for many years artistic director of Georg Jensen's workshop. Kay Fisker, an architect by profession, designed some exquisite models for the firm of A. Michelsen.

In Norway, the Functionalist style was introduced in silver by Jacob, and practised with proficiency and charm by Oskar Sørensen, head of the firm of Tostrup. The other great Oslo firm, David Andersen, produced some good Functionalist models from the designs of a team of young designers, the most talented being Torbjørn Lie Jørgensen.

Furniture 1920–40

The central position of Kaare Klint has already been mentioned. Working very much in the same spirit were the architect Ole Wanscher, Mogens Koch and others. Their designs were realized by firms like Jacob Kjær, Fritz Hansen and A. J. Iversen, whose unfailingly high standards of craftsmanship must take much of the credit for the excellence of Danish furniture of the period.

In Sweden a whole phalanx of designers followed the now broadly accepted tenets of Functionalism, and worked sensibly and well to produce good, useful and reasonably priced furniture for a mass public.

Carl Malmsten worked happily in exotic and expensive woods, with inlaid decoration, and frequently with more than a glance back to the Franco-Swedish eighteenth-century tradition.

Gunnar Asplund, active during the 1920s, was another exponent of the gently traditional 'Swedish grace', but after acting as chief architect to the Stockholm Exhibition in 1930, he accepted more radical forms, producing among other things a steel chair of great elegance. Bruno Matthson created his own technique, covering bentwood chairs with hemp webbing.

But the great exploiter of bentwood was of course Alvar Aalto. In 1930, as part of the furnishings for a sanatorium he was building, he produced his first version of the famous armchair of laminated birchwood. In 1933 came another variety, both being realized by his own firm for mass-produced furniture, Artek (founded 1935). Aalto's chairs worked on a completely new technical principle, which exploits the gentle springiness of the construction and the sitter enjoys a pleasant feeling of light movement.

Textiles 1920–40

Much excellent work was done in both woven and printed materials for use in the interior by both Swedish and Danish designers, some working in private workshops, others designing for factories, but the picture is too large and varied for single names to be mentioned. In tapestry weaving some interesting developments took place. In 1919 Märta Måås-Fjetterström opened her own workshop near Lund in Sweden, where she created a very personal kind of tapestry weaving with pictorial subjects, firmly based on folkweave techniques and traditions. She also produced furnishing fabrics. An extraordinarily powerful and original weaver was Hannah Ryggen. Born in Sweden in 1894 and trained as a painter, she settled in Norway in 1923 and devoted the rest of her life to tapestry weaving, her most notable achievement being a series of large-scale, narrative tapestries. The period also saw the beginning of the revival of rya weaving in Finland.

Decanter with stopper, designed by Oskar Sorensen for J. Tostrup, 1938.

Above Tapestry-woven wool rug from the workshop of Märta Måås-Fjetterström, Bastad, *c.* 1930.

Far left Laminated birchwood chair, designed by Alvar Aalto, 1933.

Centre left 'Lise Lotte Hermann', detail from a tapestry by Hannah Ryggen, 1938.

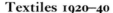

Italy and Spain

by Ian Bennett

Italy

IN ITALY, the principal influence on the applied arts at the turn of the century was French. In common with most other Mediterranean countries, Italy espoused a violent curvilinear style without, however, the restraining factors of great artistry found among the Nancy and Paris designers. It must be said at the outset that there is very little of early twentieth-century Italian applied art which is of more than passing interest. The exception, though an extremely eccentric one, being the furniture of Bugatti. Only after the Second World War did Italy begin to have a major impact on international design, especially in the fields of interiors and furniture.

The Italian showing at the Paris 1900 Exhibition was considered little short of a disaster. The pavilion itself, designed by Ceppi, was a weird amalgam of the black and white stripes of Siena Cathedral and the Byzantine extravagance of San Marco. The French critics, with the Italian exhibits primarily in mind, coined the phrase *style nouille* or 'noodle style'.

Indeed, it was largely due to the generally hostile reaction to the Italian section of the 1900 Exhibition that it was decided by Italy that the Turin Exhibition of 1902 should be as splendid an affair as possible. The architect Raimondo d'Aronco was chosen to design the principal buildings, and these again were in an ornate, Byzantine style which, despite the enthusiasm of some Italian critics, was not much of an improvement on the 1900 fiasco.

The Italian section at Turin did not, in general, fare much better at the hands of the international critics, one writer in *The Studio* remarking that 'the whole effect of it was that of a huge bazaar, rather than an exhibition of artistic work'.

Not to be discouraged, the Italian Government decided to hold another International Exhibition in Milan, which took place in 1906, an event seemingly dogged by disaster, including the destruction by fire of the Italian Pavilion of Applied Art in August. The designers of the Italian pavilion this time were Bianchi, Magnani and Rondoni, whose edifice bore a remarkable resemblance to the Turin building but without the bravura.

Italy did not lack a few architects capable of interpreting the Art Nouveau style. The best of them was probably Pietro Fenoglio of Turin, who designed a number of important buildings in the years around 1900, the most famous of which was his own house, the Casa Fenoglio, finished in 1902. In this building, the architect sought for the concept of total unity, which was the concern of many of the leading architects of the period. Other interesting architects include Alfredo Premoli of Turin, who was greatly influenced by Guimard, Giovan Battista Comencini of Udine, whose Hôtel de Londres shows an awareness of Mackintosh, Raimondo d'Aronco, who has been mentioned in connection with the 1902 Turin Pavilion and Giuseppe Sommaruga, the most important Italian exponent of the new German style of Behrens and a precursor of the Futurist concept of architecture proclaimed by Sant'Elia in his Manifesto of 1914. Even Sommaruga could not resist embellishing his work with Art Nouveau motifs.

Although no mention is made of his name, it seems possible that one of the aspects of the Italian display at the Turin exhibition of 1902 which so dismayed the English critic of *The Studio*, as it did many others, was the now famous interior designed by Carlo Bugatti, in which he achieved the height of Moresque fantasy in one of the most memorable creations of any single designer at any of the international exhibitions which took place at the beginning of this century (see p. 276).

Bugatti had been designing furniture in Milan for more than fourteen years by the time the 1902 Exhibition took place, furniture which had usually been among Italy's few successes. It was first shown in the Italian Exhibition in London in 1888; it was like no other furniture produced in Europe, the combination of painted vellum, polished copper and brass, carved and painted wood and hanging silk tassels giving it a weird and barbaric appearance.

Bugatti's furniture won a first prize at the London exhibition. In Paris and Turin, he won gold medals, despite the fact that in the former exhibition, his work was described sarcastically by Edmond de Goncourt as typifying 'the yachting style'; at Turin, it was either ignored by the critics or mauled. The German Fritz Minkus, in *Kunst und Kunsthandwerk*, described the Turin interior as producing 'the effect of a newly invented automobile, which cannot be quite comprehended at first glance, of outstanding technical refinement, together with an extremely ugly and ponderous appearance', an ironic remark in view of the fame Carlo's eldest son Ettore was to achieve as one of the greatest automobile designers and manufacturers.

In fact, 'ponderous' is not an entirely unfair description of much of Bugatti's furniture, although in the Turin Exhibition, he had begun to produce more delicate curvilinear pieces with less extravagant ornamentation, a slight change in style

due, no doubt, to the French furniture he had seen in Paris in 1900. In 1905, however, Carlo ceased to manufacture his furniture, selling the rights to do so to the Milan firm of De Vecchi.

Bugatti has become the most famous of the Italian furniture designers at the turn of the century; in many respects, he was the only one to create a unified style, which, for all its occasional excesses, remains the expression of an individual personality.

Among other Italians, the most highly regarded was probably Eugenio Quarti, who was born in 1867 and who worked in Milan until his death in 1931. Quarti's furniture is probably the most restrained attempt by an Italian designer to produce an Art Nouveau style. He was influenced obviously by the curvilinearity of the French exhibits in Paris in 1900, but his own furniture in the period between 1898, when he showed it publically for the first time in an exhibition in Turin, and 1900, is among the most florid of his whole career. There is also evidence, especially in the extraordinary sofa he exhibited in Paris, with its huge rounded back, that he was greatly impressed by his fellow Milanese, Carlo Bugatti, of whom he was a close friend.

By 1902, however, Quarti's furniture had be-

come more restrained and elegant, often painted white and with stencilled flower patterns, the inspiration for which was possibly Mackintosh or, more likely, the Vienna Secession. In the 1906 Milan Exhibition, strong elements of Art Nouveau curvilinearity were still to be seen in his pieces, but they showed the restraint of the German designers Behrens and Riemerschmid, by whom many Italians at this time were strongly influenced.

Quarti's room at the Milan exhibition was destroyed by the fire mentioned above, but it was seen by a number of international critics who found it a refreshing change from the usual eclectic extravagances of the majority of Italian designers. It should be noted that the movement towards simple furniture capable of mass-production and inspired by the German experiments, was known as 'mobile Povero' and designers of it included Ettore Bracco and Pietro Zen.

The latter was born in 1879 and continued working in Milan until 1950; he was the son of another leading Italian Art Nouveau cabinet-maker, Carlo Zen (1851–1918). Carlo's furniture, which appeared at most of the major international exhibitions, starting with Turin in 1898, exemplified the worst in the Italian commercialization of the florid French Art Nouveau style. By

Top Bedroom suite designed by Carlo Bugatti for a London private house, *c.* 1902.

Above Chair designed by Carlo Bugatti, early twentieth century.

Above Screen designed by
Carlo Bugatti, early
twentieth century.

comparison, the work of his son, which won considerable acclaim in the Milan 1906 Exhibition, is rectilinear and restrained, with strong echoes of both English and German design; a similar restraint can be seen in the work of his contemporaries Federico Tessio, A. Rigotti and the important Turin architect and designer, Giacomo Cometti, in whose work one can see the influence, above all, of Henry van de Velde. Carlo Zen's preference for the overblown may be seen also in the furniture of B. Massimino, A. Lauro, A. Vergani and A. Issel. Valabrega's room at the Milan 1906 Exhibition was, for him, surprisingly restrained, although *The Studio* critic remarked on the deplorable eclecticism of his style.

Italy also saw the development of a strongly 'rustic' or 'peasant' style of craft furniture, which was often merged stylistically with elements of Art Nouveau. These elements are seen in particular in the work of certain Sicilian designers active in Palermo, notably Ernesto Basile and Vittorio Ducrot (for whom Basile often designed furniture and wrought-ironwork). In Rome, the same approach may be seen in the furniture designed by Duilio Cambellotti and that produced by Aemilia Ars, a Secessionist group which existed from 1898 to 1903 and which included designers such as Alfonso Rubbiani and A. Pasquinelli.

The most ornate example of the 'peasant' style, however, remarkably close in feeling to the products of Russia, Hungary and Finland, was that by Giorgio Clemente of Sardinia. His furniture was exhibited in Turin in 1911, and was among the most popular exhibits.

The furniture of Ducrot and Basile is never as 'folksy' as this; the pieces, usually of mahogany, are massive and are frequently embellished with metalwork by Antonio Ugo and painting by Ettore Maria Bergler. The style seems often to have echoes of ancient Etruscan or Greek pieces, and seems prophetic of the monolithic Neo-classical style popularised by the Fascist regimes in Italy and Germany during the 1920s and 1930s. This move towards monumentality became more apparent in Italian furniture design in the years immediately before the outbreak of the First World War, especially in the work of Luigi Brunelli, Giulio Ulisse Arata of Piacenza and in the designs for the interior furnishings of the Palace of the King of Siam undertaken by Galileo Chini between 1912 and 1913.

Of the various Italian applied arts which appear in the decorative arts journals around the turn of the century, ceramics are usually singled out for particular praise. This was especially so in England, where artists and designers like William Morris and William de Morgan had paid tribute to the pioneering efforts of various Italian factories in the second half of the nineteenth century in reviving painted pottery (majolica) and lustre. Of these, the two most important were Cantagalli and Doccia, the former dating from the fifteenth century and the latter from the eighteenth.

The Cantagalli factory was inherited by Ulisse Cantagalli from his father Giuseppe in 1878. Ulisse and his brother Romeo made good copies of Italian majolica, Persian and Isnik wares and Hispano-Moresque lustre, developing a fine copper lustre which they called 'Pigeon's Blood'. A

number of talented decorators were employed by the factory, including the brothers Carlo, Giorgio and Torquato Boldrini and B. and F. Sirocchi. All these artists painted work designed by William de Morgan when he was resident in Florence for six months of each year during the 1890s.

The Doccia factory of the Ginori family had exhibited examples of its lustrewares at the Great Exhibition in London in 1851, and is credited with being one of the first to revive this ancient, but lost, art of ceramic decoration. In 1896, the factory merged with the Società Ceramica Richard, which had been founded in 1873 by Giulio Richard; the merged firms became known as Richard-Ginori and went on to become the largest manufacturers of industrial ceramics in Italy. The artistic director was Luigi Tazzini of Doccia, with a staff of designers including Giulio Richard himself and Giovanni Buffa. The factory produced ceramics of every conceivable kind, with a strong leaning towards the more florid aspects of Art Nouveau.

Another important factory in Florence was L'Arte della Ceramica, which was founded in 1896–7 by Galileo Chini. The general manager was the Ferrarese artist Vincenzo Giustiniani and the chief designer from 1902 to 1904 was the influential Domenico Trentacoste. In 1907, the factory moved to Mugello; Galileo Chini was the technical director of the new factory, with his brother Chino as artistic director. The factory lasted until 1955, changing its name in 1907 to Chini & Co.

The most important factory in one of the great traditional centres of Italian ceramics, Faenza, was the Fabricche Riunite de Faenza of Francesco Randone and Pietro Melandro, the former having been a pupil of Theodore Deck in France. The factory began production in 1910 and, mixed with a strong Japanese-Isnik leaning, no doubt derived from Deck, is a sympathy for the 'whiplash' Art Nouveau style; good pieces in both monochrome and lustre were produced by the factory.

Despite Italy's long history as one of the leading European producers of glass, with many of the great factories of Venice and Murano still operating well into the twentieth century, little of interest was produced in the period under consideration. Some delicate floral vases, in a style reminiscent of that of Koepping in Germany were produced by two Venetian factories, Pauly & C., which had been founded in 1863, and Salviati & C., which was founded around 1890 by Antonio Salviati. The latter company specialised in the production of glasses of extraordinary technical difficulty, in which the floral bowl is joined to the slightly domed base by a single incredibly thin strand of glass which follows its natural curlicues, akin to the effect made by a thin stream of treacle when it is allowed to fall on to a flat surface from a height.

Perhaps the major Italian glass designer of the inter-war years was Paolo Venini who in 1924 formed a partnership with Giacomo Cappellin, their firm being known as Vetri Soffiati Muranesi Cappellin-Venini & C. The artistic director of the firm was the Symbolist painter turned applied arts designer Vittorio Zecchin who, in 1913, had begun designing enamelled glass with another painter, Teodoro Wolf Ferrari, these pieces being made by the Murano glassworks of Artisti Barovia.

From the outset, Cappellin and Venini produced simple but elegant tableware in a style obviously based upon early Italian glass but with that emphasis on functionalism found in Philip Webb's glass designs of the 1860s, or those by Riemerschmid and Behrens in Germany in the early part of this century. Unfortunately, the partnership did not endure for long and in 1925, Venini founded his own company, Vetri Soffiati Muranesi Venini & C. Throughout the late 1920s and 1930s, Venini himself experimented with many different techniques as well as continuing his work as a designer of fine glass.

Above Carved sideboard with old Sardinian motifs, exhibited by the Fratelli Clementi in Turin, 1911.

Above left Interior by Vittorio Valabrega, shown at the Milan Exhibition of 1906.

Top Sofa designed by Carlo Zen, 1902.

Below Glass vase c. 1900 by Salviati & Co.

Spain

IN SPAIN, only the name of the architect Antoni Gaudí has become widely known, in contrast to the exceptional group of modern painters the country has produced, including Picasso, Gris, Dali and Miró.

In general, the applied arts of Spain at the turn of the century represented the extreme vulgarization found in other southern European countries, particularly Italy and Portugal. To this extreme decadence, Gaudí's work stands not so much in contrast – for no one could call it peaceful or restrained – but as an example of the fact that the style of violent curvilinearity had not been exhausted by the French and Belgian designers and, in the hand of an intuitively brilliant artist, still retained great originality and potency.

It is incorrect, although typical, to find Gaudí treated as a somewhat isolated phenomenon in Spain; he was, in fact, part of a Catalan movement in the fine and decorative arts centred in Barcelona, a movement which became the Spanish version of Art Nouveau, El Modernisme. The main force of the movement was to be seen in architecture and, as we said at the beginning, very little applied art of any note was produced. Also, the word 'modernism' suggests that the Spaniards were in sympathy with the ideals of many of the

Secessionist architects in Europe, especially in Germany, who were pioneering new methods.

This was certainly not true of Gaudí, however, whose work may, in many respects, be considered the finest flowering of the 'peasant' style of Art Nouveau, with a strong emphasis on traditional materials. Among the turn of the century Spanish architects, perhaps only Luis Domènech y Montaner may be said to represent Modernism in Spanish architecture, although in the work of others, such as Rafael Massó, there can be seen an awareness of the concepts of functionalism associated with architects such as Behrens and Loos.

It is arguable that, architecturally, Barcelona represented the most intense development of curvilinear Art Nouveau to be found anywhere in Europe. Apart from the architects already mentioned, others included Henrique Sagnier, José Puig y Cadafalch, Francesc Folguera, Raspall, Jujol, Moncunill, Granell, Artegas, and Josep Pericas; even today, more than 200 buildings in the 'modern' style still exist.

Catalonia itself was ideally suited for this major Spanish development of the new European style since it was the only area of the country which had attempted to evade the general decline into total decadence and poverty following the loss of Empire in the seventeenth and eighteenth centuries. Certainly it was the only part of Spain in which industry had managed to flourish. It is no surprise therefore that in no other area of the country is there any significant example of Art Nouveau to be found and the few examples that exist are generally by Barcelona architects or their followers.

It was Domènech who pioneered a revival in craftwork inspired by the English Arts and Crafts Movement, a revival which also had its roots in a series of books and articles written in the 1870s by such critics as Sanpere y Miquel and Miquel y Badía, who had toured the leading industrial nations.

For many of his buildings, Gaudí designed extraordinary, idiosyncratic, furniture. Among surviving examples are pieces designed for the chapel of the Colonia Güell in Santa Coloma de Cervelló, near Barcelona (1898–1914), the Casa Calvet of 1898 to 1904, in Correr de Casp, Barcelona, and for the Casa Battló (1905–7).

The style of the furniture is consistent, the Colonia Güell pieces being perhaps slightly starker than those for the Casa Calvet, in which the organic, 'shell-and-bone' forms, are most obvious. One extraordinary piece, the authenticity of which has been called into question, is the ornate prayer

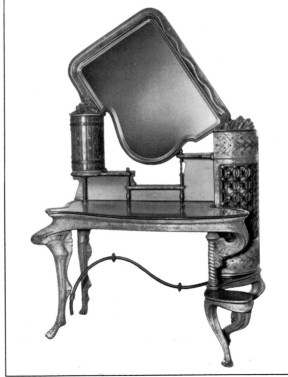

Right Dressing table designed for the Palacio Güell, Barcelona, by Antoni Gaudí, 1890.

Below Wooden armchair designed for the Casa Calvet, Barcelona, by Antoni Gaudí, 1902.

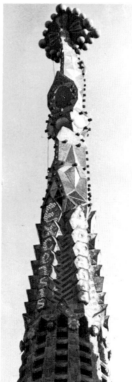

The church of the Sagrada Familia, Barcelona, begun by Antoni Gaudí in 1882 and still unfinished; its spires, façades and buttresses show a rapid movement from the precepts of the Gothic Revival to a highly individual version of Art Nouveau.

Gaudí's maturity: aspects of the park in Barcelona which Gaudí designed at the request of Eusebio Güell, a local manufacturer; the mosaics on the parapets and fountains include broken tiles and old crockery to achieve as potent an expression of the 1900 style as anywhere in Europe.

stool supposed to have been part of the furnishings of the Battló house which was sold at auction in Versailles in November 1973. The rich 'acajou et bois de loup' base of this piece, with upholstered platforms for the knees and elbows, was surmounted by an amazing edifice of stained glass and wood, embellished by five large gilt-bronze roses. Although very Spanish in feel, this piece bore little resemblance to known examples of Gaudí's furniture.

No discussion of the applied arts in Spain would be complete without mention of another Catalan, Josep Llorens Artigas, unquestionably one of the greatest potters of the twentieth century. Born in Barcelona in 1892, Artigas exhibited his first ceramics, based on traditional Spanish peasant pottery, in 1915. In 1918, he founded the Agrupacció Courbet and in the same year wrote an essay on a member of this group, Joan Miró, in *La Veu de Catalunya*. At this point in his career, Artigas began to show the same concern with understanding the methods and materials of past styles which had characterised nineteenth-century potters such as Deck and De Morgan, and in 1922 published an important book entitled *Les Pastes Ceràmíques: Les esmalts blaus de l'Antic Egipte*.

Eastern Europe

by Ian Bennett

THE DECORATIVE ARTS in Eastern Europe, those countries which today comprise the Communist block, were inspired at the turn of the century by three principal ideas. Firstly, there was a strong sense of historical nationalism. This is evident in Russian art, in Hungarian, Romanian, Yugoslavian, Czech and Polish art, and in Finnish art, which lies outside the scope of this chapter. With the exception of Russia, all the Eastern European states (the present boundaries are, of course, largely the creation of recent history) were under the domination of either Austria, Germany or Russia herself. Yet the various groups of peoples – Magyars, Croats, Slavs – living in places whose names have since disappeared from the map of Europe, such as Bohemia, Moravia, Montenegro, Croatia, Serbia and Bosnia, used their unbroken sense of national and ethnic pride to create unique artistic styles.

In many respects, therefore, the various movements in the decorative arts in these areas were political. Thus it is no surprise that another of the chief influences was the socialist work ethic of William Morris and John Ruskin. Many of the craft communities which grew up in Eastern Europe were founded in the name of these two Englishmen, whose ideas were also strong in the innumerable technical schools and art colleges which were founded in the Austrian and German spheres of influence.

Finally, since so large a part of Eastern Europe was within the Austrian Empire, the influence of Viennese design was also of great importance. French Art Nouveau influences may also be discerned, but to a lesser degree.

Russia

In Russia, the new mood in both the applied and fine arts first became apparent in the early 1880s. In 1880, a group calling itself the Nevsky Pickwickians revolted against the nationalistic, academic, school of painting. This young group included Alexandre Benois, Serge Diaghilev, Valentin Serov (later the designer of *Schéhérazade*), Konstantin Korovine and Léon Bakst. These six individuals, all of whom were to become associated with the Ballets Russes, formed a splinter group under Diaghilev's leadership in 1889, publishing their own magazine *Mir Iskustva*, which continued publication until 1905. Initially painters, they concerned themselves subsequently with the arts of the theatre, while at the same time organising exhibitions of paintings and sculptures and the applied arts, to which foreign contributors were invited. An exhibition held in Moscow in 1906, for instance, included the work of Charles Rennie Mackintosh.

The *Mir Iskustva* group was keen to awaken an interest in Russian folklore, and their aim was shared by three other groups dedicated to the revival of traditional Russian crafts – Abramtsevo, Trocadero and Talashkino. Abramtsevo, near Moscow, was the first of these groups. It was founded by Savva Mamantov and his wife to give useful work to the local young peasants during the winter months. Mamantov was a railway magnate who surrounded himself with literary and artistic personalities. His aim of making art socially useful was a deliberate challenge to the St. Petersburg Academy of Fine Arts and to the somewhat decadent cultural milieu of the Court.

The second community – Trocadero – was founded by Elena Polenova in 1884. She was a close friend of the Mamantovs and, with her considerable knowledge of Russian folk crafts, had been one of the main inspirational forces behind the founding of the first community. The third group was founded in 1887 by Princess Sviatopolk-Tchetvertynska on her estate at Talashkino. It was later reorganised and run by Princess Maria Tenicheva, who had financed the magazine *Mir Iskustva* and who was herself greatly influenced by Elena Polenova.

All four new groups attracted many of the same artists and designers and thus their joint work coalesces into the Russian contribution to new design at this time – the Russian version of Jugendstil or Arts and Crafts. One of the leading figures at Abramtsevo was Mikhail Vrübel, the son of a Polish cavalry officer in the Russian army. Vrübel had studied under Ilya Repin, the leading Russian academic painter, but showed his idiosyncratic approach to art in 1885 when he organised the building of a cathedral as a communal project, the interior and exterior of the building being covered in ceramic mosaics and tiles. Vrübel introduced the Mamantovs to another leading member of the Diaghilev group, Valentin Serov. At Abramtsevo, Vrübel painted icons and designed and painted ceramics. He became subject to violent fits of religious mania and died blind and partly paralysed in an asylum.

At Trocadero, Elena Polenova had assembled an impressive collection of old Russian crafts to be used for study purposes. She designed pieces in a similar style to be carved in wood by the boys attending her school. Among the designers and artists who worked with her were Marie Jacomichikov-Wéber, Nathalie Davidov, Victor Vaznietzov, Constantin Korovine and Serge Malioutin. Furniture, pottery, embroidery, book-binding and illustrations, wallpapers and toys were all designed and executed in the workshops. Surrounding villages well-known for particular crafts were also utilised; thus embroideries designed by the group were given to peasant women in the village of Solomenka. This village, famous for its embroideries, produced its own dyes, executing work in a characteristic palette of indigo, madder and green.

The communities at Abramtsevo and Talashkino both designed and built their own theatres, projects enthusiastically carried out by members of the *Mir Iskustva* group. These were not the usual crude and amateurish theatricals, but had scenery, costumes and accessories designed and painted by professionals.

The most important of the Russian craft communities was unquestionably Talashkino. There was a sculpture studio under Serge Malioutin, an artist deeply influenced by old Russian folk tales and legends. Malioutin designed the Talashkino theatre and painted scenic backdrops for it. Other architects and designers who taught there included A. Zinoviev and V. Beketov, and much of the furniture was designed by an artist later to become internationally famous with the Ballets Russes, Nicholas Roerich. Roerich is remembered principally today for his costume designs for the first performance of *Le Sacre du Printemps*.

Furniture was also designed by the painter Apollinaris Vaznietzov, brother of Victor; Apollinaris also designed furniture for the small avant-garde atelier in Moscow called Zemstro, where the sculptor Innokenti Joukov created works inspired by Russian historical and peasant subjects. Talashkino, obviously inspired by Vrübel's example, also built its own church in traditional Russian style.

Princess Tenicheva had an important collection of both traditional Russian crafts and also modern design, including work by Colonna, Tiffany and Gallé; the pupils, who were taught embroidery, furniture-making, woodcarving, ceramics and enamelling, were thus aware of current stylistic developments in Western Europe and the United States. The Princess herself was a skilled enameller and had her work in this medium exhibited at the Salon of the Société des Beaux-Arts in Paris. She also designed costumes for her theatre and, with other painters, produced some of the painted balalaikas which were features of all the Russian communities and which were especially admired by foreign critics.

The work produced in Abramtsevo and Talashkino was exhibited in the Paris Universal Exhibition of 1900, together with an extensive group of traditional folk crafts provided by the Russian Ministry of Agriculture, which had received instructions in 1888 to foster the continuance of these crafts among the Russian peasantry. Both the new and the old work was enthusiastically received, especially by the British who, in the true spirit of William Morris, applauded the medieval continuity of a folk tradition apparently unspoiled by industrialization (the English attitude to Japanese art was much the same).

Faced with the sturdy honesty of the Russian craft communities' work or the brilliant

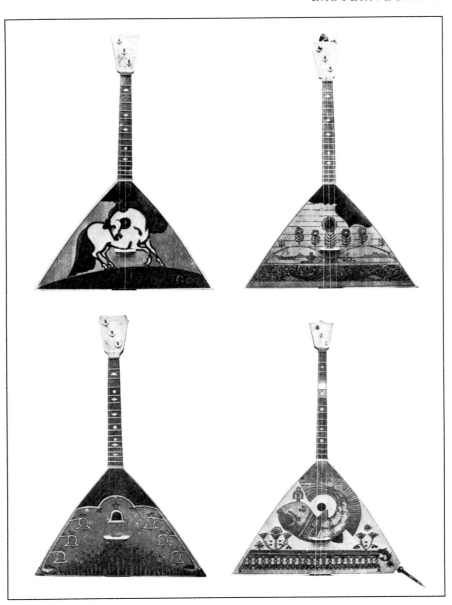

Right Decorated armchair designed by Princess Tenicheva at the Talashkino community, 1890s.

Below Settee designed by Nicholas Roerich at Talashkino, 1890s.

of extraordinary workmanship; multi-coloured and multi-textured gold was combined with semi-precious and precious stones (the former were preferred) and superb enamelling, both matt and translucent. A wide range of snuff boxes, cigarette cases, photograph frames and nécessaires were produced, as well as carved hardstone animals, birds and human figures and extraordinary sprays of flowers resting in rock-crystal vases cut so as to appear half-filled with water. There were also the famous enamelled and jewelled eggs which the Russian Royal Family exchanged at Easter.

The unquestionable technical brilliance and perfectly orchestrated use of materials act as strange counterpoints to the utter artistic sterility of almost all Fabergé's work. The agate pig, the chalcedony pigeon, the crocodilite chicken, the enamelled eggs and bejewelled flower sprays are, in many respects, the rich man's plaster ducks.

Apart from the products of the craft communities, Russian ceramics of this period are of little interest. The Imperitorskii Farfor Zavod (Imperial Porcelain Factory) had been founded in St. Petersburg in 1744 and throughout its history has been controlled by central government, first under the Tsars and latterly under the Communist régime. Some attempts were made to instil life into it in the mid nineteenth century when Tsar Nicholas I brought over the designer Derivière from Sèvres, but the Russian work remained derivative and uninspired. In the 1880s Alexander III, under the influence of his Danish wife, imported designers and painters from Royal Copenhagen, but despite some good underglaze painting in the Danish manner by Linberg, the Tsar unfortunately insisted on choosing the models the factory should produce, and the artists were allowed no freedom.

During the 1920s, some Suprematist artists turned to painting on porcelain. Most important of these artists was Nikolai Mikhailovich Suetin.

exuberance of Diaghilev and his group, it is difficult to be objective about the concurrent products of the Fabergé workshops at St. Petersburg and Moscow. The House of Fabergé was founded in 1842 by Gustav Fabergé; his son Carl Peter, born in 1846, became head of the firm in 1870. The house exhibited for the first time at the Pan-Russian Exhibition of 1882 in Moscow and won a Gold Medal. Two years later, Carl Fabergé received a Royal Warrant from Alexander III.

The principal influence on Fabergé's work was French eighteenth-century vertu. The St. Petersburg branch specialised in small jewelled objects

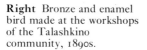

Right Bronze and enamel bird made at the workshops of the Talashkino community, 1890s.

Opposite top left Porcelain inkstand designed and painted in Suprematist style by Nikolai Suetin, 1923.

Opposite bottom Fabergé silver mounts on a Tiffany peacock vase, c. 1900.

Opposite far right Jewelled flower by Fabergé, formerly in the Strauss Collection, c. 1900.

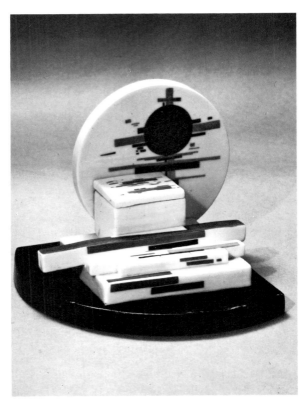

Many of his painted pieces, such as two whole tea services now in the Hermitage, Leningrad, were executed on St. Petersburg porcelain blanks, the shapes and painting making uneasy partners. However, while director of the Lomonsow Porcelain Factory, Suetin designed pieces of Suprematist shape with painted designs. Such pieces must be considered among the few successful integrations of modern art and ceramics. Other Suprematists who painted and designed porcelain were Ilja Chashnik, who also worked at Lomonsow, and the best known painter of the Suprematist group of artists and designers, Kazimir Malevich.

Hungary

If French Art Nouveau had any strong influence on the applied arts of the Eastern European countries, Hungary was the country which was most inspired by it. At the beginning of this century Hungary had assumed the unfortunate status of a province of the Austrian Empire. Magyar nationalism was, of course, fervent and many of the leading young designers were also keen to emphasise the influence of Oriental cultures on the historical Hungarian style. The combination of Byzantine and Turkish styles on traditional Magyar art thus produced a unique blend of historico-romantic symbolism seen at its most exaggerated on the Hungarian pavilion for the Turin International Exhibition of 1911, and in Aladár Körösföi-Kriesch's murals for the Academy of Music in Budapest executed at about the same time; these show historical and legendary Hungarian events in a strange stylistic mixture of Byzantine monumentality and wilting symbolism.

Pure Art Nouveau in the French manner can be seen in the Reök Palace at Szeged designed by Ede Magyar and built between 1896 and 1897; this is in contrast to the 'official' architectural style, a version of Viennese Baroque exemplified by the Török Bank in Budapest designed by Armin Hegedüs. Around 1910, the architect István Medgyaszay, an important pioneer of functionalist architecture in Hungary in the 1920s and 1930s, designed his first buildings.

Not surprisingly, the most fervent 'Magyar' style was to be seen in the pavilions erected for the international exhibitions, for these were the buildings which would generate the greatest worldwide critical response. The pavilion at the 1905–6 Milan Exhibition was designed by Geza Maróthi in the Magyar-Turco-Byzantine style. The interior and furniture were designed in a similar style by Maróthi, Odon Faragò and Ede Thorokai Wigand. Most of the furniture was inlaid with metals and upholstered in red cloth. Wigand, an

architect by profession, had been designing furniture since 1898; his first pieces were in a somewhat angular style, and with a use of costly materials, clearly influenced by Hoffmann and the Viennese school. Later pieces, such as those in Milan, were in the nationalistic peasant style.

Wigand also designed stained glass; his most famous commission in this medium is a set of six windows (four others were designed by Sándor Nagy) in the House of Culture at Marosvásárhely, Romania, executed between 1911 and 1913 and illustrating Hungarian legends and traditional ballads. Nagy, also an architect and designer of applied arts, had drawn cartoons for carpets shown in the Milan pavilion, these being executed by his wife. Other carpets in the same show were designed by Aladár Körösföi-Kriesch and made by Leo Belmonte. One of the most popular features of the Hungarian section in the Milan Exhibition was the carved wood toys, many of which had been designed by G. Weszely, head of the Royal Hungarian School of Toymaking at Hegybánya-Szélakna.

The apogee of the Hungarian nationalistic style was the pavilion for the 1911 Turin Exhibition. Designed by Emile Tory and Maurice Pogány, it was the most extraordinarily powerful mixture of traditional Magyar and Byzantine influences. The façade was ornamented with huge sculptures of crusaders by Nicolas Ligeti, the turrets were lined with dull copper and the interior light filtered through stained-glass windows designed by Miksa Róth. The hushed, cathedral-like atmosphere was carefully nurtured, as was the effect created by the historico-symbolism of the paintings and sculptures by Geza Maróthi, Eduard Telcs, Louis Greff, Louis Bansky and Aladár Körösföi-Kriesch. The pavilion and its contents were intended as a mystical, holy, symbol of an independent Hungarian people.

Unfortunately, most of the pavilion and its contents were destroyed by the fire which raged

Below A dining room in the Hungarian style designed by Ede Wigand for the Hungarian pavilion at the Milan Exhibition of 1905–6.

Below right The Hungarian pavilion at the 1911 Turin Exhibition, designed by Emile Tory and Maurice Pogány, showing an extraordinary mixture of Magyar and Byzantine influences.

through the Turin Exhibition complex. Among the most important of the destroyed Hungarian exhibits was a dining-room ensemble, including furniture, tapestries, glass and a dinner service by Zsolnay, designed on commission for Count Tivádar Andrássy by Rippl-Rónai. Only one piece, a tapestry called *Girl in a Red Dress* survived from the suite.

The most important of the Hungarian craft communities was the Gödöllö Atelier. The formation of this group was inspired by Morris and by the Russian experiments described above. One of the leaders of the group, Aladár Körösföi-Kriesch, was in regular correspondence with Leo Tolstoi. Originally only for weaving and embroidery, Gödöllö soon broadened its scope, producing designs for ceramics, glass, metalwork, sculpture and book-bindings, as well as holding regular exhibitions of paintings and undertaking commissions for murals. Indeed, much of the work previously mentioned in connection with new Hungarian design emanated from Gödöllö.

The example of Hungarian Jugendstil best-known internationally is Zsolnay pottery. The factory was founded in 1862 by Vilmos Zsolnay at Pêcs, and in its early years produced earthenware in a semi-industrial, semi-folk style. In 1893, Vinsce Wartha was appointed artistic director of an experimental studio and it was he who developed with Zsolnay the famous iridescent lustre glaze called Eosin. The inspiration for this glaze was certainly Massier's work in France.

Stylistically, Zsolnay's products can be divided into six main groups – those in traditional style, those in lustre resembling Tiffany or Loetz glass, the figures, the dishes painted with flowers and landscapes in red, green and blue, the pots with animals sculpted in high relief, and pieces made in the twentieth century which show the influence of the Vienna Secession. After 1900, many examples were made in porcelain as well as earthenware.

In artistic terms, the designer Joszef Rippl-Rónai marks the high point of the factory's history. His designs are determinedly Art Nouveau, with flowing floral patterns close in style to the work of Maurice Ranson and Walter Crane (the latter had visited the factory in 1900). Rippl-Rónai designed many pieces for execution in the Eosin glaze; the design was etched onto a ruby ground and made to stand out by the addition of gold lustre. Like Clément Massier, Zsolnay and Wartha also experimented with a muted sparkle and ruby or silver lustre through a matt or crackled base of tin glaze.

Apart from Rippl-Rónai, designers for the factory included the sculptors Sandor Apáti Abt and Lajos Mack, small figures by both of whom were exhibited by Zsolnay at the Paris 1900 Exhibition, and Vilmos' children Miklos, Terez and Julia. Another member of the family, László von Mattasovsky-Zsolnay, designed and decorated earthenware in his own studio. The factory received great acclaim at the international exhibitions, and still exists today.

Czechoslovakia

In the 1890s, the Prague Royal School of Art Craftsmanship was founded under the directorship of Professor Stribel; this was the first of many

small art and technical colleges founded throughout the country.

The leading figure in the Prague school was Jan Kotera, who was born in 1873 in Brünn, capital of Moravia. He studied architecture in Vienna under Otto Wagner and exhibited paintings at the official Prague Salon, the Rodolfinium. He continued to show work with the Vienna Secession and when the Marischer Kunstverein opened in Brünn in 1911, its exhibitions were dominated by the Viennese. Brünn became, next to Prague (the capital of Bohemia, the Czech part of the state) the leading cultural centre of what is now Czechoslovakia.

At the Prague Art School, the students were taught by a number of talented architects, painters and sculptors. The ceramic class was under Professor Kloücek, who designed earthenware for manufacture in peasant potteries; such pieces, similar to Horti's work in Hungary, were produced under the same circumstances, although Kloücek seems to have favoured raised floral decoration, not incising.

Most of Kotera's pieces were made of ash with metal inlays, and were inspired by English models, especially Baillie Scott and Voysey. Kotera also designed glass for Harrach's Glass Manufactory

A side altar and embroideries designed by Kastner at the Royal School of Art Craftsmanship, Prague, c. 1900.

Right Green lustre vase made at the Zsolnay factory, *c.* 1900.

Below Hungarian Zsolnay vase in lustred stoneware, designed by Joszef Rippl-Ronai, *c.* 1890.

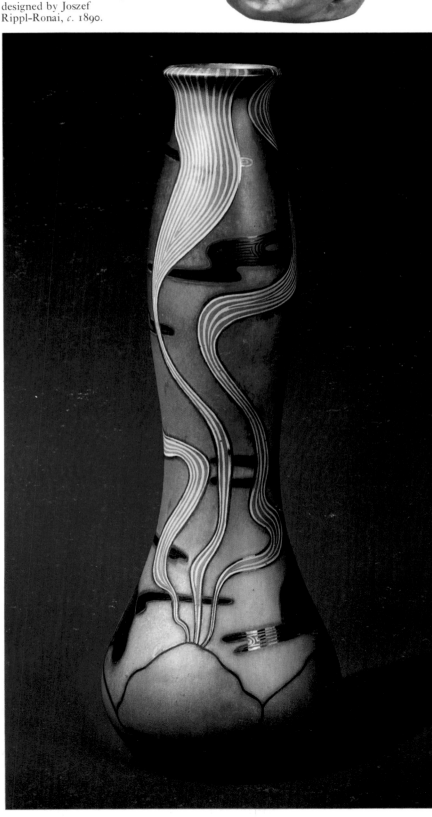

at Neuwelt. He was also one of the most important members of the Mánes Union, the principal Secessionist body in Prague, which had its journal aptly named *Volné Směry* (Free Trends).

Another extremely influential teacher at the Prague school was Jan Beneš, who devised a system of teaching design based upon plant forms which he called 'Stylisierung'. The ideas behind this was to 'replace the fruitless copying of historical forms by the study of nature as the real source of all form and colour.' Beneš was also artistic director of the Chamotte Textile Manufactory at Rakonitz, where Helená Johnová was one of the designers.

Johnová had studied at the Prague School of Arts and Crafts and in 1907 was a founder member of the Prague group of artists and designers called Artel. From 1909 to 1911 she studied ceramics under Powolny at the Vienna Kunstgewerbeschüle and in 1919 was appointed professor at the Prague School of Ceramic Art; in this capacity, she was closely involved with the development of modern ceramics in Czechoslovakia.

The Mánes Union mentioned above, included artists like Alphonse Mucha. It was concerned with new developments in modern European art. It organised the exhibition of Rodin's work in Prague in 1903, and its direction was influenced principally by French Impressionism and Post-Impressionism.

Poland and Other Countries

The main Polish dissident group of artists and designers, the Sztuka, was centred on Cracow, the German part of Poland (Galicia). It included the painters Jácek Malczewski, Ferdynand Rüszczcuz and Josef Chelmonski. The sculptor Konstanty Lászczko exhibited with this group, as did Stanislaus Wyspianski, a painter and designer of stained-glass, and Julius Makárewicz, who was responsible for the restoration of the Imperial Palace at Warsaw. The Sztuka held regular exhibitions of painting and sculpture but also placed importance on the applied arts. Kasimir Sichülski, who had exhibited with the Vienna Secession, designed tapestries, and the exhibitions included furniture, metalwork and stained glass designed by Edward Wittig and Konstanty Lászczko.

Various schools of arts and crafts were set up in Romania, including one at Craiova, founded by Gheorghe Chitu and in Bucharest (the School of Fine Arts). Probably the most famous graduate from both these institutions was Constantin Brancusi, who exhibited for the first time in Bucharest in 1908. Brancusi also exhibited in Prague in 1914 in an exhibition called 'Modern French Artists'. It need hardly be said that his influence on the development of French decorative styles is crucial, if not yet properly documented.

The Byzantine-peasant style can also be seen in the work of the various areas which today constitute most of Jugoslavia – Bosnia, Dalmatia, Croatia, Serbia. The Serbian pavilion at the Turin 1911 Exhibition was designed by Branko M. Tanásević and decorated by Ch. Inchiostu; it was in the Byzantine style, with the type of furniture familiar from the Russian craft communities (although, ironically, the Russian pavilion at Turin was in an anachronistic neo-Greek style).

PART THREE

THE
BACKGROUND
TO THE
DECORATIVE
ARTS

1890-1940

The Great Exhibitions

by Lynne Thornton

NINETEENTH-CENTURY international exhibitions were intended to be living encyclopedias of man's achievements, a balance-sheet of scientific, technical and moral progress. They were used to impress other nations with the host's political and industrial might and to act as a showcase for commerce. Each exhibition tried to surpass the one before in a gigantic, self-congratulatory display. Emphasis was laid on volume, weight, size and cost, each country in competition to produce the biggest and the best. The millions of visitors were probably rather more overwhelmed than instructed or morally elevated, after acres of Baroque palaces, Neo-classical temples, mosques, pagodas and chalets; they were, however, offered many entertainments and distractions, whipped cream on the solid pudding of worthiness. From the extensive coverage of the artistic press of the period, we today have the impression that Art Nouveau was the centre of interest. It had, on the contrary, a hard struggle amongst the heavy machinery and ostentatious objects of technical virtuosity produced by important manufacturers.

By the twentieth century, a hitherto unshakeable confidence in the future and in progress for progress's sake had been undermined by social unrest, wars and recessions, so that international exhibitions could never be the same carefree and ever-expanding affairs that they had been. The necessity of using them as an opportunity for studying the problems of urban planning was understood and there was some attempt at specialisation. The old tussle between industry and good design, artist and craftsman went on, but there was an insistence on original creation, compared to the formerly acceptable pastiches of past styles. The halls were designed by well-known architects and interior decorators and the furniture and objects were better integrated into a general Plan for Living. By 1939, however, the year of the New York World Fair, industry and science had again triumphed and the decorative arts were relegated to the background or were absorbed by production on a large scale.

Of the thirty or so international exhibitions held between 1890 and 1940 in places as far apart as Riga, Hanoi, Rio, Adelaide, Moscow and Istanbul, eight stand out as being of particular interest: the early ones, since they helped the spread of Art Nouveau, the Paris 1925 Exhibition, as an unrepeatable celebration of quality and luxury in the decorative arts, and those of the 1930s, since they had a profound influence on our habitat today.

Exhibitions before 1890

Although the first large commercial exhibition was held in Paris in 1798, it was the 1851 Crystal Palace Exhibition in London which inspired later World Fairs. Throughout the fifties and sixties, the critics complained of the slavish imitation of past styles, that the craftsman had become an animated machine and that, although the exhibits were ingenious and often technically brilliant, there were no modern creations; everything was subordinated to the clients' taste for luxury and the manufacturers' greed.

At the 1878 Paris Exposition Universelle, there were glimmerings of an artistic revival, but the glass shown by Jean, Rousseau, Gallé and Brocard and the faïence by Deck was heavily marked by their interest in Japanese, Egyptian or Persano-Arab art. At the 1889 Exhibition in Paris, the precursors of Art Nouveau were more clearly distinguishable from the mass of copyists. Chaplet showed his porcelain with flambé glazes, Taxile Doat his *pâte-sur-pâte* and Delaherche his rustic stoneware. Rousseau and his collaborator Léveillé exhibited their crackled glass and Gallé was highly praised for his enamelled, engraved and tinted vases, both for their technical innovation and their high artistic merit. Gallé and the future School of Nancy were also notable in the furniture section, although they were overshadowed by the pseudo-

La Caresse du Cygne, statuette in ivory and bronze by Philippe Wolfers, exhibited at the Exposition Internationale, Brussels, 1897.

Ethnographical room by
Paul Hankar at the
Exposition Internationale,
Brussels, 1897. The
woodwork and furniture are
in *bilinga nauclea*.

Tiffany magnolia vase in silver, gold, enamels and opals, exhibited at the World Columbian Exposition, Chicago, 1893.

eighteenth-century veneered commodes and heavy oak buffets in the Henri-Deux style. As a result of this exhibition, Gustave Sandoz created the Comité Français des Expositions à l'Etranger and a group of artists, collectors and manufacturers founded the Société d'Encouragement à l'Art et à l'Industrie, both of which helped to raise the status of creative decorative arts.

World Columbian Exposition, Chicago, 1893
The exhibition in Jackson Park, 'the biggest in the world', proved the vitality and growth of American industry. Chicago, still a village in 1830 and a city only in 1857, was famous for its flour-milling, slaughter-houses, canned meat and tanneries. The gum-chewing, tobacco-spitting public were unashamedly proud of the progress their country had made and were inclined to criticize the foreign exhibits as being too refined and namby-pamby for their taste.

Opulence was the keynote of the American exhibits (which included ice-cream soda fountains and saloon bar fixtures) sent from all over the United States by decorating and furnishing companies. Tiffany & Co. had their own pavilion, which combined Spanish and Renaissance elements, the interior resembling a Byzantine church. They showed silver and plate with Japanese, Indian, Moorish and Egyptian motifs, some of the magnificent chased and enamelled pieces being priced at $10,000. While the Tiffany furniture was composed of thousands of squares of natural woods in different colours, most pieces in the exhibition were either revivals of the Colonial 'Old World' styles or debased forms of an earlier Eastlake conception (Charles Lock Eastlake had been instrumental in introducing the ideas of William Morris and Ruskin into the United States).

These were, however, now offset by some good American arts and crafts. There were a few interesting pieces in the glass section: Thomas Webb sent cameo glass from England, and Léveillé crackled glass from France. The Daum brothers, however, had the misfortune to be badly displayed, while Gallé did not participate at all. The ceramic section was richer, with contributions from the Austrian, Ernst Wahliss, the Dane, Hermann Kähler, and Royal Copenhagen, and stoneware and faïence by Doultons and Maws. France sent Chaplet, Muller, Bigot and Delaherche; the latter was to have a profound effect on American ceramists, particularly on William Grueby. Among the American art potters of note were Mary Louise McLaughlin (who had already showed in Philadelphia in 1876 and in Paris in 1878), Maria Longworth Nichols (her Rookwood Pottery had won a gold medal at the 1889 Paris Fair) and Mrs. C. A. Plimton, a leading member of the Cincinnati pottery club. Chicago, then, was eclectic but erratic.

Exposition Internationale, Brussels, 1897 (Colonial Section)
The main part of the exhibition was situated in the Parc du Cinquantenaire and included the Palaces of Fine Arts, Sciences and Belgian Industry, as well as the foreign pavilions. The colonial section was twelve kilometres away, at

Turveren. It was destined to bring the Belgian Congo to the public's notice and to encourage artists to use imported ivory and exotic woods, in particular *bilinga nauclea*. Paul Hankar, Gustave Serrurier-Bovy, Henry van de Velde and Georges Hobé, were commissioned to design furniture and interiors to house the exhibits.

The sculpture section was especially interesting. There had been a flourishing ivory market in Antwerp since 1888 and some ivory statues were shown at the Antwerp Exposition Universelle in 1894. At Turveren, there were eighty pieces, Symbolist, Art Nouveau or traditional, some set off by silver, gold and precious stones, by thirty-eight artists, including Craco, de Rudder, Rousseau, Khnopff, Meunier and Van der Stappen. Philippe Wolfers, who had a remarkable selection of crystal and silver in the Palais des Beaux-Arts, showed fourteen pieces including a remarkable vase in ivory and bronze, *La Caresse du Cygne*. The decorative arts were completed by eight large embroidered panels by Hélène de Rudder representing the past and the future of the Congo. The quality of the exhibits was remarkably high and many are now in the Musée Royal de l'Afrique Centrale in Turveren.

Stoneware vase by Adrien-Pierre Dalpayrat with ormolu mounts by Keller, exhibited at the Paris 1900 Exhibition.

Above Interior in painted
parchment and metal by
Bugatti for the Exposizione
Internationale, Turin, 1902.

Left Mahogany display
cabinet by Bernhard
Pankok, exhibited at Turin
in 1902.

Right 'The Rose Boudoir'
by Charles R. Mackintosh
and Margaret Macdonald
Mackintosh for the Turin
exhibition of 1902.

Exposition Internationale, Paris, 1900

The 1900 World's Fair set out to embody the ideal of peace, progress and civilisation. By the time the last certificate, medal and prize had been handed out, it was already being seen as a crucial point in the decline of European optimism. More than forty nations participated, including Imperial Germany, but only the Shah and the King of Sweden accepted the official invitation; the other crowned heads saw Paris as a hotbed of anarchist plots, and there was a general anti-French feeling after the Dreyfus affair. In spite of this, nearly fifty-one million visitors filed past all the marvels of science and technology, paintings past and present, the Quai des Nations with its decorative palaces in indigenous styles and the numerous amusements, which included Loïe Fuller's dancing, Sadda Yakko's theatre and the Big Wheel. They travelled by the newly-opened Métro with entrances by Guimard, but avoided the *trottoir roulant*, the moving sidewalk destined to carry them over the 350 acres. The exhibition was breathtakingly pompous, with a mass of over-lavish ornamentation run wild.

Every well-known name in the Art Nouveau movement was there: Lalique and Vever with their Baroque jewels, furniture by the Six, Hoentschel, the School of Nancy, Bing's L'Art Nouveau and Meier-Graefe's La Maison Moderne; ceramics by Chaplet, Bigot, Cazin, Dalpayrat, Muller, Lachenal, Massier and the School of St. Amand, the American art potters, the German and Scandinavian ceramic factories and egg-shell earthenware by the Dutch firm of Rozenburg. There were Tiffany windows, Gallé symbolist vases, glass by Léveillé, Loetz and Koepping; enamels by Thesmar and Feuillâtre, silver by Cardeilhac and Christofle; tapestries after Burne-Jones, Grasset, Gustave Moreau, Lévy-Dhurmer and Rochegrosse; carpets, book bindings, pewter, medallions, embroideries, lace, and so on.

Exposizione Internationale, Turin, 1902

Breaking with tradition, the organisers stipulated that the exhibits must be original works displaying a marked tendency to an aesthetic renewal of form and that imitations of historical styles or industrial productions lacking in artistic inspiration would be refused admittance. There was a distinct bias towards Germany, artists from the Low Countries and British Arts and Crafts.

Germany had the largest section after Italy and showed thirty-eight interiors designed by Behrens, Pankok, Paul, Olbrich and Berlepsch-Valendas, with ceramics by the Berlin Manufactory, Schmuz-Baudiss, Lauger and Scharvogel. Holland exhibited furniture by the group t'Binnenhuis and Lion Cachet, textiles by Dysselhof and graphics by Nieuwenhuis.

Scandinavia sent examples of ceramics by their leading manufacturers, Kosta crystal and textiles by Alf Wallender; the United States sent Tiffany stained glass windows, lamps and Favrile glass, metalwork by the Gorham Manufacturing Co. and Rookwood pottery. France had a relatively small section, which included Lalique, the major ceramists, the School of Nancy, L'Art Nouveau and La Maison Moderne, Charpentier, Selmersheim and Plumet. English Arts and Crafts designers were there in force: Voysey, Day, Ashbee, Crane, Anning Bell, Benson, De Morgan, etc., but it was the School of Glasgow which won the day. The Scots showed furniture, objects and embroidery in three rooms decorated in mauve, rose, bright green, black and white. Many of the pieces had already been seen at the Glasgow International Exhibition and at the Vienna Secession in 1901 (the Secessionists, who had done so much to help the School of Glasgow to be better known on the Continent, did not exhibit at Turin). Although there were 250 contributors to the Italian section, they did not have much originality or sense of harmony and most of the exhibits were in a bastardised Liberty style. While the Italian architecture was influenced by the Secessionists and the Darmstadt colony, the decorative arts had all the frills of rococo Art Nouveau, without its spirit or basic form. The one exception was Carlo Bugatti, whose remarkable and highly individual furniture in parchment and metal was independent of all current styles.

Louisiana Purchase International Exhibition, St. Louis, 1904

The Fair was held to celebrate the centenary of the purchase of the State of Louisiana by Thomas Jefferson. For the occasion, St. Louis was re-landscaped, streams diverted, hills levelled off, lagoons dug and Tyrolean alps raised. The exhibition area was twice the size of Chicago's (1897), three times that of Paris (1900) and ten times Buffalo's (1901). There was a Palace of Varied Industries, a Temple of Fraternity, a Palace of Art and numerous pavilions for each state and foreign country; one palace alone cost a million dollars.

St. Louis saw the confirmation of the importance of the American art pottery movement, which had started in the 1870s. After having begun in an amateur sort of way, the ceramists had by now made great advances. Technical help had been given in the form of the treatise by the Sèvres ceramist Taxile Doat, which had been published in 1903 by Adelaide Alsop Robineau in the influential *Keramic Studio*. Until then, there had been a certain amount of artistic inspiration taken from Oriental and French ceramics seen at international exhibitions, but the work of the dozens of small American firms showed that they had now found their own style. William Grueby exhibited his matt glazes (he had won three medals at the Paris 1900 Exhibition), Mrs. Robineau her carved porcelain, Rookwood vases with vellum glazes (in contrast to their usual shiny finish), Artus van Briggle his moulded faïence with symbolist motifs, and the Tiffany Furnaces Favrile Pottery their first ivory-tinted porcelain, which was not commercialised until 1905. Besides this wealth of ceramics, Tiffany showed Favrile glass and there was a selection of American Arts and Crafts furniture, including that of Charles Rohlfs, which had been seen at Buffalo (1901) and Turin (1902).

Despite the fact that Alphonse Mucha designed a poster of a rather plump woman holding the hand of a Red Indian to advertise the Fair in France, the French section, directed by Alfred Picard, the long-suffering organiser of the Paris 1900 Exhibition, was of little interest: St. Louis remained a truly American success.

Chest of drawers in fumed oak by Charles Rohlfs, exhibited at Buffalo (1901), Turin (1902) and St. Louis (1904).

Exposition des Arts Décoratifs et Industriels, Paris, 1925

The 1925 Exhibition gave rise to a spate of books, catalogues and articles on how to appreciate and understand the contemporary decorative arts. Through these publications and recent exhibitions, notably that held in the Paris Musée des Arts Décoratifs in 1976–7, we can delight in the diversity, richness and high quality of the exhibits. The 1925 Exhibition saw the triumph of the decorators or *ensembliers*, particularly in the Pavillon d'un Collectionneur (Ruhlmann and his group), L'Ambassade Française (Groult, Dunand, Selmersheim, Dufrène, Follot) and the Pavillon de la Compagnie des Arts Français (Süe et Mare). Although some rooms in L'Ambassade Française were decorated with simplicity, even austerity, by Roux-Spitz, Chareau, Mallet-Stevens and Jourdain, the remainder were filled with furniture in shagreen, lacquer, exotic woods and ivory.

There was a series of coloured plaster boutiques built on the Pont Alexandre II for Sonia Delaunay, Lalique, Heim, Herbst, Jourdain, Cheuret and Hébrard; Paul Poiret showed his brilliantly-coloured Martine interiors on his three barges moored on the Seine, and Rateau exhibited his green-patinated bronze furniture designed for Jeanne Lanvin in the Pavillon de l'Elégance. The big department stores showed work by their studios in separate pavilions – Studium (Louvre), Pomone (Bon Marché) Primavera (Printemps), La Maîtrise (Galeries Lafayette), while other pavilions were financed by Sèvres, Christofle, Baccarat, Luce and Lalique. Although wrought-iron doors, screens, lamps and console tables by Edgar Brandt were to be found all over the exhibition, most of the applied arts, metalwork, jewellery, ceramics, glass, book binding, tapestries and lighting appliances, were shown either in the building organised by the magazine *Art et Décoration* under the heading of Artistes Français Contemporains, or in the Grand Palais, classed according to the different techniques.

Amongst this wealth of colour, comfort and luxury, the rationalism of the Pavillon de l'Esprit Nouveau (Le Corbusier, Ozenfant, Jeanneret, Cubist paintings and furniture by Thonet) seemed very cold indeed. The traditionalist organising committee had tried to ban them from the exhibition and it was only by a ruse that they were able to show their work at all.

Twenty-one foreign countries and the French colonies participated, with abstentions from the United States, Germany, Australia and Norway. Many of the buildings and their contents were a mixture of 'modern' Neo-classicism and academism, except for the striking Soviet pavilion painted a fiery red, in which the Constructivists exhibited side by side with Russian rural handicrafts. Sweden showed Orrefors glass, Denmark showed Jensen silver and ceramics by Royal Copenhagen, Jean Gauguin and Bing & Grøndahl; Austria was represented by Hoffmann's Wiener Werkstätte and Belgium by Horta's furniture, Val-Saint-Lambert crystal and 'Kéramis' ceramics. Gio Ponti, founder of the architectural revue *Domus* was the star of the Italian section, while Holland, deprived by the organisers of the collaboration of the architectural group De Stijl, sent established artists already famous in the 1900s. Britain, exhausted by the British Empire Exhibition at Wembley in 1924, half-heartedly showed eighteenth-century pastiches and furniture by Gordon Russell and Ambrose Heal.

Just as Brinkmann had done for the Hamburg Museum at the 1900 Paris Exhibition, so Edward J. Moore bought a selection of the finest Art Deco pieces, which are now in the Metropolitan Museum, New York, many of the other exhibits being in the Paris Musée des Arts Décoratifs.

After the 1925 Exhibition began the decline of a purely ornamental style for the élite and the rising influence of the modernists. Although many of the celebrated Art Deco *ensembliers* and artists were to work throughout the 1930s in a 'transatlantic liner' style, the innovators, rejected by the traditionalist Salon des Artistes Décorateurs, formed the Union des Artistes Modernes in 1930, which completed the schism between the 'decorative' and the 'functional'.

Exposition Coloniale, Paris, 1931

Reconstructions of mud huts, mosques and Far Eastern temples, animated by people in their native costume, were nothing new at international exhibitions. 'Voilà nos esclaves!' wrote Eugène Melchior de Vogüé in 1889, ironically summing up the general feeling of pride at 'owning' these strange apparitions from the far-off colonies. The 1931 Exhibition was important in showing the advance that had been made in the greater understanding of the indigenous arts and culture of France Outre-Mer. The fine arts were ahead of the applied arts in succumbing to the exoticism of the colonies. French painters and sculptors had for many years been showing their work at the Salons of various Orientalist societies and the influence of Oceania and black Africa on the School of Paris from 1905 on is well known. Although Chareau, Legrain, Coard, Dunand, da Silva Bruhns and other designers had been working in the colonial idiom during the twenties, 1931 was the first year in which there was such a large showing of furniture, ceramics, textiles and jewellery inspired by exotic prototypes.

The exhibition, directed by Maréchal Lyautey, was held in the Park of Vincennes, around Lake Daumesnil. The participating countries included Denmark, Portugal, Belgium, Italy, the Low Countries, Brazil and the United States. There were displays of every aspect of colonial life, pavilions in native styles and superb reconstructions of monuments such as the Angkor Wat, enlivened by dramatic floodlighting and coloured fountains.

The fine and applied arts were exhibited in the Musée Permanent des Colonies (now the Musée des Arts Africains et Océaniens). The façade has a magnificent frieze sculpted in low relief by Janniot; it took his two collaborators and thirty craftsmen three years to complete the sea of stylised figures representing the different colonies. The furniture designers were torn between making special exhibition pieces or catering for an expatriate clientèle. In the first case, they made full use of the exotic woods available: palissander, amaranth, teak, red padouk, bilinga, bubinga, wacapo and Macassar ebony, or Far Eastern

Above Ceramic vase by René Buthaud, exhibited at the Exposition Coloniale, Paris, 1931.

Above right Bas-relief by Alfred Janniot, symbolising the forces of the Earth, on the façade of the Palais de Tokyo at the Trocadero, Paris, 1937.

lacquer, enriched with ivory and mother-of-pearl. Furniture for export had, however, to conform to the spirit of local colonial architecture, to be easily transportable, collapsible if necessary, and to be in materials which would easily support a hot climate. Besides, the buyers from abroad had leanings towards Empire, Louis-Quinze or the Dutch Colonial style, rather than contemporary creations. The problem was solved by showing luxury pieces side by side with a cheaper range.

Among the *artistes-décorateurs* were Ruhlmann, Prou for Pomone, Guillemard for Primavera, Kohlmann for Studium, Montegnac, Renaudot, Leleu, Cheuret, Fréchet, Djo-Bourgeois, Domin for Dominique and Groult. Jean Dunand exhibited lacquer panels and inlaid metal; there were fountains and lights by Sabino, Etling, Perzel and Lalique; glass by Colotte, Sabino, Luce, Marinot, Walter, Daum, Baccarat and Saint-Louis; ceramics by Decoeur, Besnard, Massoul and Buthaud; carpets by da Silva Bruhns; textiles and wallpaper by Bonfils and Follot; metalwork by Brandt, Serrière, Linossier, Daurat and Subes. Hamm showed small objects in ivory, horn and mother-of-pearl next to cigarette cases and boxes in lacquer.

In the jewellery section, there were brooches and clasps of Algerian inspiration, onyx, coral and lapis pendants in the form of African masks, tiger and panther claws mounted in enamelled gold, and necklaces which mixed Negro Art with Cubism. Fashion, too, was touched by this vogue for exoticism: Marcel Rochas designed squared shoulders inspired by the costumes of Balinese temple dancers and the low necklines and softly draped bodices of many 1931 dresses closely followed the lines of Buddhist robes.

The critics of the time felt that this vogue would only last a short time but that the designers had made a much appreciated gesture towards the Colonies, so important to the French economy.

Exposition Internationale des Arts et Techniques, Paris 1937

The aim of the exhibition was to show that the beautiful and the useful were compatible, that art and technology should and could go hand in hand and that rationalism, simplicity, elegance and harmony in everyday life would help the spiritual well-being of man. It was a national morale-booster after the Depression, which had left so many unemployed in consumer trades.

One of the most striking features was the Palais de Chaillot, its curved Neo-classical structure replacing the ugly heterogeneous building designed by Haussmann in 1878. The Trocadero's complex of museums overlooking the Seine, the Champ de Mars and the Eiffel Tower today still offers one of the most beautiful perspectives in Paris. The two major pavilions were those of Germany and the U.S.S.R. in symbolic confrontation on either side of the Champ de Mars. Of the forty-five or so participating nations, many mixed a false 'modernism' with the rustic and traditional. Scandinavia and the Low Countries exhibited furniture and objects which were uncomplicated, and relatively cheap, being designed for a large market. Austria (whose Wiener Werkstätte had closed down in 1932 with Hoffmann's retirement), and Britain, who had a poor showing of period revival furniture, were considered too 'cosy'.

The gardens and most of the façades of both the temporary buildings and permanent museums were enriched by sculptures and bas-reliefs by Janniot (who had been prominent at the 1931 exhibition) the Martel brothers, Gimond, Orlandi, Landowski, Dejean, Drivier, Niclausse, and Sarabezolles. The interiors were decorated with engraved *verre eglomisé* panels by J. J. K. Ray and Max Ingrand and large painted decorations by some of the most representative artists of the 1930s. There were posters and publicity by

Cassandre ('Dubo, Dubon, Dubonnet'), Carlu and Cappiello, and myriads of fountains and jets which rose and fell and turned pink, mauve, blue and green according to the music played on a giant piano.

Mallet-Stevens designed the Pavillon de la Solidarité, the Pavillon de l'Hygiène and the Palais de l'Electricité (which housed Dufy's giant panorama 'La Fée Electricité'). He also presided over the avant-garde Union des Artistes Modernes, who exhibited silver, textiles, furniture, ceramics, book-binding, graphics and sculpture. The Société des Artistes-Décorateurs showed fashionable interiors of the year 1937, with sprigged wallpaper, furniture in carved oak or figured fruitwood, sideboards faced with leather, mirror glass or *verre eglomisé*, panels, quilted and fringed satin upholstery and draped curtains. Its members included many well-known names from the 1920s, Dunand, Süe, Montegnac, Dufet, Mercier, Renaudot, Groult, Rapin, Prou, Dominique, Printz, Adnet and Fréchet. They were joined by Porteneuve, Ruhlmann's successor, Arbus, antifunctionalist, who had brought back the curvilinear in the early thirties, and Jean Royère, who was to create entirely new forms during the fifties. The same feeling for discreetly lit, enveloping interiors for a chosen clientèle, was to be found in the Pavillon de l'Ile de France decorated by Dominique, Frank, Follot, Leleu, Adnet and Pascaud.

The taste in the late 1930s for Surrealism and the theatrical was most obvious in the Pavillon de l'Elégance organised by Jeanne Lanvin, the unusual disposition of the models in arcades and dramatic lighting having an equal success at the 1939 New York Fair.

We have seen that, at the exhibitions of the late nineteenth century, designers and craftsmen of originality had to struggle for recognition; even at the Paris 1900 Exhibition, the Art Nouveau artists were nearly submerged by the generally incoherent, over-ornamented mass. Although Turin (1902) was the first specialised international exhibition, it was not until Paris (1925) that the words 'Decorative Arts' found their way into the official title, from which the name of the style Art Deco was taken. Almost immediately after the status of the decorative arts had been established, there came a split between the *ensembliers* and the 'Modernists' which became definitive in 1930. In 1935, at the Brussels Exposition Internationale et Universelle, the divergence of these two movements were very clear, the Salon des Artistes-Décorateurs with their 'foyer de la famille française' on the one hand, and the Union des Artistes Modernes on the other. Even then, the U.A.M. which had done so much to change the French habitat, was criticised for not working enough with industry, as had done the members of the Bauhaus, disbanded in 1933. Although the 1937 Paris Exhibition was organised to encourage the collaboration of art and technology, the decorative was still opposed to the functional. At the 1939 New York World's Fair, however, there were few signs of individual creations. The aim: to present a synopsis of human activities and possible future developments; the theme: 'The World of Tomorrow'. The age of mass-production was on its way.

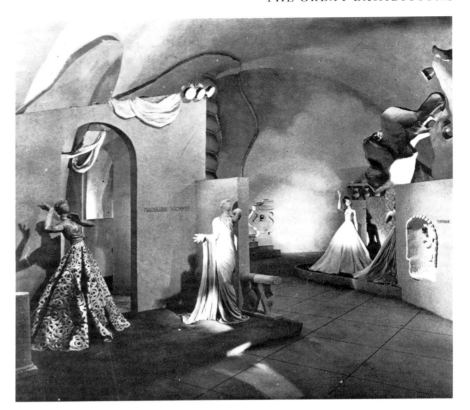

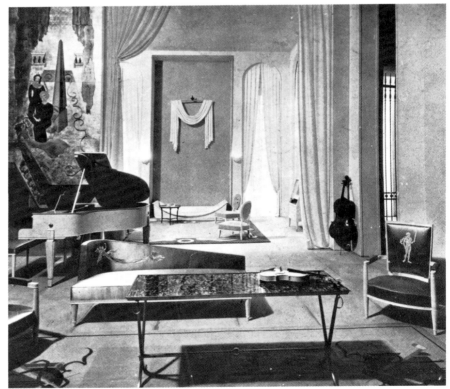

Top 'Salle de la haute couture', arranged by Jeanne Lanvin for the Paris 1937 Exhibition.

Above A music room arranged by André Arbus for the Paris 1937 Exhibition.

Photography and Cinema

by Philippe Garner

THE HISTORY OF PHOTOGRAPHY between 1890 and 1940 is both rich and varied. The fifty-year span is, of course, an arbitrary one and, if the wealth of material available for study is to be more fully explained, might more appropriately be deemed to have started in 1888. The introduction by George Eastman in August of that year of the world's first easy-to-use roll-film camera, the Kodak, marked the beginning of a significant new era of photography, an era of popularisation with the practical possibility of simple, instantaneous photography for professional and amateur alike. Amidst the almost infinite diversity of output and creativity which followed, the study of the history of photography after 1890 is perhaps best broadly divided into two parts, though overlaps inevitably occur. The subject divides itself fairly naturally between instantaneous, documentary photography and the self-conscious aesthetic evolution of photography, with its parallels and associations within other areas of the arts.

The most pertinent application of the new fast films and hand-held cameras that were now commercially available on a wide scale was in the newly-created genre of 'snapshot' photography. The freshness and spontaneity of this new genre found a notable exponent in the 1890s in the British photographer Paul Martin. An otherwise mundane professional photographer, Martin took his snapshots in his own time, as a hobby, and it is on these that his reputation has survived. It has been said of him that, 'He was content to record what he saw and pleased him, and his snapshots have more significance than much of the work of "concerned" photographers of today.' George Ruff Jnr., another British photographer, proved his talent as a gifted amateur with snapshots of unusual vitality dating from the early years of the century. In France the young Jacques-Henri Lartigue, given his first camera in 1901, entered into a lifelong devotion to capturing the everyday elements of life in snapshots imbued with a very personal warmth and *ingénu* humour.

Documentary photography had, by 1890, already established its own tradition, bringing forth the occasional spark of inspired observation amidst the sea of commercial picture-making.

The pattern continued after 1890 with such talents as Eugène Atget, Horace Nicholls, Lewis Hine and, later, Walker Evans, who distinguished themselves by their ability to instil a personal point-of-view into the subject matter of their photography.

The Frenchman Eugène Atget worked painstakingly and discreetly during the first quarter of the century documenting Paris life and architecture, the backstreets, shop-fronts, brothels and parks that other photographers overlooked. His sharp, gold-toned prints have a remarkable sense of intimacy. British photographer Horace Nicholls made lively photo-documents of Edwardian life and a vivid record, first of the Boer War and subsequently of the First World War. Lewis Hine's poignant documentation of the abuse of child labour in America in the early years of the century helped alleviate conditions.

Walker Evans came to photography in 1928. Reacting against the artiness of soft-focus pictorialism that had dominated the photographic scene, Evans gave a sharply-defined beauty to the mundane. His most notable work was his documentation of the poverty of America's mid-West in a series of some four hundred photographs taken as part of a Farm Security Administration project between 1935 and 1937.

Photo-journalism was one new facet of documentary photography to evolve in the period in question, finding its fulfilment in the 1930s in picture magazines such as the German *Müncher Illustrierte Presse,* launched in 1929, the British *Picture Post,* launched in 1938, and the American *Life,* launched in 1936; its first cover was a dynamic photograph by Margaret Bourke-White. The new breed of photographers pursued picture-stories with a human interest that would fascinate a very large public, using the new small-format 35mm cameras such as the Leica.

Amongst the most distinguished photojournalists were Henri Cartier-Bresson, Robert Capa, best remembered for his documentation of the Spanish Civil War, Felix Man, Erich Salomon, and Bert Hardy. Bill Brandt's early, stark, visual essays on industrial England were published in *Picture Post.* Brassaï's remarkable documentation of Paris night life appeared in book form in *Paris de Nuit* of 1933 and *Voluptés de Paris* of 1935. The extraordinary New York photographer Weegee slept fully dressed and with a police radio by his pillow, always at the ready, first on the scene to capture the aftermath of crime or accident with his 4 × 5 Speed Graphic and harsh direct flash.

The increased facility of the photographic process after 1890, a facility which both encouraged mass-market amateur use and allowed a new directness and realism to the professional, inspired a natural reaction on the part of those who respected photography as an art-form. Photography by no means heralded the death of painting, as had been forecast by certain critics; on the contrary, photography liberated painting from the

Snapshot by George Ruff Jnr.,
Brighton, *c.* 1905.

practical necessities of documentation and pictorialism, allowing a more rapid evolution towards abstraction.

By 1890, however, photography was in need of aesthetic revitalisation. Commercialisation had debased the idealism and achievements of the 1850s and 1860s. During the 1880s British photographer Peter Henry Emerson had fought virtually single-handed to win acceptance for his pictorial style, which he dubbed Naturalism. In the wake of an ultimately disenchanted Emerson came the establishment in 1892 in London of the Linked Ring, a society whose aim was '. . . the complete emancipation of pictorial photography . . . from the retarding bondage . . . of that which was purely scientific or technical . . . its development as an independent art.' The founder members included Henry Peach Robinson, George Davison and Henry Hay Cameron, son of Julia Margaret Cameron. Perhaps the most talented member of the Linked Ring was Frederick H. Evans, whose warm subtle-toned platinum prints are amongst the most beautiful examples of British Pictorialism.

The concept of photography as a fine art, however, found no greater advocate than the American Alfred Stieglitz. Founding the Photo-Secession in 1902 with a small group of photo-

Right Alfred Stieglitz, photographed by Alvin Langdon Coburn, published in *Camera Work*, January 1908.

Below Analytical close-up by Edward Weston, 1930s.

graphers who shared his ideals, Stieglitz created a rallying point for American Pictorialism. The galleries of the Photo-Secession at 291 Fifth Avenue became known after 1905 not only for the regular exhibitions of both American and European photography but as a showcase for the avant-garde in American and European art, Stieglitz refusing to isolate photography from the other arts. 291 displayed the work of Picasso, Matisse, Braque, Picabia, Brancusi and others and introduced examples of the primitive African carvings that were causing such excitement in Parisian artistic circles. Stieglitz exhibited the work of American artists John Marin, Arthur Dove, Marsden Hartley, Abraham Walkowitz and Max Weber and, before the Armory Show of 1913 which won the avant-garde a wider recognition, he was virtually alone in encouraging and promoting their talent.

The founder membership of the Secession included photographers John G. Bullock, Frank Eugene, Gertrude Käsebier, Joseph T. Keiley, Edward J. Steichen and Clarence White. Amongst the subsequent membership, the most distinguished talent was perhaps that of Boston photographer Alvin Langdon Coburn. The work of members and selected guests was published in fine-quality gravure reproduction in the pages of Stieglitz's quarterly journal *Camera Work*, a fifty-part work, the first issue of which appeared in January 1903.

The most characteristic Photo-Secessionist work used soft-focus effects in painterly compositions that demonstrated their status as art by imitating traditional concepts of painting. As painting, however, took rapid steps towards abstraction, the pictorialists found themselves in an impasse. A critic of 1912 remarked, 'Now, however, that it (painting) is seeking to render a vision of things not as they are palpable to the eye but as they impress the imagination, Mr. Stieglitz proves what he has known all along, that photography is powerless to continue its rivalry with painting.'

Although Pictorialism died a by no means sudden death, lingering through the twenties and thirties as the most popular style for both amateur and professional aiming at self-consciously artistic effect, by the 1920s it was no longer associated with the avant-garde. The Linked Ring dissolved in 1910, while 291 held its last show in 1917. A new direction was required and in America emerged in the analytical work of the West Coast School, finding its greatest exponent in Edward Weston and its rallying point in the f – 64 Association established in 1932.

The f – 64 group included Weston, Ansel Adams and Imogen Cunningham. They took their name from the aperture they used to achieve maximum definition. This pursuit of definition united them in a reaction to the soft Pictorialism from which some of them had evolved. Weston wrote in his daybooks that 'The camera should be for a recording of life, for rendering the very substance and quintessence of the thing itself, whether it be polished steel or palpitating flesh'. Working with a 10 × 8 plate camera he gave a philosophical dimension to landscapes, nudes or objects as diverse as seashells, vegetables or his austere and beautiful 'Bedpan' of 1930. Imogen

Cunningham specialised in the study of flowers and other natural forms, most usually in close-up, sharply analysing pattern and texture and discovering an extraordinary sensuality. Ansel Adams specialised in studies from nature and dramatically lit visions of the American landscape. Working to this day, he has made an industry of the production of his meticulously exposed and flawlessly printed images.

Minor White emerged in the late 1930s as perhaps the most intellectual exponent of the American analytical school. Frederick Sommer made analytical studies of often bizarre and distasteful subject matter using the techniques of the f – 64 group. Paul Strand was a New Yorker influenced at first by the ideals of Stieglitz but soon evolving his own principles of objective, analytical photography. His 'The White Fence' of 1916 represents an important landmark in this evolution.

In Europe, as in America, Pictorialism enjoyed popular favour. Popularisation brought about a lowering of standards, as can be seen, after the First World War, in much of the work illustrated in annual reviews such as *Photograms of the Year* and the *Salon International d'Art Photographique de Paris*. The analytical style that subsequently found favour in the United States was perhaps not

Photogram by László Moholy-Nagy, *c.* 1928.

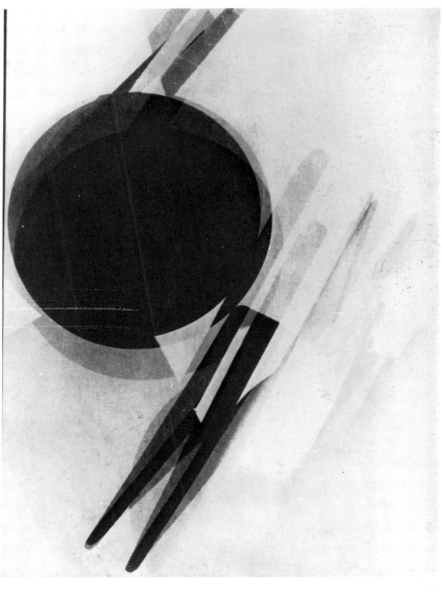

Right Kiki of Montparnasse, photographed by Man Ray, *c*.1930.

Below 'Bewegungs Studie' by Rudolf Koppitz, 1926.

Below right 'Wet Veil II' by Erwin Blumenfeld, 1937.

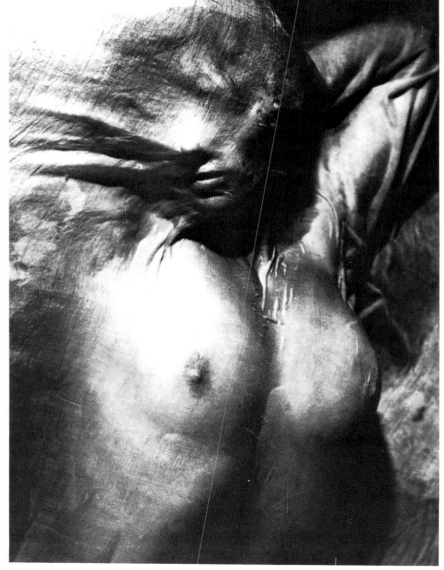

suited to the European mentality and very little distinguished work in this vein was produced in Europe. An exception was the German Albert Renger-Patzsch whose work was published in a series of books during the 1920s and 1930s. Creative photography in Europe during the inter-war years presents a multiplicity of interests, very often closely linked to other facets of the arts, notably in such manifestations as the Surrealist photography of Man Ray and the teaching of photography at the Bauhaus by László Moholy-Nagy. European trends seemed somehow more fluid, more varied and less easily defined.

Moholy-Nagy taught photography at the Bauhaus at the invitation of Walter Gropius between 1923 and 1928. He revived the photogenic drawing process of creating images on light-sensitive paper without the use of a camera, a process first used by William Henry Fox Talbot in the 1830s. Moholy-Nagy's photograms, as the results of these experiments were called, used patterns of light and shade in abstract compositions with a dynamism evocative of Constructivist paintings. He encouraged a freedom of technique that could embrace multiple exposure and montage. Perhaps the greatest exponent of this latter technique was German-born John Heartfield, co-founder in 1919 of the Berlin Dada group, but best known as the creator of virulent anti-fascist montages that incorporated both graphic and photographic elements.

A strong sense of composition often allied with a slightly ponderous symbolism characterised the work of certain mid-European photographers, such as the Austrian Professor Rudolf Koppitz, whose masterpiece is his 'Bewegungs Studie' of 1926, and the Czechoslovakian Frantisek Drtikol.

Perhaps the most central, yet enigmatic figure in creative European photography was the American Man Ray who moved to Paris in 1921 and became a key force in the Dada and Surrealist movements. Man Ray created his own version of the photogram which he dubbed the 'rayogram'; he discovered and exploited the process of solarization, giving a bizarre quality of light to his portraits, nudes and still-lifes. He recorded the features of the artistic giants of the day, Picasso, Picabia, Duchamp, Ernst and others, as well as those of various personalities related to the arts – minor poets, performers, patrons or beauties such as the young Lee Miller, who, inspired by Man Ray, took up photography herself. His portraits bring to life the rich group activity of the Paris of the twenties and thirties. If Man Ray, Lee Miller or Maurice Tabard, chose to examine the nature of objects through the camera, it was as poets, by allusion rather than analysis, in contrast to the emerging American mode. Paris created the climate in which the young German-born Erwin Blumenfeld created a remarkable series of metamorphic images of nudes, before moving to the United States in the late thirties to a successful career as a fashion photographer.

The new directions of European photography and their contrast with prevalent American work were noticeable at the show at the Julian Levy Gallery in New York in early 1932 entitled 'Modern European Photography'. The contributors comprised Man Ray, Lee Miller, Roger Parry, Eli Lotar, Ilse Bing, Ecce Photo, Florence Henri, Emmanuel Sougez, Maurice Tabard, André Kertesz and Brassaï from Paris, Walter Peterhaus, Peter Weller, Herbert Bayer, Otto Umbehr, Walter Hege, Helmut Lerski, Alice Lex, Oscar Nerlinger, Lucia Moholy and László Moholy-Nagy from Germany.

Fashion photography as a creative form came into its own in the early years of the century and, by the late 1920s, had spawned some exceptional talents. The first successful fashion photographer was the Frenchwoman Mlle. Reutlinger, though her work is formal and lacks the poetry to be found in the work of the Baron Gayne de Meyer, the first truly creative fashion photographer, who concocted a romantic fantasy world using soft, diffused lighting, halos of back-lighting, intangible surfaces, sleek and flawless models. It has been claimed that de Meyer's skilful use of artificial lighting was copied by the cinema industry. For a number of years de Meyer was the star of Condé Nast's *Vogue*.

De Meyer's top position at American *Vogue* was taken over by Edward Steichen, formerly a key figure in the Photo-Secession. Steichen worked for *Vogue* between 1923 and 1938, though his first fashion work, and the first published fashion photographs in colour, was his series published in

Nancy Cunard photographed by Cecil Beaton, *c.* 1930.

Art et Décoration in 1911, illustrating the creations of Paul Poiret. Steichen's lighting was harsh by contrast with that of de Meyer but seemed particularly effective in his modernistic images, using cut-out black-white geometric backgrounds and the aloof looks of his favourite model, Marian Moorehouse.

George Hoyningen Huené joined Paris *Vogue* in 1925 and was soon its chief photographer. A man of great taste, Huené conveyed a sleek and soft sense of movement and romance and was at his best photographing the fluid fashions of the early 1930s. Huené discovered the talent of the young Horst P. Horst who became one of *Vogue*'s foremost photographers after 1932.

English photographer Cecil Beaton evades all attempts to categorise his talent, turning with ease from travel or documentary work to society portraiture or fashion. He produced a comprehensive portfolio of portraits of all the characters that made up the elusive international *Beau Monde* of the twenties and thirties. At first influenced by de Meyer, he found his own style of fashion photography in the neo-romanticism of the mid thirties. Martin Munkasci, working for *Harper's Bazaar* in the 1930s was instrumental in bringing fashion photography from the confines of the studio into the open air.

Spectacular setting from D. W. Griffith's *Intolerance*. 1916.

The development of the movie film has its roots in two threads of nineteenth-century invention which came together in the early 1890s in Thomas Edison's first projections. The alliance was between the evolution of optical 'persistence of vision' toys, such as the Zootrope and Praxinoscope, and the refinement of rapid consecutive exposure techniques, such as those used so effectively in the documentation and analysis of consecutive phases of movement by pioneers Eadweard Muybridge, Etienne-Jules Marey and Ottomar Anschütz. The first American copyrighted motion picture was the Edison Kinetoscopic Record of a Sneeze registered on 7 January 1893. It was Louis Lumière who made the first European projection of moving pictures in 1895.

A period of some twenty years elapsed, however, before the complexity and variety of skills required to produce good-quality moving pictures were appreciated and brought together, enabling the birth of an industry that was to enjoy an ever-increasing popularity during the twenties and thirties. The cinema is a truly popular medium demanding wide public support at the box office to keep the wheels of the industry in motion. It is an industry that has evolved countless genres, but the vast majority of films, however, were spawned by the demand for entertainment, far fewer by the truly creative sensibility of author or director. Those avant-garde films that are acknowledged today as amongst the most exciting of their period often found inadequate appreciation with their contemporary public. The more commercial productions of the cinema can nonetheless, on occasion, be a marvellous reflection of tastes and styles, exaggerating fashions almost to the point of caricature and creating a distinctive celluloid style that, in turn, can be seen as the most perfect reflection of its era. There is no better mirror of a society than the fantasies it creates for itself and there is no more perfect world of illusion than the cinema.

D. W. Griffith is generally regarded as the first significant director to emerge in the history of the cinema. He started his career with the Biograph Company in 1908 but it was with *Birth of a Nation* of 1915 and his *Intolerance* of 1916 that he made his name. Griffith and, subsequently Cecil B. de Mille with spectacles such as *The Ten Commandments* (1923) greatly enlarged the technical scope of the new medium. The artistry of film production owed a great deal to European talent in the early years of the cinema. *The Cabinet of Dr. Caligari* by Robert Wiene of 1919 is an extraordinary landmark in its use of distorted perspectives and shadow patterns for dramatic effect, Sergei Eisenstein's new and imaginative editing techniques have made classics of such films as *The Battleship Potemkin* and *Ten Days that Shook the World*.

The world centre of the film industry was establishing itself positively in southern California, however, and attracting some of the best foreign talent, including Eisenstein who went under contract to Paramount, Sweden's leading director, Victor Sjöström, who changed his name to Seastrom and numerous others, including the Germans Josef von Sternberg and Fritz Lang. It was in 1926, before his move to Hollywood, that

Left Brigitte Helm in Marcel L'Herbier's *L'Argent*, 1927; jewellery design by Raymond Templier.

Far left and below Two Modernist settings for Fritz Lang's *Metropolis*, 1926.

Right The eye-cutting scene from *Un Chien Andalou*, directed by Luis Buñuel in collaboration with Salvador Dali, 1928.

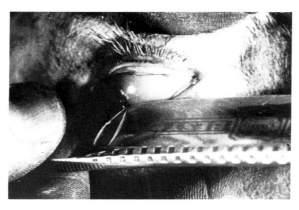

Lang made his masterpiece, *Metropolis,* a nightmare vision of Modernism as a grotesque capitalist paradise, a stylish garden of Eden atop futuristic skyscrapers, feeding on the human sacrifice to the Machine monster of the dehumanised working class.

It was, similarly, a few years later, the more artistically fertile European background that encouraged the remarkable collaboration of Salvador Dali and director Luis Buñuel in their two important Surrealist films, *Un Chien Andalou* of 1928 and *L'Age d'Or* of 1930. Julien Levy, who struggled to gain recognition in America for the best avant-garde films as well as still photography from Europe, brought both of these films to New York for projection in his gallery. Their shock value attracted a notoriety and hence the attention which his other offerings, including Man Ray's *L'Etoile de Mer,* Fernand Léger's *Ballet Mécanique* and Marcel Duchamp's *Anemic Cinema,* had failed to inspire. Out of Levy's Film Society was to grow the film library of the Museum of Modern Art.

The advent of synchronised sound in the late 1920s was a major breakthrough in the evolution of commercial film production. This factor, combined with the demand for escapist cinema after the financial disasters of 1929 and the availability of cheap labour as a result of the Crash, engendered the Hollywood genre that is associated with the early 1930s, the lavish musical. M.G.M.'s *Broadway Melody* of 1929, which won an Academy Award as the Outstanding Film of the Year, was one of the first successes in this field. Warner Bros. achieved considerable success with the series of films directed for them by Busby Berkeley whose name is synonymous with the slick and inventive choreography of large casts exemplified in his *Golddiggers of 1933.* Rival production company R.K.O. combined the talents of Fred Astaire and Ginger Rogers in a delightful series of films which include some of the most stylish sets and dance routines conceived in Hollywood.

The obvious fear of fashion overtaking filming schedules explains the general tendency for set designers to avoid the too-obviously fashionable. Producers were fully aware that the public's need for the cinema as a projection of popular dreams was perhaps best satisfied through the star system and in many cases the stars became more important than the films in which they were cast. Their appearance was imitated and their life-styles envied. The glamorous portrayal in publicity photographs of a studio's crop of stars became an important by-product of the film industry.

The beginnings of the lavishly choreographed musical: M.G.M.'s *Broadway Melody* of 1929.

Busby Berkeley's
choreography in *Golddiggers*
of 1933.

Painting and the Decorative Arts

by Marina Henderson

TO EMPHASISE THAT TOOROP'S *Three Brides* was painted only five years before Picasso's *Demoiselles d'Avignon*, that ten years separated Horta's Hôtel Solvay from Loos' Steiner House, that Marcel Breuer's tubular steel and canvas chair dates from the same year as the triumph of Ruhlmann at the Paris Exhibition of 1925, is to dramatize some of the rapid changes that took place in the fine and decorative arts between 1890 and 1940. Just as radical as these respective changes in style was the change in relationship during this period between painting and sculpture on the one hand and architecture and design on the other. Although many developments in art were absorbed after varying lapses of time into the popular decorative idiom, the progression of painting and sculpture in the first decades of the twentieth century was essentially that of a withdrawal from a mass-market society, that of architecture and design of an effort to cater for it.

The cause of this fundamental divergence was cogently stated by Henry van de Velde, the Belgian architect and designer who was one of the most influential international exponents of Art Nouveau. In an address at the Cologne Exhibition of 1914, he stated that 'the artist is a fervent individualist, a free spontaneous creator. He will never voluntarily submit to a discipline forcing on him a type, a canon.' This public protest against the direction of architecture and design towards mass-production and therefore standardization can be seen as heralding the international Modern Style, in much the same way that the 1900 Paris Exhibition heralded the decline of Art Nouveau.

Although Art Nouveau was so brief a phenomenon (when McKnight Kauffer wrote his history of posters in 1924, he did not even mention Alphonse Mucha) it is significant in the history of art as the first art movement that consciously and deliberately sought to create a new style. The 1890s, the decade of Art Nouveau, was also the height of the Symbolist movement and a peak period of Post-Impressionist activity. And although primarily associated with architectural, graphic and object design, Art Nouveau is linked in a complex and sometimes contradictory relationship to contemporaneous and future developments in painting.

In reaction to the optical realism of the Impressionists, the Symbolists aimed to depict 'the idea in sensuous form' and, in protest against the increasing industrialization of society, drew their subject matter from legend, literature, religion and the occult. Distinguished by a shared attitude rather than a common pictorial style – the movement included artists as diverse as Gustave Mo-

Below right Jan Toorop: *The Three Brides*, 1893.

Below Pablo Picasso: *Les Demoiselles d'Avignon*, 1907.

Above *The Carnation*, poster by Alphonse Mucha, 1897, showing the influence of the Symbolists' sensuous, organic painting.

Left James McNeill Whistler: *The Little White Girl: Symphony in White No. II 1864*, showing the strong Japanese influence on late nineteenth-century art, another stylistic source of Art Nouveau.

reau, Odilon Redon, Puvis de Chavannes, Ferdinand Khnopff – Symbolist painting recorded not the observation but the sensation, the intuitive experience of the artist. In both the aim to communicate emotion and in the subject matter employed to do so, much Symbolist painting, despite a totally opposed aesthetic philosophy, is allied to Art Nouveau: the use of undulating line, the proliferation of the female figure with flowing hair, as in the works of Gustav Klimt, insects, peacocks, water, decorative accessories or symbolic iconography. The work of Emile Gallé is perhaps the most direct example of Symbolist influence in applied design. Sharing the essentially literary inspiration of the painters, Gallé translated the decadence of Huysmans and the melancholy of Mallarmé into highly-wrought glass of sensuous organic form and inlaid, textured furniture, recalling the jewelled canvases of Gustave Moreau, and embodying an idea, an emotion.

The somewhat decadent elegance which typifies Symbolist painting became the hallmark of Art Nouveau in France: it informs the posters of Mucha, the jewellery of Lalique, the ironwork of Guimard, the furniture of Louis Majorelle. But the flowing, flaring, asymmetrical line employed by Art Nouveau designers was linked to a variety of art sources. In retrospect, Holman Hunt's *The Lady of Shalott* can be described as a proto-Art Nouveau painting, and the work of the Pre-Raphaelites became widely known in Europe towards the end of the nineteenth century. Later, in the work of Aubrey Beardsley, two of the main stylistic sources of Art Nouveau design were triumphantly united, the Pre-Raphaelites and the art of Japan as transmuted by Whistler in his paintings, to create the quintessence of Art Nouveau graphic design.

In the work of the Post-Impressionists, Bonnard, Seurat and Toulouse-Lautrec, the influence of Japanese prints was also assimilated to create stylistic features which became part of Art Nouveau's decorative vocabulary. Asymmetrical composition, flat, simplified areas of colour, a flowing linear surface pattern, curvilinear movement; these features, seen in Bonnard's famous screen, painted when he was exhibiting with the Nabis, Seurat's *Le Cirque* and Toulouse-Lautrec's colour lithographs, dominated Art Nouveau graphic design, especially in posters which were produced by virtually every leading artist at the time. Posters were one of the few art forms not attempted by Gauguin, although his *cloissonisme* was popularized in the designs of Grasset.

An important branch of Art Nouveau which was to persist, though transmuted, when the decorative elegance of the French school withered, can clearly be traced to him. While at Pont-Aven, between 1888 and 1891, Gauguin was inspired through the teaching of William Morris, to experiment in crafts. It is perhaps to this inspiration, helped by the influence of another William Morris disciple, Henry van de Velde, who had turned from easel painting to architectural, graphic and industrial design; that we can trace the origin of the expressive, essentially abstract use of line.

In Gauguin's *Vision after the Sermon*, the brutal and emotional use of line becomes the structural focus of the composition and, reinforced by flat areas of arbitrary colour, arouses a response independent of the subject matter. This definitive use of line rapidly spread in Belgium. Its immediate effect can be seen in Lehman's catalogue for the influential 1891 Les Vingt exhibition in Brussels. Through Van de Velde's designs for textiles, furniture, architectural accessories, lectures and writings, this influence was felt all over Europe and became a distinguishing feature of the German Jugendstil and, subsequently, the Expressionists.

When his influential book *From Delacroix to Neo-Impressionism* was published in 1899, Signac remarked that the basis of modern art must be the abstract organization of colour and line. It was not, perhaps, until Kandinsky's first purely abstract watercolour in 1910, that this was logically fulfilled, but the way had been paved by the Art Nouveau development of abstract and stylised organic forms. Van de Velde's metalwork or *Tropon* poster are essentially abstract conceptions.

The rapid decay and vulgarization of Art Nouveau lay in the contradiction that while – following the tenets of William Morris – it was meant to be a new style for a new industrial age, in practice it became one in which a handful of artist-designers created individual artifacts which shared a common decorative language for a short time. As such, it was the last coherent style in which both the decorative and fine arts found close identity. But, since it was not a style susceptible to standardization and mass-production, it was ill-suited to the demands of a mass society dominated by technological change.

One of the most flamboyant efforts in the fine arts to come to terms with this society was that of the Italian Futurists. In their Manifesto of 1910, they extolled urban life and machines, stating that the task of the artist was to 'put the spectator in the centre of the picture', to make him participate in the artistic experience which was no longer merely to be the privilege of the artist.

The Futurists employed some of the technical language of Cubism, not in an attempt to explore form but rather to arouse emotion. Glorifying speed, movement, action, crowds, the Futurists' work became rapidly known over Europe through exhibitions held from 1911 onwards in Paris, Brussels and London. As a group whose aim was direct communication, it is apt that their influence was most clearly seen in poster design, where several features of their painting became virtual clichés: the use of chaotic typography (anticipating Dada), of dramatic linear perspective, of simultaneous presentation of successive aspects of movement, first used by Balla in his charming *Dynamism of a Dog on a Lead*. In such posters as

Above The sense of curvilinear movement embodied in Georges Seurat's *Le Cirque*, 1890–1, became a major stylistic device for Art Nouveau graphic artists.

Opposite Holman Hunt: *The Lady of Shalott*, 1886, showing the flowing, asymmetrical lines later to be more closely associated with Art Nouveau.

Top Gustav Klimt: *Salome*, 1909.

Above Paul Gauguin: *The Vision after the Sermon*, 1888; the expressive use of line in this painting was taken up especially by Belgian Art Nouveau designers, as in the wood engraving (left) by Henry van de Velde, 1893.

Right Both the Futurists and the later Dadaists were fascinated by the possibilities of conveying the sense of moving streamlined forms in their paintings, as in Marcel Duchamp's *Nude Descending a Staircase*, 1912.

Below The smooth lines of the decorative sculptures of the twenties reflect the concern of the fine arts with streamlined forms; female form in bronze by V. Brecherel, *c.* 1925.

Cassandre's great *Etoile du Nord*, the Futurist faith in the new technology is combined, within a Cubist organization of space, with a dynamism and communicated sympathy that would even have satisfied Marinetti, the founder of the movement.

The Futurist extolling of speed and dynamic action also became a commonplace in object design in the later twenties and thirties. Seen at its best in Lalique's famous *Victoire* mascot, at its most commonplace in the straining lines of the decorative sculptures of improbably healthy girls popular during the twenties and thirties. The curious passion for streamlining the most inappropriate objects, radios, cookers, cocktail cabinets, may also ultimately be traced back to the Futurist example.

The most important element in early twentieth-century design, however, was the search for structural order, for form independent of accidental appearance. Cézanne had found this in 'the cone, the cylinder, the sphere'. In their early Cubist works, Picasso and Braque followed Cézanne in their analysis of the subject matter into abstract components. Their object was not to recreate pictorially the subject as it is seen at a particular moment or in a particular place, but as it is known in its many aspects simultaneously. By 1910, Cubism had resolved the subject matter into a linear geometry of interlocking planes. It was this analytical stage of Cubism that was transmitted through De Stijl, Suprematism and Constructivism to the Bauhaus, where its abstract geometry was absorbed into the development of the international Modern Style.

From 1912, when they first introduced collage, onwards, Picasso and Braque's Cubism became progressively more decorative, a trend which culminated in the lyrical elegance of Juan Gris' synthetic Cubism, the illustrative realism of Duchamp, and the colour abstraction of Kupka and Delaunay. It was these variants of Cubism that were attacked by Le Corbusier and Ozenfant in their book *After Cubism*, published in 1918, when they accused current Cubist painting of having degenerated into elaborate decoration.

De Stijl, an association of artists, architects and designers, took its name from the review founded by Theo van Doesburg and Piet Mondrian in 1917 shortly after Mondrian's return from Paris, where his painting had been revolutionized under Cubist influence. Mondrian's variant of Cubism, Neo-Plasticism, was restricted to primary colours and square or rectangular shapes, the interaction of verticals and horizontals. He considered Neo-Plasticism not as a personal conception of the individual artist, but as 'the logical development of all arts, ancient and modern' and the basis for a future rational architecture and industrial design.

Mondrian's theory that 'less is more' was most successfully applied in architecture, notably in the work of Mies van der Rohe, as in the elevation and plan for a Brick Country House in 1923, and in graphic design, such as Piet Zwart's posters. In applied design, the insistence on the limited mathematical interaction of planes paradoxically resulted in a certain fussiness. Rietveld's desk and chair of 1917 are both formally and functionally unsatisfactory. Van Doesburg himself compro-

Left Modernist interior: impersonal, geometric and devoid of ornament, c. 1930.

Below El Lissitsky; *Proun 99*, c. 1924; the teaching of El Lissitsky and Moholy-Nagy at the Bauhaus on the importance of abstract forms was of central importance in the development of the international Modern Style.

mised with the original strict tenets of the movement and his use of horizontals in the mural decorations for the Café de l'Aubiette led to a break with Mondrian.

In his Suprematist painting, *White on White*, Malevich carried Cubist geometry to its ultimate logical conclusion of complete abstraction. He applied this conclusion in his experiments with the problem of form in three dimensions, treating architecture as an abstract visual art. Developments in Suprematism and Constructivism at the Bauhaus, especially in their concern with forms in space and movements and the application of new materials to sculpture and design, followed the teaching of El Lissitzsky and Moholy-Nagy. Basic Cubist geometry was of central importance to the ultimate emergence of the international Modern Style, impersonal, geometrical, devoid of ornament. Whether executed sumptuously, as in Mies van der Rohe's Tugendhat House of 1937, or brutally, as in Le Corbusier's Weissenhoff Housing Project of 1927, the style, in architectural and applied design, parallels an earlier, fundamental, trait in the fine arts during the first decades of the century: the reduction to apparent simplicity through the exploration of fundamental form.

Art Deco was not principally concerned with form but with ornament, exquisite craftsmanship and expensive elaboration. Becoming less elaborate, though nonetheless expensive, during the twenties, the stylistic conventions of Art Deco which had been drawn from a variety of sources, including the Wiener Werkstätte.

The most obvious example is the decorative use of Cubist geometry from the mid 1920s onwards. The influence is exemplified in the textiles of Sonia Delaunay, the rugs of da Silva Bruhns and Marion Dorn, the bindings of Pierre Legrain, the silverware of Jean Puiforcat and the jewellery of Gérard Sandoz, Paul Brandt, Jean Fouquet and Raymond Templier. Reduced to bold geometrical shapes juxtaposed for visual effect and colouring which was often crude, the popular adaptations of Cubism, especially in the mass rather than designers' market, seem far removed from such achievements as Braque's profound examination of structure in even his most decorative pictures like *The Café Bar*. But even when apparently far removed from developments in the fine arts,

Above Lacquer panel by Gustave Miklos, 1922.

Right Design for a carpet by Marion Dorn, *c.* 1935.

objects intended for a mass market do display certain family relationships, as can be seen when we compare the pared-down purity of Brancusi's *Mademoiselle Pogany* with the decorative stylization of much derivative object design.

A similar visual affinity had linked the work of Art Deco artists with the paintings of Matisse. Matisse's elimination of detail and his reduction of line and colour to their elements had an immediate decorative appeal that was exploited by such designers as Lepape, Georges Barbier and (with a judicious mixture of Cubism) Charles Martin, in their immensely popular *pochoirs*, fashion plates and luxury book illustrations. Modigliani's sensuous distortion of the female form can equally be seen in much illustrative work of the time and was popularized by decorative artists such as Jean Dupas, whose posters, especially, educated the eyes of a mass audience in both France and England.

The most consistent popularizer of contemporary fine art developments, however, was the theatre. Bakst's stupendous designs for *Schéhérazade* and *Cléopatre*, which had such an immediate effect on fashionable taste, had been the West's first opportunity to appreciate the blend of Russian folk art with assimilated Western influence that had inspired the *Mir Iskustva* movement; Diaghilev continued to use outstanding artists to design décors and costumes for his ballets; these include Picasso, Matisse, Rouault, de Chirico and Cocteau. It was through a ballet, *La Chatte*, of 1927, designed by Gabo and Pevsner, that Constructivist developments were first intro-

duced to France. Similarly, Miro's whimsical abstract patterning reached a wide audience in his brilliant designs for Massine's *Jeu d'Enfants*, 1932. Conversely, in the mid 1930s, theatre designers like the neo-romantic Christian Bérard in Paris, the Bauhaus-trained Joseph Urban in New York and the whimsically nostalgic Rex Whistler in London, were amongst the most influential interior designers, contributing to the markedly theatrical flavour of chic room décors at the time.

This theatricality, emphasized by the returning fashion for Baroque, also owed a good deal to Surrealism. In 1924, proclaiming the death of Dada, a hectically vociferous movement stressing the illogical, absurd and chance elements in art, André Breton hailed the advent of an art that was 'to resolve the previous contradictory conditions of dream and reality into a . . . super-reality'. The fantasy, figurative detail and elaborate visual narrative, illustrating both the conscious and subconscious level, of Surrealist painting, were welcomed at a time when people were becoming weary of the economic austerity of the Depression and the aesthetic austerity of the international style. Truly Surrealistic designs, like the famous 'leg' console table by Robsjohn-Gittings or Dali's fantasies for Schiaparelli and Edward James (which included a room in which the furniture and décor was based on parts of Mae West's body) were produced for the delectation of a few. But through advertisements, as in the photographs of Peter Rose Pulham for Victor Stiebel, window displays like those by Artur Gumitsch and the habit of expensive fashion magazines like *Vogue* and *Harper's Bazaar* of commissioning painters to design their covers (these included Dali, de Chirico, Laurencin), Surrealist influence reached a wider public.

Van de Velde's prophecy had been correct. In an increasingly affluent and demanding urban society, which was necessarily dependent on large-scale industrial production to supply its needs for housing, furniture and every other sort of utensil, the architect-engineer, not the artist-designer or even the craftsman-designer, became the creator of style, both in architecture and design.

Above left Carpet designed for Radio City Music Hall, New York, *c.* 1925.

Left Robert Delaunay: *Hommage à Blériot*, 1914, a development of Cubism which was to have a profound influence on interior design.

Above Surrealist photograph by Angus McBean, 1930s.

Literature and the Decorative Arts

by Isabelle Anscombe

IN TRACING A RELATIONSHIP between the literature of a period and its decorative arts one immediately runs into a problem of classification. True, there are areas where a direct association can be shown, as in the line drawings of Aubrey Beardsley and the design of the *Yellow Book* or the typography used in *Blast*, where the signatories of Vorticism were putting their names as much to a style as to the Manifesto itself. However, in such cases there is only a narrow line between decorative and fine arts. Even where an attempt is made to write from a similar philosophical or aesthetic position to the artist, the problems remain, for either the philosophy stems principally from the fine arts or has little to do with the actual products of the decorative arts.

The treatment of decorative arts in writing relies on description; the problem of classification is therefore in the place of description within the body of work of a particular author. Traditionally, returning now to the rules of rhetoric, description (*ekphrasis*) is a detachable and inessential part of narrative and serves only as a jewel, highlighting the writer's skill. It is the passage in a book which can be skipped over without losing the thread of the story.

However, many of the novels of this period would all but cease to exist if that view was maintained. Proust's *A la Recherche du Temps Perdu* or Virginia Woolf's *Mrs Dalloway* or *To the Lighthouse* rely on description for the narrative to exist at all; Henry James's *The Golden Bowl* uses description as the key to the novel's themes, while James Joyce employed absolute particularity of description to heighten the narrative to a plane of anti-realism. The problem of classification is defined not in relation to placing writers in specific categories but in observing the changing role of the descriptive passage throughout the period.

The first impetus for decorative art in the nineteenth century came from John Ruskin, although the legacy of his writings gave rise to ideas which he would never have espoused himself. Ruskin saw himself as a seer who would draw attention to the infinite and essential in nature, who would bring an unhappy populace back to the truths of nature through their own moulding of their environment. He extolled the freedom of the workman's expression in Gothic edifices and denounced the cult of conventionalisation upheld by the organisers of the 1851 Great Exhibition as being the very opposite of his essential truths.

In some ways, his most apt exponent could be said to be Charles Dickens whose descriptions of the degradation of London streets and paucity of inspiration in the commercial system fully supported Ruskin's criticisms. In *Hard Times* little Sissy Jupe is ridiculed with all the force of Ruskinian scorn for preferring realistic flowers for a carpet pattern rather than the scientifically correct conventionalised motif. In fact, however, Ruskin's truest followers were the Pre-Raphaelites and William Morris.

Morris took Ruskin's advocation of medieval society to heart and combined it with his socialist theories in *News From Nowhere* to depict an England after the revolution as a society of craftsmen and agriculturalists who lived by the clean waters of the Thames. Morris wanted to persuade by the charm of his descriptions of healthy people living fulfilled lives, yet *News From Nowhere* is closer in spirit to the descriptions of medieval communities in his Prose Romances than to Karl Marx. Nor are Morris's ideas far removed from Oscar Wilde's *The Soul of Man Under Socialism* or Wilde's American lectures where he rejected socialism for the doctrine of Individualism. The ideals are the same; give the artist freedom to express himself, encourage a country to find an art among its own resources without recourse to ancient models, let man express his individuality through his surroundings, whether it be his own beloved blue and white china or Morris's bright colours of medieval heraldry.

The Pre-Raphaelites adapted Ruskin in their attention to the details of nature and the accurate depiction of medieval scenes. Dante Gabriel Rossetti was by nature, however, unsuited to the bluff innocence of Morris and his paintings and writings show a preoccupation with the prevailing sensual tastes. His *Sonnets for Pictures* are an attempt to correlate the two arts almost in the tradition of Baudelaire's Swedenborgian 'correspondances'. If material objects are uncoded symbols for spiritual values, one must attempt by the suggestion of association to penetrate the parallel spiritual world. One brief example of Rossetti's desire to marry the two arts of painting and poetry is these lines from *Lilith (For a Picture)* where the alliteration heightens the dreamy, almost mystical qualities of his own paintings:

> 'The rose and the poppy are her flowers; for where
>   Is he not found, O Lilith, whom shed scent
> And soft-shed kisses and soft sleep shall snare?'

For Rossetti, a description of colours, of scents, of dresses or landscapes, adds a depth to a painting which insinuates that there is more to one's choice of decoration than mere taste.

There is also found in Rossetti the beginnings of

Below Portrait of Georges Rodenbach by Raffaëlli.

Bottom Medallion by Lalique of Sarah Bernhardt, one of the prototypes of La Berma in Proust's *A la Recherche du Temps Perdu*, c. 1900.

Opposite top Cover design by Aubrey Beardsley for the *Yellow Book*, which began publication in 1894.

Opposite centre Helleu's sketch of Robert de Montesquiou, the original of Huysmans' Des Esseintes and Proust's Baron Charlus, 1890s.

Opposite bottom Marcel Proust (1871–1922).

the romantic leanings towards Italy which remains present not only in the English maiden tourist's predilection for the 'pensione', but in the writings of Browning, E. M. Forster and Henry James; its enduring importance for English sensibilities is summed up by T. S. Eliot:

'In the room the women come and go
Talking of Michelangelo.'

The curious mixture of virginal beauty and lush sensuality which the British find in Italy began with the publication of Walter Pater's *Studies in the History of the Renaissance*. In the Preface he defined the questions proper to the aesthetic critic as:

'What is this song or picture, this engaging personality presented in life or in a book, to *me*? What effect does it really produce on me? Does it give me pleasure? and if so, what sort or degree of pleasure? How is my nature modified by its presence and under its influence?'

In his Conclusion he answers these questions:

'To burn always with this hard gem-like flame, to maintain this ecstasy, is success in life . . . . While all melts under our feet, we may well catch at any exquisite passion, or any contribution to knowledge that seems, by a lifted horizon, to set the spirit free for a moment, or any stirring of the senses, strange dyes, strange flowers, and curious odours, or work of the artist's hands, or the face of one's friend.'

What is crucial in Pater is the passion of his writing, the quality of his descriptive passages. What Pater's aesthetic critique calls for is precisely the description, in detail, of the effect of experience upon the individual's sensibility. What the aesthetes, the later heroes of Pater's cult, were to do was to describe their reactions to objects or events. What became precious was not so much the quality of an experience, but the constant refinement of their sensibilities. From this came the cult of the artificial, the search for the exotic,

the establishment of the private world for the cultivation of the sensibility.

This development laid new emphasis, therefore, not only on the quality and type of one's surroundings, but also on the quality of one's description. In France, a parallel development had grown out of Théophile Gautier's call for 'l'art pour l'art'. There, in reaction to the successive revolutions and the rise of bourgeois politics, it was Paris itself which became the subject matter. The writer bacame the 'flâneur' described by Walter Benjamin; the *flâneur* was the man who wandered the illuminated arcades of Haussmann, who treated the city as his own interior where he could observe and spy on life; the writer became the figure of the disinterested detective reconstructing the city by reference to his own sensibilities. Thus Baudelaire, in *Le Cygne* in the Paris section of *Les Fleurs du Mal*, can mourn the passing of the Paris he admired, yet the city is *his* and the poem returns to his own sensibilities:

'Paris change! mais rien dans ma mélancolie
N'a bougé! palais neufs, échafaudages, blocs,
Vieux faubourgs, tout pour moi devient allégorie,
Et mes chers souvenirs sont plus lourds que des rocs.'

Likewise in Georges Rodenbach's *Bruges-La-Morte* the description of Bruges is a central part of the novel, reinforcing by the description of the quiet town with its still waters and humdrum streets the widower's grief:

'Une équation mystérieuse s'établissait. A l'épouse morte devait correspondre une ville morte. Son grand deuil exigeait un tel décor.'

In translating Edgar Allan Poe, Baudelaire felt that he had found a truly kindred spirit. In Poe's *Philosophy of Furniture* what begins as matter-of-fact advice on the choice of carpets and other fixtures, not dissimilar to Eastlake's *Hints on Household Taste*, turns into a description of a way of life:

'The proprietor lies asleep on a sofa – the weather is cool – the time is near midnight: we will make a sketch of the room during his slumber.'

The room is decorated in silver, crimson and gold, containing 'landscapes of an imaginative cast', portraits of 'female heads of an ethereal beauty . . . . four large and gorgeous Sèvres vases, in which bloom a profusion of sweet and vivid flowers . . . . a small antique lamp with highly perfumed oil . . . . two or three hundred magnificently bound books' and a lamp which 'throws a tranquil but magical radiance over all.' The room is almost that which one would imagine behind Baudelaire's *Le Balcon* or *Harmonie du Soir* and could be a prototype for Huysmans' Des Esseintes or Wilde's shallow copy, Dorian Gray. What is central is the weight given to objects in the description of the interior because it is those objects which create – define and place – the aesthete who inhabits it.

All these ideas find their master in Marcel Proust. In *A la Recherche du Temps Perdu* description is no longer a means to an end within the structure of the narrative, nor is it the creation in fiction of a particular 'type'; description is an end in itself. In *The Image of Proust*, Walter Benjamin

wrote that:

> 'The image of Proust is the highest physiognomic expression which the irresistibly growing discrepancy between literature and life was able to assume . . . . Proust's method is actualization, not reflection. He is filled with the insight that none of us has time to live the true dramas of the life that we are destined for. This is what ages us – this and nothing else. The wrinkles and creases on our faces are the registration of the great passions, vices, insights that called on us; but we, the masters, were not home.'

In *Le Temps Retrouvé* Proust exclaims:

> 'Ah! que le monde est grand à la clarté des lampes! Aux yeux du souvenir que le monde est petit!'

It is this making-small in the actualization of remembrance which is the central point of Proust's description, reinforced by the constant search for resemblances. Thus it is, in *Du Côté de Chez Swann*, among the Chinese porcelain, screens and Japanese silk, and the lamps, plants and orchids of Odette's room, that Swann can desire to kiss Odette because of her resemblance to a Botticelli portrait:

> '. . . while the kiss, the bodily surrender which would have seemed natural and but moderately attractive, had they been granted him by a creature of somewhat withered flesh and sluggish blood, coming, as now they came, to crown his adoration of a masterpiece in a gallery, must, it seemed, prove as exquisite as they would be supernatural.'

Here is no longer the dandy seeking new and vivid pleasures from perversity, no longer an artificial setting up the stage for a chosen experience – as Des Esseintes created the black scenario for the celebration of the death of his virility – but the weighing up of all experiences through resemblance to augment the consistency of experience.

The circle drawn by the lamplight of Proust's memory is static and given; reflection is powerless to create or produce. Therefore, like Poe's description of a room at midnight, while the occupant slumbers, the furniture, artifacts and decoration which are described have a peculiar permanence. If one sees Proust's writing as the culmination of the doctrine of 'l'art pour l'art' and the cult of the dandy it is possible to read a 'correspondance' between the qualities of Proustian description and the decorative essence of Art Nouveau. Where William Morris called his designing his 'bread and cheese work' and incorporated his own patterns in his descriptive writing, Proust is at one remove from actual production and Art Nouveau was precisely the design aspect which relied upon the linear movements of growth in the sinuous stems and unfurling leaves to give, paradoxically, an impression of a static luxuriousness, the exotic moment caught in time.

Similarly, one can look at the writings of Virginia Woolf and see an association with the art which was produced by her own sister, Vanessa Bell. Duncan Grant, whom Vanessa regarded as the superior artist, had been influenced by early visits to Italy and combined his admiration for Italian fresco with the precepts of Post-Impressionism. Many of the murals or decorative designs for furniture or needlework produced by Vanessa Bell and Duncan Grant for the Omega

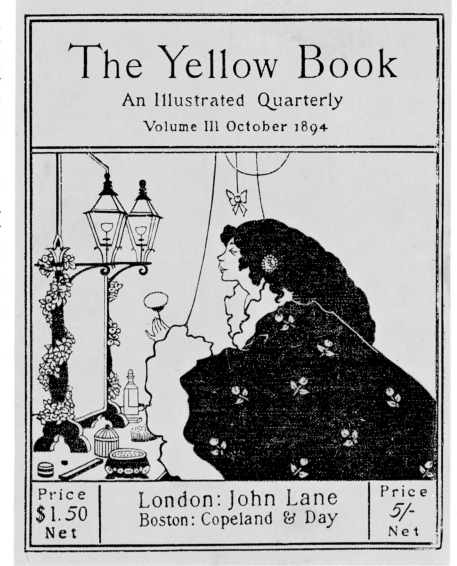

Workshops or for the Woolfs' house at Rodmell or their own house, Charleston, show an Italian appreciation of colour and form as well as theme.

The products of Omega have been criticised for their poor finish, yet what was most important was the final effect, the fact that everything in a room had been considered and decorated within the same mode. Virginia Woolf's writing can be considered from the same viewpoint. In *To the Lighthouse* is this description of an artist painting on the quay:

> '. . . in Panama hat and yellow boots, seriously, softly, absorbedly, for all that he was watched by ten little boys, with an air of profound contentment on his round red face, gazing, and then, when he had gazed, dipping; imbuing the tip of his brush in some soft mound of green and pink. Since Mr Paunceforte had been there, three years before, all the pictures were like that she said, green and grey, with lemon-coloured sailing-boats, and pink women on the beach.'

Virginia Woolf writes with the same brush and palette, creating a whole picture through the essential impression:

> 'Her voice, her laugh, her dress (something floating, white, crimson).' (*Mrs Dalloway*)

Interiors are of the utmost importance, especially

Above Scene from the film of Jean Cocteau's *Les Enfants Terribles*, 1950.

Right F. Scott Fitzgerald (1896–1940), with his wife Zelda.

in the description of women, as the odd impressions of the background are vital to the delineation of character.

How far Pater's ideals had drifted down into G. E. Moore's *Principia Ethica*, which the Apostles discussed in Bloomsbury, is impossible to say, but there remains a lingering similarity in the concluding chapter of Moore:

> '. . . personal affections and aesthetic enjoyments include *all* the greatest, and *by far* the greatest, goods we can imagine.'

When such a philosophy is here translated into descriptive prose it is no longer against the background of Beardsley and the *Yellow Book*, but amid discussions of Post-Impressionism. These are the concerns of Virginia Woolf's novels and her criticism too, in *The Common Reader*, rejected analytic examination in favour of a description of her own sensibilities amid aesthetic enjoyment. The techniques of description have changed as much as those of painting. To return to the painter on the quay in *To the Lighthouse*:

> 'But her grandmother's friends, she said, glancing discreetly as they passed, took the greatest pains; first they mixed their own colours, and then they ground them, and then they put damp cloths on them to keep them moist.
>
> So Mr Tansley supposed she meant him to see that that man's picture was skimpy, was that what one said? The colours weren't solid?'

Wyndham Lewis's hatred of Bloomsbury and his rejection of the Omega took almost the same lines:

> '. . . art-for-art's sake . . . is nothing to do with art – it is a spectator's doctrine, not an artist's: it teaches how to enjoy, not how to perform.' (*Men Without Art*)

The symbol of the Vortex was for space, for classical permanence, and not for time and the enjoyment of the romantic flux. Although concerned with the decorative arts, his writing shows no concern for the depiction of art; as *Blast* so forcefully demonstrated, it was a matter of directness, of the design of a page, not of description. The designs of Grant and Bell for the Hogarth Press show a much gentler echo of the text in contrast to Lewis's didacticism, which was designed to disturb. A writer whose descriptive prose came closest to Lewis – and also to the Surrealists – is Edward Upward, such as in *The Railway Accident*:

> 'Outside the station the air would be warm and I should remember clock-golf in the rectory garden, or there would be heavy snow recalling the voluntary ascetic life I had often planned: there would be crocuses or vultures, it would not be the same as it was here.'

Somewhere in the middle, as it were, comes the poetry of T. S. Eliot, whose meticulousness in describing objects and interiors is equally shocking, but has an internal coherence in its imagery quite unlike Upward's 'crocuses or vultures'. Eliot writes in the Prufrock Cycle:

> 'Her hand twists a paper rose,
> That smells of dust and eau de Cologne,'

In a different sense, Jean Cocteau also created whole interiors which, by their unreality, allowed for the apparent normality of fantasy actions, as in *Les Enfants Terribles*.

In the work of Henry James the importance of the object, the satisfaction of one's sensibilities in relation to artifacts, is paramount and his very style is an attempt to assimilate the completeness of the treasured object, as in *The Golden Bowl*. In the Preface to *The Spoils of Poynton*, he gives the definition of:

> '. . . life being all inclusion and confusion, and art being all discrimination and selection.'

The writer is therefore the image of the collector, the connoisseur. Adam Verver, in *The Golden Bowl*, is precisely that:

> 'Nothing perhaps might affect us as queerer, had we time to look into it, than this application of the same measure of value to such different pieces of property as old Persian carpets, say, and new human acquisitions.'

A final, and somewhat surprising, example of the last remnants of Romanticism, in discovering lost symbols and illusions of the spiritual in parallel everyday objects, is found in F. Scott Fitzgerald. Here, James's connoisseur has given way to the rich American for whom the lights of Broadway shine. Brought up on Keats, Fitzgerald believed in the romantic hero whose vision would imbue his surroundings with an inner light; but all his heroes were doomed to failure. Nevertheless, the light is there in Fitzgerald's descriptions, even if it is bound to fade again. In *The Beautiful and Damned*, perhaps his most poignant novel, is this description of Broadway on Armistice night, 1918:

> 'Under these bright lights glittered the faces of peoples whose glory had long since passed away, whose very civilisations were dead – men whose ancestors had heard the news of victory in Babylon, in Ninevah, in Baghdad, in Tyre, a hundred generations before; men whose ancestors had seen a flower-decked, slave-adorned cortège drift with its wake of captives down the avenues of Imperial Rome.'

But for the individual, as for Fitzgerald himself, the illusion fades with age:

> 'At thirty an organ-grinder is more or less a moth-eaten man who grinds an organ – and once he was an organ-grinder! The unmistakeable stigma of humanity touches all those impersonal and beautiful things that only youth ever grasps in their impersonal glory.'

Anthony and Gloria Patch are reduced to drink to conjure up the lost magic and the novel ends with their departure for Europe, too depleted now ever to enjoy it.

The fate of Anthony and Gloria Patch symbolises the end of the cult of the beautiful object. Their quest for happiness was dependent on money and at last the taint of production has entered the world constructed by Pater, Wilde, Huysmans and Proust. The description of the beautiful room, the objet d'art, is lost in the description of the struggle to attain those things. Design itself changed from the luxuries of the Paris 1925 Exhibition, the extravagances of Art Deco to a consciousness of utility and economy. The end of the great era of the decorative object, of Art Furniture, coincided with the end of the description in prose of those lost rooms and forgotten collectors.

Major Craftsmen and Designers 1890–1940

AALTO, Alvar (b. 1898)
Scandinavian architect and furniture designer, best known for his bentwood designs.

ALBERS, Josef (1888–1977)
German painter and designer who worked at the Bauhaus.

ANGMAN, Jacob (1876–1942)
Swedish architect and furniture designer.

ARGY-ROUSSEAU, Gabriel (b. 1885)
French Art Deco glass designer.

ARTIGAS, Josep Llorens (b.1892)
Spanish potter.

ASHBEE, Charles Robert (1863–1942)
British Arts and Crafts architect, designer and writer; he founded the Guild of Handicraft in 1888.

BAILLIE SCOTT, Mackay Hugh (1865–1945)
British architect and designer, he worked extensively abroad.

BAKST, Léon (1886–1925)
Russian theatre designer who introduced bright colours and oriental motifs into his sets and costumes for the Ballets Russes.

BARLACH, Ernst (1870–1938)
German sculptor, graphic artist and ceramist.

BARNSLEY, Sidney (1865–1926)
British furniture designer and craftsman working in the Cotswolds.

BAUDELAIRE, Charles (1821–67)
French poet, art critic and journalist, he also translated the works of Poe and de Quincey. *Les Fleurs du Mal* was published in 1857.

BEARDSLEY, Aubrey (1872–98)
British decadent writer and illustrator.

BEATON, Cecil (b. 1904)
British photographer.

BEHRENS, Peter (1868–1940)
Austrian architect and designer and member of the Deutscher Werkbund.

BEL GEDDES, Norman (1893–1958)
American industrial designer.

BELL, Vanessa (1879–1961)
British painter, muralist and interior designer.

BENSON, William Arthur Smith (1854–1924)
British architect, designer and metalworker; he was encouraged to start his metalwork shop by William Morris.

BERLAGE, Hendrik Petrus (1856–1934)
Dutch architect, theorist and designer.

BINDESBØLL, Thorvald (1846–1908)
Danish ceramist and designer.

BING, Samuel (1838–1905)
German writer and entrepreneur who opened his shop, La Maison de l'Art Nouveau, in Paris in 1895.

BRACQUEMOND, Félix-Henri (1833–1914)
French painter, etcher and ceramist.

BRANDT, Edgar (1880–1960)
French metalwork designer.

BRANDT, Marianne (b. 1893)
German metalwork designer who worked at the Bauhaus.

BRANGWYN, Frank (1867–1956)
British graphic artist and designer.

BREUER, Marcel (b. 1902)
Hungarian architect and designer who studied in Vienna; became director of the Bauhaus furniture design department in 1924.

BRIGGLE, Artus van (1869–1904)
American studio potter; he worked at Rookwood and subsequently set up his own pottery in Colorado.

BUGATTI, Carlo (1855–1940)
Italian furniture designer and craftsman.

CHAPLET, Ernest (1835–1909)
French ceramist.

CHARPENTIER, Alexandre (1856–1909)
French Art Nouveau designer and decorator; he was associated with Samuel Bing.

CHERMAYEFF, Serge (1900)
Russian architect and designer working in Britain.

CLIFF, Clarice (1899–1972)
British ceramic painter working in Stoke-on-Trent.

COATES, Wells (1895–1958)
Canadian architect and designer working in Britain.

COCTEAU, Jean (1889–1963)
French novelist, dramatist, critic and illustrator; he was closely connected with many of the leading theatre designers of his time.

COLENBRANDER, Theodorus A. C. (1841–1930)
Dutch ceramist.

COLONNA, Edward (1862–1948)
German designer and decorative designer working in U.S.A. and France.

COOPER, John Paul (1869–1933)
British architect, silversmith and jeweller, influenced by Henry Wilson.

LE CORBUSIER, Charles-Edouard Jeanneret (1888–1966)
French architect and designer whose work pioneered Modern Movement.

CRANE, Walter (1845–1915)
British designer, painter, illustrator and writer; a socialist, he was president of both the Art Worker's Guild and the Arts and Crafts Exhibition Society.

CZESCHKA, Carl Otto (1878–1960)
Austrian painter, architect and designer; member of the Wiener Werkstätte.

DALI, Salvador (b. 1904)
Spanish artist; the leading figure of the Surrealist movement.

DAUM, Auguste (1853–1909)
DAUM, Antonin (1864–1930)
French glass designers, brothers.

DAY, Lewis F. (1845–1910)
British arts and crafts designer and writer; he started his own business in 1870, was a founder member of both the Art Workers' Guild and the Arts and Crafts Exhibition Society.

DECK, Theodore (1823–91)
French art potter.

DECOEUR, Emile (1876–1953)
French ceramist.

DELAHERCHE, Auguste (1857–1940)
French ceramist in the Art Nouveau style; he was associated with Samuel Bing.

DELAUNAY, Robert (1885–1941)
French painter and designer, he designed sets for the Ballets Russes.

DOAT, Taxile (1851–1938)
French ceramist working at Sèvres and the University City Pottery, U.S.A.

DORN, Marion (1900–64)
American textile designer who worked in Britain 1922–38. She pioneered the Modernist rug.

DRESSER, Christopher (1834–1904)
British industrial designer; after achieving a doctorate in botany he turned to design for industrial production.

DREYFUSS, Henry (1904–72)
American industrial designer.

DUFRÊNE, Maurice (1876–1955)
French designer; worked for Julius Meier-graefe who opened his 'La Maison Moderne' in 1898. He emerged as a leading Art Deco designer.

DUFY, Raoul (1877–1953)
French painter and textile designer, he worked for Paul Poiret.

DUNAND, Jean (1877–1942)
Swiss Art Deco furniture designer, metalworker and lacquer-worker, working in France.

EAMES, Charles (b. 1907)
American architect and designer.

EASTLAKE, Charles (1836–1906)
British designer and writer; his *Hints on Household Taste* was enormously influential in America.

ELMSLIE, George Grant (1871–1952)
Scottish architect and designer working in Chicago.

ENDELL, August (1871–1925)
German architect and designer.

ERP, Dirk van (1860–1933)
American arts and crafts metalworker.

ERTÉ, Romain de Tirtoff (b. 1892)
Russian graphic artist and theatre designer working mainly in Paris. He is best known for his drawings for *Harper's Bazaar*.

FABERGÉ, Carl (1846–1920)
Russian jewellery designer; jeweller to the Russian Imperial Court.

LA FARGE, John (1835–1910)
American stained glass designer and artist.

DE FEURE, Georges (1869–1928)
French Art Nouveau decorative artist and designer.

FINCH, Alfred William (Willi) (1854–1930)
Belgian ceramist working in Finland.

FISHER, Alexander (1864–1936)
British Arts and Crafts enameller; he studied in France and subsequently set up his own school in Kensington.

FOLLOT, Paul (1877–1941)
French designer who developed his style from Art Nouveau to Art Deco.

FRANKL, Paul (1886–1958)
Austrian architect and furniture designer, he settled in America in 1914.

FRY, Roger (1866–1934)
British painter, critic and designer; he opened the Omega Workshops in 1913 to apply Post-Impressionism to the decorative arts.

FURNESS, Frank (1839–1912)
American architect working in Philadelphia.

GAILLARD, Eugène (1862–1933)
French Art Nouveau designer and writer, connected with Samuel Bing.

GALLÉ, Emile (1846–1904)
French designer; his Nancy workshops produced some of the finest productions in glass and furniture within the Art Nouveau style.

GALLEN-KALLELA, Akseli (1865–1931)
Finnish painter and designer; pioneer of nationalistic Finnish art.

GATE, Simon (1883–1943)
Swedish glass designer.

GAUDÍ, Antoni (1859–1926)
Spanish Art Nouveau architect and designer.

GAUDIER-BRZESKA, Henri (1891–1918)
French artist and designer; associated with Omega workshop.

GAUGUIN, Paul (1848–1903)
French painter, sculptor and graphic artist; leader of the Pont-Aven group.

GILL, Eric (1882–1940)
British sculptor, typographer and writer; he founded a Catholic guild to promote the revival of religious attitudes to art and craftsmanship.

GIMSON, Ernest (1864–1919)
British architect and designer; he set up his own workshops in the Cotswolds with Ernest and Sidney Barnsley and Peter Waals.

GOMPERZ, Lucie Marie (Lucie Rie) (b. 1902)
Austrian artist potter.

GRANT, Duncan (1885–1978)
British painter, muralist and designer.

GRASSET, Eugène (1841–1917)
Swiss architect, writer and designer working in France in the Art Nouveau style.

GRAY, Eileen (1879–1976)
British designer working in Paris. Known for her lacquerwork.

GREENE, Charles Sumner (1868–1957)
American architect and designer. He worked with his brother Henry, showing an eclectic appreciation of Arts and Crafts ideals.

GROPIUS, Walter (1883–1969)
German architect and designer; director of the Bauhaus 1919–28.

GRUEBY, William H. (1867–1925)
American potter known for his use of a matt glaze.

GUIMARD, Hector (1867–1942)
French architect and designer working within the Art Nouveau style to create the total environment.

GULLBERG, Elsa (b. 1886)
Swedish textile designer.

HALD, Edward (b. 1883)
Swedish glass designer.

HANSEN, Frieda (1855–1931)
Norwegian textile designer.

HEAL, Ambrose (1872–1959)
British furniture designer. He entered the firm of Heal and son in 1893. Vice-President of the D.I.A.

HENNINGSEN, Poul (1896–1967)
Scandinavian architect and designer.

HOFFMANN, Josef (1870–1956)
Austrian architect and designer; a founder member of the Vienna Secession, he founded the Wiener Werkstätte in 1903.

HOLIDAY, Henry (1839–1927)
British painter and stained glass designer; a member of the Pre-Raphaelite circle.

HORTA, Victor (1861–1947)
Belgian architect and designer in the Art Nouveau style.

HUBBARD, Elbert (1856–1915)
The founder of an arts and crafts community, the Roycrofters, in America, where he organised workshops, lectured and wrote.

IRIBE, Paul (1883–1935)
French designer and illustrator.

JAMES, Henry (1843–1916)
American novelist and critic.

JENSEN, Georg (1866–1935)
Danish silver and jewellery designer.

JOEL, Betty (b. 1896)
British furniture and textile designer.

JOUVE, Paul (1880–1973)
French designer.

KAUFFER, Edward McKnight (1890–1954)
American artist who worked in Britain between 1914 and 1938. He pioneered Cubist style in posters and designed rugs and interiors.

KLIMT, Gustav (1862–1918)
Austrian painter and designer, associated with Vienna Secession.

KLINT, Kaare (1888–1954)
Danish architect.

KNOX, Archibald (1864–1933)
British silver designer who was the inspiration behind Liberty and Co.'s 'Cymric' and 'Tudric' lines.

KOEHLER, Florence (1861–1944)
American arts and crafts jewellery designer.

KOEPPING, Karl (1848–1914)
German Jugendstil glass designer.

KROG, Arnold (1856–1931)
Scandinavian ceramist attached to the Royal Porcelain Factory of Copenhagen.

LALIQUE, René (1860–1945)
French designer, trained as a goldsmith. He was best known for his jewellery and glass designs. He opened his own glassworks in 1909.

LAEUGER, Max (b. 1864)
German architect and art potter.

LEACH, Bernard (b. 1887)
British ceramist who studied pottery in the Far East, returning in 1920 to St. Ives with Shoji Hamada.

LEGRAIN, Pierre (1889–1929)
French Art Deco designer.

LEWIS, Wyndham (1884–1957)
British painter, writer and designer, a founder of Vorticism.

LIVEMONT, Privat (1861–1936)
Belgian graphic artist and poster designer.

LÖFFLER, Berthold (b.1874)
Austrian painter, designer and graphic artist.

LOOS, Adolf (1870–1933)
Austrian architect and designer and pioneer of Modernism.

LURÇAT, Jean (1892–1966)
French painter, ceramic artist and leading tapestry designer.

MACDONALD, Margaret (1865–1933)
MACDONALD, Frances (1874–1921)
Scottish artists and designers of the Glasgow Four.

MACKINTOSH, Charles Rennie (1868–1928)
Scottish architect and designer; leading figure of Glasgow Four.

MACKMURDO, Arthur Heygate (1851–1942)
British Arts and Crafts architect and designer; he founded the Century Guild in 1884.

MAJORELLE, Louis (1859–1926)
French designer and cabinet-maker in the Art Nouveau style.

MAN, Ray (b. 1890)
American photographer who lived in Paris; an important member of the Dada and Surrealist Movements.

MARCKS, Gerhard (b. 1889)
German sculptor and potter who worked at the Bauhaus.

MARINOT, Maurice (1882–1960)
French glass designer.

MARTIN, Robert Wallace (1843–1923)
The Martin brothers (Robert, Walter, Edwin and Charles) began producing stoneware at Fulham, moving to Southall in 1878.

MATHEWS, Arthur F. (1860–1945)
MATHEWS, Lucia K. (1870–1955)
American artists and muralists, they founded the Furniture Shop and Philopolis magazine in San Francisco.

MATHSSON, Bruno (b. 1907)
Swedish designer.

MATISSE, Henri (1869–1954)
French painter and sculptor.

McGRATH, Raymond (b. 1903)
Australian architect and designer working in Britain.

McLAUGHLIN, Mary Louise (1847–1939)
American pottery and porcelain decorator.

MOHOLY-NAGY, László (1895–1946)
Hungarian designer and photographer who taught at the Bauhaus and developed the photogram.

MOORE, George E. (1873–1958)
British philosopher, mainly concerned with ethics and aesthetics.

MORGAN, William de (1839–1917)
British ceramist, closely connected with William Morris and known for his lustreware.

MORRIS, William (1834–96)
British writer, poet and designer; founder of Morris and Co. and the Kelmscott Press; leader of the Arts and Crafts Movement.

MOSER, Koloman (1868–1918)
Austrian painter, designer and graphic artist; involved in the founding of both the Vienna Secession and Wiener Werkstätte.

MUCHA, Alphonse (1860–1939)
Czech artist and poster designer.

MUNTHE, Gerhard (1849–1929)
Norwegian furniture designer.

MURRAY, Keith (b. 1893)
British architect and designer.

MUTHESIUS, Hermann (1861–1927)
German architect and designer; influenced by a lengthy visit to England. He founded the Deutscher Werkbund in 1907.

NASH, Paul (1889–1946)
British painter and designer.

NEUTRA, Richard (1892–1970)
Austrian architect working mainly in California.

NILSSON, Wiven (1870–1942)
Swedish silver designer.

NORDSTRÖM, Patrick (1870–1929)
Swedish potter, at the Royal Porcelain Factory of Copenhagen.

ORBRIST, Hermann (1863–1927)
Swiss designer working in Germany.

OBSEIGER, Robert (1884–1940)
Austrian designer and potter.

OLBRICH, Josef Maria (1867–1908)
Austrian Art Nouveau designer, architect and artist. Co-founder of the Vienna Secession.

PABST, Daniel (1826–1910)
American furniture designer and cabinet-maker, working in Philadelphia.

PARRISH, Maxfield (1870–1966)
American graphic artist and poster designer.

PATER, Walter (1839–94)
British writer, he evolved his own aesthetic critique.

PECHE, Dagobert (1887–1923)
Austrian artist and metalwork designer; co-director of the Wiener Werkstätte.

PICASSO, Pablo (1881–1973)
Spanish Cubist painter and sculptor working in France.

PICK, Frank (1878–1941)
British poster designer and typographer; he was responsible for design for the London Underground.

POE, Edgar Allan (1809–49)
American writer whose work was seized upon by French and English decadents.

POELZIG, Hans (1869–1936)
German architect and designer.

POIRET, Paul (1879–1944)
French theatre, interior designer and costumier, he founded the Atelier Martine in Paris in 1911.

PONTI, Gio (b. 1891)
Italian architect and furniture designer.

POWOLNY, Michael (1871–1954)
Austrian pottery decorator and teacher.

PROUST, Marcel (1871–1922)
French novelist; the original eight parts of *à la Recherche du Temps Perdu* were published 1913–1927.

PRUTSCHER, Otto (1880–1949)
Austrian architect, furniture designer, jeweller and designer. Worked at the Wiener Werkstätte.

PUIFORCAT, Jean (1897–1945)
French Art Deco Silversmith.

QUARTI, Eugenio (1867–1931)
Italian furniture designer working in Milan.

REDON, Odilon (1840–1916)
French painter, lithographer and etcher and an associate of the Symbolists.

RIEGEL, Ernst (1871–1946)
German Jugendstil gold and silversmith.

RIEMERSCHMID, Richard (1868–1957)
German architect and designer and founder member of the Deutscher Werkbund.

RIETVELD, Gerrit Thomas (1888–1964)
Dutch designer and architect; a member of the de Stijl group.

ROBINEAU, Adelaide Alsop (1865–1929)
American ceramist; she edited the *Keramic Studio* and worked with Taxile Doat at the University City Pottery.

ROHE, Mies van der (1886–1969)
German architect and designer and last head of the Bauhaus.

ROHLFS, Charles (1853–1936)
American furniture designer and craftsman working within the Art Nouveau idiom.

ROSSETTI, Dante Gabriel (1828–82)
British painter and poet and leading light of the Pre-Raphaelites. Also involved in the formation of Morris, Marshall Faulkner and Co.

ROUSSEAU, Clément (b. 1872)
French Art Deco furniture designer.

RUHLMANN, Emile-Jacques (1879–1933)
French designer and 'ensemblier' in the Art Deco style.

RUSKIN, John (1819–1900)
Influential British social critic, his writings were the main inspiration for the Arts and Crafts movement.

RUSSELL, Gordon (b. 1892)
British furniture designer and craftsman; began designing in the Arts and Crafts idiom, then absorbed the ideas of Modernism.

RYGGEN, Hannah (1894–1970)
Swedish textile designer working in Norway.

SAARINEN, Eliel (1873–1950)
Finnish architect and designer.

SAARINEN, Eero (1910–1961)
Finnish designer working in America.

SALTO, Axel (1889–1961)
Danish potter.

SCHIAPARELLI, Elsa (b. 1896)
Italian fashion designer working in France and America.

SCOTT FITZGERALD, F. (1896–1940)
American novelist and short story writer.

SERRURIER-BOVY, Gustave (1858–1910)
Belgian architect and designer influenced by Arts and Crafts Movement ideals.

SPARRE, Louis (1866–1964)
Swedish furniture designer.

STAITE-MURRAY, William (1861–1962)
British ceramist and teacher, influenced by Far Eastern techniques.

STAM, Mart (b. 1899)
Dutch architect; he designed the first cantilevered chair.

STICKLEY, Gustav (1857–1942)
American writer and furniture designer; he founded *The Craftsman* magazine in 1901, publicising arts and crafts ideals.

STIEGLITZ, Alfred (1864–1940)
American photographer who founded the Photo-Secession in 1902.

SULLIVAN, Louis (1856–1924)
American architect; the pioneer of the modern office block and father to the Prairie school of architecture.

TAYLOR, Ernest Archibald (1874–1951)
Scottish artist and designer, he worked within the 'Glasgow Style'.

TAYLOR, William Howson (1876–1935)
British ceramist who founded the Ruskin Pottery in 1898.

TEAGUE, Walter (1883–1960)
American industrial designer.

TIFFANY, Louis Comfort (1848–1933)
American designer and interior decorator; he specialised in stained glass and art glass as well as mosaics, jewellery and metalwork.

TOOROP, Jan (1858–1928)
Dutch painter and poster designer.

TOULOUSE-LAUTREC, Henri de (1864–1901)
French painter and poster designer.

UPWARD, Edward (b. 1903)
British writer belonging to the Marxist tradition of the 1930s.

VELDE, Henry van de (1863–1957)
Belgian theorist and designer; he helped found the Kunstgewerbeschule in Weimar in 1906.

VIOLLET-LE-DUC, Eugène-Emanuel (1814–79)
French writer and architectural theorist.

VOYSEY, Charles Annesley (1857–1941)
British Arts and Crafts architect and designer.

VUILLARD, Edouard (1868–1940)
French painter; member of Les Nabis.

WAGENFELD, Wilhelm (b. 1900)
German functionalist architect and industrial designer; he worked at the Bauhaus.

WAGNER, Otto (1841–1918)
Austrian designer; member of the Deutscher Werkbund.

WALTON, George (1867–1933)
Scottish Art Nouveau designer.

WEBB, Philip (1831–1915)
British architect and designer; he was associated with Morris and Co. from their foundation. He designed many country houses.

WHISTLER, James MacNeil (1834–1903)
American artist living in London; one of the first to recognise the importance of Japanese design.

WILDE, Oscar (1854–1900)
British poet, novelist and playwright; in both his life and his work he espoused the aesthetic ideal. His American lectures propagandized the Aesthetic movement there.

WILSON, Henry (1864–1934)
British Arts and Crafts architect, sculptor and silversmith.

WIMMER, Joseph Eduard (1882–1961)
Austrian designer and metalworker; co-director of the Weiner Werkstätte.

WOLFE, Elsie de (1865–1950)
American interior designer.

WOLFERS, Philippe (1858–1929)
Belgian Art Nouveau jeweller and sculptor.

WOOLF, Virginia (1882–1941)
British novelist and literary critic.

WRIGHT, Frank Lloyd (1867–1959)
American architect, writer and interior designer, pioneering and integral, structural style of interior decoration; he was the first major 'modern' American architect.

WESTMAN, Carl (1866–1936)
Swedish architect and decorative designer.

ZEN, Carlo (1851–1918)
Italian Art Nouveau cabinet-maker.

ZEN, Pietro (1879–1950)
Italian modernist furniture designer.

Select Bibliography

I Style and Influences in the Decorative Arts 1890—1940

ART NOUVEAU
Amaya, Mario: *Art Nouveau,* London and New York, 1966
Battersby, Martin: *The World of Art Nouveau,* London, 1968
Bouillon, Jean-Paul: *Art Nouveau, 1870-1914,* Geneva, 1985
Buffet-Challie, Laurence: *The Art Nouveau Style,* London 1982
Rheims, M.: *The Age of Art Nouveau,* London, 1966; *L'Art 1900,* Paris, 1965
Schmutzler, Robert: *Art Nouveau,* London, 1964
Tschudi Madsen, S: *Art Nouveau,* translated by R.I. Christopherson, London, 1970
Warren, G: *Art Nouveau,* London, 1972
Weisberg, Gabriel P: *Art Nouveau Bing, Paris Style 1900,* New York, 1986

ART DECO
Arwas, Victor: *Art Deco,* London, 1980
Battersby, Martin: *The Decorative Twenties,* London, 1969; *The Decorative Thirties,* London, 1971
Brunhammer, Yvonne: *The Art Deco Style,* London, 1983
Clouzot, Henri: *Le Style Moderne dans la Décoration Moderne,* Paris, 1921
Deshairs, Léon: *L'Art Décoratif Français, 1918-25,* Paris, 1925; *Intérieurs en Couleurs,* France, Paris, 1926
Duncan, Alastair *et al: The Encyclopedia of Art Deco,* London, 1988; *American Art Deco,* New York and London, 1986
Fontaines et Vauxcelles: *L'Art Français de la Révolution à nos jours,* Paris; *Encyclopédie des Arts Décoratifs et Industriels Modernes au XXème siècle,* Paris, 1926
Herbst, René: *Modern French Shop Fronts,* London, 1927
Hillier, Bevis: *Art Deco,* New York, 1969; *The World of Art Deco,* London, 1971
Hunter-Stiebel, Penelope: "Surpassing Style, Four Art Deco Masters: Ruhlmann, Dunand, Marinot and Puiforcat," *Antiques,* October 1985, 733-742
Klein, Dan, Nancy McClelland, and Martin Haslam: *In The Deco Style,* New York, 1986
Moussinac, Léon: *Etoffes d'Ameublement Tissés et Brochés,* Paris, 1925
Quénioux, Gaston: *Les Arts Décoratifs Modernes,* Paris, 1925
Rochas, Marcel: *Vingt-Cinq Ans d'Elégance à Paris,* Paris, 1951

MODERNISM
Collins, Peter: *Changing Ideals in Modern Architecture, 1750-1950,* London, 1967
Davies, Karen: *At Home in Manhattan, Modern Decorative Arts, 1925 to the Depression,* New Haven, Connecticut, 1983
Le Corbusier: *Towards New Architecture,* London, 1927 (Paris, 1923)
Mang, Karl: *History of Modern Furniture,* London, 1979
Pevsner, Nikolaus: *Pioneers of Modern Design: From William Morris to Walter Gropius,* London, 1936 (new ed. 1977); *An Enquiry into Industrial Art in England,* London, 1937

SURREALISM AND NEO-BAROQUE
Alexandrian, Sarane: *Surrealist Art,* London, 1970
Arts Council of Great Britain: *Dada and Surrealism Reviewed,* London, 1978
Chadwick, Whitney: *Women Artists and the Surrealist Movement,* London, 1985
Jean, Marcel: *Histoire de la Peinture Surréaliste,* Paris, 1959
Waldberg, Patrick: *Surrealism,* London, 1965
Wilson, Simon: *Surrealist Painting,* Oxford, revised 1982

REVIVALISM
Adburgham, Alison *et al: Liberty's 1875-1975,* Catalogue of an exhibition at the Victoria and Albert Museum, London, 1975
Battersby, Martin: *The Decorative Twenties,* London, 1969; *The Decorative Thirties,* London, 1971
Billcliffe, Roger and Peter Vergo: "Charles Rennie Mackintosh and the Austrian Art Revival," *The Burlington Magazine* 119 (1977), 739-744
Hitchcock, Henry-Russell: *Architecture: Nineteenth and Twentieth Centuries,* Pelican History of Art, London, 1958
Klein, Dan and Margaret Bishop: *Decorative Art 1880-1980,* Oxford, 1986
'The Studio' Year-books of Decorative Art, London, 1906-30

INDUSTRIAL DESIGN
Banham, Reyner: *Theory and Design in the First Machine Age,* London, 1960
Bel Geddes, Norman: *Horizons,* Boston, 1932
Buddensieg, Tilmann, *et al: Industriekultur Peter Behrens und die AEG 1907-1914,* Mailand, 1978
Bush, Donald J: *The Streamlined Decade,* New York, 1975
Eisler, Max: *Osterreichische Werkkultur,* Vienna, 1916
Giedion, Siegfried: *Mechanization Takes Command,* New York, 1948
Heskett, John: *Industrial Design,* London, 1980
Holme, Geoffrey: *Industrial Design and the Future,* London and New York, 1934
Le Corbusier: *Le Corbusier et Pierre Jeanneret: Oeuvres Completes de 1910-29,* Zurich, 1948 (5th edition); *Towards a New Architecture,* London, 1927 (Paris, 1923)
Meikle, Jeffrey L: *Twentieth Century Limited: Industrial Design in America, 1925-1939,* Philadelphia, 1979
Pevsner, Nikolaus: *An Enquiry into Industrial Art in England,* Cambridge, 1937; *Studies in Art, Architecture and Design,* London, 1968
Pulos, Arthur J: *American Design Ethic: A History of Industrial Design to 1940,* Cambridge, Massachusetts, 1983
Read, Herbert: *Art and Industry,* London, 1934
Renwick Gallery: *The Designs of Raymond Loewy,* Washington, DC, 1975
Rousselet, Louis: *L'Exposition Universelle de 1889,* Paris, 1893

Singer, Charles, Holmyard, EJ Hall, AR Williams, Trevor (editors): *A History of Technology, Volume 1, The Late 19th Century c.1850-c.1900,* Oxford, 1958
Van de Velde, Henry: *Geschichte meines Lebens,* Munich, 1962
Van Doren, Harold: *Industrial Design,* New York, 1940 (2nd edition, New York, 1954)
Wilson, Richard, *et al: The Machine Age in America 1918-1941,* New York, 1986
The Year Book of the Design in Industries Association, London, 1922, 1924-25, 1926-27, 1929-30

II Designs and Designers 1890—1940

FRANCE/Furniture and Interiors
Ancienne Collection Jacques Doucet — Mobilier Art Déco, Provenant du Studio Saint-James à Neuilly, Hotel Drouot Sale Catalogue, 8 Nov 1972
André Mare et La Compagnie des Arts Français (Süe et Mare), Exhibition Catalogue, Strasbourg, 1971
Battersby, Martin: *The World of Art Nouveau,* London, 1968
Camard, Florence: *Ruhlmann,* Paris, 1983
Deroubaix, Brigitte Loye: *Eileen Gray, Architecture, Design 1879-1976,* Paris, 1983
Dunand, Jean, Goulden, Jean: *Exhibition Catalogue, Galerie du Luxembourg, Paris, 1973*
Exposition Retrospective E-J Ruhlmann, Musée des Arts Décoratifs, Paris, 1934
Les Folles Années de la Soie, Exhibition Catalogue, Musée Historique des Tissus, Lyon, 1975
Foulk, Raymond: *The Extraordinary Work of Süe and Mare, The Foulk-Lewis Collection,* London, 1979
Gallé, Emile: *Ecrits Pour l'Art,* Paris, 1908
Garner, Philippe: *Emile Gallé,* London, 1976
Herbst, René: *25 Années U.A.M.,* Paris, 1955
Hoffman, Herbert: *Intérieurs Modernes de Tous les Pays,* Paris, 1930
Johnson, J Stewart: *Eileen Gray, Designer,* London and New York, 1979
Kjellberg, Pierre: *Art Deco: Les Maîtres du Mobilier,* Paris, 1981
L'Oeuvre de Rupert Carabin 1862-1932, Exhibition Catalogue, Galerie du Luxembourg, Paris, 1974
Olmer, Pierre: *Le Mobilier Français d'Aujourd'hui (1910-1925),* Paris, 1926; *La Renaissance du Mobilier Français,* Paris, 1927
Sanchez, Léopold Diego: *Jean-Michel Frank,* Paris, 1980
Vellay, Marc and Kenneth Frampton: *Pierre Chareau, Architecte-Meublier,* Paris, 1984

FRANCE/Glass
Bloch-Dermant, Janine: *L'Art du Verre en France 1860-1914,* Lausanne, 1974; *Le Verre en France, d'Emile Gallé à nos jours,* Osny, 1986
Catalogue des Verreries de René Lalique, Paris, 1932
Daum, Noel: *Daum Maîtres Verriers,* Lausanne, 1980; *La Pâte de Verre,* Editions Noël, 1984
Dawes, Nicholas M: *Lalique Glass,* New York, 1986
Decelle, Ph: *Opalescence, Le Verre Moulé des Années 1920-1930,* Brussels, 1986
Duncan, Alastair and Georges de Bartha: *Glass by Gallé,* London, 1984
Foucaud, Louis de: *Emile Gallé,* Paris, 1903
Garner, Philippe: *Emile Gallé,* London, 1976
Grover, Ray and Lee: *Carved and Decorated European Art Glass,* Vermont, 1970
Hilschenz, Helga: *Das Glas des Jugendstils,* Dusseldorf, 1973
René Lalique & Cie: *Catalogue des Verreries de René Lalique,* Paris, 1932, reprinted, 1980
Le Louvre des Antiquaires: *Charles Schneider, Maître Verrier,* Paris, 1984
Rosenthal, Leon: *La Verrerie Française depuis cinquante ans,* Paris, 1927
Sterner, Gabriele: *Die Vasen der Gebrüder Daum,* Munich, 1969
Warmus, William: *Emile Gallé: Dreams Into Glass,* Corning, New York, 1984

FRANCE/Ceramics
Alexandre, Arsene: *Jean Carriès,* Paris, 1895
Borrmann, Richard: *Moderne Keramik,* Leipzig, 1902
Brunet, M and T Préaud: *Sèvres, Des Origines à nos Jours,* Fribourg, 1978
D'Albis, Jean: *Ernest Chaplet, Les Presses de la Connaissance,* Paris, 1976
Jean, René: *Les Arts de la Terre,* Paris, 1911
Musée des Arts Décoratifs de Bordeaux: *Céramiques de René Buthaud,* Bordeaux, 1976
Musée National de Céramique: *L'Art de la Poterie en France, Rodin à Dufy,* Sèvres, 1971
Pelichet, E and M Duperrex: *La Céramique Art Nouveu,* Lausanne, 1977

FRANCE/Metalwork
Art-Deco, Schmuck und Bücher aus Frankreich, Exhibition Catalogue, Villa Stuck, Munich, 1975
Becker, Vivienne: *The Jewellery of René Lalique,* London, 1987
Bijoux et Orfevrerie par Jean Fouquet, Paris, c.1930
Clouzot, Henri: *La Ferronerie Moderne,* Paris, c.1925
de Gary, Marie Noel, François Mathey, Charlotte Gere, Marc Bascou, Yvonne Brunhammer, and Yvonne Deslandres: *Les Fouquet,* Paris, 1983
Flammarion, Ernest: *Jean Puiforcat, Orfèvre Sculpteur,* Paris, 1951
Hector Guimard Fontes Artistiques, Exhibition Catalogue, Galerie du Luxembourg, Paris, 1971
Le Bijou 1900, Exhibition Catalogue, Brussels, 1965
Quénioux, Gaton: *Les Arts Décoratifs Modernes,* France, Paris, c.1925
Rapin, Henri: *La Sculpture Décorative à l'Exposition des Arts Décoratifs de 1925,* Paris, 1925
Verne, H and Chavance, R: *Pour Comprendre l'Art Décoratif Moderne en France,* Paris, 1925

FRANCE/Graphic Art
Delhaye, Jean: *Art Deco Posters and Graphics,* London, 1977

Mornand et Thome: *Vingt Artistes du Livre*, Paris, 1950
Mornand, Pierre: *Onze Artistes du Livre*, Paris, 1938
Mouron, Henri: *Cassandre*, London, 1985

FRANCE/Fashion
Beaton, Cecil: *The Glass of Fashion*, London, 1954
Blum, Stella: *Designs by Erté – Fashion Drawings and Illustrations from Harpers Bazaar*,
    New York, 1976
Charles-Roux, Edmonde: *Chanel*, New York, 1975
Deslandres, Yvonne: *Poiret*, London, 1987
Erté: *Things I Remember*, London, 1975
Fashion—An Anthology by Cecil Beaton, Victoria & Albert Museum Exhibition
    Catalogue, 1971
La Gazette du Bon Ton
Horst: *Salute to the Thirties*, London, 1971
Poiret, Paul: *En Habillant l'Epoque*, paris, 1930
Schiaparelli, Elsa: *Shocking Life*, London, 1954
Vogue

UNITED KINGDOM
Adburgham, Alison: *Liberty's: A Biography of a Shop*, London, 1975
Anscombe, Isabelle and Gere, Charlotte: *Arts and Crafts in Britain and America*,
    London, 1978
Anscombe, Isabelle: *Omega and After: Bloomsbury and the Decorative Arts*, London,
    1981
Arwas, Victor: *The Liberty Style*, New York, 1979
Ashbee, CR: *Collected Letters and Journals*, in King's College Library, Cambridge, by
    kind permission of Miss Felicity Ashbee
Aslin, Elizabeth: *The Aesthetic Movement, Prelude to Art Nouveau*, London, 1969; *E W
    Godwin Furniture and Decoration*, London, 1986
Billcliffe, Roger: *Charles Rennie Mackintosh: The Complete Furniture Drawings and
    Interior DEsigns*, New York, 1979
Boe, Alf: *From Gothic Revival to Functional Form*, Oslo, 1957
Brandon-Jones, John, Joanna Heseltine, Duncan Simpson, Elizabeth Aslin, Barbara
    Morris, and Shirley Bury: *CFA Voysey: Architect and Designer 1857-1941*, London,
    1978
Crane, Walter: *William Morris to Whistler*, London, 1911
Crawford, Alan: *CR Ashbee Architect, Designer and Romantic Socialist*, London, 1985
Dresser, Christopher: *The Art of Decorative Design*, London, 1862
Eatwell, Ann: *Susie Cooper Productions*, London, 1987
Garner, Gerald and Celia: *The Glasgow Style*, Edinburgh, 1979
Haslam, Martin: *English Art Pottery 1865-1915*, Woodbridge, Suffolk, 1975
Henderson, Philip: *William Morris, his Life, Work and Friends*, London, 1967
Howarth, Thomas: *Charles Rennie Mackintosh and the Modern Movement*, London,
    1952, new edition 1977
MacCarthey, Fiona: *All Things Bright and Beautiful, Design in Britain, 1839 to Today*,
    London, 1971; *British Design since 1880*, London, 1982
Mackail, J W: *The Life of William Morris*, 2 vols., London, 1899
Naylor, Gillian: *The Arts and Crafts Movement*, London, 1971
Russell, Sir Gordon: *Designer's Trade*, London, 1968
Tilbrook, A J: *The Designs of Archibald Knox for Liberty & Co.*, London, 1976
Wentworth-Shields, Peter and Kay Johnson: *Clarice Cliff*, London, 1976
Wilde, Oscar: *Art and Decoration: Being Extracts from Reviews and Miscellanies*, London,
    1920

UNITED STATES
Andersen, Moore and Winter: *California Design — 1910*, Exhibition Catalogue,
    California, 1974
Bishop, Robert and Patricia Coblentz: *American Decorative Art: 360 Years of Creative
    Design*, New York, 1982
Brooks, H Allen: *The Prairie School; Frank Lloyd Wright and his Midwest Contemporaries*,
    Toronto, 1972
Carpenter, Charles H, Jr: *Gorham Silver: 1831-1981*, New York, 1982
Cather, David M: *Furniture of the American Arts & Crafts Movement*, New York, 1981
Clark, Garth and Margie Hughto: *A Century of Ceramics in the United States 1878-
    1978*, New York, 1979
Clarke, Robert Judson: *The Arts and Crafts Movement in America 1876-1916*, Exhibition
    Catalogue, Princeton, 1972; *Aspects of the Arts and Crafts Movement in America*,
    Record of the Art Museum, Princeton University, Vol. 34, No. 2, 1975
Evans, Paul F: *Art Pottery of the United States*, New York, 1974
Feldstin, William, Jr and Alastair Duncan: *The Lamps of Tiffany Studios*, New York,
    1983
Freeman, John Crosby: *The Forgotten Rebel: Gustav Stickley and His Craftsman Mission
    Furniture*, Watkins Glen, New York, 1966
Hanks, David A: *The Decorative Designs of Frank Lloyd Wright*, New York, 1979;
    Innovative Furniture in America: From 1800 to the Present, New York, 1981
Hennessey, William J: *Russell Wright: American Designer*, Hamilton, New York, 1983
Johnson, Diane Chalmers: *American Art Nouveau*, New York, 1979
Koch, Robert (ed and comp) with Thomas M Rosa: *Chase Chrome*, Stamford,
    Connecticut, 1978
Koch, Robert: *Louis C Tiffany, Rebel in Glass*, New York, 1974
Matthews: Masterpieces of the California Decorative Style, Exhibition Catalogue, Oakland
    Museum, California, 1972
Peck, Herbert: *The Book of Rookwood Pottery*, New York, 1968
Strover, Donald L: *The Art of Louis Comfort Tiffany*, San Francisco, 1981
Trapp, Kenneth R: *Toward the Modern Style: Rookwood Pottery, the Later Years: 1915-
    1950*, New York, 1983
Whitney Museum of American Art: *High Styles: Twentieth-Century American Design*,
    New York, 1985

GERMANY AND AUSTRIA
Apocalypse and Utopia, A View of German Art 1910-1939, Fischer Fine Art, London,
    1977
Arnold, K-P: *Gestaltete Form in Vergangenheit und Gegenwart, Möbel aus Hellerau*,
    Museum für Kunsthandwerk, Dresden, 1973
Bauhaus, Royal Academy, London, 1973
Bayer, Herbert with Walter Gropius and Ilse Gropius (eds): *Bauhaus, 1919-1928*,
    Museum of Modern Art, New York, 1938 (new ed 1975)
Behal, Vera J: *Möbel des Judendstil* (catalogue of the furniture collection of the
    Österreichisches Museum für Angewandte Kunst), Munich, 1981
Blaser, Werner: *Mies Van Der Rohe, Furniture and Interiors*, London, 1982
Bott, Gerhard (ed): *Jugendstil*, Kataloge des Hesseschen Landesmuseum Nr. 1
    Darmstadt, 1973
Burckhardt, Lucius: *Werkbund Germania, Austria, Svizzeria*, Venice, 1977; (ed): *The
    Werkbund: History and Ideology 1907-1933*, Woodbury, New York, 1977
Eisler, Max: *Dagobert Peche*, Vienna, 1925; *Gustav Klimt*, Vienna, 1920
Englehart, Josef: *Ein Wiener Maler erzählt*, Vienna, 1943
Ericksen-Firle, Ursula: *Figürliches Porzellan*, Kataloge des Kunstgewerbemuseums,
    Köln, Band V, Cologne, 1975
Fenz, Werner: *Koloman Moser: Graphik, Kunstgewerbe, Malerei*, Salzburg and Vienna,
    1984
Grimschitz, Bruno: *Osterreichische Maler vom Biedermeier zur Moderne*, Vienna, 1963
Hofmann, Helga D: *Kleinplastik und figürliches Kunsthandwerk aus den Bestanden des
    Münchner Stadtmuseums*, Munich, 1974
J P Kayser Sohn, Drefeld, Fabrik Kunstgewerblicher Metallgegenstande, Musterbuch 1907,
    Munick, 1907, reprinted 1982
Klein, Adalbert: *Moderne deutsche Keramik*, Darmstadt, 1956
Kleiner, Leopold: *Joseph Hoffmann*, Berlin, 1927
Kunsthandwerk und Industrieform des 19. und 20. Jahrhunderts, Staatliche
    Kunstsammlungen, Dresden, 1976
Löffler, Fritz and Emilio Bertonati: *Dresdner Sezession 1919-1925*, Galleria del
    Levante, Munich, 1977
Meyer, Christian: *Kolo Moser, Painter and Designer, 1868-1918*, Vienna, 1983
Mrazek, Wilhelm: *Die Wiener Werkstätte, Modernes Kunsthandwerk von 1903-1932*,
    Osterreichisches Museum für Angewandte Kunst, Vienna, 1967
Muthesius, Hermann: 'Kunst und Maschine', in *Dekorative Kunst*, vol. 9, 1902,
    pp.141-7
Natzler, Gertrude and Otto: *Ceramics*, Catalogue of the Collection of Mrs. Leonard
    M Sperry, Los Angeles County Museum of Art, 1968
Neuwirth, Waltraud: *Osterreichisches Keramik des Jugendstils*, Munich, 1974; *Wiener
    Keramik*, Braunschwig, 1974
Novotny, Fritz and Johannes Dobai: *Gustav Klimt*, London, 1968
Ozzola, Leandro: *L'Arte contemporanea all'Esposizionne di Roma*, Rome, 1911
Powell, Nicholas: *The Sacred Spring, The Arts in Vienna 1898-1918*, London, 1974
Rademacher, Helmut: *Das deutsche Plakat von den Aufgängen bis zur Gegenwart*,
    Dresden, 1965
Rossow, Walter: *Adolf Loos 1870-1933*, Berlin, 1983
Schmidt, Rudolf: *Das Wiener Künstlerhaus*, Vienna, 1964
Schweiger, Werner J: *Wiener Werkstätte Design in Vienna: 1903-1932*, London, 1984
Selz, Peter: *German Expressionist Painting*, Los Angeles, 1957
Spielmann, Heinz: *Der Jugendstil in Hamburg*, Hamburg, 1965
Tendenzen der Zwanziger Jahre, 15, Europäische Kunstausstellung, Berlin, 1977
Varnedoe, Kirk: *Vienna 1900, Art Architecture and Design*, New York, 1986
Vienna Secession, Art Nouveau to 1970, Royal Academy, London, 1971
Vergo, Peter: *Art in Vienna 1898-1918*, London, 1975
Veronesi, Giulia: *Josef Hoffmann*, Mailand, 1956
Von Hartmann, G B and Wend Fischer (eds): *Zwischen Kunst und Industrie des
    Deutschen Werkbunds*, Die Neue Sammlung, Munich, 1975
Von Hase, Ulrike: *Schmuck in Deutschland 1895-1914*, Munich, 1977
Von Treskow, Irene: *Die Jugendstil-Porzellane KPM Berlin*, Munich, 1971
Wilk, Christopher: *Thonet: 150 Years of Furniture*, Woodbury, New York, 1980; *Marcel
    Breuer: Furniture and Interiors*, New York, 1981
Wingler, Hans M: *The Bauhaus*, Boston, Mass., 1969

BELGIUM
Art Nouveau Belgium/France, Exhibition Catalogue, Institute for the Arts, Rice
    University, Houston, 1976
Borsi, Franco: *Bruxelles 1900*, Brussels, 1974
The Brooklyn Museum: *Belgian Art 1880-1914*, Brooklyn, New York, 1980
Dumont-Wilden, L: *Fernand Khnopff*, Brussels, 1972
Hammacher, A M: *Le Monde de Henry van de Velde*, Antwerp-Paris, 1967
Henrion-Giele, Suzanne: *Musée Horta*, Brussels, 1973
Hoffman Herbert: *Intérieurs Modernes de Tous les Pays*, Paris, 1930
Lenning, H F: *The Art Nouveau*, The Hague, 1951
Pionniers du XXe Siècle, Guimard, Horta, Van de Velde, Exhibition Catalogue, Musée
    des Arts Décoratifs, paris, 1971
The Sacred and Profane in Symbolist Art, Exhibition Catalogue, Art Gallery of Ontario,
    Toronto, 1969
Henry van de Velde, Exhibition Catalogue, L'Ecuyer, Brussels, 1907
Watelet, Jacques-Grégoire: *Gustave Serrurier-Bovy, architecte et décorateur 1858-1910*,
    Brussels, 1974
Wolfers, Marcel: *Philippe Wolfers*, Brussels, 1965

THE NETHERLANDS
Baroni, Daniele: *Gerrit Thomas Fietveld: Furniture*, London, 1978
H P Berlage: Nederlandse Architectuur, 1956-1935, Catalogue of an exhibition in the
    Gemeente Museum, the Hague, 1975
The Amsterdam School, Catalogue of an exhibition in the Gemeente Museum, the
    Hague, 1975

Jaffe, H L C: *De Stijl*, London, 1970
Leidelmeijer, F and D van der Cingel: *Art Nouveau en Art Déco in Nederland*, Amsterdam, 1983
Moody, C W: *Gouda Ceramics, The Art Nouveau Era of Holland*, Berkeley, California, 1970
Overy, Paul: *De Stijl*, London, 1969
Singelenberg, Peter: *H P Berlage, Idea and Style*, Utrecht, 1972

SCANDINAVIA
Boulton Smith, John: *The Golden Age of Finnish Art (Art Nouveau)*, Helsinki, 1976
Johnson, J Stewart: *Alvar Aalto: Furniture and Glass*, New York, 1984
McFadden, David Revere: *Scandinavian Modern Design 1880-1980*, New York, 1982
Møller, Jørgen E R: *Georg Jensen, The Danish Silversmith*, Copenhagen, 1985
Polak, Ada: *Norwegian Silver*, Oslo, 1972
Royal Copenhagen Porcelain, 200 years of, Catalogue of an exhibition circulated by the Smithsonian Institution, 1974-1976
Stavenow-Hidemark, Elisabet: *Svensk Jugend*, Stockholm, Nordiska Museet, 1964
Thue, Anniken: *Frida Hanse,*, Oslo, Kunstindustrimuseet, 1973
Wettergren, Erik: *Modernt scenskt glas*, Stockholm, 1943
Wollin, Nils G: *Modern Swedish Decorative Art*, London, 1931

ITALY AND SPAIN
Bairati, Eleonora, with Rossana Bossaglia and Marco Rossi: *L'Italia Liberty, Arrademento e arti decorative*, Florence, 1964
Bohigas, Oriol: 'Luis Domènech', reprinted in *The Anti-Rationalists*, London, 1973
Bossaglia, Rossana: *Il Liberty in Italia*, Milan, 1968; *Il 'Deco' Italiano, Fisionomia dello Stile 1925 in Italia*, Milan, 1975
Brosio, V: *Lo Stile Liberty in Italia*, Milan, 1967
Cirlot, Juan Eduardo: *El Estilo de Siglio XX*, Barcelona, 1952
Dalisi, Riccardo: *Gaudí Furniture*, London, 1980
De Jean, Philippe: *Carlo, Rembrandt, Ettore, Jean Bugatti*, Paris, 1981
Garner, Philippe, *et al*: *The Amazing Bugattis*, London, 1979
Il Liberty a Bologna e nell'Emilia Romagna, Galleria d'Arte Moderna, Bologna, 1977
Manifatture e Ceramisti Italiani, 1900-1960, 36 Incontri, Milan, nd
Martinell, César: *Gaudí*, Cambridge, Massachusetts, 1967
Nicoletti, Manfredo: 'Art Nouveau in Italy', reprinted in *The Anti-Rationalists*, London, 1973
Pellicer, A Cirici: *El arte modernista catalán*, Barcelona, 1951; *1900 en Barcelona*, Barcelona, 1967
Pica, A: *Storia del Triennale 1918-1957*, Milan, 1957
Pierre, José and José Corredor-Matheos: *Miró & Artigas, Céramiques*, Paris, 1974
Pirrone, G and F Scianna: *Palermo Liberty*, Rome, 1971
Prats Valles, J: *Gaudí* (with a preface by Le Corbusier), Barcelona, 1958
Sweeny, James Johnson and Josep Lluis Sert: *Antoni Gaudí*, London, 1960
Vianello, G: *Galileo Chini e il Liberty in Italia*, Florence, 1964

EASTERN EUROPE
L'Art 1900 en Hongrie, Exhibition Catalogue, Le Petit Palais, Dec. 1976-Feb. 1977
Danilovicz, C E: 'Princess Teniches' School of Russian Applied Art', *The Studio*, vol. 41, no. 172 July 1st, 1907
Die Kunstismen in Russland, 1907-1930, Exhibition Catalogue, Galerie Gmurzynska, Cologne, May-June, 1977
Fabergé, 1846-1920, Exhibition Catalogue, Victoria and Albert Museum, 1977
Gray, Camilla: *The Great Experience, Russian Art 1863-1922*, London, 1962
Levetus, A S: 'The Royal Hungarian Arts and Crafts School', Budapest, *The Studio*, vol. 38, no. 162, 1906
Pál, Miklós: *Hungarian Art Nouveau*, Washington, DC, 1977
PARCO (organiser): *Czechoslovakia Cubism: The World of Architecture, Furniture and Craft*, Tokyo, 1984
Peacock, Netter: 'The New Movement in Russian Decorative Art', *The Studio*, vol. 22, no. 98, 1901
Rowell, Margit and Angelica Zander Rudenstine: *Art of the Avant-Garde in Russia: Selections from the George Costakis Collection*, New York, 1981
Russian Avant-garde, 1908-1922, Exhibition Catalogue, Leonard Hutton Gallery, 1971
Schanzer, Hedwig: 'The Teaching of Design at the Prague Arts and Crafts School', *The Studio*, vol. 54, no. 226.
Vallance, Aylmer: 'Russian Peasant Industries', *The Studio*, Vol. 37. no. 157, 1906
Zsolnay, T M, Zsolnay, and G Sikota: *Zsolnay: A History of the Factory and the Family*, Budapest, 1974

III   The Background to the Decorative Arts 1890-1940

THE GREAT EXHIBITIONS
Allwood, John: *The Great Exhibitions*, London, 1977
Brinkmann, Dr Julius: *Die Ankaüfe auf der Weltausstellung Paris 1900*, Hamburg, 1901
Brunhammer, Yvonne: *L'Exposition Cinquantenaire de l'exposition de 1925*, Paris, 1976
Comte, Jules: *L'Art à l'Exposition Universelle de 1900*, Paris, 1900
D'Uckermann, P: *L'Art dans la Vie Moderne*, Paris, 1937
Fuchs-Newberry: *L'Exposition Internationale des Arts Décoratifs Modernes*, Darmstadt, 1902
Herbst, Rene: *25 Années Union des Artistes Modernes*, Paris, 1955
Hoentschel, Georges: *Le Pavillon des l'Union Centrale des Arts Décoratifs à l'Exposition Universelle de 1900*, Paris, 1900
Isay, Raymond: *Panorama des Expositions Universelles*, Paris, 1900
Julian, Philippe: *The Triumph of Art Nouveau, Paris Exhibition 1900*, New York, 1974

Mandell, Richard: *Paris 1900: The Great World's Fair*, Toronto, 1967
Mourey, Gabriel: *Histoire Générale de l'Art Français de la Révolution à Nos Jours: l'Art Décoratif*, Paris, 1925
Quénioux, Gaston: *Les Arts Décoratifs Modernes*, France, 1925

PHOTOGRAPHY AND THE CINEMA
Beaton, Cecil and Buckland, Gail: *The Magic Image*, London, 1975
Brandt, Bill: *The English at Home*, London, 1936
Brassaï: *The Secret Paris of the 30s*, London, 1967
Butler, Ivan: *Silent Magic*, London, 1987
The Daybooks of Edward Weston, Vols I and II, New York, 1961 and 1966
Doty, Robert: *Photo-Secession-Photography as a Fine Art*, Rochester, 1970
Eisner, Lotte H: *Fritz Lang*, London, 1976; *The Haunted Screen*, London, 1969
Gernsheim, Helmut and Alison: *The History of Photography*, London, 1969
Horst: *Salute to the Thirties*, London, 1971
Hoyningen Huene, Exhibition Catalogue, University of Southern California, Los Angeles, 1970
Jenkinson, P: *The Busby Berkeley Book*, London, 1973
Kostelanetz, Richard: *Moholy-Nagy*, New York, 1970
Krauss, Rosalind and Jane Livingston: *L'Amour Fou, Photography and Surrealism*, New York, 1985
Lambrichs, Georges: *Les Plus Belles Images du Cinema*, Paris
Lawford, Valentine: *Horst, His Work and His World*, New York, 1984
Alan Ray Photographs, 1920-34, New York, 1973
Masclet, Daniel: *Nus*, Paris, 1933
Newhall, Beaumont: *Frederick H. Evans*, New York, 1973; *The History of Photography*, London, 1969
Scharf, Aaron: *Art and Photography*, London, 1968
Taylor, John Russell: *Great Movie Moments*, London, 1987
Vickers, Hugo: *Cecil Beaton*, London, 1985
Walker Evans: *Photographs for the Farm Security Administration 1935-38*, Library of Congress Catalogue, New York, 1973
Weegee: *Naked City*, New York, 1946
Weightman, J (ed): *Masterworks of the French Cinema*, London and New York, 1973

PAINTING AND THE DECORATIVE ARTS
Alexandrian, S: *Surrealist Art*, London, 1970
Arnasan, H H: *Modern Art*, London, 1969
Bayer, H, Gropius W and Gropius I: *Bauhaus 1919-1928*, Boston, 1959
Cassou J, Langui E and Pevsner N: *The Sources of Modern Art*, London, 1962
de Lempicka-Foxhall, Baroness Kizette and Charles Phillips: *Passionby Design, The Art and Times of Tamara de Lempicka*, Oxford, 1987
Fry, E: *Cubism*, London, 1962
Jaffe, H L C: *De Stijl*, London, 1970
Pevsner, N: *The Sources of Modern Architecture and Design*, London, 1968

Contributing Authors

Philippe Garner, the consultant editor of the encyclopedia, has published several works on modern decorative arts, including *Edwardiana, Art Nouveau for Collectors* and the standard critical work on the French glass artist, Emile Gallé. He is a Director of the Department of Applied Arts at Sotheby's, London.

Roger-Henri Guerrand teaches at the Ecole Supérieure des Beaux-Arts in Paris. His books include *L'Art Nouveau en Europe*.

Martin Battersby, theatre designer and painter, was also a leading authority on Art Nouveau and Art Deco. His most notable books are *The Decorative Twenties* and *The Decorative Thirties*.

Gillian Naylor is an acknowledged expert on the Modern Movement in design and is currently writing a book on the subject. Her books include *The Arts and Crafts Movement* and *The Bauhaus*.

Malcolm Haslam is currently working on a book about the Martin Brothers, art potters. His previous publications include *English Art Pottery 1865-1915, Marks and Monograms of the Modern Movement* and *The Real World of the Surrealists*.

Stuart Durant is Senior Lecturer in the History of Design at Kingston Polytechnic, London. He has published a book on *Victorian Ornamental Design* and has organised numerous exhibitions on the decorative arts.

Lynne Thornton was formerly an expert with Sotheby's, specialising in Art Nouveau. She is now a recognised expert for the major Paris auction rooms and has made a speciality of the study of late nineteenth- and early twentieth-century ceramics.

Ian Bennett is the author of numerous books on the fine and applied arts, including the recently published *Rugs and Carpets of the World*. He is also a keen collector of modern art ceramics.

Isabelle Anscombe, after a period spent working for a London decorative arts business, now devotes herself entirely to writing on the modern applied arts. Her book on women in the decorative arts, *A Woman's Touch*, was published in 1984.

Ada Polak is the Deputy Curator in Britain of the Arts and Crafts Museum of Norway. She has published articles on the decorative arts in a number of journals, and her book *Modern Glass* is one of the standard works on the subject.

Marina Henderson, who has contributed a special essay on the relationship between the fine and applied art of the twentieth century, is the author of a book on Dante Gabriel Rossetti.

Glossary

AMBOYNA   Exotic mid-to-pale coloured wood with a rich natural grain pattern.

BIAS CUT   Garments cut 'on the bias' exploit the natural flexibility in the diagonal of the fabric, and the criss-cross pattern of the weave runs diagonally to the body as opposed to the traditional horizontal/vertical cloth pattern.

BOISERIES   Wood panelling and other fitted wooden elements of an interior scheme.

CAMEO GLASS   Glass in which the decoration stands in relief, cut or etched through layers of different coloured glass.

CIRE PERDUE PROCESS   Literally, and actually, the 'lost wax' process in which a mould is made around a wax model which is then melted and drained to be replaced by molten bronze or glass (as in Lalique's early experiments).

CLOISONNISME   A style of painting in which strongly defined outlines retaining blocks of colour evoke the technique of cloisonné enamel work.

CLOISONNÉ ENAMEL   Enamel in which the design is defined by raised outlines retaining the areas of different coloured enamels.

CRACKLEWARE (CRAQUELÉ)   Terms used to describe ceramics with glazes characterised by an intentional and controlled crazing.

DINANDERIE   Work in non-precious metals.

EBENE DE MACASSAR   A dark exotic hardwood characterised by a natural streaky marking.

ENSEMBLIER   Designer/decorator responsible for creating every element of a room setting.

ETCHED GLASS   Glass in which the relief of a cameo design, the surface texture or a monochrome graphic design is achieved by the controlled effort of corrosive acid.

FAUTEUIL GONDOLE   Tub chair.

FAVRILE GLASS   The word 'Favrile' was adopted as a trademark for Tiffany glass to remind customers of the element of craft or handwork.

FLAMBÉ GLAZES   Glazes achieved by firing at a very high temperature.

GALUCHAT   See Shagreen.

GESSO   Gesso work involves the building up of a picture in low relief using a kind of plaster, often enriched with gilding and other materials including mother-of-pearl or stones in addition to paints.

LACQUER   A resin drawn from certain Oriental trees and capable of creating a rich, even, lustrous surface when applied layer upon layer to a wood or metal base.

LIMED OAK   Oak in which the natural open grain pattern is emphasised by white lines left after rubbing lime into surface.

MARQUETERIE SUR VERRE   A process introduced by Gallé in 1897 of inlaying semi-molten glass details of decoration into the hot, soft body of a glass object.

MARQUETRY   Technique of inlaying one or more woods into another to render a graphic design on flat elements of furniture and woodwork.

MARTELÉ   A particular style of carving glass, peculiar most notably to the products of the Daum factory, giving a broad facetted surface reminiscent of hard-hammered metal.

MEUBLE D'ENCOIGNURE   Piece of furniture designed to fit into a corner.

MODELAGE À CHAUD   The process of working glass while it is still soft from the heat of the furnace.

PARURE DE CORSAGE   Elaborate jewel designed to adorn the chest.

PÂTE-D'ÉMAIL   A more brittle, more fragile variant of the *pâte-de-verre* process.

PÂTE-DE-VERRE   Glass made by the fusion at a relatively low temperature of pulverised glass bound into a paste and with an admixture of metallic oxides to give colour.

PÂTE-SUR-PÂTE   Method of decoration developed in France which consists of building up a low relief by repeated applications of layers of slip and then carving into them to form relief. Very expensive and painstaking technique.

PLIQUE À JOUR   Enamel *plique à jour* is translucent enamel fired within an openwork metal design.

POCHOIR PROCESS   A process of multiple hand-colouring using stencils, particularly popular in France in the 1920s.

RED PADOUK   Burmese wood resembling rosewood.

REPOUSSÉ METALWARE   Repoussé wares have the decorative motifs hammered out in relief.

SABOTS   Literally 'clogs', a term applied to the terminal elements of furniture legs, often in bronze or, in the case of Ruhlmann, ivory.

SALT-GLAZE   At stoneware temperature (1250–1300°C.), salt vitrified to form a glaze when thrown into the kiln.

SANG-DE-BOEUF   Term used to describe a deep blood-red colour.

SGRAFFITO   Method of decoration, scratching through a layer of slip to expose colour of clay body below.

SHAGREEN   Tough, hard skin from sharks, usually tinted pale green, very pale blue, pink or a natural shade of cream. Similar in appearance to lizard skin but with a more regular pattern.

SLIP WARES   Earthenware decorated by means of slip (clay, often tinted, diluted to the consistency of cream), applied in a manner similar to that used to decorate an iced cake. Much used by seventeenth- and eighteenth-century Staffordshire potters and modern studio potters.

SOUFFLÉ WARES   Type of glaze, usually in a single colour, occasionally with slightly mottled surfaces. Used by Edward Taylor (Ruskin).

STANNIFEROUS GLAZE   Ceramic glaze using tin-based oxides.

VERRE ÉGLOMISÉ   Term used by Gallé to describe an internal effect of white chemical inclusions in glass.

Index

Page numbers in italics refer to illustrations

Picture
Credits

(t = top; c = centre;
b = bottom; l = left;
r = right)

The editor and publishers
would like to thank the
following individuals,
museums and other institutions
which have provided
photographs and information
for this book:

Academy Editions, London 192(cl and r), 193;
ACL, Brussels 229(tl), 231(l and b and r:t and c);
Albright Knox Gallery, Buffalo, gift of Darwin Martin, courtesy of
 Smithsonian Institution 187(tl);
Anscombe, Isabelle 184, 185(c), 190, 193(tr);
Architectural Review 147(t), 148, 149(b);
Archiv für Kunst und Geschichte, Berlin 42(b);
Art et Décoration 71(t);
Art Institute of Chicago, Burnham Library, gift of Mr. and Mrs.
 James W. Howlett, courtesy of Smithsonian Institution 188(l);
The Art Museum, Princeton University, New Jersey 185(br);
Badisches Landesmuseum, Karlsruhe 217(l);
Battersby, Martin 22(r), 23(l and r), 25(r:t and b), 37, 38(t and b),
 40(l and r), 109, 112(t and b), 113, 114(l), 115(c), 117, 124(t and
 b), 125, 126, 127(t and b), 128(t and b), 129(t);
Bauhaus Archiv, Berlin 208(t), 209, 210(l), 211, 215(r), 219(tr),
 229(b);
Bennett, Ian 157(t:l and r), 159, 160, 163(l and r:t and cb), 164(t
 and b), 165(t:l and r and b), 169(t and b), 259(tr and b), 265(t
 and b), 266(t and c), 268(l and r), 269;
Berlin Museum 218(t);
Bethnal Green Museum, London 171(tr), 227(br);
Brighton Museum 155(tl);
Busch-Reisinger Museum, Harvard University 231(r);
Caisse Nationale des Monuments Historiques, Paris 280(r);
Charmet, Jean-Loup (photographer), 276(br and t), 277, 281(t and
 b);
Cheltenham Museum and Art Gallery 144;
Chicago School of Architecture 191(tr);
Christies, London 220(t), 267(r);
Courtauld Institute Galleries, London 154(t), 155(cr), 163(b);
Cincinnati Art Museum 192(cr), 193(tl); gift of Theodore A.
 Lanasbrotu 191(ct);
Cooper Bridgeman Library, London 295(tr);
Daily Telegraph 42(tl);
Deutscher Werkbund Yearbook 227(bl);
Editions Graphiques 266(b);
Elbert Hubbard Library Museum, East Aurora, New York 197(tr);
French Line 118
Fear, Michael (photographer) 9, 12(b and t:r and l), 13(t and b),
 17(t), 48(t and l:c and b), 49(l and r), 50(t:l and r and b:l and r),
 52(l: t and b and r: t and b), 53(t and b), 54(l and r and b and
 inset) 109, 112(t and b), 114(l), 117, 124(t and b), 125, 127(t),
 128(t and b), 129(t), 136(r and l), 178, 179(cr), 185(bl), 192(cr),
 195(bcr), 196(l and c), 199, 202(t and c and b), 203(t:r and l and
 b:r and l and cl), 204, 210(r), 230(b), 259(l and r:t and c and b),
 265(t and b), 266(t and c), 268(l and r), 269;
Freeman, John R. (photographer) 146(b);
Freeman, Michael (photographer) 182(tr), 186(l and b:r and l),
 187(tl), 188, 195(bc);
Garner, Philippe 10(t and b), 11, 20(b and l), 21(b), 22(l), 24(t and
 b), 25(l:c and t), 30(t and b), 31, 32, 33, 43(b), 57(t and b and l),
 59(tr and l), 58(tr), 62, 63(t and b:r and l), 65, 66, 68, 69(t and
 b), 70(l and r and b), 71(t and br), 72(t and br), 74(tr and l), 75,
 78(t and b:l and r), 79(t and b:l and r), 100(t and b), 101(l), 102(l
 and r), 105, 110(t and b), 111(t and b), 129(b), 130, 131, 132,
 133, 141(b:l and r), 149(t), 152(l), 154(b), 170(tr), 177(tl), 181,
 189, 195(tl), 205(tl), 213(br), 220(b), 225, 229(tr), 257(b),
 267(bl), 270(t), 283, 284(t and b), 285, 286(t and b:l and r), 287,
 289(tl), 296(l), 297(t), 299(r), 303(c);
Gaudí Museum, Barcelona 260(l and r);
Greenville College, Illinois, Richard W. Bock Sculpture
 Collection, courtesy of Smithsonian Institution 195(bc);
Haagsgemeentenmuseum, s-Gravenhage 241(l), 242(bl), 243(t
 and bl), 244(l and r);
Hamlyn Publishing Group 42(tr), 46(t), 47(b), 143(br), 151(tr),
 167(cl and r), 187(b), 191(tl and br), 192(cr), 193(tl);
Hapag Lloyd 47(t), 89(t and b:l and r);
Haslam and Whiteway Ltd. 163(tc);
Heal & Son Ltd, London 145(tl), 146(t and c), 153(t);
Heuser, Dr. Hans-Jorgen, Collection Maria and Hans-Jörgen
 Heuser, Marxen am Berge 89(r and l:t and b), 91(l);
Hornak, Angelo (photographer) 42(tl), 139, 143(t and bl), 151(tl),
 155(b and tl), 157(bl), 163(tc), 170(l:t and b), 171(tr), 179(b),
 182(b and t:r and l), 203(cr), 206(tl), 227(br);
Edward James Foundation, London 39(t);
Italia Line 46(b);
Jesse, John, London 219(tl), 270(b);
Jordan Volpe Gallery 193(tc), 197(tl and c);
Kölniches Stadtmuseum, Cologne 267(b);
Kröller-Muller Museum, Amsterdam 292(r);
Kunstsammlungen zu Weimar 231(l);
Kungstgewerken Museum, Berlin 276(bl);
Kunstindustrimuseet, Copenhagen 201(t);
Kunstindustrimuseum, Oslo 251(r), 255(bl and tr);
Kunstindustrimuseum, Trondheim 255(bc);
Leicester Museum 145(b);
Lewis, Philippa and Juliet Scott 157(bl);
Library of Congress, Washington 180(b);
London Transport 175(bl);
Los Angeles Municipal Art Gallery, California, courtesy of
 Smithsonian Institution 186(bl);
McMahon, Rita, courtesy of the Jordan Volpe Gallery, New York
 185(t:l and r);
Mansell Collection 300(t and b), 303(b), 304(b);

Marcilhac, Félix, Paris 58(bl), 82, 83, 88(l and r), 275;
Metropolitan Museum of Modern Art, New York, gift of Mrs.
 Winthrop Atwell 274;
Mobilier et Décoration 70(tc);
Musées des Arts Decoratifs, Bordeaux 280(l);
Musée Royal de l'Afrique Centrale, Brussels 272, 273;
Musées Royaux de Belgique 233(t);
Museum of the City of New York, The Byron Collection 44;
Museum of Decorative Art, Copenhagen 250, 254(t);
Museum für Kunsthandwerk, Dresden 213(l:t and b and r:t and c),
 221;
Museum für Kunsthandwerk, Frankfurt 230(l);
National Film Archive, London 39(b), 47(b), 288, 289(tl and c and
 b), 290, 291, 304(t);
National Gallery of Scotland 295(br);
National Portrait Gallery, London 8, 138(l), 300(c);
National Museum, Paris 295(l);
National Museum, Stockholm 253(l and tr and c), 254(br);
Nordenfjeldske Kunstindustrimuseum, Trondheim 230(t and l),
 255(bc);
Norrköpingsmuseum, Sweden 249(tr);
The Oakland Museum, California 187(tr), 188(r);
Offentliche Kunstsammlung, Basel 299(bl);
Österreichisches Museum fur angewandte Kunst 205(tr), 214(bl),
 224(r:c and b), 228(bl), 229(t);
Philadelphia Museum of Art, given by Charles T. Shenkle in
 memory of his mother, Mrs. Edna H. Shenkle 183(b),
 Philadelphia Museum of Art Collection 191(bl), Louise and
 Walter Arensberg Collection 296;
Pix, New York 72(t);
Polak, Ada 251(l), 254(l:c and b);
Poulain, Hervé 67(t and b);
Rie, Lucie, London 219(b), 224(t), 227(t);
Royal Commission on Ancient Monuments, Scotland 141(t);
Royal Commission on Historical Monuments, London 257(t);
Royal Copenhagen Porcelain Factory 253(b and cr);
Sotheby's Belgavia 16, 17(b), 18, 19, 20(c), 21(t), 25(c), 26, 29, 34,
 35(t and b), 43(t), 61(l and b and r:t and b), 59(b), 73, 74(tl and
 b:c and r), 76(l and r and b), 80, 81, 87, 93(l and r and b), 94,
 95(r and l), 96, 97, 98, 99, 101(r), 103(t:l and r and b), 104(l and
 r and b), 106, 107, 108, 115(r), 116, 119(l and r), 122 and 123,
 145(tr), 150, 152(r), 153(c:l and r and b), 155(cl and tr), 157(br),
 158, 161, 166, 167(b), 169(b), 170(br), 171(tl), 172(r), 174,
 175(r), 176(r), 177(tr), 179(tr), 192(l and cr), 195(c and tr and l:t
 and b), 197(b), 205(br), 206(tr), 214(t), 215(l), 216, 217(r),
 218(b), 222, 223, 224(bl), 228(t and br), 230(r), 233(b:l and r),
 234(l and r), 235, 242(t and br), 243(br), 249(b), 254(cr), 258,
 293(r), 298(l), 302(b), 303(t);
Stamford University, California, gift of Mr. and Mrs. Paul R.
 Hanna (courtesy of Smithsonian Institution) 186(br);
Stedelijk Museum, Amsterdam 245(t and b), 246, 247(t and b);
Sully-Jaulmes, Laurent (photographer) 58(bl), 82, 83;
Tate Gallery, London 292(l), 293(l);
Thistlewaite, H. 179(b);
Thornton, Lynne 84, 85, 86(t and b), 90, 91(r), 279;
University of Chicago, David and Alfred Smart Gallery, courtesy
 of Smithsonian Institution 186(tr);
University of Glasgow, Mackintosh Collection 143(br);
Victoria and Albert Museum 9, 12(b and t:r and l), 13(t and l and
 b), 17(t), 48(r:t and b), 136(r and l), 137(t:l and r), 139, 140(b
 and t:l and r), 142, 147(b), 151(tl), 162(l and r), 167(tl), 168,
 169(l), 172(l), 173, 175(br), 176(b), 178, 179(cr), 185(bl), 187(b),
 191(tl and br), 208(b), 196(l and c), 249(tl), 252, 255(br);
Wadsworth Atheneum, Connecticut 294;
William Morris Gallery, London 137(bl), 151(b);
Wilton Royal Carpet Factory 298(r);
Whistler, Laurence 38(c);
Wood, Trevor (photographer) 14(tl), 15(t and b), 207(t);
The Worshipful Company of Goldsmiths, London 171(b);
Wyand, John (photographer) 14(b and tr), 194, 261(t:l and r and
 b:l and r and c), 262(l and r and b), 263(l and r);
Yale University Art Gallery, New Haven, Connecticut 297(b);

ACKNOWLEDGEMENTS
The lines by Walter Benjamin on page 303 from 'The Image of
Proust', from *Illuminations*, translated by Harry Zohn, edited by
Hannah Arendt and published by Jonathan Cape, London, and
Harcourt Brace Jovanovich, New York, are quoted by kind
permission of the author, the translator, the editor and the
publishers; those on page 303 from the Scott-Moncrieff translation
of *A la Recherche du Temps Perdu* by Marcel Proust by kind
permission of Mrs. Eileen Scott-Moncrieff and Chatto and
Windus, London, and Random House, New York; those by F.
Scott Fitzgerald on page 305 from *The Beautiful and Damned* by
kind permission of Charles Scribner's Sons, New York; those by P.
Wyndham Lewis on page 305 from *Men Without Art* by kind
permission of Cassell Ltd., London; those by G. E. Moore on page
305 from *Principia Ethica* by kind permission of Cambridge
University Press, London, and New York; those by Virginia Woolf
on page 304 from *Mrs. Dalloway* and on pages 304 and 305 from
To The Lighthouse by kind permission of Hogarth Press, Angelica
Garnett and Quentin Bell, London, and Harcourt Brace
Jovanovich Inc., New York; those on page 305 by Edward Upward
from *The Railway Accident and Other Stories* by kind permission of
William Heinemann Ltd., London.